Environmental Science
Living within the System of Nature

Charles E. Kupchella
Western Kentucky University

Margaret C. Hyland

ALLYN AND BACON, INC.
Boston—London—Sydney—Toronto

*To Marge and Kup, Adele, Rick, Michele, and Jason
Mary Helen, Michael, Amy, Pete, Tony, and
Shaun*

EDITORIAL PRODUCTION SERVICE: Barbara A. Willette
SENIOR PRODUCTION ADMINISTRATOR: Jane J. Schulman
ART DEVELOPER AND COORDINATOR: Arthur Ciccone
PHOTO RESEARCHER: Louise A. Lindenberger
COMPOSITION BUYER: Linda Cox
MANUFACTURING BUYER: Ellen Glisker
COVER DESIGNER: Linda Dickinson
ARTISTS: Christy Krames, Peter Loewer, Patrice Rossi, Dennis Tasa,
          Textbook Art Associates

LIBRARY OF CONGRESS CATALOGING IN PUBLICATION DATA

Kupchella, Charles E.
    Environmental science.

    Bibliography: p.
    Includes index
    1. Ecology.   2. Pollution—Environmental aspects.
3. Human ecology.   I. Hyland, Margaret C., 1947–
II. Title.
QH541.K86   1986   304.2   85-11285
ISBN 0-205-08520-2

Printed in the United States of America.

10 9 8 7 6 5 4 3 2 1   89 88 87 86 85

Text and photo credits begin on page A-9.

Brief Contents

Detailed Contents

PART ONE
Basic Principles of Ecology 1

PART THREE

The Impact of Human Activities on Health and the Environment 257

PART FOUR
Points of View 545

Preface

Those of us who witnessed the environmental awakening marked by the first Earth Day, more than 15 years ago, are gratified by the progress made since then. We have watched the environmental movement progress from a fad to a well-entrenched part of our way of life. We have watched business and industry begin to take the environment into account as a regular part of doing business. We have seen pollution control become a very serious multi-billion-dollar commitment. We have seen the air become cleaner, we have seen some rivers get cleaner, and we have seen strip-mined land reclaimed. At the same time we watched university environmental science courses evolve from topical courses designed for the passing interest of the students of the day to serious foundation courses—courses for students interested in the environment as part of a good general education and courses for students in many different fields who might become directly involved in the great deal of environmental work that remains.

We wrote this book because we believe that the trend just described calls for a new kind of textbook. Many early environmental science textbooks, now dated, seemed to assume that students of environmental science are uninterested in facts and substance, that they want to be told how to think and what to do, that they wish simply to be moved to indignation by pictures of sewers and smokestacks. Our book is designed to take its readers beyond the superficial. It is designed to be used by college students in business, science, education, the humanities, engineering, agriculture, and other university curricula who are taking their first environmental science course. It assumes no science background other than good secondary-level courses in biology and general science.

Our approach is human-centered. Our case for concern about the environment is made on the basis of human self-interest—when the environment is harmed, humans are harmed. We focus on the places in which human beings interact with the rest of nature most intensely. Our human emphasis is superimposed on a solid framework of ecological principles. We believe that the principles of ecology are the paradigms upon which environmental science must be based. At the same time we integrate the economic, social, political, ethical, and legal aspects of our environmental problems. These are, after all, real and important components of environmental decision making.

There are no long lists of simple solutions in this book. We want our readers to appreciate that most environmental problems are too complex for such solutions. We have made every effort to present balanced, fair treatment of controversial topics, and we encourage our readers to formulate their own conclusions. We believe that the inclusion of facts and figures in the form of charts and graphs as well as the presentation of arguments on all sides of issues will stimulate independent thought and action. One of our main objectives is to provide facts that students can use in making their own reasoned decisions.

Some other aspects of our strategy and some distinctive features of this book are as follows.

ORGANIZATION

We have divided the book into four parts. The principles of ecology are considered in Part I. Separate chapters are devoted to energy flow, nutrient cycles, population and community ecology, and the origin of ecosystems.

In Part II, human needs are considered in light of the principles of ecology. Part II contains chapters covering our needs for energy, water, and mineral resources and on human population ecology. The order in which these topics are presented matches the order of earlier chapters, highlighting the connection between principles and problems. Chapters 6, 7, and 8 focus on humankind in the same way that corresponding Chapters 2, 3, and 4 treat living things in a general way.

In Part III we examine the impact of humanity on our natural support systems and on us—on humanity itself. There are chapters on air pollution, water pollution, environmental causes of cancer, pesticides and other toxic chemicals, solid and hazardous wastes, noise and crowding, and land use and abuse.

Part IV consists of two editorial chapters. Chapter 18 examines government, politics, economics, and other institutions and their general relationship to environmental problems. Chapter 19 is an editorial summary that outlines the nature of environmental problems, points to the hurdles to be overcome in dealing with them, and assesses the prospects for dealing with them effectively in the future.

BIG-PICTURE APPROACH

One of the elements in our philosophy of teaching is that learning and appreciating details comes easily if a clear framework is provided on which to hang them. This is reflected in the organization of the text and in the art program. Some of our illustrations are visual metaphors designed to give our readers working images to help keep the framework in mind.

GLOBAL SCOPE

We describe environmental problems using examples and illustrations from all over the world, and we explain the need for international approaches to global environmental problems. Although our emphasis is on the United States, we make it clear that neither problems nor solutions are limited by national boundaries.

MINI-GLOSSARIES

We define key terms associated with particular topics in clusters called mini-glossaries. Terms that might be confused with one another are defined together to help students gain a more precise understanding. We believe that definitions presented in this way favor learning over memorization. All key terms are also given in boldface the first time they are defined in context, and the locations of all key terms are again indicated by boldface in the index.

BONUSES

Optional topics that expand on points made in the text or provide interesting asides are presented throughout the text. They range from essays on how beavers influence the environment to development of an intuitive understanding for the unit "microgram per cubic meter."

CONCEPTS TO REMEMBER

In a direct outline format we have enumerated the major points at the end of each chapter so that students can easily review and reconsider them.

ACTIVITIES AND FOOD FOR THOUGHT

This end-of-chapter feature helps the reader connect the text to the real world and is intended to stimulate independent critical thinking. Here too are ideas for class discussions, outside speakers, and field trips.

REFERENCES

The articles and books listed at the end of each chapter are readily available in nearly all college libraries. They offer the reader a diversity of points of view and help identify sources of current information.

INTERPRETING TABLES AND GRAPHS

Learning how to interpret graphical representations of data is an important part of learning environmental science. Appendix A explains in a simple way how to do this. Students who have little or no background in working with scientific data may benefit from exercises in converting tabular data into histograms, pie charts, and other graphic forms of presenting data.

KEEPING UP TO DATE

Appendix B is a compact guide to finding current information. Worthwhile library exercises for scavenger hunts of recent information can be developed on the basis of this section. Mastery of this section will give the reader a textbook that is usable for a lifetime.

THINK METRIC

Because we are, as a nation, still somewhere between the English system of measurement and the metric system, both English and metric units are used throughout the text. Volumes, weights, and areas are often given in both English and metric measurements. Where only one system is used, the conversion charts in Appendix C will permit easy interconversion.

ACKNOWLEDGEMENTS

We have many people to thank. The support and encouragement of our friends, including the members of our families, were crucial. The time we spent on this project was time we would have spent with them, yet they responded to this theft of time with genuine encouragement. This project would have likewise been impossible without the support provided by the people who *are* the University of Louisville and Murray State University. We are particularly grateful to Murray State University's Committee for Institutional Studies and Research. We acknowledge elsewhere the invaluable expert assistance provided to us by our reviewers. Some of these were colleagues we asked for help, and some were identified by our editor. We very much appreciate the extra effort made by Allyn and Bacon Science Editor Jim Smith in assembling an impressive group of helpful reviewers. He managed to persuade an unusually large number of very busy people to provide us with timely, detailed, constructive criticism.

Typing the manuscript and otherwise getting it into final form required the able assistance of many typists and photocopiers. We wish to thank the following individuals, who helped generate three or four deep file drawers of drafts and redrafts and hundreds of letters sent in search of new information and permission to use copyrighted material:

Joan Pedigo	Jean Lynch
Patty Mann	Susan Vance
Joyce Johnson	Helga Keller
Janet Terry	Debbie Lynn
Michele Kupchella	Gail Raspberry
Vicki Miller	Janice Melton
Susan Johnson	Donna Marine
Donna Alexander	

All of these people brought us to the point at which a book could be made from more than a thousand manuscript pages. This is where a very able production team at Allyn and Bacon took over. We are especially grateful to Barbara Willette, Jane Schulman, Art Ciccone, and Louise Lindenberger.

We wrote this book from our unique combination of perspectives, influenced too by our many reviewers. We believe we have produced a useful teaching and learning tool. After you have been through the book, let us know what you liked or did not like about it. Your input will help us generate an even better second edition.

Review and Development

No two people could write an environmental science text alone. The subject is far too broad for anyone to be an expert in even a fraction of the areas that make up this subject. We needed and received help from many very capable people.

The individuals listed below reviewed various parts of the manuscript and made numerous valuable suggestions, corrections, and comments. Some of these individuals were and are co-workers who served quadruple duty as reviewers, sounding boards, sources of inspiration, and providers of elusive key words. Some were selected by the editor because they are outstanding teachers of environmental science courses; they ably assisted in guiding the manuscript toward the intended target. Others were chosen by the editor for their expertise in particular subject areas; they evaluated individual chapters for accuracy, timeliness, and balance. No reviewer, however, had any control after submitting suggestions and criticisms. The responsibility for any errors that may remain is ours.

Robert Anderson, Environmental Protection Agency

Kenneth B. Armitage, University of Kansas, Systematics and Ecology

John Bachman, Environmental Protection Agency

Linda R. Berg, University of Maryland, Botany

Richard J. Borden, College of the Atlantic, Human Ecology

J. Philip Bromberg, Esq., Pittsburgh, Pennsylvania

David A. Brown, Aquatic Research Consultants, Long Beach, California

William L. Brown, National Academy of Sciences, Board of Agriculture

Carl A. Carlozzi, University of Massachusetts, Fish, Game, and Wildlife Management

James E. Carrel, University of Missouri-Columbia, Biological Sciences

Ken Carstens, Murray State University, Anthropology

Bernard L. Clausen, University of Northern Iowa, Biology

John D. Cunningham, Keene State College, Environmental Studies

Edward J. Daniels, Institute of Gas Technology, Energy Development Center

Edward J. DiPolvere, National Association of Noise Control Officials, Trenton, New Jersey

Donald Duncan, Murray State University, Physics

Frank Edwards, Murray State University, Economics

Frederick I. Eilers, University of South Florida, Biology

Robert Etherton, Murray State University, Physics

Franklin B. Flower, Rutgers University, Environmental Science

Norma L. Fowler, University of Texas-Austin, Botany

Hugo D. Freudenthal, Holzmacher, McLendon and Murrell, P.C., Consulting Engineers, Environmental Scientists and Planners, Farmingdale, New York

Gene Garfield, Murray State University, Political Science

Ralph J. Gorton, Lansing Community College, Natural Science

Richard Greenberg, University of Louisville School of Medicine, Epidemiology

John P. Harley, Eastern Kentucky University, Biological Sciences

To The Student

From the beginning, the world—our ecosphere—has endured a variety of problems, from meteor showers to volcanic upheavals. Many species of plants and animals have come and gone. Now humankind faces the challenge of life on earth. That is what this book is about.

Look around you. Half the world's people live in overcrowded, polluted cities. In Jakarta, Indonesia, only one fourth of the houses have piped-in water. Lagos, Nigeria, one of the world's fastest growing cities, essentially has no sewage system. Almost all the slum children in Manila are malnourished. In cities around the world, including U.S. cities like Denver and Los Angeles, eyes water, people have trouble breathing, outdoor exercise is often unsafe.

Many of the rest of the world's people live on land that is parched, overused, and abused. As we write, Ethiopians pour out of drought-stricken countrysides into refugee camps, where many die. In China, rats eat crops meant for humans. Everywhere, insects are becoming resistant to pesticides. Thousands of lakes and acres of forests throughout North America and Europe are dying, apparently from the effects of acid rain. Precious resources grow scarce; Americans use much more oil than they can produce.

The basic necessities—clean air, adequate food, fresh water, and raw materials—are enjoyed by relatively few people. Yet over the next 30 years, the population equivalent of a thousand Clevelands will be added to the world. Population rates have slowed recently, but stabilization is still a long way off.

The world needs you. More than ever the world needs bright minds charged with idealism. There is much work to be done. A few of you will become scientists and technicians, working on technical solutions. Some of you will become, lawmakers, judges, and government workers who will legislate and enforce solutions. Others will become philosophers, psychologists, artists, and teachers who will help the rest of us learn to live with the changes associated with the new solutions. But most important, all of you are already citizens in positions to demand that environmental problems be effectively addressed.

This book is intended to help you get ready. One of its purposes is to outline what is already known about the environment and environmental problems. Another is to identify the questions that have not been answered and to point out the most important obstacles. Our ultimate objective is to involve you fully as a well-informed citizen in the effort to improve the world environment.

Although we have strong opinions on what should be done, we have tried very hard to keep preaching to a minimum. Instead, we offer facts and balanced presentations of opposing views—to give you a basis for making your own judgments and to allow you to practice making up your own minds.

HOW THIS BOOK WILL HELP YOU LEARN

We have tried to make this book easy to study. We have created several special aids to help you along.

Each chapter contains Mini-glossaries to define important concepts that are often confused or that belong together; they appear near the text where they are discussed. Concepts to Remember appear at the end of each chapter to help you review the most important points within the chapter. We have annotated the References and Further Readings so that you will be able to study further those topics that especially interest you.

At the end of the book are several appendixes to help you use this book fully. We have included an appendix on Interpreting Tables and Graphs for those of you who need a review. You will also find an appendix on conversion between English and

Review and Development

metric units of measure. You can use it to translate the units of measure found within this text and other books into the units you are most familiar with. We have also created a special appendix called Keeping up to Date. This appendix lists the names and addresses of sources of information that you can use to get the most recent information about our environment. We hope that this will save you time in the library and will encourage you to look further and dig deeper when discussing or writing about environmental topics.

We hope that you will come to see this textbook as a valuable tool that you will want to use again and again. The problems you will study in this course are not theoretical ones that will fade away after school is over. You will be called upon, in your workplace and as a citizen, to make up your minds about environmental issues. Now is the time to start practicing.

About the Authors

Charles E. Kupchella is the Dean of the Ogden College of Science, Technology, and Health at Western Kentucky University in Bowling Green.

Since 1968, Dr. Kupchella has worked as a teacher and researcher in the environmental field. At Bellarmine College in the early 1970s he developed a course called "Man and His Environment" as an offshoot of the first Earth Day observation. During this time he also formulated an environmental education program at the King Center in Nazareth, Kentucky.

From 1973 to 1979, Dr. Kupchella served as Associate Director of the Cancer Center at the University of Louisville School of Medicine. His research at the University of Louisville was in tumor biology as part of a group engaged in a cancer control program associated with the plastic industry. He taught a course on the health effects of environmental contaminants and helped to develop and coordinate a course on the biology of cancer in the School of Medicine.

From 1979 to 1985, Dr. Kupchella was Professor and Chairman of the Department of Biological Sciences at Murray State University, Murray, Kentucky, where he taught a range of courses including Human Ecology. He is a member of Sigma Xi, the American Institute of Biological Sciences, the American Association for the Advancement of Science, the American Association for Cancer Education, the North American Association for Environmental Education, and the American Society of Zoologists. He is also past president of the Kentucky Academy of Science and the Kentucky Association for Environmental Education. Dr. Kupchella received his Ph.D. in Biology from St. Bonaventure University.

Margaret C. Hyland has spent the last 12 years as a teacher, practitioner, and researcher in the environmental field.

Since 1976, she has been associated with the Kentucky Legislative Research Commission: first, as a Legislative Analyst responsible for policy research, fact finding, and drafting of legislation in the areas of agriculture, natural resources, and environmental protection; and at present, as Assistant Director responsible for coordination of legislative committee activity and issue development.

In her legislative work, Ms. Hyland has kept up to date on environmental and natural resource issues at the federal, state, and local levels; briefed legislators on pending environmental laws; and developed an ecology workshop for state legislators that explained basic ecological processes and showed how to apply biological concepts to environmental problems.

Prior to her work with the Kentucky State Legislature, she was the Director of the Environmental Education Program at the King Center in Nazareth, Kentucky, where she developed, implemented, and evaluated environmental education programs for teachers, school groups, and citizen groups.

Ms. Hyland has also served on the Board of Directors and the Environmental Studies Section of the Steering Committee of the North American Association for Environmental Education. She graduated from Ohio State University in 1973 with a Master of Science degree in Natural Resources, specializing in natural resource management and environmental education.

Basic Principles of Ecology

*E*cology is the study of how the living and nonliving things in nature relate to one another. Ecologists have discovered many truths about these relationships, principles that serve as a foundation for modern ecology and for environmental science in general. The basic principles of ecology must be the starting points in understanding any and all environmental problems. Part I of this book is devoted to a consideration of (1) the overall framework of structure and function in living systems, (2) the flow of energy through living systems, (3) the movement of chemicals within living systems, (4) the basic patterns of interaction between members of the same species and between members of different species, and (5) the basic patterns of change in living systems.

The Framework of Ecology

At first glance, nature seems almost hopelessly complex. The webs that connect every living thing to other living and nonliving elements of our world are made of countless finely drawn and far-reaching threads. Everything is connected to everything else. The poet Francis Thompson went so far as to suggest that when one touches a flower, a star is disturbed. He was essentially correct.

Consider the task we would be facing here if, in order to understand nature, we had to be familiar with *all* of its details. To completely appreciate how a rabbit relates to its world, for instance, we would have to take into account how each rabbit relates to other rabbits and how each rabbit interacts with foxes, owls, grass, humans, and other species of plants and animals. We would also have to consider the effects on each rabbit relationship of physical and chemical environmental changes, both subtle and dramatic, both human-made and otherwise. To appreciate how the entire natural world functions, we would have to do this for the millions of species, subspecies, varieties, and subtypes of living and non-living things—an impossible task.

Fortunately, there are patterns in nature. Nature functions as one big system made up of countless little systems, all with similar basic parts organized in the same basic patterns of interaction. The key to understanding the natural world is to recognize that the same types of activities go on everywhere in nature. In lakes, forests, fields, oceans, and ponds the basic story is much the same. The underlying plan will be our focus in Chapter 1. Our aim is to depict the living world in terms of its least common denominators, stripped of the differences that distinguish a desert from a jungle, an onion from a carrot, or a rabbit from a mouse. First, let's examine the basics more closely and then give some definitions.

LEVELS OF ORGANIZATION IN NATURE AND THE SCOPE OF ECOLOGY

Levels of Organization in Nature

Figure 1.1 illustrates the levels of organization in nature. Shown here are the subjects studied by chemists, physicists, geologists, biologists, hydrologists, astronomers, sociologists, and political scientists. Although ecology technically encompasses nearly all of the levels depicted in Figure 1.1., ecologists concern themselves mostly with those levels above the individual organism. **Ecologists** study how organisms interact with one another and with the nonliving environment.

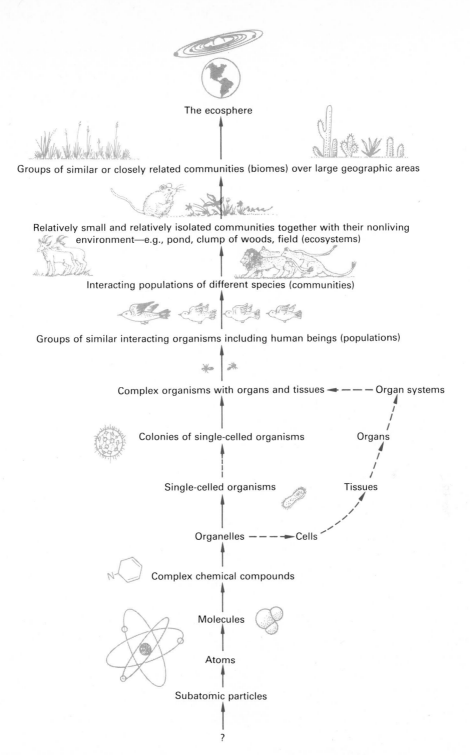

The ecosphere

Groups of similar or closely related communities (biomes) over large geographic areas

Relatively small and relatively isolated communities together with their nonliving environment—e.g., pond, clump of woods, field (ecosystems)

Interacting populations of different species (communities)

Groups of similar interacting organisms including human beings (populations)

Complex organisms with organs and tissues ◄ ─ ─ ─ Organ systems

Colonies of single-celled organisms   Organs

Single-celled organisms   Tissues

Organelles ─ ─ ─► Cells

Complex chemical compounds

Molecules

Atoms

Subatomic particles

?

Figure 1.1 Levels of Organization in Nature. The overall scope of ecology is broad, but its core begins just above the level of the individual organism and extends up through the ecosphere to include all of the plants and animals of the earth and the parts of the nonliving environment with which these interact. Ecology is the study of what goes on in the living systems called ecosystems.

Ecology, the Study of Ecosystems

Ecology is the study of the structure and function of nature. Ecology can also be defined as the study of **ecosystems** or self-regulating communities of different kinds of living creatures interacting with one another and with their nonliving setting. The words ecology and ecosystem come from the Greek *oikos*, a word meaning "house" or "place of residence."

Ecology deals mainly with the roles filled by organisms in nature and how environmental conditions affect and are affected by these roles.

The **ecosphere** is the grand system that includes *all* life forms on earth together with the parts of the earth on which, and in which, living things exist. The **ecosphere** includes parts of three "great spheres," the **atmosphere**—the earth's gases; the **hydrosphere**—the earth's water; and the **lithosphere**

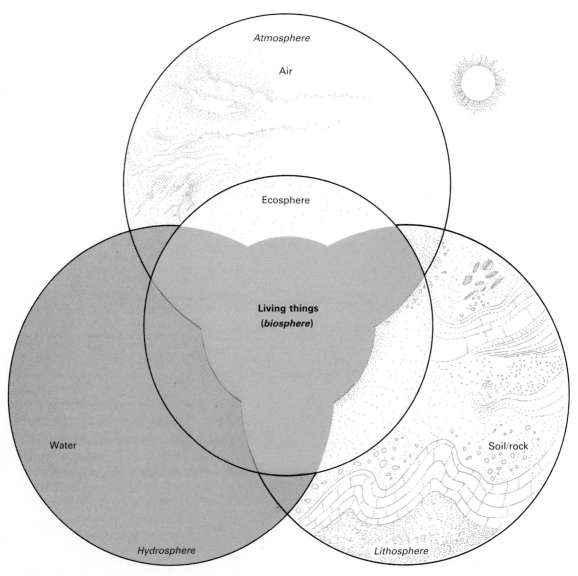

Figure 1.2 The Earth's Great Spheres. The ecosphere is made up of parts of the atmosphere, lithosphere, and hydrosphere. Other parts of each of the latter three spheres are relatively inaccessible to living things. The parts of them that *are* reached by living organisms, together with all living organisms, comprise the ecosphere.

Ecology: the study of the structure and function of ecosystems, dealing mainly with the interaction of organisms with one another and with their nonliving setting.

Ecosphere: all of the living things on earth together with the part of the nonliving world in which, and with which, they interact.

Ecosystem: a self-regulating community of plants and animals interacting with one another and with their nonliving environment.

System: any collection of interrelated parts that form a functional, defined whole.

Mini-glossaries such as this one are scattered throughout the book to highlight and show the relationship between key terms. Words and concepts found in mini-glossaries, along with many other terms indicated in **bold type,** are also defined in context throughout the text. Some of the terms introduced in this chapter are defined more completely in Chapters 2, 3, and 4.

the earth's rock and soil. The term **biosphere** is commonly used as a synonym for ecosphere, but it would make more sense to define biosphere as all of the earth's plants and animals; the ecosphere could then be defined as the biosphere plus those parts of the hydrosphere, atmosphere, and lithosphere in which, and with which, plants and animals interact (see Figures 1.2 and 1.3). Living things tend to be found at the junctions of the great spheres (Figure 1.3).

Ecosystems are real systems like forests, fields, ponds, and lakes; but the ecosystem is also an abstraction. Just as the triangle is a generalized concept applicable to many specific triangles, the ecosystem concept is a generalization about natural systems, a concept that grew out of observing what goes on in ponds, woodlots, and fields. An ecosystem has no particular size. In a sense, asking how big an ecosystem is would be like asking how big city government, an engine, a corporation, or a triangle is. All

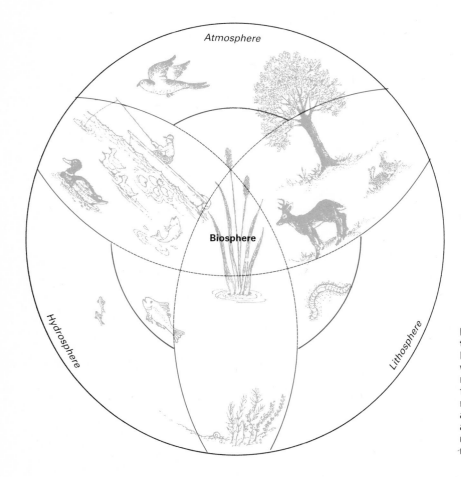

Figure 1.3 The Junctions of the Earth's Great Spheres. Most life on earth is found where land, air, and water meet. This is no accident. In fact, it tells us something fundamental about life. Living things are agents that need and use and—in the process—mix, maneuver, and manipulate the elements in air, soil, and water.

The ecosphere is the system of the earth's land, air, and water and all of its life forms.

of these things are abstractions. A pond is an ecosystem—so is an aquarium, a Pennsylvania forest, or a Colorado field. No two ecosystems, city governments, engines, corporations, or triangles are exactly alike.

THE STRUCTURE OF ECOSYSTEMS

Consider a pond and an abandoned field (Figures 1.4 and 1.5). The sun is the source of energy for both ecosystems, and both contain plants that provide food. In a pond, microscopic algae carry out most of the food making; in a field, grasses and other plants do precisely the same thing. Both ponds and meadows contain animals that eat plants. In a pond this role is filled by certain fish and insects, and by snails; in a field, mice, other kinds of insects, and rabbits play the same role. Both ponds and meadows contain animals that eat the animals that eat plants. Snapping turtles and bass eat the pond's plant eaters; in a field this same ecological role is filled by hawks and foxes.

There are actually four fundamental structural components of all ecosystems:

1. food makers or **producers**;
2. **consumers**, or eaters of plants or animals;
3. a special class of consumers that gets food from decaying plants and animals, the **decomposers**; and
4. nonliving components.

The first three of these are **biotic** (living) components; the nonliving things are called **abiotic**. Let's consider the abiotic components first.

Nonliving Components of Ecosystems

The sun provides the energy for everything going on in ecosystems, and each part of all that activity is very much affected by the *physical features* of ecosystems. Examples are the winds and weather, terrain, water currents, the amount of light, and temperature. The abiotic components of an ecosystem include all the materials that are not, for the moment, a part of an animal or plant. These include water, gases such as oxygen, minerals such as iron and sulfur, compounds such as acids, and a wide variety of other complex chemicals.

A chemical can be part of a living thing at one moment and part of the nonliving environment a moment later. The carbon in a molecule of protein can be part of a functioning enzyme of some animal, but after the enzyme is broken down and reduced to its component parts, that same carbon atom could be exhaled as a molecule of carbon dioxide and thus become a part of the *gaseous* abiotic environment. Chemicals move into and out of living organisms and are used over and over again. Some of the carbon atoms forming a protein molecule in the muscle of your left arm may have once been part of a chicken liver, the hide of a dinosaur, or even a limestone formation.

The importance of chemical substances to living systems varies with the type, location, and form of the chemical. Certain chemicals—carbon, for exam-

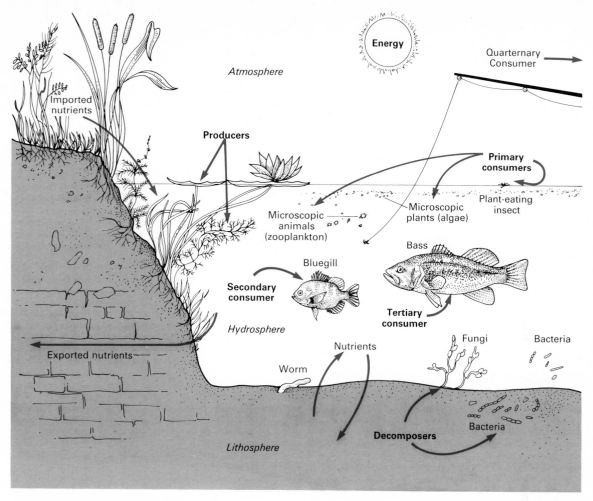

Figure 1.4 A Pond Ecosystem. Each of the roles of producer, consumer, and decomposer is filled by a number of different organisms in a pond ecosystem. For example, additional secondary or tertiary consumers might be water snakes, snapping turtles, and various birds of prey. Although ecosystems are often thought of as closed systems, none of them really are closed. Typically, both living and nonliving things are imported and exported.

ple—make up much more of the structures of animals and plants and play a far greater role in their activities than do other chemicals—for example, copper. Some chemicals may lie dormant deep within the earth's crust, for millions of years, so living organisms do not have access to them; they may be too far removed from the junctions of the great spheres (Figure 1.2). Certain other substances, because of their physical or chemical forms, may be inaccessible to living things even when they are in continuous contact with a variety of organisms. Only a small fraction of the earth's chemicals exist in forms in which plants and animals can use them.

Nitrogen and its compounds offer a particularly good example of the importance of *chemical form*. All living things need nitrogen to manufacture pro-

teins. The atmosphere is nearly 80% nitrogen, but most plants and animals cannot use nitrogen in its gaseous form; plants grown in an atmosphere of 80% nitrogen may be yellow rather than green because of a nitrogen deficiency. Most plants require their nitrogen in the form of compounds (with other elements), such as nitrates, which we sometimes provide for them in fertilizer.

The kinds and amounts of chemicals available in an ecosystem regulate the activities of the plants and thus the animals in that system, and may even determine which organisms can or cannot be part of that system. At any particular time there may be too much of one chemical substance or too little of another for a given organism or group of organisms in an ecosystem.

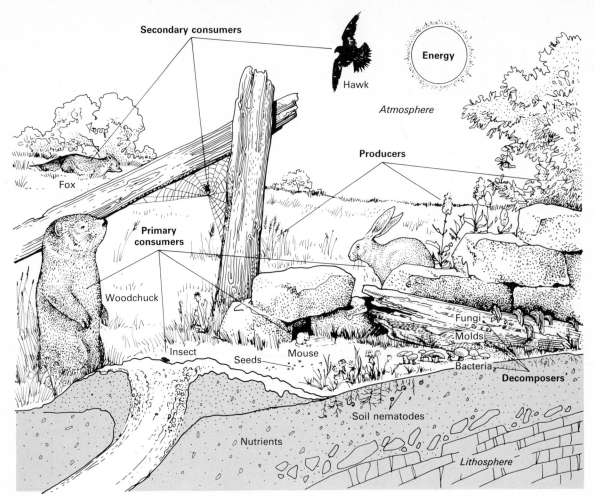

Figure 1.5 A Field Ecosystem. Each of the roles of producer, consumer, and decomposer is filled by a number of different organisms in a field ecosystem. The same funda-mental relationships exist between these classes of organisms in every ecosystem.

Nonliving components such as light, weather, and terrain help to fashion a forest ecosystem. In turn, the living components affect the forest's physical and chemical features.

Part I   Basic Principles of Ecology

Beavers

While it is easy to imagine how the environment can influence an individual organism, it may be a little more difficult to appreciate (at least for organisms other than humans) the extent to which the reverse is true. Beavers offer a particularly good example of how much organisms can influence their surroundings.

Beavers build dams that hold streams in check. These dams provide a steadier water supply (and a diminished threat of drought), reduce erosion, and somewhat stabilize silt and sediment loads. The water behind the dams provides habitat for fish, turtles, ducks, and many other aquatic organisms. Beaver dams spread out and divert water, creating marshes and other wetlands. This can increase humidity and soil moisture over a large area and have a profound impact on vegetation.

Beavers carry wood into the water. Some kinds of wood are rich in nitrogen and other potentially scarce nutrients. In this and other ways, beaver dams tend to release steady amounts of nutrients to the waters downstream, actually making it possible for certain organisms to live in the water.

Beavers cut down certain trees, making it possible for the sun to shine through the canopy to reach the forest floor. This in turn influences the humidity in the forest, increases air temperature, and increases the average temperature of the forest soil surface. Warming of the soil influences the insect and microbial populations in the soil. The reduction in shade allows sun-loving plants to grow on the forest floor and allows shade-intolerant trees such as pine and spruce to grow.

See Seastedt and Crossley (1984) for an easy to read account of how *insects* influence ecosystems.

To make matters still more complicated, the living components of an ecosystem have a great effect on chemical and physical features of the environment. One of the most important concepts of ecology is that while the physical and chemical features of an ecosystem have an impact on animals and plants, plants and animals also have an impact on their physical and chemical surroundings. Trees and grasses help form soil, and hold soil and sand dunes in place. Trees can buffer the wind and make the climate cooler. Plants, as we will see later, are generally responsible for the fact that there is oxygen in the atmosphere in the form that *we* can breathe.

Living Components of Ecosystems: Producers, Consumers, and Decomposers

Living things are made of carbon and other chemicals with a lot of water added. Living things are beautifully organized combinations of nonliving materials. The same could be said of diamonds. Although most living things are readily distinguishable from diamonds by the magnitude of their complexity, a more distinctive quality of life is that it is more or less in constant complex and dynamic action. Living organisms exchange, expel, convert, assemble, disassemble, organize, and otherwise manipulate the constituents of earth, air, and water. The energy-requiring manipulation of earth, air, and water by living things enables individual organisms to grow, repair themselves, and persist.

We have already identified producers, decomposers, and consumers as the basic kinds of *biotic* ecosystem components. As we will now see, the distinctions between these groups are based on their sources of energy and materials.

Producers. All green plants are *producers*. They produce in the sense that they **assimilate** (take in) simple chemicals from the soil and from the air (Figure 1.6) and, with the help of energy from the sun (Figure 1.7), transform them by photosynthesis into more complex energy-rich chemicals that eventually make up the substance of the plant. Obviously, plants do not produce something from nothing. Perhaps a better name for producers would be "converters" or "transformers." The term "producer" will suffice, however, as an indication of the relative role that plants have in all ecosystems. From the perspective of the consumer, producers make food.

Recently, scientists have confirmed the existence of ecosystems based on chemical energy at great ocean depths (more than a kilometer), far below the limits of light penetration. The producers in these systems are bacteria that are able to gain energy from the oxidation of hydrogen sulfide that seeps from volcanic vents in the ocean floor. Since these organisms get their energy from chemical reactions rather than light, they are called **chemotrophs** rather than **phototrophs**—literally "chemical feeders" rather than "light feeders." The roles of consumers in these ecosystems are filled by bacteria-eating relatives of the consumers that feed on organic matter derived from sunlight elsewhere in the ocean. Even more recently, chemotrophic-based systems have also been found in shallow parts of the oceans.

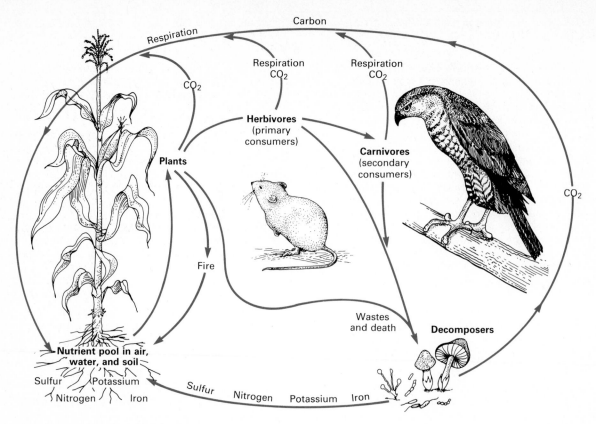

Figure 1.6 Cycling of Ecosystem Materials or Nutrients.
Several of the constituent parts of this diagram could be removed without stopping the cyclic flow of nutrients within a
functional ecosystem.

Except for a few obscure species such as those described above, all living things other than green plants are *consumers*. They must consume the chemical energy and chemical nutrients derived from other living things.

Consumers. Cattle graze. They consume plant material from which they extract energy and chemical building blocks. Some of the food energy is used as a cow moves, and some of it is used in the assembly of chemical subunits into new cells for the cow or into a calf fetus—for growth or reproduction. Similarly, an eater of cows extracts energy from some of the chemicals in beef, and in the same way that a cow breaks down plant chemicals to get energy a cow eater breaks down cow chemicals to get energy. A cow eater might use some of this energy to square dance or to swim; some is used to reassemble beef chemicals into human chemicals (if the cow eater happens to be human).

Because cows eat plants, they are called **herbivores**. They could also be called vegetarians. Because they get their food directly from producers,

cows and all other strict herbivores are also called **primary consumers**. Organisms that eat cows or that eat any other plant eater are called **secondary consumers**, since their food is one step removed from plants. They are also called **carnivores**.

The pattern we have just established predicts that an animal that eats a cow eater would be called a **tertiary consumer**, and so on. Obviously, there are organisms in ecosystems that consume plants *and* plant eaters. A person eating a steak and potatoes dinner would qualify as a *multilevel consumer* or **omnivore** (eats both plants and animals).

Decomposers. Decomposers comprise a special class of consumers that get energy and nutrients by digesting waste matter and dead plant or animal material. Decomposers are the organisms—mostly bacteria and fungi—responsible for decay, decomposition, or rotting. Sometimes animals die for reasons other than being killed and eaten by a predator. If their carcasses are not found and picked clean by scavengers, they rot. The energy-rich and mineral-rich treasure that these carcasses hold goes to bacteria and fungi. Similarly, plants die for reasons other than being picked and eaten by a primary consumer. The chemicals in dead plant material—the enormous volume of leaves that forests give up every fall, for instance—also go to the decomposers.

Decomposers fill a very important role in ecosystems. They are responsible for the completion of ecosystem mineral cycles. (In the next chapter this sentence will be qualified somewhat in discussions of ecosystem storage and ecosystem export/import.) By breaking down residual organic chemicals and by using up any "remaining" energy, decomposers figuratively "mop up"; they ensure that nutrients do not remain tied up in nonfunctioning plant or animal mass; they complete cycles.

Fire is like decomposition. Fire can also release chemical energy and nutrients held in plant and animal material. Fire also mops things up. It also completes cycles and closes circles. Fire is much

Decomposers such as fungi consume dead plant material and return nutrients to the soil.

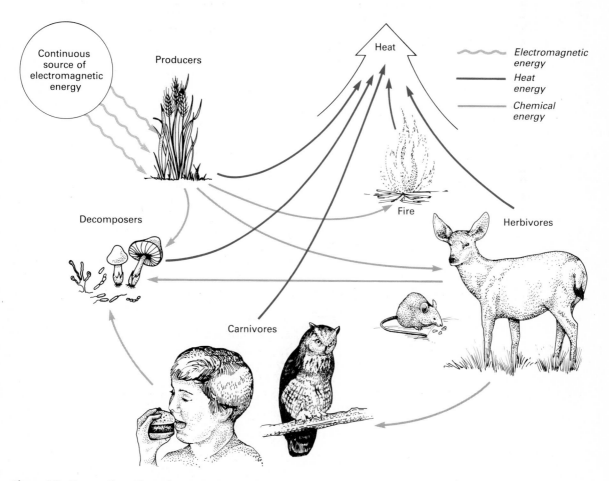

Figure 1.7 Energy Flow Through Ecosystems. Three basic kinds of energy are involved in energy exchanges within an ecosystem. These are electromagnetic energy, heat energy, and chemical energy.

Chapter 1   The Framework of Ecology

11

Fire, like decomposers, breaks down complex organic material, completing mineral cycles.

more traumatic than decomposition and is obviously different in other ways. Many kinds of ecosystems are not compatible with regular fires; others depend on them. Still, the net results of fire and decomposition are the same: Complex organic material is broken down into mineral nutrients, carbon dioxide, and water; energy is released as heat.

ECOSYSTEM FUNCTION

Given the proper physical setting—temperature, light level, slope, etc.—living organisms really require only two things from the environment: (1) *chemicals* to make up the substance of the organisms and (2) *energy,* the power necessary to make the substance "go." All of the principles of ecological interaction are concerned in one way or another with the acquisition of chemical substance (matter) and energy. Energy and matter thus form the basis of what ecologists consider to be the cardinal principles of ecology, namely:

1. energy *flows through* and propels ecosystems, and
2. chemical matter *cycles within* and/or between ecosystems.

Chemicals are used over and over again within ecosystems. Although in most real ecosystems there is a certain amount of import and export, *matter*

need not be imported from outside an ecosystem in order for the system to continue to function.

Energy cannot be used over and over. The energy that gets into ecosystems is *not* restored to its original form as ecosystems use it. Except in fireflies and negligibly few other luminescent creatures, the *chemical* energy in the herbivore or primary consumer is never restored to *light* energy. Also, energy transfers are inefficient. As energy is converted from one form to another form—from light to chemical, for instance—much of it is necessarily lost as heat. As energy passes from plants through consumers and decomposers, all of it is eventually dissipated as heat (Figure 1.7). Thus energy does not cycle. Energy comes into the ecosystem, it is used, and most of it is lost to the system forever as it is converted to heat. Ecosystems must all have continuous sources of energy.

For *all* living things an energy crisis is a crisis indeed.

POPULATIONS AND COMMUNITIES

Most ecosystems have many different kinds (species) of producers, decomposers, and consumers. This makes ecosystems lively and variably complicated. Individual organisms in an ecosystem relate to other members of their species and to members of other species in ways that range from competition for space and food to mating. Ecologists study these interactions, lumping them into the categories of **intraspecific** interactions (between members of same species), or population interactions, and **interspecific** (between members of different species), or community interactions (review Figure 1.1).

Many of the principles of ecology relate to populations and communities. A **population** is a group of interacting individuals of the same kind or species. All the gray squirrels in a clump of woods, all the bass in a pond, or all the deer mice in a field would qualify as a population. The individuals in populations relate to one another in many ways. While some animals—the lynx, for instance—lead an almost solitary existence, insects—ants, for instance—carry interaction among members of the same species to the extreme. As we will see in Chapter 4, a population is considerably more than the sum of its individual members.

A **community**, in the ecological sense, is made up of all of the interacting populations of a number of species in a given area. Examples of communities are all the plants and animals of a desert, all the plants and animals in a pond, all the plants and animals in a meadow, and all the plants and animals in an aquarium. The community is the biotic part of an ecosystem. Interaction at the community level can be extremely complex. In a pond community a bass population may feed on smaller fish, which in turn feed on minnows, which in turn eat microscopic animals, which in turn subsist on microscopic plants; larger plants provide shelter and food for other animals in the pond food web. In Chapter 4 we will see that a community is also more than the sum of its parts.

THE MOLECULAR BASIS OF PRODUCTION AND CONSUMPTION: PHOTOSYNTHESIS AND RESPIRATION

Photosynthesis is the process by which plants convert light energy into chemical energy. **Respiration** is the process by which chemical energy is released to do work in both plants and animals. This energy is used to drive the many chemical reactions collectively called anabolic or biosynthetic reactions. Photosynthesis and respiration are at the molecular "heart" of the mechanisms by which matter and energy are moved within ecosystems. A simplified summary of the processes of photosynthesis, respiration, anabolism, and the interrelationships among these processes is presented in Figures 1.8 through 1.10.

Plants, as illustrated in Figures 1.9 and 1.10a, use some of the chemical energy they derive from sunlight to make fruit, seeds, stems, and leaves. Plants synthesize molecules like glucose and starch, and from some of this they extract the energy they need for anabolism through plant respiration (Figure 1.9).

The net effect of respiration is photosynthesis in reverse. Figures 1.8 and 1.9 illustrate that the processes of photosynthesis and respiration exemplify cycling in natural systems. The chemicals used in photosynthesis are regenerated by respiration.

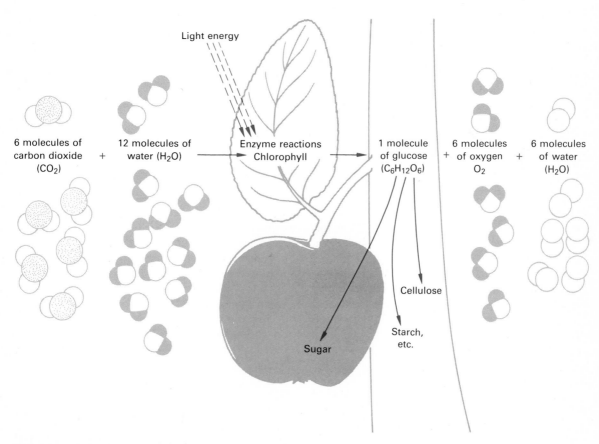

Figure 1.8 Photosynthesis Simplified. Carbon dioxide and water are consumed in the process of photosynthesis, and oxygen, water, and glucose are produced. Much more is involved than is illustrated in this diagram; only the *net* effect of photosynthesis is shown here.

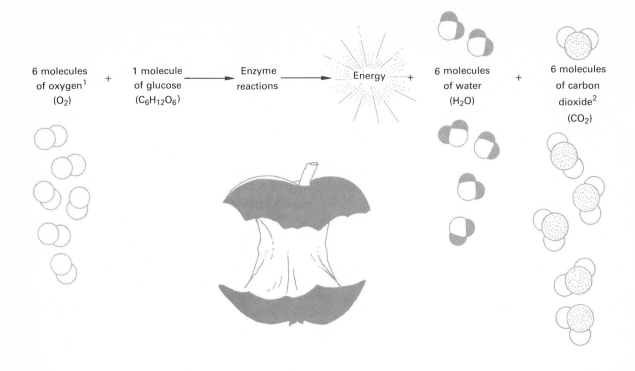

| 6 molecules of oxygen[1] (O_2) | + | 1 molecule of glucose ($C_6H_{12}O_6$) | → | Enzyme reactions | → | Energy | + | 6 molecules of water (H_2O) | + | 6 molecules of carbon dioxide[2] (CO_2) |

Figure 1.9 Respiration Simplified. In respiration, oxygen, water, and glucose are consumed; energy, water, and carbon dioxide are produced. The energy is used by the respiring organism; the carbon dioxide and water are by-products. The specific enzyme reactions that take place are not represented in this simplified diagram. Note that the *net* effect of respiration is the reverse of the *net* effect of photosynthesis.

Fortunately—for animals—plants do not themselves reverse all photosynthesis through plant respiration. It is this fact that makes it possible for consumers to exist. As shown in Figure 1.10b, herbivores and carnivores are completely dependent on plants.

Figure 1.8 shows that three major effects of photosynthesis are significant to our consideration of ecosystems. The first is that energy is converted from electromagnetic or light energy into chemical energy. This brings solar energy into another form that is useful to plants and animals. The second effect of photosynthesis is that simple chemicals are converted into more complicated ones. The third effect is that oxygen is released as a by-product of photosynthesis. All the oxygen in the atmosphere, approximately 20% of the air, probably is a result of photosynthesis that has never been reversed by respiration. Chapter 5 will explain this further.

While plants get their energy from photosynthesis and their nutrients from the soil, all animals ultimately rely on plants for both the energy and nearly all of the nutrients they require. Each species of organism satisfies its need for minerals and energy and finds a good place to live in the unique way that constitutes that species' functional role in the natural scheme. Species compete with one another, and some are dependent on others. Some organisms like it hot. Some like it wet. Some do best where it is hot and dry. Some plants flourish on slopes, and some do better in the shade than in the sun. Physical variables exist in numerous combinations over the surface of the earth, and these factors all bear on the ability of organisms to survive. Therefore we should expect great differences in species composition from one place to another, and there are indeed great differences. The differences are qualitative, however. All ecosystems, all living systems, have their equivalents of producers, consumers, and decomposers.

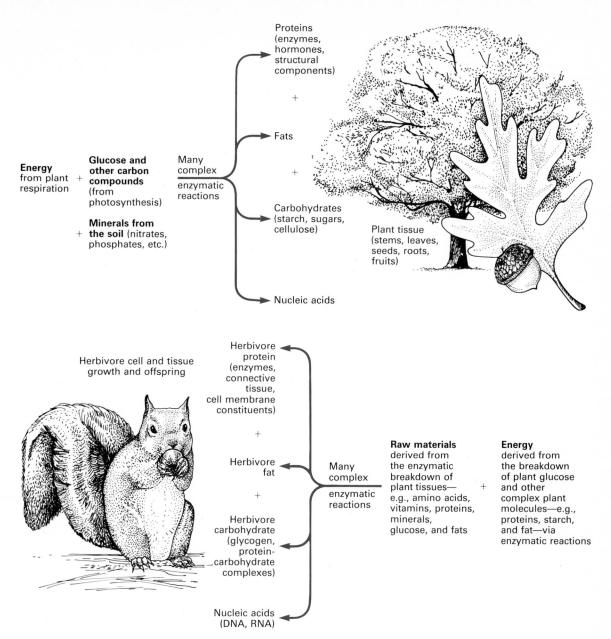

Figure 1.10 Plant and Herbivore Biosynthesis. (a) Plants use some of the chemical energy they produce to convert some of the chemicals they produce into proteins, fats, and carbohydrates. (b) Animals use some of the chemical energy they consume to convert derivatives of some of the chemicals they consume into proteins, fats, and carbohydrates.

BALANCE IN NATURE

If producers produce and give rise to more producers that also produce, how is it that the earth is not overrun by producers and production? Why isn't the earth covered by a thick tangle of brush and vines? If decomposers decompose and give rise to more decomposers, which also cause decomposition, why hasn't everything rotted? In the middle of January there may still be unrotted leaves on the ground. Why don't living things rot even before they die of other causes—they do sometimes; why not all the time? To belabor the point: If consumers consume, if they have babies that also consume, why hasn't everything consumable been consumed by now? From time to time, grasshoppers do strip areas of North Dakota clean. Why doesn't this sort of thing happen more often? How is it that photosynthesis, respiration, and the other processes happening very rapidly in most ecosystems do not seem to change very much? The answer surely lies in some system of checks and balances.

Nature certainly has its ups and downs. There are lots of apples one year and hardly any the next. There are years with large acorn crops and years in which acorns are scarce. There are cycles in game animal populations. There are algae blooms, red tides, and explosions in lemming, cicada, and grasshopper populations. There has been an incredible human population explosion.

In some years there may be drought and fire; in other years there may be too much water. In some years, frosts come late and the peach blossoms freeze. In some centuries, mountain ranges rise up where plains once stood. In spite of all these fluctuations in nature, on certain time scales (decades or even hundreds of years) things seem to stay relatively the same. Over still larger time spans, change can be dramatic. Species of dinosaurs have appeared and disappeared. Over 90% of all the species that ever lived are now extinct. Time frame is very important to the question of whether nature is balanced or not.

The numbers of individuals of each species in a community remain relatively constant. Significant changes in these numbers occur only when something upsets natural "balances." This view of balance in nature is, some ecologists say, perpetuated by popular magazines and nature films and is thus part of the lore of the person on the street. Some argue that balance is really an inaccurate term to describe what goes on in nature because population densities are continually changing. Species numbers tend to oscillate about a mean that is "relatively" stable, though subject to change over long periods of time. Other ecologists say "**balance in nature**" is a useful term—if it can be defined as the persistence of ecological systems as a result of their ability to compensate for disruptions. Perhaps the truth about balance in nature can best be illustrated by a short fictionalized tale.

Once upon a time, on an island in a large lake there was a large moose herd. On the same island there was a large wolf pack. The island had lots of succulent vegetation and some tall trees but not much else. For many, many years things stayed pretty much the same on the island. Moose were born to spend a lifetime standing knee-deep in water, browsing on vegetation, and eventually dying.

Some moose, usually the sick ones and occasionally a young one, were eaten by wolves. Wolves were born to spend a lifetime seeking out and running down old or young moose, and eventually dying. A new crop of lush vegetation came up every year, and some of it was eaten by the moose. Not much else happened.

One year there was not much rain on the island. There was even less the following year and still less the year after that. This went on until the island's ponds began to dry up, and the vegetation was not lush anymore. Six years into the drought, things really got bad for the moose. Coincidentally, things really got *good* for the wolves. More moose died than were born. More wolves were born than died. Eight years into the drought, the island's vegetation was even less lush. There were not many moose, but there were lots of sleek, healthy wolves. As the moose became increasingly scarce, things began to go badly for the wolves. Nine years into the drought, more wolves died than were born.

Eleven years after the drought began, the rains came again in abundance. The spring of the following year was glorious; ponds rose, vegetation came back, and the moose that remained experienced no decline in numbers. Because there were not many moose, they were not too hard on the vegetation that year, and lots of it "went to seed," so there was even more vegetation the next year. The wolves were still relatively few in number. Things really began to look good for the moose. The following year, many more moose were born than died. Because there were not many wolves to harass them, most of the moose that were born lived to reproductive age to produce new moose.

Soon, with large numbers of young, inexperienced moose about, things got a lot easier for the wolves, and they too eventually began a slow climb in numbers. Eventually, about 35 or 40 years after the drought began, the number of moose and the number of wolves on the island returned to the levels that existed before the drought. Nature is resilient.

Resilience is unquestionably a better term than balance to describe nature. Nature has the ability to cope with disruptions but this ability is limited. Limitations in the ability of natural systems to snap back from insult and disturbances wrought by humans are at the heart of many of our environmental problems.

In the extreme, nature is sufficiently resilient to withstand *any* human-induced disruption in nature. We need not worry about destroying nature. If we attempt to destroy nature or even inadvertently destroy some of nature, we will obviously destroy ourselves long before all of the natural system is annihilated. Humanity simply cannot survive the systems on which it depends. Some, probably most, of nature will surely remain after the last human being is gone. It is important to keep this in perspective when we talk about human ecology and environmental control. We would be wasting energy to worry about destroying nature; in fact what we worry about is destroying the particular arrangements and particular features of nature that are conducive to our survival and good health.

While ecosystems are resilient and can—within limits—compensate for disruptions, they also are subject to change. In a later chapter we will consider how natural systems drift. We will examine the factors in natural systems that determine the kinds and degrees of disruptions for which they can compensate, and we will be looking for some ideas about why natural systems sometimes collapse altogether when their elastic limits are reached and exceeded.

Human effects on an ecosystem need not be disruptive. Crown vetch planted along roadways helps to inhibit erosion.

ENVIRONMENTAL PROBLEMS AND THE PRINCIPLES OF ECOLOGY

Our species is now having tremendous reproductive success worldwide. Cultural evolution and human inventiveness have, to a large degree, overcome many of the kinds of restraints and controls previously imposed by nature on humanity. However, our current reproductive success is a temporary phenomenon. Already our species is beginning to reach new limits. We are approaching the limit of our supplies of some fossil fuels—oil, for example. Some say we have reached the point at which there are too many people, too many pollutants, too much waste, too many poisons, and too little food.

The critical question has become: Will natural controls automatically come down hard on human beings, or will we recognize how we seriously strain and disrupt the systems that support us and find ways through our inventiveness to reduce or minimize this impact? Can the human brain, which made possible the tremendous successes our species has enjoyed, also provide the means by which to avert or diminish the disaster that many say looms on the horizon? It is with these questions in mind that we will consider in more detail the ecological principles introduced in this chapter. We will specifically take a very close look at how these principles apply directly to *Homo sapiens*. Our species will not be presented as a villain or as a defiler of nature. We are an integral part of nature. Conceivably, if we can restrict our activities to the kinds and levels that are compatible with the system of which we are part, our species may persist for some time. The question to keep in mind from here on is: What level of human activity and what kinds of human activity can the ecosphere tolerate indefinitely with humankind as one of its integral components?

CONCEPTS TO REMEMBER

1. Ecology deals with organisms at the level of their interaction with other organisms and with their nonliving environment.
2. Different parts of the ecosphere (deserts, lakes, forests, etc.) may look very different, but the same basic structural and functional relationships are found in all of them.
3. The two most basic kinds of relationships in any ecosystem are those having to do with energy flow and those having to do with chemical cycles.
4. Producers, consumers, and decomposers are the basic classes of organisms that comprise ecosystems.

5. Physical/chemical features of the environment (moisture, light level, temperature, soil texture, etc.) influence the organisms that live there, but the reverse is also true: Living things influence their physical/chemical environment.
6. Nature appears to stay the same because ecosystems are self-regulating and resilient, not because populations are static. The size of the population of a particular species may vary within wide limits because of how that population relates to the other elements in the ecosystem.
7. All human environmental problems have their roots in one or more of the fundamental principles of ecology.

DISCUSSION QUESTIONS AND FOOD FOR THOUGHT

1. On a blackboard or a large sheet of paper, draw an ecosystem diagram depicting a self-sufficient, relatively isolated farm family and their farm. Include as many elements as you can, but categorize each according to the broad headings shown in Figure 1.4 and 1.5. Indicate the flow of energy and material using two different kinds of arrows.
2. Modify the diagram developed in item 1 to be applicable to a modern farm that is part of a larger system including a nearby city. List any assumptions you find it necessary to make.
3. *Discuss:* Are the levels of organization illustrated in Figure 1.1 real or arbitrary?
4. Can you think of any species that live very far from the junctions of the great spheres? What special adaptations characterize any such species?
5. Write a short essay with one of the following titles: "Producers Are Really Converters" "A World Without Decomposers" "So Who Needs Consumers Anyway" "Decomposers Are Really *Not* Like Fire"
6. Discuss: "Figure 1.8 is a gross oversimplification."
7. Choose up sides and debate: Resolved: Natural systems are not balanced, they only appear to be. Use the articles by Erlich and Birch and Slobodkin et al. in the bibliography as starting points.
8. List three current environmental problems—acid rain, for example—and discuss how they relate to the principles outlined in this chapter.

REFERENCES AND FURTHER READING

Annual Review of Ecology and Systematics, 1970– Palo Alto, Calif: Annual Review, Inc. Bound volumes of this good ongoing review of developments in ecology are published each year.

Brewer, R., 1979. *Principles of Ecology,* Philadelphia: W. B. Saunders Co. This paperback is designed for sophomore–junior level courses in general ecology. It goes into more detail than we do here (or even in the next three chapters) on the subjects of population and community ecology.

Ehrlich, P. R., and Birch, L. C., 1967. "The 'Balance of Nature' and 'Population Control,' *The American Naturalist* **101**:97–107. This is a classic article that makes the point that the idea of balance with respect to population sizes in nature is at best misleading and at worst false.

Hadley, N. F., and Szarck, S. R., 1981. "Productivity of Desert Ecosystems," *Bioscience* **31**(10): 747–753. This easy-to-read article discusses just how water limitation sets the ecological character of the desert.

Hiatt, B., 1980. "Sulfides Instead of Sunlight," *Mosaic,* July/August, **11**(4):15–21. This is a nontechnical treatment of the unusual, deep-ocean thermal vent communities that draw sustenance from chemo-synthesis rather than photosynthesis.

Houston, D. R., 1979. "Understanding the Game of the Environment: An Illustrated Guide to Understanding Ecological Principles," *Agriculture Information Bulletin No. 426.* Washington , D.C.: U.S.D.A. Forest Service.

Kormondy, E. J., 1984. *Concepts of Ecology,* 3rd ed. Englewood Cliffs, N.J.: Prentice-Hall. This is another, more advanced paperback.

Odum, H. T., 1982. *Systems Ecology: An Introduction.* NY: John Wiley & Sons, This introduction to both theoretical and applied systems ecology is written at an advanced level.

Odum, E. P., 1983. *Basic Ecology.* Philadelphia: W. B. Saunders Co. For readers interested in more detail, this is a good, up-to-date textbook designed for college courses in general ecology.

Pimm, S. L., 1982. *Food Webs.* London: Chapman and Hall Publishing Co.

Seastedt, T. R., and Crossley, D. A., 1984. "The Influence of Arthropods on Ecosystems," *Bioscience* **34**(3):157–161. This article describes the influence of insects on nutrient cycling and other aspects of ecosystems.

Slobodkin, L. B.; Smith, F. E.; and Hairston, N. G., 1967. "Regulation in Terrestrial Ecosystems and the Implied Balance of Nature," *The American Naturalist* **101**:109–124. This classic article is a response to the article by Ehrlich and Birch (also cited here) and makes the point that use of the term *balance* does in fact have utility in ecology.

Smith, R. L., 1980. *Ecology and Field Biology,* 3rd ed. New York: Harper and Row. This is another one of several good college-level textbooks used for courses in ecology.

Energy in Ecosystems

W ithout energy there would be nothing. Never has a statement made anywhere been meant more literally. Without energy, nothing could walk, fly, prowl, dive, swim, chew, slither, hiss, bark, or grow. Einstein showed that even matter is a form of energy. It should be obvious, then, why energy is central to one of the cardinal principles of ecology presented in Chapter 1. One of the most basic ways in which organisms relate to their environment is through their need for energy.

In Chapter 6 we will consider how energy is important to human beings; in this chapter we will consider how energy is important to living things in general. The material presented here has two purposes. One is to help the reader understand living systems by illustrating how energy moves through, and is used by, living systems. The second is to lay a foundation from which we can more intelligently explore the human energy "crisis."

ENERGY AND ENTROPY

Energy

Energy is difficult to define. Let's begin with a simple definition and expand on it.

Energy is the ability to do work. Energy is something that, given the right device, can be converted into a push. Energy can be used to move an object against an opposing force over some distance and thus account for work. Energy is stored work.

In the relationship of energy to work, energy must be defined in terms of space, distance, and spatial order. In a strict physical sense, work always involves movement or displacement of one body relative to another. It takes energy to move a stone away from the earth. The actual amount of **work** done against gravity to move a stone away from the center of the earth equals the force applied to the stone times the distance it is moved. Having been moved "up," the stone has acquired a certain amount of potential energy. Released and allowed to respond to gravity, the stone falls to earth, and its potential energy is converted into **kinetic energy** (the energy of motion) and other forms of energy. In this example it should be fairly obvious that the forms of energy being discussed have meaning only in terms of the spatial relationship between two or more bodies.

With other forms of energy the importance of spatial arrangement may be less obvious, but the concept still holds. Consider chemical energy—that contained in gasoline, for example. The **hydrocarbons** (chemicals that contain carbon and hydrogen in a $1:2$ ratio) in a droplet of gasoline represent a certain amount of chemical energy or chemical potential energy—but only if in the vicinity of this droplet of gasoline there are molecules of oxygen or some other potentially interreactive chemical. Under certain conditions, hydrocarbons and oxygen will combine to form carbon dioxide and water and yield heat energy.

There are actually many different kinds of energy; most of them are illustrated in Figure 2.1. All forms of energy can be expressed in terms of capacity for work or in terms of the amount of heat into which the energy could be converted.

Entropy

If a body of water, or anything else, were heated to a high temperature, the energy held by that body by virtue of its heat would not be available to do work unless another unheated body were available nearby to serve as a sink (a place to which the heat could be moved). Steam can move an engine only if there is some place to which the steam can push a piston, somewhere where there is not as much

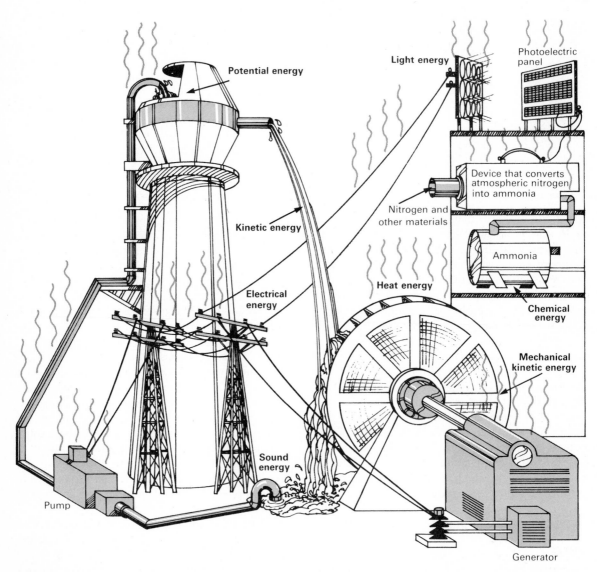

Figure 2.1 Some of the Forms of Energy and Examples of How They Can Be Converted to Other Forms. No conversion from one form of energy to another is 100% efficient; some energy is lost as heat. Actually, heat is a form of energy, and the energy it represents is not lost in the absolute sense. Heat, which tends to disperse rapidly within a system, is the least useful (harnessable) form of energy. If this were a closed system, all activity in it would quickly come to a halt; all the energy would be converted to heat evenly distributed throughout the system.

Part I   Basic Principles of Ecology

Calorie: the unit of energy needed to raise one gram of water one-degree Celsius. Any form of energy has an equivalent in calories. Calories used in connection with diets or food are actually "big" calories, equal to 1000 "little" or *gram calories*. A big calorie will raise the temperature of one kilogram (liter or 1000 cm^2) of water one degree Celsius. Big calories are also called *kilogram calories.*

Closed system: strictly speaking, a system (see Chapter 1) that is totally isolated from everything else. A closed system exchanges neither matter nor energy with its surroundings. Physicists speak of *totally* closed systems, but ecologists sometimes use the phrase "closed system" to refer to systems that do not exchange matter but do exchange energy with their surroundings. The planet Earth is a closed system in the ecological sense.

Energy: ability to do work. In common terms, energy is anything that can be used to change something by pulling, pushing, or heating it.

Entropy: a measure of the energy within a closed system that is unavailable for work within that system.

Gross primary production: total amount of solar energy converted into chemical energy by producers within a unit of time.

Kinetic energy: the energy an object has by virtue of its motion relative to another object.

Net primary production: total amount of organic matter made available by plants to consumers per unit of time; gross primary production minus plant respiration.

Potential energy: the energy an object has by virtue of its position relative to another object; for example, a stone 2 meters above the ground has a certain amount of potential energy and could be used to accomplish some work.

Solar constant or **solar flux:** the average amount of solar energy the earth gets every day from the sun, 2 gram-calories per square centimeter per minute.

Work: strictly speaking, the product of the force applied to an object and the distance that force moves the object against some opposing force. In common terms, work is the name given to what is accomplished when an object is moved against an opposing force such as gravity.

---

steam. A positive electrical charge by definition bears potential work only because there is a relatively negative charge nearby. To be harnessed, energy must flow; it must have someplace to go *to, from* where it is. Thus the usefulness of energy in doing work is directly related to how it is distributed within a system. The more uniformly heat is distributed within a closed system, the less harnessable the heat is for work. **Entropy** is the amount of energy in a system *not* available to work within that system.

Consider a bar of soap in a large volume of water. Each time the soap is used, less of it is available for soaping, even though the body of water—the system—has the same total amount of soap. What happens to soap for soaping—or energy for working—as it is used is that it becomes dispersed, unharnessable. The key to understanding entropy or the "usefulness" of energy is to see that it is related to order, dispersion, and randomness.

Heat is a relatively random form of energy because heat tends to become rapidly dispersed. Figure 2.2 depicts a system, Room A, heated to uniform temperature. If a colder room were placed next to the uniformly heated room, the two-room system would have a nonuniform distribution of heat that could be harnessed to do work as shown. Note that once the two-room system reached a uniform temperature, the heat energy would become unharnessable within that system—the air would stop moving, the fan blades would stop, and no work could be done—even though the two-room system had the same amount of heat energy that it had at the outset.

It is the tendency toward uniform distribution of energy as heat that physicists speak of when they say that the universe is running down.

The Laws of Thermodynamics

To appreciate the behavior of energy in living systems, we must become acquainted with two universal laws of energy, the first and second laws of thermodynamics. These two laws govern all energy transactions in the universe, including those of animals and plants. The laws of thermodynamics form the basis for the principles that energy flows *through* ecosystems and that ecosystems must have continuous inputs of energy.

The **first law of thermodynamics** specifies that energy can be neither created nor destroyed by any process or event but that energy *can* be changed from one form to another. Stated in other words, the total amount of energy in the universe or in any closed system is always the same, though the proportions of the various forms of energy may vary. In still other words, energy that seems to disappear from a "dead" flashlight battery is really still around somewhere, in some form.

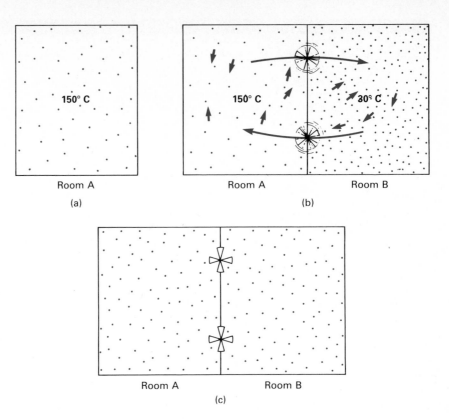

Figure 2.2 A Crude Illustration of Entropy. A room heated uniformly (Room A left) has heat energy, but none can be harnessed to do work in the room. If the room were connected to a *cold* room and holes were made between the rooms at the top and bottom of the common wall (right), the colder, more dense air from room B would flow through the lower opening into room A. The hot air in room A would tend to rise into room B. If vanes were placed in the openings, the flow of air could be harnessed to make the blades rotate as in a windmill. Once the two rooms became uniformly heated, the heat would no longer be harnessable within the two-room system. What might happen if a third room were then hooked up to this system?

Consider Figure 2.1 again. Depicted there are a number of forms of energy and some arrangements by which they could be interconverted.

The first law tells us that no matter what arrangement exists in a system like the one shown in Figure 2.1, no matter what kind of energy is converted into what other kind, the total amount of energy *in a closed system* remains the same.

The **second law of thermodynamics** says, among other things, that some heat is produced—entropy is increased—each time energy is converted from any form to any other. Regardless of the kind of energy, not all of it can be converted into work; some of it is always "lost" as heat in the process of being used. No energetic conversion is 100% efficient. The second law also specifies that spontaneous processes are those in which entropy tends to increase. Energy transformations (conversions from one form to another) in which entropy could *decrease* are not likely to occur spontaneously. The first law of thermodynamics would not be violated if a lake suddenly cooled down a number of degrees (losing heat energy) and at the same time rose several feet into the air (gaining potential energy). Some of the lake's heat energy would simply have been converted into an equal amount of potential

energy. Nothing created, nothing destroyed. The second law says not to expect such a thing because it describes a decrease in entropy, an increase in order—a conversion from a less useful to a more useful energy state. What are some implications of the second law in everyday life?

Life, including human life, is a struggle against the trends described by the second law. After the keys are turned over to the owner of a new house, the owner in effect begins a continuous response to the second law of thermodynamics. A new home is a form of order; a complex combination of chemical and potential energies is represented in its structure. Over time, the assault of weather on shingles and paint, the reaction of air pollutants with paints and fabrics, and the effects of use tend to reduce a house to a scattering of its molecular constituents. A house must be maintained, repaired, and kept up at great expense. It is because of the second law of thermodynamics that homeowners spend Saturday mornings traveling to and from hardware stores.

Think of an abandoned house. Gradually, the roof develops leaks. Gradually, water gets into the house, and weathering takes its toll. Rotting begins. Eventually, the house collapses into a heap. If such a house were located in the eastern part of the

Energy flows through ecosystems—from sunlight to plants to herbivores (like these American bison) to the organisms that consume the herbivores and eventually to decomposers.

United States, the lot on which the house stood would eventually become part of a deciduous forest. One kind of order would be replaced by another. While at first this might seem to belie the universal tendency toward disorder, forest order is made possible only by a colossal amount of solar energy. While the forest was replacing the house, the sun was losing order. The system made up of the house, the forest, and the sun actually experienced a great increase in entropy in the process.

Life is characterized by an ability to extract order from the environment, to bring about an increase in order at the expense of a decrease in order somewhere else. This violates neither the first nor the second law of thermodynamics, since these laws govern only total, closed systems. For plants and ecosystems the "somewhere else" is ultimately the sun. Ecosystems extract order from solar energy as it passes by on its way to dilution throughout the universe.

Suppose we filled a large, clean jar with a handful of humus and leaves dug from a forest floor and then sealed the jar and had some way of measuring exactly what went on in the jar from that point forward in terms of energy. If the jar were properly shielded from light or from any other energy input, we would in effect have given to the jar system a certain amount of chemical energy. We would have invariably included organisms of decay with the leaves and humus, and these decomposers would break down the chemicals in the leaves, extracting the chemical components and the energy for their activities and growth. The second law of thermodynamics says that such a closed system must inevitably wind down because every time one chemical is converted into another, some energy is converted to heat. The jar would give off heat over time. Eventually, all of the original energy would be converted to heat (entropy) and all living activity in the jar would grind to a halt (though this is a simplified description of the process).

THE EARTH'S ENERGY BUDGET

The earth is like a jar of rotting leaves in that it has a decreasing amount of chemical energy stored in the form of coal and oil. The earth is unlike a jar full of leaves in that it has a daily energy income—from the sun.

The Source

If our coal and oil reserves are like a candle, which some claim we are burning at both ends, the sun is figuratively a lifetime battery for the ecosphere. Literally, the sun is a thermonuclear fusion reactor. Every second, some 4.2 million tons of the sun's mass is converted into 10^{26} calories of energy. Although the rate of conversion of mass into energy on the sun is enormous, the sun is so large that there is enough of it left to allow this process to go on for billions of years.

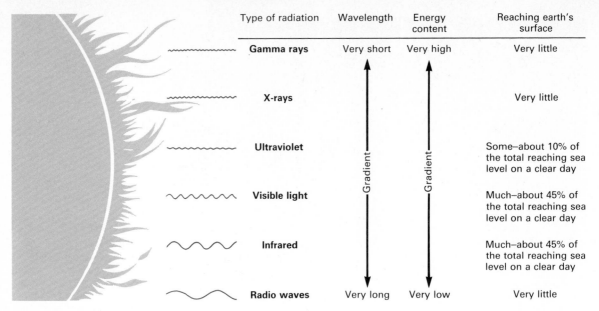

Type of radiation	Wavelength	Energy content	Reaching earth's surface
Gamma rays	Very short	Very high	Very little
X-rays			Very little
Ultraviolet			Some—about 10% of the total reaching sea level on a clear day
Visible light			Much—about 45% of the total reaching sea level on a clear day
Infrared			Much—about 45% of the total reaching sea level on a clear day
Radio waves	Very long	Very low	Very little

Figure 2.3   The Solar Emission Spectrum and the Relative Amounts of Each Type of Radiation Reaching the Earth. The earth's atmosphere is relatively opaque to most high-energy forms of radiation such as X-rays and gamma rays. Most of these get absorbed high in the atmosphere.

The specific energy-releasing reaction taking place on the sun is the fusion of hydrogen into helium. Two molecules of hydrogen are fused to form a molecule of helium, and a helium molecule weighs *almost* twice as much as two molecules of hydrogen. The difference, or the lost mass, is converted into energy according to the equation $E = mc^2$.

The energy generated from solar mass emerges in the form of electromagnetic radiation (including light), heat, and other forms of energy. Because neither heat nor sound can cross the near vacuum of space, the only kinds of energy that reach us here on earth are the electromagnetic varieties. The electromagnetic spectrum of solar radiation is presented in Figure 2.3. Though a rather wide spectrum of energy is shown in this illustration, about 99% of the radiation that reaches the earth is in the range encompassing *visible* light, near-infrared, and (a little) ultraviolet radiation.

Solar Constant

As electromagnetic energy streams away from the sun in all directions, it becomes less concentrated with distance. The earth, a small target some 150 million kilometers (93 milliion miles) from the sun, intercepts only 1/50 millionth of the sun's energy output. This amounts to about two gram calories per square centimeter per minute. Two calories per square centimeter per minute, a constant some-

times referred to as the **solar flux** or **solar constant**, is the average amount of energy the earth gets every day—some for photosynthesis, some to heat the atmosphere, and some to be expended in other ways important to living things.

Solar Energy, Weather, and Climate

As illustrated in Figure 2.4, of the energy that reaches the outer atmosphere of the earth, on the average about 42% is reflected by clouds and dust in the atmosphere. Another 10% or so is absorbed by molecules of ozone, water vapor, and other gases in the atmosphere, leaving less than half the solar flux to reach the surface of the earth. Although our primary interest in this chapter is in the tiny fraction of solar energy that is converted into chemical energy by plants, we should pause and consider some of the other things solar energy does for living systems.

Solar energy warms the earth; it causes evaporation of water and brings rain; and it drives the winds. The influences that the earth has on the absorption of solar energy by virtue of its shape, its atmosphere, its orbit around the sun, its rotation, and its topography mean the differences between night and day, the seasons, deserts and tropical rain forests, the poles and the equator, life and no life. Let's consider some of the details.

Weather and climate are the direct and indirect results of solar heating. The atmosphere is the first thing to experience the sun's rays in the morning, but actually only a little of the incident radiation heats the gases of the atmosphere as sunlight comes in. Of the energy that is absorbed by water vapor and other atmospheric gases, some is reemitted as infrared radiation, and some of this reaches and warms the ground. Some of the energy absorbed by atmospheric gases is converted directly into molecular kinetic energy (heat). However, most of the heating of the atmosphere is done from the bottom up (see Figure 2.5).

A highly variable fraction of the sunlight that reaches the earth's surface is reflected all the way back into space. Snow or white sand reflects much more than does black volcanic rock or vegetation. In any case, some of the radiant energy that reaches the earth's surface (including both direct sunlight and radiation reemitted by clouds and atmospheric

gases) is absorbed (see Figure 2.4). Some of this energy heats the ecosphere directly; some is reemitted as infrared radiation. Reemitted infrared radiation would also travel back into space except that some of the same gases that allowed the visible light *in* will not let infrared radiation *out*. The fact that carbon dioxide and other gases will not absorb much visible light but will absorb infrared radiation is the basis of the so-called greenhouse effect, which we will discuss in Chapter 10.

The atmosphere can be heated by the earth in three general ways: conduction, radiation, and heat transfer. Heat can be passed from the earth to air by direct conduction (contact). Infrared radiation emitted from the earth's surface can be absorbed by water vapor, carbon dioxide, and other gases, increasing their kinetic energy. Warming of the surface can also cause surface waters to evaporate; water that evapo-

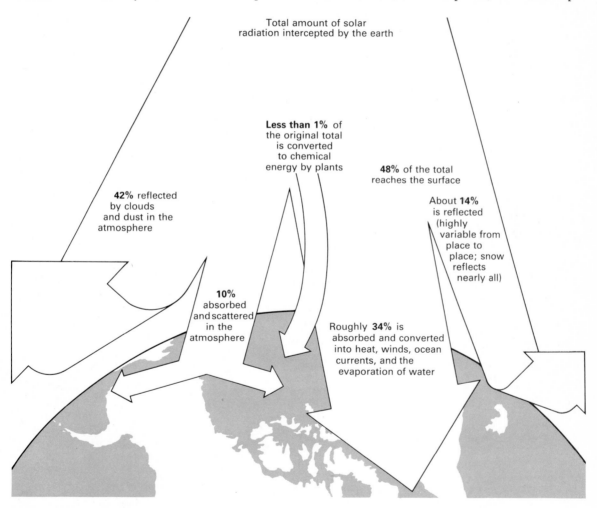

Figure 2.4 The Fate of the Solar Energy That Is Intercepted by the Planet Earth. About half of this remains in the atmosphere or is reflected back into space.

rates at the surface and later condenses in the atmosphere actually transfers heat into the atmosphere.

The atmosphere is heated unevenly. Heating causes air to expand, and uneven heating leads to uneven expansion and differential densities of air. Hot air rises, and cold air falls and moves to fill in the space left by the hot air (Figure 2.5). In other words, uneven heating leads to *wind*. The winds and other air movements can carry water vapor from warm places to cold places, where the vapor condenses and falls back to earth. Thus air movement leads to rain and snow. In Chapter 3 we will consider the role of sun-driven weathering by wind and rain in biogeochemical cycles (see also Figure 2.7).

Keep in mind that energy budgets for particular parts of the earth vary considerably. The earth ro-

---

Solar Energy and Climate

Although every place on the earth gets an average of 12 hours of sunlight per day over the course of a year, not all places get the same amount of solar energy or heat. The amount of energy delivered to a square meter of the earth's surface is a function of the angle of the sun's rays. The most energy is delivered per unit of area when the sun is directly overhead.

The plane of the earth's rotation and the plane of its orbit around the sun are such that the place on earth where the sun is directly overhead changes with both the time of day and the season. On any given day the sun will pass directly over all of the points over a certain line of latitude—a line or narrow stripe that goes all the way around the earth from east to west.

Over the course of a year the path of the overhead sun moves north and south from the extreme of the tropic of Cancer (23.5°N) in the northern hemisphere at summer solstice, gradually to the equator, which it reaches at fall equinox, past the equator to the Tropic of Capricorn (23.5°S) in the southern hemisphere at winter solstice (shortest day of the year in the northern hemisphere). The *torrid zone* between these latitudes obvi-

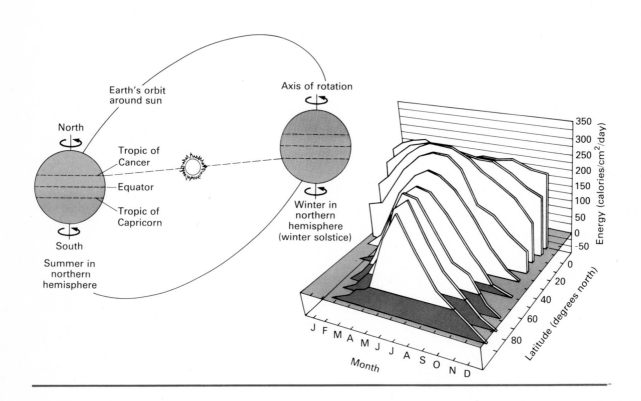

Part I Basic Principles of Ecology

tates such that half of it is in darkness at this very moment. Since the earth is a globe, solar radiation strikes it at a complete spectrum of angles with the surface ranging from perpendicular to parallel; the earth is farther from the sun at some times of the year than at others, with different parts of the earth at different angles (accounting for the seasons of the year). What all of this means is that the actual amount of radiation striking a field, pond, or lake

varies considerably from one place to the next, from one day to the next, from one season to the next, and from one hour of the day to the next. It is only *on the average* that two calories per square centimeter per minute strike the outer atmosphere and approximately one calorie per square centimeter per minute strikes the surface of the earth.

One final meteorological note in closing: Radiation equilibrium does not prevail at all latitudes.

ously gets much more solar energy during the year than other more northerly and southerly places. This accounts directly for the contrast between the richness of the flora and fauna in the tropics and the relative lifelessness of the polar regions.

The amount of energy delivered to each latitude during the course of the year is illustrated at left. Note that in certain months the northernmost latitudes lose more energy than they gain. The mean temperature of the earth decreases 4°C for every degree of latitude at sea level.

The basic air movements or wind patterns for the globe are shown in the figure below. On the average, air tends to rise directly over the equator because it is heated most and becomes relatively least dense. Air moves in from either side of the equator to replace the rising air because of the earth's rotation; this "moving in" becomes the northeast and southwest trade winds. The air that rises over the equator falls again over the 30 degrees north and south latitude, and this coupled with the air falling over the poles drives the prevailing westerlies.

Actually, because of the north-south movement of the overhead sun band, the latitude above which air rises most strongly also shifts from one side of the equator to the other during the year. The zone where the air rises most strongly is called the **intertropical convergence zone.** Shifting of the intertropical convergence zone causes seasonal rains in the tropics. It rains in the intertropical convergence zone, but to either side north and south there is no rain unless moving air is forced to go up over mountains. This brings us to another point.

Wherever air rises very far, it cools such that its water vapor eventually condenses and falls as rain. This accounts both for intertropical convergence zone rains, which fall practically every afternoon, and for the fact that where air descends, there is little if any rainfall. The latter explains why many deserts of the world are located near 30 degrees latitude. Elsewhere on the globe, air is forced to give up its moisture as rainfall when it must go up over mountains or where warm air is forced up over cooler air masses (see Chapter 3).

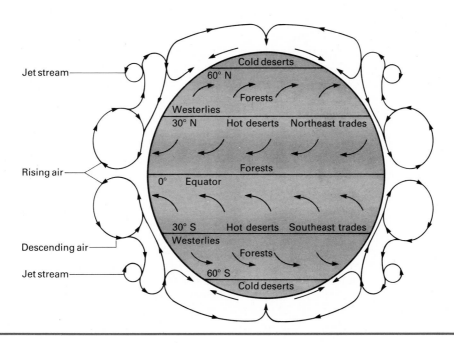

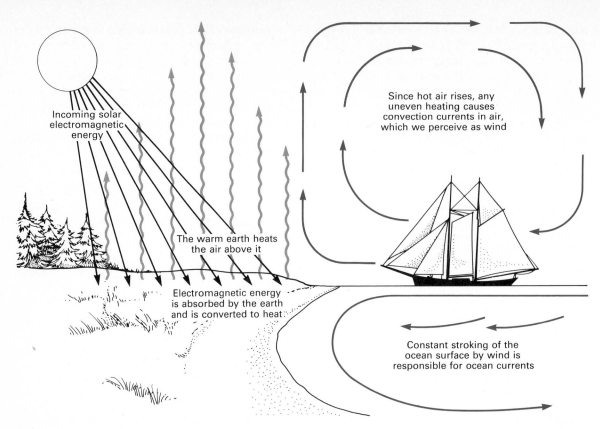

Figure 2.5 The Energy That Causes Winds and Ocean Currents Comes from the Sun by Way of the Surface of the Earth. During most of the year in many places the sun heats up the land during the day, so it is warmer than the ocean. As the air over the land is heated, it rises, and cooler air over the ocean moves in as a sea breeze to take its place. At night, the ocean is warmer than the land, so the breeze shifts from the land out to sea.

That is, not all areas of the earth radiate as much back into space as they receive from the sun. Some of the solar energy coming into equatorial regions, for instance, is dissipated into other zones via winds and ocean currents. This meteorologic distribution of heat helps moderate climate; it blends what would otherwise be distinct zones having more profound differences in climate.

ECOSYSTEM ENERGY BUDGETS

According to Odum (1983), of the electromagnetic energy striking a typical ecosystem, less than half is absorbed by the plants directly. Only a small fraction is of the right wavelengths to be absorbed specifically by chlorophyll and converted into chemical energy in photosynthesis. On the average, the efficiency of energy fixation by green plants is less than 1%.

As shown in Table 2.1, the efficiencies of energy fixation in various ecosystems actually range from a fraction of 1% up to 7% or so. During optimal growing conditions, corn, one of the most efficient energy capturers, converts about 3.2% of solar radiation into the chemical energy in kernels, cobs, silk, stalks, roots, and leaves and uses another 3.6% (for a total of 6.8%) in its own metabolic activities.

Care must be taken in interpreting "efficiency" as it is used here. We have based our figures on *total* solar energy reaching leaves, even though some portions of the visible light spectrum cannot be absorbed by plants. This, you might say, really is not fair. But we think it is, as long as we qualified what we did. The reader should realize that qualifiers are important here. Efficiency would be one thing if computed for corn that is free of disease on a hot sunny day following a soaking rain in a fertilized field and quite another if computed on a per-year basis (counting the winter, in which there might be less solar input but *no* production).

Figures 2.6 and 2.7 summarize what happens to

Table 2.1 Solar Input Versus Primary Productivity in Nature and Agriculture. Note that a direct comparison cannot be made between the natural and agricultural efficiencies here. The natural figures are computed on a year-long basis (including nongrowing season), while only the best conditions for productivity were used in calculating the agricultural efficiency. This was done to show that even with this advantage the increase over natural efficiencies is not all that great.

	Efficiency of Gross Production[1]	Efficiency of Net Production[2]	Percent Net/Gross Production
In Nature[3]			
Maximum	5%	4%	80%
Average favorable condition	1%	0.5%	50%
Average for biosphere	0.2%	0.1%	50%
With Human Intervention[4]			
Sugar cane field	7.6%	4.8%	62%
Corn	6.8%	3.2%	47%
Sugar beets	7.7%	5.4%	72%

[1] Efficiency of gross production is the percent of electromagnetic energy reaching a system that is captured by plants and converted into chemical energy.
[2] Efficiency of net production is the percent of electromagnetic energy reaching the system that is captured by plants and available to plant eaters.
[3] Long-term averages over the entire year or longer.
[4] Short-term productivity (best days) with intense cultivation.

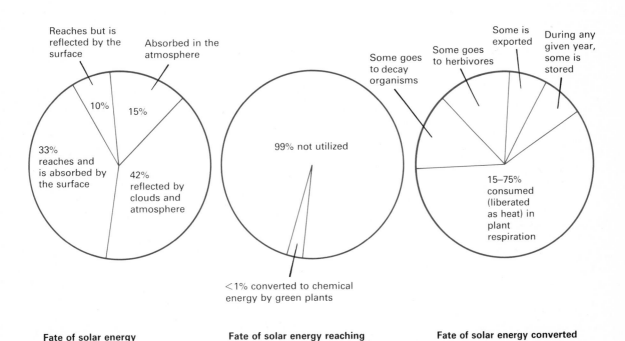

Fate of solar energy reaching earth

Fate of solar energy reaching green plants (the surface)

Fate of solar energy converted into chemical energy by green plants in any ecosystem

Figure 2.6 What Happens to Solar Energy on Its Way and Through an Ecosystem. Only one part in fifty million of the sun's energy reaches the earth. Of that amount, less than 1% is converted to chemical energy by green plants.

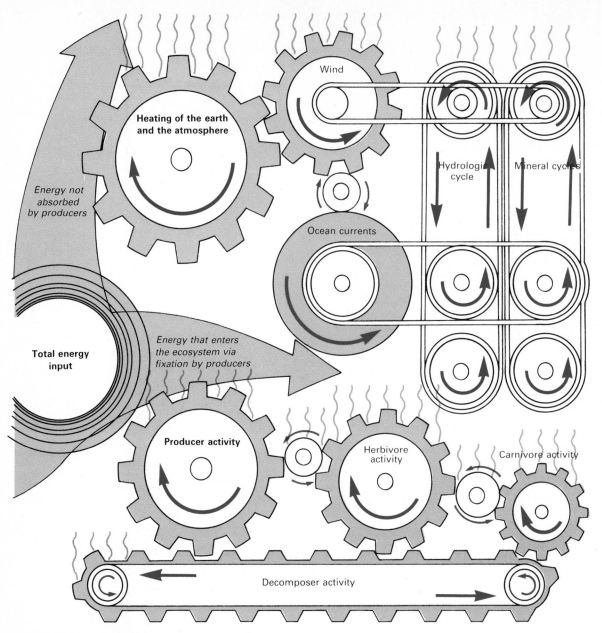

Figure 2.7 Almost Without Exception, If It Is Happening, the Sun is Making It Happen. The earth and its ecosystems can be thought of as rather inefficient interrelated engines, all powered by the sun. Mineral cycles driven by the sun are covered in Chapter 3.

energy from the time it starts out on the sun until it passes through an ecosystem here on earth.

ENERGY FLOW THROUGH LIVING SYSTEMS

About one tenth of one percent (0.1%) of the energy that the earth gets from the sun is fixed or converted into chemical energy by plants in photosynthesis (Woodwell, 1970). One tenth of one percent of what the earth receives as solar energy over a year is a considerable amount of energy. In the temperate zone the daily conversion of sunlight into chemical energy is equivalent to 300–400 calories per square centimeter (Odum, 1983).

Net Versus Gross Production

You may remember from Chapter 1 that the conversion of solar energy into chemical energy (photosynthesis) constitutes **primary production**. Primary production is the accomplishment of producers. We can also speak of **primary productivity**, the *rate* of production by plants; that is, how much production goes on per hour, per day, per minute, or per year. Primary production or productivity is the rate at which the photosynthetic equation moves from left to right:

$$6CO_2 + 12H_2O \xrightarrow[\text{energy}]{\text{solar}} C_6H_{12}O_6 + 6H_2O + 6O_2$$

In the absolute sense, productivity means the total amount of this reaction that occurs in a unit of time. Of course, not all of the sugar made in photosynthesis goes on to become plant matter; the plants oxidize (respire) some of the glucose for the energy they themselves need. In effect, in plant respiration, plants reverse some of the photosynthesis they carry out. Because the proportion of photosynthesis that leads to accumulated plant mass varies from plant to plant and with varying conditions of a plant's physical/chemical environment, ecologists have found it useful to distinguish *net production* and *gross production*.

In all the earth's ecosystem, both terrestrial and marine, about 160–170 billion metric tons of dry organic matter are produced annually (Woodwell, 1970). This amount of organic matter is presented to the earth by plants each year and constitutes *net* primary production for the ecosphere. As was stated above, plants use up some chemical energy each year for their own metabolic needs. The chemical energy plants use up plus *net* production equal *gross* production. The **gross primary productivity** of an ecosystem, then, is the total rate of the conversion of solar energy into chemical energy in that system. **Net primary productivity** is the rate at which plants make chemical energy available to consumers and decomposers or for storage or export. Depending on the type of plant and other factors, the amount of organic matter used up in plant respiration ranges from 15% to 75% of the total amount of organic matter produced by the plants (Table 2.1).

Of the net primary production in an ecosystem, herbivores and decomposers may not consume all of the organic matter produced by plants in any given period. The expression **net community productivity** or net ecosystem productivity is sometimes used to describe the rate at which organic matter is accumulated (stored) in an ecosystem. Net community production (or net ecosystem production) is equivalent to net primary production minus the organic matter respired or used by consumers and decomposers.

Sometimes the rate at which chemical energy accumulates at the level of the consumer (e.g., kilograms of rabbit per year) is referred to as **secondary production**. This is really an inappropriate term; consumers assimilate rather than produce. Henceforth in this chapter we will use the term production or productivity to refer only to plants, and we will often not use the adjective primary.

On a year to year basis, for the earth as a whole there is virtually *no* net ecosphere production (total annual added plant and animal biomass). Nearly all that is produced is consumed in the respiration of plants, herbivores, carnivores, omnivores, and decomposers. The result is the near complete annual return to the environment of carbon dioxide and water, effectively reversing the chemical effects of the photosynthesis that went on during that year.

Plant material does not pile up in a mature forest. The thickness of the deposit of leaves on a forest floor stays about the same from year to year. During any year there seems to be about as much death, decomposition, and rotting as there is new plant growth and as there are new offspring.

At certain periods in the early development of an ecosystem, however—starting from bare, burned-over land, for instance—there are periods of considerable annual production. Net production in an ecosystem varies with its age and certain other factors.

Factors That Affect Productivity

Factors other than the age of ecosystems affect both net production and gross production. The productivity of a particular plant or population of any plant species depends upon growing conditions, that is, the factors that limit plant growth: access to water and nutrients, temperature, sunlight, wind, and slope, to name a few. Still other factors include physical characteristics of the soil, humidity, and, in aquatic environments, cloudiness (transparency) of the water. With variations in any or all of these the same plant species would exhibit different annual productivities at different latitudes or even in different locations in the same field. Genetics is another factor. Different kinds of plants have different rates of production under similar circumstances; some are simply more efficient producers than others.

In general, net productivity is affected by the same factors that affect gross productivity. Some of these factors also affect the ratio of net production to gross production. Human beings long ago learned to identify plants with high *net* productivity as particularly useful for food and/or fiber. They also long ago discovered that some of the factors affecting gross and net productivity can be manipulated. The use of fertilizer and irrigation are two examples. Phosphates and nitrates are limited in most ecosystems, and adding them can enhance the rate at which plants can convert solar energy into chemical energy to human advantage.

Carbon dioxide may be another one of the limiting factors in production. Carbon dioxide, which is certainly an important ingredient in the photosynthetic equation, is a plausible limiting factor. Woodwell (1970) has suggested that the increase of about 10% in carbon dioxide in the atmosphere that has occurred since the middle of the nineteenth century may have increased net production worldwide by as much as 10%.

The development of "miracle grains" has a special relationship to the concept of net production. Plant breeding and artificial selection have been used extensively to maximize net production and also to maximize net *edible* production. Not all of what plants provide as net production can be eaten by any one species. Plant geneticists have developed plant varieties that put maximum amounts of chem-

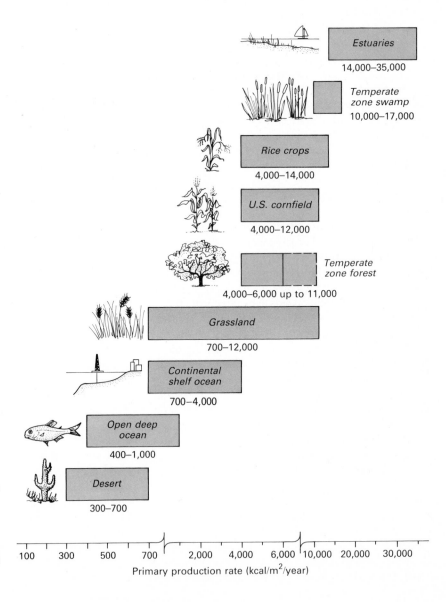

Figure 2.8 Relative Rates of Primary Production in Some Natural and Managed Systems. We have chosen to express annual production in terms of big calories or kilocalories (1000 little or gram calories) here, but we could just as easily express it in terms of grams dry weight. An approximate average conversion factor is 4 kilocalories per dry gram.

Estuaries
14,000–35,000

Temperate zone swamp
10,000–17,000

Rice crops
4,000–14,000

U.S. cornfield
4,000–12,000

Temperate zone forest
4,000–6,000 up to 11,000

Grassland
700–12,000

Continental shelf ocean
700–4,000

Open deep ocean
400–1,000

Desert
300–700

Primary production rate (kcal/m²/year)

Part I   Basic Principles of Ecology

ical energy into those parts (seeds and fruits, for example) that human beings and/or domestic animals can eat.

Productivities of the Major Subdivisions of the Ecosphere

Because the ecosystems of the world vary in almost every factor that influences net production, it is not surprising that annual rates of production vary considerably from one subdivision of the ecosphere to another (see Figure 2.8). Relatively high rates of production are characteristic of the tropics, swamps, estuaries, and marshes, places in which conditions are ideal for the growth of plants. Intensive agriculture, with its "artificial" addition of fertilizer and water and with pest and disease control, also favors relatively high plant productivity. Deserts, oceans, and tundras have low rates of primary production, attributable to combinations of limiting factors such as temperature, water, and nutrients. In the oceans, light penetration is a chief limiting factor.

The open oceans are relatively unproductive in comparison with terrestrial ecosystems. Although they cover most of the earth's surface, the oceans

Productive ecosystems like forests may contain a great variety of species. The Indian pipe plant, which lacks chlorophyll, gets its food from decaying organic matter through an association of its roots with fungi.

Ocean ecosystems have feeding levels like those on land. The man-of-war is a secondary (or higher-order) consumer.

contribute less than a third of the annual primary production on earth. With a mean productivity of 50–55 grams of dry organic matter per square (surface) meter per year (Woodwell, 1970), oceans may not represent the "vast exploitable source of food energy" described by some. Some authors, in fact, have suggested that the oceans are already being exploited for food (fish) at close to the maximum sustainable rate (based on average measurable productivity) and that the continued use of the oceans as dumps for wastes may actually bring this resource to an even lower level of productivity (see Chapter 12).

The oceans are not all the same, obviously; some parts of some oceans are highly productive. In the open sea, relatively high productivity can be found in places where there are favorable combinations of warm temperatures, upwelling of nutrients, and sunlight. Estuaries, where oceans meet land and mineral-laden rivers, are among the most highly productive places on earth.

Forests, in contrast to oceans, are quite productive. Gross production in one forest on Long Island was shown by Woodwell and Whitaker

(1968) to be in the neighborhood of 2600 grams per square meter per year. Net community production in this particular forest system approached 1200 grams per year, an amount suggesting that this ecosystem was immature, that is, it was still accumulating organic matter on a year-to-year basis. The forest in the Woodwell and Whitaker study had—in terms of solar energy availability—an efficiency of gross primary production approaching 1%. Other forests have been reported to have annual efficiencies of up to 3%.

According to the ecologist Eugene Odum (1983), on the average for all kinds of ecosystems, about 50% of gross production is available to plant eaters and decomposers. It is important to remember, however, that this is highly variable.

How Is Primary Productivity Measured?

The most important activity-determining, life-supporting characteristic of an ecosystem is primary productivity. One can derive a lot of information about an ecosystem if its level of primary productivity is known. For otherwise suitable habitats we would know roughly how many herbivores—be they cattle, rabbits, or deer—could be supported in a system of known productivity. Because of its importance, ecologists have devised a number of techniques and methods for measuring primary productivity.

All of the techniques used to measure productivity are based on the fact that the photosynthetic equation is a *balanced equation*. The net effect of the very complex photosynthetic process is that six moles of carbon dioxide (CO_2) (264.066 g) and twelve moles of water (H_2O) (216.192 g) are incorporated into every mole of glucose ($C_6H_{12}O_6$) (180.162 g) and every six moles of oxygen (O_2) (192 g) and six moles of water (H_2O) (108.096 g) produced in photosynthesis. (A **mole** is the molecular weight of a compound expressed in grams.)

Some relatively simple ways of estimating *net* productivity include (1) measuring the amount of oxygen produced in a system per unit time; (2) measuring how much carbon dioxide is consumed per unit time; and (3) harvesting, drying, and weighing the plant material that accumulates in a period of time. Estimates can also be made by determining how much chlorophyll is present in an ecosystem. For each of the methods the facts that respiration and photosynthesis are coupled in living systems (the raw material for one comes from the other) and that they are going on simultaneously must be taken into account.

Light Bottle, Dark Bottle: A Method for the Separation of the Effects of Respiration and Photosynthesis. Suppose we lowered two bottles into a pond to a level of one meter with the bottles weighted somehow so that they could be lowered to that level while empty (Figure 2.9). Suppose we also had a device for opening the bottles at the level of two feet and then resealing them. Such a device would allow water and pond organisms to enter the bottles; consumers and producers would be included. Suppose that we filled the bottles on a particular day at noon, sealed them, and permitted them to remain in place for two hours.

In both bottles, production and respiration would go on. Carbon dioxide and water would be taken up in *photosynthesis* and released in *respiration*. If we had a way of measuring changes in these substances, changes in carbon dioxide content, or changes in oxygen and glucose that were produced, we would be measuring the net effects of these two generalized equations. We would be measuring *net pond production* or *net (pond) ecosystem production*.

Suppose that we had painted one of the bottles black so that no sunlight could get to the inside. What then? Obviously, photosynthesis could not go on; only respiration could. Oxygen and carbohydrate material would be consumed, and carbon dioxide and water would be produced as a byproduct; no oxygen or glucose would be *produced*. With both a light and a dark bottle we would have a way of estimating how much gross production actually takes place.

By measuring the amount of oxygen in both bottles at the beginning and at the end of a period of time we would know two things: (1) how much oxygen was consumed in respiration (dark bottle oxygen change) and (2) how much oxygen was produced (light bottle oxygen change) in a bottle in which *both respiration and photosynthesis were going on at the same time*. Assuming that the same amount of respiration went on in both bottles, if we subtracted the change in oxygen in the dark bottle from the change in oxygen in the light bottle, we would have an estimate of the amount of oxygen that was produced as a by-product of photosynthesis per unit of time.

Net productivity can also be measured in terms of biomass, the weight of (dry) organic material accumulated over a period of time. If we have such data in grams, let's say, all we would need to do is sample some of that biomass in a device in which the caloric content of organic material can be measured, that is, by the amount of heat released when that

Light bottle

Photosynthesis
Respiration

Dark bottle

Respiration
only

Change in oxygen content
in one hour reflects
<u>net</u> production

+

Change in oxygen content
in one hour reflects
<u>total</u> respiration

=

Gross
production

Figure 2.9 Estimating Production (Gross) in a Pond by the Light Bottle/Dark Bottle Method. The equation shows how gross productivity is calculated. Net productivity during one daylight hour can be estimated from the change in oxygen content in the light bottle.

organic material is combined with oxygen. We would then have a precise measurement of the energy content of that biomass and could express the material that accumulated in an ecosystem over time as energy in calories.

Specialized Ways of Stating Production. The U.S. Department of Agriculture periodically publishes estimates of the number of bushels of corn, wheat, and other crops that will be produced in one year in the United States. This is a useful expression of net production. As we stated earlier, humans are consumers of only certain kinds of food. We are not really interested in the weight of wheat stalks produced; we are interested in the weight of the grain. As we will see in Chapter 6, the use of biomass as fuel may change that focus.

What Happens to Energy in Ecosystems Once It Is Produced?

Figure 2.10 summarizes how energy flows into, through, and out of ecosystems. As we have already discussed, plants utilize some of the chemical energy that they produce for their own activities. The same pattern applies to herbivores and to carnivores higher up in the food chain. Herbivores and carnivores take some of the energy they capture and use it to do the things that they do, that is, grow, carry out metabolic activities, and expend energy through various mechanical activities. Some of the energy assimilated or fixed at each level is available to the next level up—to the carnivores in the form of herbivores. In every case, some of it ends up going to the decomposers; decomposers use up the last bits of "useful" energy that enter an ecosystem, releasing it ultimately as heat.

Note in Figure 2.10 that not all of the energy that comes into an ecosystem comes in as solar energy; some of it is imported. Leaves blown into a pond from a forest are an example of imported chemical energy. A frog that eats an insect that flew out of a forest is importing energy. A forest bird that eats a fish from a pond is carrying energy in the opposite direction, exporting it from the *pond* ecosystem. Similarly, a raccoon that eats a freshwater

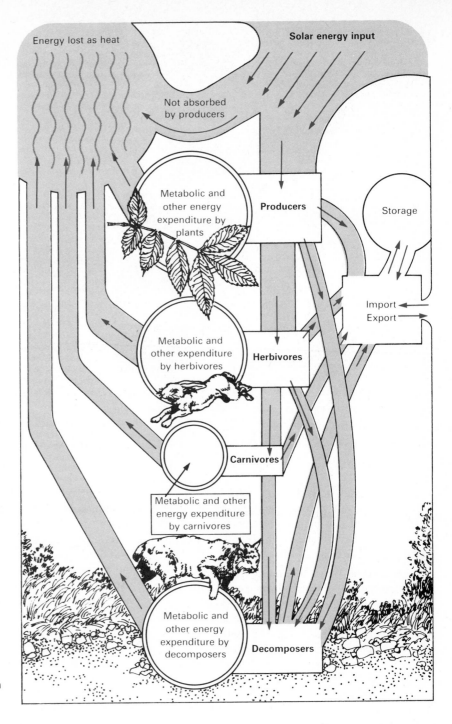

Figure 2.10 Energy Flow Through an Ecosystem. The amount of energy traveling by each path may vary greatly from one system to another, but the pathways are basically identical.

mussel from a pond is an exporter of energy from the pond ecosystem.

Chemical energy may also be temporarily stored out of the mainline of energy flow in an ecosystem. Coal is an example of a long-term version of such storage. Organic matter remaining as humus over a period of time would qualify as a short-term form of ecosystem storage.

Like the cabbage looper, all primary consumers must eat huge amounts of vegetation to satisfy their energy needs.

Efficiencies of Energy Transfers Within Ecosystems

We have already mentioned a number of times that the efficiencies of primary production are very low; less than 1% of available energy is captured by plants and ecosystems. Beyond the producers, efficiencies of transfer increase a bit. Here, too, there may be considerable variation from one ecosystem to another. Depending on the ecosystem, and certain physical/chemical factors, up to 50% of the chemical energy present in the form of producers is transferred to the primary consumers. In turn, somewhere between 5% and 30% of the energy present in the form of primary consumers makes its way to the secondary consumers or carnivores. *On the average,* about 10% of the energy entering a particular feeding level is transferred to the next level. That is, if

10% of the energy available in the form of plants ends up being incorporated into secondary consumers, then 10% of 10% of 10% is available to the next or tertiary level of consumption. The *10% law,* as it is sometimes called, is one of the reasons why if you set out to count the number of animals you see in a forest, you will count more herbivores than carnivores. It is much easier to find plants as you walk through the woods; it is somewhat more difficult to find a primary consumer; and only rarely does one encounter a secondary consumer such as a mountain lion.

Pyramids: Why There Are More Plants Than Plant Eaters

The second law of thermodynamics forces the "shape" of ecosystems into so-called ecological pyramids; the number of ecosystem components *decreases* with distance from the primary producer level (see Figure 2.11). A rapidly diminishing amount of energy is available as the number of steps away from the primary producer increases. Because of this, typically only three to five feeding levels will exist in an ecosystem. We have been referring up to this point to feeding levels, but ecologists call them **trophic levels** (trophic coming from the Latin word meaning to eat or to feed). Figure 2.11 illustrates that the higher the trophic level, the fewer organisms there are. Since some organisms are big and some are little, perhaps this relationship should more accurately be expressed in terms of mass—or even better, in terms of energy. If we dried and weighed all the organisms in a representative area of any ecosystem, we would have to infer that it takes hundreds of thousands of kilograms of (dry) producer biomass to

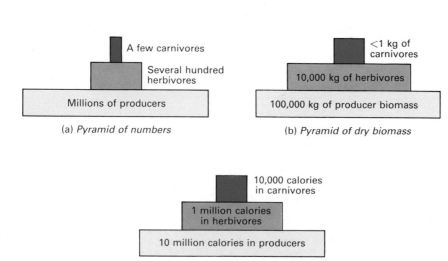

(a) *Pyramid of numbers*

(b) *Pyramid of dry biomass*

(c) *Pyramid of energy content*

Figure 2.11 The Shape of Ecosystems. Practically any way of looking at producers and consumers—in terms of numbers, weight, or energy content—yields a pyramid shape that results from the inefficiency of energy transfers, the use of some energy by the members of each trophic level, and the fact that some energy goes directly to decomposers and storage from each level.

Chapter 2 Energy in Ecosystems

support tens of thousands of kilograms of herbivore biomass to support in turn less than a kilogram of carnivore mass.

By measuring the caloric content of the different types of biomass at each level we could express biomass in terms of caloric (energy) content by assuming an average caloric value of dry organic matter. Kormondy (1984) uses the value of four kilocalories per dry gram as an arbitrary average (this, according to Kormondy, is somewhat on the low side). At any rate, tens of millions of calories in the form of producers are needed to support millions of calories in the form of herbivores, to support tens of thousands of calories in the form of carnivores, and so on. We depict just three trophic levels in Figure 2.11, but some ecosystems may have a few more. They may all have multilevel consumers. Figure 2.11 also ignores some of the dynamics of energy flow; for instance, no indication is given of the energy lost to respiration and decomposition.

Regardless of what units are used, it should be appreciated that in nature, pyramids can change shape from moment to moment. They can even become *inverted* for short periods. Fill an aquarium bowl with pond water and put it on the window sill in the sun. Cover the bowl with something to reduce evaporation. If you are lucky, the aquarium will become pea soup green and then clear up from time to time. Clear-ups are caused by algae eaters experiencing great population booms. Unfortunately for them, their populations peak just as the algae are nearly all eaten up. At that point the pyramid in the aquarium is inverted. Can this last? Obviously not.

The dynamics of biological pyramids are perhaps better illustrated in Figure 2.12, which shows that some of the chemical energy at each level is

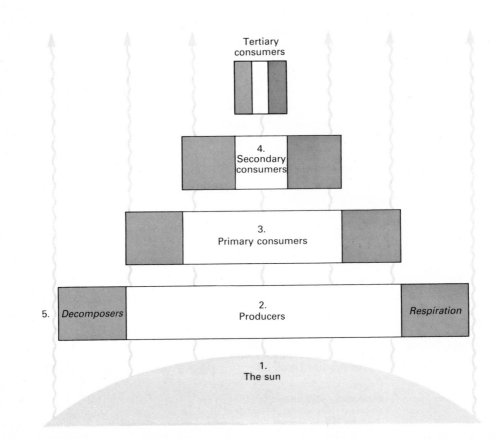

Figure 2.12 The Dynamics of the Ecosystem Pyramid. Energy dissipates as heat as it passes through an ecosystem. 1. Electromagnetic energy comes to an ecosystem from the sun. 2. A small part of solar radiation is changed into chemical energy by producers. 3. Some plant chemical energy ends up in herbivores or primary consumers. 4. Some herbivore chemicals go to carnivores. 5. Some of the chemical energy at each level goes to decomposers. The organisms at each level also use up some energy for their own metabolic activities. Because of the inefficiency of each energy transfer step, not much energy is left after four or five transfers.

Part I   Basic Principles of Ecology

destined to pass through the decomposers. In essence, Figure 2.12 illustrates the energy that comes to an ecosystem from the sun and dissipates as it moves through the trophic levels, eventually to be converted completely into heat.

Biological pyramids such as those illustrated in Figures 2.11 and 2.12, if properly derived for a given ecosystem, can provide valuable information about the nature of that ecosystem. Such data can be used to make general comparisons between ecosystems of various types in various locations. Such data provides a way of expressing the absolute natural value of a particular piece of land in terms of biological production. Such data could allow questions to be answered such as how vital a piece of territory is as a spawning ground or what the natural impact would be of diminishing the habitat for certain kinds of producers or consumers in a particular place—a swamp or an estuary that somebody wanted to fill in, for instance.

Food Webs and Food Chains

The figures mentioned above are simplified; they do not take into account that each trophic level of an ecosystem is occupied by a wide variety of species. This is illustrated in Figure 2.13. One of the characteristics of an ecosystem is the number and

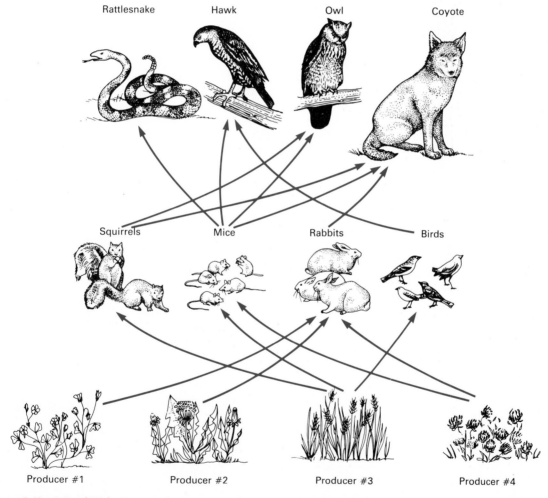

Figure 2.13 A Food Web. Many species can occupy the same trophic level in any ecosystem. Certain species may predominate, however, and some species occupy more than one level. This illustration does not capture the essence of nature in the raw. We could not possibly represent something so dynamic and ever-changing on paper. To cite just a few of the things this figure fails to show: predators change their prey from season to season; some predators and herbivores eat different things when they are young than they do when they grow up; some predators are more flexible than others when their food of choice decreases in supply.

nature of the species that occupy its various trophic levels. We generally find that although many species can occupy each trophic level in any ecosystem (for example, buffalo, grasshoppers, and field mice may all occupy the same trophic level in a prairie ecosystem), certain species may *predominate* at each level. A certain kind of grass may dominate a field ecosystem: a few species of trees may dominate a forest ecosystem; and a certain type of algae may carry on most of the photosynthesis in a stream ecosystem.

Figure 2.13 also shows that there are complex relationships between the constituents of one trophic level and constituents of adjacent trophic levels. Ecologists sometimes refer to the relationship between trophic levels as *food chains;* at other times they are somewhat more accurately described as *food webs.* The web is a much better analogy to the actual nature of the interactions between trophic level components. As Figure 2.13 shows, the occupants of a primary consumer level may eat (draw energy and material from) a number of producer species. Similarly, carnivores draw their food from a number of individual species at the primary consumer level.

Ecosystems vary considerably in the design of their energy-nutrient webs.

Complexity and Stability

Generally speaking, the more complex the combination of trophic level interrelationships in an ecosystem, the more stable the system. It would be considered a somewhat unstable condition if an industry depended on a raw material available from only one source. Any disruption at the source or in the line to the source would mean a critical problem for that industry. Similarly, if all of the herbivores in an ecosystem depended on a single species of producer, the system would not be very stable. A disease or anything else that caused the demise of that producer would be immediately felt at the consumer level. Ecosystems that are in some kind of relative equilibrium and in which many different kinds of plants and animals fill similar niches should be better able to adjust to problems with any one of the species. It does not necessarily follow from this that the more species an ecosystem has, the better it is able to withstand disruption. Many other factors go

A consumer may feed on many different species. This seven-spotted ladybird beetle has found one of its favorites—a pea aphid.

Part I   Basic Principles of Ecology

into determining the ability of an ecosystem to resist alteration or to return to its original condition after being altered. These are discussed in Chapter 4.

MOVING ON

It should be obvious that the concepts covered in this chapter have much to do with problems that face humankind in its relationship to the natural environment. There are starting points here for improving our system of agriculture, our energy policies, and our prospects for solving the world hunger problem. Arguments could be developed from the material presented here to support the development of solar power. Explanations could be developed from the material presented here for:

— why the oceans may not be the answer some say they will be to the problems of feeding the people in this world;
— why people in poorer countries eat very little meat;
— why you cannot eliminate coyotes and expect nothing else to happen; and
— why there is danger in humanity's relying on fewer than a dozen plant species for nearly all of its food.

CONCEPTS TO REMEMBER

1. There are many forms of energy; what they all have in common is the ability to do work. Work can be thought of as the larger class of actions that include all of the things that plants and animals do—running, growing, fruiting, flowering, growling, squeaking, etc. All living things must have energy sources in order to do what they do.
2. The second law of thermodynamics says, in essence, that as the energy in a closed system is used, it becomes less useful to do work—it wears out in the functional sense even though the first law of thermodynamics says that energy cannot be destroyed. A consequence of this is that all living systems need continuous supplies of new energy.
3. Practically all of the energy that drives ecosystems comes from the sun. Of the total amount of solar energy that strikes the earth's outer atmosphere, less than half reaches the surface. A significant fraction of the solar energy intercepted by the earth determines the earth's weather and climate. Because of the earth's shape, its orbit, its surface topography, and its atmospheric composition, different amounts of incident solar radiation spell the difference between tropical "paradises" and inhospitable polar regions, between jungles and deserts.
4. All of the solar energy intercepted by the earth is eventually returned to space.
5. Only a tiny fraction of the solar energy that strikes vegetation is converted into chemical energy—less than 1% on the average.
6. About half of the chemical energy fixed by green plants is available to consumers; plants use the rest themselves.
7. Productivity varies from one kind of ecosystem to another and from one time to another. The availability of water, the amount of minerals, and many other factors (in addition to incident radiation) limit productivity in different ecosystems.
8. Energy dissipates as heat as it flows through ecosystems.
9. On the average, about 10% of the energy entering a particular trophic level is available to the next level in an ecosystem.
10. The "web" is a better metaphor than the "chain" to describe the flow of energy through most ecosystems.

DISCUSSION QUESTIONS AND FOOD FOR THOUGHT

1. Why do you suppose a heat-utilizing organism has not evolved that is capable of using "waste" heat in the same way that photosynthetic organisms use light?
2. Make a list of typical menu items for one day—breakfast, lunch and dinner. Using the 10% law, a 1% efficiency for photosynthesis, and the number of calories in an average portion of each item, calculate the amount of solar energy that went into each item and the total amount of solar energy represented in that menu.
3. Using the second law of thermodynamics, explain why, kilogram for kilogram, hamburger is more expensive than cornbread.
4. On the basis of inherent productivities, discuss the relative merits of using the oceans and deserts as solutions to the human hunger problem.
5. Using the laws and concepts presented in Chapter 2, discuss the relative potential of coal, nuclear energy, and solar energy as solutions to the energy crisis.

6. Read the short story "The Final Question" by Isaac Asimov and discuss it in relationship to the concepts presented in Chapter 2.

7. As best you can, collect all of the living things present in a square meter of an abandoned field, dry the material to a constant weight, classify each item according to trophic level, weigh the items at each level, and draw a representative pyramid of biomass. Draw an equivalent energy pyramid.

8. Suppose it were possible to place a gigantic movable mirror in orbit around the earth to reflect an additional amount of sunlight to the earth, adding 25% sunlight. What might some of the consequences be?

REFERENCES AND FURTHER READING

References marked with an asterisk are cited in the chapter.

Brafield, A. E., and Llewellyn, M. J., 1982. *Animal Energetics.* London: Chapman and Hall. This advanced book on energy transactions in ecosystems emphasizes animals.

Evans, J. V., 1982. "The Sun's Influence on the Earth's Atmosphere and Interplanetary Space," *Science* **216:**467–474.

Gosz, J. R.; Holmes, R. T.; Likesn, G. E.; and Borman, H., 1978. "The Flow of Energy in a Forest Ecosystem," *Scientific American,* March. This is an easy-to-read account of the energy flow patterns in a forest ecosystem.

Jeffers, J. N., 1982. *Modeling.* London: Chapman and Hall. This book introduces the application of math and computers in ecology.

*Kormondy, E. J., 1984. *Concepts of Ecology,* 3rd ed. Englewood Cliffs, N.J.: Prentice-Hall.

Lieth, H., 1978. *Patterns of Primary Production in the Biosphere.* New York: Van Nostrand/Rinehold. This is an advanced treatise on global primary production.

Lincoln, R. J.; Boxshall, G. A.; and Clark, P. F., eds., 1982. *A Dictionary of Ecology, Evaluation, and Systematics.* NY: Cambridge University Press.

Montieth, J. L., 1965. "Light Distribution and Photosynthesis in Field Crops," *Ann. Bot. N.S.* **29**:17–37.

*Odum, E. P., 1983. *Basic Ecology.* Philadelphia: W. B. Saunders.

Woodwell, G., 1970. "The Energy Cycle of the Earth," in *The Biosphere.* San Francisco: W. H. Freeman and Co.

Woodwell, G., and Whittaker, R., 1968. "Primary Production in Terrestrial Ecosystems," *American Zoologist* **8**(1):19–30.

Material Cycles in Living Systems

The alarm has just gone off. You awaken to face another day. After pulling yourself out of bed, you wash up, relieve yourself of the wastes you accumulated through the night, dress, have a bite to eat, and depart. Already you have had some impact on the chemistry of your environment.

As you breathed, you exchanged carbon dioxide (CO_2) for oxygen (O_2). As you washed, you added chemicals to the water—hydrocarbons and oils from your skin and soap. Your wastes added other chemicals. During breakfast you took in nutrients produced by plants or animals and later you broke some of these down into materials your system could use. Big deal, you say? But over 230 million of your friends and neighbors in the United States alone were doing the same thing. Surely this *is* a big deal, chemically speaking. It would be a big deal even if we did not also have a chemically intense technology. We humans move a lot of chemicals around. It follows that if chemicals regulate ecosystems, then our chemical manipulations must be having an impact on living systems. Here are some examples of environmental problems related to the things we humans do with chemical substances.

— Nutrients in organic wastes that humans flush or drain into aquatic systems accelerate plant growth, resulting in the choking of waterways

and, as a result of the ultimate death and decay of this vegetation, the depletion of oxygen.

— Certain agricultural practices have depleted nutrients from some soils and added harmful salts to others.

— Certain human-made chemical compounds that have been released in our environment—vinyl chloride, EDB, and benzene, for example—cause cancer.

— The rapid release of carbon and sulfur from burning coal has increased the amounts of these elements in harmful chemical forms in the atmosphere—for example, as carbon monoxide (a poison), carbon dioxide (which may alter the earth's climate), and sulfur dioxide (a poison). The transport of sulfur dioxide by wind has resulted in acid rain hundreds of miles from the source of the chemical.

— We have added ozone to the lower reaches of the atmosphere, where it acts as a poison, and we have removed it from the upper reaches, where it serves to shield us from harmful ultraviolet radiation.

So that we might understand these and other problems related to the movement of materials in nature, we will review in this chapter some of the cycles particularly important in the regulation of ecosystems.

CHEMICALS IN MOTION: CYCLES IN THE ECOSPHERE

We saw in Chapter 2 that energy flows through ecosystems. Emphasis was on the word "through". Energy is generated from matter in the sun; as energy passes through living systems, enabling organisms to perform various kinds of work, all the energy is ultimately dissipated as heat. It is gone forever in terms of usefulness to the system. As we have already suggested, *matter* is quite another matter.

Of the more than 100 elements, only 20–30 are constituents of living things. Some are needed in relatively large amounts (macronutrients); some are needed only in trace amounts (micronutrients). The major macronutrients are found in all organisms. The minor macronutrients and the micronutrients are found in varying amounts in different species (see Table 3.1).

The basic chemical elements or nutrients that make up the substance of living systems need not be supplied continuously from the outside because the *substance* of ecosystems is continuously cycled. Since chemical elements are not "used up" but are rather "used over," one might wonder how they can ever be in short supply. The answer lies in the fact that the availability of an element can be limited by its chemical form, its physical location in relation to living things, and the rate at which it passes from one form or location to another.

Chemical Form

Individual chemical elements can exist in combination with other elements, that is, in different molecular forms or compounds, the smallest units of which are called molecules. Some of these compounds cannot be used by individual organisms to gain access to individual essential elements within them. Plants need carbon, for example, but they generally cannot get it from methane (CH_4), sugar ($C_6H_{12}O_6$), carbon monoxide (CO), or any of thousands of other carbon compounds. Carbon must be supplied to plants in the form of carbon dioxide (CO_2). Similarly, plants all need nitrogen, but most of them must have it in the form of soluble nitrate (NO_3^-) or ammonia (NH_3).

Location

A second general factor that limits the availability of essential chemicals for living systems is physical location. We mentioned in Chapter 1 that most organisms are found where air, water, and earth meet. Conditions that favor life diminish with distance from the thin film at the surface of the earth. Deep within the oceans there is not enough light or oxygen to support much life. Deep within the earth there is too little oxygen, little or no water, and *no* light. High in the atmosphere there is little chemical matter, and it is too cold. The point is that regardless of chemical form, key nutrients can be lost to living systems for short periods or geologi-

Table 3.1   Relative Amounts of Chemical Elements That Make up Living Things.

Major Macronutrients (> 1% dry organic weight)		Relatively Minor Macronutrients (0.2–1% dry organic weight)		Micronutrients (<0.2% dry organic weight)	
Name of Element	Symbol	Name of Element	Symbol	Name of Element	Symbol
Carbon	C	Calcium	Ca	Aluminum	Al
Hydrogen	H	Chlorine	Cl	Boron	B
Nitrogen	N	Copper	Cu	Bromine	Br
Oxygen	O	Iron	Fe	Chromium	Cr
Phosphorus	P	Magnesium	Mg	Cobalt	Co
		Potassium	K	Fluorine	F
		Sodium	Na	Gallium	Ga
		Sulfur	S	Iodine	I
				Manganese	Mn
				Molybdenum	Mo
				Selenium	Se
				Silicon	Si
				Strontium	Sr
				Tin	Sn
				Titanium	Ti
				Vanadium	V
				Zinc	Zn

Dissociation: the separation of ions from one another in water, e.g., $NaCl \rightleftharpoons Na^+ + Cl^-$.

Element: any of the more than 100 fundamental units of matter that consist of atoms of one kind. (Some examples: boron, carbon, chlorine, hydrogen, oxygen, nitrogen, sulfur.)

Essential element: an element needed by an organism, usually in some particular chemical form from the environment. Phosphorus is an essential element for plants, but the element phosphorus is poisonous. Plants usually require phosphorus in the form of phosphate (PO_4^-) salts. In this text we sometimes use the phrase **mineral nutrient** as a synonym for essential element.

Ion: an atom or group of atoms with a positive or negative charge; the charge is the result of the loss or gain of electrons. Positive and negative ions attract one another, e.g., $Na^+ + Cl^- \rightarrow NaCl$.

Molecule: the smallest unit of either an element or a **compound** (combination of two or more atoms) still having the chemical characteristics and identity of that element or compound. Molecules may contain more than one element. For example, water molecules (H_2O) contain two atoms of the element hydrogen (H) and one atom of the element oxygen (O).

---

cally long periods by being lifted high into the atmosphere, by becoming incorporated in deep ocean sediments (and eventually into rock), or by becoming embedded in silt, to give just a few examples.

Reservoirs. There are places in the ecosphere that serve as major abiotic reservoirs for chemical elements. Consider nitrogen. Though the sizes are not drawn to scale, the relationship between the various reservoirs of nitrogen might look as shown in the diagram at right.

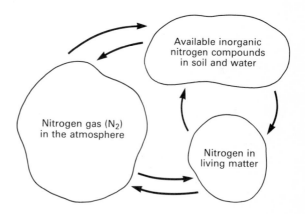

During some periods of the earth's history, enormous amounts of water have been locked up in glaciers.

Chapter 3   Material Cycles in Living Systems

The reservoirs are not uniform. There is far more nitrogen in the form of nitrogen gas than there is in the form of available nitrogen compounds in the soil or in the form of organic compounds.

Chemicals move from one reservoir to another in cycles. This means that the size of any reservoir and the accessibility of nutrients to living things depend upon the patterns of movement and the rates at which nutrients move from one reservoir to another.

Pathways and Rates

The cycling of chemicals may be long, complex loops or short loops. A short carbon loop involving plants and animals is the following:

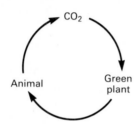

A long carbon loop also involving plants is the following:

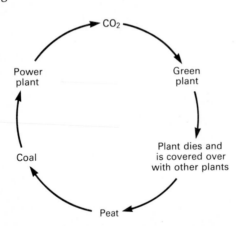

Living things participate in the movement of chemicals into and out of various reservoirs and into and out of various chemical forms, hence the term **biogeochemical cycles.**

The rate at which any particular chemical nutrient makes a complete loop is determined by the number of steps in the cycle and the nature of the specific steps involved. Again using the carbon loops illustrated above, the loop with the coal formation in it would take much longer than the one in which animals are involved. Many plants that long ago converted carbon dioxide into plant matter were themselves later converted into coal. The burning of coal releases carbon that had been tied up for millions of years. Another example of a long-term loop involves calcium. Ancient crustaceans whose shells were made of calcium carbonate have ended up as carbonate rocks, where the carbon has been held for millions of years. Living things also have important short-term effects on the availability of mineral nutrients. In certain aquatic systems, plant growth can take up the limited available phosphate, tying up the phosphate in the substance of the plants such that further plant growth is limited by the lack of phosphate.

The most ecologically important fact about the steps or stages of chemical cycles is that individual steps can be slowed, blocked, or accelerated. Throughout this book there will be examples of how blocking a portion of a cycle by interfering with it in some way can result in a harmful accumulation of materials at one point and/or a harmful depletion of a component in the cycle at some other point.

Cycles and Energy

Biogeochemical cycles are dynamic processes in which atoms are recombined and rearranged and the starting materials are regenerated. Progress through portions of all such cycles requires energy, and the principal energy source driving biogeochemical cycles is the sun. Solar energy powers the processes of evaporation and condensation that move water in cycles. "Water power" in turn becomes the mechanism for weathering and erosion, which moves minerals through long stretches of various geochemical cycles. Solar energy, converted into chemical energy through photosynthesis, powers those portions of the biogeochemical cycles that involve living things. Without the sun, all biogeochemical cycles on the earth's surface would run down and stop. It turns out that water (as a solvent and as an agent of weathering) is the principal medium through which solar energy is applied to the movement of chemicals in the ecosphere. For this reason, though water is not a nutrient in the sense of the other things we will consider here, we will begin our consideration of specific cycles with water.

THE HYDROLOGIC CYCLE

Water—A Unique Solvent

Water is the universal internal medium of all living things; living things are made of 90% or more water. Water is also the external medium of all aquatic life forms. The special relationship of life and water stems from the fact that water is a relatively universal solvent; almost anything will dissolve in water to some degree.

Water is the most essential and the most unique of all compounds. Water is clear—transparent to light. This means that photosynthesis can occur in water, at least to certain depths. Consequently, producers—green plants, the foundation of the biosphere—can grow, flourish, and serve as the nutrient source for aquatic consumers. Water has a high **heat capacity**; this means that it can absorb much heat energy with a relatively small increase in temperature in comparison with other substances. Because of this high heat capacity, aquatic life forms do not have to be adaptable to a wide range of temperatures or to rapidly changing temperatures.

Water becomes increasingly dense and thus heavier with lower temperature down to 4°C. This is why deeper water feels cooler in a lake. Because the maximum density of water occurs at 4°C, water becomes increasingly lighter at 3°C, 2°C, 1°C, and 0°C (freezing). Thus water is heavier as a liquid than as a solid; this is why ice floats in a glass of water. Another important consequence of these properties is that water freezes from the top down. This protects aquatic organisms because ice acts as an insulator to prevent further decreases in temperature in the remaining water and decreases the chances that ponds and lakes will freeze solid.

Water movement is cyclical. Surface water evaporates into the atmosphere, where it condenses and returns to the earth as precipitation, which will eventually evaporate once again.

Water Does Not Always Flow Downhill

Although we do not usually think about it, water is moving around us constantly. It is not always flowing downhill; a good deal of it is being pulled up as individual molecules into the atmosphere by the sun. Solar energy causes water on the surface of the earth to **evaporate** (change from a liquid to a gas) and enter the atmosphere. When water evaporates from the exposed parts of plants, such as leaves, the process is called **transpiration**. (Transpiration is the driving force that raises water and dissolved substances from the roots into the rest of the plant.) Once in the atmosphere, water vapor is carried by the wind and may meet any of several ends, all of which ultimately involve **condensation** (changing from a gas to a liquid) as a result of cooling. Following condensation into larger and larger water droplets or ice crystals, water returns to the surface of the earth as precipitation. Thus the complete cycle includes evaporation, condensation, and precipita-

tion—with intermediate effects and stops throughout (Figure 3.1).

The amount of water in circulation annually is only a small amount of the total. The oceans constitute a reservoir for over 97% of all the water on earth. A tiny fraction is held in the atmosphere, and the rest exists as ice, ponds, lakes, streams, and subsurface water.

Water that falls as rain or snow on land may seep into the soil, where it becomes groundwater. Some rock layers are more permeable to water than others, and if groundwater reaches a rock layer that is relatively impermeable, the water tends to collect above the layer and may form an **aquifer**—an underground water storage area. The upper surface of such underground water is called the **water table** (Figure 3.2). Some precipitation ends up as runoff carrying sediment and dissolved minerals to lakes, streams, and rivers, from which some evaporates and the rest makes its way "downhill" to the oceans.

Terrestrial organisms influence the hydrologic cycle in many ways. Plant cover diminishes the force of impact of raindrops and reduces erosion. Organic matter in soil acts as a sponge holding water in place between rains. Plants extract water from soil and give off water vapor from leaves via transpiration. Transpiration in turn has a cooling effect, which helps moderate temperature and thus climate.

Rainfall Patterns: Water, Wind, and Weather

We described the relationship between global rainfall patterns and the patterns by which the sun heats the earth's atmosphere in Chapter 2. Figure 3.3 shows how the major global wind patterns and topography combine to produce wet places. A graphic reminder that rain tends to fall on the windward side

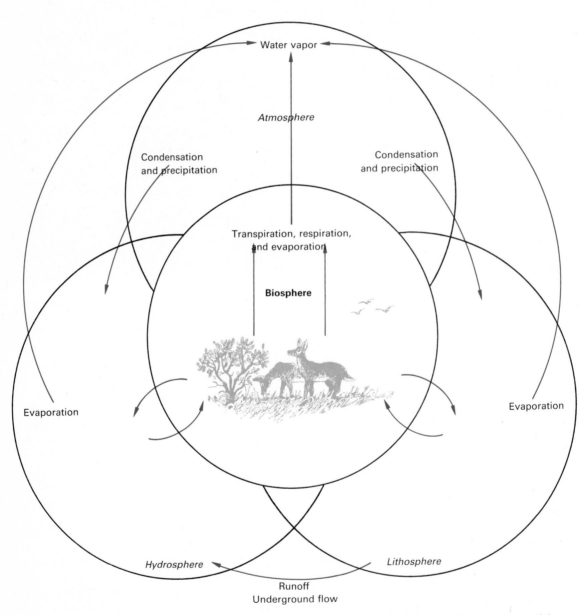

Figure 3.1 The Hydrologic or Water Cycle. This consists primarily of the processes of evaporation, condensation and precipitation. Water passes through all of the great spheres, carrying with it various mineral substances—some of them important nutrients for plants and animals.

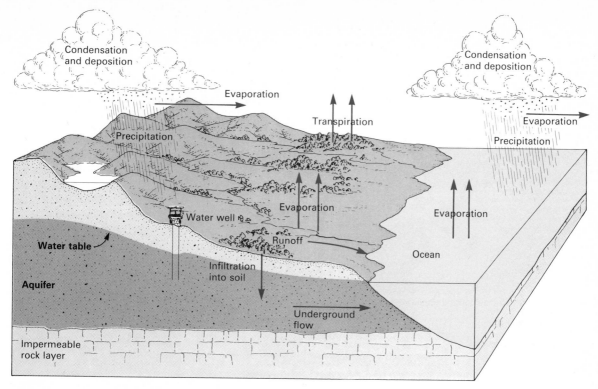

Figure 3.2 The Formation of Aquifers. Water that seeps into the ground may eventually reach relatively impermeable layers of rock. The water then tends to accumulate above this layer, forming aquifers that may be tapped for use via wells. The upper level of the groundwater, called the water table, fluctuates somewhat depending upon rainfall, rates of withdrawal by humans, and the rate at which the groundwater flows to still lower levels.

of mountains as air is forced upward and cooled is presented in Figure 3.4. Certain land-water junctions have high annual precipitation even where no mountains are involved because of the differential air temperatures over land and water (see Chapter 2) and the resultant more frequent meeting of cold and warm moisture-laden air masses.

Human Activities and the Hydrologic Cycle

Humans affect the hydrologic cycle in several ways. For example, if flowing water is pooled by dams, the evaporation rate changes. Standing water over a large surface area can absorb more heat energy from the sun to vaporize water molecules. This in turn may increase precipitation somewhere else. Clearcutting a forest or building a parking lot reduces water seepage and increases runoff, thus reducing the amount of groundwater and increasing the risk of flooding. In terms of direct human need, if water is withdrawn from a stream or an aquifer faster than it is added, a water shortage is sure to follow. As we write this, the water table in much of

the Great Plains region of the United States is falling fast, and several states are fighting over rights to the water in the Colorado River. If overuse were not bad enough, we humans continue to decrease our access to high-quality water by polluting it. There will be much more on human water problems in Chapters 7 and 12.

ATMOSPHERIC CYCLES

We will now look at the carbon cycle and the nitrogen cycle, which are good examples of *atmospheric cycles*, cycles in which the primary reservoir or source (as far as living systems are concerned) is the air.

The Carbon Cycle

The carbon cycle intimately involves all living things; a molecular carbon "skeleton" is found—by definition—in every organic chemical. Carbon is thus a key element in the chemistry of all life.

The carbon cycle is categorized as an atmo-

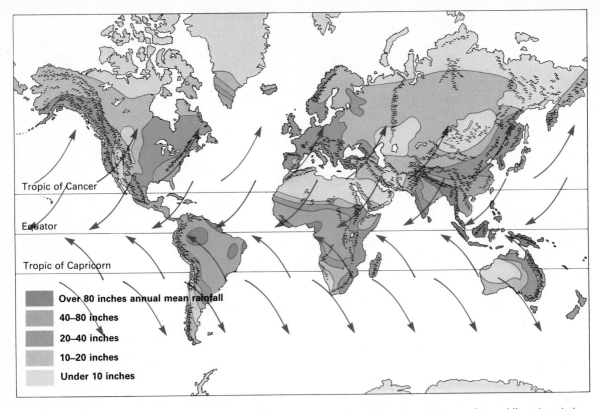

Figure 3.3 Global Wind and Rainfall Patterns. Sunlight warms the atmosphere in some places more than others, causing movement of the air or winds in predictable patterns.

The trade winds and westerlies are the world's major wind patterns. Also shown on this map is the mean annual rainfall in various parts of the world.

Tropic of Cancer

Equator

Tropic of Capricorn

Over 80 inches annual mean rainfall

40–80 inches

20–40 inches

10–20 inches

Under 10 inches

spheric cycle because most of the carbon that passes through the biosphere comes from the air. Approximately 0.03 to 0.04% of the air is carbon dioxide (CO_2), and this minute percentage is the main source of carbon for all living things. It is the reser-

voir from which plants withdraw carbon in photosynthesis, the key process by which carbon enters the biosphere (see Figure 3.5).

Through photosynthesis, green plants pick up carbon from carbon dioxide in the air and, through

Figure 3.4 The Effect of Air Flow over Mountains on Rainfall Distribution. As moist air rises and cools, its ability to hold water decreases, and the moisture falls as precipitation. As cool air is forced up and over mountains, it tends to drop its moisture going up on the windward side, creating a dry area (rain shadow) or even a desert on the other side.

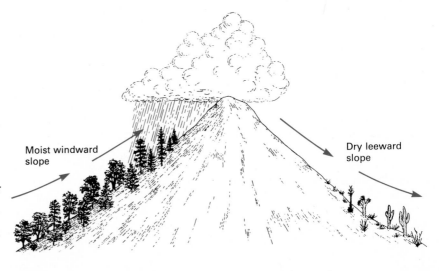

Moist windward slope

Dry leeward slope

complex chemical processes, combine and rearrange these carbon atoms into carbon skeletons of various molecular shapes and sizes. Oxygen, nitrogen, phosphorus, sulfur, and other elements are attached to carbon to produce the substance of living matter—fats, carbohydrates, proteins, and nucleic acids. In turn, this plant matter may be passed on to consumers, who rearrange the elements to suit their own specific chemical makeup.

Carbon Equilibrium

Oxides of carbon are also found in water and in the form of rock. Carbon dioxide is slightly soluble in water; in solution, carbon dioxide forms carbonic acid (H_2CO_3). Carbonic acid dissociates to form hydrogen ions (H^+) and bicarbonate ions (HCO_3^-). The bicarbonate ions in turn dissociate further to form hydrogen ions and carbonate ions ($CO_3^=$). Nega-

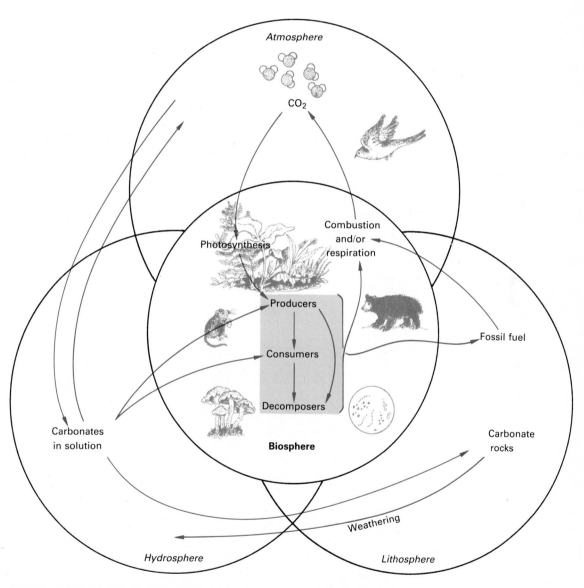

Figure 3.5 The Carbon Cycle. The chemical skeleton for the substances that compose living things is carbon. Illus- trated here are the patterns of carbon cycling through the great spheres.

tively charged ions can combine with positive ions to form various salts—calcium carbonate, for example. Some calcium salts are relatively insoluble in water and accumulate as carbonate sedimentary rock (limestone in the case of calcium carbonate). The reactions involved in carbon dioxide–carbonate equilibrium are as follows:

1)
$$\underset{\substack{\text{(carbon} \\ \text{dioxide)}}}{CO_2} + \underset{\text{(water)}}{H_2O} \rightleftharpoons \underset{\substack{\text{(carbonic} \\ \text{acid)}}}{H_2CO_3} \rightleftharpoons \underset{\substack{\text{(hydrogen)} \\ \text{ion)}}}{H^+} + \underset{\substack{\text{(bicarbonate} \\ \text{ion)}}}{HCO_3^-}$$

2)
$$\underset{\substack{\text{(bicarbonate} \\ \text{ion)}}}{HCO_3^-} \rightleftharpoons \underset{\substack{\text{(hydrogen)} \\ \text{ion)}}}{H^+} + \underset{\substack{\text{(carbonate} \\ \text{ion)}}}{CO_3^=}$$

3)
$$\underset{\text{(e.g., Ca}^{++}\text{)}}{CO_3^= + \text{positive ions}} \longrightarrow \underset{\text{(e.g., CaCO}_3\text{)}}{\text{salts}}$$

Phenomena that would tend to remove carbon dioxide from the air in a given locality would shift all of the reactions to the left, in effect replacing the carbon dioxide. Conversely, if some process or event tended to add to the CO_2 in the atmosphere, the reaction series would shift to the right, again having the effect of tending to keep the CO_2 concentration constant. The reactions are affected by pH, temperature mixing, and other factors, and on a global scale the adjustments are far from instantaneous. It is worth noting that the percentage of carbon dioxide in the atmosphere has actually increased over the last century. Because of the role of CO_2 in holding in heat, this has some potentially serious implications for the earth's climate. This problem will be discussed in detail in Chapters 9 through 11.

The Nitrogen Cycle

A basic difference between the nitrogen cycle and the carbon cycle is that while all green plants can extract the "raw material" carbon dioxide directly from the atmosphere, most green plants are dependent upon a few species of bacteria and blue-green algae to convert atmospheric nitrogen into a form they can use. The earth's atmosphere contains approximately 79% nitrogen—about four times more nitrogen than oxygen and 2000 times more nitrogen than carbon dioxide. Yet *plants that can utilize the minute amount of carbon dioxide cannot utilize the large amount of atmospheric nitrogen.*

The nitrogen cycle offers a good illustration of the complexity and fragility of nature. Figure 3.6 shows that atmospheric nitrogen can be changed into ammonia (NH_3) and nitrate (NO_3^-) (the primary forms usable by plants) by at least two processes. Lightning may serve as an energy source to cause atmospheric nitrogen and oxygen to react to form nitric acid (HNO_3), which is then carried to the soil in rainfall. However, the contribution of this reaction to the overall availability of nitrogen to organisms is minimal. Certain nitrogen-fixing bacteria and blue-green algae utilize atmospheric nitrogen in their metabolic processes and produce ammonia as an end product. Most nitrogen that is fixed naturally occurs as a fortuitous by-product of the activities of these bacteria and blue-green algae.

The most important nitrogen-fixing bacteria are those of the genus *Rhizobium,* which grow in the roots of legumes such as clover and alfalfa. *Rhizobium* reside in nodules on the roots and receive

Limestone, a form of calcium carbonate, is relatively insoluble in water. Being sedimentary, it tends to occur in layers. It has been found on all continents, in strata from every geologic age.

Part I Basic Principles of Ecology

nourishment from the plant while at the same time producing "nitrogen fertilizer," that is, usable nitrogen compounds for that plant. When such legumes decay, ammonia is released to serve as nitrogen sources for other plants. As much as 500 pounds of nitrogen per acre has been found to be fixed by such bacteria in fields of clover in New Zealand (Kormondy, 1969). This is why a farmer will periodically plant a field with a "cover" crop of legumes such as beans, alfalfa, or clover.

Anaboena is a blue-green alga capable of fixing nitrogen. It is a free-living alga sometimes found in association with a certain water fern. Farmers in China take advantage of this relationship by growing

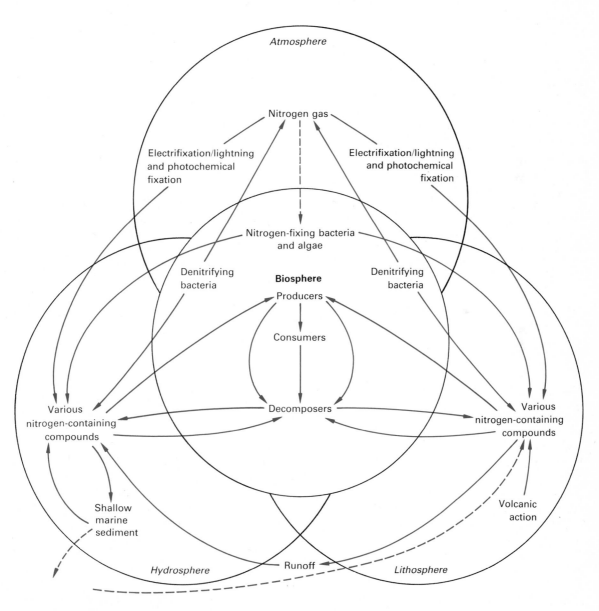

Figure 3.6   The Nitrogen Cycle. Although nitrogen comprises almost 80% of the atmosphere of the earth, most living things cannot use nitrogen as a gas. This diagram shows how nitrogen enters the biosphere primarily through the action of bacteria and algae, which convert nitrogen gas to ammonia and nitrates—usable by plants. Many types of bacteria and algae keep the nitrogen cycle moving. Each uses products from one or more of the others as raw material for its own metabolic activities. Note that there are different kinds of decomposers, some of which are bacteria.

the fern in their rice fields. Most nitrogen fixation in aquatic systems is accomplished by free-living bacteria and algae. Free-living bacteria include those of the genus *Azotobacter,* which are **aerobic** (oxygen-requiring), and the genus *Clostridium,* which are **anaerobic** (able to live in the absence of oxygen).

Most plants absorb ammonia and nitrates from the soil through their roots and incorporate the nitrogen into protein, nucleic acids, and other biochemicals. Animals acquire these various organic forms of nitrogen by eating plants and rearranging the nitrogeneous compounds to suit their own needs. When animal wastes are excreted or when plant or animal tissue dies, certain (ammonifying) decomposers convert organic nitrogen compounds into ammonia gas (NH_3) or ammonium salts (in which nitrogen occurs in the form of an ammonium ion, NH_4^+). These in turn may be acted upon by still other species of bacteria. Through a process called **nitrification**, ammonia and ammonium salts are converted to nitrites ($NH_4^+ \rightarrow NO_2^-$), and then other bacteria convert nitrites to nitrates ($NO_2^- \rightarrow NO_3^-$). Bacteria of the genera *Nitrosomonas* and *Nitrobacter* are associated with this process. There are also bacteria that reverse nitrification; they are called **denitrifying bacteria.** Some of them convert nitrates to nitrites and other nitrites to ammonia; others convert nitrates to free nitrogen or oxides of nitrogen (Figure 3.6).

The remarkable thing about the nitrogen cycle is that a few obscure species of bacteria and algae provide the only practical link between the primary reservoir of inorganic nitrogen and living systems. Each participating species in the chain is operating using raw materials that are the waste products of other species, and through it all, life as we know it is made possible. The nitrogen cycle offers an important example of the "tightness" and complexity of interrelationships in the biosphere.

Agriculture and Nitrogen

Modern farming practices include the use of commercial, synthetic, nitrogen-containing fertilizers in addition to nitrogen-building cover crops and natural compost or manure to increase crop yields. Although the effect of natural and commercial nitrates is basically identical for the crops, there are some significant problems with commercial fertilizers from an environmental and cultural perspective. For one thing, it takes a lot of energy to fix nitrogen artificially. This is relevant to the energy problems we will discuss at length in Chapter 6. Second, the availability of so much synthetic nitrate

aggravates the problem of what to do with manure and other naturally occurring organic wastes. Excess nitrates from overfertilization or improper disposal of organic wastes can be washed into waterways, where they stimulate excessive plant growth and indirectly deplete oxygen, or seep into groundwater, contaminating water supplies. Kormondy (1984) indicates that biological fixation of nitrogen produces about 54×10^6 metric tons per year compared to 30×10^6 metric tons annually fixed in the manufacture of synthetic fertilizers. However, he also states that the amount fixed synthetically is increasing at such a rate as to reach 100×10^6 metric tons by the year 2000.

LITHOSPHERIC CYCLES

Another class of cycles are the **lithospheric cycles,** cycles in which the principal and most important nutrient reservoir is the lithosphere. Lithospheric cycles are characterized by the occurrence of **sinks** or places where elements are tied up, taken out of the cycle, or removed from the juncture of the spheres for extremely long periods of time. Over long time spans, lithospheric cycles depend on geological uplifts; they are driven by weathering over the short term. The forces of erosion and weathering cause minerals to break off and dissolve in water and to be carried into rivers and streams and eventually into the oceans. These minerals may enter numerous loops or cycles in the biosphere before an ultimate redeposition as ocean sediment.

The Phosphorus Cycle

The role of phosphorus, in the form of phosphate, in reactions that store and release energy for use in cells makes it a very important nutrient. The availability of phosphate through the phosphorus cycle is one regulator of biological activity.

Through erosion and weathering of rock, inorganic phosphate is made available to plants through uptake from the soil or, in the case of aquatic plants, from the aqueous environment. Once taken into the plant, the phosphate may become part of an energy-rich molecule of ATP (adenosine triphosphate), a nucleic acid, or some other organic compound. The phosphate may be returned to the soil or sediments when the plant dies and decomposes (phosphate is also one of the constituents of the ash left following the burning of a plant or animal). Phosphorus may also be passed on to a consumer.

In the consumer, phosphorus may be incorporated into bones or teeth, in which case the phosphorus is bound for an extended period of time. Some of it is excreted as waste and is immediately accessible to decomposers; it may, by a short loop, be converted back to inorganic phosphate and be reassimilated by plants very quickly. It may become tightly bound as phosphorus salts to iron, calcium, aluminum, and clays in the soil to be washed away or "lost" in sediments. In an aquatic system, released phosphorus may eventually become part of deep sediments, where it is out of reach of organisms at the air-water interface and only geologic uplifts, shifting vertical currents, or the like will get it back into the cycle (Figure 3.7). In coastal marine ecosystems, in which the sea gull may be the ultimate consumer (or top carnivore), the fate of phosphorus—whether it goes to a long term sink or is

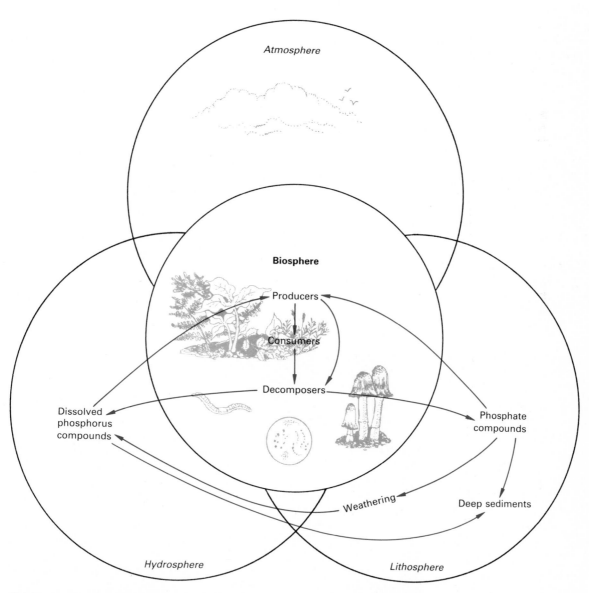

Figure 3.7 The Phosphorus Cycle. Physical and geological processes are important in the cycling of phosphorus and in all other lithospheric cycles. The rate of cycling of phosphorus is extremely important to growth and activity in living things.

quickly cycled—depends on where gull droppings fall: on the beach, the cliffs, or the ocean. Bird droppings, called guano, are actually high phosphate reservoirs and "mined" as a resource along some coastlines such as the western coast of South America.

Phosphorus is scarce in many—especially aquatic—environments, where it is the key limiting factor for biological activity. The turnover (cycling) rate for phosphorus may actually determine the level of productivity in many aquatic ecosystems. This is one reason why phosphates in fertilizer runoff can disrupt aquatic communities (see Chapter 7). This is also the reason why some states have banned the use of detergents containing phosphates. It is interesting, to say the least, that one kind of environmental problem is keeping excess phosphates out of living systems while others have to do with the need for phosphates in agricultural production.

The Sulfur Cycle

Sulfur is an important element in proteins and various protein-carbohydrate complexes. Sulfur is found in the soil primarily in the form of elemental sulfur and sulfates (compounds containing the SO_4^- group) (Figure 3.8). Sulfur is taken in by plants in the form of sulfates and is eventually returned to the soil through the decomposition of wastes or dead materials. Organic sulfur is converted into inorganic sulfate by common decomposers (bacteria and fungi). The sulfur cycle involves numerous species of bacteria and fungi that interconvert sulfates, sulfides, and elemental sulfur.

One of the most common sulfides is a gas, hydrogen sulfide (H_2S), well known for its "rotten egg" odor. The bacteria that convert sulfates to hydrogen sulfide are adapted to anaerobic (oxygen-deficient) habitats. The foul smell of hydrogen sulfide is characteristic of decomposition in an oxygen-deficient system.

Sulfur may enter the atmosphere as hydrogen sulfide or as sulfur dioxide (SO_2). Sulfur dioxide is formed in the combustion of organic material—leaves, carcasses, or *coal*. Sulfur dioxide, itself reactive and toxic to animals (including humans), reacts in the atmosphere to form sulfuric acid. When this acidic moisture condenses and falls to the ground as precipitation, the result is what is called "acid rain." Acid rain will be considered in detail in Chapter 10.

NUTRIENT CYCLES AS REGULATORS OF ECOSYSTEM ACTIVITY

We have seen that biogeochemical cycles involve complex interactions between the abiotic environment and living organisms. We have also seen that any one cycle is composed of numerous loops and steps. As we look back over Figures 3.1, 3.5, 3.6, 3.7, and 3.8, we find that the representative cycles all overlap, that they operate simultaneously in the same functioning systems. We have observed that the biosphere both regulates and is regulated by various biogeochemical cycles. The nature and speed of certain chemical interactions

In lithospheric cycles, minerals may be held out of the cycle for very long periods. These stalactites, formed from a solution of calcium carbonate in groundwater that has seeped into rock, may represent thousands of years of groundwater action on the rock.

among producers, consumers, decomposers, and the abiotic environment determine how well any given ecosystem functions.

The Law of the Minimum

In 1840, Justus Leibig expressed the idea that organisms and the living systems they comprise are held in check by the scarcest of the things they need. What we refer to today as the **law of the minimum** was derived from Leibig's observation that a plant tends to grow only to the limit of the foodstuff available to it in the most extreme minimum quantity. This would be analagous to saying that an automobile assembly plant can make cars only as fast as it can get tires during a rubber shortage. In the general world of real ecosystems the applicability of Liebig's law is far from being as simple and straightforward as this analogy might suggest.

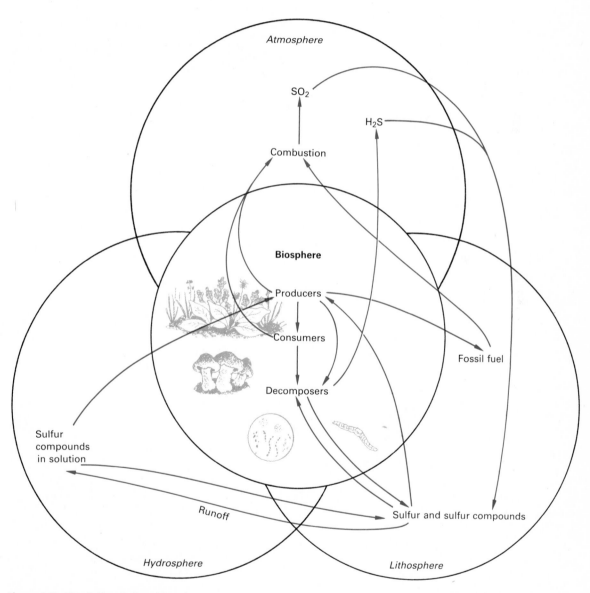

Figure 3.8 The Sulfur Cycle. Although most troublesome in its atmospheric form of sulfur dioxide, sulfur is predominantly a lithospheric cycle. Bacteria are important factors in the sulfur cycle, changing sulfur into various forms in the soil.

For one thing, the law of the minimum is a law only under steady state conditions. During periods of change, ecosystems tend to be held in check by the availability of many raw materials, the composite genetic program of the organisms involved, and many physical conditions, all at the same time. There are many potential limiting factors in any ecosystem. For example, the rate at which photosynthesis occurs depends on the availability of water, carbon dioxide, nutrients such as nitrogen, phosphorus, iron, zinc, and magnesium; the ambient temperature; and the light intensity, any one of which could be rate limiting. Even under steady state conditions these things vary over time and influence one another in complex ways. A given plant might need less rainfall when it is cool. Its need for a particular mineral might depend on the availability of one or more other minerals. A plant might very well need less of a particular mineral if it is growing in the shade.

Because conditions tend to be somewhat more constant in aquatic ecosystems, the law of the minimum tends to be more apparent in such systems. Phosphorus as phosphate is often a limiting nutrient in lakes and rivers; this is why phosphate detergents can cause a disruptive acceleration of plant growth in these aquatic systems. Nitrogen is commonly a limiting or near-limiting nutrient in terrestrial (and aquatic) systems; it is for this reason that nitrogen is such a common ingredient in fertilizers.

Factors Governing the Supply of Mineral Nutrients

There are a number of influences on the supply of nutrients within any living system. For one thing,

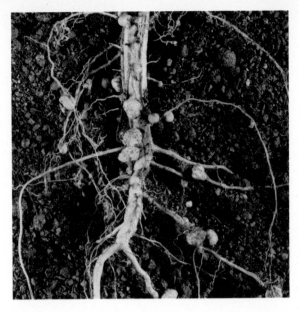

The supply of nitrogen available to plants depends on nitrogen fixers like the *Rhizobium* bacteria found in these soybean root nodules, which in turn depend on the availability of other minerals.

nutrients affect one another. Phosphorus is often a key regulator of activity in ecosystems because of its relative scarcity in the form of soluble phosphate and because of its key role in storing and releasing energy as part of the ATP molecule. In an aquatic system the supply of phosphorus to living systems may be linked to the presence of sulfur and iron. The binding of sulfur with iron under anaerobic conditions in an aqueous environment creates conditions that convert phosphorus from an insoluble form to

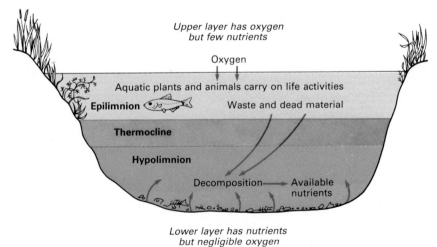

Figure 3.9 Stratification in Deep Lakes. The thermocline is a horizontal interface between less dense, warmer, upper layers of water and colder (denser) lower layers. This effectively prevents mixing of the upper (epilimnion) and lower (hypolimnion) layers of the stratified lake.

Upper layer has oxygen but few nutrients

Oxygen

Aquatic plants and animals carry on life activities

Epilimnion   Waste and dead material

Thermocline

Hypolimnion

Decomposition → Available nutrients

Lower layer has nutrients but negligible oxygen

a soluble form that can be used by living things. Bonding with sulfur may also tie up minerals such as copper, cadmium, zinc, and cobalt.

The supply of usable nitrogen is dependent primarily on nitrogen fixers, which take atmospheric nitrogen and convert it to ammonia and nitrates. The activity and reproduction in nitrogen fixers may be controlled in turn by the availability of other minerals such as phosphorus, iron, calcium, molybdenum, or cobalt.

Because of variations in geochemical influences, the amount of nitrates, phosphates, water, and other minerals available to living systems varies from one area to another and may even change from one season to another or be influenced by periodic "imports" and "exports" (see also Chapter 2). Runoff from a feedlot or a heavily fertilized cornfield may import phosphorus and nitrogen to a nearby lake and result in a large increase in the availability of these usually limiting nutrients. Erosion may export nutrients in topsoil, resulting in less fertile farmland and more fertile nearby streams.

Lakes: Spring and Fall Overturn

Changes in physical environment can also cause changes in the supply of chemicals within a system. One such example is the effect of seasonal temperature changes on bodies of water. A pattern that occurs twice yearly in certain deep lakes is known as fall and spring overturn. This phenomenon is related to the nature of water, which, as was mentioned previously, has its greatest density at 4°C.

Normally, in the summer, temperature zone lakes become stratified into layers having different temperatures (Figure 3.9 and 3.10). Being somewhat insulated, the lower layer (**hypolimnion**) stays cool while the surface layer (**epilimnion**) warms. As the temperature and density differential increase, an

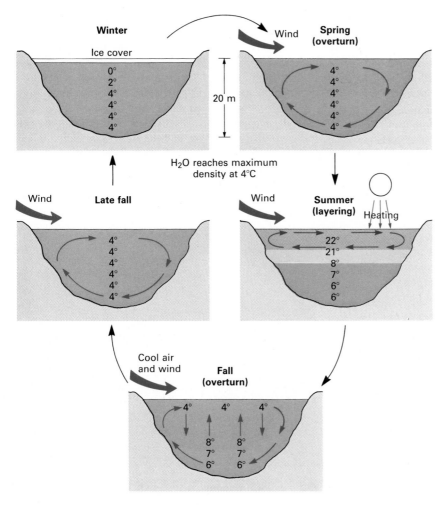

Figure 3.10 Temperature Cycles in Deep Lakes. This schematic demonstrates how the change in water temperature results in a layering or mixing of water in deep lakes. The movement of the water is the result of the fact that water is heaviest at 4°C.

area of fairly dramatic vertical temperature change forms between the upper and lower layers. It is called the **thermocline**. This stratification prevents mixing of the upper and lower layers. Algae grow best at the surface, where the light is strong. As they grow, they take up nutrients such as phosphate and nitrate; and as they (along with consumers) die, they sink to the bottom, carrying their accumulated nutrients with them. This tends to deplete the surface layer of nutrients; the depletion soon limits plant growth. Meanwhile, at the bottom, decomposers break down the organic matter slowly because of the cool temperatures and low oxygen concentration.

During the fall the surface layer gets cooler, and a point is eventually reached at which the surface layer begins to become more dense (heavier) than the lower layer, and a dramatic mixing of the layers or overturn occurs (Figure 3.10).

Going into the winter months, surface water temperatures cool to below 4°C. Toward the end of winter and into early spring, surface water temperatures begin to rise. As the surface temperature approaches 4°C, surface waters become heavier than the lower layers, and mixing occurs again.

Overturns bring nutrients from the lower level to the sunlit upper level, creating ideal conditions for plant growth. This is why algae "blooms" often occur shortly after overturns. This is not necessarily a good thing, however. The growth of algae may be so prodigious as to form a mat over parts of the lake. Plants below this mat no longer receive sufficient sunlight and begin to die and decompose. This provides a huge food source for decomposers and results in a rapid increase in the number of decom-

posers and an accelerated rate of decomposition. The increased respiration by decomposers may use up oxygen faster than it can dissolve in the water from the atmosphere and faster than the aquatic plants can release it. The lake may become oxygen deficient, and organisms unable to tolerate this condition will perish.

Note that during this entire sequence, several *different* factors (sunlight, O_2, nutrients) were limiting for *different* parts of the aquatic community. Overturn illustrates clearly that physical conditions are able to influence living systems through an impact on chemistry.

The Law of Tolerance

We have just seen that there can be problems in nature associated with both too little (law of the minimum) and too much of a chemical regulator. Figure 3.11 demonstrates this fact graphically; it applies to individual organisms and to communities of living things. Similar generalized graphs could be drawn for features of the environment other than nutrients. Temperature, light level, soil moisture, and slope are among the most important. All of this could be summarized by saying that organisms and, in the aggregate, whole systems of organisms have ranges of physical and chemical conditions within which they can flourish but beyond which they change and much beyond which they cannot exist.

Shelford's law of tolerance states, in essence, that both too much and too little of various environmental chemical and physical factors can serve as limiting factors or regulators in ecosystems. If the lowest annual temperature reached in a particular

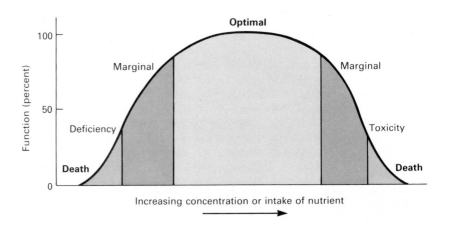

Figure 3.11 Shelford's Law of Tolerance. Both too much and too little of a chemical nutrient or given environmental factor (temperature, rainfall, etc.) can be harmful to living things.

environment is below the lowest temperature that a particular plant can tolerate, *that* plant is not likely to be found in *that* environment, even if moisture or soil type is sufficient.

As one might expect, some organisms have wider ranges of tolerance than others, and individual organisms have varying ranges of tolerance for different environmental factors (Figure 3.12). Animals and plants having the widest ranges of tolerance overall can be found in many different kinds of environments. Limits of tolerance are often interrelated. Bacteria, for instance, can tolerate higher heat longer when they are dry and when the soil or substrate is close to neutral (not too acid or too alkaline). The concepts of tolerance limits and limiting factors link the disciplines of ecology and physiology and form the basis of biogeography, the study of the abundance and distribution of species in nature.

The human species has learned to manipulate limiting factors to some extent. We cultivate plants by adding water and nutrients to the level that should be optimum for growth. We have learned to develop methods of importing nutrients for human consumption into areas that of themselves could not support many people. Humans can live in all types of temperature extremes because of the ability to heat and cool shelters and to put on and take off layers of clothing. The human species is among the most widely distributed of all species.

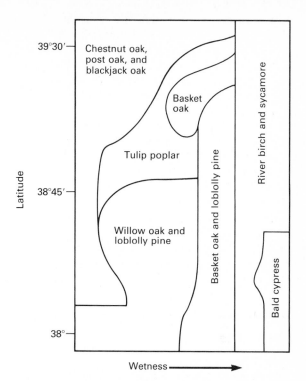

Figure 3.12 Ranges of Tolerance in Some Tree Species. The distribution of tree species can be shown to vary according to their tolerance ranges for moisture and latitude; latitude affects factors like temperature and day length. Ranges of tolerances overlap.

THE ECOLOGICAL CONNECTION

The ecosphere is in chemical motion. Elements are being taken out of the abiotic environment by plants, moved up the food chain, and excreted. As you read this, chemicals you consumed at breakfast are being incorporated into proteins and other chemicals. Yesterday's proteins are being torn down, and the constituents are being incorporated into other proteins and other chemicals. Calcium is moving into and out of your bones. You may feel stable, but you are in a dynamic chemical state with the ecosystem around you. This is true for the entire global system of which we are part. The cycling of nutrients is complex, and individual cycles are interrelated.

Human activity can alter cycles. Alterations can be for the good or for the bad, but inadvertent alterations are seldom for the good in intricate ecological systems. Many of the environmental and health problems we face today are the result of unanticipated impacts of synthetic substances on the ecosphere, overloading cycles and piling up concentrations of chemicals that exceed tolerance limits, and "revving up" natural systems by adding nutrients of which small amounts had been limiting.

CONCEPTS TO REMEMBER

1. For the most part the total amount of each chemical element in the ecosphere remains the same. Chemical elements are used over and over by living things.
2. Chemical elements are combined to form the substance of living and nonliving things.
3. At any point in time a specific chemical element in an ecosystem is distributed in various chemical forms in air, rock (or soil), water, and in some cases living things. Over time the elements move from one sphere to another in patterns called biogeochemical cycles.

4. Chemical elements that are essential to organisms are called chemical nutrients. The availability of chemical nutrients regulates growth and other activities in living systems. Plant productivity, for example, can be held in check by the lack of certain compounds of nitrogen or phosphorus.

5. The availability of specific chemical elements to living things is determined by three factors: (1) molecular form—the element must be in a form that is usable by that organism; (2) physical location—an element has to be accessible to living things; and (3) patterns and rates of cycling—how fast an element moves from one form to another and from one location to another.

6. Individual organisms and, collectively, specific communities of organisms have characteristic *tolerance ranges* for individual chemical elements and their compounds. Too much or too little can be detrimental. Living things also have tolerance ranges for physical conditions such as light and temperature.

7. Human activities have altered biogeochemical cycles in ways that are detrimental to humans and other living things. We can, and have, influenced chemical form, physical location, and the rate of cycling of chemical elements. We have discovered and have added new compounds to biogeochemical cycles. Some of these synthetic substances have had serious unanticipated effects on the ecosphere.

8. Human beings are integral components of biogeochemical cycles and share a dynamic chemical commonality with all other things, living and nonliving.

DISCUSSION QUESTIONS AND FOOD FOR THOUGHT

1. Minerals are not used up but are constantly cycled in the ecosphere. Discuss and explain the origins of mineral "shortages."

2. Draw a diagram showing the change that might occur in the hydrologic cycle if a pasture bordering a river were developed as a subdivision.

3. Trace the process by which the carbon in the charcoal you used to grill with last summer may end up in a molecule of a guppy in your aquarium.

4. Phosphate is often a limiting factor in plant growth. Because of this, phosphate deposits are mined in order to produce commercial fertilizer. What effect might this mining have on the cycling of phosphate? Where does mining fit in Figure 3.7?

5. Discuss: Modern U.S. civilization is based on a one-way mineral flow rather than on nutrient or mineral cycling.

6. Draw a diagram showing how nitrogen is cycled on a farm where manure from the feedlot is used as fertilizer. Draw a second diagram showing the cycling of nitrogen on a farm where a commercial fertilizer is used. Remember that you must still show the possible routes the unused manure might follow. Place a person in the picture as a consumer of milk containing nitrogen. Are all of the pathways closed cycles? What are the implications if they are not?

7. Debate: Air pollution, water pollution, and land pollution are different aspects of the same problem—a distortion of biogeochemical cycling.

8. What adjustments might occur in the carbon cycle to keep the amount of the carbon dioxide in the atmosphere constant as more CO_2 is released from the burning of fossil fuels. Use Figure 3.5.

9. Draw a schematic of the lithospheric zinc cycle.

10. Find out what the numbers 20:10:5 on a bag of chemical fertilizer mean.

REFERENCES AND FURTHER READING

References marked with an asterisk are cited in the chapter.

Anderson, J. M., 1981. *Ecology for Environmental Sciences: Biosphere, Ecosystems and Man.* New York: John Wiley & Sons.

Bolin, B., and Cook, R. B., 1983. *The Major Biogeochemical Cycles and Their Interactions.* New York: John Wiley & Sons.

Brush, G. S., 1982. "An Environmental Analysis of Forest Patterns," *American Scientist* **70** (January–February); 18–25.

Commoner, B., 1971. *The Closing Circle.* New York: Alfred A. Knopf.

Commoner, B., 1977. "Cost-Risk-Benefit Analysis of Nitrogen Fertilization: A Case History," *Ambio* **VI**(2–3):157–161.

Federov, E. K., 1979. "Climatic Changes," *Environment* **21** (4; May) 25–31.

Haas, R. B., 1984. "The Year of the El Nino," *Resources for the Future* **75** (Winter): 12–13.

*Kormondy, E. J., 1969. *Concepts of Ecology.* Englewood Cliffs, N.J.: Prentice-Hall.

*Kormondy, E. J., 1984. *Concepts of Ecology,* 3rd ed. Englewood Cliffs, N.J.: Prentice-Hall.

Mertz, W., 1981. "The Essential Trace Elements," *Science* **213** (September 18): 1332–1338.

Odum, E. P., 1984. *Fundamentals of Ecology.* Philadelphia: W. B. Saunders.

Sellers, W. D., 1977. "Water Circulation on the Global Scale: Natural Factors and Manipulation by Man," *Ambio* **VI**(1): 10–12.

Walker, J. C. G., 1984. "How Life Affects the Atmosphere," *Bioscience* **34**(8): 486–491.

See also the general references and textbooks cited in "References and Further Reading" at the end of Chapter 1.

CHAPTER 4

Populations and Communities

In Chapter 2 we discussed the importance of energy to living things. In Chapter 3 we considered the importance of matter. Organisms depend on one another for *both* of these commodities. Energy flows through ecosystems, from one living thing to another, in "chains" or "webs" that begin with producers and end with consumers or decomposers one or more trophic levels later. Matter cycles within ecosystems. It moves in short loops and long loops from one living thing to another, from producers to consumers and back again.

In Chapters 2 and 3 we looked at how organisms depend on one another *directly* for matter and energy. In Chapter 4 we will focus on relationships between organisms in the context of how the relationships govern energy and nutrient flow directly and indirectly and (most of the time) yield constancy in nature in the face of explosive potential for growth and change.

On the way through Chapter 4 we should find the basis for the answers to the following kinds of questions:

— How do particular groups of living things get to be what they are? For example, why are there characteristic kinds of plants and animals in nearly all North Carolina swamps?
— Why do the numbers and kinds of plants and animals in, say, a Pennsylvania forest stay about the same from year to year? Or do they?
— Why do "population explosions" occur in nature? Why don't they occur more often? Why does the explosive growth of a population go only so far?
— What happens when a new species is introduced into an ecosystem? What happens when an old one is taken out?
— What if there is a fire? Do ecosystems eventually recover—get back to their original condition? If so, why? If so, how? If not, what does happen? How long does it take in either case?
— Assuming that we all know why deserts are where they are, why are there prairies in some places, deciduous forests in some places, and evergreen forests in other places, each a characteristic community of living things?
— What is the ecological significance of territoriality and social organization in some species—packs of wolves, troops of baboons, prides of lions, beehives, and anthills?

These are all questions about regulation and regulation is the theme of Chapter 4. The cardinal question we will be addressing throughout is: *Just how do the organisms in an ecosystem influence one another so as to amount to a relatively stable community or a gradually and systematically changing community?*

We will start at the population level, the level of interaction between members of the *same* species. This will set us up to look at the more complex community level—the level of interaction of *different* species. It will help to keep in mind that the interdependence of living things is the essence of ecology.

POPULATIONS: SOME GENERAL CHARACTERISTICS

A **population** is a group of similar organisms or, more specifically, interbreeding members of the same species in a given area. The term population can apply to all the members of a species in a field or to those in larger areas such as the Atlantic Ocean. "Population" is another example of a term that is an abstraction with variable applications. Because populations are composed of many individuals, they exhibit certain patterns or traits that individuals cannot.

Patterns of Distribution

Populations can vary in the way their individual members are distributed (Figure 4.1). The individuals in populations of some species tend to be regularly dispersed with no aggregation or clumping; an apple orchard is a familiar example, though it is not wild. Such *uniform distributions* are not extremely common in nature, but they can occur, usually where there is severe competition for resources. The creosote bush of the American Southwest is thought to produce a substance in its roots that prevents creosote bush seeds from germinating and growing too close. Competition for water and other needs may also play a role. In any case there are rather uniform distributions of creosote bushes in the desert.

The distributions of the individuals in some species approach complete *randomness*. Plants with airborne seed dispersal mechanisms might follow this pattern. Random patterns are found in environments with relatively uniform conditions throughout and consequently are relatively rare.

In old fields, sassafras, hawthorn, and other shrubs exhibit a third pattern of distribution, called *clumped*. This pattern is the most common. Generally speaking, clumping is a result of short-range seed dispersal and/or nonuniform environmental conditions (remember the concept of tolerance explained in Chapter 3). Within a large, apparently uniform area, differences in microenvironment favor some species over others. Moss usually grows best on the side of a tree that is most moist. Different plant species are often found on the north-facing and south-facing slopes of the same woods. Within a plant community, plants requiring more moisture may be found in shady areas or in slight depressions or low places. Social factors can likewise cause clumping in species distribution. The formation of packs or herds by some kinds of animals serves to help them get food and protect themselves.

Density

Apart from its distribution pattern a population may exhibit various **densities**, that is, different numbers of individuals (or amounts of biomass) per unit area or volume. If there are one hundred mice in a two-acre field, the density is 50 mice per acre. Sometimes more refined expressions of density must be used when not all of a given area is suitable habitat for particular species under study. If a half-acre pond were located in the middle of the two-acre field, for example, it would make more sense to speak of 100 mice per 1.5 acres. Density per unit of *habitat* is called **ecological density** and is a more useful expression of density.

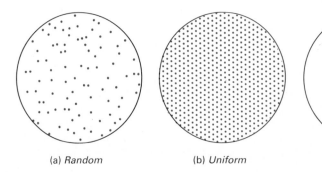

Figure 4.1 Distribution Patterns of Organisms in Nature. The range of distribution results from interactions with abiotic factors such as climate and soil type and with each other (social factors). Organisms may be distributed randomly, uniformly, or in clumps.

(a) *Random*   (b) *Uniform*   (c) *Clumped*

Social Organization

Animal populations exhibit varying degrees of social organization. Social organization can take the form of territoriality or hierarchical relationships and extends to the highly specialized divisions of labor that are found among the members of insect colonies.

Many species of animals exhibit **territoriality**, wherein individuals vie for the "rights" to units of habitat. The winner gets to use the territory; the loser is driven off. Usually, the defended territory is somewhat smaller than the **home range**, the total area in which an animal lives, eats, and functions. Territories and home ranges vary in size for different species. Territories may cover several miles in the case of large animals or birds; they may be limited to a single plant in the case of some insects. In confrontations over territory between two members of the same species, physical harm is rarely done even to the loser. Quite often the interaction consists only of scent signals and/or vocal and behavioral displays. Territoriality serves to diminish destructive competition for resources such as food or habitat by limiting the number of organisms of a species in a given area.

In the hierarchy of breeding colonies, the older male seals take the choice locations; the younger males, in their less desirable spots, can attract fewer females.

Chapter 4   Populations and Communities

65

A second form of social organization expresses itself in patterns of **hierarchy** in species in which interaction is more extensive and continuous. Perhaps the most familiar example of this is the **pecking order** among chickens. At the top of the pecking order is a chicken that can peck (dominate) all others and in turn is pecked by none. In the middle are chickens that can peck some chickens but are pecked by others. At the bottom is a chicken that all other chickens can peck but that cannot peck back. These dominant-subordinate relationships become more apparent in some animals during mating season. The result is that the more dominant and usually stronger have first choice of mates. Individuals at the lower end of the hierarchy may or may not have the opportunity to mate.

Extreme social organization is found in the structure of colonies of insects like termites, ants, and bees. Insect colonies may be so highly integrated that an individual may not be able to survive outside of the society. Bees are a prime example. So interdependent are the individuals in a beehive that a hive is more like an organism made up of cells than it is like a population made up of individuals.

GROWTH OF POPULATIONS

Factors Affecting Population Growth

To determine the growth rate of a population, one would have to look at the factors that tend to *increase* the number of individuals within that popu-

lation and those that tend to *decrease* the number of individuals in that population. There are only two ways by which new individuals can enter a population. One is by new *births* and the other is by *immigration*. The birth rate is determined by the inherent reproductive potential of the species and the number of individuals in the population capable of reproducing. The overall reproductive success of the species is also affected by environmental factors such as the food and habitat available and favorable or unfavorable climate conditions. The immigration rate is determined by species mobility and the extent of the exploitable opportunity. A population loses individuals by *death* and by *emigration* (see Figure 4.2). Death and emigration rates are determined by such things as abundance of food, environmental conditions, disease, predation, and competition for food and habitat.

For a given population in a given place we can think of growth rate as a function of the maximum reproductive rate characteristic of that species, various factors that tend to keep maximum reproductive potential from being realized, and various characteristics of the population itself. Age structure would be an example of the last of these.

Biotic Potential and Environmental Resistance

The **biotic potential** of a species is its maximum possible growth rate; it is a concept based on births per female in the "ideal" absence of any limiting

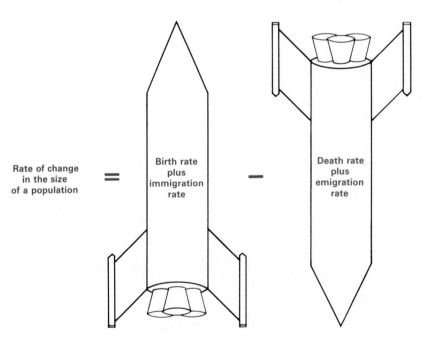

Figure 4.2 Population Change. Population growth results from the net effect of all factors adding to the number of individuals in that population (births and immigration) and those decreasing the number of individuals in that population (deaths and emigration). These factors in turn are the result of species characteristics and environmental conditions.

Rate of change in the size of a population **=** Birth rate plus immigration rate **−** Death rate plus emigration rate

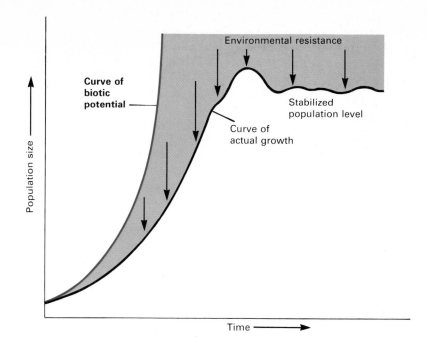

Figure 4.3 **Biotic Potential and Environmental Resistance.** Seldom does the growth rate of a population equal its biotic potential—its growth rate under ideal, nonlimiting conditions. Environmental factors such as food supply, habitat, and disease limit growth.

conditions, for example, limitations in habitat or food supply. Biotic potential differs widely from species to species but is a relatively fixed characteristic for any one species. Ideally, one female fly and her offspring could produce six trillion flies in one year. In 750 years a pair of elephants and their offspring could theoretically produce 19×10^6 elephants. Likewise, in ten years a pair of sparrows could generate 275×10^9 offspring. Biotic potentials can be expressed as population doubling times, that is, how long it takes a population to double in size. Doubling times can vary from minutes in the case of bacteria to many years in the case of elephants.

Biotic potentials are never realized for very long; in fact, most species never realize their full biotic potential. The reason? Factors such as disease, lack of food, predation, lack of space, and others come into play. These factors keep growth rates well below biotic potentials and are termed collectively **environmental resistance**. Ecologists spend a great deal of time determining which factors or combinations of them are most important in influencing population growth in specific kinds of organisms (Figure 4.3).

There are two basic types of environmental resistance factors in nature. **Density-independent factors** are those that tend to exert the same pressure on a population regardless of the number of individuals present in that population. Often climate and weather are density-independent factors. Seasonal changes and even storms and rapid temperature changes tend to exert the same basic influence on each individual regardless of how many individuals there happen to be. The same is true of chemical pollutants. Under some circumstances, density independence might be somewhat less than complete. Within certain limits, for example, the availability of shelter or social behavior might help ease the effects of certain physical environmental changes such as climate. In this case the degree of the impact might be somewhat density related and could even be called "density-vague."

Density-dependent factors are those that come into (and out of) play gradually as population size increases (or decreases). They are also called "density-governing." Density-dependent factors include such things as access to food, access to suitable habitat, and the impact of parasites, pathogens, and predators. (See the example of wolves and moose in Chapter 1.) Density-dependent control mechanisms influence population growth by influencing the probability that an individual will live to reproductive maturity or by influencing fertility. High concentrations of geese, for example, can (at the same time) attract more predators, offer conditions in which disease is more likely to spread, and create conditions in which food is scarce. Each of these effects can in turn influence the average number of viable offspring per nest and the probability that a given goose will live to reproductive maturity.

In the 1930s the American chestnut population was all but destroyed by a fungous disease. Only a few members remain of this species that was once widespread in the eastern United States.

An often cited example of predation *and* food supply limitations as density-dependent population control mechanisms is based upon data for Canadian lynx pelts and the pelts of the snowshoe hare taken over a 90-year period. It was observed that the hare population decreased every 9–10 years and that the lynx followed a similar pattern but 1–2 years behind the hare. It seems that the hare, being a principal source of food for the lynx, is playing some role in the regulation of the lynx population—and possibly vice versa. Other factors are surely involved because similar hare population cycles occur even where there are no lynx. However, one plausible partial explanation for this is that when the hare population is large, it provides a large source of food for the lynx, resulting in an increase in the lynx population. An increase in the lynx population, however, means that more hare will be taken for food. This alone or in combination with other elements of resistance to hare reproduction causes the hare population to decrease. A loss of food for the lynx means that the lynx population will have to compete for a smaller amount of food, and its population will decrease. With fewer lynx, more hare survive, their population flourishes again, and the system repeats. The length of the interval between ups and downs would be a function (at least in part) of how long it takes hares to become plentiful and lynx to become plentiful once conditions become favorable for each. In each case, density-dependent factors come into play (predation and food supply) to keep the upward growth of the populations in check.

Certain physiological and neurophysiological control mechanisms may also be operative as density-dependent growth regulators in some species, especially in vertebrates. Christian and Davis (1964) monitored dense populations of rats in the laboratory. They found that crowding resulted in an enlargement of the adrenal gland (an indication of stress) and decreased fertility (see Chapter 16).

Density-dependent factors tend to keep populations at levels that the environment can support, but the influence of these factors wanes as numbers fall, keeping populations from getting too small. For most species there are optimum densities—undercrowding as well as overcrowding may be limiting. If populations fall too low, mates may not be found, or the signals that lead to successful reproduction may be missed. For some species there may even be a threshold level of density below which a population is doomed to extinction.

Density-independent factors generally are more important in population regulation in ecosystems with *low* species diversity and regular or periodic physical disruptions such as fires or flooding; density-dependent factors tend to be more important in ecosystems with *high* species diversity and relative constancy in the physical environment. Density-independent factors are usually more important growth rate regulators when a species is first introduced into a new habitat, and density-dependent factors become increasingly important, by definition, as the population gets larger. For organisms in situations in which the density-independent factors are *not* limiting, that is, where physical factors are such that the populations are not continuously knocked off balance, density-dependent factors ultimately regulate population growth. Generally, density-dependent factors combine to increasingly suppress growth as the population gets large, and a point is reached at which growth stabilizes. A theoretical parameter known as **environmental carrying capacity** is the largest population of a given species that can be sustained indefinitely in a particular ecosystem. This is a theoretical balance point between biotic potential and environmental resistance.

Survivorship

The age-specific pattern in which the individuals in a population survive or die varies from species to species, and such patterns are important determinants of the way populations grow. Figure 4.4 shows three different kinds of **survivorship curves**. In one type of survivorship pattern (Curve A), most

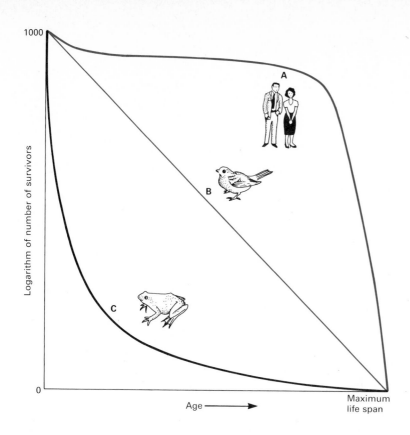

Figure 4.4 Survivorship Curves in Populations. This shows graphically three basic patterns for survivorship. The curve begins with 1000 live offspring on the left and shows the numbers of survivors with time indicated as a percentage over the normal life span. There are three characteristic survivorship curves: Most members of the species die late (Curve A); mortality is relatively constant throughout the life span (Curve B); most members die young (Curve C). The exact configuration of the curve varies from species to species. Survivorship is also affected by various factors such as food supply, density, and quality of habitat.

of the organisms survive to their maximum life spans because there are few factors to cause death among young organisms. Humans and mountain sheep tend to follow this pattern. In species exhibiting an equal probability of death at any point in a typical life span, survivorship is represented as a straight line in a logarithmic graph as in Curve B. This pattern is found in most species of songbirds and in small aquatic organisms such as hydra. In the third pattern, characteristic of organisms like frogs, oysters, and oak trees, large numbers of offspring never reach maturity but die at early ages (Curve C). Typically, the reproductive pattern of such organisms amounts to the production of extremely large numbers of offspring, only a small fraction of which then usually survive to reproduce. Organisms following this pattern have the greatest explosive growth potential if, for whatever reason, survival improves for a time.

These curves represent *basic* patterns. It is unlikely that any species has exactly a straight-line logarithmic pattern. The exact nature of a survivorship curve varies from one population to another for the same species. In humans, for example, developing countries tend to have higher infant mortality rates than developed countries. Males and females of a species have slightly different patterns of survivorship. Changing population density, food availability, and other such factors can even change the survivorship pattern for a given population for a period of time.

Survivorship curves for individual species can be derived through detailed field studies. One of the first such studies was done on Dall mountain sheep by Edward S. Deevey (1947) using data collected by Adolf Murie. Murie collected skulls from a population of Dall sheep in Alaska. He could tell the age of the sheep from annual rings on the horns of the skulls and published their ages. Deevey developed a "life table" from these (see Table 4.1) whereby he was able to show and compare the probabilities of death for various age groups.

Age Structure

The age structure of a population reflects its growth *potential* (see Figure 4.5). **Age structure** is usually represented as the percentage of individuals within incremental age ranges, for example, 0–5 years, 5–10 years, 10–20 years, and so on. In terms of potential population growth the most useful way of classifying the age structure of populations is ac-

Table 4.1 Life Table for Dall Mountain Sheep

Age* (years)	Number Dying in Age Interval out of 1000 born	Number Surviving at Beginning of Age Interval out of 1000 born	Mortality Rate per Thousand Alive at Beginning of Age Interval	Expectation of Life, or Mean Lifetime Remaining to Those Attaining Age Interval (years)
0–0.5	54	1000	54.0	7.06
0.5–1	145	946	153.0	—
1–2	12	801	15.0	7.7
2–3	13	789	16.5	6.8
3–4	12	776	15.5	5.9
4–5	30	764	39.3	5.0
5–6	46	734	62.6	4.2
6–7	48	688	69.9	3.4
7–8	69	640	108.0	2.6
8–9	132	571	231.0	1.9
9–10	187	439	426.0	1.3
10–11	156	252	619.0	0.9
11–12	90	96	937.0	0.6
12–13	3	6	500.0	1.2
13–14	3	3	1000.0	0.7

* A small number of skulls without horns, but judged by their osteology to belong to sheep nine years old or older, have been apportioned pro rata among the older age classes.

This table was constructed solely from examination of a collection of sheep skulls from Mount McKinley. It reveals that most mortality was suffered by the very young and the very old, which was as expected because wolves were the main source of mortality and they were known to hunt the weaker animals.

cording to ability or potential to reproduce. Those members of a population that have not yet matured sexually form a *prereproductive* group. The two other categories are the *reproductive* group and the *postreproductive* group. Again, by examining the age structure of a given population at one point in time *in light of current survivorship for that species* it is possible to tell whether that particular population is growing or shrinking (see Figure 4.5).

If there is a "bulge" in a population in the actively reproducing group, the prereproductive group will obviously not entirely replace those presently reproducing, and barring any surge in **fertility rate** (births per reproductive age female), that population can be expected to decline (Figure 4.5).

In many species, including humans, if the prereproductive fraction of a population is comparable in size to the reproductive fraction, if survivorship is

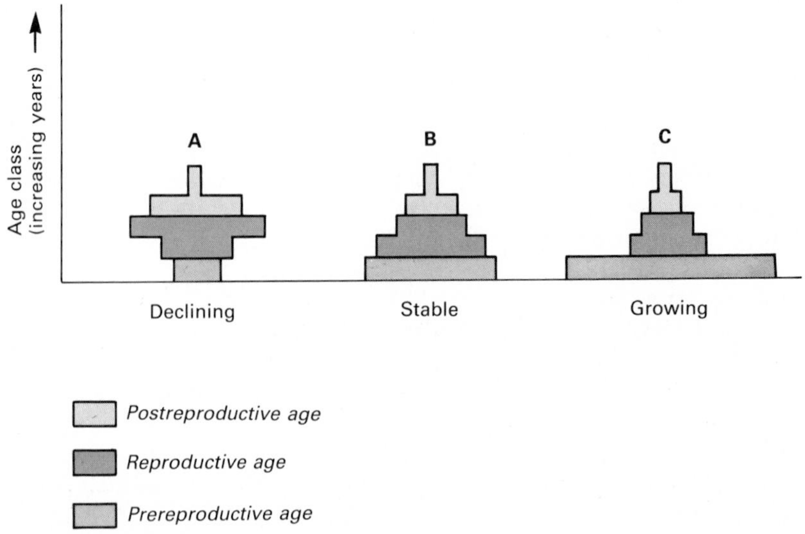

Figure 4.5 The Age Distribution Patterns and Growth Potentials in Populations. The patterns show the relative proportion of a population that is reproducing and the proportion that soon will be reproductive, assuming a certain pattern of survivorship.

□ Postreproductive age

■ Reproductive age

▨ Prereproductive age

high, and if fertility is constant, the population is in a steady state, that is, will stay the same size (Figure 4.5). If the postreproductive group comprises a very large fraction of a population, this is generally an indication that the population is in decline.

If the prereproductive class is much larger than the reproductive class and if survivorship is high, the prereproductive group will eventually more than replace those now in the reproductive stage (Figure 4.5). Of course, if survivorship is low and stays low, the configuration may well change very little if at all.

Any change in survivorship would influence just what will happen for any given population profile. These basic ecological facts have direct application to questions about human population growth (Chapter 8).

POPULATION GROWTH PATTERNS

Exponential Growth

In order to understand population growth patterns we must first examine what is meant by exponential growth. Exponential rates of growth can be interestingly deceptive. For example, if you offered to give a person one penny and to double it each day thereafter, on the seventh day you would have to pay that person 64¢, on the fourteenth day you would owe $81.92, and on the twenty-first day you would have to pay $10,485.76! (See Table 4.2.) Just for fun, estimate the number of grains of corn in a kilogram. Then calculate the weight of corn you would have coming if someone promised to give you one grain on the first square of a checkerboard, two on the second, four on the third, eight on the fourth, and so on. (Mathematically, the number of grains on the sixty-fourth square would be 2^{63} or 9.2234 ×

10^{18} or just about 9.0 million million million grains. How would this compare to the world production of corn for last year?)

When a species is introduced into a new suitable habitat, following a brief lag period its growth rate often soon becomes exponential. The growth rate is invariably something less than its biotic potential, but it may be dramatic, nevertheless. Although the *rates* of initial growth may vary considerably from one species to another, the *pattern* of lag followed by exponential growth is the same for all species. What happens after that seems to fall into one of two general patterns. Depending on the species and to some degree on circumstance, overall growth patterns assume either a J-shaped pattern or a sigmoid (S-shaped) pattern.

The J-Shaped Curve

The **J-shaped curve** (Figure 4.6) describes populations in which growth is exponential to a point at which a "crash" or a dying off of most of the population occurs. The curve that results looks (to the imaginative) like the letter J. The crash might be the result of density-dependent destruction of the environment or the abrupt change in the influence of some density-independent factor. An example of the former would be the food depletion and the accumulation of waste in a bottle of milk populated by bacteria. An example of the latter would be a first frost and its impact on flies, other insects, or annual plants. If the survivors are so few that the reproductive rate continues to be less than the death rate, that population is on the way to disappearance. If a sufficient number of the population survives that the reproductive rate again surpasses the death rate, that population may again go through a J-shaped rise and fall.

Table 4.2 Exponential Growth Rates

First Week		Second Week		Third Week	
Day	Amount	Day	Amount	Day	Amount
1	$0.01	8	$ 1.28	15	$ 163.84
2	0.02	9	2.56	16	327.68
3	0.04	10	5.12	17	655.36
4	0.08	11	10.24	18	1310.72
5	0.16	12	20.48	19	2621.44
6	0.32	13	40.96	20	·5242.88
7	0.64	14	81.92	21	10,485.76

Starting with one penny and doubling it daily result in exponential or geometric growth. The term "exponential" comes from the fact that growth is described mathematically by an exponential expression, that is, some constant raised to a power. This means that as a population gets larger and larger, it grows faster and faster in succeeding intervals of time.

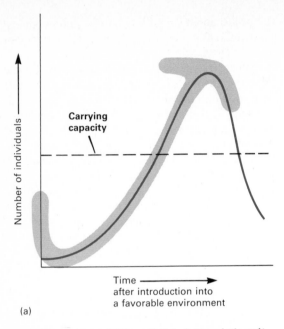

(a)

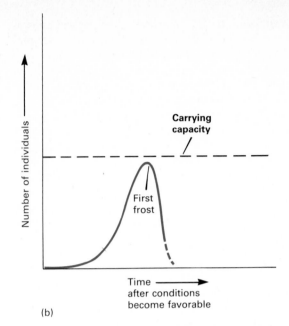

(b)

Figure 4.6 Exponential Growth Rate in Populations (J-shaped Curve). Species with this type of growth pattern are "opportunists." (a) Some are environmental opportunists that grow rapidly in response to favorable conditions and then literally eat and live themselves out of house, home, and local existence. (b) Some are seasonal or cyclic opportunists whose numbers go up during favorable conditions and fall sharply when conditions change (for example, annual plants, some insects).

The Sigmoid Curve

The more common general pattern for growth of animal and plant populations is the **sigmoid (S-shaped) growth curve** (Figure 4.7). In this case, limiting factors come into play to "put on the brakes" very gradually, and the population tends to stabilize around a given level. As we have already pointed out, the *carrying capacity* of a particular environment is the maximum population size for a given species that can be supported *indefinitely*. If the population rises above the carrying capacity, it will strain the ecosystem to such an extent that the system will not be able to support it at that level, and individuals will die from lack of food or habitat, or the population will decline because of other factors that reduce the number of viable offspring. Growth sometimes takes a population well above carrying capacity initially. When this happens, the size of the population might quickly fall back toward or even below carrying capacity, and this might be followed by a period of considerable "wobble." In other cases the environment puts the brakes on ever so gradually, and population growth tapers off more smoothly as the size of the population approaches the environmental carrying capacity. In either case, populations tend to fluctuate around or below carrying capacity unless some dramatic event causes a major change in the carrying capacity of that system.

There are many determinants of carrying capacity. Food supply is the ultimate regulator of many populations. Temperature seems to influence seasonal fluctuations in some populations, as does **photoperiod**, the amount of light in a 24-hour span. Predation, disease, and competition may limit population growth long before food supply is endangered in many species. The question of *ultimate* regulation is a complex and controversial one, and there is apparently no single answer; various factors seem to be more important for some species than others and for the *same* species under different circumstances and at different times (see Clark, 1964). Reports by Slobodkin et al. (1967), Murdoch (1960), Ehrlich and Birch (1967), and others cited at the end of this chapter illustrate the multiple complex factors involved.

THE CONCEPT OF NICHE

We are going to look at communities next, and it will help illuminate the kinds of interactions that characterize a community if we first consider the concept of *niche* (pronounced "nitch").

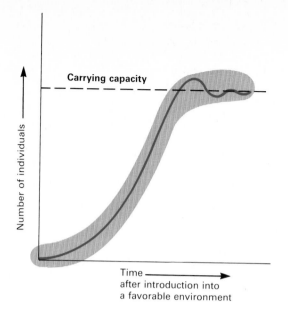

Figure 4.7 Sigmoid Growth Rate in a Population (S-shaped Curve). Species with this pattern begin with an exponential growth rate but then respond to an environmental braking effect as their numbers approach the limits of environmental support. Sometimes such populations increase slightly above carrying capacity, but they are soon brought back within supportable limits by self-regulating density-dependent factors and fluctuate around or below this level.

While the **habitat** of any given species is simply the kind of environment where one would go to find that species—its address, as it were, its niche is more complex. A species' **niche** refers to the unique, functional *role* or "place" of that species in an ecosystem. The ecologist Eugene Odum says that we should think of an organism's niche as its "profession," how it makes its living, how and when it gets its energy and nutrients, how and when it reproduces, how it relates to other species. According to Odum, to be complete in the description of the niche or "place" of a particular species, one would have to describe:

1. its physical *location* within a particular habitat, its **habitat niche**, where it "goes to work";
2. its *ecological role* within the ecosystem, e.g., the species it eats, the species with which it competes, the species that prey upon it—its **trophic or food niche**, its job or role; and
3. its preferences for temperature, shade, pH, humidity, slope, etc., its **multidimensional niche**, its working conditions.

Habitat Niche. A variety of habitat niches exist within any ecosystem. A forest, for example, can be pictured as having layers of habitat niches or *strata*. Some species are found on the forest floor (wildflowers, beetles, snails). Other species are found beneath the surface (earthworms). Still oth-

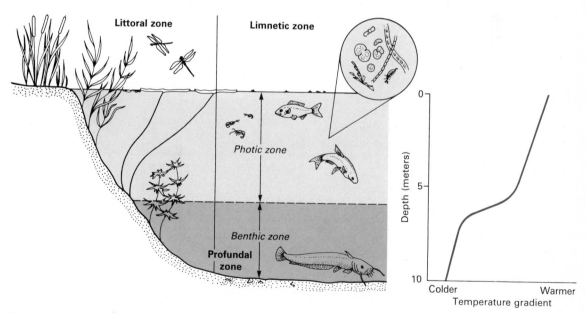

Figure 4.8 Stratification in a Lake. Differences in such factors as sunlight, temperature, and oxygen create a multitude of habitat niches or spatial niches in a lake. Terrestrial systems also exhibit stratification.

ers, such as lichens and algae, may occupy tree trunks. The lower branches and shorter trees provide habitats for some species (squirrels), and other species (birds) occupy the upper canopy area. **Stratification** is found in aquatic environments as well. In a lake, for example, variation in temperature, oxygen, and light cause different species to be found at different levels (Figure 4.8).

In fact, deep lakes can be divided into three zones—the littoral, limnetic, and profundal zones—on the basis of the types of vegetation and animal species found. The **littoral zone** extends from the shoreline to the farthest point where rooted vegetation is found. Cattails, water lilies, and various submerged vegetation live in this zone, along with such other organisms as frogs and insects. The **limnetic zone** is the open water area beyond the littoral zone. Its major vegetation are green and blue-green algae. Its animal species include fish and microscopic zooplankton. The limnetic zone extends downward as far as light penetrates. In a deep lake there is a third zone, the **profundal zone**, below the limnetic zone. Because there is no light penetration in this zone, its major species are decomposers and organisms that feed on dead organic matter.

Food Niches. Food niches may be demarcated by time. A hawk and an owl feed on the same food type, but one feeds predominantly in the daylight and the other is nocturnal. Thus there are equivalent—but different—night and day food niches. Still other species feed at daybreak and twilight (deer, fox). Food niches may also be separated by food type. Birds that feed in the same place at the same time may occupy different niches because of what they eat—different insects, seeds, etc. It is important to be aware of all of these subtleties because they bear on the general rule in nature that no two different species can occupy the same niche at the same time—for very long.

Multidimensional Niche. G. E. Hutchinson (1965) has suggested that the niche can be pictured as a multidimensional volume demonstrated by graphing the tolerance ranges of a species for various factors on a set of coordinates. For example, as shown in Figure 4.9, the range for two factors such as temperature and pH tolerance can be graphed. A third dimension can be added, such as shade tolerance (Figure 4.9). There are theoretically any number of such factors that form the ecological niche. Since we can graph only three dimensions, the ultimate multidimensional niche or hypervolume cannot be drawn, but the abstraction can be imagined.

COMMUNITIES

Communities are groups of interacting populations. For example, a field community might consist of populations of different grasses, insects, worms, birds, and mammals interacting in various ways. Grasses provide food for certain insects and mammals; insects provide food for birds; birds prey on mammals and worms. Functionally, communities are made up of organisms with interlocking niches; each species in a community depends on certain other species in the definition of its role in the community. While each species may not relate

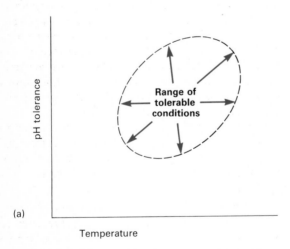

(a)

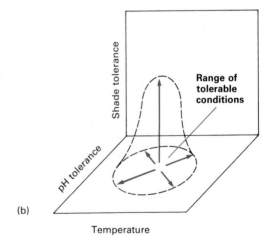

(b)

Figure 4.9 Niche as a Multidimensional Volume. The concept of niche is a complex one. Hutchinson has suggested that it can be graphed to a limited extent as a hypervolume bounded by tolerance ranges for specific factors.

Part I   Basic Principles of Ecology

directly to every other species in a community, they all are interrelated. This would be analogous to the interrelated parts in an engine or the interrelatedness of the jobs in human society. A community is the living part of an ecosystem. As is true of many of the terms and concepts considered up to this point, "community" is an abstraction. There is a biotic community of the planet earth. There is a biotic community in every woodlot. There is a biotic community in every aquarium.

Diversity and Stability Revisited

In Chapter 1 we broached the subject of the relationship between stability and species diversity and concluded that the relationship was fuzzy. Older environmental science textbooks nearly all had statements to the effect that the more **diversity** in an ecosystem, the more species it had, in other words, the more stable the system. Sometimes this was stated in the converse: the simpler an ecosystem, the more delicate it is. The delicacy of the Alaskan/Canadian environment (higher latitudes typically have less species diversity) was loudly touted as the main reason why the Alaskan pipeline should not have been built a decade ago. Now the textbooks equivocate because over the years, species diversity has not been found to be highly correlated with stability.

Odum (1984) points out that part of the problem may be semantic; there are, after all, several definitions of stability.

Relative stability is the ability to hold fast in the face of disturbance. It is also the ability to return to exactly the same place following a change induced by a disturbance. Relative stability might also be the ability to return to near normal quickly after a change induced by a disturbance. Odum suggests that some kinds of stability may be mutually exclusive. He uses the phrase "inversely related." Odum ascribes **resistance stability** to California redwood communities, indicating that they are hard to change or destroy but nearly impossible to restore once they are changed. **Resilience stability**, on the other hand, ascribed by Odum to California chaparral, means that while chaparral may burn easily, it recovers quickly.

Diversity may be one of several factors that improves *resistance* stability in nature, but it could also decrease *resilience* stability. Perhaps an analogy would help.

Consider a symphony orchestra and a three-piece jug band. Assume that one member of each group dies at random. While the jug band would be devastated, the symphony orchestra would have enough redundancy that it would sound nearly the same (because of resistance stability) as before. The remaining members of the jug band, having only the task of filling one musical vacancy, might, even allowing for training, accomplish the task in time to keep all of their engagements (resilience stability). Now assume a prolonged musician's strike and the partial disbanding of both bands. The symphony orchestra's diversity would be a drawback this time; it might never get back to its original form. The jug band's simplicity would allow it to form again fairly easily.

If diversity improved one kind of ecosystem stability and hurt another kind, this might explain why studies have failed to show a strong, positive correlation between diversity and stability.

Perhaps stability is best thought of as something ecosystems settle into. As time passes, no matter what else is true, instability is eliminated, and stability is rewarded by preservation. We should not worry nearly so much about whether or not ecosystems are simple as we should about changing them. Simple ecosystems may well be stable, after all, but arbitrarily changed ecosystems will almost certainly be less stable.

Redwood communities are fairly resistant to disease and fire. However, once destroyed, they are almost impossible to restore.

Factors Influencing Species Diversity in an Ecosystem

The Edge Effect. Although communities are sometimes depicted as distinct units, they actually merge indistinctly into one another. At the junction of two communities—a field and a forest community, for example—there is typically a zone containing species from both types of systems as well as species not found in either of the juxtaposed communities. This transition area is called the "edge" and is characterized by a great diversity and density of species. The "effect" results from the mix of microhabitats and available niches made up of the combined totals from the two systems plus some new ones created by the junction. The high level of diversity and density that occurs within these areas is called the **edge effect** (Figure 4.10).

Latitude and Diversity. Diversity also tends to increase from the colder to the warmer climates (see Table 4.3). Tropical rain forests are thought to encompass two thirds of the world's plant and animal species. One reason for this is that warmer climates encompass the ranges of tolerance of more species than cooler areas. Another reason is that many of the warm climate ecosystems are more highly stratified—they have a greater variety of habitat niches.

It is also known that diversity tends to be reduced in stressed biotic communities and with a critical decrease in the area of a given type of habitat. Too many "edges" can lead to a decrease in diversity.

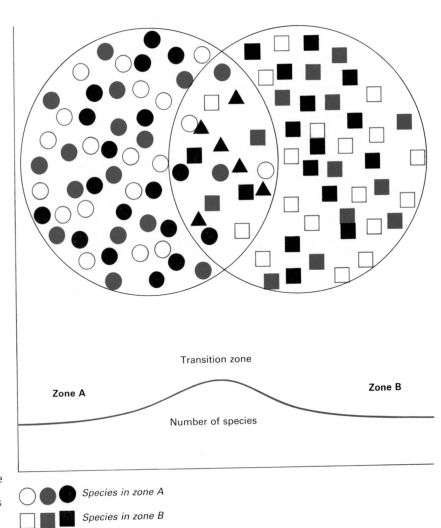

Figure 4.10 The Edge Effect. Where two community types come together, such as a forest and field, species in the zone between them include both forest and field species and some additional species that do not exist in either forest or field. The high level of diversity (and density) that occurs in these areas is called the "edge effect." Estuaries where oceans and fresh water merge exhibit this edge effect.

Transition zone

Zone A   Zone B

Number of species

○ ◉ ● *Species in zone A*

□ ◼ ■ *Species in zone B*

▲ *Species in transition zone only*

Part I   Basic Principles of Ecology

Given the importance of the relationships between diversity or changes in diversity and stability, the concept of diversity is especially important to humans and human activities. On one hand, we tend to simplify ecological systems as we create cornfields, wheat fields, timber stands, and front lawns. We human beings rely on only a few strains of grain for food. While we have grown those strains that are most productive, we have left ourselves vulnerable to disease invasions and crop failures from climatic conditions.

But humans also make biotic communities more complex. By creating fields separated by woodlots a greater diversity of habitat and an enriched diversity of biotic communities may be established. Cities tend to destroy some kinds of habitats but provide others that are quite suitable for rats, pigeons, sparrows, songbirds, and other living things.

Dominance and Stability

Although a community may have many species, one or two might be the most important with regard to the nature and overall stability of the system. Such species are said to be **dominant**.

Abundance is only one of several determinants of **ecological dominance**. In a forest, insects may exist in the largest numbers, but it may be two or three species of trees that dominate, that is, exert an overriding influence on the character and stability of the system. If the dominant trees were destroyed, the entire system might be drastically altered, whereas insect population changes would be less generally felt. One reason for the relative unimportance of numbers is that it takes a lot of insects to equal the biomass of just one oak. *Biomass* is obviously a more meaningful expression of presence than numbers. Also, because of the second law of thermodynamics

MINI-GLOSSARY

Biomes: the major community types of the world, characterized by specific climate conditions and plant types. (Examples: prairie, tundra, desert, and deciduous forest.)

Biotic community: a group of populations of different plant and animal species that interact within any prescribed area or physical unit of the ecosphere. A biotic community is all of the living portion of an ecosystem.

Climax community: the end point of ecological succession. A climax community is a community that is in a relatively steady state; the impact of each species tends to be neutralized by the other species. Climax communities do not change much, even over long periods of time.

Diversity: a measure of the number of different species in a biotic community. Diversity is high when there are many different species and low when there are few.

Ecological dominance: a measure of the degree to which one or a few species have the greatest biological impact in an ecosystem and thus characterize that system.

Interspecific relationships: interactions between the individuals of different species in a community. Interaction can be directly beneficial to one and harmful to another (predation or **parasitism**); beneficial to both (**mutualism**); or beneficial to one and neutral to another (**commensalism**). Competition is a form of interaction.

and because of their key role connecting the abiotic with the biotic, the dominance award almost always goes to plants; most terrestrial communities are named for their dominant plant species (often more than one). For example, we speak of beech-hemlock communities.

Table 4.3 Changes in Species Abundance and Diversity with Latitude. Numbers indicate approximate number of species.

	Florida (27°N)	Massachusetts (42°N)	Labrador (54°N)	Baffin Island (70°N)
Beetles	4000	2000	169	90
Land snails	250	100	25	0
Intertidal mollusks	425	175	60	*
Reptiles	107	21	5	0
Amphibia	50	21	17	0
Freshwater fishes	*	75	20	1
Coastal marine fishes	650	225	75	*
Flowering plants	2500	1650	390	218
Ferns and club mosses	*	70	31	11

*Data lacking.

The Competitive Exclusion Principle

In the 1930s, while studying two different species of *Paramecium* in the laboratory, the Soviet biologist G. F. Gause (1934) established the principle that two species cannot occupy the same niche simultaneously (Figure 4.11). This concept is termed **the competitive exclusion principle**. If two species in the same area tend to occupy the same niche, one of three things seems to happen. If one species has a greater competitive advantage due to greater reproductive potential or some other factor, this will lead to the demise and eventual "departure" of the other species from that area. If the habitats occupied by the two species are not completely identical, and an adjacent habitat is within the tolerance range of one of the species, that species may be forced into the adjacent habitat. A third alternative is character displacement. Two species that occupy the same area and are very much alike at first may develop differences from one another that tend to decrease competition (see Chapter 5). This divergence of characters was the operative principle behind what Charles Darwin saw among the finches of the Galapagos Islands in the 1800s (see Figure 4.12).

Competitive exclusion as a result of the coincidence of niches was also demonstrated in a classic study in the laboratory by Dr. Thomas Park (1954) using flour beetles of the genus *Tribolium*. Park and his associates found that whenever two different species of flour beetles were put in a jar of flour, one species always thrived and the other died out. Which species survived and which one became extinct depended not on which species was the most abundant at the outset, but rather on the abiotic factors of temperature and humidity. Alone, each species could survive at the tested temperature and humidity variables; together, one species did better under warm, moist conditions and the other under

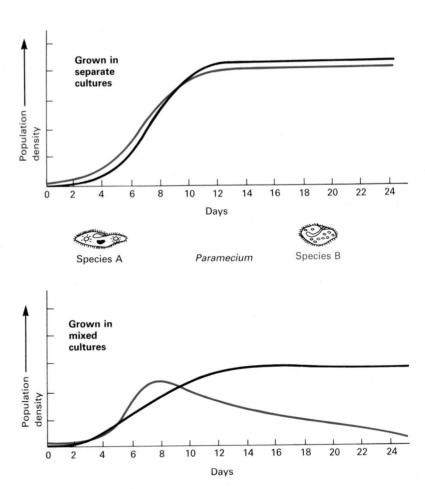

Figure 4.11 Gause's Competitive Exclusion Principle. When two species of paramecium are grown in the same culture, occupying basically the same niche, one species predominates and the other gradually declines. The Soviet scientist G. F. Gause concluded that two species cannot simultaneously occupy the same niche in the same community.

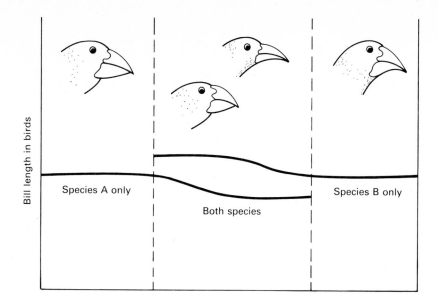

Bill length in birds

Species A only

Both species

Species B only

Figure 4.12 Character Displacement. Species occupying the same niche may undergo physical changes over many generations that lead to the development of several niches from an initially common one. Otherwise similar species of birds in overlapping habitats drift in isolation toward characteristics that displace them from one another; differences in their bills reflect differences in types of seeds or insects eaten. This phenomenon was the basis of Darwin's observations of various types of beaks on the finches of the Galapagos Islands.

cool, dry conditions. Under moderate conditions, one or the other could survive, but not both.

Not all scientists agree on the significance of competition in explaining species coexistence or lack of it. For a discussion of the application of the competitive exclusion principle in the field and the controversy over the significance of competition, see the references at the end of this chapter for Hutchinson (1959), Simberloff and Boecklen (1981), Diamond (1978), MacArthur and Levins (1967), and Schoener (1982).

Other Interspecific Relationships

Here we consider some specific common relationships between species. As will be seen in the examples that follow, interactions have become obligatory in some cases—certain species cannot exist except in very specific interspecies relationships. In other cases we will see that some such relationships are **facultative**, that is, the species may exist either within or outside of such a relationship.

One type of interspecific interaction is termed symbiotic, which means "living together." Often **symbiosis** refers to relationships between two species that are mutually beneficial (**mutualism**) or beneficial to one with the other unaffected (**commensalism**).

In **mutualistic** interactions, both species benefit. The most common example used to demonstrate obligatory mutualism is the lichen. You often see lichens growing as a greenish-grey crusty coating on

tree trunks or rocks. A lichen is composed of a fungus and an intimately associated alga. The fungus contributes moisture and minerals to the union; the alga produces food via photosynthesis. In more advanced species of lichens the fungus does not penetrate the algal cell wall, and the relationship is indeed mutualistic. In more primitive lichens, however, the algal cell wall is penetrated, and thus a parasitic relationship results. A more consistent example of mutualism is the relationship between certain fungi and other plants. The rootlike structure of these fungi, or mycorrhizae, interacts with the roots of trees or other plants, enhancing mineral uptake from the soil. Mycorrhizae are important in the growth in poor soils of some trees such as pines. Another interesting example is the termite. The termite actually owes its ability to digest wooden houses to a small protozoan that the termite carries in its gut. The protozoan secretes a substance that converts cellulose into its carbohydrate components, providing nourishment for the protozoan *and* the termite. Insect pollination of flowers is another common example of a mutualistic relationship.

Commensalism is a form of interaction in which one species benefits and the other is not affected. Epiphytes, plants that grow on the limbs of trees in tropical forests, extract no nutrients from the tree but utilize the branch as a point of attachment to obtain sunlight that does not penetrate to the forest floor. An orchid is an epiphyte. In another example of commensalism a small ocean fish called a remora attaches itself to the body of a shark. The shark provides transportation, and the remora may also consume food remnants from the shark's prey.

Two classes of species interaction wherein there is benefit for one species and harm for the other are **parasitism** and **predation**. In parasitism the organism lives *in* (**endoparasite**) or *on* (**ectoparasite**) its host; often more than one parasite infects a single host. A "good" parasite is one that has developed a relationship with its host over long generations and will not kill its host. It must at least allow sufficient time for its host to reproduce; otherwise in killing its host it destroys its own food supply. Consequently, a well-developed parasitic relationship may actually approach commensalism. This points up a very pertinent fact. All of our classification schemes are human-made; they are loose abstractions made from patterns observed in nature. Examples that do not specifically fit any category show only the weaknesses in our classification schemes, not a weakness in nature.

Another kind of interspecific interaction is *predation*. In predation the predator is free living and usually larger than its prey. A predator kills its prey for food. While predation is most definitely a "negative" for the *individual* caught and eaten, the picture is not so clear-cut when the focus is on the total prey *population*. Many studies show that in larger animals, predation is a mechanism for culling the imperfect young, the old, and the sickly. Deevey found in developing the life table for the Dall sheep (Table 4.1) that mostly the very young and the very old were killed by wolves.

A study of moose and wolves carried out on Isle Royale, Michigan (Mech, 1966), shows the role of predators in population control. When there were no wolves on the island, the moose population increased dramatically, and the moose destroyed habitat in search of food. This overpopulation resulted in a population crash; many moose died of starvation. Eventually, wolves made their way to the island, and a balance was reached between the moose and the wolves, keeping both populations in check.

For many predator-prey relationships the predator may be a relatively insignificant population control factor. To affect population size, the predator must have a significant impact either on the number of individuals able to reproduce or on those who will one day be able to reproduce. If predators take only those that are likely to die soon anyway, their effect as regulators of population size is negligible.

Generally, it would seem that in populations of *smaller animals,* predation is less discriminate, and individuals of all ages and reproductive capacity are equally subject to the predator. Consequently, predators may be one factor in regulating population size for smaller animals.

Homo sapiens is a predator of sorts, but our modern relationship to our food species, both plant and animal, comes closer to mutualism. Some plants and animals are ensured of propagation by humans, and in return humankind is supplied with a dependable food source. The development of these relationships between humans and the rest of nature is considered in Chapter 5.

Species Introductions

The practical importance of population and community dynamics in nature can best be illustrated by example. When the European hare was introduced into Australia as a game animal, it had no natural predators. The hares reproduced dramatically—perhaps close to their biotic potential—and advanced over the continent "like a swarm of locusts." No one had considered the population checks on the European hare. In 1950 a strain of virus known to be fatal to rabbits was introduced into Australia. In one year, 97–99% of the hare population was killed. Those that survived, however, passed on some immunity, and the rabbit population gradually increased again. Hares are still a problem in Australia.

Another episode occurred in the United States when the European starling was introduced in the 1890s to compete with the house sparrow, which had been released in the 1850s and was reproducing prolifically. As it turned out, both the starling and the sparrow populations prospered; the starling became the competitor of songbirds instead of sparrows. In addition, the starling damaged crops and eventually became a general nuisance, especially around airports.

The Distribution of Communities: Biomes

The distribution of various types of terrestrial communities is primarily a function of climate and soil. From the North Pole to the equator there is a gradual transition from tundra to tropical rain forest. The same phenomenon can be observed in the transition from a high to a low altitude.

Biomes are the major types of biotic communities of the world. Some major terrestrial biomes are tundra, coniferous forest, temperate deciduous forest, chaparral, grassland, desert, and rain forest.

The Major Terrestrial Biomes

Tundra has no trees. Soil is poorly drained and spongy. Permafrost (water permanently frozen in the soil) limits the growth of plant roots. Rainfall and evaporation rates are low. Temperatures are low, less than 10°C in the warmest months. Vegetation is low and hardy, consisting of grasses, sedges, low flowering herbs, and lichens. Animals are burrowers—lemmings, mice, and Artic fox. Few species are present in large numbers.

The temperature range in **coniferous forests** is cool to cold. There is more rain than in tundra. The soils are acidic and deficient in minerals. Trees are needle-leaf, cone-bearing evergreens such as spruce, fir, larch, and pine. There are some aspen, poplar, and birch in low, moist areas. Animal species are mostly fur-bearing mammals such as moose, caribou, elk, grizzly bear, wolverine, and beaver.

The **temperate deciduous forest** has a moderate climate and four distinct seasons. Trees are hardwoods such as beech, maple, oak, hickory, basswood, poplar, sycamore, and elm. There is also a rich, diverse understory and broad-leaf shrubs. Animals include deer and black bear. There may be seasonal plant and animal inhabitants.

Chaparral is found in southern Europe, southern Australia, and southern California. It is fire adapted, which means that it depends on periodic fast-burning fires to perpetuate itself and allow reproduction of low vegetation at the expense of taller trees. Chaparral is more open than deciduous forest. The precipitation rate is low. Vegetation is characterized by thick evergreens with waxy leaves. Animals are small hooved ungulates.

Grassland is characterized by irregular rainfall, a high evaporation rate, and rich soils. There is only one story of growth but a great diversity of grass vegetation. Animals are grazers and burrowing rodents adapted with sharp eyes and speed for eluding predators. Examples of grasslands are the steppes of Eurasia and the pampas of South America. Much of the original grasslands in the eastern United States is now gone.

The **desert** has a low rainfall rate and a high evaporation rate. There is a wide fluctuation in diurnal high and low temperatures. Characteristic plants are brush, cacti, and low-profile plants with reduced waxy leaves. There are few large animals. Some desert animals are coyote, fox, rodents, insects, and lizards.

Rainfall is evenly distributed throughout the year in **tropical rain forests,** and humidity is high. Temperatures range between 68°F and 82°F. Because temperature and water are not limiting factors, there is a great diversity of species. Plants are primarily evergreen species. There are usually two stories, and floor vegetation is scarce because little light penetrates the forest to reach the ground.

The map at the end of the first color insert shows the distribution of some important types of biomes about the earth.

Predators like the bald eagle may help to regulate the populations of their prey.

Each is a "megacommunity" characterized by specific plant types. Each biome is unique, and yet **ecological equivalents** (different species performing the same ecological function in different communities) are found in each. This is an illustration of the fact that the same fundamental patterns override the specific relationships in any subdivision of the biosphere.

SUCCESSION

We stated in previous chapters that living organisms are affected by their environment and in turn exert an influence on it. Organisms invading virgin territory characteristically change their environment even to the extent that they make it less suitable for themselves and more suitable for other species of organisms. The natural sequence of such changes in community structure is called **ecological succession**. It occurs in amazingly regular patterns tending toward a *climax* or steady state situation.

Succession is often referred to as being primary or secondary. **Primary succession** involves an unbroken sequence from rock or bare soil to climax vegetation. Primary succession can be found in abandoned quarries, abandoned strip mines, badly eroded slopes, and the area around Mount St. Helens and other recently erupted volcanoes. **Secondary succession** occurs where a climax or near-climax community is changed and succession from earlier stages begins again. Abandoned farmland is a good example of an area undergoing secondary succession. Foresters often speak of secondary growth timber where all the virgin growth has been cut down and the area allowed to grow to forestland again. A path or trail worn through the forest, if left untraveled for a while, would undergo secondary succession. Both terrestrial and aquatic communities undergo succession by means of a series of transitional stages called **seres** until a dynamic equilibrium is reached. Let us look at specific examples.

The transformation of rock to soil is an example of primary succession and is an inherent part of terrestrial succession (Figure 4.13). Exposed by a violent storm or exposed by the draining of a lake, bare rock immediately begins to weather. Pulverized, moisture-holding material will, in time, accumulate in small low places or in cracks in the larger rock. Seeds from trees, flowers, and/or shrubs are likely to become trapped in these areas as well, but conditions may not be right to support most of these kinds of plants at first. It does happen that

some kinds of pioneer plants—lichens, for example—that need little moisture, *can* survive and flourish under such conditions. So of all the potential colonizers that arrive and try to become established, only certain species such as lichens may find an appropriate tolerance range. Lichens are actually referred to as pioneer species in ecology. They prepare the way for others to follow. As they grow, lichens release organic acids that react chemically to further dissolve more rock, which together with accumulating organic matter from dead bits of lichens creates new conditions that may be suitable for other species. Gradually, as more water and debris accumulate in the depression and as weathering of the rock continues, moss may outdo the lichens in competition for light and other resources. Moss in turn causes still further changes in chemical and physical conditions, making the environment suitable for small plants and shrubs. As these plants provide greater shade, changes in temperature and moisture cause conditions to become more favorable for different seeds to germinate and flourish that earlier would have germinated and withered. Eventually, sun-tolerant species of trees become established. As these trees provide more and more shade, shade-tolerant species of trees will dominate.

In terrestrial systems, succession is a function of the interaction of organisms and their abiotic environment. In some aquatic systems, such as ponds and lakes, the prime factor in succession is input from the "outside."

Succession in lakes and ponds involves the gradual change to marsh and then solid land by the accumulation of sediment and debris on the lake bottom (Figure 4.14). Sediment and debris may be carried into the lake through runoff water that picks up materials as it travels through the watershed or drainage areas to the lake. In areas where the land surface has been disturbed, erosion is more severe, and the buildup of sediment occurs at a faster rate. In lakes that receive a lot of nitrates and phosphates, such as those receiving runoff from cattle feedlots or effluents from sewage plants, the rate of succession is increased. These nutrients result in more plant growth within the lake. When this plant growth dies and decays, this debris accumulates on the lake bottom, resulting slowly in a more shallow lake.

Odum (1984) describes various patterns of secondary succession. Secondary succession in a temperate terrestrial environment is as follows. Generally, the growth of annual plants is replaced by perennials, which in turn prepare the way for grasses and shrubs. Eventually, pines and fast-growing de-

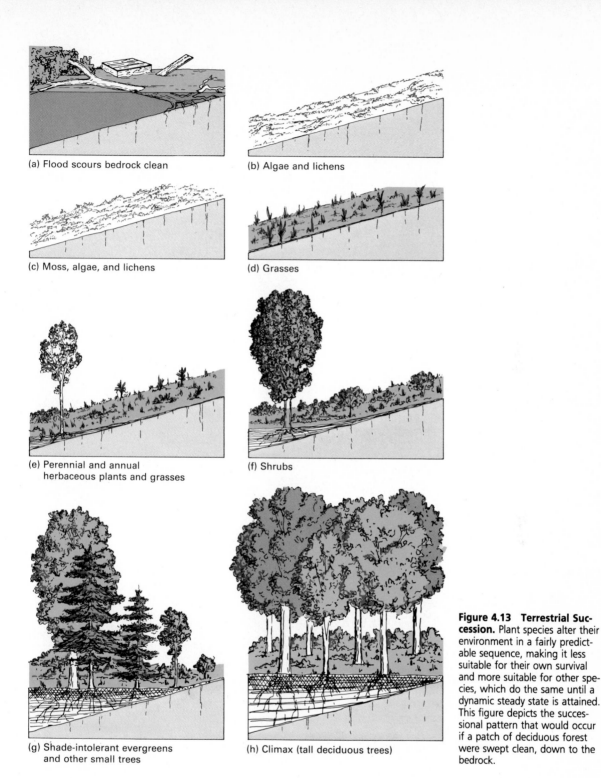

(a) Flood scours bedrock clean

(b) Algae and lichens

(c) Moss, algae, and lichens

(d) Grasses

(e) Perennial and annual
herbaceous plants and grasses

(f) Shrubs

(g) Shade-intolerant evergreens
and other small trees

(h) Climax (tall deciduous trees)

Figure 4.13 Terrestrial Succession. Plant species alter their environment in a fairly predictable sequence, making it less suitable for their own survival and more suitable for other species, which do the same until a dynamic steady state is attained. This figure depicts the successional pattern that would occur if a patch of deciduous forest were swept clean, down to the bedrock.

ciduous trees develop and change the conditions to favor the growth of shade-tolerant species such as oaks or hickories. In the southeastern United States, management practices such as fire must be used on pine tree plantations to prevent succession to shade-tolerant hardwood species.

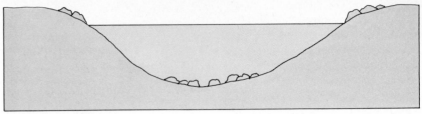

(a) Newly formed lake

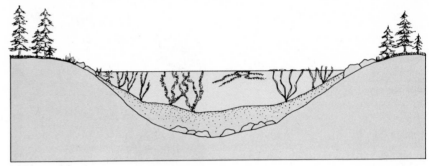

(b) Mature lake

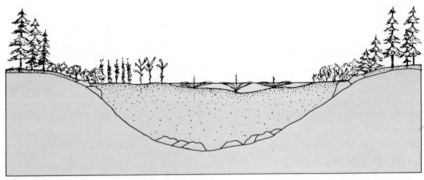

(c) Meadow/marsh

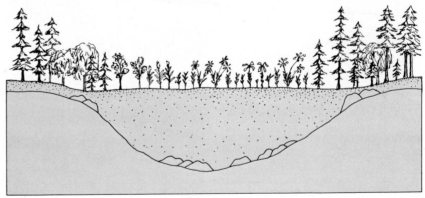

Figure 4.14 Aquatic Succession. Lakes and similar aquatic communities undergo a series of changes as over time they begin to fill with sediment and organic debris. Eventually, lakes become solid land and undergo terrestrial succession. Depicted here are the successional stages following formation of a new lake by a receding glacier.

(d) Dry land

Secondary succession on grasslands is fairly well documented. The pattern involves a four-stage development from annual weeds to short-lived grass to perennial grass and finally to climax grass. A total of 20–40 years is required for grasslands to become reestablished from plowed ground.

Changes in vegetation, whether terrestrial or aquatic, bring with them changes in the animal species that live and feed on the vegetation. Animal species in turn influence prevailing conditions by the manner in which they help distribute seeds, burrow into the soil, and feed on the vegetation, among other things.

A climax community is, by definition, relatively stable. A dynamic balance—homeostasis—results from more finely tuned self-regulating feedback mechanisms. Only a major climatic disturbance, fire, or other similar human impact is likely to disrupt a climax system or knock it back to some earlier successional stage.

The expected or normal climax stage for a particular region is not always reached in every location because of varying local conditions. For example, factors such as chronic erosion may prevent soil development, thus preventing the successful growth of vegetation that requires good soil. Many of the things we humans do serve to keep ecosystems from maturing; agricultural and forestry practices (e.g., cultivation, pasturing, logging, mowing) are perhaps the most familiar examples. Human impact has also been known to cause succession to occur at faster than normal rates. A variety of human activities tend to increase siltation in lakes, causing the sequence of successional stages to occur more quickly. Normally, the time required for the transition of a lake to a climax forest may be hundreds or thousands of years. *Homo sapiens* can cause a lake to fill in less than 100 years.

MOVING ON

Many words used in ecology are not only *not* descriptive, they are even misleading. "Producers" is one such word, as was pointed out in Chapter 1. In this chapter we have introduced some more. "Climax" is a notable example.

If one scraped a patch of virgin Montana forest clean to the bedrock, a series of stages would result until something once again resembling a virgin forest appeared. But Montana did not always look like it does now. And it surely will not always look that way. There is another dimension to succession, obviously. What we have described above are not *climaxes* in the absolute sense at all.

We are about to consider chemical and biological evolution. Evolution, as we shall see, is really a "supersuccession." It is the sum of the interactions between chemicals and the physical environment and then later between life forms and the environment. Evolution is succession extended to the very gradual impacts living things have on the composition of the atmosphere, the physical state of the earth's surface, and climate *and* the impact that these things have in turn had on which organisms will most likely survive to reproduce.

CONCEPTS TO REMEMBER

1. The patterns of interaction between living things are an important dimension of ecology. Interaction is the means of self-regulation of biotic communities, and self-regulation of biotic communities is the essence of ecology.

2. An interbreeding or otherwise interacting group of organisms of the same species is called a population. Certain features are unique to the population level of organization. Some examples are distribution, density, growth rates, survivorship, and age structure.

3. Many factors determine the growth rate of a population. These ultimately can be reduced to how many individuals are born, how many die, how many move in, and how many move out per unit of time. Among the determinants of these basic parameters are (1) the number of individuals (particularly females) of reproductive age; (2) the number of offspring per

"litter"; (3) how often births occur; and (4) the survival pattern determined by predation, disease, nutrition, shelter, and living space.

4. There is no one answer to the question of what regulates population growth. Factors that influence population size change from season to season and from species to species. Among the most important factors are food supply, availability of habitat, social interactions, and climatic changes. Some factors come into play when populations reach a certain size such as available food or spread of disease; others such as climate have impacts not directly related to population size.

5. The maximum number of individuals of a particular species that an ecosystem can support indefinitely is called the carrying capacity. The size of a stable population usually fluctuates around or below the carrying capacity.

6. The carrying capacity of a given ecological system for a particular species may change dramatically if some severe disruption occurs such as a forest fire or the introduction of a competing or predatory species. Should a population exceed the carrying capacity of the environment, the impact on the system may permanently lower the capacity of that system for that species.

7. If we could describe everything about a species, such as how it relates to every other species in the ecosystem, what type of habitat it prefers, how, when, and what it eats, when it reproduces, and how it relates to members of its own species, we would have defined the niche of that species. Every species has a niche or job description within the ecosystem.

8. A community is an interactive group of plant and animal populations. Communities have certain characteristics that individuals and populations do not have; these include diversity, food webs, and species interactions such as competitive, predatory, parasitic, and symbiotic relationships.

9. Diversity refers to the number of different species in a community. Diversity may enhance some kinds of stability and diminish other kinds. Generally, diversity increases with the stages of succession. Diversity is greater in warmer climates than it is in colder climates. Diversity is high where two different communities overlap. Diversity is reduced when areas of a given habitat are drastically reduced in size and in stressed communities.

10. The major terrestrial communities of the world are called biomes. They include tundra, coniferous forest, temperate deciduous forest, chaparral, grassland, desert, and rain forest.

11. A natural sequence of changes (succession) in communities of living things takes place over long periods of time until a highly stable community is reached called the climax stage. Before the climax stage the species in the transient communities interact with abiotic factors, changing the ecosystem so that it is less favorable to the current species and more favorable to new species. Aquatic ecosystems such as lakes eventually fill in to form terrestrial systems; terrestrial ecosystems usually move toward climax as one of the major biomes.

DISCUSSION QUESTIONS AND FOOD FOR THOUGHT

1. Discuss: Petaluma, California, passed an ordinance to limit the number of families moving into the community by limiting the construction of new housing. Is this a form of territorial behavior?

2. Debate: Resolved: Extinction is a natural end point to a natural course of events; consequently, trying to protect species in danger of extinction is pointless and unnatural.

3. Discuss: The ocean is a climax stage of succession.

4. Is habitat destruction via fire, clearcutting of forests, and/or draining of wetlands density independent or density dependent with respect to natural populations of living things? Discuss.

5. Look for the stages of succession on your campus. What is the climax plant community for the region?

6. Place double-sided tape on one side of a piece of wood. Place the block outside where it can collect airborne seeds and particles. Leave it for several days. Return and count the different seed types. Compare these with the different species types in the immediate area. Explain any difference.

7. Describe what effect modern medicine has had on the human survivorship curve (Figure 4.4).

8. Assume that you have a species of bacteria that doubles in number every 15 minutes. At midnight on day one you put X of them in nutrient media. At midnight the next day you collect them all and find you have one liter full of bacteria. At what time was there half a liter of bacteria?

REFERENCES AND FURTHER READING

References marked with an asterisk are cited in the chapter.

Allee, W. C.; Emerson, A. E.; Park, O.; Park, T.; and Schmidt, K. P., 1949. *Principles of Animal Ecology.* Philadelphia: W. B. Saunders.

Andrewartha, H. G., and Birch, L. C., 1954. *The Distribution and Abundance of Animals.* Chicago: University of Chicago Press.

Andrewartha, H. G., and Birch, L. C., 1984. *The Ecological Web.* Chicago: University of Chicago Press.

Bergerud, A. T., 1983. "Prey Switching in a Simple Ecosystem," *Scientific American* (December) 130–141.

Caughley, G., 1970. "Eruption of Ungulate Populations with Emphasis on Himalayan Thor in New Zealand," *Ecology* 51:53–72.

*Christian, J. J., and Davis, D. E., 1964. "Endocrines, Behavior and Populations," *Science* **146**:1550–1560.

*Clark, L. R., 1964. "The Population Dynamics of *Cardiaspina Albitetura (Psyllidae),*" *Australian Journal of Zoology* **12**:349–361.

Connell, J. H., and Orias, E., 1964. "The Ecological Regulation of Species Diversity," *American Naturalist* **98**:399–414.

*Deevey, E. S., 1947. "Life Tables for Natural Populations of Animals," *Quarterly Review of Biology* **22**:283–314.

*Diamond, J. M., 1978. "Niche Shifts and the Rediscovery of Interspecific Competition," *American Scientist* **66**: 322–331.

*Ehrlich, P. R., and Birch, L. C., 1967. "The 'Balance of Nature' and 'Population Control,'" *The American Naturalist* **101**:97–107.

Forrester, J., 1971. *World Dynamics.* Cambridge, Mass.: Wright-Allen Press.

*Gause, G. F., 1934. *The Struggle for Existence.* Baltimore: Williams and Wilkins.

Golley, F. B., ed., 1977. *Ecological Succession.* Hutchinson Ross Series, Benchmark® Papers in Ecology. New York: Scientific and Academic Editions, Van Nostrand Reinhold.

Goodall, D. W., ed., 1983. *Ecosystems of the World* (30-volume set). New York: Elsevier Science Publishing Co. Especially pertinent are volume 14A, *Tropical Rain Forest Ecosystems,* and volume 26, *Estuaries and Enclosed Seas.*

Hairston, N. G.; Smith, F. E.; and Slobodkin, L. B., 1960. "Community Structure, Population Control, and Competition," *The American Naturalist* **XCIV**:421–425.

Hedrick, P. W., 1984. *Population Biology.* Portola Valley, Calif.: Jones & Bartlett Publishers.

Hubbell, S. P., 1979. "Tree Dispersion, Abundance, and Diversity in a Tropical Dry Forest," *Science* 203:1299–1309.

Hutchinson, G. E., 1957a. "Cold Springs Harbor Symposium: Concluding Remarks." *Quantitative Biology* **22**:415–427.

Hutchinson, G. E., 1957b. *A Treatise on Limnology. Vol. I: Geography, Physics and Chemistry.* New York: John Wiley & Sons.

*Hutchinson, G. E., 1959. "Homage to Santa Rosalia, or Why Are There So Many Kinds of Animals?" *American Naturalist* **93**:145–159.

*Hutchinson, G. E., 1965. *The Ecological Theater and the Evolutionary Play.* New Haven, Conn.: Yale University Press.

Kormondy, E. J., 1984. *Concepts of Ecology,* 3rd ed. Englewood Cliffs, N.J.: Prentice-Hall.

Lewin, R., 1983a. "Predators and Hurricanes Change Ecology," *Science* 221:737–746.

Lewin, R., 1983b. "Santa Rosalia Was a Goat," *Science,* **221**:636–639.

*MacArthur, R. H., and Levins, R., 1967. "The Limiting Similarity, Convergence and Divergence of Coexisting Species," *American Naturalist* **101**:377–385.

*MacLulich, D. A., 1937. "Fluctuations in the Numbers of Varying Hare (*Lepus americanus*)." University of Toronto Studies, Biological Sciences no. 43, pp. 1–136.

Meadows, D. H., and Meadows, D. L., 1977. *The Limits to Growth.* New York: Universe Books. This report was published for the Club of Rome.

*Mech. L. D., 1966. "The Wolves of Isle Royale," in *U.S. National Park Fauna,* **7**:210.

*Murdoch, S. W., 1960. "Community Structure, Population Control, and Competition—A Critique," *The American Naturalist* **100**:219–226.

*Odum, E. P., 1984. *Fundamentals of Ecology.* Philadelphia: W. B. Saunders.

*Park, T., 1954. "Experimental Studies of Interspecific Competition. II. Temperature, Humidity and Competition in Two Species of *Tribolium,*" *Physiological Zoology* **27**:177–238.

Patrick, R., ed., 1983. *Diversity.* Hutchinson Ross Series, Benchmark® Papers in Ecology. New York: Scientific and Academic Editions, Van Nostrand Reinhold.

*Schoener, T. W., 1982. "The Controversy over Interspecific Competition," *American Scientist,* **70**:586–594. (Nov.–Dec.)

*Simberloff, D. S., and Boecklen, W., 1981. "Santa Rosalia Reconsidered," *Evolution* **35**:1206–1228.

*Slobodkin, L. B.; Smith, F. E.; and Hairston, N. G., 1967. "Regulation in Terrestrial Ecosystems and the Implied Balance of Nature," *The American Naturalist* **101**:109–124.

Strong, D. R., Jr.; Simberloff, D.; Abele, L. G.; and Thistle, A. B., eds., 1984. *Ecological Communities: Conceptual Issues and the Evidence.* Princeton, N.J.: Princeton University Press.

Tilman, D., 1982. *Resource Competition and Community Structure.* Princeton, N.J.: Princeton University Press.

Van Doblen, H. W., and Lowe-McConnell, R. H., eds., 1975. "Unifying Concepts in Ecology," *Report of First International Congress of Ecology.* The Hague: W. Junk B. V., Publishers.

Woodwell, G. M., and Smith, H. H., eds., 1969. "Diversity and Stability in Ecological Systems," *Pub. No. 22.* Upton, N.Y.: Brookhaven National Laboratory.

Zaret, T. M., 1982. "The Stability/Diversity Controversy: A Test of Hypothesis," *Ecology* **63**:721–731.

See also the general references cited in "References and Further Reading" for Chapter 1.

Evolution and Ecology: The Emergence of the Ecosphere

*T*here are several reasons for including a chapter on evolution in a book with an environmental/ecological theme. First, as was indicated at the end of Chapter 4, evolution is another kind of ecological "succession."

As with ecological succession, evolution is driven by selective forces derived from the interaction between and among living things and the nonliving environment. Both ecological succession and evolution encompass both the biotic and the abiotic. The nonliving environment also undergoes succession and evolves. As we discussed in Chapter 4, moss and other pioneer species generate the soil and other physical/chemical conditions that allow other plants to succeed them. A parallel example in evolution would be the way in which oxygen-*producing* organisms changed the atmosphere so as to allow oxygen-*utilizing* organisms to emerge and to thrive.

Another reason for including evolution here is that a book on any topic should include some history. Serious students of the relationship of humans and the environment must appreciate how the natural systems on which we depend came to be and how they came to function the way they do; they must also appreciate how the stage was set for humans by prehuman evolution and how our species was literally shaped by the environment. The history of

human evolution may even reveal the roots of the environmental impact our species has today.

Still another reason for including evolution is that a grasp of the concepts of adaptation, natural selection, and evolution is essential to understanding a wide range of modern environmental problems such as those relating to the development of resistance to pesticides by insects and those associated with species extinction.

Finally, by considering our species in the evolutionary context, by appreciating it as the tip of a branch having origins in common with numerous other species, it should become easier to see that we are indeed an integral part of nature.

WHAT IS EVOLUTION?

Biological evolution is change in the genetic composition of populations resulting from the unequal reproduction of genes. The basis for evolution is *variation* and *selection*.

There is considerable variation in any group of living organisms. Not all individuals in a population of squirrels, bass, or people are exactly the same (see Figure 5.1). Variation exists because of differences in environmental influences and because of individual genetic differences. Let's consider an example.

Imagine a population of mammals that in the past may have been the ancestors of the giraffe. The distance from the ground to the mouths of the members of this population ranged from six to nine feet; in other words, there were some tall animals and some short ones. Suppose that during a period of two or three years there was a dry spell, much of the vegetation on which this species subsisted did not thrive, and the population had to survive by eating the leaves of a certain type of tree. Suppose that all the low-lying branches of these trees were consumed during the first year and that after a time the lowest leaves that could be found were above the level of eight feet.

Now, assuming that some of the short organisms in this population were short because they had genes that specified shortness, imagine what would happen to "short genes." Eventually, short members of this population would be unable to obtain food and would die, and the genetic packages including the genes that specified shortness would disappear. This would, of course, constitute evolution as defined at the beginning of this section. Perhaps long before the short organisms starved to death, they would find it more difficult to reproduce, but certainly when they reached the point of starving and dying, their chances of reproducing would be zero. So under a set of circumstances in which food

was hard to reach, short organisms had a much lower reproductive rate than taller ones, and the genetic composition of that population changed. "Short genes," the genes specifying short organisms, disappeared.

Try to imagine the effects of an infinite number of more subtle influences on survival in millions of species simultaneously, each resultant genetic

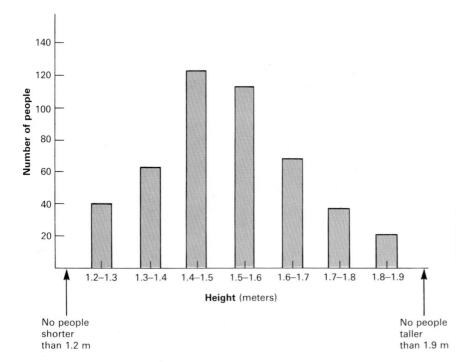

Figure 5.1 Number of Individuals within Specific Height Ranges in a Hypothetical Village. Within any group of even seemingly like individuals there is considerable variation in traits like height and weight. Variation exists in less obvious traits as well—in the ability of certain cells to synthesize enzymes that detoxify chemicals such as pesticides, for example.

change constituting one of the factors determining the course of evolution of every other species. The concept that natural selection was the basis of organic evolution was first elaborated by Charles Darwin more than 100 years ago.

The evidence that evolution accounts for the origin of species can be found summarized in almost any textbook of general biology (see also Volpe, 1977). The main elements of the evidence that evolution has occurred include the following:

1. Almost all vertebrates share very strong similarities in their internal and external organs and in the interrelationship among these organs.
2. All vertebrates have similar courses of embryonic development, that is, all species go through very similar stages of unfolding as embryos on their way to becoming what they will become (see Figure 5.2).
3. Many vertebrates have vestigial organs. Darwin and others have pointed out that the presence of the pelvic girdle in the snake, the existence of birds that cannot fly, and the human tailbone all indicate that the current forms of these organisms are the products of evolution in which selective pressures favored the gradual assumption of new characteristics and the loss of old ones.
4. Over time the fossil record shows gradual "progressive" changes. An outstanding example is the horse. The geologic evidence indicates that the horse evolved over a period of 60 million years through some 30 distinct "species" to its present-day form (Swanson, 1973) (see Figure 5.3).

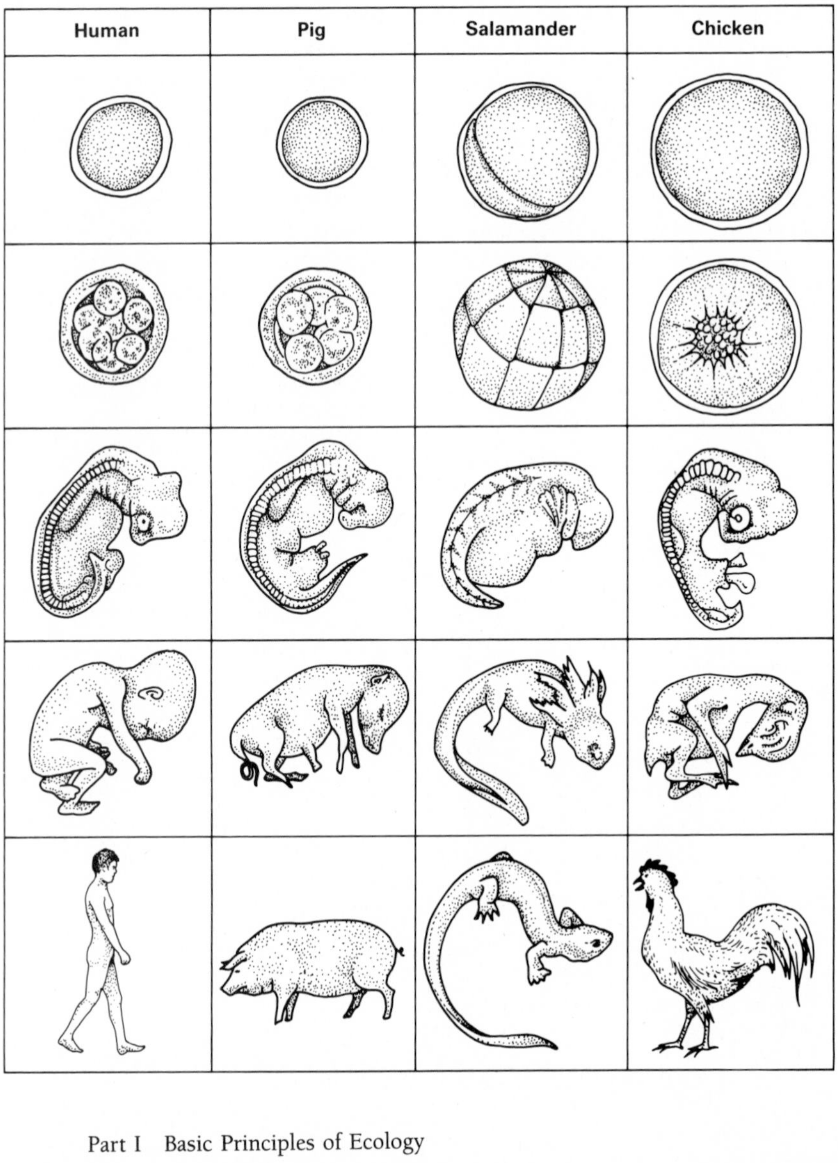

Figure 5.2 Embryonic Development of Some Vertebrates. The stages of development are quite similar for all vertebrate species. It is actually difficult to distinguish one species from another in the earliest stages. This suggests the possibility of the common origin of species.

Part I   Basic Principles of Ecology

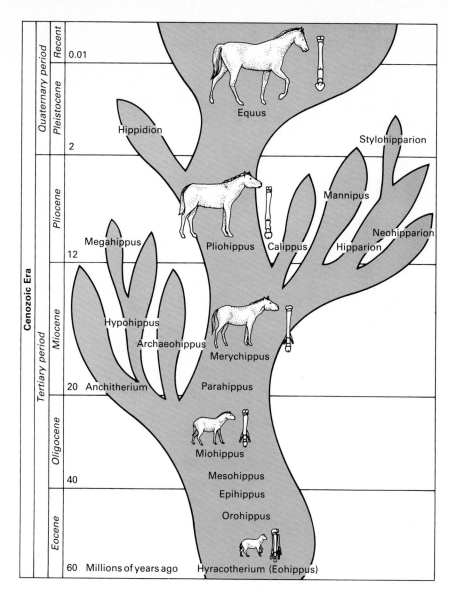

Figure 5.3 Fossil Record of the Horse over Sixty Million Years. This chart offers a striking illustration of gradual, evolutionary change. Note how evolution "tries" many things, only a few of which work. Many branches of horse evolution eventually died out; ten blind alleys are illustrated here.

5. **Biogeography**, the distribution of plants and animals over the globe, shows subtle differences in species from place to place as a result of environmental differences. This stimulated some of Charles Darwin's thinking about the origin of species. He wondered how it was that there were such differences in species and ecosystems throughout the world. The varying adaptations among the finches of the Galapagos Islands provided Darwin with his "aha!" experience. He reasoned that if slight differences in environment from one island to another could account for the differences in the finches, the wide range of changing environments of the whole earth over millions and millions of years may have accounted for the origin of all of the earth's species.

6. By comparative chemistry it has been shown that related organisms have similar sequences of subunits in analogous DNA and protein molecules. For example, closely related primates have very similar sequences of amino acids in their hemoglobin (a protein) molecules. The more closely related the primates, the more similarity.

7. Artificial selection routinely results in the evolution of special breeds and strains of both plants and animals, for example, miracle grains, short-haired terriers, and thoroughbred race horses.

Through evolution, giraffes have become the tallest mammals. A large male may reach a height of 19 feet (6 meters). Like most mammals, including humans, giraffes have just seven neck bones, though in giraffes the neck bones have become much elongated.

win knew that there is inherited variation in all populations, in all litters, and in all clusters of eggs.

A few years after Darwin, Gregor Mendel described the principles by which characteristics are transmitted from one generation to another by the male sperm and the female egg. It was not until the middle of the twentieth century, however, that it was confirmed that the chemical substance containing information specifying particular features and characteristics was in fact deoxyribonucleic acid (DNA). Chemical information contained in **DNA**, in units called genes, specifies the structure and nature of

Throughout this book we discuss the principles of ecology, mainly with the present and future in mind. However, the principles of ecology have been in effect for billions of years. By the time we emerge from the other end of this chapter it should be clear that evolution is the net effect of ecological interaction that has been going on since the beginning of time. The most profound way in which a species or a population can be influenced by the environment is through the environment's differential influence on the reproduction of organisms with different combinations of genes.

HOW DOES EVOLUTION ACTUALLY WORK?

Darwin observed, as did some of his predecessors, that all species of plants and animals produce many more offspring than are likely to survive. He further observed that the production of offspring is followed by an intense struggle for survival, the result of which is that only a few of the offspring are able to pass on their traits to future generations. Darwin viewed the millions of eggs or seeds produced in any one year as the raw material for **natural selection** with every facet of the environment determining which of the organisms originating as eggs or seeds would grow to maturity and reproduce. Dar-

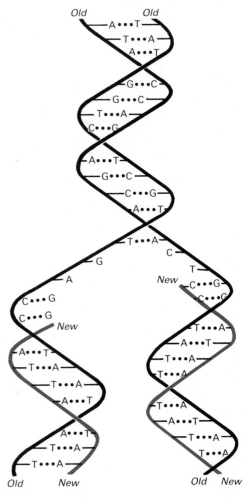

Figure 5.4 Replication of DNA. Each half of the DNA molecule serves as a template for construction of the other half. The helix unwinds and separates into halves, each half participates in forming a new complementary half, and the result is two identical strands. This phenomenon is responsible for inheritance of traits—why you may look like your mother or your father or have some features of each.

Science and Religion: Conflict?

A word is appropriate here concerning what sometimes seems to be a running battle between science and certain religious persuasions concerning evolution. Let's examine what it is that science has to say about the process of evolution, about the direction of evolution, and about metaphysics or the origin of existence and see where there exists any substantive conflict with religious views concerning these concepts and ideas.

Available scientific evidence, incomplete though it is, and the knowledge we have of atoms, molecules, and their behavior, provide the basis of the scientific view of the course of evolution that goes something like this:

Given the existence of some fundamental units of matter like hydrogen or subatomic particles like protons, neutrons, and electrons, given certain qualities of reactivity (the tendencies of these units to associate in various combinations having differential stabilities), and given lots of time, chemical and biological evolution could have accounted for the current physical, chemical, and biological state of the planet earth. Scientific evidence indicates that not all species have been present since the beginning; rather, individual species have come and gone over a 3.5-billion-year period. There is evidence that *Homo sapiens* has been around at least since 100,000 B.C. and that ancestors of ours have been walking the earth for more than 3.5 million years.

Many, if not most, believers in a supreme being accept the possibility that creation could have been set into motion to unfold over time following the creation of hydrogen. Others, however, believe that a supreme being intervened directly at each of maybe thousands or even millions of individual steps in the formation of the earth and its living species. Some believe that this was done in a few days during the year 4004 B.C. There is clearly a difference here, then, between at least some literal biblical interpretations and scientific evidence.

Some people mistakenly extend this difference to a belief that there is a difference between science and religion related to metaphysics—the origins of existence. But science has nothing to contribute to metaphysics. Science cannot go beyond the edge of that which can be measured. Science has nothing at all to say about the "who did it" and "why" questions about the origin of life and the origin of species. Science has nothing to offer to either the theistic or atheistic views of metaphysics. Scientifically, it is equally plausible—actually equally incomprehensible—that (1) a supreme being created all that exists, and this supreme being always was and always will be, or that (2) hydrogen and subatomic particles have always existed and always will exist.

---

proteins, and these in turn determine the overall character and appearance of the organism. Each molecule of DNA has the ability to replicate (see Figure 5.4), or to produce, almost invariably, exact copies of itself. The copies are passed on to sperm or eggs and thereby transmit parental traits.

One important fact about DNA that explains *some* genetic variation and was therefore a factor in evolution and the origin of species is that it does *not always* reproduce itself exactly. Rarely, but regularly, errors or **mutations** occur naturally and spontaneously. The average rate of spontaneous mutation per gene in the fruit fly is about 1 in 100,000 gametes (sperm or eggs) (Volpe, 1977). Mutations can also be caused by X-rays and mutagenic chemicals.

Most mutations are harmful. This is reasonable. If the genes of a normally functioning organism are arranged in such a way as to produce a perfectly integrated, functioning, whole organism, random change is *most likely* to be harmful. Occasionally, such mutations are neutral; that is, they specify some change that really does not make any differ-

ence to an organism's survival. Mutations that do amount to an improvement are more likely to be reproduced. Mutations are not the only way in which variation can occur in new organisms.

Most organisms above the level of simple microorganisms are **diploid**. That is, they have *two* complete sets of genes. When the sex cells are formed, there is a random sorting of these genes such that, although the offspring will receive one complete set from each parent, it may receive any combination of genes held by the parents. Having received one set of randomly sorted genes from the father and one set from the mother, an offspring almost invariably represents a unique (except in the case of identical twins) combination of genetic material. This accounts for considerable variation in any population.

Each time one set of male and female parents produces offspring, another array of genetic combinations is presented to the world. Chance and the degree of fitness of these packages will determine which of them will survive. Darwin first pointed out that evolution works because nature is able to try countless combinations. Only a tiny percentage of the experiments turn out to be "good," but the good ones will be preserved and will become part of the basis from which other experiments and combinations can be tried in an ever-changing environment.

Each of nature's creatures has emerged from this process and has come into being as a result of the fitness of cumulative mutations and genetic recombinations and, to some extent, chance.

FITNESS FOR WHAT?

The term **fitness**, as used by Darwin, refers specifically to the ability to reproduce. While the term *survival of the fittest* conjures up images of strong, powerful, and healthy individuals, it must be understood that strength, power, and health are important only to the extent that they are translated into the perpetuation of particular sets of genes. A healthy warrior who was constantly off fighting other warriors and eventually died by the sword would be infinitely less fit, biologically, than another individual who was not quite well enough to be accepted into the army but who stayed home and produced offspring instead. The success of any particular species can be measured only in terms of how successful that species is at keeping its genetic packages in existence, by having its offspring come into existence to survive to reproduce again. Fitness is a relative term; under one specific set of environmental conditions, one genetic package might be considerably more fit than another; yet in other environmental circumstances the reverse could be true.

One of the best-known examples of the way in which natural selection works is in the case of the peppered moth. A shift was observed in the relative abundance of light- and dark-colored moths around Manchester, England, during the last half of the nineteenth century. It was first observed that in certain industrial areas the number of dark moths was increasing. At that time in industrial England, much economic activity was based on coal combustion. Cities like Manchester were grimy places where even the tree trunks were sooty and black from the products of incomplete combustion and coal dust. Moths are nocturnal insects; they rest during the day on places like tree trunks. With the blackening brought by coal dust and smoke, light-colored moths would have become increasingly more visible to predators such as birds. Under these circumstances, dark-moth genetic packages would have become less visible to predators and more apt to be perpetuated.

Such differential predation has been verified in an experiment in which light and dark moths were released into dirty and clean areas. It was found that in the clean areas, survival was significantly higher for the light-colored moths than it was in darker, dirtier areas. The selective advantage was evidently so great that it accounted for a shift of from 1% dark moths in 1850 to 99% in some dirtier areas of England at the turn of the century (Swanson, 1973).

Interestingly, in recent years, with increased cleaning up of coal discharges, the percentage of light moths has begun to increase. It is not hard to imagine, though, that given a little more time or a little more selective pressure, the light-colored moths could have disappeared entirely (become extinct).

Let's consider another example, this time a hypothetical one in which a population of insects develops resistance to a particular pesticide. Suppose that a farmer, upon discovering that the barn door was covered with flies, runs to the hardware store to buy a pesticide. A plausible sequence of events for the pesticide applications is illustrated in Figure 5.5. The farmer observes that most of the insects have been killed by the first application. Among the insects originally present on the barn door, however, there may have been a few with particular genetically specified arrays of enzymes or concentrations of enzymes that enabled them to handle the pesticide just a little bit better. Suppose the pesticide in fact killed all but a very few of the most resistant types (Figure 5.5b), which also happened to be otherwise well adapted to the barnyard environment. Given the high reproductive rate characteristic of most insects, and given a few weeks, our farmer could well have been surprised to find the barn door covered once again. Although the flies looked like exactly the same kinds of insects as before, because of the selective action of the pesticide and the shifts in the genetic composition of the population that resulted from elimination of the more susceptible strains, the farmer was actually looking at a much more resistant population of insects than was seen the first time (Figure 5.5c). The farmer might find that a second spraying killed a smaller percentage than the first spraying did (Figure 5.5d) and that a third spraying three weeks later killed even fewer. Although the farmer might now go to the county extension agent and claim that the insects on the barn door had become immune to the pesticide, what in fact had happened was that the farmer had acted as an agent of selection, making it possible for pesticide-resistant genetic packages to survive. In effect, the farmer changed the genetic composition of the population toward resistance to the pesticide.

Fitness is relative and is determined by environ- mental circumstances. In the preceding example it did not matter so much that in the population of flies originally encountered on the barn door there were some that could fly faster than others, some that

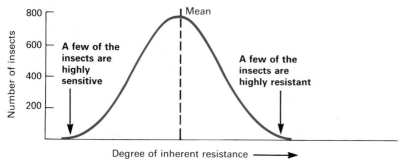

(a) Original population

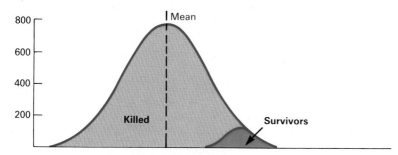

(b) Insects killed by first application of pesticide

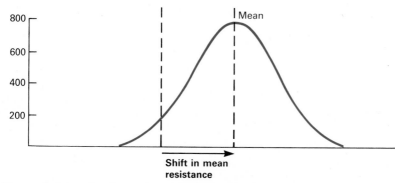

(c) Two weeks later, after the survivors have had a chance to reproduce

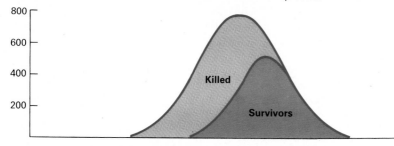

(d) Insects killed by the second application

Figure 5.5 Natural Selection of a Pesticide-Resistant Strain of a Hypothetical Insect.

The Effects of Natural Selection

Imagine a population of a species that has a particular frequency distribution for some trait—height, weight, skin color intensity, or whatever. Let's represent the population as follows:

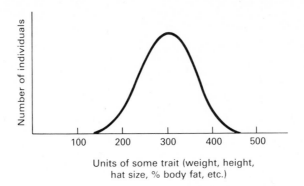

Units of some trait (weight, height, hat size, % body fat, etc.)

There could conceivably be changes in the influence of the environment that favor (1) one of the extremes, (2) the middle, or (3) both extremes (which is the same as selection against the middle).

Favoring one of the extremes results in **directional selection.** Directional selection results, over time, in the shift or *drift* of the population in the direction of the selection. This can be represented as follows:

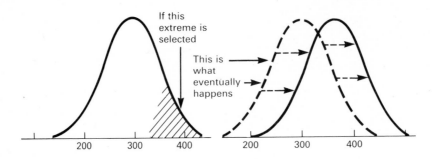

could find food better than others, some that could attract mates better than others. In the presence of the pesticide the major determinant of fitness was whether or not a fly was resistant to the pesticide.

DOES NATURAL SELECTION STILL OPERATE IN HUMAN BEINGS?

Natural selection has operated in the past, operates now, and will operate in the future on human beings. Even though we have been able to control many of the influences in our environment, there is still considerable room for natural selection among humans. Of all potential human beings, 2% die shortly after birth; of the human beings that survive infancy, 3% die before sexual maturity, 20% never

marry or have offspring, and 10% of those who do marry remain childless (McKusick, 1969). On the average, about one third of the individuals of any one generation of human beings contribute nearly 70% of the genes in the genetic packages represented by the great-grandchildren (Lerner, 1968). This is significant to any consideration of humans adapting to various environmental insults, a topic that comes up occasionally in discussions about people and their relationship to the environment.

WHY ARE THERE SPECIES? WHY NOT A CONTINUUM OF GENETIC PACKAGES?

A question posed by what we have considered up to this point is: If natural selection results in

Part I   Basic Principles of Ecology

If selection favors both extremes over the middle, this is called **diversifying selection.** Diversifying selec-tion eventually leads to a bimodal frequency distribution:

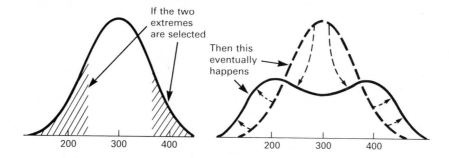

If the two extremes are selected

Then this eventually happens

If selection favors the middle, the result is called **stabilizing selection.** Stabilizing selection results in a decrease in diversity in the population. Because this would tend to decrease the likelihood of either directional or diversifying selection, its effect is to *stabilize.*

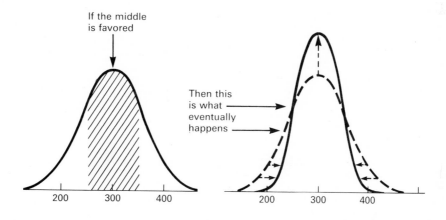

If the middle is favored

Then this is what eventually happens

gradual incremental changes in the genetic composition of populations, why isn't there one continuous spectrum of organisms all the way back to the origin of life? Well, there *was* a continuous spectrum; some parts of the spectrum simply no longer exist.

For organisms that reproduce sexually a species is a group of organisms that can or could interbreed and produce fertile offspring. More generally speaking, a species is a genetically related and genetically isolated group of organisms. The question of why there are species can be reduced to: How do genetically isolated organisms come to be? Let's consider the concept of reproductive isolation.

If a river suddenly appeared because of a shift in the earth's surface and it separated a population of any particular species into two groups (and the or-ganism could not swim), the members of the population on the two sides of the river could, over a period of time, become two separate species, unable to interbreed. With time, each of these populations would be influenced by different environmental pressures because conditions would not be exactly the same on one side of a river as they are on the other. The influences of the different environments on the two sides would cause the two populations to become increasingly dissimilar. Eventually, they might become too physically or physiologically dissimilar to interbreed even if the river dried up and they could once again associate.

There are actually a number of mechanisms by which **reproductive isolation** occurs in nature. There are physical barriers like the river, barriers

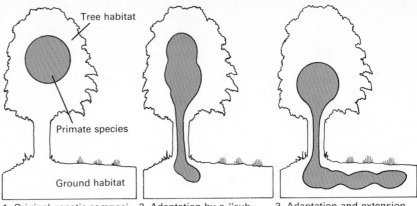

1. Original genetic composition of a tree-dwelling primate species.

2. Adaptation by a "subspecies" to life on the ground.

3. Adaptation and extension proceed.

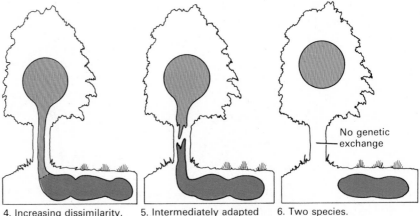

Figure 5.6 Highly Diagramatic Illustration of Speciation. The key to speciation and the definition of "species" is *genetic exchange.*

4. Increasing dissimilarity.

5. Intermediately adapted forms begin to disappear.

6. Two species.

that result from the disappearance of a land bridge, and habitat barriers that result from fluctuations in climate. There are a number of ways by which separation of ideal habitats by less ideal or more dangerous zones can occur.

Picture a population of primates well adapted to life in the trees. Imagine a long dry spell that results in clumps of trees becoming separated by prairielike grassland (Figure 5.6). Imagine some groups of tree-dwelling primates beginning to adapt to part-time life on the ground because of a shrinking **arboreal** (tree) habitat and the presence of food on the ground. Imagine this progressing to the point at which some primates become almost completely adapted to the ground-level niche, enabling them to move far from trees and their tree-dwelling cousins. The existence of successfully ground-adapted primates and the persistence of tree-adapted primates

could make it difficult for any varieties in between. Any intermediate organisms might disappear with time because of competition on both sides.

HOW DID THE EARTH AND ITS GREAT SPHERES ORIGINATE?

The cosmos originated some 10–20 billion years ago. The stars, the planets, the meteors, and other assorted bits of matter are thought to have condensed from clouds of superhot gases or mixtures of atoms and subatomic particles. Some say that the clouds of gases from which the stars and planets condensed resulted from an explosion so uniquely large that it cannot really be described by using standard superlatives, though it is sometimes referred to as the *big bang.*

Some five billion years after the origin of the

Simplified Description of the Relationship Between the Concepts of Natural Selection, Evolution, and Origin of Species

Natural Selection

All living things overproduce. For example, many more frog eggs are laid than will ever become egg-laying adult frogs. The environment and chance determine which offspring will live to reproduce. Disregarding pure chance (because over the long haul its effects even out and produce no bias), environmental pressures tend to go easier on the individuals with the "best" of certain characteristics, for example (other things being equal), the fastest rabbits, the wariest deer, the most cautious bass, the sharpest-toothed wolves, the most discerning eagles, and the most light-sensitive earthworms. The result is that the genes of these most likely to reproduce variants will be preserved, and those of the slow rabbits, dull-toothed wolves, nearsighted eagles, etc. will eventually be lost in a competitive world. Over the long haul this natural or environmental selection of favored gene combinations leads to evolution.

Evolution

Environmental pressures, which come in many forms (for example; temperature, light levels, availability of food), can come and go, intensify and ease up, change abruptly and/or gradually, change cyclically and/or linearly in nature. Because of these selective pressures, the genetic composition of every species is constantly changing, sometimes quickly, sometimes slowly, usually linearly. This process, which is manifest as change in the physical/behavioral characteristics of a group of organisms, is called *evolution*. When it goes far enough, evolution leads to the origin of species.

Origin of Species

Imagine that somehow two groups of the same species of plants or animals become isolated from one another. The environmental pressures on the two groups would differ, since no two places or circumstances are exactly alike. The two groups would evolve away from each other. When the point was passed beyond which the two groups were no longer able to interbreed and produce viable offspring, through mixed mating, the groups would technically have become two different species. Darwin imagined that all species could have come from common ancestors in just such a pattern repeated over and over and over.

---

cosmos the earth came to be as a condensed, relatively tiny bit of matter in orbit around the sun. At first the earth was too hot to have water on its surface, but gradually, and in total conformity to physical laws, the atmosphere and hydrosphere separated from the lithosphere. Over the next few billion years the earth continued to change in form, the atmosphere changed from an oxygen-free one to an oxygen-rich one, the hydrosphere changed (it became saltier), and the lithosphere underwent changes. During the Precambrian period and even later, the cooling crust continued to crack and separate into pieces that drifted atop less solid substrata, colliding with one another in cataclysmic clashes that resulted in the uplifting of mountains and produced various other wrinkles in the surface of the earth. Gradually, the planet became quieter and less chaotic.

COULD LIFE HAVE ORIGINATED ON EARTH SPONTANEOUSLY?

From the start the earth contained about 100 elements existing singly and in various combinations, all having certain potentials for still additional combinations. It is certain that many of the chemical entities in the earth's atmosphere, hydrosphere, and lithosphere during its first billion years combined with one another in all sorts of combinations. It is highly likely that organic molecules were created in this early part of the earth's history. All the right ingredients were present under the right conditions—occasional electrical discharges in the form of lightning, unique and complex mixtures of chemical substances, heat, and ultraviolet radiation. As molecules absorb energy, they enter into more excited states from which they are more apt to enter into chemical combinations with other elements or molecules.

A number of theoreticians postulate that organic chemicals appeared on prebiotic earth (Azoic era) to such an extent that the oceans were converted into a weak "organic soup." Urey (1952) postulated that this organic soup may have been as much as 1% organic matter.

A few decades ago, Stanley Miller demonstrated in the laboratory that in environments absolutely devoid of oxygen it is possible to produce amino acids, **polypeptides** (chains of amino acids), and nucleic acids from hydrogen, methane, nitrogen,

Extinction

Extinction means the disappearance of a species from the face of the earth. If extinction is bad, then things have been bad for the earth's creatures from the beginning because extinction has been the general rule. Practically all of the species that have ever existed are now extinct.

Extinction is the result of a species being unable to adapt to new environmental circumstances fast enough. The earth's environment has been constantly changing all along; the rate of change has been sometimes gradual and sometimes rapid. Gradual changes have apparently been responsible for a steady background rate of extinction. The background rate for marine organisms, for example, has been about 3–5 families or 180–300 species per million years (see Lewin, 1983a). Some of the key factors that account for relatively gradual extinction are: (1) predation, (2) competition, (3) habitat change, and (4) reproductive rates. The impact of the first three of these obviously depend to some extent on the fourth.

There *have* been periods of abrupt extinctions, and these may have been the result of cataclysmic events such as the collision of asteroids with the earth or collisions of drifting continents. The fossil record indicates that there have been at least six periods of mass extinction on land and at *least* four in the oceans. Raup and Sepkoski (1982) calculated that species disappeared at the rate of 20 families and up to 1200 species per million years during the mass extinctions in the oceans. Such mass extinctions of marine invertebrate and vertebrate families occurred in the late Ordovician, Permian, Triassic, and Cretaceous periods. There has been some recent speculation that the mass extinctions occur about every 26 million years as a result of some kind of "regular" meteor/asteroid shower.

There was an especially dramatic mass extinction at the end of the Cretaceous (65 million years ago), when a very high proportion of the oceans plankton (microscopic plants and animals) disappeared along with what was left of the dinosaurs within a relatively short time. It is now generally believed that this was caused by a collision of the earth and an asteroid. In a number of ways that we will not go into here, this collision is thought to have caused a drastic decline in incident solar radiation, depleted the ozone layer, and otherwise messed things up for a long time—tens of thousands or hundreds of thousands of years. Among the evidence for this hypothesis is the occurrence of an iridium-rich deposit at the boundary between the Cretaceous and Tertiary periods apparently laid down throughout the world at about the same time that the extinctions occurred. Iridium is relatively rare in the earth's crust but is relatively abundant in meteors. Although there is no doubt about the extinctions, the *cause* of the extinctions is the subject of ongoing debate (see Hsu et al., 1982).

Extinction can be thought of as one of the main processes in the evolution of life. The disappearance of a species changes the environmental setting as much as the appearance of a species does. Extinction has thus been one of the regular elements of change in an everchanging world. The extinction of individual species or families or wholesale extinctions has created niches that drive evolution further along.

The possible involvement of humans in mass extinctions of large mammals during the Pleistocene is discussed elsewhere in this chapter. The role of modern humans in the extinction of other species is discussed in a later chapter.

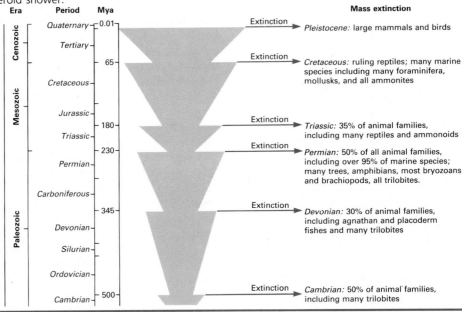

Era	Period	Mya		Mass extinction
Cenozoic	Quaternary	0.01	Extinction →	*Pleistocene:* large mammals and birds
Cenozoic	Tertiary			
Mesozoic		65	Extinction →	*Cretaceous:* ruling reptiles; many marine species including many foraminifera, mollusks, and all ammonites
Mesozoic	Cretaceous			
Mesozoic	Jurassic	180	Extinction →	*Triassic:* 35% of animal families, including many reptiles and ammonoids
Mesozoic	Triassic	230	Extinction →	*Permian:* 50% of all animal families, including over 95% of marine species; many trees, amphibians, most bryozoans and brachiopods, all trilobites.
Paleozoic	Permian			
Paleozoic	Carboniferous	345	Extinction →	*Devonian:* 30% of animal families, including agnathan and placoderm fishes and many trilobites
Paleozoic	Devonian			
Paleozoic	Silurian			
Paleozoic	Ordovician			
Paleozoic	Cambrian	500	Extinction →	*Cambrian:* 50% of animal families, including many trilobites

water, and various salts by exposing these chemicals to electrical discharges or ultraviolet radiation.

Although the process has never been carried out in a laboratory, it is not considered impossible that early life originated spontaneously out of this organic soup. Somehow, some of the constituents of the organic soup evidently acquired the organization and ability to reproduce themselves using the organic molecules that made up the organic soup.

It is postulated that while the first anaerobic bacterialike life forms were using up the primordial soup, variants appeared that were somehow able to bring energy-yielding chemical reactions and/or light energy to bear on the assembly of *new* organic raw materials.

There are many unanswered questions in the way of a clear explanation of how life may have arisen from an organic soup. Nevertheless, the spontaneous generation of life is plausible.

OXYGEN: A WASTE PRODUCT AND SOME NEW NICHES

The earth today has an atmosphere that is 21% oxygen. Chemically, this is an atmosphere that causes things to rust and to literally but slowly burn or oxidize (see Chapter 1). The atmosphere was not always this way. In fact, the earth probably began with an atmosphere containing mostly methane, ammonia, hydrogen, carbon dioxide, and carbon monoxide. Standing where you are today, four billion years ago, without a space suit, you would have died in minutes of asphyxiation.

According to various theoreticians, the earth's atmosphere began to increase in oxygen content as organisms perhaps similar to present-day algae appeared. By taking hydrogen from water molecules these phototrophs released oxygen as a by-product. In the Cambrian period, as a result of this kind of activity, atmospheric oxygen reached 1% of its present levels or about two tenths of one percent of the atmosphere (see Figure 5.7). By the end of the Silurian period, some 400 million years ago, the oxygen in the atmosphere reached about one tenth of what it is today.

The appearance of life forms able to capture light energy and use it as a source of energy for synthesizing organic subunits was a great step forward. The fact that this activity produced oxygen as a by-product made it possible for another great step forward. The stage was set for aerobic heterotrophs, those capable of getting their energy by oxidizing organic material using oxygen.

COULD LIFE ORIGINATE SPONTANEOUSLY TODAY?

What the early oxygen producers did offers a particularly striking example of how lithospheric, atmospheric, and biospheric changes all interrelate to create niches leading to new kinds of interrelationships.

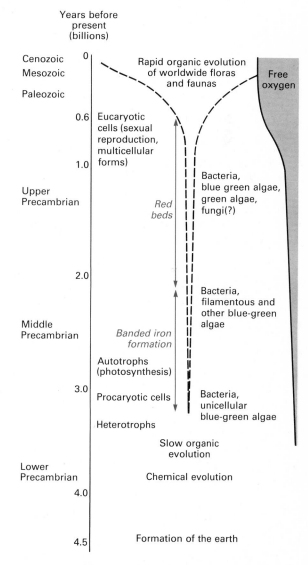

Figure 5.7 Evolution Has Been Both Chemical and Biological. Gradual chemical evolution led to the first living forms. These living forms in turn altered the makeup of the earth's atmosphere. Once sexual reproduction appeared, the resultant acceleration of recombination and evolutionary experimentation yielded much more rapid biological evolution.

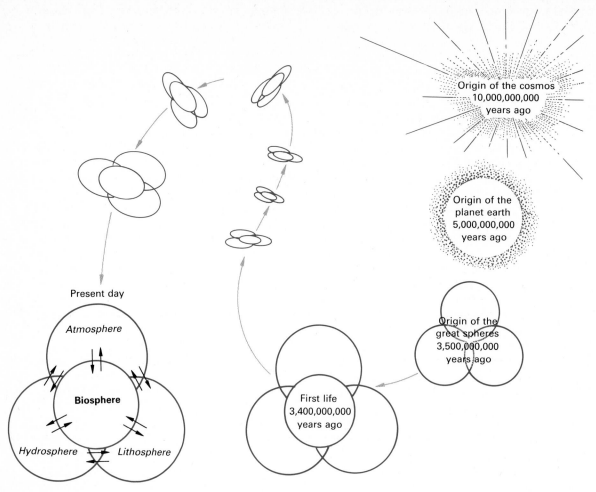

Figure 5.8 Evolution of the Great Spheres. The biosphere, the atmosphere, the lithosphere and the hydrosphere (see Chapters 1 and 3) have interactively evolved for nearly four billion years. Changes in each "sphere" have served—and continued to serve—as agents of change and/or selection in the others.

We pointed out that ultraviolet light might have played a role in the formation of some of the organic molecules in the primordial organic soup. The soup would have provided a new opportunity, one that permitted primordial heterotrophic life forms to appear and sustain themselves using the organic material as raw material. Out of these first life forms evolved other forms that were capable of using light energy and produced oxygen as a by-product. Some of the oxygen in turn was chemically converted into ozone, which began to create a shield over the surface of the earth against ultraviolet radiation. This enabled photosynthetic life forms to move into areas where there was more light energy to do still more photosynthesizing. Eventually, enough of a shield was created by the production of oxygen that even

the land was protected from ultraviolet radiation. This opened up still more opportunities, which would eventually be exploited first by terrestrial plants, then by animals. Thus the evolution of the biosphere, lithosphere, hydrosphere, and atmosphere was highly interrelated (Figure 5.8).

Interrelated changes in all of the earth's spheres explain why life probably will never be able to originate again as it once did. The combinations of conditions that existed when life first originated were changed permanently by the appearance of life itself. Even if life could originate spontaneously again, newly appearing forms would have little chance in competing with the forms already in existence. They would be gobbled up, absorbed, or otherwise outdone by organisms that have had three to four billion years to adapt with a changing environment to where it is now.

AFTER THE EARLY LIFE FORMS

According to the fossil record, a rapid rise in the number of species began about 600 million years ago. Presumably, this was made possible by all that had gone before, the result of four billion years of preparatory chemical and biological evolution. Brachiopods (clamlike organisms), sponges, and gastropods (e.g., snails) appeared in great abundance rather suddenly at the beginning of the Paleozoic era nearly 600 million years ago. On land there was a flurry of plant evolutionary activity 200 million years later (see Stormer, 1977) in the late Silurian period, which produced an enormous variety of vascular plants, providing niches that would later be filled by plant eaters. Dinosaurs originated from very early reptiles that appeared on earth just after the age of large land plants during the Permian period, two to three hundred million years ago. Dinosaurs dominated the earth for well over 100 million years, but by the time the Mesozoic era closed, a majority of them had disappeared (see the box on extinction).

THE EVOLUTION OF ECOSYSTEMS

One of the main points in all of what we have considered so far is that ecological relationships between organisms and the environment existed from the very first appearance of life on earth. Although the number of species may have increased with time, the same basic kinds of ecosystem relationships have persisted.

The sharp climb in oxygen that began about a billion years ago suggests that the earth went through an "age of producers," a time when there was more oxygen given off than consumed. A steady state was evidently reached some hundred million years or so ago because for a long time the amount of oxygen in the atmosphere has remained about the same. We saw in Chapter 1 that the net effect of respiration is the reverse of photosynthesis; as long as the two processes are coupled, there can be no net accumulation of oxygen and no net decrease in carbon dioxide. LaMont Cole (1966), an ecologist, advanced the view that the 1,200,000,000,000,000,000 kilograms of oxygen in our atmosphere plus about another 1% of this amount dissolved in the oceans of the world reflect the amount of photosynthesis that has never been reversed by respiration. This, according to Cole and others, corresponds to only a very, very small fraction of all of the oxygen that was ever produced by photosynthesis. Relatively little production has gone unmatched by decomposition, plant respiration, fire, or consumption and oxidation of plant material by herbivores. Ecosystems must have functioned much as they do now for a long, long time.

Our knowledge of early life forms comes mostly from the fossil record. By putting together the information gleaned from great numbers of fossils, scientists can trace evolutionary trends and their rates of development.

An important trend in evolution was the development of eyes on the front of the head, allowing depth perception. The ability to judge distances must have offered an advantage in the arboreal habitat.

HOW DID HOMO SAPIENS EVOLVE?

Homo sapiens now generally considers itself to be the terminal point of an evolutionary path beginning with primordial matter and extending through the appearance of life, the appearance of animal forms, and the appearance of the vertebrates. Vertebrates appeared in the early Ordovician period about 500 million years ago. Out of this group evolved the special class of warm-blooded vertebrates that suckle their young, called the **mammals**: *Homo sapiens* specifically emerged from a subgroup of mammals called primates.

The stage for *Homo sapiens* had been set by all that had gone before. Dinosaurs were on their way out when there appeared in greater numbers a shrewlike mammal. It must have been difficult being a small mammal during the final days of the dinosaurs. Most early mammals were believed to have been nocturnal, their days spent under cover and nights spent scurrying from cover to cover searching out the relatively enormous amounts of food that their active life-style and warm-blooded metabolism required. Smell would have been extremely important to such creatures.

Fossil records suggest that somewhat later in the evolution of mammals, some of the early forms took to the trees, a move that would have provided a whole new framework of selective pressures. There would have been little advantage in having an acute sense of smell high off the ground. There would have been pressures favoring abilities to walk on tree branches or to grasp branches. As the eons rolled by, any adaptation toward better grasping would have been a selective advantage.

Sometime after the early mammals moved into the trees, a tarsierlike mammal appeared. This evolutionary line favored an adaptation that would later be important to humans. The eyes of tarsiers are up front; both look at the same target. Having two such eyes, together with the brain circuitry necessary for their coordination, made possible stereoscopic vision or the ability to perceive depth. Clearly, there is some advantage to depth perception if one's life depends upon an ability to leap from limb to limb.

Tarsierlike mammals gave rise to monkeylike and catlike creatures and, eventually, *Homo sapiens*. In our monkeylike ancestors there were many additional adaptations that eventually came to characterize humans. For example, the adoption of a hand-over-hand locomotion in early tree-dwelling primates required many muscle changes and changes in the placement and orientation of internal organs. These adaptations eventually made possible other selective steps leading to the upright posture characteristic of human beings today.

Apparently, at one point in the history of primate evolution it was necessary for some of them to come down out of the trees. This move is believed to have been related to a prolonged dry spell over many parts of the habitable earth that lasted from 60 million years ago until about four million years ago. This period favored low forms of vegetation, such as those we now see in prairies. Forests receded in many locations, and clumps of trees became separated by large expanses of prairie or savanna. The climatic change is believed to have resulted from great continental drift–related upliftings that appeared in the surface of the earth, upliftings that produced the Sierra Nevada Mountains, the Andes Mountains, and the Himalayas. These, we know from our discussions in Chapter 3, would have resulted in the deflection of water-laden clouds upward, causing rain to fall on the windward side of these mountains and leaving the leeward or opposite sides dry.

As the trees receded, the arboreal habitat must have become crowded, less desirable, and less able to support the organisms that had adapted to it during earlier, wetter times. Perhaps the climatic change produced a drop in the yield of fruit, and some of the tree dwellers may have found it necessary to come down to the savanna occasionally to find food there. What happened, in effect, was that as one niche began to recede, another one expanded. This is rele-

Continental Drift and Evolution

Two hundred million years ago, there was just one big continent now called "Pangea" and only one enormous ocean. Sometime after the beginning of the Mesozoic era, Pangea began to break up into two continents, "Gondwanaland" in the southern hemisphere and "Laurasia" in the northern hemisphere. Gondwanaland split into several pieces, one that later became South America and Africa and other pieces that became Australia, Antarctica, and India. India later crashed into what became Asia, and the resulting wrinkles are called the Himalayas. Long after Africa separated from South America, it bumped into Arabia and provided a way for African primates to move up into Asia (about 16 or 17 million years ago).

Most of the earth's mountain ranges were formed when the continental plates rode over or beneath one another as they collided. These ranges permanently altered climate over many parts of the earth. Continental drift also changed the ocean currents, which became another important climatic factor. These changes were an important driving force in evolution and may have been responsible for the extinction of many species. Also important was that the breakup of the original land masses isolated many organisms. For example, the unusual animals on Australia are a result of that piece of real estate's isolation.

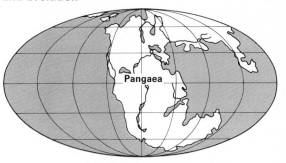

180,000,000 years ago

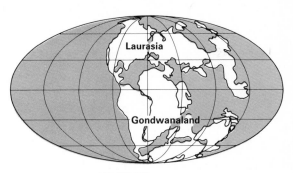

120,000,000 years ago

vant to an idea we developed earlier, namely, that because of the enormous adaptive potential of life, if there is a niche to fill, it will be filled eventually because of pressures such as competition.

Adaptive features that began to take shape in tree-dwelling preprimates underwent further adaptation in the expanded niche of the savanna. The environment was giving birth to *Homo sapiens*. Adaptations that enabled a primate to grasp a limb and to move easily from one tree to another led eventually to an ability to handle tools and to perform delicate manipulations requiring hand-eye coordination. In a very real way your ability to untie a knot in your tennis shoe is the result of pressures that favored steroscopic vision and grasping abilities in your tree-dwelling, fruit-eating ancestors.

The fossil record of the evolution of human beings is quite incomplete, and we have much yet to learn. Tentative schemes of how humans and other primates emerged during the Cenozoic era and the relationship of modern human beings to various fossil forms are given in Figure 5.9. However the sequence went, the important thing is that from the first tool users there most certainly was strong selective pressure favoring greater and greater elaboration of the use of tools and eventually the use of energy other than muscle to power them. Some time after *Australopithecus afarensis,* about 500,000 to 1,000,000 years ago, *Homo erectus* appeared as the first species to live what the fossil record indicates was definitely a human type of existence. *Homo sapiens* emerged sometime during the next two million years, perhaps as recently as 100,000 to 300,000 years ago (Figure 5.9b). *Homo sapiens* was the result of the competitive advantage conferred by better brains and tools.

Changes in the outward appearance of our human ancestors became quite subtle after *Homo ha-*

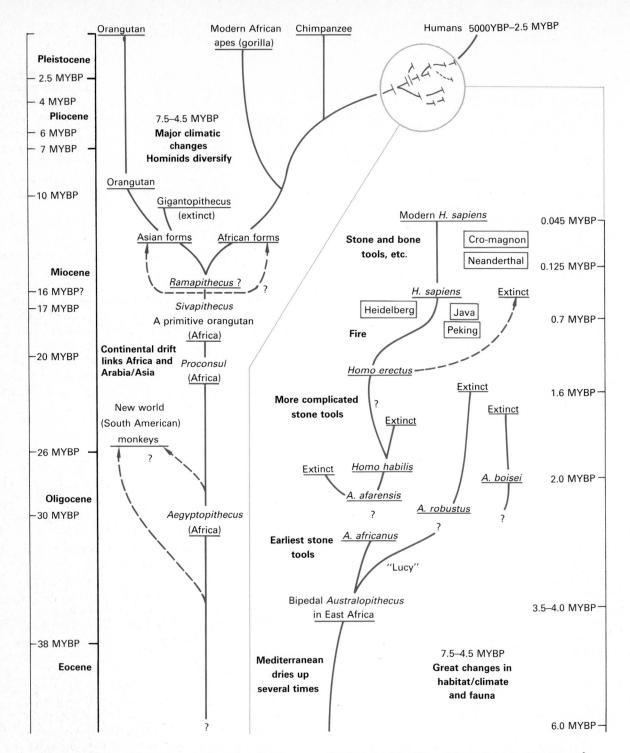

Figure 5.9 (a) Plausible Pattern of Divergence in Primate Evolution during the Cenozoic Era. (b) The Relative Temporal Position of Some Famous Ancestors of Modern Humans.

The System of Nature

*From outer space, our planet looks like [a]
schoolroom globe—but with a difference.
Without labels and national bound-
ries it is easier to see that the world [is]
one big system, one thin layer of [at-]
mosphere, one enormous oce[an]
into which all rivers drain, o[ne]
resource of minerals that [all]
living beings must share. On[ly]
by studying its parts—the e[n-]
ergy flow, the water cyc[le,]
the nutrient cycles—can [we]
understand how the s[ys-]
tem works. And only [by]
understanding the s[ys-]
tem can we make de[ci-]
sions that will allow [us]
to develop lifestyles t[hat]
are harmonious w[ith]
nature. Even from [far]
away, an observer can [see]
that the surface of [our]
planet has a comp[lex]
makeup, oceans and dese[rts,]
mountains and plains, e[ach]
with its own unique combin[a-]
tion of air, water, soil, minera[ls,]
temperature, light, and humid[ity.]
Each environment contains differ[ent]
kinds of organisms interacting with [one]
another and the environment in s[elf-]
regulating ecosystems. But although [the]
ecosystems found in deserts, ponds, tidal pools, [and]
prairies appear to be very different, they all exh[ibit]
the same kinds of fundamental relationships.*

*T*he islands of Hawaii make up an exotic ecosystem, formed by giant volcanoes that rose from the Pacific Ocean floor, far away from other land masses. But we can see here the same cycles and relationships in action that we would find in more familiar surroundings.

he islands' mineral cles are dominated by nost constant volcanic tivity that brings up nerals from deep inside e earth. Although the hot va destroys everything its path, the fresh va fields are quickly colonized by new plants, ich break up the rock d create soil for other ants to grow on.

The new rocky crust of lava is also altered by the forces of sunlight and water. As it does everywhere, the sun drives the Hawaiian ecosystem, providing almost all the energy that flows through the ecosystems. All green plants must have sunlight for photosynthesis, and solar energy also powers the process of evaporation. Water that is evaporated into the atmosphere, seen here as clouds on the mountaintops, is eventually released as precipitation. The precipitation and resultant runoff erode the surface of the land, changing its shape and bringing chemical elements into solution, where they can be used by living organisms.

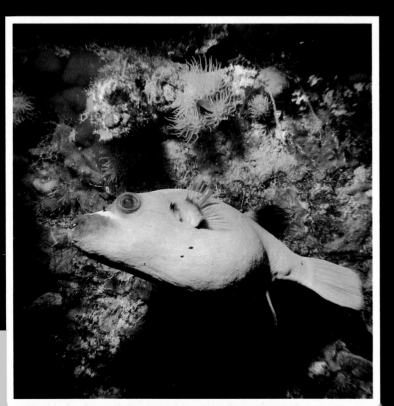

Hawaii's organisms include those that live underwater offshore. Here colonies of brightly colored coral compete for space and food. In this system, the producers are free-floating marine plants, invisible to the human eye, that are consumed by the corals as primary consumers. In turn, the corals are eaten by fish, like the smooth pufferfish. Not only do the coral's hard skeletons build up huge undersea reefs and even whole islands, those that pass through the puffer's system are ground up and excreted as pure white sand. So the corals play an important role in both the nutrient cycle and the mineral cycle on the Hawaiian islands.

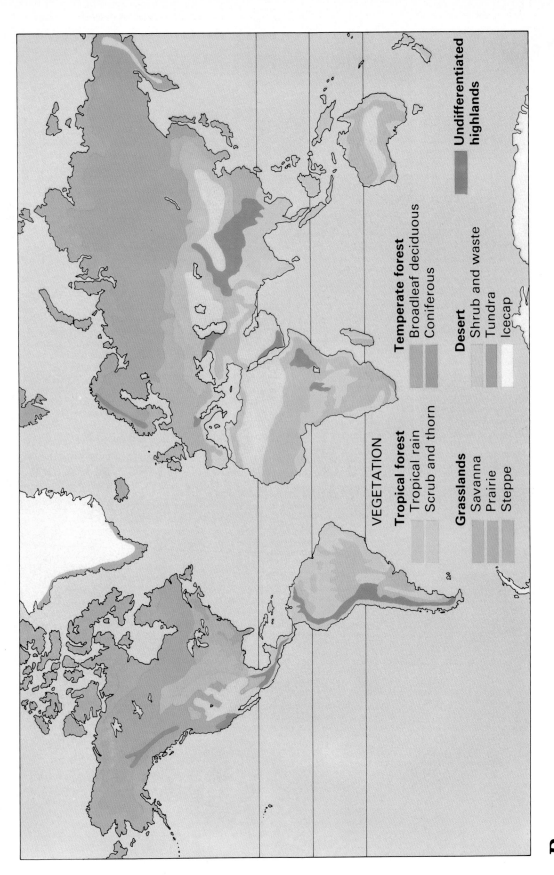

Biomes are the earth's major community types. Biomes are characterized by specific climatic conditions (of which temperature, rainfall, and evaporation rate are the most important) resulting in characteristic plant types. The plant types in turn are important determinants of the kinds of animals that can exist in each biome.

VEGETATION

Tropical forest
Tropical rain
Scrub and thorn

Grasslands
Savanna
Prairie
Steppe

Temperate forest
Broadleaf deciduous
Coniferous

Desert
Shrub and waste
Tundra
Icecap

Undifferentiated highlands

All in The Family?

A small primate that inhabited Africa 30 million years ago is now believed to be a common ancestor of both *Homo sapiens* and modern apes. Discovery of the skeletal fossils of *Aegyptopithecus,* as the creature was named, was announced in February 1980. The fossil of *Aegyptopithecus* was found in the same area of Africa in which other ancestors of *Homo sapiens* have been found. This location and the brain size, teeth, and other physical characteristics deduced for *Aegyptopithecus* place it in the line of descent for both humans and modern apes.

Because many new niches appeared and others expanded as the savanna replaced forest, the evolution of primates probably followed several directions. It is now generally believed that at least *two* major splits occurred sometime after *Aegyptopithecus. Aegyptopithecus* is believed to have given rise to *Ramapithecus.* A relative of *Ramapithecus* is believed to have given rise to African and Asian primate branches about the time that continental drift connected Africa with Asia (16 million years ago). The African branch later split into three separate

primate ancestral lines leading to gorillas, chimpanzees, and humans.

It was once thought that the hominid *Australopithecus africanus,* discovered by Ramond Dart in 1925 in Tswana, South Africa, was an ancestor of modern human beings. However, it is now rather generally agreed that *Australopithecus africanus* and the ancestors of modern human beings developed in separate branches and may even have been in competition—a competition that *A. africanus* and its relatives lost. Donald Johanson and Timothy White announced in 1979 that they had discovered *Australopithecus afarensis,* believed to be a common ancestor of both *Homo sapiens* and *A. africanus.* There is still considerable disagreement as to just how it all went, but however or whenever the splits occurred, sometime before the Pleistocene epoch came, about 3.5 million years ago, creatures with humanlike characteristics were present over large expanses of Africa, Asia, and the Middle East.

---

bilis, and it has been suggested that a Neanderthal person dressed in modern clothes might pass unnoticed on one of our city streets today. The evolution of the genus *Homo* was primarily toward attributes favoring intraspecies cooperation and culture leading to a *gradual* increase in reproductive success. It was not until human beings learned to harness fossil fuel that human reproductive success began a

sharper ascent (Figure 5.10). Modern life is a very recent phenomenon.

If we conceptually condense the history of humankind since the Stone Age, that is, the previous half million years, into one day, agriculture started in the last half hour—after 11:30 P.M.; Julius Caesar's reign would have begun around 11:55 P.M.; William the Conqueror would have invaded England at

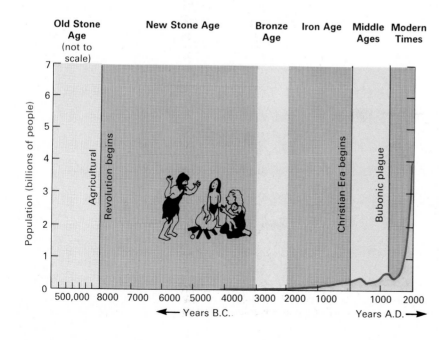

Figure 5.10 Growth of Human Population in the Last Half-Million Years. The increase in numbers of *Homo sapiens* has been mostly very slow over time. If the Old Stone Age were drawn to the same scale as the rest of the figure, it would be nearly 20 feet wide. *Very* recently, our increase in numbers has been *very* fast.

Chapter 5   Evolution and Ecology: The Emergence of the Ecosphere

11:57 P.M.; George Washington's administration would have occurred within the last half minute of the day; and humanity would have relied almost entirely on its own muscle and beasts of burden for all except the last 16 seconds.

HUMANS AS INTELLIGENT, COOPERATIVE GENERALISTS

While some species are more or less completely adapted to particular niches, ours is not. Ecological adaptability seems to have been—and still to be—a characteristic of primates in general. Primates have no outstanding features they all share except the ability to survive environmental change by being relatively flexible about their needs. As a group, the primates occupy a wide range of ecological niches. The evolutionary history of *Homo sapiens* and the sequence of adaptations that have come to characterize this species confer a little of every ability on men and women, but we are not really outstanding at any of them. Humans can swim, run, climb, and do lots of other things. There are other organisms that can swim farther, run faster, dig deeper, and climb better; most others have sharper teeth, keener sight, and better insulation. However, no other animal can do all of the things human beings can, and no other species can make up for its shortcomings with intelligent cooperative interaction the way our species does. Some say that our species' most distinctive characteristic is intelligence. But another key feature, cooperativeness, amplified the importance of intelligence by making possible shared behavior—learning from one another and even learning from those long since dead. Because of our cooperative-interactive way of life, only one of us had to invent the wheel for all to benefit from it.

Throughout the history of evolution, niches have been created and filled as a consequence of evolution. The filling of specific niches is a slow process because they can be filled only through competition and adaptation, biological processes that take time. The success of *Homo sapiens* can be attributed to an ability to circumvent these processes through intelligence and the explosive advance of learning and invention, feeding on itself in a process that has come to be called cultural evolution. Cultural evolution together with the human generalist primate heritage has enabled our species to recognize and to occupy a niche of many niches. We have become the supreme exploiters. Humans can invade any habitat and use almost anything as food. We are more than multilevel consumers; we are controllers of producers. Although we cannot convert electromagnetic energy into chemical energy (yet), we *can* make it happen. We can start, augment, or stop production; we can even alter the nature of producers.

Humans are generalists with the flexibility and intelligence to fill whatever niches are available. Alaskan Inuit and Australian Wagaitj successfully exploit vastly different ecosystems.

From Hunter to Farmer and the Origins of Culture

Born out of a heritage of cooperative bands that reached high levels of organization in our primate forebears, humanity started out gathering fruits, insects, and other miscellaneous edibles. Some say that humans turned to hunting later, possibly after finding that predators killed in self-defense were also edible. In any event, the archeological record of human campsites indicates that our branch of the order Primate spent its early years as small bands of hunters supplementing kills with things foraged and gathered. Although there have been some complex band-level human cultures with some fairly sophisticated, cooperative divisions of labor, band-level cultures supported by hunting and gathering never got very far. Some say that this type of culture was successful enough to bring about population pressures that made agriculture necessary. At the very least, these cultures set us up to exploit agriculture once it was discovered.

People began to farm seriously about 10,000 years ago, though there were probably occasional false starts before that and perhaps a long period in which hunting and gathering were combined with agriculture in various proportions. Archeological records indicate that humans began to farm seriously in 8000 B.C. in parts of the Near East and in Southwestern Asia and that there was full-scale agriculture in many places just after 4000 B.C.

Turning to crops for food was extremely important to the success of the species for many reasons, all of which have to do with the simple fact that plants are at the base of the food chain. As we learned in Chapters 1 and 2, as food energy moves from one level to another in the food chain, about 90% of available energy is lost with each transfer. It remains true to this day that many more people can be supported if they subsist on a basic diet of corn than if that same amount of corn were fed to hogs and the humans ate pork. In a very real sense, using plants as food eliminates the middle consumer—the herbivore, the rabbit, the hog or the cow—and the energy profit taken in the process of making meat. Plants also have fixed locations and are easier to find than animals, especially if they are planted in a particular location. Grain and beans are much more easily stored than meat, and this provides another kind of food energy cushion against hard times, something that hunting could not do as well.

For all of these reasons, agriculture permitted the establishment of stable population centers and time free from the business of subsisting. This added an enormously important dimension to the potential for human success. Because of the energy/survival advantage of agriculture, a primate that had already developed considerable intellectual powers and patterns of cooperation suddenly had much more time to think and to invent. This in turn led to greater opportunities for inventiveness and the development of technologies that produced more and more free time for more and more thinking and more and more inventions. The process accelerated sharply when humans learned to harness the energy derived from fossil fuels.

How Do Cultural Evolution and Biological Evolution Compare?

We defined biological evolution earlier, and we have now traced the process to the point at which there is apparently another kind of evolution, cultural evolution. Perhaps **cultural evolution** can be defined as changes passed on not by genetic transfer, but by learning.

In comparison with the time scales we have been dealing with for most of this chapter, the time scale of cultural evolution is very short (see Table 5.1). Cultural evolution occurs very much faster than biological evolution, yet both have the same result, that of producing populations more fit in relation to a given environment. Both processes can go on simultaneously.

Flight could be considered something that confers a selective advantage and increased "fitness" on *Homo sapiens*. Disregarding nuclear missiles and the like, being able to fly translates into improved survival for the species through the transport of goods or of combinations of expertise to the right place at the right time. Humankind has not had to wait for biological evolution to produce human wings, however; the Wright brothers used their highly evolved intellectual capacity to *invent* wings. There are many other similar examples. So rapid are the changes that can be effected through cultural evolution and inventiveness that they outstrip the natural tendency of life—*Homo sapiens* included—to come up with responsive biological adaptive mechanisms. Physiologically, we are cave men and women in suits and dresses.

THE IMPACT OF EARLY HUMANS ON THE ENVIRONMENTS THAT SHAPED THEM

While *Homo sapiens* was literally being formed from the primordial dust over the long course of chemical and biological evolution, there was, as we have stated often, a reciprocal interaction between forces driving evolution. Born to this heritage, humankind has had considerable impact on both its biological and its physical/chemical environment since long before there were such things as large-scale fossil fuel combustion and atomic bombs. To be sure, this impact was less in the beginning, when there were fewer of us and technological advances for the most part were not made on such a grand scale.

Because early humans subsisted by hunting and gathering, the species was controlled by relatively short control loops and simply could not hurt the environment very much. If early humans decided for some reason to cut down lots of trees or otherwise destroy vegetation, the deer and other animals they needed for food would leave and no longer be there to sustain them. The humans would have to move on or starve long before any permanent harm could be done. Textbooks cite some notable exceptions to this, some of which have come to be known collectively as the **Pleistocene overkill**.

Table 5.1 Cultural Evolution of *Homo sapiens* Since the Last Major Ice Age.

Date	Climatic Changes in Northern Europe	Old World Cultural Stages	New World Cultural Stages
10,000 B.C.	Last glacial stage (Würm-Wisconsin ice)	Last Paleolithic hunting cultures (Cro-Magnon, etc.)	
9000 B.C.	Retreat of the glaciers (preboreal period, cold dry)	Mesolithic fishing, hunting, collecting cultures	
8000 B.C.			Hunting cultures established (Folsom Man, etc.)
		?Agricultural beginnings	
7000 B.C			
6000 B.C.	Boreal period (warm, dry)		
5000 B.C.	Atlantic period (warm, moist)	Neolithic agriculture established and spreading	
4000 B.C.		Beginnings of civilization (Egyptian-Sumerian)	
3000 B.C.		Neolithic agriculture in northern Europe	
			American agricultural beginnings
2000 B.C.	Subboreal period (colder, dry)	Babylonian Empire	
		Invasions: Aryans to India; Medes and Persians to S. W. Asia and Mesopotamia	
1000 B.C.		Rise and flowering of Greek civilization	
			Early Mexican and Mayan civilizations
B.C.—A.D.	Sub-Atlantic period (cool, moist)	Roman empire	
		Invasions, Goths, Huns	Decline of Mayans
		Rise of Islam	
		Norsemen to America	
1000 A.D.		Mongol and Tarter invasions	Aztecs and Incas
		Voyages of discovery and colonization by Europe	
		Industrial revolution and modern period	
2000 A.D.			

Early humans are believed to have improved hunting techniques during the Pleistocene epoch by using fire and/or advancing lines of hunters to drive prey into traps or swampy areas where they could easily be killed. This was successful to the extent that it is believed to have contributed to the extinction of as much as 40% of the game species in parts of Africa (Martin, 1967). At about the same time, as humans came over the land bridge from Siberia to North America, the invaders encountered many large mammals that had never before seen humans and had not developed a fear of predators. Some anthropologists believe that as humanity advanced through North America and eventually into Central and South America, many of these species, some already endangered by environmental and habitat changes, were rendered extinct long before selection could produce more wary varieties.

As humankind began to develop the beginnings of today's agricultural patterns, humans began to have more chronic kinds of impact on the environment. Some of this impact was damaging, and some, though perhaps quite extensive, could be considered benign.

Scholars as early as 347 B.C. described deforestation and overgrazing around the Mediterranean Sea and how this led to the drying up of springs and erosion of soil. Both ancient and modern scholars attribute the collapse of the Babylonian Empire and other civilizations of the Middle East to such ecological disasters. There were also environmentalists in those early days. Around 40 B.C., Virgil recommended that the crops be rotated (Cole, 1966; Dorst, 1970), that legumes be planted with other crops, that land be left fallow in alternate years, and that soil be regenerated with manure, ashes, and the like. Pliny wrote of human activities and how they caused alteration in local climates—for example, by changing the course of rivers and the draining of lakes. He reported that grapes and other food crops were destroyed by frosts once the temperature-moderating effects of certain bodies of water were removed (Cole, 1966).

Early agricultural humans were known to use fire to clear land for crops and to create pasture lands. This undoubtedly resulted in the destruction of forests and produced great temporary upsets in the balance of nature in and around the Mediterranean Sea and in other parts of Europe from the Middle Ages on. In Europe, great destruction of forests began around the Middle Ages as land was cleared for agriculture and as more and more lumber was used for ship building.

As the human species picked up even more steam, its impact extended to some benign but nevertheless major changes in the flora and fauna of the world. Our ancestors moved cows and horses all over. Although wheat first arose in parts of the Middle East, it has been scattered by would-be farmers all over the globe. Today, some 600,000,000 acres of land are covered by wheat most of the year, supplanting thousands and thousands of species of natural grasses, trees, and shrubs (Brown and Finsterbusch, 1972). Human horticulturists have often acted as agents of natural selection as they learned to identify good seed and to favor those seeds that produced what was wanted. Humans have surely had quite an impact on the genetic makeup of a number of species.

Homo sapiens has also served as a passive factor in the evolution and development of other species. Many organisms have learned to exploit humans and the niches humankind has created. The rise of humanity was paralleled by an increase in success for a number of disease organisms that wreaked havoc on human populations throughout most of human history. Some of these diseases were transmitted by rodents that had adapted very well to human-made habitats. A number of organisms have adapted to live in harmony with humans in the habitats our species created without much of a direct negative effect on the humans. These include certain weeds, songbirds, field mice, squirrels, and other organisms like dogs that find some of the human-made niches very suitable, or at least not incompatible with their biological success.

Humankind has had a great impact, both positive and negative, on nature since its introduction into natural systems. Extrapolation from the past and the events of the present day seem to indicate that this pattern will persist.

THE QUESTION

We have just described what we consider to be a plausible sequence of events by which we humans arrived where we are. In a word, humans are the leading edge of an evolutionary strategy in which reproductive success is achieved through the intelligent use of tools to manipulate the environment to advantage.

We have recently come to realize that our powers bring serious threat as well as promise. Some of us feel confident that now that we have seen the problem, the same intelligence that brought it will eliminate it. Others are not so sure. Now that our intelligence has gotten us into a certain amount of trouble, will we be wise enough to use it to find the solutions to get us out? That is the question.

CONCEPTS TO REMEMBER

1. Ecological interaction has been the driving force behind both biological and geochemical evolution. In a sense, evolution is the epitome of ecological succession. Evolution is succession on million-year or billion-year time scales.
2. That humankind can be influenced by the environment is obvious if humankind is seen in terms of evolution. The changing environment literally formed us from dust in a process spanning nearly four billion years.
3. Science has nothing to say one way or the other about the existence of a supreme being. Evolution and natural selection are explanations of "how," not "who."
4. Genetic selection can be natural or artificial. Both result in evolution.
5. Environmental destruction is not an invention of modern *Homo sapiens*; even our Stone Age ancestors were good at it.

DISCUSSION QUESTIONS AND FOOD FOR THOUGHT

1. Discuss the idea that we will biologically adapt to a polluted world. Perhaps it would be enlightening to first discuss the validity of the following statement: Biological adaptation can occur only through death.
2. Choose up sides and debate the following: Resolved: Since modern human beings cannot exist as we do without having an enormous negative impact on the environment, we should return to an earlier, much simpler life-style.
3. Summarize the ways in which access to non-physiological energy has accounted for the success of *Homo sapiens*.
4. Explain how life could have originated and become increasingly complex in light of the second law of thermodynamics, which says that the universe is running down and is becoming less "ordered" with time.
5. Discuss the following concept: Life is simply a device used by DNA to preserve itself.
6. Defend or refute: Evolutionary history indicates that *Homo sapiens* is in no danger of extinction.
7. What is the relationship between "fitness" as defined by Charles Darwin and the kind of fitness associated with gymnasiums?
8. Defend or refute: Cultural evolution is artificial; technology is unnatural.
9. What are some of the reasons why the missing link (the species intermediate between man and ape) might be missing?
10. Defend or refute: If we burned all of the coal and oil on earth, all of the oxygen in the atmosphere would be converted to carbon dioxide.

REFERENCES AND FURTHER READING

References marked with an asterisk are cited in the chapter.

Bajema, C. J., ed., 1971 (Reprinted 1977). *Natural Selection in Human Populations: The Measurement of Ongoing Genetic Evolution in Contemporary Societies.* New York: John Wiley & Sons.

*Banks, H. P., 1970. *Evolution and Plants of the Past.* Belmont, Calif.: Wadsworth Publishing Company.

Bendall, D. S., 1983. *Evolution from Molecules to Men.* New York: Cambridge University Press.

Berkner, L. V., and Marshall, L. C., 1965. "On the Origin and Rise of Oxygen Concentration in the Earth's Atmosphere." *Journal of Atmospheric Science* **22**:225–261.

Bronowski, J., 1973. *The Ascent of Man.* Boston: Little, Brown and Co.

*Brown, L. R., and Finsterbusch, G. W., 1972. *Man and His Environment: Food.* New York: Harper and Row.

Caldwell, M. M., 1979. "Plant Life and Ultraviolet Radiation: Some Perspective in the History of the Earth's UV Climate." *Bioscience* **29**(9):520–525.

Cloud, P. E., Jr., 1965. "Symposium on the Evolution of the Earth's Atmosphere," *Proceedings of the National Academy of Sciences* **53**:1169–1226.

*Cole, L. C., 1966. "Man's Ecosystem," *Bioscience* **16**(4):243–248.

Crick, F., 1981. *Life Itself: Its Origin and Nature.* New York: Simon and Schuster.

Darwin, C., 1859. *The Origin of Species.* Originally published November 24, 1859, in Down-Beckenham, Kent, England; this work is now available in a paperback version through Dolphin Books, Doubleday and Company, Garden City, N.Y.

Dasmann, R., 1972. *Environmental Conservation.* New York: John Wiley & Sons.

Dobzhansky, T. and Boesiger, E., 1983. *Human Culture: A Moment in Evolution.* New York: Columbia University Press.

*Dorst, J., 1970. *Before Nature Dies.* Baltimore: Pelican Books.

Eldredge, N., and Tattersall, I., 1982. *The Myths of Human Evolution.* New York: Columbia University Press.

Gillespie, N. C., 1979. *Charles Darwin and the Problem of Creation.* Chicago: University of Chicago Press.

Gould, S. J., 1982. "Darwinism and the Expansion of Evolutionary Theory," *Science* **216**:380–387.

Grene, M., 1983. *Dimensions of Darwinism.* New York: Cambridge University Press.

Hammond, A. L., and Crabtree, M., 1983. "Tales of an Elusive Ancestor," *Science 83* (November), 37–43.

Hardin, G., 1969. "In Praise of Waste," in *Population, Evolution, and Birth Control.* San Francisco: W. H. Freeman and Co.

*Hsu, K. J., et al., 1982. "Mass Mortality and Its Environmental and Evolutionary Consequences," *Science* **216**:249–256.

Johnson, D. C., and Edey, M. A., 1981. *Lucy.* New York: Simon and Schuster.

Landau, M., Pilbeam, D., and Richard, A., 1982. "Human Origins a Century after Darwin," *Bioscience* **32**(6):507–512.

Leakey, R., and Lewin, R., 1977. *Origins.* New York: E. P. Dutton.

*Lerner, I. M., 1968. *Heredity, Evolution, and Society.* San Francisco: W. H. Freeman and Co.

Levinton, J. S., 1982. "Charles Darwin and Darwinism," *Bioscience* **34**(6):495–500.

Lewin, R., 1983a. "Extinction and the History of Life," *Science* **221**:935–937.

Lewin, R., 1983b. "What Killed the Giant Mammals?" *Science* **221**:1036–1037.

*McKusick, V. A., 1969. *Human Genetics.* Englewood Cliffs, N.J.: Prentice-Hall.

*Martin, P. S., 1967. "Pleistocene Overkill," *Natural History* **76**(4):32–38.

May, R. M., 1978. "The Evolution of Ecological Systems," in *Evolution, Scientific American,* San Francisco: W. H. Freeman.

Newell, N. E., 1982. *Creation and Evolution: Myth or Reality?* New York: Columbia University Press.

*Newman, W. L., 1977a. *Geologic Time: The Age of the Earth,* U.S. Department of Interior Geological Survey. USGS 0-240-996/31. Washington, D.C.: U.S. Government Printing Office.

Newman, W. L., 1977b. "Puzzling Out Man's Ascent," *Time,* November 7, 64–78.

Nitecki, M. N., ed., 1982. *Biochemical Aspects of Evolutionary Biology.* Chicago: University of Chicago Press. This collection of essays was presented at a 1981 symposium.

Nitecki, M. N., ed., 1983a. *Coevolution.* Chicago: University of Chicago Press. This is a collection of nine essays presented at a 1982 symposium.

Nitecki, M., 1983b. *Extinctions.* Chicago: University of Chicago Press.

Oparin, A. I., 1953. *The Origin of Life.* New York: Dover Publications. A classic!

Patterson, C., 1978. *Evolution.* Ithaca, N.Y.: Cornell University Press. This is a paperback introduction to evolution.

Penzias, A. A., 1979. "The Origin of the Elements," *Science* **205**:549–554.

Pilbeam, D., 1984. "The Descent of Hominoids and Hominids," *Scientific American* **250**(3, March):84–96.

Provine, W. B., 1982. "Influence of Darwin's Ideas on the Study of Evolution," *Bioscience* **32**(6):501–507.

*Raup, D. M., and Sepkoski, J. J., 1982. "Mass Extinctions in the Marine Fossil Record," *Science* **215**:1501–1502.

Reader, J., 1981. *Missing Links: The Hunt for Earliest Man,* Boston: Little, Brown and Co.

Rensberger, B., 1984. "A New Ape in Our Family Tree," *Science 84,* (March), 16.

Rosen, B. R., 1982. "Darwin, Coral Reefs, and Global Geology," *Bioscience* **34**(6):519–525.

Ruse, M.,1984. "Is There a Limit to Our Knowledge of Evolution?" *Bioscience* **34**(2):100–103.

Schopf, J., ed., 1983. *Earth's Earliest Biosphere.* Princeton, N.J.: Princeton University Press.

Schweber, S. S., 1978. "The Genesis of Natural Selection—1838: Some Further Insights," *Bioscience* **28**(5): 321–326.

Silver, L. T., and Schultz, P. H., eds., 1982. *Geological Implications of Impacts of Large Asteroids and Comets on the Earth.* Boulder, Colo.: Geological Society of America. This is a collection of papers from a conference.

Stanley. S. M., 1984. "Mass Extinctions in the Ocean," *Scientific American,* June **250**(6):64–72.

Steel, R., 1979. *The Encyclopedia of Prehistoric Life.* New York: McGraw-Hill.

Stebbins, G. L., 1982. *Darwin to DNA, Molecules to Humanity.* San Francisco: W. H. Freeman.

*Stormer, L., 1977. "Anthropod Invasion of Land during Late Silurian and Devonian Times," *Science* **197**:1362–1364.

*Swanson, C. P., 1973. *The Natural History of Man.* Englewood Cliffs, N.J.: Prentice-Hall.

*Urey, H. C., 1952. "The Early Chemical History of the Earth and the Origin of Life," *Proceedings of the National Academy of Sciences of the U.S.* **38**:351–363. Another classic!

Volpe, E. P., 1977. *Understanding Evolution,* 3rd ed. Dubuque, Iowa: William C. Brown.

Vrba, E. S., 1983. "Macroevolutionary Trends: New Perspectives on the Roles of Adaptation and Incidental Effect," *Science* **221**:387–389.

Waldrop, M. M., 1984. "Before the Beginning," *Science 84,* 45–51. This article describes Alan Guth's inflation theory of the origin of the universe.

Walker, J. C. G., 1977. *Evolution of the Atmosphere.* New York: Macmillan.

Weisskopf, V. F., 1983. "The Origin of the Universe," *American Scientist* **71**:473–481.

Woese, C. R., 1979. *Human Ancestors.* (This is a collection of readings from *Scientific American.*) San Francisco: W. H. Freeman.

Woese, C. R., 1984. *The Origin of Life.* Burlington, N.C.: Carolina Biological Supply.

Homo Sapiens in the Scheme of Natural Things

Although philosophers may never agree on some of the more mystical aspects of *Homo sapiens,* one thing is certain: Ours is an animal species subject to the laws of nature. In Part I we considered life in general and the laws by which life is governed. We have seen that natural systems are regulated by complex webs of checks and balances and that life has an exponentially explosive, reproductive potential; we know that seemingly insignificant biological events may have many, varied, and extensive consequences. Perhaps the reader can now appreciate the fact that life is not a *thing* so much as it is a *process* and why it is more important to be concerned with trends and potential in living systems than to be concerned with momentary status.

From the perspective presented in Part I we will now focus on *Homo sapiens*. We will consider our energy and nutrient relationships with the rest of nature. We will look at how these relationships set, and may set, the current and future limits to human population growth and human activities.

Energy in Human Affairs

SECTION A

Energy up to Now: Sources and Uses

The energy crisis of the mid-1970s was greatly overblown. Long lines at gas stations, home heating oil shortages, turned down thermostats, and sharply rising energy prices made good human interest stories but reflected little more than temporary supply problems and some long overdue price adjustments. Except for the fact that the so-called crisis *illustrated the importance of energy* to human beings, it had little directly to do with the basic ecological need of all living things and all living systems for continual sources of energy.

It is important that we see the energy crisis of the 1970s as a relatively minor part of a very real, ongoing, fundamental problem. Otherwise, the fact that this particular crisis all but ended a decade after it started could give us a false sense of security—a false view that energy problems are only minor nuisances that come and go. A decade after the 1974 Arab oil embargo that triggered the energy crisis, high energy prices and some worldwide economic problems related to expensive energy were all that remained of the crisis; energy itself became plentiful in virtually every form. Even the ability of the United States to deal with disruption in energy supplies had improved greatly, thanks to a healthy increase in our strategic petroleum reserve, conservation, reduced oil imports, and the national experience of having gone through the crisis of the 1970s. Today we are using roughly the same amount of energy as we did in the early 1970s. Oil prices have stopped rising and have even fallen in some of the last few years.

But are our energy problems over? Consider the following:

1. In a very brief period in the history of the world, in less than five centuries, we will have consumed virtually all of the coal, oil, and gas formed over a period of 500 million years (Figure 6.1).
2. We *are* running out of some of the energy sources we depend upon most, and we have no assurance that we will be able to make smooth transitions to other sources of energy already available to us, let alone to those for which technology is not yet sufficiently advanced.
3. There are many uncertainties about the economic, political, social, and other ripple effects as the world goes through the crisis of passing peak production of natural gas and oil.
4. In a world in which energy is of supreme importance, there are few energy policies or plans. Because the United States uses the greatest proportionate share of the energy, it is especially irresponsible in not having a sound energy policy.
5. Energy has long been wasted—especially in the United States.

6. In the United States and in much of the rest of the world, economics and ways of life have become shaped by the availability of cheap energy. Now energy is no longer cheap. The oil-importing developing countries will need more energy during the 1980s to sustain their progress. Rising costs will require that energy efficiency be increased significantly (Dunkerly and Ramsay, 1982).

7. Nearly every environmental problem is directly related to the production and consumption of energy. The combustion of fuel accounts for nearly all of the *air* pollution problem; the extraction, processing, and use of fuel generates much *water* pollution. Strip-mining is an obvious example of how energy use can contribute to the deterioration of land. Energy consumption is even responsible for some less generally recognized types of pollution, such as noise and hazardous wastes.

The former chairperson of the United States Atomic Energy Commission, Dixie Lee Ray, once pointed out that every American uses the electrical equivalent of 11 servants, that with electrically powered machinery one human being can do the work of 700 human beings, and that a barrel of oil has the heat energy equivalent of a person working at hard labor for two years. A direct consequence of this labor-saving access to energy is that fossil fuel is squarely responsible for delivering much of human-kind from bondage to the soil. But we have traded one kind of bondage for another. Much of civilization as we now know it is dependent, directly or indirectly, on high rates of **consumption** of what for now and the foreseeable future are nonrenewable, rapidly dwindling, and increasingly expensive sources of energy that cause problems in the environment. This is a crisis indeed.

Chapter 6 should be read with the ecological concepts covered in earlier chapters well in mind: Chapter 2 described the principles of energy use by living things and made it clear that continual energy input is crucial to all living systems. Chapter 5 reviewed the emergence of modern human beings and made it clear that access to energy has been a major factor in the past success of our species and that it will be a major factor in the quality of our future success if not our ultimate survival.

THE HISTORY OF ENERGY USE—SOME RELATIVELY RECENT NOTEWORTHY TRENDS

The History of Consumption

The trend in energy consumption from the primitive era of human history to the modern day is shown in Figure 6.2. Note that during this period of time, energy consumption increased by more than a hundredfold. Note also that energy consumption

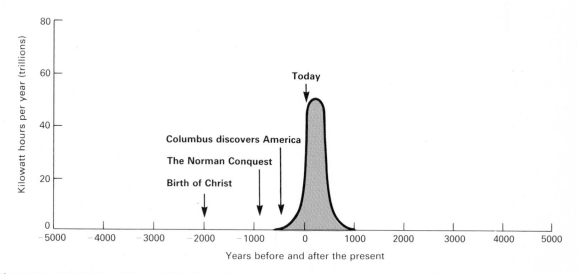

Figure 6.1 Historical and Expected Fossil Fuel Use. The use of fossil fuels will appear as just a blip even on a time scale as short as 10,000 years. After using fossil fuels for about 600 years, we are probably already on a permanent downward course in worldwide production of natural gas, at or just past the peak in production of oil, and within a few hundred years of reaching the peak in our use of coal. The "age of fossil fuels" might more aptly be called the "fossil fuel incident."

Chapter 6   Energy in Human Affairs

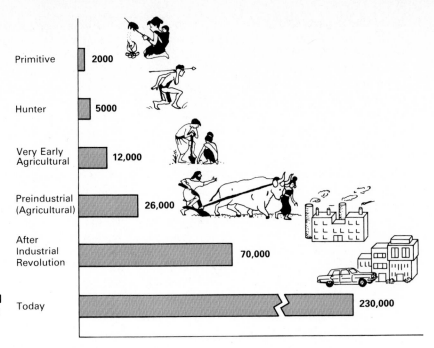

Figure 6.2 Energy Consumed at Different Stages of Human History. In kilocalories *per person* per day.

Primitive	2000
Hunter	5000
Very Early Agricultural	12,000
Preindustrial (Agricultural)	26,000
After Industrial Revolution	70,000
Today	230,000

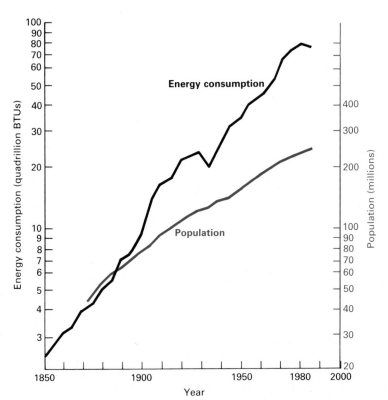

Figure 6.3 Comparison of Energy Consumption and Population Growth in the U.S. Since the Mid-nineteenth Century. These data clearly indicate that per capita consumption increased considerably from the turn of this century until recently. Note that the vertical scales are logarithmic.

Part II *Homo Sapiens* in the Scheme of Natural Things

British thermal unit (BTU): amount of heat necessary to raise the temperature of a pound of water 1°F.

Coal: solid combustible organic fuel formed by the anaerobic decomposition of vegetable matter. This material is composed of aromatic carbon compounds.

Consumption: the amount of energy or any other resource used in a unit of time by some unit of people (*Example:* In the United States we consumed about 7 billion barrels of oil in 1979. This could also be expressed as more than 30 barrels per person in 1979.)

Electrical energy: electricity; energy derived from the movement of charged particles.

Fossil fuel: any organic fuel such as coal, petroleum, or natural gas formed over millions of years from what was once living matter.

Generator: a machine that converts mechanical energy into electrical energy. Generators typically consist of a coil of wire that can be made to rotate in a magnetic field. The rotation causes electrons to flow in the wire, thus producing electricity.

Kilowatt (kw, 1000 watts): one kilowatt is equal to about 1 1/3 horsepower.

Kilowatt hour (kwh, 1000 watt hours): unit of electrical energy equivalent to the energy delivered by the flow of 1 kilowatt of electrical power for one hour; for example, a 200-watt bulb burning five hours will use one kwh of energy or enough to lift 300 pounds roughly 9000 feet into the air.

Megawatt (Mw): one million watts or 1000 kilowatts.

Natural gas: naturally occurring fossil fuel gases found in coarse geological formations, often in association with oil. The principal chemical constituent in natural gas is methane (CH_4).

Oil: a general term that is technically applicable to any of a large group of viscous, flammable liquids (e.g., whale oil, petroleum, vegetable oil) that are soluble in alcohol or ether but not in water. Petroleum is a dark-colored oil consisting of a mixture of hydrocarbons derived from once-living matter. Petroleum occurs in natural deposits scattered throughout the world and is usually recovered by drilling. The word *oil* is sometimes used as a synonym for petroleum.

Petroleum: a generic term applied to oil composed of hydrocarbons and its products in all forms.

Production: the amount of an energy or other resource mined or otherwise obtained from the earth per unit of time. (*Example:* The United States produced nearly 700 million metric tons of coal in 1979.)

Quad: one quadrillion British thermal units (BTUs). The amount of an energy resource is often expressed in terms of its heat energy content, in calories or in BTUs. This makes possible direct comparisons between different kinds of energy sources. While it would not be fair to compare barrels or even kilograms of oil to kilograms of coal, it would be fair to compare the heat content of a given amount of oil with that of a given amount of coal. One metric ton of coal has 0.0000000278 or 2.78×10^{-8} quads, and a barrel of oil has 0.0000000058 quads. In terms of energy content, then, a metric ton of coal has nearly five times as much energy as a barrel of oil. A quadrillion is equal to 1000 trillion; it is a one, followed by 15 zeros, or 10^{15} in scientific notation. One quad is thus 10^{15} BTUs!

Watt: an amount of power available from an electric current of one amp at the potential difference of one volt.

rose most sharply in recent times; even in the United States the days of iceboxes, outdoor privies, washtubs, chamberpots, horse-drawn carriages, oil lamps, and waking up to ice in one's wash basin (indoors) were simply not all that long ago.

More recent trends reflect a dramatic climb in the use of electrical energy in the American home (Table 6.1). There has been more than a doubling of total energy use in the United States every 20–25 years over the past century, and this pace has exceeded the rate of population growth for some time now (Figure 6.3). For much of the twentieth century the use of electricity, a highly desirable, somewhat inefficient form of energy, increased at nearly twice the rate of overall U.S. energy consumption, a doubling every 10–12 years.

Perhaps because of increased energy consciousness, but more likely because of increased energy bills, the demand for electrical energy and energy in general quite unexpectedly tapered off in very recent years (Figure 6.4a), falling way off the projections made in the early 1970s. Demand for

Table 6.1 Homes with Electricity from 1907 to the Present in the United States

Year	Percent of Homes with Electricity
1907	8
1912	16
1920	35
1930	68
1940	79
1950	94
1960	99
1965–present	100

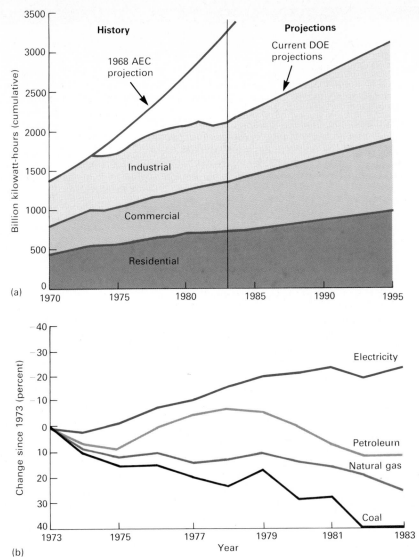

Figure 6.4 (a) Consumption of Electricity in the U.S. from 1960 Projected through 1995 for Industrial, Commercial, and Residential Sectors. Note the departure of *actual* use from projections made in the late 1960s and early 1970s. **(b) Use of Electricity Compared to Use of the Three Major Sources of Energy from 1973 through 1983.**

electricity did continue to increase during the ten years following the energy crisis, however, bucking the general trend of the use of energy during that period (Figure 6.4b).

As for *total* energy consumption in America, after the 1973–1974 oil embargo, overall energy consumption fell in five of the next nine years (U.S. Department of Energy, 1983a). Energy consumption in 1981 was actually 0.3% below what it was in 1973 (Conservation Foundation, 1982).

The unexpected downturn in overall energy consumption in the last decade was a result of (1) a sluggish economy, (2) rapidly escalating fuel prices, (3) supply problems, and (4) conservation, mostly as a result of the first three factors.

The History of Imbalance

As is illustrated in Figure 6.5, there is considerable difference in the use of energy from one country to another, and Americans account for a particularly large share of world energy consumption. For most of the last several decades the 5–6% of the world's population made up of Americans accounted for 33% of all energy consumption.

Since 1950 there have been greater proportionate increases in energy use in Western and Eastern Europe than in the United States, and it is expected that the gap between other developed countries and the United States will become narrower in years to come. Figure 6.6 illustrates how

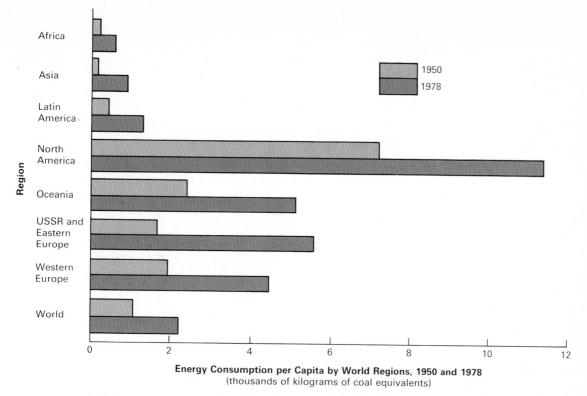

Energy Consumption per Capita by World Regions, 1950 and 1978
(thousands of kilograms of coal equivalents)

Figure 6.5   Worldwide Per Capita Energy Consumption.
While there has been a general worldwide increase in energy consumption in recent decades, the gap between the developed and developing nations has continued to widen.

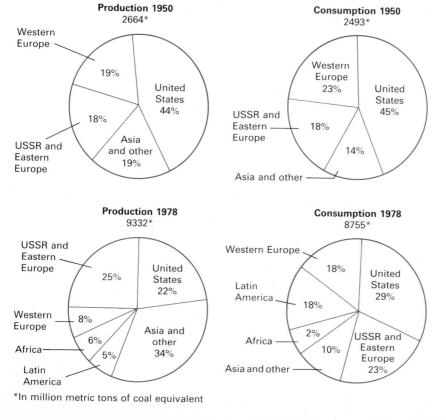

Production 1950
2664*

Western Europe — 19%
USSR and Eastern Europe — 18%
United States 44%
Asia and other 19%

Consumption 1950
2493*

Western Europe 23%
United States 45%
USSR and Eastern Europe — 18%
Asia and other — 14%

Production 1978
9332*

USSR and Eastern Europe — 25%
Western Europe — 8%
Africa — 6%
Latin America — 5%
United States 22%
Asia and other 34%

Consumption 1978
8755*

Western Europe — 18%
Latin America — 18%
Africa — 2%
Asia and other — 10%
United States 29%
USSR and Eastern Europe 23%

*In million metric tons of coal equivalent

Figure 6.6   World Trends in Energy Production and Consumption from 1950 to 1978.
In the 1950s, consumption and production were well matched in individual countries and regions. By the mid-1970s, there were significant gaps between production and consumption in many countries and regions, particularly the U.S. and Western Europe. The resultant dependencies have become very important factors in world economics and politics.

the gap between developed nations and the developing nations has widened since 1950. There has been a notable and growing disparity between production and consumption within individual countries and regions of the world (Figure 6.6), resulting in a growing dependence by energy-*consuming* countries (including the United States and many of the countries of Western Europe) on the energy-*producing* countries. We will consider the political and economic implications of this situation later in the chapter.

ENERGY SOURCES UP TO THE PRESENT

During the period we have just outlined in which energy consumption has been increasing worldwide, there have also been changes in major sources of energy. In the early stages of human energy history we relied almost entirely on wood fires. A little more than 100 years ago the United States got about three fourths of its commercial energy from wood (Figure 6.7). The increasing use of **fossil fuels** (fuels such as coal, oil, and natural gas derived from the slow physical/chemical changes in deposits of accumulated dead plant and animal materials over millions of years) in more recent times has itself been marked by notable trends. These are illustrated for the United States from 1952 to 1982 in Figure 6.8. The most notable feature in these trends is the increasing dependence on natural gas and petroleum until *very* recently.

As shown in Figure 6.8, fossil fuels currently contribute more than 90% of the energy used in the United States. Nearly half of the current energy supply for the United States is in the form of oil; another 26% is natural gas. Thus the two forms of energy that are in shortest supply are those on which the United States depends almost exclusively. If "crises" can be defined in terms of necessary, inevitable (possibly disconcerting) change, a major change in the way things are done, we can surely expect to face continued energy crises.

In the paragraphs immediately following, we will summarize the history and the status of natural gas, coal, oil, and nuclear fission as energy sources. We will consider the prospects for the future for each of these sources along with solar power, nuclear fusion, hydroelectric power, and other energy options in Section B of this chapter.

Natural Gas

Natural gas has been used for a little over a century and currently provides about one fourth of the energy used in the United States. In the 1920s, Americans used about 800 billion cubic feet of gas annually; this had risen to 22 *trillion* cubic feet by the mid 1970s for an average increase of about 6% per year (Dorf, 1978). Over the next ten years, consumption fell to around 18 trillion cubic feet. Today, about two thirds of all American homes and roughly half of our commercial enterprises use natural gas. Natural gas is the source of about one third of the energy used in manufacturing (DOE, 1983b).

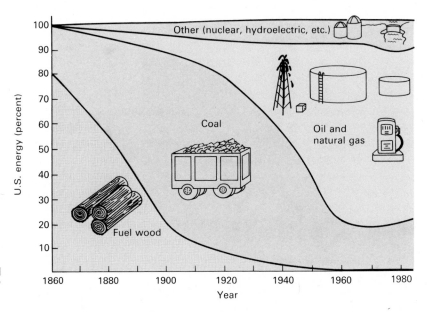

Figure 6.7 U.S. Energy Sources, 1860–1980. Since 1850 there have been several dramatic shifts in our primary energy sources.

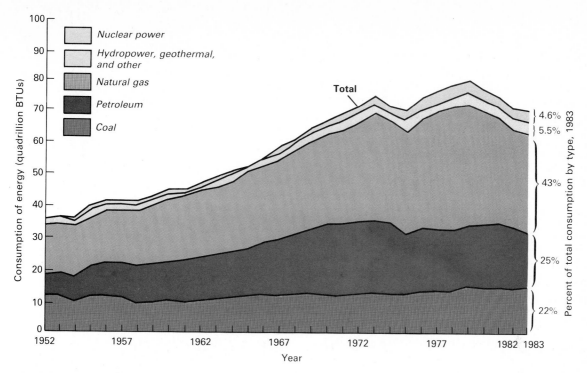

Figure 6.8 The Recent Trend: U.S. Energy Consumption. Although coal is the most plentiful energy resource in the U.S., coal consumption stayed about the same during this period while petroleum and natural gas consumption increased considerably. Much of the *recent* decline in energy use was almost entirely from a decline in petroleum consumption. More than two thirds of our energy now comes from oil and natural gas; more than 90% comes from *fossil* fuels; less than 5% comes from renewable sources.

Natural gas has been extremely popular in the United States throughout this century, particularly since the 1950s, when large-capacity pipelines linked gas-producing regions to the big population centers. Gas utilization got another boost in the 1960s, when concern for the environment began to intensify because natural gas produces very little pollution. Another reason for the popularity of natural gas is that for most of the middle of this century, gas has been about 20% cheaper than coal and about 6% cheaper than oil on an energy content basis (coal is now cheaper than gas on a BTU basis). This has been partly due to government price controls (imposed with the Natural Gas Act of 1938) on interstate shipments. Natural gas has been popular also because it is easily stored and transported through pipes. By 1974 there were already more than a quarter of a million miles of natural gas pipelines installed throughout the United States. Because of dwindling supplies, rising costs, and use restrictions imposed by the government, the use of natural gas in the United States has declined since about 1973 (see Figure 6.8). Prices are gradually being decontrolled

(following the Natural Gas Policy Act of 1978) after a long period of controlled, artificially low prices.

In the 1880s the world used about 200 billion cubic feet of natural gas per year; today about 300 times as much is used (Dorf, 1978). Natural gas provided about one fifth of the world's energy in 1982. It is a major source of energy today in the United States, in Canada, and in the Soviet Union. Despite the fact that the peak of natural gas production may have been reached or even passed worldwide, many countries of Europe and the Middle East are expected to increase their use of natural gas in the immediate future.

Coal

Both archeological and written records indicate that **coal** was used in Bronze Age Europe some 4000 years ago. The Chinese were using it at least 2000 years ago, and Hopi Indians were using coal at least 400 years before Christopher Columbus was born. Some historians say that significant coal burning began about 600 years ago, and problems with coal

The Role of Demand in Energy Production

It should become clear as we go through this chapter that energy production is governed by many factors and not simply the amount of fuel left in the ground. To be sure, production limits are ultimately set by the amount of a resource to be had. But demand plays an important role in determining production along the way until the last "drop" is gone (assuming we could ever get to that point, which we cannot).

Simply stated, unless somebody wants some, no natural gas will be produced no matter how much there is. More accurately, no natural gas will be produced unless someone wants to *buy* some. The price of gas then becomes a major determinant of production because the

more people are willing to pay for it, the harder the explorers will look for it, and the more production companies are willing to spend to get it out. This becomes complicated because the factors involved all influence one another. High prices reflect high demand, but they also tend to decrease demand. To make a long story short (at least for the time being), whenever there is a downward turn in production, it might be equally accurate to say that "gas is harder to get" or "demand is down because prices are too high." With natural gas the picture has been made even more complicated by price controls.

---

were recognized almost immediately—Edward I banned coal burning in London in 1306 (Gilbert and Kaufman, 1978).

The rate of increase in coal use was very low at first, but the Industrial Revolution produced a sharp worldwide increase resulting in a doubling of coal production every 20 years between 1860 and 1920 (Table 6.2a). Coal production has risen unsteadily in the United States over the past century (Table 6.2b), but since 1850 it has increased nearly 100-fold. Figure 6.9 gives a comparative production breakdown for the leading coal-producing countries, showing that three coal-producing nations generate over half the world's total. It is noteworthy and important to later discussion that coal is used in more heavily industrial ways than other types of fuel; the ways in which it was used as of 1982 in the United States are illustrated in Table 6.3. It is also noteworthy that

Table 6.2 Coal Production
A. World Coal Production Since 1860

Year	World Coal Production (millions of metric tons)
1860	150
1880	320
1900	780
1920	1200
1940	1700
1960	2100
1970	2500
1975	3331
1981	3834
1982	3974

B. U.S. Coal Production Since 1850

Year	U.S. Production (millions of metric tons)
1850	9
1890	145
1910	454
1930	454
1940	462
1945	544
1950	468
1960	399
1970	556
1975	594
1980	753
1982	760
1985 (projected)	900
1990 (projected)	1050

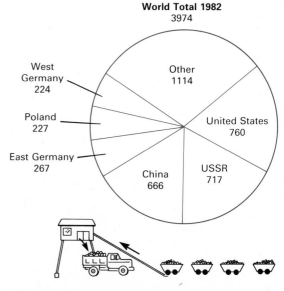

Figure 6.9 International Coal Production 1982. Numbers are in millions of metric tons.

Table 6.3 The Uses of Coal in the United States in 1982 and 1983

	Percent of Total Use	
	1982	1983
Electric utility	72	77
Industrial steam and miscellaneous	8	8
Coking coal for steel	5	4.5
Railroad fuel	<1	<1
Residential and commercial heating	1	1
Export	13	9.5
	100	100

coal is the only significant source of fuel exported by the United States (13% was exported in 1982).

Coal today supplies a little over one fifth of U.S. energy despite the fact that this energy source constitutes by far the largest fraction of proven U.S energy reserves. Coal has been held to a relatively minor role in meeting American energy needs in recent decades because of a combination of difficulties in mining it, transporting it, and burning it.

Much of the promise of the future of coal has been dimmed by the combination of (1) higher rail rates following recent deregulation, (2) delayed and indefinitely discontinued plans for coal conversion (synfuels) technology (related to both politics and to the "oil glut" that began in 1982), (3) the coming of age of the acid rain issue (Chapter 10), and (4) air pollution restrictions in general. There continue to be serious safety, labor, and environmental problems with mining operations (see Chapter 17).

Petroleum

We have known about **petroleum**, or oil, for only 100 years, but it quickly became a highly pre-ferred form of energy partly because of the ease with which it could be transported and handled.

The growth in oil production and consumption in the United States since 1920 is illustrated in Table 6.4. Notice how much faster consumption grew than production over most of this period. A comparison of trends in oil consumption for the United States and the world is made in Figure 6.10. This illustration reveals two particularly interesting facts: that the United States accounted for about 40% of world oil consumption from 1930 to 1970 and that the United States began consuming proportionately less during the 1970s.

The most important dimension of the oil energy crisis is that we are running out. The peak in world oil production will occur in the 1990s (Calvin, 1979), and some energy experts predict that oil supplies will fail to meet demand—at any price—in 20 years or so. Recent (1952–1983) trends in U.S. oil consumption are depicted in Figure 6.8 in relationship to other forms of energy.

Nuclear Power

As Enrico Fermi and his colleagues looked on anxiously, the world's very first nuclear fission reaction went critical (developed a sustained, controlled nuclear chain reaction) on December 2, 1942. More than a decade later, the first commercial-scale atomic fission reactor was turned on at Shippingport, Pennsylvania. The first *licensed* atomic power plant opened on November 15, 1957, in Vallecitos, California. Today, nuclear fission (which we will describe in some detail in Section B of this chapter) is an important energy source in many parts of the world. Although only about 1% of the world's *total* energy needs are met by nuclear fission, some 300 nuclear power plants are generating electricity worldwide. There are more than 80 oper-

Table 6.4 Annual Consumption and Production of Oil in the United States Since 1920

Year	Consumption (millions of barrels)	Domestic Production (millions of barrels)	Imports as Percent of Consumption
1920	434	443	2%
1930	862	898	4%
1940	1285	1353	5%
1950	2467	2157	13%
1960	3579	2905	19%
1973	6322	3997	37%
1980	6231	3712	40%
1982	5588	3723	33%
1983	5544	3730	33%
1990 (projected)	6200	3670	41%

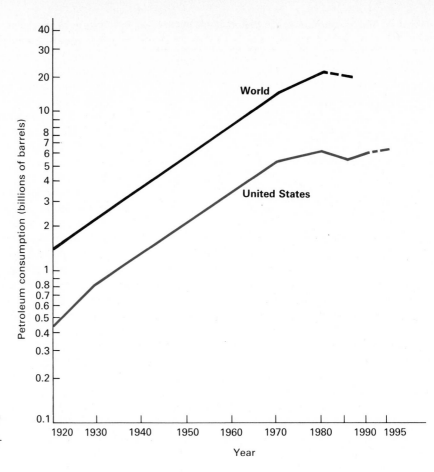

Figure 6.10 Annual Consumption Rates of Petroleum in the U.S. and the World Since 1920. Note that the vertical scale is logarithmic.

ational nuclear fission plants in the United States and nearly 20 in West Germany. France, one of Europe's most nuclear-oriented nations, had 14 plants in service and another 27 under construction toward the end of the 1970s. Japan has more than 20 reactors producing more than 10% of its electricity. As of the end of the 1970s, nuclear power provided 12–13% of U.S. electricity (note that this is not total energy, just electricity) overall. This ranged from 5% in the Southwest to 25% in New England.

Among the factors that have sustained the proliferation of nuclear power plants are the facts that, done right, nuclear power is clean, it produces no smoke, and it requires very little fuel. Among the factors limiting the further expansion of nuclear power and already responsible for a precipitous decline in the orders for new plants in the United States and elsewhere are: (1) economics (nuclear plants have become very expensive to build in comparison with plants that accept conventional fuels); (2) leveling off in the demand for electricity; (3) scarce and dwindling uranium deposits; (4) waste disposal problems (we have yet to come up with an acceptable long-term way of storing nuclear waste); and (5) nuclear accidents, particularly that at Three Mile Island. The Three Mile Island accident intensified an already existing concern (fear) over the safety of atomic power and has intensified negative public pressure, resulting in much altered (downward) projections for use of nuclear power in the future. We will return to this topic in Section B of this chapter.

Electricity as a Delivery Form

Electricity is a favorite form of energy in the United States and elsewhere largely because it can be

Table 6.5   Consumption of Electricity in the United States Since 1900

Year	Population (millions)	Generating capacity (millions Kw)	Consumption (billion Kwh)	Consumption per person per year (Kwh)
1900	76		3.7	49
1920	106		57.3	540
1930	123		115.0	935
1940	132		141.8	1,074
1950	152	68.9	329.1	2,161
1960	180.7	168.0	753.4	4,169
1970	204.8	340.4	1,529.8	7,469
1975	216.0	508	1929	8,930
1980	227	613	2311	10,180
1981	230	635	2331	10,134
1982	232	650	2275	9,806
1983	234	657	2346	10,025

delivered easily and directly to power appliances and machines. Trends in U.S. consumption of electricity are illustrated in Table 6.5. Americans used 3.7 billion kilowatt hours (kwh) of electrical energy (49 kwh per person) per year at the beginning of this century. By the end of the century this will have grown by more than *three* orders of magnitude— more than 1000-fold. Electricity now accounts for 30% of U.S. energy consumption (Bodansky, 1980). We have improved the efficiency with which we can generate electricity from fossil fuels (from about 20% in 1940 to about 35% today), and this in turn has reduced the relative cost of electricity, contributing to its popularity (Figure 6.11)

We use electrically delivered energy in many ways (Figure 6.12). Industrial uses account for nearly 40%. In the American home, refrigeration and lighting top the list, together accounting for more than 22% of the total.

Electricity will likely be with us forever as a delivery form, since a great variety of sources and uses of energy can be coupled by electrical wires. Electricity is generated (to considerably varying degrees) by burning oil, coal, natural gas, wood, garbage, and trash, as well as from flowing water, wind, the earth's heat, sunlight, and nuclear fission.

Other Energy Sources

Sources of energy of today, other than those listed above, amount to a very small percentage of

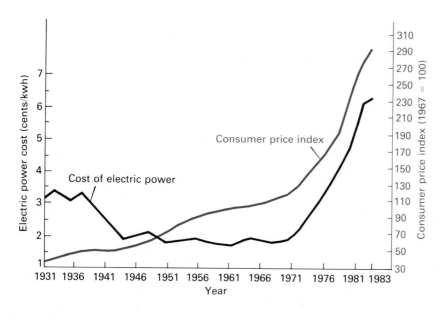

Figure 6.11   The Cost of Electric Power Compared to the Cost of Living Since 1931. It is true, as suggested by the electric utility industry, that electricity has become more of a bargain over the years. The cost of electric power actually fell during much of the period in which the consumer price index was rising.

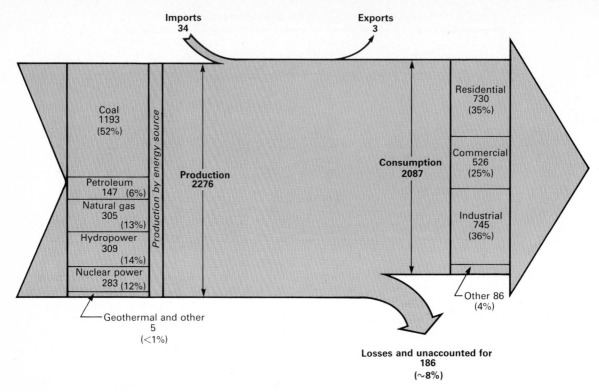

Figure 6.12 Electricity: Where It Comes from and Where It Goes in the U.S. Numbers are in billion kilowatt hours.

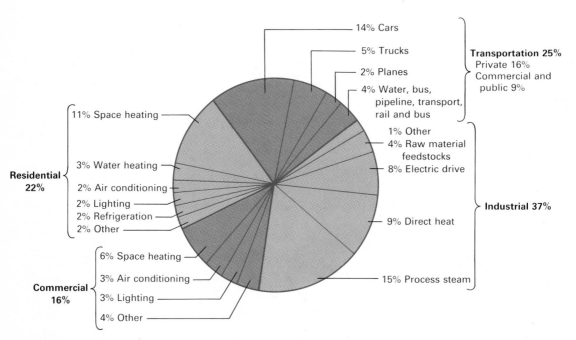

Figure 6.13 The Things We Do with Energy in the U.S. Personal energy use amounts to 37%; business, industry, agriculture, and government use 63%.

the total. We will consider these—including solar, hydroelectric, geothermal, atomic fusion, biomass, and tidal energy—in the more detailed analysis of energy sources of the future in Section B of this chapter.

MAJOR CATEGORICAL USES OF ENERGY

The things we do with energy in the United States are summarized in Figure 6.13. For comparison and to illustrate again the point that different forms of energy are used in different ways, a figure depicting the uses of oil in the United States is presented as Figure 6.14.

Some notable facts about our overall use of energy, some of which are illustrated in Fig. 6.13, are the following:

— 30% of U.S. energy is used to generate electricity;
— nearly *half* of all the energy we consume is lost through some form of inefficiency or conversion loss as a consequence of the second law of thermodynamics (Chapter 2).
— 25% of the energy we use goes for residential and commercial lighting and heating and other domestic and commercial uses;
— another 28% goes for mining, smelting, and industrial processes;
— about 6% of U.S. energy is issued as a raw material, the coal and petroleum and natural gas used in making chemicals, pesticides, plastics, and other products.

Roughly 17% of U.S. energy is used in agriculture (Pimentel and Dazhong, 1985), and it is this use of energy we would like to take up in more detail now.

Energy in Agriculture

Corn as an Example. About one in six of the calories of energy consumed or used in the United States is used in the production, processing, transportation, and handling of food. This was not always the case; in fact, energy intensiveness in agriculture is a relatively recent trend.

The extent to which energy use has increased in agriculture in the United States can be inferred from the data presented for corn in Table 6.6, covering the period from 1700 to 1983. These data show that:

— in the last 40 years, yields have increased threefold while energy input has increased fourfold;
— there has been a drastic *decrease* in manual labor;

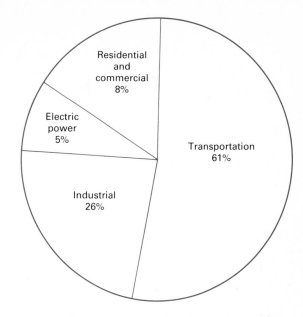

Figure 6.14 How We Use Oil (Refined Petroleum Products) in the U.S.

— the use of electricity increased 100-fold from 1920 to 1983; and
— the use of energy to make herbicides, insecticides, and fertilizers has increased dramatically in recent times.

Another remarkable fact illustrated in Table 6.6 is that the efficiency of our energy utilization (kilocalories returned for kilocalories put in) declined 30% from 1945 to 1970. There were nearly 2.5 million tractors in the United States in the mid-1940s, but there are more than double that number today. Fuel consumption in farm machinery has nearly doubled in the last 30 years.

It seems fair to assume that the general trends illustrated in Table 6.6 for corn are basically the same for agriculture in general. However, some crops are more energy intensive than corn, and some are less energy intensive (Figure 6.15).

Perhaps the most remarkable thing abut energy trends in agriculture is that human labor decreased about 60% in a 25-year period from 1945 to 1970 at the same time that yield was increasing almost threefold. Pimentel and associates (1973, 1984) claim that while 20–40% of the increased corn yield is attributable to new varieties of corn, 60–80% is due to the input of energy in the form of fossil fuel. Today only a fraction of a percent of energy consumed on the American farm comes from human labor; corn requires a little more than five hours of

Table 6.6 Energy Used in U.S. Agricultural Corn Production, 1700–1983 (in thousands of kilocalories per hectacre)

Years	1700	1920	1945	1954	1959	1970	1975	1980	1983
Labor	653	65	31	23	19	12	10	7	6
Machinery	19	278	407	648	777	907	925	1,018	1,018
Draft animal	0	886	0	0	0	0	0	0	0
Fuel									
Gasoline	0	0	1,200	1,500	1,550	1,200	600	500	400
Diesel	0	0	228	342	399	912	912	878	855
Manure	0	0							
N			168	630	966	2,625	2,478	3,066	3,192
P	0	0	50	82	113	221	410	466	473
K	0	0	15	50	85	168	188	240	240
Lime	0	3	46	39	50	69	69	134	134
Seeds	44	44	161	421	470	520	520	520	520
Insecticides	0	0	0	20	54	110	200	300	300
Herbicides	0	0	0	7	20	100	400	700	800
Irrigation	0	*	125	250	375	1,125	2,000	2,125	2,250
Drying	0	0	9	15	54	376	458	640	660
Electricity	0	1	8	24	36	80	90	100	100
Transport	*	25	44	67	79	84	82	90	89
Total	716	1,302	2,492	4,118	5,047	8,509	9,342	10,784	11,037
Ratio	10.5	5.8	3.4	2.5	2.7	2.4	2.2	2.4	2.4
Yield	7,520	7,520	8,528	10,288	13,548	20,320	20,575	26,000	26,000

* Greater than zero.
Note: The many assumptions made in deriving these data are given in the original source.

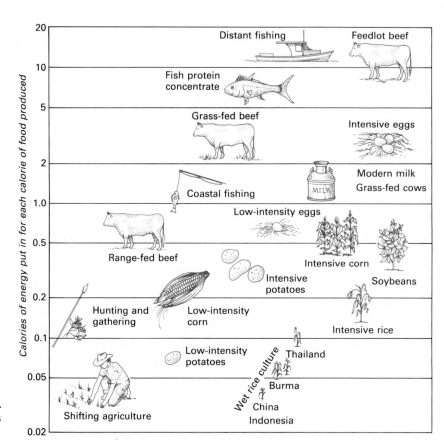

Figure 6.15 Comparative Energy Intensiveness of Various Food Crops in the U.S.

human labor per acre, according to Pimentel and Dazhong (1985). The reason for this is fairly obvious; energy has been abundant and relatively cheap during a time when labor has become prohibitively expensive. Illustrating of the degree to which this is true, Pimentel and associates (1973) calculate that while the hand planting of corn requires only about 1/60 of the energy used by a tractor and a sprayer, planting by hand would *cost* about four times more.

Sociopolitical Implications of Energy Intensiveness in Agriculture. Energy intensiveness of agriculture is highly variable throughout the world and is one of the reasons for the disparity in energy use from one country to another. China is a nation of one billion people, four times as many people as there are in the United States, and yet China grows nearly all of its own food on far less cropland than there is in the United States and with much less fuel energy—but with a lot more human labor. Human labor is much more plentiful and much cheaper in countries like China; machines, pesticides, and other energy-consuming practices are used comparatively less, although fossil fuel energy-use has increased dramatically (100-fold) in China in the last 30 years.

It goes almost without saying that the energy intensiveness of agriculture in the United States has had an enormous impact on the American way of life. It has enabled the situation to emerge in which most Americans now live in cities working at jobs that have only a very indirect relationship to food production. The application of energy in agriculture has made it possible for a demographic shift to take place in which, whereas one out of ten people lived on a farm in the early 1930s, only one out of 35 people lives on a farm today. It is energy intensiveness in agriculture that has enabled the United States to be a largely urban society and yet be a major exporter of food for the world. While many Americans have viewed the successes of the American system of agriculture as evidence of national ingenuity and hard work, the facts suggest that much of American agricultural success can be attributed to the application of relatively cheap fossil energy. American agriculture may have grown into what will become an increasingly tight corner. While the United States exports food, this is done at the expense of fuel that is to some extent imported from other countries.

Energy intensiveness raises a number of questions that have significance to the world population, to food problems, and to phenomena like the *green revolution* (see Chapter 8). Energy costs have now become extremely important to the prospects that agricultural technology will be exported to the developing nations of the world.

It has been estimated (see Pimentel and Dazhong, 1985) that to feed the entire world with an agricultural system like that of the United States, about 90% of the world's annual energy supply would be required just to supply food. During these times of increased energy costs and dwindling energy supplies this is a sobering thought indeed.

The Future of Energy in Agriculture. The foregoing discussion raises a number of important questions with regard to agriculture, food production, and the continuing energy crises in the world and in the United States. If we run short of energy sources, we run the risk of shortages of food for many of the world's people. What happens when energy supplies run short or when certain types of commonly used energy sources run short? What if energy becomes even more expensive? Steinhart and Steinhart (1974) estimate that so tightly connected is the price of oil and the price of food that if there were a four-fold increase in the price of oil, there would be a six-fold increase in the price of food. The extra increase is partly related to the second law of thermodynamics (Chapter 2). But regardless of the exact details of the economic relationships, as fossil fuels become more scarce and more expensive, agricultural practices will change. Given the premise that modern-day agricultural methods are based on cheap energy, the following kinds of changes should be anticipated in the future.

We will use less chemical fertilizers and pesticides that take significant amounts of energy to produce and will begin to rely more on natural fertilizers. We will practice more scientific forms of crop rotation and soil tillage and will develop increasing respect for the soil and what we do to it—we will gradually lose the attitude that no matter what insult we inflict on soil, we can restore it with chemicals. It should be anticipated that because of some of the principles we discussed in Chapter 2, meat will become less dominant in the diet of people in developed countries. According to Pimentel and colleagues, in order to produce one calorie of beef protein in modern agriculture, 25 calories of fossil fuel energy have to be put into the cow.

Energy in Transportation

Transporting people and goods accounts for about 25% of the energy used in the world. Total energy used in transportation in the United States, including gasoline, jet fuel, distillate fuel oil, and other fuels, has increased at the annual rate of 2.7% since 1947; the use of gasoline in transportation has increased even faster. Petroleum is obviously the energy source of choice in modern transportation. Over half the oil used in the United States (about one fourth of our total energy) is used in transportation. Passenger cars consume about one half of the total used in transport (Fig. 6.14).

Americans do a lot of traveling. According to Newman and Day (1975), we covered about 6000 miles per capita in intercity travel during the early part of the 1970s. Since commuting to and from work accounted for over 40% of the car miles traveled during the 1960s and slightly more than that as cities spread out even further during the 1970s, a little arithmetic indicates that about one tenth of all the oil consumed in the world every day is used by American motorists on their way to and from work—usually traveling alone. In America the use of cars for local travel has become exceedingly important because of our entrapment in a vicious cycle. The automobile has altered the face of America by making it possible for cities to spread out, making the automobile necessary to get almost anywhere.

A comparison of the various modes of transportation of goods and people is given in Tables 6.7 and 6.8. These data reveal that while the airplane is the most energy-intensive mode of all, the automobile is a close second in terms of BTUs per passenger mile. Far more passenger miles are traveled by automobile than by airplane, however. Automobiles account for nearly 90% of all miles traveled by people; airplanes garner a modest 9.3%. Each year, Americans fly an average of 580 miles per person in airplanes, ride about 150 miles per person in buses and trains, travel about 120 miles on the average on inland waterways, and, as we have already indicated, travel an average of more than 6000 miles per person in automobiles. What this suggests—and

Table 6.7   Estimated Freight/Energy Efficiency

Shipping Method	Efficiency (BTUs per ton mile)
Airplane (all cargo)	28,610
Truck	3,420
Barge	990
Rail	1,720
Coal slurry pipeline	1,270
Oil pipeline	500

Note: Combines energy required for propulsion, maintenance, manufacturing/construction, movement of empty carrier. A ton–mile equals one ton carried one mile.

Table 6.8   Relative Energy Efficiency of Various Modes of Domestic Transportation

Transportation Mode	Efficiency (BTUs per passenger mile)
General aviation	11,044
Airplane (carrier)	5,733
Automobile	3,498
Motorcycle	2,273
Intercity Bus	1,078
AMTRAK	1,765

we will take up the matter in some detail in a later section on conservation—is that the automobile is an obvious target in our battle to come to grips with our energy problems.

Automobile ownership is practically universal in the United States. Beyond the necessity factor, the automobile's popularity is due in part to the tremendous amount of freedom it gives the user. Perhaps no other device gives people at almost every socioeconomic level (in countries like the United States) the power to overcome natural restraints on mobility. To appreciate this power, one need only reflect on the fact that we can travel 55 miles per hour over some of the worst kinds of terrain in driving rainstorms, swirling blizzards, or intense heat, all at a comfortable 72°F with stereo music, isolated from the environment. It will be difficult at best to wrest any of this sort of freedom away. The appeal of the freedom factor is obviously a major reason why people do not use less energy-intensive forms of transportation like buses and bicycles. It seems inevitable, however, that buses, bicycles, and trains will assume an increasingly important role in the years ahead as the energy situation gets tighter and especially more expensive. This trend, modest though it may yet be, is being spurred by subsidies for bus travel. A great truth that may be emerging from the relatively poor results of nationwide efforts to get people away from their cars and into buses is that nothing beats the private automobile in terms of convenience. Perhaps the answer is to make the auto less convenient by means of higher taxes, license fees, and parking rates.

Residential and Commercial Energy Consumption

Annual residential and commercial use of energy in the United States by source is given in Table 6.9. The rise in labor-saving appliances has been largely responsible for the increasing use of energy in the American home. The comparative power consumption of various home appliances is given in

Table 6.9   Annual U.S. Residential and Commercial Use of Energy by Source

Source	Quads[1]	Percent Total
Electricity sales	2.847	10
Electricity losses[2]	7.046	24
Coal	3.556	12
Natural gas	8.198	28
Petroleum	7.439	25
Hydroelectric	0.037	<1
Other	0.066	<1
Total	29.190	100

[1] Quad = quadrillion BTUs.
[2] Energy lost in the generation of electricity for homes and commercial businesses.

Small power stations like this feed electric power to neighborhood homes from larger systems.

Figure 6.16. American homes may have 20–50 or more light bulbs, and just one 100-watt light burning around the clock for a year requires the burning of about 60 gallons of oil. The use of energy for heating and cooling is also considerable; 20% of the energy used in the United States is for space heating and cooling. A majority of American households now have air conditioning units of some kind.

The patterns of energy use in homes and commercial establishments in the United States are quite similar. The largest fraction in each case, 58% and 47% of the energy used in homes and commercial establishments, respectively, goes to space heating. Most of the remainder goes to air conditioning, water heating, lighting, and refrigeration in very roughly equal amounts.

Industrial Energy Consumption

In the United States, mining, smelting, and manufacturing activities account for 28% of total energy consumption. About 45% of the energy used industrially is used to generate steam, and 25% is used to drive motors, to light factories, and to drive chemical processes like electroplating. Nearly all of the remainder is used to heat buildings, to heat vats of various liquids, and in other direct heating applications. In the last three decades, industrial coal consumption remained constant while industrial petroleum consumption increased almost 4% annually.

An automobile	900,000,000 BTU/yr.
A home heater	180,000,000 BTU/yr.
An air conditioner	40,000,000 BTU/yr.
A stove	9,000,000 BTU/yr.
A color TV (tube)	9,000,000 BTU/yr.
A dishwasher	4,000,000 BTU/yr.
A black and white TV (solid state)	2,000,000 BTU/yr.
A hair dryer	150,000 BTU/yr.
An egg beater	50,000 BTU/yr.

Figure 6.16   Comparative Energy Use in Automobiles and Various Home Appliances (annual average). Note that one ton of coal is equal to 25,000,000 BTU; one barrel of crude oil is equivalent to 5,800,000 BTUs and one cubic foot of natural gas is equal to 1031 BTUs.

Energy Alternatives for the Future

A mong the plausible energy alternatives for the future are some very well established old standbys and some untested new ideas. Coal is perhaps the most important of our old standbys.

COAL

If—and this is a very big if—we find environmentally safer ways to mine, transport, and burn coal, it would be our best bet for the next several hundred years.

Although we humans have been using large amounts of coal lately (Figure 6.17), there is still a great deal left. In the United States a little over one fifth of current energy needs are met by coal, but coal represents about four fifths of proven U.S. energy reserves. World reserves of coal are described in Figure 6.18, where it can be seen that the United States has nearly one third of the known reserves of the entire world.

U.S. Western Coal Reserves: Promises and Problems

Coal is far from uniformly distributed. Major deposits of coal in the United States are illustrated in Figure 6.19. While we have been mining our midwestern and eastern coal since the dawn of the industrial age, only recently has our attention turned to the thick coal seams in the West. According to some sources, there is enough coal in the western United States *alone* to keep up with America's need for coal for 300 years (assuming that present rates of consumption continue).

Western coal has really not yet begun to be developed, and there are several reasons for this. One is the distance from western coal to the markets where it would be consumed—the mills and population centers of the United States. However, because western coal occurs in such thick seams and because it is close to the surface, it is estimated now that even with shipping costs included, western coal

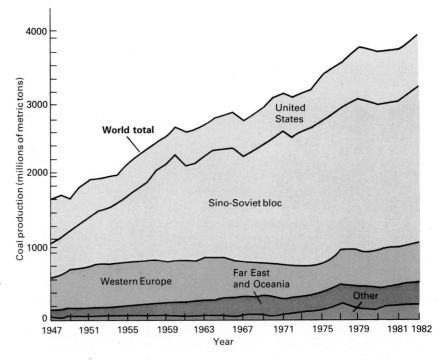

Figure 6.17 World Coal Production by Various Countries and Regions 1947–1982. (Note: One metric ton equals 1.102 short tons.) The greatest increases in coal production during this period were in the Sino-Soviet block of nations. This accounted for nearly all of the increase of world production in recent times.

Part II *Homo Sapiens* in the Scheme of Natural Things

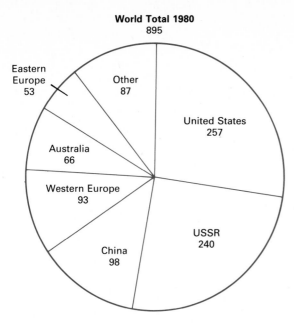

World Total 1980
895

Figure 6.18 World Recoverable Coal Reserves as of 1980. (Note: Proved or recoverable reserves are coal deposits known to be available with current technology and worth getting under current economic conditions. In 1980, world coal production was approximately four billion metric tons (one short ton = 2000 pounds = 0.907 metric tons), about 0.5% of the total recoverable. Thus if production continues at its present rate, existing reserves will continue to provide coal for several hundred years.)

will soon actually be cheaper than coal mined in eastern and central areas of the United States. An alternative to shipping would be to convert western coal to electricity and to send the electricity east. While this would shift the pollution associated with burning coal away from the population centers, there would be other problems. For example, there would be problems associated with providing right-of-ways needed for transmission lines and the reduced efficiency of electrical as opposed to direct combustion heating. Another serious technological problem with western coal is the scarcity of water (for cooling and condensing the steam that drives the generators and for irrigation related to reclamation) in the West.

The Trouble with Coal in General

If coal is to become more of a solution than an addition to our energy problems, better ways will have to be found to reduce the environmental impacts of mining, processing, transporting, and burning it. Some of the problems are as follows:

— Although strip mining practices are no longer as destructive as they once were, strip mining has a profound negative impact on land (Chapter 17).
— Mining in some areas results in acid mine water pollution of streams and rivers (Chapter 12).

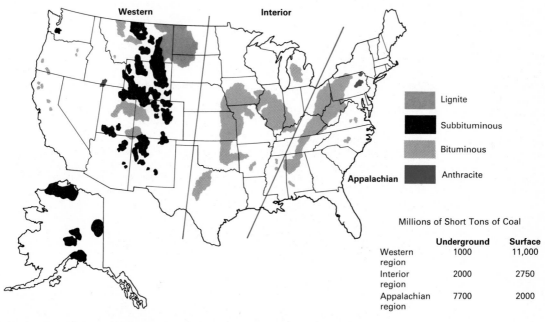

	Millions of Short Tons of Coal	
	Underground	**Surface**
Western region	1000	11,000
Interior region	2000	2750
Appalachian region	7700	2000

Figure 6.19 Estimated U.S. Coal Reserves by Region. Numbers are in billions of metric tons. It should be noted that the coal in Montana and Wyoming consists principally of lower rank bituminous coal.

— Coal cleaning is still done at the expense of clean water in many places (Chapter 12).

— Sulfur dioxide from coal has increased the acidity of rain in many areas of the world (Chapter 10).

— The burning of coal generates sulfur dioxide and particulate air pollution problems (Chapters 9–11).

— The burning of coal produces carbon dioxide, which has the potential to alter the earth's climate, and oxides of nitrogen, which contribute indirectly to ozone pollution and to acid rain (Chapter 10).

— Coal combustion also produces hydrocarbons, some of which participate in the generation of ozone and some of which cause cancer (Chapters 9–11 and Chapter 14).

— Coal may contain radioactive materials.

— Among the most serious problems with coal are

MINI-GLOSSARY

Alpha particles: positively charged particles consisting of two protons and two neutrons spontaneously emitted by certain radioactive materials undergoing decay.

Anthracite: hard coal; coal that burns with less smoke than softer varieties and is therefore more desirable.

Barrel: a liquid measure equal to 42 U.S. gallons commonly used to measure petroleum and oil products (bbl).

Beta particles: particles equal in mass to that of an electron (negative charge) or positron (positive charge) emitted by certain substances undergoing radioactive decay.

Bioconversion: conversion of one form of energy into another by plants or microorganisms. The conversion of solar electromagnetic energy into chemical energy in photosynthesis is a form of bioconversion, as is the conversion of plant mass into ethanol or methanol.

Biomass: literally, living material (or once-living material—excluding fossil fuel); in connection with energy this term applies to the use of once-living material as fuel. The most common example is wood; however, any type of dried plant material can be used as fuel.

Bituminous coal: soft coal, somewhat softer than anthracite.

Breeder reactor: a nuclear reactor that produces more fissionable fuel than it consumes. This is because once fission is underway, as each nucleus undergoes fission, it releases several neutrons. Some of the neutrons sustain the heat-yielding fission reactions, while the other neutrons render what had been relatively nonfissionable materials (uranium 238, for example) fissionable by the capture of a neutron.

Chain reaction: as the term has come into general usage, a sequence wherein one reaction leads to another. In atomic fission a neutron collides with an unstable nucleus, causing it to undergo fission, which in turn releases one or more additional neutrons, which cause still other fissionable nuclei to undergo fission, and so on.

Coal gasification: the conversion of coal to an energy-rich gas.

Coal liquefaction: the chemical/physical conversion of coal into a liquid fuel.

Continental shelf: the submerged shelf of land sloping away from the edge of continents like North America; generally defined as areas in which the ocean water is less than 200 meters deep.

Core: the central part of a nuclear reactor, i.e., where the atomic fuel is located.

Critical mass: the smallest amount of fissionable material necessary to sustain a chain reaction.

Crude oil: petroleum direct from the ground; oil before it is refined.

Deuterium: hydrogen with an extra neutron in the nucleus, i.e., an isotope of hydrogen.

Enrichment: process by which the radioactive material in uranium ore is concentrated to about 3%, the level necessary to sustain a fission reaction.

Fission: splitting of the nuclei of the atoms of certain elements into two lighter nuclei accompanied by the release of relatively large amounts of energy.

Fusion: the combining of two atoms into a single atom as a result of a collision. Because the fused mass is a little less than the mass of the two nuclei that collided, the result is the release of the amount of energy that comes from the loss of mass according to Einstein's equation, $E = mc^2$.

Gamma rays: electromagnetic radiation of the same nature as an X-ray but usually of a shorter wavelength. Gamma rays are emitted by certain materials undergoing radioactive decay.

Heat pump: a device that moves heat from colder to warmer areas, i.e., causes heat to flow in the direction opposite of that in which it would spontaneously flow. This can be done only through the expenditure of energy.

In situ: literally, "in place"; the in situ gasification of coal, for example, amounts to the conversion of coal into gas as it sits in the original coal seam.

Lignite: a very low grade of coal, intermediate in quality (energy content per pound) between peat and bituminous coal.

those having to do with human health and safety. Coal mining remains one of the most hazardous of all occupations.

While many people have been hard at work on these problems, we have a long way to go. New pollution control and coal production technologies are under development, but in all likelihood things will get *worse* before they get better; we will probably increase our reliance on coal faster then these problems are solved.

Because everything must go somewhere, there will always be problems of one sort or another with coal. For example, a by-product of scrubbing (removing) SO_2 from stack effluents is a calcium sulfate sludge. A 2000-megawatt power station burning high-sulfur coal will produce about 80,000 cubic feet of sludge per day (Eisenbud, 1979). Particulate recovery yields an ash. Both of these forms of waste are potential land and water pollutants because they can contain heavy metals and other toxic and carcinogenic chemicals.

Liquid metal cooled fast breeder reactor: a type of breeder reactor in which the coolant for the reactor core is molten sodium.

Methanol: methyl alcohol or wood alcohol (CH_3OH), the chief alcohol derived from the destructive distillation of wood. Methyl alcohol can be burned as fuel.

Neutron: a subatomic particle having a mass equal to that of a proton but having no charge. When a nucleus disintegrates (fission), the resultant free neutrons can collide with other nuclei, causing them to undergo fission, provided that the neutron is moving fast enough. Neutrons are able to crash into nuclei because they are not repelled by the positive charge of the nucleus.

Nuclear fission reactor: any device in which a fission chain reaction can be started, maintained, and controlled by the regulation of dampening rods set into the core of the reactor. A fission reactor gives off heat, converting water into steam, which then drives generators.

Oil shale: sedimentary rock (not really a shale) containing the solid hydrocarbon, kerogen. Processing of oil shale converts it into a gas or a liquid fuel.

Passive solar heating: heating that does not require special machines or devices other than structural features that allow sunlight in to be absorbed.

Photovoltaic conversion: direct conversion of solar radiation into electricity.

Plutonium: a chemical element, all of the isotopes of which are radioactive. Plutonium 239, the most important isotope of plutonium, is an alpha particle emitter. Plutonium 239 is a fissionable material that can be made by bombarding nonfissile uranium 238 with neutrons; this is what is done in a breeder reactor.

Proved reserves: a relatively accurate estimate of the amount of crude oil, natural gas, coal, or some other resource that can be obtained from the earth with existing technology and sold for a profit.

Rad: a delivered (absorbed) unit of radiation energy equal to 100 ergs per gram of tissue.

Radiation equivalent man or mammal (rem): a rad adjusted for relative biological effectiveness; 1 rem is 1 rad times the RBE of the radiation in question. Thus 1 rem of any kind of radiation does an equivalent amount of biological damage as 1 rem of any other kind.

Refining: separation and conversion of the complex mixture of hydrocarbons in crude oil into its component fractions, for example, gasoline and heating oil.

Relative biological effectiveness (RBE): term used to compare the effectiveness of different kinds of radiation to the effectiveness of beta particles. Beta particles have an RBE of 1; alpha particles have RBEs of 10-20; neutron beams have RBEs of 2-10.

Resource: any naturally occurring entity, material, or space that is useful to human beings (see Chapter 7).

Secondary recovery: a term that applies to the extraction of oil and gas by other than spontaneous means, i.e., by forcing the oil or gas out by injecting air, gas, or water into the formation where it resides.

Slow neutron: a "thermal" neutron with enough energy to cause unstable (fissionable) nuclei to undergo fission. Stable nuclei can be made to undergo fission only by impact with fast neutrons. The kinetic energy of a slow neutron is about equal to the kinetic energy of atoms and molecules of air at normal room temperature.

Thorium: Radioactive chemical element of atomic number 90, useful as a nuclear reactor fuel. Thorium 232 is used in breeder reactors because when it captures or absorbs a slow neutron, it decays into fissionable uranium 233.

Tritium: Hydrogen with two extra neutrons in the nucleus, i.e., an isotope of hydrogen. Tritium is an unstable (radioactive) isotope of hydrogen.

Uranium: a radioactive element with the atomic number of 92. Uranium occurs in natural deposits throughout the world.

New strip mining technology is being developed to meet the demand for domestic coal supplies.

ican Public Health Association study in 1979, if power plants were to increase coal generation of energy from 0.8 quadrillion BTUs to 1.1 quadrillion BTUs, SO_2 levels would rise enough to kill an average of 500 more adults with heart disease and cause 16,000 more respiratory attacks among children under five years old each year. (This is an increase of less than one tenth of one percent over present rates.)

Another part of an emerging national energy plan is to convert coal into other physical forms and to burn it in better ways. These alternatives are not without their own problems. Some of the problems are the same, of course. In order to liquify coal it still has to be mined in ways that still have significant negative environmental impacts. Also, no matter how coal is burned, CO_2 will be generated to more or less the same degree (Calvin, 1979). New anticipated problems will be unique to the processes involved, and there will no doubt also be unanticipated problems.

Emerging Coal Technology

Fluidized Bed Combustion. Among the approaches to improving the way in which coal is used as a source of energy is to convert it into forms that can be burned more efficiently. One such method under advanced testing now is fluidized bed combustion (Figure 6.20). Fluidized bed combustion is

Many government officials have called for a switch from foreign oil to domestic coal over the next few decades. *If all else stays the same,* this will have the effect of making the acid rain problem worse and increasing the health risk to smokers, pregnant women, the elderly, and those with respiratory and cardiac problems. According to an Amer-

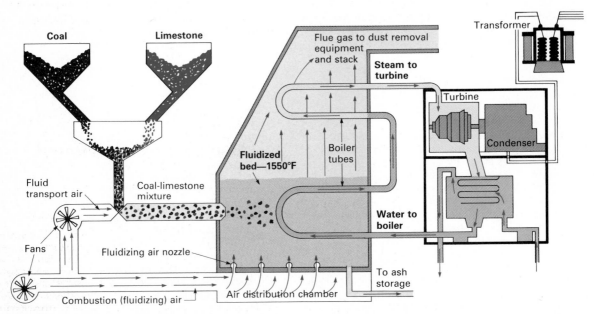

Figure 6.20 Design of a Fluidized Bed Boiler. A fluidized bed boiler is designed to minimize the pollution problems from the relatively high-sulfur coal and coal that tends to slag. A number of such designs are being tested under contract with the Department of Energy, and commercial application should occur by the year 2000.

designed both to enhance combustion efficiency and to reduce sulfur and nitrogen oxide emission. Sulfur is absorbed by the limestone mixed with the coal in this process, and lower combustion temperatures tend to produce much less oxides of nitrogen. The major problem with this approach is that it requires the disposal of relatively large amounts of solid waste or ash. Other approaches involve the conversion of coal into other forms. These include both the gasification and liquefaction of coal.

The Synfuels Corporation. Recognizing that coal is America's most plentiful fuel resource but that liquid and gaseous fuels are generally more desirable, the federal government under the Carter administration sought to stimulate the development of "synfuels" technology for coal conversion and other energy resource development technologies. A federal "Synfuels Corporation" began operation in 1981 with the purpose of bankrolling innovative projects to be designed, proposed, and carried out by private industry. By 1984 this venture had supported only a few coal gasification projects and an oil shale project. A combination of erratic political winds and the oil glut that began before the synfuels program could get started apparently resulted in a mutual loss of intense interest in synfuels by both the federal government and industry. Research in synfuels continues, nevertheless, and the prospects deserve some consideration here.

Coal Gasification. According to various sources, oil and gas production from coal will be commercially available sometime during the 1990s. The objective of **coal gasification** is to produce a fuel from coal that can be used like natural gas in the same pipes and the same appliances. The advantages would be ease in handling and cleanliness in burning. This is not a new idea. Congress appropriated $30 million in the mid-1940s to explore ways to convert coal into other forms of fuel, and coal gasification technologies have been known for some time. The main problem is that coal gasification is expensive and relatively inefficient. At present there are limitations as to the kind and sizes of coal chunks that can be gasified. Such problems are all subjects of ongoing research. Nevertheless, various gasification technologies had reached the demonstration phase toward the end of the 1970s. The basic method of converting coal into gas is illustrated in Figure 6.21.

Underground or in situ Gasification of Coal. A unique and unusual type of energy extraction from

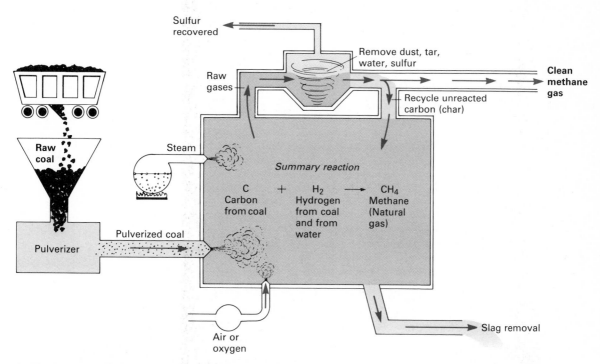

Figure 6.21 Very General Schematic Diagram of a Process by Which Coal Can Be Converted into a Gas Similar to Natural Gas. This process is about 75% efficient. With recovery of the heat generated by gasification, efficiency can exceed 96%.

coal is underground coal gasification. This process was actually first explored in the early 1930s in the Soviet Union. Wells are sunk into a coal seam some distance apart, the coal at the base of one well is ignited, and air is forced down it through the coal seam into the second well. As burning takes place, a low-energy gas comes out of the well that can be captured, stored, and used.

There are problems—both known and unknown—with **in situ** (in place) coal gasification. We do not know much about the potentials for contamination of groundwater. Once coal is burned, the coal seam can collapse; when this happens, water can seep in, or gases could escape. Another problem is that some coal beds are not permeable enough to maintain combustion and to allow the flow of gas through the coal and up the production well. There is apparently very little information available concerning the possibility of gas leakage from such processes.

Coal Liquefaction. **Coal liquefaction** is intended to generate a product that can serve in lieu of petroleum. There are a number of improved processes being studied now by which coal can be liquefied. One of the key features of liquefaction is that hydrogen is used in a process called hydrodesulfurization by which hydrogen is combined with the sulfur and then extracted, leaving a relatively sulfur-free, low-ash, synthetic fuel oil. The cost of oil derived from coal is projected to be high, in which case it will have difficulty competing with other types of liquid fuel now and in the immediate future. It is unlikely that synthetic liquid fuels will make much of a contribution to our energy supply until after the year 2000.

Among the environmental problems associated with coal liquefaction is the fact that toxic and carcinogenic compounds are generated as by-products of the production of coal-derived liquids (and gaseous fuels). Carcinogens have been measured in coal liquefaction process streams in coal liquefaction pilot plants. There is some direct evidence, too. At a coal hydrogenation (liquefaction) plant that operated in West Virginia from 1953 to 1959 the incidence of skin cancer among workers was reported to be 20 times that of other white males in the United States (Morris et al., 1979). For all forms of conversion there would be a shift in solid waste generation from the site of energy release to processing and conversion plants, which would presumably be located near the mines. An environmental advantage to conversion is that sulfur can be removed somewhat more economically in conversion processes than in the cleaning or burning of coal (Morris et al., 1979).

The Future of Coal

The future of coal is bright only because it is really the *only* fossil fuel resource that can contribute significantly to energy supplies in America's intermediate and long-range future. Even worldwide there are sufficient reserves available to last for centuries. Despite the numerous unsolved environmental problems associated with its use, coal offers the United States its only chance for achieving energy independence in the near future before more environmentally sound alternatives come of age in the more distant future. Figure 6.22 illustrates how far we have come and how far we may progress with the coal resources in the United States, given estimated and mapped desposits.

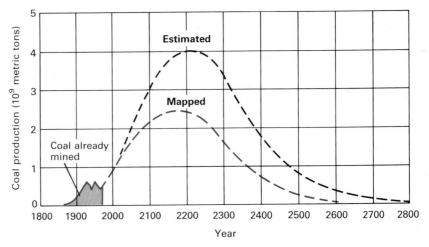

Figure 6.22 Two Estimates for the U.S. Production of Coal over the Next Several Hundred Years. This assumes that one billion metric tons are produced per year. (1982 rate = 0.748 billion metric tons.) The upper curve is based on an estimate of the amount of coal remaining in the U.S.; the lower curve is based on deposits already mapped. Each square on the grid represents $100 \times X10^9$ metric tons.

PETROLEUM

Reserves

The bad news is that estimated crude oil reserves for the world are not large. Their magnitude in the early 1980s is illustrated in Figure 6.23. The immediately striking thing about these data is that the Middle East has the greatest reserve by far. The really important fact, however, is that we are nearing the peak of oil production worldwide. At current rates of utilization we will come close to having consumed 80% of what is now estimated as the earth's total recoverable reserves in just one lifetime. The reader need only look at Figure 6.23 in light of the fact that the annual world output of oil is about 20 billion barrels (an amount equal to the total reserve of Venezuela or Libya) to get an idea of how fast we are reaching the "bottom of the barrel."

In the United States, where almost one third of the world's oil is consumed, the oil fields are yielding less and less oil. M. K. Hubbert, formerly one of the Shell Oil Company's leading geophysicists, predicts that even assuming certain levels of undiscovered oil, we have clearly passed the peak of domestic production in the United States (see Duggan and Cloutier, 1975). He projects that the United States will have consumed 80% of all the oil it "originally" had available within the 60-year period beginning in 1940 (see Figure 6.24). Already, half the oil ever consumed in the United States has been consumed

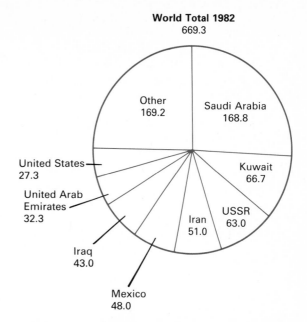

Figure 6.23 Estimated Crude Oil Reserves for the World by Region at the end of 1982. Numbers are in billions of barrels.

since people who are now middle-aged graduated from high school.

There is some disagreement about the years remaining until we exhaust our domestic supplies of oil. Depending on the estimator, we might run out

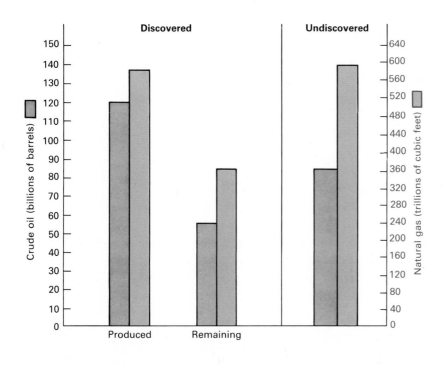

Figure 6.24 Projections of Oil and Natural Gas Resources. Recoverable conventional oil resources in the U.S. that are still undiscovered are estimated at 64.3–105.1 billion barrels; the mean estimate is 82.6 billion barrels. Natural gas resources are estimated at 474.6–739.3 trillion cubic feet.

before the turn of the century, or it might take until the year 2075, or even beyond. In any case these estimates and data on the number of truly exploratory wells now being drilled and the number of these producing seem to point to the inescapable conclusion that our supplies of oil (and natural gas) are rapidly diminishing.

In the meantime the fact that demand is expected to continue to outstrip supply by some considerable measure in the United States has serious economic implications because the difference will have to be made up by imports (Table 6.4). Although some significant progress was made in reducing oil imports from the late 1970s to the early 1980s (8 million barrels per day in 1978 down to 4.3 million barrels in 1984), imports are expected to climb again (see Table 6.4). The decline in imports was a result of conservation induced by the shock of rising prices and the general increase in oil supplies that included domestic oil, which was also spurred by higher prices.

The increased cost of oil imports has been a major contributor to the U.S. balance of payments deficits and a serious factor in the instability of world economic relationships. Many underdeveloped nations have been brought close to bankruptcy as a result of high oil bills. Many Western nations continue to be at the mercy of distant political events over which they have little influence and almost no control.

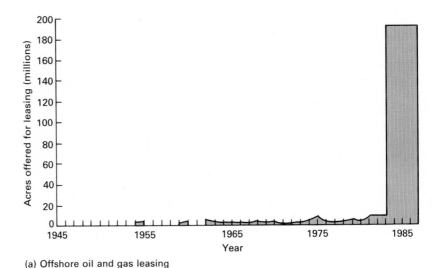

(a) Offshore oil and gas leasing

Figure 6.25 Recent Trends in Leasing of Federal Lands and Offshore Areas for Energy Exploration.

(b) Geothermal leasing

New Oil Fields Including Those Offshore

Perhaps the most direct approach to increasing oil supplies is to find more. That this approach works is indicated by the fact that the recently discovered oil field on the "north slope" of Alaska now accounts for one fourth of U.S. domestic production (U.S. Department of Energy, 1983a). Now that Prudhoe Bay has become old news, our attention has turned to the continental shelves off the Atlantic, Pacific, and Gulf coasts. In 1982, offshore oil amounted to about 15% of domestic production. This proportion is expected to rise in the future as a result of much increased offshore exploration.

In 1981 the Department of Interior announced a five-year program of leasing almost the entire continental shelf for oil and gas exploration. There was much opposition to this move by environmental interests based mainly on the threat of environmentally damaging leaks and spills associated with exploration and production (see Chapter 12). The advocates of offshore oil and gas exploration carried the day, however, their main arguments being (1) that exploration impacts have been well studied and found safe and (2) that America needed the energy. The immediate, dramatic result is presented in Figure 6.25. The Bureau of Land Management within the Department of Interior followed suit and opened up as many acres to oil and gas exploration in 1982 as were offered in the entire period from 1977 to

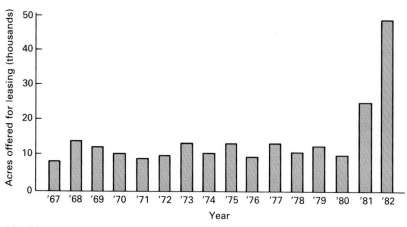

(c)   Onshore oil and gas leasing

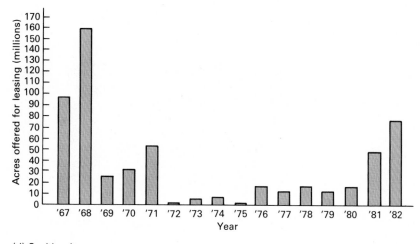

(d) Coal leasing

To transport the oil from the Alaskan fields to major refineries, a pipeline thousands of miles long was constructed.

1980. A similar pattern was followed in coal and geothermal leasing (see Figure 6.25). Although there have been some gains in domestic oil production from all this, domestic production is projected to level off again by 1985 or so and to remain flat through 1990 (1982 *Annual Energy Review*).

Enhanced Recovery

Another way of increasing domestic oil supplies is to enhance the percentage of oil recovered from *present* oil fields. Gushers come to mind when oil wells are mentioned, and gushers are illustrations of the fact that oil deposits are under pressure. If oil deposits are tapped in the right way, this pressure is enough to lift much (35–45%) of the oil out of the ground into storage tanks. Natural pressures are derived from gaseous pressure or water pressure (see Figure 6.26); oil recovery as a result of these natural forces is called **primary recovery**. It is often necessary to use pumps to get the remaining oil out of a deposit as cumulative withdrawals reduce the natural pressure. If natural forces have to be helped along by pumping or by injecting water or air into oil wells, this is referred to as **secondary recovery**.

Primary and secondary recovery combined often leave 40% to as much as 80% of the oil in the ground. Enhanced or **tertiary recovery** methods such as those illustrated in Figure 6.26 are being used—or tried—to get at the oil that is left by conventional (primary and secondary) recovery methods. In the steam-flooding or thermal recovery method, for example, oil is heated so that it will flow out of porous rock formations more easily and is then moved out by the steam pressure. Still another method is to burn some oil *in situ*. In the latter method a fire is started under one well, which then reduces the viscosity of adjacent oil, allowing it to be more easily pushed into a production well. As would be expected, enhanced recovery costs money; oil recovered in this way is generally more costly to produce than oil derived from primary recovery.

Oil Shale

Locked in oil-bearing rock formations within a relatively small area of the high desert in Utah, Wyoming, and Colorado is an estimated two trillion barrels of a solid hydrocarbon equivalent of oil called *kerogen*. Deposits are found in some of the eastern states as well. The product is not oil, and the rock in which it resides is not shale, but the term "oil shale" has stuck. If kerogen can be economically melted and extracted, it will represent a resource 50 times greater than the amount of our present oil reserve (Maugh, 1977b).

Research is underway designed to explore and refine two basic ways of getting "oil" from "shale." One is to extract the "oil" from the "shale" in an above-ground process using chemical and physical

This experimental oil shale processing plant in Colorado was built in an attempt to develop extraction methods that are both efficient and environmentally safe.

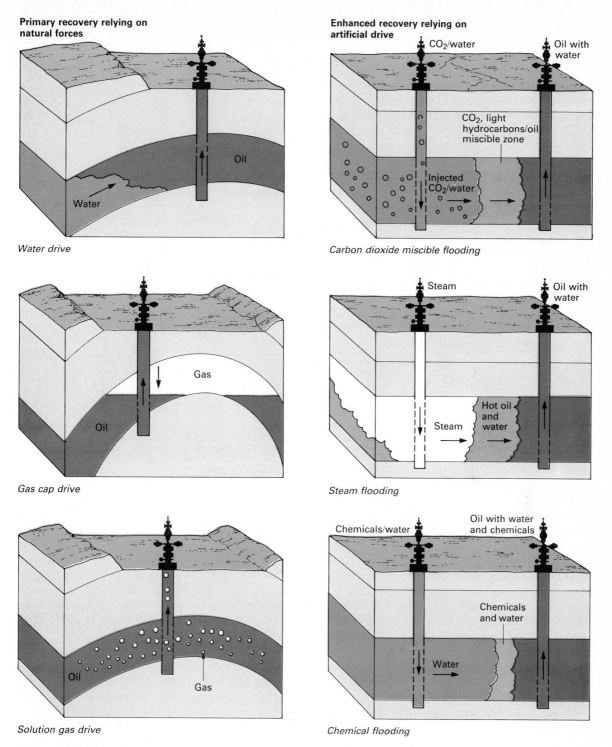

Primary recovery relying on natural forces

Water drive

Gas cap drive

Solution gas drive

Enhanced recovery relying on artificial drive

Carbon dioxide miscible flooding

Steam flooding

Chemical flooding

Figure 6.26 Three Forms of "Natural" Drive and Three Forms of Enhanced Recovery of Oil.

methods. The other is an in situ approach, which may turn out to be somewhat more economically feasible. There are a number of environmental concerns. Above-ground extraction can be done by strip mining or other forms of extraction and will tend to cause water pollution and to disturb land directly. The disposal of spent shale will present other forms of the same problems. Finding a place to put spent shale will be a problem because once stripped of its hydrocarbons in processing, the shale will take up more room than it did originally because of a swelling or popcorn effect. There will also be the potential for gaseous and particulate emissions from mining, drilling, preparation, and handling of oil shale at the site of processing. No matter how it is done, the extraction of oil from shale will be a process with a relatively high capital cost, and there are a number of uncertainties about operating costs because of a need to deal with as yet-unknown environmental impacts. There is also the possibility that carcinogenic and mutagenic materials will be included in the effluents from "oil shale" operations.

NATURAL GAS

Natural gas, with emphasis on the word "natural," apparently does not have much of a long-range future. Natural gas reserves are just about depleted, even on a worldwide scale (Figure 6.27). We are apparently past the peak of natural gas consumption in the United States. There have already been several years in which the annual rate of increase in gas production has been declining. The United States annually consumes about one tenth of its 1982 reserve. We have already seen how important natural gas is to us as a form of energy; it would obviously be quite traumatic to have to shift away from this type of fuel rapidly. Given the realities of U.S. natural gas supplies and barring any unexpected new sources, America must now rely on research aimed at producing pipeline-quality gas from other forms of fuel such as coal.

It should be pointed out that we have some very large deposits of natural gas that are uneconomical to tap at present. Some natural gas and oil deposits, for instance, are held in spongelike sand and porous rock formations. The gas can be held so tightly in "tight sand" formations that it does not flow out easily. Experiments have been performed, including some that have attempted to use nuclear explosives to break up such formations, but so far these gas deposits remain in the category of resources but not reserves (see Chapter 7). The U.S. Geological Survey

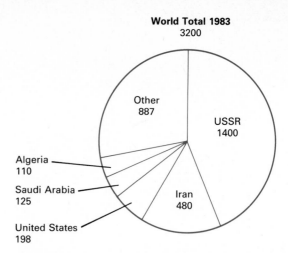

Figure 6.27 Proved Natural Gas Reserves for the World at the End of 1983. In trillion cubic feet. Note that world *annual* marketed production was approximately 54 trillion ft³ in 1982; U.S. production in 1984 was approximately 20 trillion ft³.

estimates that undiscovered natural gas resources are 63% of what has been found (see Figure 6.24).

ENERGY FROM THE SUN

History

Perhaps no form of energy has more inherent appeal than solar energy. Broadly defined, solar energy would include—in addition to direct radiant energy—wood, vegetation, heated surface water, and wind power. In this section we use a narrow definition which includes only direct solar energy. The fact that solar energy is delivered to the earth every day, whether we tap it or not, promises that we would not have to do much extra environmental manipulation to use this form of energy.

Archimedes was said to have used solar reflecting mirrors more than 2000 years ago to set fire to ships in a Roman fleet. In the mid-1880s a French scientist developed the first known solar device able to convert water into steam and power an engine. There were some rather surprising solar technological developments in the early parts of the twentieth century. Tens of thousands of solar water heaters were sold and used in California and Florida in the early 1900s, and some of these reportedly are still in operation. Bell Telephone Laboratories came up with a method for converting solar energy into electrical energy nearly 30 years ago. The world's current energy problems provide new incentive to further developments in solar technology.

Potential

Every day the sun delivers about 1400 BTUs of energy to every square foot (929 cm²) of land in the United States. In an absolute sense we get far more solar energy than we could possibly ever use. The solar energy received by the earth in one day would take care of the world's energy requirements for 30 years at present rates of energy consumption (U.S. Department of Energy, 1983a). While this serves to illustrate the potential of solar energy, many factors—technological, economic, and others—stand in the way of achieving any fraction of this potential.

Space Heating and Water Heating

All that is needed to convert sunlight into heat in a confined space is for the sunlight to be able to pass through transparent panes and be absorbed. This simple technology is now relatively well advanced, and there are some interesting possibilities for extended application. The conversion of sunlight to heat is a straightforward, efficient, direct way of using solar energy. In terms of transmission, direct solar energy is already delivered to exactly

where it is needed—everywhere—although in different amounts and, of course, not always *when* it is needed.

The solar collector can be as simple as a double layer of glass that admits light to an absorber plate painted black to maximize absorption. Air heated in such a collector can be circulated to heat a building directly, or fluid can be pumped through collectors to carry heat to storage depots, hot water tanks, and radiators (Figure 6.28).

There is no question that we already have the engineering capabilities to design, install, and use equipment of solar space and water heating. Solar water heating is already economically competitive with electrical water heating in many parts of the United States (Bezdek, Hirschberg, and Babcock, 1979). A research firm in New England tentatively concluded that solar water heating is really not yet commercially competitive with other forms of energy—in *northern* states. In this study, several hundred families participated by keeping track of the energy they saved by using solar water-heating boosters. They saved 17% of the energy that normally would go into heating water, but the saving was not high enough to offset the capital construction cost in a reasonable period of time. This will no doubt change in the future as more conventional energy sources become more expensive and as solar capital construction becomes more standard and less expensive.

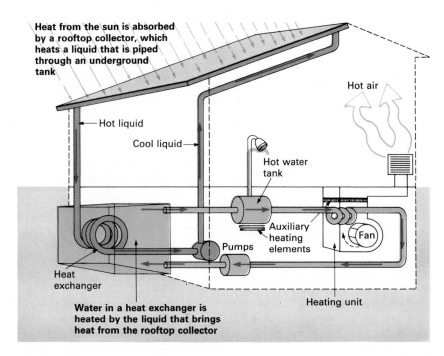

Heat from the sun is absorbed by a rooftop collector, which heats a liquid that is piped through an underground tank

Hot liquid

Cool liquid

Hot water tank

Hot air

Auxiliary heating elements

Pumps

Fan

Heat exchanger

Water in a heat exchanger is heated by the liquid that brings heat from the rooftop collector

Heating unit

Figure 6.28 System for Heating the Space and Water in a Home Using Sunlight.

The major problem standing in the way of improvements much beyond simple **passive solar space heating** is the economics of capitalization, that is, the costs of installation and the costs of equipment and structural modifications. It will take time to close the cost differential between solar energy capitalization and fossil fuel burning.

The cost of systems such as those illustrated here is not insignificant. The average solar installation cost $3235 in 1981. A telling statistic is that 70% of these installations were hot water units, and water heating typically costs about $150 per year. It would take more than 20 years to break even even if interest and maintenance costs are ignored. On the average, Americans move to a different house every seven years (Dukert, 1983).

Although simple passive solar space heating can be achieved for little or nothing by appropriate designs of windows and roof overhang, tree planting, opening and closing drapes, more elaborate systems can be costly. Solar space and water heating systems such as the one illustrated in Figure 6.28 can require structures covering up to the equivalent of half the floor space of a home and cost tens of thousands of dollars. During 1981, 150,000 solar units were installed in the United States, 95% of them into old and new single-family dwellings. Between one and two million houses are built each year, and some 80 million units already exist (Dukert, 1983).

Surveys have shown, however, that many people would be willing to establish such a system if it could be shown that the result would be sharply reduced fuel bills and consequent long-term savings. As prices of fossil fuel increase, the prospects for the realization of these conditions increase along with them. The potential benefit from solar heating is significant; the overall energy used for space heating and water heating is high; it constitutes 20% of the U.S. energy budget. Obviously, even if solar energy technology were limited to heating, it would be well worth pursuing. A high priority should be assigned to research into the design and technology of solar heating, particularly in the construction design of office buildings and homes.

Solar *cooling* technology is not nearly as well advanced as the technology for heating. However, solar energy can be used relatively directly in cooling by having the sun serve as a means of regenerating refrigerants in air conditioners.

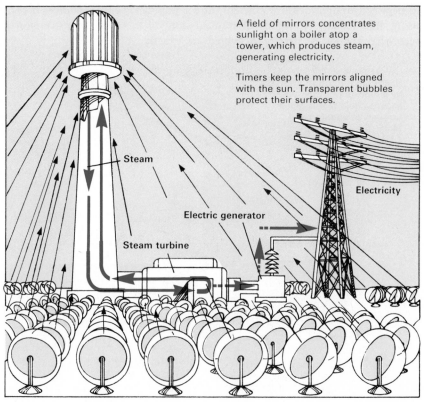

A field of mirrors concentrates sunlight on a boiler atop a tower, which produces steam, generating electricity.

Timers keep the mirrors aligned with the sun. Transparent bubbles protect their surfaces.

Steam

Electricity

Electric generator

Steam turbine

Figure 6.29 A Solar Power Plant Employing a Field of Heliostats. Each heliostat consists of a mirrorlike reflector and control system. The controls continuously focus reflected solar rays onto a central boiler mounted on a tower. Fluid heated in the tower is then expanded through a turbine, producing electricity.

Conversion of Solar Energy into Electricity via Steam

An indirect application of solar energy would be to convert it into electricity. This would in effect feed solar power into existing electrical delivery/distribution systems or power grids throughout the United States and the world. One way of generating electricity from sunlight is illustrated in Figure 6.29. In this system the sun's heat is focused on a boiler, causing water to be converted into steam used to drive a turbine. Among the problems with this type of system is that it requires a several-phase conversion of one form of energy into another, and this of course means reduced efficiency. Such systems require about 6000 m^2 per megawatt produced (Kreith and Meyer, 1983). Still, because the source of energy is free, it has been estimated (Hildebrandt and Vant-Hull, 1977) that **heliostats** like those in Figure 6.29 will be economically reasonable ways to capture and utilize solar energy. They estimate that the capital cost for construction of facilities such as those illustrated in Figure 6.29 would not (with mass production of components and systems) be dissimilar to the cost of more conventional means of generating electricity. The world's first solar plant like the one illustrated in Figure 6.29 opened near Barstow, California, in 1982. "Solar One," as this ten-megawatt plant is called, is now one of seven solar receivers undergoing tests throughout the world.

Photovoltaic Conversion

As we have already pointed out, Bell Laboratories developed a method of converting solar energy into electrical energy more than a quarter of a century ago. This is known as **photovoltaic conversion**. Hundreds of U.S. and Soviet space vehicles and satellites have been powered by solar energy since the late 1950s. One of the very first large photovoltaic arrays, one that generated 10,000 watts of electricity, was used to power the U.S. Skylab space station in 1973.

Among the problems with generating electricity with silicon solar cells is that it takes a large surface area (with present low-efficiency technology) to generate the electricity needed even within a single household. This, coupled with the fact that the solar cells are very expensive and that they would have to be kept immaculately clean, diminishes the expectations about general utilization of this type of system on any large scale in the very near future. Efficiency of conversion is apparently the key. DeMeo and Taylor (1984) estimate that expected improvements in efficiency will permit electrical utilities to use solar cells by the turn of the century.

Local Versus Central Conversion

Because sunlight reaches everywhere, it somehow seems perverted to consider collecting and focusing sunlight on one point or place or area and then shipping the energy through transmission lines or some other means to places where it is to be used. We look for solar technologic developments with emphasis on systems that are *not* central, we look for small solar conversion units that capture and make use of energy for homes, small businesses, and office buildings directly on site. An appealing feature of this decentralized concept is that it would mean a much more stable situation; individuals would not have to depend on power grids that serve large expanses of territory.

The Problem of Storage and Other Research Subjects

A key research strategy for photovoltaic conversion is finding more selective and better surfaces for absorbing solar radiation and converting it into electricity. For solar space heating and water heating, the main technological problems remaining have to do with the development of better systems of storage and improvements in architectural design of buildings to allow greater and greater utilization of this form of energy.

A common problem for all of the many applications of solar energy is "What do you do in cloudy periods and at times of the year when there is less sunlight—and at night?" We look for significant future advances in the area of energy storage (storage of heat energy, storage of electrical energy, etc). On the distant horizon, perhaps we can overcome the cloudy, nighttime problem with a system of solar energy collectors in orbit that then beam microwave radiation to the earth. These could be placed so as to provide a continuous supply of energy to the earth (see Figure 6.30). In November 1979 the U.S. House of Representatives passed a bill authorizing $25 million to explore the plausibility of such satellites.

Assessment

A study made by the U.S. National Science Foundation and the National Aeronautics and Space Administration *in the early 1970s* concluded:

1. Enough solar radiation is received in the United States to make a major contribution to future heat and power needs.

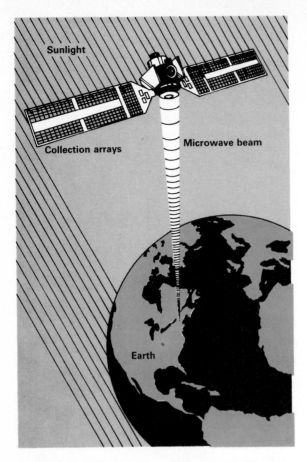

Figure 6.30 A Futuristic Way to Deal with Cloudy Days and Sunless Nights. Satellites orbiting at altitudes of 22,000 miles or more, fixed over the same point on the earth's surface, could be designed to convert sunlight into microwaves, which would then be beamed to earth and converted into electricity.

2. There are no substantial technological barriers to wider application of solar energy.
3. While solar energy is currently more expensive than some conventional types of fuel, increasing natural gas costs and increasing costs of other fuels will almost certainly make solar energy economically competitive in the not-too-distant future.
4. If developed correctly, solar energy will be available to the general public around 1980 (it was, to a limited extent).
5. Even very large scale use of solar energy would have a minimal impact on the environment.

During the 1970s the U.S. Council on Environmental Quality estimated that, given problems and the extent to which we will be able to cope with them in the near future, solar energy *could* have allowed the United States to meet about one fourth of its total energy needs by the turn of the century (Carter, 1979a). Current trends indicate that solar energy will not even come close to that, however; current estimates including those by the U.S. Department of Energy are pessimistic.

According to a panel of experts asked by then President Carter to look into the possibilities of solar power, the prospects are ultimately good, but the panel projected that by the year 2000 only 1% of U.S. electrical needs will be met by solar technology. A study reported by the U.S. Office of Science and Technology Policy projected that it would take 30–50 years before solar sources would provide even 10% of U.S. *electricity*. Solar energy apparently will not have a major impact on our energy problem for quite a few generations. Progress is being made, however (Table 6.10), and should continue at a brisk pace.

ATOMIC ENERGY

Fission

Figure 6.31 illustrates what happens when the nucleus of an atom of uranium 235 (^{235}U) absorbs a free neutron. The splitting of the uranium nucleus is called **nuclear fission**, and a number of the things produced as a result of fission are of interest to us in this book. In Chapter 14 we will discuss radiation emissions (alpha particles, beta particles, and gamma rays) that result from the decay of fission products and how these rays can cause radiation sickness, cancer, and birth defects. The heat energy released can be used to boil water to produce steam to drive turbines; this is the part of the fission process of most interest to us in this chapter. The fission reaction also produces free slow neutrons, which, if they happen to be absorbed by another nucleus of ^{235}U, will cause another nucleus to undergo fission, repeating the whole process. If enough uranium is present at a high enough density, a chain reaction can be generated, producing an explosive release of energy such as in an atomic bomb. At lower densities, such reactions can be controlled—made to proceed at much slower rates—as is done in a nuclear reactor.

How Does a Nuclear Power Reactor Work?

The basic design of a nuclear fission reactor is almost identical to that of any steam boiler. In a

Table 6.10   Production of Solar Collectors, 1974–1982

Year	Low-Temperature Collectors[1]		Medium-Temperature, Special, and Other Collectors[2]	
	Number of Manufacturers	Quantity Manufactured (million square feet)	Number of Manufacturers	Quantity Manufactured (million square feet)
1974	6	1.14	39	0.14
1976	19	3.88	203	1.92
1978	81	5.87	180	4.99
1980	73	12.23	245	7.16
1982	61	7.48	247	11.14

[1] Low-temperature collectors are used almost exclusively for swimming pool heating.
[2] Medium-temperature collectors are used primarily for space heating and domestic water heating. Special collectors include evacuated-tube collectors and concentrating collectors; uses include domestic water heating, space heating, and space cooling.
Note: Manufacturers producing more than one type of collector are accounted for in the respective listing.
Sources: 1974–1976: Federal Energy Administration, *Solar Collector Manufacturing Activity*, semi-annual; 1977–1981: Energy Information Administration, *Solar Collector Manufacturing Activity, July through December, 1981*. March 1982 (semi-annual).

nuclear reactor the heat from fission is transmitted to water, causing it to be converted to steam, which is then used to drive turbines and generate electricity. A typical nuclear power reactor is illustrated in Figure 6.32. The rate of fission in nuclear reactors is controlled by moving dampening or control rods in or out from between rods of ^{235}U. Control rods are made of materials that absorb neutrons and thus regulate the rate at which neutrons strike and are captured by ^{235}U.

Because the world's ^{235}U reserves are quite limited even in the United States, which has a relatively abundant supply, there is considerable interest in alternatives to simple fission for the extraction of energy from atoms. One such alternative is the breeder reactor.

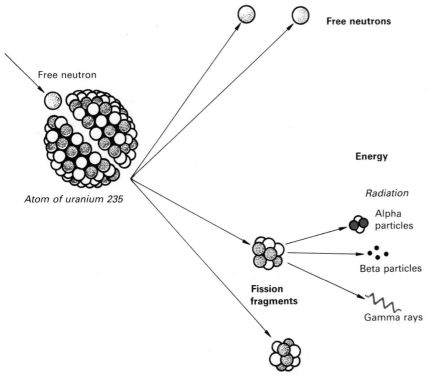

Figure 6.31 The Products of Nuclear Fission.

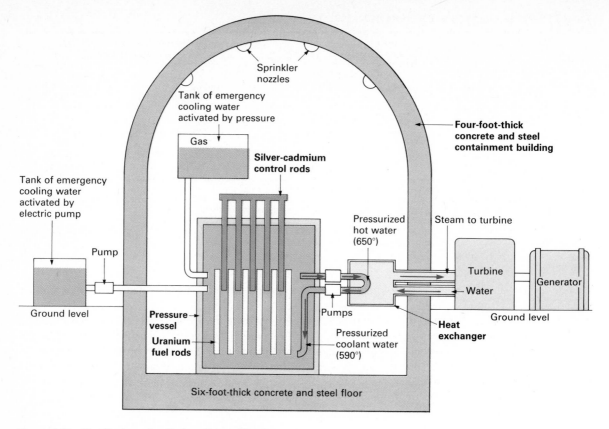

Figure 6.32 The Design of a Nuclear Power Reactor.

Breeder Reactors

The **breeder reactor** starts with fissionable fuel, but as it operates, it converts nonfissionable materials into those that are fissionable. In a sense—not in the absolute thermodynamic one, of course—breeders produce more fuel than they consume, hence the term "breeder."

Plutonium 239 is a byproduct of the interaction of neutrons with uranium 238 (^{238}U). Although (unlike its isotope, ^{235}U) ^{238}U is not readily fissionable, it can be converted into fissionable plutonium 239. This actually occurs to some extent in conventional fission reactors—reactors in which the principal reaction is the fission of ^{235}U. Breeders are actually special fission reactors in which, by allowing the fission reactor to run "hotter," fast neutrons produce more than one atom of fissionable material for every one consumed.

The vanguard of breeder reactor technology is the **liquid metal cooled fast breeder reactor (LMFBR)**. In these reactors the breeding of ^{239}Pu is accomplished by arranging a blanket of ^{238}U around the core of a reactor in which fissionable material is undergoing fission. This is done in such a way that 1.2 or more atoms of ^{239}Pu are made from ^{238}U for every atom fissioned in the core. As the ^{239}Pu is made, it can be processed and returned as core fuel, and some can be used to fuel another reactor. LMFBRs must be cooled by liquid sodium rather than by water as in conventional reactors. The main reason is that the water would slow the fast neutrons too much, thereby preventing them from converting ^{238}U into ^{239}Pu. This also makes breeder reactors somewhat more efficient because liquid sodium is a better conductor of heat from the reactor core to the water that is to be converted to steam.

The principal advantage of the breeder reactor over the traditional and currently much more prevalent light water reactor is that there is considerably more ^{238}U in the world than ^{235}U. Actually, nearly all (>99%) of the uranium in uranium ore is in the form of ^{238}U. According to Dorf (1978), there are currently some 20,000 tons of discarded ^{238}U at Oak Ridge, Tennessee, and at other processing sites. This "waste" (in terms of conventional light water reactor technology) is 70% usable as fission energy in terms of LMFBR technology (see Kulcinski et al., 1979). Because a 1000-megawatt LMFBR power plant would consume only one ton of uranium annually, that stockpile alone could supply 400 LMFBR plants for some 500 years.

At least two experimental breeder reactors are already operating in the United States, one in Idaho and one in Richland, Washington. Breeder reactors have been reliably producing electricity for a number of years in England and the Soviet Union; a French plant that began operation in 1967 ran until 1982, when it was shut down permanently because of an internal leak.

For a variety of technical, political, and economic reasons the breeder programs in both Britain and France have been slowed way down from earlier projections. The U.S. Congress declined to continue to fund the Clinch River Breeder reactor project in Tennessee in 1983, partly because the Tennessee Valley Authority said it did not need the power in the foreseeable future and at least partly because of the decline in demand for uranium as a result of the general demise of the nation's nuclear power program. Technological development continues, and while some experts believe that commercial orders for breeder reactors will be possible by the turn of the century, some economists claim that breeders will not be competitive with conventional light water reactors for a half century (*Science,* 1982, **218**:1094).

Consensus on the *positive* side of the breeder reactor is perhaps expressed best by Zaleski (1980):

> With breeders . . . the world will have a major and almost inexhaustable source of energy which will allow enough time to find and develop complementary and perhaps better energy sources.

Opposition to the further development of the breeder in the United States runs high because of the security problems associated with plutonium. Plutonium is one essential ingredient in the manufacture of atomic bombs, and it is one of the most toxic substances produced by humankind. The potential for use of plutonium by terrorists (see below) would be greatly expanded with the increased use of breeder technology.

Atomic Fusion

At normal earthly temperatures, if two atoms were on a collision course with one another, their nuclei would not ultimately collide because of the repulsive forces that would come into play. If atoms can be made to collide in a situation in which they have high thermal/kinetic energy—that is, extremely high energy of motion at very, very high temperatures such as exist on the sun—they can be made to fuse because once the nuclei get close enough, the very strong but short-range attractive *nuclear* forces can then overcome the repulsive *electrical* forces. When this reaction, known as **fusion**, occurs between hydrogen atoms, the sum of the masses that go into the fusion product is larger than the mass of the final product (helium). The difference is converted into energy according to Einstein's equation, $E = mc^2$. (Note that it is the conversion of mass to energy that yields the energy in fission reactions also.) Our sun loses four million tons of mass per second in generating energy via atomic fusion. The sun is a fusion reactor.

Although we have been realizing energy benefits from atomic fusion in the sun from day one, harnessing controlled atomic fusion generated here on earth will not be easy. The trick in atomic fusion will be to create and sustain **plasmas** or conditions of matter in which the heat is so extremely intense that atoms cannot exist as atoms. Part of the problem is how to *contain* matter at such high temperatures. What on earth could be used as a container for something as hot as a star? Experiments are underway using magnetic fields to contain superhot plasma in fusion research.

It should be pointed out here, perhaps, that there is no danger from such plasmas. If these super fires did happen to touch the wall of a vessel, they would go out. Unlike stars, the density of fusion-type plasmas is quite low; as a result, they have very little heat content. The problem is not how to keep the plasmas from burning up labs, exploding, etc.; it is how to keep plasmas hot enough.

In 1978, Princeton University scientists reported that they were able for the first time to produce the temperatures necessary to support sustained fusion. This report was later described as a "media event" (Metz, 1978) because although the temperatures reached were high, the density of the heated plasma was very, very low, and the temperature lasted only 15 thousandths of a second. In 1983, however, scientists at MIT achieved the minimum plasma density and confinement needed for the fusion break-even point. All of the criteria for fusion are expected to be achieved together in one place in the late 1980s—indeed, the Magnetic Fusion Engineering Act of 1980 specifically calls for a fusion engineering device by 1990.

In search of an almost limitless energy source, scientists study atom fusion in devices like this one at Oak Ridge, Tennessee.

Fusion reactors would be somewhat safer and would have other advantages over fission reactions. The fusion reaction is theoretically very efficient, producing 180 times more energy than it consumes. Furthermore, fusion would have relatively little adverse environmental impact, and plenty of the fuel needed to keep the process going is available. Of the possible products of the fusion of hydrogen, for example, only **tritium**, radioactive isotope of hydrogen, is produced as a by-product. Tritium emits no gamma rays, and its radiations are easily shielded; its **half-life** (the time required for half of any amount of radioactive material to undergo radioactive decay) is about 12 years. Tritium *is* dangerous; but even though it may well be very difficult to contain the large amounts of tritium that would be involved, the tritium problem is thought by many experts to be considerably less than that of the radioisotopes produced as by-products of fission.

Although a number of fuels could be used in fusion, a likely fuel for fusion reactors of the future is heavy hydrogen or deuterium. Although it is rare, deuterium occurs as 1 part in 7000 of ordinary hydrogen. One gallon of seawater contains the deuterium fusion energy equivalent of several hundred gallons of gasoline.

The advantages of fusion over fission, in summary, are as follows:

1. Fusion would provide a relatively inexhaustible source of cheap fuel; fission cannot.
2. Fusion would generate comparatively less serious radioactive waste disposal problems than fission.

The problems with fusion are as follows:

1. We have not solved the problem of confining the proper reaction mixture (containing 100 billion ions per cubic centimeter for one second) at the right temperature (above 44 million degrees).
2. Fusion reactors will probably be complicated, large structures without application in certain areas like propulsion; it is not likely that there will be fusion reactor atomic submarines, for example.

Kulcinski et al. (1979) give a more detailed comparison of the environmental impacts of fission and fusion.

The Trouble with Nuclear Energy

There are problems with the use of nuclear energy; we have touched on some of them already. The problems, all of which have to do with various real and feared health and environmental impacts of radiation, can conveniently be divided into four categories, maybe five. First, there is the controversy over whether or not routine operation of nuclear power plants adds significant amounts of radioactivity to the general environment. Second, there is the very real problem of what to do with radioactive waste. Third, there is the controversy over the possibility of a core meltdown—a colossal nuclear accident. Fourth, there is the problem of security. How can uranium and plutonium be kept out of the hands of the wrong people? All of these are related to a fifth item: cost. Nuclear power plants have become very expensive to build. Final estimated construction costs (*not* inflation adjusted) for many nuclear power plants were 1.5–4 times higher than the preconstruction estimates. Most of this can be attributed to a sharp rise in interest rates; some of it is a result of changes in technical designs and is related to more rigorous safety and environmental standards (U.S. Department of Energy, 1984a).

Before we go into each of these problems with nuclear power we would like to review some important facts about radiation.

The Effect of Radiation. In 1927 the Nobel Laureate H. J. Muller found that high-energy radiation could damage genetic material—the chromosomes of living organisms. Most of what we have found out since then about the specific, direct effects of radiation on the human body comes from studies of survivors of the atomic bomb blasts in Japan and studies of Marshall Islanders who were exposed to radiation during atomic tests in the early 1950s. Data about chronic exposure come from X-ray technicians and radiologists who received large doses in the years before the dangers of radiation were recognized. Still other data come from uranium miners. A considerable amount of additional basic information has come from experiments with laboratory animals.

Death can occur in just a few days to a few weeks from a whole-body dose of more than 500 rads. As few as 300 rads might be fatal for some people.

While we know a lot about acute effects of radiation above the levels of 150 rems, we have less information about the effects of short-term radiation in smaller doses. We do know that doses of radiation below 150 rems can have important genetic effects leading to birth defects and cancer. In Chapter 14 we will see that radiation may be responsible for some cancer deaths—some of these from radiation used in medicine for medically indicated reasons. A small percentage of cancers are no doubt due to background radiation in the environment. The implication is that if background radiation goes up, the number of cancers induced by radiation will increase proportionately.

Studies of the health effects of extremely small doses of radiation are difficult if not impossible to conduct and interpret (see Chapter 14). As a result, the effects of very low doses of radiation are not known. There are two possibilities: (1) that below some threshold level, genetic damage can be *repaired* before it becomes "expressed" or (2) that genetic damage is directly proportional to radiation all the way down to zero. The latter is called the linear hypothesis and is favored by most experts. Most informed nonexperts believe that if the experts disagree, we should err on the safe side. But as is plainly illustrated in Table 6.11, it is *impossible* to avoid all radiation whether on, above, or beneath the earth.

The National Council on Radiation Protection has established the "maximum permissible doses" (MPD) for radiation workers and for the general public from artificial sources of radiation other than those related to medicine. The MPDs have been reduced over the years to their current levels of 5 rems per year for radiation workers and 170 millirems (1000 millrems = 1 rem) per year for the average citizen. The National Academy of Sciences continues to urge that the MPDs be lowered substantially, even though actual exposure of the general public is well below the current limit.

Table 6.11 Background Radiation and Other Chronic Sources of Radiation in the United States

Source	Dose (millirems per year except as noted)
Cosmic rays:	
Sea level	41
Denver (5000 ft)	70*
Leadville, Colorado area (10,500 ft)	160*
20,000 ft	400*
Commercial jet (35,000 ft)	0.7 millirems per hour
U.S. average from cosmic rays	44
γ Rays from rocks, soil—U.S. average	26
Internal radionuclides:	
^{40}K	16
^{14}C, Ra, and decay products	2
Total	18
Grand total U.S. environmental average gonadal dose (Oakley, 1972)	88 ± 11
Human-made sources:	
Fallout (1970)	4
Nuclear power	0.003
Medical diagnostic	72
Medical radiopharmaceuticals	1
Occupational	0.8
Miscellaneous	2

* These illustrate the shielding effect of the earth's atmosphere.

Radiation Hazards and Nuclear Energy. Measurements of radioactivity made in waters and areas surrounding correctly functioning nuclear power plants by state health departments, nuclear power facility operators, and the EPA have in most cases revealed *no* increase in environmental radiation near these plants. It has been estimated by many sources that, overall, nuclear power contributes insignificantly to background radiation. According to McBride et al. (1978), coal contains radioactive material and radiation doses from coal-burning electrical-generating plants may be greater than those from a properly operated nuclear plant. According to one source, nuclear power installations add no more than 0.0001 millirad per year to background radiation. But there is far from universal agreement on the significance of the radiation "leak" problem.

In 1979, two major National Academy of Sciences studies were made public. The studies indicated that nuclear power would account for some 2000 cancer deaths by the year 2000 (100 people per year). The projection was not arrived at easily or with complete agreement; five of the 16 commission members filed a dissenting opinion that the estimate was far too high.

Nuclear power proponents argue that the danger associated with nuclear power is greatly exaggerated. They argue that overly alarmist negative publicity has given the public an overwhelming distorted view of the past record. They claim that even educated people believe that nuclear power kills more people than automobile accidents. In actual fact, the number of deaths including cancer deaths related to nuclear power has so far been very small. Bernard Cohen (1983), physics professor at the University of Pittsburgh, points out that the 100 or so accidents from the transport of nuclear material, many of which were front page stories, produced less than a 1% chance of causing *one* death from escaped radiation. He points out that the historical record indicates that the risk from nuclear power to the average American is equivalent to the risk of smoking one cigarette in a lifetime, an overweight person gaining a fraction of one ounce, crossing the street one extra time every three years, or increasing the national speed limit to 55.003 mph.

Despite the fine points of the controversy, there *are* real reasons for concern. The fact that some radiation materials have extremely long half-lives militates in favor of a very careful and extensive consideration of all risk factors before nuclear power is allowed to proliferate beyond its present state. This becomes obvious when one considers the magnitude of the problem of what to do about nuclear waste.

The "Chronic" Problem of Radioactive Waste. The word "chronic" has a special meaning in connection with atomic wastes. **Plutonium**, one of the by-products of atomic fission, has a half-life in excess of 24,000 years. What this means is that half of the radioactivity in any given amount of plutonium will remain after 24,000 years; half of the remaining half will be around after another 24,000 years. Where do you put something you want to keep safely tucked away for 100,000 years or longer? Nuclear proponents argue that while it is true that radioactive wastes remain radioactive for thousands to hundreds of thousands of years, most of the harmful high-energy radiation will have been dissipated after a few hundred years (R. P. Hammond, 1979). Obviously, even if this point is conceded, the disposal of atomic waste is a serious problem, and despite the fact that waste is currently being generated in significant amounts the problem has not been solved. ("Significant" is a judgment word, and it refers in this context more to the nature of the waste than to its volume or weight. The U.S. Committee for Energy Awareness points out that the total volume of all of the high-level radioactive waste produced by all 80 of our nuclear power plants up to 1984 was equal to that of a rectangular solid as large as a tennis court 45 feet deep. Most of the radioactive waste we generate is generated by the military.)

Storing spent fuel rods under water at reactor sites is generally thought to be unsatisfactory. The reactor sites are simply not permanent enough. But what then? No matter where waste is put, that place will have to remain a repository for the waste in a relatively undisturbed condition, practically speaking, for all eternity. We know more about the world than to expect that things will stay the same for very long in any one particular place even on a human time scale, let alone on the geologic scales appropriate to radioactive waste. It is not surprising that many states have put the Department of Energy on notice that they will not welcome deep repositories or any other kinds of repositories of radioactive wastes within their borders. Between March 1977 and the spring of 1980, more than 15 states passed laws that had the effect of tightly controlling or banning the disposal of radioactive waste within their borders.

This "not me" chorus undoubtedly had something to do with the nature of the Nuclear Waste Policy Act passed by both houses of Congress in 1982 and signed by Ronald Reagan in January of

The China Syndrome: A Nuclear Meltdown

A **meltdown** is what could happen if a nuclear reactor core cooling system and all backup systems fail. The core would melt right through the floor of the reactor into the ground and "head in the general direction of China" (thus the term China Syndrome). The molten core would actually come to rest something less than 100 meters down as a boiling, seething mass of molten materials. Any water coming into contact with the molten core would be instantaneously converted into contaminated steam, which could carry radioactive gases and particles over a wide area. Radioactivity would cause water molecules to split into hydrogen and oxygen. This mixture could explode, possibly further rupturing the containment building and spreading even more radioactive material around.

The following scenario has been developed and expanded as the likely or possible consequence of a meltdown:

1. An area perhaps as large as several states would become contaminated.
2. Agricultural or human activity in the area might be restricted or forbidden altogether for thousands of years.
3. Five hundred thousand people might have to be evacuated from the immediate area; outside this range, another three and a half million people would have to restrict outdoor activities for a while to keep from receiving high doses of radiation.
4. Several thousand people would die from acute radiation exposure, and as many as 50,000 more might die later from radiation-induced cancer.
6. General panic and a hysterical state of affairs might exist for some time following an accident—perhaps leading to a shutdown of all nuclear power plants and numerous other unforeseen problems.

1983. The bill required the Department of Energy to nominate five sites as possibilities for the first permanent radioactive waste repository by January 1985 and a second group of five by 1989. The bill provided for interim federal storage sites until the permanent sites were selected and ready. A key provision in the bill is that states (and tribes) can object to the placement of a repository on their territories, but both houses of Congress can *override* the objection.

Environmental interests generally express unhappiness over the Nuclear Waste Policy Act, claiming (among other things) that safe forms of permanent storage have yet to be defined by the studies of storage techniques going on in the United States, West Germany, Sweden, Belgium, Australia, Canada, and elsewhere.

Although the method is not without controversy, some scientists and scientific bodies such as the National Academy of Sciences have expressed the belief that high-level nuclear waste blended into a glasslike material in a process called **vitrification** can safely be disposed in deep, geologically secure depositories thousands of feet underground. The Nuclear Waste Policy Act of 1982 itself specifically calls for lowering sealed-up waste in a glasslike or ceramiclike form about 2500 feet underground into the geological formations such as granite, basalt, or salt.

What About Old Reactors? Old reactors present a special kind of atomic waste problem (see Olson, 1984). Reactors have a lifetime of 20–40 years; they wear out and become obsolete. Already, 20 plants have been closed in the Western world, 15 in the United States and five in Western Europe. By the year 2000 there will be 100 inactive plants. It is claimed that it will be hundreds or even thousands of years before these plants cease being dangerously radioactive. This is a long time to resist the second law of thermodynamics. There are currently only three options—all imperfect—for dealing with closed plants: (1) mothballing (weld them shut and place them under guard); (2) entombment (bury them); and (3) dismantlement (and then do something safe with the hot parts).

Nuclear Power Plant Accidents. Quite apart from the consideration of low-level leaks of radiation from routinely operating nuclear plants is the spectre of the nuclear accident. It must be made clear that when nuclear accidents are discussed, it is *not* an atomic explosion as in a nuclear bomb that is feared. Atomic power plants cannot explode like an atom bomb. There is some finite possibility of a meltdown, however (see Bonus 6.2).

A U.S. government report published in 1975, commissioned by the then Atomic Energy Commission and generally known as the Rasmussen Report (the study was directed by Norman Rasmussen), concluded that there was essentially no chance of an atomic power plant disaster. In January 1979, some two months before the Three Mile Island accident, the Nuclear Regulatory Commission (NRC) declared the Rasmussen report to be misleading and

In 20–40 years when this plant is obsolete, what will society do with it?

unreliable and stated that the risk was probably higher.

In a report released late in 1982 (done by Sandia Labs for the NRC) the worst possible nuclear accident was projected to take more than 100,000 lives and cost $300 billion dollars. The study projected that the possibility of a meltdown and failure of all safety systems was about 1 in 100,000 reactor years—a 2% chance that such an event would happen before the year 2000. The study went on to point out that the consequences would be much less severe in *most* of the locations where there are functional nuclear power plants. The highest death toll would occur if such an accident occurred at Salem, New Jersey (102,000 early deaths); the greatest damage would occur if the meltdown happened at Indian Point 3 Reactor on the Hudson River ($314 billion).

In the 1950s the U.S. Senate passed the Price Anderson Act, which exempts facilities engaged in nuclear power generation from liability for accidents and guarantees that the government would pay up to $560 million to help take care of nuclear accidents. This act did little to inspire public confidence in the safety of nuclear power. In late 1983 the NRC recommended to Congress that the limit on the utilities' liability for damages resulting from an accident at a commercial atomic power plant be lifted and that the statute of limitations be increased from 20 to 30 years.

Naturally, since nuclear engineers have long been aware of the possibility of a meltdown, there are multiple safeguards in nuclear power plants to prevent them. There are backup cooling systems; containment buildings are designed to hold fission products in place; and there are neutron-absorbing materials that can be inserted into the core automatically to turn off the fission reaction.

There has never been a full-scale meltdown as far as we know, but there have been a few close calls and at least one partial melt. There have certainly been some accidents. According to a report by Klaus Hopfner in *Nature* (1979), the principal environmental protection groups in Germany (Bundesverband Bürgerinitiativen Umweltschutz) claimed —on the basis of data gleaned from the files of the German Reaction Safety Society—that an incident or accident occurred in German nuclear plants every three days from 1977 to 1979. There have been many relatively minor escapes of radioactivity from plants in the United States and in other countries as well. And, of course, there was the Three Mile Island accident (see Bonus 6.3).

Some say that the Three Mile Island plant came close to a meltdown. Technically, it was a *partial* meltdown, since about 1% of the metal cladding that holds the uranium fuel pellets melted. The Three Mile Island problem started when the cooling system failed, and this was followed by a compounding of human errors, mechanical collapses, bad luck, design flaws, and administrative negligence. There was a real threat of a hydrogen explosion, and some radiation was vented into the environment. No one was seriously overexposed to radiation, injured, or killed at Three Mile Island, but there were some major consequences.

— The President of the United States (Jimmy Carter) appointed an investigative commission,

Three Mile Island

In terms of its negative impact on the development of nuclear power worldwide, and in terms of how close it came to unequivocal disaster, it was the worst commercial nuclear accident in U.S. history. The story is still fresh in most memories. On March 28, 1979, at Three Mile Island near Harrisburg, Pennsylvania, the failure of a faulty water pump in a nuclear reactor and then the malfunction of a valve were followed by a chain of further mechanical and human failures. The results were the release of radioactive water from the emergency cooling system into the Susquehanna River; the venting of radioactive steam into the atmosphere; the conversion of water into hydrogen gas, which raised the possibility of an explosion; and, for a time, a very real danger of a reactor meltdown (see Bonus 6.2). The accident released some radioactivity that would have resulted in a dose of only about 70 millirads (see Table 6.11) of radiation to an individual at the plant boundary (half the allowable annual exposure to a member of the general public). Some experts claim that the radiation that eventually did escape was never a threat to health. Others have warned that there will yet be cancers, genetic defects, and other long-term outcomes. The net effect of the accident in terms of danger to health is still a subject of controversy. The cleanup, which is expected to cost $1.5 billion dollars, was incomplete six years after the accident.

---

which found that the main problems were bureaucratic complacency regarding departures from standard safety and maintenance procedures and insufficient operator training. The report was critical of the NRC and actually recommended that it be abolished and replaced, a recommendaton that was not carried out. The commission made numerous additional recommendations regarding operator training, nuclear plant siting, evacuation plans, and operating procedures, nearly all of which have been and are being implemented.

— The cleanup was still going on as of 1985 and is expected to cost more than a billion dollars.
— We have learned that even nonlethal nuclear accidents are very difficult to deal with.
— The Tennessee Valley Authority ordered a review of the design and modes of operation of all its nuclear facilities.
— There were stepped-up efforts to scrutinize construction and to block the construction of nuclear power plants in Phoenix, Sacramento, Cincinnati, Madison (Indiana), and Hannover, West Germany. Some of this eventually led to discontinuation of projects.

There have been other incidents since the Three Mile Island accident. In February 1983 the Salem 1 reactor in New Jersey failed to stop a fission reaction when ordered to do so by a safety control system—something that was supposed to happen only once in a million reactor years. This was the *third* record of such an occurrence in commercial nuclear history. While very few of the accidents associated with atomic power have caused any problems, they have had a combined devastating effect on public confidence and comfort with nuclear power.

Public Opinion. Nuclear energy has become a social issue. We have all seen pictures of, heard about, or maybe even gotten involved in the protests. People have picketed, held rallies, and even placed themselves in front of cement trucks, trying to halt the construction of nuclear power plants throughout the world. There is a clear negative public attitude toward nuclear power that had already become a significant factor in the proliferation of nuclear power plants even before the Three Mile Island accident. The attitude of a large sector of the public is perhaps summed up best by Dr. Hannes Alfvén (1972), who says,

> Fission energy is safe only if a number of critical devices work as they should, if a number of people in key positions follow all their instructions, if there is no sabotage, no hijacking of the transports, if no reactor fuel processing plant or repository anywhere in the world is situated in a region of riots or guerrilla activity, and no revolution of war— even a "conventional" one—takes place in these regions. The enormous quantities of extremely dangerous material must not get into the hand of ignorant people or desperados. No acts of God can be permitted.

Well-informed scientists can be found on both sides of the nuclear question. Proponents cite the need for atomic energy "if our way of life is to be maintained" and the relatively good safety record of the nuclear industry. The "on-the-other-hand" opponents claim that:

1. Small amounts of radioactivity may well leak into the air and water, and we do not know what effects these low levels of radiation will have on the incidence of diseases like cancer.

NUCLEAR POWER: Perhaps the final solution to the earth's energy problem.

The negative public attitude toward atomic energy is often reflected in the work of editorial cartoonists. (A) Don Wright, Miami News. (B) H. Haynie, The Courier Journal. Reprinted with permission.

2. There is no safe, permanent system for disposal of nuclear wastes at the present time.
3. The probability of meltdown, even if small, is intolerable.
4. We really do not have good systems for preventing the diversion of nuclear material into the wrong hands (terrorist groups), which could lead to blackmail or even to the destruction of whole cities.

It is generally conceded that almost anyone can make a nuclear explosive once he or she has a critical amount of uranium or plutonium 239—about 10 or 11 pounds. **Uranium** occurs naturally in many deposits throughout the world, but it must be enriched before it can be used in a bomb. Plutonium is made in nuclear reactors as a by-product of nuclear fission. For a long time the U.S. government has been reluctant to let commercial enterprises reprocess reactor fuel elements to extract plutonium from them for fear that this would increase access to plutonium by groups and individuals with mayhem on their minds. Likewise, opposition to the breeder reactor is often based on its potential for increasing the amount of ^{239}P available for subversive activities.

The Status of Nuclear Energy in America

The U.S. nuclear power industry is in trouble. After a fast start, things have pretty much ground to a halt. Worldwide, some 300 nuclear plants now generate electricity; 200 more are under construction. In the United States there are 82 plants at some level of operation. According to an Atomic Industrial Forum, Inc. survey, U.S. nuclear generating capacity was about 81,000 megawatts in 1984. If all 50 of the U.S. plants then under construction eventually come on line, our nuclear power should double by 1990.

This may be impressive, but it is far short of the 1200 nuclear power plants projected for the United States by the year 2000 as recently as *1970* (see Figure 6.33).

Between 1972 and 1982, 100 nuclear power plants under constuction or on order were canceled at a total cost of 10 billion dollars (U.S. Department of Energy, 1984a). Six plants were canceled in 1983. Only two of the plants ordered in the ten-year period ending in 1985 have *not* subsequently been canceled. The Tennessee Valley Authority (TVA) offered to sell eight nuclear reactors to China in April 1984, all left over from plant cancellations in 1982. Most recently, the half-finished Marble-Hill plant in Indiana was canceled with some 2.8 billion dollars already spent; and after $1.7 billion had been spent, the Zimmer nuclear power plant near Cincinnati was marked for conversion to a coal-fired plant at a cost of another $1.7 billion. These actions have had a chilling effect on an industry already in trouble. There have been no new orders for nuclear plants since 1978. Although the pace of nuclear power development has slackened in some other countries as well, nuclear power abroad has flourished in comparison to that in the United States (see Figure 6.34). The question is—why?

In its annual report to Congress in 1983 the Department of Energy cited five principal factors responsible for the demise of nuclear power in the United States:

1. Lower forecasted growth in the demand for electricity.
2. High interest rates and other constraints on long-term financing.
3. Reversal in nuclear power's cost advantage over coal in many places.

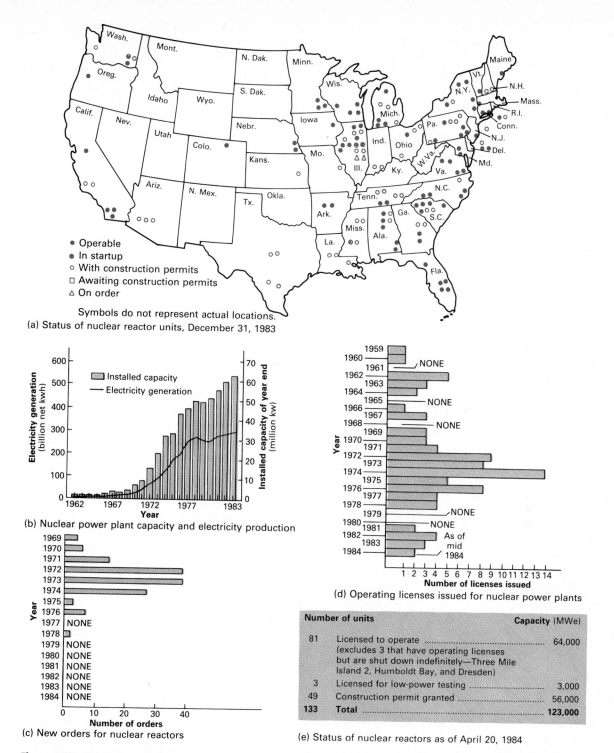

Operable
In startup
With construction permits
Awaiting construction permits
On order

Symbols do not represent actual locations.

(a) Status of nuclear reactor units, December 31, 1983

(b) Nuclear power plant capacity and electricity production

(c) New orders for nuclear reactors

(d) Operating licenses issued for nuclear power plants

Number of units		Capacity (MWe)
81	Licensed to operate .... (excludes 3 that have operating licenses but are shut down indefinitely—Three Mile Island 2, Humboldt Bay, and Dresden)	64,000
3	Licensed for low-power testing	3,000
49	Construction permit granted	56,000
133	**Total**	**123,000**

(e) Status of nuclear reactors as of April 20, 1984

Figure 6.33 The Status of Nuclear Power. (a) The location of proposed, planned, and operational nuclear power plants in the U.S. as of December 31, 1983. (b) There has been an increase in the generation of electricity by nuclear power in recent decades. But (c) the record of new orders for nuclear power plants and (d) new operating licenses issued suggests that this will level off and may even decline in the future. (e) The status of nuclear power generation.

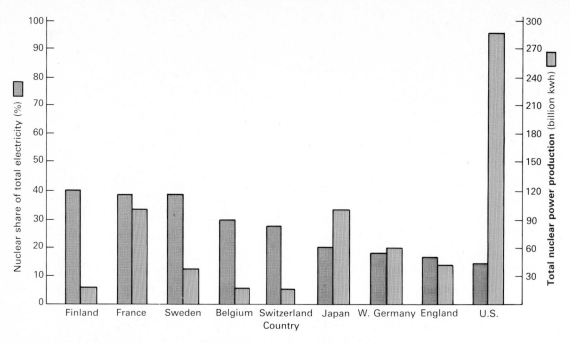

Figure 6.34 Total Electricity Generated by Nuclear Power in 1982, by Country.

4. Changes in and uncertainties about the regulatory climate.
5. Denials of nuclear power plant certification by some states.

The U.S. Office of Technology Assessment issued a report in 1984 that came to the same general conclusions. Items 2, 3, 4, and 5 on the above list are related to one another and can ultimately be traced to an overwhelming decline in public confidence in nuclear power.

While the Office of Technology Assessment's 1984 report concluded that government regulation had little to do with the nuclear industry's problems, the NRC itself accepted some of the blame. In an April 1984 report the NRC said that it failed to screen utility companies closely enough to determine whether they were competent to deal with the complexities of nuclear power.

France and Switzerland have single companies or organizations developing plants. In Japan, only a few companies are involved in nuclear power plant construction and operation. While the pattern in these countries has tended to generate standard designs, dozens of U.S. utilities have gotten into the act, each "inventing wheels" in its own way.

Inexperience with nuclear power by utilities and by construction companies and changing federal regulations have, no doubt, contributed to the nu-clear industry's problems. In Japan it takes five years to build a plant; here it takes ten. With interest rates as they are, delays mean huge costs. The Zimmer plant, to give just one example, was budgeted at 240 million dollars in 1969; by 1984 it would have cost a total of 3.1 billion dollars to complete.

All of this raises the question, What is the future of nuclear energy in the United States?

The Future of Nuclear Energy in the U.S.

Public opinion and the events of recent times will preclude the headlong development of nuclear power that was once envisioned, and the future of nuclear fission is nowhere near as bright as it once was. The limited world reserves of ^{235}U used in conventional nuclear fission reactors makes fission a stopgap measure for energy production until other sources are developed. Any long-range energy strategy should depict *conventional* fission as being phased out. The fate of the breeder reactor lies in the answer to the question, Is it worth the risk of making plutonium more plentiful? For both conventional fission and the breeder the question remains, What about the wastes? While nuclear fusion would have considerably fewer of these problems, its barriers are primarily technological. Perhaps fusion holds the most promise for the long-range future of nuclear power. Logic may not dictate what will happen with nuclear energy. Unknown variables and intangibles appear to be the controlling factors. Public pressure and safety considerations are two of the most important intangible factors. Their influence is variable and in the future will be determined in part by the perceived risks associated with the use of other energy sources (including the risk of dependence on foreign oil). Another important factor is economics. This is equally variable. The capital cost per kilowatt went up twice as fast for nuclear plants as for coal plants during the 1970s (Lewis, 1980). Because of the uncertainties surrounding nuclear plants, utilities have been, and are likely to continue to be, reluctant to invest in atomic power.

In summary, nuclear power has an uncertain place in our energy future. Technological breakthroughs in waste management and in fusion would improve its future, as would steps to improve public confidence. But, for the moment anyway, the main question, to which there are many different responses, is, What is the rush—and is it worth it?

HYDROELECTRIC POWER

The electricity generated via turbines as water passes through holes in dams is really a form of solar energy. Hydroelectric power generation takes advantage of that portion of the hydrologic cycle in which the water is flowing back to its lowest point after the sun lifts it into the atmosphere by evaporation and it returns to the earth as precipitation. According to various sources, somewhat less than 20% of the world's hydroelectric capacity is currently being tapped. Overall, about 40% of the generating capacity of hydroelectric power in the United States had been developed by 1975.

Hydroelectric power is not without negative environmental impacts, and there have been controversies over almost every dam built in the United States in the last several decades. The lakes created behind hydroelectric dams cover land, including good agricultural bottom land, and all ecosystems behind dams are altered, including the aquatic one. Deep lakes with low flows simply support different aquatic ecosystems than do "wild" rivers. Also, the development costs of hydroelectric projects are relatively high. This is partly because the life of such projects is limited by the tendency of dams to fill up with silt.

Various informed sources indicate that despite the fact that a significant percentage of hydroelectric potential has yet to be developed in the United States, this will be done slowly if at all because (1)

Developing hydoelectric resources is limited by the financial and environmental costs of constructing dams and reservoirs.

the major sites close to population centers have already been developed and (2) the costs of establishing reservoirs is high in comparison to the benefits received. It is generally expected that the relative contribution of hydroelectric power to the total U.S. energy budget will decrease in the years ahead.

GEOTHERMAL ENERGY

Geothermal energy is energy derived from the heat of the earth itself. The earth has the basic structure illustrated in Figure 6.35. The central core is very hot; on the average the temperature increases about 1°C for every 100-foot drop from the surface. This is an average, however, and in some places the temperature increases much more sharply. In some locations it is very hot very near the surface. The world has some 600 active volcanoes, nearly all of which are located in the ring of fire around the perimeter of the Pacific Ocean from Asia to the west coasts of North and South America. In these locations, molten lava and the heat from the earth's core come close enough to the surface to be useful in generating electrical energy. In the United States it is believed that Hawaii and Alaska, particularly the Aleutian Island chain, are good possibilities. Where geothermal hot spots come into contact with near-

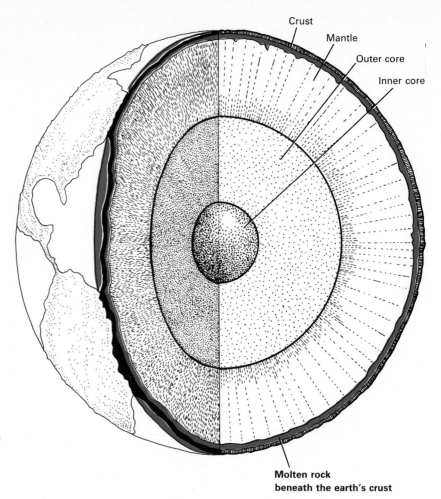

Crust

Mantle

Outer core

Inner core

Figure 6.35 The Structure of the Earth. The heat in the earth's core and mantle is another source of energy that can be tapped to provide power.

Molten rock beneath the earth's crust

surface water, the result is hot springs and geysers, which can be tapped directly as steam. Hot water reservoirs can also be reached by drilling.

There are actually two types of subsurface geothermal fields; one is the hot water type to which we have just referred, and the other is the dry, hot rock that could be used to heat piped-in water. Although there would obviously be the problem of keeping the hot water from cooling on the way out of the earth, it is believed that wherever there is dry, hot rock within 25,000 feet, systems are technically feasible whereby water can be injected down to the rocks, converted to steam, and then brought back up as steam to drive turbines. One of the beauties of this suggestion is that it will require hardly any new technologies; we already have drilling rigs that can reach at least that far.

Some new technology might be needed to develop the so-called hydrofracturing method to pro-

duce porous areas in which water can be heated as it passes through (see A. L. Hammond, 1973; see also Figure 6.36). Hydrofracturing is a technique in which water is injected into the heated layers of rock at 7000 pounds of pressure per square inch, cracking the rock over a large area. The idea would then be to infuse or inject into these cracks some sort of agent that would keep the hole open and allow water to be pumped through the cracks from the bottom and recovered as steam from the top. It is believed that such hot rock could be used to heat water for many years before cooling off and that the cost of building and operating hydrofracture geothermal plants would be somewhat less than that of conventional power plants burning coal.

There is some disagreement about the environmental problems related to geothermal energy, and controversy still rages over how extensive this source of energy really is. Axtmann (1975) reviewed some of the problems, which include the chemical (and even thermal) wastes that would be brought to the surface as geothermal power is tapped. He cites experience with New Zealand's Wairakei geothermal plant, which produces about six and a half times as much heat, five and a half times as much water vapor, and about half as much sulfur pollution per unit of power produced as coal-fired electric generating plants. Axtmann admits that the plant in New Zealand is an old one and uses out of date technology, but his review does suggest that there may well be environmental problems in the use of geothermal energy that must be taken into account in any projection about the use of this source of energy in the future.

The significance of geothermal energy in the overall picture is somewhat uncertain at the moment. In a cooperative, U.S. government/Union Oil project at the Baca geothermal field in New Mexico there have been numerous drilling problems and problems in finding porous areas with enough hot water to supply even a single power plant. Similar problems have been encountered in "La Primavera"

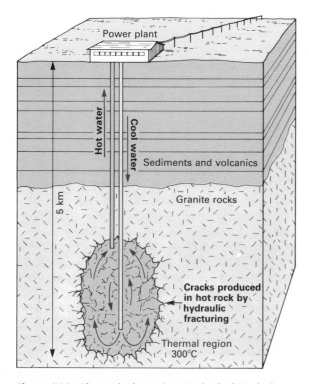

Figure 6.36 The Hydrofracturing Method of Producing Steam in Hot, Dry Rock. Water forced into the hot rocks causes cracking. Some agent (e.g., beads or grains) holds the cracks apart. Water can then be pumped through the cracks, and steam is produced to be recovered at the top and used to generate power.

field in Mexico. Finding porous strata in which to reinject spent water has been a problem in many geothermal fields. Some say the hot rock is much more prevalent and much closer to the surface of the earth in many places than was previously thought. Places where geothermal energy is being explored include Albuquerque, El Paso, and Klamath Falls (Oregon), as well as other locations in Hawaii, Alaska, South Dakota, Louisiana, and Texas. Geothermal energy has been used for years in scattered locations such as Iceland and parts of Idaho. While geothermal energy may well make significant contributions in these and other locations in the future, it will not contribute much to the overall energy needs of the world.

ENERGY FROM BIOMASS

Green plants are natural solar collectors that convert solar energy into chemical energy as plant matter. Wood and other plant materials are therefore forms of solar energy. Since coal and oil are formed from plant matter, they are also forms of solar energy. Yet while wood is considered a *renewable* energy source, coal and oil are considered *nonrenewable*. Why? The difference has to do with the time required for coal and oil to form—literally millions of years. In terms of energy the important thing going on during these millions of years is that chemical energy is being *concentrated*. Terrestrial plants have a mean energy content of about five kwh per kilogram dry weight; petroleum products have the equivalent of slightly less than 12 kwh per kilogram (Bjork and Graneli, 1978); coal has the equivalent of about nine kwh per kilogram. All of this suggests a strategy of using plant mass or **biomass** as energy. The trade-off involved would be using fuel with a lower energy content (having more weight to handle) in exchange for its being renewable and available relatively immediately.

Far from being a new idea, biomass has been used as fuel for centuries, its most familiar form being firewood. In some places, biomass as firewood is still heavily exploited today. In fact it is probably fair to say that *most* human beings in the world still rely on biomass for their energy needs. According to D. Hayes (1977) and many others, biomass directly derived from photosynthesis may have a significant role to play in providing energy on a worldwide basis in the future. There have been various proposals, some involving the deliberate cultivation of plants to be used for fuel (**energy farming**) and some involving the use of waste or scrap biomass.

A proposal for the use of the common reed as fuel and a description of some of the spin-off benefits of large-scale reed cultivation for the purpose of generating energy are given by Bjork and Graneli (1978) (see Figure 6.37). Various other common and trou-

If some of this municipal refuse could be used for biomass energy, two problems would be lessened.

blesome plants have been discussed as possibilities; some of these include the water hyacinth and certain varieties of algae (D. Hayes, 1977).

There are still other sources of biomass. Perhaps the most advantageous source is waste in municipal refuse and agricultural and forestry residues. Pimentel et al. (1981) claim that residues after forest and agricultural crop production amount to nearly one fifth of the total of U.S. biomass production with a gross heat energy equivalent of 12% of the fuel consumed annually in the United States. They estimate that only about one fifth of this is potentially harvestable and usable, but this is still equivalent to a significant fraction of our electrical energy consumption.

Alcohols from Biomass

Biomass can be burned directly, or it can be converted to other forms of fuel. Two related examples of liquid fuels derivable from biomass are *methanol* (CH_3OH) (wood alcohol) and *ethanol* (CH_3CH_2OH) (grain alcohol).

The nice thing about methanol is that it can be made from almost any kind of existing fuel. It can be made from fossil fuels as well as from a number of forms of biomass ranging from wood harvested es-

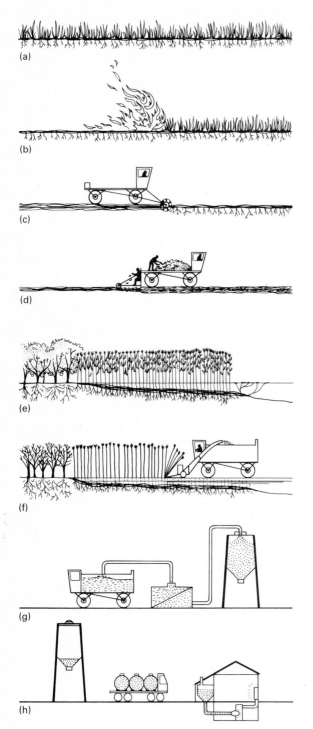

(a)
(b)
(c)
(d)
(e)
(f)
(g)
(h)

Figure 6.37 Biomass in Energy Production. A Scheme for Cultivating the Common Reed as a Source of Energy. (a) Drained lake or wetland overgrown by sedges, (b) cutting and collection or direct burning of sedge detritus, (c) destruction of sedge root and preparation of the bottom by roto-cultivator, (d) planting of reed rhizome pieces, (e) establishment of reed plantation combined with wildlife management, (f) reed harvesting during the winter, (g) grinding of chopped reed stems in a mill, (h) transport of a powder for heating purposes.

pecially for the conversion to the cellulose-based scrap in municipal, agricultural, and forestry wastes (Figure 6.38).

Ethanol is produced in other forms of bioconversion. Just as yeast makes ethanol from grape juice, a variety of anaerobic microbes, including yeast, can make ethanol from sugar (Figure 6.39) and other carbon compounds. Many of us have used this energy product in **gasohol**, a mixture of gasoline and ethanol.

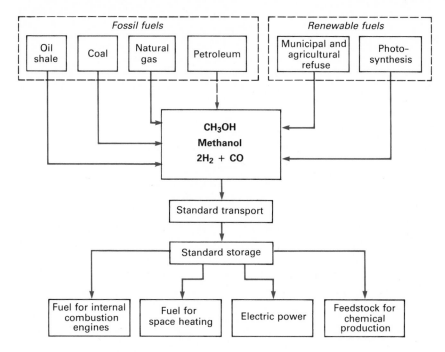

Figure 6.38 Some Sources and Uses of Methanol.

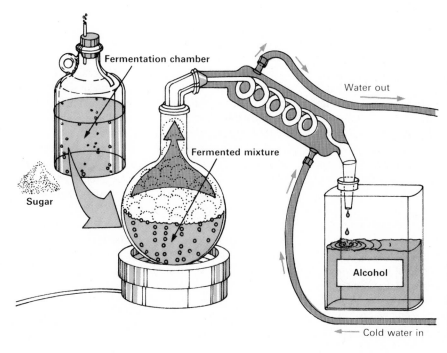

Figure 6.39 The Efficiency of Alcoholic Fermentation Producing Alcohol as a Liquid Fuel. It is claimed that the conversion is relatively efficient. The reader can calculate cost efficiency based on current prices of sugar and gasoline.

Natural "Gas"

A company in Oklahoma is reported to already be manufacturing gas from cow manure. The methane (CH_4) produced in this way can be used in the same way as natural gas. According to one estimate, if all manure produced in the United States every year by our cattle and hogs were used to produce this kind of energy, it could provide 5% of our total gas consumption. Of course, there is no way that *all* manure could be used for this purpose. In theory, it would take about 30 head of cattle to supply the heat needs of an average household. Sewage and other wastes can also be fermented to yield usable gas (see Chapter 12).

Petroleum from Plants

Certain shrubs have sap containing hydrocarbons similar to those found in petroleum. Calvin (1979) claims to have demonstrated the economic feasibility of producing oil from hydrocarbon-producing species of the genus *Euphorbia*. These plants are especially appealing because they grow in semiarid areas and thus are not in competition with food crops.

Energy Balances for Biomass Conversion

It takes energy to grow biomass. In the conversion of biomass deliberately grown for energy—corn into ethanol for gasohol, for example—a key question is, Can more energy be gotten out than is put in (in the forms of fertilizer, pesticides, and gasoline)?

Chambers et al. (1979) conclude that if *conventional* agricultural techniques and *conventional* distillation techniques are used, the net energy balance for gasohol production and use is negative—more energy has to be put in than is gotten out. They acknowledge that with some generous assumptions concerning energy-efficient agricultural practices and using crop residues there *could* be a "modestly positive energy balance." They also acknowledge that if the goal is to produce fuel that can substitute for petroleum and if more plentiful fuels such as coal provide the energy to produce gasohol, energy from biomass might not be a bad idea. Even with this, however, gasohol turns out to be a rather inefficient method of converting coal to liquid fuel.

Da Silva et al. (1978) report "very favorable" energy balances for the conversion of sugar cane and sorghum to alcohol. They emphasize the importance of evaluating specific crops *individually*. Calvin (1979) points out that sugar cane is one of the world's most efficient converters of solar energy into chemical energy and indicates that sugar cane can be converted to alcohol with very little energy loss. He drives home his point by describing a sugar plantation as a completely energy self-sufficient system. The waste remaining after sugar juice is extracted can be burned, yielding more than enough steam to generate all the electricity needed to run the sugar mill and the fermentation process and to generate the fertilizer required for sugar cane production. Still, Calvin admits that the United States cannot grow enough sugar cane on the scale required to end our dependence on foreign oil.

Advantages, Problems, and Disadvantages with Biomass as Fuel

Several advantages are commonly cited in using biomass for energy. For one thing, some of the starting materials already exist, unused, in some cases amounting to waste disposal problems. The chief advantage is that biomass is a *renewable* energy source. Neither the use of waste biomass nor the use of biomass derived from energy farms is without problems and limitations, however.

Pimentel et al. (1978) conclude that the potential for biomass conversion from waste and energy farming is quite limited. Acknowledging that the total harvest of agricultural and forestry products amounts to 5.8×10^{15} kcal of net energy (equal to 32% of our fossil fuel consumption), Pimentel and colleagues (1984) report that biomass-derived energy currently amounts to only 3% of the total energy consumption in the United States. However, they project that biomass *could* provide as much as 11% of gross U.S. energy by the year 2000.

The prospect of large-scale agricultural production of biomass materials to be used as sources of gaseous and liquid forms of energy raises many important questions relative to the environment. The large amounts of land needed would raise many land–use questions, not the least significant of which would be, Should land now used for food production, in a world short of food, be used to grow "energy" in a world short of *energy*? The use of marginal or otherwise currently unused lands would bring with it various environmental problems such as habitat destruction and erosion (see Chapter 17). Energy farms will, in either case, tend to produce the same kinds of environmental problems found in other types of agricultural or forestry production, namely, erosion, ecosystem simplification, ecosystem disruption, and fertilizer runoff. Collecting, transporting, processing, and ultimately burning biomass will generate air pollution and other pollution problems as well (see Pimentel et al., 1984).

In summary, it can be said that both biomass produced for fuel and biomass wastes can be converted into easily handled fuels such as methane, methanol, ethanol, and even powders. While this is an interesting possibility, one that might provide some *fraction* of our energy needs in the future, the potential of this source is not known. There have as yet been no large-scale tests of such energy systems that would indicate cost and technical difficulty. Energy farming would have much the same environmental impact as food farming and forestry, and there may well be environmental impacts yet to be discovered.

OTHER ENERGY SOURCES

There are two kinds of other energy sources. First, there are sources that have yet to be imagined or conceived. While there are sure to be novel energy sources and novel ways of extracting energy from old sources in the future, we obviously cannot describe them. Another category is really a miscellaneous category. It includes some old sources and some new sources, none of which are likely to provide anything more than a small fraction of our overall energy needs in the future. Three of the latter are wind, ocean thermal gradients, and tides.

Wind

It has long been known that fanlike structures can be used to harness the wind. Relatively recently, it has been discovered that such structures can actually drive turbines and generate electricity. The advantages of wind energy conversion are that the wind is free and does not pollute. The chief disadvantages of wind-derived energy are that wind is intermittent and there is not much of it in many places. Environmental problems are relatively minor, but they do include visual pollution, hazards to airplanes and migrating birds, noise, and interference with television and radio. Already a number of experimental wind generators have been built, and other projects are now on the drawing boards. Money being spent in the United States on this type of wind turbine research is now in the tens of millions of dollars annually. Feasibility studies by the Department of Energy (DOE) in cooperation with the National Aeronautics and Space Administration (NASA) have shown that prototype wind-driven generators can produce enough electricity for 30 homes in a 14 mph wind. In 1979 a 150-foot wind

The blades on the world's largest wind turbine, in North Carolina, are as long as the wing span of a Boeing 707.

turbine boasting 100-foot blades able to produce 2000 kilowatts of electricity (enough for 500 homes) at an ideal wind speed of 25 mph began operation in Boone, N.C. The structure funded by DOE and NASA cost $5.8 million.

NASA has optimistically predicted that wind turbines may one day provide as much as 10% of the electrical power needs of the United States—perhaps as soon as the year 2000 (Wade, 1974). More recent estimates are much lower, ranging from 10% down to a fraction of a percent.

Ocean Thermal Energy

It has been suggested that vertical temperature gradients within the oceans can be harnessed with devices like the one shown in Figure 6.40. The device would work as follows: In a reservoir at the top, warm water would evaporate. The increase in pressure resulting from the conversion of the liquid to a gas would push vapor past the turbine blades, rotating them as the vapor moved toward a lower, cooler area of the system, where the gas would condense into a liquid in a vapor sink. Meanwhile, more liquid would move toward the top and evaporate. This would be, in effect, a closed system. Figure 6.40b is an artist's conception of a structure proposed by Lockheed's Ocean Systems Division in Sunnyvale, California. The structure includes a platform with area quarters. Attached around the outside are turbine generators and pumps. The proposed structure is 250 feet in diameter and 1600 feet long and would weigh 300,000 tons. In theory, such a structure in the right location could supply the power needed by a city of 100,000 residents.

The Department of Energy is evaluating the feasibility of this nonpolluting renewable (solar, really) resource. The idea is appealing because the oceans cover seven tenths of the earth's surface and absorb enormous amounts of solar energy. The National Academy of Sciences has looked into the matter and has determined that while the concept is technologically feasible, there are numerous developmental problems to be overcome. Because seawater is extremely corrosive, for example, corrosion will be a big technological problem.

Tidal Power

Tidal energy was used as early as the eleventh century along the Atlantic coasts of France, Britain, and other Western European countries (Dorf, 1978). Despite the fact that there are several prototype generating stations in the world using the power of tides, this form of energy generation is not likely to be very significant in the future.

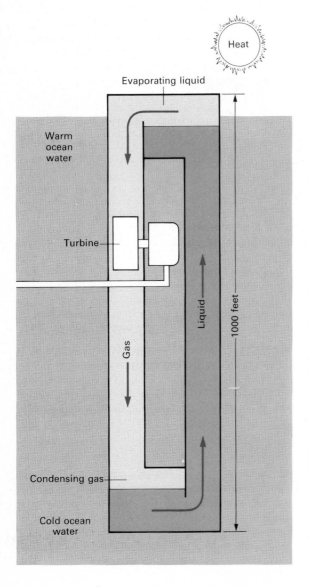

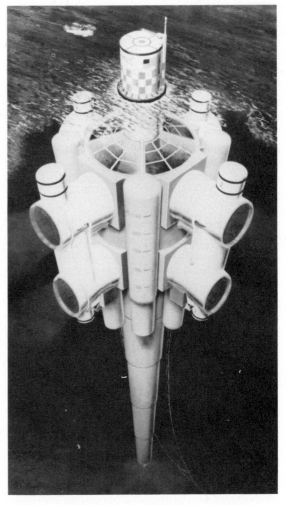

Figure 6.40   Ocean Thermal Energy. The photograph and accompanying diagram show a device to convert ocean temperature gradients into electricity.

Tides are produced by the gravitational effects resulting from the interaction between the earth, moon, and sun. The magnitude of tides varies in cycles depending on the relative positions of the earth, moon, and sun. Tidal power is harnessed by taking advantage of the moving of water in and out of bays much like the generation of power in a hydroelectric dam.

According to various sources, the total potential rate of energy extraction from tides in shallow seas (where the tides are greatest and where the energy is most accessible) is just a little over a billion kilowatts. Only a small fraction of this could be harnessed with existing technology. The chief advantages of tidal power are that it is clean and free; the chief disadvantages are that (1) it is expensive to build and maintain the structures to harness the free energy and (2) building dams across harbors or inlets would create navigational problems.

After indicating that the potential of waves, tides, currents, and salt and temperature gradients *could* provide energy on a "significant scale," Isaacs and Schmitt (1980) conclude that the most important relationship of the oceans to power needs will continue to be the use of seawater for cooling and possibly the use of the sea floor for disposal of nuclear wastes. This fairly accurately sums up the prospects of ocean-derived energy—at least as it stands now.

THE PROSPECTS OF IMPROVED ENERGY STORAGE AND ENERGY TRANSMISSION

Once energy is produced, by whatever means, it must be delivered or stored until it is needed. Electricity will become more important as a delivery form of energy in the future, but for the moment a major technological problem relative to electricity is storage. Storage of electricity is important for two reasons. One is that electricity generated via some of the newer forms of energy—solar energy and wind, for example—is available only intermittently. Quite simply, if solar- and wind-derived electricity are to go far, provision will have to be made for energy needs at night and when the wind is not blowing. A second need for storage is related to the facts that demand for electricity is intermittent and some types of electrical generation produce electricity best at relatively constant rates; nuclear energy is a notable example.

Electricity as such cannot be stored. To be stored, electrical energy must first be converted into some other energy form such as chemical energy—

in a battery, for example. Another alternative would be to pump water uphill and to allow it to come back through turbines during periods of peak demand. Because of the second law of thermodynamics, much energy will be lost as these transfers take place.

Hydrogen as Stored Electricity

Electricity can be used to split water molecules (H_2O) into hydrogen (H_2) and oxygen (O_2) gas. Hydrogen generated in this way can be saved and used later as a fuel, in effect amounting to a way of storing electrical energy.

Hydrogen is a flammable material that can exist as a gas or a liquid under various conditions of temperature and pressure. Hydrogen gas has about one third fewer BTUs per cubic foot than natural gas; however, liquid hydrogen has a much higher energy content than gasoline. Thus if a way were found to produce it cheaply, hydrogen would represent a useful form of energy, one that would be adaptable to many of the ways in which we use energy today.

It should be no surprise that it takes more energy to produce energy in the form of hydrogen than one would get if hydrogen were burned. Hydrogen is a means of improved storage and transmission; it is not a primary solution to the energy crisis. If we were to substitute electrically derived hydrogen only for natural gas, for example, the demand for hydrogen would require four times as much electrical power as we now generate in the United States.

A major disadvantage to the use of hydrogen is that it is explosive. The major advantage of hydrogen is that it pollutes very little when it is burned; it simply reverts back to water when combined with oxygen, sometimes producing small amounts of nitrogen oxide pollution. Because it can be transported as a gas or a liquid, hydrogen is relatively inexpensive to transport, and it is much more efficiently transported than electricity.

Electrical Transmission in the Future

Another major problem with electrical energy is the inefficiency of transmission lines. Transmission lines also have a certain amount of danger associated with them. As we discussed earlier, over half of the energy used to generate electricity is lost in generation and transmission inefficiency. In the future we will look for more underground transmission of electrical energy and for the development of more superconducting materials that can transmit electricity with minimal losses of energy. We also look for improved ways of generating electricity so as to reduce waste heat.

CONSERVATION IN OUR ENERGY FUTURE

We learned two fundamental principles about efficiency of energy utilization by living systems in Chapter 2. One of these principles was that the shorter the energy chain, the more energy is available to the elements in the chain (Figure 6.41). More energy, as you recall, is available to primary produc-

ers than to consumers. Another principle we illuminated in Chapter 2 was that energy efficiencies are variable. Some living things are more efficient than others. Extending these fundamental principles to the human condition, we find that the use of energy in the form of fossil fuels by civilization is subject to the second law of thermodynamics just as is energy use by the primary and secondary consumers in an ecosystem.

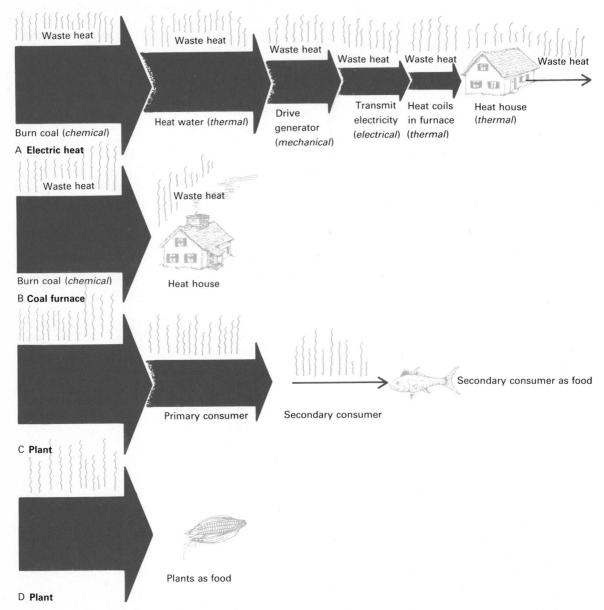

Figure 6.41   The Energy Chain. The shorter the chain of energy transfer, the fewer energy conversions and the less energy waste. This is true for ecosystems and for the uses that civilizations make of energy. Which is best in terms of heating a house, A or B? Which is better for providing food energy, C or D?

Efficiency is obviously central to the issue of energy utilization by human beings. We have already seen that nearly half of the energy released in the burning of fossil fuel ends up serving no useful purpose whatsoever. It is wasted. The purpose of this section is to consider the possibility, plausibility, and potential significance of energy conservation—doing less and doing it more efficiently.

Energy Efficiency Around the World

A comparison of the efficiencies of energy use throughout the world suggests that the potential for energy conservation in some countries is very great. The United States is the world's outstanding example of energy inefficiency. Many nations of the world achieve comparable standards of living on just a little more than *half* the amount of energy used in the United States per capita. The Swedes, for example, use less than two thirds of the energy per capita and half the energy per dollar of gross domestic production used by Americans (Johansson et al., 1983). Reviewers of the energy situations in the United States and Sweden suggest that the Swedes are able to accomplish greater efficiency because of higher energy prices, which encourage more efficient energy use (Schipper and Litchtenberg, 1976). The Swedes also have more energy conservation construction codes and other incentives for energy conservation in housing. Johansson et al. (1983) project that even with a 50% increase in the consumption of goods and services in the future, Sweden will be able to reduce energy consumption by 35% through the use of even more efficient transportation and building technologies. Gasoline and other fuel taxes also have a strong energy-conservative effect on Swedish transportation. There are still more factors responsible for energy efficiency in Sweden. These bear looking into to see how they might apply to other societies.

Conservation Potential

There are many areas in which the potential for conserving energy is very great. Included among these are lighting, home heating, home air conditioning, the use of appliances and packaging, and energy use in industry and agriculture. Significant amounts of energy could be saved in every category in which energy is used, though the potential for conservation is much greater in some categories than in others.

Lighting. During the coal miners' strike in early 1978, many institutions reduced lighting in all

Someday solar homes like these, called zomes, may reduce our energy demands.

buildings, disconnecting every other fluorescent light, as an energy conservation measure. Some energy was saved, but the amazing thing was that no one seemed to mind. This raised questions about how much light is actually needed. It is difficult to get at the truth.

Some critics claim that the lighting industry has pushed for standards of lighting in construction that are two to three times higher than that required for good vision. The critics claim that largely because of lobbying, lighting standards for schools have been increased from 30 footcandles (*A footcandle is a measure of brightness.*) in the early 1950s to more than double that by the mid-1970s. Where we have been able to find estimates of what is needed for good vision, it seems that 20–25 footcandles are considered adequate for schools. If this is true, it is doubly profound because more than 10% of all electricity generated in the United States goes for lighting. Eight million tons of coal must be burned each year to provide the lighting in the United States.

If nothing else, the lighting question makes one wonder how such things are decided. How do we go about deciding how much light we actually need for different purposes in different places? Do highly motivated special interest groups have the most to say about such things? Obviously, it takes money to buy, install, and power lighting systems; one would think—naively perhaps—that economic pressure would quickly locate the borderline of good vision and low costs. But then again, perhaps not. Perhaps when government becomes involved by establishing standards for light levels in all public buildings, the economic competitive factors that would normally favor efficiency no longer operate very well.

Politics aside, better lighting efficiency is possible even if light levels are kept constant. A 40-watt fluorescent bulb gives off more light than a 100-watt incandescent bulb, and it uses about half the energy. In other words, fluorescent light gives off three to four times more light per unit of energy input than incandescent light. Light bulbs are now being developed that fit into regular incandescent light sockets but that are actually fluorescent lamps.

Heating and Cooling. According to Hirst and Carney (1978), the potential for conservation of energy in the American household is very great indeed—as much as $27 billion (in mid-1970s dollars) in energy costs could be saved between now and the end of the century. Heating and cooling are the biggest consumers of energy in the home. Approaches to conservation here include:

1. tightening up existing homes,
2. adapting to lower temperatures in winter and higher temperatures in summer,
3. developing improved systems for heating homes,
4. improving the design of newly constructed houses to conserve temperature more efficiently, and

5. using landscaping and external factors to improve the conservation of energy.

For existing homes the obvious strategies are insulation, storm windows, and weather stripping. A quarter-inch gap at the bottom of a 36-inch-wide door provides the same potential for escaping heat as a nine-square-inch (three-inch by three-inch) hole in the wall. It is estimated that fuel bills can be cut almost 4% by just adding weather stripping to the average existing home.

Computer simulation research and actual measurement have shown considerable energy savings by reducing temperature in homes during the winter—maybe as much as 3% for every degree the thermostat is turned down in a cold climate.

The Heat Pump. There are a number of relatively new ways of heating and cooling homes; one of these is the **heat pump**. The heat pump is a device that collects heat from air and pumps it into or out of a house or a building. In winter, such pumps actually collect heat from outside and pump it in; in the summer they do the reverse. The ability of the heat

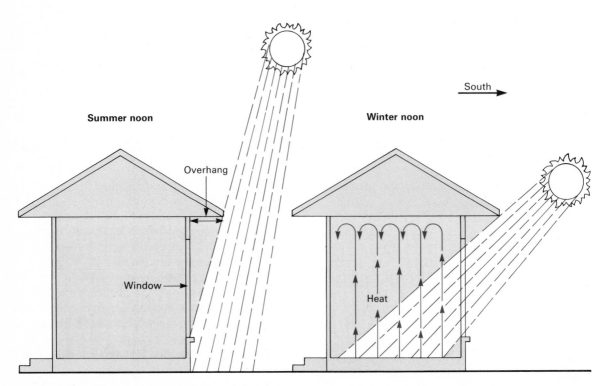

Figure 6.42 Using Housing Design to Save Energy. The sun is higher in the sky during the late spring and summer than it is in winter. In the northern hemisphere a south-facing house with a properly designed overhang can keep the sun's rays from coming through the south-facing windows during the summer but let them in during the winter, when they are more welcome. In the southern hemisphere the overhang is needed on north-facing windows.

pump to pump heat in decreases as the outside air temperature drops, and at 32°F a balance is reached at which supplemental heating must be used to heat the house. When one considers that 80% of U.S. heating occurs in the temperature range of 32–65°F, this is not much of a problem. In the solar-assisted heat pumps that are now being developed, solar energy is used to lower the break-even point.

Construction Codes. The community of Davis, California, is often cited as an example of energy efficiency. This community has a number of ordinances that promote the conservation of energy through building codes. The codes limit the proportion of window to wall area, favor houses that come with trees, set insulation standards, and the like. According to one source, these ordinances reduced electric consumption in Davis by 18% during a time when electric consumption increased 8% nationally. Housing design changes obviously have a great deal of conservation potential. Most existing houses were not designed for expensive energy; in the late 1970s it cost over $1000 a year to heat the average American home. When we speak of design, we mean

things like the amount of insulation in walls, the ratio of window to wall space, and the design of overhanging roofs (Figure 6.42) as well as the use of more efficient heating systems and the more widespread use of heat pumps. A number of anticipated energy conservation effects on housing design as given by Snell, Achenbach, and Petersen (1976) are listed in Table 6.12.

Trees and Things. Deciduous trees located near a house shade the house from the sun's rays during the summer, decreasing the air-conditioning burden. Leaves fall off in the autumn, allowing the sun's rays through during the winter to help heat the house. This effect can be accentuated if a house has a properly designed overhang.

The use of evergreen trees in landscaping can also make a difference. It takes twice as much fuel to heat a house when the outside temperature is 32° and the wind is blowing at 12 mph as it would for the same temperature with a wind of only 2 mph. The windbreak effect of evergreen trees can really make a difference. In many places, it is estimated that the economy potential exceeds 30%.

Table 6.12   Expected Impacts of Energy Conservation on Housing Design

Housing type

Smaller, higher density, fewer detached houses
Increased shift to townhouse and low-rise from single-family detached
Diminished relative attractiveness of mobile homes in life-cycle cost terms
Improved designs with lower unit demands will keep fossil fuel economically competitive in
    many areas for years to come

Architectural features

Thicker wall (cavity and sandwich) and roof construction for more insulation
Fewer picture windows, more double- and triple-glazed windows, some specially coated glass
More functional windows—designed as passive solar collectors
Tighter, better sealed joints, higher performance sealants, better workmanship
Better control of moisture to protect insulation
Attention to shape, orientation, landscaping in design
Control of air movement between floors—fewer open stairwells and split-level designs
Insulated foundation walls in cold climates
Greater thermal resistance for more expensive fuels, such as electric heating
Better thermal comfort and greater acoustical privacy

Mechanical systems

Smaller, more efficient equipment, better load matching
Customized ventilation to provide outdoor air when and where needed
Widespread use of heat pumps in moderate climates—integrated heat pump and solar heating
Solar space heating in selected climates where gas and oil are in short supply
More zoning and multipoint control systems in larger residences
Electrical load management control options for hot water and appliances
Solar water heating in the south

Institutional

Life-cycle cost-based performance standards (voluntary or mandatory) for new housing design
Labeling of houses, equipment, and appliances for energy use, cost, and performance
Householders knowledgeable of how to operate homes efficiently

Appliances. A significant amount of energy is used in dishwashers, gas and electric stoves, televisions, stereos, and hot water tanks. Energy can be saved with existing appliances by taking shorter showers, lowering the temperature of water in a hot water tank, using cold water in the washing machine, and hanging clothes on clotheslines on nice days instead of using the dryer. There is also a great deal of conservation potential in design. It is estimated, for example, that as much as half of the gas consumed in a gas stove is used in the pilot light. Turn back to Figure 6.16 to assure yourself that the potential for energy savings in appliances is significant.

Commerce. The advances in home building design discussed above are applicable to commercial buildings and stores as well. Changes have already begun to take place in big building design. Manhattan's new 59-story Citicorp Tower is an example. Although it has an aluminum and glass exterior, the aluminum panels contain twice the insulation found in similar older buildings; the glass is double and is coated to reflect the rays of the sun. In a federally funded demonstration project it was shown that if lighting were cut from the usual level, which requires 5 watts per square foot, to a lower level requiring only 1.65 watts by focusing light to where it is needed and not providing it everywhere at once, a significant amount of energy could be saved. The results of this experiment have been confirmed by a number of other studies.

Industry. As is illustrated in Figure 6.13, industry uses nearly a third of America's energy. Perhaps big industry can be expected to be the bellwether of energy conservation, being the most sensitive to and quickest to react to economic pressures. In 1977, according to one source, American industry reduced its energy consumption by 4% over the previous year while turning out nearly 6% more products. Many conservation steps were taken in industry during recent periods of energy cost escalation simply to save money. In the past when natural gas and other forms of energy were not expensive, it apparently did not pay to try to save. Now it pays. The 31% jump in the price of natural gas from 1975 to 1976 was a big incentive indeed.

It is interesting that recycling has proven to be an industrial energy saver. According to one source, producing copper from recycled copper requires only a tenth of the energy as it would starting from ore. For aluminum the saving is even greater. The net energy savings from the use of scrap in making steel is less impressive. Hannon and Brodrick (1982) claim that while increased use of scrap would reduce energy use, it is not economical mainly because of the high volatility of scrap prices. They further claim that even if all steel were made from scrap, the energy savings would only be 6%.

Packaging. Consider the following:

— One source estimates that the Oregon law providing that all bottles be redeemable for a deposit saves enough annually to heat 50,000 homes for an entire winter.

— A 100-watt bulb could give light for five hours on the same amount of energy needed to make a single disposable can or bottle.

— It takes the output of several nuclear power plants to produce the energy needed to make the throwaway containers used in the United States each year.

— The EPA estimates that the banning of disposable bottles could save the equivalent of 125,000 bbls of oil per year.

Although there are some energy-based arguments that favor throwaway containers (one being that owing to the weight difference, a truck can carry twice as much beverage in aluminum cans as in returnable glass bottles), there is little doubt that in the overall analysis, throwaway packaging contributes to our energy problem.

It is generally conceded that in the United States, nearly all goods are overpackaged. There must be a significant energy conservation potential in the manufacturing and transport of packaging materials.

Electricity. Only about 30% of the heat generated in an electric power plant makes its way to the consumer. The rest is lost through the inefficiency of energy transformation and transfers. Earlier in the chapter we reviewed some of the ways being explored to improve the efficiency of the generation and transmission of electricity.

Transportation. About a fourth of the energy consumed in the United States is used in transportation. Obviously, the potential for conservation here is significant. The system of personal transportation in the United States is outlandishly inefficient in every way. Considering the objective of getting people from one point to another, nearly all of the energy consumed in the automobile is wasted. Should we abolish the automobile immediately? This is obviously not practical or possible, so we must address ourselves to a long-range strategy for finding and using substitutes for the automobile.

To begin with, it has been pointed out repeatedly that perhaps as much as half of the gasoline consumed in the United States is consumed in trips of less than three miles—trips within walking distance or easy range of a bicycle. Second, gas mileage is far poorer than need be because our cars are still too big and unnecessarily powerful. Apparently, economic and legal incentives have already begun to make a difference, however. Gas mileage in the 1977 automobiles reportedly improved as much as 30% over that in 1974 models. Some 1979 and 1980 cars got as much as 70% better gas mileage than their counterparts made in 1974 (see Figure 6.43).

While many observers expect to see continued improvement in the efficiency of the automobile, many of us advocate a long-range solution in which we gradually do away with automobile transportation as we know it today. Automobile driving should be both allowed to and made to become very expensive. Normal economic pressures should be accentuated through systems of taxation such as we will discuss later in the chapter. Clearly, much of what we get from the automobile we could get with some less convenient form of mass transportation. Although we acknowledge that the concept is somewhat simplistic given present-day attitudes toward mass transportation, we cannot help but think that even if a small part of the large fraction of the gross national product related to the automobile were diverted to mass transit, the United States could construct and operate one of the most efficient, pleasant, desirable, and spectacular transit systems in the world within a short time.

Agriculture. We have already alluded to a number of energy-conservative practices that might be adopted in agriculture. While there may be complex reasons for it, Amish farmers use far less fuel energy (but much more human energy) per pound of produce, getting almost as much per acre as their non-Amish counterparts. According to data gathered by investigators from San Diego State University, Eastern Illinois University, and Columbia University, Amish farmers in Pennsylvania used 83% less energy to produce milk than did their neighbors on adjacent farms. The same study showed that the

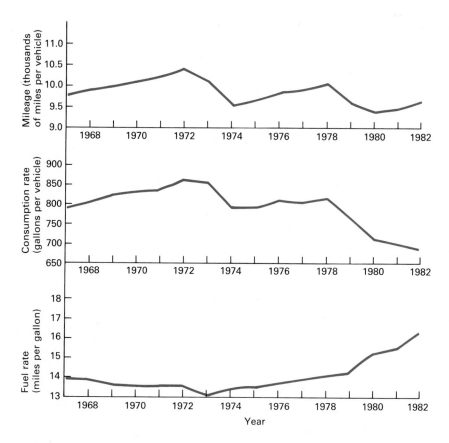

Figure 6.43 Average Annual Motor Vehicle Use, Fuel Use, and Fuel Efficiency.

Can Energy Really Be Conserved?

It has been pointed out by more than one observer that energy conservation may be an illusion. A homeowner who turns off some lights and saves $10 during any given month will most likely spend the $10 on something else, and the something else may cause at least the same amount of energy to be consumed as the lights would have.

A more specific example: If you were to insulate your house, you might have to spend $3–4 in insulation costs for every unit volume of oil you save during the lifetime of your house. If oil cost $12 per unit volume, economics favors the insulation; you end up spending $3 instead of $12. Would you actually save $9 worth of energy? Probably not if you take your $9 and treat yourself to a couple of movies, causing oil to be burned to heat the theatre, project the film, produce the film, fly the film crew to Cairo and back, grow popcorn, ship popcorn, etc. This dilemma illustrates the tightness of the relationship between money and energy. We will explore the nature of this relationship in Section C.

Amish produced 115 bushels of corn per acre using organic fertilizer, while their neighbors who used much more energetically expensive chemical fertilizers got 165 bushels per acre. While there are other data showing similar things, we do not think the definitive studies have been done to show realistically how much energy could be saved by changing agricultural practices in the United States. Because the use of energy in agriculture is significant, energy conservation in agriculture must be explored further.

What Can We Do?

A number of specific energy-saving suggestions have been made throughout this section on conservation. Obviously, a great deal of potential impact can be made on our energy problem through conservation. The beauty of this strategy is that it will help solve some of our air and water pollution problems at the same time.

Great potential for conservation can be found in all of the modes of energy use, including:

1. space-heating,
2. transportation,
3. lighting,
4. packaging,
5. generation and transmission of electricity,
6. running of appliances,
7. the operation of commercial enterprises,
8. industry, and
9. farming.

Although the Reagan administration brought the federal energy conservation effort to a virtual standstill, numerous specific proposals have been considered, debated, and implemented. The following is a list of proposals summarized by Newman and Day (1975) in the mid-1970s; those with an asterisk have already been implemented to some degree:

*1. Establish loan program to provide incentives for repair and energy-conserving rehabilitation of homes.
2. Establish loan program for builders of new homes whose designs are energy conservation oriented.
*3. Establish programs to improve housing design.
4. Require public utility commissions to insist on rate structures that do not promote energy use and establish systems of pricing to eliminate peak loads, evening out demand.
5. Prohibit promotional practices by public utilities.
*6. Establish programs to label appliances so that the public knows how efficient they are.
*7. Fund research programs to improve the technological efficiency of appliances and establish required performance ratings.
8. Establish a heavier tax on cars based on weight such that the tax is prohibitive for very heavy cars (over 2500 pounds); have the tax go into a public transit trust fund.
9. Add a tax to gasoline based on the weight of cars.

Clearly, a number of things can and should be done about conservation. As we will see in Section C, these things *are* in fact worth doing.

The Economics and Politics of Energy

Our use of energy in the future will not be determined solely on the basis of environmental considerations. At best, environmental factors will be given more and more weight in what will no doubt continue to be a struggle involving economic and political considerations in all environmental matters. Those who care most about the environment cannot afford to ignore economics and politics. These must be embraced, understood, and dealt with as if they were as real as ecosystems.

DOLLARS AND WATTS: THE ECONOMICS OF ENERGY

Economics is, among other things, the science of how value is determined. Economists concern themselves with the factors that go into determining the value of commodities such as energy. It will become apparent throughout the remainder of this book that economics is a major dimension of each and every environmental problem. Here we wish to explore briefly some economic dimensions of the energy problem. (Some of the fundamental principles of economics are covered in detail in Chapter 18. It might be useful to read the section on supply and demand in that chapter before going on with this section.)

At the philosophical end of the spectrum of questions we will consider are the following: How basic is energy as a commodity in our value system worldwide? Is money really a symbol for energy? Is money really only a means of trading in energy, such that a dollar spent is equivalent to a unit of energy consumed? A related question is: What is the relationship between economic growth and the consumption of energy? Other specific and somewhat more practical—and perhaps more answerable—questions we will explore are the following:

1. To what extent does the *price* of energy determine the *use* of energy?
2. What effect have higher energy prices had on world economics?

3. What impact does the regulation of energy prices have on the use of energy?

Is Money a Symbol for Energy?

Hannon (1975) points out that when people double their income, they just about double their use of energy. Hannon has gone so far as to suggest that energy be made the coin of the realm. He thinks of energy as a much more realistic basis for wealth than the gold in Fort Knox. Energy, according to Hannon, is the basis for all value in our economic and legal system, and therefore we should embrace this reality and structure our financial systems accordingly. While there is some truth to this, the fact that countries having similar standards of living consume quite different amounts of energy per capita suggests that the relationship between economics and energy is not fixed. There apparently are ways for dollars to be spent in which a "bigger energy bang can be gotten for a buck." The relationship between **gross national product (GNP)** (the value of all goods and services produced by a nation per year) and energy consumption in the United States has been rather close over most of the period since 1920, but there has been a discernible slow but steady increase in the efficiency of the GNP. Since 1973 there has been a 20.3% **real growth** in the GNP (growth after adjustment for inflation) and a slight *drop* in energy consumption (Conservation Foundation, 1982). This indicates clearly that while GNP and energy consumption are related, they are *not* tightly coupled (see Figure 6.44). GNP *can* increase without increased energy consumption.

One other factor allowing slippage to creep into the relationship between energy and dollars is that the profit margin for oil is highly variable and often quite large. Since one gets what one can for a barrel of oil in a world in which certain countries have most of the oil, prices can be controlled and can far exceed the cost of production. This fact has many implications. A group of countries in control of oil prices could strategically undercut the emergence of new energy technologies, essentially stifling them.

Consumer price index: the cost of an array of typical goods (market basket) expressed as a multiple of the cost of the same or equivalent items in some base year. For example, if a list of items costs $251 in 1983 and if the equivalent items cost $100 in 1961, the consumer price index would be said to have risen by 151% from 1961 to 1983.

Efficiency: yield divided by input, usually expressed as a percentage. (*Example:* If 10 quads of coal were converted to electricity and then to 1 quad of electric heat, the entire process could be said to be 1/10 or 10% efficient.)

Gross national product: the total value of goods and services produced by a nation in a one-year period.

Per capita: per person.

ances that they do have tend to be models that consume less energy; low-income people have fewer frost-free refrigerators and automatic as opposed to nonautomatic washers. While there are data that can be interpreted to mean that energy consumption does *not* rise quite as rapidly as income, some who have looked at these data suggest that not all the energy consumed in producing certain goods and services is accounted for; that is, we do not have good data on how much indirect energy is consumed in producing the things well-off people tend to have. The truth seems to be that while cost or price is a major factor controlling energy consumption, the connection is less than absolute.

Oil prices held constant from 1952 to 1972 and then gradually began to outdistance inflation. During the period when oil prices were increasing substantially, U.S. dependence on oil actually *increased* even though the price of oil was passed along to consumers. Apparently, even with the increase in price, people felt they could derive more economic good—more value, if you will—from the product they purchased than it cost them to buy it. This suggests that, over the short term at least, energy cost has little impact on how much is used.

To What Extent Does the Price of Energy Affect Its Use?

This is somewhat the reverse of the question raised in the previous section. As is true of much that we have discussed so far, the picture is not crystal clear. In the extreme it is obvious that there *is* a relationship between how much energy costs and how much of it is used. Studies have shown that the better off an individual is, the more energy he or she tends to use. People whose incomes are low tend to own fewer energy-consuming devices. The appli-

What are Some of the Effects of Energy Price Regulation?

The U.S. government has long regulated the price of energy transported across state lines and energy imported from foreign countries. The effect of regulation has been to hold prices low for certain domestic energy commodities, in effect shielding consumers from the realities and full costs of oil and

For example, they could cut oil prices to the extent that new technologies like oil shale or coal gasification are uneconomical; oil would still do quite well because of the large margin between the price of a barrel of oil and the cost of producing it.

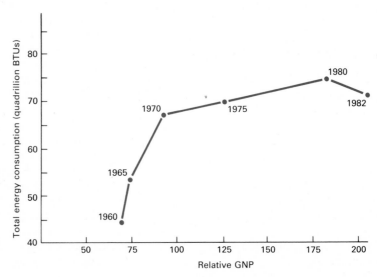

Figure 6.44 Relationship Between Gross National Product and Energy Use Since 1960. Note that the units used for the GNP are relative. For purposes of this graph, the 1972 GNP is given the value 100, and GNP in other years is measured in relation to that value.

natural gas. At one point, domestic gas and oil prices were regulated such that foreign oil cost four times as much. Some observers have argued that this has been harmful and has tended to aggravate and accelerate the onset of energy crises. Clearly, if economics is to come into play so as to favor conservation and to slow down our consumption of energy, the marketplace must be allowed to indicate to consumers the true price of energy—the price the world feels is appropriate for a barrel of oil.

It can be argued easily that price regulation brings on shortages. To keep the price low for a particular commodity is in effect promoting the use of that substance because people derive more economic value than they must pay in terms of dollars or in trade. This not only favors the using up of the resources in question, it also retards the development of alternative resources because a primary stimulus for the development of alternatives is economic pressure. This is not to say that an abrupt departure from price regulation would be without problems. Because of the inertia of the way we have done things in the past, abrupt deregulation would have a disproportionate impact on the poor. The poor would suffer most from a rapid rise of the cost of fuel; indeed this has happened in the last decade. Even so, it seems that all things considered, the price of energy should not be regulated. Other solutions must be found for the problem of the impact of energy costs on the poor.

What Impact Have Rising Energy Prices Had on the World Trade Balance?

The United States has had a serious balance of payments deficit over the past decade largely because of our dependence on foreign oil. While this is a direct problem for the United States and other user countries, it has also created ripples that have affected the economics of the world as a whole. We cannot help but wonder what sorts of economic horrors lie in wait for us in the future if imbalance becomes even greater. We also wonder about the effect this will have on world political stability.

THE POLITICS OF ENERGY

Energy and World Politics

The fact that recoverable world energy reserves are far from evenly distributed ensures that energy reserves and resources will continue to be an important factor in world politics. Even though the United States has a considerable fraction of the

When OPEC price increases caused petroleum shortages, more than transportation was affected.

world's total recoverable energy reserves, it has had a negative balance of trade in fossil fuels since the late 1950s. Many industrialized countries of the world, notably countries of Western Europe and Japan, have had relatively stable levels of energy production since 1960 while undergoing considerably increased consumption during the same period. Japan now imports nearly every drop of petroleum it consumes and nearly three quarters of its coal. In contrast, many of the members of the Organization of Petroleum Exporting Countries (OPEC) and some developed nations have experienced increased rates of consumption. OPEC countries have had an even faster rate of increase in production than consumption, resulting in the surplus which is the main export of many of these countries.

Some time ago, the oil-producing nations came to a collective realization that it was not in their own economic or political interests to deplete their oil reserves quickly in response to the demands of the industrialized nations and that it would be better for them to prolong the period of depletion by raising prices and imposing taxes on their energy resources instead. This presents another important dimension to the political-economic side of the world's energy picture. It is noteworthy that the Sino-Soviet block of nations has been energy self-sufficient for the last two decades and is expected to continue to be self-sufficient at least for the near term.

The U.S. Domestic Politics of Energy

When this textbook was being written, U.S. energy policies were still in the very earliest stages of emergence. The Reagan administration, apparently believing that the answer to our energy problems was deregulation and opening up federal lands and offshore areas to the recovery of traditional energy sources, did not follow the Carter administration's lead in subsidizing the development of solar energy or even coal conversion technologies by industry. The Reagan administration took government out of the conservation picture almost completely, offering a 1983 budget that cut funding for conservation programs by 97%. The administration also proposed the liberalization of coal, gas, and oil leasing policies on federal lands, *including wilderness areas*. Understandably, this has provoked much opposition and debate.

The special interest groups in the United States, almost without exception, have spoken out on the energy crisis, declaring that a strong program is needed and adding, implicitly or explicitly, *only if it does not hurt them or threaten them in any way*. Obviously, the United States cannot break away from old patterns and chart a new course without some rather general sacrifices and some degree of universal pain. Blame for the fact that we have had no policy at all for so long rests squarely on the shoulders of the American people. It has been said by many that the American public made the key decisions that led to U.S. withdrawal from Vietnam and that this is how most major decisions are made. Because of their short terms of office, nearly all elected officials tend to respond to real and/or perceived public sentiment on almost any issue. Why doesn't the public feel that an energy policy is needed? Apparently, many Americans have for too long believed that there is no energy problem. Numerous surveys done in the thick of the energy problems of the late 1970s determined that almost half of the people interviewed were not aware that the United States had to import oil to meet current energy needs. The U.S. system of government fails—by design—to get very far ahead of public opinion. While this may have served the country very well in the past, the future is likely to bring problems for which such a response time may be critically too long.

The Problem of Lag. It takes time to develop alternative sources of energy. The first nuclear reactor in the United States went critical in 1943, and by the mid-1970s, nuclear energy accounted for only about 1% of the nation's energy consumption. It takes 5–8 years to open a new coal mine. A nuclear electric plant can take more than 10 years to put into operation. It can take as long as 12 years to make a new oil field productive. This lag is part of the reason why crisis management, management by public opinion, and the lack of a positive natural energy policy are less than ideal in responding to energy crises.

An energy bill was passed by the 95th Congress in October 1978. Some important provisions of that energy bill were the following:

1. Prices of newly discovered natural gas—not old or stored natural gas—will be permitted to rise 10% per year until 1985, when the price controls would be lifted altogether. (The deadline was later extended.)
2. New industrial and new utility plants are required to use coal or fuels other than oil or natural gas. Plants already existing before the bill took effect were required to switch to alternative fuel supplies by 1990.
3. Utility commissions were required to consider revamping utility rate structures in favor of conservation, for example, establishing lower prices during off-peak hours.
4. Utilities were required to provide their customers with information about energy savings, and provisions had to be made for the public to be able to borrow money—to be paid off through utility bills—to pay for conservation improvements. Grants and government-backed loans were to be available to families. Mandatory efficiency standards were authorized for many types of home appliances.

Several factors seemed to stand in the way of implementing stronger measures than those in the original (1978) energy bill. Kash et al. (1976) point out that there are three reasons for government inaction or weak action in energy matters. One of the factors is *institutional uncertainty*, that is, the fuzzy relationship between the government and the energy production establishment. There is a great contrast, for example, between the relationship that exists between government and the nuclear power industry and that between government and the coal industry. A second factor is *performance uncertainty*, that is, the unknowns associated with future energy sources and what they will and will not be able to do. Third, there is uncertainty about future demand.

The Need for a Federal Energy Policy

Government must play more of a major role in energy affairs. The responsibility for doing so clearly falls to the *federal* government under directives having to do with general welfare, interstate commerce, and a host of other specific constitutional provisions. The federal government must force decisions that consider the big picture and the long-range picture—something that market forces are rarely able to do very well.

The federal government must establish improved national energy policies that encompass (1) the use of federal lands, (2) regulation of electric rates (the federal government owns an electric company, TVA), (3) the strategic petroleum reserve, and (4) other aspects of energy bearing on national security. The federal government is already involved in mine safety, mine regulation, and regulation of interstate commerce, including energy prices, energy import regulation, and pollution control. It should get back into the conservation promotion business; it should develop a bipartisan national energy plan, and this plan should have major provisions for the continued support of energy research.

Government has an important role in the support of energy research and development. The current research program of the U.S. Department of Energy is extensive. About $58 million was spent in fossil fuel programs alone in fiscal 1973, and by fiscal year 1978, about $700 million was spent—more than a ten-fold increase in just six years. In the fall of 1983, President Reagan signed a bill that provided $10.1 billion for the Department of Energy, $600 million of which was for energy research.

There is a substantial role for government in the exploration of new sources of energy and improved ways of using energy. The role is essentially one of speeding up research that might have been conducted later in response to immediate economic forces. The Atomic Energy Commission subsidized the building of atomic power plants well before such plants were economically competitive. Problems with that venture not withstanding, the government should continue to fill this role in the future.

OUR ENERGY FUTURE: PROJECTIONS REGARDING ENERGY USE AND ENERGY SOURCES

Future Trends in Energy Use

The fact that the future cannot be known applies to energy consumption as it does to everything else. Throughout the mid-1970s, many estimates were made of future trends in energy utilization. Nearly all of them forecast continued increasing universal consumption. Although energy use will most likely continue to grow throughout the world for the fore-seeable future, the rate of increase in countries like the United States has already fallen off sharply. After decades of growth in energy consumption in excess of 7% annually, energy consumption in the United States actually *fell* in four of the eight years following the Arab oil embargo of 1973—1974. In 1981, total energy consumption was 0.3% below 1973 levels (Conservation Foundation, 1982). Many factors, including the depressed economy, higher energy prices, temporary shortages, and conservation laws and programs, combined to cause this downturn, but it was *not* foreseen. There is no way to tell just what will happen in the future. A number of factors are working against further decline in energy use. The U.S. population will continue to grow, and our consumption of energy is likely to become increasingly inefficient, owing mostly to an expected switch to electrical heating of homes. Some observers predict that Americans may well be using more than 100% more fuel by the turn of the century. But who knows?

Future Trends in Energy Sources

Projections by the U.S. Department of Energy (DOE) of energy sources in the free world are given in Figure 6.45. For the United States specifically, petroleum and natural gas use will decline. Coal utilization is expected to increase significantly. In a DOE study published in 1983 it was projected that the combination of solar, geothermal, and wind energy will account for only 2.5% of the energy we use in the year 2000. The contribution of nuclear energy is expected to rise from the current 4% to about 8% (Dukert, 1983).

The use of electricity will increase in the world overall in the next few decades. Many countries will be catching up to the United States in terms of electrically powered technology, and in the United States, consumption will move from the present 25% of total energy toward 50%. Some of this will be caused by a decline in the number of homes heated by natural gas and a switch to electrical heating systems. Transportation costs and environmental considerations will tend to make the increased use of coal take the form of electrical energy. A summary review of our short-range and long-range energy alternatives is presented in Table 6.13.

What Must Be Done?

The technologically advanced countries of the world must do two things very soon:

1. Reduce their degree of dependence on other

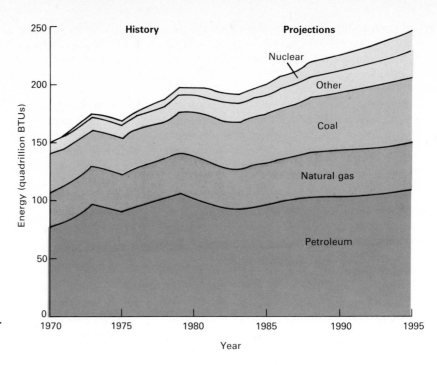

Figure 6.45   Free World Energy Sources Projected Through 1995.

Table 6.13   Comparative Estimated Short-term and Long-term Value and Potential Environmental Impacts of Future Energy Resources

| Energy Source | Prospect for providing a significant fraction of the world's energy needs | | Relative Environmental Impact | Spheres Significantly Affected | Type of Impact and Chapter in Which Covered |
	Short-term (1980s)	Long-term (beyond 1990)			
Coal					
(in general)	very good	very good	high	air, water, and land	
Deep mining	very good	very good	high	water and air	Deep mining produces acid mine water problems (Chapter 12)
Strip mining	very good	very good	high	air, water, and land	In addition to above, strip mining can have significant negative impact on land (Chapter 17)
Liquefaction and gasification	poor	good	high	air, water, and land	Burning of coal produces hydrocarbon products, some of which are carcinogenic (Chapter 14) Liquefaction and gasification processes may constitute additional source of carcinogens Mining, especially deep mining, is associated with occupational dust disease

Table 6.13 *(Continued)*

Energy Source	Prospect for providing a significant fraction of the world's energy needs		Relative Environmental Impact	Spheres Significantly Affected	Type of Impact and Chapter in Which Covered
	Short-term (1980s)	Long-term (beyond 1990)			
					such as pneumoconiosis (Chapter 10)
Oil					
Wells	good	poor	moderately high	water	Marine pollution from offshore wells and ocean transport (Chapter 12)
Shale	poor	good	high	air, water, and land	Solid waste problem from spent shale (Chapter 6)
					Processing oil shale may yield carcinogens (Chapter 14)
					Combustion of hydrocarbon products produces mutagenic and carcinogenic chemicals (Chapter 14) and contributes to ozone pollution (Chapters 9–11)
Natural Gas	moderate	poor	low		
Nuclear					
Fission	poor?	uncertain	high	principally land but also air and water	Problems are related to radioactive waste disposal and, to a much lesser extent, escape of radioactive materials from power plants (Chapter 14) Possibilities of colossal accidents (reactor core meltdown) and theft of plutonium that could be used by radical groups or individuals to make nuclear weapons also exist
Fusion	poor	unknown	low to moderate	water	Impact problems limited to tritium control
Geothermal	poor	poor	moderate	water	
Solar	poor	fair (space heating)	low	land (use)	
Wind	poor	fair	low	land (use)	
Biomass	poor	fair	moderate to high	land, water	Energy farms would have problems in common with other types of agriculture (Chapters 12, 17) Burning biomass will generate hydrocarbons and potentially carcinogenic compounds (Chapters 9–10, 14)
Hydroelectric	poor	poor	low to moderate		
Conservation	fair	good	very low	indoor air	

Note: Environmental impacts of current energy sources are described in chapters on pollution in Part III. The impacts of many new energy sources can only be speculated on at present.

countries in the interest of world stability, both political and economic.

2. Prepare for transition to new energy sources working on *both* the supply and demand sides of the problem.

Reducing demand is a straightforward task. The problem is that conservation has no constituency, and many governments have policies that hinder conservation. Working on the supply side is less straightforward. So what is the best course?

Bodansky (1980) claims that we do not have any basis on which to put all of our eggs into coal, nuclear power, solar power, or any other basket. It is important, says Bodansky, that we explore and exploit all options, especially the emotionally endangered nuclear option. This exploration will bring risk as well as potential new energy sources.

Lovins (1976, 1977, 1978) and others have advocated what has become labeled the "soft energy path" for the future. The **soft energy path** is cast as an alternative to the so-called "hard energy path" of trying to do more and more of what we have been doing in the face of increasing economic, social, political, and environmental resistance. The soft path would be based on a reordered match-up between the sources of energy and their end use. Strategically, the soft path would move us through a period of much more efficient energy use toward a system based on the decentralized generation of renewable energy sources. Specifically, soft energy technologies, including such things as solar heating, biomass conversion, small-scale hydroelectric plants, and electric plants would come into prominence over a 50-year period during which the strategy would be to improve the efficiency (including conservation) and cleanliness of traditional fossil fuel sources of energy.

Is There Room for Optimism?

Although there seems to be little doubt that adequate energy at a noneconomically devastating cost will be among the most difficult and serious problems for *Homo sapiens* in the next half century, perhaps there is room for some optimism. We find at least three sources of hope.

First, the Demand and Conservation Panel of the National Research Council's Committee on Nuclear and Alternative Energy Systems (CONAES) optimistically projects that the prospects of improving our lot through conservation are good because:

— Much greater efficiency is already in reach either with currently available technology or with technology that is now on the drawing boards. Up to 1% improvement in efficiency per year is possible, the panel claims.
— High energy costs will stimulate responsive technological innovation.
— Growth in energy consumption is not tightly coupled to prosperity.

Past excesses in energy consumption reflected

— a steadily declining cost of energy relative to other commodities,
— rapid increases in energy-intensive products,
— major increases in disposable income, and
— increased labor costs.

Cost-conscious businesses like this bank are already using soft energy technology—solar panels.

None of these factors can be expected to continue to increase at their historic paces (Committee on Nuclear and Alternative Energy Systems, 1978).

Second, it may be comforting to know that much of humankind is *not* dependent upon fossil fuel. Most of the people in the developing nations (which comprise 75% of humanity) are completely separated from, or are only marginally involved with, modern fuels and electricity. It is ironic that many developing nations have tried to match economic models based on nonrenewable resources, although more and more of them have begun to see this as a two-edged sword. For these people and these nations there is still time and increasing incentive to tie future development to improved uses of *renewable* energy sources.

The third source of optimism (or hope, if optimism is too strong a word) is expressed in a report issued in early 1980 by the U.S. National Academy of Sciences Committee on Nuclear and Alternative Energy Systems:

It is important to keep in mind that the energy problem does not arise from an overall physical scarcity of resources. There are several plausible options for an indefinitely sustainable energy supply, potentially accessible to all the people of the world. The problem is in effect a socially acceptable and smooth transition from gradually depleting resources of oil and natural gas to new technologies whose potentials are not now fully developed or assessed and whose costs are generally unpredictable. This transition involves time for planning and development on the scale of half a century. The question is whether we are diligent, clever, and lucky enough to make this inevitable transition an orderly and smooth one.

The report went on to say that the prospect of our being diligent, clever, and lucky enough will be based on social and political factors. Is there room for optimism? Do you think that the resolution of the conflicting values and special interests we have touched on in this chapter will be orderly and smooth?

CONCEPTS TO REMEMBER

1. Energy as food is fundamentally important to human beings in the same way that it is for all organisms. But human civilization requires several orders of magnitude more energy than its members require in food. Civilization allows us to sustain a much larger population than could be sustained otherwise, but civilization brings an enormous extra dependence on energy.

2. The energy crisis of the 1970s was caused by temporary supply problems and overdue price adjustments, not on any absolute shortage of energy. It did, however, point up the importance of energy and helped bring the broader, more fundamental, and continuing crisis into clearer focus.

3. We are running out of oil and natural gas and should expect continuing problems in making transitions to other sources.

4. Energy use accounts directly for many of our environmental problems.

5. The use of all forms of energy has increased dramatically in the United States during this century, electricity leading the way as a delivery form.

6. We Americans use more oil than we produce. This situation, which is not expected to improve, creates balance-of-payment problems and other political and economic tensions. It also creates national security problems.

7. The fossil fuels oil, coal, and gas at present account for more than 90% of energy used in the United States.

8. Residential use (mainly heating), transportation, industry, and commerce are the big–four energy–use categories. Personal use amounts to about 37% of the total; business, industry, agriculture, and government use the rest.

9. Coal is the only energy resource currently available to the United States in large amounts. However, increased dependence on coal would mean an intensification of the environmental problems associated with the use of coal.

10. At current rates of utilization we will have come close to using 80% of the world's total petroleum reserves in just one lifetime.

11. We have apparently passed the peak of production of natural gas.

12. Solar energy will not have much of an impact on U.S, or world energy needs for quite a few generations into the future.

13. The immediate future prospects of atomic energy are poor; the long-range future is uncertain. Nuclear power currently provides about 5% of our energy needs. Although the promise

of breeder and fusion technology is great, the real and especially the *perceived* threat of nuclear power appears to be even greater.

14. Geothermal energy may have some local significance but will contribute little to our overall energy needs in the intermediate future.

15. Conservation and increased efficiency offer the greatest potential for impact on U.S. energy problems in the foreseeable future.

16. Americans use far more energy per unit of gross national product than other countries with comparable standards of living. This indicates that our standard of living need not be compromised by energy conservation.

17. The cost of energy has some impact on its use but not as much as might be expected. This indicates that energy is undervalued and suggests that there may be some room for inducing conservation by increasing taxes or otherwise passing along to consumers more of the actual cost of using energy.

18. Regulation of energy prices to keep costs low has the effect of promoting the use and even the waste of energy.

19. We need a sound energy policy, and because of the nature of energy use and impact, the responsibility falls to the federal government.

20. In the next quarter of a century, coal, oil, and natural gas will continue to supply the bulk of our energy. Our task will be to conserve; to perfect new, environmentally sound, energy use technologies; and to make smooth transitions to the substitutes for gas and oil, whatever they may be.

21. We need continuous sources of energy, but this need must not be allowed to supersede the need for a functional, clean, and healthy environment.

22. There is room for optimism. We are *not* going to run out of energy; the problem will continue to be to learn to use it, in whatever form, without harming the environment.

DISCUSSION QUESTIONS AND FOOD FOR THOUGHT

1. Have one member of your class to look up his or her family's gas and electric bills for the past several years and present the data to the class in the form of a graph. Have another class member ask the administration to provide data on the cost of energy for your college or university over the last 5–10 years and present these data in the form of a graph (taking into account the obvious correction factors—changes in numbers of buildings, changes in the number of students, etc.).

2. Discuss the implications of the fact that more than a quarter of a million barrels of crude oil are needed to produce the polystyrene containers in which McDonald's sells its Big Macs and other hamburgers.

3. Keep a log of your driving record over a period of time, indicating trips made, their purpose, and the number of miles. Compare in class and generate some class statistics.

4. Choose sides and debate: Resolved: Because petroleum serves as chemical feedstock for plastics and other types of manufactured materials, oil should not be used as a fuel, (i.e., burned); we should wean ourselves from the use of petroleum as a fuel as soon as possible.

5. Draw up a comprehensive list of energy conservation steps or habits that might be adopted at home. Use some of the following headings: (1) insulation and weather proofing, (2) lighting, (3) summer weather energy savers, (4) heating systems, (5) kitchen, (6) laundry, (7) bath, (8) workshop, (9) yard and garden, (10) transportation, (11) vacationing, (12) buying a home.

6. Choose up sides and debate: Resolved: Because behavior is highly correlated with economic pressure, the cost of electricity and the cost of oil and natural gas should be allowed to float in an economic system free of government control.

7. Discuss some of the simplest, least expensive methods that might be used to convert an existing home into one in which solar energy assists the heating system.

8. Have a brainstorming session in which you draw up as many resolutions related to the use of energy that you can come up with in a defined period of time. Then see how many of these get 100% approval by the class, faculty members, or other groups.

9. List as many energy advantages you can related to the planting and management of a good home vegetable garden and an associated compost pile.

10. Design a solar-heated home using whatever information you can gather from local and library sources.

11. Using some of the energy efficiency data given for different types of ecosystems in Chapter 2, discuss some of the best locations and types or characteristics of crops that might be used to produce biomass for conversion into alcohol or to be burned directly as fuel.

12. Research and determine whether there are any laws governing the location of nuclear power plants or nuclear waste disposal sites in your state. Are either of these types of facilities already functioning in your state?

13. Arrange a site visit to a surface coal mine, an oil refinery, or a power plant.

14. The United States may accept nuclear waste from all other countries in the world in order to be the "keeper" of plutonium 239 and other by-products that have potential for misuse. Discuss some of the pros and cons of this proposal.

15. Make a list of all of the electrical appliances you use in a year. Assume that your electrical energy consumption must be cut in half and that you must eliminate half of the items on your list. For the purposes of this exercise, assume that each item uses the same amount of electricity. Make your selections. Now assume that you must cut your list in half again. Make your selections.

16. Have someone from your local energy utility come to discuss past, present, and future trends for energy use in your area.

17. Run a school survey and a community survey to determine the general attitude and awareness of the current energy situation.

18. List ways that energy consumption can be decreased without a major change in the so-called standard of living.

19. Assuming all things not mentioned being equal, would it pay to buy a new car that got 60 mpg if you now own one that gets 8 mpg even assuming that you present car, worth $1800, would simply have to be discarded with 50,000 good miles on it? Assume that gas costs $1.50 per gallon and that you would have to borrow the $12,000 (payable over four years) for the new car at 12% annual interest (you could also use prevailing figures in your area) and that you drive 20,000 miles per year.

20. Convert the following tables in this chapter into figures: Table 6.1, 6.2B, 6.3, 6.5, 6.6. For Table 6.5, use different kinds of lines or symbols for each of the four items to be graphed in the same figure.

21. Choose sides and debate: Resolved: The marketplace, not the government, should determine energy policy. A free market will stimulate the right amount of conservation and the right amount of energy production.

22. Try some of the available microcomputer programs on energy. Science Software Systems, Inc. in Los Angeles publishes Apple II and TRS-80 diskettes with accompanying sound filmstrips covering "Home Energy Conservation," "The Solar Option," and "Energy and the Environment."

REFERENCES AND FURTHER READING

References marked with an asterisk are cited in text.

Abelson, T. H., ed., 1974. *Energy: Use, Conservation, and Supply,* Washington, D.C.: American Association for the Advancement of Science.

Alexander, T., 1978. "New Fears Surround the Shift to Coal," *Fortune* (November 20): 50–60.

*Alfvén, Hannes, 1972. "Energy and the Environment," *Bulletin of the Atomic Scientists* 28(5):5–15.

Allar, B., 1984. "Atmospheric Fluidized Bed Combustion: No More Coal-Smoked Skies?", *Environment* 26(2):25–31.

Axtmann, R. C., 1975. "Environmental Impact of a Geothermal Power Plant," *Science* 187(4179):795–803.

Behrman, D., 1976. *Solar Energy: The Awakening Science.* Boston: Little, Brown.

Bernard, H., 1981. *The Greenhouse Effect,* New York: Harper and Row.

*Bezdek, R. H., Hirshberg, A. S., and Babcock, W. H., 1979. "Economic Feasibility of Solar Water and Space Heating," *Science* 203:1214–1220.

*Björk, S., and Graneli, W., 1978. "Energy, Reeds, and the Environment," *Ambio* 7(4):150–156.

*Bodansky, D., 1980. "Electricity Generation Choices for the Near Term," *Science* 207(4432):721–728.

Boffey, P. M., 1975. "Energy Plan to Use Peat as a Fuel Stirs Concerns in Minnesota," *Science* 190:120–122.

Brace Research Institute, 1973. *How to Build A Solar Water Heater.* Leaflet No. L-4, Brace Research Institute, Macdonald College of McGill University, St. Anne Dr., Bellevue 800, Quebec, Canada.

Bungay, H. R., 1982. "Biomass Refining," *Science* 218:643–646.

Butler, E. W., and Pick, J. B., 1982. *Geothermal Energy Development: Problems and Prospects in the Imperial Valley of California.* New York: Plenum Press.

*Calvin, M., 1979. "Petroleum Plantations for Fuel and Materials," *Bioscience* 29(9):533–538.

*Carter, L. J., 1979a. "Policy Review Boosts Solar as a Near-Term Energy Option," *Science* 203:252–253.

Carter, L. J., 1979b. "Radioactive Waste Policy Is in Disarray," *Science* 206:312–314.

Carter, L. J., 1980. "News and Comment. Academy Energy Report Stresses Conservation," *Science* 207:385–386.

Chambers, R. S.; Herendeen, R. A.; Joyce, J. J.; and Penner, P. S., 1979. "Gasohol: Does It or Doesn't It Produce Positive Net Energy?" *Science* 206:789–795.

Cheney, E. S., 1981. "The Hunt for Giant Uranium Deposits," *American Scientist* 69:38–48.

Cohen, B.L., and Lee, I.S., 1979. "A Catalog of Risks," *Health Physics* 206:707–795.

*Cohen, B.L., 1983. *Before It's Too Late: A Scientist's Case for Nuclear Energy.* New York: Plenum Press.

*Committee on Nuclear and Alternative Energy Systems, 1978. "U.S. Energy Demand: Some Low Energy Futures." *Science* 200:142–152.

Commoner, B., 1976. *Poverty of Power: Energy and the Economic Crisis.* New York: Alfred A. Knopf.

Congressional Budget Office, 1982. *Energy Use in Freight Transportation.* Washington, D.C.: U.S. Government Printing Office.

*Conservation Foundation, 1982. *State of the Environment 1982: An Assessment at Mid-Decade.* Washington, D.C.: Conservation Foundation.

Cook, E., 1971. "Energy for Millenium Three," *Technology Review,* December, 16–23.

Council for Agricultural Science and Technology, 1984. *Energy Use and Production in Agriculture,* Report 99. Ames, Iowa.

Council on Environmental Quality, 1979. *Environmental Quality 1979.* 10th Annual Report. Washington, D.C.: U.S. Government Printing Office.

Council on Environmental Quality, 1981. *Global Energy Futures and the Carbon Dioxide Problem,* Washington, D.C.: U. S. Government Printing Office.

Council on Environmental Quality, 1982. *Environmental Quality 1982*. 13th Annual Report. Washington, D.C.: U.S. Government Printing Office.

Cox, K. E, ed., 1977. *Hydrogen: Its Technology and Implications* (5 vols.). Boca Raton, Fla.: CRC Press.

*DaSilva, G. J.; Serra, G. E.; Moreira, J. R.; Conclaves, J. C.; and Goldenberg, J., 1978. "Energy Balance for Ethyl Alcohol Production from Crops," *Science* 201:903–906.

*DeMeo, E. A., and Taylor, R. W., 1984. "Solar Photovoltaic Power Systems: An Electric Utility R&D Perspective," *Science* 224:245–251.

Dienes, L., and Shabad, T., 1979. *The Soviet Energy System: Resource Use and Policies.* New York: Halstead (Wiley).

Dolton, G. L., et al., 1982. *Estimates of Undiscovered Recoverable Conventional Resources of Oil and Gas in the United States,* Geological Survey Circular 860. Reston, Va.: U.S. Geological Survey.

*Dorf, R. C., 1978. *Energy Resources and Policy.* Reading, Mass.: Addison-Wesley Publishing Company.

Duffie, J. A., et al., 1974. Bulletin 21: *Analysis of the World Wide Distribution of Solar Radiation.* Madison, Wis.: Engineering Experiment Station, University of Wisconsin.

*Duggan, J. L., and Cloutier, R. J., eds., *Symposium on Energy: Sources for the Future.* (A symposium conducted by the training division of the Oak Ridge Associated Universities, July 7–25, 1975, Oak Ridge, Tenn.)

*Dukert, J. M., 1983. *Analyzing Future Energy Use,* Exxon Corporation. 4th Quarter, pp.24–29.

*Dunkerley J., and Ramsay, W., 1982. "Energy and the Oil-Importing Developing Countries," *Science,* 216:590–595.

*Dupree, W.; Herman, E.; Miller, S.; and Hillier, D., 1976. *Energy Prospectives 2.* Washington, D.C.: U.S. Department of the Interior.

Eccli, E., 1976. *Low-Cost Energy Efficient Shelter for the Owner and Builder.* Emmaus, Pa.: Rodale Press.

*Eisenbud, M., 1979. "Reassessing Our Environmental Imperatives," *Exxon USA,* 2nd Quarter, pp. 8–11.

Energy: The Next Twenty Years, 1979. A report sponsored by the Ford Foundation. Cambridge, Mass.: Ballinger Publishing Co.

Eskridge, K., 1978. "Congress High on Alcohol Fuels," *BioScience* 28(7):469–470.

Ferrey, S., 1984. "Electric Power in America," *The Amicus Journal* Winter.

Fennelly, P., 1984. "Fluidized Bed Combustion," *American Scientist* 72:254–261.

Gail, J. J., 1976. *Energy and Transportation,* Englewood Cliffs, N.J.: Prentice-Hall.

Garrison, A. J., 1981. *Solar Projects,* Philadelphia Pa.: Running Press.

*Gilbert, B., and Kaufmann, E., 1978. "The Second Reign of Old King Coal," *Audubon* (Nov.): 52–74.

Goldemberg, J., 1984. "Energy Problems in Latin America," *Science* 223:1357–1362.

Gomes da Silva, J; Serra, G. E., Moreira, J. R.; Goncalves, J. C.; and Goldenberg, J., 1978. "Energy Balance for Ethyl Alcohol Production from Crops," *Science* 201:903–906.

Greenberger, M., 1983. *Caught Unawares: the Energy Decade in Retrospect.* Cambridge, Mass.: Ballinger Publishing Co.

Gundlach, E. R., 1983. "The Fate of Amoco Cadiz Oil," *Science* 221:122–129.

*Hammond, A. L., 1973. "Dry Geothermal Wells: Promising Experimental Results," *Science* 182(5):43–44.

Hammond, A. L., 1978. "Energy: Elements of a Latin American Strategy," *Science* 200:753–754.

Hammond, A. L., and Metz, W. D., 1978. "Capturing Sunlight: A Revolution in Collector Design," *Science* 201:36–39.

*Hammond, R. P., 1979. "Nuclear Wastes and Public Acceptance," *American Scientist* 67:146–150.

*Hannon, B., 1975. "Energy Conservation and the Consumer," *Science* 189(1497):95–102.

*Hannon, B., and Brodrick, J. R., 1982. "Steel Recycling and Energy Conservation," *Science* 216:485–491.

Hannon, B.; Stein, R. G.; Segal, B. Z.; and Serber, D., 1978. "Energy and Labor in the Construction Sector," *Science* 202:837–847.

Harrison, J., 1984. "Disposal of Radioactive Wastes," *Science* 226:11–14.

Harte, J., and El-Gasseir, M., 1978. "Energy and Water," *Science* 199:623–634.

*Hayes, D., 1977. "Biological Sources of Commercial Energy," *Bioscience* 27(8):540–546.

Hayes, E. T., 1979. "Energy Resources Available to the United States, 1985 to 2000," *Science* 203(4377):233–239.

Heiken, G., et al., 1981. "Hot Dry Rock Geothermal Energy," *American Scientist* 69:400–407.

Heller, A., 1984. "Hydrogen-Evolving Solar Cells," *Science* 223:1141–1148.

Henig, R. M., 1979. "BEIR Comes to a Head on Low-Level Radiation Risks," *BioScience* 29(6):381–382.

*Hildebrandt, A. F., and Vant-Hull, L. L., 1977. "Power Heliostat," *Science* 197(4309):1139–1146.

Hirsch, R. L.; Gallagher, J. E.; Lessard, R. R.; and Wesselhoft, R. D., 1982. "Catalytic Coal Gasification: An Emerging Technology," *Science* 215:121–128.

Hirst, E., 1976. "Transportation Energy Conservation Policies," *Science* 192(4234):15–20.

*Hirst, E., and Carney, J., 1978. "Effect of Federal Residential Energy Conservation Programs," *Science* 199 (4331): 845–851.

Hohenemser, C., 1983. "Surprises, Surprises (What's in Store for Our Energy Future)," *Environment* 25 (10):30–35.

*Hopfner, K., 1979. "West Germany: A Nuclear Incident Every Three Days," *Nature* 281:418.

Hoyle, F., and Hoyle, G., 1980. *Common sense in Nuclear Energy.* San Francisco, Calif.: W. H. Freeman.

Hubbert, M. K., 1962. *Energy Resources.* National Research Council Publication 1000-D, p. 91. Washington, D.C.: National Academy of Sciences.

Hubbert, M. K., 1974. *U.S. Energy Resources: A Review as of 1972.* Serial No. 93-40 [92–75]. Washington, D.C.: Senate Committee on Interior and Insular Affairs.

Inhaber, H., 1979. "Risk with Energy from Conventional and Nonconventional Sources," *Science* 203:718–723.

*Isaacs, J. D., and Schmitt, W. R., 1980. "Ocean Energy: Forms and Prospects," *Science* 207(4428):265–273.

*Jansson, A., and Zucchetto, J., 1978. "Man Nature, and Energy Flow on the Island of Gotland," *Ambio* 7 (4):140–149.

*Johansson, T. B., et al., 1983. "Sweden Beyond Oil: The Efficient Use of Energy," *Science* 219:355–361.

Johnson, W. A.; Stoltzfus, V.; and Craumer, P., 1977. "Energy Conservation in Amish Agriculture," *Science* 198: 373–378.

Kane J.W., and Sternham M.M., 1978. *Physics.* New York: John Wiley.

*Kardsell, L., 1978. "Ecological Aspects of the Swedish Search for More Wood," *Ambio* 7(3):84–92.

*Kash, D. E., et al., 1976. *Our Energy Future.* Norman, Okla.: University of Oklahoma Press.

Kelley, H., 1978. "Photovoltaic Power System: A Tour through the Alternatives," *Science* 199:634–643.

*Kreith, F., and Meyer, R. T., 1983. "Large-Scale Use of Solar Energy with Central Receivers," *American Scientist* 71:598–605.

*Kulcinski, G. L.; Kessler, G; Holdren, J; and Hafele, W., 1979.

"Energy for the Long Run: Fission or Fusion?" *American Scientist* **67**:78–89.

Landsberg, H. H., 1982. "Relaxed Energy Outlook Masks Continuing Uncertainties," *Science* **218**:973–975.

LaPorte, T. R., 1978. "Nuclear Waste: Increasing Scale and Sociopolitical Impacts," *Science* **201**:22–28.

Lee, K. N., 1980. "A Federalist Strategy for Nuclear Waste Management," *Science* **208**:679–684.

Lehman, R. L., and Warren, H. E., 1978. "Residential Natural Gas Consumption: Evidence That Conservation Effort Today Has Failed," *Science* **199**:879–882.

Leighton, F. A., et al., 1983. "Heinz-Body Hemolytic Anemia from the Ingestion of Crude Oil: A Primary Toxic Effect in Marine Birds," *Science* **220**:871–873.

*Lewis, A., 1980. "Shaking the Assumptions on Nuclear Production of Electricity," June. New York Times News Service.

Lilienthal, D. E., 1980. *Atomic Energy: A New Start.* New York: Harper and Row.

Lockeretz, W., ed., 1984. *A.A.A.S. Selected Symposium: Agriculture as a Producer and Consumer of Energy.* Boulder, Col.: Westview Press.

*Lovins, A. B., 1976. "Energy Strategy: The Road Not Taken?" *Foreign Affairs* **55**:65–96.

*Lovins, A. B., 1977. *Soft Energy Paths: Toward a Durable Peace.* New York: Harper and Row.

*Lovins, A. B., 1978. "Soft Energy Technologies," *Ann. Rev. Energy* **3**:477–517.

Lovins, A. B., 1979. *Soft Energy Paths.* New York: Harper and Row.

Lucas, T., 1975. *How to Build a Solar Heater: A Complete Guide to Building and Buying Solar Panels, Water Heater, Pool Heaters, Barbecues and Power Plants.* Pasadena, Calif.: Ward Richie Press.

Marshall, E., 1979a. "News and Comment. Kemeny Report: Abolish the NRC," *Science* **206**:796–798.

Marshall, E. 1979b. "The Crisis at Three Mile Island: Nuclear Risks Are Reconsidered," *Science* **204**:152–153.

Marshall, E. 1980. "News and Comment: NRC Takes a Second Look at Reactor Design," *Science* **207**:1445–1448.

Marshall, E., 1983. "Clinch River Dies," *Science*, **222**:590–592.

Matthews, D., 1982. "Let's Decontrol All Natural Gas," *Exxon, USA,* **21**(4)24–31.

Maugh, T. H., 1976. "Natural Gas: United States Has It If The Price Is Right," *Science* **191**:549–550.

Maugh, T. H., 1977a. "Underground Gasification: An Ultimate Way to Exploit Coal," *Science* **198**:1132–1134.

*Maugh, T. H., 1977b. "Oil Shale Prospect on the Upswing," *Science* **198**:1023–1027.

Maugh, T. H., 1980. "Work on U.S. Oil Sands Heating Up," *Science* **207**:1191–1192.

*McBride, J., 1978. "Radiological Impact of Airborne Effluents of Coal and Nuclear Plants," *Science* **202** (4372):1045–1050.

McDaniels, D. 1979. *The Sun: Our Future Energy* Source, New York: John Wiley.

*Metz, W. D., 1978. "Report of Fusion Breakthrough Proves to Be a Media Event," *Science* **201**:792–794.

Metz, W. D., and Hammond, A. L., 1978. *Solar Energy in America.* Washington, D.C.: American Association for the Advancement of Science.

*Morris, S. C.; Moskowitz, P. D.; Sevian, W. A.; Silberstein, S.; and Hamilton, L. D., 1979. "Coal Conversion Technologies: Some Health and Environmental Effects," *Science* **206**:654–662.

Morse, R. N., 1977. "Solar Energy in Australia," *Ambio* **6**:209–215.

National Academy of Sciences, 1977. *Implications of Environmental Regulations for Energy Production and Consumption.* A report to the U.S. EPA from the Committee on Energy and the Environment-Commission on Natural Resources, Natural Research Council.

National Academy of Sciences, 1980. *Energy in Transition: 1985–2010.* A Final Report of the Committee on Nuclear and Alternative Energy Systems—National Academy of Sciences. San Francisco: W. H. Freeman. This is a look by the National Academy of Sciences at the next 25 years.

National Academy of Sciences, 1984. *Energy Use: The Human Dimension.* San Francisco: W. H. Freeman.

Natural Resources Defense Council, 1982. *The Reagan Energy Plan: A Major Power Failure,* Washington, D.C.

Nelkin, D., and Fallows, S., 1978. "The Evolution of the Nuclear Debate: The Role of Public Participation," *Ann. Rev. Energy* **3**:275–312.

*Newman, D. K., and Day, D., 1975. *The American Energy Consumer: A Report of the Energy Policy Project of the Ford Foundation.* Cambridge, Mass.: Ballinger Publishing Company.

Nielsen, P. E.; Nishimura, H; Otvos, J. W.; and Calvin, M. 1977. "Plant Crops as a Source of Fuel and Hydrocarbon-like Material," *Science* **198**:942–944.

Norman, C., 1984. "High-Level Politics over Low-Level Waste," *Science* **223**:258–260.

Norton, T. W., 1977. *Solar Energy Experiments.* Emmaus, Pa.: Rodale Press.

Nuclear Power: Issues and Choices, 1977. Cambridge, Mass.: Ballinger Publishing Company.

Odum, H. T., 1970. *Environment, Power, and Society.* New York: Wiley Interscience.

Office of Technological Assessment, 1982. *Energy Efficiency of Buildings in Cities.* Washington, D.C.: U.S. Government Printing Office.

*Olson, S., 1984. "Nuclear Undertakers," *Science 84,* Sept., 50–59.

Othmer, D. P., and Roels, O. A., 1973. "Power, Fresh Water, and Food from Cold, Deep-Sea Water," *Science* **182** (4108):121–125.

Parisi, A. J., 1980. "Nation's Appetite for Electricity Falls Below Utility Predictions," *The (Louisville) Courier Journal,* April 13, B12.

Park, J., 1981. *The Wind Power Book.* Palo Alto, Calif.: Cheshire Books.

Pauly, D., with Henkoff, R.; Lindsay, J. J.; Hager, M.; and Monroe, S., 1979. "Nuclear Power on the Ropes," *Newsweek,* April 16, 41–44.

Perry, H., 1983. "Coal in the United States: A Status Report," *Science* **222**:377–384.

Perry, H., and Streiter, S. H., 1977. *Multiple Paths for Energy Policy: A Critique of Lovins Energy Strategy.* New York: National Economic Research Associates.

Pimentel, D., ed. 1980. *CRC Handbook of Energy Utilization in Agriculture,* Boca Raton, Fla.: CRC Press.

Pimentel, D., ed., 1983. "Biomass Energy: Review Article by the Biomass Panel of the Energy Research Advisory Board," *Solar Energy* **30** (1):1–31.

*Pimentel, D., and Dazhong, W., 1985. "Technological Changes in Energy Use in U.S. Agricultural Production," in Gliessman, S., ed., *Research Approaches in Agricultural Ecology: An Introduction.* New York: Springer.

*Pimentel, D. L.; Hurd, E.; Bellotti, A. C.; Forstar, M. J.; Oka, I. M.; Sholes, O. D.; and Whitman, R. J., 1973. "Food Production and the Energy Crisis," *Science* **182**:443–449.

*Pimentel, D.; Nafus, D.; Vergara, W.; Papaj, D.; Jaconetta, L.; Wulfe, M.; Olsvig, L.; Frech, K.; Loye, M.; and Mendoza,

E., 1978. "Biological Solar Energy Conversion and U.S. Energy Policy," *Bioscience* **28**(6):376–382.

*Pimentel, D., et al., 1981. "Biomass Energy from Crop and Forest Residues," *Science* **212**:1110–1115.

*Pimentel, D., et al., 1984. "Environmental and Social Costs of Biomass Energy," *Bioscience* **34**(2):89–94.

Probstein, R. L., and Hicks, R. E., 1982. *Synthetic Fuels.* New York: McGraw-Hill.

Ramsay, W., 1979. *Unpaid Costs of Electrical Energy: Health and Environmental Impacts from Coal and Nuclear Power.* Baltimore, Md.: Johns Hopkins University Press.

Reed, J. W., 1975. *Wind Power Climatology of the U.S.* Albuquerque, N.M.: Sandia Laboratories.

Reed, T. B., and Lerner, R. M., 1973. "Methanol: A Versatile Fuel for Immediate Use," *Science* **182**(4110):1299–1304.

Roberts, L., 1982. "Ocean Dumping of Radioactive Waste," *BioScience* **32**(10):773–776.

*Schipper, L., and Litchtenberg, A. J., 1976. "Efficient Energy Use and Well Being: The Swedish Example," *Science* **194** (4269):1001–1012.

Schriesheim, A., and Kirshenbaum, I., 1981. "The Chemistry and Technology of Synthetic Fuels," *American Scientist* **69**:536–542.

Schurr, S.; Darmstadter, J.; Perry, H.; Ramsay, W.; and Russell, M., 1979. *Energy in America's Future: The Choices Before Us.* Baltimore: John Hopkins University Press.

Schwarz, J., 1982. "Learning About Life in an Oil Seep," *Exxon USA*, **21**(4):12–15.

Shapely, D. 1975. "Senate Study Predicts U.S. Oil Exhaustion," *Science* **187**:1064.

Sheils, M., with Buckley, J., 1979. "Welcome to 'the Monster,'" *Time*, July 23, p. 66.

Smil, V., 1984. "On Energy and Land," *American Scientist* **72**:15–21. Describes how switching from fossil fuel to renewable energy will change our patterns of land use.

*Snell, J. E.; Achenbach, P. R.; and Petersen, S. R., 1976. "Energy Conservation in New Housing Design," *Science* **192**:1305–1311.

Sorensen, B., 1979. "Nuclear Power: The Answer That Became a Question," *Ambio* **8**(1):10–17.

Sorensen, B., 1981. "Turning to the Wind," *American Scientist* **69**:500–508.

Stein, R. G., 1977. *Architecture and Energy.* Garden City, N.J.: Anchor-Doubleday.

*Steinhart, J. S., and Steinhart, C. D., 1974. In Abelson, P. H., ed., *Energy: Use Conservation and Supply.* Washington, D.C.: American Association for the Advancement of Science.

Stobaugh, R., and Yergin, E., eds., 1979. *Energy Future: Report of the Engineering Project of the Harvard Business School.* New York: Random House.

Swift, H. E., 1983. "Fuels and Chemicals from Single-Carbon Sources," *American Scientist* **71**:616–620.

Teller, E., 1979. *Energy from Heaven and Earth.* San Francisco: W. H. Freeman.

A Time to Choose, 1974. Cambridge, Mass.: Ballinger Publishing Co.

United Nations, 1974. *United Nations Statistical Yearbook.* New York: United Nations.

United Nations, 1975. *Selected World Demographic Indicators by Countries 1950–2000.* New York: United Nations.

United Nations, 1976. *World Energy Supplies, 1950–1974.* New York: United Nations.

United Nations, 1979. *World Energy Supplies 1973–1978.* U.N. Statistical Papers, Series J, No. 22. New York: United Nations.

U.S. Department of Energy, 1975. *Energy Conservation,* Washington, D.C.: Federal Energy Administration (now Department of Energy).

*U.S. Department of Energy, 1977. *Fossil Energy Research Program of the Energy Research and Development Administration,* April, FY-1978. Washington, D.C.: U.S. Government Printing Office.

U.S. Department of Energy, 1979a. *Annual Report to Congress, 1979.* DOE/EIA 0173 (79)/2 (annual). Washington, D.C.: U.S. Government Printing Office.

U.S. Department of Energy, 1979b. *International Energy Annual.* DOE/EIA-0219 (79) August 1980, Washington, D.C.: U.S. Government Printing Office.

U.S. Department of Energy, 1981. *Coal Conversion and the Environment: Chemical, Biomedical, and Ecological Considerations.* Springfield, Va.: National Technical Information Service.

U.S. Department of Energy, 1982. *Nuclear Power from Fission Reactors.* Washington, D.C.: U.S. Government Printing Office.

*U.S. Department of Energy, 1983a. *1982 Annual Energy Review.* Washington, D.C.: U.S. Government Printing Office.

*U.S. Department of Energy, 1983b. *1982 Annual Energy Outlook,* Washington, D.C.: U.S. Government Printing Office.

U.S. Department of Energy, 1983c. *Atoms to Electricity.* Washington, D.C.: U.S. Government Printing Office.

*U.S. Department of Energy, 1984a. *Annual Report to Congress 1983.* Washington, D.C.: U.S. Government Printing Office.

U.S. Department of Energy, 1984b. *1983 Annual Energy Outlook.* Washington, D.C.: U.S. Government Printing Office.

U.S. Department of Energy, 1984c. *1983 Annual Energy Review.* Washington, D.C.: U.S. Government Printing Office.

U.S. Department of Transportation, 1983. *National Transportation Statistics: Annual Report.* Washington, D.C.: U.S. Government Printing Office.

Wade, N. 1974. "Windmills: The Resurrection of Ancient Energy Technology," *Science* **184**:1055–1058.

Walton, S., 1980. "Coal Conversion Will Increase Acid Rain Damage," *BioScience* **30**(5):293–295.

Wentorf, R. H., and Hanneman, R. E., 1974. "Thermochemical Hydrogen Generation," *Science* **185**:311–319.

Weinberg, A., and Spiewak, I., 1984. "Inherently Safe Reactors and a Second Nuclear Era," *Science* **224**:1398–1402.

Whicker, F. W., and Schultz, V., 1982. *Radioecology: Nuclear Energy and the Environment* (2 vols.). Boca Raton, Fla.: CRC Press.

Wise, D. L., ed., 1981. *Fuel Gas Production From Biomass* (2 vols.). Boca Raton, Fla.: CRC Press.

Wymer, R. G., and Blomeke, J. O., 1975. *Radioactive Wastes: Sources, Treatment and Disposal,* In: Duggan and Cloutier, New York.

*Zaleski, C. P., 1980. "Breeder Reactors in France," *Science* **108** (4440):137–144.

CHAPTER 7

Mineral and Water Resources

SECTION A
Minerals: Essential Nutrients of Civilization

*E*arly humans needed chemical nutrients just as all living things need them. They had to have calcium for bones and teeth; iron for hemoglobin; and hydrogen, oxygen, phosphorus, potassium, iodine, nitrogen, sulfur, copper, zinc, molybdenum, and magnesium, for their basic structure and function. Later, *Homo sapiens* began to rely on inorganic chemical substances for purposes other than food. They beat elements into spears and plowshares, so to speak. In doing so, *Homo sapiens* began to use water and certain minerals in ways designed to help get the chemical elements needed as food (Figure 7.1). Humans have mined minerals and transformed them into fertilizers, farm machinery, and other equipment. We extended food production into dry areas as metals derived from minerals became the components of water pipelines, pumps, and irrigation systems. Shipping food into places where it could

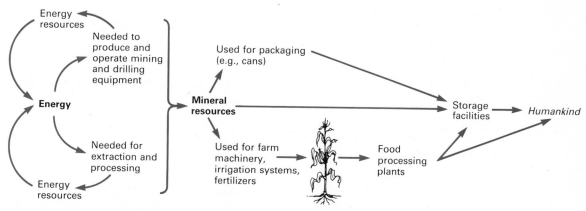

Figure 7.1 The Expanding Role of Minerals in Getting Food to Humans. Humans have long used minerals to improve access to food. Human societies have become nearly as dependent on food-getting systems made from minerals as the individual person is on food. We also use minerals in other ways—to provide shelter, for example, which also improves our prospects for survival and gives us a higher quality of life.

Element: a substance composed of just one kind of atom. There are only 106 different elements; in various combinations they make up all the materials in the universe.

Mineral: a chemical element, a specific inorganic compound, or a specific complex aggregation of elements and compounds. (Examples: iron—an element, asbestos—a mixture of compounds.)

Ore: a mineral-containing substance or mixture from which that mineral can be extracted. For example, bauxite can be mined and processed to extract the aluminum it contains. If the amount of aluminum per given volume is high, it is a *high-grade ore;* if the amount is low, it is a *low-grade ore.*

Reserve: deposits of a mineral that have been located and are recoverable under existing or imminent economic and technological conditions.

Resource: the total amount of a mineral on the earth (or potentially in the universe). Includes material whose location may or may not be known and material that may not now be economically or technically recoverable.

not be produced was made possible by minerals that had been transformed into transportation systems. And so it went.

The expanding use of minerals and the use of energy to power mineral-derived machinery long ago brought us to the point at which civilization is absolutely dependent upon nonfood mineral (and energy) resources. Minerals other than those humans eat have become essential to human civilization.

Just as the human need for energy has significance that extends well beyond the energy (calories) that individual humans must eat every day, the need for minerals has significance that extends beyond minimum daily requirements printed on the sides of cereal boxes. It is the requirements of civilization, not those of individuals, on which the reader is asked to focus in this chapter.

RESOURCES AND RESERVES: SOME DEFINITIONS

Despite the fact that, practically speaking, elements are neither created nor destroyed, minerals are generally regarded as nonrenewable resources. **Nonrenewable resources** are those not naturally regenerated at rates comparable to their rates of depletion. We learned in Chapter 3 that the great spheres differ in chemical composition, both qualitatively and quantitatively (Table 7.1). While the chemicals that make up the atmosphere and hydrosphere tend to be relatively well dispersed, minerals in soil and rock (the lithosphere) vary from one area to another; they tend to occur in deposits of varying richness. These deposits are the result of physical-chemical phenomena like crystallization that produce a given mineral. The solid state of the earth's crust keeps such deposits from scattering once they have been formed. The deposition of most minerals occurs slowly, in geologic time frames. For some minerals the conditions may no longer exist that caused or permitted a given combination of elements to become concentrated in mineral deposits. This is why mineral ores are considered nonrenewable. Once they are mined and used, they are gone as ores.

Mineral **resources** are the minerals that are important to human beings. **Mineral reserves** are mineral deposits that are recoverable at a profit under existing or imminent conditions of technology and economics. A schematic relationship between mineral resources and reserves is shown in Figure 7.2. It should be noted that linear use (extract, use, and discard) tends to *decrease* reserves; discoveries and new recovery technologies tend to *increase* them; recycling tends to hold them constant.

SUPPLY AND DEMAND, RESOURCES AND RESERVES

The relationship between resources and reserves changes with supply and demand. As supply goes down and/or as demand goes up:

Table 7.1 Mineral Distribution in the Great Spheres. Some examples showing that the distribution of the elements varies considerably from one sphere to another.

	Hydrosphere (oceans) (% composition)	Atmosphere (% composition)	Lithosphere (% by weight)
Hydrogen	10.67	0.01	0.14
Nitrogen	<0.002	78.03	trace
Calcium	0.05	trace	3.63
Sodium	1.14	trace	2.83
Magnesium	0.14	trace	2.09

1. Reserves become more valuable—cost goes up.
2. The search for new deposits intensifies because of the economic incentive.
3. Resources or deposits that had previously been uneconomical may become economical and thus shift into the category of reserves. (During the coal boom of the late 1970s in the United States it became economical for a time to mine coal/rock refuse piles for coal.)

4. The search for more efficient technologies of mineral extraction intensifies.
5. The search for substitutes intensifies.
6. Recycling and reuse become more desirable practices.
7. Conservation increases, and wasteful practices decrease.

As the limits are reached and the gap between supply and demand makes cost too high for a particular

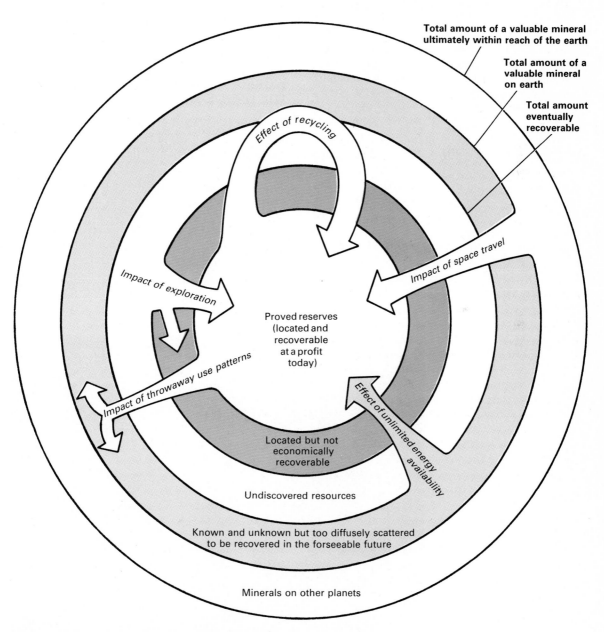

Figure 7.2 The Difference Between Reserves and Various Categories of Resources.
Technically speaking, even the minerals on other planets can be considered resources.

mineral, cost serves as a feedback influence causing demand to level off. Demand may actually fall off as people decide to do without or to settle for less desirable substitutes (where substitution is possible). All of the foregoing is grossly simplified, but it should illustrate some of the complexities of the human relationship to natural resources, which we will explore in this chapter.

MINERALS AND LIMITING FACTORS

If we accept the premise that the total amount of nearly every chemical element on earth is constant and that all minerals can be synthesized from the elements, the ultimate limiting factor in obtaining minerals is energy. One cubic kilometer of surface rock contains 2×10^8 metric tons of aluminum, over 1×10^8 metric tons of iron, 800,000 metric tons of zinc, and 200,000 metric tons of copper (Brooks and Andrews, 1974). If we had unlimited energy, trace elements could be accumulated from such rock or even from air, soil, and water. We could mine anything—even landfills—and we would never run short. But we do not have unlimited energy.

Problems are arising today because many of the highly concentrated deposits have been mined out, leaving more low-grade (less concentrated) deposits to be mined. Because needed minerals are now only to be found in more dispersed **low-grade deposits**, more energy is needed to mine and concentrate them. In a 1978 report the National Academy of Sciences indicated that by the year 2000 the grade of copper ore available at *that* time will likely require "three times as much energy to yield one ton of copper in the form of concentrate as is employed today" (U.S. General Accounting Office, 1979). Industry accounts for about 40% of all fuels and electricity used in the United States, and of this, 25–50% is used in the extraction and processing of minerals (U.S. General Accounting Office, 1979). This percentage is likely to increase in the future.

WORLD TRENDS AND IMBALANCES IN THE USE OF MINERAL RESOURCES

There is no question that we have been using up our mineral resources at faster and faster rates. The entire metal production of the world before World War II was about equal to what has been consumed since 1969. Figure 7.3 illustrates the substantial increase in material consumption in the United States and other countries in the twentieth century. Some of the increased rate of consumption can be attributed to increases in population, but increases in per capita consumption have had a greater effect. Total consumption and per capita consumption in the United States increased at similar rates through the

We are consuming our mineral resources at a great rate. Every aluminum bumper that is made to satisfy our desire for new cars uses up resources that cannot be replaced.

mid to late 1900s. Projections through the year 2000 indicate a sustained positive rate of increase of 3–5% for most nonfuel minerals.

It is important to note that there have also been changes over time in the things we have used in support of civilization. There has been a relative increase in the use of nonrenewable materials (including minerals) since 1900. There has also been a trend toward increased use of materials that require energy in their extraction and processing.

It seems worth noting that some nations of the world use up mineral resources more quickly than

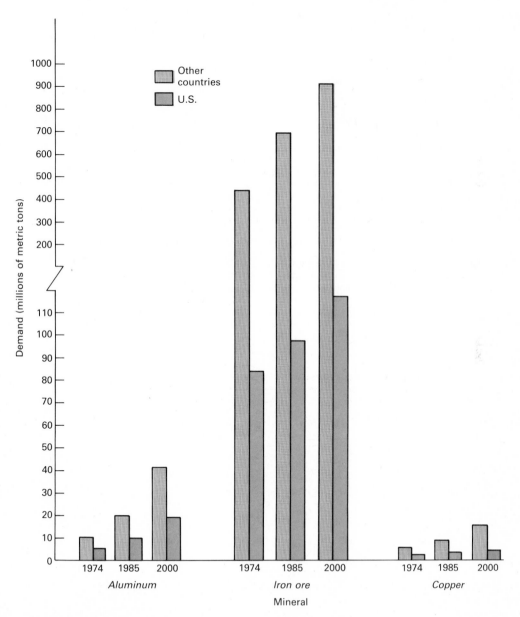

Figure 7.3 Mineral Consumption in the Twentieth Century. Total consumption of minerals has increased dramatically in the U.S. and other industrialized countries since 1900. This chart shows how demand for three minerals is expected to change up to the year 2000. A steady rise is expected over the remainder of the twentieth century and beyond.

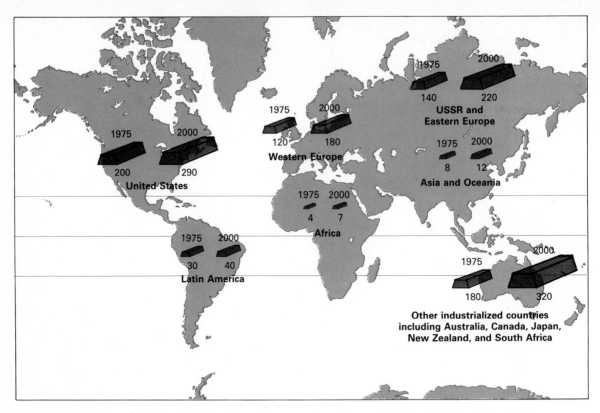

Figure 7.4   Metal Consumption Per Capita—World. The rate of consumption of nonfuel minerals varies from country to country. This figure compares metal consumption per capita for 1975 and projected figures for per capita consumption for 2000 based on moderate growth projections. Numbers are constant 1975 dollar values of crude steel, primary aluminum, and refined copper. It is expected that by the year 2000 the industrialized countries, with no more than one fourth of the world's population, will consume over three fourths of the world's nonfuel mineral production.

Table 7.2   Life Expectancies of World Reserves of Selected Minerals.

	1976 Reserves	Projected Demand Growth Rate (percent)	Life Expectancy (years)*	
			Static at 1976 level	Growing at Projected Rates
Fluorine (*million short tons*)	37	4.58	18	13
Silver (*million troy ounces*)	6,100	2.33	20	17
Zinc (*million short tons*)	166	3.05	26	19
Mercury (*thousand flasks*)	5,210	0.50	22	21
Sulfur (*million long tons*)	1,700	3.16	34	23
Lead (*million short tons*)	136	3.14	37	25
Tungsten (*million pounds*)	4,200	3.26	52	31
Nickel (*million short tons*)	60	2.94	86	43
Platinum (*million troy ounces*)	297	3.75	110	44
Phosphate rock (*million metric tons*)	25,732	5.17	240	51
Manganese (*million short tons*)	1,800	3.36	164	56
Iron in ore (*billion short tons*)	103	2.95	172	62
Aluminum in bauxite (*million short tons*)	5,610	4.29	312	63
Chromium (*million short tons*)	829	3.27	377	80
Potash (*million short tons*)	12,230	3.27	470	86

*Assumes no increase to 1976 reserves.

others (Figure 7.4). Figure 7.4 shows metal consumption per capita for the world. Without question, industrialized nations are the major users of nonfuel minerals. The *Global 2000 Report to the President* (Council on Environmental Quality, 1980) projects that the use of nonfuel minerals in Latin America, Asia, and Africa will increase only slightly by the year 2000. Even with 75% or more of the world's population in 2000, these countries are expected to use only 8% of the aluminum produced in the world, 13% of the copper, and 17% of the iron ore. The 25% of the population in industrial countries in the year 2000 will continue to use 75% of the world's nonfuel mineral production. Currently, the United States alone, with 5% of the world's people, uses more than 33% of the world's mineral resources. The United States happens to have abundant mineral resources, but it already imports nearly all of the chromium, most of the aluminum and manganese, and more than half of the tin, tungsten, zinc, and nickel that it uses.

WHERE DO WE STAND TODAY?

Inventory

Table 7.2 summarizes world mineral reserves and the number of years they will last, calculated on the basis of current trends and projected changes in rate of use.

It should not be surprising that growth in the demand for phosphate rock is projected to be one of the highest. The demand for all mineral commodities used for the production of fertilizers is expected to grow at a rate of increase greater than 3%. Even if the rate of consumption remains static, the world is within 50 years of exhausting its reserves of lead, mercury, silver, sulfur, tin, and zinc. A mineral is considered to be depleted or used up when 80% or so of its known reserves have been mined. Total depletion of a mineral resource deposit is an unrealistic end point because of economics. In any case, if a particular mineral were indeed critical, the most severe impact that would result from running short would be reached as supplies became *very* tight, well before the end.

Since there is no way to know for certain whether future rates of consumption will rise, drop, or stay the same, all that predictors can do is state and explain the assumptions upon which their predictions are based. The assumption that future rates will remain constant produces a **static reserve index** (0% increases in the rate of consumption). If one assumes some degree of exponential (faster and faster) increase in the rate of utilization (a given percentage each year), the result is an **exponential reserve index**. Figure 7.5 illustrates these indices for certain important metal resources.

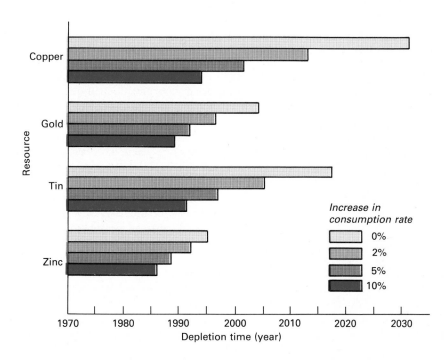

Figure 7.5 Depletion Times.
Depletion times for minerals can be calculated on the basis of assumptions about changes in the rates at which the material will be used. This chart shows four possible depletion times for copper, gold, tin, and zinc.

U.N. Conference on the Law of the Sea

In the summer of 1980, after eight years of meeting, the U.N. Conference on the Law of the Sea appeared to have reached an agreement on who controls the ocean and its resources. The treaty

1. establishes a 12-mile territorial limit for coastal nations and a 200-mile exclusive economic zone (EEZ) in which the coastal nation controls all fishing, marine life, and mineral rights;
2. prescribes fines for those who pollute the sea; and
3. establishes an International Seabed Authority to oversee the mining of deep seabed minerals. The authority will set policy consistent with the treaty, and license companies to mine outside the EEZs. The authority will collect taxes on the minerals produced. The authority can also do its own mining. Revenues from its mining and tax collection will go to the United Nations to be used for developing nations (developed nations will lend the authority money to support its initial mining activities).

On December 10, 1982, 119 nations signed the treaty in Montego Bay, Jamaica. The treaty will become effective when 60 nations ratify it; this is expected to take several more years. The United States, under the Reagan administration, has not signed the treaty, nor have several other industrialized nations including the Soviet Union. Although the United States did not vote for or sign the Law of the Sea Treaty, President Reagan, by Executive Order on March 10, 1983, established the U.S. Exclusive Economic Zone (EEZ), extending U.S. jurisdiction over minerals found within 200 nautical miles of the U.S. coast and that of its island territories. In late 1983 a draft Environmental Impact Statement was completed for a proposal to lease several tracts for mining on the Gorda Ridge, an area of ocean bottom 140 miles off the Oregon/California coast.

Although this formal action by the government may help to settle questions of mineral rights within the boundaries of the EEZ, unless there is an international agreement signed by the major industrialized nations the question of mineral rights in the open seas is likely to remain unsettled.

The Trouble with Inventories

Estimating resources and reserves is difficult because so many factors are involved. Finding new deposits would extend the life of a given mineral, as would increased recycling of products that contain the mineral. The development of new technologies to rework old deposits or to work known deposits previously considered too poor to be economical could increase the supply of a given mineral. The rate of use of a mineral could change because of the availability of a substitute material (which would result in a decrease in use) or the expansion of uses for a mineral (which would result in an increase in use). Consequently, it is often more realistic to talk about several alternative estimates of how long a mineral may be available based on specific assumptions about changes in rates of use and available reserves.

INCREASING OUR RESOURCE RESERVES: PROMISE AND PROBLEMS

Finding New Deposits

Many human beings are gainfully employed scouring the globe looking for new mineral deposits. All sorts of technologies are employed, ranging from prospectors with picks to satellites. Using satellites to identify areas of likely deposits is termed **remote sensing** (see Chapter 17). Since many deposits have been found already, what is left to find will be harder and harder to locate. The law of diminishing returns has been operative for some time. Deposits that are being found now are of generally lower quality than those we have tapped in the past. Recently, increasing attention has been given to the last of the least explored portions of the earth—the oceans and the ocean floor.

Mining the Deep Sea

It is already known that concentrations of nickel, cobalt, manganese, and perhaps copper are located on the ocean floor in sufficient quantities to be mined economically. Some problems with the development of a sea mining industry are related to the political uncertainties involved—who owns the deep sea and its contents? There have been attempts to reach international agreement on deep-sea mining, and the U.S. Congress has considered legislation. The industrialized countries are concerned with assuring supplies for themselves, while developing countries seek also to be included in the benefits of mining international waters.

Whether the cost of deep-sea minerals will undersell the current market is also a problem, leaving countries with land reserves in a major slump. Some agreement is needed (see Bonus 7.1) before much development is likely in this area. Should development come, only a few types of minerals are likely to be commercially recoverable in the near future.

Finding Better Ways to Extract Minerals

Research financed by private industry and government is underway that would develop improved technologies for mineral extraction. Improved efficiencies would have the effect of improving the cost-selling price ratio for marginal deposits. Such deposits might then move into the category of reserves (see Figure 7.2). What do we mean by improved extraction methods? We refer mainly to reduction in the number of dollars needed to extract a unit of resource—dollars per kilogram of iron, let's say. We mean reduction in the amount of energy required to extract the mineral, reduction in the environmental impact of mining and processing, and reduction in hazards in the work place, all of which are involved in calculating the cost of extracting minerals.

Problems with the Strategy of More

As resources become harder to find and harder to extract, more and more energy must be used in the finding, mining, and extraction of minerals. This shifts part of our mineral resource problem into the category of the energy resource depletion problem addressed in Chapter 6. In turn, the use of more energy generates more pollution (see Chapters 6, 9, 10, 11, 12, and 17). There are also a number of direct environmental impacts to consider.

A 1978 study by the National Academy of Sciences indicated that the mining of low-grade copper deposits in the year 2000 not only would use three times as much energy per ton, but would also require the disposal of three times as much **overburden** (the rock layers overlying the copper, which must be removed to mine) and **tailings** (what is left after the copper is extracted)—about two billion tons a year (U.S. General Accounting Office, 1979). The area of land disturbed will be greater per ton of mineral extracted. Extra processing will add still more pollutants to the air and water. Impacts on health and worker safety are additional factors to be considered in calculating the trade-offs for mineral supply. The environmental impacts of mineral resource extraction and use are summarized in Figure 7.6.

Elsewhere in this text (Chapter 15), we will review in detail the many environmental problems associated with errant (wasted) mineral resources. Mercury, nickel, sulfur, chromium, lead, and cobalt escape into the environment to poison fish, birds, and people. There is also the problem of solid waste, which can include aluminum, iron, copper, nickel, and much, much more. We would like to review one environmental problem here to underscore the point that minerals can be used in ways that bring harm to the environment. To help avoid simplistic thinking patterns, we have chosen an example wherein the use of minerals is good *and* bad.

Minerals in Food Production: An Example

In Chapter 3 we examined the concept of limiting factors and pointed out that nitrates and phosphates are the essential nutrients in least supply in many natural systems. Their availability limits the growth of plants and hence governs the activities of natural systems overall. It has long been known in agriculture that if limiting nutrients can be supplied in larger amounts, yield will increase. Farmers have

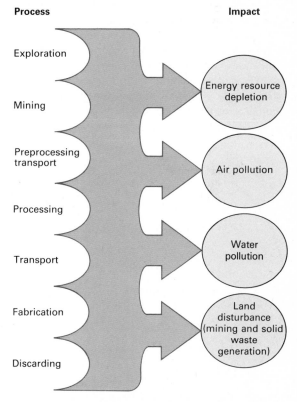

Figure 7.6 The Relationship Between Mineral Utilization and Environmental Problems. Many stages in the extraction and use of minerals have considerable real or potential negative impact on the environment. Although there are likely to be more nonpolluting technologies in the future, it is generally true that the lower the grade of a mineral ore, the greater the potential negative impact from extraction and processing on the environment.

long practiced rotation of crops so that a cover crop of legumes could periodically enrich the soil with nitrates. This has been supplemented by use of manure. However, there have always been problems with these methods. Crop rotation eliminates a cash crop in some fields every year; manure is difficult to apply, and its concentrations are difficult to regulate.

During World War I the technology was developed to extract nitrogen from the atmosphere and convert it into nitrates and ammonium salts—the forms of nitrogen usable by plants. This technology involves using fossil fuel–derived energy to copy the natural activities of the nitrogen fixing bacteria in the nitrogen cycle (Chapter 3). This together with the discovery that rich natural deposits of phosphorus and potassium salts *can be mined* resulted in the use of inorganic or synthetic fertilizers in ever-increasing amounts. Inexpensive energy supplies made the use of inorganic fertilizers much more profitable to the farmer than the older methods of crop rotation or organic fertilizers. But this innovation has had some side effects on natural systems.

The net increase of nitrates in the soil increases the risk of contamination of groundwater and, in some cases, surface water. Nitrates may reach the groundwater by leaching, and nitrates can be harmful to people and other animals (see Chapter 12). Though phosphates tend to adhere to soil particles,

they can be carried into surface waters, where they can stimulate plant growth, which is followed by plant death and decomposition, resulting in oxygen depletion (see Chapter 12). The mining of phosphates brings these substances back into the cyclic process at a much faster rate than geologic uplift and weathering. This means that more of this limiting factor is available overall, which is not always a good thing.

The availability of synthetic fertilizers has aggravated the problem of what to do with natural fertilizers like manure. Much manure ends up in surface water and groundwater or as a nuisance in lagoons (Figure 7.7).

There are alternatives to solving mineral problems, other than finding more minerals.

STRATEGIES TO REDUCE RATES OF MINERAL COMSUMPTION

Repeated Use of Minerals: Recycling

One of the environmentally ideal solutions to the problem of mineral supply would be one that would increase the availability of a given mineral while using less energy, disturbing less land, and polluting less air and water. It has been calculated

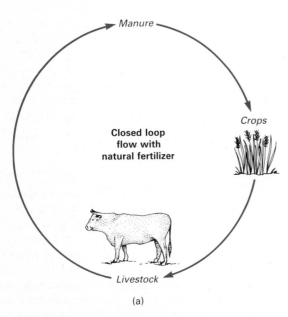

(a)

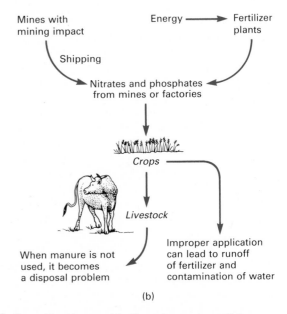

(b)

Figure 7.7 Material Flow Patterns for Natural and Synthetic Fertilizer. By failing to take into account the big picture, humans have often progressed in one area while creating havoc in another. A prime example is in the use of fertilizers. (a) With natural fertilizer, there was an efficient closed loop. (b) Synthetic fertilizers are easier to mix and apply but can disrupt cycles with problematic results.

Part II *Homo Sapiens* in the Scheme of Natural Things

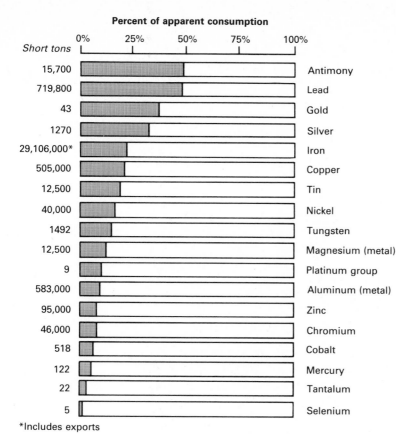

Percent of apparent consumption

Short tons	Material
15,700	Antimony
719,800	Lead
43	Gold
1270	Silver
29,106,000*	Iron
505,000	Copper
12,500	Tin
40,000	Nickel
1492	Tungsten
12,500	Magnesium (metal)
9	Platinum group
583,000	Aluminum (metal)
95,000	Zinc
46,000	Chromium
518	Cobalt
122	Mercury
22	Tantalum
5	Selenium

*Includes exports

Figure 7.8 Scrap Reclaimed in the U.S. as a Percent of Total Consumption. (One short ton equals 0.91 metric ton.) Although recycling provides an ideal solution to some of the problems of mineral shortages, only a small percentage of scrap materials is recycled. The potential for increasing supplies of some minerals through recycling is great.

that to make aluminum from scrap instead of from virgin material requires 95% less energy. This kind of processing results in an 89% energy savings for copper, 55% for steel and 46% for paper (Case, 1980). Virgin materials require more energy for extraction and processing as well as transportation. If recycling increased by 50% in the steel industry and tripled in the paper industry, energy equivalent to 500,000 barrels of oil could be saved daily. This amounts to more than the daily energy output of 14 nuclear power plants. Likewise, recycling of steel cuts air pollution by 76%. If the amount of paper recycled were tripled, $750 million could be saved annually in disposal costs (Case, 1980).

Though the recycling of paper, metals, and glass is already an established part of the U.S. economic system, it is not widely practiced. Figure 7.8 shows the amount of scrap recycled in the United States.

The question then arises, Why don't we recycle? The answer has many facets. Basically, relatively rigid institutional forces encourage use of raw materials and discourage use of scrap or waste materials.

Institutional policies such as tax breaks for depletion of a mineral resource and higher transportation rates for scrap material than for virgin materials were established at a time when development of resources was a national priority and resources were plentiful. The institutional policies have carried over into our patterns of using convenience products and throwaway materials. We have not yet changed to adjust to the current circumstances in which wise use of resources and resource conservation should be national priorities.

A shift to an economic system emphasizing secondary (as opposed to virgin) materials industries would be no simple matter (see Figure 7.9). Most industrial machinery is designed for processing virgin materials. The collection and sorting of used materials for recycling requires costly labor. Products have not been made with recycling in mind; consequently, the complex mixtures of metals in automobiles require expensive separation techniques and so are poor reserves. Products that are made basically of one mineral—such as aluminum

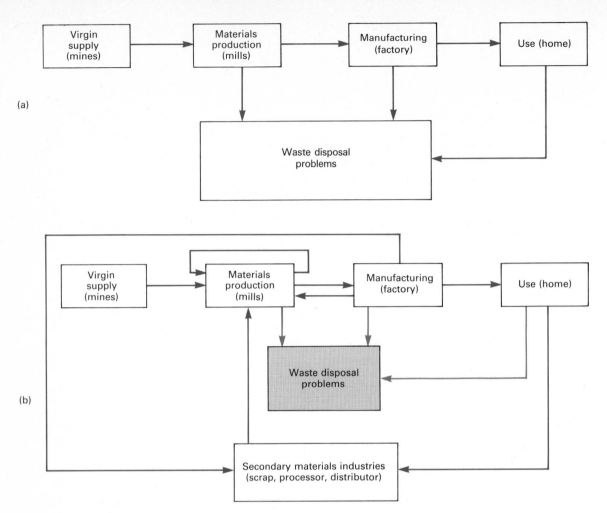

Figure 7.9 Secondary Materials Industry in the Grand Scheme of Material Flow. (a) The most common pattern for materials use has been the one-way flow from virgin materi-als to product to disposal. (b) The development of a second-ary materials industry changes the pattern to a cycle.

or steel—are actually rich reserves, but such prod-ucts are hard to find. As in any system, changing one cog—such as the way materials are used—disrupts the operation of the interlocking wheels of civiliza-tion.

In 1976, Congress passed the Resource Conser-vation and Recovery Act (RCRA) to provide funds for extensive research and development projects in the areas of resource recovery and conservation. This act authorized special studies, including a de-tailed analysis of the type of wastes and path of waste flow in our present system of operation and the potential for utilization of simple, small-scale recov-ery facilities for communities. The economics of re-source recovery and separation of wastes by type (paper, metal, glass) at the point of production and the marketing of recovered material were also in-

cluded (see Chapter 15). The act specified that fed-eral agencies were to begin to buy items composed of significant amounts of recovered material within practical and economically competitive limits. The impact of this legislation still remains to be seen. Of special interest to those of us who are aware that everything is connected is the fact that the increased cost of waste disposal, especially for hazardous waste, is making recycling more economically com-petitive.

Extended Use of Products: Antiobsolescence

In a society in which obsolete and old-fashioned things are collected once a week and buried, a shift toward products designed to last longer would de-crease the demand for the materials from which those products are made. Such a shift will not come easily. Obsolescence is partly related to the fact that cheaply made and rapidly worn-out products are not expensive in the short run, as are more soundly made products. There is a real demand for such inexpensive things.

Even if this could be overcome, major economic changes and adjustments would be required by any movement toward antiobsolescence. Labor-intensive activities would replace energy- and mineral-intensive activities. For instance, the production of fewer cars each year would decrease the use of minerals and the energy required to transport and process them, but the work force would have to shift from assembly work into repair and maintenance. Cars would cost more, since manufacturers would be selling fewer and better products. Perhaps not many people could afford cars. Repercussions would spread to the steel industry, sales, and other related enterprises. Imagine this sort of domino effect over the entire spectrum of manufacturing! Still, this is an approach that deserves consideration.

Substitutes: Let Them Eat Cake?

Another approach to solving mineral shortage problems is to work toward decreased demand—beyond that which results from rising prices.

First of all, technology can find substitutes for scarce minerals. In specific instances we have already seen a shift from copper to aluminum and from iron and steel to aluminum. Chromium on automobiles has largely been replaced by aluminum and plastic. There might well be more alternative materials that can be modeled to fit the function of the mineral in short supply. Figure 7.10 indicates that the creation of new types of materials has been an increasingly popular alternative in the twentieth century. However, new synthetic materials such as plastics have created other problems, such as that of disposal. Also, these materials have been based on petroleum.

What about substitutes that are not only in greater supply, but also less environmentally harmful? The advantages must be weighed along with numerous other considerations on a case-by-case basis. A shift from metal or plastic to a renewable resource—wood—is possible in some cases. However, forests are already being used faster than they are produced. At the moment, renewable wood happens to be a lot more expensive than plastic made from nonrenewable petroleum. Policies and practices governing renewable resources must be examined closely if demand is to shift in their direction.

Small-scale community recycling is just the beginning. It is vital that industry also make resource recovery a priority.

We humans live mostly for the moment. We could say that economic natural selection *should* already have brought us to the point at which we are using the best mineral (in terms of suitability for the job and low cost). However, new substitutions can be found only through painstaking research. Once found, it takes a while for substitutes to be placed into the manufacturing system—machines and whole factories have to be retooled. Now, though, as equipment and processes in industries are upgraded and replaced, we must look for environmentally sound substitutes for scarce minerals and for minerals that hurt us as we use them.

MINERALS AND WORLD POLITICS

The uneven distribution of mineral deposits through the world adds a political dimension to the whole question of mineral supply. Of the 74 non-energy minerals designated by the U.S. Department of Interior as essential to our industrial economy, about 22 are imported at least partly if not entirely. After the mid-1980s, this will probably rise to 50% of all raw materials (U.S. General Accounting Office, 1978). Figure 7.11 indicates U.S. mineral requirements for 1978 and the amounts imported from other countries. Given the essential nature of most of these minerals, they are important factors in U.S. foreign policy considerations.

We are all aware of the dependence of the United States on imported oil from the OPEC cartel. Although it is generally thought that a cartel for nonfuel minerals is unlikely because of the erratic

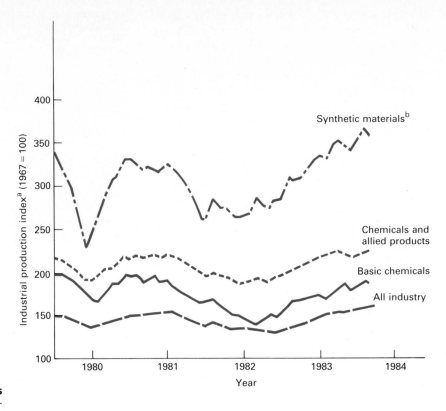

Figure 7.10 Changing Trends in the Use of Materials. Different types of synthetic materials are continually being developed. The use of synthetic materials is increasing dramatically.

[a] Seasonally adjusted.
[b] Includes plastics, synthetic rubber, and man-made fibers.

distribution patterns of the deposits and because of the potential for substitutes, mineral resources are factors in our foreign policy. For example, in 1966 the United States was party to a U.N. action placing economic sanctions on Rhodesia (now Zimbabwe). Imports from that country were banned. In 1971 the United States revised its position on the sanctions. Figure 7.11 shows that chromium was imported from Rhodesia by the United States. Low stockpiles and the concern that we would become dependent on the Soviet Union for an essential mineral contributed to this policy reversal (Council on Environmental Quality, 1977). Chromium is used by the steel industry producing stainless steel, among other things. In 1977 the United States joined the boycott again after stockpiles were replenished and improved technology and increasing exports by other countries made supplies more available.

A related problem arises when supplies are curtailed for reasons other than an embargo. For example, in 1978, internal problems in Zaire prevented ample production of cobalt. Prices soared, and there were major disturbances in the marketplace.

There is increasing international competition for mineral resources. Currently, some European countries and Japan have entered into international commodity agreements with mineral-producing countries. Producer countries bargain for premium prices and technical assistance. User countries are willing to give generous terms to prevent supply disruptions. All of this, of course, affects the mineral market system worldwide and strains political allegiances. Energy will continue to be one of the biggest issues in world politics in the future, but mineral supplies will be close behind. Water will be another continuing problem.

Part II   *Homo Sapiens* in the Scheme of Natural Things

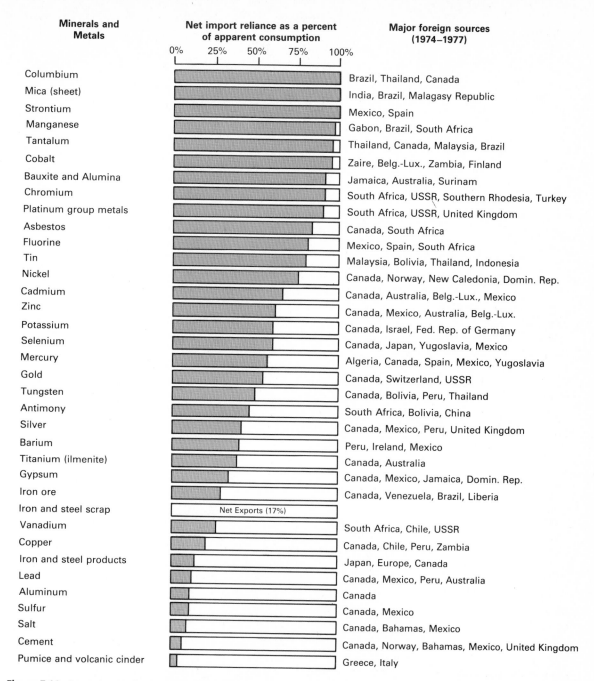

Minerals and Metals | **Net import reliance as a percent of apparent consumption** | **Major foreign sources (1974–1977)**

Minerals and Metals	Major foreign sources (1974–1977)
Columbium	Brazil, Thailand, Canada
Mica (sheet)	India, Brazil, Malagasy Republic
Strontium	Mexico, Spain
Manganese	Gabon, Brazil, South Africa
Tantalum	Thailand, Canada, Malaysia, Brazil
Cobalt	Zaire, Belg.-Lux., Zambia, Finland
Bauxite and Alumina	Jamaica, Australia, Surinam
Chromium	South Africa, USSR, Southern Rhodesia, Turkey
Platinum group metals	South Africa, USSR, United Kingdom
Asbestos	Canada, South Africa
Fluorine	Mexico, Spain, South Africa
Tin	Malaysia, Bolivia, Thailand, Indonesia
Nickel	Canada, Norway, New Caledonia, Domin. Rep.
Cadmium	Canada, Australia, Belg.-Lux., Mexico
Zinc	Canada, Mexico, Australia, Belg.-Lux.
Potassium	Canada, Israel, Fed. Rep. of Germany
Selenium	Canada, Japan, Yugoslavia, Mexico
Mercury	Algeria, Canada, Spain, Mexico, Yugoslavia
Gold	Canada, Switzerland, USSR
Tungsten	Canada, Bolivia, Peru, Thailand
Antimony	South Africa, Bolivia, China
Silver	Canada, Mexico, Peru, United Kingdom
Barium	Peru, Ireland, Mexico
Titanium (ilmenite)	Canada, Australia
Gypsum	Canada, Mexico, Jamaica, Domin. Rep.
Iron ore	Canada, Venezuela, Brazil, Liberia
Iron and steel scrap	Net Exports (17%)
Vanadium	South Africa, Chile, USSR
Copper	Canada, Chile, Peru, Zambia
Iron and steel products	Japan, Europe, Canada
Lead	Canada, Mexico, Peru, Australia
Aluminum	Canada
Sulfur	Canada, Mexico
Salt	Canada, Bahamas, Mexico
Cement	Canada, Norway, Bahamas, Mexico, United Kingdom
Pumice and volcanic cinder	Greece, Italy

Figure 7.11 Imports as a Percentage of Total U.S. Consumption in the Mid-1970s. Because minerals and mineral deposits are not equally distributed worldwide, there is a political dimension to mineral consumption. The *net import reliance* is imports and exports plus adjustments for government and industry stock changes. *Apparent consumption* is U.S. primary and secondary production plus net import reliance.

Chapter 7   Mineral and Water Resources

Water Resources

Just as minerals are the essential "nutrients" for modern industrial civilization, water has been civilization's essential solvent. Water has been the vehicle for extending the range available to humans for settlement and development. Water has turned deserts into farmland by irrigation; water has provided major transportation routes; water has been used to cool people, float boats, and carry off the garbage and sewage wastes of concentrated populations of people; water has even been used to produce energy.

Throughout recorded history and even before, *Homo sapiens* has increased water supplies by various technological means—some simple and some highly complex. In other locations, humankind has eliminated water by draining, damming to prevent flooding, or filling in marshes with soil.

Bringing water to arid or semiarid regions opens the way for agriculture, additional settlements, and eventually business and industry—all of which become dependent on the continued flow of artificial streams. Obviously, extending water resources to areas that are otherwise not suitable for large human settlements carries with it the risk of overextension and is not without other problems.

Like mineral shortages, water shortages can be solved only by increasing supply and/or decreasing demand. In this section we examine world and U.S. water distribution and consider the approaches that have been used and those that have been proposed for increasing water supply and decreasing demand. As with mineral resources, the impact of a civilization on its water resources is much greater than the sum of the impacts of its individual members.

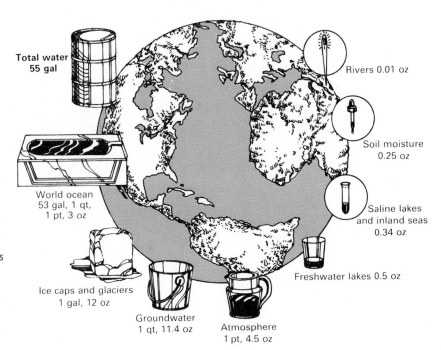

Figure 7.12 A Drop in the Barrel. Though the earth contains vast water resources, only a small part of the water in the hydrosphere is available at any one time for use by people. This figure indicates the world's distribution of water, treating the whole supply as if it were 55 gallons. The primary sources of water for human use are from groundwater, freshwater lakes, and rivers.

Total water 55 gal

Rivers 0.01 oz

Soil moisture 0.25 oz

Saline lakes and inland seas 0.34 oz

World ocean 53 gal, 1 qt, 1 pt, 3 oz

Freshwater lakes 0.5 oz

Ice caps and glaciers 1 gal, 12 oz

Groundwater 1 qt, 11.4 oz

Atmosphere 1 pt, 4.5 oz

WORLDWIDE WATER RESOURCES

There are 400 billion billion gallons (1520 billion billion liters) of water above, on, and in the earth, but it is not evenly distributed. Water "deposits" occur as rivers, lakes, streams, and oceans. Water is also found in the soil as groundwater and is bound up as ice in glaciers. Figure 7.12 shows the earth's reservoirs of water in proportion to one another. If our entire supply of water were equal to 55 gallons, the oceans would comprise over 53 gallons (97%). Of the remaining two gallons, more than one gallon would be tied up in glaciers and ice caps. Much of the rest of the water would be found in underground aquifers or in the soil (only about 50% of this is within one mile of the surface, and only about 25% can be extracted with current technologies). Less than one fluid ounce would be left for surface waters such as lakes, rivers, and inland seas or estuaries. So although there are 400 billion billion gallons of water in the ecosphere, only a small part is directly available to human beings. At any one time, only about five of every 100,000 gallons of water in the world supply is in motion as precipitation, running streams, or atmospheric vapor. The rest is stored underground, in lakes, in glaciers, or in the oceans (U.S. Geological Survey, 1977). Water may be held or stored in the ground for thousands of years, in a lake for a hundred years, or locked in a glacier for 40 or so years (U.S. Geological Survey, 1977). Eventually, however, stored water will find its way into the hydrologic cycle again.

Precipitation obviously plays a major role in water supply, since it is precipitation that replenishes or **recharges** reservoirs that have been diminished through evaporation, runoff into the oceans, or human withdrawals from the ground or the surface. If the water loss or withdrawal exceeds the rate of water recharge in a particular area for very long, the water supply in that area is obviously in jeopardy. In certain localities in the United States, withdrawals already exceed recharge (Figure 7.13). Later, we will discuss some additional problems that result from overuse.

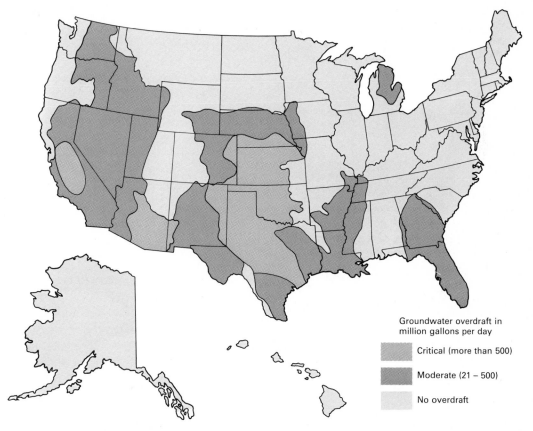

Groundwater overdraft in million gallons per day

Critical (more than 500)

Moderate (21 – 500)

No overdraft

Figure 7.13 U.S. Groundwater Withdrawals in Excess of Recharge, 1975. Total withdrawal for all regions in the United States was 82,328 million gallons per day; withdrawal in excess of discharge was 20,902 million gallons per day.

Water is used for many purposes throughout the world. These purposes can be broadly defined as domestic (cooking, cleaning, bathing) and industrial (manufacturing and cooling). Domestic water use may range from 76–270 liters per person per day for European countries to as low as five liters per person per day in some developing countries.

WATER SUPPLY AND USE IN THE UNITED STATES

The average annual rainfall for the United States is 30 inches, or about 4200 billion gallons per day (bgd). About 70% of this (2750 bgd) is lost in evaporation before it can be "used"; approximately 1450 billion gallons per day become runoff into surface bodies of water or seep into the soil to become groundwater (Figure 7.14).

Approximately 75% of the available runoff water in the United States is in the eastern states. Figure 7.15 indicates the differences between water distribution in the East and the West. Water shortages have already become reality in the highly populated areas of the West when rainfall is below normal. In 1980, drought conditions in the Southwest resulted in water rationing. In the winter of 1980–1981, drought conditions prevailed throughout the North-

east, resulting in water rationing in New York and many other cities. In the summer of 1983 a prolonged drought in the Midwest resulted in an estimated loss of one billion bushels of corn. In 1984, profound drought conditions in Texas led 72 cities to put water conservation plans in effect.

It should be noted that water shortages can be of two types. Shortages may result from low supply or from poor water quality. Chemical spills in the Kanawha and Ohio rivers have caused alerts requiring boiling of water and curtailment of water use until the "slug" of toxic materials passed through or became sufficiently diluted. Thus even if the supply is sufficient, water of the quality needed for human consumption, municipal, and industrial uses may not be available. Water quality and water quantity are aspects of the same problem of water supply.

Water for Drinking, Washing, and Flushing

Figure 7.16 indicates the domestic water consumption of the average U.S. family in a day. Although the amount of water needed per person per day for biological survival purposes (in food and water) is less than half a gallon, actual water use per person may range from less than 100 gallons to more than several hundred gallons. Residents of Tucson average 160 gallons of water a day; residents of

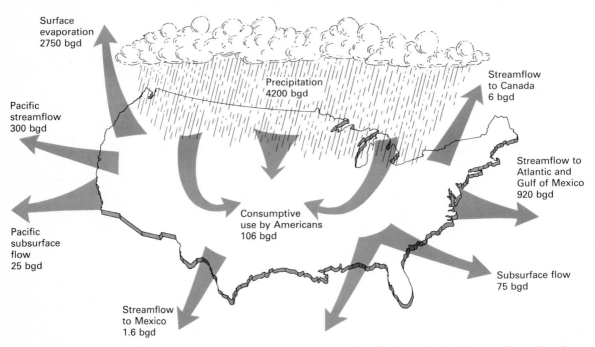

Figure 7.14 U.S. Water Budget. What happens to the rain that falls daily on various parts of the U.S.? The 4200 billion gallons per day (bgd) are mostly evaporated back into the at-mosphere (70%), the remainder drain to surface and underground reservoirs.

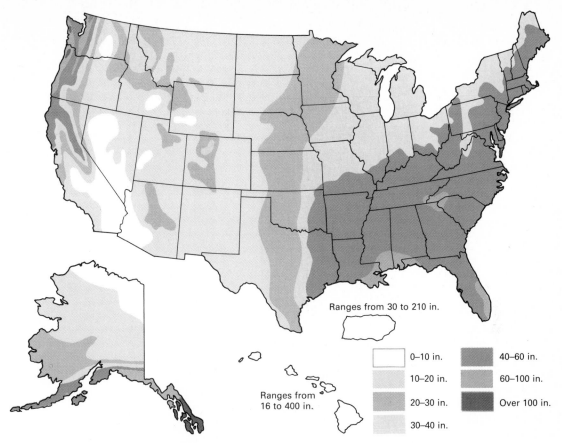

Ranges from 30 to 210 in.

Ranges from 16 to 400 in.

☐ 0–10 in.	☐ 40–60 in.
☐ 10–20 in.	☐ 60–100 in.
☐ 20–30 in.	☐ Over 100 in.
☐ 30–40 in.	

Figure 7.15 Average Annual Precipitation Pattern for the U.S. Because water is scarce in the West and abundant in the East, different policies and procedures for water use have developed in these areas. However, as water quality limitations in the East cause water shortages, the needs, policies, and practices of the East and West may move closer together.

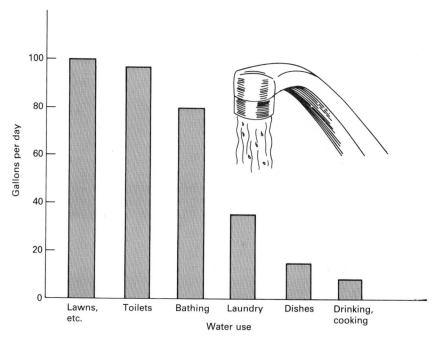

Figure 7.16 Estimated Daily Use of Water by a U.S. Family of Four. Total usage per day will run in excess of 300 gallons. Per capita usage can be figured by dividing each number by four.

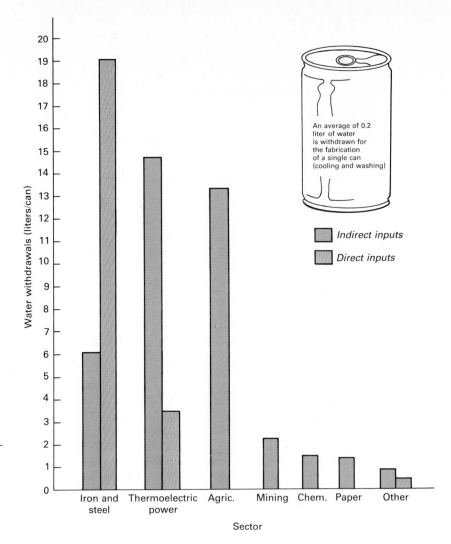

Figure 7.17 Water in a Can of Root Beer. To calculate the water input per unit of product made, we need to consider not just water used in the manufacturing process itself, but also water used in the mining or harvesting of the raw materials used in the manufacturing process. How many other products do you use daily that directly or indirectly have used or consumed water? (Note: One liter = 1.06 quarts).

Phoenix average 260 gallons per day (Alexander, 1984). Note that lawn watering and toilet flushing are the leading domestic activities in volume of water used. Water is also used in numerous industrial and agricultural ways. When these other uses are averaged over the entire population, per capita use increases to more than 2000 gallons per person per day.

To better illustrate this indirect water use, let's consider a 12-ounce can of root beer. Figure 7.17 indicates that the water required to produce the can, from mining to manufacture of a single finished can, amounts to about 63 liters per can (James, Kammerer, and Murray, 1976).

Withdrawals Versus Consumption

In most water uses, water quality is altered; either the temperature is changed or materials are added. In many cases, however, water is *used* but not *consumed.* This is true of both municipal and industrial uses. Water from industry may be drawn from its source (lake, river, reservoir, or underground aquifer) and used to carry away heat, to "scrub" products during manufacturing, or to carry away industrial waste materials. Water is also used by cities to carry away wastes, though industrial and municipal wastewater can be treated and returned to a surface or groundwater reservoir and made available again for other uses. Agricultural water is not immediately recyclable; 60% or more of the water used in irrigation is "consumed" in evaporation and transpiration and thus is not immediately available as surface or groundwater supply. Figure 7.18 shows withdrawals and consumption for various functions for 1975 and projected for the year 2000 in the United States.

INSTREAM USES OF WATER

There are also *nonwithdrawal* uses of water. These are called flow uses, onsite uses, or instream flow uses. Such uses include navigation, commercial and sport fishing, habitat protection, dilution of wastewater, and recreational or aesthetic uses. Instream uses have for many years been taken for granted. However, as surface supplies become more and more overextended, the need to keep and allow for a minimum instream flow to protect the navigational and recreational potential, the quality of the stream, and the survival of instream organisms has taken on a new importance.

Federal water policies are beginning to recognize the need for federal and state planning to preserve instream flows. In 1976 a federal multiagency group called the Cooperative Instream Flow Service Group was formed under the sponsorship of the U.S. Fish and Wildlife Service with monies from the U.S. Environmental Protection Agency. It was charged with promoting education and research into instream flow requirements and determining critical times of year and water volumes for fish species and for water-related recreational purposes. Instream

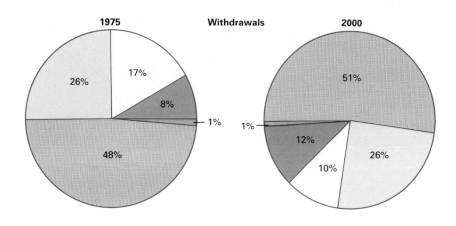

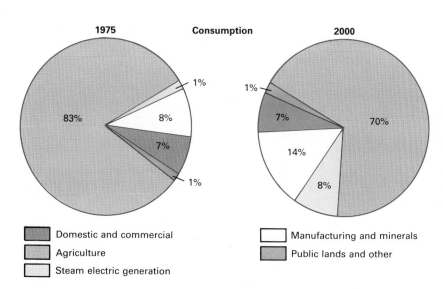

Figure 7.18   U.S. Water Withdrawal Versus Consumption, 1975 and 2000. These graphs show the activities that use and consume water. Agriculture is not only a large withdrawer of water but also a large consumer. Much of the water used in irrigation is lost to further immediate use owing to evaporation. On the other hand, steam electric generation uses water primarily for cooling, and the water is returned to its source for reuse. The decrease in consumptive use by agriculture in 2000 is based on an assumption of increased efficiency in irrigation.

use versus out-of-stream use compete for the available water supply. As supplies become more and more committed, this competition will increase.

Groundwater

Almost 13–20 times as much water is in the ground as is available on the surface. This water may be contained in the soil or in **aquifers**—areas underlain by impermeable rock (unconfined) or areas between two impermeable rock layers (confined or **artesian**) (see Figure 7.19). About one fourth of this water is extractable by using today's technology (U.S. General Accounting Office, 1978). Currently, 22% of all fresh water used in the United States is

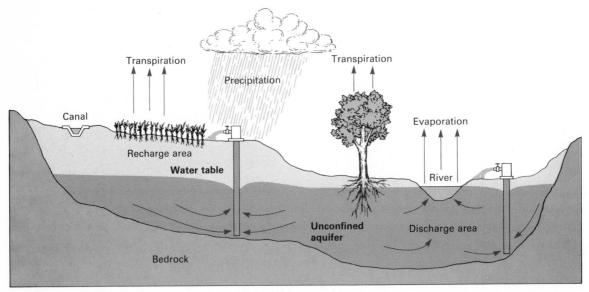

(a) Unconfined aquifer

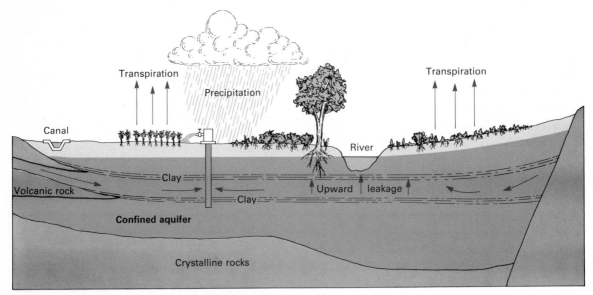

(b) Confined aquifer

Figure 7.19 Groundwater. Rainwater infiltrating the soil collects in aquifers as groundwater. The upper surface of an unconfined aquifer is the water table. The water table shifts upward when water accumulates after rain, recharging the aquifer; it shifts downward as water is withdrawn by plants or human activities, as it flows to lower levels, or as it is discharged to the surface.

supplied from groundwater. About 50% of the United States population relies on groundwater for domestic water supply. Groundwater reservoirs are recharged by rainfall; however, with increasing demands on groundwater supplies, the risk increases of pumping more water than is recharged in any given time.

When withdrawals exceed recharge, several things may happen. The water table levels drop. The **water table** is the upper surface of an unconfined aquifer. This may result in subsidence of the ground surface, that is, a lowering of the ground surface from the voids left because of reduced amounts of groundwater. Subsidence permanently diminishes the size of the aquifer. Near Eloy, a town in Central Arizona, land has subsided 10 feet in the last 30 years from groundwater overdraft. As much as a 30-foot drop has occurred in areas of south central California. Along with subsidence in Arizona, large fissures 25 feet wide and 50 feet deep have been measured. Subsidence in the Houston area has caused structural damage and damage to sewers and other drainage systems. Lower water tables are becoming more and more characteristic in western and southwestern dry states.

This phenomenon is not limited to the West, however. Florida has over 50 inches of rain per year, but overuse of its groundwater supply is resulting in lower water tables. This is resulting in the intrusion of salt water into the water table, making the groundwater brackish. **Saltwater intrusion** can be a groundwater problem in any coastal area. On May 11, 1981, a sinkhole 37.5 meters deep and 120 meters wide appeared in Winter Park, Florida, swallowing a house, six cars, a camper van, and part of a swimming pool. The water level in the aquifer beneath the area had dropped and left the roofs of limestone caverns unsupported. The roofs caved in, resulting in the massive subsidence.

Other problems arise when cities begin to rely on groundwater supplies. Urbanization, which covers soil with asphalt, causes increasing runoff and less percolation of rainfall into the land. This decreases recharge and lowers the water table. Tucson is the largest city in the United States relying entirely on groundwater. Currently, Tuscon withdraws water five times faster than it is recharged. Figure 7.20 shows groundwater withdrawals by state in 1975.

The Ogallala Aquifer

The Ogallala Aquifer underlies the High Plains States from Kansas and Nebraska to Wyoming, including Texas, New Mexico, Oklahoma, and Colorado. The agricultural economy of the Texas High Plains has been built from the overdrafting of the Ogallala Aquifer. The water level is dropping 2–5 feet a year. In Gaines County, Texas, the cost of pumping one acre-foot of water has increased from $1.50 to $60 in ten years. The cost increase is due to increased energy prices and increases in the amount of energy required to pump the water up. Over the years, federal policies have encouraged use of water from the aquifer by providing price supports for water-intensive crops like cotton. Even now, High Plains farmers are eligible for a depletion allowance on pumped groundwater from the Ogallala Aquifer. In Kansas alone this amounts to benefits estimated at one billion dollars. Congress has mandated a study of the Ogallala Aquifer. To date, the study indicates that the aquifer can supply the Plains States with water for the next 40–50 years. The problem is, What happens after that?

WATER RIGHTS AND WATER ECONOMICS

Water economics has had an interesting history. Throughout early history, water was free. There were no charges for using water, diverting water for use, or depositing materials in bodies of water.

It is interesting to note that although water was free, the rights to water developed differently in the eastern and western parts of the United States. In the East the **doctrine of riparian rights** (that is, rights relating to the bank of a watercourse) developed, which said that a landowner adjacent to a stream had the right to the water in the stream undiminished in quantity and/or quality. This placed responsibility on upstream users and was directed toward protecting private rights in streams and lakes. In the West, where water was scarce, the old adage "first come, first served," applied. The **doctrine of appropriation** states that the right to water is acquired when water is diverted from the watercourse for a "beneficial" use, and in all cases the water right that was acquired first takes priority over those acquired at a later time. "Beneficial" was interpreted as economic; thus diversions for economic purposes were the only uses that carried with them recognized rights. Instream uses of water or diversions for wildlife or other "uneconomic" purposes were not recognized historically as beneficial uses. It is likely that in both the East and the West, sophisticated accounting systems will have to be developed in order to ensure that public water needs are met, even at the expense of private needs.

Today, the cost of water varies with the system of acquisition, purification, and transportation. Pricing is generally not strictly proportionate to the amount used. In fact, in many places the more an industry uses, the cheaper the rate. Not surprisingly, this subsidization of waste has created situations wherein it is cheaper to draw clean, fresh water than to reuse the old. For domestic use, charges may be based on volume, but they are often based on such things as number of taps, property frontage, or even property value. Overall, our systems of pricing developed when water shortage was not a concern. With increasing water shortages and continued population and industrial growth, the need to increase supply or decrease demand arises. A change in the way we charge for water would be one mechanism for influencing water use. There are others.

INCREASING SUPPLY: OLD WAYS AND NEW

The most common method used for increasing water supply has been diverting water to where it is needed. Also, streams have been dammed to control water fluctuation, and groundwater supplies have been tapped by means of wells. In recent times, new methods have been tried or proposed for increasing

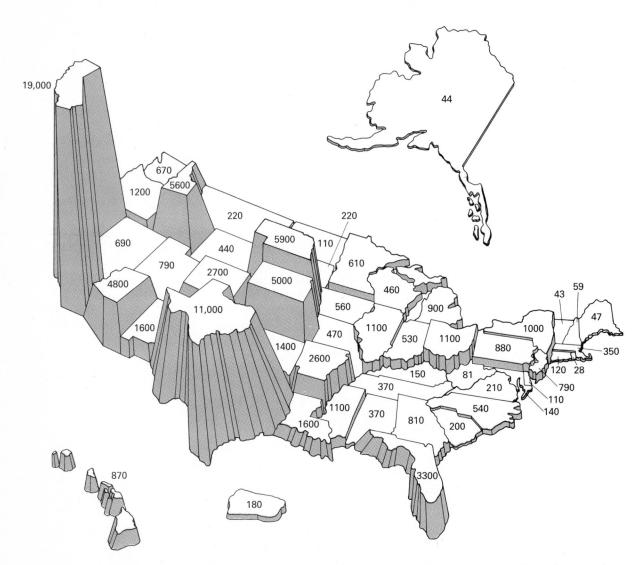

Figure 7.20 Groundwater Withdrawals, by State, in Millions of Gallons per Day. The raised map gives a better perspective on which states rely most heavily on their groundwater supplies.

the supply of fresh water. These include desalination of seawater, melting of glaciers, and seeding of clouds. Each of the ways of increasing supply carries with it some ecological and other implications.

Diversions

Homo sapiens has often seen fit to base its technology on models found in nature. It is not surprising then that one of the major ways of redistributing water is through human-made diversions. Artificial streams such as channels or pipelines have been constructed to take water to where it is wanted.

The western United States provides several examples of major diversion projects developed to carry water to the growing population centers in the Western states. The California State Water Plan outlines a system of diversions from the Colorado River and other streams to the north. The Central Arizona Project currently underway will pipe water 250 miles from the Colorado River to cities and land areas of Central Arizona.

Diversion projects are major undertakings often subsidized by federal taxpayers. In earlier times, when water supplies were plentiful, diversions were hardly opposed. Today, diversion projects are mired in political, social, and environmental problems. Shortages are widespread, and people with water are becoming more and more possessive.

Northern Californians oppose plans to divert water from Northern California to Southern California, for example. There are, in fact, real problems with giving up water apart from the obvious one of not keeping enough. Lower supplies in the donor area eventually means higher water prices there. Diversions may affect instream flows and species in the area from which volumes of water are taken. Likewise, future industrial development may be threatened. Then what about droughts? When these occur, which users—direct or diversion—get how much water?

Also, diversions do not necessarily have only positive effects at the receiving end. Dry areas into which water is brought usually have high evaporation rates. In normally arid regions, evaporation pulls water from deep in the soil to the surface. As it does, the salts it carries are deposited on the surface of the land. This may lead to an accumulation of salts that leaves the land unfit for further agricultural uses. The San Joaquin Valley in California provides a good example of this very phenomenon; once a fertile valley, it is now endangered by salt accumulated from irrigation waters. A similar situation has occurred in California's Imperial Valley.

Then, too, water availability spurs population growth and further development, requiring even more water. A large portion of the people in the world are totally dependent upon "engineered streams" or diversions for their water needs. The future management of these areas is of vital importance as prolonged droughts bring increasing potential for catastrophe.

This open, lined section of the Los Angeles Owen-River Aqueduct runs approximately 40 miles, providing water to the Los Angeles area.

Dams

Another method for increasing water supplies in a given area is to impound water in dams. Dams have been around as long as the beaver and probably from the first time a tree fell across a stream, causing a pileup of debris and a backup of water. Human-made dams are large-scale versions with controls for varying water level.

Dams serve human need in several ways. First, dams collect water, hold back the excess water during flooding, and release it gradually during low-flow periods. This means that the floodplain below the dam is now available for farming and development with less chance of flooding. Second, the large pool of water in the reservoir provides a constant supply and continuous flow for human consumption, farm irrigation, and industrial uses. Third, the pool has recreational potential. A dam may also generate electricity.

But there are ecological problems with dams. Damming produces a large pool area in the river or tributary. As the moving water enters the pool area, it slows down. This causes sediment to settle out. Eventually, silt buildup makes reservoirs practically nonfunctional because of the decrease in volume of the reservoir.

Another problem is that some plants and animals that flourish in streams are not adapted to and will not survive in reservoir impoundments. Lake flora and fauna will take over the niches. Furthermore, the land area flooded by the reservoir is no longer available for land uses; in some cases this has meant relocation of the human as well as other inhabitants. The potential for new human inhabitants with different skills in the area served by the reservoir may well be increased, so a sort of "niche" exchange takes place as a dam is built. Such exchanges can have far-reaching negative as well as positive effects.

A classic example of the good news and the bad news about dams is the case of the Aswan Dam in Egypt. In 1960, construction was begun on the Aswan Dam, which was to turn the Sahara into a rich farming area. However, a number of major adverse side effects have become apparent since the dam's completion in 1970. Lake Nasser, the reservoir produced by the dam, is filling with silt at a faster rate than was expected. The nutrients carried by the Nile are enriching the lake and causing problems with eutrophication. Before the dam was built, the nutrients and silt were deposited annually downstream in the Nile Delta. Because this source of fertilizer for the Delta has been cut off, the productivity of the Delta area has decreased. The newly irrigated Sahara is also plagued with problems of increasing salinity. Another hazard that was overlooked relates to human health. Diseases involving vectors that breed in standing water are on the rise.

Glaciers and Ice Mining

What is the potential for utilizing the fresh water that is tied up in glaciers for human water needs? Proposals have been made to pull icebergs to major coastal cities and mine them for water. The logistics of such a project are probably feasible; however, there are a number of unanswered questions. What effect would the ice have on the surrounding waters near the coast? How would it affect climate? When the ice was replaced by water in the arctic area, less sunlight would be reflected, and more would be absorbed. Would this warm the arctic waters enough to cause melting of the ice remaining there? Every action may have enormous environmental repercussions because, after all, everything is connected to everything else.

Desalination

Almost 97% of the earth's water is salty. Because of the amount, it is only logical to consider the feasibility of utilizing salt water for human needs. Salt water can be used directly for power plant cooling along coastal areas. However, it is too salty to be used for most industrial processes, agriculture, or drinking. Before sea water can be used for these purposes, the salt must be removed. This is known as **desalination**.

There are three methods by which salt can be removed from sea water—distillation, electrolytic and osmotic separation, and freezing.

1. In distillation the water is boiled or heated, and pure water is collected as it evaporates. The salt is left behind. Proposals have been made that would tie nuclear power plants to distillation plants. Waste heat from the power plant would provide the energy for heating the water.

2. In electrolysis, positive and negative electrodes attract the charged salt and leave the water away from the electrodes less salty. In a process called reverse osmosis, seawater is pushed under pressure through a membrane that allows the water to pass through but not the salt.

3. In freezing technology the salt forms crystalline pockets as the ice freezes.

As predicted by the second law of thermodynamics, all of these methods require energy.

Although the technology for desalination exists, it is now used only in small-scale plants. About 70–80 desalination plants are in operation on Florida's west coast. For a medium-sized plant the cost of desalting averages $3–6 per 1000 gallons. Desalination is economical in arid regions where there are no other water sources to compete with it. In Israel, desalted water costs around $1.00 per cubic meter. This is about five times the cost of domestic water in some areas of the United States.

Even if cost could be brought into a more competitive range, there is another problem. What do we do with all of the salt? Every million gallons of fresh water that is produced from seawater leaves about 150 tons of salt behind.

Cloud Seeding

Another source of fresh water is the clouds. **Cloud seeding** is used to cause rain. Chemicals are sprinkled into the clouds to serve as surface agents on which water can condense.

How successful cloud seeding actually is has been difficult to verify scientifically. There is no sure formula for producing rainfall at will from cloud seeding. Investigations have been going on since the late 1940s and continue today. Cloud seeding poses interesting legal questions. Who owns the water in the clouds? If clouds are seeded, they may drop their water in Washington State rather than in the Rocky Mountains. There is only a given amount of water in

the condensation phase; if it is used in one place, it will simply not be available to users downwind.

DECREASING DEMAND

In the discussion of minerals we noted that the demand for any one mineral could be shifted by the development of substitutes. There could be other mineral deposits in more abundant supply or new synthetic materials. Other methods for decreasing demand involve longer-lasting mineral products and life-style adjustments.

In the case of water, most of these alternatives are not available. There are no substitutes to which demand can shift. There is nothing like water. However, demand can be decreased by improving the efficiency of water use. This would be directly comparable to recycling and somewhat comparable to the development of longer-lasting products in the case of minerals. Let us look at some examples for improved water resources management.

Water Resources Management

We can conveniently classify water uses as agricultural, industrial, and domestic, and there is room for improved water resources management in all of these areas.

Irrigation, being a major consumptive use, can be much more efficiently executed. Irrigation can be carried out via underground pipelines, which decrease the amount of evaporation and consequent water loss. Drip and sprinkler irrigation systems

Efficient irrigation systems like this center pivot sprinkler can increase crop yield while conserving water.

conserve water. Lined trenches for water transportation prevent seepage loss. Plant hybrids requiring less water have been developed. Improved timing of water deliveries, avoidance of over-deliveries, and control of weeds or competing vegetation focus water on the desired crop. All of these can increase the agricultural output per unit of water used.

As water resources become scarce and prices increase, industry will find more efficient ways to control its water use. Industry has already begun to reuse its water, particularly water used primarily for cooling. Leakage and water pressure controls are other ways of decreasing industrial uses.

Every flush of human waste in the bathroom ordinarily carries 4–7 gallons of water with it. Devices are on the market now that cut down on the volume of water used in each flush. These devices are a little more sophisticated than the brick-in-the-tank technique, though the brick still works. (In the early 1970s, environmentalists encouraged people to put a brick in the toilet tank to take up some water space; when the tank refilled after each flush, not as much water was needed to fill the tank to the desired water level.) Devices for showers and faucets are available that reduce water flow.

Changes are also gradually occurring in the system of charging for water use. Individual metering of homes is increasing. Incentives for water use at off-peak times is an interesting possibility. Several states have approved the use of waterless sewage waste systems in which human wastes and kitchen wastes are used to form compost.

Water quality is another issue to be considered. For the most part, the same quality of water is used for all activities, whether domestic, industrial, or agricultural. This again is a reflection of earlier times in which water was abundant and free. In the home the same quality of water is used for sewage disposal as for drinking. Because of shortages, sequential use of water may become the pattern at home and work. Human wash water can be used to clean the car and then to flush sewage wastes. This leads to another mechanism for decreasing demand—an alteration of life-style.

Bluegrass Versus Rock

Lavish and inefficient use of water resources is a feature of the American standard of living. It seems to have developed from the axiom that "cleanliness is next to godliness." Use of waterless systems for sewage wastes and reuse of domestic water will require fundamental adjustments. Removing swimming pools as status symbols and learning to appreciate the beauty of a rock garden instead of a carpet of green front lawn—especially in places like the Southwest—will require changes in values and attitudes. Setting priorities among essential uses and distinguishing them from luxuries will have to be done when water becomes an increasingly scarce commodity.

Institutional Adjustments

For change to occur, institutional policies and practices in the area of water resources management must be altered. There must be economic incentives to conserve. This can be brought about by a change in pricing structure. Some method of compensating for water *not* used is a possibility—just as we have compensation for land not used—and for providing this unused water to a water user in need. A clearinghouse for information on tested conservation practices and devices would be valuable. The U.S. General Accounting Office (1978) has concluded that a major reason that water-conserving techniques are so little used is a lack of knowledge of their effectiveness.

The relationship between water *quality* and water *quantity* needs to be fully understood. Shortages stem from overloading water supplies with sewage or industrial wastes. Why use water of drinking quality to flush toilets or even for cooling processes? Methods for sequential water uses need to be explored—with, of course, all caution to prevent negative health effects. Related to water quality is good land management to prevent sedimentation, increased siltation, and the filling of water reservoirs.

THE FUTURE

Humans and human civilization depend on water and minerals. Interestingly, water and mineral resources are interlinked. Water is used in the extraction, processing, and shipping of minerals. In the future, as poorer grades of minerals are mined, the percentage of our water resources used in mining and industry is expected to increase significantly. Water and mineral resources have been exploited, and the time has now come—or it may have passed—for them to be better managed. There are ecologically sound ways to approach the management of these essential resources, but they have yet to be implemented. Water and mineral resource problems will be among our most important environmental problems in the future.

CONCEPTS TO REMEMBER

1. Access to mineral resources has become as crucial to modern civilization as food is to the individual person.

2. Mineral *resources* are minerals that are important to human beings. Minerals that are accessible under existing economic and technical conditions are called *reserves*. The relationship between resources and reserves changes with the relationship between supply and demand.

3. Nonrenewable resources are those being used up faster than they are regenerated. A small number of countries, the so-called industrialized nations, use up a disproportionate share of the world's mineral resources. Worldwide, nonrenewable mineral resources are being used at faster and faster rates.

4. Although the life of our mineral reserves can be extended by finding new deposits, mining the sea, finding substitutes, and developing more efficient extraction processes, none of these strategies makes as much ecological sense as consuming less.

5. As highly concentrated deposits of minerals are depleted, lower-grade deposits are mined, requiring more energy for mining and processing per unit of usable mineral produced, resulting in more environmental disturbance.

6. Rates of mineral consumption can be reduced by recycling, by extended use of products (antiobsolescence), and by substituting other materials. Various institutional factors work against the large-scale adoption of these practices in the United States.

7. The uneven worldwide distribution of mineral deposits adds a political dimension to mineral supplies. The foreign policies of industrialized nations reflect, at least in part, their mineral supply needs.

8. Access to water has extended the range of land available to humans for settlement and development. Many people worldwide now depend on the availability of water supplied by human engineering projects.

9. Only a very small percentage of the total water in, on, and above the earth is accessible to humans at any one time as fresh water.

10. Usable water reservoirs are recharged by precipitation. If water is withdrawn faster than it is replenished, the water supply is in jeopardy. In many places in the United States, water withdrawal exceeds recharge. Lowering of the water table can lead to other problems such as saltwater intrusion.

11. Water withdrawn for *use* may or may not be *consumed*. Water used for cooling will be returned to a water reservoir and be immediately available for another use; much of the water used for irrigation will be "consumed" by evaporation.

12. Instream uses of water are also important and can be jeopardized by excessive withdrawal. Instream uses include navigation, recreation, support of aquatic life, and waste dilution.

13. Water rights developed differently in the eastern and western United States. In the eastern United States, where water is relatively plentiful, laws tend to protect the rights of all users along the stream course. In the West, with scarcer water resources, the doctrine of appropriation or "first come, first served" has prevailed. As water in the East becomes less available because of pollution and drought, more exact water use accounting procedures are emerging. Water shortages can be the result of low supply or poor quality.

14. Methods for increasing water supply have included the building of dams and diversion projects, desalination of ocean water, cloud seeding, and ice mining. All of these bring major environmental impacts directly or as a result of increased energy use.

15. Decreasing demand for water can be achieved by greater efficiency in its use.

DISCUSSION QUESTIONS AND FOOD FOR THOUGHT

1. Numerous social, political, and economic factors help to determine whether or not something is a resource, that is, has value. Minerals become resources as a function of cultural evolution. Aluminum, silica, and iron ore would have been valueless to early humans. Name some shifts in mineral values that have occurred in the last ten years. Do you foresee any shifts in the near future? What might precipitate them?

2. Discuss the advantages and disadvantages of recycling, substitution, and simplification of life-styles as solutions to mineral shortages. Base your reasoning on the principles of cycling presented in Chapter 3, and include economics in your analysis.
3. Compare the mineral vulnerability of developed and developing countries. What impact might a shortage of minerals have in each case? Using the data in Figure 7.11, hypothesize the most vulnerable mineral resource for the United States.
4. What is the role of supply and demand in directing changes in the mineral market?
5. "Technological fix" refers to the idea that technology can solve all of our problems. What are some basic underlying differences in "technological fix" and "simplification of life-style?" How are they compatible?
6. As shortages become more and more a reality in areas that have previously had an abundant water supply, what changes do you predict will occur in the existing system of water rights?
7. Debate the following: Most of our shortage problems are the result of too many people.
8. Design a flowchart for water use that involves intake and then three distinct uses before the water is returned to the surface water system.
9. Using the numbers in Figure 7.16, estimate your daily water consumption, direct, and indirect. If you had to decrease your daily water consumption by 20%, decide where you would cut back. Do the same for a 50% decrease. Consider alternatives for combining efforts with neighbors to cut down on water use.

10. Investigate the recycling facilities in your community. Ask local representatives to speak on the market fluctuations for recycled goods.
11. Survey industries in the area for their mineral needs. Interview officials concerning location of their mineral resources, number of years minerals will be available from their current source given current rates of consumption, changes in quality of available mineral (high or low grade) over the last 10–20 years, and plans to change the use of minerals via substitution of another mineral or recycling.
12. Talk with the water treatment plant manager for your town. Find out about peak load times, daily use (using population figures to determine per capita usage), plant capacity (what restrictions this will place on growth), and major pollutants for which water is treated.
13. If there is a major reservoir in your area, trace its development and the impact it has had. Try to find photos depicting the land now covered by the reservoir, interview any former residents, and collect news items.
14. Explain how we can be "running out" of some minerals when the total amount of a given mineral in the ecosphere is constant.
15. Go back to Figure 7.2. Discuss what would happen if all of the deposits of a mineral were brought into the category of reserves? What would happen after that if all recycling stopped?
16. Discuss the economic implications of longer-lasting products in terms of higher costs versus wider distribution and labor versus mineral input.

REFERENCES AND FURTHER READING

References marked with an asterisk are cited in the chapter.

*Alexander, G., 1984. "Water: Making Do with Less," *National Wildlife,* Feb./March, **22**(2):11–13.

Balon, E. K., 1978. "Kariba: The Dubious Benefits of Large Dams," *Ambio* **7**(2):38–48.

Boddé. T., 1981. "Quality vs. Quantity: Is a U.S. Water Crisis Imminent?" *BioScience* **31**(7, July–Aug):485–488.

*Brooks, D. B., and Andrews, P. W., 1974. "Mineral Resources, Economic Growth and World Population," *Science* **185** (4145):13–19.

Burroughs, T., 1984. "Ocean Mining: Boom or Bust," *Technology Review* **87**(April):55–60.

*Case, C.P., III, 1980. "Recycling Is a Painless Way to Save Our Energy," *The Washington Post,* June.

Castle, E. N., and Price, K. A., eds., 1983. *U.S. Interests and Global Natural Resources: Energy, Minerals, Food.* Washington, D.C.: Resources for the Future.

Cloud, P. E., Jr., 1968. "Realities of Mineral Distribution," *Texas Quarterly* **11**:103–126.

Cloud, P. E., Jr., 1969. "Mineral Resources from the Sea" in *Resources and Man.* San Francisco: W. H. Freeman and Company, 135–156.

Cloud, P. E., Jr., 1971. "Resources, Population, and Quality of Life" in S. Fred Singer, ed., *Is There An Optimum Level of Population?* New York: McGraw-Hill.

Coats, R., 1984. "The Colorado River: River of Controversy," *Environment* **26** (2, March):6–13ff.

Commission on Critical Choices For Americans, 1977. *Vital Resources,* Volume I. Lexington, Mass.: Lexington Books.

Conservation Foundation, 1982. *State of the Environment 1982: An Assessment at Mid-Decade.* Washington, D.C.

Cooke, R., 1984. "Metals in the Sea," *Technology Review* **87**(April):61–66.

*Council on Environmental Quality, 1977. *Annual Report.* Washington, D.C.: U.S. Government Printing Office.

*Council on Environmental Quality, 1980. *The Global 2000 Report to the President. Entering the Twenty-First Century.* Washington, D.C.: U.S. Government Printing Office. This report was prepared by the Council on Environmental Quality and the Department of State with Gerald O. Barney as Study Director. It was published in two volumes: Volume I, Summary; and Volume II, Technical Report.

Dasmann, R. F., 1972. *Environmental Conservation,* 3rd ed. New York: John Wiley and Sons.

*James, I.C.; Kammerer, J. C.; and Murray, C. R., 1976. *Annual Report: How Much Water in a 12-ounce Can? A Perspective on Water Use Information.* Reston, Va.: U.S. Geological Survey.

Kerr, R. A., 1982. "Cloud Seeding: One Success in 35 Years," *Science* **217** (August 31)519–521.

Kneese, A. V., 1976. "Natural Resources Policy 1975–1985," *Journal of Environmental Economics and Management* **3**:253–288.

Lacey, W. C., ed., 1982 *Mineral Exploration.* New York:Van Nostrand Press.

Lacey, W. C., 1984. "Water: A Treasure in Trouble," *National Wildlife* Feb./March:7–21.

"Materials," *Science* **191**(February 10, 1976):4128. This entire issue was devoted to discussion of the subject of materials.

National Academy of Sciences, 1969. *Resources and Man: A Study and Recommendations.* San Francisco: W. H. Freeman and Company.

National Commission on Materials Policy, 1973. *Final Report: Material Needs and the Environment Today and Tomorrow.* Washington, D.C.: U.S. Government Printing Office.

Schumacher, E. F., 1973. *Small is Beautiful.* New York: Harper and Row. Chapter 3, pp. 110–125, is especially pertinent to this chapter.

Sheridan, D., 1981. "The Desert Blooms—At a Price," *Environment* **23**(3, April)7–20.

Tilton, J. E., 1977. *The Future of Non-Fuel Minerals.* Washington, D.C.: The Brookings Institution.

U.S. Bureau of Mines, 1970 and 1975. *Minerals Facts and Problems.* Washington, D.C.: U.S. Government Printing Office.

U.S. Bureau of Mines, 1979a. *Status of the Mineral Industries.* Pittsburgh, Penn.: Publications Distribution Branch, U.S. Department of the Interior.

U.S. Bureau of Mines, 1979b. *Mineral Trends and Forecasts.* Washington, D.C.: U.S Government Printing Office.

*U.S. Environmental Protection Agency, 1980. *Environmental Outlook 1980.* EPA-600/8-80-003. Washington, D.C.: Office of Research and Development.

U.S. Fish and Wildlife Service, 1977. *Cooperative Instream Flow Service Group: The First Year.* Washington, D.C.: U.S. Government Printing Office.

*U.S. General Accounting Office, 1978. *Review of the President's June 6, 1978, Water Policy Message.* Washington, D.C.: U.S. Government Printing Office. CED-79-2.

*U.S. General Accounting Office, 1979. *Learning to Look Ahead: The Need for a National Materials Policy and Planning Process.* EMD-79-30, April 19.

U.S. Geological Survey, 1975. *Rain—A Water Resource.* Washington, D.C.: U.S. Government Printing Office.

*U.S. Geological Survey, 1977. *The Hydrologic Cycle.* Washington, D.C.: U.S. Government Printing Office.

U.S. National Water Commission, 1973. *Final Report: Water Policies for the Future.* Washington, D.C.: U.S. Government Printing Office.

U.S. Water Resources Council, 1968. *The Nation's Water Resources.* Washington, D.C.: U.S. Government Printing Office.

U.S. Water Resources Council, 1978. *The Nation's Water Resources 1975–2000. Second National Water Assessment.* Washington, D.C.: U.S. Government Printing Office.

U.S. Water Resources Council, 1980. *Bulletin 16: Essentials of Ground Water Hydrology Pertinent to Water Resources Planning.* Rev. ed. Washington, D.C.: U.S. Government Printing Office.

Walsh, J., 1980. "What Do We Do when the Well Runs Dry?" *Science* **210**(November 14)754–756.

CHAPTER 8

Population, Food, and Hunger

SECTION A
Population in Perspective

*O*nce upon a time, a great many people were invited to a banquet. Even though none of the guests had any idea who was giving the banquet or why *they* had received invitations, they all made plans to come.

It came to pass that on the night of the banquet, more guests appeared than were anticipated. Perhaps some of the guests had failed to comply with the RSVP request, or perhaps there was some failure of coordination among the planners, inviter, and cooks. At any rate the result was too little food for the number of guests that appeared. To make matters worse, the problem did not become apparent to the kitchen and serving staff until they had already distributed standard portions to the people at the first few tables. After that point the waiters adjusted by serving smaller and smaller portions until those at the last few tables were actually underfed.

Naturally, there was a mixed reaction to the whole state of affairs. In the kitchen the collective impression was: *There are too many people out there!* In the dining room the predominant impression was: *There isn't enough food here!* Of course, those who had been underfed felt much more strongly that the problem was lack of food.

We introduce this chapter on population and hunger with this story to emphasize at the outset that the concept of "overpopulation" is relative (Fig-

ure 8.1). If the problem is that there are too many people, the problem is not completely stated until the following questions are answered: Too many people in relation to what? To available food? To nonrenewable resources? To the assimilative capacity of the biosphere? To personal preference?

OVERPOPULATION?

Wayne H. Davis (1970) once stated that overpopulation is a fact when "people by virtue of their numbers *and activities* are most rapidly decreasing the ability of the land to support human life" (emphasis added). By this definition the world is already grossly overpopulated. Polluted water and air, loss of good farmland, contamination of land by chemical spills, and improper disposal of wastes are all degrading our life-support system.

Walter E. Howard (1969) cited three characteristics of overpopulation among animals in general: mass suffering, a high rate of premature death, and deterioration of the environment. Some intelligent people argue that such conditions characterize *Homo sapiens* at this very time. Other intelligent people argue that these problems are not simple consequences of numbers of people; they are a result of the *way* people do things. They say that the earth is far from overpopulated.

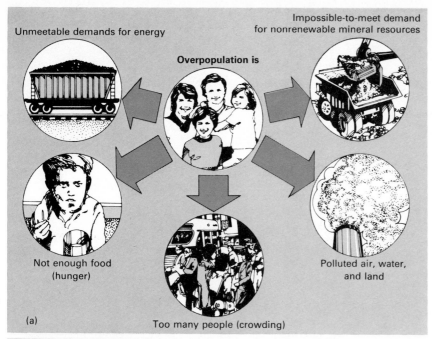

Unmeetable demands for energy

Impossible-to-meet demand for nonrenewable mineral resources

Overpopulation is

Not enough food (hunger)

Too many people (crowding)

Polluted air, water, and land

(a)

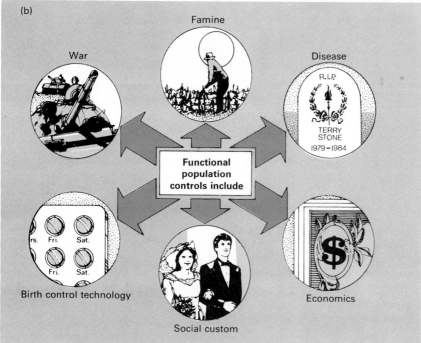

(b)

War

Famine

Disease

Functional population controls include

Birth control technology

Social custom

Economics

Figure 8.1 Overpopulation is More Than a Big Number.
(a) The carrying capacity of the earth is related not only to numbers of people but also to impact of their life-styles. A few people with a highly consuming life-style can have a much greater impact on the ecosphere than a larger number of people with a simpler life-style. (b) Likewise, population control is much more than birth control technology. Economic, cultural, and religious factors also come into play.

Throughout the world, 15–20 million people die each year because of malnutrition or starvation. Is this a problem of overpopulation or a problem of the inequitable distribution of food and wealth?

It has been calculated that one U.S. citizen has an impact on the biosphere equal to that of 25 citizens of India. Thus we would need to multiply the population of the United States by 25 to compare it to the population of India in terms of effect on the biosphere. For other comparisons, other relationships might apply. For example, with 5% of the world's population the United States consumes over 33% of the mineral resources of the world. By the single standard of mineral resource consumption the

The population problem is not just a question of numbers. The different environmental impacts of the world's cultures, customs, and life-styles must be considered in dealing with it.

population of the United States is six or more times larger than actual numbers indicate.

The point? One's concept of overpopulation depends on personal values, societal standards, the life-style to which one is accustomed, or the life-style one thinks *everyone* should have. The population problem is more than a problem of numbers.

LIMITS TO GROWTH

The enormous potential for human population growth has been known and discussed for hundreds of years. In the sixteenth century, Thomas More specified in *Utopia* "that the city neither be depopulated or grow beyond measure." In the eighteenth century, Robert Wallace wrote, "Under a Perfect Government . . . mankind would increase so prodigiously that the earth would at last be overstretched and become unable to support its numerous inhabitants." Thomas Malthus (1766–1834) started a controversy that is still raging with his observation that population will always expand to some limiting situation in which misery is the general condition. Malthus sets forth an explanation of why, in his estimation, "the power of population is indefinitely

greater than the power in the earth to produce subsistence for food." (Malthus, 1982 reprint of 1816 publication). The basis of his argument is his hypothesis that population increases geometrically whereas subsistence increases only arithmetically (see Chapter 4).

War, Famine, and Disease

Historically, the three most important factors serving as checks to human population have been death by war, famine, and disease. Throughout history, although human population was increasing gradually, there were many "booms" with subsequent "crashes" attributable to one or more of these factors.

A war affects population in two ways. Directly, it kills people. Indirectly, it sets up conditions in which famine and disease can occur.

Famine and disease may also result from other factors. One of the most notorious of famines occurred in Ireland in 1845. The success of the potato as a crop in Ireland (beginning around 1588) contributed to a population increase from two million in 1687 to over eight million in 1841. It is estimated that in 1845–1846, when the potato blight occurred, over one million people died of starvation or related diseases; many more people moved to other countries. Today, Ireland's population fluctuates between four and five million.

The outstanding example of disease as a population control factor was the fourteenth century's Black Death, the plague during which one quarter of the population of Central Europe died. England's population was cut in half by the plague between 1348 and 1379.

War, famine, and disease are still at work today, smoldering and flaring with an ever-increasing potential for impact on human numbers (Table 8.1). A quick examination of almost any newspaper or weekly news magazine will corroborate this point.

Self-Regulatory Mechanisms

Do other factors limit growth in *Homo sapiens*? Scientists have found that there are factors other than lack of food, predation, and disease that serve as limits to population growth in various animal species. For example, the males of many species stake out territories. Territoriality limits the numbers that can breed in a given area (see Chapter 4). Physiological effects of crowding lead to hormone imbalances in some animals, which result in diminished reproductive potential and even death (see Chapter 16).

How much of this applies to humans is not known, but many scientists hold that such self-regulation is *not* physiologically innate in humans. They believe that in our species, similar regulatory control is achieved by culture and social custom. Lack of food may, among other things, trigger the social regulation of population growth. Various other socioeconomic factors are also important. The scientific and industrial revolutions seem to have led to population decrease rather than increase. In an agrarian society, children are unquestionably assets—as workers. In an industrial setting this is not necessarily so. Children may in fact reduce mobility and make accumulation of goods more difficult. This is the basis of an anti-Malthusian theory stating that poverty increases breeding while plenty decreases it.

Physical Laws and Population Growth

J. H. Fremlin (1964) once calculated the absolute limit of the earth's population. He assumed that if all political, sociological, medical, and other human problems resulting from an expanding population could be solved, the final limit would be a physical heat limit. He projected that world population would be absolutely (physically) limited after it reached the point at which the earth was covered over its entire surface by a single 2000-story building. The upper 1000 floors would be devoted to the machinery to keep the lower 1000 going. Ducts and wires, elevator shafts, and conveyor belts would leave 3–4 square yards for each individual in the lower 1000 stories. A plate on the roof would be kept at the melting point of iron to radiate away all of the earth's heat. This world would support 100 million billion people. On the bright side, Fremlin points out, such a population might have as many as ten million William Shakespeares. The dark side is not hard to imagine. Fremlin's exercise points up the absurdity of the ultimate extension of always trying to solve the problems brought on by increasing population and never coming to grips with the fact that population growth itself may be a problem.

Models of Growth and Limits to Growth

The first practical attempt to develop a model for how the systems of the earth interact was made by Jay Forrester (1971). On the basis of this model, another group headed by Donella and Dennis Meadows attempted in 1972 to project the factors that would eventually check human population growth. Although the assumptions and methodologies used in this projection continue to be controversial, some of the factors involved in checking population limits and industrial growth were defined, and a first step was taken toward expressing their interrelationships in a model.

Using a computer, the Meadows team attempted to show the interactions of five factors affecting the ability of the world system to continue intact. These factors were population growth, agricultural production, nonrenewable resource utilization, industrial output, and pollution. Conservative assumptions about future technological advancements were

Table 8.1   Countries Experiencing Famine Since 1950

Year	Location	Estimated Deaths
1960–1961	China	8,980,000
1968–1969	Nigeria (Biafra)	1,000,000
1971–1972	Bangladesh	430,000
1972	India	830,000
1973	Sahelian Countries	100,000
1972–1974	Ethiopia	200,000
1974	Bangladesh	330,000
1979	Kampuchea	450,000
1983	Ethiopia	30,000
1984	Ethiopia	1,000,000

The Haves and the Have Nots

The nations of the world are often classified into some major groups based on largely economic factors that also seem to parallel certain demographic factors (population growth rate, fertility rate, etc.). Generally, **industrialized nations** such as the United States are characterized by *high* gross national product (GNP) and *low* birth rates. Industrialized nations are also called **developed countries** (DCs). Nonindustrialized nations are characterized by *low* GNP and *high* birth rates. Nonindustrialized nations are also called *developing countries* and *less-developed countries* (LDCs). **Developing coun-** tries are classified as low-income or middle-income depending on whether the GNP is less than $360 per capita (low-income) or more than $360 per capita. As a group these countries are also referred to as the **Third World Nations,** distinct from Western countries and from communist countries, which are also known as **centrally planned economies.** The World Bank provides the following breakdown on the nations of the world. Industrialized nations are broken down into the Western world, capital-surplus oil exporters, and centrally planned economies.

Low-income countries

1. Kampuchea, Dem.	20. Sierra Leone
2. Bangladesh	21. Zaire
3. Lao PDR	22. Niger
4. Bhutan	23. Benin
5. Ethiopia	24. Pakistan
6. Mali	25. Tanzania
7. Nepal	26. Afghanistan
8. Somalia	27. Central African Rep.
9. Burundi	28. Madagascar
10. Chad	29. Haiti
11. Mozambique	30. Mauritania
12. Burma	31. Lesotho
13. Upper Volta	32. Uganda
14. Vietnam	33. Angola
15. India	34. Sudan
16. Malawi	35. Togo
17. Rwanda	36. Kenya
18. Sri Lanka	37. Senegal
19. Guinea	38. Indonesia

Middle-income countries

39. Egypt	53. Papua New Guinea
40. Ghana	54. El Salvador
41. Yemen, PDR	55. Morocco
42. Cameroon	56. Peru
43. Liberia	57. Ivory Coast
44. Honduras	58. Nicaragua
45. Zambia	59. Colombia
46. Zimbabwe	60. Paraguay
47. Thailand	61. Ecuador
48. Bolivia	62. Dominican Rep.
49. Philippines	63. Guatemala
50. Yemen Arab Rep.	64. Syrian Arab Rep.
51. Congo, People's Rep.	65. Tunisia
52. Nigeria	66. Jordan

67. Malaysia	79. Brazil
68. Jamaica	80. Uruguay
69. Lebanon	81. Argentina
70. Korea, Rep. of	82. Portugal
71. Turkey	83. Yugoslavia
72. Algeria	84. Trinidad and Tobago
73. Mexico	85. Venezuela
74. Panama	86. Hong Kong
75. Taiwan	87. Greece
76. Chile	88. Singapore
77. South Africa	89. Spain
78. Costa Rica	90. Israel

Industrialized Countries—Western

91. Ireland	100. Netherlands
92. Italy	101. Belgium
93. New Zealand	102. Canada
94. United Kingdom	103. Norway
95. Finland	104. Germany, Fed. Rep.
96. Austria	105. United States
97. Japan	106. Denmark
98. Australia	107. Sweden
99. France	108. Switzerland

Capital-surplus oil exporters

109. Iraq	112. Saudi Arabia
110. Iran	113. Kuwait
111. Libya	

Centrally planned economies

114. China	120. Bulgaria
115. Korea, Dem. Rep.	121. Hungary
116. Albania	122. Poland
117. Cuba	123. USSR
118. Mongolia	124. Czechoslovakia
119. Romania	125. German Dem. Rep.

made and included in the formula. Depending on the assumptions that were made about changing rates of growth, food production, resource development, and environmental deterioration, one or another of these factors proved limiting to the continuation of the world system over specific periods of time. For example, in the "standard run," which assumed "no great changes in human values nor in the functioning of the global population/capital system as it has operated for the last one-hundred years," nonrenewable resource depletion was projected to cause the collapse of the world economic/

political system well before the year 2100 (Meadows, Meadows, Randers, and Behrens, 1972). When the assumption was made that twice as many nonrenewable resource reserves are available as were used in the standard run, system collapse again was projected before 2100, but in this run the limiting factor was pollution. No doubt other models attempting to predict the future of global society will emerge and be scrutinized and disputed. Although a model is only as good as the accuracy of the assumptions upon which it is based, modeling does help to clarify the factors to be considered in assessing the vulnerability of the world system and defining the variables—some of which are under the control of world decision makers.

DEMOGRAPHY

Demography is the study of the vital and other social statistics of human populations. A study of certain key indices over time can be used to project future trends in human population growth. Let's look at some of these significant statistical factors.

Population Growth Indices: A Review

As we discussed in Chapter 4, growth rate is a function of birth rate, death rate, and net migration. Birth rate and death rate can be expressed in terms of births and deaths per thousand people per year. In 1982, when there were about 229,900,000 people in the United States, there were 3,704,000 births and 1,986,000 deaths.

The birth rate was:

$$3{,}704{,}000 \text{ divided by } \left[\frac{229{,}900{,}000}{1000}\right] = 16.1$$
births per 1000 people.

The death rate was:

$$1{,}986{,}000 \text{ divided by } \left[\frac{229{,}900{,}000}{1000}\right] = 8.6 \text{ deaths}$$
per 1000 people.

If migration is ignored, the growth rate for that year was $16.1 - 8.6 = 7.5$ per thousand people. This is the *rate of natural increase*. It is usually expressed as the *annual percentage increase*. Thus 7.5 per thousand becomes 0.75 per hundred, so the natural rate of increase was 0.75%.

To determine the actual *net growth rate* for a given year, one would also have to consider migration. Assuming a net U.S. migration of 400,000 in 1982 or a percentage increase of 0.17, the actual rate of population increase was 0.92% (0.75% + 0.17%) in 1982.

These births and death rates are crude because they do not provide certain relevant information. A less crude, more information-rich term is *fertility rate*. The **general fertility rate** is the number of births per year per 1000 women ages 15–44 (the reproductive group); it is used to measure changes in overall fertility in a population. For predictions of more long-range trends, other fertility factors may be used. The **age-specific fertility** rate is the number of births per year per 1000 women at a given age—say, 28. By comparing such specific rates over a period of time, general trends in population growth can be determined.

The rate of natural increase is a function of fertility and of the number of women of reproductive age. If the fertility rate remains constant but there are more women entering the reproductive age, there will be more babies. This illustrates the importance of age structure within a population (see Chapter 4). Generally speaking, developed countries are characterized by a bell-shaped profile, which indicates a stable population (see Figure 8.2). Developing countries exhibit an age structure like a broad-based pyramid. In a developing country, 40–50% of the population may be 15 years of age or younger. Such countries have an explosive potential for further growth should death rates decline quickly (see Chapter 4).

Age structure is related to the survivorship curves we discussed in Chapter 4. The human survivorship curve has changed dramatically with improvements in, and accessibility of, medicine. The decrease in infant mortality in both developing and developed nations has contributed significantly to the population increases of the last several decades.

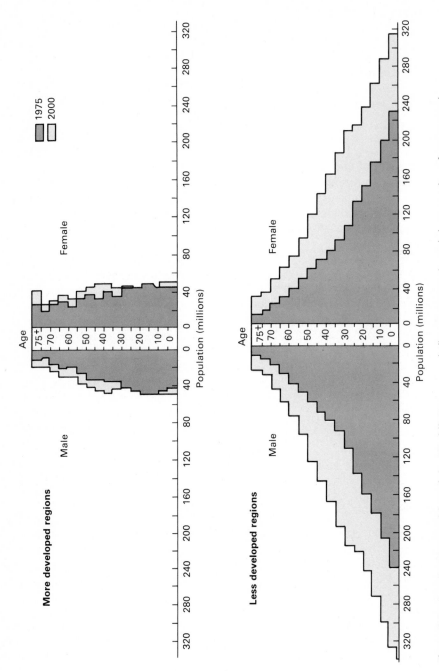

Figure 8.2 Age-Sex Composition of the World's Population, 1975 and 2000. These two pyramids of age structure of populations typify the difference between developed and developing countries. The broad base of developing countries indicates a proportionately large number of young people, which means a potentially explosive population. The profile of the developed countries indicates a decreasing birth rate and a stable population.

Zero Population Growth (ZPG)

If crude birth rate is equal to crude death rate for a long enough time, the result is **zero population growth**. For human beings an average of 2.1 children per female is the theoretical replacement rate, the rate at which ZPG is eventually reached (if immigration is disregarded). The extra tenth of a percent over 2—the rate one might expect to be the replacement rate—takes into account deaths prior to reproduction, the fact that fewer females are born than males, and similar factors.

In any growing population it may take a number of years for growth to stop, following the achievement of 2.1 births per female. This will be true, for example, in a population in which the proportion of women of reproductive age is increasing. In other words, replacement rates must be maintained for some time before ZPG can be attained.

Figure 8.3 indicates that if the *world* attained replacement rate fertility between 2000 and 2005, the *total* population would continue to increase by 2.6 billion people and would eventually stabilize around 8.5 billion. If replacement rate were not reached until around 2020, world population would stabilize eventually around 10.7 billion. If the world did not attain fertility replacement rate until the middle of the twenty-first century, population would grow to 13.5 billion because of the lag resulting from the age structure of the world population.

Lag is extremely important in determining the meaning and effects of changes in population growth rates. Population control is a long-range phenomenon that cannot be achieved instantaneously at the time of an impending crisis. In Figure 8.3, even before replacement rate is reached in the most optimistic scenario (lowest curve) the curves have split to reflect a gradual change in population growth. There is a lag from the time population growth begins to slow to the point at which replacement rate is reached. There is another lag from the time replacement rate is reached to the achievement of ZPG.

HISTORICAL PERSPECTIVES AND TRENDS

Now that we are familiar with some of the terms and indices used to gauge population trends, let us look at the historical growth of human population. Two major factors permitted substantial human population increases. One was the increased ability to produce food through agriculture. The second was the substantial lowering of the death rate achieved through improved sanitation and medicine.

World Population

World population reached one billion in 1850, two billion in 1930 (80 years later), three billion in 1960 (30 years after), and four billion in 1975 (15 years later). The next billion is expected in 1989 (14 years). Most projections put world population around six billion in the year 2000. The momentum of population growth is immense.

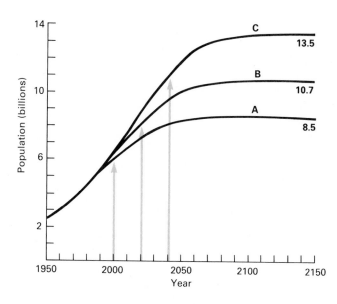

Figure 8.3 World Population Growth Projections. Even if a replacement rate of fertility could be reached immediately worldwide, total population would continue to grow for many years because of the broad base of young women already born and about to enter their reproductive years. This graph indicates three projections for ultimate world population based on when replacement rate is achieved (see arrows). For example, if the world attained replacement fertility between 2000 and 2005, the population would then stand at 5.9 billion, and the world population could be expected to stabilize eventually at 8.5 billion.

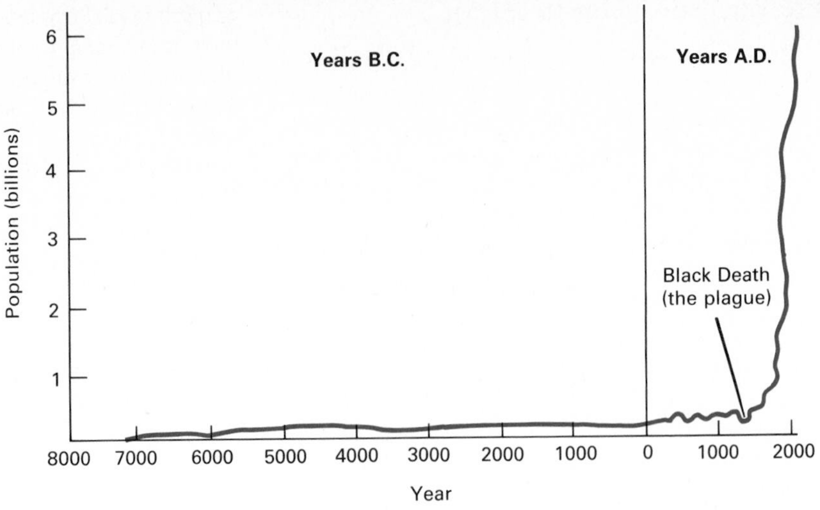

Figure 8.4 What Goes up Might Come down. The growth of human population has been dramatic in the last 100 years or so. Providing an ever-increasing number of persons with clean air, water, nourishing food, and shelter is becoming more and more difficult. Will we follow a J-shaped curve or an S-shaped curve as time goes on?

Figure 8.4 shows world population growth over time. It is impossible to gauge from this figure whether we are following a J-curve or the first part of a sigmoid curve. A J-shaped curve is characteristic of species that increase exponentially and then, because of the lack of density-dependent feedback control, overshoot carrying capacity and go through a population "crash" (see Chapter 4). In the S-shaped pattern characteristic of other species, population growth levels off gradually and stabilizes somewhere below carrying capacity. Some feel that humankind's adoption of an S-shaped or a J-shaped curve is still a matter of collective choice. Others fear that carrying capacity has already been seriously exceeded and that this will lead to a considerable wobble or even a crash in the future.

At an annual percentage growth rate of 1% the human population will double in 70 years; at 2% the doubling time in 35 years; and so on. Average annual growth rates for the world declined to 1.7% in 1984 from a high of 2.0% in the previous decade.

Although the *rate* of human population growth has declined, the decade of the 1970s still had a greater number of births worldwide than any previous decade. In mid-1983 the world recorded its largest 12-month increase in human population to that time—82,077,000 persons. The reproductive rate was lower than rates in previous decades, but there were more people reproducing. The United Nations estimates that as a result of the large existing population base in prereproductive or reproductive groups, about 90 million people will continue to be added to the world population annually to the year 2000.

Developed Versus Developing Countries

Since 1950, the fertility rates in developed countries have decreased significantly. Many of the developed countries have reached replacement fertility levels, and in East and West Germany, death rates now actually exceed birth rates. For all developed countries the fertility rate is just about at the replacement rate (Mauldin, 1980). Should these rates continue, these countries will soon achieve stable populations or possibly decline. Although no one knows for certain, it is generally thought likely that once low fertility rates are reached, they will be maintained around replacement levels with periodic fluctuations (Mauldin, 1980). The population problems facing many of the developed countries in the future will stem from increased immigration, urbanization, and unequal distributions of goods.

What about the developing countries? Figure 8.5 shows that crude birth rate has also declined in many of the developing countries since 1950, the most significant declines being in Asia, the Pacific, and Central and South America. Although fertility rates in some developing countries are on the decline, there is in the age structure of the populations of these countries tremendous momentum for continued growth.

Almost 90% of current world population growth can be attributed to the developing countries. It has been predicted that of the six billion people expected to occupy this planet in the year 2000, five billion will live in developing countries. According to a recent U.S. government study, developing countries had 66% of the world's population in 1950, had 72%

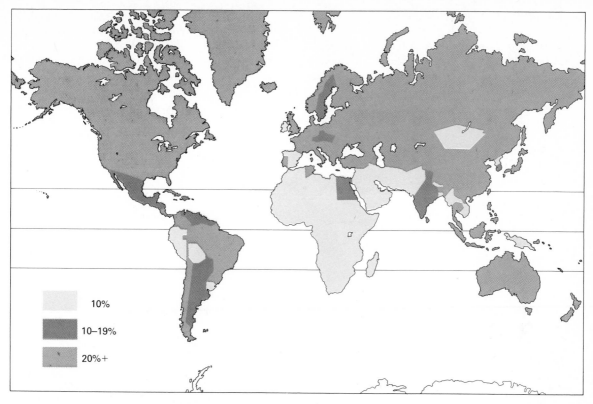

Figure 8.5 Percentage Decline in Crude Birth Rate 1950–1955 Through 1975 for Various World Regions. Although world population is still increasing, worldwide rates of population increase are coming down. We expect further decline in the rate of growth both in developed and developing nations.

10%

10–19%

20%+

in 1975, and are likely to have 79% in the year 2000 (Council on Environmental Quality, 1980b) (See Figure 8.6.)

Population problems in developing countries include the same problems as are associated with urbanization and distribution of goods in developed countries, but in developing countries these problems will continue to be overshadowed by poverty, hunger, and the need to increase economic output faster than population growth. Historically, population growth in the developing countries has far outstripped resource development and improvement in the quality of life. It has been predicted that to simply maintain present, sometimes very low standards of living in developing countries, economic output must double by the year 2000.

World Trends

Although *total world population* will continue to increase for many decades, most *population growth indices* are on the decline and are expected to con-tinue to decline. Crude birth and death rates, gross and net reproductive rates, and general fertility are all expected to decline. The world birth rate appears to be declining at a faster and faster rate. The drop in birth rate in developing countries from 1970 to 1977 was reported to be three times as great as the drop from 1950 to 1970. This dramatic drop in birth rate in developing countries has, since the mid-1960s, exceeded their continuing declining death rate, resulting in an overall decline in the population growth rate (Coale, 1983) (see Figure 8.7). We must keep in mind, however, that even with these promising trends, *population growth* overall will continue well into the twenty-first century because of the lag effect.

It appears that trends toward urbanization will continue. Cities, of course, are places of high population density that carry with them advantages in employment, access to food and shelter, and the trappings of civilization. Apparently, these more than offset the disadvantages of urban life for an ever increasing number of the earth's people.

Population in the United States

Figure 8.8 shows the historical changes in U.S. population growth. We would like to draw the reader's attention to several important points. There was a decrease in the *rate* of population growth in the 1930s, a time of economic depression. A "baby boom" followed World War II and is reflected in the sharp rise in the population growth rate prior to 1950. Population growth since the 1970s appears to

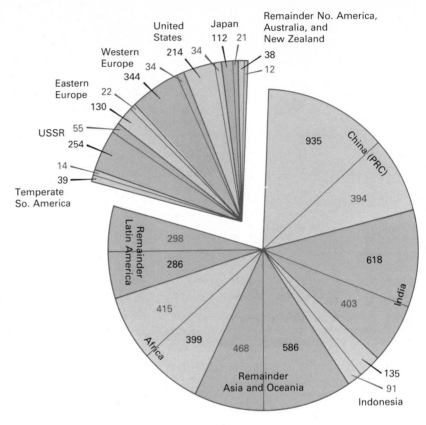

Figure 8.6 Twenty-five Years of World Population Growth. Less-developed nations with higher birth rates will contribute a larger and larger portion to the world population in the next quarter century. Numbers are in million persons. Those in black indicate population in 1975; those in color indicate projected growth from 1975 to 2000.

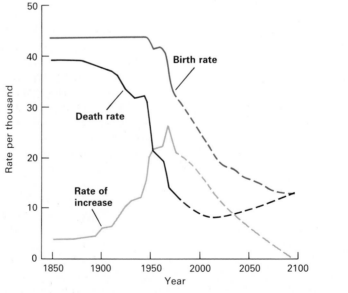

Figure 8.7 Birth Rate, Death Rate, and Rate of Population Increase in Developing Countries, 1850–2100. Since the mid-1960s, the rate of increase in population in developing countries has decreased significantly owing to a dramatic decrease in birth rate. The dashed curves after 1983 are projections. The increase in death rate shown for the mid to late twenty-first century is due to the large number of older people in the population at that time.

Part II *Homo Sapiens* in the Scheme of Natural Things

be slowing down, but the full effect of the baby boom—as the baby boom babies have babies—has yet to be seen (Figure 8.8b). It is thought that this boom generation is either delaying childbirth or will have a much lower fertility rate, resulting in a continuation of the population growth rate decline. Only time will tell.

Since the 1950s the birth rate has declined

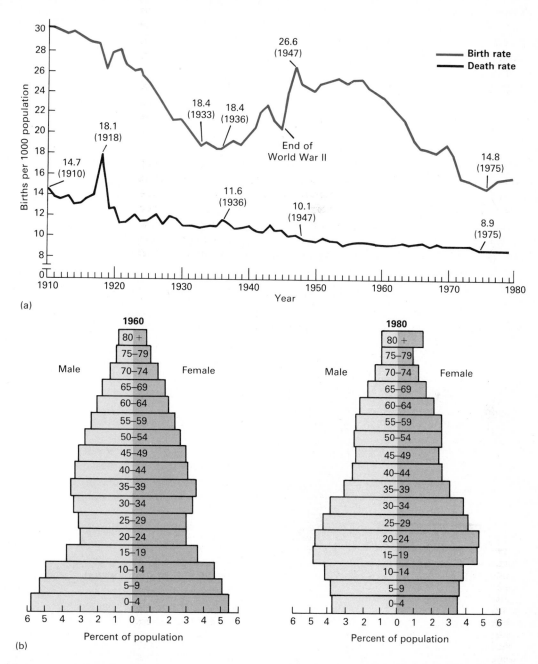

(a)

(b)

Figure 8.8 U.S. Population Profiles. (a) Birth and death rates per thousand from 1910 to 1980. Birth rates slowed in the 1930s, then picked up again after World War II. The beginning of a new leveling out period is apparent; its duration will depend on the reproduction patterns of the "baby boom" children now in their reproductive years. (b) U.S. Population by Age and Sex, 1960 and 1980. The "baby boom" bulge has had a significant impact on the economics of American life from education to job seeking. Even more changes are likely as this predominant portion of the population enters the middle and late years.

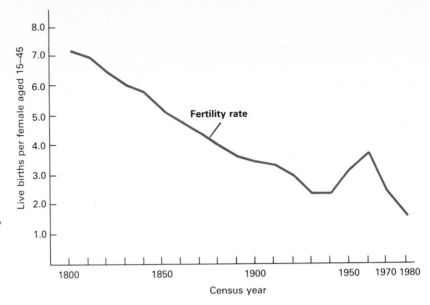

Figure 8.9 U.S. Fertility Rate, 1800–1980. The fertility rate in the U.S. has been decreasing fairly steadily since 1800 except for a "baby boom" associated with World War II and the post–Great Depression era.

Since most of the people in the U.S. live in urban areas, the advantages of city life must appear to most to outweigh the crowding, noise, and lack of green space.

significantly more than death rate. This decline accounts for a slowdown in the rate of population growth. Figure 8.9 shows that fertility rate in the United States is also on the decline. The net population growth rate in the United States has averaged 0.7–0.9% in the last several years.

Immigrants account for 25% of present U.S. population growth (Council on Enviromental Quality, 1977). This does not include illegal aliens, who add another significant (but unknown) percentage.

The U.S. Census Bureau has projected U.S. population growth on the basis of high (2.7), medium (2.1), and low (1.7) fertility rates. The Census Bureau estimates that the earliest the population size will stabilize or decline under any of the estimates is around the year 2030.

U.S. Population Distribution Trends

Where are the people? In 1900, approximately 40% of the people in the United States lived in urban areas; in the 1980s, approximately 75% lived in **standard metropolitan statistical areas** (SMSAs) (urban areas of 50,000 or more together with the county containing the urban area and adjacent counties with employment ties). Nearly 50% lived in 36 metropolitan areas with populations of one million or more.

The center of population in the United States has been moving steadily westward. In 1980 it was projected to be 40 miles south of St. Louis, Missouri, reflecting population shifts to the south and west.

U.S. Immigration Policies and Trends

Immigrants are "nonresident aliens" admitted to the United States for residence of one year or longer. As far back as 1882, Congress limited immigration into the United States by enacting the Chinese Exclusion Law (repealed in 1943). In 1917, Congress passed an act barring certain peoples from Asia and the Pacific Islands. In the 1920s the U.S. Congress enacted a quota law consisting of complicated formulas for determining the number of immigrants to be allowed from various countries. In 1965 the quota law was abolished, and 170,000 was set as the annual number of immigrants allowed from the Eastern Hemisphere with no more than 20,000 coming from any one country. A limit of 120,000 was imposed for the Western Hemisphere. Exemptions were allowed in both cases for relatives of U.S. citizens.

The Immigration Act of 1965 emphasized family reunification, refugee asylum, and needed skills and professions rather than national origin as immigration criteria (President's Commission on Population Growth and the American Future, 1972). The annual quota now runs about 400,000 (Mauldin, 1980).

Between 1945 and 1965, 43% of all U.S. immigrants came from Europe. From 1966 to 1970 this figure was reduced to 33 1/3% with another third coming from Canada and Latin America and the remaining third from West India, Asia, and Africa (President's Commission on Population Growth and the American Future, 1972). This pattern of increased migration from Asia and South America has continued in recent years (Mauldin, 1980).

Above and beyond its quotas the United States also provides asylum for refugees. This figure varies depending on world events. The shiploads of "Marielitos" from Cuba in 1980 added over 100,000 persons to the U.S. population. In a "normal" year, however, refugees may average only 100,000–150,000 (Mauldin, 1980).

People do not just immigrate to the United States; some also emigrate. About 125,000–150,000 persons leave the United States each year. Although numbers vary, substantially more migrants come into the United States than leave annually. Typically, there is a net of 300,000 *legal* migrants coming in (Mauldin, 1980).

The contribution of illegal aliens is growing. In 1971 and subsequent years, more illegal aliens were expelled than legal immigrant aliens were admitted. Actual numbers of illegal aliens entering the United States are unknown. Estimates range from 150,000 to 250,000 a year, but some think it is much more. Some estimates for 1977 run as high as 2,000,000 illegal immigrants. The total population of illegal aliens in the United States in 1984 was estimated to be about six million. In 1984, Congress considered but did not agree upon legislation to address the issue of illegal aliens.

POPULATION GROWTH AND ECONOMICS

What is the relationship between population growth and economic growth? What impact can birth control programs have on the overall economic development of a country? Is a growing population a requirement for continued economic growth?

Economic Growth and Population

The report of the President's Commission on Population Growth and the American Future published in 1972 states:

> We have looked for, and have not found, any convincing economic argument for continued national population growth. The health of our economy does not depend on it. The vitality of business does not depend on it. The welfare of the average person certainly does not depend on it.

The study cites the fact that because, in the past, periods of rapid population growth have also been periods of rapid economic expansion, we tend to assume that the two go hand in hand: The more people, the more consumption of goods and services, the higher the GNP. The report went on to suggest that "the diminished burden of providing for dependents and for the multiplication of facilities should make more of our national output available for many desirable purposes" such as human resource investments and expenditures for *qualitative* improvements and environmental objectives.

In the third world, population growth characteristically has the effect of *decreasing* the economic welfare of the individual or, at best, greatly retarding improvement in individual welfare. Many studies show that developing countries would make more progress faster by investing in slowing population growth rather than accelerating industrial growth. The *World Development Report 1984* (World Bank, 1984) states that rapid population growth is impeding development. In other words, over time the cost of implementing birth control programs is recovered many times over as extra income per capita for the population. In fact, the rate of return on population control programs is greater than that on investment in capital construction such as railroads and factories.

Since the mid-1970s, China has embarked on a population control program and has set a goal of reaching replacement birth rate by the year 2000. China's population control program is aimed at reducing population in order to increase capital accumulation, public education levels, and overall improvements in the standard of living (Mauldin, 1980). Strategies used there to reduce population growth include encouraging late marriages, encouraging family planning, providing contraceptive devices and abortive services, and promoting the concept of the one-child family.

Although some gains are being made in efforts to slow population growth in developing countries, absolute increases in total numbers due to the lag effect will keep per capita GNP levels low for many decades. Predictions are that the gap between GNP in developed and developing countries will continue to widen. Figure 8.10 shows the predictions of GNP per capita for various regions of the world for 1975 and 2000.

Differences in quality of life throughout the world lead to tensions, which can be the seeds of rebellion and conflict. The instability caused by these tensions in turn makes it difficult to sustain programs of economic development and population control, and the imbalances become even greater. All countries, developing and developed, have a stake in bringing about worldwide **demographic transitions** and otherwise working to improve the lot of individuals throughout the world.

Economic Birth Control

In industrialized societies where the rate of economic development has exceeded the rate of population growth, childbearing tends to decrease as income rises. In modern American society, in which both parents generate income, children may be more of an economic liability than an economic asset. While it might be argued that the answer to the world population problem is to give everyone a

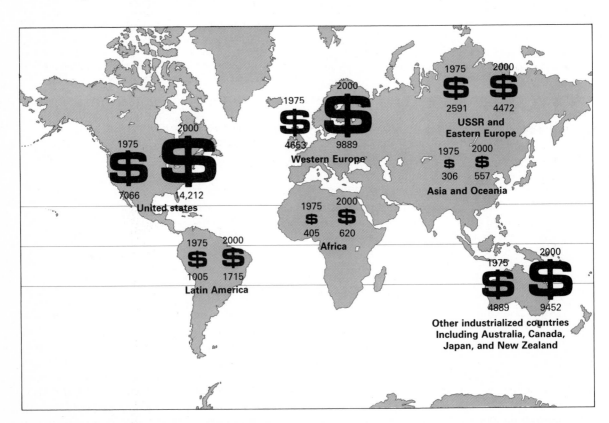

Figure 8.10 World GNP's per Capita 1975 and 2000. This figure shows the Gross National Product (GNP) per capita for various regions of the world. Numbers (in constant 1975 U.S. dollars) are for medium growth. Developing countries are having difficulty increasing economic output at levels commensurate with population increases. The gap between developed and developing countries will probably continue to widen.

chance at a good-paying job and a comfortable life, this strategy would generate enormous environmental pressures. As we have pointed out often, affluent countries such as the United States have a far greater impact on the global ecosystem via increased pollution and increased resource depletion than do many less developed countries. To quote the Worldwatch Institute (1978),

> As the effort to improve the welfare of a growing world population places ever greater stresses on resource supplies and on the stability of ecosystems . . . pressure will have to be brought to bear on those whose activities and habits account for incongruously high proportions of . . . the stresses.

POPULATION GROWTH AND CULTURE

In a 1978 report to the Council on Environmental Quality, the Worldwatch Institute stated

> whatever the physical carrying capacity of the earth and the possibilities for technological gains that promise to raise it, the most basic limits to growth may well be social. Most societies will likely be unable to make the awesome and rapid social transformations necessary to absorb the projected population increases and resource stresses without experiencing human disasters.

Determining Family Size

There are cultural reasons for high fertility in the Third World countries. They include high infant mortality, the importance of family and kin in subsistence, education, care of the elderly (all functions that fall to other institutions in industrialized countries), and the importance of a male heir. All of these tend to encourage more childbearing. An important contributor to the present population problem is the fact that cultural norms have not yet adjusted to the decrease in infant mortality. Previously, higher birth rates were required to compensate for early death. The problem is that birth rates have not yet fallen in many countries in proportion to the decline in infant mortality and death rates in general. Old ways fade slowly.

A number of things operate to keep birth rates low in the *developed* countries. They include:

1. a lower infant mortality rate,
2. compulsory education, which reduces or eliminates economic productivity by children,
3. mechanization, which diminishes the need for human labor,
4. social programs for the elderly,

5. the advancement of birth control technology, and
6. shifts in social status symbols.

Status has become associated with affluence and occupation, not family size; women are finding satisfying roles in society other than child rearing.

Birth Control: Methods and Programs

Egyptian papyruses dating back to 1900 B.C. show that contraception was known even then. However, information on contraception has not always been easily available. The subject was taboo for centuries. One of the earliest American advocates of disseminating birth control information was Margaret Sanger (1883–1966). Sanger's experiences as a nurse convinced her of the need to provide contraceptive information to those who wanted it. Objections from religious organizations and the failure of the medical profession to acknowledge the need made her task an uphill fight. (The American Medical Association gave its first endorsement of birth control in 1937.)

Technological approaches to contraception are varied. Researchers continue to look for methods that are safe, reliable, convenient, and reversible. Recent efforts have centered on the development of a vaccine to immunize a female against sperm, against certain hormones needed to maintain pregnancy, or even against her own eggs. Pills for males are also under investigation, as is the use of sex hormones to halt sperm production.

Having the means leaves the question of motivation. As we have already seen, the motivation to limit births apparently comes fairly automatically to the individuals in highly industrialized societies. The question we would like to explore now is how motivation can be manipulated or influenced. A related question is, *Should* motivation be influenced?

GOVERNMENT INVOLVEMENT IN POPULATION CONTROL

There is power in numbers. Italy under Mussolini and Germany under Hitler attempted to increase the birth rate by taxing bachelors, giving married people preferential job treatment, reducing taxes for large families, and granting marriage loans. France developed a family allowance scheme in the 1930s; the amount of the allowance increased with the size of the family. Sweden enacted a program in the 1930s based on assisting those families who really wanted children by providing services rather than actual monetary allowances.

A society has many ways—some subtle, some obvious—to influence people's motivation to have or not have children. In China, billboards are part of a campaign to convince couples to have just one child.

In the United States, federal influence on birth rates has been indirect. During certain periods, military draft policies have encouraged early marriage and provided incentives for childbearing. Tax breaks are given for each added dependent. One of the few federal laws dealing with contraception was the Comstock Act of 1873, named after Anthony Comstock, founder of the Society for the Suppression of Vice. This act prohibited the importation, transportation in interstate commerce, and mailing of any article whatever for the prevention of conception. This law was not repealed until January 8, 1971, although it was widely ignored long before that.

The effectiveness of such programs may be questionable, but the precedent they set for government involvement in procreation is important. In recent years the key questions have had to do with limitation rather than promotion of reproduction.

Proponents of government intervention in population control cite examples of government intervention in other personal, individual matters. The government mandates one spouse at a time, enforces compulsory education, and may require that critically ill children be treated even if treatment goes against religious beliefs.

Incentives and Coercion

Table 8.2 summarizes some of the possible ways governments might influence population control. These proposals include involuntary fertility control, educational campaigns, and legal and social reforms. Not many of them have ever been implemented or even seriously considered. The proposals vary widely in their scientific readiness, political viability, administrative feasibility, economic feasibility, ethical acceptability, and presumed effectiveness.

Berelson (1969) characterizes as ideal birth control programs those that permit maximum freedom and diversity, that consider goals other than birth control (such as improved health care), and that do not weigh heavily on the disadvantaged. But Berelson concludes that "what will be scientifically available, politically acceptable, economically justifiable and morally tolerated . . . depends on the people's perception of consequence."

India: A National Program of Birth Control

We often read of famine and disasters in India, but their impact on population growth has been negligible. A great famine occurred in Bengal in the 1940s when India's population was 310 million; in 1951 the population was 360 million, and in 1971 it was 548 million. Gulhati (1977) concluded that Malthusian checks on population "while causing misery and pain, are unlikely to reduce India's population significantly."

India was the first country to initiate a national family planning program in the 1950s (although it was not pursued vigorously until 1965–1966). In the mid-1970s, India was the first nation to advocate compulsory sterilization as a national policy.

India's family planning program is credited with about a 50% reduction in all births, due primarily to its stress on sterilization. Although the Indian government's policy of compulsory sterilization resulted in dramatic increases in sterilizations in 1976, this policy was one of the prime factors leading to the overthrow of Indira Gandhi's government in the late 1970s.

PROSPECTS FOR THE FUTURE

In "Tragedy of the Commons," Garret Hardin (1968) makes the point very plainly that "no action" relative to population control *is* action. Doing nothing is an endorsement of the status quo. The World-

Table 8.2 Alternatives for Controlling Birth Rates

Proposal	Scientific Readiness	Political Viability	Administrative Feasibility	Economic Capability	Ethical Acceptability	Presumed Effectiveness
Extension of voluntary fertility control	high	high on maternal care, moderate-to-low on abortion	uncertain in near future	maternal care too costly for local budget, abortion feasible	high for maternal care, low for abortion	Moderately high
Establishment of involuntary fertility control	low	low	low	high	low	high
Intensified educational campaigns	high	moderate-to-high	high	probably high	generally high	moderate
Incentive programs	high	moderately low	low	low-to-moderate	low-to-high	uncertain
Tax and welfare benefits and penalties	high	moderately low	low	low-to-moderate	low-to-moderate	uncertain
Shifts in social and economic institutions	high	generally high, but low on some specifics	low	generally low	generally high, but uneven	high, over long run
Political channels and organizations	high	low	low	moderate	moderately low	uncertain
Augmented research efforts	moderate	high	moderate-to-high	high	high	uncertain
Family-planning programs	generally, high, but could use improved technology	moderate-to-high	moderate-to-high	high	generally high, but uneven, on religious grounds	moderately high

watch Institute (1978) states that the question is not whether population growth in the Third World will slow down, but how? At stake in the population question are basic human freedoms, which will be diminished either by the increasing regulation that will be necessary to care for a growing population or by the use of coercive measures for population con-

trol. It is an ecological reality that the population growth of *Homo sapiens* will be checked somehow. Should we let it happen naturally, or will human intervention to check population growth be less traumatic? Should we work on means or on motivation? Shall we educate or legislate? Shall we provide incentives or penalties?

Food, Hunger, and Nutrition

Despite all the advances in human knowledge that have taken place, somehow or other we have failed to solve the very basic problem of hunger. Even in the United States, the 1985 report of the Physician Task Force on Hunger in America estimates that up to 20 million Americans may go hungry at least some part of each month. Hunger is worse in other countries.

What is the essence of the food, hunger, and nutrition problem? Is it the need for increased production? Is it the need for better distribution of food? Is it related to food habits? Is it a problem of too many people too fast? Is it a problem of poor technology or the inappropriate transfer of technology? Is it a problem of priorities that place food production and agricultural research behind other developments? Is it a problem of lack of overall economic development? Is it a problem of culture? Is it a problem of politics and trade? The answer to all of these questions is "yes."

FOOD PRODUCTION: CURRENT SITUATION

Where do we stand after several decades of intense effort to increase worldwide food production? After World War II, technological advances such as chemical fertilizers and hybrid crops resulted in ma-

Even in the United States, a land of plenty, some people are going hungry.

jor increases in food production worldwide. From 1950 to 1973 the worldwide production of grain more than doubled (Brown, 1984a). While population was growing at a rate of about 1.9% annually during this period, grain production was increasing at a rate of over 3% annually. The year 1973 is a landmark because it was the year that energy prices began to rise dramatically. Because many of the agricultural practices responsible for the major increases in food production up to that time were energy intensive (increased use of fertilizer, pesticides, gasoline-powered farm equipment), the high cost of energy was a major factor in slowing the increase in per capita food production. Since 1973, world grain production has increased less than 2% annually (Brown, 1984a), while the world's population has been growing at about 1.7%. There has been little if any gain in improving food supplies per capita in recent years.

Another significant indicator of how well we are doing in meeting the demand for food is how nations overall are becoming more or less self-sufficient in food production (see Figure 8.11). Although there are other exporter countries, including Argentina and Brazil in recent years (not reflected in Table 8.3), the United States and Canada remain the major grain exporters today. Should any prolonged climatic change or other phenomenon cause crop failure or even decreased production in North America, this too could change. It almost changed in 1983. In 1983 the United States had the smallest corn harvest since 1974. A combination of factors brought this about. The Reagan administration initiated a farm program in 1983 to reduce grain surpluses in storage in the United States. The program was designed to award surplus stored grain to farmers who voluntarily kept their farmland out of production that year. The "Payment-in-Kind" (PIK) program resulted in a loss in production of about 2.2 billion bushels of corn. That same year a severe drought in the Corn Belt in the United States resulted in the loss of another billion bushels of corn. The combined impact of these events reduced world carryover stocks of grain to a level that was one of the lowest

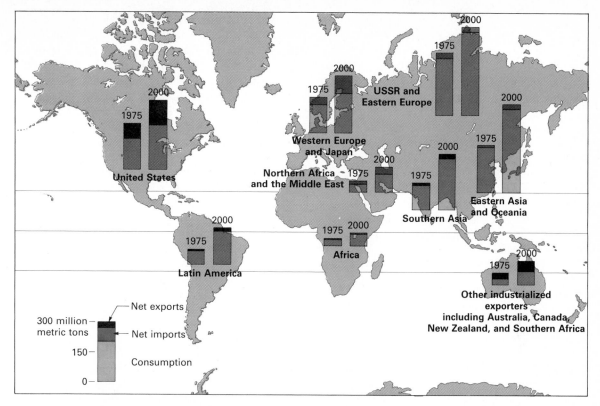

Figure 8.11 Patterns in Grain Exports and Imports. The U.S. and Canada are the two major grain exporters in the world. Other exporters include Australia and New Zealand. Although Latin America as a whole is not an exporter, the countries of Brazil and Argentina are exporter nations. Grain consumption figures include grain used for livestock.

that had been experienced in several years (Brown, 1984a). Drought in the United States in 1980 caused world carryover stocks to fall below the amount needed for 50 days of consumption.

The world fish catch was nearly three times as great in 1970 as in 1950 but turned downward for several consecutive years in the early 1970s. In 1976 it increased, but between 1979 and 1984, worldwide fish harvests decreased again. There is concern that overfishing of the oceans is occurring and that pollution of the oceans is also taking its toll.

In the 1970s, world grain output per **hectare** (a unit of measure equal to 2.47 acres or 10,000 square meters) was down for all grains except rice (Brown, 1975). The reasons for this included poor weather, the high cost of energy and fertilizer, general soil deterioration, and the use of more marginal, less productive lands.

Table 8.3 The Changing Pattern of World Grain Trade, 1950–1983 (in million metric tons)

Region	1950[1]	1960	1970	1980	1983[2]
North America	+23	+39	+56	+131	+122
Latin America	+ 1	0	+ 4	− 10	− 3
Western Europe	−22	−25	−30	− 16	+ 2
Eastern Europe and Soviet Union	0	0	0	− 46	− 39
Africa	0	− 2	− 5	− 15	− 20
Asia	− 6	−17	−37	− 63	− 71
Australia and New Zealand	+ 3	+ 6	+12	+ 19	+ 9

Plus sign indicates net export; minus sign indicates net imports.
[1] Average for 1948–1952.
[2] Preliminary.

The *Global 2000 Report to the President* (Council on Environmental Quality, 1980b) predicted a 90% increase in food production in the year 2000 compared to 1970. This increase will depend upon the use of high-yield crops, energy-intensive technologies including pesticides and fertilizers, and irrigation. The report indicates that these increases will be made but in many cases with diminishing returns (more energy and effort will be put in per unit of food produced). Although the *Global 2000 Report* predicted that food production will increase at a greater rate than population, per capita consumption will vary considerably from country to country. The less developed countries have a poor outlook for improved diets. According to the World Bank, the number of malnourished people could rise to 1.3 billion by the year 2000.

THE POTENTIAL AND LIMITS OF THE LAND

There are only three ways by which more food can be made available to the world market. One is by bringing new lands into production; the second is by increasing the yield on existing land; the third is by improving the use of existing supplies.

New Lands

There seems to be some general agreement that increased food supplies will not come from bringing into production land that has not been used for crop production before. In 1973 the U.N. Food and Agriculture Organization (FAO) announced that most of the 11% of the world's land that is suitable for cultivation is already in use (Pimentel, Dritschilo, Krummel, and Kutzman, 1975). Africa and Latin America have the greatest potential for cultivating new lands. Eventually, on a worldwide scale the law of diminishing returns will render this strategy of new lands ineffective. Land under cultivation is expected to increase by only 4% by the year 2000. The shortcomings of this approach are intensified by the daily loss of farmland by conversion to other uses, by loss of topsoil, and by conversion of farmland into desert by improper management. (See Chapter 17.)

Desertification

Almost 78 million people live on lands that are relatively barren because of human activities; the southern boundary of the Sudan moved 90–100 kilometers further southward between 1958 and 1975 (Worldwatch Institute, 1978). In addition, almost 125,000 hectares of cropped land is lost annually because of poor irrigation practices in arid lands, resulting in soil waterlogging and salinization (salt accumulation) (Worldwatch Institute, 1978). This process of improper management of arid or semiarid land to the extent that it is no longer suitable for range or cropland is called **desertification**. It is a serious and growing problem, not just for developing countries but even for the United States. Extensive irrigation, poor soil drainage, overuse of groundwater, overgrazing, and urban development are all contributors to soil erosion, salinization of topsoils and irrigation water, and destruction of native vegetation. In the United States the primary problem areas are the San Joaquin Valley in California, the Wellton-Mohawk Irrigation District in Arizona, the Santa Cruz and Pedro River basins in Arizona, the counties of Kiowa and Crowly in Colorado, and the High Plains in Texas (Council on Environmental Quality, 1980a). Actual global losses to desertification are estimated to run about six million hectares annually, an area about the size of Maine (Council on Environmental Quality, 1980b). This includes 3.2 million hectares of rangeland, 2.5 million hectares of rain-fed cropland, and 125,000 hectares of irrigated farmland. Ironically, the trend toward desertification may accelerate as population growth puts additional pressures on land for food, energy, and shelter.

Increasing Yields

Sound land conservation techniques must be used to maintain soil fertility. What about the prospects for increasing yields from existing farmland? The *Global 2000 Report* indicated that whereas one hectare of land supported 2.6 people in 1970, a hectare will have to support four people in the year 2000.

One way to increase yield is to use fertilizer. Eventually, the law of diminishing return will also prevail here, however. The United States is already reaching the limit, and most of the potential for increased yields through fertilization is in the developing countries. However, energy requirements for fertilizer production will keep the costs of fertilizer high and out of reach of those who need it most. In addition, many developing countries are the very ones where, even with sufficient fertilizer, water may be the limiting factor. But water is scarce, and irrigation also requires energy.

Yields can also be increased by growing more crops on the same land in any given year. Varieties of crops with shortened growing seasons are now available. However, more crops will require more resource and energy inputs.

Pimentel and his colleagues (1975) calculated the agricultural energy requirements of a population of four billion if it were to eat at the U.S. dietary level. Fuel consumption would be 5 trillion liters annually; fuel reserves would be gone in 31 years. We cannot escape the fact that increases in food production in the past were made possible in part by energy (see Figure 8.12). The world's simultaneous food and energy crises present a profound dilemma indeed.

The Green Revolution

In the mid-1960s a technological breakthrough in the development of improved pure-line varieties of rice and wheat resulted in such an optimistic outlook for food production that it was called the **Green Revolution.** New wheat varieties were shorter and stiffer; this allowed them to respond to fertilizer without growing tall and falling over from their own weight. They had proportionately more grain than

straw. The varieties appeared to be more adaptable to diverse environments and showed some resistence to diseases and insects. They required shorter growing seasons and matured over wide ranges of day length. The prognosis looked good. Between 1967 and 1969, miracle grain–based food production increased by 27% in India and Pakistan.

In the early 1970s, however, some of the gloss began to fade. For one thing, the new strains performed best with large amounts of fertilizer, even though without fertilizer their yields exceeded those of traditional varieties. The wheat required much water, and the rice did not do well in flooded fields. The new varieties were genetically very similar to one another, and this increased pest susceptibility. In the early stages of the "revolution" the miracle varieties were highly subsidized, so the high costs of production were somewhat masked. Even so, the new varieties often were not economically available to the poorest rural people. Socially, because the Green Revolution technology tends to use machines instead of human labor, it presents problems in

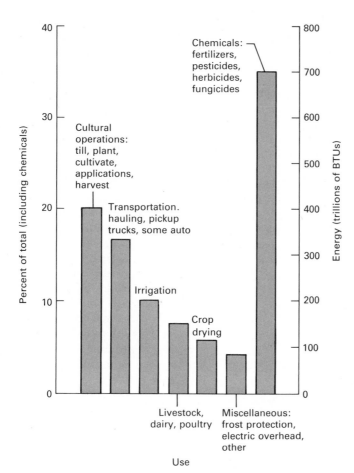

Figure 8.12 Energy in Agriculture. Modern agriculture is energy intensive. Energy is used directly in running farm machinery, but the largest single energy consumer in modern agricultural practices is fertilizer and herbicide production (see also Chapter 6).

many countries for the farm labor market and the millions of landless laborers in rural areas. Good technology out of the context of social and economic norms cannot solve the problem of food production in developing countries.

The technology of the Green Revolution *has* increased crop yields. Nevertheless, adoption of the high-yield varieties by Third World countries has not come as quickly or as broadly as was originally predicted. Attempts to develop more resistant strains and more culturally acceptable strains will be necessary.

Improving the Use of Existing Supplies

What about the third alternative? What kinds of changes would improve the percentage of food produced that *actually reaches and is consumed by people*. Less meat production and more direct consumption of grain, better preservatives and storage techniques, and better distribution systems are all possibilities.

Meat Versus Grain for Human Consumption. The second law of thermodynamics tells us that far more people could be supported on grain than on the meat of grain-eating animals. While this suggests a simple partial solution to the hunger problem, it is not really so simple. The economics of current demand worldwide will probably hinder a voluntary decline in meat production. The pressure for food is coming not just from growing populations in the Third World but also from rising demands for meat in industrialized nations. From 1960 to 1970, meat demand increased 31% in the United Kingdom, France, West Germany, Italy, the Soviet Union and 265% in Japan (Brink, Densmore, and Hill, 1977). Likewise the increased buying power of the OPEC nations will result in greater food imports. Currently, the consumption of grain in affluent countries is proportionally four to five times that of poorer countries owing to the use of grain for poultry and livestock to produce meat, milk, and eggs (Worldwatch Institute, 1978). In developing countries, about 450 lb. of grain are consumed per capita per year; in the United States, almost one ton of grain (2000 lb.) is consumed per capita per year. Of this, only 200 lb. is consumed directly; the rest is fed to livestock.

Worldwide, of the protein consumed by humans, 47% comes from cereals, 20% from legumes, 5% from fish, and 25% from livestock (Pimentel, Dritschilo, Krummel, and Kutzman, 1975). Of the livestock protein, 60% is produced by the conversion of forage crops and rangeland proteins that are *not* usable by humans. In this way, by converting unusable protein into usable protein, *livestock can actually increase the amount of protein available to human beings*. The problem is that the remaining 40% of livestock protein is produced from feed that is usable by humans. Efficiencies are such that 5 kilograms of vegetable protein suitable for human consumption but fed to livestock instead results in only 1 kilogram of livestock protein for human consumption. It should be noted that chickens convert more plant protein to animal protein per unit consumed than do cattle. The net effect, however, whether grain is fed to chickens or to cattle, is a decrease in calories for human consumption. Pimentel and his colleagues calculate that almost 29% of the world's supply of protein suitable for human consumption is fed to livestock. A forage-fed-only system for livestock would release around 135 million tons of grain for human consumption, an amount capable of feeding 400 million people—a large number but less than 10% of the world population (Pimentel et al., 1980). Worldwide, one third of the fish harvest is used to feed animals other than humans (Council on Environmental Quality, 1980b).

Because of the increasing demand for meat, it is unlikely that we will soon see production systems using only feed that is unsuitable for humans. It is likely, however, that the limiting factor at least for beef production will ultimately be energy. As we have seen, increases in food production require increases in energy consumption. "There are no low energy options for producing beef in the quantities approaching these currently consumed in this country" (Ward, Knox, and Hobson, 1977). Already, higher costs of beef resulting from increased costs of production are causing a shift to poultry and eggs.

Increased demand for U.S. grain, the need for grain exports to help the balance of payments, and the resulting greater costs of grain-fed beef are all likely to result in a decrease in the production of grain-fed livestock. Increased forage feeding of livestock could utilize lands not suitable for crop production. Forage-fed cattle also have a lower fat content, less waste, and a higher protein content—producing a more healthy meat for the consumer (Abelson, 1980).

Storage and Preservation

An unbelievable amount of grain headed for human consumption is "lost" to rodents, insects, mold, and fungi. In the 1960s, rodents were reported to have consumed 20–30% of India's stored grain (Panel on World Food Supply, 1967). Rodent-proof storage bins would obviously increase India's food supply immediately. Proper ventilation and improved preservation technology would help prevent loss of grain from molds. So great is the food loss problem today that if harvest losses could be reduced by 30–50%, food supply would increase 10–15% (Ennis, Dowler, and Klassen, 1975).

FOOD FROM THE SEA

Since ancient times, humans have harvested food from the seas. Webber (1968) suggests that 200×10^9 metric tons of living matter are produced by green plants in the ocean annually. This is at least as great as plant production on the land. Schaeffer (1965) has suggested that this converts into 200×10^6 metric tons of fish that might be available on a sustained basis. Ackefors (1977) places the harvest potential of fish at 200–400 million metric tons annually.

Currently, the global harvest of fish from the sea runs from 65 to 73 million metric tons each year (Worldwatch Institute, 1978). Thus the potential harvest is estimated at two to three times the current harvest (Figure 8.13). There are, however, some problems in the way of achieving greater yields. Numbers of various species of fish have peaked and declined from overfishing (Worldwatch Institute, 1978). Lower catches per boat and a dominance of

smaller fishes are indicative of the fact that certain fish species in certain areas are being overfished, that is, being harvested faster than the supply can be replenished. The take of cod in the northwest Atlantic has decreased by 50% since 1968 (Worldwatch Institute, 1978). Squid and krill appear to offer the greatest "fish" reserves (Ackefors, 1977).

Artificial production of fish through **aquaculture**, in both fresh and salt water, provides about six million metric tons of food annually (Ackefors, 1977). Much of this is in the form of delicacies such as lobsters and clams (Locke, 1978). Many of these operations are economically marginal because of high feed and labor costs. Likewise, only the waters over the continental shelves appear to be sufficiently productive for **mariculture** (salt-water aquaculture).

Although total marine productivity may in fact equal total terrestrial productivity, marine food resources are scattered over a much larger surface and have a third dimension—depth. This makes harvesting difficult. About a billion liters of seawater would have to be processed to yield one ton of plankton (Morris, 1970). Given the energy involved, larger fish can concentrate protein more efficiently than humans, a fact that might save us from plankton dinners.

What about fertilizing the ocean, increasing plankton, and then harvesting fish higher up the food chain? The problem again is diffusion and economics. It would take a large amount of energy to pull nutrients from the ocean bottom or to produce enough fertilizer otherwise to have a significant ef-

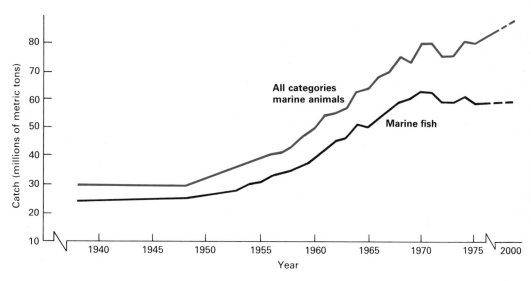

Figure 8.13 World Fish Catch Trends.

The oceans are rich sources of food. We must take care not to harvest them faster then they can renew themselves.

fect. Also, long aquatic food chains yield calories available for human consumption less efficiently than does land production. It takes as much protein in the form of plankton to produce one annual world catch of fish as is contained in 40 world harvests of wheat or 75 world harvests of rice (Ackefors, 1977).

As we will see in Chapter 12, the protection of high fish concentrations near shorelines and estuaries is extremely important in sustaining yields, yet it is these areas that are most susceptible to pollution. The need to travel farther and farther out to sea for a fish catch results in increased energy consumption. Another problem is that while fish provide more protein per gram than many other foods, access to seafood inland is limited in poorer countries where transportation and storage services are not available.

The bottom line is that "increases in . . . marine protein . . . can no longer be taken for granted" (Worldwatch Institute, 1978). This may even be a gross understatement. The *Global 2000 Report* indicates that on a per capita basis the oceans may contribute less to human nutrition in the year 2000 than they do now (Council on Environmental Quality, 1980b).

FOOD AND HEALTH

There are a half billion people in the world who do not have enough to eat. In some cases they are **undernourished**, which means they do not have sufficient intake of calories. In other cases they are **malnourished**, that is, they lack sufficient protein. Proteins are complex substances composed of basic units called amino acids. Humans require different types of amino acids. Vegetable or animal protein entering the digestive tract is broken down into individual amino acids, which are then absorbed and later reassembled to form human body protein. Most plant protein is typically deficient in one or two of these necessary amino acids. Since different plants are deficient in different amino acids, a proper mix of plants will yield a sufficient amount and variety of amino acids. Malnutrition is most common in cultures in which the diet consists predominantly of plant material of only a few different types.

Caloric intake quite obviously varies from country to country and from one income level to another within the same country. Those groups that are most vulnerable to nutrition problems are the very young, the very old, and pregnant and nursing women.

Marasmus is a disease caused by insufficient calories and protein; it affects children less than one year old most acutely and is characterized by progressive emaciation, extreme loss of weight, and wasting away. We are all familiar with pictures of children suffering from **kwashiorkor**, a disease caused by a lack of protein. Kwashiorkor affects predominantly 12 to 36-month-old children. It is characterized by an enlarged liver, accumulation of abdominal fluid contributing to a "pot belly," skin discoloration, retarded growth, loss of hair, and the accumulation of fluid in other tissue. Both marasmus and kwashiorkor result in apathy and apparent mental slowness.

Nutrition in pregnant women is important to both mother and child. Lack of proper nutrients during the first six months of pregnancy can result in mental defects in the child because of impairment of brain cell development. Malnutrition in the sixth to seventh month may affect the child but may be reversed, since only brain cell size is stunted. Generally, poorly nourished mothers give birth to higher-risk premature and underweight babies.

Many diseases are caused by a lack of vitamins: Some important ones are **beriberi** (lack of thiamine), **scurvy** (a vitamin C deficiency), **pellagra** (a niacin deficiency), and **rickets** (a lack of vitamin D and/or calcium). Lack of vitamin A causes a drying out of the eye membranes and may lead to blindness. Anemia results from a lack of folic acid, B_{12}, or iron. A lack of iodine in a pregnant woman may lead to a mentally deficient child.

Overall poor nutrition lowers the resistance of an individual and makes one more susceptible to infection and disease. The 1985 report of the Physician Task Force on Hunger in America notes that some clinics in poor areas of the United States are reporting cases of marasmus, kwashiorkor, and vitamin deficiency diseases.

FOOD DISTRIBUTION AND ECONOMIC DEVELOPMENT

The Worldwatch Institute (1978) observes that the unequal distribution of food is a reflection of the unequal distribution of income within and among nations and is a primary cause of undernourishment. A Presidential Commission on the World Food Problem in 1967 stated, "The world's increasingly serious nutritional problem arises from the uneven distribution of the food supply among countries, within countries, and among families with *different levels of income.*" And again in 1978 a Presidential Commission was formed specifically to look at reasons why, even when there are world grain surpluses, still 50% of the world is malnourished.

The basic reason for this is obviously related to the fact that the hungriest people in the world are usually the poorest. The demand for food by the hungry is simply not recognized in a worldwide economic system in which food is a commodity—it is bought and sold and only rarely given away. What this means is that the most logical strategies for eliminating hunger are aimed at economic development, giving the hungry the means to buy food and not just giving them food.

The Politics of Food

Through the 1960s, U.S. agricultural policy was directed toward dealing with the problem of surplus. It promoted holding land *out* of production. Food exports were relatively low because of their high prices. All of this changed in the 1970s. Devaluations of the dollar in 1971 and 1973 made U.S. prices more competitive in the world market and

Nutrition during pregnancy is important to both mother and baby. This undernourished Ethiopian woman gave birth to a undernourished child, whose chances of survival are low.

resulted in increased food exports. At the same time, bad weather abroad in 1972 and 1973 caused more demand for U.S. exports (U.S. General Accounting Office, 1979).

The importance of economics and politics to food distribution became quite clear in the late 1970s when President Carter imposed an embargo on grain sales to the Soviet Union (intended as a rebuke for Soviet intervention in Afghanistan). This forced a decline in demand, which along with the decline in grain exports resulting from the strengthening dollar led to huge surpluses and plummeting grain prices. U.S. grain surpluses were such in 1982–1983 that the Reagan administration paid farmers for keeping land out of production not in dollars, but in surplus grain, which in turn could be sold in the marketplace. Such is the capriciousness of politics and economic demand in a world in which hunger is rampant.

According to a U.S. General Accounting Office report issued in 1979, of U.S. grain exports, about 40% go to developed countries, 30% to developing countries, and 30% to centrally planned economies like the Soviet Union. Asia is the largest customer, followed by Western Europe, and then Latin America and the Soviet Union (U.S. General Accounting Office, 1979).

The 1978 Presidential Commission on Hunger found that U.S. aid to developing countries amounts to less than 0.25–0.3% of the U.S. GNP (O'Toole, 1979). The goal set by the United Nations for aid to developing countries by developed countries is 0.7% of GNP. At least 12 nations have exceeded this goal; the United States is not one of them. Estimates of food aid shipments from the United States to developing countries in 1983 are around four million tons—down from 15.3 million tons in the mid-1960s. Some think we should do more.

According to the 1978 Commission on Hunger (Mayer and Dwyer, 1980), the U.S. should take the following actions:

1. Base foreign policy regarding developing countries on the primary goal of alleviating hunger and developing self-sufficient agricultural programs in those countries. The Commission was explicit in its insistence that the U.S. should not try to feed the world but rather to assist it in learning to feed itself. Besides foreign trade in agricultural products the United States has programs to assist developing countries via foreign economic assistance and technical aid.

2. Double its nonmilitary assistance to developing countries in the next three years and triple it within a decade (U.S. General Accounting Office, 1979).

That the "help them feed themselves" approach works is exemplified by India. A World Bank report in 1980 indicated that India was beginning to reach food self-sufficiency (Rowen, 1980). Increased yields are attributed to nonfood aid and technical assistance, which resulted in increased use of fertilizer and more land under irrigation. The Indian government provided price supports for crops and fertilizer to encourage production in India by locals. The report predicted that India might become an exporter of wheat and rice at some time in the future. Some sources cite India as a grain exporter today.

Appropriate Technology

Any strategy to transfer technology to less developed countries must take into account the prevailing social, economic, and cultural patterns. In other words, the technology to be transferred must be appropriate and realistic. High-protein food that people will not eat will not solve a protein deficiency problem. High crop yields from intricate mechanized farming techniques may not be transferable to small family farmers who cannot get machinery. Food that does not reach the hungry because of bureaucratic red tape has no impact on the hunger problem. As we saw in Chapter 6, agricultural practices that are highly energy intensive will be less and less useful to poorer nations, which are simply unable to afford fossil fuels.

An appropriate strategy for enhanced livestock production in developing countries (see Ward, Sutherland, and Sutherland, 1980) might include the implementation of multiple-cropping systems that leave the land in cover crops for a period, replenishing the soil and also providing forage; intensive cropping of fertile land and use of less fertile land for forage production; maximum use of livestock—for draft, transportation, food, and energy (from manure); and use of manure as fertilizer. Since a good amount of land that is unsuitable for cropping is suitable as pasture, this land has considerable potential for increased animal production in developing countries. Developing countries already have large numbers of cattle, buffalo, sheep, and goats. What has not been done is to maximize their full potential for work, food, energy, and fertilizer through appropriate methods that are compatible with the prevailing customs and practices. Animal production requires resources that are abundant in most developing countries—forage crops and human labor.

Another example of the application of appropriate technology is the promotion of aquaculture in China, where demonstration projects growing carp have been immensely successful (Culliton, 1979a). One variety of carp eats waste vegetation from farms or grass cut along the side of the pond; other varieties eat phytoplankton; others feed on the organic matter on the pond bottom. Human and animal excrement is fermented to remove pathogens and then used to fertilize the pond. In a complete cycle, humus from the bottom of the pond is returned to the fields as fertilizer. These aquaculture projects are conducted under the auspices of the Pearl River Fisheries Research Institute in Canton. Representatives from other Asian countries have been trained in these techniques, which are simple, basic, low in energy and capital input, high in output, and certainly appropriate for the needs of many developing countries.

In the past, developing countries have been somewhat suspicious of the concept of appropriate technology, labeling it a method to keep developing countries from entering the high technology markets of the West and sharing a similar standard of living. Such suspicions are being somewhat allayed by successes in using appropriate technology especially when the government of the receiving nation is involved in identifying and promoting appropriate agricultural technology. For example, the Indian Institute of Science supports the project AS-TRA (Application of Science and Technology to Rural Areas). This project has done research not just on agriculture but on rural energy systems, housing technology, water projects, and the processing of agricultural wastes and residues (Holden, 1980). In addition a system of International Agricultural Research Centers is distributed worldwide in countries such as Mexico, the Philippines, Columbia, and Nigeria; these centers are dedicated to increasing yields and protein levels in staples grown in the Third World.

RESEARCH

Where is science headed in improving world food supplies? To date, the greatest advances in increasing crop yields have come from using fertile soils in favorable climates. Research since the Green Revolution has focused on the need to address some of the problems associated with the high-yield varieties of crops such as decreased resistance to pests. However, future research must look at improving yields in areas with less than ideal soil and climate. This means developing varieties of crops that can better tolerate saline soils, acidic soils, and soils with high levels of toxic minerals, as well as varieties that are drought tolerant or flood tolerant.

Because of all the analysis of the Green Revolution's success and failures, the direction of research has broadened to include considerations such as the applicability in tropical areas of small-scale, low-capital, low-machinery solutions as well as more technological approaches. Induced genetic mutations, gene splicing, and plant hybridization could possibly produce plants with the ability to feed on nitrogen from the atmosphere.

Scientists are looking at food substitutes for livestock, freeing grains for human consumption. Finding ways of decreasing nitrification (the conversion of nitrate to nitrite), which releases volatile nitrogen gases from the soil, to maintain fertility longer is another goal of agricultural research. Losses by denitrification and volatilization may be as much as 10–30% of the nitrogen applied (Huber, Warren, Nelson, and Tsai, 1977). Another problem arises here, however; the known nitrification inhibitors are also long-lived, generally toxic substances.

Research on nutrition and diet is also going on. We know less than we need to know in this area. For instance, the possible efficacy of breast feeding as a means of improving nutrition and providing some immunity against disease has been overlooked. Instead, prepared formula, which is costly and can become contaminated by impure containers or impure water, has been promoted in the developing nations.

Certain techniques such as remote sensing of the environment via satellite may be used to provide information that will make crop predictions more reliable and might help stabilize the economics of food. These same techniques have proved helpful in determining appropriate irrigation schedules to prevent too much or too little watering. Weather control, although controversial, will no doubt continue to be studied.

Should there be greater emphasis on food commodities over nonfood commodities (tobacco, cotton, biomass for energy conversion) in allocating the research dollar? Can the protein content of such staples as rice, maize, yams, and cassava be improved? Should we teach more tropical agriculture to foreign exchange students? Can family farming survive, or are agribusiness and market farming the only way to go? Numerous ecological, economic, and social questions need answers.

Saint and Coward (1977) conclude that "efforts to increase productivity will depend for the most part on the success with which new agrotechnologies and appropriate organizational and institutional arrangements can be incorporated into systems of traditional agriculture especially those in which small farmers predominate." A total systems approach including ecological, technical, and social considerations seems to be surfacing. As Wendell Berry (1974) states, "A healthy farm culture can only be based on familiarity; it can only grow among a people soundly established upon the land; it would nourish, and protect a human intelligence of the land that no amount of technology can satisfactorily replace."

CONCEPTS TO REMEMBER

1. Historically, war, famine, and disease have served as checks to human population growth. Today, by and large, the mechanisms that serve to regulate population growth in humans are economic, social, and institutional.

2. Demography is the study of the vital and other social statistics of human populations. Indices such as birth rate, death rate, rate of natural increase, and fertility rate can be used to project trends in human population growth.

3. If constant age-specific death rates (e.g., constant infant mortality rates) are assumed, the age structure of a population and its fertility rate are the two key factors in predicting its long-range growth trend. When an expanding population's fertility rate falls to the replacement rate, it will still take a number of years for the population to stop growing, that is, to reach zero population growth (ZPG). Although the U.S. fertility rate has been at or below the replacement level for some years, ZPG will probably not be reached until at least the year 2030.

4. The lag effect in stabilizing population growth is highly significant. At an annual growth rate of 2%, the world population would double in 35 years. Currently, world population growth is 1.7% annually. Even though fertility rates are generally on the decline worldwide, total popu-

IN CLOSING

The problems of population, food, and hunger will be with us for some time. Although fertility rates in the developing world have been declining since the late 1960s, total populations will continue to increase significantly because of the large numbers of women of prereproductive age. Although new environmentally appropriate technologies and economic development strategies will help improve food distribution and alleviate hunger, the ultimate solution to the food problem is to limit the demand for food. Some fear that by continually finding the means to produce more food we are short-circuiting one of the mechanisms of population control. If we fail to see the ultimate need for control of population, we will find ourselves up against the ecological carrying capacity of our planet. We must never forget that "Economically and socially sound development will also be ecologically sound, or it will be neither sustained or socially beneficial over time." (Worldwatch Institute, 1978).

lation will continue to increase for many decades. This means continuing strain on food resources from the land and sea and on other life-supporting resources.

5. While nearly all nations of the world have experienced a declining death rate, the industrialized nations have had a greater decline in birth rate than the developing nations. A shift from high fertility and high mortality to low fertility and low mortality is called the demographic transition. While the industrialized countries have made it all the way through such a transition, many of the developing countries have not. Modern health care and improved nutrition have brought improved survival, especially decreased infant mortality, to these countries, but the countries have not yet managed low fertilities to match.

6. Worldwide, especially in developing nations, governments are becoming involved in population control programs. As long as population is increasing rapidly, it is difficult to make improvements in the standard of living per capita; the gap widens between the haves and the have nots.

7. The world or a nation can be overpopulated in relation to available food, nonrenewable re-

sources, the assimilative capacity of the biosphere, or the quality of life desired.

8. Since the mid-1970s, food production worldwide has increased less than 2% annually—barely ahead of population growth. Per capita consumption of food varies considerably from country to country. People may be undernourished (lack sufficient calories) or malnourished (lack sufficient protein).

9. Mechanisms for bringing more food to the world market are limited and will require expensive energy inputs.

10. Improper management of cropland is reducing the amount of land available for agriculture on a sustained basis. Desertification of cropland is a worldwide problem. Extensive irrigation and poor soil drainage in arid and semiarid regions, including parts of the United States, have led to salt accumulation, and some of this land is no longer suitable for agriculture or livestock.

11. The Green Revolution, technological advances made in the development of high-yield varieties of rice and wheat, has improved yields, but not to the extent originally predicted. Part of the problem lies in the fact that the new grains cannot be easily obtained or grown by developing countries on a large scale because of their high cost and need for mechanization.

12. Grain-fed livestock reduces the calories available to feed people. Forage-fed livestock increases the calories available to feed people.

Complex cultural and economic factors prevent these two facts from being used in practice on a large scale to increase human food supply.

13. The hungriest people in the world are usually the poorest. From an economic perspective, food is a commodity to be bought and sold. U.S. aid to developing countries amounts to less than 0.3% of the U.S. GNP. The United Nations has set a goal of 0.7% of the GNP of wealthy nations to be given to developing nations.

14. The long-term policy in food distribution should be to provide developing nations with the skills and resources to grow their own food. Any strategy to transfer technology to developing countries must take into account prevailing social, economic, and cultural patterns if it is to succeed.

15. Research to improve world nutrition and food supply includes developing crop varieties that will grow in saline or acidic soils and drought- and flood-resistant strains. Food substitutes for grain-fed livestock and methods of preventing nitrogen loss from soils are other areas of study.

16. Although new environmentally appropriate technologies and economic development strategies will help improve food distribution and alleviate hunger, the ultimate solution to the food problem must include limiting the demand for food.

17. It has yet to be determined whether the human population growth curve is J-shaped or sigmoid.

DISCUSSION QUESTIONS AND FOOD FOR THOUGHT

1. Debate: The most likely scenario is that in the future the human population will crash; our growth curve will not take a sigmoid shape.
2. Grain yields can be increased if denitrification can be inhibited. However, the methods for controlling denitrification may involve the use of persistent toxic chemicals. How would you go about deciding whether to use persistent chemicals to inhibit denitrification?
3. Debate: Beef production should be converted to forage feeding only.
4. Define in your own words: "appropriate technology." Give examples.
5. Choose one of these statements and defend it:
   a. There are too many people in the world to feed.
   b. There is not enough food for all the people in the world.
6. Define the relationship between economics, food, and population.
7. Explain the following: "The population bomb is everyone's baby."

8. Debate: Resolved: The United States is overpopulated.
9. Write an essay describing conditions in 2025. What do you think will have happened to world population?
10. Conduct a survey to determine what students, faculty, wealthy people, poor people, or other groups feel is the ideal family size.
11. Go to the county courthouse and use birth and death statistics for one year to determine birth and death rates for your county and rate of natural increase. How does your community reflect national trends?
12. Discuss one of the following:
   a. Technology alone cannot solve the food problem.
   b. Increasing food production only aggravates the population problem.
13. Define overpopulation.
14. List as many checks or limiting factors to human population growth as you can. Which do you think will ultimately control human population size?

15. List the various sources of food for humans and summarize their potential for increasing food supplies.
16. Develop a list of U.S. domestic policies that may directly or indirectly influence family size.
17. Develop a list of acceptable social customs or mores in the United States that have an impact on population growth.
18. The ability of U.S. farmers to continue to produce the food necessary to feed the world is heavily based on fossil fuel supplies. What implications do you see in the long run because of this dependence?
19. Debate one of the following:
    a. The current American standard of living cannot be maintained indefinitely.
    b. American technology is appropriate technology.
20. Find news articles and reports making the case that war, famine, and disease still have an impact on human population growth.

REFERENCES AND FURTHER READING

References marked with an asterisk are cited in the chapter.

*Abelson, P. H., 1980. "Beef Production and Consumption," *Science* **208**(444):555

*Ackefors, H., 1977. "Production of Fish and Other Animals in the Sea," *Ambio* **6**(4):192–200.

Batie, S. A., 1983. *Soil Erosion: Crisis in America's Croplands?* Washington, D.C.: The Conservation Foundation.

*Berelson, B., 1969. "Beyond Family Planning," *Science* **163**(3867):533–543.

*Berry, W., 1974. "On Farms and Food and Rural Culture," *Courier Journal and Times,* October 6, E-3.

Biological Sciences Curriculum Study, 1975. *Food for Humanity,* Environmental Resource Papers, Book III. Reading, Mass., Addison-Wesley Publishing Co.

Biological Sciences Curriculum Study, 1975. *Human Population,* Environmental Resource Papers, Book IV. Reading, Mass: Addison-Wesley Publishing Co.

Boyer, J. S., 1982. "Plant Productivity and Environment," *Science* **218**(October 29):443–448.

Brady, N. C., 1982. "Chemistry and World Food Supplies," *Science* **218**(November 26):847–853.

*Brink, R. A.; Densmore, J. W.; and Hill, G. A., 1977. "Soil Deterioration and the Growing World Demand for Food," *Science* **197**:625–638.

*Brown, L. R., 1975. "The World Food Prospect," *Science* **190**:1053–1059.

Brown, L. R., 1983. "The Changing Global Economic Context," *Environment* **25**(6, July/August):28–34.

*Brown, L. R., 1984a. "Putting Food on the World's Table," *Environment* **26**(4, May):15–20ff.

Brown, L. R., 1984b. *State of the World.* New York: W. W. Norton.

Bulatao, R. A., and Lee, R. D., eds., 1983. *Determinants of Fertility in Developing Countries.* New York: Academic Press.

Callahan, D., ed., 1971. *The American Population Debate.* New York: Doubleday & Company.

Carter, L. J., 1974. "Green Revolution(I): A Just Technology, Often Unjust in Use," *Science* **186**:1093–1098.

Chang, T. T., 1984. "Conservation of New Genetic Resources: Luxury or Necessity?" *Science* **224**(April 20):251–256.

Cleveland, H., 1978. "The Management of Weather Resources," *Science* **201**(4354):339.

*Coale, A. J., 1983. "Recent Trends in Fertility in Less Developed Countries," *Science* **221**:828–832.

Connell, K. H., 1975. *The Population of Ireland 1850–1945.* Westport, Conn.: Greenwood Press.

Conservation Foundation, 1982. *State of the Environment 1982.* Washington, D.C.: The Conservation Foundation.

*Council on Environmental Quality, 1977. *Eighth Annual Report.* Washington, D.C.: U.S. Government Printing Office.

Council on Environmental Quality, 1979. *Tenth Annual Report.* Washington, D.C.: U.S. Government Printing Office.

*Council on Environmental Quality, 1980a. *Desertification of the United States,* Washington, D.C.: U.S. Government Printing Office.

*Council on Environmental Quality and the Department of State, 1980b. *The Global 2000 Report to the President: Entering the Twenty-First Century.* Washington, D.C.: U.S. Government Printing Office.

*Culliton, B. J., 1979a. "Aquaculture: Appropriate Technology in China," *Science* **206**:539.

Culliton, B. J., 1979b. "China's New Birth Policy: One Baby Is Enough," *Science* **206**:429.

Cushing, D. H., 1975. *Marine Ecology and Fisheries.* Cambridge, England: Cambridge University Press.

*Davis, W. H., 1970. "Overpopulated America," *The New Republic* **162**(2):13–15.

Day, P. R., 1977. "Plant Genetics: Increasing Crop Yield," *Science* **197**:1334–1339.

Ehrlich, P. R., 1968. *The Population Bomb.* New York: Ballantine Books.

Ehrlich, P. R. and Ehrlich, A. H., 1972. *Population, Resources, Environment.* San Francisco: W. H. Freeman & Co.

Enke, S., 1968. "Raising per Capita Income through Fewer Births," *General Electric—TEMPO*(Publication 68TMP-9), from G. Hardin, *Population, Evolution and Birth Control.* San Francisco: W. H. Freeman and Co.

*Ennis, W. B., Jr.; Dowler, W. M.; and Klassen, W. 1975. "Crop Protection to Increase Food Supplies," *Science* **188**(4188):593–598.

"Food," *Science* 1978, **188**(4188).

*Forrester, J. W., 1971. *World Dynamics.* Cambridge, Mass.: Wright-Allen Press.

*Fremlin, J. H., 1964. "How Many People Can the World Support?" *New Scientist* **415**:285–287.

Greenland, D. J., 1975. "Bringing the Green Revolution to the Shifting Cultivator," *Science* **190**:841–844.

*Gulhati, K., 1977. "Compulsory Sterilization: The Change in India's Population Policy," *Science* **195**:1300–1305.

*Hardin, G., 1968. "The Tragedy of the Commons," *Science* **162**:1243–1248.

Hardin, G., 1969. *Population, Evolution, and Birth Control,* 2nd ed. San Francisco: W. H. Freeman and Company.

Holden, C., 1978. "Government Seeking Ways to Encourage Aquaculture," *Science* **200**:33–35.

*Holden, C. 1980. "Pioneering Rural Technology in India," *Science* **207**:159.

Hoskins, B. B.; O'Connor, J. T.; Shannon, T. A.; Widdus, R.; and Danielli, J. F., 1977. "Application of Genetic and Cellular Manipulations to Agricultural and Industrial Problems," *Bioscience* **27**(3):188–191.

*Howard, W. E., 1969. "The Population Crisis is Here Now," *BioScience* **19**(9):779–784.

*Huber, D. M.; Warren, H. L.; Nelson, D. W.; and Tsai, C. Y., 1977. "Nitrification Inhibitors: New Tools for Food Production," *Bioscience* **27**(8):523–529.

Idso, S. B.; Jackson, R. D.; and Reginato, R. J., 1977. "Remote-Sensing of Crop Yields," *Science* **196**:19–24.

Jensen, N. F., 1978. "Limits to Growth in World Food Production," *Science* **201**:317–320.

Keyfitz, N., 1984. "The Population of China," *Scientific American* **250**(February):38–47.

Kormondy, E. J., 1984. *Concepts of Ecology,* 3rd ed. Englewood Cliffs, N.J.: Prentice-Hall.

Lappe, F. M., 1973. "The Politics of Protein," from *The World Food Problem: The Hastings Center Report,* **3**(5, Nov.):11–13.

Leeper, E. M., 1977. "End Hunger by 2000—A Possible Dream," *Bioscience* **27**(8):571–573.

*Locke, R., 1978. "The Unseized Seas." *Courier Journal,* September 10, D-4.

*Malthus, T. R., 1982. *Essay on the Principle of Population,* Totowa, N.J.: Biblio Distribution Center. This is a reprint of the 1816 edition.

Marx, J. L., 1978. "Contraception: An Antipregnancy Vaccine?" *Science* **200**:1258.

Mathews, J., 1980. "Breeding-control Ideas Are Surfacing in China," *The Washington Post,* July.

*Mauldin, W. P., 1980. "Population Trends and Prospects," *Science* **209**(4452):148–157.

*Mayer, J. and Dwyer, J., 1980. "Study Shows Half-million Hungry," *The Courier Journal,* April 27, G-16.

*Meadows, D. H.; Meadows, D. L.; Randers, J.; and Behrens, W. W., III, 1972. *The Limits to Growth: A Report for the Club of Rome.* New York: Universe Books; A Potomac Associates Book.

Meadows, D.; Richardson, J.; and Bruckmann, G., eds. 1982. *Groping in the Dark: The First Decade of Global Modeling.* New York: John Wiley & Sons.

McDermott, W., 1980. "Pharmaceuticals: Their Role in Developing Societies," *Science* **209**:240–244.

*Morris, I., 1970. "Restraints on the Big Fish-in," *New Scientist* Dec. 3, 1970.

National Academy of Sciences, 1983. *Genetic Engineering of Plants: Agricultural Research Opportunities and Policy Concerns.* Washington, D.C.: National Academy Press.

New York Times News Service, 1978. "Illegal Aliens Boost U.S. Population," *The Courier Journal,* October 22.

*O'Toole, T., 1979. "U. S. Urged to Lead Fight to Wipe out World Hunger," *The Washington Post,* December.

"Panel Calls for Global Food and Nutrition Research Drive," *Science* **197**(1977):140.

*Panel on World Food Supply, 1967. *The World Food Problem: A Report of the President's Science Advisory Committee.* The White House, May 1967, as reported by R. Revelle, A. Khosla, and M. Vinovskis, eds., *The Survival Equation: Man and His Environment.* Boston: Houghton Mifflin.

*Pimentel, D.; Dritschilo, W.; Krummel, J.; and Kutzman, J., 1975. "Energy and Land Constraints in Food Protein Production," *Science* **190**:754–761.

Pimentel, D. et al., 1976. "Land Degradation: Effects on Food and Energy Resources," *Science* **194**:149–155.

*Pimentel, D., et al., 1980. "The Potential for Grass-fed Livestock: Resource Constraints," *Science* **207**:843–848.

Planned Parenthood Federation of America, 1980. Publication No. 1253. New York: Planned Parenthood Federation of America, Inc. This is a brochure on available birth control methods.

Plucknett, D. L., and Smith, N. J. H., 1982. "Agricultural Research and Third World Food Production," *Science* **217**(July 16):215–220.

Population Reference Bureau, 1978. "World Population: Growth on the Decline," *Interchange* **7**(2):1–3. *Interchange* is published quarterly and sent to educators free on request; the address is The Population Reference Bureau, 1337 Connecticut Ave., N. W., Washington, D. C. 20036.

President's Commission on Population Growth and the American Future, 1972. *Population and the American Future.* New York: Signet, New American Library.

Radmer, R., and Kok, B., 1977. "Photosynthesis: Limited Yields, Unlimited Dreams," *Bioscience* **27**(9):599–605.

Rawitscher, M., and Mayer, J., 1977. "Nutritional Outputs and Energy Inputs in Seafoods," *Science* **198**:261–264.

Resources for the Future, 1984. "Twenty-first Century Agriculture—Critical Choices for Natural Resources," *Resources* **75**(Winter 1984):14–16.

*Rowen, H., 1980. "India Achieving Food Self-sufficiency," *The Washington Post,* August.

Sai, F. T., 1984. "The Population Factor in Africa's Development Dilemma," *Science* **226**(16):801–805.

*Saint, W. S., and Coward, E. W., Jr., 1977. "Agricultural and Behavioral Science: Emerging Orientations," *Science* **197**:733–737.

Sanger, M., 1938. *An Autobiography.* New York: W. W. Norton.

*Schaeffer, M. B., 1965. "The Potential Harvest of the Sea," *Transactions of the American Fishery Society* **94**:123–128.

"Scientists Report Drop in Fertility Worldwide," (Louisville) *Courier Journal,* February 15, 1978. New York Times and AP Dispatch.

Short, R. V., 1984. "Breast Feeding," *Scientific American* **250**(April):35–41.

Spooner, B., and Mann, H. S., eds., 1982. *Desertification and Development.* New York: Academic Press.

Trenkle, A., and Willham, R. L., 1977. "Beef Production Efficiency," *Science* **198**:1009–1014.

U.S. Department of Commerce, Bureau of the Census, 1977, 1978, and 1984. *Statistical Abstract of the United States.* Washington, D.C.: U.S. Government Printing Office.

U.S. Department of Commerce, 1980. *Census of the Population. General Population Characteristics. U. S. Summary.* Washington, D.C.: U.S. Government Printing Office.

*U.S. General Accounting Office, 1979 and 1980. *Food, Agriculture, and Nutrition Issues for Planning.* CED 79-36(January 29, 1979) and CED80-94(June 11, 1980). Washington, D.C.: U.S. Government Printing Office.

Wagar, J. A., 1970. "Growth versus the Quality of Life," *Science* **168**:1179–1184.

Walsh, J., 1984. "Sahel Will Suffer even if Rains Come," *Science* **224**(May 4):467–471.

*Ward, G. M.; Knox, P. L.; and Hobson, B. W., 1977. "Beef Production Options and Requirements for Fossil Fuel," *Science* **198**:265–271.

*Ward, G. M.; Sutherland, T. M.; and Sutherland, J. M., 1980. "Animals as an Energy Source in Third World Agriculture," *Science* **208**:570–573.

*Webber, H. H., 1968. "Mariculture," *Bioscience* **18**(10):940–945.

Winikoff, B., 1978. "Nutrition, Population and Health: Some Implications for Policy," *Science* **200**:895–902.

Wittwer, S. H., 1978. "The Next Generation of Agricultural Research," *Science* **199**(4327):375.

World Bank, 1980. *World Development Report 1980.* New York: Oxford University Press.

*World Bank, 1984. *World Development Report 1984.* New York: Oxford University Press.

"World Food: The Next Presidential Commission," *Science* **199**(1978):866.

*Worldwatch Institute, 1978. *The Global Environment and Basic Human Needs: A Report to the Council on Environmental Quality.* Washington, D.C.: Worldwatch Institute.

The Impact of Human Activities on Health and the Environment

The age of ecology, which began sometime during the late 1960s, started with the realization that modern human life can have some undesirable side effects. Much of our dislike for what has been happening to our environment is associated with esthetics: Pollution looks bad! Much more comes from a realization of how our activities harm other species and upset natural balances. Perhaps most generally appreciated is the fact that deteriorating environmental quality can and does have direct effects on human health.

That there is a relationship between human health and the environment is not a new idea. In his work "Air, Water and Places," Hippocrates said,

> Whosoever wishes to investigate medicine properly should proceed thus: in the first place to consider the seasons of the year and what effects each of them produces . . . then the winds, the hot and the cold . . . such as are peculiar to each locality. We must also consider the qualities of the waters, for as they differ from one another in tastes and weight so also do they differ in their qualities.[1]

This passage has even more meaning today than it did twenty-four hundred years ago. We still have the waterborne diseases caused by the same bacteria and viruses that existed in Hippocrates' day; but to these, modern civilization has added diseases caused by the waterborne toxins stirred up by human technology. To the ancient list of airborne diseases, most of which were also caused by bacteria and viruses, modern technology has added chemically induced health problems including dust diseases, respiratory problems caused by pollutants, and even some diseases caused by noise.

In Part III we look at pollution from each of the "who, what, when, where, and why" perspectives. We consider pollution's esthetic impacts and the impact of pollution on species other than our own. We concentrate on its human health effects.

---

[1]From an excerpt: Hippocrates, "Air, Water, and Places," in Adams, F. (transl.), *The Genuine Works of Hippocrates*, 1939, Williams and Wilkins Co., Baltimore, quoted in: Carnow, B.S. 1971. "Air Pollution and Physician Responsibility," *Archives of Internal Medicine*, Vol. 27, p. 91.

Air Pollutants and Their Sources

The atmosphere, presented in Chapter 1 as one of the great spheres, is a mixture of gases that forms a layer about 400 kilometers (km) (250 miles) thick around planet earth. The bottom 16–19 km (10–12 miles) is the most important part of the atmosphere in terms of weather and other aspects of biogeochemical cycles (Chapter 3). The lowest 600 meters (2000 feet) of the atmosphere constitutes nearly all of the atmospheric portion of the ecosphere (Figure 9.1; see also Figure 1.2).

Normal air contains about 78% nitrogen and 21% oxygen, the remaining 1% being made up of carbon dioxide and several other trace gases. Both carbon dioxide and oxygen are absolutely vital for nearly *all* living systems; for most living things, oxygen is the most immediately important part of the nonliving environment. Human beings can live for weeks without food, for several days without water, but for only minutes without oxygen.

The average adult human exchanges about 16 kilograms (kg) (about 35 pounds) of gases per day, about six times the weight of food and water consumed. In a lifetime a human being exchanges many millions of cubic feet of air in hundreds of millions of breathing cycles. This is one of the principal reasons why the quality of air is so important.

Curiously, air does not seem to be considered to be as much a resource as water. What is worse, we tend to think of air as the *absence* of something. You must have often heard such naive statements as "This box is empty!", "The room didn't have a thing in it.", "As far as we could see . . . nothing." Many of the problems we address in these next three chapters stem from this kind of attitude toward air.

Air *is* a resource, and air quality is something that must be preserved. Just as there are watersheds, there are airsheds. Although airsheds are far less distinct entities than **watersheds** (regions drained by a river or other body of water), an **airshed** can be defined as the land area that contributes to the air—and the things found in the air—that flows over or through a particular geographical area. Fairly regular wind flow patterns and land contours are what give airsheds their definition. As is true of watersheds, airsheds do not necessarily coincide with political or other artificial boundaries. This presents various sociopolitical problems, which we will consider in Chapter 11.

THE AIR POLLUTION PROBLEM DEFINED

The concept of air pollution we will use has to do mainly with the things that humans add to air that impair its usefulness as a resource. Although we will discuss natural sources of air contaminants, our principal focus will be on the extra measure of deterioration in the quality of the air that comes from *the things we humans put into the air*. **Air pollution** is thus the transfer of harmful amounts of natural and synthetic materials into the atmosphere as a direct or indirect consequence of human activity. Air pollution is the dust, gas, and droplets we stir up in doing what we do as human beings. Most air pollution is generated where people live, breathe, and work.

Air pollution is a complex problem because a pollutant can be any of a number of chemical substances existing in gaseous, liquid (aerosol), or solid form (roughly 90% of the weight of all pollutants in the air is gas, however). Furthermore, pollutants can be added to the air directly (**primary pollutants**), or they can be created in the air (**secondary pollutants**)

Concentrated human activity is what causes the air we breathe to become polluted.

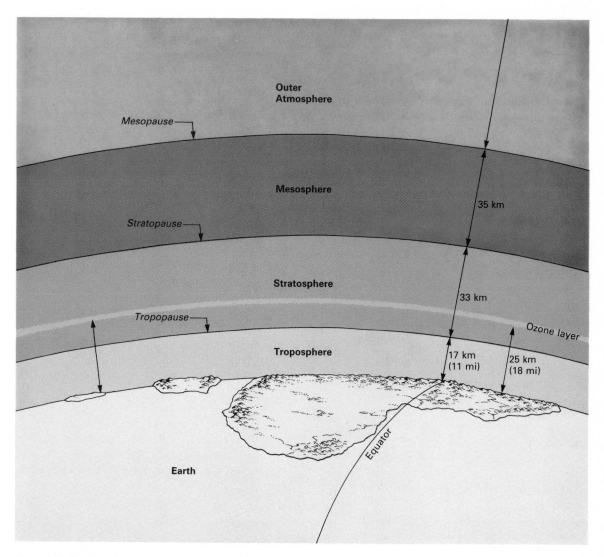

Figure 9.1 Major Subdivisions of the Atmosphere.

from other pollutants under the influence of electromagnetic radiation from the sun and through combinations with other air pollutants.

The effects of pollutants vary considerably because of differences in their concentrations and their chemistry. Some are far more toxic than others, and some have far greater impacts than others on materials and ecosystems.

Air pollutants have many different kinds of effects on *Homo sapiens* and other components of the natural world. Air pollution can have a psychological impact; it can make the environment unpleasant. Air pollutants can erode statues and painted surfaces, cause things to become soiled, and damage property in other ways. Air pollution can impair human health and the health of other organisms. Air pollution can also alter climates and the chemistry of lakes, streams, and soil. All of these things make air pollution profoundly important in the most basic ecological sense.

Because there are established ways of preventing many kinds of pollutants from getting into the atmosphere, air pollution is more of a sociopolitical and economic problem than it is a scientific one. Scientifically, the challenge seems to be to define more clearly the relationships between specific pollutants, specific sources, and specific impacts. The problem with this is that the effects of some pollutants are subtle; even profound effects are sometimes separated from exposure by long time lags and may be difficult to pin down. Sociopolitically, the problem is related to our relative inability to deal with subtle impacts, our failure to appreciate cause-and-effect connections that are not obvious, and our reluctance

to focus political attention on difficult chronic problems. Our sociopolitical system (maybe humankind in general) seems to be designed to respond best (if not only) to abrupt *unmistakable* disasters.

We will now consider some classic air pollution disasters. We do this reluctantly because we hesitate to dignify these episodes by calling them disasters and seeming to give them preeminence over the much more important *chronic* air pollution disaster.

The real impact of air pollution on *Homo sapiens* is caused not so much by the isolated alerts or incidents that kill people or make them ill for a day or two as it is by the chronic, day-to-day pollution that leads to lung disease and acid rain.

The disasters we are about to consider were really meteorological or toxicological accidents. They were episodes that attracted attention because people died as a direct effect of bad air. But as we shall see, most of those who died were older people or people with preexisting respiratory and/or heart conditions. Most of those who died were pushed beyond their physiological limits of compensation and adaptation.

We wonder what fraction of the people who died during these *acute* air pollution episodes were first weakened by chronic background air pollution. How many were brought to the point of high risk by exposure to air pollution over an entire lifetime?

A SHORT HISTORY OF SOME NOTABLE AIR POLLUTION DISASTERS

In the history of air pollution there have been some notable historic events. These episodes are instructive in that they demonstrate that

This photograph taken in 1910 shows the effects of over 400 years of weathering on this grotesque decorating Lincoln Cathedral in England.

1. many air pollutants are poisons,
2. weather, topography, and air pollution are very closely related, and
3. pinpointing the exact relationship between air pollutants and health can be quite difficult.

Meuse Valley, Belgium, 1930

In early December 1930, while the world was in the throes of the Great Depression, stagnant weather conditions and a cold mist covered most of the Northern European country of Belgium. The mist was particularly concentrated along the Meuse River Valley, an industrial valley not unlike the Ohio River Valley and parts of the Mississippi River Valley in the United States. Because the air was not moving, the valley held the combustion products of its factories and mills; these pollutants together with water in the air turned the valley air into a stronger and stronger solution of poisons.

Several thousand people became quite ill simultaneously, from one end of the valley to another, and there were approximately 60 deaths over and above the number normally expected in a three-day period. Practically all of the deaths resulted from acute heart failure. Coughing, shortness of breath, and vomiting were among the reported symptoms. It was noted that most of the deaths were among elderly people and those with preexisting heart conditions and respiratory diseases. But many young, healthy people became ill. Cows, rats, birds, and other animals were also noticeably affected.

While the Meuse Valley episode was notable, it received little attention in 1930; air pollution was not exactly an idea whose time had come. Today, very little is actually known about this disaster or about the details of the relationship between the health effects and the pollutants that were present in the air. As often happens in the history of humankind, when such lessons go unheeded, they are repeated.

At the same time of year, 18 years later, another disaster occurred in a Monongahela River Valley town in Western Pennsylvania—under almost identical weather conditions.

Donora, Pennsylvania, 1948

Western Pennsylvania is cool in late October, and autumn rains bring a chilling dampness. On such a day in 1948, in the small industrial valley town of Donora, the winds died down and the air became still. Like a large soup tureen, the valley held the emission products from factories and trains, and the "soup" was incubated together with people for several tragic days. Nearly half of the people of Donora were stricken with severe eye, nose, and throat irritation, chest pains, and labored breathing. Twenty people died over and above the number expected during that period. Here, too, animals as well as people got sick. Here, too, people with preexisting illnesses—most asthmatics, nearly everyone with heart diseases, and most others with diseases like chronic bronchitis and emphysema—suffered serious illness. But a world caught up in the postwar recovery had little room for air pollution in its order of priorities. Air pollution was apparently still not a concern whose time had come.

In 1984, only 74 years later, atmospheric pollution had worn the figure to a barely recognizable remnant.

Acid rain: rain that is more acidic than normal because it contains sulfuric acid and nitric acid derived from oxides of sulfur (SO_x) and nitrogen (NO_x) in the atmosphere. Acidity can also come out of the atmosphere as dry deposition (particulates). Acid rain is sometimes included under the more general label, "acid deposition," which includes the deposition of solid (particulate) acid-forming materials, gaseous acid-forming materials, and all forms of acid precipitation.

Acute: immediate, brief, and severe—in reference to the *duration* of exposure or to the *effects* of pollutants, those effects that follow exposure more or less immediately as a direct reaction to exposure. (*Example:* Acute exposure to even low levels of ozone may result in acute damage to the lungs.)

Adsorption: the adherence of a gaseous substance or a substance in solution onto the surface of a solid.

Aerosol: a gas that contains suspended solid particles or droplets of liquid able to stay suspended in air because of their very small size (usually less than one micrometer in diameter).

Air pollution: the presence of contaminants in the air to such a degree that the air causes problems or the use of air as a resource is impaired.

Air pollution episode: a striking surge of high levels of air contamination resulting in notable problems such as discomfort, illness, or even death.

Ambient air: outside air, the air around us.

Chronic: long-lasting or long-term in reference to either *duration* of exposure or *effect* of exposure to a pollutant. (*Example:* Continued (chronic) exposure to even low levels of ozone can result in permanent scarring of the lungs, i.e., chronic lung disease.)

Convection: the movement of air or water upward as a result of heating, which causes a decrease in the density in the air or water and makes it rise. Convection currents in air tend to disperse air pollutants as the pollutants are carried up and away from the surface of the earth.

Dust: solid particles that can be suspended temporarily in the air because of their weight.

Emission: discharge of a pollutant from some source into the environment.

Fly ash: gas-borne solid particles resulting from the combustion of fuel and other materials.

Particulate: (adjective) in small pieces, as in particulate matter; (noun) a small particle of solid matter or a droplet of liquid of a size that allows it to remain suspended in air.

Photochemical process: chemical or physical changes brought about by the action of sunlight.

Photochemical smog: collection of harmful materials in the air resulting from the action of sunlight on nitrogen oxides, hydrocarbons, and other chemicals in the air. Automobile exhaust is the major source of photochemical smog in urban areas.

Pollutants: in a strict *general* sense a pollutant is anything that changes air, water, or any other resource in some way such that use of the resource is impaired.

Pollutant Standard Index (PSI): a calculation by formula of the degree to which air quality relates to the standards set by the EPA for each of the major pollutants (see Chapter 11).

ppm (parts per million): the number of parts of a given substance in a million parts of a mixture by volume (see Bonus 9.1).

Smog: a term that combines the words "smoke" and "fog," coined originally in Los Angeles to characterize a visible combination of smoke and fog. One type of smog is that due to a high concentration of smoke particles and fly ash. Photochemical smog, on the other hand, is the result of the interaction between nitrogen oxides and hydrocarbons under the influence of sunlight.

Smoke: a combination of solid and liquid particles under one micrometer in diameter emitted from burning materials.

Synergism: a phenomenon in which the effect of a combination of materials is different from (usually greater than) the sum of the separate effects of the individual substances.

Thermal inversion: an atmospheric meteorological condition in which a layer of warm air acts like a lid to trap a layer of cold air beneath it. This frustrates the normal convection of air upward as the surface of the earth is heated; the air and any pollutants being vented into it are trapped.

London, 1952

Four years after the episode in Donora, a disaster of a slightly different sort struck London, England. A high-pressure mass dominating the weather picture for four or five days caused the air to stagnate and allowed pollutants to build up. Within a week there were almost 3000 more deaths than expected, and an additional 1200–1500 excess deaths occurred in the weeks following the episode. During the four or five days in which stagnant conditions persisted, hospital admissions were 40% greater than normal. Sickness claims filed with health insurance systems more than doubled. Supposedly, home fireplace (coal) smoke mixed with the moisture of the London fog generated a deadly sulfuric acid mist.

A similar disaster occurred again in London in 1956. This time there were about 1000 deaths above normal, even though the conditions that caused the problem lasted only about 18 hours.

There were some significant differences between the London disasters and those of Donora and Belgium. In London in 1952 the problem was believed to be precipitated by a highly synergistic combination of water vapor, carbon monoxide, sulfur dioxide, and tar—all of which are generated by the combustion of sulfur-containing coal in home fireplaces. Much of the blame for the disaster in Belgium was initially and still is placed on sulfur dioxide in factory smoke; however, some scientists think that gaseous fluoride compounds were the cause of the problem. While some investigators stated that sulfur dioxide was one of the main ingredients in the Donora disaster, others think that zinc ammonium sulfate may have been a major cause (see Waldbott, 1978). The most generally accepted conclusion about the Donora case in particular is that *several* toxic agents were responsible, none of which would have caused the problem alone.

We draw the reader's attention to this disagreement to suggest that if it was difficult for scientists and physicians to identify the cause of disasters involving a large number of *sudden* deaths, it must be even more difficult to identify the cause or causes of

illnesses that are *chronic*—diseases like cancer, lung disease, and heart disease. These chronic diseases develop gradually and insidiously with vague, inconspicuous symptoms until, at some point, respiratory and cardiovascular systems are compromised to the extent that any extra stress can push them beyond their limits of compensation. When death finally occurs, it may have no *apparent* connection to air pollution. Or, as we have just seen, the death of a person with a chronic disease could be blamed on a single acute air pollution episode.

We turn now to the nature of particular air pollutants and the difficulty of linking each of these, singly or in combination, to specific sublethal effects on health and quiet, less dramatic disasters.

THE PROPERTIES OF AIR POLLUTANTS

Some General Considerations

The major air pollutants are those produced in significant amounts and those having documented health and/or other environmental effects. The chemical composition and characteristics of some of the most important air pollutants are given in Table 9.1. While these pollutants all have effects, sources, and control strategies in common, each is chemically unique.

Table 9.1   Molecular Composition and Characteristics of Major Pollutants

Pollutant	Composition	Characteristics
Sulfur dioxide	SO_2	colorless, heavy, water-soluble gas with a pungent, irritating odor
Particulates	variable	solid particles or liquid droplets including fumes, smoke, dust, and aerosols
Nitrogen dioxide	NO_2	reddish brown gas, somewhat water soluble
Hydrocarbons (and other volatile organic compounds)	variable	many and varied compounds of hydrogen and carbon
Carbon monoxide	CO	colorless, odorless toxic gas, slightly water soluble
Ozone	O_3	pale blue gas, fairly water soluble, unstable, sweetish odor
Hydrogen sulfide	H_2S	colorless gas with a very offensive "rotten egg" odor, slightly water soluble
Fluorides (example: hydrogen fluoride, HF)	variable	pungent, colorless, water-soluble gases (hydrogen fluoride)
Nitric oxide	NO	colorless gas, slightly water soluble

Oxides of Sulfur

A number of oxides of sulfur (SO_x) have deleterious environmental effects. The most notable, and the one on which we will focus in this section, is *sulfur dioxide* (SO_2). (The subscript x is sometimes used to designate *all* of the oxides of a pollutant. SO_x is a symbol for all of the oxides of sulfur, for example, sulfur dioxide (SO_2), sulfur trioxide (SO_3). NO_x is a symbol for all of the oxides of nitrogen, for example, nitric oxide (NO), nitrogen dioxide (NO_2).) Coal-burning electrical power plants are blamed for producing most of the sulfur dioxide problem in the United States. On the average, 70% of the sulfur dioxide in the air over our cities comes from these utilities.

Fuels vary greatly in their sulfur content. High-sulfur coal from certain locales might have as much as 5% sulfur (**low-sulfur fuels** are those with less than 1% sulfur content). Natural gas contains only trace amounts of sulfur; this is why, when controls were first placed on sulfur dioxide emissions, many plants, factories, and power-generating stations switched from coal to natural gas. The energy crisis of the mid-1970s and the increased cost of low-sulfur fuels caused a reversal of the trend toward use of gas and oil and stimulated a search for new solutions to the sulfur dioxide problem.

Sulfur dioxide is itself a poison, but it can also react with ozone, hydrogen peroxide, water vapor, and other substances in the atmosphere to form sulfuric acid (H_2SO_4). Sulfuric acid is one of the strongest acids known; it is able to corrode limestone, metal, and clothing, and it has a devastating effect on delicate respiratory tissue. Sulfuric acid derived from sulfur-containing air pollutants is a major contributor to the acidity in acid rain (see Chapter 10).

In terms of amounts emitted into the air and toxicity, sulfur dioxide may be the most toxic and dangerous air pollutant for the United States as a whole. For every ton of high-sulfur (say, 4%) coal (see Chapter 6) burned without benefit of modern smokestack scrubbers, as much as 160 pounds (63 kg) of sulfur dioxide are released into the air. Our power plants, factories, and other sources have been emitting around 20 million metric tons of sulfur oxides per year since well before 1940 (U.S. Environmental Protection Agency, 1984b). (Emission *trends* for oxides of sulfur and other air pollutants will be presented in Chapter 11.) In the early 1980s, more than one fourth of the American people lived in areas where emission densities of oxides of sulfur exceeded 100 tons per square mile per year. Largely as a result of the Clean Air Act, only about 2% of the U.S. population now lives in counties where SO_x levels are *occasionally* an acute threat to health (see below). The main problems with the oxides of sulfur now appear to be acid deposition (including acid rain) (see Chapter 10) and impairment of visibility by sulfates formed from SO_2.

We will discuss the health effects of sulfur dioxide in more detail in Chapter 10. For the moment, let's put the health effects of SO_2 into perspective vis-à-vis its concentrations in polluted air. The following figures were compiled from various sources including Waldbott (1978), publications of the U.S. Environmental Protection Agency (see 1982d), and Lippmann and Schlesinger (1979):

Atmospheric background	0.2–0.4 ppb
Nonindustrial city air	0.01 ppm
EPA's 24-hour primary standard (see Chapter 11)	0.14 ppm
Asthmatics begin to experience distress (see Smith, 1981)	0.5 ppm (min.)
Odor threshold	0.5–1.0 ppm
Level at which even normal people experience bronchial spasms	1.0 ppm (1 hr.)
Threshold of taste	0.5–1.01
Impaired lung function, occupational limit (8 hours exposure)	5.0 ppm
Water-logged lungs (pulmonary edema) and permanent damage (see U.S. Environmental Protection Agency (1982d) for detailed analysis of studies of both human and animal exposures).	20.0 ppm

How well we do in controlling the SO_2 problem during the rest of this century will depend on the energy strategy we adopt. If the use of coal increases faster than the application of SO_2 controls, there will be an increasing sulfur dioxide pollution problem. Energy conservation will also make a great deal of difference.

Oxides of Nitrogen

When air is fed into a combustion mixture, particularly when the combustion is occurring at a temperature above 2000°F, the oxygen and nitrogen present in the air as O_2 and N_2 combine to form nitric oxide, ($N_2 + O_2 \rightarrow 2NO$). Nitric oxide is *not* thought to be very harmful and does *not* do much damage because it cannot readily dissolve in water

Trace Concentration Units in Perspective

The terms parts per million, parts per billion, and parts per trillion are used often in discussions of air and water pollution. This table will help to put these terms into perspective.

Unit	1 part per million (ppm)	1 part per billion (ppb)	1 part per trillion (ppt)
Length	1 inch/16 miles	1 inch/16,000 miles	1 inch/16,000,000 miles (a six-inch leap on a journey to the sun)
Time	1 minute/2 years	1 second/32 years	1 second/320 centuries
Money	1¢/$10,000	1¢/$10,000,000	1¢/$10,000,000,000
Weight	1 ounce salt/31 tons potato chips	1 pinch salt/10 tons potato chips	1 pinch salt/10,000 tons potato chips
Volume	1 drop vermouth/80 fifths gin or 1 drop vermouth/50 liters gin	1 drop vermouth/500 barrels gin or 1 drop vermouth/50,000 liters gin	1 drop vermouth in a pool of gin covering the area of a football field 43 feet deep (about 50,000,000 liters) or 1 drop vermouth in 520 30,000 gal. tank cars of gin
Area	1 square foot/23 acres or 1 m²/1 km²	1 square inch/160 acre farm	1 square foot in the state of Indiana
Action	1 bogey stroke/3500 golf tournaments 1 lob/1200 tennis matches	1 bogey stroke/3,500,000 golf tournaments 1 lob/1,200,000 tennis matches	1 bogey stroke/3,500,000,000 golf tournaments 1 lob/1,200,000,000 tennis matches
Quality	1 bad apple/2000 barrels	1 bad apple/2,000,000 barrels	1 bad apple/2,000,000,000 barrels
Rate	1 dented fender/10 car lifetimes	1 dented fender/10,000 car lifetimes	1 dented fender/10,000,000 car lifetimes

or in tissue. However, through the action of sunlight, nitric oxide can combine with oxygen to form nitrogen dioxide ($2NO + O_2 \rightarrow 2NO_2$). Nitrogen dioxide is a reddish-brown toxic gas that has considerable environmental impact. Nitrogen dioxide is similar to sulfur dioxide; through various reactions with substances in the atmosphere, nitrogen dioxide is converted into inorganic nitrates, peroxyacetyl nitrate (PAN), and an equivalent of sulfuric acid called nitric acid (HNO_3). Nitric acid may do even more harm to materials and to health than the oxidant NO_2, and it is implicated in the formation of "acid fogs" recently observed in Southern California.

Natural agents like soil bacteria produce far greater *total* amounts of the oxides of nitrogen than humanity does by its fires. The problem with the oxides of nitrogen that humans generate is that the oxides are generated in and around cities, where they reach harmful concentrations, sometimes 10–100 times greater than those found in rural areas.

Nitrogen dioxide is produced in the combustion of coal, oil, natural gas, and motor vehicle fuel and wherever temperatures are high enough to cause atmospheric nitrogen and oxygen to combine. Twenty million metric tons of nitrogen oxides are emitted annually in the United States, though only the people of Southern California are exposed to occasionally unhealthful accumulations (see Chapter 11) (Conservation Foundation, 1984). As was true of SO_x, NO_x is an important part of the acid precipitation problem affecting many locations throughout the world.

As might be expected, the health effects of the oxides of nitrogen (see Chapter 10) are similar although not identical to those of oxides of sulfur. For oxides of nitrogen (NO_x), again from the World Health Organization, the U.S. Environmental Protection Agency (1982b), and other sources:

Atmospheric background   4 ppb
City air background   a few to 80 ppb

EPA's air quality standard (annual mean) (see Chapter 11)	0.05 ppm
Increased respiratory rate in rats	0.8 ppm (a few hours)
Pungent odor noticed	1–3 ppm
Increased airway resistance in humans	2.5 ppm (1 hour)
Occupational limit (8-hour day)	5 ppm
Reversible increase in airway resistance	5 ppm (10 min.)
Pulmonary edema, fatal	100–150 ppm (1 hour)

Note that the effects of NO_x (and all other pollutants) vary both with concentration *and* with duration of exposure. See U.S. Environmental Protection Agency (1982b) for more detailed information.

Because of the role of ultraviolet radiation in converting nitric oxide into nitrogen dioxide (more on this coming up), there is a daily pattern in nitric oxide and nitrogen dioxide concentrations in cities (see Figure 9.2).

Gaseous Hydrocarbons and other Volatile Organic Compounds

Hydrocarbons form a miscellaneous category; the term **hydrocarbon** has come to mean any compound composed of carbon and hydrogen. The properties of hydrocarbons vary over a wide spectrum of chemical reactivity. Some hydrocarbons— for instance, certain **polycyclic hydrocarbons** (hydrocarbons that occur in multiple-ring structures)— may have a considerable direct effect on humans by virtue of chemical **carcinogenicity** (ability to cause cancer) (see Chapter 14). Literally tons of the carcinogenic hydrocarbon benzopyrene are dumped into the air each year in the United States. Most of this is generated in the states of Kentucky, Ohio, Indiana, Pennsylvania, Michigan, Illinois, and Virginia, where it is produced as a by-product of the burning of coal, the production of **coke** (a product of the destructive distillation of coal used as a fuel in

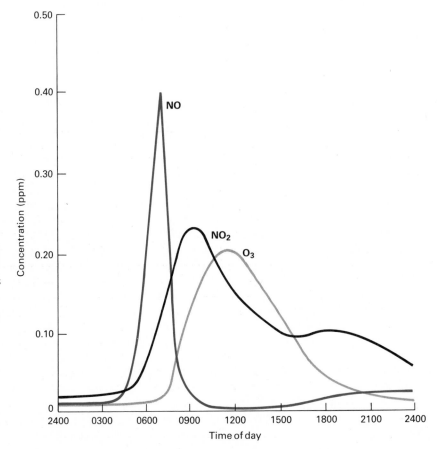

Figure 9.2 Typical Daily Pattern of Nitric Oxide, Nitrogen Dioxide, and Ozone Levels. Shown here is the pattern in Los Angeles on July 19, 1965. NO levels rise with morning traffic. A few hours later NO_2 levels rise as NO_2 is generated from NO. Still later, ozone levels rise as ozone is generated from NO_2, hydrocarbons, and sunlight. NO all but disappears first as it is converted to NO_2 then because it reacts with ozone. Ozone levels eventually drop as ozone reacts with the NO generated by afternoon rush-hour traffic.

Microgram per Cubic Meter

This is an important unit of expression for the concentration of a pollutant in air. A microgram (μg) is one millionth of a gram (there are 454 grams in one pound) or one thousandth of a milligram. A sheet of typing paper weighs about 4 grams, and one fourth of a sheet weighs about one million micrograms. The paper covered by a period having a diameter of 0.5 millimeter and an area of 0.196 mm^2 ($\pi r^2 = 3.14 \times 0.25^2 = 0.196$) would represent 1/76,428 of the area of a fourth of a sheet of paper

(140×107 mm $= 14980$ mm^2). The paper under a period would therefore weigh about 13 micrograms or 1/76,428 of one gram.

A cubic meter (m^3) is about the size of a typical desk. Thus if you scattered the molecules that make up the paper under a period throughout a volume of air equal in size to a desk, you would have a concentration of 13 μg/m^3.

---

making steel), and the smoldering of refuse piles near coal mines.

Aside from this sort of direct, chemically specific problem, atmospheric hydrocarbons or the more general category of volatile organic compounds (VOCs) which are emitted at the rate of 18 million metric tons per year in the United States are a problem largely because they participate in the formation of ozone as described in a later section.

Human-produced sources of ozone-generating hydrocarbons include unburned gasoline and evapo-

rated solvents especially from refineries. Figure 9.3 illustrates a sequence of petroleum production, refining, distribution, and use and indicates numerous points in this sequence at which hydrocarbons escape into the atmosphere.

Humans produce only about 15% of total global atmospheric hydrocarbons, but again the problem is accentuated by the pattern of concentration of human emissions in cities and industrial centers and, to some extent, by the nature of the specific hydrocarbons emitted.

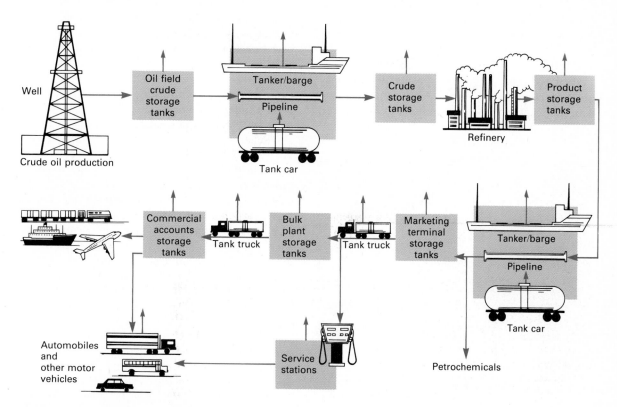

Figure 9.3 The Patterns of Petroleum Production, Refining, and Distribution. This diagram shows sources of evaporation of volatile organic compounds including hydrocarbons.

Carbon Monoxide

Since carbon monoxide poisoning has been a common method of suicide over the years, nearly everyone is aware that an idling automobile produces considerable amounts of this pollutant. Human beings contribute only about 10% of the carbon monoxide load dumped into the atmosphere, and nearly all of this comes from incomplete combustion—largely in the automobile—of fuels. Naturally produced carbon monoxide comes mixed with methane and other substances in marsh gases and other gases emitted from decaying material. Carbon monoxide also escapes from forest and grass fires and volcanoes. Some is formed through chemical reactions in the upper atmosphere.

In keeping with the pattern already described in our consideration of specific pollutants, human-generated carbon monoxide is a problem because most of what we generate is dumped into the areas in which we also live and breathe. In cities, 95–98% of the carbon monoxide in the air is from human sources, and the levels of CO are many times higher than the average levels in the natural world. Overall, carbon monoxide is the single most abundant pollutant known to affect human health that we vent into the atmosphere—just over 70 million metric tons per year in the United States (U.S. Environmental Protection Agency, 1984a).

While background levels of carbon monoxide average about 0.1 mg/m^3 of air, concentrations may reach levels of 80–150 mg/m^3 in heavy traffic. Prolonged exposure to concentrations as low as 58 mg/m^3 (50 ppm) can impair judgment and reflexes (see Chapter 10). Such levels can impair vision, produce headaches, and exert strain on the heart. This last effect is a result of the fact that the oxygen-carrying capacity of the blood is reduced by carbon monoxide when it binds to hemoglobin; this is carbon monoxide's most important health effect. Carbon monoxide is otherwise relatively innocuous, with none of the effects on *materials* that the oxides of nitrogen and sulfur have.

The technology for controlling carbon monoxide emission involves adjustments in combustion processes to allow more complete combustion of fuels. For example, carbon monoxide can be decreased by increasing the air-to-fuel ratio in the internal combustion engine. This solution is not quite as incredibly straightforward as it sounds.

Carbon Dioxide

Carbon dioxide is a colorless gas (at common temperatures and pressures) with a very faint odor. It is a relatively minor normal component of the atmosphere (0.03%), but it plays a major part in the carbon cycle discussed in Chapter 3. Carbon dioxide is produced in respiration and fermentation as sugars and other foods are oxidized. Plants use carbon dioxide as a starting material in photosynthesis. Carbon dioxide is one of the basic end products of the burning of wood, coal, tobacco, leaves, paper, and other carbon-containing materials. When carbon dioxide is generated in this way, it is generally thought of as a much *more desirable* end product than the more toxic combustion product, carbon *monoxide.*

Relative to the other air pollutants, carbon dioxide is unreactive and is not really considered a pollutant in the most common sense of the word because it has no direct *health* effects. Although it is slightly soluble in water, producing the weakly acidic carbonic acid, carbon dioxide makes this list of pollutants because of neither its chemical reactivity nor its solubility. It makes the list because as a constituent of the atmosphere, carbon dioxide absorbs infrared radiation, keeping some of the earth's heat from being radiated quickly into space. Carbon dioxide has a large share of the responsibility for the "greenhouse effect" (see Chapters 2, 6, and 10).

The relationship between the facts that (1) CO$_2$ *has* been increasing for some time, at least partly as a result of fossil fuel combustion; (2) the earth *does* appear to be getting warmer, and (3) even slight warming might upset delicate energy balances (Chapter 2), melt polar ice, and cause ocean levels to rise, inundating coastal cities, means that carbon dioxide is an air pollutant in every sense.

Among the pollutants entering our air from automobile exhaust are lead, nitrogen dioxide, volatile hydrocarbons, carbon monoxide, and particulate matter. The hydrocarbons and nitrogen oxides may react with sunlight to form smog.

Oxidation, Oxidants, and Photochemical Oxidants

For our purposes we can define oxidation generally as the *loss of electrons.* Thus when an atom or molecule loses some electrons, it can be said to have undergone oxidation or to have been *oxidized.* That which takes the electrons is referred to as an *oxidizing agent, oxidizer,* or *oxidant.*

The oxidation of hydrogen can be depicted as follows:

$$H_2 - 2e^- = 2H^+$$

Everything must go somewhere, of course, and when something like hydrogen loses electrons, something like oxygen has taken them:

$$O + e^- = O^-$$

The gain of electrons is called *reduction;* that which does the gaining is said to be *reduced.* Thus oxidizing agents become reduced as they oxidize; conversely, *reducing agents* are oxidized. Oxidation and reduction are always coupled, so the examples given above can also be expressed as follows:

$$H_2 + O_2 \rightarrow H_2O_2$$

or

$$2H_2 + O_2 \rightarrow 2H_2O$$

In both cases, hydrogen is oxidized, and oxygen is reduced. Both are called oxidation-reduction reactions.

High-energy wavelengths of light (e.g., ultraviolet) can cause the formation of rather powerful oxidants (chemicals that can readily take electrons from other chemicals) from chemicals that were originally less powerful or from nonoxidants.

Ozone is a powerful oxidant; because of the way it is produced, the term *photochemical oxidant* applies. Any oxidizing agent created in a photochemical reaction is technically a photochemical oxidant.

Photochemical Oxidants (Ozone)

The story of how Los Angeles came to be nearly synonymous with photochemical smog is an interesting one. At first the problem of watering eyes was thought to be due to particulates; later it was attributed to sulfur dioxide. Reductions in the emission of these substances had little effect on smog, however. Later, the notion that hydrocarbons were responsible for the problem came into vogue, and the source was believed to be mainly refineries. Control programs for refineries were also ineffective. Eventually, the suggestion was made that the villain was the automobile, that the combination of hydrocarbons and oxides of nitrogen in automobile exhaust and sunshine leads to the formation of ozone and other photochemical oxidants. (Although we speak of ozone here, a host of products are generated in the atmosphere through the interaction of nitric oxide, sunlight, and hydrocarbons. These include ozone, peroxyacetyl nitrate (PAN), and acrolein (there are other products as well). Of these, ozone is the one chosen for measurement as an indicator of the presence of the family of photochemical oxidants that make up photochemical "smog." This is because ozone may account for as much as 90% of the oxidant chemicals in smog.)

Although oxygen molecules can absorb ultraviolet radiation directly, causing them to split into two oxygen atoms ($O_2 = 2O$) that eventually go on to form ozone ($O + O_2 = O_3$), this occurs to a significant extent only high in the atmosphere. Short-wavelength ultraviolet radiation capable of doing this does not reach the earth's surface. Another mechanism is necessary to create the highly reactive atomic form (O) of oxygen and then ozone in the air that people actually breathe. It turns out that nitrogen dioxide is a very efficient absorber of the ultraviolet light that does reach the earth's surface. As NO_2 absorbs such radiation, it is broken down (**photolyzed**—split by light) into NO and O. In a subsequent reaction, O combines with O_2 to form O_3 or ozone (see Figure 9.4a). Fortunately, the NO produced by the initial photolytic reaction can react with O_3 and cause a reversion back to NO_2 and O_2. The interrelationships of these reactions are shown in Figure 9.4a.

As suggested in Figure 9.4a, if no other factors were involved, ozone would break down as quickly as it is formed. However, there are apparently two pathways other than the one shown in Figure 9.4a by which NO can revert to NO_2:

$$A) \quad RO_2 + NO \rightarrow NO_2 + RO$$

where R may be hydrogen or an organic radical (**radicals** are atoms or groups of atoms that are chemically important constituents of molecules; they give the molecule certain reactive characteristics) and

$$B) \quad 2NO + O_2 \rightarrow 2NO_2$$

Note that both of these reactions spare ozone from having to react with NO and thereby allow ozone to

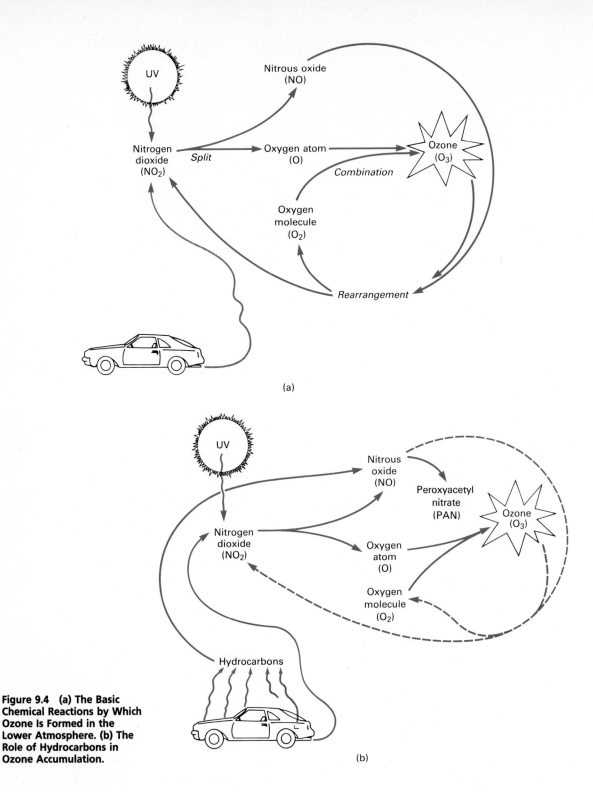

Figure 9.4 (a) The Basic Chemical Reactions by Which Ozone Is Formed in the Lower Atmosphere. (b) The Role of Hydrocarbons in Ozone Accumulation.

stay in existence—or to build up if it is being actively generated (see Figure 9.4b). Reaction B is actually too slow to spare much ozone. Reaction A, on the other hand, *is* fast enough to spare ozone. It is this reaction that becomes increasingly important in the presence of hydrocarbons.

The reader should be aware that the chemistry involved is quite a bit more complicated than is suggested by these generalizations, and the details of the mechanisms involved are still quite controversial. The generalized reactions do, however, describe the *basic* relationship between hydrocarbons and ozone.

Although we are most concerned with the 18 million metric tons (U.S. Environmental Protection Agency, 1984b) of volatile organic compounds emitted via human activity every year, it may be that volatile organics emitted from trees and other vegetation are also factors in the generation of surface-level ozone. It has been shown, for example (Sandberg, Basso, and Okin, 1978), that in the San Francisco Bay, summer violations of federal ozone standards correlate well with precipitation during the preceding two winters. The hypothesis is that hydrocarbons released from growing trees and vegetation participate in the formation of ozone. The original haze of the Great Smoky Mountains is believed to have been the result of an interaction between sunlight and forest-derived organic compounds in the air. Today, most of the grayish haze associated with these mountains is apparently caused by sulfates derived from human activity.

The reaction process that produces photochemical smog is such that the ozone concentration peaks 40–60 km downwind (the actual distance depending on topography, wind speed, and other meteorologic conditions) of major sources of the reaction ingredients. Ozone concentrations in the air entering New York are about equal to the concentration in the air leaving New York (Cleveland and Graedel, 1979); however, metropolitan New York appears to be the source of the starting materials that are responsible for the higher levels of ozone in Connecticut. This obviously has some significant implications for air pollution control, which we will consider later.

Ozone as a Problem. Some people feel the effects of ozone when it is present at only 0.001 ppm. At 0.05–0.1 ppm, some people experience impaired eye muscle coordination and a drop in visual acuity. Pulmonary edema can be produced in human test subjects at less than 1 ppm.

According to the U.S. Environmental Protection Agency (EPA), the probable median health effects on which the ozone standard of 0.12 ppm was based are that 0.15 ppm produces chest discomfort, irritation of the respiratory tract, and reduction of pulmonary function; at 0.17 ppm, asthma, emphysema, and chronic bronchitis are aggravated; and at 0.18 ppm there is reduced resistance to bacterial infection. The above figures are **median** points, meaning

that at these points half of all people exposed to these levels will experience the effect and half will not. The 0.12-ppm standard (see Chapter 11) is considered by the EPA to provide an adequate margin of safety.

The allowable concentration of ozone in industry (for 8-hour exposures) is 0.05 ppm. However, in some industries, concentrations of ozone can occasionally reach nearly 1 ppm; this level is also sometimes reached in acute air pollution episodes in places like Los Angeles. At times there are relatively high concentrations of ozone in cabins of airplanes flying above 30,000 feet. Above 80,000 feet, ozone concentrations in (outside) air reach 12 ppm, which is lethal even when exposure time is very short.

As a powerful oxidizing agent, ozone can damage crops and other vegetation and can cause the premature deterioration of rubber, fabrics, and other materials (see Chapter 10). By promoting the formation of light-scattering particles, ozone and other oxidants contribute to the kind of lessened visibility that makes it difficult to see across the Grand Canyon.

Atmospheric Ozone as a Protector in Jeopardy. Ironically, ozone is also an important, useful constituent of the atmosphere because of its role in protecting life from ultraviolet radiation (see Chapters 5 and 14). The ozone in the stratosphere (see Figure 9.1) screens out all but a fraction of a percent of the harmful (cancer- and mutation-causing) radiation having wavelengths (see Chapter 2) shorter than 340 nanometers (a **nanometer** is one billionth of one meter).

The problem is that certain human-produced pollutants (chlorine and halogenated hydrocarbon refrigerants, for example) tend to remove stratospheric ozone via a catalytic cycle involving free chlorine atoms. The reaction goes as follows:

$$CF_2Cl_2 + \text{ultraviolet radiation} \rightarrow CF_2Cl + Cl$$
$$Cl + O_3 \rightarrow ClO + O_2$$
$$O_3 + \text{ultraviolet radiation} \rightarrow O_2 + O^{\cdot}$$
$$ClO + O^{\cdot} \rightarrow Cl + O_2$$

Although chlorofluorocarbons are inert at ground level, they can be made to release chlorine by the action of ultraviolet radiation, and the chlorine then acts as a catalyst to destroy ozone.

This reaction is called catalytic because chlorine is not changed in the reaction; thus a little chlorine as a free radical can be responsible for the conversion of much ozone into oxygen.

Various sources yield the broad general consensus that for each 1% decrease in stratospheric ozone, there will be a 2–5% increase in basal cell skin cancer and a 4–10% increase in squamous cell skin cancer (see Chapter 14). Maugh (1984) indicates that this multiplier is partly derived from the fact that each 1% drop in ozone might increase the amount of ultraviolet radiation that reaches the surface by as much as 3%.

Two satellites (Nimbus 4 and Nimbus 7) collected data from 1970 through 1979 showing that at an altitude of 25 miles (40 km), ozone is decreasing at the rate of 0.5% per year. In a report released in March 1982 the National Research Council estimated that there would be a 5–9% reduction in stratospheric ozone late in the next century if chlorofluorocarbon production continued at its current pace.

Solomon, de Zafra, Parrish, and Barrett (1984) measured levels of chlorine monoxide in the stratosphere (about 30 km) and determined its daily variation. They concluded that the chlorine *already in* the stratosphere will result in an ultimate decrease of 3–5% in stratospheric ozone.

A National Academy of Sciences report released in 1984 indicated that stratospheric ozone was unlikely to fall more than 4%. This latest NAS prediction was considerably less than the 18.6% decline predicted in a 1979 report. The difference is attributed to better understanding of what goes on in the atmosphere and *not* to a decline in the use of chlorofluorocarbons. A 4% reduction in stratospheric ozone will, other things staying the same, mean a significant increase in skin cancer rates.

The United States continues to work with other countries in attempting to resolve the ozone depletion problem. The forum for this international approach is the United Nations Environmental Program (UNEP) and the Organization for Economic Cooperation and Development (OECD). The United States banned all nonessential uses of chlorofluorocarbons (CFCs) as aerosol propellants in 1978, and similar steps are under consideration in other countries. CFCs are still widely used as refrigerants in the United States and elsewhere, however, because no suitable substitute has been found for this application.

Particulate Matter

The category of particulate pollutants, which includes about 5% of the weight of all air pollutants, is a miscellaneous category. The term "particulate" itself implies a single kind of gritty entity. However, particulate pollution has multiple components, including sulfate salts, sulfuric acid droplets, salts of metals (like lead or oxides of iron), dust from finely divided particles of carbon or silica, liquid sprays and mists, and a host of uncataloged substances.

The size of particulate matter is an important characteristic. Individual particles are measured in units called **micrometers** (μm), one million of which add up to one meter. Particulates range in size from 0.005 μm to about 100 μm (U.S. Environmental Protection Agency, 1982a). While *natural* dusts constitute half the total mass of particulate matter in the atmosphere at any one time, this dust has a relatively small impact because it is in the form of coarse particles. Being heavy, these particles settle out of the atmosphere quickly and otherwise do not get to delicate lung tissue. Because of their small size (80% are less than 2 μm), transportation-derived particulates have a greater impact on health even though they make up only about 1% of the particulate load in the atmosphere. Fine particulate matter (less than 2.5 μm in diameter as defined by the EPA) is generally considerably more hazardous to human health than coarse (diameters greater than 2.5 μm) particulate matter.

Although particles as large as 15 μm in diameter can reach the nonciliated portion of the lung and even the alveoli (see Chapter 10), particulate matter having diameters less than 10 μm reach the alveoli with greatest efficiency. (The peak in efficiency of alveoli deposition for mouth and nose breathing occurs in the range 2–4 μm.)

Although rain generally tends to clean particulate matter out of the air, it is not very effective in removing pieces smaller than 2 μm in diameter. Particulates in this category tend to remain suspended and, depending on turbulence and wind conditions, can be transported over long distances. Very fine particles behave almost identically to gases.

Particulates occur as sprays, mists, and dusts from spraying and grinding activities, land clearing, and highway building. Soot and fly ash are emitted from electrical power plants and factories. Significant amounts of particulates also come from forest fires and agricultural fires. Secondary particulate particles can be created in the atmosphere by the reaction of gases producing a solid or droplets or by one chemical acting as a nucleus onto which other chemicals condense to produce new chemical entities. Hydrocarbons, for example, can react with oxidants in the atmosphere to produce peroxide radicals, which, through chemical chain reactions, eventually form large organic molecules, which in

Parts per Million (ppm) and Micrograms per Cubic Meter: The Relationship

Sometimes the concentration of a pollutant is expressed in terms of micrograms (μg) per cubic meter (m³). Sometimes the concentration is expressed in terms of parts per million (ppm). The expression μg/m³ is a weight per volume expression; it indicates how much all of a particular pollutant in a unit volume of air weighs. The ppm expression defines a volume per volume relationship. It is an expression of the fraction of a unit volume of air occupied by a pollutant.

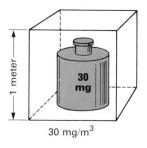

30 mg/m³

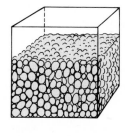

If half of any given volume of air were taken up by pollutant molecules, the pollutant would be at a concentration of 500,000 parts per million.

It so happens that a **mole** (the molecular weight of a compound expressed in grams) of any gas takes up 22.414 liters at standard conditions of temperature (0°C) and one atmosphere (760 mmHg) of pressure. One fifth of a mole would occupy one fifth of 22.414 liters and so on. What this means is that the conversion of ppm to μg/m³ is a function of the molecular weight of a particular compound. There is no *constant* that can be generally used to convert ppm to μg/m³. There is a formula, however:

If You Have	Multiply by		To Get
ppm	the compounds $\dfrac{\text{molecular weight} \times 1000}{22.4}$ or	the compounds $\dfrac{\text{molecular weight}}{0.0224}$	μg/m³
μg/m³	$\dfrac{0.0224}{\text{molecular weight}}$		ppm

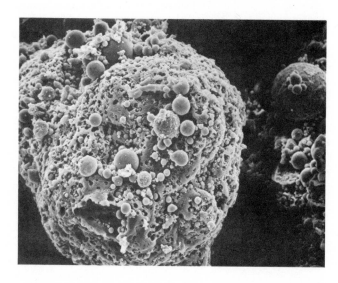

This is a particle of fly ash from a coal-fired power plant (magnified 100X).

Chapter 9   Air Pollutants and their Sources

273

turn join together to form small droplets or solid particles (Fenneley, 1976).

Once a particle gets inside the lungs, its effect depends on its chemical nature; and, as we said above, there are many chemically different particulates. Particulates do, however, have several *general* effects on humans and the environment. First, some of them are actually forms of dirt, which simply make things dirty. As they become absorbed onto the surface of materials, particulates can promote rust and corrosion by attracting water. Sulfates and sulfuric acid are particularly **hygroscopic** (tend to take up water). Particulates such as carbon can also cause complicated health effects by carrying into the lungs various gaseous substances absorbed on their surfaces. The cancer-causing chemical **benzopyrene** has been found to be associated with particles of soot in just such a way.

Since the advent of tougher clean air laws in the late 1960s, particulate pollution has been *relatively* effectively controlled. There was a 58% decline in particulate emissions from 1970 to 1982 (U.S. Environmental Protection Agency, 1984b). In the mid-1980s, only 25% of the U.S. population were exposed to levels of particulates that begin to have health effects (Conservation Foundation, 1984). Most of the progress made in keeping particulates out of the air since the early 1970s was made by removing the large particles from large stationary sources, for example, power plants and mills. Some additional "progress" in the early 1980s is attributed to decreased industrial activity of the economic slump.

Under consideration at the time of this writing is an EPA proposal to apply air quality standards and thus control only to particles that are less than 10 μm in diameter, the most damaging to health.

Metals: Lead and Mercury

Lead. Lead is fairly well known as an environmental problem related to its use in paint. This has been a serious problem in rundown old housing where very young children eat leaded paint chips, apparently because they taste sweet, and suffer lead poisoning. Lead has also been a problem in occupational settings, for example, in and around lead smelters and where lead-based solder is used. The *general* problem of atmospheric lead contamination comes largely from the automobile and the high-compression engine.

Tetraethyl lead was introduced as a motor fuel additive in the 1920s as a means to slow gasoline combustion to reduce engine knock and engine

wear. Nearly all of that lead gets back into the environment through the air (Figure 9.5). That leaded gasoline is the main source of atmospheric lead was made clear by the impact of unleaded gasoline. According to the Conservation Foundation (1984), there was a 64% decline in the average concentration of atmospheric lead between 1977 and 1982—paralleling a 68% decline in the use of leaded gasoline over roughly the same period.

Because the automobile has been and still is a major source of lead pollution (almost half the gas used today still contains lead), urban air has concentrations of lead 5–10 times those of sparsely populated areas and several thousand times more than would be found in the air over midocean (Figure 9.6). The lead content in the air and in the blood of people in remote reaches of Nepal is substantially lower (3.4 μg/dl in adult males) than it is in the industrialized areas (the U.S. normal range is 15–25 μg/dl) of the world (Piomelli et al., 1980). Typical body burdens of lead are some 500 times higher today than they were in people living before the industrial age (Marshall, 1984). (Ancient Romans may have been exceptions. Their bones typically have high lead levels, and lead poisoning linked to lead food and beverage vessels used by the upper class is believed to have contributed to the eventual fall of Rome.)

Paralleling the decline in use of leaded gasoline and the general decline in per capita lead consumption (in the resource use sense), a survey by the National Center for Health Statistics and the Center of Disease Control involving 27,801 people aged 6 months to 74 years showed a 38% decrease in blood lead levels from 1978 to 1981 (*Conservation Foundation*, 1984). According to a report by the National Academy of Sciences, surveys of children living in large cities in recent decades have commonly revealed blood lead levels of 40–60 μg per 100 ml or deciliter (dl) whole blood. This is one fifth to one third of what it would take for a doctor to write "lead poisoning" on a chart.

Human beings acquire lead mainly by ingestion and inhalation. The way in which humans are exposed to lead is important because not all routes are equally open to lead. Roughly half of inhaled lead is absorbed; a smaller (variable) fraction of the lead ingested in food is absorbed (Goldsmith and Hexter, 1967). After lead gets into the blood, it is gradually excreted, and some of it may be stored in bone. Depending on the rates of storage and excretion relative to the amount absorbed, blood levels may reach the limits of toxicity. Hormone changes and

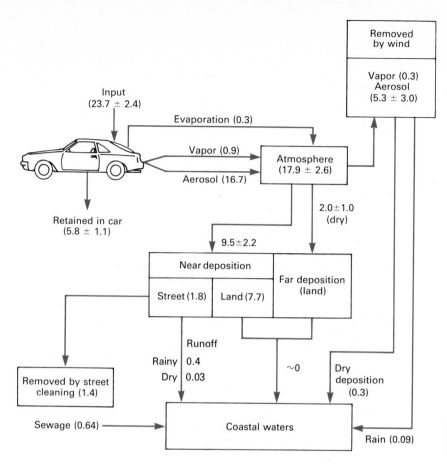

Figure 9.5 **The Fate of Lead in Leaded Gasoline in Los Angeles.**

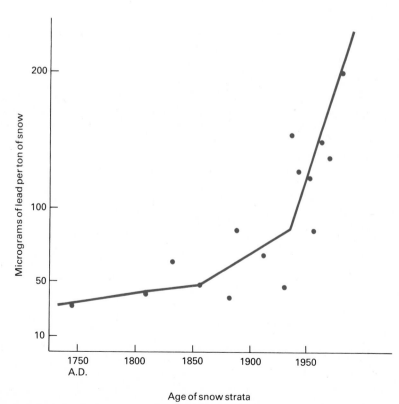

Figure 9.6 **Changing Lead Content in the Snow of the Ice Sheet in Greenland over the Past 200 Years.** The first sharp rise in the curve probably reflects the lead stirred up by the Industrial Age. The second, sharper rise, in 1950 or thereabouts, undoubtedly reflects the lead used as an antiknock ingredient in gasoline.

stress may cause the lead in bone to be released, causing surges in blood lead and health problems in individuals who previously carried blood lead burdens near threshold.

Until very recently it was thought that a blood lead level of 50 µg/dl (40 µg/dl in children), where a reduction in blood hemoglobin began (*Ambio*, 1977), was right at the health effect threshold, but new evidence indicates that the threshold may be much lower. The recent recommendation by the EPA that the amount of lead in gasoline be reduced from 1.1 grams per gallon to 0.1 gram per gallon by 1986 was based on observations that brain wave changes occur in children with blood lead levels as low as 15 µg/dl and that lower IQs, mental retardation, and behavioral changes have been associated with 40–60 µg/dl levels in preschool children.

As a heavy metal, lead causes biochemical, then physiological, then health effects as a consequence of its reactions with enzymes, other proteins, and other chemical constituents of cells. Apparently, two of the most lead-sensitive types of tissue are those of the brain and the bone marrow cells that normally give rise to hemoglobin-filled red cells. Interaction between lead and the brain—particularly the developing brain—takes the forms of mental retardation, lowered IQ, and behavioral abnormalities. In red blood cell precursors, lead inhibits one of the key steps leading to the synthesis of hemoglobin. This manifests itself as microscopically stippled red blood cells and the appearance in the urine of two chemicals (delta-amino-levulinic acid and coporphyrin III) that would normally have been incorporated into hemoglobin. The ultimate manifestation of the blood effect is an impaired ability of the blood to carry oxygen to the tissues—a kind of anemia.

Lead has other effects. Both benign and malignant tumors have been produced in rats and mice exposed to lead acetate (a lead salt) (*Ambio*, 1977). Lead can also affect the kidneys by damaging renal tubules and by inducing fibrotic changes in the space between tubules.

As was mentioned above, the EPA recommended (in mid-1984) a 91% reduction in the amount of lead in gasoline by 1986. At the same time the EPA indicated that an outright ban by 1995 was under consideration. One reason given for the recommended reduction was that the unleaded gasoline strategy had not worked well enough. Because of the widespread illegal use of leaded gas in cars designed for unleaded gas and for other reasons, 45% of gas is still leaded. This together with recent evidence (cited above) that lead was an even more serious health problem than had earlier been feared made additional action necessary.

It was estimated that the proposed reduction would cut in half the amount of impaired mental development in children being caused by lead in 1984; 50,000 children would be saved from brain damage in only two years. While it was acknowledged that the reduction would cost refiners $575 million dollars or more, William Ruckelshaus (then EPA administrator) pointed out that this would be much more than offset by the 1.8 billion dollars that would be saved in 1986 alone in the consequent reduction in medical bills, rehabilitation costs, increased fuel efficiency, and other benefits. As for the absolute ban, it was estimated by the EPA that the IQs of four million children could be raised by 2.2 points if lead were removed from gasoline altogether. Earlier, the Director of the U.S. Center for Environmental Health estimated that there would have been 80% fewer cases of lead toxicity among children if lead had been eliminated from gasoline entirely between 1977 and 1981 (Marshall, 1984).

A number of research questions remain concerning the effects of lead. We need to know more about the relative effects of organic and inorganic lead compounds, and we need to know more about how much lead we get from air versus diet. We also need to know more about the environmental variables that can affect human responses to lead.

Mercury. Most of us were unknowingly introduced to the concept of mercury poisoning by Alice on her way through Wonderland. The Mad Hatter was apparently a parody of hatters in Lewis Carroll's day, who did tend to go mad as a consequence of the mercury (mercuric nitrate) used in the curing of furs and felt used in making hats.

Today, as in Alice's time, a major source of atmospheric mercury is the natural degasing of the earth's crust. This produces between 25,000 and 125,000 tons of mercury per year. Geothermal steam used for power production contains significant amounts of mercury, which escapes into the atmosphere as cooling tower exhaust. Mercury emissions from geothermal plants are comparable to the emission of mercury (a contaminant in coal) from coal-fired power plants (Robertson, Crecelius, Fruchter, and Ludwick, 1977). In industry, mercury is used primarily in paper, chemical, and paint manufacturing. From these industries and from agricultural sources (pesticides and fungicides), mercury escapes into the air and soil and reaches human beings by a number of routes (see Figure 9.7). The concentration of mercury in the air is usually below

50 μg per cubic meter, and the average is about 20 μg per cubic meter (World Health Organization, 1978). Mercury escapes into the environment as a vapor, as a solute in water, or as a solid particulate in various chemical forms having different degrees of toxicity. Pure metallic mercury is relatively harmless in comparison to, say, mercuric chloride ($HgCl_2$), which is a very deadly poison. The ingestion of as little as a gram (1/454th of a pound) of mercuric chloride can cause death.

Mercury kills cells by causing the denaturation of proteins. In episodes of acute mercury poisoning, mercury tends to kill cells of the organs with which it comes into contact and thus impairs those organs. When mercurial compounds are eaten, for example, they affect the digestive tract and the kidney (because some of the mercury is absorbed from the gastrointestinal tract and is filtered from the blood by the kidney). Chronic exposure causes lesions of the mouth and skin and neurological problems like those suffered by the Mad Hatter. Air pollution is more important than ingestion to the *chronic* kinds of mercury toxicity.

The classic symptoms of poisoning by mercury vapor are irritability, excitability, loss of memory, insomnia, tremor, and gingivitis (gum disease). Such symptoms do not occur below a average mercury concentration in air of 0.1 mg (100 μg) per cubic meter, although loss of appetite and psychological problems have been reported to occur at levels slightly below 0.1 mg/m^3 (World Health Organization, 1978). Adverse health effects in workers have not been known to occur below the level of 0.05 mg (50 μg) per cubic meter of air (World Health Organization, 1978). The effects of methyl mercury in adult human beings becomes noticeable in sensitive individuals when levels of mercury in the blood reach 20–50 μg per 100 ml.

Much more research on mercury and its effects is needed, particularly with respect to various *forms* of mercury and its conversion products in air, food, and water and with respect to dietary intake and the dose/response relationship for certain health effects of mercury.

Mercury as a water pollutant will be discussed in Chapter 12.

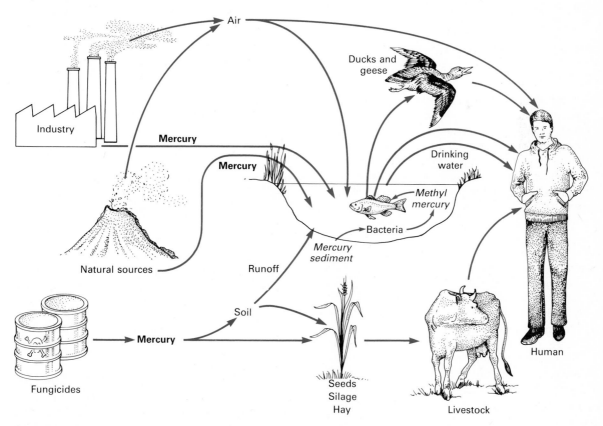

Figure 9.7 How Mercury Can Get into Human Tissues Through Water, Air, Soil, and Food Chains.

Radioisotopes

We have chosen to cover the details of the sources and effects of radioactive pollutants, both those transported in water and those transported in air, in Chapters 6, 13, and 14. Here we emphasize only the following points.

Most of the radiation to which humans are exposed comes from natural (background) sources (see Chapter 6). Radioactive gases and solids are found naturally in soil and rocks. The sun creates still more through the interaction of solar energy with materials in the atmosphere. We receive about 100 millirems (Chapter 6) of radiation per year from natural sources. We receive another 100 or so millirems on the average from artificial sources; most of this comes from medical and dental X-rays. We receive about 5 millirems per year from artificially made atmospheric pollutants derived from activities such as nuclear weapons testing. Fallout containing the radioisotopes plutonium-239, strontium-90, and others has added about 10% to the dose of radiation we humans receive in a given year. The EPA indicates that nuclear power plants contribute less than 0.01 millirem to the radiation each of us receives from air, water, and soil (Chapter 6).

Other Air Pollutants

There are pollutants other than those described above; some of them are included in Table 9.1. We will discuss still other pollutants in greater detail in other chapters. Asbestos, for example, will be discussed in the chapter on cancer (Chapter 14). Asbestos continues to be important because hundreds of thousands of buildings throughout the United States and other countries were sprayed with it for fireproofing and to improve acoustics. It was not until 1973 that the EPA began to restrict the use of materials containing fractions of asbestos exceeding 1%.

The fluorocarbons that we mentioned in the section on ozone represent just one group of fluoride compounds that have health effects. Other *fluorides,* inorganic compounds such as those released into the atmosphere from the smelting of iron and aluminum and the processing of phosphate fertilizers, can severely damage plants and have been reported to adversely affect human as well as animal health (Waldbott, 1978). Fluorine is a very reactive oxidant that is capable of reacting with and impairing enzymes and other chemicals. The biological effect of fluorine gas and gaseous fluoride compounds that has received most attention is its ability to affect the calcification of bones and teeth. A little fluoride helps strengthen teeth (hence fluoride toothpaste and fluoridated water), but too much can cause disruption of phosphocalcium crystal formation and produce mottled teeth. In excess, fluoride actually decalcifies bones and teeth, making them brittle.

THE SOURCES AND CAUSES OF AIR POLLUTION

Only part of the air pollution problem comes from the *amount* of pollutants that get dumped into the air. There are also important considerations having to do with space, time, and circumstances. We would like to bring these aspects into sharper focus.

Space is part of the air pollution problem because most air pollutants are released into the very air we breathe. Residential areas or cities occupy about 1% of the land area in the United States, and it is the air over this 1% that receives emissions in highest concentration.

Time is part of the problem because the rate of polluting is important. In every major American city there is a monumental exodus of automobiles from the suburbs in the morning and the reverse late every afternoon. The result is a sharp peak of effluent release twice each day. There are also similar patterns that amount to surges of effluent—output at rates that exceed the ability of the environment to disperse or otherwise neutralize the pollutants.

Still other temporal pollution patterns are the result of patterns in circumstance. For reasons related to weather, for example, the "ozone season" occurs in the summer (May–October). As we mentioned earlier and as we will discuss in the last portion of this chapter, *circumstances* of weather and topography are important factors in air pollution. Keep *space, time,* and *circumstance* in mind.

Natural Sinks and Overloading

Before we get deeply into sources, we would like to crystallize a concept touched upon indirectly in several places earlier. To begin with, it is obvious that the contaminant level in the atmosphere at any one time falls very short of the cumulative amounts released into the atmosphere. This indicates that there are *sinks* for various pollutants; something happens to sop them up.

According to Schlesinger (1979), sinks for atmospheric pollutants (and other types) fall into three broad categories:

1. spontaneous chemical transformation—for example, oxidation;

2. microbial degradation in soil and in water; and
3. physical processes such as solubilization and sedimentation.

The degree to which these processes operate varies from place to place, from pollutant to pollutant, and from time to time. In other words, the amount of time any chemical remains in the environment is highly variable and depends on the various chemical, physical, and biological features of the environment and on the chemical in question.

The main removal mechanisms for atmospheric particulates are physical; particles are cleared by either dry or wet deposition. Wet deposition refers to the ability of rainfall, for example, to sweep particles out of the atmosphere. Dry deposition is of primary importance in the troposphere (see Figure 9.1), where sedimentation or settling out increases as particles get bigger.

Atmospheric gases are removed by both physical and chemical processes. Gases either are adsorbed onto solids or undergo chemical reactions in the air. A summary of the sinks for various selected atmospheric gaseous pollutants (as presented by Schlesinger, 1979) is given in Table 9.2.

Natural Sources of Air Pollution

The rest of nature puts more things and greater quantities of bad things into the air than humans do. Sulfur dioxides, oxides of nitrogen, carbon monoxide, methane, hydrocarbons, and particulates emanate from volcanoes, swamps, forests, natural fires, and the action of wind on soil not covered by vege-tation. Volcanoes contribute great amounts of dust and particulate matter as well as noxious gases. Organic decay in tropical forests and other places puts a variety of gaseous compounds like methane into the atmosphere, and forests contribute various organic compounds including ketones, aldehydes, and other complex hydrocarbons, which, as we have already discussed, can participate in the generation of ozone. Somehow the fact that there is a lot of naturally occurring air pollution seems to offer little comfort in light of the seriousness of the highly concentrated, largely *human-derived* air pollution problem in our cities today.

Humans and Air Pollution: Technology as a "General Source"

In his book *The Closing Circle,* Barry Commoner (1971) made the point that modern technology is more costly, is more energy-consuming, and tends to pollute more than the technologies it has replaced over the years. Beyond the impression that we do lead somewhat better and happier lives today, close inspection seems to reveal that we have to pay more, in terms of energy and deterioration of the environment, for equivalent units of economic "good" produced than we did in decades past. Commoner offers aluminum as an example; he points out that aluminum takes more energy to produce than steel. While there are unarguable advantages to using aluminum in packaging, construction, and other areas, the fact is that to make an aluminum beer can requires about six times more energy and generates several times more pollution than to make a steel one.

Table 9.2   Sinks for Selected Atmospheric Gaseous Pollutants

Pollutants	Sink	Estimated Residence Time
CO	uptake by soil and conversion to CO_2 by microbes	0.09–2.7 years
CO_2	dissolves in oceans; taken up by plants in photosynthesis	2–10 years
H_2S	oxidation to SO_2	0.08–2 days
SO_2	precipitation scavenging then oxidation to sulfate particles	20 min–7 days
NO	atmospheric oxidation to NO_2	4–5 days
NO_2	precipitation scavenging and oxidation to nitrate	3–5 days
Hydrocarbons	oxidized to CO_2; absorption on soil then microbial degradation; photochemical degradation	1.5–2 years (methane)
Ozone	Photochemical reaction (reversion to O_2) in atmosphere	2 hr–3 days

Table 9.3 Sources of Major Air Pollutants

Sulfur dioxide	combustion of coal, oil, and other sulfur-containing fuels and in petroleum refining metal smelting, paper making
Particulate matter	many sources; fuel combustion, industrial processes, construction, forest fires, refuse incineration, automobile traffic
Nitrogen dioxide	produced by combinations of atmospheric nitrogen and oxygen at high combustion temperatures such as those in automobile engines; also a by-product in the manufacturing of fertilizers
Volatile organic compounds (e.g. volatile hydrocarbons)	motor vehicles—evaporate from gasoline tanks carburetors; industrial processes involving solvents
Carbon monoxide	combustion of fuel, e.g., gasoline
Photochemical oxidants	produced via complex photochemical reactions in the atmosphere involving hydrocarbons, nitrogen dioxide, and sunlight
Hydrogen sulfide	various processes in many kinds of chemical industries; oil wells, refineries
Fluorides	fertilizer manufacture, ceramics manufacturing, and aluminum smelting
Lead	combustion of leaded gasoline; solder, lead-containing paint; lead-smelting operations;
Mercury	paper, chemical, and paint manufacturing; pesticides; fungicides

Electrical power generation is responsible for a significant fraction of the air pollution problem. As we saw in Chapter 6, while our increasing use of electrical power has unquestionably added to the quality of life, the improvement/power ratio has remained rather small: Very little of the power we consume is translated quantitatively into improved living. We saw in Chapter 6 that much electrical power is wasted through inefficiency. The automobile, which by now the reader may have recognized as a major villain in this chapter, offers another particularly profound example of the fact that sometimes it is not *what* we do that matters, or even *how much* of it we do, as it is the *way* we do it.

For many years, pollution by automobiles increased much faster than the number of automobile miles traveled in America (Commoner, 1971). Various design changes in the automobile were responsible for this. Escalation in the power of internal combustion engines in the 1950s and 1960s was achieved through engineering based on increases in engine displacement and in the compression of the gasoline-air mixture before ignition. While this produces more power per stroke, it also results in higher combustion temperatures and, consequently, greater quantities of NO_x and other pollutants. There are other examples, to be sure, but the foregoing will serve to illustrate that part of the air pollution problem has to do simply with the *way* we do things.

Let's now take a look at some general categories of specific human generators of air pollution in preparation for considering source-based control strategies in Chapter 11. A summary of the sources of major pollutants is given in Table 9.3.

The major contributors of air pollution, in decreasing order, are transportation, electric power generation, industry (including fuel combustion and materials processing), forest and agricultural fires, and incineration. Each source of pollution is a way of burning some kind of fuel rapidly.

Transportation and Air Pollution: The Mobile Sources

Human-generated air pollution is sometimes divided, for the purposes of discussion, into *mobile* and *stationary* sources. **Mobile sources** are automobiles, buses, trains, airplanes, and other fossil fuel–powered modes of transportation. **Stationary sources** include factories, incinerators, and other kinds of nonmobile sources. There is a practical reason for making such a division; it has to do with the differences in the pollution control problems presented by these two categories. Mobile sources tend to be much smaller, much more plentiful, and much more widely dispersed and are therefore more difficult to monitor than stationary sources.

Automobiles and trucks (highway vehicles) are the main mobile source problem with respect to air pollution because (1) to carry the same load, trucks and cars emit about six times as much pollution as railroads (see Chapter 6) and (2) automobiles produce many more times the amount of pollution per gallon of fuel consumed than diesel-powered trucks or trains and/or jet aircraft. Overall, highway vehicles generate roughly ten times more air pollutants than other mobile sources (U.S. Environmental Protection Agency, 1984). We will ignore for the moment the facts that the building of highways takes many times the energy needed to lay railroad track on a per-mile basis and that railroads take up less right-of-way than do highways (Commoner, 1971).

Disregarding the relative *toxicity* of pollutants, automobiles alone produce about two thirds of the *weight* of air pollutants that are human derived, and this fraction can reach 90% in certain U.S. cities (Waldbott, 1978). In the United States, transportation accounts for over two thirds of the carbon monoxide emissions, over one third of the volatile organic compounds, about half of the oxides of nitrogen, less than 5% of the oxides of sulfur, and about 17% of the particulates (mostly diesel engines) (U.S. Environmental Protection Agency, 1984) (see Table 9.4). Automobiles continue to contribute most of the hundreds of thousands of tons of

lead that are introduced into the atmosphere each year.

Stationary Sources (Electric Utilities, Industry, Agriculture, and Construction)

The burning of coal and other fuels is the principal cause of air pollution coming from stationary sources. Coal combustion in electrical utilities and in smelting generates oxides of sulfur, oxides of nitrogen, hydrogen fluoride, carbon monoxide, and particulates such as carbon, silica, aluminum, and iron oxides in addition to assorted hydrocarbons and metals such as lead, mercury, cadmium, selenium, vanadium, and zinc (Waldbott, 1978). Electric utilities together with other industrial, commercial, and residential *stationary* fuel combustion sources contribute one third of particulate emissions, about 80% of SO_x emissions, half the NO_x, 10% of volatile organics, and less than 10% of CO emissions (U.S. Environmental Protection Agency, 1984b).

Solid Waste Disposal and Incineration

Packaging for products ranging from food to toys contributes significantly to the air pollution problem (Chapter 15). First, pollution is generated

Table 9.4 Summary of Emission Patterns by Source Category (in millions of Metric Tons)

Source Category	Particulate Matter	SO_x	NO_x	Volatile Organic Compounds	CO
Highway vehicles	1.1	0.5	7.8	4.8	46.3
Aircraft	0.1	0.0	0.1	0.2	1.0
Railroads	0.0	0.1	0.7	0.2	0.2
Other transport	0.1	0.3	1.1	0.9	5.8
Total transportation	1.3 (17)	0.9 (4)	9.7 (48)	6.1 (34)	53.3 (72)
Electric utilities	1.0	14.3	6.2	0.0	0.3
Industrial fuel combustion	0.4	2.3	2.7	0.1	0.5
Commercial/ institutional	0.1	0.6	0.3	0.0	0.1
Residential	0.9	0.2	0.4	1.9	5.7
Total fuel combustion	2.4 (32)	17.4 (81)	9.6 (48)	2.0 (11)	6.6 (9)
Industrial processes	2.4 (32)	3.1 (14)	0.6 (3)	7.1 (39)	4.8 (7)
Incineration	0.2	0.0	0.0	0.3	1.2
Open burning	0.2	0.0	0.1	0.3	0.9
Solid waste (total)	0.4 (5)	0.0 (0)	0.1 (<1)	0.6 (3)	2.1 (3)
Miscellaneous	1.0 (13)	0.0 (0)	0.2 (1)	2.4 (13)	6.8 (9)
Total all sources	7.5 (100)	21.4 (100)	20.2 (100)	18.2 (100)	73.6 (100)
Percent of total emissions	5%	15%	14%	13%	52%

Note: 0 = less than 50,000 metric tons. Numbers in parentheses are percents of total for particulate pollutant. The "grand total" is 140.9 million metric tons.

Stationary sources such as power plants are easier to monitor than mobile sources, which tend to be small and dispersed.

in making all packaging. Then, after a package is opened and the product is removed, the package must be disposed of, often by incineration. Americans have accepted the extra cost that packaging has brought to various goods almost without realizing that they pay for packaging at least twice. The second time is the cost to health and the environment and the real cost of solid waste disposal as packaging is picked up, transported, and burned, releasing its combustion products into the atmosphere. Incinerators emit carbon monoxide, aldehydes, hydrocarbons, particulates, and a variety of miscellaneous gases. The shift in composition of packaging from paper to plastics has brought about changes in the character of the emissions from incinerators. Among the things that now appear in significant amounts in effluents from burning refuse are chlorine and chlorides. The chlorides are derived from plastics made from polyvinyl chloride and other chloride-containing components of plastic.

Leaves and refuse burned in residential areas obviously also contribute to the air pollution problem. Many American cities have banned the burning of leaves because it adds particulates and assorted noxious gases to the atmosphere, usually at a time of year when there are stagnant air conditions. Leaf burning offers a particularly poignant example of people causing deterioration of a resource through the acceleration of a natural process to the point at which products accumulate more rapidly than they can be dispersed. An ecological paradox here is that leaves could be composted (many cities now have leaf collection/composting programs) and used to enrich garden soil in the same way that commercial fertilizer and peat moss add to the quality of soil.

Thus in addition to polluting the air, burning the leaves deprives the leaf burner of the moisture-holding, soil-improving qualities of compost.

Incineration and open burning account for roughly 5% of particulate emissions, 3% of volatile organics and CO, and negligible fractions of total SO_x and NO_x emissions (U.S. Environmental Protection Agency, 1984b). Emission fractions unaccounted for come from forest fires and other miscellaneous sources.

THE INFLUENCES OF WEATHER AND OTHER SYNERGISTIC FACTORS ON AIR POLLUTION

There is no city on earth where the level of air pollution is harmful on a continuous basis, although Mexico City and Los Angeles come very close. Variation in pollution is a result of irregularity in the emission of pollutants and a number of factors that determine where pollutants go and whether or not they will accumulate. Weather and meteorologic conditions relevant to the pollution problem include light, humidity, temperature, wind, thermal inversions, and rain. Other factors include topography and interactions between chemical pollutants (Table 9.5). Biological magnification of certain pollutants is still another factor, one that depends on the nature of the food chains in a particular location (see Chapters 2 and 13). As we will see later, the effect of pollutants on health varies not only with the levels of pollutants themselves and their interaction, but also with a number of host factors such as age, the presence of respiratory or cardiovascular illness, genetic predisposition, degree of physical activity, and level of stress.

Synergism Defined

When the effects of two things are **synergistic** (noun = **synergism**), they have an impact, together, that is different from the sum of their separate impacts. A particle of asbestos becomes harmful when it reaches the alveoli of the lung. Fortunately, most particles are caught in the upper respiratory tract and are carried back out on a layer of mucus fanned by tiny cilia (Chapter 10). Smoking interferes with the action of the cilia, paralyzing them. Smoking thus increases the chances that asbestos or other particulate material will reach and remain in the delicate lower respiratory tract. As will be discussed in Chapter 14, medical researchers found that asbestos workers who smoked had far more lung cancers than nonsmokers or nonasbestos workers and had

Table 9.5 Summary of Factors Affecting the Distribution of Air Pollutants

Increase in	Pollution	Typical effect
Precipitation	−	cleanses the air (but brings acid rain)
Humidity	+	dissolves many pollutants; renders pollution more visible
Fog	+	remains the same
Sunshine	+	initiates oxidation
Wind velocity	±	less pollution near the source but faster and wider distribution
Wind direction from contaminating source	+	greater contamination
Increasing temperature with increasing height	+	less dispersion
Barometric pressure	+	lighter wind; less dispersion
Height of emitting source	−	enhances dispersion and dilution of contaminant
Mountains, hills	+	break force of winds; but promote light winds
Valleys	+	trap pollutants
Plains	−	greater dispersion
Distance from contaminating source	−	remains the same

A minus sign means less pollution; a plus sign means more pollution.

far more cancers than smokers who were *not* asbestos workers. They also found that nonsmokers who worked with asbestos had actually no greater risks of developing lung cancer than did nonsmokers who did *not* work with asbestos. Asbestos and cigarette smoking are thus **positively synergistic**. The combination of the two things is much more effective in producing lung cancers than the sum of the separate effects of the two apart. Nobody knows what the asbestos does exactly, but asbestos *is* known to be able to stimulate the production of certain enzymes, one or more of which might be able to convert one of more of the chemicals in cigarette smoke into carcinogens. Such an effect would not be apparent in the absence of tobacco smoke.

There are many other examples of positive synergism. Gaseous pollutants that are highly reactive and/or that are extremely soluble and that would normally react and be absorbed in the upper respiratory airway can reach deep into the lungs by being adsorbed onto the surface of particulates and carried into the lungs. Sulfur dioxide exposure in the presence of certain particulates is a more serious problem than sulfur dioxide exposure alone. Similarly, sulfur dioxide with water vapor is much more toxic than the same levels of sulfur dioxide in a dry environment. This is because sulfur dioxide can dissolve in water and subsequently become oxidized, forming sulfuric acid, which can be carried into the lower respiratory tract as a mist.

There is also *negative* synergism or **antagonism**. During the air pollution disaster in London in the 1950s, animals housed in dirty pens did not seem to suffer nearly as much as did animals housed in clean pens. The reason for this is believed to have been the neutralization of sulfur dioxide by the ammonia being released from waste materials in the dirty pens. The combination of ammonia and sulfur dioxide is actually less harmful than the effects of either ammonia or sulfur dioxide alone. This is **negative synergism**.

In a survey conducted in the early 1960s the United States government found that nearly 40 different substances not present in natural air *were* present in the air of many American cities. The potential for synergistic interactions between any or all of these compounds makes impossible any simple determination of the cause-and-effect relationship between specific air pollutants. Attempts to sort out specific effects often end up in a hopeless tangle because of the many complex chemical interactions that are possible.

Another Reason to Complain About the Weather

Normally, as the sun peeks over the horizon in the morning, the temperature of the atmosphere is warmest near the ground and drops slightly with distance from ground level. (Normally, every 1000-foot increase in altitude brings a temperature drop of about 5.4°F. In Celsius and metric terms there is a 1–3°C drop for every 100-meter rise.) As the sun begins to beat down, the ground becomes warm and heats the air immediately adjacent to it. As it is heated, surface air becomes less dense and be-

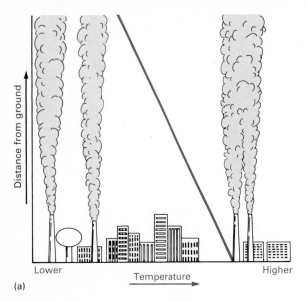

(a)

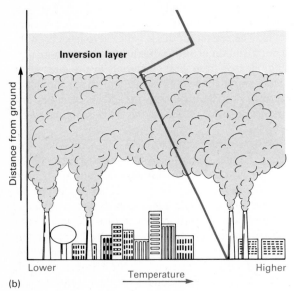

(b)

Figure 9.8   A Thermal Inversion. (a) Air usually gets cooler with altitude; temperature drops about 1–3°C for every 100 m in elevation. (b) Sometimes layers of air occur in which this relationship is inverted. Inversion layers act like lids; the air that rises from below (as the sun warms the ground and the air just above it) stops when it reaches the inversion layer. Hot air rises only as long as the air around it is cooler; in other words, at the inversion layer, rising air stops if the air in that layer is as warm as or warmer (and thus less dense) than it is.

gins to rise. Normally, such an air mass cools as it rises, but the rate of cooling usually does not quite allow the temperature (or, more accurately, the density) of the rising air mass to match that of the ambient air at each new height that it reaches. The air mass might continue rising for 11–16 km (7–10 miles), all the way to the end of the troposphere (Figure 9.1), before its density does match that of the surrounding air.

This phenomenon by which dirty air can be moved away from the earth's surface vertically is blocked whenever there is a temperature inversion. A temperature inversion or **thermal inversion** is defined as a condition wherein temperature actually increases with altitude within a layer in some part of the troposphere. In other words, there is a layer of warm air over some cold air. The effect of this is that surface-heated air rises through the lower levels only until it reaches the inversion layer. There the rising air is suddenly *not* warmer (less dense) than the air above or around it, and so it stops rising. Convection is thus halted, and air is effectively trapped together with any pollutants it carries as long as the inversion persists. Figure 9.8 depicts such a thermal inversion, showing the pattern of temperature change with height.

Meterologists say that thermal inversions can come about in several ways. In a **radiation thermal inversion** (synonym: **ground inversion**) the ground is cooled at night by thermal radiation and cools the air above it, but not the air farther up; this causes an inversion. These are normal nighttime phenomena and are usually destroyed by the morning sun. If the ground air is cooled too much or if, because of clouds, the sun cannot reverse an inversion, it hangs on.

Another kind of inversion is called a **subsidence inversion**. In this case, upper air masses compress (in high-pressure areas) lower air masses such that the upper portion of the lower air mass is compressed more and thus *heated* more. This sets up high-pressure doldrums, which might last several days or longer. Stationary highs are rather common over the northern continents during the winter months. They are also fairly common in late summer over the eastern United States, creating air stagnation conditions. Stationary highs are common over the West Coast of the United States practically all year long.

If a city generates pollutants (they all do) and if it is located in an area with prolonged thermal inversions, which block vertical air movement, it will almost invariably have a serious air pollution problem. These factors converged on Donora, Pennsylvania, in 1948; they converge on Los Angeles *almost constantly*. Los Angeles is unique in that it has very frequent inversions. It has about 250 days each year when its air is unhealthful or very unhealthful. In 1981, Los Angeles had around 110 days of air quality alerts and 140 days air quality warnings (Council on Environmental Quality, 1983). (See Chapters 10 and 11.)

The Creation of Pollutants in the Atmosphere

We have already discussed how ultraviolet radiation from the sun would have a much more intensely adverse effect on life on earth if it were not for an ozone shield high in the atmosphere. The direct negative or harmful effect of ultraviolet radiation on living things is that it can be absorbed by DNA (Chapter 5) and other chemicals that make up living things. Chemicals that absorb energy become activated; they are more likely to react with some other chemical and become changed, almost inevitably for the worse. ultraviolet radiation and other light energy can also cause pollutants to react with one another and thus change them from one form to another. This adds considerable complexity to the air pollution problem. Several of the most important examples of radiation-induced chemical reactions in the atmosphere were discussed earlier under the heading "Photochemical Oxidants."

Temperature and Wind

Temperature affects the formation of, the action of, and the interaction between pollutants in several ways. Part of the influence of temperature on pollution is related to the fact that chemical reaction rates tend to increase with temperature. Also, the warmer the air, the more water the air can hold. Many air pollutants dissolve in water to form acids. This effect is at least partially offset (as an air pollution problem, anyway) when water vapor in the atmosphere condenses and returns to earth as rain, sleet, or snow, cleaning the atmosphere.

Temperature is also important because of its effect on wind (Chapter 2). Wind cleans by diluting

and dispersing. While this can be a great boon to the residents of the city that generates pollutants, it can be a problem for people who live in small towns and cities downwind. Wind can, and does, also bring in pollutants. According to some reports, smog generated in Los Angeles has been linked to ill effects in places 200 miles away. According to a report by Cleveland and colleagues (1976), air pollution from New York is carried by west winds through Connecticut and as far as Massachusetts. Some parts of Connecticut have the highest ozone concentrations in the Northeast, largely as a consequence of the pollutants carried there from New York.

Topography

The disasters we considered in the first part of this chapter illustrate the importance of topography in air pollution. Cities at the bottoms of topographic depressions or nestled in mountains are especially prone to dangerous levels of pollution when inversions put lids on these depressions. But mountains can also help to *create* inversions. This happens because heat is radiated from the tops of mountains faster than it is from valleys. As air next to cool mountain slopes is cooled, it pours down the sides of the mountains and fills the valley up with cool air, aggravating and often creating inversion conditions that are favorable to the buildup of air pollution.

On to Health

In the next chapter we will see that while chemists have a great deal of difficulty keeping track of pollutants in the atmosphere under all kinds of variable conditions, biomedical scientists often have the even more difficult task of trying to link specific pollutants to specific health effects. Part of the reason this is so difficult is that in addition to variations in dose and length of exposure, the actual impact of a given pollutant on a human being depends on the human being, his or her age and genetic heritage, whether or not other illnesses are present, the degree of physical activity, and stress. In Chapter 10 we will look in some detail at these factors and describe what is known about the health effects of air pollutants.

CONCEPTS TO REMEMBER

1. Although there have been some particularly notable, even spectacular, acute air pollution disasters, these are insignificant in comparison to the impact that air pollution has on all of us over many years of *chronic* exposure.
2. The properties of air pollutants are highly variable. Their chemical properties are summarized in Table 9.1. (Biochemical and health effects are covered in Chapter 10).
3. The oxides of sulfur and the oxides of nitrogen have similar chemical properties. Beyond their harmful effects on lung tissue, both of these

classes of air pollutants also contribute to the acid rain problem and damage materials.

4. Many hydrocarbons are important individually as toxic substances (Chapters 13 and 14); hydrocarbons are important as a class of compounds in the generation of ozone (summarized in Figure 9.4).

5. Carbon dioxide is *not* a human health problem. Its standing as a pollutant stems from its contribution to the "greenhouse effect."

6. Carbon monoxide is toxic by virtue of its ability to compete with oxygen for hemoglobin. It does not damage materials.

7. The health effects of ozone and its effects on materials are derived from its strong oxidizing properties.

8. Particulate matter is a chemically miscellaneous category of pollutants. The size of suspended particles is a major determinant of their health effects. Large particles settle out quickly; generally, only particles less than 10 μm in diameter can stay suspended in the air. Particles less than 1 μm in diameter are difficult to filter and are most likely to get by air defenses and to reach the lungs.

9. There are natural sinks for air pollutants, but these can be overloaded rather easily.

10. The *rate* at which pollutants are emitted, the size of the *space* into which they are emitted, and the *circumstances* under which they are emitted are all critical determinants of pollutants' impact.

11. Our technology is a source of many pollutants.

12. *Stationary* and *mobile* are the two categories of sources of air pollution from the point of view of control strategy.

13. Most air pollution (in terms of weight) comes from automobiles and other forms of transportation.

14. Weather has a particularly profound effect on air pollution. The effects of wind, rain, and other factors on air pollutants are summarized in Table 9.5.

15. Inversions limit the vertical movement of polluted air; mountains limit horizontal movement.

16. Although air contaminants are generated from natural sources in significant amounts on a global scale, these are of little importance in relation to human-generated air pollutants in cities, where emissions are highly concentrated.

DISCUSSION QUESTIONS AND FOOD FOR THOUGHT

1. Find out what the major pollutants are in your city or region and compare your problems with those of other major cities. Find out if your region has particular air pollution problems at different times of year.

2. Consider the facts that (1) trains can carry the same load with one sixth of the energy used by automobiles and trucks (and emit about one sixth as much pollution in the process), (2) railroads take up one fourth the amount of right-of-way space as does a highway, and (3) it takes almost four times as much money, energy, and time to produce a mile of highway as it does to produce a mile of railroad. Look up the efficiency of barge transportation. Then design a system of transportation for freight *and* passengers that capitalizes on the advantages of a railroad system and also incorporates some of the advantages of the personal automobile and the truck.

3. Discuss the philosophical significance of the fact that our society permits the power of engines for passenger cars to be increased well beyond that necessary to get people from point A to point B under a legally mandated speed—and at the same time produce poisons that decrease the quality of life for all citizens.

4. One of the major causes of air pollution is obviously the automobile. Choose sides and debate the following: Resolved: Because of the problems of air pollution and energy, Americans should no longer have the individual personal freedom to own and drive an automobile; automobiles should be phased out over the next 25 years and then banned outright.

5. Make a long list of things an individual can do to reduce air pollution. For example (from an American Lung Association pamphlet), (1) don't burn leaves, (2) dry your clothes outside instead of using a clothes dryer, (3) buy unpackaged foods and liquids in returnable containers whenever possible, (4) set thermostats at 68° or 70° and wear a sweater if you are chilly, (5) have your heating system checked annually for efficiency, (6) keep your car tuned, ...

REFERENCES AND FURTHER READING

References marked with an asterisk are cited in the chapter.

*Ambio, 1977. "W. H. O.(World Health Organization) Environmental Health Criteria for Oxides of Nitrogen," *Ambio* **6**(5):290–292.

Ambio, 1978. "W. H. O. Environmental Health Criteria for Mercury," *Ambio* **7**(1):28–30.

Baes, C. F., and McLaughlin, S. B., 1984. "Trace Elements in Tree Rings: Evidence of Recent and Historical Air Pollution," *Science*, **224**:494–496.

Brodine, V., 1973. *Air Pollution.* New York: Harcourt Brace Jovanovich.

Callis, L. B.; Natarajan, M.; and Nealy, J. E., 1979. "Ozone and Temperature Trends Associated with the Eleven Year Solar Cycle," *Science* **204**:1303–1305.

*Cleveland, W. S., and Graedel, T. E., 1979. "Photochemical Air Pollution in the Northwest United States," *Science* **204**: 1273–1278.

Cleveland, W. S.; Kleiner, B.; McRae, J. E.; and Warner, J. L., 1976. "Photochemical Air Pollution: Transport from the New York City Area into Connecticut and Massachusetts," *Science,* **191**:179–181.

*Commoner, B., 1971. *The Closing Circle.* New York: Bantam Books.

*Conservation Foundation, 1984. *State of the Environment: An Assessment at Mid-Decade.* Washington, D.C.: The Conservation Foundation.

Council on Environmental Quality, 1979. *10th Annual Report: Environmental Quality—1979.* Washington, D.C.: U.S. Government Printing Office.

*Council on Environmental Quality, 1983. *Environmental Quality 1982,* 13th Annual Report. Washington, D.C.: U.S. Government Printing Office.

*Fennelly, P. F., 1976. "The Origin and Influence of Airborn Particulates," *American Scientist,* **64**:46–55.

*Goldsmith, J. R., and Hexter, A. C., 1967. "Respiratory Exposure to Lead: Epidemiological and Experimental Dose-Response Relationships," *Science,* **158**:132–134.

Grandjean, P., ed., 1984. *Biological Effects of Organolead Compounds.* Boca Raton, Fla.: CRC Press.

Kramer, P. J., 1981. "Carbon Dioxide Concentration, Photosynthesis and Dry Matter Production," *Bioscience.* **31**:29–33.

*Lippmann, M., and Schlesinger, R. B., 1979. *Chemical Contamination in the Human Environment.* New York: Oxford University Press.

Lynam, D. R.; Piantanida, L. G.; and Cole, J. F., eds., 1981. *Environmental Lead.* New York: Academic Press.

*Marshall, E., 1984. "Senate Considers Leaded Gasoline Ban," *Science* **225**:34–35.

Maugh, T. H., 1975. "Air Pollution: Where Do Hydrocarbons Come From?" *Science,* **189**:277–278.

*Maugh, T., 1984. "What is the Risk from Chlorofluorocarbons?" *Science* **223**:1051–1052.

*National Academy of Sciences, 1984. *Causes and Effects of Changes in Stratospheric Ozone: Update 1983.* Washington, D.C.: National Academy Press.

National Commission on Air Quality, 1981. *To Breathe Clean Air.* Washington, D.C.: U.S. Government Printing Office.

National Research Council Board on Atmospheric Sciences and Climate, 1983. *Changing Climate: Report of the Carbon Dioxide Assessment Committee.* Washington, D.C.: National Academy Press.

Perea, F. P., 1978. "Fine Particles in the Atmosphere," *Natural Resources Defense Council Newsletter* March-April-May-June, 1978.

Peterson, G., and Salvia, J. P., 1968. "Lead in the Modern Environment," *Environment* 19:66–79.

*Piomelli, S., et al., 1980. "Blood Lead Concentrations in a Remote Himalayan Population," *Science* **210**:1135–1136.

Reisner, M., 1977. "It's 1977, Why Don't We Have Cleaner Air?" *Natural Resources Defense Council Newsletter* **6**: 2–3.

*Robertson, D. C.; Crecelius, E. A.; Fruchter, J. S.; and Ludwick, J. D., 1977. "Mercury Emissions from Geothermal Power Plants," *Science* **196**:1094–1097.

Sandberg, J. S.; Basso, M. J.; and Okin, B. A., 1978. "Winter Rain and Summer Ozone: A Predictive Relationship," *Science* **200**:1051–1054.

*Schlesinger, R. B., 1979. "Natural Removal Mechanisms for Chemical Pollutants in the Environment," *Bioscience* **29**(2):95–101.

Shapley, D., 1977. "Will Fertilizers Harm Ozone as Much as SST's?" *Science* **195**:658.

Solomon, P. M.; de Zafra, R.; Parrish, A.; and Barrett, J. W., 1984. "Diurnal Variation of Stratospheric Chlorine Monoxide: A Critical Test of Chlorine Chemistry in the Ozone Layer," *Science* **224**:1210–1214.

Smith, J., 1981. "Utilities Choke on Asthma Research," *Science* **212**:1251–1254.

Stern, A. C., ed., 1968. *Air Pollution,* 2nd ed.(three volumes) New York: Academic Press.

U.S. Environmental Protection Agency, 1973. *Compilation of Air Pollution Emission Factors,* 2nd ed.(supplements 1–15, released 1973–1984). Research Triangle Park, N.C.: U.S. Environmental Protection Agency.

U.S. Environmental Protection Agency, 1977a. *National Air Quality Monitoring and Emission Trends Report.*(EPA-450/1-77-002).

U.S. Environmental Protection Agency, 1977b. *Compilation of Air Pollutant Emission Factors.* Supplement 72, 2nd ed., April 1977.

*U.S. Environmental Protection Agency, 1982a. *Office of Air Quality Planning and Standards Staff Papers.* Research Triangle Park, N.C.: U.S. Environmental Protection Agency.

*U.S. Environmental Protection Agency, 1982b. *Review of the National Ambient Air Quality Standards for Nitrogen Oxides: Assessment of Scientific and Technical Information.* EPA 450/5-82-002. Washington, D.C.: U.S. Government Printing Office.

U.S. Environmental Protection Agency, 1982c. *Review of the National Ambient Air Quality Standards for Particulate Matter: Assessment of Scientific and Technical Information.* Washington, D.C.: U.S. Government Printing Office.

*U.S. Environmental Protection Agency, 1982d. Review of the National Ambient Air Quality Standards for Sulfur Oxides: Assessment of Scientific and Technical Information. EPA 450/5-82-007. Washington, D.C.: U.S. Government Printing Office.

*U.S. Environmental Protection Agency, 1984a. *Revised Evaluation of Health Effects Associated with Carbon Monoxide Exposure: An Addendum to the 1979 Air Quality Criteria Document for Carbon Monoxide.* Washington, D.C.: Office of Health and Environmental Assessment.

*U.S. Environmental Protection Agency, 1984b. *National Air Pollutant Emission Estimates, 1940–1982.* Research Triangle Park, N.C.: Office of Air Quality.

*Waldbott, G. L., 1978. *Health Effects of Environmental Pollutants,* 2nd ed. St. Louis: C. V. Mosby.

*World Health Organization, 1978. "Air Quality in Selected Urban Areas in 1975–1976." *W. H. O. Publication No. 41.* Geneva: World Health Organization.

Young, W. A.; Show, O. B.; and Bates, D. V., 1964. "Effects of Low Concentrations of Ozone on Pulmonary Function in Man," *J. Applied Physiol.* **19**:765–769.

Zimmerman, P. R.; Greenberg, J.; Wandiga, S.; and Crutzen, P., 1982. "Termites: A Potentially Large Source of Atmospheric Methane, Carbon Dioxide, and Molecular Hydrogen," *Science* **218**:563–565.

Other general air pollution references are given after Chapters 10 and 11.

The Effects of Air Pollution

This chapter is about the effects of air pollutants on people, places, and things. More specifically, it covers the effects of air pollutants on human health, trees and crops, fish and other animals, climate, statues and paintings, buildings, fabrics, rubber gaskets, and other material things. All of these effects ultimately influence human welfare, in a way making this a chapter about the effects of air pollutants on things humans care about. Some humans care more than others about buildings, paintings, and statues; probably the greatest proportion of our fellow men and women care most directly about people. This assumption seems to suggest that we should begin with human health even though some of the other effects may prove to be far more important, even to people who care only about people.

THE EFFECTS OF AIR POLLUTION ON HUMAN HEALTH

There is an impressive amount of evidence linking air pollutants to respiratory disease in humans. In the first part of this chapter we review the effects that air pollutants have on cells and tissues, and we look at data linking air pollution and specific pollutants with diseases like emphysema, chronic bronchitis, lung cancer, dust diseases, and other respiratory diseases. In the middle of the chapter there is a special section on **epidemiology**, an investigative approach to medicine that looks at patterns of disease in groups or populations in relationship to various environmental factors. In the last part of the chapter we will look at the effects of air pollutants on things other than human beings.

Let's begin our consideration of the health effects of air pollutants by reviewing some basic anatomy and physiology of the respiratory tract, focusing on the built-in defense mechanisms against environmental insult.

The Respiratory Tract and Its Defenses

The basic anatomy of the respiratory tract, the lung, and the interface or the junctures of pulmonary blood vessels (capillaries) and air sacs (**alveoli**) is presented as Figure 10.1. The *alveolar sacs,* shown at the ends of tiny air ducts called *bronchioles,* serve collectively as the organ of gas exchange with the environment. In human beings the total surface area of the alveoli is approximately that of a tennis court. An area this large is required for the oxygen–carbon dioxide exchange serving the trillions of cells that make up the human body. (The reader may consult a textbook on human physiology to review the physiology of gas exchange.)

The respiratory tract contains built-in defense mechanisms against both particulate and gaseous air pollutants. These defenses are spread out along the passage leading from the nostrils to the most delicate portion of the respiratory tract, the alveoli.

The first line of defense is the nostril, especially the nasal hairs just inside. The hairs function like the air filters found in automobiles, air conditioners, and furnaces. Most *large* particles are caught in this first part of the respiratory tract and end up in the alimentary canal after being swallowed or are blown into handkerchiefs. Even some *gaseous* pollutants do not travel farther than the nasal passages because they are quickly absorbed. At high concentrations, some of these very same pollutants can cause damage in the upper respiratory tract, but here the damage is less important than it would be in the alveoli or the delicate bronchioles.

The sense of smell is another important defense mechanism. When we get a whiff of a pungent

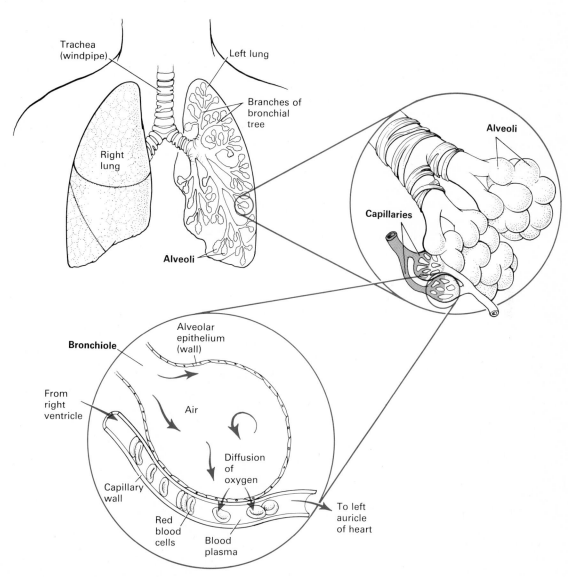

Figure 10.1 The Gross Anatomy of Respiratory Tract and the Microanatomy of the Site of Gas Exchange. The exchange of gases between a red blood cell and alveolar air depends in part on the distance between them. Pollutants cause an increase in the distance by stimulating the accumulation of fluid and thus impairs gas exchange.

chemical, we reflexively turn away, and the brain insists that it be taken away. This is an often overlooked defense mechanism—perhaps because not all dangerous airborne substances smell bad.

Particulate matter can be caught in the mucous membranes lining the respiratory tract from the nose into the upper portions of the bronchial tree. Particulate matter is thus entrapped is eventually blown out or is swallowed and passed into the gastrointestinal tract, from which it is either excreted directly or absorbed and then excreted by the kidney. The mucus or washout defense mechanism can be stepped up in the face of especially severe environmental insult. Tears and running noses (both of which serve to wash irritants away) are often reactions to irritating gases, as are the cough and the sneeze. Both of the latter irritation-initiated reflexes are also parts of the air pollution defense system. They are quite a bit more dramatic than the normally smooth, quiet, and unnoticeable action of the respiratory cilia.

Lining the upper and lower portions of the respiratory tract are cells with tiny hairs that beat in a coordinated rhythmic pattern so as to move toward the outside anything that becomes caught on them (Figure 10.2). These cilia carry mucus and trapped particles up and out of the respiratory tract to where they can be expelled or swallowed. Cigarette smoke retards the action of the cilia lining the respiratory tract and thereby acts as an important cofactor in the damage caused by many air pollutants. Smokers deprived of the action of the cilia are left only with a cough, which they sometimes suppress with lozenges.

Particles that make their way to the ends of the bronchioles into the alveoli must face the **alveolar macrophages**. These *phagocytic* (engulfing) cells are the last line of defense. They engulf particulates and work to digest them or to move them back up the respiratory tract to be carried out by cilia (ciliated cells do not extend down into the alveoli of the lung). While this system of phagocytes is particularly good at disposing of invading bacteria (which macrophages can also kill), the macrophages do not do very well with certain kinds of particulate material. As a result, certain kinds of particulate matter can become lodged in the lung more or less permanently. Smoking is also significant at the alveolar macrophage level; it has been shown that cigarette smoke can inhibit the action of these scavenger cells. A summary of the body's total "air defense" system is given in Figure 10.3.

Once they dissolve in tissue fluids and reach cells, the effects that pollutants have depend on their chemical properties (see Table 10.1) and consequent biochemical action (Table 10.2). Some pollutants are so reactive that they do their damage in the first

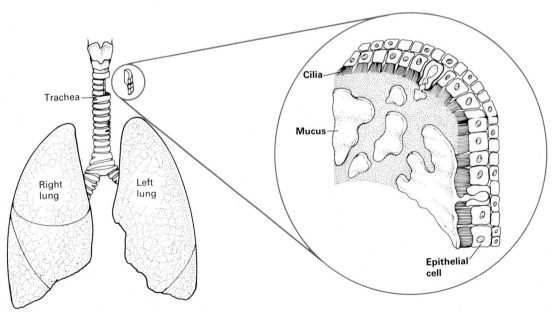

Figure 10.2   The Ciliated, Mucus-Covered Epithelium of the Human Airway. The respiratory tract is lined, except for the lower reaches, with cells bearing tiny hairlike cilia that undulate in a coordinated fashion, carrying debris caught in the mucus up and out of the respiratory tract.

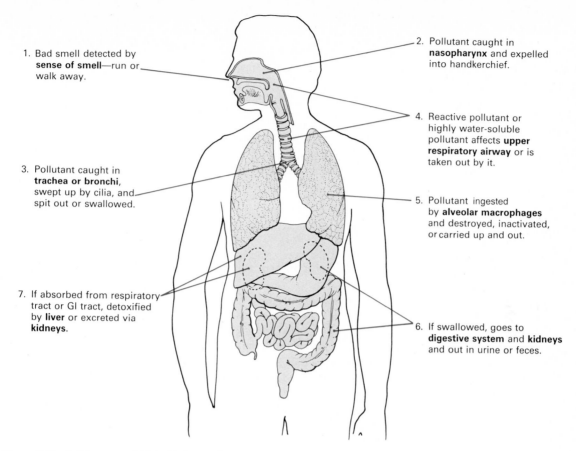

1. Bad smell detected by **sense of smell**—run or walk away.

2. Pollutant caught in **nasopharynx** and expelled into handkerchief.

3. Pollutant caught in **trachea or bronchi**, swept up by cilia, and spit out or swallowed.

4. Reactive pollutant or highly water-soluble pollutant affects **upper respiratory airway** or is taken out by it.

5. Pollutant ingested by **alveolar macrophages** and destroyed, inactivated, or carried up and out.

6. If swallowed, goes to **digestive system** and **kidneys** and out in urine or feces.

7. If absorbed from respiratory tract or GI tract, detoxified by **liver** or excreted via **kidneys**.

Figure 10.3   A Summary of Air Pollution Defense Mechanisms in the Human Body.

cells they encounter. Pollutants that are less reactive can be absorbed into the bloodstream and be carried in an active form to organs of detoxification and excretion like the liver and the kidney. Some may not be excreted or detoxified very rapidly and may accumulate in certain organs or tissues (for example, strontium-90 in bone, radioiodine in the thyroid, DDT in fat, lead in bone), where they may have cumulative, latent effects (see Chapters 13 and 14).

The Effects of Pollutants on Enzymes and Other Vital Parts of Cells   To have a health effect, pollutants must get at some crucial structural or functional substance in the body. Many of the effects of pollutants are the result of their ability to damage vital cell structures or to interfere with enzyme function.

Cells can do what they do only because of the enzymes that promote most biological reactions. In many enzymes, metals are integral parts of their structure. Zinc as a pollutant can interfere with enzymes that normally contain magnesium if zinc becomes substituted for magnesium in those enzymes. Metals and other kinds of pollutants can destroy enzymes by binding to them indiscriminately, causing various structural changes. Enzymes function only as long as they have a particular molecular shape. *Anything* that reacts with an enzyme can distort the enzyme's shape such that it can no longer combine with its substrate. Then vital reactions fail to occur. With the functionally impaired enzymes, cells die.

Pollutants that eventually react with structural components of the cell membrane or with other parts of the structural and chemical makeup of a cell can also result in cell death. A chemically damaged cell membrane may allow essential cellular constituents to escape or allow things normally kept out to get in. In either case the cell is likely to die. Pollutants that react with DNA, though they may most often kill the cell, can also cause mutation and cancer.

Table 10.1 Chemical Reactivities of the Major Air Pollutants

Pollutant	Effects
Sulfur dioxide	A water-soluble, rapidly diffusing, acid-forming oxidizing agent. Through various reactions in water, can form sulfurous acid and sulfuric acid, both of which react with organic matter as well as with metals and other materials.
Particulate matter	Airborne particles vary in properties depending upon their chemical nature. Droplets of sulfuric acid behave as sulfuric acid, for example. Solid particles can absorb various chemicals onto their surfaces.
Nitrogen dioxide	An oxidizing agent. Can react in water to form nitric acid. Being less soluble in water, NO_2 tends to travel further into the respiratory system. Nitric acid is a very powerful oxidizing agent capable of reacting with nearly all metals and most organic compounds, particularly lipids. NO_2 is also involved in production of ozone in the atmosphere.
Hydrocarbons (volatile hydrocarbons sometimes included in a larger group of volatile organic compounds)	Combine with many kinds of compounds; products have varied reactive properties. For example, carcinogenic hydrocarbon compounds can combine with DNA, causing mutations and cancer. Volatile hydrocarbons and other organic compounds also participate in atmospheric reactions generating ozone.
Carbon monoxide	Though only slightly soluble in water, extremely dangerous because it has a greater affinity for hemoglobin than does oxygen.
Ozone (and other photochemical oxidants)	Ozone is an unstable, very reactive oxidizing agent able to combine with many organic compounds in cells and tissues as well as with rubber and other materials.
Hydrogen sulfide	Behaves like a weak acid and can also act as a reducing agent, making it mildly reactive with various organic compounds and metals.
Fluorides	Very reactive reducing agents, can combine with many otherwise nonreactive inorganic and organic compounds.
Nitric oxide	Has little direct effect, being insoluble in water (tissue), but it can be converted to nitrogen dioxide.

Table 10.2 Biochemical Effects of the Major Air Pollutants

Pollutant	Effects
Sulfur dioxide	Tends to be absorbed quickly and acts in the upper respiratory tract; reacts with cellular constituent chemicals, e.g., enzymes. Sulfuric acid (H_2SO_4) lowers pH, impairing enzyme function, and/or destroys various functional molecules.
Particulate matter	Effect varies depending on the nature of the particles. Carbon particles and other particles cause scarring of lungs via complex walling off and fibrogenic reactions. Particles carrying absorbed mutagens lead to damaged DNA in the lung and elsewhere.
Nitrogen dioxide	Direct effects include the oxidation of cellular lipids; some nitric acid–mediated effects are similar to those described above for H_2SO_4.
Hydrocarbons (and volatile organic compounds in general)	Some can react with constituents of cells, for example, the carcinogenic hydrocarbons like benzopyrene (see Chapter 14) react with DNA, causing mutations.
Carbon monoxide	Competitively inhibits combination of oxygen and hemoglobin.
Photochemical Oxidants (e.g., ozone)	Oxidize cellular constituents.
Heavy metals	Can take the place of metals that are normal parts of enzymes or otherwise bind to enzymes, rendering them inactive. Other effects depend on the chemical nature of particular metals.

Tissue Reactions to the Death of Cells

The number of cells killed or altered will determine how generally felt a reaction to a pollutant will be. Cells die all the time in small numbers. The body's cells are replaced completely every six or seven years. However, when lots of cells die in an organ system in a short time, there may be drastic local and bodywide (**systemic**) effects.

As cells become damaged and die, they release substances (like histamine) that cause capillaries to **dilate** (expand) and become more permeable to water. As this happens, fluid is able to escape from the capillaries, causing localized tissue fluid accumulation. This is part of the reason why a wound or a bruise swells. Bruises become warmer because the blood supply to that area is increased. All of this serves to concentrate repair mechanisms in the injured area. But these mechanisms can go too far. Secretion of fluid in an irritated bronchiole, up to a point, can help wash out a pollutant; after that point, the accumulated fluid impairs gas exchange and causes respiratory distress.

Another outcome of the injury and death of cells is the scar. The body responds to the death of cells by replacing them with scar tissue, which serves to reinforce the injured area. While scars are good for many kinds of wounds, if scars develop beyond a certain point in organs that must be perfused (continually washed through by blood or air), such as the liver and the lung, these organs become less elastic and less functional. A less resilient lung or liver cannot be as well perfused with air or blood, respectively. As a consequence, lung and liver functions decrease. Impaired lung perfusion causes stress on the right heart and generalized stress on body tissues as the cardiovascular and respiratory systems' ability to deliver oxygen to the tissues decreases.

The buildup of scar tissue takes time (resulting from repeated injury), whereas the localized inflammation and swelling described above is an immediate effect of pollutants. We refer to scar formation as a **chronic effect** and to the irritation reaction as an **acute effect**. What air pollutants ultimately do to a human being physiologically is summarized in Table 10.3.

Table 10.3   Acute and Chronic Physiological Effects of Major Air Pollutants on Human Beings

Pollutant	Effects	
	Acute	Chronic
Sulfur dioxide	Gives rise to irritation reactions, which cause capillaries to dilate and exude fluid; this leads to tissue fluid accumulation and swelling (edema), bronchial spasms, and shortness of breath. General physiological reaction to SO_2 is similar to allergic asthma, i.e., with impaired pulmonary function via increased airway resistance, impaired lung clearance, and increased susceptibility to infection.	Contributes to and aggravates lung diseases like chronic bronchitis, pulmonary fibrosis via irritation leading to decreased pulmonary function and increasing stress on the heart.
Particulate matter	Depending on nature and size, particulate matter can cause irritation, altered immune defense, or systemic toxicity.	Again depending on the nature and size of the particles, particulate matter can cause decreased pulmonary function and stress on the heart.
Nitrogen dioxide	Incompletely understood, although cell membrane disruption appears to be the principal reasons for respiratory tract edema.	Cell membrane damage and acid-induced irritation leads to or contributes to diminished pulmonary function and right heart stress.
Carbon monoxide	Asphyxiation, heart and brain damage, impaired perception.	Increased red blood cells (polycythemia) in blood, leading to increased resistance to blood to flow; weakness, fatigue, headaches.
Photochemical oxidants (e.g., ozone)	Decreased pulmonary function and right heart stress as above.	Emphysema, fibrosis, right heart failure, aging of lung and respiratory tissue.
Hydrocarbons	The primary harm of hydrocarbons is in their participation in ozone production. Cancer is one kind of direct primary effect of some organic compounds.	

Major Classes of Air Pollution–Related Diseases

The following is one of many possible classification of diseases related to the general problem of community exposure to air contaminants:

1. pulmonary irritation and acute impairment of lung function (breathing);
2. cancer
3. structural changes;
4. systemic toxicity (e.g., lead poisoning)
5. suppression of host defense mechanisms, leading to increased susceptibility to infection; and
6. other types of reduced tissue oxygenation such as carbon monoxide asphyxiation.

This classification scheme is far from being clean and neat, since the categories overlap. However, it will serve as a useful framework within which we can consider some of the specific health effects of air contaminants.

Acute and Chronic Irritation Diseases and Impaired Lung Function

With even brief exposures to the oxides of sulfur (5 ppm for a few minutes), to nitrogen (e.g., 2 ppm for 10 minutes), or to ozone (see U.S. Environmental Protection Agency, 1982), breathing and gas exchange can be impaired because of **edema** (tissue fluid accumulation), mucus production, and bronchospasms (see Figure 10.4) secondary to irritation and inflammation. Bronchospasms, edema, and mu-

cus production impair air flow, decrease lung capacities, and decrease rates of gas exchange between blood and alveolar air because of the extra fluid the gases have to pass through. All of these tend to reduce the amount of oxygen delivered to the tissues throughout the body and tend to make the heart work harder. *Chronic* lung irritation, whether induced by air pollutants, cigarette smoking, living with cigarette smokers, allergic reactions, or *all* of the above, may lead to chronic conditions and ultimately to permanent structural alteration of the lungs.

Human beings who have asthma, chronic bronchitis, and/or emphysema get them principally through variable combinations of hereditary predisposition, smoking, and/or occupational exposures, helped along by exposure to air pollutants in the general environment. However they may come by their lung diseases, these individuals are some of the highly susceptible (to air pollutants) groups of people (along with the elderly and children) who are taken into account in establishing air quality health standards (see Chapter 11). Increased airway resistance has been reported in asthmatics with exposures to 0.1 ppm NO_2 for an hour. The same effect in healthy adults might not occur until NO_2 levels reach 2.5 ppm for several hours. With SO_2, asthmatics can show increased airway resistance at 0.1–0.5 ppm for a few hours or even minutes, whereas it might take up to 5 ppm for the same amount of time to produce equivalent effects in normal individuals (U.S. Environmental Protection Agency, 1982).

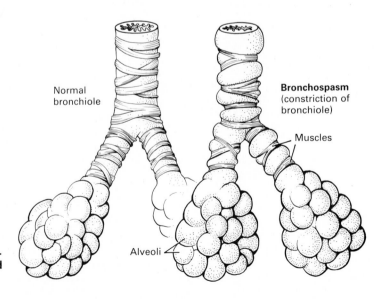

Normal bronchiole

Bronchospasm (constriction of bronchiole)

Muscles

Alveoli

Figure 10.4 Diagrammatic Representation of the Bronchial Muscle Spasms Caused by Irriation.

Alveolus: very small, thin-walled sac of the vertebrate lung. The alveoli are the sites of gas exchange between blood and air.

Chloroflurocarbons: a family of chemically stable compounds made up of hydrocarbons to which either chlorine or fluorine atoms are attached.

Cohort: in epidemiology a cohort is any defined group of people under observation, for example, those being checked periodically for the development of disease.

Enzyme: a protein or a principally proteinaceous molecule that catalyzes a chemical reaction, that is, facilitates conversion of a chemical substance from one form into another.

Epidemiology: an investigative approach to disease that looks for the factors that account for the frequency and patterns of disease within defined populations.

Hepatotoxin: a liver poison; any chemical substance that causes injury to the liver.

Macrophage: large cells found throughout the body that are capable of engulfing (by phagocytosis) invading particles or bacteria. (Literally, **macro** = big, **phage** = eater.)

Mutagen: any chemical or thing capable of altering cellular DNA such that a mutation results.

National Academy of Sciences: a nongovernmental American organization of scientists and engineers established by Congress in 1863. The Academy serves as an official adviser to the U.S. government in matters of science and technology.

National Research Council: a body established by the U.S. National Academy of Sciences in 1916 to coordinate the activities of scientists and engineers in government, industry, and universities.

Phagocyte: any of the cells of the human body that serve as a means of defense against invading bacteria by engulfing the bacteria.

Right heart: the right side of the heart. The right atrium receives blood from the venous system and ejects it into the right ventricle, which in turn pushes the blood into the lungs. It is the right heart that is stressed first in certain types of lung disease.

Substrate: that which enzymes act upon. Enzymes usually react with only specific substrates.

Vinyl chloride: a chemical substance that is polymerized to yield polyvinyl plastic.

Therefore it is important to note that bronchitis and emphysema have doubled in importance as diseases every five years for the last 20 years. In the mid-1980s, Americans were dying of emphysema, bronchitis, and bronchial asthma at the rate of 50,000 per year. Today, emphysema remains the fastest-growing cause of death in the United States. Emphysema, chronic bronchitis, and related chronic lung conditions are among the most significant causes of disability now compensated by Social Security.

Aggravated Asthma. Asthma is an allergic reaction in which the membranes of the bronchioles are irritated by inappropriately severe reaction to foreign materials such as pollen. The disease is marked by narrowing of airways caused by bronchospasms (see Figure 10.4), edema of bronchial linings, and oversecretion of mucus. There are various forms of asthma: **extrinsic asthma** is precipitated by external factors; **intrinsic asthma** can be precipitated, apparently in the absence of external factors, by such things as emotion and exercise. In an asthmatic attack, air literally becomes trapped in the lungs because it cannot be expelled. Breathing may, in severe cases, become so impaired as to result in oxygen starvation and death. Air pollutants in the class of

irritants are known to aggravate asthma; pollutants (such as certain particulate pollutants) may also be involved in the actual precipitation of asthma attacks.

Chronic Bronchitis. The problem in chronic bronchitis is inflammation and edema of the linings of the bronchi, resulting in increased mucus production and chronic coughing. The cough and continued mucus secretion cause more irritation and more mucus secretion and coughing, ultimately leading to the actual destruction of small bronchioles. Cigarette smoking and air pollution in industrial environments seem to be the major causes of chronic bronchitis. Air pollution in the more general environment can make matters worse by impairing clearance of mucus, impairing defense mechanisms that lead to infection, and adding to the irritation. Chronic bronchitis affects about one in five American males between the ages of 40 and 60.

Emphysema. As if it were not bad enough by itself, chronic bronchitis can lead to emphysema. Bronchospasms and accumulated mucus can in time conspire to trap air in the alveoli. The obstruction acts like a one-way valve allowing air to come in

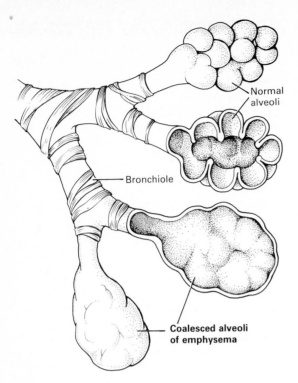

Figure 10.5 Diagrammatic Representation of Emphysema. This is a disease in which the walls of the alveoli break down, coalescing individual alveoli into larger sacs having an overall smaller total surface area. The effect is to decrease the ability of the lung to exchange gases.

during deep inspiration but keeping it from being expelled. Eventually, the walls of overinflated alveoli rupture, and several alveoli coalesce into fewer, bigger sacs. This irreversible phenomenon leads to emphysema. Because small sacs have larger surface-to-volume ratios than large sacs, emphysema amounts to a structural condition in which the surface area of the lung is reduced, resulting in reduced breathing efficiency—the lung cannot exchange gases normally (see Figure 10.5).

Cancer

Among the things that can be present in polluted air are certain chemical substances called **carcinogens**, which are able to react with DNA in such a way as to cause cancer. Inhaled carcinogens may cause cancer in respiratory tissues directly, or they may be picked up by the bloodstream and cause cancers in other body tissues. We have devoted Chapter 14 to cancer; we will not discuss it further here.

Dust Diseases

We have already discussed how irritants in contaminated air may eventually help bring about structural impairment and loss of lung function. The **pneumoconioses**, or dust diseases, are caused by a special class of air pollutants that bring about structural changes in lungs. The term pneumoconiosis applies to *all* of the dust diseases of the lungs. Two examples of dust disease are **silicosis**, in which the active ingredient is silicon dioxide, and **black lung** (or coal workers pneumoconiosis), in which the active ingredient is coal dust. Through a mechanism that is only poorly understood, dust in the lungs causes a response in which fibrous tissue is deposited around dust particles, creating "macules." The dusts that cause the pneumoconioses (see Table 10.4) are relatively inert and tend to stay in place over many, many years. The fibrotic reaction eventually decreases the function of the lungs; this in turn puts stress on the heart. While pneumoconioses tend to cause diffuse lung changes, certain fibrous tissue–generating agents such as beryllium and hair spray produce granular knots or lumps called granulomas (see Walbott, 1978). Granulomas also have an adverse effect on pulmonary function.

Systemic Toxins

Chemicals picked up from the environment by the lungs may cause disease in organs other than those of the respiratory tract. Air pollutants that get into the bloodstream via the lungs to cause problems in various other parts of the body (Figure 10.6) are called systemic toxins. Lead and mercury are prime examples of systemic toxins that can be picked up from the air. These were discussed in Chapter 9.

The Effect of Air Pollution on Resistance to Disease

A number of studies have shown that one of the most important effects of air pollution on health may be that it makes an individual more susceptible to infection. This possibility has been raised by many experiments with animals. In such studies, one group of animals is exposed to pollution while another is not; each group is then equally challenged with an infectious microorganism of some sort—the disease organism that causes pneumonia, for example. In one study it was shown that one third of the animals *not* exposed to pollution came down with pneumonia and died when challenged by a causative disease organism, but *all* of the animals previously exposed to nitrogen dioxide for just a short time died of pneumonia.

Colfin and Blommer (1967) showed that if mice were exposed to irradiated exhaust (irradiated to mimic the effects of solar radiation), they had much greater death rates due to subsequent challenges by streptococcal pneumonia than did controls (mice not subjected first to the exhaust). The study utilized concentrations of auto exhaust fumes that were somewhat *lower* than those found in heavily polluted city air. Experimental evidence like this indicates that many pollutants, for example, metals, organic pesticides, and gaseous pollutants, can in fact impair our immune defenses and make us more susceptible to infectious disease (Caren, 1981).

Asphyxiation

Carbon Monoxide. The chief environmental problem with carbon monoxide is that it combines with hemoglobin, competing with oxygen. In an atmosphere with more than 10 ppm carbon monoxide, even in the presence of normal amounts of oxygen, the blood can be rendered unable to carry sufficient oxygen to tissues. If as little as 5% of the hemoglobin in the blood is carrying carbon monoxide, the oxygen-carrying capacity of the blood is reduced to the extent that certain kinds of performance tests begin to reveal physiological impairment.

Because the affinity of carbon monoxide for hemoglobin is more than 200 times that of oxygen, there is some doubt that even extremely low levels of carbon monoxide are safe. As yet, there is no experimental evidence, or even any theoretical basis, for establishing a threshold level for carbon monoxide problems. The impairment of oxygen transfer by carbon monoxide is probably a continuum that ranges from severe impairment and death at very high concentrations down to no impairment at zero concentration.

It appears that most people suffer no problems when inhaled air contains concentrations below 10 ppm of carbon monoxide. At 100 ppm, however, nearly all humans experience headache, dizziness, and impaired perception. At 300–400 ppm even for a few minutes, vision is impaired, and there may even be nausea and abdominal pain. Exposure to 1000 ppm carbon monoxide for less than an hour is fatal. It is important to note that the key parameter is the percentage of blood hemoglobin in the form of *carboxyhemoglobin* (COHb). This percentage is related to the level of CO in ambient air, to the duration of exposure, and to the ventilation rate (which increases with exercise). In terms of carboxyhemoglobin, 3–4% COHb has been associated with reduced work efficiency in some people. Numerous studies have demonstrated decreased vigilance, altered perception, and decreased manual dexterity when COHb levels are 5–7% or greater (see U.S. Environmental Protection Agency, 1984).

Groups at special risk from CO exposure are fetuses and young infants, the elderly (especially those with heart and/or lung problems), and individuals with heart disease, lung disease, or anemia (including sickle-cell anemia) (U.S. Environmental Protection Agency, 1984).

Hydrogen Sulfide. Another major asphyxiant, hydrogen sulfide, is sometimes encountered in high concentrations in sewers and in various oc-

Table 10.4 Agents That Cause Scar Formation in Lung Tissue

Material	Disease Designation
Inorganic fibers and dusts	
Crystalline silica	Silicosis
Asbestos	Asbestosis
Talc	Talcosis
Coal (pure)	Coal workers' pneumoconiosis
Kaolin	Kaolinosis
Graphite	Graphite lung
Organic fibers and dusts	
Cellulose	Bagassosis
Cotton	Byssinosis
Flax	Byssinosis
Hemp	Byssinosis
Metallic Fumes	
Tin oxide	Stannosis
Iron oxide	Siderosis
Beryllium oxide	Berylliosis

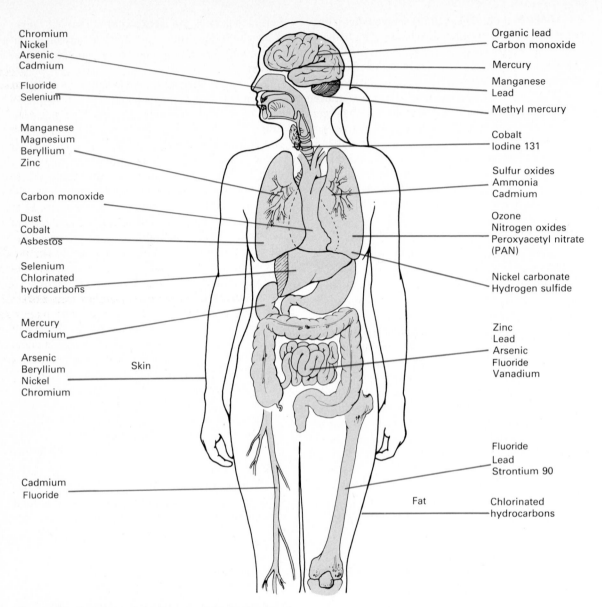

Chromium
Nickel
Arsenic
Cadmium

Fluoride
Selenium

Manganese
Magnesium
Beryllium
Zinc

Carbon monoxide

Dust
Cobalt
Asbestos

Selenium
Chlorinated
hydrocarbons

Mercury
Cadmium

Arsenic
Beryllium
Nickel
Chromium

Skin

Cadmium
Fluoride

Organic lead
Carbon monoxide

Mercury

Manganese
Lead

Methyl mercury

Cobalt
Iodine 131

Sulfur oxides
Ammonia
Cadmium

Ozone
Nitrogen oxides
Peroxyacetyl nitrate
(PAN)

Nickel carbonate
Hydrogen sulfide

Zinc
Lead
Arsenic
Fluoride
Vanadium

Fluoride
Lead
Strontium 90

Fat

Chlorinated
hydrocarbons

Figure 10.6 Summary of the Targets of Air Contaminants.

cupational settings. This toxic gas impairs tissue oxygenation indirectly by paralyzing the breathing control center in the brain. Although hydrogen sulfide's characteristic "rotten egg" odor gives it away at low concentrations, at higher concentrations it rapidly paralyzes the sense of smell and prevents any warning. Hydrogen sulfide apparently affects neurons by decreasing their ability to conduct impulses.

Metal Fume Fever

Fumes of certain metals—particularly manganese and zinc but also oxides of antimony, arsenic, cadmium, cobalt, copper, iron, lead, magnesium, mercury, nickel, and tin—can cause temperature elevations in those who breathe them. **Metal fume fever**, as this is called, is also accompanied by a dry throat, chest constriction, fatigue, headache, back pain, nausea, and muscle pain (Waldbott, 1978). Although primarily an occupational problem, metal fume–related health problems have also been reported in people living adjacent to metal processing plants.

Air Pollution and Feeling Good

According to some reports, people do not function very well on smoggy days—they suffer from impaired efficiency. For some people, at least, pollution brings a decrease in the internal feeling of well-being. Studies have shown that there are more absenteeism, higher accident rates, and higher suicide rates during unfavorable weather and on overcast and smoggy days. Some people believe that smog is at least *partly* responsible for *some* of these effects. Certain studies have suggested that smog leads to personality changes and accentuates traits such as forgetfulness and irritability. Such effects seem to be most pronounced on the first day of a pollution episode.

Since, as the World Health Organization defines it, **health** is a state of complete physical, mental, and social well-being and not merely the absence of disease or infirmity, effects on these kinds of conditions must be included in any discussion of the health effects of pollutants. While feeling good may be more subjective than a disease like emphysema, not feeling good may have indirect impacts that equal or surpass the negative impact of specific disease. For instance, the California Department of Public Health reports that as the level of photochemical oxidants rises, so does the accident rate. As another example, carbon monoxide at low levels may not have much of a direct impact on mortality rates, but in its negative effects on perception, particularly among people driving automobiles at high rates of speed, it may ultimately have considerable impact.

EPIDEMIOLOGY: A POPULATION-BASED APPROACH TO ENVIRONMENTAL DISEASE

The Place of Epidemiology in Understanding Disease

As was pointed out by Mausner and Bahn (1974), there are three fundamental ways of studying human disease. They are

1. the basic science approach (studies using experimental animals, biochemicals, etc.),
2. the clinical approach (studies of sick people and volunteer experimental subjects), and
3. the epidemiological approach.

The *basic science approach* is concerned with every detail of the causes (**etiology**) and the biochemical, biological, and physiological steps involved in the progression (**pathogenesis**) of the disease in question. What is the causative factor? How does it get in? Where does it go? How is it metabolized? How is it excreted? What tissues are affected? What happens to the factor in water? In air? What exactly does it do at first? What happens then?

The *clinical scientist* is more directly concerned with the impact on the individual human. What measurable changes occur in the exposed human that might be used to detect the presence and determine the extent of disease? What are the physiological symptoms? What will arrest the disease? What will relieve the symptoms?

The third approach, the community, population, or *epidemiological approach,* examines the relative frequency of disease within a defined population and within subgroups of that population. What kinds of people are getting sick? Is the disease more prevalent among the young? The old? Factory workers? Does the disease exhibit a pattern that indicates that it is communicable?

Another way of saying all of this is that epidemiology is one of several important ways of studying the relationship between environmental contaminants and disease. First, animals, plants, living cells, and even biochemicals can be exposed to the environmental contaminants under investigation to see what happens. Second, human volunteers can (under some circumstances) be exposed to see what happens to people directly. Third, the patterns of relationship between disease and exposures can be systematically observed in large groups of people. In the real world, all the three approaches are almost always employed in concert. For example, epidemiology might discover that those who work with a particular chemical have relatively high rates of cancer. Laboratory scientists might then expose experimental animals to a suspected causative agent to confirm or refute the connection experimentally. If and when a connection is confirmed, clinicians would begin to look more carefully for the symptoms of disease among people who have been exposed to the agent. The order of the involvement of the three approaches is variable; any one of the approaches might initially lead to the suspicion that there is a connection between specific agents and a disease.

In 1974 Dr. John Creech, a physician in Louisville, Kentucky, observed that an unusual number of vinyl chloride workers had died of a rare liver cancer (hepatic angiosarcoma). Subsequent epidemiologic checks of death certificates confirmed the significance of this relationship. Almost simultaneously, scientists in Italy confirmed that vinyl chloride caused cancer in animals. Laboratory scientists and clinicians throughout the world then went to work investigating just how vinyl chloride "caused" liver cancer and how the cancer might be detected, diagnosed, and treated.

For reasons that may not become entirely clear until after we get through Chapter 14, we have singled out epidemiology for emphasis here. One reason for this is that epidemiology is a bit more abstract and less straightforward than experiments with animals or people. The most important reason for the emphasis, however, is that epidemiology has special importance in connection with environmental diseases. Epidemiology can help make up for the facts that animals do not always react the same as humans to environmental contaminants and humans cannot ethically be deliberately exposed to any amount of, say, suspected cancer-causing agents. In some cases, epidemiology—which is really a way of collecting data from exposures that are going on anyway—may be the only way to document the effect of a particular contaminant on human beings.

What Do Epidemiologists Do?

Epidemiologists study the patterns of disease (incidence over time, spatial distribution, etc.) within defined groups of people (a county, a state, a metropolitan area, etc.) and the relationships of these patterns to *other* patterns within that group (for example, occupational patterns, residential patterns, who drinks water coming from what sources). Epidemiologists try to match up patterns of disease with other patterns in an effort to identify possible cause-and-effect relationships. More often, epidemiologists try to *confirm* or *refute* match-ups already under suspicion. For example, after the initial observation that "an unusually large number of vinyl chloride workers died of liver cancer," epidemiologists went to work to assess just how much greater the risk of liver cancer is to vinyl chloride workers with varying degrees of historical exposure. Another way of defining **epidemiology** is that it is the study of patterns of disease within defined populations and the factors that are responsible for, or that influence, those patterns.

One of the key words in the preceding definition is the word "defined." Perhaps the most easily missed or the most readily misunderstood feature of the epidemiological approach to studying disease is that epidemiology is dependent on *rates* of disease. The importance of the word *defined* (as a modifier of group or population) lies in the need for a denominator to give meaning to expressions of magnitude. Three hundred cancer deaths in a year would be high in a group of 6000 people. The same number might be normal in a group of 100,000 people and low in a group of one million. The point is that the numbers of people with a certain disease can have meaning only in terms of the number of people who might have developed the disease. Further, this is only meaningful in terms of the rate of disease in some standard or control population. Time is another important dimension here. Epidemiologists can work with "morbidity" expressed in terms of time, that is, the percent of people who have the disease at one particular point in time or the number who are diagnosed within a given period of time (e.g., per year). If **mortality** (death) is used, this must also be qualified in terms of some defined period of time.

In terms of our earlier example, if someone came up to you and reported finding three cases of liver cancer, you might reply, "So what? A lot of people die of liver cancer each year—especially in Africa." If someone came up to you and reported the discovery of three cases in two years of a rare form of liver cancer in a single group of 1200 American vinyl chloride workers, you might be more impressed. You might be moved to ask the key question, "How prevalent or how common is liver cancer among people in general?" Suppose someone came forward and reported finding three cases of a certain type of liver cancer among 1200 vinyl chloride workers in a single plant and added that only 25 or 30 cases of this type of liver cancer had been reported in the whole world that year. In such a case, you could be fairly sure that an occupational disease had been discovered.

Although the vinyl chloride–hepatic angiosarcoma relationship was discovered in just such a way, differences in relative rates are usually not nearly so impressive. Epidemiologists usually work with small relative differences in rates of disease between the group of people exposed to some agent and those not exposed.

In epidemiological investigations, precise mathematical analyses are required, and extreme care must be given to the methods by which disease is observed, measured, and cataloged in well-defined groups. Great caution must be exercised to ensure that "apples are always being compared to apples." Chemical workers may have significantly greater or less risk of developing certain diseases than people in general. But these rates might be identical to rates in groups of nonchemical workers with similar distributions of age, sex, race, and/or socioeconomic status. Let's consider the concept of controls in a bit more detail.

Control Groups

As was pointed out by Lave and Seskin (1979), if an association is found between "exposure to air pollution in cities" and "lung disease," say lung cancer, there would be four possible explanations. Assuming that there was no bias in the way the sampling of city and noncity dwellers and smokers and nonsmokers was carried out:

1. the observation is a false, chance occurrence resulting from the way the sampling was done;
2. air pollution causes or contributes to lung disease;
3. lung disease causes or contributes to air pollution; and
4. there is some third factor that is responsible for *both* lung disease and air pollution.

To conclude that air pollution is a cause or contributing factor in lung disease, the other three explanations have to be ruled out. Generally the first possibility is ruled out by repeating the study a number of times, and the third possibility is usually ignored. It is the fourth possibility that gives epidemiologists the most trouble, and this is where controls come in. The selection of a control group is intended to minimize the possibility that other factors might line up on one side or the other side of the comparison being made. If cities have high proportions of smokers, old people and males and if old people, smokers, and males have high rates of lung cancer, it could be falsely concluded that cities cause lung cancer.

Age offers a particularly good case showing that great care must be taken to compare apples with apples in epidemiology research. Since cancer is largely a disease of the relatively old, investigators must be sure that differences in cancer rates between two populations is not a result of the fact that one population has proportionately more old people in it. This does not mean that comparisons cannot be made between populations having different age pro-

files; it does mean that if such comparisons are made, the data have to be *age adjusted*. Typically, this is done by comparing the age-specific rates of the two populations in some way. If a particular population is being compared to a large standard population, say, that of the whole United States, then the age-specific rates for the standard population can be used to calculate an "expected" number of cancers for the number of people in each age bracket of the population being evaluated. This expected number of cancer cases can then be compared to the actually observed number, any difference or ratio then being subjected to a statistical test of significance. This indirect method or other methods of making mathematical adjustment in populations being compared can also be applied to sex, race, and other factors that might influence rates of cancer in populations.

Epidemiologists work very hard to find control groups that are matched for as many other factors as possible. The effects of benzopyrene on lung cancer would best be studied (epidemiologically) by comparing the rates of lung cancer in a city having high benzopyrene levels with the rates in a city that has low levels but is otherwise identical."

Obviously, no two cities or groups of any sort are identical, and this is the curse with which all epidemiologists must live. The task then amounts to controlling confounding variables to the extent possible. Among the most common variables controlled in epidemiological studies are age, sex, race, and socioeconomic status.

Retrospective and Prospective Epidemiology

Epidemiology has the advantage of being able to look forward and backward. Suppose, by way of example, that we were concerned that a certain type of skin cancer was possibly caused by exposure to a certain pesticide. One of the first steps we might take would be to identify as many people as possible in whom the cancer was diagnosed within a certain (large enough) period of time. These would then be matched with an equal number of similar people who have never had the cancer and do not have it now. We could then look into the histories of the two groups and determine the proportion of those *with* the cancer exposed to the pesticide versus the proportion of those *without* the cancer exposed to the pesticide. If it turned out that a very high proportion of those with the cancer in question were exposed to the pesticide and relatively few of those in the control group had ever been exposed to the chemical, we might hypothesize that there was a connection. This type of backward-looking study (**retrospective study**) is called a *case-control study*.

Our second step might be to watch groups of exposed and nonexposed people over time to see how many of each group develop skin cancer, for example. This would be a forward-looking or **prospective study**. Prospective studies start with exposure and look into the future for disease; retrospective studies generally start with disease today and look back for exposure (Table 10.5). Retrospective studies may also look back for both exposure and disease. Perhaps we should describe and contrast *prospective* and *retrospective* studies, cohort studies, and case-controlled studies more carefully.

Retrospective case-control studies are those in which people with the disease in question are compared to similar people who do not have the disease (controls). Epidemiologists look to see whether members of the two groups were exposed differently to various environmental or other factors, that is, if more of those *with* the disease were exposed to something suspected as a cause of the disease.

In retrospective studies it is important that criteria establishing the study groups be delineated as precisely as possible and that the number of cases of disease include all of those that appear in a specified (and long enough) time period. This is necessary in order to avoid missing patients with a very short disease course (because they die rapidly or because they are cured quickly). Controls must be very carefully selected in such studies. If the control group is not matched with the disease group for everything other than exposure to the factor under suspicion, then it is possible that some factor could confound any relationship between the suspected factor and the disease.

Incidence rates cannot be derived in case-control studies because the number of people who were at risk is not known (that is, there is no basis on which to determine the size of the group from which the identified cases arose). Once a case-control study is completed, however, the relative degree of extra risk for those exposed can be estimated. Case-control studies can yield a **relative risk factor** or **odds ratio**, defined as the ratio of the odds of a person with disease having been exposed to the odds of a person free of disease having been exposed. We might learn from such a study that a person who smoked more than two packs of cigarettes per day is roughly 24 times more likely to have died of lung cancer than a matched nonsmoker.

The main advantage of case-control studies is that they are inexpensive because the number of subjects evaluated can be relatively small. The main disadvantages of all retrospective studies are that information about past exposure may not be available and that if it is available, it may be inaccurate. Information provided by an informant about the past may be biased as well. Another serious disadvantage is the difficulty in selecting an appropriate control group. More on this problem later.

Cohort studies are really organized ways of collecting data from inadvertent "experiments" with

Table 10.5 Comparison of Retrospective and Prospective Studies of the Relationship Between Disease and Causative Agents

Study	Past	Present	Future
Retrospective Case-control study	Look for differences in exposure to various "factors" in the disease cases and in the controls ←	Find documented cases of disease and match these with an equal or larger number of people who are similar but free of disease	
Cohort study	Go back to document exposure in a cohort of people and then look for subsequent disease rates in their medical records ←	Find out about a suspicious relationship	
Prospective Cohort study		Select a group of people free of disease and classify them according to degree of exposure to a factor (or factors) under suspicion →	Follow the groups over time and observe the frequency with which disease develops in groups exposed to various levels.

human subjects. Such studies start with a group of people (usually a much larger one than a case-control study would require) free of disease but with known exposure to some suspicious agent. This group is then followed to see which people in the group develop disease and/or whether those who have higher exposure to the suspected agent are more likely to develop the disease. The group (cohort) selected for a prospective epidemiological study may either be heterogeneous with respect to previous exposure to the factor under study or be restricted to those having high (or low) exposure only. Cohort studies may be retrospective or prospective, as long as the starting point is exposure and not disease.

The size of the cohort to be studied depends on a number of factors, not the least of which is the expected incidence or, reciprocally, the relative rarity of the disease. The study group would obviously have to be very large if it were expected at the outset that only a small percentage would develop the disease. Other size-determining factors include the availability of subjects, access to medical records, and the size of the group that has been exposed to reasonably high levels of a particular agent.

Cohort studies allow investigators to determine the absolute as well as the relative risk of developing disease in people exposed to a factor under question. Data derived from cohort studies can be expressed as either relative risk or attributable risk. **Relative risk** is an expression of how many times more likely one group is to develop disease than another. **Attributable risk** is the absolute difference in incidence rate between the exposed group and the nonexposed group. Attributable risk is literally the number of deaths per unit number of people that can apparently be directly attributed to exposure to a factor (e.g., smoking) under consideration.

A major advantage of cohort studies over case-control studies is that there are fewer opportunities for bias to creep in. The people under study are classified as to exposure before anything is known about disease. One other major advantage of the cohort approach is that any kind of relationship between exposure and disease can be discovered. That is, in addition to confirming or refuting a specific relationship under suspicion, prospective studies offer a chance to discover other relationships as well (since a large number of people will be followed very closely).

The main disadvantage of the cohort approach is that it involves large numbers of people over a long period of time and is therefore very expensive.

The Trouble with Controls and the Trouble with Epidemiology

We mentioned earlier that there is no such thing as a perfect control group. A consequence of this and some other limitations inherent in the epidemiological approach is that conclusions derived from epidemiological investigation are far from absolute. This much may be obvious to the sophisticated reader who knows that absolute answers really do not come even from much more precise and more completely controlled laboratory investigations. Epidemiologists can be fairly exacting in establishing the degree of correlation between a disease and suspected etiologic agent. But even when correlations are nearly perfect, nothing can really be *absolutely* inferred in the way of cause and effect.

In science, as in courtrooms, association is considered circumstantial evidence, although "guilt" can eventually become established through consistent association. Proof of the sort that comes from elegantly constructed laboratory experiments does not happen in epidemiological investigations. Proof usually emerges only gradually. Often it does not emerge fast enough. This is one of the major reasons why despite large volumes of circumstantial evidence, pollution control and the relationship between smoking and health continue to generate controversy.

Epidemiological Evidence That Air Pollution Is Indeed a Real Health Problem

Much of the general information we have about the relationship between air pollution and disease has come from epidemiological studies. Some of these studies have focused on air pollution in general rather than on one specific pollutant because of the difficulty of sorting out specific pollutants in the air where people live. In an early study reported in the *British Journal of Preventive Social Medicine* (Fairbairn and Reid, 1958), for example, postmen who lived in the northeast part of London, the most heavily polluted part of the city, had a higher rate of respiratory disease, greater frequency of earlier retirement, and greater numbers of deaths from chronic lung disease than postmen who lived in other areas. In another study it was determined that in Erie County, New York, children living in areas of the county with low levels of pollution were hospitalized for asthma at a lower rate per 100,000 people than children in more heavily polluted areas of the same county.

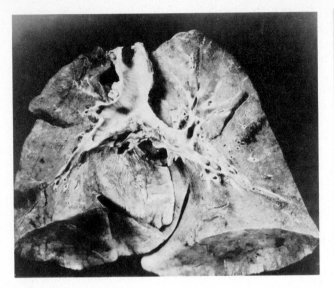 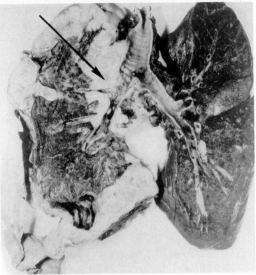

The link between cigarette smoking and lung cancer is clear. At left are the healthy lungs of a non-smoker; at right are the lungs of a heavy smoker with lung cancer (the arrow indicates the area of cancer).

An American Lung Association pamphlet describes another county showing that of the 38,200 deaths in Nashville, Tennessee over a 12-year period, more people died of breathing ailments in parts of the city that were heavily polluted than in less polluted areas. The same pamphlet also describes a British study based on observations of a cohort of 3866 children followed from birth to the age of 15. This study determined that there was a definite relationship between the rates of lower respiratory tract infection and life in high-pollution environments.

A later chapter of this book is devoted to cancer, but it is appropriate to mention here that one of the most well-documented connections between pollution and health has to do with the relationship between air pollution and lung cancer. While acknowledging that cigarette smoking is the main culprit, the National Research Council has blamed the rising tide of lung cancer at least partly on the quality of the air over American cities. Lung cancer is *the* greatest cause of cancer deaths in cities. In some cities the incidence of lung cancer is twice that in rural regions. The link between lung cancer and smoking may account partially for this; that is, there may be differences in the smoking habits of city folk and rural dwellers. It is more likely, however, that the increased risk of lung cancer comes from the combination of cigarette smoking and the unhealthful elements of city air and/or exposure to other things

characteristic of cities. Lave and Seskin (1970), who evaluated a number of studies done in England comparing rural and urban air, claim that there is significant evidence of an association between air pollution and lung cancer. Their report went further, however, suggesting that for both males and females the incidence of more than 16 different kinds of cancer was higher in cities than it was in rural areas.

Episodic studies have been done attempting to find correlations between days of high air pollution levels and admissions to hospitals for respiratory problems. Close correlations have generally been found between bad air days and respiratory diseases, including bacterial infection, influenza, bronchitis, allergic disorders, and cardiovascular diseases.

Some studies have attempted to relate respiratory disorders to more specific air pollution measurements. In New York City, young children were found to have greater respiratory disease problems in areas or on days in which there were high levels of particulate matter and carbon monoxide in the environment. In a classic Chicago study of air pollution and its relationship to disease it was determined that serious respiratory disease or aggravation of disease in individuals with chronic lung disease—especially in older age groups—was much higher when sulfur dioxide levels were high. This relationship was found to exist on the day on which the exposure occurred, and it was even stronger for disease problems observed on the day *following* exposure (Carnow, Lepper, Shelelle, and Stamler, 1969).

A number of difficulties are associated with episodic studies of the kind just described; not the least of these is the fact that by looking at death rates during a particular high excursion of certain air pollutants, one is really singling out those members of the population most highly susceptible to disease, those already weak or sick.

In their comprehensive look at the literature concerning the relationship between air pollution and disease, Lave and Seskin (1970) concluded that abatement of air pollution could bring about a 10–15% decrease in death due to heart disease. They say that there is a strong relationship between death due to bronchitis and air pollution and that mortality due to bronchitis could be reduced up to one half in certain places by eliminating air pollution episodes and reducing levels of pollution overall. They further suggested that a 10% overall decrease in particulate matter would decrease the infant death rate overall by seven tenths of a percent, the neonatal death rate by six tenths of a percent, and the fetal death rate by nine tenths of a percent. The National Research Council has estimated that if air pollution were reduced in and around U.S. cities by half, the lung cancer rates might be reduced by as much as 20%. Recent EPA criteria documents (e.g., U.S. Environmental Protection Agency, 1978) and staff papers (U.S. Environmental Protection Agency, 1982) document numerous epidemiological studies linking air pollution and human disease. The reader is referred to these documents for an up-to-date account.

THE EFFECTS OF AIR POLLUTION ON OTHER ANIMALS, PLANTS, MICROORGANISMS, AND ECOSYSTEMS

We presented the effects of air pollution on human health first, not because this is necessarily the most important effect of air pollution on the planet earth, but simply because they relate most directly to the organisms reading these pages and because they are among the most direct kinds of effects. Another important problem may well be the effect that air pollution has on life forms in general. Unfortunately, difficult as it is to establish tight connections between human health and pollution, the effects of pollution on the balance in nature and on ecosystems are considerably more difficult to establish.

The Effects of Air Pollution on Animals Other Than *Homo sapiens*

There *have* been studies showing harmful effects of air pollution on animals; not surprisingly, most of these involved species in which humans have an economic interest. Fluorides, for example, have been shown to cause more worldwide damage to farm animals than any other kind of pollutant. We described the health effects of fluorides on humans in Chapter 9. In other animals, similar kinds of effects have been documented by Lillie (1970). Most fluoride problems in animals have occurred among livestock pastured in and around aluminum smelters. Waldbott (1978) described several cases of lead poisoning in animals allowed to graze near lead smelters. Other air pollutants that have been shown to have an adverse effect on farm animals are selenium, molybdenum, and mercury. Though it has not been well documented, we must assume that wildlife and domestic animals are affected by air pollutants in the same general ways as humans and domestic animals.

The Effects of Air Pollution on Plants

Damage to plants by air pollutants has been known since the beginning of the twentieth century, but what were once only isolated episodes have become more general and more widespread. A list of air pollutants and the plants they affect is given in Table 10.6.

According to reports published by the EPA, the air pollutants most responsible for plant damage are oxidants such as ozone, sulfur dioxide, acids derived from the oxides of both sulfur and nitrogen (see the section on acid rain), and various particulates; misapplied herbicides have also been reported to damage crops. Plants that are susceptible to these kinds of pollutants include vegetables, fruits, other kinds of agricultural crops, grasses, shrubs, trees, and commercial flowers (see Marx, 1975). The susceptibility of plants to pollutants is influenced by such variables as temperature, wind, light intensity, soil fertility, and relative humidity. High soil moisture and atmospheric humidity actually intensify the damage (McLaughlin and Taylor, 1981).

A particularly poignant example illustrating the extent to which pollutants can affect crops was the severe damage to the potato crop on the Eastern Shore of Virginia in the summer of 1971, which was linked to oxidant pollution (Marx, 1975). This was a profound episode in that up to half the potato crop was lost during that summer. In the United States,

Table 10.6   Effects of Air Pollutants on Plants

Chemical	Symptom	Sensitive Plants*	Examples of Concentration for Sensitivity
Chlorine	Bleaching, leaf tip and margin browning, dropping of leaves, yellow spots	Radish, alfalfa, peach, buckwheat, corn, tobacco, oak, white pine	Radish, 1.3 ppm
Fluorides	Leaf tip and margin yellowing (chlorosis), dwarfing, leaf abscission, decreased yield	Gladiolus, tulip, apricot, blueberry, corn, grape, blue spruce, white pine	Gladiolus, apricot, 0.1 ppb
Nitrogen oxides	Brown spots on leaf, suppression of growth	Azalea, sunflower, mustard, tobacco, pinto bean	Pinto beans, 3 ppm
Sulfur dioxide	Bleached spots on leaf, chlorosis, suppression of growth, early abscission, reduced yield	Barley, pumpkin, alfalfa, cotton, wheat, lettuce, apple, oats, aster, zinnia, birch, elm, white pine, ponderosa pine	Alfalfa, barley, cotton, 0.3 ppm
Ozone	Reddish brown flecks on upper surface of leaf, bleaching, suppression of growth, early abscission, premature aging	Alfalfa, barley, bean, oat, onion, corn, apple, grape, tobacco, tomato, spinach, aspen, maple, privet, white pine, ponderosa pine	Tomato, tobacco, 0.05 ppm
Other oxidant gases, e.g., peroxyacetyl nitrate (PAN)	Glazing, silvering or bronzing of lower surface of leaf	Pinto bean, mustard, oat, tomato, lettuce, petunia, blue grass	Petunia, lettuce, 0.2 ppm
Unsaturated hydrocarbons, e.g. ethylene	Leaf abscission, dropping of flowers, loss of flower buds, chlorosis, suppression of growth	Orchid blossom, carnation blossom, azalea, tomato, cotton, cucumber, peach	Orchids, 0.005 ppm Tomatoes, 0.1 ppm

*Certain varieties of these plants are sensitive.

ozone is believed to be responsible for 90% of all air pollution–related crop damage, amounting to some one to two billion dollars each year (Skarby and Sellden, 1984; Heck et al., 1983; and Adams et al., 1982). Discussion of the economic impact of air pollutants on crops will be extended in Chapter 11.

Air pollution affects plants in many of the same chemically fundamental ways that it affects animals—by the oxidation of cellular constituents and enzymes, for example. Some of the primary symptoms that appear in plants are **chlorosis** (yellowing, which reflects an impaired ability by plants to manufacture chlorophyl) and the destruction of leaf tissue. As with animals, the influence of pollutants on plants extends to weakening them to the point at which they are more susceptible to attack by infectious agents or other natural enemies. Oxidants like ozone, for instance, are believed to weaken ponderosa pines to the extent that the trees are more susceptible to the western bark beetle. The pine dies of complications of bark beetle infection rather than

the oxidant directly—but dead is dead. There are other examples of disease in plants that are aggravated by oxidant injury. Air pollutants may also be responsible for some other subtle effects on plants such as impaired reproduction and germination through increased mutation rates (Marx, 1975).

Some see damage to crops by air pollutants as an enormous problem with worsening implications for the future. To others this is only a remote concern. Most farmers see the damage due to SO₂ as only one of a number of problems with their crops. The effects of things like SO₂ are in fact difficult to distinguish from the effects of insects, nutrient imbalances, and weather. For an extended general discussion of the effects of acid deposition on vegetation, including agricultural crops and forests, see the work of Helvey, Kunkle, and Dewalle, (1983) and Irving (1984) and various EPA criteria documents and staff papers (U.S. Environment Protection Agency, 1982) specific for each pollutant. See also the upcoming section on acid rain.

Air Pollution As Fertilizer?

Most fertilizers contain phosphorus, nitrogen, and potassium but no sulfur, even though sulfur is the fourth most important plant nutrient. In the early 1950s it was shown that plants absorb sulfur directly from the atmosphere and incorporate it into the materials that make up the plant (Maugh, 1979). This has led to the suggestion (see Maugh, 1979) that agricultural crops in the United States may have become dependent on the sulfur in air pollution. It is conceivable that where soils are locally deficient in sulfur, atmospheric inputs may in fact help fertilize plants. Given the many negative impacts of sulfur oxide air pollution, this is not much of an argument in favor of air pollution. It does perhaps suggest a future use of the sulfur scrubbed from smokestacks.

Plants as Early Warning Systems

Some plants are very sensitive to pollutants (Table 10.6), and it has been suggested that plants can serve as warning systems for chemicals in the air, much as canaries were once used in coal mines. One can easily imagine a system in which the plants that are most sensitive to a particular kind of pollutant are planted in particular locations and checked periodically as indicators of the recent history of air pollution in that area. While a problem with this is that it would give after-the-fact information, this kind of biological assay has the advantage that it would integrate and sum the effect of pollution on living things.

The Effects of Air Pollution on Ecosystems

Although the effects of air pollutants on ecosystems would represent a kind of bottom line in our consideration of the effects of such pollutants, unfortunately, we still know very little about effects at this level.

We do know a few things. We know, for instance, that air pollutants can inhibit nitrogen fixation. Ozone and sulfur dioxide reduce the ability of bacteria to fix nitrogen at or just below the levels that are known to have some *health* effect. Ozone has been found to reduce ammonia-nitrogen in some soils, possibly having an adverse effect on the growth of trees and other plants.

It has been shown that oxides of nitrogen can also be a problem for ecosystems through enrichment. According to a report based on a study done in New Jersey, in one episode, rain brought 25 pounds of nitrogen to the ground per acre, the source of the nitrogen being oxides of nitrogen gen-erated industrially. While this could actually benefit ecosystems through increased production, nitrates accumulated too rapidly can cause ecosystem imbalances.

The 1983 Annual Report of the Council on Environmental Quality lists the federal agencies involved in research at the ecosystem level. Included are the National Science Foundation, the Environmental Protection Agency, the Department of Energy, the Department of Agriculture, the Forest Service, and the National Ocean and Atmospheric Administration. Among the things being studied are:

— the best indication of human-induced changes in ecosystems;
— predictive models of ecosystem function;
— the nature and extent of the ability of ecosystems to adapt to insult;
— the fate of things put into ecosystems by human beings—acidity, for example; and
— the assimilative capacity of ecosystems for various kinds of wastes.

Most of the ongoing studies are relatively recent in origin and have produced little as yet in way of solid information. The acid rain problem has stimulated a greatly intensified interest in the impact of pollutants on ecosystems. This promises to yield information about the general workings of systems and their responses to impacts of many kinds.

ACID RAIN: WHAT GOES UP MUST COME DOWN—SOMEWHERE, SOMETIME, IN SOME FORM

The earliest published reference to acid rain was made by an English chemist, Robert A. Smith, in 1872, in a book entitled *Air and Rain: The Beginnings of a Chemical Climatology* (Cowling, 1982). Modern scientific awareness of acid rain began with agricultural scientist Hans Egner in the late 1940s and limnologist Eville Gorham and meteorologists Carl Rossby, Christian Junge, and Erik Eriksson in the 1950s. A comprehensive picture was developed by Svante Oden, a Swedish soil scientist, beginning in the late 1960s, providing the outline of the acid rain picture we have today.

In the early 1970s it became widely noticed that lakes without any known source of acid (such as coal mine seepage) in Canada, the northeastern United States, and Scandinavian countries were becoming increasingly acidic and that fish were disappearing from them. Acidification of lakes was reported at about the same time in England, Brazil, and Scotland (Reisner, 1977). Acid from the sky seemed to be the only explanation, and monitoring demonstrated that rainfall and even snow did indeed carry notable acidity. Today's acid rain issue was born.

We appear to be stuck with the term *acid rain* even though the problem is really a more general acid deposition problem. Acid or acid-forming materials may be deposited from the air in the form of snow, sleet, fog, or even as gases or dry particulate matter—as well as in the form of rain.

Acid rain should have been no surprise. Everything, and there are no exceptions, must go somewhere. For a hundred years or more we have been burning enormous quantities of coal and oil and smelting enormous quantities of ore. Coal (and to a lesser extent oil) and the ores of many metals (e.g., copper, nickel, lead, and zinc) contain sulfur. In the presence of oxygen at high combustion temperatures, sulfur compounds are oxidized to become sulfur oxides (SO_x). Combustion at high temperatures in power plants, smelters, and automobiles also creates oxides of nitrogen, mostly as atmospheric nitrogen combines with oxygen. In Chapter 9 we described how the oxides of both sulfur and nitrogen undergo chemical reactions in air to form some of the most powerful acids known.

Gravity keeps the things in the atmosphere from moving off into space, and this leaves only two possibilities: either sulfur and nitrogen compounds come down in some form, most probably as acids, or they are all still up there somewhere. It is much more than likely that nearly all has come back down—along with almost everything else that has ever been vented into the atmosphere. Almost all has probably returned to earth as dry deposition or acid precipitation somewhere downwind of the spots where it was formed.

Why Acid Rain Now?

We have already cited a published reference to acid rain dated 1872, but there was acid rain long before there were dinosaurs. As long as there has been carbon dioxide in the atmosphere, some of it has dissolved in rainwater to form carbonic acid (see Chapter 3). Even "pure" rainwater can have a pH of 5.6 or even lower. Over the eons, nature, without any help from humankind, has even made acid rain from the oxides of sulfur vented by volcanos and from other gases vented into the atmosphere from natural sources. Acid soils have been around since before there were terrestrial plants. There is nothing new about any of these things.

What is new is that human beings have been adding significantly to acid deposition at faster and faster rates in many parts of the world. Forests in North America and Europe may now be receiving as much as 30 times more acidity than they would if precipitation fell from or through clean air (Postel, 1984). Apparently, this has rather recently begun to cause obvious damage to the animals and plants in susceptible waters and soils where it falls most heavily. Intensification of the acid rain problem in recent decades (Figure 10.7) is probably related to some combination of several factors.

First of all, most of the coal burned by electric utilities has been burned relatively recently. Much oil and gasoline has been burned at high, nitrogen dioxide–generating temperatures in recent decades (see Figure 10.7; see also Chapters 6 and 11). Although total SO_x emissions have not changed much since the turn of the century, enormous amounts of SO_x were already being emitted in 1900. For a hundred years or more, human generation of SO_x has roughly equaled natural emissions. Some perspective is offered by Postel's (1984) observation that the International Nickel Co. smelter in Sudbury, Ontario, generates more than twice the sulfur that Mount St. Helens did in its biggest sulfur-emitting year. In West Germany, NO_x emissions rose 50% between 1966 and 1978. Since the 1950s, NO_x emissions have roughly doubled in the United States and tripled in Canada (Postel, 1984). A major point here is that the acid rain problem does not correlate strictly with the amount of coal used; it correlates better with the type of use, particularly the methods of combustion and with the accelerated, high-temperature combustion of oil (Patrick, Benetti, and Halterman, 1981).

A second contributing factor can reasonably be presumed to be the tall stack strategy adopted in the early 1970s and late 1960s (Figure 10.7). We used to be concerned only about the local human health effects of air pollutants like SO_2. At first we thought that we could deal with SO_2 by using tall smokestacks to lift the pollutants up and over the populations surrounding power plants. We thought that the pollution would be sufficiently diluted by the time it came back down and no health standard would be violated (see Chapter 11). Only very recently have we begun to pay more attention to other impacts like acid rain.

Finally, the recent overt appearance of damage from acid rain may, in part, be a consequence of an intensifying "conspiracy" of environmental insults. Acidity from air pollution, oxidation by air pollut-

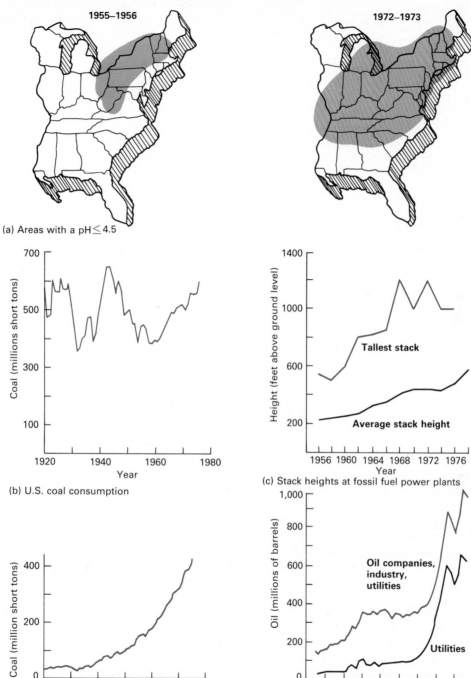

Figure 10.7   Trends Related to Acid Rain. (a) areas in the eastern U.S. that had rainfall with a pH of 4.5 or lower (1950's and 1970's); (b) overall coal consumption; (c) stack heights at fossil fuel–burning power plants; (d) coal consumption by electric utilities; (e) oil consumption. Conclusion: It is not just coal consumption that causes acid rain.

Tall smokestacks were built to solve air pollution problems by lifting pollutants high into the atmosphere to be diluted. This practice is now known to contribute to acid rain.

10,000 additional Swedish lakes have been damaged. In recent years the growth of spruce has declined 50% on Camels Hump in Vermont; there has been a 40% decline in the growth of dozens of other species. Perera (1978) links decreased hardwood growth to acid rain in New Hampshire, and acid deposition is believed to be a major factor if not the whole story in recent widespread damage in German forests.

Overt forest damage related to acid rain in Central Europe seems to be well ahead of damage in the United States. Only on a few mountain peaks in New England does damage rival the widespread destruction in the forests of West Germany, Poland, and Czechoslovakia. Forests with damage linked to air pollutants now cover an area of Central Europe equivalent to half the size of Austria—some 3.5–4 million hectares (Postel, 1984). Damage to pines and other trees has been documented in the Netherlands, Italy, Sweden, the Soviet Union, France, Switzerland, Romania, England, Austria, and Yugoslavia (Postel, 1984). In the United States, acid rain has caused problems in the Colorado mountains, in the forests and waters in many parts of New England, in lakes of California's Sierra Nevada, and in the Shenandoah National Park, where streams are holding their own but at the expense of soil buffering capacity (buffering is discussed shortly).

There are several specific mechanisms by which acid rain is thought to influence living systems. An obvious mechanism is that involving pH itself. In Chapter 3 and elsewhere we discussed the concept of tolerance limits, and we mentioned pH specifically. Living things have optimal pH levels and pH limits. Departure from near-optimal pH means suboptimal reproduction, growth, and survival. Acid rain can change the pH of lakes directly and through the soil acids it mobilizes as it runs over and through soil on its way to streams and lakes. A National Academy of Sciences panel in 1984 indicated that the acidifying effect of acid deposition is magnified in bodies of water surrounded by acid soils because deposited acidity can mobilize hydrogen ion–donating materials from the soil.

In aquatic systems, acidification can also cause toxic metals (e.g., aluminum and mercury) to be leached from sediment—in a lakebed, for example—and from soil as acid water percolates through it. Acidified water may even be able to leach metal from pipes on the way to faucets in houses.

While many studies of the effects of acid rain to date have focused on lakes and other aquatic systems, the effects of acid deposition on terrestrial

ants, insects, drought and other factors may simply have ganged up on forests, for example. Nature has a finite capacity to absorb insult, and perhaps limits are being exceeded in the most sensitive of lakes and forests suffering the most intense combinations of insults.

The acid rain problem itself now boils down to a few basic questions: Just how far can the elements of acid rain travel? What exactly are the impacts of acid deposition on lakes, soil, crops, forests, animals, and ecosystems? What level of emission control makes sense in light of damage and the cost of emission control? What factors other than the burning of coal contribute to acid deposition? Just what is the best technology to keep the oxides of sulfur and the oxides of nitrogen out of the air?

The Effects of Acid Rain

In the eastern provinces of Canada—Ontario, Quebec, and Nova Scotia—acid rain has apparently rendered hundreds if not thousands of lakes fish-free and has had considerable impact on other forms of aquatic life. In this same area the 24 billion dollar forest industry is jeopardized by acid rain. Crops and other plants have apparently also been affected. In Norway, acid rain is believed to have rendered many southern lakes and rivers nearly fish-free. Sweden is reported to have some 3000–4000 so-called "dead" lakes—lakes without fish, frogs, or lily pads, where algae are the only grossly visible form of life. Some systems—forests in particular—are being studied with increasing intensity. There is still more uncertainty than certainty about the mechanisms by which acid deposition affects plants. Among the possibilities and likely contributing factors (See Figure 10.8) are (1) the acidification of soil; (2) the leaching of nutrients from the soil and/or from leaves; (3) mobilization of toxic metals in the soil; (4) the inhibition of nitrogen fixation in the soil; and (5) the stimulation of growth directly by nitrates, forcing growth and making trees more susceptible to freezing.

An example of the kinds of complications that preclude simple explanations is that nitric acids and nitrates may act as fertilizers in the summer and as poisons in the winter. Clouding the picture is the fact that many different kinds of air pollutants act together in different combinations. Even in rural areas, ozone levels get into the ranges known to damage trees, and sulfur dioxide levels high enough to diminish tree growth are not uncommon (Postel, 1984). Sulfur dioxide concentrations in ambient air as low as 25–50 μg/m^3 can apparently reduce tree growth (see U.S. Environmental Protection Agency, 1982; Postel, 1984). The National Ambient Air Quality Standard based on human health consid-

Studies are now under way to determine the effects of acid rain on vegetation. These pachysandra plants show tissue damage from acid rain.

erations is 80 μg/m^3 as an annual average; some trees are apparently more sensitive to SO$_2$ than sensitive people are.

Gaseous oxides of sulfur and nitrogen, acid-forming sulfate particles, and ozone act directly on leaves, causing yellowing and needle loss at the same time that acid-forming pollutants act on roots directly and indirectly, all conspiring to reduce growth

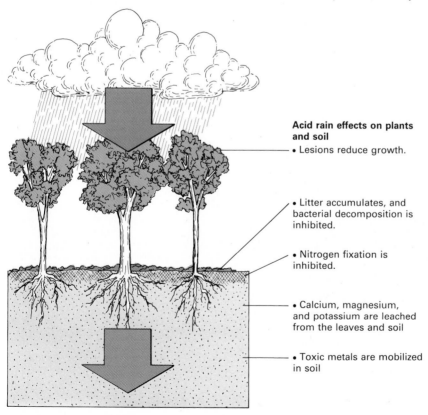

Acid rain effects on plants and soil
• Lesions reduce growth.

• Litter accumulates, and bacterial decomposition is inhibited.

• Nitrogen fixation is inhibited.

• Calcium, magnesium, and potassium are leached from the leaves and soil

• Toxic metals are mobilized in soil

Figure 10.8 Some Possible Effects of Acid Rain on Vegetation and Soil.

or kill the plant. As was discussed earlier, the action of pollutants can weaken trees, making them more susceptible to freezing, drought, insect damage, and other stresses. Complicating the picture still further is the fact that some forest species are much more susceptible to pollutants, particularly acid deposition, than others. It will take many years of research to sort out the relative importance of all of the relevant factors summarized in Figures 10.8 and 10.9.

Not All Soils and Bodies of Water Are Equally Sensitive to Acid Rain

Acidity is a measure of the effective concentration of hydrogen ions (see Chapter 12). These ions come directly from the dissociation of compounds that have hydrogen ions to donate (e.g., $H_2SO_4 \rightarrow 2H^+ + SO_4^=$). But hydrogen ions can be tied up by various compounds and chemical reactions called *buffering reactions* (Figure 10.10).

If soils or bodies of water have buffers in or around them, they can maintain their pH in the face of continual hydrogen ion loading. Limestone, for example, acts like an antacid tablet. The principal

ingredient in limestone is calcium carbonate ($CaCO_3$); in an antacid tablet the ingredient is usually sodium bicarbonate ($NaHCO_3$). In both of these cases the carbonate forms carbonic acid in the presence of hydrogen ions, and this in turn is converted to carbon dioxide and water (see Chapter 3).

There may even be other ways in which the effects of acid rain can be neutralized. It has been suggested, for example, that lakes and streams with a lot of organic material may suffer less from metals because organic material is able to bind the metals, reducing their toxicity (see Patrick, Benetti, and Halter, 1981).

The susceptibility of a body of water to acidification due to acid deposition, then, depends upon

1. the amount of acid-contributing material that falls into the watershed;
2. the path that the material takes on its way to the body of water (over the surface or filtered through soil or bedrock);
3. the ability of the soil to contribute additional acid when flushed by acid-containing precipitation;

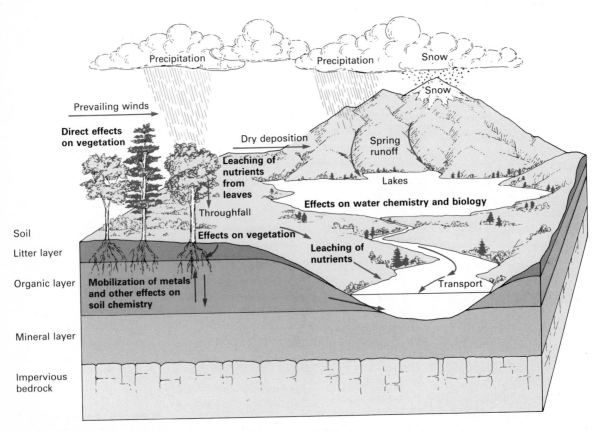

Figure 10.9 Sources of Acid Deposition and a Summary of Its Effects.

Part III   The Impact of Human Activities on Health and the Environment

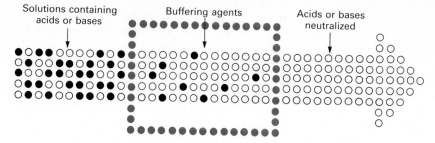

Solutions containing
acids or bases

Buffering agents

Acids or bases
neutralized

Figure 10.10   Buffering.

4. the buffering capacity of the soil; and
5. the rate at which buffers are released to the soil from underlying bedrock.

All of these factors vary tremendously from place to place, even from slope to slope around the same lake. Soils that can buffer acid precipitation can ultimately lose this ability if demand for buffering exceeds the weathering rates by which buffers are made available. Figure 10.11 illustrates the most sensitive areas of North America.

Surges may be a problem even in lakes of rela-

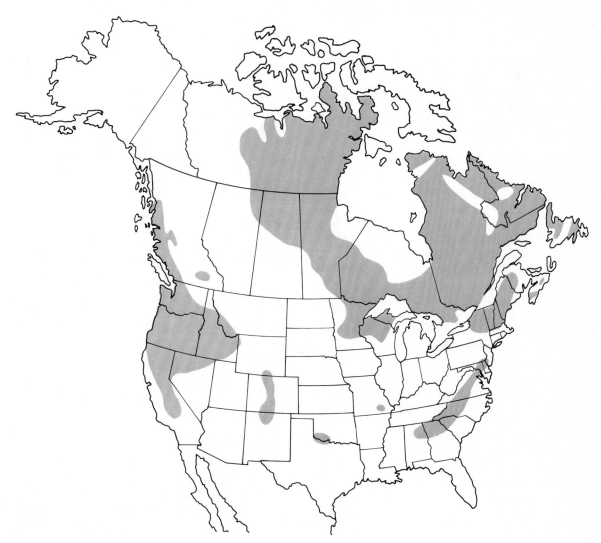

Figure 10.11   Areas of North America with Lakes Particularly Sensitive to Acid Deposition.

Chapter 10   The Effects of Air Pollution

tively low sensitivity. Even if a lake is eventually able to buffer the acidity and neutralize the metals it receives over the course of a year, aquatic life could be damaged severely by the surges in acidity and toxic metals that occur during heavy rains or spring thaws. Melting snows, for example, could bring a cumulative winter's deposition to a lake—right at the time egg laying, egg fertilizing, and egg hatching are beginning.

How Much Deposition Is Too Much?

The aquatics subgroup of a joint U.S. and Canadian working group on acid rain concluded that when acid deposition reaches 20–30 kg per hectare per year, moderately sensitive lakes begin to exhibit chemical and biological changes. This group found consistent evidence that effects were negligible below 17 kg per hectare per year and that changes were long-term when deposition of sulfur oxides exceeded 30 kg per hectare per year. Allegedly because of pressure, this group came up short of recommending that emission controls be targeted to achieve a 20 kg per hectare per year limit (Roberts, 1983). Reducing deposition to the 20-kg limit would require roughly a 50% decrease in emissions.

Acid Rain As an International Issue

The acid in acid rain apparently can come from far away. Airborne sulfate originating in England and elsewhere in northwestern Europe has been linked to increased acidity in the rain coming down in Scandinavia (Ottar, 1977). Some of the acid rain in New England and New York is believed to originate in coal burned along the Ohio River. American oxides of sulfur and nitrogen end up in Canadian acid rain; to a lesser extent, Canadian oxides end up in American acid rain.

Up until now the connections between acid rain and its sources have been derived primarily via computer models and by correlations between emission and deposition. Only recently have atmospheric scientists begun to follow tracer substances put into the atmosphere to see just how they travel (see Rahn and Lowenthal, 1984). Most of these studies are still in the evaluation stages, and some are still in planning stages. But those that have been conducted tend to support computer models (qualitatively if not quantitatively) (see Blair, 1984). But even as we wait for direct confirmation, transboundary pollution has already raised some delicate political issues throughout the world.

In August 1980 the United States and Canada signed an agreement to work on transboundary pol-

lution, but the United States has since balked at following through. The Reagan Administration was at first reluctant to concede that air pollution was a cause of acid rain. It has continued to be reluctant to impose the cost of emission control on industry. Although a joint scientific working group was formed, the group released its report a year late with considerable disagreement as to the degree of emission control needed. Canadian officials have accused the American government of stalling and even blatant interference with the work group (Roberts, 1983). Critics of the Canadian position point out that Canada has an economic stake in driving up the price of American electricity; that a Sudbury, Ontario, plant is still the largest generator of SO_2 in the world; and that Canada's SO_2 emissions per capita are greater than those of the United States.

What Can Be Done?

In some parts of the Northeast, lime is being put into acidified lakes. Although this strategy works—it has been shown to return aquatic life to some semblance of normal—it has been described as about as effective as distributing a few antacid tablets during an epidemic of chronic hyperacidic indigestion (when a more effective approach would be to tell everyone to avoid highly acidic foods). Liming lakes might work up to a point, but it makes better sense in the long run to minimize the insult.

A panel of the National Research Council concluded in a 1983 report that a 50% reduction in emissions of sulfur gases throughout the East would probably bring about a 50% reduction in acid deposition. The report was based on theoretical considerations, laboratory evidence, and the tightness of the correlation between changes in emission and changes in deposition over the last several decades (as well as tests of the alternative hypothesis that the relationship between emissions and acid formation is nonlinear). The panel indicated that at present it is impossible to relate reduction of emission in particular locations to specific sites of acid deposition because the computer models are not good enough to do that.

Current Trends

The acid deposition problem has apparently been getting worse, and many expect it to continue to worsen unless something is done. The demand for electricity continues to rise, and we are increasingly turning to coal as an electrical energy source (see Chapter 6). Because of declining natural gas and domestic oil resources and because of our desire to decrease our dependence on foreign oil, coal is our "ace in the hole." Unless new coal combustion technologies and emission control technologies are refined and adopted, SO_x emissions could conceivably increase as a consequence of an expected increase in coal use over the next few decades (Carter, 1979). NO_x emissions are likely to increase even more. A bill (H.R. 300) that would have reduced SO_2 emissions by some ten million tons through 1993 failed to make it out of committee (House Subcommittee on Environment and Health) in the spring of 1984.

Perhaps the effort to curb acid rain is making little headway because it is seen by many as a regional issue. Although the problem is clearly most serious in the East (Figure 10.12), the acid rain issue has recently spread to the West. Acid deposition problems in the West include acid fog problems in Los Angeles and acidification of lakes in the Colorado Rockies. Acidity is measurable in the rainfall in some places in California and elsewhere in the West (Oppenheimer, 1983) and at least some of this appears to be unnatural. Some areas of the West are equally sensitive to acid rain as the most sensitive areas of the eastern United States (Figure 10.11). It is clear that far from being a regional issue, acid rain is a global issue.

We now give an answer to the question of what needs to be done and reiterate some conclusions from Chapters 6 and 7: We should obviously stop wasting energy; we should continue to refine technologies for the burning of high-sulfur fuels and use more low-sulfur fuels; and we should adopt recycling as a way of life. According to Postel (1984), one third of Canada's copper is made from scrap rather than ore, and this alone keeps about one million tons of sulfur dioxide out of the air each year. Each ton of paper made from waste paper reduces energy use by one third to one half and reduces air pollution by as much as 95%. Producing aluminum from scrap rather than ore cuts nitrogen oxide pollution by 95% and sulfur dioxide by 99%. However we go about it, we must continue on the strategic course of reducing sulfur oxide and nitrogen oxide emissions even as we work to determine the limits of harmfulness.

The acid rain issue is a classic case of ecology at odds with the private market, financial analysis view of economics (see Chapters 11 and 18 and Hitzhusen and Hemphill, 1984). As with other similar issues, the control costs are far more easily figured than the cost of no control. Achieving the degree of control that will bring us close to the 20 kg per hectare per year deposition standard (assuming that this can be figured and that this standard is indeed the one that will protect all but the most sensitive aquatic systems) will cost four to five billion—some say as much as eight billion, others say as much as 20 billion—dollars per year. Except perhaps in the context of national defense, 20 billion dollars is a lot of money. No one can say for sure just how much the damage related to acid deposition is worth. No one knows for sure how much momentum the damaging effects will have when they are speeded up. No one knows how much of the damage is relatively irreversible.

Should we pay billions of dollars every year in control costs to save the fish in thousands of lakes and streams—and maybe crops and trees? Should we protect all of the lakes and streams, or should we set less stringent, less costly standards and save all but the most sensitive? What about related consequences of sulfur and nitrogen oxides other than acid rain? Where do they fit in?

Politicians have a very difficult time dealing with issues and questions such as these because action on pollution issues might well carry them too far from the basic concerns of most of their constituents. Also, the most appropriate actions can be translated into large costs to special interest groups; the translation into general welfare is much less clear-cut.

West Germany and the rest of Europe, Canada, Japan, and much of the rest of the world are out in front of the United States on the acid rain issue. With respect to this and many other environmental issues, these countries seem to have a deeper realization than does the United States that if we destroy ourselves and what we live on, there can be no economic progress—or any kind of progress.

THE EFFECTS OF AIR POLLUTION ON MATERIALS

The Bavarian Monuments Protection Office in Germany has documented an alarming deterioration rate of buildings and monuments made of stone and plaster and even of painted glass works dating from the Middle Ages. Particularly striking examples are the statues of the Augsburg Cathedral. These badly damaged sandstone statues are literally covered by a black coating that contains large amounts of gypsum (a product of the reaction between limestone and sulfuric acid). Heating systems and power-generating stations have been identified as the source of the sulfur dioxide that is believed to cause the problem.

Figure 10.12 Where Acid Falls and Will Fall in the U.S. (a) Average annual pH of rainfall in 1980; (b) Particulate sulfate pollution predicted for 1990.

Pollutants affect health because they are reactive. Because they are reactive, pollutants can and do react with almost every living and nonliving thing. The oxides of sulfur can react with aluminum to form aluminum sulfates and thus corrode aluminum surfaces. Dilute acid solutions formed from a variety of air pollutants can etch limestone and even marble. In its reaction with limestone, sulfuric acid (as well as other sulfur compounds) cause gypsum ($CaSO_4:2H_2O$) to be formed. When this occurs on surfaces, coatings such as those described above are formed; when gypsum forms in cracks, the expansion of gypsum crystals causes the limestone to crumble away.

Hydrogen sulfide can combine with silver to form silver sulfide and tarnish silverware. Ozone can cause the oxidation of fabrics directly, causing them to age faster. Most pollutants that have a health effect also have some effect on materials, though carbon monoxide does not. A summary of the material effects of air pollutants is given in Table 10.7. Economic impacts will be considered in Chapter 11.

Pollutants react with almost every material. On this statue of Thomas Jefferson at Columbia University in New York, the dark coating was formed by atmospheric pollution reacting with the stone of the statue.

Table 10.7 Effects of Major Air Pollutants on Materials

Chemical	Primary Materials Attacked	Typical Damage
Carbon dioxide	Building stones, e.g., limestone	Deterioration
Sulfur oxides	Metals	
	Ferrous metals	Corrosion
	Copper	Corrosion to copper sulfate (green)
	Aluminum	Corrosion to aluminum sulfate (white)
	Building materials (limestone, marble, slate, mortar)	Leaching, weakening
	Leather	Embrittlement, disintegration
	Paper	Embrittlement
	Textiles (natural and synthetic fabrics)	Reduced tensile strength, deterioration
Hydrogen sulfide	Metals	
	Silver	Tarnish
	Copper	Tarnish
	Paint	Leaded paint blackened due to formation of lead sulfide
Ozone	Rubber and elastomers	Cracking, weakening
	Textiles (natural and synthetic fabrics)	Weakening
	Dyes	Fading
Nitrogen oxides	Dyes	Fading
Hydrogen fluoride	Glass	Etches, opaques
Solid particulates (soot, tars)	Building materials	Soiling
	Painted surfaces	Soiling
	Textiles	Soiling

THE EFFECTS OF AIR POLLUTION ON CLIMATE: THE GREENHOUSE EFFECT

We mentioned the role of carbon dioxide in the so-called "greenhouse effect" in Chapters 6 and 9. We will reiterate a few points and expand our consideration here.

Carbon dioxide and other constituents of the earth's atmosphere are transparent to visible light but are relatively opaque to long-wave, infrared radiation (see Chapter 2). This is the basis of the greenhouse effect. Greenhouses, even unheated ones, are much warmer inside than the air outside. The reason for this is that glass will transmit light but is relatively opaque to infrared radiation (Figure 10.13). Everyone is somewhat familiar with the heating of automobiles by the sun. The interior of an automobile standing for a time in the sun will be much

warmer, summer or winter, than the air outside even if the engine and the heater have been off for hours.

So it is with the earth and its atmosphere. The temperature of the earth is determined by the presence in the atmosphere of infrared-absorbing molecules like water, carbon dioxide, and ozone. According to Wang, Yung, Lacis, Mo, and Hanse (1976), there are also a number of *trace* gases in the atmosphere such as methane, ammonia, sulfur dioxide, and certain chlorinated hydrocarbons that may also have a significant effect on the overall heat-retaining properties of the earth's atmosphere. The combination of water vapor, ozone, carbon dioxide, and trace gases behaves like glass in a greenhouse. The heat these materials absorb and hold accounts for the earth's surface temperature. This being the case, there is reason for concern that we humans continue to increase the amount of CO_2 in the atmosphere through the burning of fossil fuels.

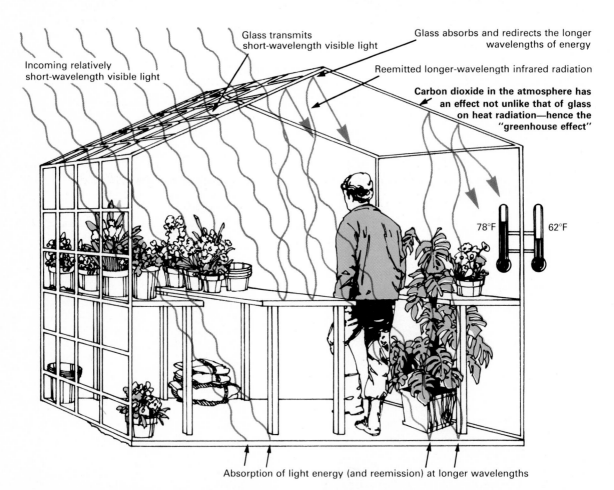

Figure 10.13 The Greenhouse Effect—How It Happens in a Greenhouse. Constituents in the earth's atmosphere— mainly carbon dioxide—do the same thing for the earth's atmosphere and surface as the glass does for a greenhouse.

In the last hundred years, human activity has added about 360 billion tons of carbon dioxide to the atmosphere, increasing the overall concentration of this gas in the atmosphere about 13%. The difference between what we have generated and what has actually been added to the atmosphere is that amount of CO_2 that has dissolved in the oceans or that has been absorbed by plants and animals in biomass. From theoretical considerations this atmospheric increase in carbon dioxide should have caused an average increase in the earth's temperature of about 1°F; this is not far from what has actually occurred. We are still adding billions of tons of carbon dioxide to the atmosphere each year (Figure 10.14). (An interesting fact: The use of fossil fuels has increased in such a short time that the average age of fossil fuel–derived CO_2 in the atmosphere in the late 1970s was only 28 years (Kerr, 1977).) Measurements show that the average carbon dioxide content of the atmosphere has risen more than 8% since 1958. The current rate of increase is one part per million per year, equivalent to

2.3 × 10^{15} grams of carbon. If this rate continues, there will be some 660 ppm of CO_2 in the earth's atmosphere by the middle of the next century. This is twice as much as there was in 1900 (Woodwell et al., 1983).

Not all of the increase in atmospheric CO_2 in recent years has come from the burning of coal and oil. Stuiver (1978) (see also Bolin, 1977; Woodwell et al., 1983) claims that from 1850 to 1950 land use practices reduced terrestrial biomass some 7% and that this has contributed to increased atmospheric CO_2. The earth's plants do, after all, exchange 100 billion metric tons of carbon as CO_2 each year; any net increase in biomass would mean a net consumption of CO_2, any net decrease would mean a net release.

It is noteworthy that we seem to be putting antagonists into the air simultaneously. While CO_2 tends to hold heat in and to increase the temperature of the earth, *particulate matter* tends to reflect solar energy and bring about a cooling of the earth. Although the majority of people involved in the debate

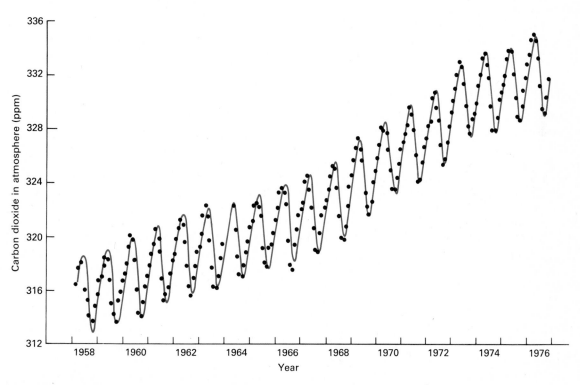

Figure 10.14 Trends in Atmospheric Carbon Dioxide.
These trends have been measured since 1958 at the Mauna Loa Observatory on the island of Hawaii by Charles D. Keeling of the Scripps Institution of Oceanography. The dots show the monthly average concentration of carbon dioxide. Not

shown are seasonal oscillations caused by removal of carbon dioxide by photosynthesis during the growing season in the northern hemisphere and the subsequent release during fall and winter.

come down on the side of net heating, nobody seems quite sure which of these effects will predominate and what will happen to the climate of the earth as a result of our burning fossil fuel. In this context it is also worth noting that in the face of dramatic, *naturally* occurring fluctuation in atmospheric chemistry, it is not really clear how much of a relative effect humans have had and will have on climate. In 1883, to cite one classic example, a volcano 700 miles west of Bali spewed enormous quantities of dust and debris all the way into the stratosphere (Figure 9.1), where it remained for several years. For several annual cycles thereafter the earth was cooler because much of the normal solar flux was blocked out. Recorded history also indicates that in the seventeenth century, volcanic eruptions caused a series of little ice ages in which glaciers advanced in some places almost as far as they did in the big ice ages.

In any case, the average annual temperature of the northern hemisphere rose about half a degree for the 60-year period ending in 1970. James Hansen and his fellow atmospheric physicists at the Goddard Space Flight Center reported that the earth's average temperature rose 0.2°C from the mid-1960s to 1980. There has been a rise in world mean sea level of 12 cm in the past century—due mostly to the ocean's thermal expansion paralleling the rise in surface air temperature (Gornitz, Lededeff, and Hansen, 1982). Robert Etkins and Edward Epstein of the National Ocean and Atmospheric Administration claim (1982) that this rise in sea level cannot be entirely due to thermal expansion and suggest that "significant discharges of polar ice must also be occurring."

There is some disagreement as to how fast the carbon dioxide content of the atmosphere will increase from this point forward as we continue to burn fossil fuel. Had the rates of increase in fossil fuel combustion from the mid-1950s until 1973 held at 4.3% per year, the atmospheric concentration of CO_2 would have doubled in less than 60 years and was estimated to eventually cause a rise in global mean temperature of 3.0°C (more than 5°F). (Note: $1°C = 5/9°F$; $1°F = 9/5°C$.) If recent less dramatic trends hold, however, the doubling and the warming will take longer.

In mid-October 1983, both the National Academy of Sciences (NAS) and the EPA released reports on CO_2-induced global warming. The EPA report predicted temperature increases of 4°F by the year 2040 and 9°F by 2100 (27°F in polar regions), with a 1- to 2-foot rise in sea level as early as 2025. This was projected to cause inundation of low places in

Charleston, South Carolina, Galveston, Texas, and other coastal cities and to alter rainfall patterns in the Midwest. The NAS report reached basically the same conclusion, predicting a doubling of atmospheric CO_2 sometime late in the next century with a 7°F rise in global temperatures. It is noteworthy that the waxing and waning of the ice ages of the past involved temperature changes of only 11–12°F (Kerr, 1983a).

Can the increase in atmospheric CO_2 be stopped? Maybe. Given the source of this CO_2, the increase can be halted by reducing total energy consumption and/or by switching from fossil fuels to solar energy, fusion, and other sources of energy that cause no net increase in CO_2 (see Chapter 6).

It has been suggested that the increase in atmospheric carbon dioxide may soon taper off anyway because the increase will be consumed by increased photosynthesis. While it is true that increasing CO_2 levels do in fact increase production in experimental systems, there is no direct support for the notion that this applies on a global scale, where most plant communities are already limited by the scarcity of water and nutrients (see Kramer, 1981). Kramer points out that we particularly need to know how forests will react to increased CO_2 because they carry out about two thirds of global photosynthesis.

The picture is still unclear. A World Meteorological Organization panel of experts indicated recently that trace gases such as methane, nitrous oxide, and certain chlorofluorocarbons may have as much of an impact on global warming as the much more abundant CO_2 (Kerr, 1983b).

AIR POLLUTANTS AND VISIBILITY

According to the EPA, impairment of visibility is "perhaps the most noticeable and best documented effect of particulate matter in current U.S. atmospheres" (U.S. Environmental Protection Agency, 1982). Visible smoke plumes are obvious examples of this problem. Urban and even multistate regional haze is another dimension for those of us who value visual range, the color of the sky, and the ability to see stars at night. In socioeconomic terms the fact that air pollution has reduced visibility in recent decades in the United States (particularly in the East) has considerable impact on air travel, property values, and psychological well-being. Many different air pollutants are involved in reactions that yield haze-generating fine particles in the atmosphere. These include ozone, sulfur dioxide, and nitrogen dioxide. Both the reactions and the fate of the hazes they form are influenced a great deal by meteorologic conditions including wind, rain, sunlight, temperature, and humidity.

CONCEPTS TO REMEMBER

1. The respiratory tract defenses against air pollutants include nasal hairs; ciliated cells lining the upper airway; moist, mucus-coated, contorted airways; coughs and sneezes; the sense of smell; and alveolar macrophages. These defenses can be overwhelmed.
2. To have a health effect, a pollutant must get at and react with some structural or functional element in cells. Contact with cells may be direct or indirect. Some pollutants are absorbed into the bloodstream and are carried to sensitive organs, where they do their damage.
3. Two of the most general consequences of air pollutants for tissue are scar formation and tissue fluid accumulation. The latter result from blood vessel dilation that is secondary to cellular damage as in a bruise.
4. The major classes of air pollution–related diseases are pulmonary irritation, dust diseases and other structural changes, systemic toxicity, asphyxiation, and cancer.
5. Air pollution can make an individual more susceptible to infections and other diseases that are seemingly unrelated to air pollution.
6. Epidemiological or population-based investigation is one of the principal ways by which we

learn about the connections between air pollutants and human disease. Epidemiology is the study of patterns of disease in populations in relation to environmental exposures and various other patterns within those populations. Epidemiological investigations tend to produce circumstantial rather than hard evidence.

7. Air pollutants affect living things other than humans in the same fundamental ways that they affect humans, that is, through chemical interference.
8. Acid rain is principally a result of the venting of oxides of nitrogen and the oxides of sulfur into the atmosphere. Acid rain is part of the more general problem of acid deposition, which includes dry deposition as well as wet.
9. Acid rain affects living systems through pH changes directly, by causing the mobilization of toxic metals such as mercury and aluminum, and possibly by other mechanisms currently under investigation.
10. Carbon dioxide is classified as an air pollutant because human activity is increasing the amount of this gas in the atmosphere and this trend is expected to cause global warming via the greenhouse effect.

The very same pollutants that reduce visibility may also affect climate via reduction of net solar radiation, enhanced cloud formation, and fog formation. Carbon dioxide is not the only pollutant that affects climate.

DISCUSSION QUESTIONS AND FOOD FOR THOUGHT

1. The very young and the very old are most susceptible to the effects of air pollution. Is this pattern true for any other types of environmental disease or insults? Discuss the reasons why this might be so. How is air pollution like a predator?
2. Write to the American Lung Association for some of their pamphlets on things that can be done about air pollution.
3. Write to or visit your state's Office of Vital Statistics for a copy of the latest annual report. Find out if your state or region has any notable pattern of causes of death or sickness. If you get lost in the numbers, invite a epidemiologist from the state Health Department in to give a talk.
4. Defend or refute: Physicians should treat the sick and leave the well alone; physicians have no time to worry about the prevention of disease caused by pollution.

5. If you live in a coal-mining state, invite a retired coal miner in and ask him to describe the conditions he worked under over the years.
6. Get copies of the January 1981 report by the Council on Environmental Quality entitled *Global Energy Futures and the Carbon Dioxide Problem*. Read and discuss the report.
7. Get a small group of brainstorming classmates together and suppose that you suspected that a certain brand of hair spray caused a skin disorder—let's say you heard five scattered reports over a two-week period. How would you go about studying the problem? Make a list of all of the important considerations associated with each approach.
8. Indoor air pollution presents a serious risk to the health of nonsmokers. It has been known for a long time that children of smokers suffer higher rates of respiratory dieases. The relationship has recently

been extended to cancer. According to a Japanese study released in January 1981, nonsmoking women who lived with smoking husbands developed lung cancer at a higher rate than the wives of non-smokers. This was found to be directly related to the degree of exposure, that is, the number of cigarettes smoked by the husbands and the total number of years of marriage. Give a talk entitled "Four Reasons for Not Smoking" based on the material in this chapter and the section on smoking in Chapter 14.

9. Have one member of the class or an outside speaker give a status report on acid rain as it affects your region.
10. Invite an asthmatic in to describe asthma and how it is affected by polluted air.
11. Debate: Resolved: Cigarette smokers should have no complaints about air pollution.

REFERENCES AND FURTHER READING

References marked with an asterisk are cited in the chapter.

Abelson, P., 1983. "Acid Rain," *Science* **221**:1.

"Acid Rain—How Great a Menace?" *National Geographic,* November, 1981, 652–680.

*Adams, R. M., *et al.,* 1982. "An Economic Assessment of Air Pollution Damages to Selected Annual Crops in Southern California," *Journal of Environmental Economics and Management* **9**:42–46.

Barrett, L. B., and Waddell, T. E., 1973. *Cost of Air Pollution Damage: A Status Report.* Research Triangle Park, N.C.; National Environmental Research Center, Environmental Protection Agency.

*Blair, G., 1984. "Chasing Acid Rain," *Science 84,* 64.

*Bolin, B., 1977. "Changes of Land Biota and Their Importance for the Carbon Cycle," *Science* **196**:613–616.

Bower, F. A., and Ward, R. B., eds., 1982. *Stratospheric Ozone and Man* (Volumes I and II). Boca Raton, Fla.: CRC Press.

Bromberg, J. P., 1983. *Clean Air Act Handbook.* Rockville, Md.: Government Institutes.

*Caren, L. D., 1981. "Environmental Pollutants: Effects of the Immune System and Resistance to Infectious Diseases," *Bioscience* **31** (8):592–596.

Carnow, B. W., 1971. "Air Pollution and Physician Responsibility," *Archives of Internal Medicine* **127**:91–95.

*Carnow, B. W.; Lepper, M. H.; Shelelle, R. B.; and Stamler, J., 1969. "Chicago Air Pollution Study: SO$_2$ Levels in Acute Illness in Patients with Chronic Clinical Pulmonary Disease," *Archives of Environmental Health* **18**:768–776.

Carter, L. J., 1979. "Uncontrolled SO$_2$ Emissions Bring Acid Rain," *Science* **204**:1179–1182.

Chapman, R.; Hasselbald, V.; Hayes, C.; William, J.; Simon, J.; and White, R., 1974. "Ventilatory Function in Elementary School Children in Two Southeastern Cities, 1971–72," Presented at the American Medical Association, Air Pollution Medical Research Conference, December 5–6, 1974, San Francisco, Calif.

Clark, W. C., 1982. *Carbon Dioxide Review 1982.* New York: Oxford University Press.

*Colfin, D. L., and Blommer, E. J., 1967. "Acute Toxicity of Irradiated Auto Exhaust," *Archives of Environmental Health* **15**:36–38.

The Conservation Foundation, 1984. *State of the Environment: An Assessment at Mid Decade.* Washington, D.C.: The Conservation Foundation.

Council on Environmental Quality, 1979. *10th Annual Report: Environmental Quality—1979.* Washington, D.C.: U.S. Government Printing Office.

Council on Environmental Quality, 1981. *Global Energy Futures and the Carbon Dioxide Problem.* Washington, D.C.: U.S. Government Printing Office.

Council on Environmental Quality, 1982. *12th Annual Report.* Washington, D.C.: U.S. Government Printing Office.

Council on Environmental Quality, 1983. "Acid Rain," *13th Annual Report* 211–217. Washington, D.C.: U.S. Government Printing Office.

Council on Environmental Quality, 1984. *14th Annual Report: Environmental Quality 1983.* Washington, D.C.: U.S. Government Printing Office.

*Cowling, E. B., 1982. "International Aspects of Acid Deposition," in Herrmann and Johnson, 1983, pp. 3–12.

Cowling, E. G., and Linthurst, R. A., 1981. "The Acid Precipitation Phenomenon and Its Ecological Consequences," *Bioscience* **31**(9):649–654.

The Debate Over Acid Precipitation: Opposing Views, States of Research. Washington, D.C.: General Accounting Office. (1981)

De Wispelaere, C., 1983. *Air Pollution Modeling and Its Applications 2.* New York: Plenum Press.

Doll, R., and Hill, A. B., 1956. "Lung Cancer and Other Causes of Death in Relation to Smoking: A Second Report on the Mortality of British Doctors." *Brit. J. Med. 2:*1071.

Economic Implications of Regulating Chlorofluorocarbon Emissions from Nonpropellant Applications. Santa Monica, Calif.: Rand Corporation. (1980)

Electric Power Institute, 1983. "Acid Rain Research—A Special Report," *Electric Power Research Institute Journal,* **8**(9, November Issue).

*Etkins, R., and Epstein, E. S., 1982. "The Rise of Global Mean Sea Level as an Indication of Climate Change," *Science* **215**:287–289.

*Fairbairn, A. S., and Reid, D. D., 1958. "Air Pollution and Other Factors in Respiratory Disease," *Brit. J. Prev. and Soc. Med.* **12**:94–103.

Fennelly, P. F., 1976. "The Origin and Influence of Airborne Particulates," *American Scientist* **64**:46–55.

Glass, G. E., and Loucks, O., eds., 1981. *Impacts of Airborne Pollutants on Wilderness Areas Along the Minnesota-Ontario Border.* Washington, D.C.: Environmental Protection Agency.

Gorham, E.; Martin, F.; and Litzau, J., 1984. "Acid Rain: Ionic Correlations in the Eastern United States, 1980–1981," *Science* **225**:407–409.

*Gornitz, V.; Lededeff, S.; and Hansen, J., 1982. "Global Sea Level Trend in the Past Century," *Science* **215**:1611–1614.

Graves, C. K., 1980. "Rain of Troubles," *Science 80* (July/August) 75–79.

Grennfelt, P., and Schjoldager, J., 1984. "Photochemical Oxidants in the Trophosphere: A Mounting Menace," *Ambio* **13** (2):61–67.

Hansen, J.; Johnson, D.; Lacis, A.; Lebedeff, S.; Lee, P.; Rind, D.; and Russell, G., 1981. "Climate Impact of Increasing Atmospheric Carbon Dioxide," *Science* **213**:957–966.

*Heck, W. W. et al., 1983. "A Reassessment of Crop Loss from Ozone," *Environmental Science Technology,* **17**(12): 573A–581A.

*Helvey, J. D.; Kunkle, S.; and DeWalle, D., 1983. "Acid Precipitation: A Review," *Journal of Soil and Water Conservation* (May/June) **37**:143–148.

Herrmann, R., and Johnson, A. I., 1982. "Acid Rain: A Water Resources Issue for the 80's," *Proceedings of the American Water Resources Assn., International Symposium of Hydrometerology.* Bethesda, Md.

Hitzhusen, F., and Hemphill, R., 1984. "The Economics of Acid Rain," *Socioeconomic Information.* Cooperative Extension Service, No. 667, May. Columbus Ohio: The Ohio State University.

Howard, R., and Perley, M., 1982. *Acid Rain: The Devastating Impact on North America.* New York: McGraw-Hill.

Hutchinson, T. C., and Havas, M., eds., 1980. *Effects of Acid Precipitation on Terrestrial Ecosystems,* published in coordination with NATO Scientific Affairs Division by Plenum Press, NY.

Indoor Pollutants. (1981) Washington, D.C.: National Academy Press.

*Irving, P. M., 1984. "Acid Rain Research: A Review and Analysis of Methodology," *Trends in Electric Utility Research,* April, 3–4.

Kagawa, J.; Toyama, T.; and Nakaza, M., 1974. *Pulmonary Function Tests for Children Exposed to Air Pollution,* presented at the American Medical Association, Air Pollution Medical Research Conference, December 5–6, San Francisco.

*Kerr, R. A., 1977. "Carbon Dioxide and Climate: Carbon Budget Still Unbalanced," *Science* **197**:1352–1354.

*Kerr, R. A., 1983a. "Carbon Dioxide and a Changing Climate," *Science* **222**:491–492.

*Kerr, R. A., 1983b. "Emission Control Will Control Acid Rain," *Science* **221**:254–255.

Kerr, R. A., 1983c. "Trace Gases Could Double Climate Warming," *Science* **220**:1364–1365.

Kerr, R. A., 1984. "Carbon Dioxide and Control of Ice Ages," *Science* **223**:1053–1054.

Kozlowski, T. T., 1980. "Impact of Air Pollution on Forest Ecosystems," *Bioscience* **30**(2): 88–93.

*Kramer, P., 1981, Carbon Dioxide Concentration, Photosynthesis, and Dry Matter Production, *Bioscience,* **31**(1):29–33.

Krug, E., and Frink, C., 1983. "Acid Rain on Acid Soil: A New Perspective," *Science* **221**:520–525.

Lacasse, N. L., and Treshow, M., eds., 1978. *Diagnosing Vegetation Injury Caused by Air Pollution.* Washington, D.C.: Superintendent of Documents. (EPA 450/3-78-005).

*Lave, R. J., and Seskin, E., 1970. "Air Pollution and Human Health," *Science* **169** (3947):723–733.

*Lave, L. B., and Seskin, E. P., 1979. "Epidemiology Causality and Public Policy," *American Scientist,* **67**:178–186.

*Lillie, R. J., 1970. *Air Pollution Affecting the Performance of Domestic Animals: A Literature Review.* Agricultural Handbook, No. 380. Washington, D.C.: U.S. Dept. of Agriculture.

Lippmann, M. and Schlesinger, R. B., 1979. *Chemical Contamination in the Human Environment.* New York: Oxford University Press.

Longo, L. D., 1976. "Carbon Monoxide: Effects of Oxygenation of the Fetus *in Utero,*" *Science* **194**:523–525.

*McLaughlin, S. B., and Taylor, G. E., 1981. "Relative Humidity: Important Modifier of Pollutant Uptake by Plants," *Science* **211**:167–169.

*Marx, J. L., 1975. "Air Pollution Effects on Plants," *Science* **187**:731–733.

*Maugh, T. H., 1979. "SO_2: Pollution May Be Good for Plants," *Science* **205**:383.

*Mausner, J. S., and Bahn, A. K., 1974. *Epidemiology: An Introductory Text.* Philadelphia: W. B. Saunders.

National Commission on Air Quality, 1981. *To Breathe Clean Air,* Washington, D.C.: U.S. Government Printing Office.

National Research Council, Committee on the Atmosphere and the Biosphere, 1981. *Atmosphere–Biosphere Interactions: Toward a Better Understanding of the Ecological Consequences of Fossil Fuel Combustion.* Washington, D.C.: National Academy Press.

National Research Council, Committee on Transport and Chemical Transformation in Acid Precipitation, 1983. *Acid Deposition, Atmospheric Processes in Eastern North America.*

Oden, S., 1968. "The Acidification of Air and Precipitation and Its Consequences in the Natural Environment," *Ecology Committee Bulletin, No. 1.* Stockholm; Swedish National Science Research Council. English-language edition published by Translation Consultants, Ltd., Arlington, Va.

*Oppenheimer, M., 1983. "Acid Rain Has Spread to the West," Louisville *Courier Journal,* August 28.

*Ottar, B., 1977. "International Agreement Needed to Reduce Long-Range Transport of Air Pollutants in Europe," *Ambio* **6** (5):262–269.

*Patrick, R.; Benetti, V. P.; and Halterman, S.G., 1981. "Acid Lakes from Natural and Anthropogenic Causes," *Science* **211**:446–448.

*Perera, F. P., 1978. "Fine Particles in the Atmosphere," *Natural Resources Defense Council Newsletter,* March-April-May-June, pp. 1–16.

Plass, G. M., 1959. "Carbon Dioxide and Climate," *Scientific American*(July) **201**(1):41–47. Reprinted in Ehrlich, P. R., et al., eds., 1971. *Man and the Ecosphere,* San Francisco: W. H. Freeman and Co., 173–179.

*Postel, S., 1984. "Air Pollution, Acid Rain and the Future of Forests," *Worldwatch Institute Paper 58.* Washington, D. C. This paper is also reprinted as a series beginning in the July 1984 issue of the magazine *American Forests.*

Price, S., and Wilson, L. 1982. *Pathophysiology,* 2nd ed. New York: McGraw-Hill.

*Rahn, K. A., and Lowenthal, D., 1984. "Elemental Tracers of Distant Regional Pollution Aerosols," *Science* **223**:132–139.

Rampino, M. R., and Self, S., 1984. "The Atmospheric Effects of El Chichon," *Scientific American* (January 1984):48–57.

*Reisner, M., 1977. "It's 1977, Why Don't We Have Cleaner Air?" *Natural Resources Defense Council Newsletter* **6**:2–3.

*Roberts, L., 1983. "Acid Rain Clouds U.S. and Canadian Relations," *Bioscience* **33**(7):418–422.

Sanders, C. L., et al., eds., 1980. "Pulmonary Toxicology of Respirable Particles," *Department of Energy Symposium Series.* Washington, D.C.: National Technical Information Service.

Schlesinger, R. B., 1982. "Defense Mechanisms of the Respiratory System," *Bioscience* **32**(1):45–50.

Sievers, R. F.; Edward, T. I.; Murray, A. L.; and Schrenk, H. H., 1942. "Effect of Exposure to Known Concentration of Carbon Monoxide," *Journal of the American Medical Association* **118**(VIII):585–588.

*Skarby, L., and Sellden, G., 1984. "The Effects of Ozone on Crops and Forests," *Ambio* **13**(2):68–72.

Solomon, P. M.; de Zafra, R.; Parrish, A.; and Barrett, J. W., 1984. "Diurnal Variation of Stratospheric Chlorine Monoxide: A Critical Test of Chlorine Chemistry in the Ozone Layer," *Science* **224**:1210–1214.

Stern, A. C., ed., 1968. *Air Pollution,* 2nd ed.(three volumes). New York: Academic Press.

*Stuiver, M., 1978. "Atmospheric Carbon Dioxide and Carbon Reservoir Changes," *Science* **199**(4326):253–258.

Sulman, F. G., 1982. *Short-and Long-Term Changes in Climate* (volumes I and II) Boca Raton, Fla.: CRC Press.

Treshow, M., 1984. *Air Pollution and Plant Life.* New York: Halstead Press.

Ulrich, B., and Pankrath, J., eds., 1982. *Effects of Accumulation of Air Pollutants in Forest Ecosystems.* Boston: Reidel.

*U.S. Environmental Protection Agency, 1978. *Air Quality Criteria for Ozone and Other Photochemical Oxidants.* Washington, D.C.(EPA-600/8-78-004)

U.S. Environmental Protection Agency, 1980. *Acid Rain,* Washington, D.C., Office of Research and Development. EPA-600/9-79-036.

*U.S. Environmental Protection Agency, 1982. *Review of the National Ambient Air Quality Standards for Nitrogen Oxides: Assessment of Scientific and Technical Information; Review of the National Ambient Air Quality Standards for Particulate Matter: Assessment of Scientific and Technical Information; and Review of the National Ambient Air Quality Standards for Sulfur Oxides: Assessment of Scientific and Technical Information.* Research Triangle, N.C.: Office of Air Quality Planning and Standards Staff Papers.

*U.S. Environmental Protection Agency, 1984. *Revised Evaluation of Health Effects Associated with Carbon Monoxide Exposure: An Addendum to the 1979 Air Quality Criteria Document for Carbon Monoxide.* Office of Health and Environmental Assessment.

*Waldbott, G. L., 1978. *Health Effects of Environmental Pollutants,* 2nd ed. St. Louis: C. V. Mosby Co.

*Wang, W. C.; Yung, Y. L.; Lacis, A. A.; Mo, T.; and Hanse, J. E., 1976. "Greenhouse Effects Due to Man-Made Perturbations of Trace Gases," *Science* **194**:685–689.

Wilson, R., 1980. *Health Effects of Fossil Fuel Burning: Assessment and Mitigation.* Cambridge, Mass.: Ballinger Publishing Co.

Woodwell, G. M., 1978. "The Carbon Dioxide Question," *Scientific American,* Jan. 1978, *238*(1):33–43.

Woodwell, G. M.; Whittaker, R. H.; Reiners, W. A.; Likens, G. E.; Delwiche, C. E.; and Botkin, D. B., 1978. "The Biota in the World Carbon Budget," *Science* **199**:141–146.

*Woodwell, G. M., et al., 1983. "Global Deforestation: Contribution to Atmospheric Carbon Dioxide," *Science* **222**:1081–1086.

Young, W. A.; Shawn, D. B.; and Bates, D. V., 1964. "Effects of Low Concentrations of Ozone on Pulmonary Function in Man," *J. Applied Physiol.* **19**:765–769.

CHAPTER 11

Control of Air Pollution

I n this chapter we turn our attention to the economic, legal, and technical aspects of air pollution control. We consider both the costs associated with air pollution control and the costs of not controlling air pollution. The costs of *not* controlling pollution can be thought of as the dollar value of the negative effects of air pollution discussed in Chapters 9 and 10. We looked at the technical aspects of the *effects* of air pollutants in Chapter 10; here we look at the technical aspects of air pollution *control*. We also look at air pollution control laws and how well they have worked so far. All of these things are closely related, of course; economic and technical factors have much to do with the kinds of laws we have and with how well they work.

THE ECONOMICS OF AIR POLLUTION

Our resolve to control air pollution is determined in part by cost. Perhaps it would be more accurate to say that our resolve is determined by our perception of the difference between the cost of controlling pollution and the cost of not controlling pollution. Assessing the cost of *not* controlling air pollution is difficult because it is subjective; assessing the cost of air pollution control is relatively straightforward. Let's start with the cost of control.

The Cost of Air Pollution Control

Expenditures for air pollution control in the United States had already approached 20 billion dollars annually by 1978 (Figure 11.1), and we spent some 60 billion dollars in the decade ending in 1982. These figures include money paid by both public and private sectors to control both mobile and stationary pollution sources. According to the Council on Environmental Quality, air pollution control expenditures will exceed 42 billion dollars in 1987, and for the decade 1978–1987 the cumulative total cost for control will exceed 300 billion dollars. Federal legislation will be responsible for 37 billion dollars and nearly 280 billion dollars of these amounts, respectively. In a report released in 1984 the EPA projected that a half trillion dollars could be spent for all forms of pollution control during the 1980s (about half of that for air pollution control). Figure 11.2 illustrates past and projected trends in emission control costs for automobiles. Figure 11.3 shows the cost of all forms of pollution control in relation to the Gross National Product. Although the annualized cost of pollution control is just over 1% of the gross national product today (Figure 11.3), obviously money *is* being spent to control pollution, and the sums of money being spent are large.

As costs have increased, the debate has intensified over the need for air pollution controls and the

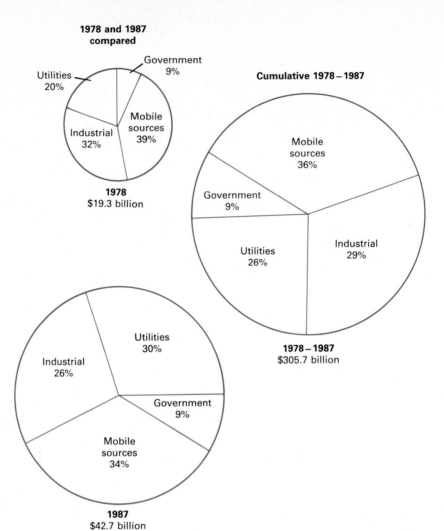

1978 and 1987 compared

Cumulative 1978–1987

1978
$19.3 billion

Mobile sources 39%
Government 9%
Utilities 20%
Industrial 32%

Mobile sources 36%
Government 9%
Utilities 26%
Industrial 29%

1978–1987
$305.7 billion

1987
$42.7 billion

Utilities 30%
Industrial 26%
Government 9%
Mobile sources 34%

Figure 11.1 Estimated Total Air Pollution Control Costs 1978–1987 (1978 dollars). These reflect both annual operation and maintenance costs and annualized capital costs (interest charges plus cost of equipment averaged over the number of years it is expected to last). They also include both incremental costs (those required by federal clean air legislation) and the cost of controls required by state and local governments, plus the cost of controls that would likely have been added even in the absence of specific legislation.

laws requiring them. The spectre of lost jobs adds further complexity to the debate.

Pollution control costs can and do result in higher prices and thus lower demand for products. Diminished demand for consumer goods in turn leads to lost jobs. The closing of plants unable to meet emission standards also means lost jobs. Some 155 plants closed between 1971 and 1984, all at least partially because of the cost of meeting emission standards. These shutdowns alone amounted to more than 30,000 lost jobs (U.S. Environmental Protection Agency, 1984).

Of course, since someone must make, install, and maintain pollution control equipment, pollution control also means a certain increase in jobs— different jobs. The EPA estimates that the net impact of pollution control legislation will be an increase,

not a decrease, in employment (Figure 11.4). According to an EPA report, employment in the pollution control manufacturing industry in 1978 was nearly 36,000; it was projected then that this would grow to 44,000 by 1983. Furthermore, about a half million people were employed nationwide in the mid-1980s to operate and maintain pollution control equipment.

What about the impact of air pollution control on the cost of things in general? Does pollution control contribute to inflation? The consumer price index (CPI) was estimated to be 2.7% higher in the late 1970s because of all forms of pollution control. This is expected to rise to 3.6% by 1986 (U.S. Environmental Protection Agency, 1979) (Figure 11.5). But the EPA points out that the methods used in deriving the CPI fail to take into account most of the *benefits* of air pollution control. Thus these methods exaggerate the costs and minimize the benefits.

Clearly, to answer the tough questions being asked about the need for air pollution control, we need more and better information about the costs of *not* controlling pollution. But while the costs of pollution control are rather easily translated into dollars, doing the same thing with pollution control benefits is much more difficult, and the results are more controversial.

The Overall Cost of Air Pollution Damage

To date, there have been two relatively thorough attempts to establish the costs of air pollution damage. The first was by Barrett and Waddell; their report, published by the U.S. Environmental Protection Agency, is entitled *The Cost of Air Pollution Damage: A Status Report* (published in 1973). There was also a 1979 report by A. M. Freeman, prepared for the Council on Environmental Quality (see Freeman, 1979). Both reports looked at the impact of air pollution in terms of the costs associated with health and with damage to vegetation, materials, and residential property. An interesting difference in the two reports is that while Barrett and Waddell estimated the total cost of the impact of air pollution, Freeman estimated the dollar benefit of an assumed 20% improvement in air quality that occurred between 1970 and 1978.

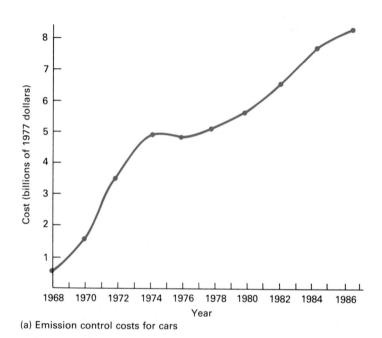

(a) Emission control costs for cars

(b) Pollution control costs

Figure 11.2 (a) Emission Control Costs for Light Duty Passenger Cars. The curve of increased air pollution control costs on American automobiles has been steep since 1968 and is projected by the EPA to continue to rise at least through 1986. The figures given here include annualized capital costs, maintenance costs, and fuel consumption penalties (the reduced fuel consumption economy caused by the air pollution control devices). **(b) Cost of All Forms of Pollution Control, 1972–1982.**

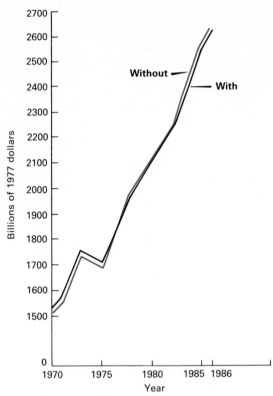

(a) GNP with and without pollution controls

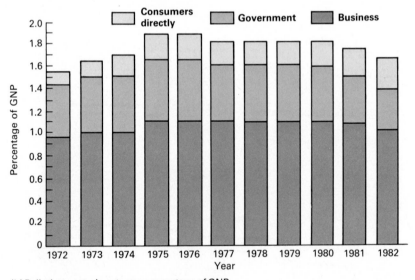

(b) Pollution control costs as a percentage of GNP

Figure 11.3 (a) Real Gross National Product with and without Environmental Controls. (b) Pollution Control Expenditures as a Percentage of the GNP, 1972–1982.

We would like to consider both of these reports in some detail here because they illustrate many of the universal features—and problems—associated with studies of this kind. We should point out there have also been a number of other studies that have focused on specific individual categories of impact such as health effects (Carpenter, LeSourd, Chromy, and Bach, 1977; Bhagia and Stoevener, 1978; Blom-

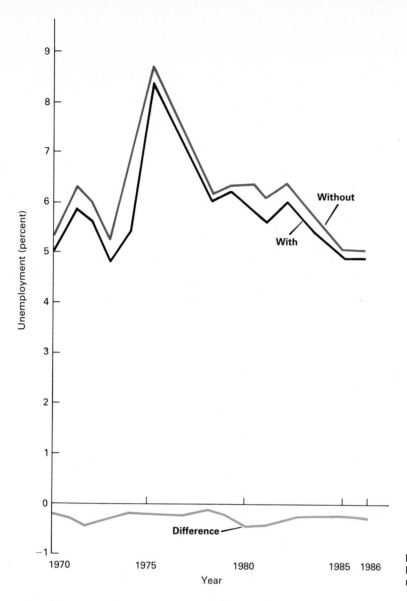

Figure 11.4 Unemployment Rate with and without Environmental Controls.

quist, 1979; Finklea et al., 1977; Lave and Seskin, 1970, 1973, 1977; American Lung Association, 1977), the effects of air pollution on crops (Adams, Thanavibulchai, and Crocker, 1979), materials damage (Gillette, 1975), and the value of aesthetics (Brookshire Ives, and Schultz, 1976). Other studies were being reported and still others were underway as we went to press. It would be a good class exercise to find, compile, and review some of them.

Each of these studies is based on some set of assumptions concerning such things as the cost of being sick, the cost of missing work, the value of a human life, and the relationships between pollution and sickness and pollution and materials damage.

Literally hundreds of specific assumptions had to be made in coming up with the estimates that came from these studies, and the reader is referred to the original reports for a description of these assumptions and the justification for making them.

As is illustrated in Figure 11.6, Barrett and Waddell concluded that the annual economic impact due to air pollution in 1968 was 16.1 billion dollars.

Freeman estimated that the *benefits* of air pollution control enjoyed ten years later amounted to 21.4 billion dollars (Figure 11.7). Freeman assumed 1978 economic conditions, 1978 population, and an improvement in air quality of 20% between 1970 and 1978. Freeman concluded that the annual eco-

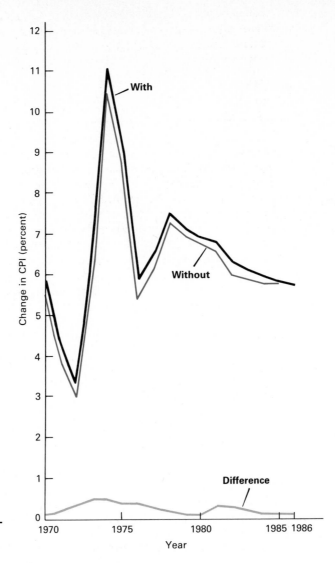

Figure 11.5 Percent Annual Increase in Consumer Price Index with and without Environmental Controls.

nomic benefit of the Clean Air Act was actually somewhere between 4.6 and 51.2 billion dollars in 1978. The size of this range suggests that the data base is poor and that we really do not have the basis for an exacting determination of the benefits of clean air (or conversely the cost we pay if we do not keep the air clean). We should emphasize that Freeman did not estimate the total cost impact of dirty air, he estimated what it was worth to us in 1978 to have air 20% cleaner than it was in 1970.

Freeman's numbers obviously cannot be directly compared to those of Barrett and Waddell simply by adjusting for inflation. Nor can the estimates be made comparable by multiplying by five.

The reasoning that if 20% of pollution costs x dollars, all of it should cost $5x$ dollars does not apply because the benefit of removing the first 20% is not necessarily the same as that derived from removing the *next* 20%.

Although all of the studies that have been done do not agree and the data we have are far from exacting, it is safe to conclude that there *is* a cost associated with dirty air and that the cost is highly significant. We will now examine briefly some of the specific categories of impact. Again our purpose is to illustrate the kinds of things that go into assessing the economic impact of air pollution on health, vegetation, and materials.

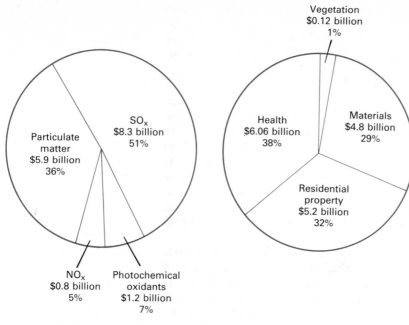

(a) Impact of individual pollutants

(b) Impact of pollution by category

Figure 11.6 The Cost of Not Controlling Air Pollution. One of the earliest estimates of the cost of air pollution damage. Shown here are the fractions of a total estimated annual 1968 cost of $16.132 billion (1968 dollars) (a) attributable to the major pollutants and (b) assigned to various categories of impact.

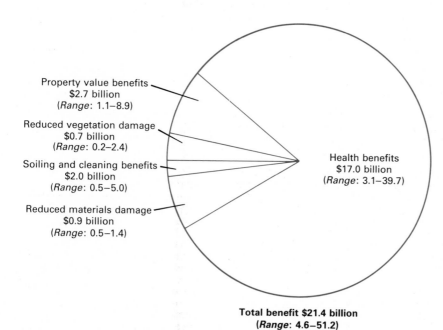

Total benefit $21.4 billion
(*Range*: 4.6–51.2)

Figure 11.7 Benefits of Pollution Control. One estimate of the economics of air pollution control benefits enjoyed in 1978. Numbers here express the 1978 dollar value of an assumed 20% lower level of air pollution brought about by clean air laws.

Health Costs of Air Pollution

Barrett and Waddell's estimates of the overall impact of air pollution on health with respect to selected diseases are given in Table 11.1. They estimated that the health costs of air pollution exceeded 6.06 billion dollars per year in the late 1960s. Their data were derived from one of the earliest attempts to estimate the cost of damage to health from air pollution, published by Ridker in 1967. Table 11.1 illustrates the need to include many *indirect* factors in determining the health cost of pollution damage, that is, the cost of absenteeism due to sickness as well as the cost of premature death (wages lost) and the cost of treatment.

As is indicated in Figure 11.7, Freeman concluded that the 1978 health benefit of the 20% reduction in air pollution that occurred between 1970 and 1978 was somewhere between 3.1 and 39.3 billion dollars (with a best estimate of 17.0 billion dollars).

A 1979 EPA report estimated the total annual impact of air pollution on health was 5–16 billion dollars in increased mortality (earlier death) and 36 billion dollars in sickness (health care and lost work).

The Economic Impact of Air Pollution on Vegetation

Summarizing a host of studies of the economic impact of air pollution on vegetation, Barrett and Waddell concluded that the value of the air pollution damage that occurred in 1968 was 120 million dollars. Barrett and Waddell noted that their estimate included only the major pollutants and their effects on only agricultural, horticultural, and forest crops.

There have been other reports. A 1969 report by the Stanford Research Institute (SRI) estimated a 113 million dollar annual vegetation loss due to air pollution. Food, crops, ornamentals, noncommercial forests, and parks were considered. A 1978 EPA training manual (450/3-78-005) projects that the SRI estimate could be adjusted to 200 million dollars per year for 1978.

According to Freeman, early studies largely failed to consider the buildup of photochemical oxidants downwind of the sources. They also (1) failed to consider the effect of reduced crop output on food prices, (2) ignored the cost of a farmer having to move to a new location, and (3) disregarded the cost of switching to more resistant varieties or less profitable crops.

Freeman identified a study by Heintz et al. (1976) as the most complete as of the early 1970s. Adjusted to 1978, this gave a range of loss of 1.2–12.2 billion dollars per year for plant damage *due to photochemical oxidants pollution*. To this Freeman adds 500 million dollars as the cost of damage to vegetation due to SO_x pollution (including estimated plant damage from acid rain).

Freeman assumed a 20% improvement in oxidant pollution between 1970 and 1978; he assumed *no* improvement in SO_x pollution for the same period and concluded that we were enjoying a benefit of 0.2–2.4 billion dollars in vegetation saved by air pollution control in 1978 (see Figure 11.7). (Here again, it would be an interesting class exercise to find and consider any more recent reports.)

The Economic Impact of Air Pollution on Animals

No thorough study has ever been conducted of the economic impact of air pollution on animals. Notable episodes of damage to animals by air pollution have been highly localized, and any economic consequences were relatively unimportant on a national scale.

Table 11.1   An Early Estimate of the Cost Associated with Selected Air Pollution–Related Diseases in the U.S.

Type of Cost	Costs Associated with Selected Diseases (in millions of dollars)							
	Cancer of the Respiratory System	Chronic Bronchitis	Acute Bronchitis	Common Cold	Pneumonia	Emphysema	Asthma	Total
Premature death	518	18.0	6.0	N.A.	329	62	59	992.0
Treatment	35	89.0	N.A.	200	73	N.A.	138	535.0
Absenteeism	112	52.0	N.A.	131	75	N.A.	60	430.0
Total	665	159.0	6.0	331	477	64	257	1957.0

The Economic Impact of Air Pollution on Materials

Barrett and Waddell cited a number of reports, most notably one by Uhling (1950) in which it was estimated that in the 1950s, corrosion due to air pollution would cost the United States up to 5.4 billion dollars annually. In still another report published by the Rustoleum Corporation, annual corrosion losses due to air pollution were estimated to be in the neighborhood of 7.5 billion dollars in the 1960s. Studies have been conducted more recently by the Stanford Research Institute, the Midwest Research Institute, and Battelle Laboratory. These studies yielded the data summarized in Figure 11.6.

Freeman concluded that air pollution damage to materials amounted to 2.4–7.2 billion dollars in 1978. Again assuming a 20% improvement in air pollution between 1970 and 1978, he projected a 1978 annual benefit (in the form of undamaged materials) of 0.5–1.4 billion dollars.

Soiling is a specific kind of effect of air pollution on materials. It has to do mainly with the settling out of particulates or the absorption of particulates on fabrics and structures like windowsills. The cost of cleaning up made necessary by soiling was not included in the estimates referred to above, but the results presented in one (early) soiling study are given in Table 11.2. This table shows that a number of things must be included in any consideration of the economic impact of soiling. The study cited in Table 11.2 revealed that the costs of keeping things clean in polluted areas of England were twice those in relatively unpolluted areas.

The Impact of Air Pollution on Property Values

Barrett and Waddell also estimated the cost to society that comes from decreases in residential

The cost of cleaning soiled buildings is one of many costs to be considered in comparing the relative economics of pollution and pollution control.

property value due to pollution. Again, they cite a number of studies in which estimates were made of various kinds of damage, pointing out that each study involved a number of specific assumptions. Citing numerous limitations in how they derived their own summary estimate, Barrett and Waddell concluded that air pollution's impact on residential property values amounted to 3.4–8.4 billion dollars annually in 1968. Although it is beyond the scope of this book to explain in detail their exact methodology, Barrett and Waddell estimated how much people were willing to pay to live in an unpolluted

Table 11.2 Cost of Air Pollution–Related Soiling. Summary of a report by H. Beaver in London. The results of more recent studies are summarized in the criteria documents and staff papers listed in Chapters 9 and 10.

Category	Cost (million dollars per year)
Direct	
Laundering	70
Painting and decorating	84
Soiling and depreciation of buildings (other than houses)	56
Corrosion of metals	70
Damage to textiles and other goods	147
Indirect (loss of efficiency)	280
Total	707

The cost per person was $14 per year in nonpolluted areas and $28 per year in polluted areas.

area. This was then converted into the estimated economic impact of incremental amounts of pollution.

In his estimate, Freeman added a special adjustment for the decrease in willingness to pay as air quality got better; this compensates for the fact that it is more important to people to remove the first half of the pollution in the air than it is to remove the last half. Freeman estimated that the 1978 annual property value benefits derived from a 20% improvement in air quality from 1970 to 1978 amounted to 1.1–8.9 billion dollars. This implies that the residual impact in 1978 amounted to 5.5–44.5 billion dollars from mobile and stationary source pollution combined. Freeman notes that the impact on property values is also counted in other categories (for example, deterioration of paint is a material impact as well as a property value impact). Accordingly, he counts only 30% of the property value impact in his grand total (see Figure 11.7).

In the above paragraphs and in the reports by Barrett and Waddell, Freeman, and others, many qualifications are given in the cost estimates. Many things are left out of estimates simply because there is very little if any basis on which to make a dollar cost estimate. For certain materials this problem is profound indeed. What about the deterioration of materials of historical or aesthetic significance? What about rare paintings and books, for example? How would one assess the value of a beautiful vista that can no longer be appreciated because of air pollution? What about reduced visibility as a highway safety factor? What about the depressing psychological effect of air pollution (Chapter 16)? How does one assign a value to the deterioration in life that comes from the presence of noxious odors—without regard to the effect they might have on health? These problems have all been pointed out by Barrett and Waddell and by Freeman and others, and we can all probably think of more.

The Economic Impact of Air Pollution on Ecosystems

How can we begin to assess the economic impact of air pollution on the smooth functioning and/or probability of the stable continued functioning of an ecosystem? We only poorly understand the effects, never mind assigning a value to them. Obviously, it will be difficult to fit *ecosystems* into our *economic* systems, to sort out, scrutinize, and pin down values in enough economically exacting detail to allow us to identify the factors that should go into this analysis. We hope that the future will bring better ways of approaching this problem.

DETERMINING THE COST-BENEFIT RATIO FOR AIR POLLUTION CONTROL

The two foregoing sections give us some idea of the costs and benefits of controlling pollution. An idea is really all we have. It is obvious that we will never have all of the exact information we need, but we must start nonetheless to obtain more and better economic information. Without such we will be unable to assess the cost-benefit ratio for controlling air pollution (see Chapter 18).

Figure 11.8 contains a number of generalized curves illustrating some plausible relationships between the cost of uncontrolled pollution, the cost of pollution control, the benefit of pollution control, and the value of retained resources. The only thing certain about the curves is the direction of their slopes. Whether the curves should be straight lines or not remains to be seen, although there may be more of a basis for defining some curves than for others. If we had *accurate* curves of the sort presented in Figure 11.8, we would have a better handle on the air pollution problem. We would have completed the next necessary step toward solutions, that step being the determination of the nature and the degree of the problem.

A major premise in the last paragraph is that it takes more than statements that something is bad to bring about correction. As difficult or nearly impossible as the task may be, environmentalists must be able to express badness in terms of dollars or some other commonly understood unit and to do this with good data. Only then will it be possible to get corrective action that will subsequently withstand ever-present economic pressures. (In Chapters 18 and 19, we will explore in greater detail the difficulties associated with expressing the economic impact of pollutants.)

We call the reader's attention again to Figure 11.8, which shows that the cost of removing or stopping pollutants increases in an exponential way with the percentage of the pollutant removed. In other words, it may be relatively easy to remove the first few tons of a pollutant from the air, but it would be impossible to deal with the last few molecules.

Another curve in Figure 11.8 illustrates how society might perceive the benefit of pollution control or how much pressure there might be to spend money to do something about pollution. The curve

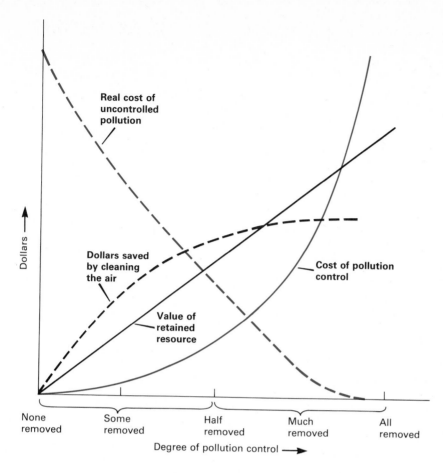

Figure 11.8 Cost Versus Benefit. Some of the generalized relationships between the cost of controlling pollution and the cost of not controlling pollution. Note that the curve of cost of not controlling pollution and the curve of pollution control costs intersect. This occurs at the theoretical point beyond which it is not worth cleaning the air any further.

shows that while the public might want very much to do something about the worst of the pollution, it would be increasingly less willing to pay for removing the last bits of pollution. One economic concept has to do with the fact that curves such as the two we have just described intersect at some point, a point at which the cost of controlling pollution matches the price people are willing to pay for controlling it. The point of intersection would obviously depend on such things as the technology available for pollution control and the magnitude of the real and perceived effects of air pollution.

AIR POLLUTION AND THE LAW

The modern history of clean air legislation began with the Motor Vehicle Act of 1960, which was eventually followed by the Clean Air Act of 1970. The 1970 Clean Air Act was really a compilation of amendments to earlier legislation, and the Clean Air Act has itself been amended twice, once in 1974 and again in 1977. A third set of amendments is under consideration in Congress as we go to press. The Clean Air Act of 1970 was tighter than earlier legislation in that it required that standards for ambient air be established and set up somewhat more restrictive criteria for granting delays and variances in achieving these standards. The Act also for the first time specified that the federal government would determine the best available technologies to be used in achieving performance standards for industrial plants, automobiles, and other sources of air pollution. The Act also established federal control of particularly hazardous substances like asbestos.

The **Environmental Protection Agency (EPA)** was established in 1970 as an umbrella agency in charge of the environmental programs previously scattered through many branches of the U.S. government. The Clean Air Act gave the EPA responsibility for implementing the provisions of the Act and certain regulatory and enforcement powers. Although many of the responsibilities and authorities are intentionally delegated to individual states, many other authorities are ultimately retained by the EPA.

Ambient air quality standard: federal limit for a pollutant in ambient air that serves as a target in local air quality improvement or protection programs. The *primary standard* protects public health; the *secondary standard* protects public welfare. The federal government establishes air quality standards, but more strict standards may be established by state governments.

Emission standard: limit in the amount of a pollutant that can be legally discharged into the environment from a particular source. Under the Clean Air Act of 1970, emissions from *existing* sources are controlled by the states under State Implementation Plans approved by the EPA. The federal government retained control over *new* (construction begun after 1972) sources, establishing maximum emission standards for any new plants built in any state. This is intended to preclude the development of "pollution havens," that is, to remove any temptation for any state to try to attract new industry by having low pollution control standards.

Environmental Protection Agency (EPA): the federal agency charged with the enforcement of all federal regulations having to do with environmental pollutants. The address is 401 M Street N.W., Washington, DC 20460.

Indirect source: a facility, road, building, structure, or other installation that causes air pollution to be generated through associated mobile source activity such as automobile, bus, and truck traffic. (Examples of indirect sources are a sports complex and a shopping center.)

Ringlemann charts: a series of charts that simulate various pollution densities by presenting different degrees of darkness used for estimating the opacity (density) of smoke rising from stacks and other sources.

Variance: permission by a legal body for a company or an individual to operate outside the limits prescribed in a law or standard, usually to allow the person or company to develop the means to bring its activity into compliance

---

The Act empowers the EPA to take any necessary action to stop or correct any air pollution emergency. The EPA can also levy fines, as can state or local environmental control agencies.

The Clean Air Act implied that areas of the United States that were cleaner than the standards would not necessarily be allowed to be made dirtier. However, it was later recognized that there had to be a compromise between the desire to preserve cleanliness and the development of relatively undeveloped areas of the country. Using its broad authority, the EPA established three classes with regard to just how dirty clean air (cleaner than the standard) would be allowed to become. In Class I areas the quality of air can be degraded slightly, moderate deterioration will be allowed in Class II areas, and dirtiness will be permitted to reach the national standard in Class III areas. Class III regions are so designated only upon appeal and only when it has been shown that the designation will optimize the economic growth and environmental objectives of the people affected.

Air Pollution Standards

The Clean Air Act of 1970 required that the Environmental Protection Agency set ambient air quality standards with a margin of safety such that the most sensitive people would suffer no adverse health effects. These standards were to be the goals in cleaning up the air, and they would be the limits beyond which the air would not be allowed to deteriorate. Using the data available at the time, in April 1971 the Environmental Protection Agency identified six pollutants as requiring some National Ambient Air Quality Standard. These six were particulate matter, sulfur dioxide, carbon monoxide, photochemical oxidants, nitrogen dioxide, and hydrocarbons. They were singled out because they were known to have effects on human mortality and morbidity and to have effects on vegetation, material, visibility, and other things that would fall within the realm of public welfare. Studies that served as the basis for setting these standards originally are described in the respective criteria documents issued by the EPA.

The Making of a Standard

Because it was recognized that setting a standard at almost any level would generate controversy over whether that standard was too high or too low, the procedure for setting a standard is rigorous and involves multiple reviews. The standard-setting process, in summary, involves:

1. reviewing all available data on the health and environmental effects of a pollutant and/or conducting studies to generate data;
2. preparing a *criteria document* summarizing all relevant data followed by the preparation of a *staff*

paper (by the EPA's Office of Air Quality Planning and Standards) in which the key studies of the criteria document are evaluated and the critical elements to be addressed in setting the standard are identified (Jordan, Richmond, and McCurdy, 1983);

3. conducting an open review of the staff paper, followed by staff recommendations for a standard to the EPA Administrator (these recommendations are published in the *Federal Register*);

4. publicizing the Administrator's decision regarding a standard in the *Federal Register* for the purpose of seeking comments from the general public and inviting individuals and organizations to submit comments within a certain time period; and

5. promulgating a final standard in the *Federal Register* to become effective and enforced after a specified length of time.

National Ambient Air Quality Standards

In the early 1970s the EPA issued air quality standards for the pollutants described above. Lead has since been added to the list, and hydrocarbons have since been deleted. The National Ambient Air Quality Standard for lead is 1.5 $\mu g/m^3$ as a quarterly average. It is anticipated that the major strategies for complying with the newer lead standard will have to do with lead smelters, petroleum refiners, and the automobile—the latter two because leaded gasoline is the primary source of atmospheric lead pollution. At its discretion, the EPA may add to the list.

Standards for each of the pollutants listed above were established in two categories, primary standards and secondary standards. Primary standards are set with public health in mind. The limit established as a **primary standard** is intended to identify a safety limit with respect to human health. The **secondary standard** is intended to take in all non-health effects of a pollutant and is a kind of public welfare standard. The secondary standard, where different, is more stringent.

Current primary and secondary National Ambient Air Quality Standards are given in Table 11.3. Also given in that table are (1) the levels of each of the major pollutants set as limits by the American Conference of Governmental Industrial Hygienists (for exposures in a 40-hour work week in occupational settings) and (2) the levels of each pollutant considered to constitute a hazardous or emergency situation.

It should be noted that there are pollutants in Table 11.3 other than those for which primary and secondary standards have been set. It should also be noted that the *ozone* standard originally set in 1971 was 0.08 ppm for a one-hour average. In June 1978 the EPA proposed to raise this to 0.10, but in 1979 the standard was actually set at 0.12 ppm for a high hourly average. The deadline for meeting the revised ozone standard is December 31, 1987.

Of 105 urban areas in the United States in 1978, only Honolulu and Spokane, Washington, met the health standards for ozone set in 1971. Raising the standard to 0.12 ppm meant that 20 cities rather than two had clean air as far as photochemical oxidants go. The EPA estimated that the annual cost of meeting the new standard for ozone would be 4.5 billion dollars compared to 6 billion dollars for the 0.08-ppm standard.

Setting standards is only one of the steps in the program for reaching and maintaining an appropriate quality of air nationwide specified in the Clean Air Act of 1970. Implied in the setting of the standard is that there have to be ways established for *measuring* the amounts of pollutants in ambient air, plans devised for *bringing existing air quality levels into compliance* with the standard, and ways of *enforcing compliance.*

The EPA has set air quality standards, but there is no guarantee that they will be met. The smog problem in Los Angeles, caused by frequent atmospheric inversions and an automobile-oriented culture, will not be easy to clear up.

Measuring and Monitoring Pollutants in the Air

Measuring air pollutants is no simple matter. First, methods for making measurements must be identified, established, and refined, and there must be systematic ways of sampling air so as to obtain the most accurate representation of environmental concentrations in a given large area. Under the provisions of the Clean Air Act the EPA specified the methods to be used to measure air pollutants (see Hoffman et al., 1975). Local agencies charged with monitoring air pollution must place measuring instruments in logical locations and determine—if

Table 11.3 National Ambient Air Quality Standards and Occupational Limits of Exposure for the Major Air Pollutants

Pollutants	Toxicity Rank	Primary Standard (to protect human health)	Secondary Standard (to protect public welfare)	Limits of Exposure Set for 40-Hour Week by the American Conference of Governmental Industrial Hygienists	Pollutant Levels Considered Hazardous
Sulfur Dioxide	3	80 μg/m^3 annual arithmetic mean (0.03 ppm) 365 μg/m^3 (0.14 ppm) maximum 24-hr. avg.[b]	1300 μg/m^3 maximum 3-hr. avg. (0.5 ppm)	5 ppm	2100 μg/m^3 24-hr. avg.
Particulate matter measured as "total suspended particulate"	4	75 μg/m^3 annual geometric mean 260 μg/m^3 maximum 24-hr. avg.[b]	60 μg/m^3 annual mean 150 μg/m^3 Maximum 24-hr. avg., 1300 μg/m^3 (0.5 ppm)- 3hr. avg.[b]	—	875 μg/m^3 24-hr. avg.
Nitrogen Dioxide	5	100 μg/m^3 annual arithmetic mean (0.05 ppm)	equal to primary	5 ppm	3000 μg/m^3 1-hr. avg.
Hydrocarbons[a] (excluding methane)[c]	8	160 μg/m^3 (6 to 9 AM) (0.24 ppm)	equal to primary	varying limits set for certain chlorinated, and other, derivatives	—
Carbon monoxide	9	10 mg/m^3 maximum 8-hr. avg. (9 ppm)[b] 40 mg/m^3 (35 ppm) maximum 1-hr. avg.[b]	equal to primary	50 ppm	46,000 μg/m^3 8-hr. avg.
Ozone	1	235 μg/m^3 maximum 1-hr. avg. (0.12 ppm)	equal to primary	0.1 ppm	1000 μg/m^3 1-hr. avg.
Hydrogen sulfide	7	none		10 ppm	
Hydrogen fluoride	2	none		3 ppm	
Metals	6	—	—	50 μg/m^3– 150 μg/m^3	—
Lead	—	1.5 μg/m^3 (monthly avg.)	equal to primary	0.15 mg/m^3	

[a] Since deleted; non-health related standard used as a guide for ozone control.
[b] Not to be exceeded more than once per year.
[c] A natural pollutant produced in swamps via anaerobic decay.

measurement is not to be continuous—how often to take readings.

Once it has been determined that the air in a particular region falls short of meeting clean air standards, control strategies (state implementation plans) must be devised by the states (and approved by EPA) to bring that air into compliance, for example, by setting and enforcing limits on how much of each pollutant can be discharged from pollution sources. **National Ambient Air Quality Standards (NAAQS)** are limits set on the amount of pollutants permitted to be in the air around us; **emission standards** are limitations on the amount of pollutant that may be discharged from specific sources.

For new plants the EPA sets national minimum emission standards. The states may set more stringent emission limitations than the federal minimums on new plants. The states set limits on pre-1972 plant emissions in the form of permit limitations designed to achieve the national ambient air quality standard.

In addition to the requirement that the EPA set National Ambient Air Quality Standards for the major air pollutants, the Clean Air Act (Section 112) requires that the EPA control any other substances that "may reasonably be anticipated to result in an increase in serious, irreversible, or incapacitating reversible illness." The EPA must first list suspected hazardous materials and then set emission standards for point sources (or clear the suspect) within one year of listing. To date, asbestos, benzene, inorganic arsenic, radionuclides, vinyl chloride, and beryllium have been listed; a total of 37 chemicals are on an informal list of potentially hazardous chemicals at some stage of review.

According to present laws, authority to enforce NAAQS and emission standards is to be delegated to the states by the EPA, but the EPA retains the authority to step in when the Administrator of the EPA finds that a state is not being strict enough in fulfilling its responsibility. The EPA also requires states to establish performance standards for new sources.

New Source Performance Standards are emission standards for different classes of new factories and plants. Such standards are to be based on the best available pollution control technology for controlling emissions from plants and other pollution sources of varying technological types; they are expressed in terms of maximum amounts of pollutant emitted per unit of activity, for example, tons of product produced. Performance standards may be different for different kinds of emission sources to the extent that they may be different for plants producing the same product by different processes. "Standards of performance" established by EPA for asphalt plants, concrete plants, refineries, sewage treatment plants, iron and steel plants, lead smelters, and certain other sources are described in the March 8, 1984, *Federal Register*. Other standards have been published since.

The Bubble Policy

In 1979 the EPA adopted a *bubble policy* with respect to emission control. Before this policy was adopted, emission control regulations were applied to every individual source of air pollution within an industrial plant. For the purposes of emission control, the bubble policy treats an entire plant as if all of its emissions came from a single port or stack coming out of an imaginary bubble covering the entire plant. Under this policy a facility that has several sources of pollution may be brought into compliance (with a state implementation plan) by a larger than required reduction in emission from one stack within the imaginary bubble and a lesser than required reduction in some other stack within the same bubble. Such flexibility allegedly allows a more cost-effective mix of pollution control measures without compromising clean air.

Enforcement: Giving Meaning to Air Quality Standards.

Most of the enforcement of the Clean Air Act has been delegated by the federal government to the states. As was noted above, the law required the states to submit implementation plans describing how emissions would be reduced and what steps would be taken to meet, maintain, and enforce the NAAQS. Such plans were to be approved by the EPA, and following approval, the states had to come up with a timetable for *reaching* the air quality standard.

At the federal level, violation of emission or performance standards can bring fines up to $25,000 each day of violation and one year in prison. Subsequent convictions can bring fines up to $50,000 for each day of violation and two years in prison. The law authorizes the EPA to shut down plants during especially severe episodes. These emergency powers were used by the EPA for the first time in late 1971 when a serious air pollution episode occurred in Birmingham, Alabama. Penalties whereby a non-complying firm is charged an amount equal to the savings gained from delaying compliance have put more teeth into the enforcement effort.

Compliance Trends

The national trend in bringing air pollution or air quality into compliance with the standards set in 1971 has been generally downward; that is, there *has* been a reduction in emission and an improvement in the last 15 years. The movement was fairly rapid up until 1976, when energy considerations led to a relaxing of some of the provisions of the Clean Air Act and slowed the rate of progress being made. The trends for total suspended particulate matter (TSP), NO_2, SO_2, CO, and O_3 levels during the late 1970s and early 1980s is given in Figure 11.9. Emission trends are depicted in Figure 11.10. Monitoring of NAAQS and emission trends is made possible through the existence of a uniform network, the State and Local Air Monitoring System (SLAMS), and a subset of this established in 1979 called the National Air Monitoring System (NAMS). Both systems monitor different numbers of high-pollution sites for different pollutants.

During the latter half of the 1970s, improvement continued (though not to the same degree for all pollutants). In its annual report released in January 1981 the Council on Environmental Quality said that in the 23 cities for which it had

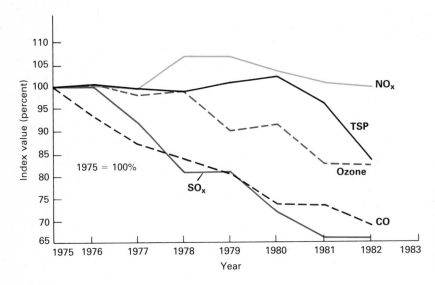

Figure 11.9 Pollution Trends. Trends in the ambient levels of total suspended particulate matter (TSP), oxides of nitrogen (NO_x), oxides of sulfur (SO_x), carbon monoxide (CO), and ozone (O_3).

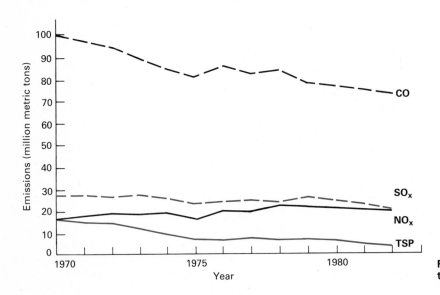

Figure 11.10 Trends in National Air Pollutant Emissions.

good data the overall quality of the air improved 18% between 1974 and 1978. Further improvement is expected.

The Air Pollution Index and Air Pollution Alerts

Before 1976, air pollution indices varied from city to city. In 1976 the Council on Environmental Quality established a task group to come up with standardized air pollution indices to be used across the country. The task group recommended that an index be established on the basis of five principal pollutants: sulfur dioxide, carbon monoxide, total suspended particulate matter, oxidants, and nitrogen dioxide. **The pollutant standard index (PSI),** illustrated in Table 11.4, assigns the value of 100 to a concentration of a pollutant when it is at the NAAQS level set by the EPA. If a pollutant reaches half the level of the NAAQS, its PSI is reported at 50. At higher levels of the index the numbers have the same kind of significance in terms of human health. For example, a PSI of 500 for any one of the five pollutants means that that level of that pollutant brings significant risk or significant harm. Another key feature of this index now in general use is that each pollutant elevated above the NAAQS is reported separately; any pollutant exceeding the value of 100 is reported. It is expected that additional pollutants will be added to this index in years to come. National trends with respect to the Pollutant Standard Index are illustrated in Figure 11.11.

Stay Indoors?

Sometimes during air pollution alerts, people are advised to stay indoors and to minimize physical activity. Human studies have shown that a subject's level of exercise during ozone exposure is directly related to the magnitude of diminished lung function. Restriction of physical activity would obviously reduce gas exchange and lessen exposure of lung tissue to ozone and other damaging pollutants.

The reason for advising people to stay indoors is perhaps less obvious. Some recent evidence indicates that there may be an ironic twist to this advice. The advice is based on observations that for a variety of complicated reasons pollutant levels are usually much lower indoors during outdoor air pollution episodes. This is due partly to the fact that there are things in indoor air that react with pollutants and neutralize them.

The irony is that indoor pollution may be more of a problem than outdoor pollution *most of the time.* People spend anywhere from 70% (Gold, 1980) to 90% (Repace and Lowrey, 1980) of their time indoors and another 5–10% of their time in an automobile or other vehicle (Spengler and Colome, 1982). This is significant in light of recent studies in which formaldehyde, nitrogen dioxide, asbestos,

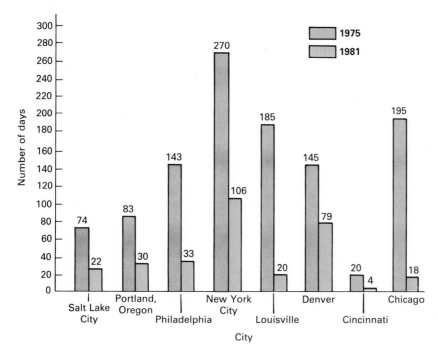

Figure 11.11 Air Quality Improvement in Eight Metropolitan Areas, 1975 and 1981 as Reflected in the Number of Unhealthful Days.

Table 11.4 Nationwide Standardized Air Pollution Index

PSI Index Value	Air Quality Level	Pollutant Level					Health Effect Descriptor	General Health Effects	Cautionary Statements
		TSP (24-hr.), $\mu g/m^3$	SO_2 (24-hr.), $\mu g/m^3$	CO_2 (8-hr.), mg/m^3	O_3 (1-hr.), $\mu g/m^3$	NO_2 (1-hr.), $\mu g/m^3$			
500	Significant Harm	1000	2620	57.5	1200	3750	hazardous	Premature death of ill and elderly. Healthy people will experience adverse symptoms that affect their normal activity.	All persons should remain indoors, keeping windows and doors closed. All persons should minimize physical exertion and avoid traffic.
400	emergency	875	2100	46.0	1000	3000	hazardous		
300	warning	625	1600	34.0	800	2260	hazardous	Premature onset of certain diseases in addition to significant aggravation of symptoms and decreased exercise tolerance in healthy persons.	Elderly and persons with existing diseases should stay indoors and avoid physical exertion. General population should avoid outdoor activity.
200	alert	375	800	17.0	400[c]	1130	very unhealthful	Significant aggravation of symptoms and decreased exercise tolerance in persons with heart or lung disease, with wide-spread symptoms in the healthy population.	Elderly and persons with existing heart or lung disease should stay indoors and reduce physical activity.
100	NAAQS	260	365	10.0	160	—[a]	unhealthful	Mild aggravation of symptoms in susceptible persons, with irritation symptoms in the healthy population.	Persons with existing heart or respiratory ailments should reduce physical exertion and outdoor activity.
50	50% of NAAQS	75[b]	80[b]	5.0	80	—[a]	moderate		
0		0	0	0	0	—[a]	good		

a. No index values reported at concentration levels below those specified by "Alert Level" criteria.
b. Annual primary NAAQS.
c. 400 $\mu g/m^3$ was used instead of the O_3 Alert Level of 200 $\mu g/m^3$.

carbon monoxide, (radioactive) radon, particulate matter, and various other components of tobacco smoke have been implicated as airborne health hazards in many homes and other buildings.

Formaldehyde apparently escapes from plywood, particle board, and certain types of foam insulation. The type of insulation known to emit formaldehyde was installed in more than 100,000 homes per year during the late 1970s. Gold (1980) reports that levels of formaldehyde high enough to cause dizziness, rashes, nosebleeds, and vomiting have been measured in some homes.

Nitrogen dioxide is emitted from gas stoves. Particulates come from tobacco smoke, cooking, aerosol sprays. Radon apparently escapes from stone, concrete blocks, and even water. Carbon monoxide comes from cars in garages and other sources of incomplete combustion.

A Harvard School of Public Health study revealed that homes in five of six cities studied had particulate levels that were double the levels outdoors. In at least a few homes with two-pack-a-day smokers, particulate levels exceeded the EPA outdoor limit. Tobacco smoke includes particulate matter, carbon monoxide, and assorted carcinogens. It has long been known that cigarette smoke had health effects on nonsmokers. Recently, the link was extended to cancer in a Japanese study (see Chapter 14). If it can be inferred from the 90% of the time people spend indoors that 90% of all cigarettes are smoked indoors, American buildings receive the combustion products of 554 billion cigarettes each year.

A double irony to all of this is that the problem is getting worse because of efforts to save energy. Weather stripping and other means of tightening up buildings reduce the rate of air exchange and increase the buildup of pollutants indoors. The EPA estimates that there would be 20,000 more cases of cancer (mainly lung) per year from radon exposure if ventilation rates were cut in half (Gold, 1980).

The matter of indoor air pollution raises an important point. Indoor pollutants should be taken into account in epidemiological studies that attempt to measure the relationship between health and air pollution. It is not simply what can be measured in outdoor air that people are being exposed to; indoor exposure may have an overriding effect. To be technically correct in assessing the health effect of exposure to whatever pollutant, the levels of that pollutant should be measured in all of the places where people spend time and then their exposure weighted accordingly in relation to the amount of time they spend in each place. This is actually done by having representative people carry samplers around with them all day.

Amendments to the Clean Air Act (1977)

As the Clean Air Act was implemented, it became obvious that some of its provisions had to be tightened and others had to be relaxed. Some of the reasons for the 1977 amendments included:

1. Poor fuel comsumption efficiencies in cars equipped with air pollution control devices.
2. Failure of the auto industry to reach the target dates set by earlier versions of the Act.
3. Failure of many regions of the country to achieve the primary standards by 1975 and secondary standards by 1977 as required in the original legislation.
4. Pressure to postpone implementation of transportation control plans required of urban communities.

The amendments to the Clean Air Act became effective on August 9, 1977. Among the things the amendments did were the following:

1. Extended the deadline for achieving tailpipe emission standards for two years. These standards are given in Table 11.5. These were extended again for some models in 1980.
2. Required states to submit revised plans for those pollutants for which standards have not been attained by January 1, 1974, to reach the primary standards by July 1, 1982.
3. Encouraged establishment of auto inspection and maintenance programs; the EPA can require such programs if standards were not reached by 1982.

Table 11.5 Emission Standards for Motor Vehicles Established by the Amendments to the Clean Air Act of 1977. Numbers are in grams generated per mile of operation.

Model Year	Hydrocarbons	Carbon Monoxide	Nitrogen Oxides
1978–1979	1.5	15.0	2.0
1980	0.41	7.0	2.0
1981	0.41	3.4	1.0

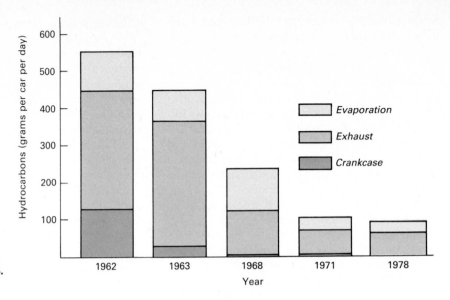

Figure 11.12 Trend in Hydrocarbon Emissions in U.S. Automobiles.

4. Required that if a new pollution-worsening development occurred in an area currently exceeding the national standard, an offsetting reduction must be made elsewhere.
5. Required the EPA to review and, if necessary, modify the existing standards by the end of 1980.
6. Required the EPA to consider setting a short-term NO_2 standard (see Table 11.3).
7. Extended to all auto repair facilities the anti-tampering prohibition with regard to automobile emission control devices.

The Effectiveness of the Clean Air Act and Its Amendments

In some respects the Clean Air Act has been successful; in other respects, accomplishment has fallen short of expectations.

On the plus side, much of the trend of increasingly dirty air before 1970 has been halted and reversed; standards have been set, and progress toward achieving these standards has been significant. As we pointed out earlier, emissions of most pollutants have been reduced by various control technologies and regulations. Reduction in particulate emissions are attributed to the installation of control equipment in industry. Sulfur dioxide emissions have been reduced through the use of low-sulfur fuels, scrubbers (see below), and new combustion technologies despite increased electric power generation. Hydrocarbon levels have been reduced as a direct result of emission controls on highway vehicles (Figure 11.12). In short, most areas of the United States have better air than they had in 1970 (see Figures 11.9, 11.10, and 11.11).

On the negative side, progress has been slow; many of the amendments to the Clean Air Act in 1977 simply extended the deadlines for reaching clean air goals. Deadlines for achieving automobile emissions standards had already been pushed back twice at the end of 1977; in the late summer of 1979 the EPA granted five automobile manufacturers two-year delays in having some of their engines meet 1981 standards for carbon monoxide emissions. The EPA admits that the average new car violates federal clean air standards during its first year on the road, 70% of the new cars violate at least one pollution emission standard by the end of the first year; 9% violate two standards after two years.

As for the negative side of the bigger picture, roughly 20 American cities still had air in the unhealthful and hazardous range 50 or more days in the late 1970s (Council on Environmental Quality, 1980). Emission compliance as of the beginning of the 1980s is illustrated in Table 11.6.

In summary, the Clean Air Act and its amendments have brought cleaner air, but the air we are breathing is still *dirty;* it is causing cancers in some of us and emphysema in others and is aggravating asthma in still others. At least part of the reason for this is that as a narrowly focused piece of legislation, the Clean Air Act does not regulate such clearly relevant things as planned obsolescence, transportation inefficiency, and the wasting of energy in other ways. Perhaps other crises will make it more

Table 11.6 Compliance Status of Major Air Pollution Sources, 1980

Industry	Number of Total Sources	Number in Compliance with Emission Limitations	Meeting Compliance Schedule	Violating Emission Limitations	Violating Compliance Schedule	Other (Unknown)
Power plants (coal, oil)	700	559	54	67	3	17
Iron and steel	204	110	34	56	4	0
Municipal incinerators	72	60	2	7	3	0
Petroleum refineries	214	170	15	21	0	8

generally obvious that we need laws that are ecologically comprehensive—laws able to modify social inertia in significant ways—to take on things that are for the moment sacred cows. We must continue to address both *what* we do and *how* we do it.

AIR POLLUTION CONTROL STRATEGIES AND TECHNOLOGIES

As we have just concluded, many American cities still exceeded primary standards by a considerable amount more than 100 days out of each year. While a little of this problem could be blamed on the need for better control technologies, the primary reasons for our failure to achieve clean air in the United States has been the failure of strategies other than technological ones. There are obviously a number of very fundamental technological *and* nontechnological approaches to the control of air pollution, all of which are being used to some degree. These might be enumerated as follows.

1. *Alternatives.* A number of kinds of alternatives could be used: (a) we could change our lifestyles to those requiring less of the energy that brings pollution with it, (b) we could find alternative ways to get our life-style—find different technologies that are less polluting, or (c) we could use alternative sources of energy that do not have as much pollution as a by-product.

2. *Reduction.* We could continue to do the same sorts of things but less of them. For instance, we could switch to still smaller cars, modify our technology to make cars still more efficient, and/or make our overall expenditure of energy more efficient by insulating houses (and finding ways to neutralize indoor pollutants).

3. *Remove pollutant generating materials from fuels.* An example of this kind of technological fix would be to remove sulfur from coal before it is burned.

4. *Keep pollutants from escaping into the air as fuels are burned.* This can be done by putting catalytic converters in automobiles and installing scrubbers (see Figure 11.13).

5. *Remove the pollutant from ambient air.* We include this absurd strategic element for the sake of completeness (we say absurd though it has been proposed (Maugh, 1976) that small concentrations of pollution-scavenging chemicals could be added to the air over cities on days of high pollution). The second law of thermodynamics tells us that it would be more efficient to approach the problem of minimizing air pollution by getting at the offending material before it is scattered throughout the environment.

6. *Change the affected receptors to protect them.* For example, we could coat statues with protective materials, breed resistant plant species, and add lime to lakes.

The range of strategies and plans adopted around the country for controlling pollutants have included most of this spectrum. Implemented and planned approaches involving the automobile, for example, have included

1. reduction in size, horsepower, and compression ratios of the internal combustion engine;
2. improvements in the technology of controlling the emission of pollutants from automobiles;
3. reduction of the number of automobiles by improving mass transit, encouraging carpooling, establishing downtown parking restrictions, and establishing bicycle paths;
4. periodic inspections of automobiles; and
5. replacement of the gasoline engine with electric or steam engines.

Strategies for reducing sulfur dioxide pollution by power plants have included

1. substituting low-sulfur fuels for high-sulfur fuels,

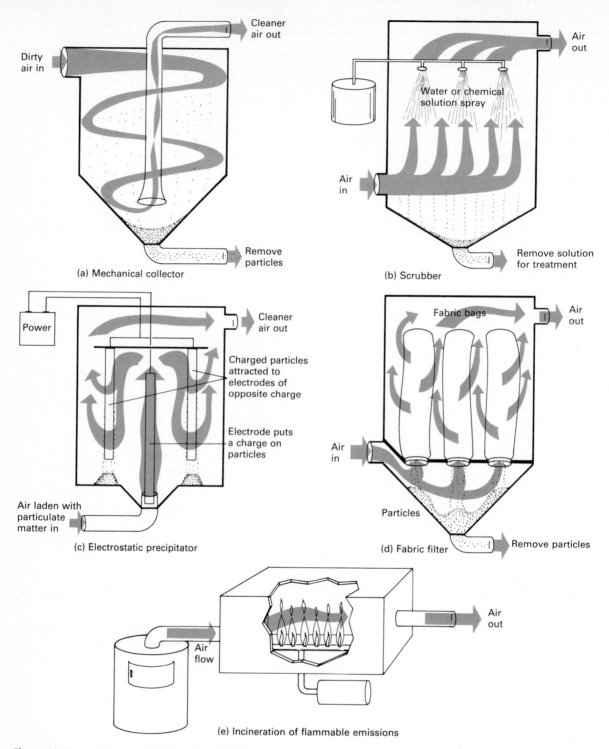

Figure 11.13 **Common Air Pollution Control Devices.**

2. using smokestacks high enough to poke through inversion layers (as we discussed earlier, this is a false, "dump it on somebody else" type of strategy; it results in acid rain somewhere downwind),
3. chemically scrubbing sulfur dioxide and other compounds of sulfur from the effluent going up stacks, and
4. removing sulfur from the coal and oil and gas before it is burned—in addition to reducing the demand for electric power.

Let us look at each of the approaches to air pollution individually and see which of them seem to hold the most promise. We will editorialize a bit; see if you agree.

Changing Life-Styles

If the environmental movement up to this point has done anything at all, it seems to have revealed at least one great truth—namely, that appeals to human reason to change life-styles and reduce consumption are exercises in energy-wasting rhetoric. Perhaps human beings respond only to physical or financial pain. Even then it might be argued that humans can perceive relationships between pain and pollution only when the pain is immediate. Unfortunately, it appears that we must rely on some combination of law, significant economic pressure, and education to bring about necessary, pollution-reducing changes in life-style. A law that requires that cars get at least 30 miles per gallon and an economic system that requires that the cost of pollution control be passed on to consumers are obviously much more effective than saying "please." In this regard we think it somewhat ironic that the *energy crunch,* which resulted in legislation that weakened the Clean Air Act, may—because of the expense of energy—ultimately prove to be *the* most important effector of clean air by bringing about reductions in fuel consumption.

Alternative Technologies

Alternative types of solutions often bring alternative problems. The Clean Air Act legislation in the early 1970s brought about a gradual but profound switch from coal to natural gas, natural gas being a much cleaner fuel. Unfortunately, we will soon run short of natural gas—a different kind of problem. Replacing gasoline-powered engines with electric engines, for another example, would simply change the source of pollution from the automobile to the plants where electricity is generated. Such a switch

At top, fumes pour from the basic oxygen furnace stack at Bethlehem Steel Corporation's plant in Bethlehem, Pa. At bottom, the same stack emits almost no fumes after installation of an electrostatic precipitator control system.

might at least make the pollution more controllable by consolidating source locations. Furthermore, legislation would probably be required to effect a switch to electric automobiles. Our technology can already produce electric automobiles, we would have to get used to stopping every so often to be recharged, and we might not be able to go as fast. Americans are not likely to switch to this kind of alternative willingly and on the basis of appeals to reason.

Perhaps the key element in the strategy having to do with alternative technology is *efficiency.* Most air pollution comes from the combustion of fossil fuels. Obviously, any gain we make in the efficiency would have direct payoff in terms of reducing the pollution problem. Reducing energy consumption by half would produce about a 50% reduction in the air pollution problem.

Alternative Energy Sources

Most of what we had to say about different sources of energy for our society was presented in Chapter 6. Suffice it to say here that not all of the ways of producing energy pollute the air to the same

Afterburner: an air pollution control device that keeps undesirable organic compounds from escaping by burning them.
Bag house: an air pollution control device that traps particles by forcing air containing dust and other particles through large filter bags usually made of fiberglass.
Catalytic converter: an air pollution control device that removes organic compounds from a stream of exhaust by completing their oxidation into carbon dioxide and water in the presence of a catalyst.
Cyclone: an air pollution control device that removes heavy particles by causing the particle-containing gas to swirl and removing the particles through centrifugal force.
Electrostatic precipitator: an air pollution control device that removes particulates by putting an electric charge on them and then attracting them to an electrode of opposite charge.
Scrubber: an air pollution control device that uses a liquid spray to remove aerosol and gaseous substances from an airstream. The principle is that the gases are removed either by absorption, by dissolving the liquid, or through chemical reaction with a chemical in the liquid spray.

Several kinds of particulate control devices are illustrated in Figure 11.13. It should be noted that each of them produces a product that must be disposed of in some way so as not to produce a substitute environmental problem. Modifications of the scrubbers shown in Figure 11.13 can effectively remove gaseous pollutants from the air. Highly water-soluble gases, for instance, can be removed in water sprays or in chemical sprays that neutralize the pollutants. Here too there must be ways of disposing of the resultant solutions. Another type of scrubber is a combustion chamber or afterburner. Hydrocarbons can be removed from gases in such devices through combustion.

The control of automobile emissions is now largely effected by the catalytic conversion of pollutants to relatively harmless reaction products.

The state-of-the-art catalytic converter uses metals such as platinum, palladium, and more recently rhodium. Platinum and palladium act as catalysts in the conversion of hydrocarbons and carbon monoxide in automobile exhaust into carbon dioxide and water. Rhodium, a reducing catalyst, converts oxides of nitrogen into nitrogen gas and oxygen. Seventy percent of the 1975 automobiles and 85% of the 1976 models sold in the United States were equipped with catalytic converters. According to the 1976 report of the Council on Environmental Quality, catalytic converter technology, together with the trend toward smaller cars and better gas mileage, made 1976 cars 13% better than the 1975 models and 30% better than the 1974 fleet in terms of reduced air pollution.

Although improved and more economical control technologies are needed, the most important limiting factors in cleaning up air appear to be sociopolitical and socioeconomic factors. Perhaps the following will illustrate this point.

degree. Each form of energy generation has its unique problems and lends itself in slightly different ways to the control of air pollution. This must be taken into account in the consideration of various solutions to our air pollution problem and our energy crises.

Cleaning Fuel

It is possible to remove inorganic sulfur from coal. The basic technology for doing this already exists, but only recently have economic pressures, legal pressures, and scarcity-of-fuel pressures combined to focus our technological attention on more economical ways of doing such things. The point we wish to make here is that it is possible to reduce air pollution by taking chemicals like sulfur out of the fuel. Naturally, this costs money.

Trapping Effluents

The technologies for cleaning effluent gases extend from "tightening up" (no open tanks, no leaky valves or joints) to keeping things like hydrocarbons from leaking into the environment to chemically or physically scrubbing gaseous or particulate pollutants from the effluents going up stacks and out exhaust pipes.

The Scrubber Controversy

When the need to control SO_2 emissions first became apparent, the technology for removing SO_2 from stack gases was far from well developed. At first, electrical utilities stayed away from scrubbers and went for other strategies open to them as options by the Clean Air Act. For example, many switched to oil as a fuel; some went for low-sulfur coal; and some decided simply to build higher stacks. The initial tall-stack theory was that SO_2 would be lifted over the areas immediately downwind of coal-fired plants and become dispersed to the point of being below the limits set by the EPA before it came back down.

Unfortunately, the acid rain problem apparently results in part from this strategy.

In any case, because of many factors—including the energy crises, the scarcity of low-sulfur coal, the difficulty of linking SO_2 emissions to acid rain hundreds of miles downwind, loopholes in the Clean Air Act governing old plants, the expense of scrubbers, inflation, and the fact that scrubbers produce a solid waste that must be disposed of in some way—a scrubber controversy raged during most of the 1970s. The EPA worked hard to persuade utilities to develop and use scrubbers. The utility industry fought the idea with appeals to consumers (mostly through threats of higher utility rates) and ridicule of the EPA. The battle was waged through ads in newspapers and magazines and in the courts.

Ironically, it was a federally supported agency, the Tennessee Valley Authority (TVA), that waged *and lost* the longest and most celebrated court battle against a coalition of environmental groups. The EPA indicated that the mandated installation of scrubbers by the TVA would keep 970,000 tons of sulfur dioxide and thousands of tons of dust out of the Tennessee Valley each year. The TVA countered that this would cost consumers 9–12% more in utility bills each year for 5 years.

Scrubber technology has advanced considerably in the last decade. Models have been around since the late 1970s that are supposed to be operable 90% of the time, removing 95% of SO_2 emissions (Reisner, 1977). Scrubbers that can be regenerated rapidly and that produce a more easily handled sludge should soon be available.

IN SUMMARY

Scattered throughout this chapter were defined and implied tasks for science and technology. There are some things we need to know, and there are other things we must learn to do more economically. Perhaps the most glaring things we do not know are the effects that low levels of pollutants alone and in combination have on human beings. Perplexing problems in this regard have to do with

1. varying sensitivity to pollutants among test species and human beings,
2. the dynamic chemistry of pollution under the influence of sunlight,
3. the varying stability of pollutants,
4. the chronic, slow, insidious nature of air pollution–related diseases, and
5. the variable biological magnification of different pollutants (see Chapter 13).

Many states require cars to pass an inspection to ensure that their emission control equipment is working properly.

Although these will translate into many hours of scientific work, far more of the task of dealing with air pollution falls to institutions other than science and technology.

Studies can be designed, and laborious, elegant, time-consuming, expensive studies can and surely will add to what we know as facts. Research can pinpoint health effects, establish more precise thresholds (if there are thresholds), and differentiate very toxic from not-so-toxic pollutants. Both political and economic value judgments will obviously be required not only because our data will always be somewhat short of complete but because there will always be at least a little room for choice and interpretation.

In closing this chapter we would like to remind the reader of one simple fact and point to the connection between this chapter and the earlier chapters on energy and biogeochemical cycles. The fact is that *there will always be pollution.* We have defined pollution as the sum total of those effects we have on our environment that have an adverse effect, and so, as with all environmental problems, the task is to learn more and to work to diminish the effects. A connection between this chapter and Chapter 3 is that pollutants are constituents of biogeochemical cycles. Air pollution is a result of our kicking up the lithosphere too fast and furiously for the ecosphere to handle it. When this happens in nature, pollution *becomes* the environment, and we have to live in our own waste.

There is a profound connection between these chapters on air pollution and the chapter on energy. Air pollution is largely a phenomenon related to the combustion of fossil fuels. The statement by some that we may have to choose between energy and the environment simply is not true. What we have to choose between is the waste and socially costly uses of energy and the environment. As more of us recognize this simple fact, significant things should begin to happen more quickly.

CONCEPTS TO REMEMBER

1. The cost of controlling air pollution is significant. Some 300 billion dollars will have been spent to control air pollution between 1978 and 1987, nearly all of it because of the Clean Air Act. Annual costs of all forms of air pollution control amount to just over 1% of the gross national product.

2. By some measures, more jobs have been gained than lost because of the Clean Air Act. Things in general cost a little over 3% more in the mid-1980s because of the cost of all forms of pollution control.

3. Determining the cost of *not* controlling air pollution is much more difficult than determining the costs of pollution control. One estimate of the benefits of cleaner air mainly brought by the Clean Air Act in the late 1970s placed dollar values on prevented damage to health, vegetation, materials, and property values, giving a range of 4.6–51.2 billion dollars with a best guess of 21.4 billion dollars.

4. If all things had a dollar value, our air pollution control task would simply be to balance or match the costs of air pollution control with the cost of not controlling air pollution. Not all things impacted by air pollution have universally agreed dollar values, however.

5. National Ambient Air Quality Standards (NAAQS) have been set for particulate matter, sulfur dioxide, nitrogen dioxide, ozone, carbon monoxide, photochemical oxidants, and lead.

6. Emission standards are the maximum rates set by the EPA at which relatively new pollution sources are allowed to emit pollutants. States may set more stringent emission limitations for new plants, and they set limitations for old plants for which there are no federal standards. According to a state's plan to achieve the NAAQS, the EPA also sets emission standards for especially hazardous substances such as asbestos and mercury and for automobiles.

7. A bubble policy permits the EPA to consider a plant's emission sources as if they were all emitted through a common vent.

8. A pollutant standard index now in effect rates each pollutant on a common scale based on a value of 100 when a pollutant is right at its NAAQS level.

9. Although staying indoors does in fact lessen exposure to bad outside air, the indoors has characteristic air quality hazards of its own, notably particulate matter, asbestos, nitrogen dioxide, radon and formaldehyde.

10. Although there was a federal Air Pollution Control Act in 1955 (PL 84-159) and local air pollution laws that go back to the 1890s, modern clean air legislation started with the Motor Vehicle Act of 1960 and began to assume its present form in the Clean Air Act of 1970.

11. The Clean Air Act *has* resulted in improvements in air quality, but we still have a long way to go.

12. Clean air strategies range from scrubbing stack gases to energy conservation; the latter helps solve energy, land use, and water resource problems as well as the air pollution problem.

DISCUSSION QUESTIONS AND FOOD FOR THOUGHT

1. It has been said many times that air pollution control is very costly, and this is true. However, proponents of strict air pollution control state that the cost of uncontrolled air pollution is even greater. List some of the indirect costs that have to be paid by a society in which individuals and groups are relatively free to release pollutants into the atmosphere.

2. Obtain copies of the legislation governing air pollution in your city, state, or county. What agencies are involved in enforcing these laws? Discuss the degree to which air pollution laws are enforced where you live.

3. Pick any pollutant from those discussed in this chapter and determine and list all of the ways in which a reduction in this pollutant could be brought about.

After the list is complete, try to reach agreement on the most important problem standing in the way of each of the approaches you identified.

4. Discuss: Could it be that despite antitrust laws, the automobile industry, the product of which is based entirely on the internal combustion engine, is now so large and so highly capitalized that it is virtually impossible for any new automobile technology to gain a foothold? Many people believe that new developments in transportation should be left to private enterprise; such a strategy implies that competition will bring about necessary changes. How do you feel about the view that new automobile or new transportation technologies will come only if automobile manufacturers are forced by law to develop them? Must the government help bring new technology along with some form of subsidy?

5. The following are articles or excerpts clipped from newspapers, journals, and other sources. Read and discuss each one. If similar articles appeared in your newspaper today, you may prefer to use them.

Pennsylvania was able to woo the Volkswagen Manufacturing Corporation of America into establishing a plant in the heavily polluted and economically depressed southwestern portion of the state by a tradeoff with its own Department of Transportation (Penn-DOT). Under EPA's offset policy, new sources of pollution may enter an area where air pollution standards are not being met only if existing polluters are able to reduce their output of noxious emissions to a degree that an overall decrease in pollution results. It was estimated that the VW plant would release approximately 810 tonnes of hydrocarbons into the atmosphere a year. Penn-DOT has been releasing some 923 tonnes a year from the asphalt it used to pave roads in the area around New Stanton, where VW will begin to manufacture Rabbits. A recent issue of *Conservation News* (Vol. 42, No. 15), published by the National Wildlife Federation, reported that Penn-DOT was able to effect a net reduction in emissions by switching from a petroleum-based asphalt to an emulsion or water-based asphalt, which releases only water vapor when it is being laid. With this decrease in pollution, EPA permitted the VW plant to move into the area. (From *Bioscience* 27(12):832, 1977. Copyright © 1977 by the American Institute of Biological Sciences.)

Political factors cannot be discounted in the review process. In this connection it is worth noting that the much less publicized Volkswagen plant in Westmoreland County in Western Pennsylvania (about 20–30 miles from Pittsburgh) which is presently producing some 1000 Rabbits a day was located in an area which is non-attainment for hydrocarbons. The final permit was obtained, at least in theory, by changing the formula of a state asphalt plant to provide the "offset." To a large extent the offset was fake, and that was probably not the determining factor. The major issue was the fact that the local populace wanted the plant; the governor of Pennsylvania wanted the plant, and had even made several trips to West Germany to convince Volkswagen to build the plant at that site; all the members of the Pennsylvania Congressional delegation wanted the plant; the U.S. Department of Commerce wanted the plant; in short, everybody wanted the plant built, and little if any opposition was raised by any environmental intervenor group. Given that set of circumstances there was little doubt that a way would be found to approve the plant. Proposed projects encounter problems only when objections are raised to the projects. If no objections are raised, there are no problems.

The offset policy has given rise to a new vested property interest in the right to pollute. Thus, for example, ABC Corporation might own an existing plant which, subject to the SIP [State Implementation Plan], is legally emitting say 1,000 tons of SO_2 per month. The plant can be sold to XYZ Corporation which can shut the plant down and build a new plant which emits 999.9 tons of SO_2 per month (or some lesser amount, depending upon the state plan). The right to emit would be a major factor in the sale price of ABC's plant. Alternatively, XYZ might pay for the installation of a scrubber at ABC to reduce the emissions at ABC to 100 tons per month, freeing up the remaining 900 tons per month of emissions for its own use. In either case, XYZ has in essence purchased a right to emit from ABC. (From J.P. Bromberg, *Clean Air Act Handbook*, Government Institutes, Inc., Rockville, Md., 1983. Used with permission.)

Air pollution reached 'very unhealthy' level

Louisville's air-pollution level yesterday reached 201 on the pollutant standards index—a "very unhealthy" level.

John Tate of the Jefferson County Air Pollution Control District said the problem was caused by increased amounts of ozone, one of a family of photochemical oxidants. The ozone is created by warm weather and bright sunlight reacting with automobile exhaust fumes and smoke from industries.

Yesterday was the first day since January that the pollution index exceeded 100. The index goes up to 500, which Tate said is a nearly impossible and fatal level.

Tate said yesterday's level could aggravate respiratory and heart problems. He advised Louisville residents to try to avoid driving their cars or exercising, and to remain indoors with the windows closed if the problem occurs again today.

Louisville had two ozone alerts last year. Tate said an alert was not called yesterday although the ozone was at an alert level, because the prospects for today looked good.

However, the Louisville office of the National Weather Service says relief is not in store until tomorrow at the earliest. Forecaster George Sickels said the warm, sunny weather would continue through today with very little chance of precipitation to clear the air.

The General Hospital emergency room reported no noticeable increase in cases of respiratory problems yesterday, although high levels of pollution usually lead to such an increase. (From *Louisville Courier Journal and Times*, May 17, 1977. Copyright © 1977. The Courier-Journal. Reprinted with permission.)

Increase Jobs Not Clean Air

The district job picture has finally gotten some good news.

Bethlehem Steel Corporation has recently announced plans to resume production of hot steel and the employment of 8,000 workers at its Johnstown plant by the end of the month. This represents an increase of about 500 workers from the figure Bethlehem had said would remain at the Johnstown plant (down from the 11,500) pre-flood level) if all governmental pollution-control device requirements were to be suspended for the next two years.

Now there is a possibility, according to Thomas

Crowley, local plant manager, that employment at the Johnstown works may rise to as high as 8,500 depending on the outcome of negotiations between the firm and the federal Environmental Protection Agency.

The addition of even 500 more jobs will mean a lot to a district struggling [in] the aftermath of a devastating flood. A district where jobless projections for the near future range from 17 to 20 percent.

It is for this reason that we urge the EPA yield to the demands of Bethlehem pertaining to the Johnstown plant.

Government was formed to act in the best interests of the public. In the situation now facing the Cambria County area, the public (Cambria County) can best be served by relaxing the pollution-control standards formerly required of the Johnstown works of Bethlehem Steel.

An increase in jobs, not clean air, is the most important priority for the district. (From: *Nanty Glo Journal* (Pennsylvania) Sept. 14, 1977. Used with permission.)

5,000 steelworkers to lose their jobs in Youngstown

NEW YORK—Citing import competition and environmental restraints, Youngstown Sheet and Tube Co. yesterday announced a major cutback in its steel operations at Youngstown, Ohio.

R. C. Rieder, chairman of Youngstown Sheet, a subsidiary of Lykes Corp., said some of the operations would be relocated from the old Campbell Works to the newer, more modern Indiana Harbor Works on Lake Michigan near Chicago.

Youngstown's headquarters will also be moved to the Chicago area, Rieder said.

The layoffs and cutbacks affect 5,000 of the company's 9,000 workers in the Youngstown area.

In addition, U.S. Steel Corp. the nation's largest steel producer, has said it is planning to consolidate its Youngstown area operations with severe cuts in a work force that ranges from 5,400 to 6,400.

The announcement came on the heels of a decision by the 3rd U.S. Circuit Court of Appeals that invalidated a March 1976 decision of the Environmental Protection Agency to exempt eight steel mills in the Mahoning River Valley of Ohio from federal water-quality standards.

Youngstown Sheet and Tube's Campbell Works was one of those affected by the decision. Other companies with plants involved were U.S. Steel and Republic Steel, the nation's fourth largest steelmaker.

When the original decision was handed down in 1976, the steel companies said the plants involved, all on the Mahoning River, were not profitable enough to justify spending about $140 million for pollution controls to meet federal standards. (From *Louisville Courier Journal and Times,* Sept. 20, 1977, p. B4. Used with permission.)

6. Discuss the need for, and the potential impact of, each of the following items (together with the others you come up with) relative to the air pollution problem.
   a. Carefully document the health effects of air pollutants.
   b. Set Emission Standards and Ambient Air Quality Standards for *all* pollutants.
   c. Establish a strict Auto Inspection Program with severe penalties for noncompliance.
   d. Tax all big cars.
   e. Encourage bicycle riding.
   f. Limit the speed and power of auto engines.
   g. Ban all big cars.
   h. Design new cities with getting around in mind.
   i. Build good interurban transit systems.

   After your discussion, rate each item from 1 to 5 (1 being low and 5 being high) in importance and urgency.

REFERENCES AND FURTHER READING

References marked with an asterisk are cited in the chapter.

*Adams, R. M.; Thanavibulchai, N.; and Crocker, T. D., 1979. *Methods Development for Assessing Air Pollution Damages for Selected Crops within Southern California.* Washington, D.C.: Environmental Protection Agency.

*American Lung Association, 1977. *The Health Costs of Air Pollution.* New York: American Lung Association.

Bachmann, L. J., and Richmond, H., 1983. *Protecting Public Welfare: The Role of Environmental Effects Information in Air Standards Development.* Research Triangle Park, N.C.: Environmental Protection Agency.

*Barrett, L. B., and Waddell, T. E., 1973. *Cost of Air Pollution Damage: A Status Report.* Research Triangle Park, N.C.: National Environmental Research Center, Environmental Protection Agency. (Publication No. AP-85)

Bhagia, G. S., and Stoevener, H., 1978. *Impact of Air Pollution on the Consumption of Medical Services.* Corvallis, Ore.: Environmental Protection Agency.

*Blomquist, G., 1979. "Value of Life Saving: Implications of Consumption Activity," *Journal of Political Economy* **87** (3):540–558.

Brodine, V., 1973. *Air Pollution.* New York: Harcourt Brace Jovanovich.

Bromberg, J. P., 1984. "The Use of Coal Cleaning in Bubbles Trade-offs and Acid Rain Applications," *Proceedings of the First Annual Pittsburgh Coal Conference and Exhibition.* Washington, D.C.: U.S. Department of Energy.

*Brookshire, D. S.; Ives, B. C.; and Schulze, W. D., 1976. "The Valuation of Aesthetic Preferences," *Journal of Environmental Economics and Management* **3**(4):325–346.

*Carpenter, B. H.; LeSourd, D. A.; Chromy, J. R.; and Bach, W. D., 1977. *Health Costs of Air Pollution Damage, A Study of Hospitalization Costs.* Research Triangle Park, N.C.: Environmental Protection Agency.

"Cleaner Air and Water: Can We Afford 690 Billion Dollars?" *U.S. News and World Report,* February 28, 1983.

The Conservation Foundation, 1984. *State of the Environment: An Assessment at Mid-Decade,* Washington, D.C.: The Conservation Foundation.

The Costs and Benefits of Sulfur Oxide Control. Washington, D.C.: OCED. (1981)

*Council on Environmental Quality, 1980. *10th Annual Report: Environmental Quality—1979.* Washington, D.C.: U.S. Government Printing Office.

Council on Environmental Quality, 1982. *The 12th Annual Report: Environmental Quality 1981.* Washington, D.C.: U.S Government Printing Office.

*Council on Environmental Quality, 1983. *13th Annual Report: Environmental Quality 1982.* Washington, D.C.: U.S. Government Printing Office.

Council on Environmental Quality, 1984. *14th Annual Report: Environmental Quality 1983.* Washington, D.C.: U.S. Government Printing Office.

Economic Implications of Regulating Chlorofluorocarbon Emissions from Nonpropellant Applications. Santa Monica, Calif.: Rand Corporation. (1980)

Data Resources, Inc., 1979. *The Macroeconomic Impact of Federal Pollution Control Programs: 1978 Assessment.* Submitted to EPA and CEQ.

*Finklea, J. F., et al., 1977. "The Role of Environmental Health Assessment in the Control of Air Pollution," in J. N. Pitts, R. L. Metcalf, and A. C. Lloyd, eds. *Advances in Environmental Science and Technology.* New York: John Wiley & Sons.

*Freeman, A. M., 1979. *The Benefits of Air and Water Pollution Control: A Review and Synthesis of Recent Estimates.* A report prepared for the Council on Environmental Quality. Brunswick, Me.: Bowdoin College.

*Gillette, D. G., 1975. "Sulfur Dioxide and Material Damage," *Journal of the Air Pollution Control Association* **25** (12):1238–1243.

*Gold, M., 1980. "Indoor Air Pollution," *Science '80,* March/April, 30–33.

*Heintz, H., Hershaft, A., and Horak, G., 1976. "National Damages of Air and Water Pollution Control. A report submitted to the EPA.

*Hoffman, A. J.; Curran, T. C.; McMullen, T. B.; Cox, W. M.; and Hunt, W. F., Jr., 1975. "EPA's Role in Ambient Air Quality Monitoring," *Science* **190**:243–248.

*Jordan, B. C.; Richmond, H.; and McCurdy, T., 1983. "The Use of Scientific Information in Setting Ambient Air Standards," *Environmental Health Perspectives* **52**:233–240.

*Lave, L. B., and Seskin, E. P., 1970. "Air Pollution and Human Health," *Science* **169**(3947):723–733.

*Lave, L. B., and Seskin, E. P., 1973. "An Analysis of the Association Between U. S. Mortality and Air Pollution," *Journal of the American Statistical Association* **68**(342):284–290.

*Lave, L. B., and Seskin, E. P., 1977. *Air Pollution and Human Health,* Baltimore: Johns Hopkins University Press.

*Maugh, T. H., 1976. "Photochemical Smog: Is It Safe to Treat the Air?" *Science* **193**:871–873.

The National Commission on Air Quality, 1981. *To Breathe Clean Air,* Washington, D.C.: The National Commission on Air Quality.

On Prevention of Significant Deterioration of Air Quality, 1981. Washington, D.C.: National Academy Press.

Padgett, J., and Richmond, H., 1983. "The Process of Establishing and Revising National Ambient Air Quality Standards," *Journal of the Air Pollution Control Association* **33** (1):13–16.

*Reisner, M., 1977. "It's 1977, Why Don't We Have Cleaner Air?" *Natural Resources Defense Council Newsletter* **6**: 2–3.

*Repace, J. L., and Lowrey, A. H., 1980. "Indoor Air Pollution, Tobacco Smoke, and Public Policy," *Science* **208**: 464–472.

*Ridker, R. G., 1967. *Economic Costs of Air Pollution.* New York: Fredrick A. Prager Co.

The Rust Index and What It Means. Evanston, Ill.: Rust-Oleum Corporation. (1964)

Schwartzman, D.; Liroff, R. A.; and Croke, K. G., eds., 1982. *Cost–Benefit Analysis and Environmental Regulations: Politics, Ethics, and Methods.* Washington, D.C.: Conservation Foundation.

*Spengler, J. D., and Colome, S. D., 1982. "The In's and Out's of Air Pollution," *Technical Review,* **85**(6):32–44. SRI International, 1981. An Estimate of the Non-Health Benefits of Meeting the Secondary National Ambient Air Quality Standards, Report to the National Commission on Air Quality, Washington, D.C.

*Uhling, H. H., 1950. "The Cost of Corrosion in the United States," *Corrosion* **51**(1):29–33.

*U.S. Environmental Protection Agency, 1979. *The Cost of Clean Air and Water: Report to Congress.* Washington, D.C.: (EPA 230/3-79-001) Office of Planning and Management.

U.S. Environmental Protection Agency, 1984. *National Air Quality, Monitoring, and Emission Trends Report, 1982.* (EPA-450/4-84-002) Washington, D.C.: U.S. Government Printing Office.

Walsh, P., *et al.,* eds., 1984, *Indoor Air Quality.* Boca Raton, Fla.: CRC Press.

Watt, K. 1982. *Understanding the Environment.* Boston, Mass.: Allyn and Bacon.

Also see "References and Further Reading" at the ends of Chapters 9 and 10.

CHAPTER 12

Water Pollution

*B*ecause many kinds of chemicals dissolve in it, water is sometimes called the universal solvent. This remarkable property of water makes its contamination inevitable in the technical sense. After water is purified by evaporation and as it condenses and begins to fall back to the earth, it immediately begins picking up dissolved gases and particulates. Stretching the point a bit, even hundreds of feet above the earth's surface this water would be contaminated from the point of view of a biologist needing ultrapure water for a study of the effects on an organism of the absence of trace elements. Once a raindrop strikes the earth, it picks up materials like calcium, magnesium, iron, and zinc, and becomes contaminated at a more rapid rate.

One way to look at water and how living things use it is to note that water serves to carry away waste. Single-celled aquatic organisms discharge wastes directly into surrounding water. More complicated organisms have circulatory systems (carrying mostly water) that bring nutrients to cells and carry away waste. This role of water at the cellular level is closely analogous to the uses of water at the "civilization" level of organization (see Figures 12.1 and 12.2). Major cities are typically located on important waterways, which serve to carry nutrients and other needs *in* and to carry manufactured products and wastes *out*.

Years ago, when populations were less dense, water pollution was much less widespread. While this may be obvious, it is important to note that water pollution has accelerated more quickly than population densities; this apparently is a result of modern ways of doing things.

It has been estimated that every American now uses about four times as much water as Americans living at the turn of the century (see Chapter 7). A typical U.S. household uses over 200 gallons (roughly 760 liters; 1 gallon = 3.786 liters) of water each day, well over half of it for flushing away wastes and for showers and baths. Twenty-five gallons pass through the average washing machine or dishwasher. Another five or so gallons are used for miscellaneous things like hosing down driveways and watering gardens (Greenwood and Edwards, 1973).

As our factories became larger, they required increasing amounts of water to remove both chemical wastes and waste heat. About 1,000,000 gallons (roughly 3.8 million liters) of water are needed in the production of a ton of copper; 200,000 gallons are dirtied in the production of a ton of rayon; over 300,000 gallons of water are polluted in the production of a ton of aluminum; over a half million gallons are "used" in the production of a ton of synthetic rubber (Lavaroni, O'Donnell, and Lindberg, 1971).

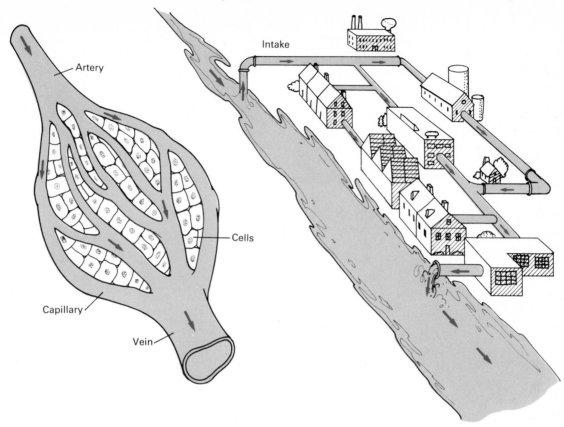

Figure 12.1 Of Cells and Cities. The use of water by humans to flush away or dilute waste parallels one of the major functions of blood at the cellular level.

According to the U.S. Department of the Interior, it takes 82,000 gallons of water to make a ton of medium-quality paper and 184,000 gallons for the same amount of fine book paper. Thus about one gallon was used in the production of the paper that makes up this page.

Agriculture also makes a signficant contribution to water pollution. About 40% of the water supply in the United States goes to agriculture, and some of this water ends up as polluted water carrying various types of agricultural wastes and contaminants.

Water pollution comes then from industrial, agricultural, and domestic sources and is the result of both the way things are done (technology and lifestyle) and the number of people doing them in a given area (population density).

In this chapter we look at types of water pollutants including biological agents, salt, chemicals that enrich, chemicals that poison, sediment, heat, and radioactive waste. We will see that nearly all bodies of water suffer from several different pollutants. We also look at water pollution from the perspective of sources because control strategies and laws are tailored to sources. We will see that industry, agriculture, and municipal sources all make significant characteristic contributions. Because energy is so important to us, we focus on the problems of oil pollution and acid mine waste later in the chapter. Still later, we examine the overall magnitude of the water pollution problem and try to get at some of the reasons why one out of every two or three miles of streams in the United States is significantly polluted. We will focus on one river (the Ohio), one lake (Lake Erie), and one ocean (the Mediterranean). We also consider the problem of groundwater pollution in the United States. We examine various technological and nontechnological alternatives for the control or reduction of water pollution. We review some economic factors involved in water pollution and water pollution control, and we conclude with a review of the history and status of water pollution and the law.

WATER POLLUTION: A DEFINITION

We need a working definition of *water pollution* for the reading that lies ahead. Precise definitions will be developed as we move along, but for the time being, let our definition be: Any change in water caused by *Homo sapiens* and considered by *Homo sapiens* to be unfavorable to *Homo sapiens* and/or to other forms of life. Basically, water pollution is any human action that impairs the use of water as a resource. It should become clear by the time we finish this chapter that the term "water pollution" is a relative one. Pollution is relative to the intended use of a water. Nearly pure water may be unsuitable

for making beer. Water of lesser quality may satisfactorily be used for drinking, recreation, fishing, navigation, or irrigation. The problem is that there is much water in the world that might be used for some purpose but that is not used because it is polluted.

Water pollution is the red, lifeless, acid mine drainage water of Blacklick Creek, which runs through Nanty Glo, Twin Rocks, and Vintondale, Pennsylvania; it is the sometimes raw sewage–laden waters of the Ohio River at Louisville, Kentucky; it is the detergent-derived phosphate in Lake Erie, the asbestos fibers in Lake Superior off Duluth, Minnesota, the mercury in the coastal waters of the harbors of Japan, and the heated water from the cooling

Figure 12.2 How Water Gets Polluted. Water gets polluted because it is used to wash away wastes, including heat.

towers of the large electric-generating plant in Seward, Pennsylvania. Water pollution is the pesticide-laden silt in the Missouri River; it is the oil on the beaches of Brittany, Texas, Chile, and Massachusetts. Water pollution is a major global environmental problem.

TYPES OF WATER POLLUTANTS

Although there might well be a hundred ways to subdivide the pollutants of water, all water pollutants fall into one of four *general* categories. Water can be polluted by: (1) biological agents, (2) dissolved chemicals, (3) nondissolved chemicals and sediment, and (4) heat.

Small amounts of certain chemicals that sometimes cause pollution actually can be neutral or even *beneficial* to water quality and aquatic ecosystems (curve A in Figure 12.3). Other chemical agents are harmful in practically any amount (curve B in Figure 12.3). Because of the importance of this concept, the following more specific classification will be used from this point on:

1. biological agents,
2. chemicals that enrich and overenrich (both organic and inorganic chemicals),
3. chemical toxins,
4. physical agents (including heat and suspended solids),
5. radioactive wastes,
6. salts

Biological Agents

Many ancient civilizations had rules about water sanitation, so we know that the relationship between human disease and water has been known for centuries. A severe outbreak of cholera that occurred in the middle of the last century in London was traced to a contaminated well on Broad Street. The pump handle was removed and the epidemic ended, even though it was not known at the time that a particular microorganism, *Vibrio cholerae,* was the causative agent. This was an early triumph of epidemiology (Chapter 10). Other epidemics of this very dangerous waterborne disease have occurred over the centuries in every part of the world.

Epidemics of another waterborne disease, typhoid fever, have also occurred worldwide throughout recent centuries. Notable epidemics occurred in Pennsylvania in 1885, New York State in 1890, and Massachusetts in 1890. In each of these epidemics the disease was eventually determined to be spread by drinking water.

Near the end of the nineteenth century, after it was demonstrated that cholera could be prevented by water purification and sanitation—keeping *Vibrio cholerae* out of drinking water—there was an abrupt disappearance of this and other waterborne diseases. The curve has flattened out now to the point at which there are only about 4000 known or documented cases of waterborne disease in the United States every year. In countries with less well-developed public health programs and water puri-

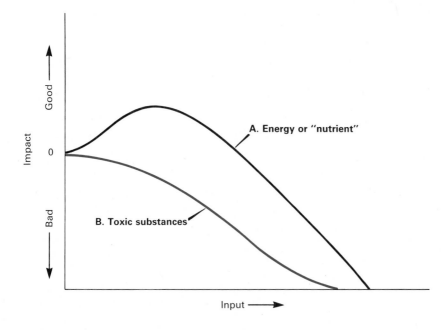

Figure 12.3 Too Much of a Good Thing Is as Bad as Being Poisoned. Some pollutants are actually beneficial to aquatic ecosystems in small amounts (curve A). Other types of pollutants are harmful at almost any level (curve B).

Table 12.1 Examples of Biological Agents of Human Disease in Polluted Water

Types of Organisms	Agent	Disease
Bacteria	*Vibrio cholerae*	Cholera-paracholera
	Salmonella typhi	Typhoid fever
	Other salmonellas	Enteritis (intestinal inflammation)
	E. coli of pathogenic types	Enteritis
	Shigella dysenteriae	Dysentery
	Clostridium botulinum	Botulism
	Clostridium perfringens	Enteritis
Protozoans	*Entamoeba histolytica*	Amoebic dysentery
Helminths (multicellular parasites)	*Schistosoma* of different types (trematodes) (flukes)	Schistosomiasis (Bilharziasis)
	Diphyllobothrium latum (fish tapeworm)	Diphyllobotriasis
	Taenia saginata (beef tapeworm)	Taeniasis
	Ascaris (round-worm)	Ascariasis
	Anchylostoma (hookworm)	Anchylostomiasis
Viruses	Poliovirus	Fever, headaches, nausea, diarrhea, muscular pains, meningitis, paralytic polio
	Coxsackievirus	
	Echovirus	
	Adenovirus	Fever, acute upper and lower respiratory tract infections, inflammations of the eyes
	Reovirus	Virus has been demonstrated in connection with common cold and other upper and lower respiratory tract infections, with diarrhea, and hepatitis, especially in children
	Hepatitis virus A ("infectious hepatitis" virus)	Fever, nausea, diarrhea, hepatitis (acute or chronic)

fication systems, however, current rates are much higher; typhoid fever, dysentery, cholera, and viral hepatitis continue to be serious problems.

The incredible thing about many countries today and about all countries in the days before good sanitation is that there are not and were not *more* epidemics. Waters contaminated by human waste are and were often directly connected to drinking water supplies, but the relative scarcity of epidemics can probably be explained in part by immunity. People who are chronically exposed to certain microorganisms build up some degree of immunity to them. This is the basis of the gastrointestinal problems people often have when visiting another country; it is also the reason why explorers of long ago sometimes caused epidemics in the countries they visited. In both of these examples, people are exposed to microbes to which their immune systems are not acclimated.

In any case, the problem of waterborne disease can be simply and somewhat grossly stated as the contamination of humans' drinking water with humans' disease organism–bearing bodily waste. There is a long list of human **pathogens** (organisms that cause disease) that can remain viable in raw

wastewater. Lund (1978) lists four categories of such pathogens and summarizes the more important representatives in each category as shown in Table 12.1.

Hepatitis is a viral disease; another potentially important waterborne virus is the polio virus. Chlorination, which kills most of the bacteria that make their way into water, has little effect on viruses. More than a hundred different kinds of viruses have been identified in human wastes, and many of these can remain viable for some time in domestic sewage waste.

Microorganisms other than those found in human waste can also be a problem. According to Nemerow (1978), this extends to microorganisms that make their way into water supplies as by-products of the processing of fruit and vegetables and as discharges from canneries and slaughterhouses. However, most of the bacterial contaminants that get into water from these sources are relatively harmless and, in fact, may help to degrade organic matter discharged along with the bacteria. Potentially **pathogenic** (disease-causing) microorganisms might also be transmitted from animals in this way. *Anthrax* bacilli or parasites originating from diseased animals in canneries and slaughterhouses, for example, can enter water supplies and infect animals and people downstream.

Energy-Rich Organic Chemicals

Certain chemicals in the right concentrations can distort and disrupt aquatic ecosystems by over-feeding certain components of such systems. Overfeeding (**eutrophication**) of aquatic ecosystems can occur in two basic ways via two kinds of chemical pollutants. One way is through the addition of inorganic nutrients that are normally limiting for plants (Chapter 3). Another way, the one we will discuss first, is through the addition of organic chemicals that serve as food for decomposers.

Biochemical Oxygen Demand

The addition of dissolved organic matter to an aquatic ecosystem gives a boost to the decomposers, organisms that use organic materials as sources of energy and nutrients. The problem comes when this activity increases to the point at which the decomposers use up all of the available oxygen as they oxidize organic matter (see Chapter 1).

The degree to which pollution by organic matter will remove oxygen from water depends on a number of factors, including the amount of oxygen in the water and the amount of water receiving the waste discharge. It would be better from the point of view of a stream community if organic matter were discharged (if it had to be discharged at all) into a very large, rapidly running, cool stream that is saturated with oxygen. Being cool helps in two ways: decomposition is slower and oxygen dissolves better in cool water. The degree to which oxygen will be depleted by sewage obviously also depends on how much sewage is discharged in a given time. The oxygen-depleting strength of organic matter is a rather precise parameter called biochemical oxygen demand.

Biochemical oxygen demand, sometimes referred to as biological oxygen demand or BOD, is a

Large amounts of organic matter in a body of water can increase the activity of decomposers, which may use up so much available oxygen that fish and zooplankton die.

quantitative expression of the oxygen-depleting impact (via the action of decomposers) of a given amount of organic matter. It is an expression of how much oxygen is needed for microbes to oxidize that organic matter. (Organic matter will undergo chemical oxidation even in the absence of decomposers; there is also a straight *chemical* oxygen demand or COD.)

In the extreme, large amounts of organic matter could result in a near-absolute depletion of oxygen in a given body or stretch of water. This would clearly make life impossible for the species that need oxygen. Fish and zooplankton die under such circumstances, and even among the bacteria themselves there is a rise in **anaerobic species**—species that can live in the absence of oxygen. This in turn leads to the production of foul-smelling toxic end products of anaerobic respiration such as those listed in Table 12.2.

Table 12.2 Chemistry of Aerobic and Anaerobic Decomposition

Chemical Element in an Organic Compound	Compounds in Which Each Element Ends up	
	In Aerobic Decomposition (where oxygen is present)	In Anaerobic Decomposition (where oxygen is absent)
Carbon	Carbon dioxide (CO_2)	Methane (CH_4)
Sulfur	Sulfate salts (SO_4^-)	Hydrogen sulfide (H_2S) (stinks, is poisonous)
Nitrogen	Nitrate salts (NO_3^-)	Ammonia (NH_3) (is poisonous, stinks)

Short of absolute oxygen depletion, the reduction of oxygen in water can still seriously disrupt natural systems. For most aquatic systems, dissolved oxygen should never be lower than 3 ppm at any time and should actually be above 5 ppm for the greater part of every day. (Remember that since respiration is carried out by both plants and animals at night, there is a nocturnal drop in oxygen content, which is restored in the morning when plants begin photosynthesizing.) Changes in species composition in aquatic ecosystems varies with average oxygen concentrations because different species can tolerate different oxygen limits. Trout require *at least* 5 ppm of oxygen, whereas certain scavenger fish like carp can survive in water having as little as 1 ppm.

Inorganic Chemicals That Enrich

A second way in which aquatic ecosystems can be overenriched (and thus polluted) is through the addition of *inorganic* matter, for example, phosphates and nitrates. While these substances can be added to aquatic ecosystems indirectly in the form of phosphorus- and nitrogen-containing *organic* pollutants, phosphates and nitrates can also be added as pollutants directly. Some detergents contain large amounts of tripolyphosphates, and as much as 10–25% of the nitrate and phosphate fertilizer used in agriculture makes its way into water, contributing to eutrophication. Phosphates and nitrates can get into water supplies from other sources; we will consider some of these in the next section.

Phosphate pollution is an especially serious problem because in many if not most parts of the world, including the United States, this form of the element phosphorus is often the plant growth limiting nutrient in aquatic environments; that is, phosphorus (as phosphate) is the controlling nutrient in terms of Liebig's Law discussed in Chapter 3. What this means is that when phosphate is added to water supplies, it triggers a rapid growth of plants. Somewhat ironically, perhaps, while this plant growth results in an increase in oxygenation due to the increased photosynthesis, plant respiration and decomposition of dead plant material create a problem similar to the one we just described for organic pollution of water.

The addition of inorganic or organic matter as sewage can have a devastating effect on a pond or a lake. Although these materials tend to have the same kind of oxygen-consuming effect on rivers, the impact there can be quite variable. Rivers vary considerably in flow, and consequently they have different rates of reoxygenation, mixing, and sediment load,

which limits penetration by sunlight (and consequently plant growth). These factors all determine the impact of **eutrophicants** (agents that lead to overenrichment) (see Figure 12.4).

We point out again that what happens when water becomes polluted by overenrichment is not so much a complete wiping out of life forms as it is a change in the forms of life and the qualities of water that are perceived to be detrimental and harmful. Sewage-polluted streams are often described by the uninitiated as devoid of life, dead, when in fact they may support much larger populations of living things than clean water. The problem is that they tend to support microscopic organisms to the exclusion of other "desirable" organisms in the aesthetic and economic sense. In terms of the concepts introduced in Chapters 1–4, *biomass* may stay the same or increase with eutrophication; *species diversity* is usually decreased significantly. Protozoans often exist in great numbers in sewage-polluted waters because food chains become shortened (Chapter 2) by the elimination of upper trophic levels.

Among the most common organisms of polluted water is the *Tubifex* worm. The presence of *Tubifex* worms in water is almost a certain indication that the water is polluted to some degree. The worms are good sources of food for fish and other aquatic life; they are found in large numbers in polluted water because conditions are unsuitable for the consumers that feed upon them.

In summary, small amounts of either organic matter or certain inorganic chemical compounds can actually be beneficial to an aquatic ecosystem in the same way that fertilizers are beneficial in small amounts to gardens, wheat crops, and terrestrial ecosystems. The problem comes when too much is added too soon in too small a space, pushing the ecosystem beyond the point of resilience.

Chemical Poisons

Many of the chemicals that get into water with an assist from *Homo sapiens* are poisons. Poisons are poisons, of course, no matter in what subsphere of the ecosystem they happen to be located. We have already reviewed the properties of some of the poisons found in the atmosphere. Many of these poisons are found in water as well. In the next two chapters we will review the properties and health effects of pesticides and other long-lived poisons. Still other water poisons will be discussed in detail in Chapter 15. Here we will simply summarize the poisons found in water and discuss mercury and PCBs briefly.

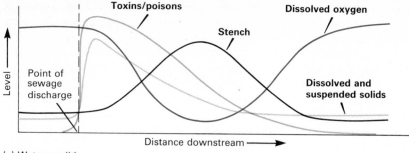

(a) Water qualities

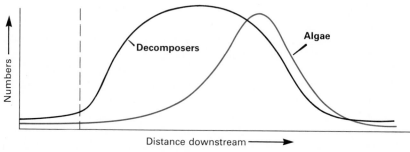

(b) Abundance of decomposers and algae

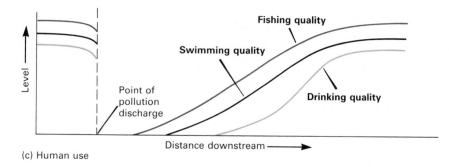

(c) Human use

Figure 12.4 The Impact of Sewage. This graph shows the impact of sewage on some of the important qualities of a stream of water and how this impact varies from the point of discharge to various points downstream. No distance units are given because the impact at a given distance varies according to stream flow and amount of discharge.

Among the inorganic toxic chemicals found in water supplies are arsenic (which comes from many types of insecticides), cadmium (which comes from electroplating operations), chromate (from various kinds of industrial processes), cyanide, lead, selenium, and mercury. Others are copper, chromium, and zinc. These substances are toxic to fish and other aquatic organisms as well as to human beings because they interfere with the action of enzymes and other biochemicals as we discussed in Chapter 10. Metal toxicity problems are often compounded by the biological magnification of biometallic compounds (metal-organic complexes) in aquatic ecosystems (see Chapter 13).

The Minimata Bay incident in Japan has become the classic example of the impact of water contamination by mercury. During one period in the 1950s there were more than 50 deaths in the seacoast village of Minimata, more than three times that many cases of brain damage, and two dozen children born with neurological problems, all linked to the ingestion of mercury introduced into the food chain. The source of the mercury was effluent from a local factory. Nearly all of the victims, it was found, ate fish from the bay three times a day. Cats and other household pets also showed signs of mercury poisoning. This incident established mercury as a bona fide environmental problem and set off a mercury scare that eventually led people to avoid eating swordfish and tuna.

The **methylation** of inorganic mercury (the incorporation of mercury into an organic methyl (CH_3) compound by microorganisms) in the sediment of lakes, rivers, and waters of other types is apparently the key to the transport of mercury in aquatic food chains leading to human beings. Because inorganic mercury is relatively insoluble in water, the organic variety is much more important. Its organic character makes it lipid-soluble and thus soluble in body tissues; it is therefore subject to biological magnification (see Chapter 13). Methyl mercury accumulates in organisms in aquatic environments according to their placement in the trophic level, the highest concentrations being found in top carnivores. As we discussed in Chapter 9, the greatest effect of inorganic mercury compounds seems to be on the kidney and digestive organs; organic mercury compounds, on the other hand, affect neural tissue, principally the brain, and also cause digestive system problems and even birth defects.

Many types of organic toxins also get into water supplies as pollutants. Examples of these are pesticides such as DDT and chlordane, chemicals that are actually made to harm living things (see Chapter 13); hydrocarbons such as benzene that cause cancer (see Chapter 14); and a host of chemicals that cause genetic damage and birth defects. Certain organic chemicals—phenols, for instance—give an off-taste to water.

A particularly interesting class of organic water pollutants, one that has generated considerable discussion in recent years, is the family of **polychlorinated biphenyls** (PCBs). PCBs are chlorinated compounds similar to DDT in their extreme stability. Because highly chlorinated PCBs are very sta-ble and are usually present in only trace amounts, they are not a biochemical oxygen demand problem for aquatic ecosystems; they are extremely toxic, however. PCBs originate in a variety of manufacturing processes including the manufacture of brake linings, grinding wheels, glass, ceramics, various types of coatings, flame-proofing paint, varnishes, sealants, electrical equipment, tires, plastic coatings, soap, and (ironically) water treatment chemicals, just to name a few (Nemerow, 1978). Over 400,000 tons of PCBs were produced in the United States from 1948 to 1973. Because of their stability, PCBs that escape the manufacturing process or that escape from the products into which they have been incorporated make their way into aquatic ecosystems.

The maximum PCB levels accepted by the FDA in fish to be eaten by human beings is just 2 ppm. Ingestion of larger concentrations of PCBs causes death due to various physiological disturbances (Chapter 13). We do not yet know the long-term effects of chronic ingestion of low levels of these compounds.

Heat

Water has a high heat capacity; that is, it is able to absorb large amounts of heat with relatively small increases in its own temperature while remaining liquid, making it an ideal cooling medium. For this reason, many industrial plants are located on rivers, where water is available to carry away waste heat. As heat-laden water is discharged back into the main

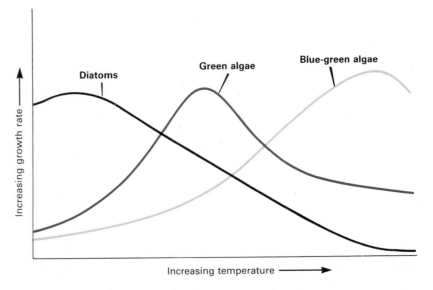

Figure 12.5 Temperature Preferences. Different species have different temperature optima and tolerance ranges. *Diatoms* are single-celled algae characterized by transparent silica shells or cases and a golden brown pigment in addition to chlorophyll. Blue-green algae are distinguished from green algae by a much more primitive cell type and the presence of bluish-green and other pigments in addition to chlorophyll.

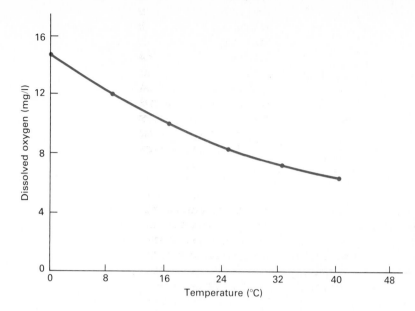

Figure 12.6 Oxygen Solubility and Water Temperature. The quantity of oxygen that can dissolve in water is inversely related to temperature. The lower the temperature, the more oxygen can be held in solution. Thermal pollution thus influences the oxygen content of water.

water supply, it raises the temperature of the aquatic environment. As much as 80% of the water used in industry in the United States is used for cooling purposes. Electric utilities alone use billions of gallons of water for cooling each day, trillions of gallons each year.

Heat affects the life found in water in several ways. First, every life form has a temperature tolerance range, as we discussed in Chapter 3. At some point in the life cycle of every organism there is a most temperature-sensitive stage—hatching eggs, for example. All individual organisms have ranges of temperature within which they can survive and specific temperatures at which they function best (Figure 12.5). Changing water temperatures can therefore result in change in species composition. Waste heat can also adversely affect aquatic ecosystems by increasing temperature *variability,* keeping the natural system off balance. The most important direct effect of heat on organisms that do not have constant body temperature is the acceleration of metabolic reactions; the warmer it is, the faster the metabolic reactions. Because heat accelerates some kinds of reactions more than others, temperature changes tend to disrupt the chemistry of living things.

Heat also disrupts and changes the chemistry of the *abiotic* environment. Heat increases the solubility of certain chemicals and generally decreases the solubility of gases.

Heat can actually affect the amount of oxygen and other gases dissolved in water in several ways. First, gases dissolve more readily in cold water than in warm water (Figure 12.6). Second, because higher temperatures accelerate metabolism, heat can accelerate decomposition, making BOD more of an immediate and acute problem while at the same time increasing the need for oxygen by fish and other organisms. A third way in which higher water temperatures can affect dissolved oxygen and ·other gases is in the stratification that can occur when hot water is discharged into a cooler body of water. The effects of stratification on chemical mixing were discussed in Chapter 3.

Getting back to the *direct* effects of heat, temperature changes of only 2 or 3 degrees under certain circumstances can have a very serious effect on fish and aquatic life. Trout eggs, for example, take 165 days to hatch in cool water (3°C or 37°F) but will hatch in only a month if kept at 12°C (54°F). They will not hatch if temperatures reach 15°C (60°F). Since temperature is a major key to spawning and reproduction for many species (Table 12.3), increased heating can result in such important problems as the hatching of fish eggs out of synchrony with normal peaks in food supply for the hungry hatchlings. Another problem is that blue-green algae tend to do better in warmer water than other types of algae; population explosions in these types of algae are often accompanied by significant levels of the

Table 12.3 Recommended Maximal Water Temperatures for Various Species of Fish

Temperature	Fish Species
32.2°C (90°F)	Growth of largemouth bass, drum, bluegill, and crappie
28.9°C (84°F)	Growth of pike, perch, walleye, smallmouth bass, and sauger
26.7°C (80°F)	Spawning and egg development of largemouth bass, white and yellow bass, and spotted bass
20.0°C (68°F)	Growth of salmon and for egg development of perch and smallmouth bass
12.8°C (55°F)	Spawning and egg development of salmon and trout (other than lake trout)
8.9°C (48°F)	Spawning and egg development of lake trout, walleye, northern pike, and sauger

toxins they produce. There will be more on pollution by heat in the upcoming section on sources.

Floating Solids and Liquids

Oil, grease, and a number of other materials that float on the surface of water are another kind of pollutant. The effects of these substances can be aesthetic, of course, since they occur where they can be seen, but certain types of organic materials that float are also toxic. Some of the materials in oil, for example, are flammable, creating the kind of fire hazard that resulted in Cleveland's famous Cuyahoga River fire in 1969. Floating materials also decrease light penetration and can retard the diffusion of gases such as oxygen. Floating materials may also contribute to biochemical oxygen demand. If floating materials break up and become suspended in water, they can concentrate toxins (for example, oil droplets can accumulate fat-soluble toxins such as DDT) in water and deliver these to filter-feeding organisms such as clams and mussels.

Suspended or Sedimentary Solids

Among the things that affect water physically are undissolved solids, some of which dissolve over long periods of time and some of which practically never go into solution. Both types of solids decrease water quality in a physical way; silt and other types of insoluble materials clog waterways, fill up dams, and make water cloudy or muddy. Such solids can also be physical problems for gill breathers (fish) and filter feeders (such as clams). By adsorption and in other physical and chemical ways, suspended organic and mineral solids can also concentrate metals and other toxins and then deliver them to various organisms in the food chain. Pesticides can be concentrated in and on suspended solids, for example.

Sediment, which gets into streams naturally through runoff, is also contributed by agriculture and industries like the china (clay) industry, construction, and steel.

Color

Some pollutants change the color of water. Perhaps the most outstanding example of this is the red and yellow colors in acid mine discharges derived from iron oxide and sulfate. Although these discharges are harmful because of the chemicals, which are only incidentally related to color, coloring agents are among the most objectionable types of pollutants as far as the public is concerned. People seem to be raised to indignation most by things they can see. The problem is that funding has a way of going to things that raise public indignation, often before it goes to truly serious problems.

Chemicals That Make Foam

Some of the chemicals that get into water make it more apt to foam. This was an extremely serious problem back in the 1960s and earlier, when detergents were **nonbiodegradable** (not broken down by microorganisms) but is less of a problem now that nonbiodegradable detergents are no longer made. There are still other pollutants that cause foaming in water supplies and, as with color, this visible form of pollution discourages recreational use and is often a more politically important form of pollution than many more serious pollutants are.

Radioactive Substances

Extensive discussions of the problems of radioactive materials in water supplies can be found in Chapters 6, 14, and 15. Chapter 14 contains a detailed description of the nature of radionuclides and the problem of biological magnification. Suffice it to say here that radioactive materials make their way into water supplies from

1. the processing of uranium ore,
2. the laundering of contaminated clothing from laboratories where radioisotopes are used,
3. wastes from research laboratories,
4. wastes from hospitals using isotopes in diagnostic and therapeutic procedures,
5. the processing of fuel elements from uranium ore,
6. water from nuclear power plants, and
7. fallout generated by nuclear weapons testing.

Low-level waste from hospitals and other laboratories can get into water by leaching from what may have been thought to be secure low-level waste depositories. Some is simply dumped illegally.

Inorganic Salts, Acids, and Alkalis

While some inorganic salts dissolved as ions cause overenrichment, others are chemical agents of hardness—calcium salts, for example. The **hardness** of water is the degree to which certain dissolved salts make it difficult to produce a soapy lather in that water. These salts are present naturally in water supplies, and they are present in high concentrations in certain types of wastes. They can also come out of solution under certain circumstances and become deposited within pipes and water-handling equipment, causing industrial maintenance problems. Agents of hardness also interfere with dyes in the textile industry and cause special problems in the beer-brewing industry. Still other inorganic salts in water pose human health problems. For example, magnesium sulfate, which cannot be absorbed from the digestive tract, has a **cathartic** effect, causing a chronic chemical type of diarrhea when it is present in significant amounts.

Acids and alkalis represent another kind of chemical pollution problem that has to do with ranges of tolerance for particular associations of living things in aquatic ecosystems. While only a few organisms can survive very high acidity and only a few can withstand very high alkalinity, the acidity of water supplies varies over a broad range; this has an effect on aquatic life and limits the uses of water by humans. Chemical neutrality is pH 7; pHs below 7 reflect increasing acidity, and pHs above 7 reflect increasing alkalinity. Fish can tolerate a pH range from about 4.5 up to 9.5. Discharges from industrial sources have been known to range from as low as 2 to as high as 11. Acids are produced as a by-product of many kinds of industries including mining and those that contribute the starting materials for acid rain (see Chapter 16). Alkalis such as sodium hy-

Pollutants that cause foaming in water supplies may be less dangerous than other forms of pollution, but they tend to attract more public attention.

droxide are produced as a by-product of soap manufacturing, textile manufacturing, and the tanning of leather.

Acids and alkalis influence the chemistry of organisms directly by influencing the shape and function of key cellular molecules. Indirect effects include changes in water chemistry via influences on solubility of abiotic chemicals.

WATER POLLUTION SOURCES

We have just considered the characteristics of major water pollutants. Ahead, we are going to consider strategies for controlling these pollutants. Before we discuss control strategies, we should know a bit more about the sources of water pollution.

The sources can be generalized as follows. First, U.S. industrial plants and electrical utilities discharge more than a hundred billion gallons of used water each day. Much of this water is not adequately treated. Some is not treated at all. Imperfect American public sewage systems contribute another 40 billion gallons a day. There are still several thousand fair-sized communities and towns in the United States that treat sewage very little if at all. Fifty billion gallons of water containing pollutants come from U.S. agricultural runoff. These wastes include pesticides and fertilizers as well as the organic waste that come from hog and cattle feedlots. Accidental oil spills and acid mine drainage also contribute to the water pollution problem.

Electrical utilities use billions of gallons of water every day for cooling, contributing to thermal pollution. Construction sites and farms contribute millions of tons of sediment through runoff. Millions of tons of garbage, sludge, chemicals, miscellaneous dirt, and debris are dumped each year into the ocean. Still another important source of water pollution is leaching from chemical and solid waste dumps (Figure 12.7) (see also Chapters 13 and 17).

The EPA has found it convenient to distinguish point sources from nonpoint sources of pollution, mostly for purposes of control and regulation. A **point source** is a discernible port or channel through which wastes are discharged, including pipes, ditches, channels, sewers, tunnels, and even floating barges from which pollutants are discharged. Nonpoint sources of pollution include the runoff from urban areas, agricultural runoff, and the like.

It should be noted that there are *natural sources* of water contaminants. These include silt and sediment from natural erosion, natural oil seeps, and organic material (e.g., leaves) flushed into streams by heavy rains and flooding.

Municipal Sewage

A wastewater discharge inventory completed in 1975 by the National Academy of Sciences indicated that municipal sewage constituted one of the largest sources of BOD and suspended solids. Despite significant progress in municipal sewage treatment in the last ten years, municipal discharges are still one of the major sources of water pollution. It seems that the problem here is the existence of combined storm sewers and wastewater sewers in many American cities. When there are heavy rains, the combined flow exceeds treatment plant capacity, and bypass mechanisms operate to allow the sewage to pass directly into the receiving stream *without* treatment. Another part of the problem is that many towns and cities still have inadequate sewage treatment systems. The result is that several billion pounds of BOD and several billion pounds of suspended solids annually pass from the nation's city sewer pipes into waterways.

An extension of the domestic waste problem is the problem of waste discharge by pleasure boats and other craft. There are more than eight million pleasure boats in the United States, and the number is growing by a quarter of a million boats each year. Until the Water Quality Improvement Act was passed in 1970, boats simply discharged wastes directly in the waters on which they floated. Now standards of performance and marine sanitation devices are supposed to prevent the discharges of inadequately treated sewage from boats. However, the standards are often ignored, and there is little enforcement.

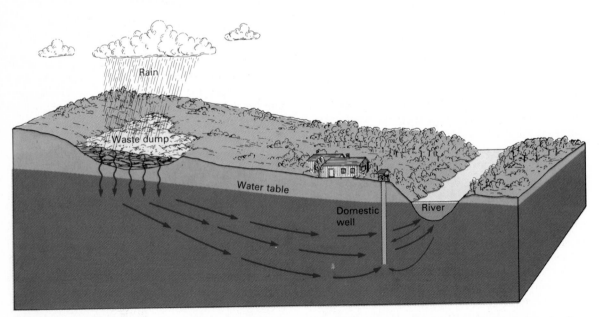

Figure 12.7 Landfill Leaching. Groundwater that seeps from landfills and dumps can reach wells and rivers to become sources of contamination. Especially important in this regard are metals, other persistent toxic chemicals and radioisotopes.

　Part III　The Impact of Human Activities on Health and the Environment

The concentrated wastes of cattle kept in feedlots have more of an impact on water supplies than would the wastes of the same number of cattle scattered across rangelands.

Water Pollutants from Farms

Agricultural sources of pollution include the body wastes of farm animals, the runoff of inorganic fertilizers and pesticides, sediment, and salt. Fertilizers and animal wastes both contribute to eutrophication.

The total farm animal population in the United States exceeds 700 million (Table 12.4). The waste these animals generate is equivalent to that of about *two billion* people (Table 12.5). Within the last generation or so it has been found that, rather than allowing cattle to roam the open range up to marketing time, it is economically beneficial to concentrate them during the last stages of their growing in feedlots, where they can be fattened before being sent to market. American feedlots now hold more than 500 million cattle and more than one million hogs. These concentrated sources alone generate a biochemical oxygen demand equivalent to that of almost 100 million people.

The use of commercial fertilizers has grown considerably since the dawn of the modern age of chemistry in the early 1940s. Unheard of before World War II, nitrate fertilizers are now applied at 50 pounds per planted acre in the United States.

Table 12.4 Production of Waste by Livestock in the U.S.

Livestock	U.S. Animal Population, 1982 (millions)	Approximate Total Production of Solid Waste (million tons/yr)	Total Production of Liquid Wastes (million tons/yr)
Cattle	115	1078	419
Hogs	53	57	34
Sheep	13	6	3.5
Chickens	379	29	—
Turkeys	165	30	—

Table 12.5 The Human Population Equivalent of Fecal Production by Animals

Biotype	Fecal (gallon per capita)	Relative BOD per Unit of Waste	Population Equivalent
Human	150	1.0	1.0
Horse	16,100	0.105	11.3
Cow	23,600	0.105	16.4
Sheep	1,130	0.325	2.45
Hog	2,700	0.105	1.90
Hen	182	0.115	0.14

According to some, these fertilizers are the main reason why this country is able to produce enough to feed all Americans and a considerable number of people in the rest of the world. A problem with this is that such fertilizer is sometimes washed into water, where it contributes to eutrophication; some of it leaches into groundwater, polluting wells.

Our review of the available data indicates that although intensifying economic pressures may well take care of the problem (fertilizer costs much more than it once did), the potential and actual seriousness of the environmental problem warrants significantly more attention to better timing and improved methods of fertilizer application. We have very little good data on the fate of fertilizer applied to farm fields, and we need more. In the meantime, since doing away with inorganic fertilizers is not very likely, a solution would be to control the runoff by using and applying fertilizers in ways that would minimize this problem.

Things are interconnected, and simple solutions are rarely *the* answers. It has been argued that banning commercial fertilizer could conceivably cause more water pollution than it would prevent. If the alternative selected was to bring additional marginal acreage into production, this would add to runoff, silting, and other types of pollution. According to some responsible authorities, if inorganic fertilizers

The Relationship Between pH, Hydrogen Ion Concentration, Some Common Expressions of Acidity, and Some Common Acidic and Alkaline Liquids

The pH of a solution is defined as the effective hydrogen ion concentration of that solution expressed as a negative logarithm. The equation looks like this:

$$pH = -\log_{10}[H^+]$$

A one-molar concentration of H^+ ions would have a pH of 0 because the logarithm of 1 is zero ($10^0 = 1$). A solution with a pH of 7 would have a 10^{-7} molar concentration because the logarithm of 10^{-7} is -7, and $-(-7) = +7$. The relationship between pH and acidity is such that as pH goes up, acidity is less.

Quantitative Description	pH	Moles of Hydrogen Ions per Liter	Example
Extremely alkaline	14	10^{-14}	Household lye
	13	10^{-13}	Bleach
	12	10^{-12}	Ammonia
Strongly alkaline	11	10^{-11}	
	10	10^{-10}	
	9	10^{-9}	
Slightly alkaline	8	10^{-8}	Baking soda / Seawater
Neutral	7	10^{-7}	Blood / Distilled water / Milk
Slightly acidic	6	10^{-6}	
	5	10^{-5}	
Strongly acidic	4	10^{-4}	Orange juice
	3	10^{-3}	Vinegar
	2	10^{-2}	Acid mine water
	1	10^{-1}	Lemon juice / Concentrated lab. acids
Extremely acidic	0	10^0	Battery acid

Common range for most natural waters (from 10^{-8} to 10^{-6})

Acidity is measured in terms of pH units, which inversely reflect hydrogen ion concentrations; pH values go down as the acidity or hydrogen ion concentration goes up (gets stronger).

Note that pH is really the *negative* exponent of the effective hydrogen ion concentration. Another way of saying this is that pH is the negative logarithm of the effective hydrogen ion concentration. A logarithm of any number is the power to which 10 must be raised to yield that number. Hydrogen ions (H^+) are the "active" components of acids. These positive ions influence chemistry by reacting with negatively charged groups on biotic and abiotic chemicals.

---

were banned, productivity would drop to half of what it is now, and food prices would skyrocket.

Industry

Water is used in four basic ways by industry: cooling, processing, boiler feed, and sanitary service. The problems of using water for sanitary service are identical to the problems of sewage discharged as municipal sewage. Boiler feedwater is a relatively minor problem. Here we will discuss a few specific examples of the industrial use of water for food processing and the processing of paper.

Fruit and Vegetable Processing. Water is used in the fruit and vegetable industry in cleaning, sorting, cooking, and other forms of processing. In some industries, lye solutions are used to dissolve vegetable skin; and in some cases, vegetables have to be dipped into hot water to loosen the skins or to denature the enzymes that would later produce off-colors and off-tastes.

Pulp and Paper Industry. The paper industry produces pollutants in a number of ways beginning with forestry practices (including the use of pesticides and the practice of clearcutting, which increases erosion and siltation). Water is used in the processing of wood to remove the fibers that go into the manufacturing of paper. These processes yield biochemical oxygen–demanding sulfide liquors. Ironically, even the processing of recycled paper has potential for pollution in the de-inking and bleaching processes.

Electrical Utilities

Electric utilities generate most of the waste heat discharged into water supplies in the United States; however, other industries make significant contributions. As was discussed in Chapter 6, after steam has pushed the blades of turbines, causing them to spin, it must be cooled and condensed before it can be returned to the boiler for another cycle. For this to happen, the steam must give up its heat energy, and water is almost always the medium used to carry such heat away. A single 1000-megawatt plant requires two to three million gallons of cooling water every minute.

Water Pollution from the Production of Coal

Coal production presents water pollution problems at two different stages. The first is during mining, and the second is in the processing of coal once it is mined.

The first coal mine in the United States opened in Pennsylvania a decade or two before the Declaration of Independence was signed. Since then, streams throughout the coal-producing regions in the United States have become polluted from acid drainage to the extent that many are absolutely de-void of any semblance of normal aquatic life. Acid mine wastes originate as water passes through mines and various iron compounds (particularly iron sulfide compounds) are oxidized. The agent of oxidation is the oxygen dissolved in water or in the air pumped through the coal mines. The acidification processes is accelerated by **chemosynthetic bacteria**, microorganisms that oxidize inorganic chemicals (iron sulfides in this case) as chemical energy sources and use the energy in the same way that photosynthetic organisms use sunlight. The equation for the reaction is as follows:

$$2FeS_2 + 7O_2 + 2H_2O \xrightarrow{\text{enzymes}} 2FeSO_4$$
$$+ 2H_2SO_4 + \text{energy}$$

As can be seen from the equation, the active ingredients are sulfides of iron, oxygen, and water. Iron sulfide ($FeSO_4$) can be further oxidized to yield still more sulfuric acid (H_2SO_4). The overall effect of these reactions is the conversion of sulfur compounds into sulfuric acid, one of the most powerful acids known (Chapter 9). The most important offending microorganism is the bacteria *Thiobacillus thiooxidans*. Coal mining can be thought of as the creation or expansion of habitat for this microorganism.

Although acid is the most important constituent in acid mine drainage, other chemicals are present in mine effluents as well, and the composition varies considerably from one location to another. A chemical analysis of an acid mine–polluted stream in comparison to natural waters is presented in Table 12.6.

Acid drainage can also come from piles of waste removed from coal mines. Leachates coming from such gob piles can be very similar to the drainage that comes from coal mines directly.

Table 12.6 Chemical Analysis of a Stream in Pennsylvania Containing Acid Mine Drainage and the Chemical Properties of Natural U.S. Waters. Data for mine drainage (in which pH averages between 3 and 4) can also be compared to U.S. Public Health Service and World Health Organization Drinking Water Standards of pH 7.0–9.0, 0.3 ppm for iron, 200 ppm for calcium, 150 ppm for magnesium, 250 ppm sulfate, and 500 ppm dissolved solids. All numbers are in parts per million.

	Average Value Over 5–11 Sample Sites	5% of Natural Waters Contain Less Than	95% of Natural Waters Contain Less Than
Total dissolved solids	1444	72	400
Bicarbonate	0	40	180
Sulfate	1012	11	90
Calcium and magnesium	200	18.5	66
Iron	1.0	0.1	0.7

Control of Acid Mine Drainage. Acid mine drainage presents a unique problem of control. Nemerow (1978) gives a number of methods for preventing the formation of acid mine water and neutralizing the acid in these waters. His strategies include

1. using landscaping to control the amount of water that flows into mines;
2. sealing coal mines so that water cannot flow in or out;
3. flooding the mines with water and holding it there to keep oxygen out;
4. using lagoons to impound acid mine water, then feeding this into streams gradually in proportion to the amount of flow in the receiving stream;
5. using the acid mine water for washing coal (this, according to some proponents, neutralizes the acidity at the same time the coal is cleaned);
6. using limestone or lime to neutralize the acid;
7. covering strip mines with earth; and
8. disposing of waste rock from coal mines in layers sandwiched between layers of earth.

It is difficult, though possible, to clean up a stream after it is polluted by acid drainage. One case in point is the Youghiogheny River. Pennsylvania embarked on a ten-year program to clean up this river in the late 1960s. The task was to cost an estimated 500 million dollars, 200 million of which was to go toward stopping mine drainage into the river system. Coal veins and mine shafts were sealed, and the river began to become noticeably cleaner in the early 1970s. The water in the Youghiogheny is now considered by some to be safe to drink.

Waste from Coal Preparation. After coal is mined, it is usually brought to a coal-cleaning plant, where it is processed by first breaking it into small pieces and then washing out impurities. Many coal-cleaning operations produce significant amounts of sediment and suspended solids containing calcium, magnesium, sulfates, iron, and other minerals found in coal and shale (Nemerow, 1978). These problems can be partially solved by treating and reusing water used in the coal-cleaning process.

Water Pollution from the Production, Transport, and Use of Oil

The problem of oil pollution of the ocean is not new. Conferences were held as early as 1926 on the pollution of navigable waters by oil, and another such conference was held at the League of Nations in 1935.

The history of oil pollution in most minds begins with the wreck of the *Torrey Canyon.* This infamous tanker, a small one by today's standards, ran aground on what were supposed to have been well-charted rocks in broad daylight in 1967. The ship released over 100,000 metric tons of oil (more than 700,000 barrels; 1 bbl = 42 U.S. gallons or 159 liters), most of which eventually washed ashore to pollute the beaches of southern England and northern France. There have been a host of similar incidents involving larger ships since 1967.

The world's oil production is approximately three trillion gallons per year, well over half of which is moved over the ocean from wellhead to consumer. Although less than 1% of this oil ends up as a pollutant, mostly in the oceans, this amounts to considerable contamination. Thousands of oil spills contaminate coastal waters every year, and many other spills occur in inland waters. In its landmark study published in 1975 the U.S. National Academy of Sciences estimated that 6.1 million metric tons of oil enter the world's oceans each year. Figure 12.8 shows the amounts of oil reaching the oceans from the various sources.

While some of the chemicals in oil spills are very volatile, escaping into the atmosphere rapidly, other components are very stable and can remain in the aquatic environment for many years. Some of the latter effectively disappear via dispersion and emulsification (division into very fine droplets). Some is oxidized by sunlight. Some is degraded by microorganisms. Some is deposited in ocean sediment.

On an evening in March 1978 the supertanker *Amoco Cadiz* lost its steering and ran aground near Portsall on the Brittany coast of France. Nearly a quarter of a million metric tons of oil were lost, contaminating 300 km of seacoast. An accounting of the oil after the first few months showed that 13% was incorporated into the **water column** (water between the surface and the bottom); another 4.5% degraded quickly in the water; 8% ended up in tidal sediments; 28% washed into the intertidal zone; 30% evaporated; and a little more than 20% was not accounted for (Gundlach et al., 1983). After three years, little evidence of oil remained, although estuaries and marshes still had elevated hydrocarbon levels (Gundlach et al., 1983).

Much more of the oil pollution in the world's waters results from routine operations than from high-visibility accidents such as the blowouts (oil escaping under pressure from the bore hole into the water) in the North Sea and off Mexico and the breakup of tankers like the *Torrey Canyon,* the Am-

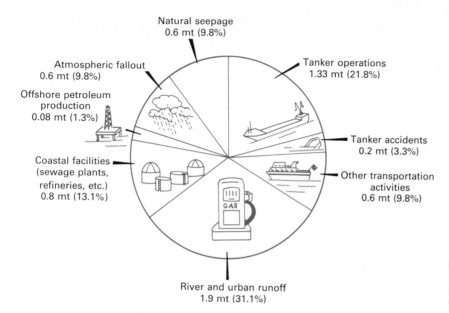

Natural seepage
0.6 mt (9.8%)

Atmospheric fallout
0.6 mt (9.8%)

Offshore petroleum
production
0.08 mt (1.3%)

Coastal facilities
(sewage plants,
refineries, etc.)
0.8 mt (13.1%)

Tanker operations
1.33 mt (21.8%)

Tanker accidents
0.2 mt (3.3%)

Other transportation
activities
0.6 mt (9.8%)

River and urban runoff
1.9 mt (31.1%)

Figure 12.8 Oil Pollution.
Sources of the oil that ends up
in the world's oceans in millions
of metric tons (mt) per year.

oco Cadiz, the *Argo Merchant,* and others (Atlas, 1978). Routine operations include a practice in which oil wastes mixed with seawater that had been taken on as ballast are dumped from oil tankers when the ships return to the sources of oil for refills. While technology is available for recovering oil from the ballast tanks, sometimes the crews of outmoded oil tankers ignore international law and simply dump this mixture of seawater and oil overboard as soon as they are out of danger of detection.

Two other sources of oil pollution are the occasional accident in offshore wells and inadvertent leakage from oil deposits through cracks developed in the ocean floor offshore as side effects of the drilling and capping processes. There is also a considerable amount of natural oil pollution in the

More oil pollution comes from
the routine operation of tankers
than from highly publicized oil
spills. Many tankers flush oil
wastes directly into the sea, year
after year.

ocean. When the oil washes ashore, there are obviously some immediate physical, aesthetic, and even toxic chemical effects.

The Effects. So what happens when oil gets dumped into the oceans? One episode that was studied quite a bit was the Santa Barbara incident of the early 1970s. A leaking offshore well polluted miles of beaches and had dramatic effects on shorebirds, coating their feathers with oil, preventing them from feeding or flying, and killing them. Despite this tragedy, the oil spill apparently had only minimal long-range effects and very few important short-range effects on the marine environment. The earlier *Torrey Canyon* incident was also studied, and it was determined that some of the detergents used to try to disperse the oil may have actually done more harm to marine life than did the oil itself.

Oil floats, and it coats things. Thus it can kill quickly by coating marine and freshwater life, interfering with gas exchanges necessary for life. Benthic (bottom) organisms may be particularly susceptible. Much damage to the benthic community—the organisms in the tidal zone and just below—was caused by the oil pollution that occurred when the

When oil coats their feathers, birds are unable to fly, and their feathers lose the capacity to retain body heat. Most affected birds die of exposure.

supertanker *Metula* went aground off the coast of Chile in August 1974, releasing 54,000 tons of oil. Studies showed that the benthic community began to recover within several months. None of this is to say that the overall effects of oil on aquatic systems are not significant. The full story on chronic effects is not yet known, and the acute effects can be significant. A February 1976 barge accident dumped one million gallons of heating oil into the Chesapeake Bay and resulted in the deaths of some 20,000 birds, a notable effect indeed (Council on Environmental Quality, 1976). Some of the chemicals in crude oil and in partially refined products are known to be carcinogens; we will discuss these in some detail in Chapter 14.

As yet, there are practically no data on the effect of oil pollution on human health. Oil pollution seems to have little long-range effect on fish, and there does not yet seem to be evidence for food chain magnification of the hydrocarbons in oil. Although many microscopic marine animals appear to take them up, the general fate of these hydrocarbons is to be rather quickly converted (photochemically and metabolically) to oxygenated metabolites (some of which may be more toxic than the parent compounds) and then to simple, harmless compounds. If there are indeed long-term effects on aquatic communities, they have yet to be documented.

Strategies for dealing with oil pollution once it has occurred have not been very effective. The failures include using detergents to disperse oil that can do more harm than the oil and using absorbants like straw to hold the oil, creating a new disposal problem. Burning the oil is usually not very effective because flammable materials escape quickly and leave the more fire-resistant chemicals behind. Various new containment methods are being tried and tested, for example, deploying barriers that contain the oil so that it can be siphoned up, skimmed off, or recovered in some other way. In general, all of these approaches have been found to be ineffective.

Some of the latest methods being considered include the use of microorganisms that can degrade oil. According to Atlas (1978), microorganisms can attack the hydrocarbons in petroleum at temperatures that range from less than 0°C to well above 60°C. He suggests that a combination of adding microorganisms and enhancing the environment for the action of microorganisms might be the best way to deal with oil spills once they have occurred. It is clear, however, that the *best* way to deal with this problem is to prevent it from happening in the first place. This can be done by better enforcement of regulations governing bilge pumping and tanker cleaning operations, better control of loading and unloading operations, maintenance and controls in the construction of supertankers, better training of tanker crews, and better training and methods for managing offshore drilling rigs.

Water Pollution as a By-Product of Refining. Many millions of gallons of oil wastewater are generated every day in petroleum refining. Water is used in many ways in petroleum refining, chiefly to remove salts and other impurities from oil. According to the U.S. Department of the Interior, 10 liters of water are used to refine a liter of gasoline.

POLLUTED WATER: SOME NOTABLE EXAMPLES

Having considered the *types* of pollutants and some of the more important *sources* of water pollution, we would like to consider the magnitude of the water pollution problem by looking at what it has done to one river, one lake, and one small ocean.

We have chosen a lake, a river, and an ocean as representatives of the major types of bodies of water affected by pollution; there are different considerations for each. Because the flow in rivers tends to increase oxygenation, for example, rivers can handle biological oxygen demand more readily than lakes. The differences between rivers and lakes in this regard are becoming less now that many major rivers are being converted into chains of long lakes by construction of flood control, recreational, and navigational dams. The Ohio River offers a good example of this trend. Coastal problems are the main problems in oceans; the open oceans tend to minimize the impact of pollution by their sheer volume. That is why we picked a little sea, the Mediterranean. Lakes as a group, though they too vary considerably in size, are especially prone to damage from pollutants because of their low flow and stratification. Lake Erie in North America is an outstanding example of the problems of lake pollution.

The Trouble with Lake Erie

North America's Great Lakes are the largest reservoir of fresh water on earth. If all the fresh water in the world were reduced to a gallon, the Great Lakes would have a volume equal to that of a fifth of Kentucky bourbon. The natural resources of these lakes include water for drinking, navigation, recreation, and industrial uses; fish as sources of food; and the kinetic energy of water as hydroelectric

power as the water spills from one lake into another on its way to the sea.

The Great Lakes are like tubs connected by very small pipes to one another and eventually to the ocean. Things dumped into them tend to settle out or accumulate in other ways rather than washing into the Atlantic Ocean. This presents a problem for all the Great Lakes, and it is most serious in Lake Erie. Lake Erie is both the shallowest of the Great Lakes and the lake serving the greatest number of people and industrial centers.

In the 12,000 years since it was born as a gouge left by a receding glacier, Lake Erie has suffered many abuses. In addition to natural crises, Lake Erie has long been receiving pollutants created as byproducts of the Industrial Age. Lake Erie drains some 30,000 square miles of North America; 70% of the drainage comes from the American side. Eleven and a half million Americans dump their sewage (after various degrees of treatment) into Lake Erie, and the wastes from a million Canadians comes in from the other side. Even on normal days the Detroit River alone brings nearly 5000 cubic yards of mostly agriculturally derived sediment into the lake. On stormy days the same river delivers 50,000 cubic yards of soil from Michigan and Canada. A hodgepodge of industries dump hundreds of millions of gallons of spent water into the Cuyahoga River each day.

Pollution has changed the biological character of the lake, and detergents and other eutrophicants have apparently caused significant oxygen depletion. Sturgeon and other commercially important fish began to disappear from the lake at the beginning of this century. Contrary to much that has been said about Lake Erie's death, the eutrophication has not brought about a decrease in the *amount* of life in the lake. It has brought about a change in the *character* of that life.

What has happened to Lake Erie has been described as accelerated aging. By some estimates, the lake looks twice its age. We know from one of the first few chapters of this book that lakes do not last forever. They gradually become shallower and shallower as sediment falls into them and begins filling the lake in from the edges. Eventually, lakes become marshes and advance toward some kind of terrestrial community (Chapter 4). Through overenrichment from phosphates, nitrates, organic matter, and other by-products of civilization and through erosion-derived sediment, Lake Erie has become shallower and contains more organic matter and less oxygen. It should be pointed out that Lake Erie is not uniformly polluted. The shallow, heavily industrial western basin is in worse shape than the eastern basin.

There is no question that the impact of water pollution on Lake Erie has been considerable or that the many and varied users and potential users of the lake have a problem. The hope is that the problem is not irreversible or at least that the slope of aging can be made less steep. There is cause for some optimism.

By early 1980, three fourths of the more than 100 industrial polluters on the American side of Lake Erie cited for violation in the 1960s were meeting minimum treatment requirements. Municipal sewage treatment has also improved. Major cities, including Detroit and Windsor, Ontario, banned phosphate-containing detergents in the early 1970s; in 1977, Michigan became the fourth Great Lake state to outlaw detergents containing phosphates. Billions of dollars have been spent cleaning up the effluents that spill into Lake Erie. Restocking and fish management programs have started to bring the fish back.

There is still room for improvement. It has been proposed that extending the limitation on phosphates would be a step in the right direction. Chapra and Robertson (1977) reported that a 1 mg/l effluent restriction for point sources would cause a significant improvement in the entire Great Lakes system. However, they indicated that even more stringent controls of *nonpoint sources* might be necessary if this effect is to be extended to Western Lake Erie. A 1982 Army Corps of Engineers study of wastewater management in Lake Erie determined that the present phosphorus influx for Lake Erie is still 16,500 metric tons per year, despite a significant decline in municipal phosphate loading following the banning of phosphates in detergents. It has been estimated that the largely nonpoint source effluent will have to be reduced at least to 11,000 metric tons annually to restore oxygen levels to most of the lake (Council on Environmental Quality, 1982).

No sooner had Lake Erie begun to show signs of recovery from its eutrophication problems than its pollution by persistent toxic chemicals became increasingly apparent. Toxaphene, DDT, dioxin, and PCBs (see Chapter 13) have been reported in significant levels in fish throughout the Great Lakes system (Council on Evironmental Quality, 1982b). These toxic chemicals are apparently making their way into the lakes from farm fields and from leaky disposal sites in the drainage system. The *Thirteenth Annual Report* of the Council on Environmental Quality (1983) put this problem in some perspective by describing the 18–20 mg/kg levels of PCBs in Lake Michigan lake trout as follows:

> Even though residue levels (roughly 20 mg/kg) of PCB's in Great Lakes fish are decreasing, if the loading of PCB is not changed, it will take until the turn of the century to achieve acceptable PCB residues and residues of PCB metabolites in fish and 5–15 years later for the human population consuming those to maintain acceptable levels in their body tissues.

The Ohio River

In 1936 a Kentucky congressman called the Ohio River a "cesspool." Everything was dumped into the river; pollution control was decades into the future. The Ohio River is a good example of what water pollution has done and can do to a river.

The Ohio River basin includes nearly 200,000 square miles of Indiana, Kentucky, Ohio, West Virginia, Illinois, Virginia, North Carolina, Tennessee, Maryland, Pennsylvania, and New York. About 20 million people live and work in this basin, and it has about 2000 major industrial operations. The valley produces about 75% of the nation's coal and more than one third of its steel. Obviously, a proportional share of the water pollution related to these activities end up in the Ohio River. The Ohio River is already polluted at its source, where it is formed by the confluence of the far-from-pure Allegheny and Monongahela Rivers at the Golden Triangle in Pittsburgh, Pennsylvania. Things get worse as the Ohio flows some 981 miles to the southwest, where it joins the Mississippi at Cairo, Illinois. The urban centers along the Ohio River include Paducah, Covington, Newport, Owensboro, Louisville, and Ashland, Kentucky; Evansville, Indiana; Cincinnati, Portsmouth, Ironton, Marietta, and Stubenville, Ohio; Huntington, Parkersburg, Weirton, and Wheeling, West Virginia; and Pittsburgh, Pennsylvania.

According to some sources, less than 40% of the industries along the Ohio meet current emission standards. Numerous reports have identified hundreds of errant chemical compounds in Ohio River water; many of these chemicals are known to produce cancer in humans and other animals.

Some of the Ohio River pollution problem stems from the fact that the Ohio has been converted over the years into a series of long lakes created by dams built by the Army Corps of Engineers to ensure navigation depths along the entire length of the river. A related problem is that the percentage of oxygen saturation during the summer drops considerably from Pittsburgh to Cairo.

According to Environmental Protection Agency's Office of Water Planning and Standards, pollution problems of the Ohio River include (1) low alkalinity (high acidity)—a result of the fact that the Ohio drains many coal-mining areas in Pennsylvania, West Virgina, and other states; (2) a high total fecal coliform count (**coliforms** are bacteria that inhabit the digestive tract of *Homo sapiens* and other animals and are used as indicators of contamination by human waste)—indicating that sewage treatment in a number of cities along the Ohio is inadequate at best; (3) a high iron and manganese concentration—reflecting the character of the industry along the Ohio; and (4) some toxic substances—DDT and chlordane, for example. (Although coliform bacteria are not usually in themselves pathogenic, they are used as indicators of waste contamination of water and warn of potential for infection from other less common but more virulent inhabitants of the human gastrointestinal tract—for example, the causative agents of cholera and hepatitis.)

Iron and manganese levels continued to rise during the early and mid-1970s, and levels already exceed the EPA's limit of the 50 μg of manganese per liter of drinking water and the limit of 300 μg of iron per liter of drinking water.

The Ohio has a PCB pollution problem (see Chapter 13) that got worse through the mid-1970s. Catfish caught at six of eleven collection points along the Ohio contained more than what was then a 5-ppm limit established by the U.S. government. The limit is now 2 ppm, set by the FDA.

Some of the things that get into the Ohio River cancel some other things out. For instance, the Ohio has high levels of suspended solids, apparently the result of sediment being washed into the stream during high flows along its length. Although the Ohio also has a great potential for algae growth, the cloudiness of the water, caused by suspended solids, blocks out sunlight, inhibiting algal growth.

As late as 1948, still 99% of the raw sewage from toilets, slaughterhouses, and similar sources went directly into the Ohio—untreated. Although there was some very slow progress in the 1950s, significant improvement did not begin until the environmental movement in the late 1960s. Because of the Clean Water Act and other legislation, much of the raw sewage and odor of the Ohio are gone now. Many of the cities along the river are fast approaching the EPA standard of reduction of sewage by 85%. Many of the coal mines have been closed and sealed; operational mines are better controlled. Today, the Ohio also has less cyanide, arsenic, lead, and cadmium that it did a decade ago. Also on the comeback trail are sauger, crappie, white bass, and freshwater drum and paddlefish. According to ORSANCO, an organization of the states that border the Ohio, Ohio River fish now carry less heavy metal. More than four billion dollars have been spent on the clean-up of the Ohio and its tributaries (Tye, 1983).

Largely as a result of clean water legislation of the early 1970s, the 700 industrial plants along the Ohio have sharply reduced the amount of waste they dump into the river over the last decade. But plants are relatively easy to monitor and to regulate. The greatest unresolved problems now come from farms, construction sites, septic tank leakage, and the like—nonpoint sources and sources otherwise difficult to regulate. Silt from cultivated farmland along the Ohio gives the river a "coffee with cream" appearance during rainy periods; the silt brings pesticides and fertilizers along with it.

Even the point sources have considerable room for improvement. Fewer than half of the 200 sewage treatment plants along the Ohio and its feeder streams meet the federal standard of 85% removal of pollution (Tye, 1983). Because of combinations of technical problems, design problems related to the connection of storm drains to sewage systems, and other problems, some Ohio River towns are removing less than half the contaminants from their sewage.

There has been dramatic though incomplete success with other of the world's great rivers. The Potomac River, which runs through Washington, D.C., used to smell of human excrement; today, the cities that affect the Potomac remove more than 85% of pollutants from the sewage they generate before the Potomac gets it. It was 0% not very long ago, but Congress has apparently acted to get its own house in order. Other notable success stories include the Willamette River in Oregon and the Thames in England—both of which, like the Ohio and the Potomac, were once virtual cesspools and are now *relatively* clean.

The Mediterranean Sea

The Mediterranean Sea is of interest because it has enjoyed a delicate balance with humankind for thousands of years. Areas along the Mediterranean are highly populated and have been for some time; there were reportedly 50,000,000 people in the Mediterranean basin when the Roman Empire was

People have lived in towns and cities in the Mediterranean basin for thousands of years, but the pollution problem in the open parts of the small, shallow Mediterranean Sea appears to be no worse than that in the open oceans of the world.

at its peak (Helmer, 1977). Today, more than 200,000,000 people live in the countries that border the Mediterranean Sea; some 44,000,000 of these live adjacent to the sea and interact with it directly.

The Mediterranean is of special interest because of the questions: Can humankind pollute the oceans? Has it already? The Mediterranean is a small sea; it is relatively shallow, and for all practical purposes it is isolated. If humans have truly had an impact on oceans, nowhere should this impact be more evident than in the Mediterranean Sea.

Many of the nations ringing the Mediterranean and many others whose rivers empty into it are now highly industrial. Helmer (1977) describes an inventory made by the U.N. Environmental Program in which pollution of the Mediterranean was cataloged according to the broad categories of (1) domestic sewage, (2) industrial waste (including pollution by the petroleum industry), (3) agricultural runoff, (4) radioactive waste, and (5) river discharge (rivers coming into the Mediterranean treated as point sources). A summary of the findings of this study follow.

Domestic sewage comes into the Mediterranean in great volumes both directly and in the rivers that empty into it. Although the situation has improved since the early 1970s, virtually none of the communities along the Mediterranean bothered to treat sewage as recently as the mid-1970s. An Italian cholera epidemic in 1973 has been blamed on sewage contamination of shellfish, but relatively few other sewage-related health problems have been documented along the Mediterranean coast. The main

incentive for cleaning things up even today seems to be the potential health impact and the aesthetic impact on the tourist trade in places like the French Riviera.

Industrial waste comes from many types of Mediterranean industry, and it comes in great volumes. The Mediterranean is actually one of the most highly industrialized areas in the entire world; its industrial spectrum includes iron and steel, food processing, pulp/paper, leather, textiles, and petroleum-based chemical operations. Industrially derived metals including mercury, cadmium, copper, lead, and zinc have been measured in the open Mediterranean and have been found to be present in amounts no greater than the background levels in the world's major oceans (Osterberg and Keckes, 1977). As in other oceans, however, there are high concentrations at various localized spots along the coast. High concentrations of copper have been measured in the coastal waters off Marseilles, for example.

Oil pollution is a problem of yet uncertain dimension in the Mediterranean. Much oil is spilled in the Mediterranean, as would be expected from its role as one of the major highways linking the oil-rich Middle East with the rest of the world (nearly 400 million tons of petroleum are transported over the Mediterranean each year). Most spilled oil comes from the routine tanker petroleum refining and drilling operations that ring the Mediterranean. At the time of this writing, dumping oil is actually legal in two central areas of the Mediterranean, one east of Malta and the other about midway between Alexandria and the Turkish coast.

The impact of spilled petroleum on the marine environment is similar to that reported along other shipping lanes of the world. The most visible problem is that of tarry lumps that wash up on beaches. Tainting of commercial species of fish and even decimation of populations of some species have been blamed on oil (LeLourd, 1977). Spain has reported the tainting of grey mullet and mussels in oil-polluted harbors. Both France and Italy have reported polluted shellfish and fish that taste bad to the point of being inedible. Turkey has reported that the reproduction of bonita and mackerel has been negatively affected by oil pollution (LeLourd, 1977). Nearly all of the oil problems are in harbors and coastal areas rather than in open areas.

The Mediterranean also receives considerable *farm-related pollution*. Rivers carrying nutrient run-off from the farming areas of Southern Europe contribute most to this problem. The Rhine and Po Rivers are particularly bad (Helmer, 1977).

Although there are nuclear reactors in Spain, France, and Italy and although there are medical and research installations all along the Mediterranean, *radioactive waste* does not appear to be a problem at present. However, considerable expansion of the atomic power industry in the Mediterranean basin is projected over the next few decades, and the situation may change.

If marine pollution is defined as the introduction into the oceans by *Homo sapiens* of materials and/or energy that have the effect of harming living resources, harming human health, hindering marine activities such as fishing, and/or limiting any use of seawater (including recreation), then the Mediterranean Sea is polluted—in some places more than in others. Most of what we know about so far is localized and coastal in nature. Data collected to date show little if any pollution of the open Mediterranean Sea. Despite its long-term, intense insult by humans (relatively speaking) and despite its being much smaller in volume than the earth's major oceans, there is little if any difference between the levels of contamination in the Mediterranean and in other larger oceans. This suggests that the pollution of the *open* oceans of the world may be, at this time, one of the least significant of our environmental problems.

The Oceans in General

It is almost incomprehensible to think we could pollute the oceans. They make up 70% of the earth's surface and are seemingly inexhaustible sinks for waste. Perhaps this is why we continue to dump thousands of tons of garbage into them every year (see Figure 12.9). Although the point can be argued at great length, it is perhaps impossible to pollute the

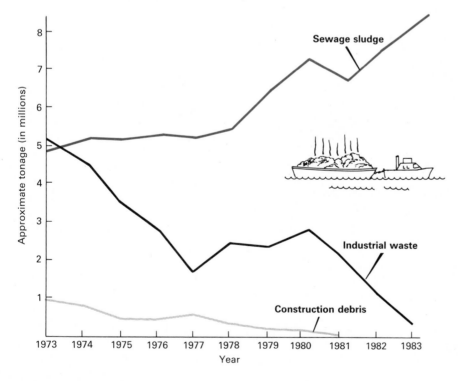

Figure 12.9 Trends in Ocean Dumping in the U.S.

oceans to a uniformly dangerous level. Although the dynamics of biomagnification may indeed lead to the contamination of high-trophic-level organisms over wide expanses of world's oceans (see Barber and Warlen, 1979; Gossett, Brown, and Young, 1983), the most serious problem for the moment is localized pollution.

Already very serious is the pollution of coastal areas of the oceans such as that caused by oil spills, sewage, and other wastes (see Chapter 15). Coastal pollution affects some of the most important natural systems on earth—the estuaries—and extends over much of adjacent continental shelves in many locations. Estuaries are important because they serve as breeding areas for species that hold key positions in many oceanic food chains and marine ecosystems. We saw in early chapters that estuaries are among the most productive ecosystems on earth; they constitute an optimal life support interface between the atmosphere, lithosphere, and hydrosphere. Obviously, we should be concerned about the pollution of estuaries. *Environmental Quality—1982* contains a short description of the pollution problems in the Chesapeake Bay, "one of the word's largest and most productive estuarine systems." This account describes nutrient enrichment as *the* major threat to the productivity and environmental quality of the Chesapeake Bay (Council on Environmental Quality, 1983, p. 57).

The Pollution of Groundwater

Groundwater, which we defined in Chapter 7, is also subject to pollution. Since a great deal of this water source is tapped for various uses, groundwater pollution has important implications. Indeed, the contamination of groundwater by toxic chemicals is listed by the Council on Environmental Quality as one of the three most important environmental problems for the 1980s (desertification and extinction are the other two). Consider the following:

— Half the people of the United States depend on groundwater for their drinking water (Ableson, 1984), and one quarter of the water consumed for all purposes in the United States is drawn from the ground (Rogers, 1983).
— Between 1950 and 1975 the demand for groundwater increased 140% (Rogers, 1983).
— Groundwater is the source of fully half the irrigation water used in the American West.
— Seventy five percent of American cities depend upon groundwater for most of their supply (Pye and Patrick, 1983).

— Groundwater is the next largest reservoir of water on earth after the oceans.
— Thirty percent of the stream flow in the United States starts as groundwater (springs, etc.).
— Once contaminated, groundwater may remain contaminated for hundreds of years or more (Council on Environmental Quality, 1981b).

Obviously, groundwater is important. Even so, an understandable first reaction to the notion of groundwater pollution might well be: How can groundwater become polluted? It's underground! Figure 12.7 illustrates how contaminants can get into surface water from waste dumps by being carried by groundwater. Any such groundwater would itself be polluted, as would groundwater that receives other contaminants from above. It is not difficult to imagine that the 10,000 or more toxic waste dumps identified by the EPA (see Chapter 15) are an enormous source of potential groundwater contamination. In even more quantitative terms, Rogers (1983) cites government statistics indicating that 28–54 million tons (EPA) or as much as 255–275 million tons (Office of Technology Assessment in Congress) of federally regulated hazardous waste are released into the environment each year. Much of this has ended up in leaky landfills and ordinary garbage dumps from which there has been seepage into groundwater. Agriculture wastes, domestic waste, and deliberate deep-well disposal are additional sources of groundwater contamination (Figure 12.10). Septic tanks alone are the source of 800 billion gallons of waste discharged into the ground each year (Rogers, 1983).

There is considerable evidence that wastes do contaminate groundwater. In the last several years, between one fourth and one third of all cities relying on groundwater for drinking experienced some form of contamination, mainly from leachate from toxic waste dumps (Rogers, 1983). Groundwater contamination has been reported in every state (Pye and Patrick, 1983), and the EPA has reported contamination of drinking water wells by toxic organic chemicals in virtually every state (Council on Environmental Quality, 1981b). Although only about 1% of underground aquifers are badly polluted at present, many of these are in large population centers.

The following specific cases are described in the volume *Contamination of Groundwater by Toxic Organic Chemicals* published by the Council on Environmental Quality in 1981:

— Thirty-nine public wells in the San Gabriel Val-

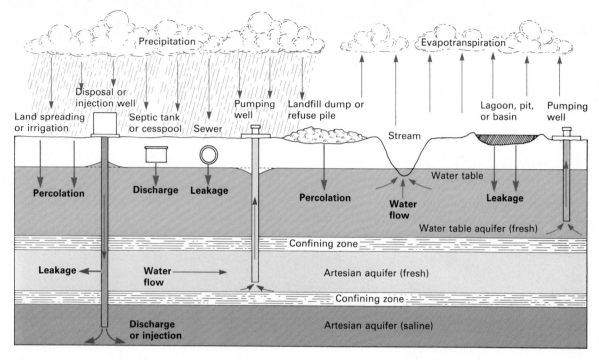

Figure 12.10 Sources of Groundwater Contamination.

ley were closed by California public health officials because the wells were contaminated by trichlorethylene, a chemical known to cause cancer in laboratory animals. These wells had provided water to some 400,000 people in 13 cities.

— Hazardous waste disposal was blamed for the contamination of the groundwater supply in South Brunswick, New Jersey. Several carcinogenic chemicals were found in high concentrations in a number of wells.

— Thirty square miles of a shallow aquifer between Denver and Brighton, Colorado, at the Rocky Mountain Arsenal, were contaminated by chemical by-products of a manufacturer of pesticides and herbicides. Domestic, stock, and irrigation wells had to be abandoned.

— Phenols, phenanthrene, chrysene, and pyrene, all by-products of creosote production, were found in drinking water wells a mile away from a creosoting company in a suburb of Minneapolis.

— One hundred drinking water wells were closed in 1972 in Jackson Township, New Jersey, because of organic chemical contamination. Apparently, chemicals were being dumped illegally in a landfill licensed to take sewage sludge and septic tank wastes. Deaths, kidney disease, and other health problems were blamed by local residents on the contamination.

— The *Eleventh Annual Report* of the Council on Environmental Quality (1981a) cites similar examples of contaminated drinking water wells in Bedford, Massachusetts, in two counties on Long Island, and in Gray, Maine, and cites an EPA claim that there are serious contamination of drinking water supplies in more than 30 states.

The four most common pollutants of groundwater are chloride, nitrate, heavy metals, and hydrocarbons (Pye and Patrick, 1983). The specific health effects of these and other individual compounds and classes of compounds are described in Chapters 9, 10, 13, and 14.

The problem of groundwater contamination is especially difficult because of the out-of-sight nature of the problem; we know comparatively little about what goes on "down there." We know that the groundwater flows relatively slowly, but we know little about the pathways. We know that wastes can in fact be effectively taken out of groundwater by (1) surface adsorption; (2) dilution; (3) mechanical filtration; (4) precipitation following chemical interaction; (5) buffering, (6) chemical neutralization; (7) microbial degradation; and (8) plant uptake; we do not know to what extent these occur in different locations. Very few groundwater sources have ever been tested. Nor have many, if not most, of the chemicals contaminating groundwater today been adequately tested, particularly at low levels, for health effects; no standards exist for their allowable concentrations.

WASTEWATER TREATMENT AND OTHER TYPES OF WATER POLLUTION CONTROL

One way to control pollution is not to generate pollutants or to generate less. This is more applicable to some sources than to others, however. Except for long-range population control, there really is no way to reduce the amount of human and animal bodily wastes generated. These must be dealt with by using some kind of strategy to keep them from becoming water pollution problems. Industry is another story. There *are* ways to reduce industrial waste, and we will discuss some specifics shortly.

Self-Purification of Water

As indicated in Table 12.7, there are natural mechanisms of water purification; some of these are physical, some are chemical, and some are biological in nature. Physical purification includes obvious things such as dilution and some less obvious ones like the absorption of chemical contaminants into suspended clay particles that eventually settle out. As a result of absorption and sedimentation, some

Table 12.7 Sinks for Water Pollutants in the Hydrosphere and in Soil

Chemical Group	Some Sources	Major Sinks	Examples
Pesticides	agricultural operations; public health programs	photoxidation on surface of soil or water	dieldrin; 2,4-D
		hydrolysis in waterways	DDT
		oxidation and reduction catalyzed by organic and mineral fractions in soils and sediments	organophosphate pesticides
		adsorption on particles in soil or suspended in water	DDT
		microbially mediated degradation in soils and sediments	organophosphate pesticides; carbamate insecticides
Hydrocarbons	industrial operations; petroleum spills	photoxidation on surface of soil or water	some petroleum components
		adsorption on particles in soil or suspended in waterways	polycyclic aromatic hydrocarbons (see chapter 14)
		evaporation	low boiling point materials
		microbially mediated degradation	polycyclic aromatic hydrocarbons; naphthalene
Halogenated hydrocarbons	industrial operations	adsorption onto particles suspended in waterways	polychlorinated biphenyls (PCBs) (Chapter 13)
Synthetic polymers	industrial operations	autooxidation on surface of soil or water	butyl rubber
		microbially mediated degradation in sediments and soils	cellulose nitrate, cellulose acetate, styrene polymers
Fertilizers	agricultural operations		
Nitrogen		chemodenitrification	nitrate
		volatization from topsoil to air	ammonium
		microbially mediated reactions; production of nitrous oxide and nitrogen gas, which may diffuse into atmosphere	nitrate, ammonium
Phosphorus		microbially mediated reduction of phosphate; precipitation from solution in ground and surface waters	phosphate

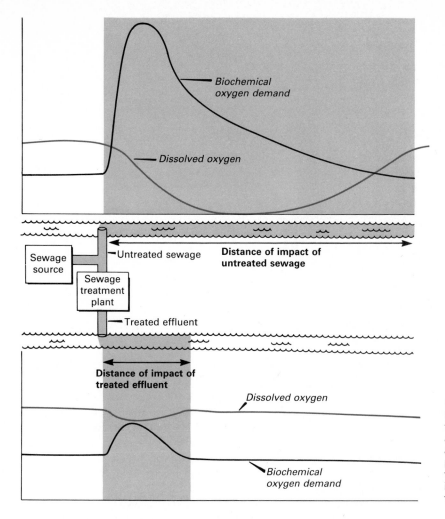

Figure 12.11 The Impact of Sewage Treatment. Sewage treatment plants compress into a very small space the cleansing action that would normally take place over much longer distances in a flowing river. The ideal treatment plant reduces the impact to near zero.

pollutants end up as deep-ocean sediment and are more or less permanently sequestered from the biosphere. Chemical purification also occurs naturally; organic and inorganic acids may be neutralized by reaction with lime (calcium carbonate) in limestone creekbeds, for example. Biologically, many naturally occurring microorganisms are able to degrade the organic matter that reaches waterways.

All of the natural sinks described in Table 12.7 can be overloaded. They are variable in how well they work, and many circumstances affect them. The amount of suspended clay available for absorption varies, as does the amount of calcium carbonate dissolved in water; microorganisms work better at some temperatures than others; and so on. Even the most optimally functional natural sinks can become overloaded by the sheer volume of pollutants.

We have tried to develop water treatment sys-

tems to help solve this problem. At first our efforts were largely engineering-intensive and ecologically inappropriate. Lately, we seem to be discovering that dealing with this problem by gently helping nature along (Figure 12.11) may be the best answer.

Primary Sewage Treatment

Primary sewage treatment is the simple removal of the solids from wastewater. As illustrated in Figure 12.12, the basic primary treatment system includes some combination of screens, filters, grit chambers, and sedimentation tanks connected in series. Some primary treatment systems also utilize grinders, which shred solid materials to be collected later in a sediment tank. Primary treatment systems often include a chlorinator, which is designed to kill all or most of the bacteria present in wastewater. It has been suggested that chlorination may be a

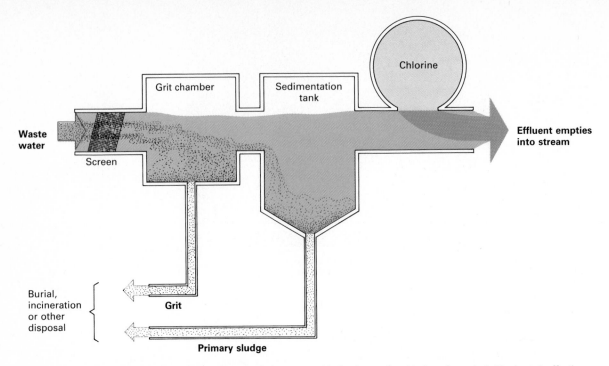

Figure 12.12 Primary Treatment. This involves physical screening and physical removal of grit and sedimented solids. Chlorine is usually added at the end of this short, ineffective process to kill potentially harmful bacteria.

double-edged sword. It may kill bacteria and some, though not all, viruses, but it also causes the chlorination of certain organic chemicals, perhaps creating compounds such as trihalomethanes, which are carcinogenic (see Chapter 14).

The final product of primary treatment is wastewater containing assorted toxic substances and a large amount of dissolved organic matter and salts. These can constitute a considerable BOD and potential for eutrophication. Thus primary treatment alone is generally inadequate.

The captured products of primary treatment, the sludge and solids, must be used or disposed of by some means. Common methods include allowing the sludge to dry and then spreading it in a landfill or incinerating it. Primary treatment does little more than help slow down the aging of waterways by keeping out grit and solids that would tend to fill them up. The problems that remain in wastewater after primary treatment can be reduced considerably by secondary treatment.

Secondary Sewage Treatment

Secondary treatment employs the kinds of decomposers discussed in Chapter 1 to break down the organic matter in sewage before it gets to a river or lake. The target for this stage of treatment is the dissolved organic matter that constitutes the BOD in sewage. There are several types of secondary treatment processes, two of which are the activated sludge process and the trickling filter.

In the **activated sludge process**, illustrated in Figure 12.13, aerobic microorganisms decompose the organic matter in wastewater; as they do so, they increase in numbers. Some of the enriched or biologically activated material thus generated is used to reseed the incoming wastewater. In a **trickle filter**, which is usually a big vat filled with crushed stones on which aerobic decomposers become established, wastewater is trickled downward over the stones while air (oxygen) is being forced upward, creating an enormous oxygen-rich surface on which organic material is reduced to carbon dioxide, water, and mineral salts. Both of these processes work on the liquid portion of sewage from which the solids have been removed. Secondary treatment of solids is accomplished by allowing it to be digested in an **anaerobic digester** (Figure 12.13) at relatively high temperatures. Here microorganisms that do not use oxygen break down the organic matter in sludge, producing gases like methane, which have a potential to be used as a source of energy to heat sewage treatment plants. Sludge residence time in a sludge digester is about 15 days, and the product that emerges is not markedly different for organic humus. In some places it is even packaged and sold as a soil conditioner.

While primary sewage treatment is basically *physical* in nature, secondary treatment is *biological*. The biological nature of secondary treatment makes it susceptible to poisons that can kill decomposers. Chromate polluters have been known to shut down secondary treatment systems for long periods of time.

A comparison of primary and secondary treatment in the removal of wastewater components is made in Table 12.8. Note that secondary treatment removes nearly all the biochemical oxygen demand.

While secondary treatment systems are very effective in reducing organic matter, they are not effective in removing the inorganic salts that can also cause eutrophication. This is where tertiary treatment comes in.

Tertiary Sewage Treatment

Primary treatment is physical, secondary treatment is biological, and tertiary treatment is basically chemical. The nature of **tertiary treatment** is complicated because it varies from location to location, but it is basically the use of chemical methods to remove some of the chemicals remaining in sewage wastewater after primary and secondary treatment. An example is the precipitation of phosphorus compounds through the addition of iron or aluminum salts. Nitrogen compounds including ammonia can also be removed by chemical processes.

It goes without saying that as we improve the quality of water by increased degrees of treatment, the treatment becomes more and more expensive. Now even more expensive ways of treating sewage are emerging.

Table 12.8 Performance of Primary and Secondary Stages of Sewage Treatment

Component Removed	Percent of Pollutants Removed by	
	Primary Treatment	Secondary Treatment
Biological oxygen demand (BOD)	30	90
Suspended solids	60	90
Nitrogen compounds (total)	20	50
Phosphorus compounds (total)	10	30

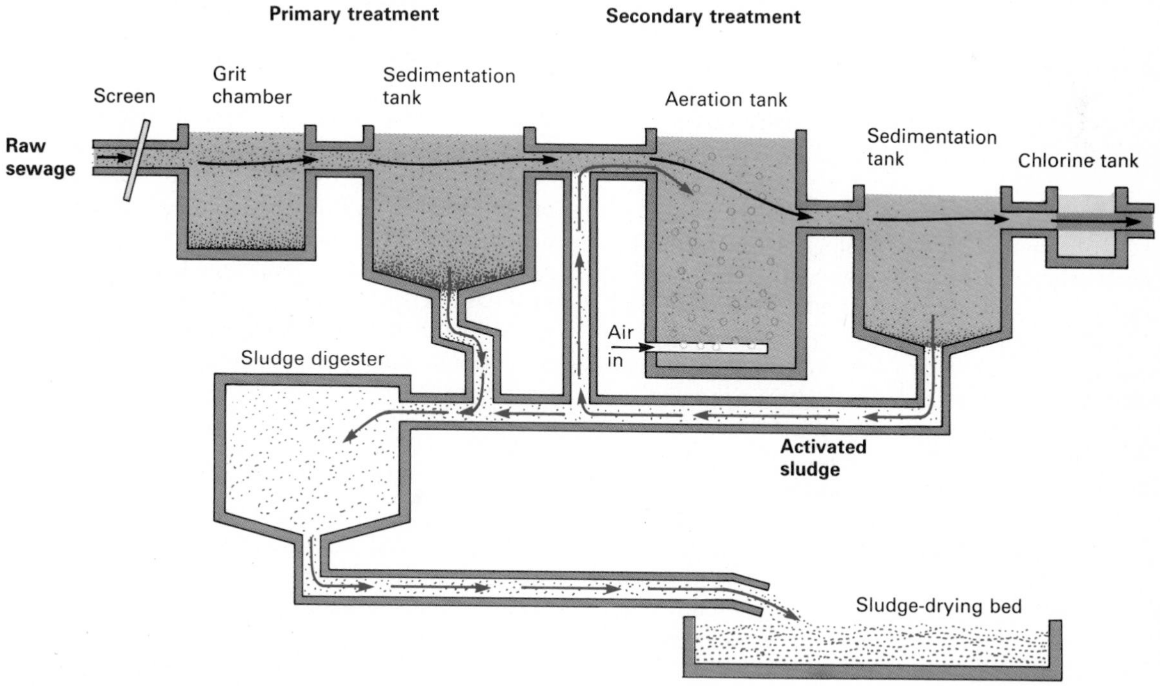

Figure 12.13 Secondary Treatment. Such systems involve biological oxidation of wastes using, for example, an activated sludge system (shown here). In other secondary systems, sludge is subjected to anaerobic biological digestion; the treated sludge is dried and disposed of by incineration or land disposal.

Activated sludge: a process that removes organic matter from sewage by saturating it with air and adding biologically active sludge.

Adsorption: an advanced way of treating wastes in which activated carbon removes organic matter from waste water.

Aeration tank: serves as a chamber for injecting air into water.

Algae: plants which grow in sunlit waters. They are a food for fish and small aquatic animals and, like all plants, put oxygen in the water.

Bacteria: small living organisms which often consume the organic constituents of sewage.

Biochemical oxygen demand (BOD): the dissolved oxygen required by organisms for the aerobic decomposition of organic matter present in water. It is used as a measure in determining the efficiency of a sewage treatment plant.

Coagulation: the clumping together of solids to make them settle out of the sewage faster. Coagulation of solids is brought about with the use of certain chemicals such as lime, alum and iron salts.

Combined sewer: carries both sewage and storm water run-off.

Comminutor: a device for the catching and shredding of heavy solid matter in the primary stage of waste treatment.

Diffused air: a technique by which air under pressure is forced into sewage in an aeration tank. The air is pumped down into the sewage through a pipe and escapes out through holes in the side of the pipe.

Digestion: takes place in tanks when sludge materials decompose, resulting in partial gasification, liquefaction, and mineralization of pollutants.

Effluent: the liquid that comes out of a treatment plant after completion of the treatment process.

Electrodialysis: a process that utilizes direct current and an arrangement of permeable-active membranes to achieve separation of the soluble minerals from the water.

Flocculation: the process by which clumps of solids in sewage are made to increase in size by chemical, physical, or biological action.

Incineration: burning the sludge to remove the water and reduce the remaining residues to a safe, non-burnable ash. The ash can then be disposed of safely on land, in some waters, or into caves or other underground locations.

Lagoons: ponds, usually human-made to rigid specifications, in which sunlight, algae, and oxygen interact to restore water to a reasonable state of purity.

Mechanical aeration: uses mechanical energy to inject air into water, causing the waste stream to absorb oxygen from the atmosphere.

Mixed liquor: a mixture of activated sludge and waters containing organic matter undergoing activated sludge treatment in the aeration tank.

Organic matter: the carbonaceous waste contained in plant or animal matter and originating from domestic or industrial sources.

Oxidation pond: a human-made lake or body of water in which wastes are consumed by bacteria. It is used

Modern Physical-Chemical Treatment Systems

New physical-chemical treatment systems do not rely on any type of biological treatment. The basic components are filtration/pretreatment, clarification, filtration, absorption, and disinfection. Clarification is a process by which chemicals such as alum or lime are used to precipitate wastes into particulate masses that settle out. Filtration is a step that removes any remaining suspended solids. Absorption removes dissolved organic matter by chemical charge attraction using such materials as activated carbon. Some physical-chemical treatment systems use **electrodialysis**, a system in which charged poles attract negatively and positively charged ions from wastewater, causing them to pass through tiny pores in membranes and then allowing the water to move on relatively free of dissolved ions.

Physical-chemical systems are not affected by toxins that occasionally neutralize or disrupt secondary treatment plants, and they are relatively un-affected by cold weather. Physical-chemical treatment systems are in operation or will be soon in Niagara Falls, New York; Garland, Texas; Pittsburgh, Pennsylvania; Fitchburg, Massachusetts; and Cleveland and Plainsville, Ohio. These systems are expensive to build and operate because they are material-intensive and energy-intensive. In the perspective of the total environment, some of them may actually cause as much environmental difficulty as they prevent.

Package Treatment Plants

In wide use these days in many parts of the suburban United States are the so-called package treatment plants. These are small wastewater treatment systems, usually less than a few hundred square feet in size, that treat the waste from small subdivisions and small communities. When present in large numbers in urban areas, package plants are a problem because they require considerable maintenance and attention. Regulation and monitoring of most frequently with other waste treatment processes. An oxidation pond is basically the same as a sewage lagoon.

Primary treatment: removes the material that floats or will settle in sewage. It is accomplished by using screens to catch the floating objects and tanks for the heavy matter to settle in.

Salts: the minerals that water picks up as it passes through the air, over and under the ground, and through household and industrial uses.

Sand filters: remove some suspended solids from sewage. Air and bacteria decompose additional wastes filtering through the sand. Cleaner water drains from the bed. The sludge accumulating at the surface must be removed from the bed periodically.

Sanitary sewers: in a separate system, pipes in a city that carry only domestic waste water. The storm water runoff is taken care of by a separate system of pipes.

Secondary treatment: the second step in most waste treatment systems in which bacteria consume the organic parts of the wastes. It is accomplished by bringing the sewage and bacteria together in trickling filters or in the activated sludge process.

Sedimentation tanks: help remove solids from sewage. The waste water is pumped to the tanks where the solids settle to the bottom or float on the top as scum. The scum is skimmed off the top, and solids on the bottom are pumped to incineration, digestion, filtration or other means of final disposal.

Septic tanks: used for domestic wastes when a sewer line is not available to carry them to a treatment plant. The wastes are piped to underground tanks directly from the home or homes. The bacteria in the wastes decompose the organic waste and the sludge settles on the bottom of the tank. The effluent flows out of the tank into the ground through drains. The sludge is pumped out of the tanks, usually by commercial firms, at regular intervals.

Sewers: a system of pipes that collect and deliver waste water to treatment plants or receiving streams.

Sludge: the solid matter that settles to the bottom, floats, or becomes suspended in the sedimentation tanks and must be disposed of by filtration and incineration or by transport to appropriate disposal sites.

Sterilization: the destruction of all living organisms. In contrast, disinfection is the destruction of most of the living organisms.

Storm sewers: a separate system of pipes that carry only runoff from buildings and land during a storm.

Suspended solids: the small particles of solid pollutants which are present in sewage and which resist separation from the water by conventional means.

Trickling filter: a support media for bacterial growth, usually a bed of rocks or stones. The sewage is trickled over the bed so the bacteria can break down the organic wastes. The bacteria collect on the stones through repeated use of the filter.

---

the effectiveness of these plants are difficult. Many of them discharge partially treated waste into very low-capacity streams and have been known to present health hazards in highly populated areas.

Industrial Water Pollution Control

Some of the especially toxic substances produced by industry—metals and toxic organic chemicals, for example—can be removed from effluents chemically. Nemerow (1978) summarized these methods and presents a number of strategies other than directly removing waste from the effluent. These include (1) volume reduction, (2) strength reduction, (3) neutralization, and (4) equalization of discharge. The first three of the strategies are self-explanatory and have to do with changing processes and procedures within plants. **Equalization of discharge** means using a holding system for pollutants that allows them to be discharged in proportion to the amount of flow or capacity of the receiving waters to absorb and neutralize them.

Figure 12.14 illustrates two common methods for dissipating waste heat. The wet tower and dry tower work by dissipating heat into the atmosphere instead of into the hydrosphere. The *wet tower* works by removing the most kinetically active water molecules by evaporation. The natural draft up and out of such towers carries away heat as evaporated water. The problems with this method are that (1) water is lost in this process and (2) the addition of water vapor to the air in the vicinity of such cooling towers makes the area foggier than normal; under certain conditions this vapor can also lead to highway icing and altered patterns of precipitation.

The *dry tower* works on the same principle as the automobile radiator. The kinetic energy of hot water passing through coils is transferred to air molecules surrounding the coils, which are removed rapidly by a fan. Because this system requires power to run the fan, it is slightly more expensive to operate than the wet tower.

Another solution to the thermopollution problem is the holding or cooling pond. In this system,

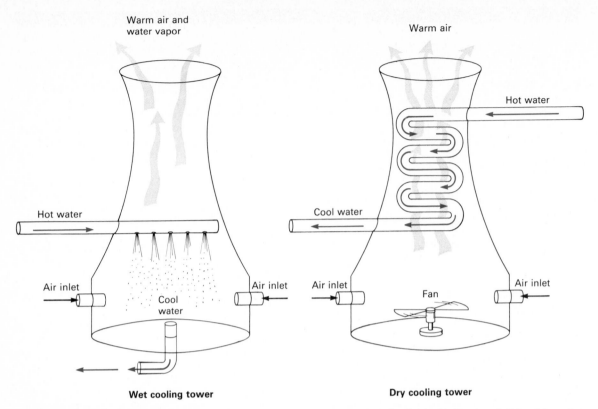

Figure 12.14 Cooling Towers. Two of the methods by which heat can be removed from water used in industrial cooling are illustrated. The wet cooling tower is a device in which hot water is exposed to air, which takes the heat away via evaporation. The dry tower uses the principle of the automobile radiator; heat is given off by convection to air forced over coils containing the hot water.

warm water is simply held in a pond for a certain time before it is released into a stream. Natural cooling by evaporation and radiation dissipate the heat before it gets into the natural aquatic ecosystem. Ponds take up space, of course, and this can be a problem in areas where there is little land. The most ecologically sensible way to reduce thermopollution is the adoption of technologies and practices that reduce the need for energy.

Deep-Well Injection: Waste Under the Rug

One way of dealing with hazardous waste is to inject it into limestone or sandstone strata. Ideally, this is done where such permeable strata are sandwiched between relatively inpermeable layers (Figure 12.15) well below the water table so that contamination of the water table is prevented. While some say that perhaps half of the surface of the United States may be suitable for deep-well injection disposal, others say that the dangers of leakage and contamination are too great and this method should not be used.

Near Denver, Colorado, it has been shown that there is a high correlation between deep-well injections and earthquakes, presumably a result of the transmission of the pressure of injected liquids into subsurface strata.

There are already several hundred deep-well injection operations in the United States, and the number is increasing by about 30–40 per year. Millions of barrels of wastes are being injected into such wells each day.

Recycling Water and Waterborne Wastes: An Ecologically Sensible Water Pollution Control Strategy

More and more companies, particularly those that need large quantities of water, are adopting systems in which water is used over and over. A steel-manufacturing operation employing recycling methods can cut the need for water from 65,000 gallons per ton of steel produced to about 1000 gallons per ton. This is certainly a big difference. Such recycling methods will make ever-increasing sense as clean water becomes increasingly scarce and more expensive.

Another dimension to water recycling is the fact that pollutants are resources out of place. At least some industrial pollutants can be recovered profitably. The recovery of zinc from wastewater generated in the production of rayon is one such example. First, zinc is a dwindling resource (Chapter 7). Second, zinc is harmful to fish in concentrations of 1 ppm. Processes have now been developed whereby much of the 50 million pounds of zinc sulfate used annually in the rayon industry can be recovered rather than lost as a water pollutant. (In the manufacture of rayon, zinc is used to create conditions necessary for the spinning of rayon; the zinc is not used up.)

Still another dimension of water conservation strategy is using water for more than one thing in the same use cycle or use stream. You may have had the experience of cleaning something in the kitchen sink while looking out the window at a rather dry garden and wondering why there couldn't be a system whereby the water being used in the sink could somehow be diverted to the garden, where it would serve a good purpose and reduce the burden of water to be treated at the local sewage treatment plant. There are many other such examples of possible multiple uses of water. For instance, water from the kitchen sink could be diverted for flushing toilets. We do not need drinking-quality water to flush away wastes. It has been estimated that such multiple uses of water could reduce the water to be treated in sewage treatment plants by 40% or more.

What about carrying this a step further? What about directing the water carrying human wastes in shorter loops? Although this is somewhat a less aesthetic concept, it is already been demonstrated to be practicable. Sewage enrichment farming has been practiced in many countries of the world for centuries. Now sophisticated systems for utilizing wastewater both as a source of water and as a source of organic and inorganic nutrients are well on their way to being a practical reality in the United States.

As early as 1962, scientists at the Pennsylvania State University began evaluating the use of sewage for irrigation and enrichment of forests and other types of land. They studied the application of partially treated wastewater—water free of suspended solids—to fields, forests, and pastures at rates that allowed the water to be absorbed by these terrestrial systems. They found that soil functioned as a perfect filter and that clean water percolated through to the water table. Some of the water and most of the nutrients dissolved in the wastewater were picked up by vegetation, increasing its yield.

This practice has been used to solve the problem of revegetation of strip-mined areas. Even when returned to contour, the spoil piles that result from strip mining remain nonfertile, acidic, and very hot. Spraying partly treated wastewater onto such surfaces leaches the acid out of the topsoil rather quickly, provides a wet environment, and adds organic matter. The effect is to accelerate ecological succession (Chapter 4). Strip-mined land in the Shawnee National Forest in Southern Illinois, which once resembled the surface of the moon, has been restored to grass and brush with the aid of Chicago sewage.

A major problem with this approach is the risk of chemical contamination and infection of water-

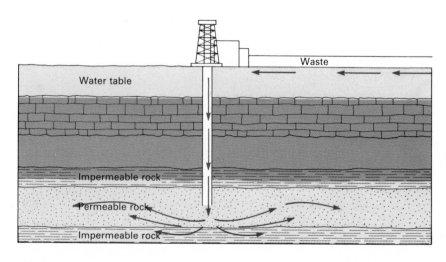

Figure 12.15 Deep-Well Injections. One method of disposing of hazardous waste is the deep-well injection system. Ideally, waste fluids are deposited well below the water table into permeable layers of rock sandwiched between impermeable layers of rock.

Water table

Waste

Impermeable rock

Permeable rock

Impermeable rock

borne human pathogens. Wastewater and solid residuals carry variable chemical loads and may carry a full complement of pathogenic organisms (see Table 12.1). The degree of risk depends upon the treatment process employed before the sewage is applied and the survival of the pathogenic viruses, parasite eggs, and bacteria in soil, crops, groundwater, and runoff. The problem is a very real one, since—for example— shellfish can accumulate human viruses and *Salmonella* has been shown to survive both aerobic and anaerobic digesters and to be viable for more than a year in sludge spread on grassland (Hess and Beer, 1975).

Although the risk of contamination and infection are serious indeed, they can be avoided. Tertiary treatment of municipal sewage, control of industrial water pollution, and the strict control of persistent toxic chemicals could eliminate or greatly diminish chemical contamination. New technologies for disinfecting wastewater should all but eliminate the risk of disease. An economically feasible method of disinfection described by Trump (1981) passes thin streams of watery sludge through intensely ionizing beams of electrons. Obviously, even with such technologies in place, wastewater on its way to recycling will have to be carefully monitored.

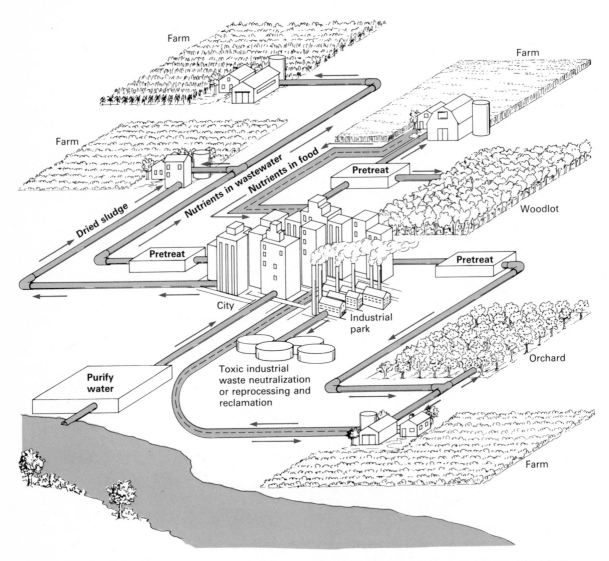

Figure 12.16 Wastewater Recycling. Perhaps much of the wastewater problem could be solved by an improved system of recycling and reuse. Such systems could also help solve other problems, for example, the need for irrigation water and the need for energy in the manufacture of chemical fertilizer.

Why not large-scale systems for multiple use of water such as that depicted in Figure 12.16? Apparently, they are on the way. A wastewater system in Michigan that is to be completed sometime before the turn of the century may be a model of things to come. When finished, the Michigan system will collect 43 million gallons of raw sewage and industrial wastes every day. Rather than running into Lake Michigan, the wastes will be pumped 15 miles eastward, where bacteria will be allowed to work on it for a while in aerated lagoons. Some of the sludge will be allowed to settle out to be collected and used as soil conditioner later. The supernatant—the water left after the sludge settles out—will be sprayed on 6000 acres of cropland, which will then presumably take out some if not all nutrients in the water as the water makes it way through the soil back to Lake Michigan. It has been estimated that this system will generate agricultural profits that will eventually more than pay for the establishment of the system.

We would like to summarize by saying that the deficiencies in nearly all the methods used for treating the effluents, the energy that it takes to treat and/or dispose of sewage, our dwindling water supplies (Chapter 7), and the increasing value of some of the materials discarded as wastes seem to suggest that the *real* solution to the wastewater problem in the future is the tightening of water use loops, reduction of the volume of the waste stream, and recycling. Sewage treatment through the tertiary stage is expensive. It is expensive precisely because this type of solution is linear rather than cyclic. The cycling of wastewater makes profound ecological sense because it conforms best to several major ecological principles, which we will paraphrase here as

1. all parts of the environment are interrelated anyway, and
2. the system is closed—nothing can really be disposed—everything must go somewhere. We expect to see increasing use of recycling systems and procedures that are more in harmony with natural systems than the technologically heavy systems we have relied upon in the past.

THE PURIFICATION OF DRINKING WATER

The treatment of water for drinking is much like the treatment of wastewater but the process is more intense and more complete. While purer sources of water require very little treatment or monitoring of quality, river water such as that used in many cities throughout the world for drinking receives a variety of more energy-intense treatments. These procedures involve some combination of the following:

1. Spraying the water into the air to release dissolved gases like hydrogen sulfide that give water a bad taste.
2. Treating the water chemically, using coagulants like aluminum sulfate (alum), a compound that clumps together finely suspended particles, protein, and other material having electrical charges.
3. Allowing the suspended solids and the coagulated solids to settle in sedimentation basins.
4. Passing the water through a system of filters such as sand filters and adsorbants that take out previously unsedimented materials as well as bacteria and even viruses.
5. Using chlorination to kill any remaining microorganisms.

Systems such as this serve nearly every community in the United States.

While we have come to rely on the safety of water treated by these systems, a study of drinking water supplies in the early 1970s showed that 36% of tap water samples evaluated had one or more bacteriological or chemical contaminants that exceeded limits established by law. Furthermore, over half the systems tested showed various deficiencies related to equipment design, construction, or condition of the treatment plant; more than three quarters of water purification plant operators were found to be inadequately trained in microbiology; and almost all of the systems had not been inspected by the proper authorities during the year preceding the survey (U.S. Environmental Protection Agency, 1976). Research into the safety of drinking water has been intensified recently because of the discovery of carcinogens in drinking water supplies in many communities in the United States and other parts of the world (see Chapter 14). In the United States the federal government has attempted to improve the situation by the Safe Drinking Water Act of 1974 (Public Law 93-523). This law (described later in the section on water pollution and the law) directed the EPA to establish minimum drinking water standards for the nation.

On a worldwide scale, a conference on water was held in Argentina in March 1977. There the delegates of 116 nations developed recommendations to deal with the worldwide problem of drinking water quality. The conferees set a goal of safe water for every individual in the world by 1990 (Goldblat, 1977) and recommended that the decade 1980–1990 be designated as the International Drinking Water Supply and Sanitation Decade.

THE ECONOMICS OF WATER POLLUTION AND WATER POLLUTION CONTROL

Proposals to control water pollution have included abolishing the free enterprise system, apparently because in the minds of some, water pollution is an inevitable consequence of free enterprise capitalism. It is true that water pollution, like all environmental problems, has an interesting economic aspect, but the relationship between water pollution and enterprise has nothing directly to do with whether or not the enterprise is free. Water pollution has been a problem in countries like China, the Soviet Union, all of Europe, and indeed all of the countries of the world from at least the beginning of recorded history.

An interesting account of the pollution of Lake Baikal in the Soviet Union is given by Goldman (1970), who concludes that there is water pollution in the Soviet Union for many of the same economic reasons that there is water pollution in the United States. The fact is that water has rather uniformly been considered by all societies as a free medium that can be used to carry waste away. In economic terms, this means that in nearly all economic systems the pollution of water is and has been treated as an external cost (Chapter 18). In other words, it does not cost anything to dispose of waste in water because, in the attitude of most human beings, water is inexhaustible; therefore it does not need to be paid

for or taken into account in the cost of doing business. The roots of the water pollution problem go back to times when no one or very few people were affected in any economically determinable way. As population densities have increased, the negative economic impact of pollution has correspondingly increased. More people are now concerned about the cost of *not* controlling pollution.

Action must now be based on a consideration of both the cost of water pollution control and the cost of *not* controlling pollution. Let's begin by looking at some of the costs of water pollution control.

The Cost of Water Pollution Control

While it is difficult to establish the economic impact of water pollution in all of its various aspects, determining the cost of water pollution control is relatively simple and straightforward.

The cost of treating sewage varies with the sophistication of the equipment and the energy required to operate it. At one end of the spectrum are relatively cheap means of treating sewage like the waste stabilization pond. At the other end of the spectrum are the very highly sophisticated tertiary treatment systems we described earlier. Secondary treatment costs two or three times more than primary treatment; tertiary treatment can cost up to six times as much. Sophisticated tertiary treatment systems that produce drinkable water push the cost even higher.

There has been a great increase in sewage treatment plant construction in the United States since the mid-1950s. Much of the increase has come since

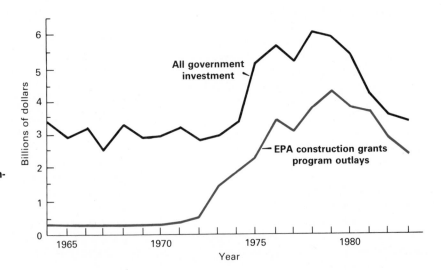

Figure 12.17 Government Investment in Wastewater Treatment Facilities, 1964–1983. EPA outlays are funds the agency transfers to states and localities as reimbursement for constructing facilities.

Part III   The Impact of Human Activities on Health and the Environment

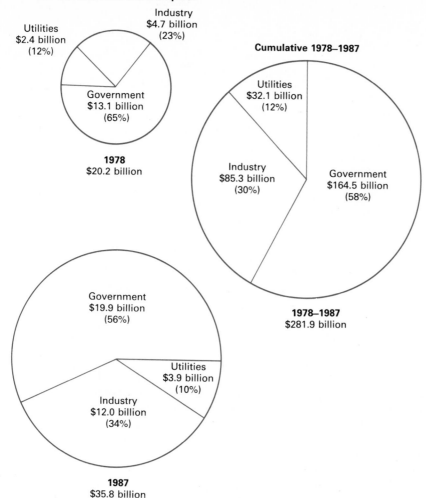

1978 and estimated 1987 compared

Utilities
$2.4 billion
(12%)

Industry
$4.7 billion
(23%)

Government
$13.1 billion
(65%)

1978
$20.2 billion

Cumulative 1978–1987

Utilities
$32.1 billion
(12%)

Industry
$85.3 billion
(30%)

Government
$164.5 billion
(58%)

1978–1987
$281.9 billion

Government
$19.9 billion
(56%)

Utilities
$3.9 billion
(10%)

Industry
$12.0 billion
(34%)

1987
$35.8 billion

Figure 12.18 Estimated Total Water Pollution Control Costs 1978–1987. The figures given here (in 1978 dollars) reflect both annual operation and maintenance costs and annualized capital costs.

the early 1970s and the passage of the Federal Water Pollution Control Act, which had a provision for partially financing the construction of sewage treatment facilities (Figure 12.17).

A summary of costs and expected costs for capital construction and operation of industrial and municipal sewage treatment facilities is given in Figure 12.18. For the decade ending in 1987 the United States is expected to spend 282 billion dollars (1978 dollars) for operation and maintenance (as well as capital cost) of water pollution and control facilities.

The Cost of Not Controlling Water Pollution

In Chapter 11 we discussed in considerable detail the difficulties in assigning dollar values to the negative impact of air pollution. The problem is nearly as difficult for water pollution. We could say

that the economic impact of uncontrolled pollution can be estimated from the degree to which we are now willing to pay for controlling pollution. We could also deduce the negative economic impact from the benefits of minimizing the wastewater problem.

The benefits of industrial waste treatment given by Nemerow (1978) range from the value of the resources recovered to the value of the water that is recycled or reused. Nemerow gives a whole range of secondary benefits including increased economic growth of the area served by a particular industry or municipal sewage treatment plant. There is also a host of intangible benefits such as the public relations factor for industry and a potential for development of land areas that could not be developed if there was polluted water.

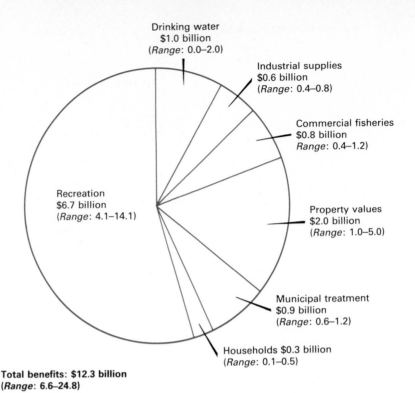

Drinking water
$1.0 billion
(*Range*: 0.0–2.0)

Industrial supplies
$0.6 billion
(*Range*: 0.4–0.8)

Commercial fisheries
$0.8 billion
Range: 0.4–1.2)

Recreation
$6.7 billion
(*Range*: 4.1–14.1)

Property values
$2.0 billion
(*Range*: 1.0–5.0)

Municipal treatment
$0.9 billion
(*Range*: 0.6–1.2)

Households $0.3 billion
(*Range*: 0.1–0.5)

Figure 12.19 Benefits of Water Pollution Control. An estimate of the benefits derived in 1985 from the removal of conventional water pollutants (in billions of 1978 dollars). Some of the limitations of these estimates are given in the text.

Total benefits: $12.3 billion
(*Range*: 6.6–24.8)

Using his own set of assumptions and parameters, Freeman (1979) derived the annual value of water pollution control benefits as shown in Figure 12.19. Freeman's estimates were based on 19 individual reports by others published between 1966 and 1979. In Figure 12.19 the ranges are the estimates from different sources using different assumptions; the single values above the ranges are best estimates. Freeman indicated that there were many problems with his summary report. He cited difficulties related to the fact that water quality varies considerably on a national scale, making it nearly impossible to generalize about water quality for the nation as a whole or about the degree of cleanup that has occurred. Freeman also cited difficulty in coming to economic conclusions about the effect of legislation because (1) the principal legislative tools have tended to focus on point sources and (2) most of the data he had to work from were based on the benefits to be enjoyed after 1985—after all of the stages of the implementation of the best available technology were completed as specified in the Clean Water Act.

Finally, Freeman indicates that his conclusions may grossly underestimate true water pollution control benefits because early estimates tended to focus on such items as fecal coliform bacteria and BOD,

largely failing to take into account the fact that the 1977 amendments (discussed below) redirected attention to toxic substances.

The Balance Sheet

It is tempting to note that 28.2 billion dollars is projected to be spent on water pollution control each year from 1978 to 1987 (Figure 12.18) and that Freeman's high estimate of the annual benefit to be enjoyed during 1985 is 24.8 billion dollars (Figure 12.19), but there are many reasons, technical and otherwise, why Figures 12.18 and 12.19 cannot be directly compared.

Despite the problems of doing an exacting cost-benefit analysis, it is obvious that economic factors in the solution to the water pollution control problem will force industry and municipalities to treat the cost of dealing with pollutants as a direct cost of doing business—as every bit as much of a direct cost as raw materials and labor.

WATER POLLUTION AND THE LAW

Although water pollution has had a worldwide legislative history going back to prehistoric times, we will focus on the United States and begin with the Refuse Act of 1899.

Refuse Act of 1899

The Refuse Act of 1899 is of more than historical interest. Although it was originally intended to address only problems of navigation, disease, and oil discharges in navigable waters, the act was broad enough to be useful, particularly in the years 1970–1972, in halting many of the worst water pollution atrocities.

The Water Pollution Control Act of 1948

The 1948 Act was a weak, ineffectual piece of legislation. Although it looked good on paper, with provisions for new water pollution control programs, research, funds for the construction of waste treatment facilities, construction loans, and planning grants, many of the provisions were never implemented because much of the money authorized by the Act was never appropriated. Although the Act contained a provision that permitted suits to be filed in federal courts against states over the pollution of interstate waterways, another provision was that states had to consent to such suits.

The 1956 Water Pollution Control Act

The 1956 Act was a tougher law; among its provisions were authorization of funds for the construction of treatment facilities and funds for research and wastewater treatment as well as for worker training. It also provided for the collection and dissemination of water quality data and provided grants to states for the establishment and maintenance of water pollution control programs. The 1956 Act provided for an enforcement process and allowed suits to be brought against a state in federal court without that state's consent.

The Water Pollution Control Act Amendments of 1961

Amendments to the 1956 Act passed in 1961 included provisions for (1) extended coverage to all navigable waterways, whether or not they were interstate, and (2) more funding for construction of waste treatment facilities.

The 1965 Amendments

The 1965 amendments are notable in that they introduced the concept of *water quality standards* for interstate waters. The Act provided for different water quality goals depending upon the intended or actual use of the waterway. The law also established the Federal Water Pollution Control Administration, an agency that was transferred into the Environmental Protection Agency in 1970.

Under the 1965 amendments, all the states and territories were permitted the option of preparing their own water quality standards for interstate streams, rivers, lakes, and coastal waters, or they could ask the federal government to set these standards for them. All of the states eventually decided to draft their own water quality standards, which were then to have been approved by the Secretary of the Interior.

The 1966 Amendments

The 1966 amendments nearly tripled the amount of money authorized for the construction of waste treatment facilities—from 450 million dollars in 1968 to 12.5 billion dollars in 1971 (U.S. Environmental Protection Agency, 1973). The amendments also increased the federal share of construction and increased the amount of funds available for research into better methods of wastewater treatment and water purification.

The 1970 Amendments

The 1970 amendments went further into the problems of oil pollution, sewage from boats, mine drainage, lake eutrophication, worker training, and pesticides.

The 1972 Federal Water Pollution Control Act

The Water Pollution Control Act of 1972 was a great leap forward. Reflecting the deep public interest in the environment born in the late 1960s, this Act clearly expressed a serious national interest in water quality and reflected strong public commitment to end water pollution. The 1972 amendments contained some of the ultimate steps that had emerged only gradually in preceding legislation. There were more strict deadlines for terminating pollution, stronger enforcement provisions by federal, state, and local governments, and a greater federal degree of control over the quality of the nation's waters. The concept of standards of water quality were extended to cover even intrastate waters.

The 1972 amendments spelled out a five-point strategy intended to largely eliminate the nation's water pollution problem by the year 1985. The five elements of the strategy in the 1972 amendments are as follows:

1. Determine the quality of the water in the United States for the present and on a continuing basis.
2. Establish effluent limitations, that is, limits as to what can be discharged into waters from fac-

tories, sewage treatment plants, and other point sources of water pollution.

3. Establish an improved discharge permit system aimed at forcing polluters to establish schedules for reducing pollutants and complying with the effluent limitations.
4. Establish performance standards for new plants and industries; they should not be permitted to be built unless they take into account the very latest technology for water pollution control.
5. Install sewers in all municipalities in the United States.

A national system of water quality surveillance has been set up as required under the first element of strategy outlined above. The intention was for this surveillance system to be the means by which priority problem areas could be identified. As of the present day, effluent limitations have been established for most if not all types of factories and water-polluting installations. This part of the law had a flexible provision for *feasible* (best practicable technology currently available) limitations by 1977 and an *absolute* (best available technology) limitation by 1983.

An example of the difference between *best practicable technology* and *best available technology* was given by the EPA in its booklet *First Things First* (1974), describing the beet-sugar industry. The law required the beet industry to come into compliance with effluent standards by July 1977 *provided that suitable land owned by the company was available for disposal of wastes*. If such land was not available for a particular plant, some discharge would be permitted into water. However, all beet sugar plants would have to meet the no discharge requirement by July 1, 1983, regardless of whether or not land was available in 1977. The idea was that if they did not have land in 1977, six years was time enough to get some.

The permit system was intended to be more than bureaucratic red tape. When a permit is applied for, the polluting company must furnish data on the kinds of discharges it makes and provide a careful plan of how it intends to bring them into compliance with the effluent standards set by the EPA. While the EPA and the federal government retained the ultimate authority in this permit system, the Water Pollution Control Amendments of 1972 gave the states the power and responsibility for conducting the permit program. For industries and operations that discharge sewage into the municipal waste treatment systems, the 1972 amendments required that industrial waste be pretreated before being discharged into the municipal system.

Concerning the problem of municipal sewage, the 1972 amendments again increased the funding available for construction of waste treatment facilities. Twenty billion more dollars were made available in 1972. The amendments also increased the federal share for such construction to 75% and provided help to local government to raise the other 25%.

The 1972 amendments required that new municipal plants have *at least* secondary treatment if constructed before mid-1974 and that after that date, the best practicable treatment methods had to be included in new construction. Another clause provided that all municipal plants, regardless of when they were constructed, had to provide a minimum of secondary treatment by mid-1977 and that all treatment plants regardless of where and what type had to have the best practicable treatment system in place by mid-1983.

The 1972 amendments also had provisions for areawide planning for water pollution control in problem areas like large cities. Section 303 of the amendments covered river basin plans, which were to be developed by all involved political and geographic subdivisions. An example would be the Ohio River basin, for which the bordering states formed the Ohio River Sanitation and Navigation Commission (ORSANCO). Special agencies (to be identified under Section 208 of Public Law 92-500) were to deal with problems in improving water quality in a large area. Agencies to be identified under the Section 208 of the 1972 amendments were to deal in a comprehensive way with the problems of waste reduction and waste treatment and to coordinate such diverse factors related to water pollution as zoning, development, transportation, and solid waste management. The agencies are to serve a planning function, which will take into account various economic constraints and other very real social and economic problems in coming up with recommendations and plans for making and keeping water clean.

As we stated earlier, initial responsibilities for enforcing provisions of the 1972 amendments fell to individual states. However, if the states failed to assume this responsibility, the EPA was empowered to enforce laws. States have the authority to set water quality standards for waterways within their borders, but if it is found that the standards are not strict enough or that none are set, the federal government may establish standards for that state via the Department of Interior. Enforcement powers specified in the Act also provide that those violating the permit conditions can be fined $10,000; negligent or willful violations can bring $25,000 fines for each day of violation. The Act also gives the EPA the power to enter and inspect any potentially polluting facility.

1977 Clean Water Act

Implementation of certain provisions in the 1972 legislation was slower than anticipated. One of the things that the 1977 amendments did was make adjustments in timetables for this fact. For example, target dates established for compliance with effluent limitations for point sources were no later than three years after limits are established by a state—but in no case later than July 1, 1987 (Section 301 as amended). Some other notable features of the 1977 amendments and the sections amended are as follows:

— *Section 101* reaffirmed that states have primary rights and responsibilities regarding water quality.
— *Section 104* established a national clearinghouse for information on water pollution control.
— *Section 208* further specified the role of the Departments of Defense, Interior, and Agriculture in areawide planning.
— *Section 301* extended to 1984 in some cases the deadline for establishing effluent limits for various classes of pollution sources.
— *Sections 304 and 307* detailed the EPA's responsibility for developing *water quality standards,* for example, preparing lists of toxic substances and proposing standards.
— *Section 311* established liability for damage from oil and hazardous substances. This provision makes owner/operators liable up to $50,000,000, and if willful negligence is proven, there is no limit.
— *Section 404* added regulations governing the addition of dredged/fill material to navigable waters.
— *Section 405* established provisions for emergency assistance with "spills" of dangerous chemicals and the like.

The 1977 amendments also indicated a shift in policy toward the control of toxic pollutants and somewhat away from conventional pollutants like fecal coliforms and BOD. The 1977 amendments

also encouraged increased land disposal of sewage (Section 405). In addition, money was made available to promote innovative and alternative technologies for sewage disposal in rural areas.

The Clean Water Act was up for renewal as we went to press.

The National Environmental Policy Act of 1970

Because it contained some legislation relevant to water pollution, we will include a brief discussion of the National Environmental Policy Act here. As its name implies, this act actually encompasses all kinds of pollution. The National Environmental Policy Act (NEPA), which was signed into law on January 1, 1970, established the **Council on Environmental Quality** and charged this group with the study of the condition of the nation's environment on a regular basis. (The annual reports of the Council on Environmental Quality contain summaries and compilations of statistics on environmental quality. The annual reports come out early each year and cover the previous year. Budget reductions under the Reagan administration have curtailed CEQ activities in this area.) This act also required every federal agency to take into account environmental factors in its decision making and to show how the environment was taken into account by publishing an **environmental impact statement** in advance of each major activity that uses federal money and potentially affects the environment. The Council on Environmental Quality is the main force in the federal government behind the development of every impact statement. The EPA, in contrast, is charged with reviewing and commenting in writing on the environmental impact statements made by any other federal agency.

The environmental impact statement clause in the NEPA had an enormous impact on the environmental scene. It has been called the most important piece of environmental legislation ever passed. *When done properly,* environmental impact statements must assess the potential impact any project will have on the environment. They must also analyze in straightforward terms the cost-benefit ratios of all legitimate alternatives to proposed actions. If statements are not done properly, the agency can be sued and the project halted. A flood of suits have been filed since NEPA was passed, raising charges that it is too easy to sue and that all progress has become mired in red tape. Others feel that it is about time that a lot of the reckless disregard for the environment mislabeled as progress is regularly dragged into the light and more carefully considered from all angles.

Safe Drinking Water Act of 1974 (P.L. 93-523)

We include this piece of legislation for obvious reasons. The provisions of the Safe Drinking Water Act include the following:

1. the establishment of regulations covering taste, odor, and appearance of drinking water;
2. the development of measures to protect underground drinking water sources;
3. the provision of funds for research on health, economic, and technological problems related to drinking water supplies and their purity; and
4. provision for a survey of the quality of water and the quality of the water treatment system in rural as well as urban areas.

Public Law 92-523 was intended to standardize the purity of water throughout the United States. By 1982 the EPA had established standards for maximum contaminant levels for 11 chemicals, 6 pesticides, bacteria, radioactivity, and turbidity.

As with other forms of pollution control, national drinking water quality standards are based on available scientific evidence about threshold levels of pollutants. The states have primary responsibility for enforcement (**primacy**) provided that they have acceptable standards, regulations, surveillance and enforcement procedures, provisions for variances, and reporting and record-keeping systems.

Basic monitoring, employing state and EPA-sanctioned procedures, is usually conducted by individual water systems (companies). Special testing for such things as low-level organic compounds is done by state laboratories. In 1982, only 65% of water companies were conducting all required tests, and many state laboratories were still not able to measure certain low-level organic contaminants (Council on Environmental Quality, 1982a).

THE IMPACT OF WATER POLLUTION CONTROL LEGISLATION

Before we summarize the effectiveness of clean water legislation, let's restate its intent in summary form. Basically, clean water laws were designed to clean up our water resources and to keep them clean. The laws specifically

1. directed the states to establish criteria for mean-

ingful water quality standards based on the intended use of the water;
2. gave the federal government (the EPA) the job of developing guidelines for setting water quality standards and the authority to set technology-based upper limits on what could be dumped into water by municipal and industrial sources, without regard to the intended use of the receiving water;
3. gave the EPA the job of setting performance standards for new water pollution sources, mainly industrial and sewage treatment plants; and
4. authorized the regulation or control of water pollution via a permit system until pollution of navigable water is halted altogether.

The implementation strategy in all clean water legislation was, in essence, to define polluted water (or, conversely, to set water quality goals) and then to encourage the prevention, reduction, and eventual elimination of water pollution. Encompassed in this strategy of implementation were (1) programs of research into pollution control and monitoring technology, (2) grants to states and municipalities for the construction of wastewater treatment facilities, and (3) grants to states to help them carry out their water resource management responsibilities over the full spectrum, from setting standards to enforcing them.

Assessments of the effects of water pollution control legislation in the last generation or so have spanned the entire spectrum from those saying that the laws have tried to do too much too soon to those saying that laws have not done enough soon enough.

How well has clean water legislation worked? Success has been mixed. We should qualify this answer by pointing out again that there are literally dozens of ways of assessing water quality and that any given degree of pollution has varying importance depending on how the water is to be used and the relative scarcity of water in a location.

By some standards—for example, the removal of total contaminants from sewage—there has been considerable progress; as a result of this and other gains, the quality of water in some lakes, rivers, and estuaries has been improved considerably. However, most lakes, rivers, and estuaries have about the same quality of water now as they did in 1972; some have actually deteriorated.

Considering the overall negative trend throughout most of this century, the fact that some water pollution problems have stopped getting worse is an element of considerable progress. The *Tenth Annual*

Report of the Council on Environmental Quality (1980) summed up progress in the 1970s by saying that water quality *was not getting any worse* throughout that decade and that water pollution was still widespread coming into the 1980s. Recent water quality inventories by the EPA and assessments made by environmental organizations indicate that this state of affairs persisted through the mid-1980s. Serious problems remain with treatment plants that have overflows of combined sewer and rainwater runoff (Figure 12.20), and new problems with toxic substances in water seem to appear every day. There are still eutrophication and toxic chemicals in the Great Lakes, and groundwater contamination has become one of the most important environmental issues of the day.

Much remains to be done about toxic chemicals. We need to know much more than we do about the threshold levels (assuming that there are such) of most of the compounds that are now found as water contaminants. (Chapter 14 discusses the problems of determining the threshold of carcinogenicity and the broad philosophical questions associated with acceptable risk.) The setting of specific effluent standards has been a major problem of implementing clean water laws throughout the last ten years. The 1972 Water Pollution Control Act specified that the federal government set specific effluent standards for toxic substances, standards based not on the intended use of the water but on toxicity. Economic, political, and legal pressures have generated considerable drag on this part of the law. As late as 1977,

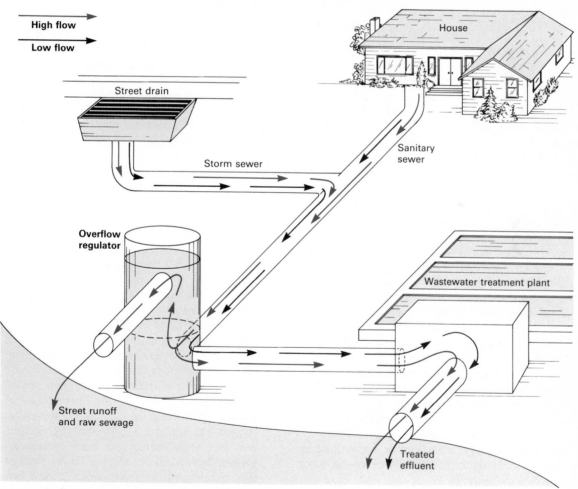

Figure 12.20 Storm Sewers and Sanitary Sewers. The sewer systems in U.S. municipalities are of two types. The combined type carries both rain runoff and waste. In other systems these two functions are separate. Combined systems present a problem at times of heavy rainfall, the common solution being to allow the flow to bypass the treatment plant—rainwater, wastewater, and all. Separate systems are much more amenable to good water pollution treatment.

only six effluent standards had been set, and a coalition of citizens took the EPA to court to order the agency to get busy setting guidelines. This contributed to Congress's amending the legislation to set up three categories of pollutants with respect to effluent standards: conventional pollutants—bacteria, BOD, etc.; toxic pollutants; and nonconventional pollutants—nitrates, phosphates, and other chemicals not falling into either of the other two categories. Toxic pollutants now number some 129 different chemicals, 65 of them established as a result of the 1977 suit against the EPA and the remainder added by the EPA since. The best available technology for limiting effluents of the substances was to be implemented by 1984.

WHAT NEEDS TO BE DONE: THE ROLE OF THE CITIZEN

We have a long way to go. While some progress has been made in controlling certain point sources of water pollution, much remains to be done. Legislation now on the books seems adequate; major programs of implementation and conforming with the laws are now needed. Water quality standards and water pollution laws, like any laws or standards, are absolutely useless unless put into practice and enforced. Implementation plans are just so much paper until they are carried out. We would like to close with the point that it is here where the citizen will play a major role in the future.

We can all do something about water pollution. Individually, we can obviously stop dumping garbage into water supplies and change habits at home that generate wastewater. In a complex society, however, the effectiveness of each one of us is limited by the degree to which we are able to work with other members of our communities to bring about adequate treatment systems for wastewater and to establish new patterns that minimize water pollution problems. The key is education. To be effective, a citizen must be well informed. Armed with solid information and a solid understanding of the problem of water pollution, citizens and citizens' groups can then effectively make their interest in clean water known to elected officials and administrators. Such individuals and groups can exert pressures by notifying candidates for public office that their votes will go to candidates who support clean water.

Any citizen awed by feeling like a little fish in a big pond should remember that the pond water is being polluted.

CONCEPTS TO REMEMBER

1. The properties of water make it an ideal cleaning agent and heat remover. The problem is that when water is used in these ways, it gets dirty and warm.
2. Water pollution is any change in water quality brought about by human activity that impairs the use of water as a resource or that adversely affects other forms of life.
3. Water pollutants come principally from domestic, agricultural, and industrial sources. The four most general kinds of water pollutants are biological agents, dissolved chemicals, non-dissolved chemicals and sediment, and heat.
4. Many kinds of diseases can be transmitted by drinking water, and such diseases are still major world health problems.
5. Organic chemicals added to aquatic ecosystems can lead to oxygen depletion of the water as the decomposers oxidize the organic matter. Inorganic chemicals that serve as nutrients for aquatic vegetation can indirectly cause oxygen depletion by causing the overgrowth of plant material, which is then later oxidized by decomposers.
6. Many toxic substances are soluble in water, and many of those that are not can be carried on the surface of particles suspended in water.
7. Heat disrupts aquatic ecosystems in several ways. Heat makes gases less soluble in water and drives certain solids into solution; both of these things amount to changes in the chemistry of water. Heat accelerates the metabolism of aquatic organisms at the same time that it makes oxygen less available for metabolism. Accelerated metabolic activity can carry certain organisms beyond their tolerance limits; short of that, accelerated metabolism can disrupt balances in aquatic systems, for example, by causing egg hatching to speed up.
8. The effects of certain contaminants of water can be magnified as they pass through food chains.
9. A point source of water pollution is any discern-

ible port or channel through which pollutants enter the water. Point sources are generally easier to control than nonpoint sources such as farm fields and construction sites.

10. Oil spills in coastal areas can be great ecological disasters, but their most profound effects seem to be limited to the short term; so far, at least, only minimal long-range effects have been documented. Strategies for dealing with oil spills after the fact have not been very effective.

11. By far the most serious water pollution problems in the oceans occur in coastal areas.

12. Groundwater pollution is a major environmental issue today partly because about half of the people of the United States now use groundwater for drinking.

13. In sewage treatment plants, water pollutants are removed by physical (sedimentation), biological (oxidation), and chemical (stripping) methods.

14. The most ecologically effective water pollution control methods are volume reduction, short-loop recycling, and using water more than once in the same use stream (for example, irrigating forestland with dirty water).

15. It costs a lot to control water pollution (nearly 300 billion dollars in the decade ending in 1987), but it also costs money not to control water pollution.

16. There are some very good laws on the books for water pollution control and safe drinking water; citizens can help the clean water effort by insisting that these laws be enforced.

DISCUSSION QUESTIONS AND FOOD FOR THOUGHT

1. Find out how to measure some of the important qualities of water, that is, dissolved oxygen, dissolved carbon dioxide, acidity, hardness, nitrate content, bacterial contamination, suspended solids, and/or dissolved solids. Then make some measurements.

2. Discuss: Lake Erie is more alive now than ever.

3. Draw energy and nutrient flow diagrams for a trickling filter ecosystem.

4. If the biological elements in a secondary sewage treatment plant can remove the organic matter in sewage, why can't biological systems remove salts? Or can they?

5. Why not simply make rivers wider and shallower below sewage outfalls and then bubble oxygen through the water as a means of reducing biological oxygen demand? How would this be like a sewage treatment plant's trickling filter?

6. Pollution is a case of resources out of place. List some of the water pollutants described in this chapter and indicate how these could be useful if they somehow reached the right place.

7. Discuss: Water is such a good medium that it will wash away nearly every form of dirt and there is so much water.

8. Debate: Water pollution is inevitable, and the key to minimizing it is resource recovery.

9. List some of the reasons why treated sewage sludge and manure do not have more of a market.

10. How are thermal pollution and pollution by acids alike in their effects on living systems?

11. Visit a sewage treatment plant near you; then make a diagram of the plant, labeling all ecologically relevant components of the system. How does your system compare with the ideal?

12. Visit a nearby stream or lake. Examine a sample of water in a clear glass or bottle. How does it smell?

13. Design an experiment to show the effect that phosphates have on the growth of algae. Carry out the experiment.

14. Find out if storm sewers and sanitary sewers are separate in your community. If they are not separate, how does your community handle large volumes of runoff during intense rainstorms?

15. Find out what the drinking water sources are for your community and find out how water is treated before you drink it.

16. Find out how water supplies in your community, once treated, are protected from subsequent contamination before you drink the water. Find out the policy where you live for the use of septic tanks.

17. Research the status of some innovative technologies related to sewage treatment including compost toilets and individual onsite sewage disposal units other than septic tanks (mechanical systems, vacuum systems, etc.). Explain the ecological and social pros and cons of such systems.

REFERENCES AND FURTHER READING

References marked with an asterisk are cited in the chapter.

*Ableson, P., 1984, "Groundwater Contamination," *Science* **224**(4650):1.

*Atlas, R. M., 1978. "Microorganisms and Petroleum Pollutants," *Bioscience* **28**(6):387–391.

*Barber, R. T., and Warlen, S. M., 1979. "Organochlorine Insecticide Residues in Deep Sea Fish from 2500 m in the Atlantic Ocean," *Environmental Science Technology* **13**:1146–1148.

Barth, T., 1984. "Weathering of Crude Oil in Natural Marine Environments: The Concentration of Polar Degradation

Products in Water under Oil as Measured in Several Field Studies," *Chemosphere* **13**:67–86.

Bascom, W., 1982. "The Effects of Waste Disposal on the Coastal Waters of Southern California," *Environmental Science Technology* **16**:226A–236A.

Bell, J. A., 1973. *The Physicians Guide to Water Pollution*. Chicago, Ill.: American Medical Association.

Berg, G., ed., 1983. *Viral Pollution and the Environment*. Boca Raton, Fla.: CRC Press.

Bitton, G., and Gerba, C., eds., 1984. *Groundwater Pollution Microbiology*. New York: John Wiley and Sons.

*Chapra, S. C., and Robertson, A., 1977. "Great Lakes Eutrophication: The Effect of Point Source Control of Total Phosphorus," *Science* **196**:1448–1450.

The Clean Water Act Showing Changes Made by the 1977 Amendments. Washington, D.C.: U.S. Government Printing Office. (Dec. 1977; Serial No. 95-12.)

Coan, E., 1971. "Oil Pollution," *Sierra Club Bulletin* **56** (3):12–16.

The Conservation Foundation, 1982. *State of the Environment 1982*, Washington, D.C.: The Conservation Foundation.

The Conservation Foundation, 1984. *State of the Environment: An Assessment at Mid-Decade*. Washington, D.C.: The Conservation Foundation.

*Council on Environmental Quality, 1976. *Environmental Quality: The Seventh Annual Report*. Washington, D.C.: U.S. Government Printing Office.

Council on Environmental Quality, 1979. *Environmental Quality—1978: The Ninth Annual Report*.

*Council on Environmental Quality, 1980. *Environmental Quality—1979: The Tenth Annual Report*.

*Council on Environmental Quality, 1981a. *Environmental Quality—1980: The Eleventh Annual Report*.

*Council on Environmental Quality, 1981b. *Contamination of Ground Water by Toxic Organic Chemicals*.

*Council on Environmental Quality, 1982a. *Contamination of Ground Water by Toxic Organic Chemicals*.

*Council on Environmental Quality, 1982b. *Environmental Quality—1981: The Twelfth Annual Report*.

*Council on Environmental Quality, 1983, *Environmental Quality—1982: The Thirteenth Annual Report*.

Council on Environmental Quality, 1984, *Environmental Quality—1983: The Fourteenth Annual Report*.

Dean, R., and Lund, E., 1982. *Water Reuse: Problems and Solutions*. New York: Academic Press.

Dickson, K.; Maki, A.; and Cairns, J., eds., 1983. *Modeling the Fate of Chemicals in the Aquatic Environment*. Woburn, Mass.: Butterworths. Ann Arbor Science.

*Freeman, A. M., 1979. *The Benefits of Air and Water Pollution Control: A Review and Synthesis of Recent Estimates*. A report prepared for the Council on Environmental Quality. Brunswick, Me.: Bowdoin College. (See also Freeman, 1983.)

Freeman, A. M., 1983. *Air and Water Pollution Control: A Benefit–Cost Assessment*. New York: Wiley-Interscience.

*Goldblat, J., 1977. "UN Water Conference: Agreement on Goals and Action Plan," *Ambio* **6**(4):222–227.

*Goldman, M. I., 1970. "From Lake Erie to Lake Baikal: Russians and Americans Face Similar Environmental Problems," *Science* **170**:37–42.

*Gossett, R. W.; Brown, D. A.; and Young, D. R.; 1983. "Predicting the Bioaccumulation of Organic Compounds in Marine Organisms Using Octanol/Water Partition Coefficients," *Mar. Poll. Bull.* **14**:387–392.

*Greenwood, N. H., and Edwards, J. M. B., 1973. *Human Environments and Natural Systems: A Conflict of Dominion*. North Scituate, Mass.: Duxbury Press.

*Gundlach, E.; Boehm, P.; Marchand, M.; Atlas, R.; Ward, D.; and Wolfe, D., 1983. "The Fate of Amoco-Cadiz Oil," *Science* **221**(4606):122–129.

*Helmer, R., 1977. "Pollutants from Land-Based Sources in the Mediterranean," *Ambio* **6**(6):312–316.

Hermann, R., and Johnson, A. I., 1983. "Acid Rain: A Water Resources Issue for the 80's," *Proceedings of the American Water Resources Association, International Symposium on Hydrometeorology*. Bethesda, Md.: American Water Resources Association.

*Hess, E., and Beer, C., 1975. "Sanitary Effects of Gamma Irradiation on Sewage Sludge," in *Proceedings of the IAEA Symposium on Radiation for a Clean Environment*, 203–208. Vienna: IAEA.

*Lavaroni, C. W.; O'Donnell, P. A.; and Lindberg, L. A., 1971. *Water Pollution*. Reading, Mass.: Addison-Wesley Publishing Co.

*LeLourd, P., 1977. "Oil Pollution in the Mediterranean Sea," *Ambio* **6**(6):317–320.

Lippman, M., and Schlesinger, R. B., 1979. *Chemical Contamination in the Human Environment*. New York: Oxford University Press.

*Lund, E., 1978. "Human Pathogens as Potential Health Hazards in the Reuse of Water." *Ambio* **7**(2):56–61.

McLusky, D., 1981. *The Estuarine Ecosystem*. New York: Halstead Press.

McWilliams, L., 1984. "Groundwater Pollution in Wisconsin: A Bumper Crop Yields Growing Problems," *Environment* **26**(4):25–34.

Malins, D. C., 1977. "Metabolism of Aromatic Hydrocarbons in Maine Organisms," *Ann. N.Y. Acad. Sci.* **298**:482–496.

Middleditch, B., ed., 1981. *Environmental Effects of Offshore Oil Production*. New York: Plenum Press.

Murphy, C. B., 1973. "Effects of Restricted Use of Phosphate-based Detergents on Onondaga Lake, *Science* **182**:379–381.

*National Academy of Sciences, 1975. *Petroleum in the Marine Environment*. Washington, D.C.: National Academy Press.

National Academy of Sciences, 1977. *Drinking Water and Health*. Volumes 1, 2, and 3 were published in 1980; Volume 4 was published in 1982; and Volume 5 was published in 1983. Washington, D.C.: National Academy Press.

National Academy of Sciences, 1984a. *Studies in Geophysics: Groundwater Contamination*. Washington, D.C.: National Academy Press.

National Academy of Sciences, 1984b. *Groundwater Contamination*. Washington, D.C.: National Academy Press.

National Academy of Sciences, 1984c. *Ocean Disposal Systems for Sewage Sludge and Effluent*. Washington, D.C.: National Academy Press.

Natural Resources Defense Council, 1983. *Citizens Guidebook to Water Quality Standards*. Washington, D.C.: National Resources Defense Council.

*Nemerow, N. L., 1978. *Industrial Water Pollution: Origins, Characteristics and Treatment*. Reading, Mass.: Addison-Wesley Publishing Co.

Nriagu, J., ed., 1983. *Aquatic Toxicology*, New York: John Wiley & Sons.

Nriagu, J., and Simmons, M., eds., 1984. *Toxic Contaminants in the Great Lakes*. New York: John Wiley & Sons.

Office of Technology Assessment, 1984. *Protecting the Nation's Groundwater from Contamination*. Washington, D.C.: U.S. Government Printing Office. Summaries are available at no charge from the Office of Technology Assessment.

*Osterberg, C., and Keckes, S., 1977. "The State of Pollution of the Mediterranean Sea," *Ambio* **6**(6):321–326.

Peterson, S., 1983. "Lake Ontario's Fish—How They Almost Got Away," *Environment* **25**(9):25.

*Pye, V., and Patrick, R., 1983. "Ground Water Contamination in the United States," *Science* **221**:713–718.

Rickert, D. A., and Hines, W. G., 1978. "River Quality Assessment: Implications of a Prototype Project," *Science* **200** (4346):1113–1118.

*Rogers, P., 1983. "The Future of Water," *The Atlantic Monthly,* July, 80.

Schelske, C., Stoermer, E.; Conley, D.; Robbins, J.; and Glover, R., 1983. "Early Eutrophication in the Lower Great Lakes: New Evidence from Biogenic Silica in Sediments," *Science* **222**:320–322.

Schlesinger, R. B., 1979. "Natural Removal Mechanisms for Chemical Pollutants in the Environment," *Bioscience* **29** (2):95–101.

Smith, J. E., 1968. *Torrey Canyon, Pollution and Marine Life."* Cambridge, England: Cambridge University Press.

Teal, J. M., and Howarth, R. W., 1984. "Oil Spill Studies: A Review of Ecological Effects," *Environmental Management* **8**:27–44.

*Trump, J. G., 1981. "Energized Electrons Tackle Municipal Sludge," *American Scientist* **69**:276–284.

Tye, L., 1983. "The Ohio's Comeback." (Three-part series.) *Louisville Courier-Journal,* Louisville, Ky., Aug. 21, 22, 23.

U.S. Department of the Interior, 1972. *Water and Industry.* Washington, D.C.: Superintendent of Documents (0-457-795.)

U.S. Department of the Interior, 1983. *Federal Offshore Statistics: Leasing, Exploration, Production, Revenue.* Washington, D.C.: U.S. Government Printing Office.

U.S. Department of the Interior, 1984. *Annual Report Fiscal Year 1983: Outer Continental Shelf Oil and Gas Leasing and Production Program.*

U.S. Environmental Protection Agency, 1971. *A Primer on Waste Water Treatment.* Washington, D.C.: U.S. Government Printing Office.

*U.S. Environmental Protection Agency, 1973, *Clean Water: Report to Congress.*

*U.S. Environmental Protection Agency, 1974. *First Things First: A Strategy Against Water Pollution.*

U.S. Environmental Protection Agency, 1974. *National Water Quality Inventory: 1974 Report to the Congress.*

*U.S. Environmental Protection Agency, 1976. *A Drop to Drink.*

U.S. Environmental Protection Agency, 1977. *Water Quality Management Accomplishments, Compendium I.*

U.S. Environmental Protection Agency, 1978. *National Water Quality Inventory: 1978 Report to Congress.*

U.S. Environmental Protection Agency, 1981a. *Construction Costs for Municipal Wastewater Conveyance Systems: 1973–1979.* Washington, D.C.

U.S. Environmental Protection Agency, 1981b. *Operation and Maintenance Costs for Municipal Wastewater Facilities.*

U.S. Environmental Protection Agency, 1983. *Conveyance, Treatment and Control of Municipal Wastewater, Combined Sewer Overflows, and Stormwater Runoff: The 1982 Needs Survey.* Cost estimates are covered in an addendum, also published in 1983.

U.S. Environmental Protection Agency, 1984a. *Financial Capability Guidebook.* This publication explains to communities the cost implications of constructing waste treatment facilities.

U.S. Environmental Protection Agency, 1984b. *Report to Congress, January 1981–1983, on Administration of the Marine Protection, Research and Sanctuaries Act of 1972 as Amended (P.L. 92-532) and Implementing the International London Dumping Convention.*

U.S. Environmental Protection Agency, n.d. "Zinc, Precipitation and Recovery from Viscose Rayon Wastewater," *EPA Report 12090 ESG.* Washington, D.C.: Superintendent of Documents.

Viets, F. G., 1971. "Water Quality in Relation to Farm Use of Fertilizer," *Bioscience* **21**(10):460–467.

Wagner, R. H., 1971. *Environment and Man.* New York, Norton.

CHAPTER 13

Pesticides and Other Chemicals in the Biosphere

Pesticides, stable toxic chemicals, and radio-active materials are not such strange bedfellows. The environmental impacts of these substances are similar, and they pervade living systems in some of the same ways. They are all poisons that can disrupt living systems with injury, disease, or death as a result. Some materials in each group are very stable or environmentally persistent. Many are able to pass from one ecosystem component to another, their concentrations becoming magnified as they pass from one trophic level to another.

We have already considered pesticides, stable toxic substances, and radioisotopes as air pollutants and as water pollutants; in Chapter 14 we will en-counter them again as cancer-causing agents. In this chapter we examine them from the perspective of the general ecological principles that explain just why these materials get mixed up with living things in ways that were never intended.

THE ECOLOGICAL CONNECTION

The Problem of Persistence

Rachel Carson, in her classic 1962 book *Silent Spring*, alerted the public to the possibility of envi-ronmental disruption by pesticides and other persis-tent, human-made chemicals. Evidence accumulated over the last two decades confirms that the eco-sphere is indeed contaminated with human-made chemicals and that these do have a negative impact. Metals, pesticides, and other synthetic chemicals that are degraded very slowly, if at all, are caught up in the flow of materials in the ecosphere. They end up in organisms that are very distant and very differ-ent from their original location or target.

Because by definition **synthetic chemicals** have not evolved in the ecosphere—they are created in laboratories—biological systems have not naturally developed the enzymes to break them down, except by coincidence. The breakdown of such chemicals often depends on physical-chemical processes that may take a long time to bring about complete deg-radation. The persistence of certain chemicals in-creases the chance that they will inadvertently enter organisms through food intake, water use, or gas-eous exchanges with the atmosphere.

Living organisms are likewise unable to handle many naturally occurring substances, such as met-als, in some of the concentrations and chemical forms that are now common because of human ac-tivities. Lead poisoning and mercury poisoning are all too familiar examples in humans and other spe-cies.

The persistence of radioactive materials is pre-dictable. The half-lives of various radioactive isotopes are known. Half-lives range from a few seconds to tens of thousands of years. Human activities that may cause radioactive materials to be released into the environment include weapons testing that has produced fallout, uranium mining, burial of radioactive materials in poorly suited disposal sites, and nuclear-powered electric-generating stations.

Biomagnification

Perhaps the most significant impact of metals, persistent chemicals, and radioactive materials on ecosystems and human health stems from their magnification in food chains. As living things break down the complex molecules of carbohydrate, fat and protein in their food, they assimilate some components and excrete others. Still other components move into storage compartments such as fat and bone. Chemicals that are stored in this way accumulate over time and are passed up the food chain in higher and higher concentrations.

At each link in the chain the amount of pesticide passed on to an individual organism is increased. For example, earthworms may ingest a pesticide by eating contaminated organic matter. A single earthworm will consume many times its own weight in

organic matter and accumulate much of the pesticide residue that the organic matter contains. The more it eats, the more pesticide it accumulates. At the next level a robin eats numerous earthworms. The accumulated pesticide in all the earthworms ingested by a robin may reach a level at which there are negative, even fatal, effects. This is exactly what happened with the pesticide DDT in 1963 in Hanover, New Hampshire. Seventy percent of the robin population died after a spraying of DDT for Dutch elm disease. Events like this were the basis for Rachel Carson's concern about a silent spring. Logically, top carnivores such as *Homo sapiens* are particularly vulnerable to biomagnification.

A classic example of biomagnification was reported in California's Clear Lake (see Figure 13.1). DDD, a derivative of DDT, was used to spray for gnats around the 46,000-acre lake in 1949, 1954, and 1957. Concentrations in water reached 0.02 ppm. In 1960, studies of the biota in the lake indicated that the plankton contained 250 times the amount of DDD in the water; frogs contained 2000 times more; sunfish contained 12,000 times more; and grebes, the top carnivores, contained up to 80,000 times more. This resulted in numerous

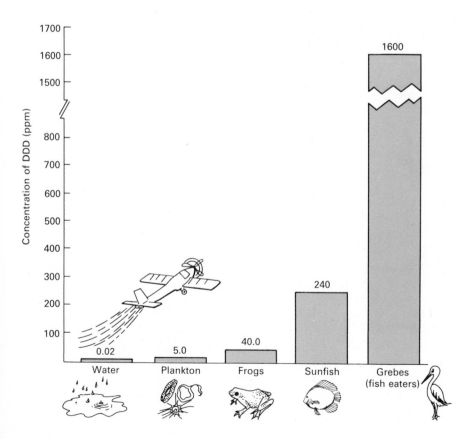

Figure 13.1 Biomagnification. This graph shows how various species studied in California's Clear Lake, north of San Francisco, accumulated DDD, a metabolite of DDT, through the food chain.

deaths among the grebes in 1954 and 1957. Edible fish caught ten years later were found to have concentrations of DDD above FDA standards.

A similar occurrence was reported in the Long Island tidal marshes (Woodwell et. al., 1967). DDT, used here for mosquito control for 20 years, was found in the following concentrations:

— Plankton: 0.04 ppm
— Shrimp (which feed on plankton): 0.16 ppm
— Minnows (which feed on plankton): <1.0 ppm
— Predatory fish (which feed on minnows): 1.0–2.0 ppm
— Fish-eating birds: 13–26 ppm

Note that DDT has been shown to be lethal to shrimp at levels as low as 0.0055 ppm (Battista, 1973). Concentrations of DDT in the brains of birds at levels of 30 ppm or greater present a lethal threat (Battista, 1973). DDT is stored in fat in living things. Under cold conditions or poor diet conditions, such as during hibernation, when energy is needed, fat is oxidized; as this happens, DDT residue reenters the bloodstream. DDT residues of 10 ppm in fatty tissues of birds can concentrate under these conditions to as much as 20 ppm in the bloodstream (Battista, 1973).

Agricultural pests like corn borers are not simply nuisances; they can affect the world's supply of food. Still, the environmental side effects of pesticides must be carefully considered in dealing with pests.

These examples show biomagnification to be a straightforward, real environmental problem, the basis of which lies in the way organisms interact ecologically. This phenomenon of biomagnification or bioaccumulation is especially significant in attempting to set standards for contamination in air, soil, or water.

Air, water, and soil are all vehicles that transport pesticides, stable toxic chemicals, and radioactive materials. The rate and distance of transport are influenced by climatic factors, the characteristics of the specific chemical, and how the chemical is applied or released.

Little is known about the impact of long-term low-level exposure to many of these substances. What we do know is that any stable substance released in the environment can and probably will make its way into the nutrient cycles that include *Homo sapiens* and other organisms. Pesticides make up the bulk of persistent synthetic chemicals deliberately released into the environment. We will start with them as we scrutinize the overall environmental toxin problem and the choices we face.

PESTICIDES

Defining Terms

A **pest** is any organism that is unwanted (by human beings) for one reason or another. It may be an annoying gnat, a dandelion in an otherwise homogeneously grassy yard, or a borer on a corn plant. In some cases—the dandelion, for example—the pest is a social or cultural one. Corn-borers are more important pests. They and their kind have great economic impact and even affect human survival in a hungry world. Cultural and socioeconomic factors are important in any discussion of the necessity of pest control.

There are several categories of pesticides based on the type of target organism that a particular pesticide has been developed to eliminate. For example, **herbicides** are plant killers, **insecticides** are insect killers, and **fungicides** kill fungi. We may refer to all of these as *biocides*.

Insecticides: A Closer Look

The best known pesticides are the insecticides. There are three principal chemical subgroups of these: chlorinated hydrocarbons, organophosphates, and carbamates.

Chlorinated hydrocarbons contain specific arrangements of atoms of hydrogen, carbon, and chlorine. Insecticides in this class include aldrin, dieldrin, endrin, heptachlor, DDT, DDE, DDD, methoxychlor, lindane, toxaphene, and mirex.

As their name implies, all **organophosphates** contain carbon, hydrogen, and phosphorus. Representatives of this group include diazinon, malathion, methyl-parathion, parathion, and phorate.

The carbamate insecticides contain arrangements of carbon, hydrogen, and nitrogen. **Carbamates** are not so numerous, and the most common one is carbaryl. Here we will focus primarily on the chlorinated hydrocarbons and the organophosphates.

The chemistry of the two major groups of insecticides causes them to behave very differently in the ecosphere. Organophosphates are water soluble and usually break down rather rapidly in the ecosphere. They are often less persistent but may be more toxic than chlorinated hydrocarbons to humans and other mammals. They represent much more of an acute health concern and require special precautions when they are applied. Chlorinated hydrocarbons are the more persistent of the two; they do not break down rapidly in the environment, and they tend to accumulate. For example, DDT in soil may persist ten years or longer under certain circumstances. Chlorinated hydrocarbons are fat soluble and not water soluble; they accumulate in the fatty tissue of animals.

Persistence

Table 13.1 illustrates some of the residence times of pesticides in soil. Among other things, the persistence of a given pesticide in a given situation depends on how the pesticide was applied, the type of substratum it landed in or on (soil, water, etc.), temperature, humidity, and whether or not it becomes stored in living organisms.

Pesticides may be broken down by the action of microorganisms, by sunlight, or by the physical-chemical actions of weathering. In the degradation processes, both inside large organisms and in the environment, conversion to substances that are even more toxic is possible. For example, substances containing mercury or arsenic may be transformed by the addition of carbon and hydrogen as a methyl group (CH_3) resulting in methyl mercury or methyl arsines—both of which are much more toxic to living things than the unmethylated forms (see Chapter 12).

Patterns of Pesticide Use

There *were* pesticides before the so-called age of chemistry, which began shortly before World War II; however, they were few, and nearly all of them were natural derivatives of plants. Pyrethrins are produced from chrysanthemums, nicotine sulphate from tobacco, and rotenone from a tropical plant. After World War II the use of synthetic chlorinated hydrocarbons for pest control increased dramatically.

Today over a billion pounds of synthetic organic pesticides are being used annually in the United States.

The actual amount of pesticides used varies regionally, with greater use in more pest-prone regions such as the warm and humid South (Pimentel et al., 1978). Overall, agricultural applications account for 60% of the pesticides used in the United States; the remaining 40% is used in public health, industry, commercial pest control, and home applications.

The Impact of Pesticide Use: A Clouded Record

At first glance, insecticides appear to have had, in the short term, a significant positive impact on agriculture and health. Some scientists say that pesticides may have been directly responsible for a doubling of food productivity in the first half of the twentieth century. DDT has been successful in controlling mosquitos that transmit malaria. DDT is also directly credited with controlling such other insect-

Table 13.1 Persistence of Various Pesticides

Designation	Chemical Group	Residence Half-Life (years)
Degradable	Organophosphate insecticides	0.02–0.2
	Carbamate insecticides	0.02
Moderately degradable	Urea herbicides	0.3–0.8
	2,4-D; 2,4,5-T herbicides	0.1–0.4
Persistent	Chlorinated Hydrocarbon insecticides	2–5
Permanent	Lead, arsenic, copper pesticides	10–30

borne diseases as yellow fever, viral encephalitis, typhus, plague, cholera, and various tick-borne diseases. For developing countries, even now, disease control is a major problem favoring the continued use of chemical insecticides.

However, the record is not really so cut and dried. The emergence of resistant strains of insects threatens the progress made by use of synthetic pesticides. We may find ourselves back where we started. Outbreaks of insect-borne diseases are occurring again. In the case of agricultural insecticides, overall losses due to pests have remained constant since the introduction of synthetic pesticides; however, the losses attributable to insects have nearly doubled (Pimentel et al., 1977). Pimentel calculates that total current world crop loss (to pests) run 40–48% (a 10–20% postharvest loss and a 33–35% preharvest loss).

Pests are indeed a significant human problem. Insecticides have helped us win an occasional battle, but the war is far from over and the enemy may be getting stronger.

The Emergence of Resistant Strains

We need to make the point that insect resistance to insecticides is a real problem, not just a theoretical one. As we saw in Chapter 5, certain insects in a population may have greater resistance to a pesticide than other members of that population because of genetic variation. The resistant insects tend to survive spraying and reproduce, passing on their resistance. Thus over time the proportion of relatively resistant individuals increases as less resistant individuals are killed off.

The EPA reports that over 300 species of insects, mites, and ticks worldwide have genetic strains that are resistant to one or more pesticides.

Smith (1979) reports malaria resurgence in more than a dozen countries (including the United States) that is attributed to mosquito resistance to pesticides. A similar phenomenon has been reported in a number of other pest species in the United States. The EPA reports that 75% of the most serious agricultural insect and mite pests in California are resistant to one or more insecticides. In a few cases the development of resistance has had an unusual twist. It was found, for example, that spraying a pesticide for pests on cotton in Central America caused the emergence of larger numbers of mosquitos that were resistant to the insecticide (Farid, 1975, and Provost, 1972). Pesticide resistance in plant pathogens (viruses, bacteria, fungi) has also

been reported (McEwen, 1978). It should be no surprise, then, that various weeds have also been reported to have developed *herbicide* resistance.

There are also indications that replacing one type of pesticide by another type in the same group, one organophosphate for another, for example, preserves and extends previously selected resistance (Luck et al., 1977). Thus the use of chemicals to improve public health and control agricultural pests must be carefully considered; there is real potential for disease epidemics caused by resistant strains and crop losses from resistant pests.

Nonspecificity

Being nonspecific, insecticides kill beneficial insects along with pests. In a very real way, spraying DDT on a forest to kill bark beetles is like dropping a bomb on a city to stop urban crime. Competitors and predators of the target pest may be diminished in numbers along with the pest. There is the possibility that the pest will recover long before the predators that helped keep it in check, creating a problem worse than the original. Insects that may have held still another pest in control (through predation, competition, etc.) may be eliminated, and a secondary pest invasion may result. An example of a combination of such problems occurred in the Canete Valley in the late 1940s.

The Canete Valley is a cotton-producing area in Peru. Before 1949, older pesticides such as nicotine sulphate and arsenic compounds were used. Soon thereafter, chlorinated hydrocarbons were introduced to the area, and yields increased tremendously for a while. Then the increase slowed somewhat, and problems began to arise as resistant pest strains and new pest types appeared. This resulted in a disastrous crop failure in the mid-1950s. A 1977 U.N. report on the consequences of pesticide use in cotton-growing areas of Central America indicates similar problems. After several seasons of pesticide use, the primary pests were controlled, but previously minor insect pests increased in numbers, resulting in severe crop damage.

The message in all of this is that the indiscriminate use of nonselective pesticides causes natural selection of resistant strains (see Chapter 5) and disturbs natural predator-prey relationships (see Chapter 4). This in turn sets the stage for an increase in resistant strains and invasions by strains normally held in check by predators. The result is that more intense and more frequent applications of pesticides become necessary, and these result in increased costs, increased pressure for selection and resistant strains, and increased opportunity for contamination and disruption in the ecosphere.

PATHWAYS IN THE ECOSPHERE

Synthetic organic pesticides are produced and sold in a concentrated form that must be diluted for application. Dilution not only decreases pesticide strength, it also facilitates an even distribution of the chemical over a large area. Different materials that are used as carrier materials for pesticides include dusts, impregnated granules, solutions, emulsions, and suspensions of wettable powders. Diluting agents include clays, talc, water, and nonaqueous solvents. These are dusted or sprayed onto plants or worked in the soil. The pesticides then follow various transport routes elsewhere (see Figure 13.2).

Air

Spraying and evaporation are the two major ways for pesticides to enter the atmosphere; smaller amounts may enter from improper incineration of pesticide containers. In air spraying, the climatic factors of wind, temperature, and humidity are extremely important. Naturally, spraying when winds are light will reduce drifting. For efficiency in getting pesticides to the target, air spraying is preferable to air dusting. Dust particles are smaller than spray droplets. This decreases gravitational pull and allows dust particles to stay in the air longer, increasing the chances of drifting. Of pesticides used for agricultural purposes, 60–65% are applied by air; a little over 50% of the pesticide applied in this way may actually reach the target crop. Pesticides worked into the soil may also get into the air by volatilization (evaporation). Pesticides in the air may be broken down by oxidation and photolysis by

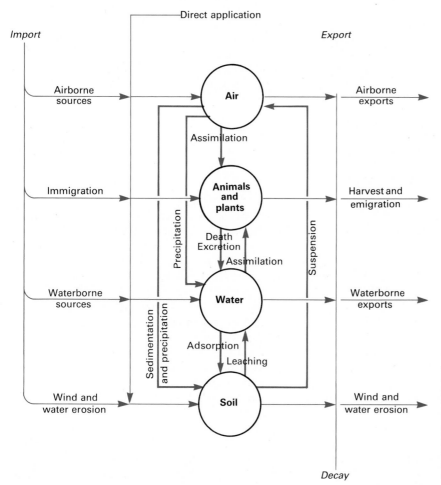

Figure 13.2 Pesticide Pathways. The routes by which pesticides spread through the ecosphere are many and varied. Besides direct application they may be imported from (and exported to) other ecosystems. Specific chemical characteristics of the pesticide and various means of application determine the pathways taken.

The helicopter is spraying a fungicide on an orange grove in Florida. A helicopter can spray small and irregularly shaped fields more efficiently than an airplane can.

sunlight. They may also be washed out by rain or fall by gravitational pull and land in places they were not intended to reach.

Water

Water contamination may result directly from pesticide application for insect or weed control. In other cases, runoff may carry soil particles laden with pesticides into bodies of water. Pesticides in the air may also drift over and be deposited on the water surface. Leaching of pesticides from soil occurs primarily with water-soluble pesticides (organophosphates) and may lead to contamination of groundwater. Improper disposal of used pesticide containers may contribute residues that are carried off in runoff. One of the major problems of pesticides in waterways is their presence in the bottom sediments of surface waters. Chlorinated hydrocarbons tend to adhere to soil particles; in deep lakes that stratify, fall and spring overturns (Chapter 3) can cause resurgences of previously sedimented residues. As long ago as 1969, the American Chemical Society reported that most surface waters in the United States contain chlorinated hydrocarbon insecticides especially DDT, dieldrin, and the herbicide 2-4D (Figure 13.3).

Soil

Adsorption of pesticides into the soil and their persistence in soil varies with the composition, pH, and temperature of the soil. Soils that have more humus tend to hold pesticides more strongly. Sandy soils tend to lose pesticides to crop absorption. At cooler soil temperatures, less pesticide volatilizes,

and thus more is absorbed. Soil moisture influences the type of microorganisms present; this, in turn, influences breakdown of the pesticide by bacteria. Pesticides such as aldrin and heptachlor are displaced from soil particles by moisture and evaporate. What about pesticides in the soil taken up by crops? Most organophosphates can be degraded by plants, but chlorinated hydrocarbons are not; plants can change chlorinated hydrocarbons into more toxic substances, however. Aldrin and heptachlor, for example, can be converted within plant cells to forms having greater persistence.

PESTICIDES AND HEALTH

Exposure Routes

Pesticides may enter the bodies of animals, including humans, by ingestion, inhalation, or absorption through exposed surface areas. Fish can absorb pesticides through their gills or body surfaces or by ingesting contaminated food. Land-dwelling wildlife ingest pesticides primarily in food but may ingest some in contaminated water and may pick up some from the air (for example, in licking their fur, rabbits may ingest pesticide adsorbed onto the fur from the air). Low-level exposure to pesticides over a long period of time can result in selective accumulation in living organisms.

Storage itself is not the problem. Problems come (1) when accumulated doses are activated, moving out of storage in high concentrations and causing one kind of health effect or another, or (2) when accumulated pesticide is further magnified as it passes up food chains. Lethal concentrations and doses (see Table 13.2) may be reached, and short of these there may be important sublethal effects.

Chlorinated Hydrocarbons in Animals Other Than Humans

Lethal effects of chlorinated hydrocarbons on fish, birds, and mammals usually involve the central nervous system, and the ultimate effect—death—may be preceded by symptoms such as respiratory difficulty, sluggishness, and neurological complications.

The sublethal effects of chlorinated hydrocarbons on fish include lowered reproductive potential, which is partly the result of the accumulation of pesticides in the yolk sac of fish eggs. As the developing fry absorb the yolk sac for nourishment, the pesticide is released and may kill the fry. Other effects have been documented as well, including liver and kidney damage, damaged gills, and modified (usually increased) metabolism (U.S. Department of Health, Education and Welfare, 1969). In addition, behavioral changes such as seeking warmer waters have been noted (U.S. Department of Health, Education and Welfare, 1969; Lassahn, 1975). Other studies showed that in the presence of endrin, minnows tended to abandon their protective behavior of staying under rocks during daylight hours (Mount, 1962).

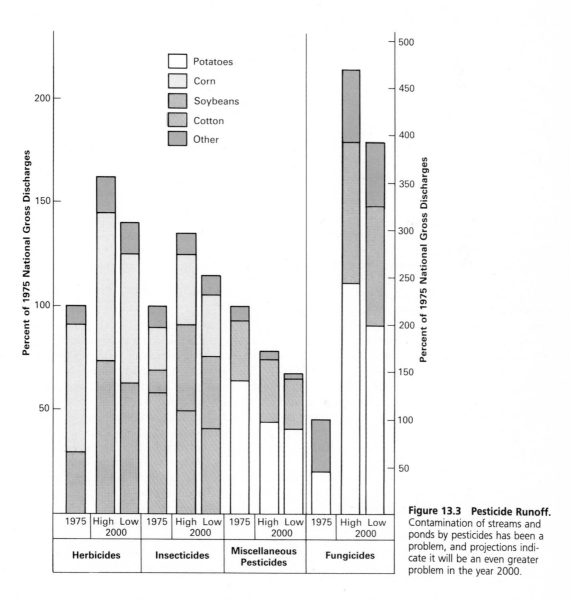

Figure 13.3 Pesticide Runoff. Contamination of streams and ponds by pesticides has been a problem, and projections indicate it will be an even greater problem in the year 2000.

Table 13.2 Toxicity to Insects. The amount of specific pesticides lethal to half the test organisms exposed to that dose are shown here. LD50 is the lethal dose for 50% of the test organisms; LC50 is the lethal environmental concentration for 50%. LD50's and LC50's are standard toxicological terms reflecting the fact that not all of the organisms in a test group will be equally susceptible.

	LD 50 (mg/kg in white rats)	LC 50 at 11°C. (mg/l in fish)
Chlorinated hydrocarbons		
Aldrin	40.0	0.0082
Dieldrin	46.0	0.0055
DDT	250.0	0.005
Endrin	12.0	0.0044
Heptachlor	90.0	—
Lindane	125.0	no effect at 0.03
Toxaphene	69.0	0.0022
Endosulfan	110.0	—
Telodrin	4.8	—
Organophosphates		
Malathion	1500.0	0.55
Parathion	8.0	0.065
Methyl parathion	15.0	irritation at 1.0
Azinphosmethyl	15–25	0.055
TEPP	1.6	—
Mevinphos	6.0	0.83
Ethion	208.0	0.42
Temik	1.0	—
Trichlorphon	450.0	no effect at 1.0
Carbamates		
Carbaryl	540.0	—
Zectran	15–36	no effect at 1.0

The sublethal effects of chlorinated hydrocarbons on birds include lowered reproductive potential due to the failure of eggs to survive to maturity. Thin shells have been identified as the cause of this problem, and they apparently result from abnormal calcium metabolism in some birds affected with pesticides, notably birds of prey such as the bald eagle, the osprey, and hawks (see Figure 13.4). DDT has been shown to lead to thinner shells in ducks and falcons but not in pheasants and quail (U.S. Department of Health, Education and Welfare, 1969). Other biochemical health effects include changes in the metabolism of certain substances and changes in liver functioning. Behavioral changes include delayed nesting due to alterations in hormone balances, which may cause delayed ovulation (Lassahn, 1975).

The effects of chronic low-levels of persistent insecticides on land mammals are not well known. More work is clearly needed in this area.

Thus chlorinated hydrocarbons can in fact alter an ecosystem by negatively affecting its components. Even the base of the food chain may be affected. One study demonstrated that photosynthesis in marine phytoplankton was diminished in the presence of DDT. Since such phytoplankton are the base of all aquatic food chains and are a major source of oxygen in the ecosphere, such effects can be very important.

Organophosphates in Animals Other Than Humans

Organophosphates are also toxic. However, because they break down rather quickly, they are less likely to become chronic problems for fish and wildlife. Strict safety precautions are, nevertheless, necessary to guard against inadvertent acute exposure of animals during pesticide application. Should a wandering animal be exposed to organophosphates or carbamates, these pesticides may affect the animal's nervous system by inhibiting an enzyme called cholinesterase, which regulates the transmission of nerve impulses at nerve endings.

At many nerve-nerve junctions, nerve impulses are transmitted by the release of a chemical called **acetylcholine**. Acetylcholine released by the stimulating neuron stimulates the next nerve fiber in line. Once acetylcholine triggers the impulse in the receiving nerve cell, the acetylcholine is usually destroyed quickly by the enzyme **cholinesterase**. Without cholinesterase, a single stimulus would be greatly amplified and would be sustained for much longer. Organophosphates and carbamates inhibit the activity of cholinesterase, resulting in tremors or even death. Enzymes that are important in metabolizing foods may also be affected by these pesticides.

How severe the effects of organophosphates are depends on many factors including the *synergistic* effects. The effects of two or more pesticides acting at the same time may be different from the effect of one of the pesticides acting independently. For example, the organophosphate malathion is normally detoxified by enzymes from the liver and so may not be considered extremely harmful to mammals. However, if other organophosphates inhibit the action of the liver enzyme system, the malathion's toxic effects will be greater (Niering, 1968). Experiments on fish and wildlife have been geared primarily to exposure to one specific pesticide. Because species are likely to be exposed to several pesticides at a time in nature, the synergistic effects of pesticides need further investigation.

Human Health and Pesticides

The validity of comparing pesticide effects on animals to effects on humans might be questionable. However, there *have* been direct studies of the effects of pesticides on people. Case reports of overexposure in the workplace or accidental ingestion have provided opportunities for direct study. In addition, epidemiological studies of groups of people who are chronically exposed to pesticides at work have provided some data, as have studies of pesticide residues in the general population.

General Effects. The fate of a pesticide inside the human body varies with the pesticide. Chlorinated hydrocarbons tend to be stored in body fat and in the fat portions of the blood and human milk. Normally, organophosphates and carbamates are metabolized and excreted rather quickly. Certain herbicides pass through mammalian systems intact.

The immediate effects of organophosphate poisoning on humans include stomach cramps, dizziness, vomiting, and heavy sweating. Direct exposure of humans to organophosphates is also reported to cause symptoms of mental derangement, memory loss, sleepwalking, speech difficulties, and depression (Lassahn, 1975). Generally, organophosphates affect the activity of certain enzymes. As we mentioned earlier, cholinesterase is inhibited, and this affects the transmission of nerve impulses. Other enzymes that metabolize foods, food additives, drugs, and other chemicals are also inhibited, as are enzymes that detoxify other organophosphate compounds.

There are complications with the breakdown products of some organophosphates. Some data indicate that in the presence of high ozone concentrations, parathion produces 30 times as much paraoxon as under normal conditions. Paraoxon, a compound in which the sulfur atom in parathion is replaced by an oxygen atom, is 10–100 times more toxic to human red blood cells than parathion. Poi-

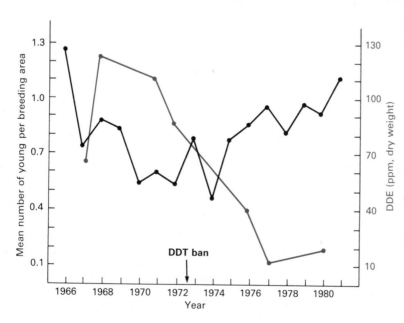

Figure 13.4 Eagle Eggs and DDT. Since the DDT ban, there has been an increase in survival of bald eagles matched by a decline in DDT residues in eagle eggs.

sonings of farm workers in central California may have resulted from this process (Spear, Lee, Leffingwell, and Jenkins, 1978).

Food intake is the major route by which chlorinated hydrocarbons enter human systems. Some studies indicate that perhaps 50% of a person's food intake may contain measurable residues of persistent insecticides (Pimentel et al., 1977). Generally, the chlorinated hydrocarbons affect the central and peripheral nervous systems, perhaps by interfering with the transmission of nerve impulses. The symptoms of acute DDT poisoning include facial numbness, **malaise** (not feeling well), headache, vomiting, dizziness, confusion, and tremor. As we shall see in Chapter 14, many chlorinated hydrocarbons are suspected carcinogens; these include DDT, chlordane, aldrin, dieldrin, and heptachlor.

Accidental poisoning by chlorinated hydrocarbon pesticides is not rare. Perhaps one of the most noted occurred in Hopewell, Virginia where in 1976 a chemical company was found to be discharging wastes into the James River. These wastes contained residues of kepone, a persistent water-insoluble insecticide. The James River and the Chesapeake Bay were substantially polluted by these dis-

charges. Plant workers began to exhibit symptoms of poisoning, including tumors, skin discoloration, blurred vision, memory loss, coordination problems, and joint and chest pain (Council on Environmental Quality, 1977). Kepone is also suspected to be a human carcinogen; it causes tumors in animals.

Body Burdens. We all carry the residues of pesticides in our bodies. Table 13.3 shows for some common pesticides (1) the important residue-containing foods, (2) the **tolerance level** (the concentration in parts per million that may be present in food considered safe for human consumption, (3) the primary toxic effects, and (4) the **acceptable daily intake (ADI)**, the amount considered to be safe for human consumption on a daily basis. Tolerance levels and ADIs are set by the World Health Organization (WHO) and the Food and Agriculture Organization (FAO) on the basis of the best available data from manufacturers and the scientific literature. Table 13.4 compares the estimated daily per capita intake of insecticides for a 50-kg person with FAO/WHO standards.

The EPA runs a program called the National Human Monitoring Program for Pesticides to deter-

Table 13.3 Selected Pesticides Whose Residues May be Present in Foods

Pesticide	Major Food Source	Typical Tolerance (ppm)	FAO/WHO Acceptable Daily Intake (mg/kg body weight)*
Organochlorine	Many agricultural products; concentrate in fat: fish, animal tissue, milk, eggs		
Dieldrin		0.1	0–0.0001
Lindane		1	0–0.01
Toxaphene		7	
Heptachlor		0	0–0.0005
DDT		1	0–0.02
Organophosphorus	Fruits, vegetables, grains		
Malathion		8	0–0.02
Parathion		1	0–0.005
Diazinon		0.75	0–0.002
Carbamate	Fruits and vegetables		
Carbaryl		10	0–0.01
Carbofuran		0.1	0–0.01

Occurrence indicated by Food and Drug Administration residue monitoring; see Duggan, R.E., Corneluissen, P.E., Duggan, M.B., McMahon, B.M., and Martin, R.J., "Pesticide Residues Levels in Foods in the United States from July 1, 1969 to June 30, 1976," published jointly by Food and Drug Administration and Association of Official Analytical Chemists, 1983; and Podrebarac, D.S., *J. Assoc. Off. Anal. Chem. 67*, 1984, 166–185.

*Vettorazzi, G., ed., *Pesticide Reference Index, JMPR 1961–1984*, Geneva, Switzerland: World Health Organization.

Table 13.4   Estimated Daily per Capita Intake of Insecticides for a 50-kg Person Compared with FAO/WHO ADI Values

Insecticide	ADI (μg)	Country	Total Intake (μg)
Total DDT	250	U. S.	55.0
		England	44.0
		Spain	78.4
Lindane	625	U. S.	3.0
		England	6.6
		Spain	13.8
Dieldrin	5	U. S.	3.4
		Britain	4.7
		Italy	1.9

mine environmental levels and trends in human contamination. Samples of adipose (fatty) tissue, blood, and urine are collected and analyzed (see Figure 13.5). A number of interesting observations have been made as a result (Kutz, Strassman, and Yobs, 1977):

1. DDT was stored in larger amounts than any other organochloride found in the survey; it was in virtually all tissue examined.
2. Although consistently present, DDT residues have tended to be reduced in recent years. (Agricultural use of DDT was banned in the United States in 1972; only limited use by permit is still allowed.)
3. Dieldrin also occurred in low levels in almost every tissue examined, and its levels did not change greatly over five years. Dieldrin also reflects exposure to aldrin, since the body rapidly converts aldrin to dieldrin.

4. Metabolites of heptachlor and chlordane were found in low levels in nearly all tissues.
5. Residues of lindane, mirex, and other pesticides were also found but at low frequencies.

Results of urine sample analyses by the EPA also indicate the presence of pesticides including organophosphates, chlorinated hydrocarbons, and carbamates. A few of the samples contained carbaryl, parathion, and the herbicides 2,4,5-T (Kutz, Strassman, and Yobs, 1977).

The presence of pesticide residues in human milk is of particular concern. The results of studies of insecticide residues in human milk are shown in Table 13.5. Several types of residues are found in human milk; DDT and its derivatives are found in higher concentrations than any of the other pesticides. Another study of pesticide residues in human milk was conducted in Sweden from 1967 to 1977. The average concentrations of DDT, DDE, and

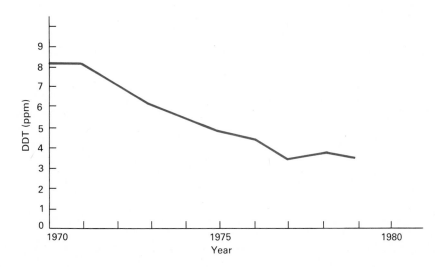

Figure 13.5   DDT in Human Adipose Tissue. The amount of DDT in human fatty tissue samples has decreased, but the number of samples containing DDT residues has remained high.

Table 13.5 Pesticide Residues in Human Whole Milk

Country or Region	Sampling Year	Residues (ppb) Total DDT	(Minimum–Maximum) Dieldrin
United States	1973–1974	344 (20–2760)	12 (Trace–50)
	1973–1975		
	High use area	719 (69–4801)	6 (1–52)
	Low use area	83 (51–130)	4 (1–7)
	1976		
	Northeast	82 (7–408)	3 (1–16)
	Southeast	146 (6–4936)	7 (1369)
	Midwest	83 (6–1140)	4 (Trace–54)
	Southwest	180 (5–7464)	5 (1–113)
	Northwest	87 (7–418)	4 (1–79)
	Average	122 (5–2813)	5 (1–126)
Central America	1971	3100	
Guatamala	1973		
	Cotton area	4070	
	Noncotton area	1830	
Sweden	1967–1969	120	
England	1965	130	6
Germany	1973	300	
USSR	1970	190	
Ghana	1972	29	
Australia	1973	64	5

dieldrin decreased over this time period (see Figure 13.6).

Although several studies indicate that people in lower socioeconomic classes seem to be more exposed to pesticides because of greater prevalence of pest problems, bug-conscious Americans in all classes are exposed to home pesticides. Pest strips, bugproof shelf paper, termite control, rodent poisons, lawn treatments, and garden applications all mean considerable human exposure.

A study of soils from 1968 to 1974 showed that urban soils actually tend to have a higher occurrence of pesticide residue than agricultural soils (see Table 13.6) (Carey, 1978). The only exceptions were in some areas of the South where DDT was used heavily on cotton crops. Over the short term, pesticide residues that are monitored apparently present little or no direct danger to human health. The effect of long-term low-level exposure, however, is largely unknown. Residues from unmonitored pesticides are also unknowns.

The most recently published report on pesticide residues in food for human consumption was conducted and published in 1984 by the Natural Resources Defense Council (NRDC). The NRDC conducted a survey of California-grown fruits and vegetables sold in San Francisco. Of the 71 samples taken, 44% contained detectable residues of 19 different pesticides, 18% contained residues of more than one pesticide, and three samples contained four

pesticides. Four of the pesticides detected were DDT, dicofol, endosulfan, and trifluralin. There are several hypotheses as to where the DDT comes from. Some conjecture that the DDT is simply residue still in the soil from use before the ban. Others hypothesize that DDT is obtained illegally from Mexico and is used actively on crops today. In addition, dicofol (kelthane) contains DDT as a contaminant.

We have no way to measure the real impact of pesticides on human health. We do not test for all possible pesticides present at one time. We know little about the synergistic impact of pesticide residues. The validity of the standards set for many pesticide residues is now questionable. In 1983 the EPA invalidated over 200 laboratory tests on pesticides and toxic chemicals that were conducted by a single private laboratory for the purpose of setting maximum safe residue limits. The same firm was responsible for the test data used to support licensing of 15% of all pesticides (*Environment Reporter*, 1983). In 1984, the National Academy of Sciences stated that industry has provided EPA with only 10% of the information it needs to assess the hazards of known pesticides. Not until 1984 were data on EPA pesticide registration applications made available to the public. The disclosure was mandated by the 1978 law, but legal maneuvers prevented its implementation until June 1984, when the Supreme Court ordered pesticide data to be released.

So how safe are we? No one really knows. We

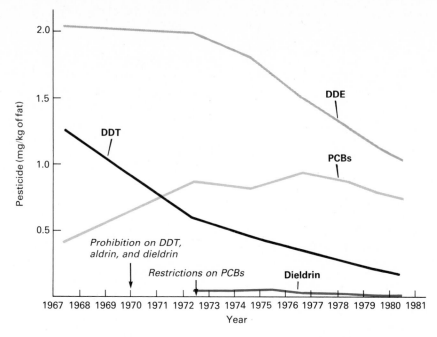

Figure 13.6 Persistent Chemicals in Mother's Milk. The graph indicates that the DDT ban resulted in a decrease in DDT and DDE concentrations from 1967 on. The 1970 ban on dieldrin resulted in a decrease in dieldrin concentrations. Such was not the case with PCBs, which were not banned but only restricted for use. A decline in PCB residues was not noted until 1978–1980.

continue to pour chemicals into our environment and make them part of ourselves with little knowledge of their effects (see Figure 13.7).

PESTICIDE BANS AND RESTRICTIONS

An Overview

Questions and concerns about the long-range effects of pesticides on humans and the rest of the biosphere have led to bans or restrictions on the use of specific pesticides. Such bans and restrictions have been hard fought because agriculture, forestry, and manufacturing depend so much on particular pesticides and because there is little solid scientific data on the health and environmental effects of pesticide use.

The following case studies illustrate many of the real problems in regulating pesticide use. It takes years for pesticides to be reviewed. Even after they are shown to be carcinogenic in the laboratory, it is years before any restrictive action is taken; public concern has forced many governmental actions in this area. Once action is initiated, it can be held up for years in the courts, and emergency exemptions can be granted to allow some uses. Once a substance

Table 13.6   DDT and Chlordane in Urban and Agricultural Soils

	DDT And Its Analogs (percent occurrence)	Chlordane (percent occurrence)
Pittsfield, MA		
Urban	55.6	11.1
Agricultural	26.3	5.3
Washington, DC		
Urban	59.1	33.3
Agricultural	20.0	ND
Greenville, SC		
Urban	61.6	9.3
Agricultural	75.0	ND
Tacoma, WA		
Urban	34.7	14.7
Agricultural	30.2	ND

ND = not detected.

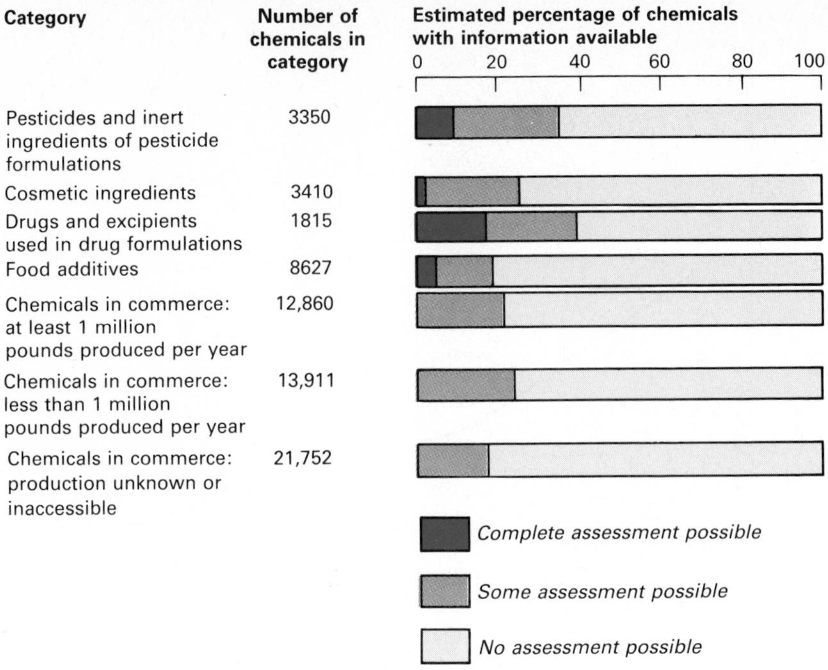

Category	Number of chemicals in category	Estimated percentage of chemicals with information available
Pesticides and inert ingredients of pesticide formulations	3350	
Cosmetic ingredients	3410	
Drugs and excipients used in drug formulations	1815	
Food additives	8627	
Chemicals in commerce: at least 1 million pounds produced per year	12,860	
Chemicals in commerce: less than 1 million pounds produced per year	13,911	
Chemicals in commerce: production unknown or inaccessible	21,752	

■ Complete assessment possible

▨ Some assessment possible

□ No assessment possible

Figure 13.7 Adequacy of Toxicity Information for Assessing Human Health Hazards. A National Academy of Sciences committee estimates that humans may be exposed to almost 66,000 chemicals; we know very little about the effects of most of them on human health.

is restricted or cancelled, it may be found that substitutes are equally hazardous or have unknown effects.

Agent Orange

The most infamous of the herbicides is 2,4,5-T or **Agent Orange** as it was called when it was used as a defoliant in Vietnam. Agent Orange contains contaminants called **dioxins**. Though dioxins are extremely toxic, their long-term effects are currently only suspected. Dioxins are carcinogenic and cause birth defects in laboratory animals (Henig, 1979). They have also been found to end up in the livers and fatty tissues of beef.

In 1966, dioxin residues were found in fish, shellfish, streams, deltas, and mothers' milk in the Vietnam target areas. In 1978–1979, Vietnam veterans in the United States began complaining of a variety of symptoms such as numbness, skin rashes, liver problems and birth defects in their children, all allegedly linked to exposure to Agent Orange. Although the relationship of these symptoms to Agent Orange is still under study, several damage suits were filed by alleged victims. One major suit was settled out of court.

The U.S. Department of Agriculture restricted use of 2,4,5-T near waterways and homes and on food crops in the 1970s. However, the use of 2,4,5-T continued in forest areas, along highway and power

line right-of-ways, and on lawns and golf courses. In March 1979 the EPA suspended most uses of 2,4,5,-T when a study indicated a possible link between dioxin and human miscarriages in Oregon. Miscarriages and infant deformities were found to occur with frequencies more than three times greater than expected in Alsea, Oregon, a mountain community located near a National Forest that had been heavily sprayed with 2,4,5-T. Although the U.S. Forest Service and the timber industry supported the continued use of 2,4,5-T, its suspension was upheld by the courts. EPA hearings on the cancellation of 2,4,5,-T continued. In October 1983, Dow Chemical withdrew its protest of the EPA's plan to cancel registration of 2,4,5,-T and silvex for use. Dow cited the emotional and political concern about dioxin contamination as the reason for withdrawing its protest. Four days later, the EPA issued the cancellation notice.

In 1984 the EPA announced plans to survey dioxin contamination nationwide from numerous sources, to assess human exposure risks, and to develop clean-up measures.

Mirex and the Fire Ants

Another controversial ban has been on the use of the pesticide mirex, which was used throughout the South from 1958 to 1978 to combat the fire ant. The fire ant does not attack crops but is a pest because it creates large mounds for its homes in the farm fields. The ant does have a sting and is considered a general nuisance. The federal government has contributed close to one billion dollars in a 20-year campaign against the fire ant, yet the problem remains.

Mirex is a persistent chlorinated hydrocarbon. When it decays, it degrades into kepone, a substance that is neurotoxic in humans. Mirex and kepone have been associated with cancer in laboratory animals. An EPA survey conducted in 1976 showed 23% of all samples of human tissues contained mirex.

In 1977 the EPA ordered the phasing out of mirex by the end of June 1978 and approved the use of ferriamicide in its place. Although ferriamicide breaks down more quickly in sunlight than mirex, it contains some mirex and may have health effects of its own. In 1982, the EPA issued a temporary restraining order on the sale and use of ferriamicide pending further investigations. Several requests for emergency exemptions to use ferriamicide have been denied on the ground that there is no evidence of significant economic or health problems arising from *not* using it on cropland.

EDB

Ethylene dibromide (EDB) is a halogenated hydrocarbon pesticide in the same family as DDT, chlordane, heptachlor, aldrin, and dieldrin. It has been used since the 1940s for fumigating soils before planting to kill such things as fruit fly larvae and roundworms and for fumigating stored grains, milling machinery, and logs. EDB is also used to fumigate citrus, tropical fruits, and vegetables.

In the 1970s, federal government studies indicated that EDB is a carcinogen. It also causes gene mutations and reproductive damage in animals species. In 1977, the EPA first moved to control the use of EDB, but strong industry lobbies and lack of initiative under the Reagan administration resulted in no formal action.

In the summer of 1983, reports from California, Georgia, Florida, and Hawaii indicated groundwater contamination by EDB. In September 1983, the EPA ordered the immediate suspension of the use and sale of EDB for soil fumigation. In March 1984, the EPA announced that as of September 1, 1984, citrus fruit and papaya with EDB residues could not be sold in the United States.

The most recent substitute for EDB is methyl bromide. Methyl bromide has also been around since the 1940s, but it has only recently been tested. Tests now indicate that methyl bromide is also a carcinogen.

Wood Preservatives

Pesticides are used not only in agriculture and forestry but also in manufacturing. In July 1984, after six years of special review, the EPA placed restrictions on three pesticides used as wood preservatives on items such as railroad ties, telephone poles, picnic tables, and desks. The restricted pesticides are creosote, pentachloro-phenol ("penta"), and inorganic arsenicals; they account for 97% of wood preservatives used. These pesticides are used to deter fungi, insects, bacteria, and marine borers in wood; they extend the service life of wood by up to five times. However, creosote was found to cause cancer in laboratory animals and skin cancer in workers regularly exposed to it. "Penta" has a dioxin impurity shown to cause cancer in animals. Epidemiological studies have shown arsenic to be associated with cancer in humans. "Penta" and the

These veterans suffer from bone and muscle deterioration, which they believe resulted from their being sprayed directly with Agent Orange in Vietnam in the late 1960s.

Chapter 13   Pesticides and Other Chemicals in the Biosphere arsenicals caused birth defects in test animals; creosote and the arsenicals caused mutations in bacteria and lab animals. The restrictions are basically designed to protect workers but will require the wood industry to initiate a consumer awareness program on the handling and disposal of treated wood. Limits are placed on the use of treated wood indoors. Manufacturers were to have significantly reduced the dioxin contaminant in "penta" within 18 months.

THE LAWS REGULATING MANUFACTURE AND USE OF PESTICIDES

Pesticide regulation began in 1947 when pesticides were lumped together with other chemicals in legislation dealing with "economic poisons." The **Federal Insecticide, Fungicide, and Rodenticide Act (FIFRA)** of 1947 addressed itself to pesticides but only to those being shipped across state lines, all of which were to be registered and appropriately labeled. The use of pesticides was not specifically addressed. When attention was drawn to the dangers of pesticides in the 1960s, the public pressed for more comprehensive laws. In 1972 and again in 1975 a number of far-reaching amendments to FIFRA were enacted. These amendments extended the regulatory aspects of the 1947 law to all pesticides whether or not they were shipped across state lines. The amendments required that the EPA classify all pesticides as either general or restricted. **Restricted-use pesticides** can be used only under the supervision of a certified applicator, and there are specific testing requirements for certification. States administer these programs if the state certification program is approved by the EPA. The intent is for pesticides that are potentially harmful to the biosphere to be applied only under supervision by individuals with some sense of the potential for harm as well as for good.

The 1972 and 1975 amendments also require registering of all pesticides intended for sale in the United States regardless of place of production. In addition, all pesticide producers must now register and keep detailed production and distribution records.

Under the amendments to FIFRA it is illegal to use pesticides improperly. The EPA has the authority to inspect establishments and private property with the owner's consent or, if there is some basis for believing that there is wrongdoing, with a warrant. The EPA may recall pesticide products, stop their sale or use, seize illegally used products, or seek court injunctions. Both civil and criminal penalties are specified in the amendments.

Because pesticides fall under the jurisdiction of numerous federal agencies, the federal act now also calls for cooperation among the agencies involved. This includes, among others, the EPA, Food and Drug Administration, Occupational Safety and Health Administration, Federal Aviation Administration, and Fish and Wildlife Service.

There are other federal laws that affect pesticide regulation. The Federal Water Pollution Control Act and its amendments set effluent limits for toxic pollutants including aldrin, dieldrin, endrin, and DDT. These laws are described in Chapter 12, where we also outline the standards for inorganic and organic pesticides based on the Safe Drinking Water Act of 1974. The Federal Food, Drug, and Cosmetic Act regulates the types and amounts of pesticide residues allowed on raw agricultural commodities and specifies labeling requirements. Many of the provisions of the Toxic Substances Control Act of 1976 (see Chapter 14) also cover pesticides, since it provides for broad control of the production, distribution, and use of all potentially hazardous chemicals (Council on Environmental Quality, 1977). All of these acts address individual facets of the overall production, transportation, use, and disposal of pesticides and other chemicals that are potentially harmful to humans and to ecosystems.

THE ECONOMICS OF PESTICIDE USE

The Cost of Using Pesticides

Pimentel and colleagues (1977) have attempted to work out the costs of agricultural pesticide use in the United States. They conclude that it cost about $4.50 a pound for materials and application in 1977. Given this figure and the more than one billion pounds of pesticides used annually, the price tag for pesticide use in American agriculture approaches five billion dollars annually. Pimentel calculated that the energy needed for pesticide production ranges from 11,000 kcal/lb for the cheaper types such as DDT and 2,4-D to 12,500 kcal/lb for others. In addition, energy is required to produce the solvent (9,500 kcal/lb) and to produce the steel cans for holding the pesticide (2500 kcal for a quarter-gallon can). Transportation and distribution involve another 500 kcal/lb. Application with ground equipment accounts for another quarter-gallon of fuel (9,500 kcal) per pound applied. The net result is that it takes about 33,000 kcal to apply one pound of pesticide to one acre. For the entire United States this amounts to the equivalent of almost a billion gallons of fossil fuel per year.

Because 80% of all pesticides are petroleum based, the energy crisis has caused production costs to increase dramatically. Thus the direct dollar cost of pesticide use is high and continues to rise sharply even if we fail to consider the indirect costs of impact on fish and wildlife, other nontarget species, and human health. This increased cost may turn out to have more impact than laws or reason in bringing about more rational use of pesticides.

The Cost of Not Using Pesticides

Estimates vary as to the overall impact on food production and food prices of foregoing chemical pesticides entirely. Pimentel and colleagues (1978) estimate that preharvest crop losses in the United States would increase from 33% to 42% if chemicals were banned and only alternative types of pest control were used, and food prices would increase 12%. Dorfman (1979) takes issue with Pimentel; using the same basic figures with different economic multipliers and methodology, Dorfman predicts a 13.5% increase in crop loss, resulting in a 40% increase in food prices. According to others, specific crops would be hit harder than the general figures indicate. Tomato losses would increase 31–87%, loss of beans would increase 26–76%, and potato losses would be 17–53%. While the fine points of the debate continued to be argued, the fact remains that under current treatment conditions, about one third of U.S. crops are lost to pests before harvest.

ALTERNATIVES TO INSECTICIDES

The University of California Biological Control Division releases more than ten million natural enemies of pests every year (Stevenson, 1978). University of California scientists claim that the program has probably saved more than 300 million dollars in the past 50 years.

In 1944, Klamath weed, which had been imported from Europe inadvertently, was taking over prime rangeland in California. After the strategic release of natural enemies, leef beetles from Australia, the weed disappeared. The resultant savings to the livestock industry are estimated to be 3.5 million dollars a year, totalling nearly 90 million dollars through 1978.

In 1981 the cotton crop in Nicaragua cost more to produce than was returned for selling it. A good 30% of the production cost was attributed to pesticides. In 1982 the government initiated a program to reduce pesticide use by using cotton stubble in the field baited with a sex attractant for the boll weevil. Only the baited areas were sprayed with pesticide. Preliminary data in 1983 indicated a healthy cotton crop, increased acreage in the program, and a 60% decline in pesticide use, comprising 10–15% of production costs.

Cotton growers in Arkansas claim to be cutting pest control costs by $480,000 a year by utilizing fewer pesticides and filling in with natural predators. Biological control agents used in management strategies also include viruses, bacteria, and fungi. There is an accelerating trend toward using combinations of some of the above strategies, the particular combination being based on the characteristics of the pest species in question. This combination approach is called **integrated pest management**.

Controlling Versus Eradicating

Given the economic and environmental effects of large-scale pesticide use, a new effort is being made to promote integrated pest management (IPM). IPM is a pest *control*, not a pest *eradication* program. It tries to keep pests at an economically tolerable level by using a combination of good agricultural practices and chemical and biological control agents. In IPM the most effective use of pesticide application is related to such things as the life cycle of the target organism, size of the target pest population, and weather. IPM takes into account as many strategic factors as possible.

The key to successful use of IPM is knowledge of the ecology of a pest species, including the microecosystem of which it is a part. The basic idea is to make the system unfavorable for successful reproduction of the pest species. An IPM program may be developed as a combination of physical, chemical, and biological techniques used at strategic times in the life cycle of the pest. These techniques range from the simple to the highly sophisticated.

Simple Forms of Integrated Pest Management

IPM may use simple agricultural practices like crop rotation to prevent a buildup of pests year after year or tilling a field at an appropriate time to expose insect eggs to drying by the air or to crush eggs and immature stages of the pest. It may involve stripcropping to break up a large expanse of a single crop. For example, some pests that may attack cotton prefer alfalfa as a food source. If alfalfa is planted in strips between rows of cotton, the pest will tend to stay on the alfalfa and feed on it. Some pests, of course, will spread to the cotton, but the infestation and the damage to the cotton will not be as severe. As long as alfalfa is available, the pest will tend to leave the cotton alone. Experiments with corn, beans, and squash in Costa Rica have also demonstrated the effectiveness of this type of strategy.

The development of resistant strains of crops continues. One strategy is to breed strains with better natural defenses. Another is to create strains with shorter growing seasons so that when pests reach the most harmful point in their life cycles, the crop has already been harvested (Figure 13.8).

Sterile Male Technique

A direct method aimed at decreasing the reproduction of pests is the sterile male technique. One of the earliest uses of this technique was in the 1950s against the screwworm fly, which attacks cattle. Releasing radiation-sterilized males to mate with the female flies results in infertile eggs. This plan works because females mate just once, whether or not they are fertilized. Initial attempts were successful, and even now the screwworm fly is kept under control in many places by this technique. Control costs are estimated to be about one fifteenth of the cost of potential annual losses due to fly infestations.

Pheromones and Juvenile Hormones

Many animals, including insects, communicate with members of their own species by secreting chemical substances called **pheromones**. Sex-attractant pheromones can be used to draw insects into traps, disorient insects, or otherwise decrease reproduction. This technique has been successful against the gypsy moth. Pheromones are most effective in controlling low-density populations. They are also useful in monitoring and defining infected areas; the extent of infestation can be determined on the basis of the number of insects trapped over a specific period of time. **Juvenile hormones** are substances produced by insects that maintain them in an immature state. Chemicals that have similar effects can prevent insects from reaching sexual maturity and reproducing.

Biological and Natural Enemies

We have cited previous instances of importation of natural insect predators or parasites to control a pest population. In the early 1970s a wasp parasite was imported into Connecticut to help control elm spanworms which were destroying elm trees. The parasites lay their eggs in the spanworm eggs. The parasite eggs then develop at the expense of the spanworm eggs. Fortunately, the wasp parasite does not sting humans (U.S. Department of Agriculture, 1975).

In a similar success story a small fish introduced into California's Clear Lake appears to be controlling its gnat problem without repeated use of pesticides. Both bacteria and viruses have also been used successfully to control specific pests. Bacteria have been used to control Japanese beetles, for example. Programs are testing the effectiveness of these biological pesticides and improving the efficiency of use and production so that their costs and control effects are comparable to those of their synthetic chemical counterparts. Like chemical pesticides, these alternatives are monitored and controlled by the EPA.

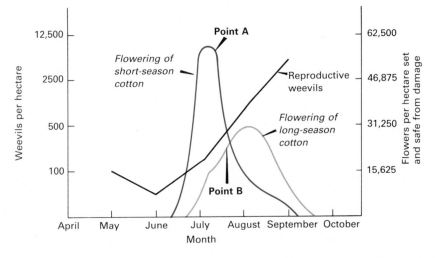

Figure 13.8 Outfoxing the Boll Weevil. This graph shows how a variety of cotton that has a short growing season can be used to prevent substantial crop loss from the boll weevil. Point A shows when second-generation weevils begin to emerge in short-season cotton; by this time, most flowers have set and are safe from damage. At point B, second-generation weevils begin to emerge in long-season cotton; only a small percentage of flowers are safe by then.

Other Natural Approaches

There are numerous other approaches to pest control. Research into natural anti-insect chemicals from plants has produced some good leads. Genetic engineering is being used to replace the genes that make pest species resistant to chemical controls.

The most important lesson in all of this is that intimate knowledge of each insect pest and its niche is extremely important to finding the most efficient, effective, economic, and environmentally sound integrated control strategies. An awareness of basic principles of ecology is essential. Chemical agents must be compatible with biological agents.

SOCIOLOGICAL AND CULTURAL ASPECTS OF PESTS

Monoculture: An Invitation to a Feast

As we mentioned early in the chapter, social and cultural factors determine what is and what is not a pest. Many of our traditional practices ignore ecological realities and actually invite major pest problems. For example, the large farm with its huge expanse of one or two crops favors the invasion of pests and the development of diseases. Where there are large expanses of corn, large numbers of corn eaters will tend to move in to exploit the expanded food supply. In 1970, 15% of the U.S. corn crop was wiped out by southern corn leaf blight because of the lack of resistance in the varieties of corn used and the habitat provided by large, unbroken fields. Lawns of pure bluegrass or other grasses may be more susceptible to damage by sod webworms or other pests.

Beautiful Tomatoes

In recent years, pesticide use has become more important because of a demand for aesthetically pleasing raw foods. Some pesticide use is for producing cosmetically flawless fruits and vegetables that chain stores will select and shoppers will purchase. Our culture has put so much emphasis on what we see, on looking good, that we forget that invisible chemicals can be much more harmful than a slightly blemished piece of fruit.

The FDA sets **defect action levels (DAL)** for foods to limit the number of insects or insect parts in various kinds of food. Pimentel and his colleagues (1977) cite several examples:

— Shelled peanuts: 5% insect infested
— Tomato paste and pizza: 30 fruitfly eggs per 100 grams or 15 fruitfly eggs and one larva per 100 grams or 2 larvae per 100 grams
— Frozen broccoli: 60 aphids, thrips, and/or mites per 100 grams

DAL tolerances have become more strict in recent years mainly because of cosmetic considerations. Meeting the standards generally means additional pesticide use. The agricultural community is being pushed for quality control while at the same time being squeezed by increased pest control costs and environmental interests.

PROBLEMS WITH PERSISTENT CHEMICALS OTHER THAN PESTICIDES

Although our discussion so far has focused on pesticides, the ecosphere is bombarded by numerous other persistent chemicals that carry the same dangers of bioaccumulation and toxicity. We would now like to look at a few nonpesticide examples.

Polychlorinated Biphenyls (PCBs)

In June 1979 an electrical transformer was damaged in a hog-slaughtering and processing plant in Billings, Montana. This damage resulted in the leakage of 200 gallons of a coolant contaminated with PCBs into the plant's drainage system. The contaminated material from the drainage system was mixed with other wastes from the plant and processed into animal feed and grease. In July 1979 a routine inspection of a wholesale poultry plant in Provo, Utah, produced a sample from a barrel of chicken fat showing five times the tolerance level allowable for PCBs (at that time 3 ppm). The source of PCBs was traced to the chicken feed and back to the plant in Montana. By this time, however, contaminated materials had been distributed to 19 states, Canada, and Japan. The cost of the federal investigation, chemical analyses and recall, and destruction of animals, food, and feed products amounted to over $3.5 million dollars. Unfortunately, this was not an isolated incident of persistent chemical contamination in the food chain.

The effects of PCB contamination in humans and other species are several. In 1968 an accidental poisoning from contaminated rice oil occurred in southern Japan; analysis of the oil showed that it contained 2,000–3,000 ppm of PCBs. Affected people developed darkened skin, nails, lips, and gums. There were also eye discharges, severe acne, numbness, neuralgic pains, swelling of joints and eyelids, jaundice, temporary hearing or visual disturbances, liver disturbances, and general weakness. The presence of some of the pigment and eye conditions in newborns indicated placental transfer.

PCBs were first produced on a commercial scale in the 1930s as insulation in transformers or capacitors and also as plasticizers, solvents in adhesives, and sealants for hydraulic or heat transfer purposes. World production of PCBs is estimated at about one million tons since 1930 (*Ambio,* 1978).

PCBs enter the environment primarily from disposal in waterways, incineration, and leakage. PCBs are stable and persistent in the environment, and they can be biologically magnified. Small amounts may be degraded by biological activity or sunlight, but by and large, PCBs dumped into the environment remain there for a long, long time. Most PCBs in the environment end up in the sediments of waterways, although measurable concentrations can also be found in air, water, and soils. PCBs are fat-soluble substances, and in the United States they are commonly detected in human **adipose** (fat) tissue. Of 683 human fat samples analyzed in 1976, only 1.9% did *not* show PCB contamination, 59.3% showed 1 ppm, 29% showed 1–3 ppm, and 9% showed over 3 ppm. Some studies on the presence of PCBs in the Baltic indicate that although PCB use has been restricted in Sweden since 1971, in Denmark since 1973, and in Finland, environmental levels of PCBs there did not decline until 1978 (Kihlstrom and Berglund, 1978). The study of human milk in Stockholm indicated that PCB levels did not decline until 1978–1980 (see Figure 13.6). Global transfer from countries where PCBs are not restricted may explain this occurrence (Westöö and Norén, 1977). In the United States, PCBs have been banned for sale, manufacture, or use in other than closed systems since 1978 and for all uses since 1979. In May 1983 the EPA reported that the level of PCBs in humans in the United States had dropped. From 1972 to 1977 the percentage of people contaminated with greater than 3 ppm PCB rose to over 9%; in 1981 this dropped to less than 1%. Old electrical transformers and capacitors still in use today contain large amounts of PCB. Unless the EPA directs otherwise, this equipment will be replaced only as it wears out.

Heavy Metals

We discussed the health effects of lead, mercury, and other heavy metals in earlier chapters. Here we will only reemphasize several points in the context of persistence and biomagnification. Metals tend to be stirred up by human activity and end up in water, air, and soil. The EPA's National Soils Monitoring Program indicates that concentrations of the heavy metals cadmium, lead, and mercury in urban and suburban areas of the United States are much greater than background concentrations (Carey, 1978). Sources of such heavy metals include industrial processes and the burning of fossil fuels.

Many heavy metals are poisonous because they interfere with cellular metabolism (see Chapter 9). Many metals can be magnified in food chains just like pesticides. We discussed mercury as a particularly important example in Chapters 9 and 12.

Radioisotopes

Here, as with metals, we wish only to reemphasize (see Chapter 6) one or two points about radioisotopes in the context of persistence and biomagnification. Persistence is reflected in the half-lives of radioisotopes. A number of radioisotopes can be stored in various tissues and become magnified in food chains. Radioisotopes differ from other persistent chemicals in one very important way. Persistent chemicals become problems when they leave storage sites and enter the bloodstream in significant concentrations. Radioisotopes are problems even in storage because they emit damaging radiation (see Chapter 14).

THE OVERALL PROBLEM OF REGULATION AND CONTROL OF PERSISTENT CHEMICALS

The United States

Pesticides are regulated by FIFRA; other persistent chemicals are regulated primarily by the Toxic Substances Control Act (TOSCA) (see Chapter 14). However, as Figure 13.9 shows, many other pieces of legislation have been enacted to deal with synthetic chemical production and exposure.

International Considerations

The United States is not alone in its attempts to regulate toxic substances. Canada, France, Norway, and Sweden have all passed similar legislation. The problem of persistent chemicals is clearly multinational. The need for international cooperation becomes even more obvious when we realize that international trade in chemicals amounts to at least 80 billion U.S. dollars every year (Huisman, 1978). The American chemical industry exports 600 million of the 1.6 billion pounds of chemicals it produces each year (Smith, 1979). An important ethical question for America is, Should we export chemicals banned for use in the United States? This issue has been debated at length among the Department of Commerce, the State Department, Congress, the chemical industry, and interested citizens.

Data Banks

The United Nations Environment Program (UNEP) has developed an International Register of Potentially Toxic Chemicals that serves to (1) compile and facilitate access to data on the effects of toxic chemicals in the environment, (2) point up data needs, and (3) catalog various policies, practices, and guidelines relating to control and standards for chemicals.

In 1967, the European Economic Community (EEC) passed a directive on the classification, packaging, and labeling of toxic materials. Additions to this directive have been proposed to parallel the requirements of U.S. TOSCA for the marketing of new chemicals. In 1977 the EEC began a review of the toxicity, persistence, and bioaccumulation of existing chemicals in order to update its policies on certain chemicals. The EEC has a toxics data base program called the European Chemical Data and Information Network.

The Organization for Economic Cooperation and Development (OECD), with Germany, Japan, the Netherlands, the United Kingdom, Sweden, and the United States as lead countries, has initiated a chemical-testing program to develop consistency in test methods and an information exchange program. At a meeting of the representatives of 16 countries in Stockholm in 1978 a number of common needs and concerns were cited; these included needs for consistency in laboratory practices, information exchange, confidentiality for industries involved, methods for evaluating economic and trade impacts, and an international glossary of terms.

For pesticide and persistent toxin problems, as for the others we have reviewed, there are obviously

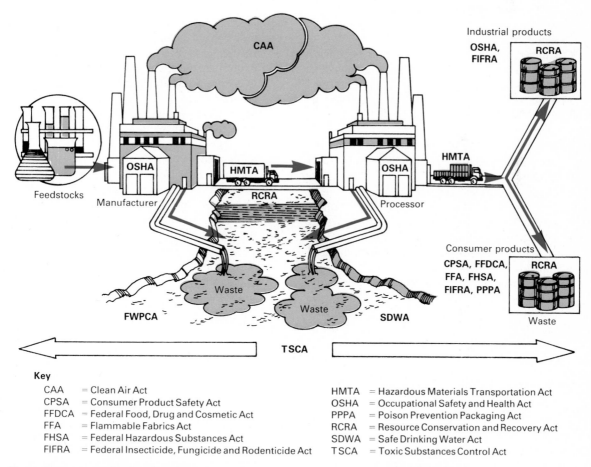

Key

CAA	= Clean Air Act		HMTA	= Hazardous Materials Transportation Act
CPSA	= Consumer Product Safety Act		OSHA	= Occupational Safety and Health Act
FFDCA	= Federal Food, Drug and Cosmetic Act		PPPA	= Poison Prevention Packaging Act
FFA	= Flammable Fabrics Act		RCRA	= Resource Conservation and Recovery Act
FHSA	= Federal Hazardous Substances Act		SDWA	= Safe Drinking Water Act
FIFRA	= Federal Insecticide, Fungicide and Rodenticide Act		TSCA	= Toxic Substances Control Act

Figure 13.9 Laws Affecting the Life Cycle of a Chemical. Each piece of legislation is directed toward a different aspect of the problem from generation to consumption to disposal. There is obviously some overlap.

no simple answers. Numerous cultural, economic, political, and international implications must be considered. Some very basic questions remain to be answered, and while the debates rage, the chemicals we produce continue to infiltrate the materials-cycling system of the ecosphere of which humans are a part. Among the more important general questions we face is just how much of what kind of chemistry is compatible with these living systems.

CONCEPTS TO REMEMBER

1. Materials cycle in the biosphere. Any stable substance that enters the biosphere can and probably will make its way into the nutrient cycles of humans and other organisms.
2. Synthetic chemicals did not evolve in the ecosphere but have been created in the laboratory; biological systems have not generally developed enzymes to break down many synthetic chemicals. Physical-chemical breakdown is much slower; thus these chemicals may remain in the ecosphere for a relatively long time.
3. Organisms cannot handle many naturally occurring substances such as metals in some of the high concentrations and chemical forms in which humans stir them up.
4. Chemicals may inadvertently enter organisms through food intake, water use, or gaseous exchanges with the atmosphere.
5. Persistent chemicals may affect organisms in ways and amounts not anticipated because of biomagnification, that is, the fact that small amounts are passed up the food chain and concentrate in ever higher amounts in individuals at each trophic level.
6. Pesticides are classified into the major groups of chlorinated hydrocarbons and organophosphates. Chlorinated hydrocarbons are generally more persistent than organophosphates and are fat soluble and thus may accumulate in the fatty tissue of organisms.
7. One danger of sustained pesticide use is the development of pests that are resistant to the pesticide. The emergence of resistant strains of insects jeopardizes the progress made by use of synthetic pesticides.
8. Most pesticides are nonspecific and kill organisms other than the target pest. They are biocides.
9. Pesticide residues are present in the fatty tissues, blood, urine, and milk of humans.
10. Integrated pest management (IPM) is an approach to pest control designed not to eradicate pests but to keep damage minimal. IPM minimizes the use of pesticides and gears pest control to the life cycle and habits of the pest species. It consists of good agricultural practices used in concert with chemical and biological control agents.
11. Alternatives to using synthetic pesticides for pest control include timely planting and harvesting, crop interspersal, use of biological and natural enemies, use of pheromones and juvenile hormones, and genetic breeding for pest resistance.
12. Many farm practices such as monoculture ignore ecological realities and invite major pest problems.
13. Radioisotopes differ from other persistent chemicals because radioisotopes emit damaging radiation even in storage in tissue.
14. Control of persistent chemicals is a global problem, since air transports contaminants around the earth.
15. Further data must be obtained on the health effects of toxic chemicals, and governmental regulatory programs must be improved to control toxic chemicals in the ecosphere.

DISCUSSION QUESTIONS AND FOOD FOR THOUGHT

1. Visit a local gardening supply store. Read some of the labels of herbicides and insecticides. See if you can find any chemicals that have been banned for home use.
2. Ask a pest control company representative to speak to your class, giving his or her views on pesticides use.
3. Choose one statement and defend it:

a. It is not fair to burden future generations with persistent chemical contamination problems as a by-product of solutions to present-day problems.
b. Future generations inevitably inherit problems from their predecessors. They will find some way to cope.

4. Design a public relations campaign directed at en-

couraging homeowners to accept dandelions and abandon the struggle for a perfect lawn.

5. Compare these two caution statements. Analyze them on the basis of what you know about chlorinated hydrocarbons and organophosphates. Which at first appears more dangerous? Write a long-term caution for the DDD container.

A. *Dichlorodiphenyl dichloroethane* (DDD)
   1. Technical, emulsions, and wettable powders above 25%. *Caution:* Harmful if swallowed. Avoid skin contact with solutions. In case of skin contact, wash with soap and water. Avoid breathing dust and spray mist. Avoid contamination of feed and foodstuffs.
   2. Self-propelled sprays. *Caution:* Do not spray on skin or on animals. Wash with soap and water after using. Avoid inhalation of mist. Avoid contamination of feed and foodstuffs. Remove birds, pets, and fishbowls from room being sprayed. Keep out of reach of children.

B. *Parathion* above 2% (except aerosols). *Antidotes: If swallowed.* Give a tablespoonful of salt in a glass of warm water and repeat until vomit fluid is clear. Have victim lie down and keep quiet. Call a Physician Immediately! *If on skin.* In case of contact, remove contaminated clothing and immediately wash skin with soap and water. *Warning:* Poisonous If Swallowed, Inhaled, or Absorbed through Skin! Do not get in eyes, or skin or on clothing. Wear natural rubber gloves, protective clothing and goggles. In case of contact, wash immediately with soap and water. Wear a mask or respirator of a type approved by the U.S. Department of Agriculture for parathion protection. Keep all unprotected persons out of operating areas or vicinity where there may be danger of drift. Vacated areas should not be reentered until drifting insecticide and volatile residues have dissi-

pated. Do not contaminate feed and foodstuffs. Wash hands, arms, and face thoroughly with soap and water before eating or smoking. Wash all contaminated clothing with soap and hot water before use.

6. If all pesticides appeared as indelible colored residues on fruits, grain, and vegetables, what impact do you suppose this would have on:
   a. pesticide use?
   b. public opinion?
   c. product consumption?

7. Go through weekly news periodicals and find some recent examples of contamination of foodstuffs with persistent toxic chemicals. Bring the examples to class and discuss (a) the nature of the contaminant, (b) the source and means of transport of the contaminant, (c) the manner in which the contaminant was discovered, (d) short-term impacts, and (e) potential long-term impacts.

8. Imagine that a chemical company has just invented a chemical that laboratory tests show can kill Mediteranean fruit flies, a citrus fruit pest.
   a. How long will it take to meet government testing requirements?
   b. What tests *must* be done before the chemical can be sold?
   c. What tests do you think *should* be done?
   d. Who should pay for the tests?

As the chemical company employee responsible for marketing that chemical, how will you label it (and in what languages?) How will you package it to ensure adequate shelf life? What factors will you consider in pricing the product? If the need for the chemical is immediate and great, will you maximize the price? Why or why not? What if the need for the chemical is even greater in a poor Third World nation? Now how will you price it?

REFERENCES AND FURTHER READING

References marked with an asterisk are cited in the chapter.

Adkisson, P. L.; Niles, G. A.; Walker, J. K.; Bird, L. S.; and Scott, H. B., (1982). " Controlling Cotton's Insect Pests: A New System", *Science* **216**(4541, April 2): 19–22.

*Ambio, 1978. "WHO Environmental Health Criteria for Polychlorinated Biphenyls and Terphenyls," *Ambio* **7**(1, 1978): 31–32.

American Chemical Society, 1969. *Cleaning Our Environment: The Chemical Basis for Action.* Washington, D.C.: American Chemical Society.

American Chemical Society, 1978. *Cleaning Our Environment: A Chemical Perspective.* Washington, D.C.: American Chemical Society.

Anagnostakis, L., 1982. "Biological Control of Chestnut Blight," *Science* **215**(January 29): 466–471.

Balls, M., Riddell, R., and Worden, A., 1983. *Animals and Alternatives in Toxicity Testing.* New York: Academic Press.

Barrons, K. C., 1981. *Are Pesticides Really Necessary?* Chicago: Regnery Gateway.

Batra, S. W. T., 1982. "Biological Control in Agroecosystems," *Science* **215**(4529, January 8): 134–139.

*Battista, G. S., 1973. "The Conviction of DDT," *Environment Reporter.* Monograph 14, **3**(39): 1–21.

Berardi, G. M., 1983. "Pesticide Use in Italian Food Production," *BioScience.* **33**(8): 502–506.

Biological Sciences Curriculum Study (B.S.C.S.), 1975. *Pesticides: Environmental Resource Papers.* Reading, Mass.: Addison-Wesley. This book includes articles by U.S. Fish and Wildlife Service, R. Chu, P. Lassahn, M. Beroza, and E. F. Knipling.

*Carey, A. E., 1978. "Monitoring Pesticides in Agricultural and Urban Soils of the United States," Presentation at the 11th Congress of the International Society of Soil Science, Edmonton, Alberta, Canada, June 19–27.

*Carson, R., 1962. *Silent Spring.* Boston: Houghton Mifflin.

*Chasan, D. J., 1979. "How Ya Gonna Keep Bugs Down (on the Farm)?" *Smithsonian* **9**(10, January): 78–84.

Cooke, S. F., 1981. "The Clear Lake Example: An Ecological Approach to Pest Management," *Environment* **23**(10): 25–30.

*Council on Environmental Quality, 1977. *Environmental Quality, 1976.* Washington D.C.: U.S. Government Printing Office.

Dahlsten, D. L., 1983. "Pesticides in an Era of Integrated Pest Management," *Environment* **25**:45ff.

*Dorfman, R., 1979. "Pesticides and Food," *Bioscience* **29**, (8): 448.

Dunlap, T. R., 1981. *DDT: Scientists, Citizens and Public Policy.* Princeton, N.J.: Princeton University Press.

Environment Reporter, 1983. "Bio-Test Officials Found Guilty of Falsifying Lab Test Results." **14**(29):1325. Washington, D.C.: Bureau of National Affairs.

*Farid, M. A., 1975. "The World Malaria Situation," paper presented at the UNEP/WHO Meeting on the Bio-environmental Methods of Control of Malaria, Lima, Peru, 10–15 December.

Flint, M. L., and Van den Bosch, R., 1981. *Introduction to Integrated Pest Management.* New York: Plenum Press.

Further Federal Action Needed to Detect and Control Environmental Contamination of Food. Washington, D.C.: General Accounting Office. (CED-81-19; December 31, 1980)

Graham, F., Jr., 1975. *Since Silent Spring.* Boston: Houghton Mifflin.

Grier, J. W., 1982. "Ban of DDT and Subsequent Recovery of Reproduction in Bald Eagles," *Science* **218** (December 17: 1232–1234.

*Henig, R. M., 1979. "Congress Calls for 2,4,5,-T Ban after Dramatic Herbicide Hearing," *Bioscience,* **29**(8): 453–454.

*Huisman, J. W., 1978. "The International Register of Potentially Toxic Chemicals (IRPTC): Its Present State of Development and Future Plans," *Ambio,* **7**(5–6): 275–277.

*Kihlstrom, J. E., and Berglund, E., 1978. "An Estimation of the Amounts of Polychlorinated Biphenyls in the Biomass of the Baltic," *Ambio* **7**(4):175–178.

Kriebel, D., 1981. "The Dioxins: Toxic and Still Troublesome," *Environment* **23**(1, Jan./Feb.):6–13.

Kutz, F. W.; Murphy, R. S.; and Strassman, S. G., 1976. *Estimation of Exposure to Specific Pesticides in the U.S. Population: A National Survey Approach.* Presentation at 104th Annual Meeting of the American Public Health Association, Miami Beach, Fla., October 21. Washington, D.C.: Ecological Monitoring Branch (WH-569). For updated information, write: National Soils Monitoring Program, Technical Services Division, Office of Pesticide Programs, U.S. EPA, WH-569, Washington, D.C. 20460.

*Kutz, F.; Strassman, S.; and Yobs, A., 1977. "Survey of Pesticide Residues and Their Metabolites in the General Population of the United States," paper presented at the International Workshop on Biological Specimen Collection, Luxembourg, April 18–22. Washington, D.C.: Ecological Monitoring Branch, U.S. Environmental Protection Agency.

*Lassahn, P. L., 1975. "The Sublethal Effects of Insecticides," from *Pesticides, B.S.C.S. Environmental Resource Papers.* (Book VI, 14–18.) Reading, Mass.: Addison-Wesley.

Leisner, R. S., and Kormondy, E. J., 1971. *Pollution.* Dubuque, Iowa: William C. Brown. This book contains articles by William A. Niering, Bruce Ingersoll, Thomas Jukes, and Shelia and William Moats.

*Luck, R. R.; Van den Bosch, R.; and Garcia, R., 1977. "Chemical Insect Control: A Troubled Pest Management Strategy," *Bioscience* **27**(9):606–611.

*McEwen, F. L., 1978. "Food Production—The Challenge for Pesticides," *Bioscience,* **28**(12):773–777.

McEwen, F. L., and Stephenson, G. R., 1979. *The Use and Significance of Pesticides in the Environment.* New York: John Wiley & Sons.

Mott, L., 1984. "Bad Apples: Pesticides in Food," *Amicus Journal,* Summer 1984, 34–37.

*Mount, D. I., 1962. *Chronic Effects of Endrin on Bluntnose Minnows and Guppies.* Washington D.C.: U.S. Fish and Wildlife Service.

Nash, R. G., and Woolson, C. A., 1967. "Persistence of Chlorinated Hydrocarbon Insecticides in Soils," *Science* **157**: 924–927.

National Research Council, 1969. *Report of the Committee on Persistent Pesticides.* Washington, D.C.: National Research Council.

*Niering, W. A., 1968. "The Effects of Pesticides," *Bioscience* **9**(9): 869–875.

Perkins, J. H., 1984. *Insects, Experts and the Insecticide Crisis.* New York: Plenum Press.

*Pimentel, D.; Terhune, E. C.; Dritschilo, W.; Gallahan, D.; Kinner, N.; Nafus, D.; Peterson, R.; Zareh, N.; Misiti, J.; and Harber-Schaim, O., 1977. "Pesticides, Insects in Foods, and Cosmetic Standards," *Bioscience* **27**(3): 178–185.

*Pimentel, D.; Krummel, J.; Gallahan, D.; Hough, J.; Merrill, A.; Schreiner, I; Vittum, P.; Koziol, F.; Back, E.; Yen, D.; and Fiance, S., 1978. "Benefits and Costs of Pesticide Use in U.S. Food Production," *Bioscience,* **28**(12):772, 778–784.

*Provost, M. V., 1972. "Environmental Hazards in the Control of Disease Vectors," *Environ. Entom.* **1**:333–339.

Shaikh, R. A., and Nichols, J. K., 1984. "The International Management of Chemicals," *Ambio,* **13**(2):88ff.

*Smith, R. J., 1979. "U.S. Beginning to Act on Banned Pesticides," *Science* **204**:1391–1394.

*Spear, R. C.; Lee, Y.; Leffingwell, J. T.; and Jenkins, D., 1978. "Conversion of Parathion to Paraoxon in Foliar Residues: Effects of Dust Level and Ozone Concentration." *Journal of Agricultural and Food Chemistry.* **26**(2, March/April): 434–436.

*Stevenson, T., 1978. "Often, Pest Control Centers on Finding Good Guy Insects," *The Washington Post,* March.

Strassman, S. C., and Kutz, F. W., 1977. "Insecticide Residues in Human Milk from Arkansas and Mississippi, 1973–74," *Pesticides Monitoring Journal,* **10**(4): 130–133.

*"A Threat to Restore a Hazard," *Louisville Times.* (October 17, 1979)

*U.S. Department of Agriculture, 1975. *That We May Eat: The Yearbook of Agriculture.* Washington, D.C. This is an annual publication.

*U.S. Department of Health, Education, and Welfare, 1969. *Report of the Secretary's Commission on Pesticides and Their Relationship to Environmental Health* (Parts I and II).

U.S. Environmental Protection Agency, 1978. *Pesticide Monitoring: Semi-Annual Report, Number 9, April 1978–September 1978.* Washington, D.C.: Ecological Monitoring Branch.

U.S. Environmental Protection Agency, 1980. *Environmental Outlook 1980.* Washington, D.C.: Office of Research and Development. (EPA 600/8-80-003)

Van den Bosch, R., 1979. "The Pesticide Problem," *Environment* **21**(4):13–16f.

Walsh, J., 1976. "Cosmetic Standards: Are Pesticides Overused for Appearances Sake?" *Science* **27**:744–747.

Ware, G. W., 1982. *Pesticides: Theory and Application.* San Francisco: W.H. Freeman & Co.

*Westöö, G. and Norén, K., 1978. "Organochlorine Contaminants in Human Milk, Stockholm 1967–1977," *Ambio* **7**(2):62–64.

*Woodwell, G. M.; Wurster, C. F.; and Isaacson, P. A., 1967. "DDT Residues in an East Coast Estuary: A Case of Biological Concentration of a Persistent Insecticide," *Science* **156**:821–824.

Human Beings in the System of Nature

In the last few hundred years the power of human beings to alter their environment has increased dramatically. Our population has exploded, and cities like Chicago grow ever larger. Water used by thousands of homes and factories pollutes the lake and destroys fish and wildlife. The exhaust pipes of all the cars and trucks on the busy city streets pump lead and other chemicals into the atmosphere, where it poisons the children who live on those streets and drifts as far away as the Greenland ice cap.

Recently, we have begun to notice the harmful effects of our modern life-style on the natural world. We have taken the first slow, difficult steps to changing our environmentally bad habits. And we have had some successes. Watersheds are being cleaned up. Factories are installing scrubbers on their smokestacks. We are taking the lead out of gasoline. Our goal should not be to return Lake Michigan (and the rest of the world) to its original pristine state, but rather to continue to find ways to live as human beings without disrupting the natural systems upon which we depend. We need both a healthy Chicago and a healthy Lake Michigan.

*T*he Midwestern United States provides homes for millions of people, hosts heavy and light industry, and supplies food for tables around the world. People in the Midwest must meet the needs of their modern life-style without compromising nature.

*T*he industries that we depend upon to manufacture the toys and tools of our modern life have had a tremendous impact upon our mineral, air, and water resources. Factories like this one in Indiana consume enormous amounts of mineral resources and fossil fuels. Through pollution they change the composition of the air and water. The people who work in and live near factories have begun to demand a cleaner environment, but the cost will continue to be high.

*A*griculture is at the heart of the human relationship to the environment. In Ohio, Amish farmers practice small-scale farming using animals and avoiding fossil fuels. In Nebraska, fallow farming, irrigation, and mechanical harvesting allow for efficiencies of scale without waste. Each approach has both benefits and drawbacks.

*C*ities, like factories, require huge amounts of energy and generate tons of waste. Plastics and metals decompose very slowly. We must find ways to safely move the resources trapped in our trash back into the resource stream. With care and planning, our cities can be clean, comfortable places to live.

*P*lanning should also allow for some wilderness to remain. We have an obligation to preserve some of the habitat of all of the living things with which we share this planet. Not only does this enrich our world and the world of those to come after, but we may well depend on the creatures who depend on the habitats we preserve.

What use are satellite images? Besides being fascinating pictures, satellite images can be used to pinpoint different kinds of terrain and to help analyze patterns of use and development in an area. This ERTS photo shows mining operations in Belmont County Ohio in September 1973. The light blue parts are water, green is forestland, red is strip-mined land, brown is reclaimed land, and gold is rangeland.

Cancer: The Ultimate Environmental Insult

The World Health Organization and other sources estimate that up to 95% of all cancer is caused by environmental factors. This may seem to imply that pollutants such as agricultural and industrial chemicals are the culprits, but many other environmental factors—radiation, diet, tobacco smoking, and sunlight included—are largely responsible for the fact that nearly one in three Americans will develop cancer and almost one in five will die of it. Nearly 60 million people now living in the United States will get cancer in their lifetimes; hardly a family will be untouched. If current trends continue, about 40 million Americans now alive will die of cancer; nearly 400,000 die of it each year. This *annual* figure exceeds the total U.S. military deaths in both Korea and Vietnam many times over. The direct cost of cancer care exceeds one half billion dollars annually, and it has been estimated that total direct and indirect costs, including such things as lost earnings, may exceed 25 billion dollars annually. Obviously, cancer is a serious environmental problem. And it is getting worse.

The incidence of cancer has been increasing by about 1% per year for several decades (see Figure 14.1). Some of this can be attributed to gains made against other diseases and the resultant increase in the number of people living long enough to develop cancer; some of the increase can also be attributed to improved detection and diagnosis. There is evidence that much of the increase in cancer is the result of a greater number of environmental causes of cancer (Figure 14.2).

CANCER DEFINED

Cancer cells differ from normal cells in that they divide in an out-of-control fashion, producing tissue disorder; they tend to leave their sites of origin and spread to other parts of the body; and they produce effects on the host that include lowering of immune defenses, fever, disruption of blood coagulation, and weight loss.

A major clue to the nature of cancer is that when cancer cells divide, the daughter cells are also cancer cells. The daughter cells, in turn, pass the transformed traits along to their daughter cells and so on. Thus cancer must have something to do with genes (Chapter 5). Cancer must be a result of some kind of permanent alteration in the genes or in factors that control the expression of genes.

Recently discovered cancer genes, called **oncogenes**, are now believed to be at the root of cancer. Oncogenes are thought to be present in all normal cells, where they serve the normal function of keeping cell division turned on during early stages of development of the organism, after which they are

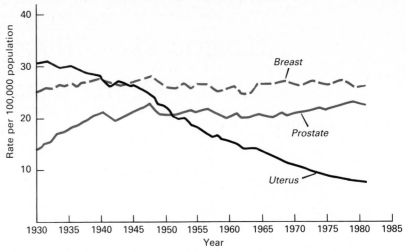

(a) Age-adjusted death rate for cancer of the breast, prostate, and uterus

Figure 14.1 Trends in Cancer Mortality Rates by Site. Much of the increase in cancer mortality in males since 1930 has been due to lung cancer; this trend did not occur in females in the same way with time. However, lung cancer mortality rates for females have recently begun to rise dramatically. Deaths due to stomach cancer and cancer of the uterine cervix have declined significantly since the 1930s.

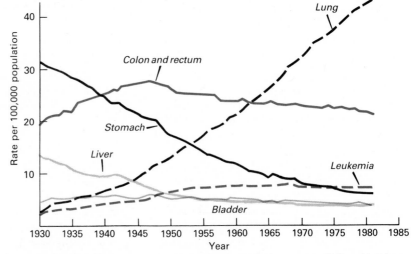

(b) Age-adjusted death rate for leukemia and cancer of the lung, stomach, liver, bladder, colon, and rectum

permanently shut off or turned way down. At least some oncogenes keep cells dividing by means of oncogene products that in various ways mimic the action of natural growth factors that stimulate cell division during processes such as wound repair. According to the **oncogene theory** (see Bishop, 1982; Marx, 1984; Weinberg, 1983), the induction of cancer amounts to inappropriate reactivation or enhanced expression of oncogenes in one or more of several possible ways. Some examples are

1. mutations (Chapter 5) in regulator genes that can then no longer hold oncogenes in check,

2. mutations in oncogenes that enable them to escape control and produce more products,
3. mutations in oncogenes that specify more powerful or possibly more stable oncogene products,
4. the introduction by viruses of uncontrollable oncogenes into what had been normal cells,
5. derangement of control of oncogenes in ways not involving mutations, for example, via chemically or physically induced chromosome breaks that separate oncogenes from genes that control them.

Cancer-causing agents are all of those things that can cause mutations in oncogenes or related

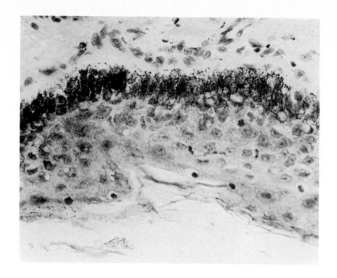

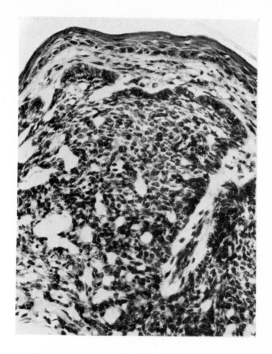

At left is normal heavily pigmented skin (magnified 290x). At right is malignant skin cancer (magnified 180x), showing the disruption of normal patterns by the cancer cells.

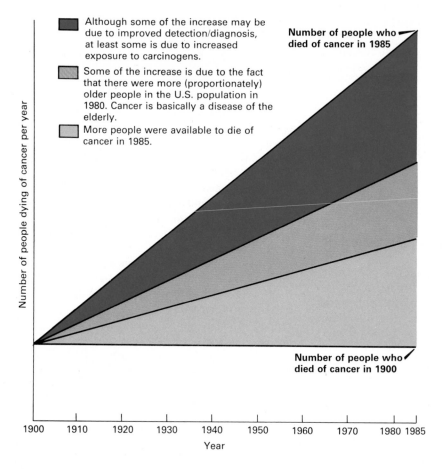

Although some of the increase may be due to improved detection/diagnosis, at least some is due to increased exposure to carcinogens.

Some of the increase is due to the fact that there were more (proportionately) older people in the U.S. population in 1980. Cancer is basically a disease of the elderly.

More people were available to die of cancer in 1985.

Number of people who died of cancer in 1985

Number of people who died of cancer in 1900

Number of people dying of cancer per year

Year

Figure 14.2 Increase of Cancer with Time. This shows cancer mortality in absolute numbers. Some of the increase in cancer that we see today can be accounted for by the fact that there are more people alive today to die of cancer. Also, because cancer is a disease of the old, some of the increase is due to increased life expectancy. Although some of the rest of the increase may be due to improved detection/diagnosis, much of the excessive increase most likely results from an increase in the barrage of environmental insults that cause cancer.

Cancer

Cancer is a family of diseases in which cells (of nearly any tissue) behave as if they were not part of an organized whole organism. Ordinarily, cells in any tissue grow in an orderly fashion and stop dividing and moving when they are surrounded by other cells. Such normal cell-to-cell relationships are missing or greatly reduced in cancer tissue. Cancer cells are in an important sense antisocial; they behave as independent entities dividing and crowding out normal tissue and leaving the site of their origin to travel, become established, and continue dividing in sites remote from where they began. Such remote colonies are referred to as **metastases**.

---

genes or that can cause other gene control problems. There are many such things in the natural environment, and human beings have added many more.

Present theories of **carcinogenesis** (the initiation of cancer) are based on the idea that a number of changes must occur in a cell before it becomes a cancer cell. The increase of cancer with age in human beings probably reflects the fact that the conversion of a normal cell to a cancer cell requires a number of permanent alterations in a cell's genetic makeup (see H. Land, Parada, and Weinberg, 1983). The more time goes by, the greater the likelihood that all the events will have occurred. Similarly, the more carcinogens in the environment, the more likely that the required number of carcinogen-mediated events will occur in a given amount of time.

THE RISE OF ENVIRONMENTAL INSULT

In 1900 the environment was in many ways much simpler than it is today. Since the turn of the century, humans have generated the most significant rise in technology in the history of the world. We are now well into the age of agricultural chemicals, antibiotics and drugs, and "better living" through chemistry. Ironically, the things that we generally consider to have brought about an overall improvement in the quality of life are also partially responsible for a rise in cancer.

For the past 40 years, humans have been exposed to chemicals and chemical combinations that never before appeared on earth. Many of these can alter genetic material or give rise to gene-altering compounds and thus can be responsible for changes that lead to cancer.

THE CAUSES OF CANCER

Three classes of agents can cause cancer and are present in the environment—chemicals, radiation, and viruses. Each of these can interfere with genes by damaging or otherwise altering DNA or by inter-fering with the control of DNA expression. This fits in well with the unified concept that cancer involves genes—through either direct changes in genes or permanent changes in control of genes.

The evidence indicates that chemicals are the biggest part of the cancer/environment problem. Most of this chapter is devoted to chemicals. The rise of nuclear power and atomic testing make it mandatory that we include radiation carcinogenesis as well. For the sake of completeness and because virus-cancer relationships constitute a special kind of interspecies interaction, we also consider viral carcinogenesis.

Viruses and Cancer

One of the most intriguing aspects of cancer being studied today is the involvement of viruses in human cancer. It has been known for nearly a century (Rous, 1910; Ellerman and Bang, 1908) that viruses can cause cancer in animals. For a number of years the search has gone on for a viral agent in *human* cancer. Investigators have looked with their electron microscopes and other tools for viruses that might be associated with certain kinds of cancer. There have been searches for outbreaks of cancer within families and for other cluster patterns that would indicate an infectious agent. These studies have turned up only limited evidence linking human cancer to viruses.

An insurmountable technical problem is that the isolation of a virus from a human neoplasm, even if accomplished on a regular basis, will not prove that the virus actually caused the tumor. Since one cannot ethically inject suspicious viruses into healthy humans to see whether cancers are indeed produced by the viruses, *Koch's postulates* really cannot be tested. In 1884, Robert Koch established postulates for conclusively linking a specific infectious agent to a particular disease. The postulates are: (1) the microbe must be present in every case of the disease; (2) the microbe must be isolated in pure culture; (3) on inoculation from culture into a susceptible host, the microbe must produce the disease with all its symptoms; and (4) the microbe must be isolated again from the experimentally infected organism. Nevertheless, viruses cause literally hundreds of cancers in animals, and since humans are animals, it is highly likely that there are also human cancer viruses.

Even though we cannot perform the ultimate test, several types of viruses have been strongly implicated by circumstantial evidence. These include warts (benign papillomas of the skin), Burkitt's lymphoma (Epstein-Barr virus) (see Figure 14.3), cervical cancer (herpes type II and certain papilloma viruses) (see Rapp, 1978), and hepatocellular cancer (hepatitis B virus) (see Blumberg and London, 1982), and some types of leukemia and lymphoma (see Gallagher and Gallo, 1975; Poiesz et al., 1981; Guroff et al., 1982).

Radiation and Cancer

Before Wilhelm Roentgen discovered X-rays in 1895, human beings were exposed only to the radiation that came from natural sources. Radiation from human activities has increased since 1900, most precipitously since the advent of the atomic bomb and the harnessing of nuclear energy. Human activity now contributes significantly to the radiation pollution of the atmosphere, the hydrosphere, the lithosphere, and—unavoidably—the biosphere.

There are many kinds of ionizing radiation. Different sources produce radiation with different energies and different biological effects. It is beyond the scope of this book to include a detailed discussion of ionizing radiation and its effects on cells and tissues here. Good reviews of this topic exist elsewhere, however (see Scott, Craig, and Iype (1976) and the 1981 report *Problems in Assessing the Cancer Risks of Low Level Ionizing Radiation Exposure* prepared by the U.S. General Accounting Office). Periodicals such as *Radiation Research* and *Current Topics in Radiation Research Quarterly* regularly contain articles on these topics.

For the discussion that follows, it is important to know the following:

1. Ionizing radiation is radiation of sufficient energy to convert uncharged chemicals into charged ion pairs (one negative part and one positive part). This can be very disruptive if the chemicals so affected are in living cells.

2. Ionizing radiation comes from radioactive decay of the nucleus of atoms. There are more than 1000 different **nuclides** (atoms with different total

Figure 14.3 Burkitt's Lymphoma. The fact that Burkitt's lymphoma is common to low parts of central Africa is one of the bits of evidence suggesting that a virus transmitted by mosquitoes inhabiting low marshy areas may be important in causing this type of cancer.

numbers of protons and neutrons in the nucleus); some are stable, and some spontaneously split into parts and give off radiation in the process. The latter are called radioactive nuclides or **radionuclides**. The spontaneous disintegration of the nucleus is termed **radioactive decay**.

3. All nuclides that have the same number of protons (and therefore are forms of the same element) but different numbers of neutrons are called **isotopes** of one another. Isotopes are not equally stable; those that undergo spontaneous fission are called radioactive isotopes or **radioisotopes**. For example, iodine-131 is a radioisotope of nonradioactive iodine.

On the sun, atomic fission, atomic fusion (Chapter 6), and other processes give off all types of electromagnetic radiation including both ionizing and nonionizing forms (Chapter 2). Fortunately, little harmful radiation reaches the earth's surface; most of what does reach the earth is absorbed in the upper atmosphere (Chapters 2 and 9). Two exceptions are gamma radiation, which can be a problem for crews of high-altitude, supersonic jets (Waldbott, 1978), and ultraviolet radiation. The relationship between ultraviolet rays and skin cancer is now well documented (Elwood et al., 1974; Blum,

Viruses

Viruses are very small. Thousands of them could be stuffed into a bacterial cell. Depending on one's definition, viruses may be considered to be the simplest of living things or nonliving complex chemicals. Viruses can be crystallized and reconstituted like chemicals. They consist only of a protein coat surrounding one strand of nucleic acid. However, if viruses are provided with a living cell that the virus can infect, the viral nucleic acid enters and controls the host cell's metabolic machinery, causing the cell to make more viruses. The cell then releases new infective viruses. Because this is the only way that viruses can reproduce, they technically fail to demonstrate one of the key characteristics of life—the ability to reproduce sexually or asexually. Viruses must have the cell of another organism in order to reproduce.

Viruses are usually able to infect only certain kinds of cells. Many viruses are species specific.

One of the mysteries about viruses is that their infection may be latent; the nucleic acid that comes into a host cell sometimes simply becomes incorporated into the host's own genetic material. This viral genetic material would then be replicated each time the host cell divides, and all progeny cells would also contain the latent viral genetic material. This material may later cause the cell to begin making viruses. It may also be that the viral gene is somehow able to cause a normal cell to begin to behave like a cancer cell. In this respect, viruses may interfere with host genetic material in the same (or similar) way that certain chemicals can react with DNA to produce a malignant transformation.

1976); it is an important part of the natural cancer-environment problem.

Radioisotopes like radium-228 and uranium-238 occur naturally and can be purified from ores. Other natural sources of radiation (e.g., radon-222 and thorium-220) can be released from soil, from rocks, and from coal when it is burned (Waldbott, 1978). Certain kinds of useful radioisotopes can be made in **cyclotrons** (devices in which a nuclide can be made from larger nuclides by bombarding them with high-speed charged particles).

Most of the radiation received by the general population comes from medical uses of radiation and from natural background radiation (see Table 6.11). Most radioactive pollution comes from atomic testing. This source has added 15% to natural radiation worldwide since the 1940s. Among the nuclides produced and released into the atmosphere in atomic explosions are cesium-137, iodine-131, and strontium-90 (Table 14.1).

While the greatest potential for pollution from nuclear reactors is the accident, perhaps the greatest practical problem related to atomic power is in the reprocessing of spent reactor fuel and the disposal of low-level and high-level radioactive wastes (Chapters 6 and 15). Normally, negligible amounts of radioactivity are produced by activation of non-radioactive substances present in the cooling water in nuclear reactors.

Some of the artificial (human-made) radionuclides used diagnostically in medicine and as tracers in research end up in sewage and in water supplies (because of illegal disposal and because of leaching from supposedly secure landfills). From water they can be transmitted to humans directly or through the food chain.

Biochemistry of Radionuclides. Radioactive isotopes of carbon, hydrogen, iodine, phosphorus, and other elements behave chemically exactly like their

---

Table 14.1   Some Important Radionuclides and Their Half Lives.

Radionuclide	Target Tissue	Half-Life
Calcium-45	bone	165 days
Carbon-14	whole body	5760 years
Cesium-137	soft tissues, genital organs	27 years
Iodine-129	thyroid	17 million years
Iodine-131	thyroid	8 days
Plutonium-239	bone, liver, spleen	24,400 years
Radium-226	bone	1620 years
Strontium-90	bone	28 years
Tritium (^{3}H)	whole body	12.3 years

Alpha particle: a positively charged particle emitted by certain radioactive substances, consisting of two protons and two neutrons. Because of their mass, alpha particles are not very penetrating.

Antibody: a protein produced by an animal's immune system in response to a specific antigen (normally a foreign protein). Such antibodies then are able to combine with the antigen, helping to neutralize it.

Antigen: any substance capable of stimulating the formation of an antibody.

Benign neoplasm: neoplasm that does not spread to other sites and that will cause death only rarely.

Beta particle: a particle, equal in mass to an electron, emitted by the nuclei of certain radioactive substances.

Burkitt's lymphoma: a lymphoma of the jaw endemic to Central Africa, first described by Dennis Burkitt.

Cancer: synonym for malignant neoplasm.

Carcinogen: an agent that can initiate the development of a malignant neoplasm.

Carcinoma: a malignant neoplasm originating in any epithelial cell.

Gamma ray: a ray similar to an X-ray but with a shorter wavelength; these very pentrating rays are emitted in the decay of certain radioactive substances.

Host: the organism infected by a disease-causing organism.

Initiator: an agent that can convert a normal cell into a cancer cell; *initiation* is the first step of a process of cancer induction. All carcinogens are initiators (see *promoter*).

Lymphoma: malignant neoplasm of certain kinds of cells of the lymphatic system.

Malignant neoplasm: a neoplasm of uncontrolled character that has some possibility of spreading and that usually will eventually kill the host.

Mesothelioma: a malignant neoplasm arising from cells of mesodermal origin in the chest or abdominal cavity.

Neoplasm: literally, new growth; a mass of cells produced by abnormal cell division.

Promoter: an agent that cannot initiate a cancer but that can push it along by inducing cell division once cancer has been initiated. Promotion is the second step in the process that leads to the expression of some cancers (see *initiator*).

Proximate carcinogen: a chemical that can be metabolically converted into an active carcinogen.

Sarcoma: a malignant neoplasm originating in any mesodermal cell.

Tracer: any readily detectable substance that can be attached to a compound, allowing the compound to be traced or followed as in synthesis or metabolism. Example: radioactive sulfur (^{35}S) could be introduced into an organism to monitor the rate of synthesis of sulfur-containing compounds.

Tumor: any abnormal swelling or lump; this is a nonspecific term that is *not* synonymous with cancer or neoplasm.

Ultimate carcinogen: a carcinogenic agent derived by metabolic activation from a proximate carcinogen through one or more steps.

---

stable counterparts. Radioactive nuclides end up in tissue wherever their nonradioactive isotopes would end up. Carbon is a constituent of all organic molecules by definition and is present in all tissues and organs. Carbon-14, a radioactive isotope of carbon-12, also distributes itself relatively uniformly throughout any living organism. The same would be true of hydrogen and its radioisotope. Radioactive iodine-131 is concentrated in the thyroid gland because the thyroid normally concentrates iodine. Strontium 90 concentrates in bone because strontium is chemically very similar to calcium and mimics that element. Some of the more important radionuclides and their half-lives are listed in Table 14.1.

The Cancer Connection. The experience of painters of watch dials early in this century established the relationship between radium and bone cancer in humans. So that our grandparents could see their watches in the dark, painters were employed in watch factories to dab radium-containing, glow-in-the-dark pigments on the hands of watches.

Imagine them using their lips to bring the tips of their tiny, radium-contaminated brushes to fine points. In this and other ways the painters absorbed radium, which lodged in their bones. Years later, a significant number of watch dial painters—many of them long since retired from watch painting—developed **osteogenic sarcoma**, a form of bone cancer.

The story of the watch dial painters raises the important point that there are two distinctly different ways of getting radiated. One is to be hit by rays that come from some *external* source. The other is to be hit by rays emitted from some *internal* source—a radioactive isotope that is breathed in, eaten, or absorbed through the skin.

Tumors found in animal studies to be caused by bone-seeking radionuclides include *osteosarcoma* (arising from the cells lining the bone surface), *fibrosarcoma* (tumors characterized by the proliferation of connective tissue cells and collagen synthesis), *chondrosarcoma* (tumors of cartilage), *lymphoma* (arising from blood-forming elements of

---

bone marrow), carcinoma of the sinuses (tumors of the soft tissues of the skull), and *reticulum cell sarcoma* (arising from cells in the bone marrow (Vaughn, 1976). Radium-226 and radium-224 have been linked to the same kinds of tumors in humans (Vaughn, 1976).

Other radiation-related tumors have been reported in humans. These include cancers that have resulted from the radiation produced by the atomic bombs dropped on Hiroshima and Nagasaki in 1945 and some that have resulted from occupational exposure. Some of the important radionuclides that cause damage to health are listed in Table 14.1.

Hiroshima and Nagasaki. An Atomic Bomb Casualty Commission was set up in 1947 to study the late effects of radiation exposure on the people of Hiroshima and Nagasaki. Studies to date have revealed an increased frequency of several cancers in these populations, including leukemia, thyroid cancer, breast cancer, and lung cancer.

Thyroid Cancer. It became evident in the 1950s that thyroid cancers developed in some children who had received therapeutic radiation to the neck in infancy (Pochin, 1976). Thyroid tumors also may be environmentally important because thyroid-seeking radioiodine is a byproduct of nuclear fission and is present in fallout occurring after atomic tests (Pochin, 1976). Radioactive isotopes of iodine are also used in a number of diagnostic and therapeutic procedures in medicine.

Uranium Mining. Nearly a third of the deaths that occur in uranium miners are due to cancer of the lung (Epstein, 1976). Presumably, this is mainly a result of cigarette smoking compounded by inhalation of radioactive uranium and other radioisotopes.

Low-Level, Long-Term Exposure. In 1943, Hanford Works, an atomic plant in Richland, Washington, began to monitor its workers. In a 1977 report, Mancuso, Stewart, and Kneale compared the long-term radiation exposure of the workers with the causes of death reported on their death certificates. The results indicated that the plant workers receiving exposure rates *below* the annual dosage established as safe by the federal government had more than double the normal expectancy of certain types of cancer.

However, this study and its methodologies have been the subject of some controversy. The reader is referred to the report *Problem in Assessing the Cancer Risk of Low Level Ionizing Radiation Exposure*, prepared by the U.S. General Accounting Office (1981). As of now, there really has been no generally accepted definitive study of the impact on humans of long-term, low-level exposure to radiation. Data gathering continues as the U.S. government tries to prescribe standards for exposure well within an acceptable risk level. Summaries of 52 studies involving humans are presented in the GAO report just cited.

The reasons for the disagreement over the risks from low doses of ionizing radiation are nicely summarized by Charles Land (1980), a statistician with the Environmental Epidemiology Branch of the National Cancer Institute:

> First, precise direct estimation of small risks requires impracticably large samples. Second, precise estimates of low dose risks based largely on high-dose data . . . must depend heavily on assumptions about the slope of the dose-response curve, even when only a few of the parameters of the theoretical form of the curve are known.

The reader is referred to Figure 14.9.

Biological Magnification of Radionuclides. Generally, when radionuclides are released into the environment, they are dispersed. We say "generally" because there are radioactive waste disposal sites where high concentrations are accumulated. Biologically, as we have seen with iodine-131 and the bone-seeking radionuclides, radioactive substances can become concentrated in particular organs, reversing the tendency toward dilution. Radionuclides can also become concentrated in food chain transfers.

Chemicals and Cancer

Because both naturally occurring and human-made chemicals are the major cause of cancer in humans, most of the rest of this chapter is devoted to them. In the next section we will summarize the kinds of chemicals that are known to cause tumors in animals and in humans. In later sections we will review what is known about human cancer and the chemicals we encounter where we live, where we work, and in what we eat and drink. Later in the chapter we will review some of the reasons why it is so difficult to determine the relationship between cancer and chemicals—why, for instance, of 1400 chemicals suspected of causing human cancer, we are relatively sure of only about 30.

Table 14.2 lists the major specific chemical carcinogens, chemical mixtures, and classes of chem-

Table 14.2   Major Known or Suspected Human Chemical Carcinogens

Chemical or Industrial Process	Main Type of Exposure[a]	Target Organs in Humans	Main Source of Exposure[b]
4-Aminobiphenyl	Occupational	Bladder	Inhalation, skin, oral
Arsenic compounds	Occupational, medicinal, environmental	Skin, lung, liver[c]	Inhalation, skin, oral
Asbestos	Occupational	Lung, pleural cavity, G.I. tract	Inhalation, oral
Auramine manufacturing	Occupational	Bladder	Inhalation, skin, oral
Benzene	Occupational	Hemopoietic system (blood cell forming)	Inhalation, skin
Benzidine	Occupational	Bladder	Inhalation, skin, oral
Bis (chloromethyl)-ether	Occupational	Lung	Inhalation
Cadmium-using industries (possibly cadmium oxides)	Occupational	Prostate, lung	Inhalation, oral
Chloramphenicol	Medicinal	Hemopoietic system	Oral, injection
Chloromethyl ether (possibly associated with bis(chloromethyl) ether	Occupational	Lung	Inhalation
Chromate-producing industries	Occupational	Lung, nasal cavities[c]	Inhalation
Cyclophosphamide	Medicinal	Bladder	Oral, injection
Diethylstilbesterol (DES)	Medicinal	Uterus, vagina	Oral
Hematite mining	Occupational	Nasal cavity, larynx	Inhalation
Isopropyl oil	Occupational	Nasal cavity, larynx	Inhalation
Melphalan	Medicinal	Hemopoietic system	Oral, injection
Mustard gas	Occupational	Lung, larynx	Inhalation
2-Napthylamine	Occupational	Bladder	Inhalation, skin, oral
Nickel refining	Occupational	Nasal cavity, lung	Inhalation
N, N-bis (2-chloroethyl)-2-naphthylamine (chlornaphazine)	Medicinal	Bladder	Oral
Oxymetholone	Medicinal	Liver	Oral
Phenacetin	Medicinal	Kidney	Oral
Phenytoin	Medicinal	Lymphoreticular tissues	Oral, injection
Soot, tars, and oils	Occupational, environmental	Lung, skin, scrotum	Inhalation, skin
Vinyl chloride	Occupational	Liver, brain[c], lung[c]	Inhalation, skin

a. The main types of exposure mentioned are those by which the association has been demonstrated.
b. The main routes of exposure given may not be the only ones by which such effects could occur.
c. Denotes indicative evidence.

ical carcinogens that have been linked to cancer in humans or are strongly suspected of being linked. The first purified chemical carcinogens were *polycyclic hydrocarbons*. It has since been determined that most polycyclic hydrocarbons are noncarcinogenic. Those that are carcinogens include derivatives of benzene and anthracene and various products of fossil fuel combustion. Unfortunate experiences with bladder cancer in the dye industry established that a number of azo dyes and other *aromatic amines* were carcinogenic. *Nitrosamines* are well-established carcinogens, having been shown to produce cancer in dogs, monkeys, parakeets, rats, mice, hamsters, guinea pigs, and rainbow trout (Shapley, 1976). A number of miscellaneous organic compounds, including the pesticides DDT, dieldrin, chlordane, aldrin, endrin, heptachlor, and chlorodecone (kepone), and the artificial sweeteners saccharine and cyclamates, are capable of causing tumors in animals. Vinyl chloride, estrogens, and (ironically) certain anticancer drugs are all strongly implicated in human cancer. A number of metals—some of which are essential nutrients in small amounts—and other inorganic compounds have also been implicated in human lung and skin cancer. These include arsenic, chromates, asbestos, beryllium, nickel compounds, and cobalt. Rounding out the list of kinds of carcinogens are a number of *natural products* including the aflatoxins produced by the mold *Aspergillus flavus,* certain plant alkaloids, and saffrole, an extract of sassafras bark (Table 14.3).

A quick glance at the kinds of tumors produced in humans by the agents listed in Tables 14.2 and 14.3 reveals that the skin and lungs—the places where humans are in direct contact with the environment—and the organs of excretion and detoxification are common sites of environmental cancers.

EPIDEMIOLOGY OF HUMAN CANCER

A lot—maybe most—of what we know about the relationship between environmental factors and cancer has come from epidemiology (Chapter 10). In humans, long-term exposure to pure carcinogens rarely occurs. Epidemiology can help sort out the major factors related to carcinogenesis from a complex combination of factors.

Patterns of Cancer Mortality Worldwide

The estimate that 90–95% of all cancers are environmentally related is based on epidemiologic data for cancer worldwide. There are great differences in the kinds of cancer that predominate from country to country. There is good evidence (from observations of immigrants) that these patterns are related to environmental differences rather than genetic differences. Theoretically, if the mortality rate for each specific cancer could be reduced worldwide to the level found in the country in which it is presently *lowest*—by making some appropriate environmental change—cancer mortality could be reduced tenfold.

Japan has the highest death rate for stomach cancer and among the lowest for lung cancer. Nearly the reverse is true for U.S. whites. There are fourfold differences in mortality due to uterine cancer worldwide; U.S. whites and nonwhites are almost at opposite ends of the spectrum. These and other observations indicate that America is apparently *not* the land of equal opportunity when it comes to cancer (see Figure 14.4).

The Patterns of Cancer Mortality in the United States

The importance of the environment is also suggested by the distribution of cancers of various types throughout the United States. The U.S. Department of Health, Education and Welfare has published an extensive series of maps (two of which are included as Figures 14.5 and 14.6) in which the mortality due to various types of cancer has been presented by county or economic subunits of the states. Among the more notable observations that can be made from these maps are the following:

Table 14.3 Natural Products Associated with Cancers in Humans

Carcinogen	Source	Target organ
Aflatoxins	*Aspergillus flavus* (a mold)	liver, kidney
Alkaloids	plants	liver (suspect)
Cycasin	plants	liver, kidney
Saffrole	plants (sassafras)	liver
Tobacco smoke products	cigarettes, pipe, cigars	lung, bladder, mouth esophagus, pharynx, larynx

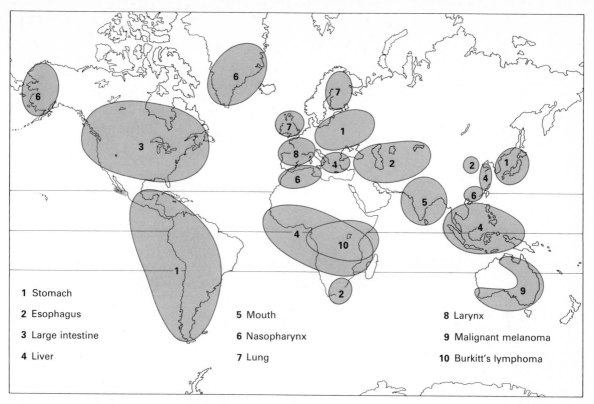

Figure 14.4 Cancer Hotspots Around the World.

1 Stomach

2 Esophagus

3 Large intestine

4 Liver

5 Mouth

6 Nasopharynx

7 Lung

8 Larynx

9 Malignant melanoma

10 Burkitt's lymphoma

Figure 14.5 Significantly High Cancer Mortality, 1950–1969 by County, White Males. Cancer death rates for males in the Northeast, in older eastern and midwestern cities, and along the Gulf Coast were so much higher than elsewhere that rates in most U.S. counties are statistically significantly below average.

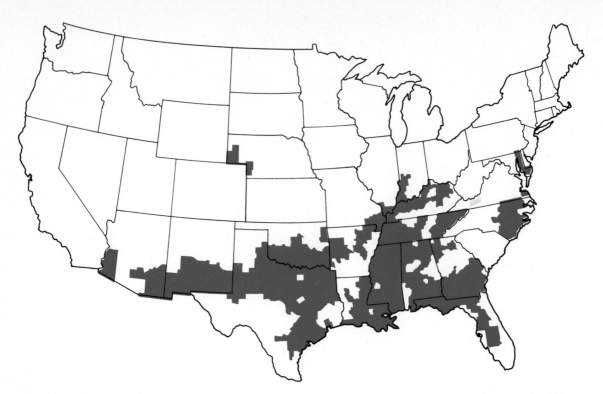

Figure 14.6   Significantly High Cancer Death Rates, 1950–1969, by U. S. Economic Area for Skin Cancer

Other Than Malignant Melanoma, White Males. This gives a different kind of meaning to the term "sunny South."

1. The mortality due to cancer of all types is extremely high in the Northeast—the most heavily industrialized and most heavily populated part of the country (Figure 14.5).
2. In this same map showing mortality for the period 1950–1969 for all sites combined in white males, it is evident that cities present an especially high risk of cancer; nearly all of the major old cities, particularly those of the eastern United States, stand out in the map as having cancer mortality in the highest decile.
3. The Northeast has a high death rate for cancer of the female breast.
4. Cancer of the cervix yields a particularly high mortality pattern in Appalachia.
5. Figure 14.6 illustrates the effect of a natural environmental carcinogenic agent—sunlight. Skin cancer (including malignant melanoma) mortality is particularly high in the Sunbelt states.
6. Stomach cancer mortality is high in certain states of the upper Midwest. It has been suggested that mortality for stomach cancer there closely matches the rate found in the countries from which the people of the Upper Midwest migrated. Cultural habits that have persisted—such as

diet—might account for the high rate of stomach cancer there (Mason et al., 1975).

The fact that there are unusually strong patterns for some types of cancer is highlighted by the observation that for some other cancers—pancreatic cancer, for example—there appears to be no unusual distribution pattern. An average amount of pancreatic cancer is found just about everywhere in the United States.

Heredity or Environment?

Cancer is obviously a product of the interaction of the host and the environment. However, epidemiologic observations of the sort we have just considered indicate that in general the environment is a much more important contributor to cancer than is heredity. Considerable support for this comes from cancer data for immigrants and their children. The children of immigrants have death rates from cancer that match those prevailing in the country to which their parents have immigrated. Those who do the immigrating, however, get cancer at rates prevailing in their homeland.

In one study it was shown that people born in

Israel, whether they were Jewish or not, had about the same **cancer mortality** (cancer deaths per 100,000 population). Jewish and non-Jewish Israelis living in Israel who were born in Europe or the United States had stomach cancer mortality equivalent to that in Europe or the United States. These immigrants to Israel apparently carried with them the effects of the environmental exposures in the countries from which they emigrated.

A study of immigrants to California from Japan revealed that over successive generations the incidence of several different kinds of cancer gradually approached the incidences of those kinds of cancer in California (Figure 14.7). The transition required several generations, perhaps because it takes that long for a family of immigrants to fall completely under the influence of a new environment (Cairns, 1975). It would obviously take a few years for Japanese immigrants to be influenced by those parts of the environment that are cultural in origin—diet, for instance.

Most kinds of cancer that have been observed in experimental animals have had different effects on different species and even on different strains of one species. We should expect that this same sort of thing will be found in human beings; there may be certain physiological types that have a higher risk than the population at large of developing certain kinds of cancer. There is evidence of a familial risk of developing cancer of the breast, stomach, large intestine, lining of the uterus, prostate, lung, and possibly ovary. It is not possible to completely separate the genetic factors from environmental factors, however. Families tend to be exposed to the same environment as well as to carry common genetic characters. So the question of the relative importance of genetics in cancer is still somewhat open.

Urban Cancer: The Mystery of Increased Cancer Among City Dwellers

Cancer is an urban disease in many respects. Figure 14.5 shows that many major cities have had significantly high mortality associated with all types of cancer combined. The differential between cities and rural areas seems to be especially striking for

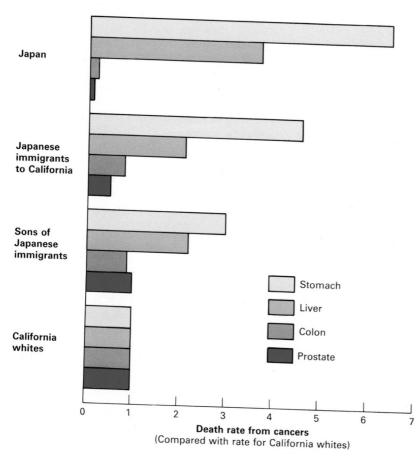

Figure 14.7 Incidences of Various Cancers in Japanese, Californians, and Immigrants from Japan to California. The death rates for stomach, liver, colon, and prostate cancer in California white males are normalized here to one so that the rest of the figure can be read as a multiple or fraction of one. The gradual shift to California rates of death from cancer following immigration suggests both that the environment, not heredity, is most important here and that persistent cultural habits may be important in cancer.

(Chart legend and axes:)

Japan

Japanese immigrants to California

Sons of Japanese immigrants

California whites

Legend:
- Stomach
- Liver
- Colon
- Prostate

Death rate from cancers
(Compared with rate for California whites)

Chapter 14 Cancer: The Ultimate Environmental Insult

certain kinds of cancer. For instance, the incidence of cancer of the lower digestive tract in urban areas of the United States is nearly twice as high as it is in rural areas; the overall incidence for U.S. cities is about ten times greater than it is in Uganda, a relatively rural country (Commoner, 1975). Lung cancer is another example. People who move from the country to the city tend to have higher lung cancer rates than those who stay in rural areas. The presence and concentrations of certain pollutants in cities is undoubtedly at the heart of this urban/rural differential, most likely because air pollutants act synergistically with cigarette smoke.

In a study reported in the *British Journal of Cancer* (Stocks, 1960) the concentration of hydrocarbons in the air over certain cities in England was highly correlated with lung cancer, even after social factors were considered. In the same study, lung cancer mortality was found to be correlated with atmospheric smoke density in more than 25 areas in northern England and Wales. Cancer of the stomach was also related to smoke in various boroughs. The hydrocarbon benzo[a]pyrene was implicated as a prime suspect.

Nitrosamines are also prime suspects in urban cancer. Nitrosamines come from a great variety of sources and can be found almost everywhere in the urban environment. Nitrous oxide and nitrogen dioxide can combine with water to form nitrous acid, which can then combine with amines under certain conditions to form nitrosamines. Such a reaction might account for the statistical correlation between nitrogen dioxide and cancer in urban areas (Shapley, 1976).

The causes of urban cancer probably extend to greater uses of tobacco and alcohol among city dwellers. Stress, which has been shown to be an important immune system suppressor, may also be a factor here.

Overall, there are many potentially cancer-related differences between city dwellers and rural residents. There are industrial pollutants in the air, and they occur in pockets of exotic and intense combinations. City dwellers take in between 500 and 1000 liters of city air every day. City dwellers might also be drinking water that is less pure or that in some cases is contaminated from various sources like cities upstream. Urban cancer is even more of a complex problem than occupational cancer, which we will take up next. Obviously, it should be easier to identify and control cancer-causing agents at their sources. Even so, occupational cancer is emerging as a major problem.

Occupational Cancer

The first connection between an occupational exposure and a cancer was made more than 200 years ago when Percival Pott described the occurrence of testicular cancer in chimney sweeps. Since then, many epidemiologic studies have indicated that occupational factors are important in the **etiology** (cause) of cancer (Table 14.4). Some of the cancers prevalent in the Northeast, for instance, have been significantly high in men but not in women; this finding strongly suggests that the exposure occurs at the workplace (Mason et al., 1975). Changing working patterns for men and women may eventually alter this disparity.

Although only a few specific chemical agents have been implicated in occupational cancer, various estimates indicate that up to 38% of all cancer deaths in males may one day be occupational in origin (Epstein, 1976). Occupational cancers now include lung cancer and pleural mesotheliomas (a cancer of the lining of the thoracic cavity between the lungs and the chest wall) in insulation workers and others exposed to asbestos; bladder cancer in aniline dye workers; a number of cancers in rubber industry workers exposed to such chemicals as 2-napthylamine, benzidine, and certain nitrosamines (Mancuso and Brennan, 1970); lung cancer in coke oven workers; skin cancer in cutting oil workers; nasal sinus cancer in woodworkers; cancer of the pancreas and lymphomas in organic chemists; and angiosarcoma of the liver and perhaps brain cancer in workers in the polyvinyl chloride manufacturing industry (Epstein, 1976).

About half of long-term asbestos workers die of cancer. Reflecting the complexity of carcinogenesis and the importance of cofactors is the fact that the specific risk to lung cancer has *not* been shown to be significantly increased among nonsmoking asbestos workers. A study by Selikoff, Hammond, and Churg (1968) showed that workers who did smoke had a far greater risk of developing lung cancer than those who smoked cigarettes but did not work with asbestos. Asbestos workers who smoke, according to the study, have nearly 100 times more risk of a death from lung cancer than an age-matched individual who neither smoked nor worked with asbestos. Asbestos workers who did not smoke had no greater risk that the normal population, a finding that indicates a strong synergistic effect of tobacco smoking and exposure to asbestos.

Another kind of cancer associated with exposure to asbestos—mesothelioma—exhibits no such

Table 14.4 Some Common Occupational Carcinogens

Agent	Organ Affected	Occupation
Wood	Nasal cavity and sinuses	Woodworkers
Leather	Nasal cavity and sinuses, urinary bladder	Leather workers
Iron oxide	Lung, larynx	Iron ore miners; metal grinders and polishers silver finishers; iron foundry workers
Nickel	Nasal sinuses, lung	Nickel smelters, mixers, and roasters; electrolysis workers
Arsenic	Skin, lung, liver	Miners; smelters; insecticide makers and sprayers; tanners; chemical workers; oil refiners
Chromium	Nasal cavity and sinuses, lung, larynx	Chromium producers, processers, and users; acetylene and aniline workers; bleachers; glass, pottery, and linoleum workers; battery makers
Asbestos	Lung (pleural and peritoneal mesothelioma)	Miners; millers; textile, insulation, and shipyard workers
Petroleum, petroleum coke, wax, creosote, anthracene, paraffin, shale, and mineral oils	Nasal cavity, larynx, lung, skin, scrotum	Contact with lubricating, cooling, paraffin or wax fuel oils or coke
Vinyl chloride	Liver, brain	Plastic workers
Coal soot, coal tar, other products of coal combustion	Lung, larynx, skin, scrotum, urinary bladder	Gashouse workers, stokers, and producers; asphalt, coal tar, and pitch workers; coke oven workers; miners; still cleaners
Benzene	Bone marrow	Explosives, benzene, or rubber cement workers; distillers; dye users; painters; shoemakers
Auramine, benzidine, alpha-Naphthylamine, beta-Naphthylamine, magenta, 4-Aminodiphenyl, 4-Nitrodiphenyl	Urinary bladder	Dyestuffs manufacturers and users; rubber workers (pressmen, filtermen, laborers); textile dyers; paint manufacturers

relationship; that is, the increased risk of developing this rare cancer is equally great in smokers and non-smokers and may be a risk even to members of the families of asbestos workers (Selikoff, 1975; Nicholson, 1977).

Lung cancer is also an occupational hazard in some other manufacturing and mining industries. About a third of the deaths among uranium workers are attributed to cancer of the lung (Epstein, 1976). Lung cancer also occurs with high frequency in occupational exposure to talc, chromates, arsenic, nickel-carbonyl, fluorspar, and beta-chloromethyl-ether. The frequency of lung cancer is about 15 times higher among coke oven workers than among non-coke oven workers (Schneider, 1975).

Vinyl chloride is an interesting occupational carcinogen for two reasons. First, vinyl chloride is a very simple molecule unlike nearly all other carcinogens, and it is apparently an example of a carcinogen

that must first be metabolically activated (Elmore et al., 1976). Second, the carcinogenic potential of vinyl chloride was recognized in humans and in animals almost simultaneously. Viola (1970; see also Viola, Bigotti, and Caputo, 1971) first reported the relationship between vinyl chloride and cancer in animals. Maltoni and Lefenine (1975) have since presented some data with differential and low doses of vinyl chloride and cancer in experimental animals. About the same time Maltoni's experiments were being completed, Creech and Johnson (1974) reported three cases of angiosarcoma of the liver among a group of workers at B.F. Goodrich Company's polyvinyl chloride–manufacturing plant in Louisville, Kentucky. Although vinyl chloride causes a number of kinds of tumors in animals, its main effect on humans seems to be the initiation of rare hepatic angiosarcoma (a vascular tumor believed to be the result of carcinogenic transformation

Asbestos fibers may be trapped in the lungs of people who work with asbestos. There is a strong correlation between asbestos and cancer, particularly in smokers.

of endothelial cells lining the sinuses in the liver). It was only because of the rarity of angiosarcoma that the relationship between this disease and vinyl chloride was discovered in humans. Had vinyl chloride caused a common cancer like lung cancer in the same numbers, the relationship would likely never have been discovered. Other examples of rare tumors associated with occupation include cancer of the scrotum in chimney sweeps and tumors of the sinuses among wood workers (Acheson, Cowdell, and Rang, 1972).

Various estimates indicate that 5–15% of current cancer deaths in males may be occupational in origin. In addition to this direct problem, industrial settings are obviously important in linking environment to cancer in humans because these settings provide relatively controlled, though inadvertent, exposure of human beings to potential carcinogens. Workers are intimately exposed to relatively high concentrations of the very same agents to which the general population is exposed at lower concentrations. Although the overall problem of occupational cancer may be relatively small, evaluation of the experiences of occupational groups should provide valuable information and allow us to identify suspected cancer agents in the general environment.

Diet, Food Additives, and Drugs

Another important part of our environment is what we eat and drink, and cancer has been linked to the overall quality of diet. There is an association between some cancers (e.g., breast and colon) and fat intake and obesity (Hill et al., 1977; Lowenfels

and Anderson, 1977). This is probably related to fat's ability to affect certain hormones that may be cancer **promoters** (substances that accelerate the development of tumors). Worldwide, overall cancer mortality by country correlates directly with red meat consumption (Figure 14.8). Countries that consume more meat have more cancer. It is not known, however, whether this is due to the meat itself, to something in the meat, or to the fact that when one eats meat, one eats less cereal or plant material. There may be other factors that parallel meat and cereal consumption patterns that are really responsible for this correlation.

Food additives also have an environmental cancer connection. Food additives are chemicals added to food to enhance color or to preserve it. Such items fall under a clause of the 1958 Pure Food, Drug, and Cosmetic Act. The clause, usually referred to as the **Delaney Amendment** (because it was sponsored by Representative James J. Delaney of New York), specifically bans the use of any food additive found to cause cancer when eaten by humans or animals or when subjected to any other test appropriate for evaluating the safety of food additives. The clause has been used in recent years in the banning of such things as cyclamates and saccharin, saffrole (root beer flavoring), diethylstilbesterol (DES, an estrogenlike dietary substance fed to livestock to accelerate meat production), and red dye No. 2. All of these produced excess numbers of cancers in experimental animals.

The Delaney Amendment is controversial because it admits no threshold level. It is based on the assumption that there is no low level of any carcinogenic substance that is completely harmless when in food or drink. Sometimes this produces results that are difficult for the general public to understand. The study on which the banning of saccharin was originally based, for instance, involved feeding about 100 rats a diet of 5% pure saccharin from the time they were born until they died. Fourteen of these rats developed bladder cancer compared with only two such animals in a group of 100 animals given no saccharin. Although a human being would have to drink several hundred 12-ounce diet sodas a day for life to accumulate an equivalent dose, strict application of the Delaney Amendment called for the removal of saccharin from the consumer market.

The banning of saccharin offers a particularly poignant example of the complexity of our society and the difficulty of regulating carcinogens in the environment. If there is indeed a relationship between obesity and cancer, if the banning of saccharin

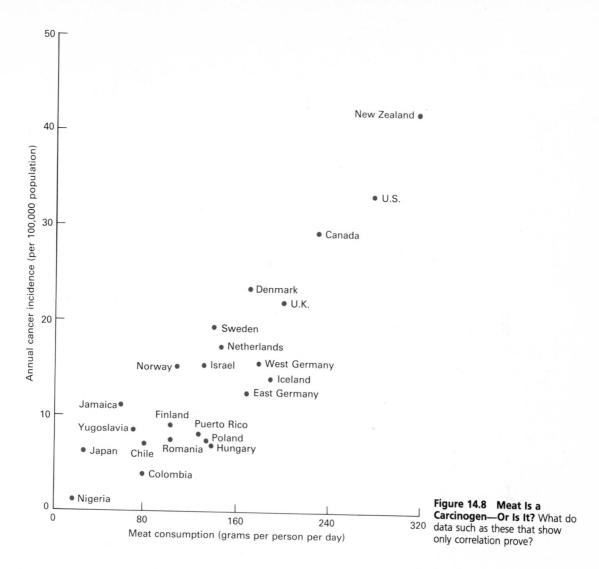

Figure 14.8 Meat Is a Carcinogen—Or Is It? What do data such as these that show only correlation prove?

results in a return to natural sweeteners like sugar, and if this produces in some people a weight increase that predisposes them to certain fat-related cancers, the banning of saccharin might produce more cancers than would have been produced if saccharin were left on the market—if, of course, saccharin would indeed cause tumors in human beings.

It must be pointed out that there is no scientific evidence to suggest that there *is* a carcinogenic threshold—that is, a dose of any carcinogenic substance that will not produce tumors if given to enough people in a large population. It therefore seems prudent that the Delaney Amendment be strictly applied until more substantial information to the contrary is available (Figure 14.9).

Perhaps the biggest problem with the Delaney Amendment is that it can miss many carcinogens. The food additives sodium nitrate and sodium nitrite are not themselves carcinogenic, but there is evidence indicating that they may be converted into nitrosamines under acidic conditions in the stomach (Lijinski and Epstein, 1970) or perhaps by bacteria in the digestive tract. Nitrosamines, as we indicated earlier, have carcinogenic potential in many species of animals. It has been suggested that a high incidence of stomach cancer in Japan is due to nitrosamines that are present in fish and other smoked foods common in the Japanese diet.

Some other dietary relationships to cancer are even more indirect. For example, one study revealed that there was a history of a higher consumption of

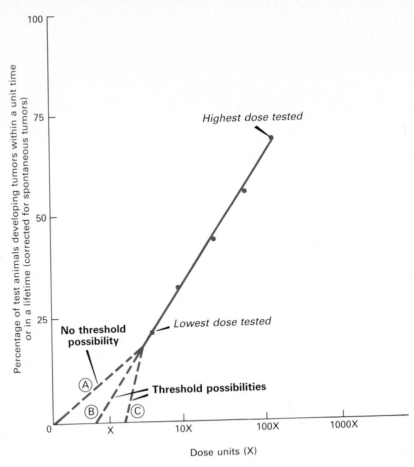

Figure 14.9 Low-Dose Wobble. Animal tests for carcinogenic potential are usually done by using several relatively high-dose regimens. Testing at very low doses becomes increasingly less feasible economically because as zero dose is approached, extremely large number of animals must be exposed to produce even a few tumors for counting.

starches among gastric cancer patients, and it was suggested that the long-term consumption of starchy foods may affect gastric secretion in such a way as to render the stomach lining more susceptible to ingested carcinogens (Modan, et at., 1974).

In a recent report by a Committee on Diet, Nutrition, and Cancer of the National Academy of Sciences (1982) a number of specific recommendations were made about what to eat and what to avoid in order to minimize the risk to cancer:

— Reduce fat consumption from the 40% in the typical American diet to 30%. Colon, breast, and prostate cancers have been linked to fat intake in epidemiological studies.
— Reduce consumption of salt-cured, pickled, and smoked foods. Diets that are heavy in these items have been linked to cancer of the stomach and of the esophagus. The smoking of foods is known to produce nitrosamines and other proven carcinogens.
— Include whole-grain cereals, fruits, and vegetables, especially those rich in vitamin C and beta-carotene (precursor to vitamin A), in the diet. The recommendations specifically mention the vegetable family Cruciferae—cabbage, brussels sprouts, broccoli, and cauliflower—as being especially rich in vitamins A and C and other chemicals believed to inhibit the formation of the active forms of cancer-causing chemicals.
— Avoid excess alcohol consumption especially if you smoke. Cancers of the mouth, larynx, esophagus, and respiratory tract have been linked to smoking and drinking together; heavy drinking even without smoking has been linked to colorectal cancer.

Water and Other Drinks. If you like bourbon and water or scotch and water, you may be in double jeopardy. As we have just pointed out, alcohol predisposes one to oropharyngeal cancer in smokers, to cancer of the esophagus, and maybe even cancer of the liver (Lowenfels and Anderson, 1977). Of possibly more interest to all of us, carcinogens can be carried in drinking water.

A curious but perhaps necessary pattern in America and perhaps in other countries is that we take our drinking water from the same rivers that we use as dumps for human and chemical waste. To be sure, we purify drinking water; but just as surely, we do not get absolutely everything out during the purification process. Drinking water supplies are subject to contamination by carcinogens from industrial plants, parking lots, accidental spills, and pesticides in agricultural runoff. Petroleum refinery wastes also find their way into our lakes and rivers. Other miscellaneous chemical carcinogens find their ways into our water supplies from gas plants, coke ovens, distilleries, and wood processing plants. Tars, pitches, and creosote are washed into our water supply from a variety of sources (Harris, 1975). Interestingly and ironically, water purification may lead to the formation of chlorinated hydrocarbons that have carcinogenic potential. In December 1980 the Council on Environmental Quality issued a report linking rectal, colon, and bladder cancer to the chlorination of drinking water (see Chapter 12). According to one source, 50 chlorinated hydrocarbons have been identified in chlorinated domestic sewage effluents (Jolley, 1973).

In an EPA study of 80 cities in which water supplies were sampled for halogenated compounds, chloroform was found in all of them (Harris, 1975) (Figure 14.10). In light of these things it is perhaps not surprising that a significant relationship was found between cancer death rates in Louisiana and drinking water obtained from the Mississippi River. The population whose drinking water came from the Mississippi had higher total cancers, as well as more cancers of the urinary organs and cancer of the gastrointestinal tract (Page, Harris, and Epstein, 1976).

Drugs. Perhaps the chemicals we consume as drugs are even more important than food additives; the doses of drugs we take are generally higher. The most important cancer-related drugs are the estrogens. As many as 15–20 million women today take some form of the hormone estrogen (Marks, 1976). Men and women alike are exposed to some extent—at least they were in the past—to a derivative of the same hormone called diethylstilbesterol

The waterways that serve as dumps for our wastes are also sources of our drinking water.

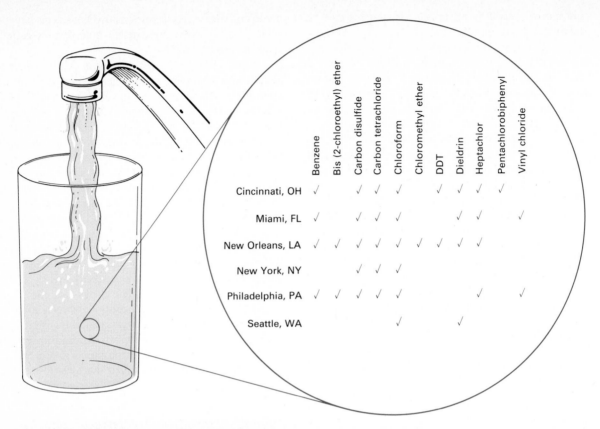

Figure 14.10 Some of the Carcinogens Found in the Drinking Water of Six U.S. Cities.
Many other suspected carcinogens have also been found.

(DES), once widely used in animal feed for increasing meat production. At one time, DES was also given to women during pregnancy for certain disorders. Now a strong association has been made between pregnant women's use of DES and vaginal cancers in their daughters. To date, several hundred such daughters have been found to have vaginal cancer. The Food and Drug Administration now requires labeling on all estrogen preparations, warning of increased risk of certain cancers (Marks, 1976). Although recent reports seem to have cleared birth control pills as a factor in breast cancer, cancer of the uterine lining, and ovarian cancer, there is still believed to be an excess risk to cancer of the uterine cervix in women who use the pills regularly. Birth control pills have also been linked to certain benign neoplasms of the liver. Male hormones used therapeutically have also been related to liver cancer (Antunes and Stolley, 1977). Another class of drugs that apparently has some carcinogenic potential is, ironically, certain anticancer drugs. Some of these drugs act by binding to DNA, which normally kills cancer cells. They have been shown to cause cancer in experimental animals. Actinomycin D, for instance, is carcinogenic in some doses and under some circumstances (Curtis, 1976).

LINKING SPECIFIC ENVIRONMENTAL AGENTS TO HUMAN TUMORS: THE DIFFICULTY

Although we can conclude that there are numerous agents in our environment that can cause cancer, at present we are *certain* about less than 30 chemical-human tumor relationships and only a few radionuclide-human tumor relationships. Many problems stand in the way of conclusively demonstrating whether any single chemical agent is or is not carcinogenic in humans.

First of all, the ultimate experiments cannot be done. One cannot inject suspect chemical agents into humans and see directly whether or not cancer results. Second, cancer takes a very long time to develop. Even if the above experiments could be done, 20, 30, or even more years might pass between the exposure to a carcinogen and the appearance of a tumor in humans. Even experiments with animals take a long time, and they are very expensive. Third (as we will see a bit later), the results of studies on laboratory animals are not uniformly and unequivocally applicable to humans. Fourth, it is difficult to generalize about carcinogens because they do not share many general reactive or structural features. Fifth, many chemical agents are moving targets; they must be converted to carcinogens by the enzymes in human tissues or by the bacteria in the human digestive tract; others may be converted to carcinogens in the air by sunlight or by interaction with other pollutants. It is even possible for two individually noncarcinogenic agents to be carcinogenic together or in the right sequence. Before we conclude our consideration of environmental cancer and before we summarize what can be done about the problem, we will review some of these difficulties individually.

Carcinogens Are Quite Dissimilar Chemically—Or Are They?

Chemicals that we call carcinogens can cause a normal cell to be converted to a cancer cell. One would think that such chemicals might all share some obvious chemical feature that would give us a clue as to which to worry most about and which to ignore. Such is not the case. Table 14.2 shows that there is a wide variety of chemical carcinogens. Some are polycyclic hydrocarbons, some are aromatic amines, and there are a host of other miscellaneous chemicals that are carcinogenic in animals.

Very slight changes in chemical structure can spell the difference between a chemical that is carcinogenic and one that is not (Figure 14.11). Carcinogenic polycyclic hydrocarbons and aromatic amines all seem to be able to react with protein and with DNA; but as we will see in one of the next sections, even if this were not true, we could not pronounce a chemical safe, since it might be converted by metabolism into a compound that could

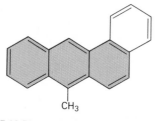

7,12-Dimethyl-Benz(a)anthracene

Anthracene

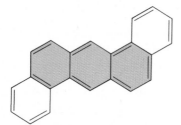

3,4-Benzyprene

1,2-Benzyprene

1,2:5,6-Dibenzanthracene

1,2:3,4-Dibenzanthracene

Figure 14.11 Polycyclic Hydrocarbons. The chemical structures on the left are moderate or strong carcinogens; those on the right are weakly carcinogenic or have no carcinogenic properties at all. Apparently even very small changes in chemical structure can mean the difference between carcinogenicity and noncarcinogenicity.

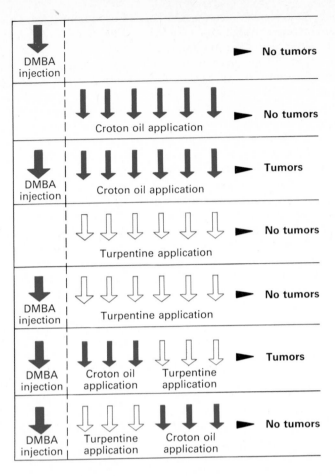

Figure 14.12 A Summary of the Experiments of Berenblum, Boutwell, and Mottran. While neither a subthreshold dose of DMBA or repeated applications of croton oil individually will produce tumors, they do produce tumors when applied together in a certain sequence. Though turpentine, another kind of irritant, does not have the same effect when substituted for croton oil, it does when substituted for late applications. This suggests that carcinogenesis may be a highly complicated process with a number of different stages.

react with DNA or a key protein and produce the same effect. At any rate, it is not possible to look at a new chemical on the basis of its chemical structure and say with a high degree of certainty whether it is or is not carcinogenic.

Synergism, Promotion, and Initiation

Experiments by Mottram and later by Berenblum and Boutwell showed that if mice were injected with a dose of a hydrocarbon like dimethylbenzanthracene (DMBA) in doses that were insufficient to induce cancer during the normal life span of the mice and if the backs of the mice were then painted repeatedly with croton oil, an irritating oil extracted from the seed of a tropical plant, neoplasms appeared within several weeks (Suss, Kinzel, and Scribner, 1973). Croton oil is not a carcinogen and applying it alone without prior DMBA treatment produced no cancer. Thus the combination of a carcinogen in a dose too small to produce skin cancer and a noncarcinogen was able to produce cancer. This resulted in the concept of a two-step hypothesis

for carcinogenesis, the first being an initiation of cancer and the second being promotion. To complicate matters still further, Boutwell found that croton oil promotion could further be subdivided into two components. He found that if he substituted turpentine for croton oil, no cancer resulted. However, he also found that cancer *could* be produced if turpentine were substituted for the last few applications after croton oil but not the first few applications (see Figure 14.12). This multistep/multifactor mechanism does not seem to be the rule for many other kinds of cancer, and it would be beyond the scope of this book to go into any more details of carcinogenesis here. The example illustrates the difficulty of identifying carcinogens and noncarcinogens and the potential importance of combinations of chemicals and other factors.

Some Carcinogens Must First Be Activated

Many substances that are called carcinogens actually cannot induce cancer directly. For example, most of the aromatic amines are apparently not carcinogenic *as* aromatic amines. They must first be converted to hydroxy esters. They must be converted from noncarcinogens or **precarcinogens** through intermediate **proximate carcinogens** to the **ultimate carcinogens** (These terms were coined by James and Elizabeth Miller of the University of Wisconsin.) (Suss, Kinzel, and Scribner, 1973). Enzymes are obviously involved in the conversion of precarcinogens to ultimate carcinogens, and it appears that the culprits are in fact enzymes that normally break down toxic chemicals. Apparently, because of the historical lack of any selective pressures to the contrary, carcinogens are inadvertently made in the process of detoxifying substances that might be more acutely toxic but that are far less harmful in the long run. This has happened because the long run carries the ultimate effect—death from cancer beyond the reproductive years and hence out of the reach of natural selection (see Chapter 5).

The Problem of Time Lag

If the rise in cigarette consumption is compared to the rise in lung cancer in the United States, the two curves are practically identical—but 20 years apart (Figure 14.13). This suggests that the cellular and molecular events that eventually lead to cancer might occur many years before the cancer is diagnosed—as much as 20 years in the case of tobacco and lung cancer. A group of individuals who begin smoking at age 16 or 20 would not experience

any great increase in lung cancer until the mean age in the group moved to age 55–65 and perhaps even later. This kind of pattern is likely to hold true for most cancers. The connection between vinyl chloride and angiosarcoma offers another case in point. Of the workers identified as having vinyl chloride–related hepatic angiosarcoma as of June 1974, most were exposed to the greatest amounts of vinyl chloride before 1950. Most human cancers probably occur 20–40 years after the initial precipitating event or events (Selikoff and Hammond, 1973). The cancers that will appear in us and in our children 30 years from now are being caused by the things we eat, drink, smoke, and breathe today.

From Mice to People: The Problem of Species Specificity

Because many carcinogens must first be metabolically activated, an evaluation of a carcinogen in one species is not necessarily applicable to another species. Metabolic activation is accomplished by enzymes, and the enzymes present in one species are not necessarily the same as those in other species. For this and other reasons that we shall discuss in the next section, testing for carcinogenic activity is far from straightforward.

The Many Faces of Life-Style

We must point out once again that when we speak of chemicals, we are using the term in the broadest possible sense. We certainly do not mean to

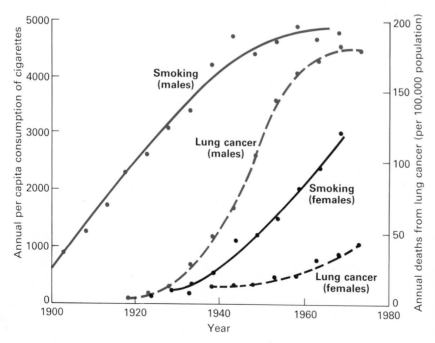

Figure 14.13 The Correlation of Cigarette Smoking and Lung Cancer. A considerable lag time apparently comes between exposure to tobacco smoke and the onset of cancer.

include only synthetic chemicals. We certainly *do* mean to include chemical hormones such as estrogen that are normal human secretions. We even mean to implicate any yet unknown balances or states in body chemisty brought about by particular cultural and social customs—or life-style. Life-style may even be a more important cause of environmental cancer than all synthetic chemicals combined. As the reader well knows, this is all complicated by the fact that life-style is undoubtedly highly correlated with chemical exposure. In a study that compared Mormons and non-Mormons (and thus Mormon and non-Mormon life-styles) in Utah (Lyon et al. 1976) it was found that cancer incidence rates were much higher for the non-Mormons (see Figure 14.14). For cancers known to be associated with tobacco and alcohol the incidence rates were 30–800% higher for the non-Mormons.

The point is that it is ultimately one's total life-style that specifies one's risk to cancer. This means that defining this risk, the factors involved, and the degree of involvement will be at least as difficult as describing all the many aspects of life-style.

Do unto Others

A new dimension was added to the list of problems in linking environmental agents to human tumors when a 1980 report of a Japanese study indicated that the nonsmoking wives of smokers had a risk of lung cancer that was one third to one half the risk to the smoker himself and that the risk increased in proportion to how much the smoker smoked. The implication is that we not only bear the burden of what we do to ourselves, but we also bear the burden of what our loved ones (and close associates) do—in more ways than one.

LINKING ENVIRONMENTAL FACTORS AND CANCER: PROSPECTS FOR THE PRESENT AND THE FUTURE

The point was made in an earlier section that if 90–95% of most cancers are environmental in nature, we ought to be able to identify the environmental factors and eliminate them, thereby bringing about an enormous decrease in the mortality due to cancer. This, of course, presumes that we can actually test a substance and show whether or not it has carcinogenic potential. Evidently, an even bigger presumption is that we can in fact do something about the carcinogens we do identify.

Testing for Carcinogenic Potential: Where Do We Stand and What Is Happening?

Of the millions of known chemical compounds, only a few thousand have been adequately tested for carcinogenicity (Wade, 1976). About 1000 of these have been shown to produce tumors in experimental animals, and many times this number are under suspicion for one reason or another. Not all of the mil-

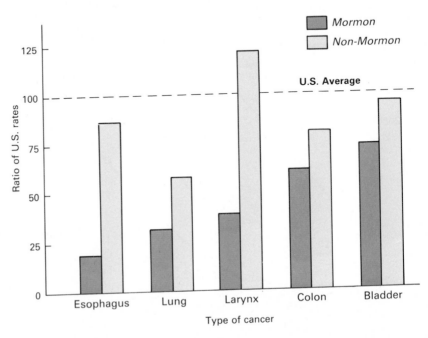

Figure 14.14 Cancer in Mormons and Non-Mormons in the State of Utah, 1966–1970. Note that while incidence rates are generally higher for non-Mormons, they are much higher for those cancers (esophageal and laryngeal) associated with alcohol and tobacco. Mormons do not use either of these substances.

Life-style can lead to environmental cancer. In seeking a perfect tan, sunbathers increase their risk of getting skin cancer.

lions of chemicals already in existence need to be tested, of course, because many of them are not in common use; however, in the 1970s we were producing about 120 billion pounds of 9000 or so synthetic chemicals in large-scale commercial manufacturing (Wade, 1976). In addition, the number of chemicals to which workers and the population as a whole are exposed is growing rapidly. Hundreds of new compounds are mass produced each year.

A carcinogenesis bioassay program has been under way for some time at the National Cancer Institute. The protocol for the testing there requires lots of animals, lots of time, and lots of money. Testing a single chemical may take up to three years and as much as several hundred thousand dollars. Although many chemicals are being tested, there are not enough qualified testing specialists or testing facilities in the United States to test all appropriate chemicals. New chemicals are created faster than the old ones can be tested. Various factors such as the presumed likelihood that a chemical is carcinogenic and the use to be made of the chemical are considered in deciding which chemicals to test first.

During recent years, chemical screening systems that are relatively fast, very cheap, and fairly reliable have been developed. Bruce Ames of the University of California (see Ames, 1979) developed a test that assesses carcinogenic potential via a mutagenic assay using microbes. One version of the Ames test makes use of the bacterial species *Salmonella typhimurium*.

The parent, or natural, strain of this species is able to make the amino acid histidine, but a mutant tester strain is unable to make this essential amino acid. Billions of mutant organisms are exposed to a test chemical; if the chemical is able to change DNA, some of the exposed mutants experience a reversal of the very mutation that made them unable to make histidine. They signify that this back-mutation has occurred by growing on an agar medium that lacks histidine—something they could not do if the back-mutation had not occurred. The beauty of Ames-type tests is that they are quick (overnight) and cheap (roughly $500 per test). But such tests miss some known carcinogens, presumably because they fail to replicate certain features of what can happen in a mammalian organism.

For example, this system fails in its basic form to take into account any species-specific metabolic activation of carcinogens. Humans and other mammals have metabolic enzymes that bacteria do not have. In view of this limitation, testing protocols have been used in which test chemicals are first exposed to mammalian liver enzymes before the chemicals come into contact with bacterial DNA. Mammalian cell culture systems that will do the same sorts of things that the Ames bacterial systems will do are being developed, but these are more expensive and more time consuming. Despite their limitations, Ames-type tests serve as valuable prescreening tests for chemicals, identifying chemicals that are mutagenic and thus should be subjected to more expensive, time-consuming, whole animal carcinogenicity tests.

The Toxic Substances Control Act (P.L. 94-469)

Cancer is not the only problem caused by chemicals in the environment. Environmental toxins are responsible for such other things as birth defects, heart disease, spontaneous abortions, emphysema, and central nervous system afflictions. However, cancer is the most feared environmental disease and it has understandably been at the heart of the effort to control toxic substances. We review here some of the promises and problems of the current laws of the land governing toxic substances.

Nearly everybody knows at least one toxic substance horror story. Chemically notable train derailments, evacuated neighborhoods, chemical dumps like Love Canal, vinyl chlorides, kepones, and asbestos have all had their share of the headlines of the 1970s and 1980s. Congress, in a characteristic zigzag approach to the problem, passed no fewer than eight laws designed to control toxic substances during the first six years of the 1970s. (These were the Clean Air Act, 1970; the Occupational Safety and Health Act, 1970; the Federal Insecticide, Fungicide and Rodenticide Act, 1972; the Federal Environmental Pesticide Control Act, 1972; the Federal Water Pollution Control Act, 1972; the Safe Drinking Water Act, 1974; the Resource Conservation and Recovery Act, 1976; and the Toxic Substances Control Act, 1977.) Of these, the Toxic Substances Control Act (TOSCA), which became law on January 1, 1977, is the most significant. As is suggested by the fact that six years of debate spanning three Congresses preceded the law, TOSCA is surely the most complex and the most far-reaching.

TOSCA is unique because it for the first time gave a regulatory agency (EPA) the power to insist that new chemicals be considered guilty until proven innocent. The reverse had been true until TOSCA.

TOSCA provides for (1) the development of procedures for testing chemical substances and mixtures, (2) the standardization of manufacturing process notices, (3) the regulation of hazardous chemical substances and mixtures once identified, and (4) the definition of procedures for reporting and retaining information on workers' health and chemical exposure.

The law provides that if a chemical carries a risk of injury to health or the environment or if such risk

is uncertain—that is, if (1) data are insufficient to determine whether it is risky or not, (2) a chemical substance is going to be produced in substantial amounts, (3) it may enter the environment in substantial amounts, and/or (4) humans may be exposed to it—the Administrator of the Environmental Protection Agency may require information regarding its possible carcinogenesis, mutagenesis, **teratogenesis** (initiation of birth defects), and other health effects. The burden of developing solid information is to be borne by the manufacturer. The law gives the Environmental Protection Agency power to prohibit the making of certain chemical substances or to limit their manufacture pending the outcome of safety tests. The statute provides up to $25,000 in penalties per day for violations related to failure to conduct proper tests, failure to post proper notices, or failure to handle toxic substances properly.

Actually, TOSCA recognizes two broad categories of chemicals—old ones and new ones. Old chemicals are those already in use when TOSCA became law, new chemicals are those that have or will come into use after January 1, 1977. The EPA was given the primary burden of assessing the risk associated with the old ones. The law intended that the burden for evaluating new ones should fall to industry.

Implementation of TOSCA has been slow. There were the usual bureaucratic delays and problems in gearing up to handle an enormous regulatory task for the EPA. The language of the law leaves considerable room for legal interpretation, so it may still be legitimate to question whether it is possible to administer TOSCA.

U.S. regulatory agencies have traditionally been slow and at times downright reluctant to enforce laws governing toxic substances. The average time for laws to be interpreted into specific rules by the EPA has been about four years (Smith, 1979). A spokesperson for a citizen's group is credited in a 1974 issue of *Science* (Smith, 1979) with the statement that public interest groups are the initiators of action by EPA, OSHA, or the FDA much more often than not. For one example, by 1978, the Natural Resources Defense Council had sued the EPA three times over missed deadlines (Smith, 1979). At the end of the 1970s there were many examples of a great lag between the identification of hazards and specific rules to control them. By 1979 the EPA had estimated that up to one third of the 1500 active constituents of registered pesticides are toxic and that nearly as many are carcinogenic (Smith, 1979), yet only five had been restricted. Of the commonly

How Much is a Human Life Worth?

In several places in this book we have glossed over the question of how much a human life is worth. It bothers most people even to consider the notion that human lives might fall short of invaluable. Yet we tolerate many kinds of activities that clearly *will* take a small number of randomly selected lives prematurely. Coal mining, automobile racing, war, hunting, shipping, driving, and football are but a few examples of essential and nonessential activities in this category. With environmental chemicals the question somehow seems more important.

In the case of benzene, for example, OSHA attempted to set new low limits on exposure in the workplace on the basis of a study showing that of 748 workers exposed to benzene in two chemical plants in Ohio between 1940 and 1949, nine died of leukemia. This was roughly eight more than would be expected in such a group. Of course, nobody knows exactly what levels of benzene were involved for any of the workers. Although even the orders of magnitude are in dispute, exposure could have been as high as several hundred parts per million (Carter, 1979). This is a central point in the debate over a proposed reduction from 10 ppm to 1 ppm, which is reported to cost somewhere between $500,000,000 and one billion dollars.

Even if we knew for a fact that a certain number of lives would be saved by lowering exposure limits to benzene—or to anything, for that matter—we could still be faced with having to make decisions like: *Just how many lives saved would justify the expenditure of even one million dollars?* Keeping in mind that everyone will die eventually of something (though it seems heartless to bring this up) and that a chemically induced cancer death really means a shortened life span, how much is 10 years of a randomly selected life worth?

Perhaps some consensus could be derived from what we actually do pay to save otherwise randomly taken lives. The U.S. government, for example, is apparently willing to spend about $140,000 to save one life in highway construction costs (Fischhoff, Slovic, and Lichtenstein, 1979). But even this seems to leave us hanging.

---

used chemicals studied by the EPA, 20% were suspected carcinogens, but permanent standards (limits) had been set for only ten chemicals (Smith, 1979).

One problem has been staffing. It takes time to build a bureaucracy. Many of the kinds of people needed to staff a unit like the Office of Toxic Substances are not available in great numbers. It takes 8–10 years (counting college and graduate school) to train some of them. An ironic twist is that industry has been hiring the very kinds of people the EPA needs (further tightening the market) in order to help *industry* deal with TOSCA.

Legal challenges occupy a great deal of EPA's time, and the threat of lawsuits demands a great deal of caution. At one point in 1979 the EPA was busy defending itself against 68 court suits. It can take years to go through appeals procedures and congressional efforts to rewrite troublesome passages.

The overall task specified in TOSCA is enormous, and some of the greatest difficulty was in getting started. During the first few years, two sections of TOSCA were the keys. One of these required that an inventory of chemicals be drawn up. The other was the establishment and definition of procedures to be used for premanufacturing notification.

It turned out to be an unexpectedly large problem that an inventory of existing chemicals had to be completed *first*. Since the law deals with new chemicals and with significant new uses of old ones, a list of the old ones had to be compiled first. Four to five million chemicals are already in existence, 63,000 of which are in common use in the United States (Culliton, 1978). By some estimates, as many as three or four *new* chemicals would have to be reviewed by an understaffed EPA every day!

Clearly, the setting of priorities will continue to be an important problem. As if this were not enough, when asked to provide lists of the chemicals they used, some companies claimed that such information was a trade secret and that providing it would tip off their competitors.

The magnitude of it all makes data compilation, record-keeping, and data management a monumental problem. It has been proposed that a colossal "Chemical Substances Information" network be established with the Council on Environmental Quality, the EPA, and the then Department of Health, Education and Welfare as the involved agencies. This network would be designed with many kinds of potential users in mind, and the data base would include:

1. information on health effects gathered under provisions of TOSCA,
2. a system of nomenclature and a chemical identification system,
3. a system for assessing toxicological data including a literature scanning system,

4. a laboratory animal data system to provide information on lab animals suitable for use in designing test systems,
5. information on standards and regulations governing each chemical.

For such data bases to be useful, old data will have to be compiled, and new data will have to be generated.

One problem is that in the language of the law itself testing is *not required*. Industry can decide when and when not to test. This was apparently built into the law because of our reverence for free enterprise. The way the law works, however, is that anyone intending to introduce a new chemical (or to use an old one in some new way) must file notice with the EPA at least 90 days in advance. Upon notification the EPA can

1. do nothing,
2. ban the chemical,
3. limit its use,
4. or ask for more information.

The EPA can go to court to get the more information it needs. The facts that it must do this and that testing cannot be required create the problem. The EPA is in the process of developing guidelines spelling out what kind of information it will usually consider necessary.

A second part of this problem is that the methods available for testing chemicals are far from perfect. For cancer-causing chemicals, for example, standard testing protocols are designed to establish any cancer-causing *potential*—not to predict the frequency with which cancer will appear in humans for a given exposure. The fact that we have decided to assume that there is no threshold for carcinogens does not mean that all carcinogens are equally potent. Some carcinogens may be a thousand times more potent than others. This obviously has profound regulatory implications.

Economic considerations become extremely important here. TOSCA acknowledges the importance of economic considerations and in doing so adds another dimension to the complexities of implementation. The timing of TOSCA in conjunction with rampant inflation started things off on the wrong foot. Experience with earlier laws provides a basis for expecting continued difficulty. According to the 1970 Occupational Safety and Health Act, standards proposed by OSHA have to be reasonable, necessary, and appropriate. OSHA "shall set standards which must adequately assure, to the extent *feasible* . . . that *no* employee will suffer impairment of health. . . ." *Feasible* is a key word.

A clause in TOSCA expected to bring much litigation is one qualifying the authority of the EPA:

> this authority should be exercised . . . as not to impede . . . or create . . . barriers to technological innovation while . . . assur(ing) that such innovation . . . do not present an unreasonable risk.

Neither "impede" nor "unreasonable risk" is defined in the act. The reader will see at once how this clause might be subject to legal interpretation.

At the time of this writing, the eventual impact of TOSCA still cannot be predicted. The effectiveness of the law will be determined by interpretation and enforcement. Even given a rigorous application of the act, it is far from perfect. There will be chemicals that screens will miss, and humans will continue to be at risk. This brings us to our closing statements about environmental cancer.

The Future

One of the main points we tried to make in this chapter is that cancer is caused to a large extent by factors in the environment; because this is so and because cancer is an enormous human problem, it falls well within the scope of human ecology. We also wanted to present evidence indicating that the potential of accomplishing something by working at the cancer/environment problem is very great—theoretically equivalent to all of the gains made against infectious diseases during the age of antibiotics in the 1930s and 1940s.

We have pointed out that some environmental carcinogens have been identified, though not many of them have been specifically linked to human cancers. We have emerging technology such that prospects appear reasonably good for finding and eliminating still more carcinogens. Although we might proceed with the ideal in mind of identifying and eliminating all carcinogenic factors, we should expect that *we will never have an environment that is free of carcinogenic agents*.

Even if we could identify all carcinogens, we would not be able to prevent exposure totally; the best we can hope for is reasonable control. Our society will gradually come to accept risk factors for cancer as we do risk factors that come from working in coal mines and other dangerous conditions. Environmental carcinogenesis will surely continue to be a chronic problem as we move into the future at-

Cost Versus Benefit

Consider a new gimmick (which we just made up), called *coffeemore*. Coffeemore is a chemical that loosens the "goodies" in coffee beans and, at the same time, holds the "bitters" in place, increasing the yield of good coffee per unit weight of beans to nearly double—two cups instead of one, in other words. Unfortunately, coffeemore also causes kidney inflammation in animals given the equivalent of 20 pots of coffee per day and causes bladder cancer in female mice (but not males). Mathematical extrapolation indicates that in a 10-year period of using coffeemore, for a group of 100,000 people, two will die of kidney disease, ten will be hospitalized for kidney disease for an average of 10 days, and 20 will die of bladder cancer after a long illness. A cost-benefit analysis might go as follows:

Benefits		Costs	
Improved (not bitter) coffee for 100,000 people for 10 years: assume a 10% improvement per cup, 30¢ per cup average over 10 years, and 10,000 cups per person in 10 years (3¢ per cup improvement × 10,000 cups per person × 100,000 people).	$ 30,000,000	Cost of 10-year supply of coffeemore (it's not expensive)	70,000,000
		Cancer in 20 people at 2,000,000/case	40,000,000
Cash savings over what would otherwise have been 50¢ per cup (20¢ savings per cup × 10,000 cups per person × 100,000 people)		Kidney death in two people at two million/case	4,000,000
	$200,000,000	Illness in ten people at $8000 per case	80,000
	$230,000,000		$114,080,000

We are assuming an average shortening of life of 10 years and that human life is worth $200,000 per year (so *you* come up with a better number!).

Although we clearly risk offending our friends in economics by the things we did with numbers in this analysis, it seems to illustrate a number of points and allows us to pose some legitimate questions. Do you see places in this analysis where subjective declarations of value could allow someone else to come up with a different outcome? Think about what your inclinations might be if you were a tea-drinking executive in the company that invented coffeemore. Now assume that you own no stock in the company and drink 12 cups of coffee per day. Suppose these figures were found to be an exact representation of the truth; should people be allowed to take a chance of being the one in 10,000 to die of bladder cancer in exchange for better coffee and a cash savings of $200 per person per year?

Incidentally, we picked coffee here because coffee is a nonessential product that a lot of humans use. How would you take the "essential" nature of a product into account in relation to the questions above? How do your answers bear on cigarette smoking? What if, rather than these nonessential, voluntary activities, you were considering the involuntary exposure of people to contaminants in drinking water? What about chemical workers and farm workers exposed to carcinogenic pesticides?

tempting to balance costs and benefits related to all kinds of human activity. It will be part of our struggle with such things as the value of a human life, the value of human illness, the ethics of suffering, questions like who should make decisions about how small a risk is small, and the inequity of risks going to some and benefits going to others.

The individual has considerable control here, however. If lung cancer is ignored, cancer is *not* increasing dramatically overall. Since lung cancer is a problem associated with smoking, this is largely an environmental problem amounting to a personal problem for those who choose to smoke and their associates. Despite the volumes of publicity given to the link between cancer and environmental chemicals, most cancers it seems are caused by the sun (exposure to which can be individually controlled) and by smoking and other things that people do to themselves. The media has somewhat distracted us all from the fact that cancer is one environmental problem whose solution is largely in individual hands.

Chapter 14   Cancer: The Ultimate Environmental Insult

CONCEPTS TO REMEMBER

1. Epidemiological evidence indicates that most human cancer is caused by factors in the environment. These include—in addition to synthetic chemicals, radioisotopes, and other pollutants—such things as tobacco smoke, sunlight, naturally occurring chemicals, and natural sources of radiation.

2. Cancer is a family of diseases in which the regulation of cell division is deranged by gene mutation or other things that impact genetic control of cell division.

3. There are three classes of agents that can cause cancer: chemicals, radiation, and viruses.

4. Evidence linking viruses and a few human cancers is strong but circumstantial; hundreds of different kinds of cancer in animals and plants are known to be caused by viruses.

5. Most of the radiation received by the general public comes from medical uses of radiation (X-rays, etc.) and from natural background radiation.

6. Radioactive isotopes behave chemically like their nonradioactive counterparts.

7. Chemicals, both natural and synthetic, are the most important class of environmental carcinogens.

8. The basis of the statements attributing up to 95% of cancers to environmental factors are the dramatic differences in cancer patterns from country to country and from place to place throughout the world. The fact that the descendants of immigrants exhibit the patterns of cancer death of the countries to which their parents move indicates that the differences are more geographical than genetic.

9. In general, we know more about the connections between environmental cancers related to occupation than we do about any other environmental source. This is because occupational exposures have tended to be relatively easier to document and because patterns within small, distinct groups of people are easier to identify.

10. We ingest carcinogens in even totally natural foods; food additives, food processing, and drugs add still more.

11. The drinking water of many cities contains measurable amounts of carcinogens.

12. It is difficult to link cancers with specific environmental causes because (a) suspected agents cannot be given to people to see what happens; (b) cancer takes a very long time to develop—20, 30, even 40 years in some cases; (c) the results of animal studies are not entirely applicable to humans; (d) it is difficult to generalize about chemicals because carcinogens do not share general reactive features; (e) chemical agents can be moving targets—some carcinogens must be converted through several steps before the ultimate carcinogen appears; (f) combinations of chemicals may be important; and (g) there are literally millions of chemicals already in existence, very few of which can be tested because of the amount of work and expense involved.

13. The Toxic Substances Control Act (TOSCA) requires that new chemicals be shown not to be harmful before they can be used.

14. There will never be an environment free of carcinogens, but the number of carcinogens can certainly be reduced. This is indeed a goal worth working toward.

15. Of all of the environmental problems covered thus far in this book, environmental cancer is the one for which an individual can make the most difference in his or her own environment whether anyone else does anything or not.

DISCUSSION QUESTIONS AND FOOD FOR THOUGHT

1. What is the likelihood that there will one day be a single, simple test to identify carcinogens?

2. Discuss the following statement: "Cancer is a social disease."

3. Why can't the same kinds of experiments that have been used to establish links between specific microorganisms and infectious diseases be used in the conquest of cancer?

4. How is it that cancer, at least forms caused by certain chemicals, is really the result of errors of detoxification?

5. Discuss the irony in the fact that (a) there are rather strict regulations governing the exposure of humans to carcinogens in the workplace and (b) human beings are free to smoke or not as they choose.

6. What are the three major types of environmental factors that produce tumors in both animals and humans?

7. Defend or refute the following statement: "If a chemical is known to produce a tumor in any experimental animal, not even one part per billion should be permitted in food." Defend or refute the same

statement in light of the fact that the U.S. government has long provided price supports for tobacco.

8. Ask a cancer researcher from a nearby university or cancer center to set up a morning or afternoon seminar in which four to six scientists present summaries of current research activities related to environmental cancer. Be sure to provide time for questions and discussion.

9. Ask your local, regional, or state air pollution control agency for information on the kinds of pollutants characteristic of your town or city's air and water and determine which of these have carcinogenic potential.

10. Review copies of the Atlases of Cancer Mortality (see the reference list) and determine where your county stands in relation to each cancer site.

11. Obtain, watch, and discuss films on cancer and carcinogenesis available from the American Cancer Society and other sources. Some examples: *From One Cell,* a 14-minute sound, 60-mm color film designed for high school and college students. A film depicting cells and embryos and cells undergoing regeneration as well as abnormal cellular behavior. This film should be available free on loan from your local American Cancer Society. *Sense in the Sun,* a 14-minute, 60-mm color film on skin cancer. This should also be available from your local unit of the American Cancer Society.

REFERENCES AND FURTHER READING

References marked with an asterisk are cited in the chapter.

*Acheson, E. D.; Cowdell, R. H.; and Rang, E., 1972. "Adenocarcinoma of the Nasal Cavity and Sinuses in England and Wales," *Brit. J. Ind. Med.* **29**:21.

American Cancer Society, 1983. "The Geography of Cancer," *Cancer News,* Autumn 1983.

*Ames, B. N., 1979. "Identifying Environmental Chemicals Causing Mutations and Cancer," *Science* **204**:587–594.

Ames, B. 1983. "Dietary Carcinogens and Anticarcinogens," *Science,* **221**:1256–1264.

*Antunes, C. M. F., and Stolley, P. D., 1977. "Cancer Induction by Exogenous Hormones," *Cancer* **39**:1896–1989.

Asbestos and Health: An Annotated Bibliography of Public and Professional Education Materials. Washington, D.C.: U.S. Department of Health, Education and Welfare. (PHS, NIH, DHEW Publication No. 79-1842, 1978)

Assessment of Technologies for Determining Cancer Risks from the Environment. Washington, D.C.: Office of Technology Assessment. (OTA-H-137, 1981)

Becker, F. F., Ed., 1975. *Cancer: A Comprehensive Treatise. Vol. I—Etiology: Chemical and Physical Carcinogenesis; Vol. II—Etiology: Viral Carcinogenesis.* New York: Plenum Press.

Beebe, G. W., 1982. "Ionizing Radiation and Health," *American Scientists* **70**:35–44.

*Bishop, J., 1982. "Oncogenes," *Scientific American* **246**(3):80–92.

*Blum, H. F., 1976. "Ultraviolet Radiation and Skin Cancer: In Mice and Men," *Photochem. Photobiol.* **24**(3):249–254.

*Blumberg, B., and London, W., 1982. "Hepatitis B Virus Pathogenesis and Prevention of Primary Cancer of the Liver," in *Accomplishments in Cancer Research, 1981,* Fortner, J., and Rhoads, J., eds., 1982. Philadelphia: J.B. Lippincott.

Bodde, T., "Nitrite Report Stirs Little Controversy: Alternatives Being Explored," *Bioscience,* **32**(2):90–91.

*Cairns, J., 1975. "The Cancer Problem," *Scientific American* **233**:64–79.

*Carter, L., 1979. "Dispute Over Cancer Risk Quantification," *Science* **203**:1324–1325.

Clark, M.; Gosnell, M.; Shapiro, D.; Bishop, J., Jr.; and Clark, E., 1976. "What Causes Cancer?" *Newsweek,* January 26, 62–67.

Clifton, K. H., 1983. "Ionizing Radiation Carcinogenesis in Man," in Kahn, *et al.,* eds., *Concepts in Cancer Medicine.* New York: Grune and Stratton. (67–85)

Council for Agricultural Science and Technology, 1982. *Diet, Nutrition, and Cancer: A Critique.* Ames, Iowa. (Special Publication No. 13)

*Commoner, B., 1975. "Cancer as an Environmental Disease," *Hosp. Pract.* February, 82–84.

Council on Environmental Quality, 1978–1984. *Annual Reports.* Washington, D.C.: U.S. Government Printing Office.

*Creech, J. L., and Johnson, M. N., 1974. "Angiosarcoma of the Liver in the Manufacture of Polyvinyl Chloride," *J. Occup. Med.* **16**:150–151.

*Culliton, B. J., 1978. "Toxic Substances Legislation: How Well Are Laws Being Implemented?" *Science* **201**:1198–1199.

Curtis, C., 1976. "The Carcinogenicity of Anti-cancer Drugs in Man," *Cancer* **37**:1014–1023.

Dominguez, G., ed., 1977 (Volume 1) and 1983 (Volume 2). *Guidebook: Toxic Substances Control Act.* Boca Raton, Fla.: CRC Press.

Drinking Water and Cancer: Review of Recent Findings and Assessment of Risk. Springfield, Va.: National Technical Information Service, U.S. Department of Commerce.

Duplan, J. F., 1976. "Some Illustrative Systems of Radiation-induced Carcinogenesis: (1) Neoplasms of Hematopoetic Tissues," pp. 444–455 in *Scientific Foundations of Oncology,* T. Symington and R. L. Carter, eds. Chicago: William Heinemann Medical Books.

*Ellerman, V., and Bang, O., 1908. "Experimentelle Leukamie bei Huhern," *Z. Hyg. Infekt. Kr.* **63**:595.

*Elmore, J. D.; Wong, J. L.; Lumbach, A. D.; and Streips, U. N., 1976. "Vinyl chloride mutagenicity via the metabolites chlorooxirane and chloroacetaldehyde monomer hydrate," *Biochem. Biophys. Acta* **442**:405.

*Elwood, J. M.; Lee, J. A.; Walter, S. D.; Mo, T.; and Green, A. E., 1974. "Relationship of Melanoma and Other Skin Cancer Mortality to Latitude and Ultraviolet Radiation in the United States and Canada," *Int. J. Epidemiol.* **3**:325–332.

"EPA and Toxic Substances Law: Dealing with Uncertainty," *Science* **202**(1978):598–600.

*Epstein, S. S., 1976. "Cancer and the Environment: A Scientific Perspective, Facts and Analysis," *Occupational Health and Safety, Industrial Union Department AFL-CIO.* No. 25 (February):1–13.

Epstein, S. S., 1978. *The Politics of Cancer.* San Francisco: Sierra Club Books.

Finsh, S., and Hamilton, H., 1976. "Atomic Bomb Radiation Studies in Japan," *Science* 191(4242). Editorial.

First Annual Report on Carcinogens. Washington, D. C.: Dept of Health and Human Services. (1980)

*Fischhoff, B.; Slovic, D.; and Lichtenstein, S., 1979. "Weighing the Risks," *Environment* 21(4):17–20.

Fraumeni, J. F., Jr., ed., 1975. *Persons at High Risk of Cancer—An Approach to Etiology and Control*. New York: Academic Press.

Frazier, R. T.; Couch, G.; Crumb, G.; Durst, H.; and Ransom, J., 1966. *A Guide to Science and Cancer*. U.S. Department of Health, Education, and Welfare Publication No. 1162A. Washington, D.C.: U.S. Government Printing Office.

*Gallagher, R., and Gallo, R., 1975. "Type C (RNA) Tumor Virus Isolated from Cultured Human Acute Myelogenous Leukemia Cells," *Science* 187:350–353.

Gori, B. G., 1980. "The Regulation of Carcinogenic Hazards," *Science* 208:256–261.

*Guroff, M.; Nakao, Y.; Notake, K.; Ito, Y.; Sliski, A.; and Gallo, R., 1982. "Natural Antibodies to Human Retrovirus HTLV in a Cluster of Japanese Patients with Adult T-Cell Leukemia," *Science* 215:975–978.

*Hammond, E. C., 1975. "The Epidemiological Approach to the Etiology of Cancer," *Cancer* 35(3):652–654.

*Harris, R. H., 1975. *The Implications of Cancer-causing Substances in Mississippi River Water*. Washington, D.C.: Environmental Defense Fund.

Harris, R.; Page, T,; and Reiches, N., 1977. "Carcinogenic Hazards of Organic Chemicals in Drinking Water," in H. Hiatt et al., eds., *Origins of Human Cancer*. Cold Spring Harbor, N.Y.: Cold Spring Harbor Laboratory.

Harvey, R., 1982. "Polycyclic Hydrocarbons and Cancer," *American Scientist* 70:386–392.

Heidelberger, C., 1973. "Current Trends in Chemical Carcinogenesis," *Fed. Proc.* 32(12):2154–2161.

*Hill, P.; Chan, P.; Cohen, L.; Wynder, E.; and Kuno, K., 1977. "Diet and Endocrine-related Cancer," *Cancer* 39:1820–1826.

"Industry Council Challenges HEW on Cancer in the Workplace," *Science* 202(1978):602–603.

*Jolley, R. L., 1973. *Chlorination Effects on Organic Constituents in Effluents from Domestic Sanitary Sewage Treatment Plants*. Oak Ridge, Tenn.: Environmental Science Division, Oak Ridge National Laboratory. (Publication no. 565)

Karpas, A., 1982. "Viruses and Leukemia," *American Scientist* 70:277–285.

Kessler, D. A., 1984. "Food Safety: Revising the Statute," *Science* 223:1034–1040.

Kolata, G. B., 1976. "Chemical Carcinogens: Industry Adopts Controversial 'Quick' Tests," *Science* 192: 1215–1217.

*Land, C. E., 1980. "Estimating Cancer Risks from Low Doses of Ionizing Radiation," *Science* 209:1197– 1203.

*Land, H.; Parada, L.; and Weinberg, R., 1983. "Cellular Oncogenes and Multistep Carcinogenesis," *Science* 222:771–778.

Lave, L., and Seskin, E., 1979. "Epidemiology, Casuality and Public Policy," *American Scientist* 67:178–186.

LeServe, A.; Vose, C.; Wigley, C.; and Bennett, D., 1980. *Chemicals, Work, and Cancer*. New York: Van Nostrand.

Levin, D. L.; Devesa, S. S.; Godwin, J. D.; and Silverman, D. T., 1974. *Cancer: Rates and Risks*, 2nd ed. Washington, D.C.: U.S. Department of Health, Education and Welfare. (Publication No. NIH 74-691) This compilation of statistics covers various types of cancer by age, sex, and race.

Lewin, R., 1981. "New Reports of a Human Leukemia Virus," *Science* 214:530–531.

*Lijinski, W., and Epstein, S. S., 1970. "Nitrosamines as Environmental Carcinogens," *Nature* 225:21–23.

*Lowenfels, A. B., and Anderson, M. E., 1977. "Diet and Cancer," *Cancer* 39(4):1809–1814.

*Lyon, J.; Klauber, M.; Gardner, J.; and Smart, C., 1976. "Cancer Incidence in Mormons and Non-Mormons in Utah 1966–1970," *N. Eng. J. Med.* 294(3):129–133.

*Maltoni, C., and Lefemine, G., 1975. "Carcinogenicity Bioassays of Vinyl Chloride: Current Results," in "Toxicity of Vinyl Chloride–Polyvinyl Chloride," *Ann. N.Y. Acad. Sci.* 246:195–218.

*Mancuso, T. F., and Brennan, J. J., 1970. "Epidemiological Considerations of Cancer of the Gall Bladder, Bile Ducts and Salivary Glands in the Rubber Industry," *J. Occup. Med.* 12:333–341.

*Mancuso, T.; Stewart, A.; and Kneale, G., 1977. "Radiation Exposures of Hanford Workers Dying from Cancer and Other Causes,". *Health Physics* 33:369–384.

Marshall, E., 1982. "EPA's High-risk Carcinogen Policy," *Science* 218:975–978.

Marshall, E., 1984. "EPA Regulators Take on the Delaney Clause," *Science* 224:851–852.

Marx, J., 1978, "Tumor Promoters: Carcinogenesis Gets More Complicated," *Science* 201:515–518.

*Marx, J., 1984. "What Do Oncogenes Do?" *Science* 223:673–676.

*Marx, J. L., 1976. "Estrogen Drugs: Do They Increase the Risk of Cancer?" *Science* 191:838.

*Mason, T. J.; McKay, F.; Hoover, R.; Blot, W. J.; and Fraumeni, J. F., 1975. *Atlas of Cancer Mortality for U. S. Counties 1950–1969*. Washington, D.C.: U.S. Department of Health, Education, and Welfare. (Public Health Service Publication No. NIH 75-780)

Mason, T. J.; McKay, F.; Hoover, R.; Blot, W. J.; and Fraumeni, J. F., 1976. *Atlas of Cancer Mortality Among U. S. Nonwhites 1950–1969*. Washington, D.C.: U.S. Department of Health, Education and Welfare. (Public Service Publication No. NIH 76-1204)

Maugh, T., 1974. "Chemical Carcinogenesis: A Long-neglected Field Blossoms," *Science* 183:940–944.

Miner, S., 1969. *Air Pollution Aspects of Radioactive Substances*. Bethesda, Md.: U.S. Department of Commerce, National Bureau of Standards. (PD 188092 Litton Industries, Inc.) Miner is quoted in Waldbott, p. 243.

*Modan, B.; Lubin, F.; Barell, V.; Greenberg, R. A.; Modan, M.; and Graham, S., 1974. "The Role of Starches in the Etiology of Gastric Cancer," *Cancer* 34:2087– 2092.

Moore, C., 1970. *Synopsis of Clinical Cancer*. St. Louis, Mo.: C.V. Mosby.

National Academy of Sciences, 1981. *The Health Effects of Nitrate, Nitrite, and N-Nitroso Compounds*. Washington, D.C.: Committee on Nitrite and Alternative Curing Agents in Food, National Academy Press.

*National Academy of Sciences, 1982. *Diet, Nutrition, and Cancer*. Washington, D.C.: National Academy Press.

National Cancer Institute, 1975. *Third National Cancer Survey*. Washington, D.C.: U.S. Government Printing Office. (No. NIH 75-787; Monograph 41)

Neel, J., 1981. "Genetic Effects of Atomic Bombs," *Science* 213:1205–1211.

*Nicholson, W. J., 1977. "Cancer Following Occupational Exposure to Asbestos and Vinyl Chloride," *Cancer* 39:1792–1801.

*Page, T.; Harris, R. H.; and Epstein, S. S., 1976. "Drinking Water and Cancer Mortality in Louisiana," *Science* 193:55–57.

Payne, L. N., 1976. "Some Illustrative Systems of Viral Carcinogenesis: (5) Marek's Disease," pp. 404–414 in *Scientific Foundations of Oncology*, Symington, T., and Carter, R. L., eds. Chicago: William Heinemann Medical Books.

*Pochin, E. E., 1976. "Some Illustrative Systems of Radiation Carcinogenesis (3) Thyroid Neoplasia," pp. 467–475 in *Scientific Foundations of Oncology,* Symington, T., and Carter, R. L., eds. Chicago: William Heinemann Medical Books.

*Poiesz, B.; Ruscetti, F.; Gazdar, A.; Bunn, P.; Minna, J.; and Gallo, R., 1981. "Detection and Isolation of Type C Retrovirus Particles from Fresh and Cultured Lymphocytes of a Patient with Cutaneous T-Cell Lymphoma," *Proc. Nat. Acad. Sci.* **77**(12):7415–7419.

*Rapp, F., 1978. "Herpes Viruses, Venereal Diseases, and Cancer," *American Scientist* **66**:670–674.

Reif, A. E., 1981. "The Causes of Cancer," *American Scientist* **69**:437–447.

Rook, J. J., 1974. "Formation of Haloforms in the Chlorination of Natural Waters," *J. Soc. Water Treat. Exam.* **23**:234–243.

*Rous, P., 1910. "A Sarcoma of Fowl Transmissible by an Agent Separable from the Tumor Cells," *J. Exp. Med.* **13**:397.

*Schneider, M. J., 1975. "The Fatal Byproduct," *The Sciences,* July 26–31.

*Scott, D.; Craig, A. W.; and Iype, P. T., 1976. "Effects of Ionizing Radiation on Mammalian Cells," pp. 427–443 in *Scientific Foundations of Oncology,* Symington, T., and R. L. Carter, eds. Chicago: William Heinemann Medical Books.

Segi, M., and Kurihara, M., 1972. *Cancer Mortality for Selected Sites in 24 Countries, No. 6 (1966–67).* Nagoya, Japan: Japan Cancer Society.

Segi, M.; Noye, H.; Hattori, H.; Yamazaki, Y.; and Segi, R., 1979. *Age-Adjusted Death Rates of Cancer for Selected Sites in 51 Countries in 1975.* Nagoya, Japan: Segi Institute of Cancer Epidemiology.

Selkirk, J., and MacLeod, M., 1982. "Chemical Carcinogenesis: Nature's Metabolic Mistake," *Bioscience* **32**(7):601–605.

*Selikoff, I. J., 1975. "Recent Perspectives (1975) in Occupational Cancer," *Ambio* **4**(1):14–17.

*Selikoff, I. J., and Hammond, E. C., 1973. "Environmental Cancer in the Year 2000," *Seventh National Cancer Conference Proceedings.* New York: American Cancer Society, 687–696.

*Selikoff, I. J.; Hammond, E. C.; and Churg, J., 1968. "Asbestos Exposure, Smoking, and Neoplasia," *JAMA* **204**(2):106–112.

*Shapley, D., 1976. "Nitrosamines: Scientists on the Trail of Prime Suspect in Urban Cancer," *Science* **191**:268–270.

Shubik, P., et al., 1984. "Criteria for Evidence of Chemical Carcinogenicity," *Science* **225**:682–687.

*Smith, R. J., 1979. "Toxic Substances: EPA and OSHA Are Reluctant Regulators," *Science* **203**:28.

Smoking and Health: An Annotated Bibliography of Public and Professional Education Materials. Washington, D.C.: U.S. Department of Health, Education and Welfare. (PHS, NIH, DHEW Publication No. 79-1841, 1978)

*Stocks, P., 1960. "Atmospheric Pollution and Mortality," *Br. J. Cancer* **14**:397–418.

*Suss, R.; Kinzel, V.; and Scribner, J. D., 1973. *Cancer—Experiments and Concepts.* New York: Springer Verlag.

Symington, J., and Carter, R. L., eds., 1976. *Scientific Foundations of Oncology.* Chicago: Yearbook Medical Publishers.

Thé, G.; Geser, A.; and Munoz, N., 1976. "Viruses and Human Neoplasia," in *Scientific Foundations of Oncology,* Symington, T., and Carter, R. L., eds. Chicago: William Heinemann Medical Books, pp. 414–425.

Tomatis, L. 1985. "The Contribution of Epidemiological and Experimental Data to the Control of Environmental Carcinogens," *Cancer Letters* **26**:5–16.

U.S. General Accounting Office, 1981. *Problems in Assessing the Cancer Risks of Low-Level Ionizing Radiation Exposure. A Report to the Congress of the United States by the Comptroller General.* 2 vols. Gaithersburg, Md.: U.S. General Accounting Office.

U.S. Public Health Service, 1984 and annually. *Annual Report on Carcinogens* (Summaries). Research Triangle Park, N.C.: Department of Health and Human Services, National Toxicology Program.

*Vaughn, J., 1976. "Some Illustrative Systems of Radiation Carcinogenesis (2) Bone-Seeking Isotopes and Neoplasia," pp. 456–466 in *Scientific Foundations of Oncology,* Symington, T., and Carter, R. L., eds. Chicago: William Heinemann Medical Books.

*Viola, P. A., 1970. "Pathology of Vinyl Chloride," *Med. Lavaro* **61**:180.

*Viola, P. A.; Bigotti, A.; and Caputo, A., 1971. "Oncogenic Response of Rat Skin, Lungs, and Bones to Vinyl Chloride," *Cancer Res.* **31**:516–519.

*Wade, N., 1976. "Control of Toxic Substances: An Idea Whose Time Has Nearly Come," *Science* **191**:541–544.

*Waldbott, G. L., 1978. *Health Effects of Environmental Pollutants,* 2nd ed. St. Louis: The C.V. Mosby Co.

*Weinberg, R., 1983. "A Molecular Basis of Cancer," *Scientific American,* October, 126–143.

Weisburger, J., and Williams, G., 1981. "Carcinogen Testing: Current Problems and New Approaches," *Science* **214**:401–407.

World Health Organization, 1976. *Cancer Publications of the World Health Organization and the International Agency for Research on Cancer.* Geneva, Switzerland.

Young, J. L.; Asise, A. J.; and Pollack, E. S., 1978. *SEER Program: Cancer Incidence and Mortality in the United States, 1973–1976.* Washington, D.C.: U.S. Department of Health, Education and Welfare, PHS, National Institutes of Health. (NIH-78-1837)

Land Pollution: Solid and Hazardous Wastes

Every year, Americans generate about four billion tons of waste. This includes residential and commercial waste, industrial waste, and waste from mining and agriculture. Disposal of this unwanted material is a monumental environmental problem with many dimensions.

Waste amounts to lost mineral resources; we covered this aspect of the problem in Chapter 7. Waste hastens the exhaustion of valuable energy resources because it generally takes more energy to make things from scratch than to make them from recycled material, and it takes more energy and dollars to process lower-grade ores as the higher-grade ores are exhausted. These dimensions of the problem were explored in both Chapters 6 and 7.

If waste is incinerated, it contributes to the air pollution problem; if it is buried, it contributes to the water pollution problem and takes up land and space; if it is dumped at sea, it diminishes marine resources and may wash up on beaches. Regardless of what is done with waste—short of not generating it in the first place—valuable energy resources are consumed in collecting, transporting, and disposing of it. These things are all well known, and yet the problem keeps getting worse; waste generation in the year 2000 is expected to be twice what it was in 1975.

In this chapter we explore the problem of waste in all its dimensions with an emphasis on the problems of disposal and solutions to those problems. It should quickly become apparent that we have waste problems because our socioeconomic system fails to take into account some of the most basic principles governing material cycles. Although some recycling of waste is done in manufacturing places (like cullet in the glass industry) and some municipalities separate and recycle paper, aluminum cans, and glass, by and large, industry and consumers generate a one way flow of materials (see Figure 15.1).

THE ORIGIN AND NATURE OF SOLID WASTE

What Is Solid Waste?

Solid waste may not be a solid at all. As defined by federal law, **solid waste** may be a liquid, a semi-liquid, or even a liquefied gas. It may be generated from industries, municipalities, businesses, or homes. It may be a discarded article that is worn out, broken, or no longer of use; it may be packaging or organic food wastes; it may be a toxic substance produced as a by-product in some industrial process.

From location to location, the composition of solid waste differs significantly. For example, rural communities may have more food and other organic wastes, while cities tend to have more paper wastes. Figure 15.2 gives a breakdown of municipal wastes

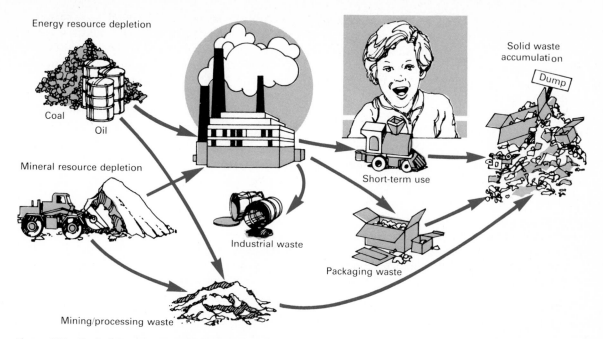

Figure 15.1 Typical One-Way Materials Flow. The bulk of our packaging and manufactured products have a one-way flow from resource extraction to disposal. This results in re-source scarcity at one end and disposal problems at the other.

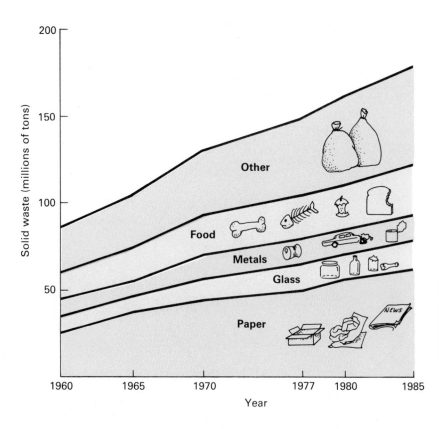

Figure 15.2 Estimated Municipal Solid Waste Including Residential and Commercial Wastes. It consists of paper, glass, metals, yard wastes, food, and other materials such as plastics, rubber, leather, textiles, and wood. The total amount of municipal solid waste generated annually has increased steadily over the years.

by millions of tons for 1960–1985. On the average, 70–80% of residential and commercial solid waste is combustible. It is worth noting that combustible solid waste yields about nine million BTUs per ton compared to 24 million BTUs per ton for coal (Council on Environmental Quality, 1976).

Where Does Waste Come From?

According to a 1979 report by the U.S. Environmental Protection Agency, of the four billion tons of waste produced annually in the United States (see Figure 15.3):

— 3000 million tons come from mining,
— 475 million tons come from agriculture,
— 380 million tons come from industry,
— 145 million tons come from municipalities, and
— 5.5 million tons come from sewage sludge.

Estimates of how much of this could be classified as hazardous waste have increased greatly over the years. In 1984 the EPA estimated that 264 million metric tons of waste were subject to regulation as hazardous waste in 1981.

The Role of Culture and the Economy

Some estimates say that each person in the United States produces about 1500 pounds of domestic solid waste per year—or four or more pounds per day. Domestic solid waste includes residential household waste and waste from commercial businesses. India, which has a much less affluent but larger population, generates less than one seventh as much waste per capita—200 pounds per person annually (Skilling, 1977). Per capita industrial and domestic waste loads vary considerably among the industrialized nations. Although estimates of waste generation vary, one source can be used for comparative purposes. For example (in pounds of domestic and industrial waste per capita annually):

— United States: 3600
— Japan: 800
— Netherlands: 600
— West Germany: 500

These numbers (Skilling, 1977) suggest that solid waste is far from inevitable and that more is involved than simple affluence. With a standard of living not much higher than that of West Germany, the United States produces more than seven times the waste per capita. Perhaps the legacy of the seemingly unlimited space and resources of the frontier sets the United States apart from many other industrial nations. Being younger, with lower population densities and endowed with a lot of space and an immense material resource base, the United States has been able to prosper even with an inefficient materials system. Rapidly escalating costs of mineral imports, energy imports, and solid waste disposal should change this rather abruptly.

Although a comfortable standard of living does not have to produce a high volume of solid waste, there does seem to be some relationship between affluence and waste generation in the United States.

During the recession of 1974–1975 the volume of solid waste in the United States decreased (see

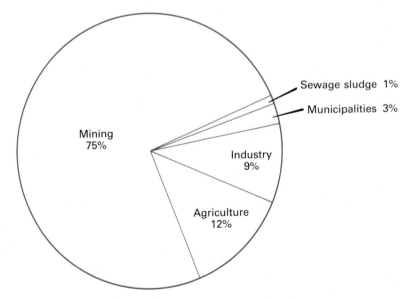

Figure 15.3 Solid Waste Sources. The major sources of solid waste by weight are mining and agriculture. Proper disposal of sewage sludge is an ever growing problem. Sewage sludge is an example of a secondary solid waste, that is, a waste resulting from the removal of other pollutants from the air or water.

Figure 15.4). Paper and board waste seem to be the best indicators of a direct relationship between affluence and waste. Nonfood wastes decreased from 84.8 million tons in 1974 to 77.5 million tons in 1975. Likewise, in 1975, container and packaging waste volumes decreased to the 1971 levels, and the volumes of discarded newspapers, books, and magazines decreased below the 1971 level. Some combination of the production of fewer items, corner cutting, increased scavenging, and attempts to get more out of everything apparently accounted for such trends.

Composition Trends

The composition of solid waste has changed over the years. An increase in plastic waste and paper used as packaging and a decrease in food wastes have

Does an affluent society have to generate so much waste?

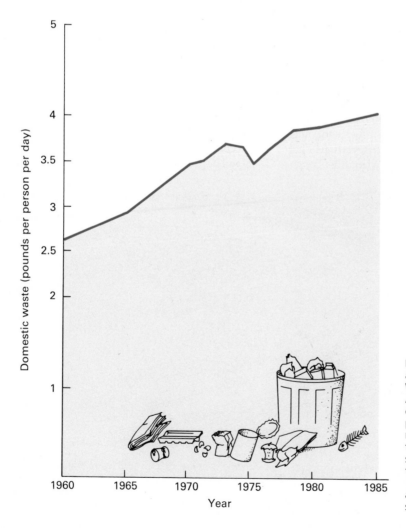

Figure 15.4 Estimated Average Individual Domestic Waste Generated, 1960–1985. Although the number of pounds of solid waste generated daily per person cannot be determined exactly, estimates indicate that per capita generation of solid waste has increased over the years. The dip in the mid-1970s reflects a recession, which apparently resulted in more conservative use of materials.

Chapter 15   Land Pollution: Solid and Hazardous Wastes   463 characterized the change in the United States. Since plastics and paper comprise most of the combustible components of solid waste, today's waste would seem to be more burnable than waste in the past.

SOLID WASTE DISPOSAL

If materials are not reused directly or recycled, there are only three places for the wastes to go: into or onto the land, into the air, or into the water. There are no other options.

Disposal on and in the Land

As of 1975, the most common way to dispose of solid waste in the United States was still the open dump (Skilling, 1977). It was not until October 1976 that Congress passed the Resource Conservation and Recovery Act, which, among other things, prohibited open dumps and required a national inventory of dumps and a compliance schedule for converting open dumps into sanitary landfills (see Figure 15.5).

Sanitary Landfills. Very noticeable to travelers to Virginia Beach on the Norfolk Expressway is a recreational area known as Mount Trashmore. In 1969 the U.S. Department of Health, Education and Welfare funded the building of this hill, which is 72 feet high, 800 feet long, and 100 feet wide and is composed of 85% solid waste. It is perhaps one of the most publicized of all sanitary landfills. It was to serve as an innovative approach to useful solid waste disposal. Once they are complete and topped off, properly managed landfills may be used for parks, playgrounds, golf courses, and other purposes that do not require heavy construction.

Figure 15.5 illustrates the most common procedures for operating sanitary landfills. Some states are now setting more stringent requirements for operation of solid waste landfills, including liners, leachate and gas collection systems, and cover seals. The cost of disposal by landfill is low in comparison to the cost of incineration. Only open dumping is cheaper. However, there are problems with landfills that will continue to increase costs. New federal regulations require landfills to be upgraded to meet more strict standards to protect groundwater aquifers and to address other environmental and health factors. Land costs are constantly rising. Land in and near metropolitan areas is expensive, and urban areas are the most concentrated sources of wastes. As one moves away from the city, the cost of land decreases, but the cost of transportation increases.

A major social problem with landfills is the siting of new ones. Communities selected as sites for landfills often oppose them because of concerns about safety, health, property values, truck traffic, odors, litter, rodents, and insects. Sites that are suitable geologically may be passed over for political reasons; sites that are not suitable geologically may be chosen for political reasons.

The technical problems of landfills include im-

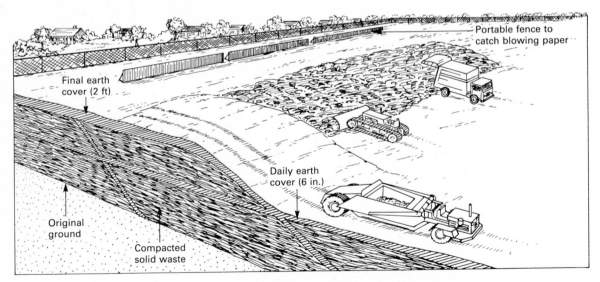

Figure 15.5 A Sanitary Landfill. Proper management requires that the waste be compacted and that a cover of earth be placed over the waste daily. If done properly, this eliminates rodents and blowing trash and reduces odors. If other mechanisms are used for solid waste disposal, including incineration and resource recovery, some residue remains. Sanitary landfills are needed for burial of such residues.

Hazardous waste: useless, unwanted, or discarded material that may pose a threat to human health or the environment.

High-level radioactive waste: spent fuel or solidified waste from reprocessing spent fuel.

Leaching: the process by which nutrient chemicals or contaminants are dissolved and carried away by water or are moved into a lower layer of soil. The contaminated liquid is called *leachate*.

Residue: material that remains after gases, liquids, or solids have been removed. Incineration residue refers to solid material collected after an incineration process is completed.

Resource recovery: the process of obtaining material or energy from waste. Several processes are used to convert ash and other solid waste into solid, liquid, or gaseous fuels.

Sewage sludge: the concentration of solids removed from sewage during wastewater treatment.

Solid waste: useless, unwanted, or discarded material. *Agricultural waste* results from the rearing and slaughtering of animals and the processing of animal products and orchard and field crops. *Commercial waste* is generated by stores, offices, and other activities that do not actually turn out a product. *Industrial waste* results from manufacturing and industrial processes. *Municipal waste* is residential and commercial waste generated by a community. *Residential waste* is domestic solid waste.

Solid waste management: the purposeful, systematic control of the generation, storage, collection, transport, separation, processing, recycling, recovery, and disposal of solid waste.

Source reduction: the alteration of processes, practices, and policies to reduce the amount of waste generated.

---

proper management and improper selection of soil types; both of these may lead to health and pollution problems. Leaching of materials from the infiltration of rain and surface water may lead to pollution of groundwater. The accumulation of methane gas from the anaerobic decomposition of waste may lead to a fire or explosion.

Composting. **Composting** is a method of land disposal that sets up ideal conditions for decomposition and for the return of organic materials to the soil as a conditioner and fertilizer. Composting has been used much more extensively in European countries than in the United States largely because cheap commercial fertilizer has made the market for compost a very limited one here. Figure 15.6 illustrates composting. The basic principle involves a mix of organic material, bacteria, and oxygen to allow rapid decomposition. Unfortunately, composting is not suitable for industrial refuse, and changes in the composition of municipal wastes to include more and more nonbiodegradable waste and less organic waste also make composting less efficient. Bacteria do not work on plastics and synthetics, and they are very slow to break down rubber and cellulose wastes such as lumber and pressed boards.

In the Air

Solid waste that does not end up on or in the land may end up in the air. Incineration is a relatively common method of solid waste disposal in

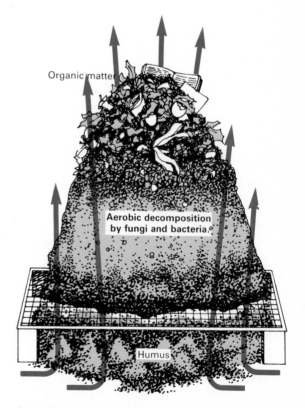

Figure 15.6 A Compost Heap. Compost heaps may be large-scale operations or backyard projects. The critical mix includes organic matter, oxygen, and decomposers. Decomposers feast on the organic matter and break it down in the presence of oxygen into simpler, partly degraded organic and mineral components. Compost may then be used as a soil conditioner.

In some places, routing sewage into the ocean is still practiced. But the oceans cannot flush away our wastes indefinitely.

areas with concentrated populations. In these areas, scarce land and transportation costs make incineration an economical alternative. Combustion of organic matter produces carbon dioxide, water, particulate matter, various gases, and ash. Particulate matter and gases that enter the air cause both health and economic problems (see Chapters 9–11). Ash causes a residual solid waste disposal problem.

The coupling of waste incineration with energy recovery is gaining increasing attention as a compelling solution to two environmental problems. It will be explored in detail in a later section.

In the Water: Ocean Dumping

Solid waste that does not end up in or on the land or in the air ends up in the water. Water can be contaminated by waste through runoff and leaching. For many years the dumping of wastes into surface waters, in particular ocean dumping, was practiced as an inexpensive and convenient method of waste disposal. More stringent and expensive on-land requirements for incineration or other disposal further encourage ocean dumping. Today approximately 50 million tons of wastes a year are discharged into the oceans worldwide. This waste consists of 80% dredge spoils (materials scraped from bottoms of bodies of water to improve channel flows), 10% industrial wastes, 9% sewage sludges, and 1% miscellaneous. Since much of the discharging takes place near the shore, the dilution benefits of the large, open sea are not available.

The 1983 report of the Council on Environmental Quality (CEQ) cites field studies at ocean sewage outfalls in California showing high concentrations of some metals in sediments and in marine fish and shellfish, eutrophication, and alteration of ocean bottom habitats. Some organisms did seem to flourish near the discharge areas; others disappeared or showed infections. Studies on the East Coast show that in one acid dump site off New York, used since 1948 for so-called nontoxic chemical wastes, sediments are contaminated, and marine organisms show concentrations of contaminants. Infections and fin rot are common.

The dump site used by Philadelphia from 1973 to 1980 was located off the coast of Maryland. Studies show effects on sediments and bottom dwelling organisms, but no long-term effects on the water column have been noted. A 106-mile dump site off the New York coast used since 1961 for chemical wastes is characterized by depths of 1700–2750 meters and shifting water masses; the CEQ report cites the size and dynamic exchange of water in this area as important factors to be considered in ocean disposal. Field studies have shown little impacts on marine life here; elevated concentrations of pollutants have been temporary and limited to the dumping area.

Changes in waste content and volumes, including increased amounts of nonbiodegradable and hazardous chemical wastes, have made ocean dumping ever less satisfactory. Coastal seafood operations are affected by chemicals and by potential pathogens from sewage sludge that get into the food chain. Floating debris from ocean dumping tends to wash back onto beaches, causing both health and aesthetic problems.

The 1972 Marine Protection and Sanctuaries Act requires that a permit be obtained for dumping in the ocean. This legislation also prohibited any further dumping of sewage sludge in the oceans after December 31, 1981. **Sewage sludge** is the solid residue from wastewater-settling tanks. Today it is often composed of toxic heavy metals and synthetic organic compounds as well as other organic materials, pathogens, nutrients and water. However, as of 1983, sewage sludge was being dumped in ever increasing amounts in the oceans, and the prospect was for a continuation of that trend.

What happened to the deadline? New York City, having run into numerous problems—one of which was cost—in attempting to convert to land-based sewage sludge disposal, challenged the deadline in court. The court held the ban to be invalid and said that New York City had to be given the opportunity to show that its dumping would not "unreasonably degrade" the marine ecosystem.

Because of the low cost of ocean dumping, other municipalities are considering it, including Philadelphia, Baltimore, Boston, Washington, D.C., and Jacksonville, Florida. Consideration is also being given to using more deep-water sites. Although that involves higher transport costs, such sites might provide for more rapid dilution and less bottom accumulation of materials.

So a decade after the proposed phase-out of ocean dumping of sewage sludge, the prospect now is for vastly increased use of this method. In late 1982, Congress did place a two-year moratorium on the ocean disposal of low-level radioactive waste.

Table 15.1 compares the effects of using various types of disposal technologies including ocean disposal for sewage and industrial wastes containing certain contaminants.

Going a step further, Lahey and Connor (1983) attempted to compare the health risks associated with ocean disposal with those associated with land disposal. For residents of Nassau County, Long Island, they compared the cancer risk associated with soluble chemical compounds that are likely to leach from land disposal sites and contaminate groundwater with the cancer risk of compounds that are likely to be absorbed and stored by fish eaten by humans (Figure 15.7). They calculated that the additional cancer risk over a lifetime for a 155-pound person who drinks 2 liters of water per day is 34 in a million. If the same individual eats 6.5 grams of

Table 15.1 Comparison of Contamination Potentials for Three Types of Disposal

Contaminants	Effects of Ocean Disposal	Effects of Land Disposal	Effects of Incineration
Pathogens (bacteria, viruses, and parasites)	Contamination of shellfish	No problem if sludge is stabilized; should not apply sludge on crops grown for raw consumption	Destroyed by incineration
Metals	Mostly nontoxic as a result of chemical changes after dumping	Absorption of cadmium, zinc, nickel, and copper potentially toxic to plant growth; potential hazard to human health from eating crops contaminated with cadmium	Metals in air emissions and ash
Organic chemicals	Bioconcentration by fish, a potential health hazard	Potential absorption by cattle grazing on land where sludge has been spread; potential groundwater contamination by smaller, more soluble compounds	Largely degraded by incineration; possible formation of suspected carcinogens

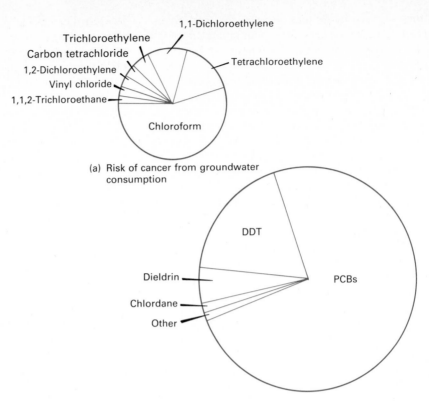

(a) Risk of cancer from groundwater consumption

(b) Risk of cancer from fish consumption

Figure 15.7 Risks of Getting Cancer from Drinking Tap Water Versus Eating Locally Caught Fish. (a) The risk from drinking water is about 34 in a million; more than half of the risk comes from chloroform contamination. (b) The risk from consuming fish is about 65 in a million; more than 75% of the risk comes from PCBs.

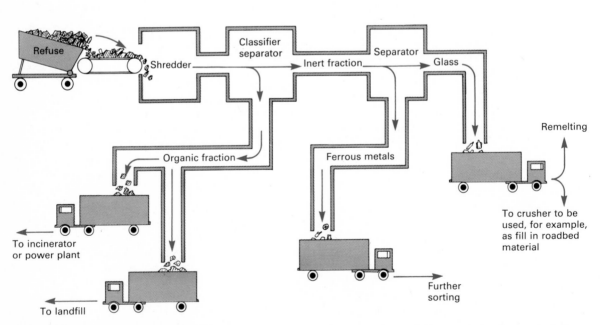

Figure 15.8 Generalized Resource Recovery. In general, all high-technology facilities involve the same basic processes. The refuse is shredded; metals and glass are separated and recovered for sale or use. The organic fraction may be incinerated, buried, or used in an energy recovery facility.

fish per day, the lifetime cancer risk is 65 in a million. Both levels are greater than the risk threshold considered acceptable by the EPA. The authors conclude that there should be as much concern about disposal of pollutants such as PCBs in shallow ocean water as there is about dumping them on the land.

RESOURCE RECOVERY

When Is a Waste Not a Waste?

One way to diminish the problem of disposal is to reuse the waste. Very simply, **resource recovery** is a method for turning wastes into resources by recovering usable products—both materials and energy. Resource recovery may involve simple facilities such as aluminum and paper sorting and recycling centers or complex automated materials recovery facilities. In any case, as the cost of disposal continues to rise because of land prices and pollution controls, resource recovery may well become more and more common.

Resource recovery can begin at home. Sorting wastes into paper, glass, and aluminum to be delivered to the nearest recycling center primarily involves human energy. Placing organic wastes in a backyard compost heap reduces the volume of waste put into trash cans and saves valuable nutrients. The sorting of materials is the preliminary step in most resource recovery operations.

Resource recovery can involve high-level technology as shown in Figure 15.8. This is often referred to as mixed waste recovery. Ferrous (iron-containing) metals are extracted by using magnets. Separation at the source is the most common separation technique for glass; mechanical recovery of glass is possible, but it is not economical if glass is the only recovery product. Table 15.2 lists the useful products that can be made from a variety of reclaimed materials.

The economics of high technology facilities increasingly requires that energy recovery be an inherent part of these systems. Because of the quantity of waste required for economic feasibility, energy recovery facilities are generally located near high concentrations of wastes and industrial markets to purchase the recovered products, which may include heat (steam), electricity, synfuels, methane gas, methanol, or ammonia.

The energy potential in solid waste is reported to equal at least 28% of that expected from the oil in the Alaska Pipeline (U.S. Code, 1976). Generally, about 70–80% by weight of municipal solid waste (domestic and commercial, not industrial, agricul-

Table 15.2 Waste-Product Matchups

Waste Material	Product
Paper	Printing paper
	Writing paper
	Sanitary paper
	Packaging
	Insulation
	Construction paper
	Hardboard
Sludge	Compost
	Roadbeds
Rubber (tires)	Pavement
	Retreads
	Reefs
Plastic	Pipes
Glass	Ceramic bricks
	Glasphalt
	Concrete
Iron and steel	Bars
	Cast-iron pipes
	Structural shapes
Aluminum	Siding
Slag	Cement
Fly and bottom ash	Roadfill
	Roadbase stabilizer
	Asphalt
	Concrete additive
	Cement
	Aggregate
Sulfur	Asphalt cement
Oil	Oil
Refuse-derived fuel	Energy
Various wastes	Automobiles
	Hand Tools
Various chemicals	Paint
	Soap and wax
Wood, metal, textiles	Office furniture
Kiln, lime, and gypsum dust	Chemical waste neutralizer
	Fertilizer

tural, construction or sewage) is combustible. Table 15.3 compares the energy values of solid waste and other fuel sources. One ton of municipal solid waste is approximately equal to nine million BTUs, 65 gallons of No. 1 (kerosene) fuel oil, or 9000 cubic feet of natural gas (U.S. General Accounting Office, 1979). Figure 15.9 shows that although the percentage of resource recovery from municipal waste is increasing, still only a small percentage is recovered.

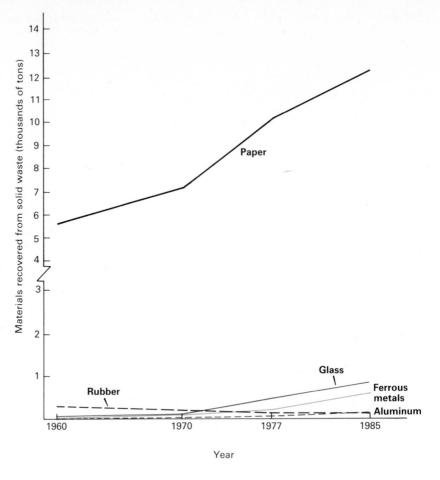

Figure 15.9 Recovery of Materials from Solid Waste. Only a small fraction of municipal solid waste is now recovered; paper is clearly in the lead. Most of what is recovered is separated at the source—before it is hauled away as mixed trash. The percentage of waste recovered almost doubled from 7% in 1960 to 13% in 1985. Note the different scales on the two parts of the graph.

Table 15.3 Approximate Energy Content of Wastes in Comparison with Standard Fuels

Fuel	Heating Value
Solid	
Coal (standard)	100%
Bark	37
Wood waste (general)	46
Sawdust	54
Coffee grounds	46
Corncobs	59
Liquid	
Oil (standard)	100
Oil waste	97
Paints/resins	54
Dirty (used) solvents	86
Old grease	76
Gaseous	
Natural gas (standard)	100
Coke oven gas	78
Refinery waste gas	271

Based on maximum values from wastes and standard fuels.

Energy Recovery Through Incineration

Many communities incinerate solid waste. Usually, the heat produced by the burning of waste simply dissipates and is lost. However, the heat produced from burning wastes can be used to convert water into steam (Figure 15.10), and the steam can then be used for heating or for running a turbine to produce electricity. This has been done since World War II in Europe, where land and resource scarcity made this an economically feasible approach.

Frankfurt, West Germany, produces 7% of its electricity by this means, and Amsterdam produces 6%. A heat recovery incinerator plant was completed in Nashville, Tennessee, in 1974. By 1977 this plant was burning an average of 400 tons of municipal solid waste daily. The plant, which is designed to handle 720 tons per day, reduced landfill space requirements by 90%. Steam produced from the burning of the waste is used for district heating and cooling.

A plant in Saugus, Massachusetts, is processing about 1300 tons of solid waste per day. In its first 7 years of operation (1975–1982) the facility processed well over two million tons of waste. Steam generated by the process is piped to a local industry. As of 1983, 22 waste-to-energy incineration facilities were in operation, undergoing testing, or under construction in the United States.

Co-disposal

An emerging technology called thermal **co-disposal** involves the simultaneous disposal of solid waste and sewage sludge. Because of its volume and the presence of persistent chemicals such as heavy metals, use of sewage sludge as a soil fertilizer has been questioned. However, because of its high water content, it does not burn readily. Thermal co-disposal involves the use of energy from burning solid waste to dry the sludge to a point at which it will burn without supplemental fuel or in combination with more refuse. Rising land costs, which make land disposal of sludge more and more expensive, and rising fossil fuel costs, which make incineration of sludge more expensive, combine to make this technology look promising.

Co-disposal has been used in Europe for several years, and in early 1980, disposal projects were underway in Concord, California; Duluth, Minnesota; Glen Cove, New York; Harrisburg, Pennsylvania; and Memphis, Tennessee. The facility in Duluth is designed to incinerate 66 tons of sludge and 460 tons of solid waste daily. Approximately 45,000 pounds of steam are produced every hour from the burning of dried sludge and solid waste. The steam is used to dry other sludge and to operate the associated waste-to-fuel system. In Harrisburg a waste-

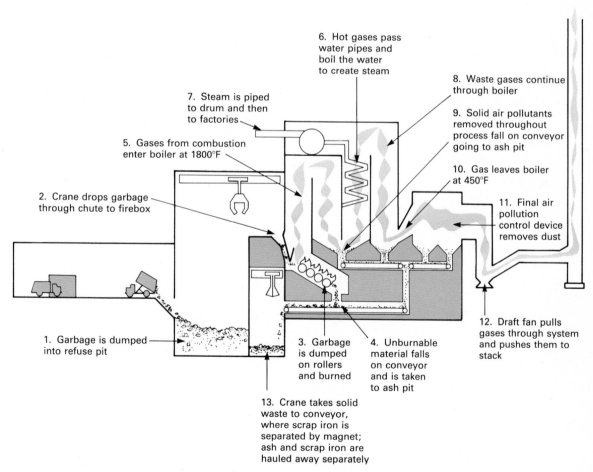

6. Hot gases pass water pipes and boil the water to create steam

8. Waste gases continue through boiler

7. Steam is piped to drum and then to factories

9. Solid air pollutants removed throughout process fall on conveyor going to ash pit

5. Gases from combustion enter boiler at 1800°F

10. Gas leaves boiler at 450°F

2. Crane drops garbage through chute to firebox

11. Final air pollution control device removes dust

1. Garbage is dumped into refuse pit

3. Garbage is dumped on rollers and burned

4. Unburnable material falls on conveyor and is taken to ash pit

12. Draft fan pulls gases through system and pushes them to stack

13. Crane takes solid waste to conveyor, where scrap iron is separated by magnet; ash and scrap iron are hauled away separately

Figure 15.10   The Operation of a Refractory-Wall Incinerator. This incinerator recovers the heat energy from burning municipal solid waste by converting it to a more usable form as steam.

water treatment plant and a solid waste incinerator located within half a mile of each other were combined. The sludge from the wastewater plant is pumped to a drying building at the incinerator site. Dried sludge is then combined with municipal solid waste for incineration. This facility has produced 92,500 pounds of steam per day, equal in a year to 8.4 million gallons of fuel oil or one million barrels of crude oil. Part of this steam powers the sludge-drying equipment; the rest is sold to a utility company for nearby buildings at a return to the city in 1979 of about one million dollars.

Energy Recovery Through Synthetic Fuel Generation

Refuse-Derived Fuel Systems. In some municipal solid waste–processing facilities, combustibles are separated from noncombustibles. The combustibles are shredded and burned in utility and industrial boilers as a primary fuel or as a supplement to fossil fuels. This type of solid waste processing operation is called a refuse-derived fuel or RDF system.

From 1972 to 1976 a refuse-derived fuel demonstration plant was operated in St. Louis, Missouri. The city, Union Electric Company, and the EPA cooperated in the venture. The plant converted 300 tons of municipal solid waste to RDF daily, and this was used in boilers initially designed for the combustion of pulverized coal. The RDF provided approximately 10% of the heat for the boilers.

In 1983 there were 29 RDF systems in the United States. These facilities had various economic difficulties primarily because there were no firm markets for their RDF. Some facilities avoided the market problem by constructing boilers onsite to use the RDF and then using or selling the energy produced from onsite combustion. Currently, an RDF system in Ames, Iowa is processing about 180 tons per day of waste. RDF is used to supplement other fuel sources in a ratio of 20% RDF to 80% fossil fuel. A plant in Dade County, Florida can process 18,000 tons of waste per week and has electricity as a final energy product.

Incineration and RDF technologies appear to be competitive in cost. In the late 1970s and early 1980s, RDF plant disposal fees were projected to range from $1.53 to $9.90 per ton. This compared to $5.89–$13.00 a ton for nonenergy recovery incineration and about $7.00 a ton for other conventional methods of disposal (U. S. General Accounting Office, 1979). Collection costs are the same regardless of the method of disposal.

Methane Recovery. As organic wastes decompose in landfills, they produce gases, predominantly methane and carbon dioxide. A buildup of methane can be dangerous, since it can cause fire or explosion. It has been found, however, that such methane is a commercially recoverable fuel. From April 1974 to February 1985 the city of Los Angeles used gases vented from a landfill in Sun Valley to produce enough electricity for 350 homes. A landfill in Menlo Park, California, has provided sufficient gas to provide electricity to 1000 homes. The EPA estimates that over 38 billion cubic feet of methane may be recoverable annually from landfills located near large metropolitan areas in the United States.

Pyrolysis. Pyrolysis is the process of heating refuse in a nearly oxygen-free environment to produce oil, gas, and/or a char as an end product. A ton of solid waste processed in this manner yields the energy equivalent of about one barrel of oil, a little more or less depending on the recovery efficiency. Although this technology is still being developed, the city of Baltimore began operating a commercial-scale facility in 1975 to produce gas from municipal solid waste. The plant was to produce 4.8 million pounds of steam daily from the low-BTU gas produced from pyrolysis. This would accomplish a savings of 357,000 barrels of oil annually. Other revenue would be available from the sale of ferrous metals that had been sorted out and the sale of glassy aggregate used in concrete manufacturing and street paving. However, after numerous modifications the process is being replaced by a mass burning system.

A demonstration unit for refuse gas pyrolysis began operating in South Charleston, West Virginia, in June 1974 and operated through 1977. The economic viability of a full-scale commercial facility at this time appears questionable. Pyrolysis to oil is even less well demonstrated. It should be noted that energy recovery efficiencies range from 37% to 62% for pyrolysis compared to 62–71% for direct combustion. The advantage of pyrolysis is that a more generally useful and transportable form of energy is produced.

A Special Problem: Old Rubber Tires. Rubber tires continue to be disposal problems. Incineration of rubber must be done in specially equipped facilities to prevent air pollution and to accommodate the intense heat released by the burning rubber. Tires tend to cause problems in landfills because they spring back into shape and do not decompose well. Some systems for burning rubber for fuel have been successful; they are small-scale operations because of the limited tire supply. However, the BTU content of burning rubber is approximately equal to that of coal. Pyrolysis has been used successfully on a small scale to produce fuels from rubber.

Bioconversion. Although solid wastes decompose to methane and carbon dioxide under landfill conditions, this process can be accelerated artificially by means of an anaerobic digester. Sewage sludge containing decomposers is mixed under anaerobic conditions with shredded combustible components of municipal solid waste. The mixture is heated in a digester for about a week. A demonstration bioconversion plant has been in operation in Pompano Beach, Florida since 1978. Methane is being produced from a mixture of RDF and sewage sludge.

The Bottom Line

The U.S. General Accounting Office estimates that if U.S. waste-to-energy projects that were in operation or at some stage of development or feasibility study as of early 1980 proceeded as projected and operated at 66% energy recovery efficiency, they would process 36 million tons of municipal solid waste. The energy they generated would be equivalent to 37 million barrels of oil annually. In addition to the energy recovery the projects would recover materials with a market value of 235 million dollars and would indirectly save around eight million barrels of oil by not having to use virgin materials. In other words, 36 million tons of waste could become more than a $900,000,000 resource annually (U.S. General Accounting Office, 1979).

Successful Resource Recovery: Some General Considerations

Many factors are involved in successfully initiating, constructing, and operating a high-technology resource recovery facility. More research and development are clearly needed for resource recovery prototypes both large and small. Once there is public acceptance of a resource recovery project, the most crucial factor is securing a market for recovered materials in business and industry.

A stable and dependable market is an economic must in resource recovery. Creating markets for recycled materials will be a function of economics and federal encouragement and a shift in federal policies that have an impact on recycled products. Virgin materials have traditionally been given economic advantages over recycled goods in transportation costs. This type of barrier must be removed. As we shall see, legislation passed in 1976 requires the federal government to increase its use of products containing recycled materials.

Other policy changes and incentives may accelerate the growth of the recycling industry. Dwindling resources may provide additional pressures to make these adjustments occur more rapidly.

Resource recovery facilities must be tailored to the characteristics of particular locations, that is, to the volume of waste available and to the needs of the industries that will buy the products. To ensure that the necessary volume of waste from the community actually goes to the facility, mandatory participation may be necessary. Individuals, businesses, and waste collection services may be required to take their waste to that facility and not to any other waste disposal facilities.

Another problem is that there is an 18- to 40-month lead time in getting high-technology resource recovery facilities operational. As demand for such facilities increases and as research and development make the technology more reliable, the lag time should decrease. However, the need for site-specific design will continue to make the design and planning phase extremely important.

There are other institutional and financial constraints to resource recovery. Generally, solid waste has been considered a local problem. Disposal is paid for from general funds or from specific fees. Local governments may not have the expertise to examine and administer resource recovery facilities or to evaluate small-scale alternatives. Small municipalities may not generate enough waste to support a large resource recovery facility. Although regional approaches to resource recovery may be needed to produce a sufficient volume of waste, there are few if any defined channels for such cooperation between governments. Also, cities must become better able and willing to enter into long-term agreements in order to justify investments in high-technology resource recovery facilities.

WASTE COLLECTION

One cost that is similar for all waste management systems is the cost of collection—getting the waste from its source to the point of disposal or processing. The average cost of collecting and disposing of one ton of municipal waste in the early 1980s was projected to be approximately $30, of which $22 went toward collection (U.S. Environmental Protection Agency, 1977); collection cost was expected to increase to $38 a ton by 1985 (U.S.

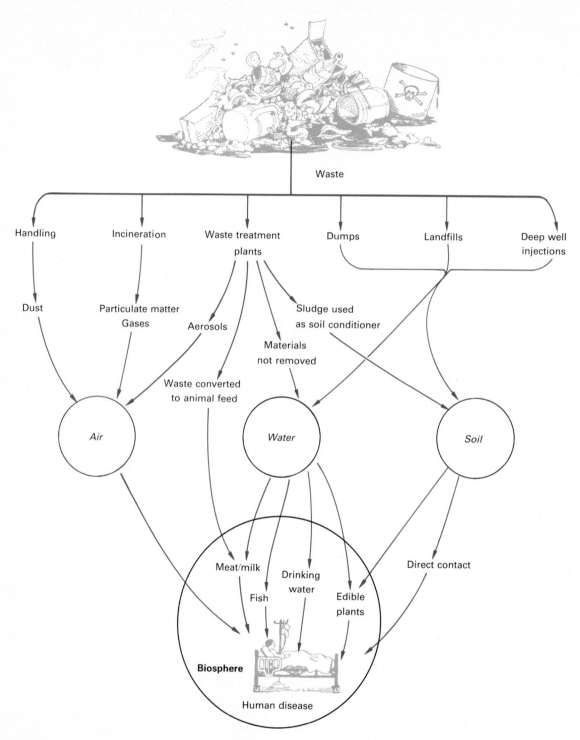

Figure 15.11 Waste and Disease. The impact of waste on human health may be direct or indirect. Everything must eventually go somewhere, and some pathways eventually lead to people. This flowchart shows how the trash you dispose of today may come back to you later in an even less desirable form.

General Accounting Office, 1979). Costs have exceeded these projections in some places. Collection accounts for 50–80% of the total three to four billion dollars spent annually in the United States on solid waste management (Skilling, 1977).

WASTE AND HEALTH

Leaching

Improper disposal of solid waste can generate health hazards (see Figure 15.11). Groundwater pollution from leaching from landfills is a major health concern. About 50% of the domestic water supply in the United States comes from underground sources. Trace metals and improperly disposed toxic waste could contribute greatly to groundwater contamination problems. Identifying leaching-related health problems is difficult, and correcting such problems once they arise is extremely difficult and costly—if possible at all.

Leachate is formed from the infiltration of rain through the soil covering. As the water seeps through the buried waste, water-soluble chemicals may be picked up and carried along. (See Figure 12.7.) This leachate then follows the normal hydrologic flow and may enter the groundwater system. The constituents of the leachate and their concentrations vary depending on local conditions. However, there are certain common problems.

Carbon dioxide is produced from the decomposition of the solid waste. In solution, carbon dioxide forms carbonic acid. This acid may increase the dissolution of the rock that forms the groundwater aquifer and thus increase the amount of minerals in the groundwater.

An even more dangerous situation arises because of lack of control over the types of materials placed in sanitary landfills and open dumps. Many wastes that are now classified as hazardous have been buried in dumps and landfills over the years. The potential for groundwater contamination and subsequent health problems is very great. Safeguards now required for hazardous waste landfills such as the use of water-impermeable liners and leachate collection systems have not yet generally been applied to sanitary landfills.

Other Health Considerations

Gases that are generated in and escape from landfills include methane, carbon dioxide, hydrogen sulfide, and hydrogen. As such gases migrate laterally, they may kill vegetation. Methane mixed with air is explosive. Hydrogen sulfide is toxic (Chapter 10), and it smells bad. Decaying organic matter may serve as food or as a breeding habitat for rats and flies. Less degradable solid waste may shelter rodents. In addition, runoff may carry litter and dissolved waste into surface waters, adding limiting nutrients that overenrich. Stray solid waste can generate navigational and flooding hazards (by clogging drainage ways). Wood and paper wastes are fire hazards.

Solid wastes along roadsides can cause accidents from falls or cuts; blowing paper has on occasion blocked a driver's vision. Roadside mowers can turn waste into lethal projectiles. Livestock and other animals may be harmed if they swallow litter.

HAZARDOUS CHEMICAL WASTE

With the advance of technology and the development of new industrial processes has come the rise of chemical wastes, some of which are toxic or poisonous. As we have already seen, these can cause serious air and water pollution problems. They can also be problems if dumped onto or into land.

What Is Hazardous Waste?

According to the federal definition, **hazardous waste** is any waste that because of its quantity, concentration, or physical, chemical, or biological nature may cause mortality or irreversible or incapacitating illness or pose a threat to either human health or the environment. Practically speaking, proposed federal regulations allow a generator of wastes to use two different approaches to tell whether the waste produced is hazardous. A generator may test according to EPA standards for ignitability, corrosiveness, reactivity, or toxicity. The law itself requires that persistence, degradability in nature, and potential for bioaccumulation also be considered, but these properties are not as easily determined, and testing of them has not yet been required. Or the generator may check to see whether the waste under consideration is on the list of federal hazardous wastes. Wastes considered hazardous under the federal law amounted to 264 million metric tons in 1981. This does not include hazardous wastes that were not regulated at that time. Examples of these are wastes from small generators producing under 1000 kg per month, agricultural wastes, and wastes from cleanup of some illegal dump sites.

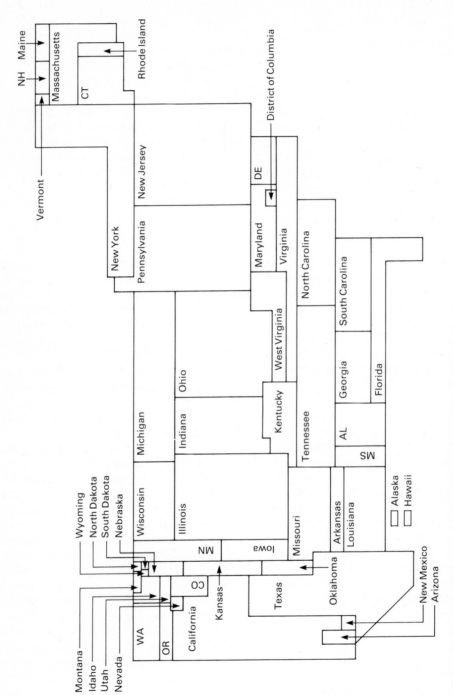

Figure 15.12 Comparative Generation of Hazardous Wastes, 1980. This schematic drawing of the U.S. shows each state and its size in proportion to the approximate amount of hazardous wastes generated in that state in 1980.

Where Does It Come From?

Most hazardous waste is generated by industry. The EPA lists over 125 industrial processes that may generate hazardous wastes. Of the hazardous waste handled in 1981, 71% was generated by the chemical and petroleum industries, 22% by metal-related industries, and 7% by all other industries. Certain products and the types of hazardous waste generated by their production are shown in Table 15.4. Figure 15.12 illustrates the comparative generation of hazardous wastes by state for 1980.

There are two very distinct problems associated with the management of hazardous waste. One is the management of wastes generated now and in the future; the other is how to deal with wastes that were improperly disposed of in the past.

The Love Canal

In August 1978 the President of the United States declared the Love Canal in Niagara Falls, New York, a federal emergency disaster area. Federal assistance became available to evacuate some of the families in the area. This disaster, the result of improper disposal of hazardous waste, was the first national emergency ever to be declared for such a reason.

For several years until 1952 the Hooker Chemical Company disposed of some of its wastes by burying them in 55-gallon drums in a ditch known as the Love Canal. When the burial area was filled, it was capped with clay. The land was sold for $1.00 to the Board of Education of Niagara Falls, and a school and some residences were built on the site. Twenty-five years later the wastes began to leach. Construction caused the clay caps to crack; water infiltrated the trenches containing the waste. Leachate penetrated basement walls in the area, surfaced in backyards, and volatized in the air. Over 300 different chemicals were identified, many of them known or suspected carcinogens.

The cost of stabilizing the area by clay capping and drainage ditches was estimated to run between 8 and 10 million dollars. Cleanup of the canal could run over 30 million dollars. Hooker Chemical has been sued for claims amounting to over 2 billion dollars.

Time has proved that the Love Canal experience is not an isolated one. A 1985 report by the Office of Technology Assessment estimates that as many as 10,000 sites in the United States may need federal cleanup assistance over the next 50 years at a cost of 100 billion dollars. This estimate takes into account

Table 15.4 Sources of Hazardous Waste

Product	Hazardous Waste
Plastics	Organic chlorine compounds
Pesticides	Organic chlorine compounds, organic phosphate compounds
Medicines	Organic solvents and residues, heavy metals (mercury and zinc, for example)
Paints	Heavy metals, pigments, solvents, organic residues
Oil, gasoline, and other petroleum products	Oil, phenols, and other organic compounds, heavy metals, ammonia salts, acids, caustics
Metals	Heavy metals, fluorides, cyanides, acid and alkaline cleaners, solvents, pigments, abrasives, plating salts, oils, phenols
Leather	Heavy metals, organic solvents
Textiles	Heavy metals, dyes, organic chlorine compounds, solvents

surface impoundments, closed solid waste landfills, and leaking licensed hazardous waste facilities.

Treatment and Disposal Alternatives

Of the hazardous waste generated and regulated under federal law in 1981, 96% was handled onsite, that is, where it was generated. This left 4% that was disposed of by commercial storage, treatment, or disposal companies. Figure 15.13 shows how the commercial facilities handled this waste. Large generators find it economically feasible to treat onsite; small generators tend to use commercial facilities. More than 80% of all generators ship at least some waste to off-site facilities.

In 1979 it was estimated that only about 10% of all of the hazardous waste produced was being disposed of properly; the remaining 90% was disposed of in unlined lagoons, nonsecure landfills, and in miscellaneous ways such as by dumping into sewers or deep wells and by incineration (Maugh, 1979d).

Although there is disagreement on the best ways to deal with hazardous wastes, they can clearly be handled better than they are now. Table 15.5 compares some of the advantages and disadvantages of various management technologies. The technology and policies associated with the storage, treatment, and disposal of hazardous waste are similar to those for solid waste but provide for detoxification or more stringent containment requirements.

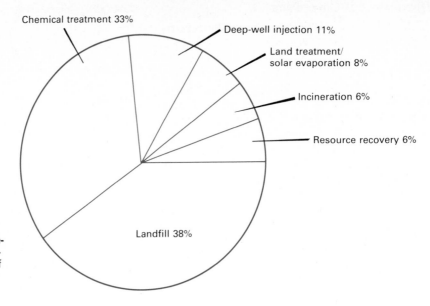

Figure 15.13 Waste Management Methods Used by Commercial Facilities. Only 12% of these wastes were recovered or incinerated.

Chemical treatment 33%

Deep-well injection 11%

Land treatment/ solar evaporation 8%

Incineration 6%

Resource recovery 6%

Landfill 38%

Table 15.5 Comparison of Some Hazardous Waste Reduction Technologies

	Disposal		Treatment		
	Landfills and Impoundments	Injection Wells	Incineration and other Thermal Destruction	Emerging High-Temperature Decomposition[a]	Chemical Stabilization
Effectiveness: How well it contains or destroys hazardous characteristics	Low for volatiles, questionable for liquids; based on lab and field tests	High, based on theory, but limited field data available	High, based on field tests, except little data on specific constituents	Very high, commercial-scale tests	High for many metals, based on lab tests
Reliability issues:	Siting, construction, and operation Uncertainties: long-term integrity of cells and cover, liner life less than life of toxic waste	Site history and geology; well depth, construction and operation	Monitoring uncertainties with respect to high degree of DRE; surrogate measures, PICs, incinerability[c]	Limited experience Mobile units; onsite treatment avoids hauling risks Operational simplicity	Some inorganics still soluble Uncertain leachate test, surrogate for weathering
Environmental media most affected	Surface and ground water	Surface and ground water	Air	Air	Ground water
Least compatible wastes [b]	Liner reactive; highly toxic, mobile, persistent, and bioaccumulative	Reactive; corrosive; highly toxic, mobile, and persistent	Highly toxic and refractory organics, high heavy metals concentration	Some inorganics	Organics
Costs: Low, Mod, High	L-M	L	M-H (Coincineration = L)	M-H	M
Resource recovery: potential	None	None	Energy and some acids	Energy and some metals	Possible building material

a. Molten salt, high-temperature fluid wall, and plasma arc treatments.
b. Wastes for which this method may be less effective for reducing exposure, relative to other technologies. Wastes listed do not necessarily denote common usage.
c. DRE = destruction and removal efficiency. PIC = product of incomplete combustion.

Source Reduction, Reuse, and Exchange. As with other wastes, the best method of managing hazardous waste is simply to produce less of it, that is, **source reduction**. As the requirements for proper disposal of hazardous waste are enforced, industry will find it more economical to change its processes to decrease the volume of hazardous waste it produces or to find mechanisms for reusing it. The EPA estimates that perhaps 20% of the hazardous waste currently generated could be reused or recycled (Maugh, 1979b). In other cases, when one industry cannot reuse its own waste, another industry can. About 20 waste exchange programs are in operation in the United States under the direction of trade associations, chambers of commerce, universities, and state or local governments. Industries provide information on the wastes they have available for reuse; this information is advertised, and inquiries from industries wanting to use the waste are returned to the generator for follow-up. The exchange program seems most appropriate for solvents, oils, and surplus chemicals.

Simple **volume reduction** methodologies are also useful and will become more important as disposal costs increase. Evaporation from holding ponds, for example, is a simple means of reducing the volume of hazardous chemicals that happen to be in aqueous solution.

Chemical Treatment. If hazardous waste cannot be reused, then the next preferred treatment is detoxification before disposal. **Detoxification** is the conversion of a toxic substance into something that is not hazardous. There are numerous ways to detoxify wastes; many of them are expensive. A common detoxification process is the neutralization of wastes by adjusting the pH. Acidic wastes can be neutralized by the addition of lime. This has the side benefit of precipitating out heavy metals. The iron and steel industry, the electroplating industry, and other metal-finishing industries use this process (Maugh, 1979b). Some wastes can be detoxified by oxidation-reduction reactions. For example, cyanides oxidized with sodium hypochlorite produce carbon dioxide and nitrogen. Carbon absorption can be used to remove organics from wastes. It has been used, for example, in the textile industry for removing dyes from effluents.

Biological Treatment. Most organic hazardous waste can decompose and thus is amenable to biological treatment such as composting. Precautions must be taken, however, to prevent the disposal of heavy metals or nonbiodegradable wastes in this manner, since they could accumulate in the soil and be taken up by plants, be carried into streams by runoff, or leach into groundwater. **Land farming** is a particular kind of composting involving the incorporation of the waste into the soil surface and mixing to provide aeration; decomposition is ideally taken care of by microorganisms. Land farming is suitable for more voluminous hazardous wastes such as petroleum refinery sludge. Composting is a more efficient method of biological treatment because decomposition occurs at higher temperatures. Composting requires protection from precipitation

The best way to manage hazardous waste is to produce less of it.

and usually some kind of bulking agent to provide a texture that is porous to ensure aerobic decomposition.

Incineration. Incineration of hazardous waste is a treatment that may or may not result in a hazardous residue. If the residue is hazardous, it must be properly disposed of by some other means. Hazardous wastes may be burned alone or with supplemental fuel. Traps for particulates, air pollution equipment such as scrubbers for toxic gases like hydrogen chloride, and high burning efficiencies are required. Several hazardous waste incinerators operate in the United States.

Several companies have developed systems for the incineration of hazardous wastes on ships at sea. Two such incineration ships are the *Vulcanus I* and *Vulcanus II,* which are owned by a U.S. waste management company. Incineration ships have proved to be efficient burners if properly operated. In 1977 *Vulcanus I* burned surplus quantities of the herbicide Agent Orange. The EPA monitored the air during the incineration and found that hazardous by-products were not released in significant amounts. As of 1984, permits for incineration at sea had not been issued, pending the adoption of regulations on ocean incineration by the EPA. The environmental impact of incineration at sea has yet to be fully determined.

Land Disposal

The last resort for hazardous wastes is to store them underground in deep wells or in landfills. It is the last resort because the waste remains toxic and the potential remains for premature or unexpected release into the environment; thus continual long-term monitoring and maintenance are required. Eventually, the waste will surely leach or make its way through landfill barriers. A basic premise in this strategy is that release will occur at such a slow rate as to be negligible in its effects or will occur after the waste itself has had time to be degraded. It is an undesirable approach, since it may postpone until future generations the handling of hazardous wastes.

Deep-Well Injection. Deep-well injection has been used for years in the oil fields to dispose of brine, and it has also been used for toxic waste disposal. Essentially, it involves pumping wastes into sandstone or limestone formations that are 1000–3000 meters deep (see Chapter 12). Opponents of this technology claim that it has caused earthquakes because of the increased underground pressures and

that it has a potential for contaminating ground-water. Proponents claim that such episodes have been the result of poor engineering.

Landfills. The **hazardous waste landfill** is very similar to a solid waste landfill except that greater precautions must be taken to prevent leaching, to separate incompatible wastes, and to check for migration of the hazardous waste from the trench. Wells are dug at strategic depths to check for leaching or migration of the waste. Knowing exactly where and when to monitor is crucial and requires information about subsurface geology and water movement.

Figure 15.14 shows the general scheme for a hazardous waste landfill. Usually several barriers are used to ensure that the waste will be contained as long as possible. These barriers include impermeable clay liners and synthetic liners. Both may be used to line the trench and to cap it to retard infiltration of rainwater. A leachate collection system is constructed to collect any water that may infiltrate the trench. Sometimes two leachate systems are used as a safeguard, one in the bottom of the trench and one beneath the liner. As the trenches are completed, they are capped with clay and contoured to allow for rapid runoff of rainwater and to decrease infiltration.

The technology associated with liners for hazardous waste landfills is only now emerging. No research projects have been underway for long enough to determine the life span of such liners under field conditions.

The EPA restricts the disposal of liquids in landfills. Liquids in trenches pose a problem not only because they can migrate but because sufficient quantities can build up like water in a bathtub. This accumulation of liquid can then produce pressure that pushes the liquid downward and outward. There are ways to solidify liquid waste. These include cement- or lime-based solidification; use of thermoplastic binders such as bitumen, asphalt, paraffin, and polyethylene; and use of organic polymers. Cement- or lime-based binders can be used with wet waste, but they are subject to leaching by acidic solutions. Thermoplastic binders may be susceptible to breakdown by organic solvents. They are, however, resistant to aqueous solutions, and they do lower migration caused by rainfall infiltration.

The EPA regulations require that landfills be insured against damages that could result from leaching and that a fund be established to pay for cleanup or closure and to cover monitoring and maintenance of the site for a given period of years after closure. Implementation of these requirements

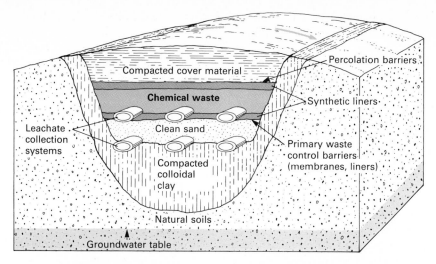

Figure 15.14 Hazardous Waste Disposal. Because of major health implications of groundwater contamination from hazardous waste landfills, numerous checkpoints are required in their design. The fill must be in an area of tight clay soils, or such clays must be imported to line the trench. Pipes and conduits to collect any leachate are required. The leachate can be pumped out and its composition tested. Synthetic liners can be another barrier between the waste and the environment or part of the cap to prevent water infiltration. The problem is to design a system that will work as long as the wastes remain hazardous—an indefinite period for some of these wastes.

should make use of other treatment and disposal technologies more attractive economically.

Integrated Hazardous Waste Management: European Style

European nations have relatively advanced technologies for managing hazardous waste. Because of the scarcity of land in Europe, detoxification and destruction of hazardous waste are favored over land disposal. In Denmark, nearly all hazardous waste is destroyed or detoxified; in West Germany, 60% is detoxified. Although some destruction and detoxification technologies yield residues that must be placed in secure land disposal sites, the volume is much reduced.

A good example of an integrated system for hazardous waste management is the Kommunekemi or "community chemical" plant in Denmark located near Nyborg. Its hazardous waste management system consists of industrial waste collection stations operated by municipalities. There are also dropoff stations for household hazardous wastes. Wastes collected at both types of stations are funneled into the Nyborg plant. The plant itself consists of three rotary kiln incinerators. The heat from the incineration process is used to generate steam to provide more than 60% of the heating demand for the 12,000 inhabitants of Nyborg. The chemical and physical processes onsite include destruction of cyanides by oxidation-reduction reaction using sodium hypo-

chlorite, neutralization of acids and bases, chemical reduction of chromium, and precipitation of heavy metals. Solid residues from incineration and treatment are disposed of in a landfill near the plant. The residues are relatively nontoxic and are in an immobile form.

Unless industries have special permission for onsite management, they are required by law to take their wastes to the municipal transfer and collection stations. Industries are charged for disposal of their wastes, costs being dependent on the technology used.

Similar integrated arrangements are found in other European countries. In West Germany, Bavaria has seven collection stations that separate oil and water, neutralize acids and bases, and thicken sludges. The wastes are then sent on to one of three destruction facilities that include incineration and other treatment technologies. Bavaria's facilities are totally owned by local government in some cases and are government-private cooperative ventures in other cases.

Sweden is developing a centralized hazardous waste treatment network similar to Denmark's that is expected to be completed in the mid-1980s.

Financing Cleanup

Besides regulating the proper disposal of hazardous waste, the United States faces the problem of the cleanup of existing dumps and spills of oil and chemicals. **The Comprehensive Environmental Response, Compensation, and Liability Act (CERCLA)**, also known as the **Superfund Act**, was passed by Congress in December 1980. It established a 1.6 billion dollar fund for emergency cleanup of spills and abandoned or inactive hazardous waste sites through industry fees and federal appropriations. To qualify for Superfund monies, a site must be placed on the National Priority List. Sites are ranked according to their potential for impact on human health and the environment; each state may designate one site to be placed on the list. Reauthorization of CERCLA is expected to increase the size of the fund to around 5–10 billion dollars to be expended through 1990.

Industry initially opposed this approach to financing cleanup as unfair. Companies with a responsible history of waste disposal do not wish to pay for the irresponsibilities of others. However, proponents claim that an assessment on hazardous waste generators will be passed on to consumers in the cost of the products. Thus consumers pay who use products that generate hazardous wastes. This is one approach to directing a shift in consumer patterns away from such higher-priced commodities and providing an impetus for industry to find ways to produce a product with less hazardous side effects.

Waste Facility Siting

A major problem in waste management is deciding where to put the treatment and disposal facilities. For many reasons, no one wants to live near waste facilities. Locating facilities in remote areas means higher transportation costs and increased danger of a spill, derailment, or other accident. Policies for siting such facilities are being sought at all levels of government. Although attention has been focused on the siting of hazardous waste facilities, similar problems exist for siting solid waste and radioactive waste facilities.

The federal government leaves questions of siting to the states and local governments. States have used different approaches to the siting of waste facilities. Some have given the authority for siting decisions to local governments; some have required local governments to follow certain state-level regulations in their decision making; some have prohibited local siting and have made it exclusively a state function. Several states have set up siting boards composed of government, expert, and citizen members (in some cases representing the local community) to make the final decision. Some states have made the

siting board an appeals board; some use it as a board for final arbitration if the negotiation process between the industry and the local community becomes stalled. Some states have established state-owned facilities.

Incentives to local communities to allow such facilities in their areas have been suggested (Table 15.6). Special taxes on such facilities to be returned as revenue to the county is a possibility in some states. Linking waste facilities with industrial parks as has been proposed in Kentucky would provide jobs, a buffer zone between the facility and the community, and an increased tax base. Public education, public involvement from the initial phases of site planning, and establishing credibility with the public in the area of waste disposal technology are other objectives being pursued.

Public relations problems associated with siting today are the result of poor waste disposal practices in the past, increased public awareness, and lack of public trust that industry will act responsibly in handling waste or that government can properly monitor and enforce hazardous waste regulations.

The siting of new facilities slowed in the late 1970s and early 1980s for other reasons as well. Industry was waiting to see what federal requirements would be for certain types of hazardous waste facilities. As landfills started to become more expensive and their long-term liabilities made them less desirable, industry began to examine its waste stream for more economic handling methods. This transition to more environmentally sound technologies for handling waste will take time.

What exactly is the role of government and industry in waste disposal? Government certainly has a responsibility to provide protection for its people. The question is how far it should go in satisfying industries' waste disposal needs when industry retains the authority to contol the volume and type of waste and to decide how and where the waste will be disposed. Who should bear the financial risk for new hazardous waste facilities? Some see government's role as to set the parameters for waste disposal, such as prohibiting the land disposal of certain wastes and requiring other wastes to be treated before land disposal. This type of regulation makes treatment technologies more economically competitive and allows the marketplace and the private sector to construct and finance new facilities. California has used this approach. Federal activity along these lines is also anticipated. The other alternative is state-owned and -operated facilities with flow control that requires industry to take its waste to certain facilities.

Table 15.6 Compensations and Incentives for Allowing Hazardous Waste Facilities in a Community

Impact issue	Compensation	Incentive
Truck traffic	Improve or partly maintain roads; provide traffic light(s)	Completely maintain roadways
Aesthetic impact	Offer direct cash payments to affected individuals/groups	Build an aesthetically pleasing park
Groundwater pollution risk	Provide liability insurance	Develop additional water supplies
Loss of wildlife area	Provide fund for endangered wildlife	Build additional recreation area
Property value decline	Provide land value guarantees and direct payments	Buy and provide additional property to affected residents
Uncertainty about potential damages	Provide performance bond liability insurance, emergency response fund; provide tipping fees to community	Purchase or provide guarantees or backing of municipal bonds
		Donate to local charitable organizations
		Provide free disposal service to local industry
		Clean up existing waste site

Obviously, there is no simple answer. The track record of waste generating and waste disposal industries must be improved; enforcement actions by government must be strong. Facilities that do not involve land disposal should be easier to site. However, both government and industry will have to work long and hard to restore their credibility with the public when it comes to proper handling of hazardous waste and enforcement of hazardous waste regulations.

RADIOACTIVE WASTE DISPOSAL

The bulk of radioactive wastes are not covered by the federal definition of hazardous waste, since they are regulated under the Atomic Energy Act. They are a subset of "solid wastes" and certainly constitute a special environmental problem. As we noted in Chapter 6, one of the problems of the nuclear industry has been the lack of a sound radioactive waste disposal program.

Radioactive wastes are classified as low-level and high-level wastes. **High-level wastes** are basically the spent fuel (fuel already used) from power reactors. Should reprocessing of commercial waste, which was halted under a presidential directive, be started again, high-level waste would be produced from fuel reprocessing (see Figure 15.15).

Low-level wastes are any radioactive wastes that are not, by definition, high-level wastes. The terms "low-level" and "high-level" refer to how the waste is generated and not to what it is or how radioactive it is. Low-level wastes include a broad spectrum of radioisotopes and are produced by the mining and processing of uranium, by nuclear power facilities, and by medical and research activities. They include radioactive isotopes used for cancer treatment and contaminated glass, pipes, clothes, animal carcasses, dry trash, and other laboratory equipment.

High-Level Radioactive Waste Disposal

Research is going on to find suitable technologies for the disposal of high-level wastes. In the meantime, wastes are being stored at power plant sites, awaiting safe ultimate disposal. Alternatives being considered include deep geologic disposal in salt beds or salt domes or in rock such as granite,

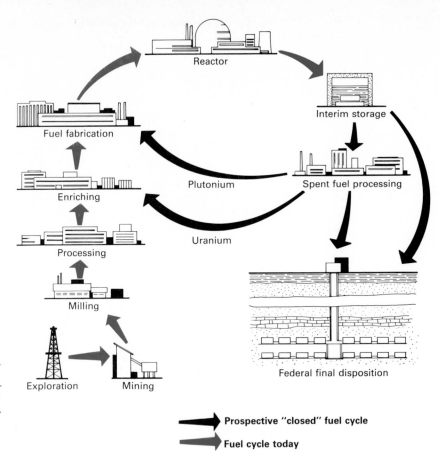

Figure 15.15 The Nuclear Fuel Cycle. Radioactive wastes are generated at each step in the cycle from uranium mining to processing, to use as reactor fuel, to reprocessing or disposal. Spent fuel is called high-level waste. Any other wastes or contaminated material have historically been classified as low level. Permanent disposal facilities for high-level wastes are still in the pilot stage.

Reactor

Interim storage

Fuel fabrication

Plutonium

Spent fuel processing

Enriching

Uranium

Processing

Milling

Exploration   Mining

Federal final disposition

➡ **Prospective "closed" fuel cycle**

➡ **Fuel cycle today**

basalt, shale, or volcanic ash. Disposal in deep ocean beds, island disposal, antarctic disposal, and even disposal in outer space have been considered. So far, the most feasible technology currently appears to be geologic disposal.

In its ideal form, **geologic disposal** involves placing waste so that there are multiple barriers between the waste and the general environment. The first barrier might be the chemical form of the waste. In one example, radioactive waste is processed into glass or ceramic blocks. Although the glass (or vitrification) technology is more highly developed, recent studies favor the use of ceramics (Carter, 1979). A second barrier might be the canister in which the vitrified waste is contained. The third barrier is the disposal medium itself (salt, rock, etc.).

Several attempts have been made to site such permanent high-level disposal facilities. A salt mine site in the late 1960s near Lyons, Kansas, was abandoned after technical problems arose from the presence of old wells and the potential for water seepage from nearby mining operations. The Waste Isolation Pilot Plant Project (WIPP) in New Mexico has had

many technical delays caused by problems such as pockets of brine in the sand. If the brine migrates toward the canisters, the heat of the waste could cause the formation of magnesium chloride, which would increase the corrosiveness of the brine. The waste itself could be converted from an insoluble oxide form to soluble chloride and hydroxide forms. Cooling the waste before emplacement is one remedy; sealed glass cylinders is another. Further studies point out the danger of groundwater intrusion at the proposed site as a result of a band of potash above the repository and the possibility of hydrocarbon deposits below the repository. There is also a problem with pressurized brine pockets.

Studies of the WIPP facility are being conducted during the construction process. The facility is authorized for use only for military transuranic (containing long-lived isotopes such as plutonium) wastes. Experimentation with military high-level waste is authorized, but the WIPP is not to be its ultimate disposal site; the waste must be retrieved.

Salt has many advantages as a disposal medium. It tends to be *self-healing*, that is, it fills open spaces around emplaced canisters. Its limitations come from the fact that it is highly soluble and, should groundwater intrude, it is chemically corrosive. Salt is also usually associated with other natural resources such as oil, gas, potash, and gypsum. At a waste disposal site, these associated resources could not be extracted.

Other geologic formations are not self-healing, and rock fractures could provide an outlet for migration of the wastes. However, even rock formations do have some capacity to adsorb the waste elements and hold them.

Disposal in deep ocean sediments is being explored. A bullet-canister could be projected a depth of about 30 meters into the so-called red clay of the deep ocean sediments. This technology is limited primarily by lack of information on the effect of heat and radiation on such sediments.

Other methods of ultimate disposal are in more preliminary stages. Disposal by melting into the antarctic icecaps has been discounted because of transportation problems and problems associated with the unknown impact of such melting on the stability of the ice formations. Shooting waste into the sun or into outer space is limited by questions of its safety, practicality, cost, and soundness as a long-term policy, among other things.

The first thousand years of disposal are thought to be the most critical, since intermediate-lived products such as cesium-137 and strontium-90 will have disintegrated over this time period. No available canisters will last that long; therefore the key is to find a disposal medium that can contain such waste for the necessary length of time.

Retrievability of radioactive waste is important. One advantage would be that if a containment system failed, the waste could be removed. Retrievability would also allow future generations having more advance technologies to use the waste as a resource or to transfer it to more advanced disposal facilities. The disadvantage of a retrievable waste disposal system is that it provides a window in the containment system that could be a weak point in the long-term integrity of the system.

Siting a Disposal Facility for High-Level Radioactive Waste

In December 1982, Congress enacted the **Nuclear Waste Policy Act**, which established a procedure and timetable for siting a permanent underground repository for high-level waste. The law requires the U.S. Department of Energy to recom-

mend three sites to the President by 1985. The President must then recommend a site to Congress by March 31, 1987, and a second site by March 31, 1990. The law provides for a state or Indian tribe veto of the facility. The veto can be overridden only by a vote of both houses of Congress. In December 1984 the U.S. Department of Energy recommended sites in the states of Washington, Nevada, and Texas for further study. It is not likely that the timetable envisioned in the law will be followed. A likely date for a permanent repository to come on line is around the year 2000. Other provisions of the law require the Department of Energy to conduct a feasibility study of a monitored retrievable storage facility for both waste and spent fuel, authorize the department to construct and operate a deep geologic test and evaluation facility, and provide for interim storage of spent fuel from nuclear power reactors. This accelerated timetable for siting a permanent facility satisfies the political need for a facility but may be unrealistic in terms of technological know-how.

Low-Level Radioactive Waste Disposal

Low-level wastes have largely been disposed of by **shallow land burial**. Originally, the intent was to have the waste permanently contained in the trenches by the impermeability of the rock in which it was buried. Consequently, artificial liners were

Low-level radioactive waste was buried in unlined trenches as late as 1981 in Los Alamos, New Mexico. Because this method proved inadequate for safety, artificial liners are now required.

not required; wastes were buried in cardboard boxes, and even liquid wastes were buried. These practices caused many problems. Criteria for siting and managing of such low-level facilities have been tightened over the years.

Six such commercial low-level nuclear waste disposal facilities have been located in the United States. Most of these facilities are currently not accepting commercial wastes or have been temporarily closed at one time or another because of water management problems, mismanagement by site operators, or inadequate enforcement of packaging and transportation requirements. The federal government operates several such facilities, but these have not been open to burial of commercial wastes. Experiences with low-level commercial sites have not been good overall. The impact this has had on the public credibility in the area of waste disposal technology is apparent in the growing opposition to the siting and operating of such facilities.

Federal Policies on Low-Level Radioactive Waste Disposal

In December 1980 Congress enacted Public Law 96–573, the **Low-Level Radioactive Waste Policy Act**, which established the policy that states shall be responsible for providing the disposal capacity for the low-level nuclear waste. The legislation authorizes states to establish multistate compacts. These would have a board or commission composed of representatives of the states with powers set out in the compact relating to siting of low-level nuclear waste disposal facilities and responsibilities of member states. Compacts are subject to ratification by the state legislatures and by Congress. The law also provides that after 1986, compacts may prohibit use of their facilities by noncompact states. This gives impetus to the states to find alternatives for handling their own wastes or to join compacts by 1986.

THE LEGISLATIVE HISTORY OF SOLID AND HAZARDOUS WASTE

Beginnings

The problems of solid waste, like many of our environmental problems, have been compounded by the political, social, and economic legacies of a time when air and water were abundant, free, and clean resources; when land was plentiful; and when energy and materials were cheap.

In 1965 the first national solid waste legislation was enacted. The **Solid Waste Disposal Act of 1965**

(PL–89–272) provided money to the states to develop solid waste management plans and to survey current disposal practices. In 1970 the **Resource Recovery Act** (PL–91–512) marked a significant policy change from focusing on *disposal* problems to examining *recovery* processes for materials and energy. However, the program was basically a nonregulatory program. In 1975, hearings on the issue of solid waste were held by Congress. In October 1976 the **Resource Conservation and Recovery Act (RCRA)** was enacted. This was an omnibus bill with regulatory implications. It was an important addition to federal comprehensive air and water laws passed earlier in the 1970s (see Chapters 9–12).

RCRA

The RCRA addresses the problems of both solid and hazardous waste. The law requires states to develop solid waste management plans and prohibits open dumps. All dumps were to be closed or upgraded to landfills by the mid-1980s. In addition, federal procurement agencies were directed to begin purchasing materials that utilize the greatest amounts of recycled materials. Recognizing the need for market promotion, the law directed the Department of Commerce to assist in developing specifications for recovered materials to ensure good-quality products. The department was also directed to look at developing markets for recycled materials and help promote them. The Department of Mines and Minerals was directed to focus on mineral waste problems, including recovery from industrial wastes and junk car processing. Freight rates and their implications for recycled materials were to be examined by the Interstate Commerce Commission. The Department of Energy was directed to promote research and development for production of energy from solid waste.

In the area of hazardous waste, RCRA provides for the development of criteria for identifying and listing hazardous waste and of standards for generation, storage, treatment, and disposal of such waste by the EPA. The law also calls for the development of a system to track wastes from point of generation to point of disposal by means of a *manifest*.

The manifest is a multicopy form (similar to a bill of lading or shipping voucher) that identifies, among other things, the origin, quantity, composition, and destination of the hazardous waste. The form is completed and signed by the waste generator. The generator retains a copy and gives the original and remaining copies to the transporter. The transporter signs and retains a copy and gives the original and remaining copies to the disposer on delivery of the waste. The disposer signs the manifest, keeps a copy, and returns the original to the generator. Such a system is intended to track the wastes from "cradle to grave." All parties are required to report periodically to the regulatory agency and to notify them if manifests are not properly received.

States may administer and enforce the hazardous waste program if they receive EPA authorization to do so. For full authorization the state program must be at least equivalent to the federal program, consistent with other federal programs, and comparable to programs in other states and must demonstrate adequate enforcement. To assist the states in developing hazardous waste policies, the EPA has set this order of priorities for disposing of hazardous waste:

1. Reduce the generation of hazardous waste.
2. Separate out and isolate hazardous waste from other industrial wastes to keep the volume small.
3. Utilize the waste through exchange and recovery.
4. Incinerate the waste; detoxify or neutralize where possible.
5. Dispose in secure landfills

RCRA was reauthorized by Congress late in 1984. Basically, the new legislation brings small generators of hazardous waste (100–1000 kg/month) under regulation and places substantially greater restrictions on land disposal of hazardous waste. The new legislation also bans land disposal for some types of wastes and establishes more strict standards for landfills and surface impoundments. A new program for the regulation of underground storage tanks is also established. There may be 100,000 such tanks leaking gasoline, pesticides, or industrial solvents underground.

CERCLA

The **Comprehensive Environmental Response, Compensation and Liability Act (CERCLA)** of 1980 was designed primarily to address the problem of financing cleanup of abandoned or illegal hazardous waste sites. Because of delays in getting criteria for designating eligible sites and because of foot dragging in the early part of the Reagan administration, only four sites on the national priority list had been cleaned up by January 1984; emergency removals had taken place at 196 sites. One of the problems in implementation is determining when a site is clean. How are cleanup costs and the degree of cleanup related to long-term care costs? As was mentioned

earlier, the original 1.6 billion dollars designated for the Superfund is likely to be increased severalfold if the Superfund is reauthorized. The reauthorization is also likely to put the EPA on a schedule for cleaning up sites and establishing mandatory cleanup standards.

OTHER SOLUTIONS

The ideal solutions to our waste problem in the long run appear to be resource recovery and reduction in the actual amount of waste produced. Both approaches conserve resources and energy. Given that waste cannot be eliminated altogether, resource recovery at least helps to alter what has been a one-way flow of materials. Resource recovery is the complement to source reduction, and both are essential to a more efficient materials system— ecologically speaking. More and more economists, business executives, and citizens are beginning to agree.

Changing the materials system is basically a problem of changing consumer patterns. For the most part, this is a question of economics. How does one convince a person to separate his or her own waste?

How can people be motivated to use products that are most easily disposed of or recycled or simply to use less? How can they be encouraged to use recycled materials? How does one encourage manufacturers, processors, packagers, and distributors to change what they do so as to produce less waste? Here are some alternatives that have been proposed or attempted.

Bottle Bills

One of the most controversial approaches to the problem of solid waste is the so-called **bottle bill** (see Figure 15.16). A bottle bill simply imposes a deposit of several cents on most types of beverage containers. The deposit is returned to the purchaser when the empty beverage container is returned to the place of purchase. Bottle bills have the effect of returning potential solid waste to the source; they also tend to shift beverage packaging from nonreturnable containers to returnable bottles.

Several countries have mandatory beverage container deposit programs, including Sweden, Denmark, Norway, and the Netherlands. Several provinces in Canada have deposit programs. Bottle bills have also been enacted in such U.S. states as Connecticut, Delaware, Iowa, Maine, Massachusetts, New York, Michigan, Oregon, and Vermont and in

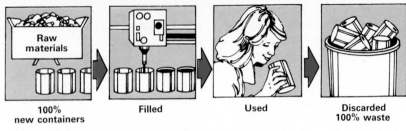

(a) Simplified present beverage container system

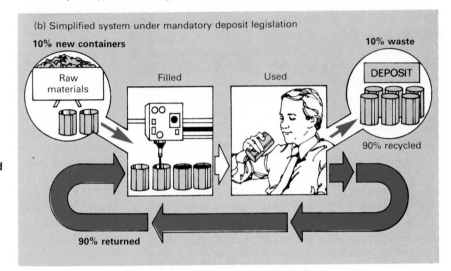

(b) Simplified system under mandatory deposit legislation

Figure 15.16 Managing Used Beverage Containers. Proponents of bottle bills claim that such legislation significantly reduces litter. Opponents claim that bottle bills are ineffective and discriminatory, since beverage containers compose only 25% of all litter.

Fairfax County, Virginia. Federal military installations have initiated deposit requirements. Other states have bottle bill legislation pending.

Pros and Cons. Bottle bill proponents claim that such laws reduce litter, reduce the total volume of solid waste, and conserve energy by promoting a shift to refillable containers and forcing recycling. Bottles can be refilled ten times or more; cans can be recycled, eliminating the energy-intensive process needed to produce aluminum from bauxite. Both practices reduce air and water pollution and help conserve natural resources.

Opponents claim that bottle bills are discriminatory, since beverage containers constitute only 25% of all litter. They further object to increased labor costs from the additional handling of containers and possible sanitary problems. Opponents say that bottle bills that do not put an equal deposit on all beverage containers influence competition. Such bills, they state, result in undue hardships on beverage industries that produce nonreturnables or throwaways, since their product cannot be refilled or recycled and thus, when returned, are of little economic benefit to the company.

Proponents counter that the impact of throw-away containers on small business was such that the number of breweries decreased from 300 in the 1950s to fewer than 100 in the 1970s. Soft drink bottling plants decreased from 4500 in the 1960s to 2300 in the 1970s (U.S. General Accounting Office, 1977). Because throwaways did not need to be returned to the bottling plant, bottlers could ship beverages over longer distances. Large national brewers and bottlers took advantage of this potential by building larger bottling facilities and expanding their markets. Smaller bottlers could not compete with the economies of scale of the larger operators.

Perhaps the best way to examine the pros and cons of a bottle bill is to look at the experience in Oregon.

Oregon: Impacts of the Bottle Bill. Oregon's bottle bill went into effect on October 1, 1972. It required a five-cent minimum deposit on beverage containers. Pull-tops on cans were banned.

Total litter was reduced by 11–26% in the first year and by 39% in the second year. Beverage container litter decreased by 66–88% in the first year.

If disposable beverage container bottles (brought in from out of state) were subtracted from the count, beverage container litter actually dropped

90%. Data from Vermont indicates a 76% decrease in beverage container litter during the first year of that state's bottle bill implementation. Michigan reported a 5% reduction in total solid waste and translated that into a 15 million dollar savings in pickup and disposal costs the first year after enactment of their bottle bill.

In 1973, beverage prices in Oregon did increase; they also increased in neighboring Washington, which did not have a bottle bill. Beer sales in Oregon increased 1.4% in 1973, down from an historical annual increase of about 5%. However, increases occurred again in following years amounting to 5.7% in 1974, 3.8% in 1975, and 3.7% in 1976.

There was a net increase of jobs in Oregon as a result of the bottle bill; estimates range from 348 to 410 more workers.

The return rate was 92% on bottles and 80% on cans.

A National Bottle Bill. The Oregon experience has been a positive one. However, opponents of the bottle bill argue that the results in Oregon cannot be extrapolated to other states because of the different mix of industry in each state and the fact that Oregonians are generally a more environmentally aware citizenry. Proponents dispute both of these assumptions and point to the fact that bottle bills have been successful in other states. Since national beverage container legislation has been initiated several times, the General Accounting Office studied the potential impact of such legislation on the nation. They concluded that such a bill would:

1. reduce beverage container litter and total litter and reduce postconsumer solid waste, thus reducing demand on landfill space and cleanup and disposal costs;
2. increase the cost of handling empty containers, since four times as many containers would have to be handled;
3. increase industry income because not all of the containers would be returned for the deposit refund.

The study concluded that a bottle bill for the nation could result in both reduced consumption of raw materials and reduced energy use. A changeover to returnables would result in an increase in associated labor costs. However, there would be a decrease in new container purchases and an increase in income from retained deposits that would more than offset the increased capital and labor costs. The study concluded that maintaining the deposit system once the changeover occurs would be considerably cheaper than continuing the present trends.

Industry still contends that the energy saved in a deposit system is very small, amounting to about only 0.2% of the total U.S. energy demand. Others believe that every little bit of energy conserved adds up. In addition, recycling aluminum cans may decrease bauxite imports and help the national balance of payments. Currently, the United States imports 90% of the bauxite it uses.

The GAO study concludes that there would be a decrease in container manufacturing industry jobs and an increase in beverage and retail store industry jobs, resulting in a net increase of 20,000–32,000 jobs.

The study also recommended some provisions to be included in a bottle bill. The deposit should be equally applied to all beverage containers. A phase-in period is advisable. A public education program should accompany implementation of the bill. Provision should be made to assist individuals displaced by the changes in types of jobs needed. Some of the unredeemed deposits should go to cities or counties to fund litter and solid waste management programs. Prelaw and postlaw studies should be conducted to provide solid data on the impact of the law.

Litter Bills

The beverage industry proposes community beautification and litter pickup programs in lieu of beverage container legislation. Along with this the industry supported the enactment of a "litter law." The **litter bill** approach first took form in Washington state. An assessment is placed on industry in the state to cover the cost of litter cleanup. The assessment is levied on industries that generate the products that often end up as litter. The Washington approach is supported by the beverage industry; they see it as more equitable than bottle bills, since it deals with paper, plastics, and throwaways in general and not just beverage containers. Public education is a major consideration here. The beverage industry is also organizing in many states to promote the development of recycling centers.

Although the litter bill and recycling programs have been promoted as an alternative to the bottle bill, the two are not mutually exclusive and in fact may be complementary. The bottle bill is concerned with stopping the production of litter; the litter bill is concerned with cleaning up litter. Some states are now considering enactment of both types of bills. The litter bill approach does seek a remedy for the aesthetic and economic issues related to solid waste collection and disposal. However, it does not address the ecological issues associated with the conversion of resources and energy, as the bottle bill does.

TECHNOLOGY AND NATURE'S WAY

There are obviously many ways to deal with the problem of waste. We can use high-technology facilities to recover, recycle, detoxify, or incinerate wastes. We can look for processes that generate less harmful waste and less waste overall. We could simply do with less.

Any solution should be measured against knowledge and understanding of the basic ecological principle that everything must go somewhere. To continue to use resources linearly is to continue to burden ourselves and future generations with the spectre of scarce resources, mounting waste disposal problems, and the long-term monitoring of waste disposal sites. Alternatives will require economic and perhaps social adjustments; some will be the result of individual decisions by consumers.

One fact is certain. The laws of nature cannot be ignored for very long.

Washington state has been active in promoting litter cleanup and recycling. Among its programs has been the hiring of summer Job Corps workers to pick up litter along highways.

CONCEPTS TO REMEMBER

1. Once waste has been generated, it must go somewhere. It goes into either the land, the air, or the water.
2. For regulatory purposes, waste is usually classified as solid, hazardous, or radioactive.
3. The amount of waste generated per capita by a nation is not necessarily related to affluence or a certain standard of living. The United States generates much more waste per capita than many other industrialized nations.
4. The composition of waste has changed over the years. In the United States there has been an increase in plastic wastes and packaging wastes and a decrease in organic wastes.
5. Land disposal of wastes in landfills or dumps has been the traditional method of waste disposal in the United States. With land disposal there is the likelihood of leaching from the landfill or dump site. From a long-term perspective it is the least desirable disposal method.
6. European nations are far ahead of the United States in developing waste disposal technologies that do not center on land disposal. This has been necessary because of the density of population and scarcity of land in Europe.

7. As long as land disposal is the most economical method of waste disposal, it is likely to remain the most commonly used method. Factors that will raise the cost of landfills include the high cost of land, the enforcement of long-term liability, the requirements for upgrading landfill operations by requiring liners and leachate collection systems, and groundwater monitoring.
8. Ocean dumping as a disposal option must be examined carefully.
9. Resource recovery is a method of turning wastes into resources by recovering usable energy and material products.
10. One ton of municipal solid waste is equivalent to nine million BTUs, 65 gallons of No. 1 (kerosene) fuel oil, or 9000 cubic feet of natural gas.
11. For a resource recovery facility to be successful, a community must plan it well. There must be some assurance that the waste stream will not change dramatically in volume and type and that there is a market for the recovered materials or energy.
12. Pollution of groundwater from leaching of landfills is a major health concern. Because of lack of control over the types of materials placed

in sanitary landfills and open dumps over the years, many wastes currently classified as hazardous have been buried in landfills. Safeguards required for hazardous waste landfills to control leaching have generally not been applied to sanitary landfills.

13. Estimates of the volume of hazardous waste generated in the United States seem to increase yearly. In 1976, Congress passed a federal law to regulate large generators of hazardous waste. In 1984, legislation was enacted to regulate small generators. Improper disposal of hazardous waste in the past has resulted in many costly cleanup problems and will continue to haunt our nation for years to come.

14. The siting of new facilities for waste management has become difficult because of improper management practices in the past and lack of government enforcement. All levels of government and industry are seeking new and equitable methods for facility siting that involve compensation to and negotiation with the host community.

15. The primary method of disposal of low-level radioactive waste has been shallow land burial. There is still no repository for high-level radioactive waste, and none is likely before the year 2000.

16. Changing a throwaway society is basically a problem of changing consumer patterns. Some methods of changing consumer patterns include full-cost pricing (include the cost of disposal in the cost of the product); deposit requirements on beverage containers to encourage their return for reuse or recycling; and incremental user charges (the more waste you produce, the more you pay for collection).

17. Waste reduction is one part of the solution to the waste problem. Reuse and recycling are other options. Detoxification by chemical and biological treatment is also desirable. Incineration in most cases reduces the combustible components of the waste to ash. Land disposal via landfills, lagoons and ponds, and deep-well injection may cause more serious environmental problems for future generations; these practices should be the disposal methods of last resort.

18. Any solutions to the waste problem should be grounded solidly in the ecological principles that materials cycle in the ecosphere and everything must go somewhere. To continue to use resources linearly is to continue to burden ourselves and future generations with the spectre of scarce resources, waste disposal problems, and long-term monitoring of waste sites.

DISCUSSION QUESTIONS AND FOOD FOR THOUGHT

1. Find out how your community disposes of its solid waste. Talk to the people in charge of disposal to determine your community's long-range plans for waste disposal.
2. Keep a list for a week of solid waste materials you dispose of. Calculate the percentage of paper, glass, metal, and organics. What amount of the waste is composed of renewable resources (paper, wood)? What amount comes from nonrenewable resources (e.g., plastic from petroleum).
3. Start a compost heap.
4. Debate: Resolved: Resource recovery is the best— maybe the only—solution to solid waste disposal.
5. Trace the social, economic, and ecological impacts of waste reduction as a solid waste disposal alternative.
6. You are a member of a city governing body. The city is running out of landfill space. Design a plan of action for the governing board to consider alternatives for further solid waste disposal. Base the plan on all appropriate factors.
7. Design a TV commercial to arouse public action concerning litter.
8. If you were a benevolent dictator, what actions would you take to eliminate the problem of solid waste disposal? Compare these actions with the plan developed in question #6 above. Are there any differences?
9. Discuss: Litter is basically an energy and resource problem, not an aesthetic one.
10. Find out about the hazardous waste program in your state. Are there any hazardous waste facilities? Can they be visited? Find a guest speaker from industry, from a state regulatory agency, and from the local community in which the facility is located.
11. Debate: Resolved: Litter bills and bottle bills are not either/or approaches to the problem of litter and solid waste.
12. Discuss the list of priorities on page 487 for managing hazardous waste and methods for encouraging alternatives to landfills.
13. Choose one statement and defend it:
    a. Because American consumers want products whose production results in hazardous waste by-products, the cost of treatment and disposal of such wastes and cleanup of abandoned sites should come from general tax funds.
    b. Only industry can choose to alter manufacturing processes to decrease the amount of hazardous waste it generates. An assessment on generators of waste will be passed on to the con-

sumers of their products, and this should reduce consumption, causing the generator to find ways to reduce the volume of hazardous waste produced. Thus the cost of treatment, disposal, and cleanup of abandoned sites should come from a fee on generators.

14. Discuss: The current standard of living in the United States cannot be maintained without the production of hazardous wastes.

15. Obtain a map of your state. Divide the state into waste management districts with each district to be served by a centralized regional waste management facility. What factors will you need to consider in addition to volume of waste and transportation? What problems do you foresee? How will the facility be paid for?

REFERENCES AND FURTHER READING

References marked with an asterisk are cited in the chapter.

Alvarez, R. J., 1983. "Waste to Energy Update," *Waste Age,* April, 106–114.

Archer, T., and Huls, J., 1981. *Resource Recovery from Plastic and Glass Wastes.* Cincinnati: Municipal Environmental Research Laboratory.

Bureau of Mines, 1984. *Mineral Commodity Summaries.* Washington, D.C.: Bureau of Mines.

Burks, S., and Page, C., 1979. "Resource Recovery: Is it for your city?" *Nations Cities* **15**(7, July):9–14.

*Carter, L. J., 1979. "Academy Squabbles Over Radwaste Report," *Science* **205**(July 20):287–289.

Carter, L. J., 1983. "The Radwaste Paradox," *Science* **219** (January 7):33–36.

Commission on Natural Resources, 1975. *Mineral Resources and the Environment Supplementary Report: Resource Recovery from Municipal Solid Wastes.* Washington, D.C.: National Research Council, National Academy of Sciences.

Congressional Research Service, 1977. *Materials Policy Handbook: Legislative Issues of Materials Research and Technology.* No. 90-4430. Science Policy Research Division. Washington, D.C.: U. S. Government Printing Office.

Conservation Foundation, 1984. *State of the Environment: An Assessment at Mid-decade.* Washington, D.C.: The Conservation Foundation.

Conservation Foundation. *State of the Environment 1982.* Washington, D.C.: The Conservation Foundation.

*Council on Environmental Quality, 1976. *Report to Congress.* Washington, D.C.: U.S. Government Printing Office.

Council on Environmental Quality, 1979. *Tenth Annual Report.* Washington, D.C.: U.S. Government Printing Office.

*Council on Environmental Quality, 1983. *Annual Report.* Washington, D.C.: U.S. Government Printing Office.

Council on Scientific Affairs, 1982. "Health Effects of Agent Orange and Dioxin Contaminants," *JAMA* **248**: 1895–1897 (October 15, 1982).

Deese, P. L.; Hudson, J. F.; Innes, R. C.; and Fundkouser, D., 1981. *Options for Resource Recovery and Disposal of Scrap Tires.* Cincinnati: Municipal Environmental Research Laboratory.

Edwards, B. H.; Paullin, J. N.; and Coghlan-Jordan, K. 1982. *Emerging Technologies for the Control of Hazardous Waste.* Cincinnati: Municipal Environmental Research Laboratory.

Frankiewicz, T. C., ed., 1980. *Design and Management for Resource Recovery. Volume I: Energy from Waste.* Ann Arbor, Michigan: Ann Arbor Science Publishers.

Franklin Associates, 1979. *Post-consumer Solid Waste and Resource Recovery Baseline.* Washington, D.C.: Resource Conservation Committee.

Hamlin, C., 1980. "Sewage: Waste or Resource?" *Environment* **22**(8):16–20f.

Hansen, W. G., and Rishel, H. L., *Cost Comparisons of Treatment and Disposal Alternatives for Hazardous Materials.* Cincinnati: Municipal Environmental Research Laboratory.

Hibbard, W. R., Jr., 1982. "The Extractive Metallurgy of Old Scrap Recycle," *Journal of Metals,* July, 50–53.

Kenne, J. C., 1983. "Managing Agricultural Pollution," *Ecology Law Quarterly* **11**(2):135–188.

Kerr, R. A. 1979a. "Geologic Disposal of Nuclear Wastes: Salt's Lead is Challenged," *Science* **204**(May 11):603–606.

Kerr, R. A., 1979b. "Nuclear Waste Disposal: Alternatives to Solidification in Glass Proposed," *Science* **204**(April 20):289–291.

*Lahey, W., and Connor, M., 1983. "The Case for Ocean Waste Disposal," *Technology Review,* August/September, 60–70.

Lash, T., 1979. "Radioactive Waste," *Amicus,* Fall 1979, 24–34.

McKinney, J. D., ed., 1981. *Environmental Health Chemistry: The Chemistry of Environmental Agents as Potential Human Hazards.* Ann Arbor, Mich.: Ann Arbor Science.

Maugh, T. H., II, 1979a. "Burial Is Last Resort for Hazardous Wastes," *Science* **204**:1295–1298.

*Maugh, T. H., II, 1979b. "Hazardous Waste Technology is Available," *Science* **204**:930–933.

Maugh, T. H., II, 1979c. "Incineration, Deep Wells, Gain New Importance," *Science* **204**:1188–1190.

*Maugh, T. H., II, 1979d. "Toxic Waste Disposal: A Growing Problem," *Science* **204**(May 25): 819–823.

Maugh, T. H., II, 1982. "Just How Hazardous Are Dumps?" *Science* **215**(January 29):490–493.

National Research Council, 1985. *Reducing Hazardous Waste Generation.* Washington, D.C.: National Academy Press.

Office of Technology Assessment, 1979. *Beverage Container Deposit Legislation: Materials and Energy from Municipal Waste.* (Report No. OTA-M-93; GPO v.1, Stock #052-003-00692-8.) Washington, D.C.: Office of Technology Assessment.

*Office of Technology Assessment, 1985. *Superfund Strategies.* Washington, D.C.: Office of Technology Assessment.

Piasecki, B., and Davis, G. A., 1984. "A Grand Tour of Europe's Hazardous Waste Management Facilities," *Technology Review,* July, 21–29.

Rodgers, W. H., Jr., 1970. "The Persistent Problem of the Persistent Pesticide: A Lesson in Environmental Law," *Columbia Law Review* **70**(4):567–611.

Seldman, N., and Huls, J., 1981. "Beyond the Throwaway Ethic," *Environment* **23**:25–36.

Shrader-Frechette, K. S., 1980. *Nuclear Power and Public Policy.* Hingham, Mass.: D. Reidel Publishing Co.

*Skilling, K., 1977. "Solid Waste Programs and the Resource Conservation and Recovery Act of 1976," *Environment Reporter* **8**(22):1–26.

Swanson, R. L., and Devine, M., 1982. "Ocean Dumping Policy," *Environment* **24**(5):15–20.

*U.S. Code, 1976. *Congressional and Administrative News, 94th Congress Second Session* **5**:6238–6354.

U.S. Department of Energy, 1979. *Management of Commercially Generated Radioactive Waste* (Summary). (DOE/EIS-0046-D.) Washington, D.C.: U.S. Government Printing Office.

U.S. Environmental Protection Agency, 1976. *The Resource Recovery Industry: A Survey of the Industry and Its Capacity.* Washington, D.C.: EPA Office of Solid Waste.

U.S. Environmental Protection Agency, 1977. *Resource Recovery and Waste Reduction.* Washington, D.C.: EPA Office of Solid Waste.

U.S. Environmental Protection Agency, 1978. *Considerations of Environmental Protection Criteria for Radioactive Waste.* Washington, D.C.: EPA Office of Radiation Programs.

*U.S. Environmental Protection Agency, 1979. *EPA Activities Under the Resource Conservation and Recovery Act: Fiscal Year 1978.* Washington, D.C.: EPA Office of Water and Waste Management.

U.S. Environmental Protection Agency, 1980. *Environmental Outlook 1980.* EPA-600/8-80-003. Washington, D.C.: EPA Office of Research and Development.

*U.S. General Accounting Office, 1977. *Potential Effects of a National Mandatory Deposit on Beverage Containers.* (PAD-78-19). Washington, D.C.: U.S. Government Printing Office.

U.S. General Accounting Office, 1978. *How to Dispose of Hazardous Waste—A Serious Question that Needs to be Resolved.* (CED-79-13) Washington, D.C.: U.S. Government Printing Office.

*U.S. General Accounting Office, 1979. *Conversion of Urban Waste to Energy: Developing and Introducing Alternate Fuels from Municipal Solid Waste.* (EMD-79-7) Washington, D.C.: U.S. Government Printing Office.

*U.S. General Accounting Office, 1980. *Federal Industrial Targets and Procurement Guidelines Programs Are Not Encouraging Recycling and Have Contract Problems.* (EMD-81-7) Washington, D.C.: U.S. Government Printing Office.

Urban Land Institute. "Solid Waste Management," *Environmental Comment,* February, 1977.

Weir, D., and Shapiro, M., 1980. "Pesticide Pollution Goes Multinational," *Bus. Soc. Rev.* Spring 1980–81:47–53.

White, I. L., and Spath, J. P., 1984. "Low Level Radioactive Waste Disposal: How are States Setting Their Sites?" *Environment* **26**(8):16–20ff.

Noise, Crowding, and Ugly Surroundings

"It is much too crowded here, let's move to the country". . . . "The air looks so bad it makes you want to hold your breath!" . . . "Would you believe that this stream was once full of trout, turtles, and other things that were alive?" . . . "What? You'll have to speak up!" . . . "My eyes were watering so badly I could barely read the newspaper, and it was impossible to carry out any kind of conversation because of the noise, especially people coughing!" . . . "The junkyard was an unbelievable eyesore, but the fence isn't much of an improvement!" . . . "The exhaust fumes are beginning to get to me." . . . "The city was gray and depressing. There were miles and miles of concrete and dilapidated red brick buildings, and there wasn't a tree to be seen anywhere."

Our purpose in this chapter is to look at some of the effects of pollutants that are often not recognized as pollutants and less well characterized in terms of their effects than the ones we have considered thus far. Most of our discussion will be devoted to noise and crowding, but we will also consider the effects of ugly surroundings on human beings.

NOISE REALLY IS A POLLUTANT

Julius Caesar reportedly barred chariots from certain parts of Rome during certain hours of the day and most of the night. Chariot wheels on cob-blestones must have made quite a racket. Although there are other such references to noise throughout ancient literature, noise, like other pollution problems is by and large a modern problem. In our stampede for bigger and better we have literally set the environment vibrating with misspent energy.

Although estimates vary, some say that background noise levels have been increasing for decades by as much as 1 decibel per year. There is general agreement among the experts that background noise long ago passed the point of causing significant harm. We have jackhammers, power mowers, demolition equipment, air compressors, generators, cars and trucks (including some without mufflers), aircraft, washing machines, dishwashers, food processors, stereos, meat grinders, chain saws, and much, much more. Most of these are associated with urban life, but even in what used to be secluded, quiet areas we have minibikes, snowmobiles, and other appliances that disturb the serenity of the outdoors, damage the hearing of the operators, and adversely affect wildlife.

Noise is a pollutant by any measure of the term. Noise hurts, and it is a by-product of human activity. Noise can be diminished, but only at some cost. As with the effects of other pollutants, the effects of noise are difficult to measure.

We do know that very loud sounds and unwanted sounds affect humans in three general negative ways. First and foremost, loud sounds can impair hearing and thus interfere with the functioning of our bodies in a manner not unlike the effect of ozone on the lungs. Second, very loud sounds and unwanted sounds can also have other negative physiological effects—for example, change in blood vessel diameter, heart rate, and blood pressure. Third, unwanted or startling sounds can affect humans psychologically.

SOUND AND HEARING

Because our definition of noise and our discussion of its effects require some understanding of the nature of both sound and hearing, we must consider each of these before moving on.

The Nature of Sound

Sound is produced whenever objects are set to vibrating in air, water, or other media. The back-and-forth movement elicited when something like a tuning fork is struck sets up a series of compression waves in the medium around the vibrating object. These waves travel away from the source at speeds related to the density of the molecules of the medium carrying the compression wave.

Imagine a line of rubber balls, each suspended from a string in a line as shown in Figure 16.1. It should be easy to imagine how striking the first rubber ball in the line would lead to its impact with the second, which would in turn strike the third, and so on. The compression wave would travel all the way to the end of the line. Though they are not suspended from strings and though they are not ordered in any particular way, molecules of air in random motion behave like the rubber balls shown in Figure 16.1, except that compression waves travel out from the source in every direction rather than in one straight line.

This is a good point at which to reflect back on the concept of efficiency of energy transfer and the second law of thermodynamics. Since each collision results in some net loss of useful energy (and gain in entropy), it is understandable that noise gets weaker with distance from the source. Sound is a disturbance within a material medium (air, water, etc.), and this is why screams cannot be heard in the vacuum of outer space.

Sound has several physical properties. Two that are relevant to our discussion here are frequency (*pitch*) and *intensity* (loudness). Before we consider these properties as interpreted by humans, let's consider their physical meanings.

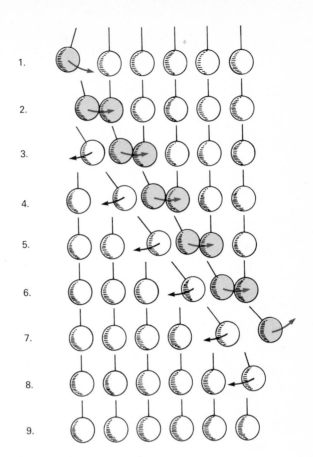

Figure 16.1   A Compression Wave. A transfer of kinetic energy via collision. Compression waves may occur in any medium made up of molecules; they cannot be transmitted through a vacuum.

Frequency. As the arm of a tuning fork moves in one direction, it sweeps molecules of air ahead of it and leaves behind it a rarified area or a vacuum. Molecules struck by the tuning fork collide with other molecules, and compression waves are propagated away from the tuning fork. With each succeeding back-and-forth motion of the tuning fork a new wave of compression is started. The rate at which a sound source vibrates determines the rate at which compression waves pass a point at some distance from the tuning fork, or the **frequency** of that sound wave. One kind of tuning fork might send 300 such compression waves per second past a point ten feet away, while a higher-frequency fork might send 420 waves each second. The vibration frequency of a particular object is related to the elastic or tensile properties of the object; these properties determine how rapidly it moves back and forth when struck. **Pitch** is the human perception of sound frequency.

Decibel: a relative measure of sound intensity; ten times the logarithm of the ratio of two sound intensities, one being a reference sound level.

Frequency: rate; sound frequency is the rate at which compression waves arrive at or pass a fixed point. Frequency is perceived as pitch.

Hearing threshold shift: a change in the loudness of the quietest sound that can be heard. Exposure to loud sound can cause the threshold to become elevated.

Hertz (Hz): cycles per second; a measure of sound frequency.

Infrasound: sound too low in frequency to be heard (below 20 Hz).

Intensity: loudness; acoustical power (the energy that sound delivers) per unit area.

Loudness: the human perception of the intensity of sound. Loudness is actually determined by both intensity and frequency; a 20-db sound will not necessarily sound equally loud at different frequencies.

Noise: sound of a duration, intensity, and/or other quality that causes some kind of physical, physiological, or psychological harm or stress to a human being.

Pitch: the human perception of sound frequency (and to some extent intensity).

Sonic boom: human perception of the shock wave generated by an object traveling faster than the speed of sound.

Ultrasound: sound too high in frequency to be heard (above 20,000 Hz).

White noise: sound generated at all audible frequencies at the same time.

Intensity. Sound waves can also vary with respect to how bunched up molecules are in each zone of compression and how relatively widely scattered they are in each rarified zone. The greater the difference between the rarified and compressed regions of the sound wave (the greater the **amplitude** of the sound wave), the more intense the sound at a given distance from the source and the louder the interpretation of the sound. Striking a tuning fork harder does not cause the tone produced by the fork to change in frequency. Only its loudness changes. (**Intensity** means power per unit area; the intensity of any sound wave is proportional to the square of its amplitude).

Both frequency and intensity are highly important in determining what makes sound noise. Loudness is clearly a factor in what makes sound noise. Frequency is also a factor because humans can hear only those sounds ranging from 20 cycles per second (**Hertz** or **Hz**) to about 20,000 Hz. For hu-

man beings, sounds above 20,000 Hz are referred to as **ultrasound**, and those below 20 Hz are called **infrasound**. Humans seem to hear best in the frequency range from 200 to 3000 Hz, the range of frequencies that includes human speech. This means that we can hear only certain frequencies, and of those we do hear we are more sensitive to some than to others.

How We Hear

Noise is a problem for human beings and other species only because we have sense organs that are capable of receiving the information in sound in various survival-related ways. Animals use sound to stake out territories and to call the attention of all members of the same species to the fact that a territory has been staked out. Sound has other types of reproductive significance, mating calls being the most obvious example. Some animals—bats, for instance—use high-frequency sound to locate prey. For every species of animal, humans included, sound is an important means of alerting individuals to danger.

The sense of hearing is subserved by the three parts of the ear illustrated in Figure 16.2. The outer ear collects and funnels sound waves to the eardrum, and sound waves set the eardrum into a vibrating motion corresponding to the intensity and frequency of the sound. The bones of the middle ear (incus, maleus, and stapes) then transfer this mechanical motion to the delicate fluid-filled inner ear (cochlea). The inner ear contains a spiral membrane, different parts of which vibrate in patterns that depend upon the frequency and intensity profile of the incident sound. Particular groups of hair cells along this basilar membrane become depolarized (lose their electrical charge) to a degree that depends on how much the membrane is moving (and stressing the hairs on the hair cells) in the particular place where those hair cells are located. The depolarization of hair cells in turn initiates frequency- and intensity-specific patterns of nerve impulses in the nerve cells associated with each hair cell, and these then carry news of noise or other sounds to the brain along the auditory nerve (Figure 16.3).

WHEN IS SOUND NOISE?

The word *"noise"* has the same Latin root as the word "nausea." This leaves little doubt as to what the originators of the term noise had in mind, and it sets the stage for our definition.

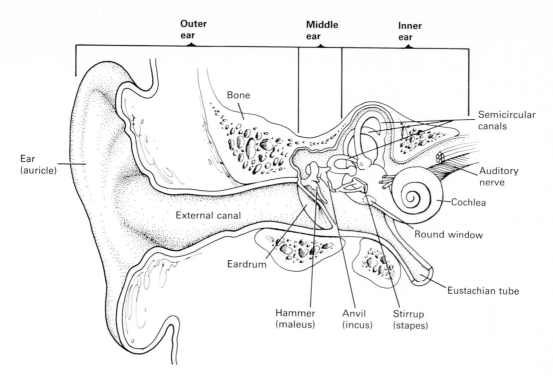

Figure 16.2 The Human Hearing Apparatus. The outer, middle, and inner ears.

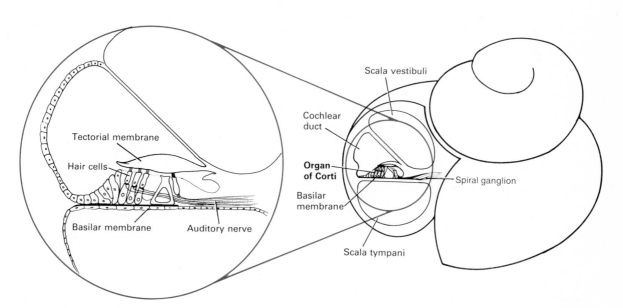

Figure 16.3 The Organ of Corti. If the cochlea illustrated in Figure 16.2 were cut away, the Organ of Corti would be as shown here. Within the inner ear the Organ of Corti runs along the entire length of the basilar membrane, which is wound within the spiral cochlea. The basilar membrane vibrates in particular patterns with particular sound frequencies, thus causing distortion of particular groups of hair cells to different degrees. This in turn is responsible for the generation of characteristic patterns of nerve impulses that travel along auditory nerve fibers to the brain.

The American National Standards Institute defines noise as any "undesired" sound. Noise has also been described at times as "unwanted" sound or sound without value. As such, these terms and expressions do not define noise adequately; they fail to take into account the fact that harmful sounds are not always *perceived* as harmful. Any definition of noise should include words like "hurt" or "harm."

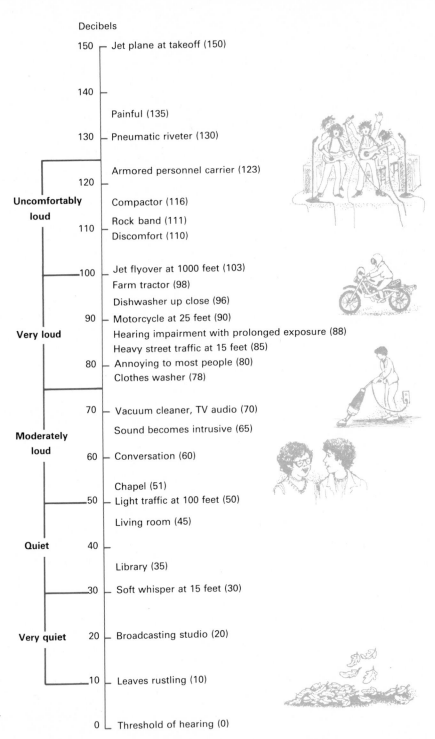

Decibels

150	Jet plane at takeoff (150)
140	
	Painful (135)
130	Pneumatic riveter (130)
	Armored personnel carrier (123)
120	
Uncomfortably loud	Compactor (116)
110	Rock band (111)
	Discomfort (110)
100	Jet flyover at 1000 feet (103)
	Farm tractor (98)
	Dishwasher up close (96)
90	Motorcycle at 25 feet (90)
Very loud	Hearing impairment with prolonged exposure (88)
	Heavy street traffic at 15 feet (85)
80	Annoying to most people (80)
	Clothes washer (78)
70	Vacuum cleaner, TV audio (70)
	Sound becomes intrusive (65)
Moderately loud	
60	Conversation (60)
	Chapel (51)
50	Light traffic at 100 feet (50)
	Living room (45)
Quiet 40	
	Library (35)
30	Soft whisper at 15 feet (30)
Very quiet 20	Broadcasting studio (20)
10	Leaves rustling (10)
0	Threshold of hearing (0)

Figure 16.4 The Decibel Scale. The locations of familiar sound sources are shown on the scale. Note that many common sound sources fall within the range of psychological and physical harm.

Our definition of **noise** is *unwanted sound or sounds of a duration, intensity, or other quality that cause some kind of physiological or psychological harm* to humans or other living things. Under this definition, "noise" would apply to any loud sound above 90 decibels (see Figure 16.4), no matter how "beautiful" it happened to be.

While loudness is relatively nonsubjective—at least in terms of the limits of physical damage—many factors are involved in the individual determination of other characteristics of sound. These include, in addition to frequency and intensity, the complexity or irregularity of the sound, the rate at which sound gets louder or quieter, and even more complex psychological factors such as whether sound is perceived by a listener as being necessary. Still other factors include the relationship of a sound to sounds people are accustomed to hearing and—believe it or not—the listeners' age, degree of training and education, and socioeconomic status. More on this later.

THE EFFECTS OF NOISE

The Auditory Effects of Noise: Hearing Loss

The magnitude of noise-induced hearing loss in the United States can be estimated from occupational hearing loss, worker compensation claims, and the number of Americans with impaired hearing. There are hundreds of thousands of workers between the ages of 50 and 59 eligible for worker's compensation because of hearing impairment caused by their jobs. Studies have shown that factory workers have double the rate of hearing loss that white-collar workers have at comparable ages. It has been estimated that maybe half of the machinery used in industry operates at levels that can impair hearing. But workplaces are by no means the only source of hearing impairment. A 1977 EPA study showed that about one in ten people in the United States are exposed to noises of duration and intensity sufficient to cause hearing impairment.

The problem of noise-induced hearing impairment begins to occur somewhere between 80 and 90 decibels. Regulatory agencies continue to struggle with where to set limits for noise levels in industry. Some studies have shown that sound at 80 decibels (on the A-scale) can produce a temporary elevation in the threshold of hearing that becomes permanent with repeated exposure. Studies in both industrial and military situations have shown that progressive noise-induced hearing impairment can

Job-related noise is a major cause of hearing impairment. Federal regulations now require companies to protect their employees from the effects of sustained high-decibel noise.

be caused by exposure to sound levels slightly above 80 decibels if exposure occurs repeatedly over an eight-hour day (Kupchella, 1976).

While we once accepted hearing loss as an inevitable consequence of old age, it is now apparent that it might instead be due to the cumulative effects of noise over one's life span. It may in fact *not* be natural to lose one's hearing—at least not at the rate we lose it in our society. L. K. Smith (1970) states that noticeable hearing losses can be measured among 12-year-old Americans (5% of them to be exact), in 14% of 15-year-olds, and in 20% of 18-year-olds. Studies have shown that people living in environments that are relatively free of noise do not have hearing loss even at advanced ages. Very old Mabaans, for example, members of an African tribe in the southeastern part of the Sudan, have about the same hearing acuity as American children (Rosen et al., 1962).

Studies of young people listening to rock music have shown that such music, generated at over 92 decibels throughout the 500- to 8000-Hz range and sustained over one hour or so, can produce a 40-decibel *threshold shift* in about 10% of the listeners—and somewhere between a 20% and 30% threshold elevation in the remainder. Though most of this threshold shift is usually temporary, repeated exposure can make it permanent. A **threshold shift** is an elevation in the threshold of hearing—that is, the quietest sound that can be heard, becomes a louder sound.

Where Does the Auditory Damage Occur?

A number of years ago, researchers found that when guinea pigs were exposed to loud noises—rock music, to be exact—the hair cells of the inner ear, cells responsible for the conversion of mechanical energy into nerve impulses, collapsed and shriveled. It is believed that loud sounds destroy these hair cells. Once destroyed, hair cells are not replaced. As we have pointed out, the hair cells of the ear are organized in rows along a thin membrane wound in a spiral fashion through the cochlea of the inner ear, and the structure of this organ is such that certain parts of the basilar membrane vibrate (resonate) with particular frequencies of incident sound. Distortion of the hair cells by movement of the membrane results in generation of nerve impulses to carry traffic sounds, symphonies, and news about other vibrating objects to the brain. The hair cells that enable us to perceive the characteristic frequencies of human speech are often the first to be destroyed. Thus as hearing loss proceeds, the first sounds to go are those by which human beings communicate (Figure 16.5).

Other Physiological Effects of Noise

Anyone who has experienced sound near the threshold of pain would not be surprised to learn that sound in the range of 120–150 decibels can affect the respiratory system and affect balance to the extent of dizziness, disorientation, nausea, and vomiting. But even sounds as quiet as 70 decibels can have measurable physiological effects. Such effects may not result in any immediate impairment, but they do emphasize the remarkable magnitude and variety of effects noise has on human beings. Let's examine some reasons why a relationship between noise and physiology might exist.

Nerve fibers that leave the inner ear carry impulses elicited by sirens, trumpets, or Linda Ronstadt to the medulla of the brain stem, where they meet other fibers going to other parts of the brain. Nerve pathways permit both ears to communicate with numerous parts of both sides of the brain, including the centers of consciousness and the control centers that regulate breathing, blood pressure, and other bodily functions below the level of con-

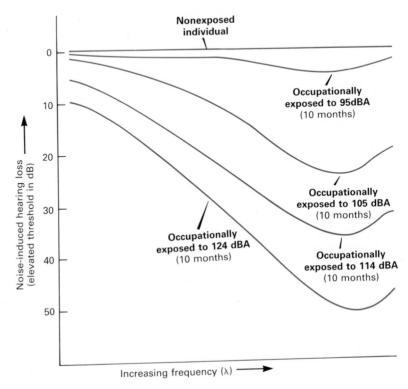

Figure 16.5 Hearing Loss in the Workplace. Occupational hearing loss over a range of frequencies is shown as a function of both frequency and duration. These data clearly show that hearing loss is a function of noise level *and* frequency.

The Decibel Scale

"Deci" comes from the Latin word for ten, and a "bel" is "the logarithm of a ratio" of any two acoustical (sound) or electrical intensities. In terms of sound, a **decibel** is ten times the logarithm of the ratio of two sound intensities, one being the intensity of any sound of interest and the other being a reference sound. In the United States the reference sound intensity is 10^{-12} watts per square meter; this is the intensity of a sound barely audible to a human being. A sound 100,000 times louder (more intense) than the reference level would be called a 50-decibel sound. Why? Because the logarithm of $(100,000 \times I_o)/I_o$ or 100,000 is 5, and 10 times 5 is 50. Sound with 10 times the intensity of the reference level would be a 10-decibel sound because the logarithm of $(10 \times I_o)/I_o$ or 10 is 1, and 10 times 1 is 10. A jet plane at takeoff generates—up close—a sound intensity 1000 trillion times that of a barely audible sound. The logarithm of 1000 trillion is 15, and 10 times 15 is 150; a jet plane at takeoff—up close—produces a 150-decibel sound (see Figure 16.4).

The really important thing to remember about the decibel scale is that it is a reference scale, meaning that it is a logarithmic way of expressing how many times louder a particular sound is than a sound level chosen arbitrarily. This scale is very appropriate to human hearing because we also happen to hear in a logarithmic way. That is, we actually perceive an increase from 10 to 20 decibels as about a doubling of sound intensity, even though it is really a tenfold increase.

The A-Scale

Sometimes sound levels are expressed according to the decibel-A(dbA)-scale. In this scale the frequencies to which humans are most sensitive are given more weight or more importance in the assessment of effects on human hearing.

---

sciousness. Figure 16.6 illustrates the influence of noise on blood flow as measured by the strength of the pulse in a fingertip. Figure 16.7 illustrates the pathways connecting the ear and key glands and organs of the body.

As part of the body's "Strategic Air Command," ears never really sleep; they are connected to the brain's arousal center and can wake us up. They are also able to muster glands like the thyroid and the adrenal gland to secrete hormones that prepare the body for fight or flight in the so-called startle reaction. Loud noises and explosive sounds can cause what physiologists call the *sympathetic reaction* because most of the characteristic physiological changes are controlled by the **sympathetic nervous system**. This is a division of the nervous system that controls many bodily functions below the level of consciousness, for example, heart rate, blood pressure, glandular secretions, and digestive tract motility. Generally speaking, when the sympathetic nervous system is activated, the things that support a flight-or-fight reaction are turned on; unessential activities, such as digestion, are shut down.

Overall, loud sounds can cause an increased production of most hormones of the pituitary gland; among the most important of these is the adrenocorticotropic hormone (ACTH). ACTH in turn stimulates the adrenal gland, which secretes several different hormones. Through a variety of influences, these hormones in turn (1) enhance the body's sensitivity to adrenalin, (2) increase blood sugar levels, (3) suppress the immune system, and (4) decrease the liver's ability to detoxify blood (Moller, 1975).

In that evolutionary period during which ears and their relationships with various organs and glands of the body were emerging, very loud sounds were rare; when loud sounds occurred, they almost always indicated danger. This connection could well have served as a selective pressure (see Chapter 5) leading to the "wiring" that now prepares human

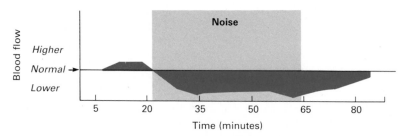

Figure 16.6 Noise and Pulse. Sound can affect the diameter of peripheral blood vessels. Shown here is a change in finger pulse that results from noise exposure. Constriction of blood vessels results in lower blood flow and a weaker pulse.

Chapter 16   Noise, Crowding, and Ugly Surroundings

beings to react automatically to loud sounds. Somewhat surprising perhaps is the fact that noise can elicit a number of automatic responses even at rather low levels. It has been shown that constriction of blood vessels in the skin can occur at only 70 decibels on the A-scale, the level of sound found on the average residential street.

The physiological responses and problems we have with noise and sound, then, may be the result of the fact that we have dragged a body shaped for a quiet, primitive environment into the bustling modern world. As we are besieged by noises, part of each of us wants to run and hide, while another part is saying, "Don't worry!" Perhaps this conflict is responsible for some of the psychological effects of noise.

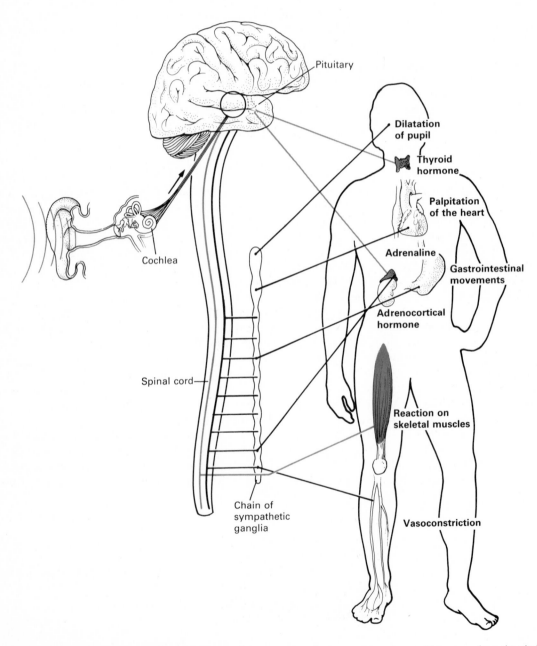

Figure 16.7 The Auditory Connection. This illustrates how noise might affect various important body functions via the sympathetic nervous system and hormones from the pituitary gland.

Psychological Effects of Noise

The German philosopher Arthur Schopenhauer long ago said, "I have long held the opinion that the amount of noise which anyone can bear . . . stands in inverse proportion of his mental capability. . . . Noise is a torture to all intellectual people." Perhaps Schopenhauer was emphasizing the fact that noise interfers with high-order mental function. Certainly, to some extent, noise is a torture to all people.

In the previous section we reviewed some of the connections between the ears and various parts of the brain including the centers of consciousness. We alluded to the fact that since evolution assigned a sentry role to the ears, impulses coming in from these organs are, by nature's design, not to be ignored. All of us are aware that noise can interfere with speech, thinking, and studying and that it can be a source of stress. Noise can have psychological effects on humans ranging from mild distress to complete unhinging. Noise has been used as a form of torture for centuries.

Noise and Speech. The ability of noise to interfere with speech may be its most important psychological effect in terms of sheer numbers of people affected. ReVelle and ReVelle (1974) estimate that some 30–40 million Americans are exposed to noise levels that interfere with normal speech. Thus noise interferes with communication in our species, and since communication is one of our biological specialties, such interference is a rather widespread source of stress. Perhaps largely because of this impact on communication, noise might have something to do with high divorce rates and various forms of social conflict as well as with indigestion, nervous breakdown, heart failure, high blood pressure, and insanity. Zuremstehung (1959) found that steel workers assigned to the noisiest parts of steel mills had significantly more social difficulty, both at the plant and at home, than workers in less noisy parts.

Noise, Sleep, Rest, Relaxation, and Mental Stability. Because sleep is important to emotional stability, it is worth noting that a study in Philadelphia some years ago showed that city noises interfered with sleep both by prohibiting a deep sleep and by interrupting sleep, especially among elderly people.

It seems plausible that through some combination of its effects on sleep, its interference with communication, and other forms of noise-induced distress, noise may contribute to emotional disturbances. A study done in France (see Smith, 1970) suggested that noise may cause as much as 70% of the neuroses found in major cities like Paris. A study

reported in *Lancet* (Abey-Wickrama et al., 1969) showed that for certain categories of mental illness, admissions to psychiatric hospitals in London occurred at significantly higher rates for people living in areas of maximum noise levels near Heathrow Airport. The authors suggested that while noise might not actually be the cause of mental illness, it might aggravate conditions leading to mental illness.

Despite data such as those cited above and what seems to be true from personal observation and common sense, an occasional writer will suggest that humans are able to adapt to noise. We suspect that the truth is that while humans may well be able to adapt to noise to some extent, the importance of noise as an alarm signal precludes complete or even very extensive adaptation. Studies have shown that the *physiological* effects of noise are independent of culture and adaptation, and we suspect that the same is true of its psychological effects.

Psychological Impact and the Ear of the Beholder. Below the levels of sound intensities that are known to be physically harmful, human beings seem to be able to tolerate certain kinds of noise more than others. As we stated earlier, human beings are least able to tolerate sounds they consider unnecessary. An example is the unnerving tapping of a foot. Obviously, sounds that are considered necessary are less likely to be bothersome. Almost any kind of sound could variously be described at the same time by different people as pleasant, irritating, annoying, beautiful, terrible, disturbing, cruel, or unbelievable. A sports car climbing through the gears to a high rate of speed might be one such an example. Subjectivity is what makes it so difficult to quantify the annoyance or the psychological impact of noise on human beings. There is simply too much variation from one human being to another. We are pretty much stuck with having to make inferences from what we see and observe. This puts those who advocate lessening noise levels in our environment in the position of having to prove a point that is at best extremely difficult to prove.

The Effects of Noise on Wildlife

The Clean Air Act has provisions calling for more research on the effects of noise on wildlife and the effects of noise on people. We know something about the latter; we know little if anything about the former.

Not only do many animal species seem to tolerate human noises quite well, some appear to seek out noisy places. Subway rats, milling plant mice, city street pigeons, and airfield birds are a few examples. Perhaps, like humans, such creatures have elected to take the bad with the good. They may be trading away peace and quiet for food and a place to live. In any case, such animals must not perceive noise as directly threatening their lives; it certainly is not a strong enough stimulus to cause them to move on.

In 1977 an attempt was made to bring into focus all that had been learned up to then about noise and wildlife (and domestic animals as well); a symposium on that topic was held as part of the Ninth International Congress on Acoustics held in Madrid (see Fletcher and Busnel, 1978). Although few definitive conclusions were reached, the conference did focus attention on the problem and revealed a number of difficulties with methodology such as the lack of standardization of experimental "noise sources."

Payne and Webb (in Fletcher and Busnel, 1978) suggest that noises made by ships might interfere with communication between whales over large ocean ranges. The actual extent of impact is unknown. Other reports suggested that noise does *not* interfere with communication among animals, citing the failure of deliberate attempts to fool bats, lovebirds, and other animals with masking noises.

At the same conference, Cottereau reported that horses, cattle, turkeys, broilers, sheep, and pheasants all "show behavioral startle, when they first experience a sonic boom . . . reaction is usually slight and they seem to adapt readily to further booms." (A **sonic boom** is a sound resembling an explosion that results when the shock wave produced by something traveling faster than the speed of sound reaches an ear.) Lynch and Speake (in Fletcher and Busnel, 1978) reported that sonic booms did *not* cause abnormal behavior that would result in decreased productivity in wild turkeys. Ames (also in Fletcher and Busnel, 1978) concluded that domestic sheep responded to noise physiologically in the same way that sheep would respond to stress in general. The effects of white noise on sheep varied with level, intensity, and duration, and the animals became acclimated (gave no response) after 10 days of experience with noise. (**White noise** is sound produced by all audible frequencies being generated at the same time.)

Busnel states that "published reports of well controlled experiments on the sonic boom problem make it plain that the behavior of domestic animals and some very shy wild species like turkeys is *un*-affected by repeated sonic booms" (Fletcher and Busnel, 1978). Busnel suggests that whatever effects

noise has on wildlife may simply reflect the lack of acclimation.

Sure, helicopters scare caribou. They scare people who aren't expecting them, too. But crows initially frightened off by gun discharges in farm field quickly become acclimated and ignore the guns (Fletcher and Busnel, 1978).

In summary, the reports in the literature are of neither the quality not the quantity to let us make any kind of solid generalization about the effects of noise on wildlife. In other words, we do not know *what* the effects of noise on wildlife are; and as far as we know, nobody else does either. At least one of the keys to more definitive work will be the standardization of noise stimuli.

SOME IMPORTANT SOURCES OF NOISE

Cars, Trucks, and Buses

Sometime around 1900, mufflers had to be put on automobiles so that they would be less noisy and thus less of a threat to horses. Over the years, additional noise control steps related to the automobile have been taken, but they have not quite kept pace with the number of automobiles, with changes in engine and tire design, or with higher speeds.

Noise generated by automobile traffic varies with the number of cars on the highway and the speed with which they travel. According to ReVelle and ReVelle (1974), highway noise measured a few feet away from a highway increases by 3 decibels for every doubling of traffic flow and by 6 decibels for every doubling of speed.

Tire noise is a major part of the noise generated by automobiles and trucks, offering a good example of problems that come with trade-offs. Tires with a crossbar design generate the most tire noise. Such tires are reported to be more durable and safer than tires with the more conventional continuous rib design, however. Do we want safety and durability or quiet?

Most subways and railroad cars are noisy largely because of the metal-to-metal contact between wheels and rails. This is accentuated by (1) severe wear problems, (2) being enclosed in the case of subway trains, (3) weight, and (4) the speed of the vehicles.

Air Transportation

There are well over 100,000 airplanes in the United States, and they sometimes all seem to be in the air at once. Because the noises jets and other kinds of airplanes produce are sporadic and concentrated in residential areas, they are perceived by many people as irritating. It should be emphasized that the problem does not have to do solely with jet aircraft, since numerous small private planes use airport facilities in or near every city. Jets present a special problem because they fly by force rather than by finesse. Even without sonic booms, jets can produce well over 110 decibels, even a quarter of a mile away.

Part of the problem would be reduced or eliminated altogether if airports simply were not located where they are. Many of them are in the hearts of major cities, so overflights, landings, and takeoffs impinge on the personal space of millions of people in all parts of the world. The issue is complicated because many of the airports surrounded by residential areas were originally built in the country. Cities grew out around many of these airports because the airport was there. Increases in jet travel over the years have also contributed to the problem. The problem has grown to such an extent that some elementary and secondary schools have been closed because of interference by airplane noises with teaching and learning. Another part of the airport-airplane noise problem and controlling land use near airports is that there are many so-called metropolitan airports that serve very large geographic and political entities. Sometimes the airport is completely outside the jurisdiction and beyond the political boundaries of the population most affected. The Cincinnati, Ohio, Airport, for instance, is actually located in Kentucky, just across the Ohio River.

Since every political jurisdiction has its own ideas about how land should be used and how activities upon it should be regulated, there is a good argument for the federal regulation of noise. However, even with federal control, there may be problems. Noise was one of many problems identified by environmentalists when the decision was being made in the early 1970s as to whether the supersonic transport planes (SSTs) would be built and operated in the United States. Because of such pressures, the U.S. government decided not to support the construction of the SST, but governments in England, France, and the Soviet Union went ahead with construction. Despite the initial action, the U.S. government eventually authorized the British-French Concorde to land at the Kennedy Airport in New York and at Dulles Airport near Washington, D.C. Somehow this was allowed even though the levels of noise generated by the Concorde exceed noise standards for aircraft established in the late 1960s by the Federal Aviation Administration.

Jet traffic is a noise problem mainly because most large airports are located near residential areas.

The control of noise generated by air traffic has been approached and will continue to be approached through a number of strategies—for example, changes in the way jets take off and land and the adoption of flight patterns that avoid residential areas. Long-range comprehensive solutions have been proffered that would locate airports in low-impact areas, control land use around new airports, design less noisy jet engines, and perhaps insulate houses and other buildings so that they are not so easily penetrated by compression waves coursing through the air.

At Home

Throughout the early parts of this chapter we cited numerous noise sources in the home. Three household noise centers that are particular problems are the kitchen, workshop, and entertainment center. Motorized gadgets in the kitchen, for example, can generate the same levels of noise found in many factories.

If you are home now, listen for a moment. What major centers can you identify? Contributing to the racket may be garbage disposals, lawn mowers, food blenders, sewing machines, knife sharpeners, vacuum cleaners, hair dryers, automatic washers, electric can openers, exhaust fans, window fans, and air conditioners. No doubt you can name more.

The City

The city is mentioned here because it concentrates all of the sources of noise we have discussed up to now. Traffic noise levels measured on the sixteenth and seventeenth floors of New York City hotels ranged up to 100 decibels in the most important (our most sensitive) frequency ranges (Still, 1970). In many studies, heavy city traffic has been measured at decibel levels well beyond those known to cause hearing damage. Concerning the psychological and physiological effects of city noise, in a survey done in New York toward the end of the 1920s—in one of the very first city-wide noise surveys ever undertaken—New Yorkers classified noise sources in terms of how much of a bother they were. Automobile and truck traffic was number one followed by public transportation, radios, and garbage collection.

Noise is clearly an important part of the extra measure of stress suffered by city dwellers.

THE PROSPECTS FOR NOISE CONTROL

One of the ways in which noise is unique as a pollutant is that we have the technology by which to control nearly every kind of noise. We know more about noise control than we know about the effects of noise. This suggests that the main problem with noise is that people are not aware that it *is* a problem.

Noise may be unique as a pollutant not only in that it is far less generally recognized as a pollutant than ozone and the like, but also in that human beings actually seek out noise. Motivational studies suggest that human beings equate noise with power. Manufacturers of appliances designed to do powerful things have found that the public develops an impression of how powerful and therefore how good an appliance is partly by how much noise it makes (Brody, 1979). This means that while noise may be *the* most controllable pollutant, social motivation for its control actually runs in the wrong direction. Little wonder that there has not been more progress with noise control.

Engineering Quiet

Basically there are four ways to control noise:

1. modify the ways things are done so as to generate less noise;
2. shield the noise-generating devices or processes at the source;
3. shield the receiver; and
4. move noisy things away from people.

Examples of the first approach would be reducing automobile traffic, outlawing sirens, making it impossible for sound to come out of a stereo except

through headsets, and using glue instead of rivets. An example of the second approach would be the use of vibration-damping or absorbing materials in dishwashers and automobiles. Earplugs and control booths are examples of the third approach. Isolating new jet ports from people would be an example of the fourth.

We have already identified a major problem associated with controlling sound in appliances, tools, and equipment by direct engineering—namely, that the public seems to equate noise with power. Perhaps this could be changed somewhat by education, but it could certainly be changed by laws requiring noise sources to meet certain standards. Possible improvements in machinery and appliances would be sound-absorbing motor mountings, better installation, motor enclosures, and other improvements in design. Sound-absorbing materials have long been used to cut down on the noise produced by electric motors, engines, and machinery; these just need to be applied more generally. There is hardly a machine that could not be better designed with noise reduction in mind. Though some say that building codes must be changed to permit more flexible use of noise-absorbing materials, there is not a house, office building, restaurant, terminal, or public building that could not now be constructed so as to reduce noise.

Legislating Quiet

As with other environmental pollutants, the control of noise pollution can conveniently be divided into two categories, occupational and nonoccupational. We will consider laws covering the general environment first.

The number of local ordinances and local noise control laws have increased in the United States almost as fast as the seriousness of the noise problem. Many of these laws are ineffective because they are based on subjective criteria and are very difficult to enforce. Because many of the most notable sources of noise (automobiles, trucks, trains, machines) are made or imported for distribution throughout the United States, noise control logically falls under the general welfare responsibility of the federal government. Federal laws tend to be more effective because they can more effectively deal with noise at its sources.

The present law of the land regarding noise control in the general environment is the Noise Control Act of 1972 as amended by the Quiet Communities Act of 1978. By this legislation the U.S. Environmental Protection Agency was directed to

1. coordinate the noise research and noise control efforts of all federal agencies;
2. establish criteria for concern about noise, that is, document the effects of noise on health and welfare;
3. give a running account of the status of harmful noise in the environment;
4. identify major sources of noise; and
5. establish performance standards for noise emission for the sources it identifies based on the "degree of noise reduction achievable through the application of the best available technology and the cost of compliance."

This legislation specifically directed the EPA to look at the noise problem as it relates to air and rail traffic. The Quiet Communities amendments also directed the EPA to develop a system of product labeling relative to noise. Still other provisions of the legislation included production of public education materials; support for noise research, and help for communities trying to implement quiet communities legislation. It should be noted that the EPA's office of Noise Abatement and Control was disbanded in 1982, and the EPA no longer furnishes direct technical assistance on noise problems.

The EPA has developed noise regulations for interstate motor carriers, other medium and heavy trucks, portable air compressors, motorcycles and motorcycle exhaust systems, and interstate rail carriers. General labeling of some products was begun in 1979, as was a labeling program for products designed to reduce noise. Criteria are being developed for such notable urban noise sources as garbage trucks, buses (bus noise is expected to be cut in half), front-end loaders, bulldozers, and pavement breakers. Garbage trucks made after October 1, 1980, were to be quieter than 79 db measured at 7 meters, and the level was to be reduced to 76 db by July 1, 1982 (Walton, 1980). Apparently more help of this sort is on the way.

The very first federal standards for occupational noise levels were established in 1969. In 1974 the Occupational, Safety and Health Administration (OSHA) set the current standards at 90 decibels over an eight-hour day with the duration of exposure to be cut in half for every 5 decibels over 90. The National Institute for Occupational Safety and Health (NIOSH) and the EPA have proposed an 85-decibel limit in the work place over eight hours. Economic and technical difficulties involved in achieving an 85-decibel limit apparently has kept OSHA, the agency charged with establishing regulations, from lowering the limit, although the Hearing Conservation Amendment to the Occupational Safety and Health Act now requires companies to have a hearing conservation program for employees exposed to 85 decibels or more. Such programs are to include annual hearing tests, provision of personal protective equipment, and area monitoring.

Controversy was still raging at the time of this writing; thousands of statements had been presented by federal agencies, universities, labor, and industry to support one standard or the other. The main argument for the 90-decibel limit is that it would cost billions of dollars more to achieve an 85-decibel limit over 5 years of complying with the law. Recently, the Council on Environmental Quality presented data showing that a period of 40 years of compliance with an 85-decibel standard would result in *benefits* of 12.8 billion dollars in reduced absenteeism and lower worker compensation rates alone—not considering some of the other intangibles we have mentioned elsewhere in this chapter.

THE ECONOMICS OF NOISE CONTROL AND THE IMPACT OF NOISE

How does one weigh the relative costs and benefits—for example, a sonic boom versus getting passengers from California to New York as fast as technologically possible? How does one compare a poorly understood, slight negative effect on thousands of people in relationship to a benefit—which may also be slight—derived by 100 passengers? How does one measure how much a worker's productivity will decrease in a noisy environment? How would one bring into a cost-benefit analysis such things as days off due to an illness that may never be perceived to be connected to noise? How would one go about determining the cost of a sleepless night? Of a fight in a family? Of indigestion? You may have heard questions such as these before; they are only partly rhetorical. They are a real challenge to those who would make the case that money must be spent to control noise. With noise, as with other pollutants, environmental cost-benefit analysis is largely an art form.

Clearly, the cost of noise pollution is not insignificant. One source places the cost of lost production and impaired efficiency due to noise at well over $4,000,000,000 per year (Environmental Education Group, 1973). It has been estimated that noise in occupational settings has produced a potential for worker compensation claims exceeding $500,000,000 (Detwyler and Marcus, 1972). The World Health Organization estimates that industrial noise costs billions of dollars annually worldwide in absenteeism, inefficiency, and accidents as well as in direct compensation. Studies in England have shown that workers exposed to continuous noise in the 90-decibel range, not far beyond the limits now currently set for U.S. industry, made more errors and were generally less productive. Only when we have a better grip on these kinds of cost can they be measured against the costs associated with restricting jet traffic in airports during certain times of day, the costs of modifying jets to make them less noisy, the costs of changes in automobile design and maybe even in highway design, and in general the costs of making environments less noisy.

PSYCHOPHYSIOLOGICAL EFFECTS OF CROWDING AND ENVIRONMENTAL UGLINESS

Crowding and ugly environments are oppressive, subjective, and highly complicated problems. Crowding and ugliness are related in that crowding is one form of environmental ugliness. Components of crowding and ugliness are found in almost every environmental problem. There are many who feel that overpopulation and crowding are the ultimate causes of all of the various forms of environmental ugliness. To be sure, the sheer weight of numbers of people is a factor in all the kinds of environmental

deterioration we have discussed throughout this book. If pollution is the extra measure of environmental deterioration of air brought about by humans, it seems logical that, other things being equal, the more people there are, the more environmental deterioration there will be.

How Many People Make an Ugly Crowd?

Crowding and ugliness are almost equally subjective in nature and interpretation. One person's crowd is another person's party; beauty and ugliness are in the eye of the beholder. Crowding is subjective in that it depends on circumstances and on what an individual has on his or her mind. While allowing 500 people in a movie theater to watch a movie or jamming 50,000 spectators into a stadium to watch the Cincinnati Reds play the Pittsburgh Pirates might be satisfactory, the same amount of space obviously could not accommodate these crowds if the individuals were going to toss Frisbees, listen to their radios, or practice their musical instruments. While a swimming pool could hold several hundred people who just wanted to stay cool and splash about, the same pool would be crowded to any wishing to swim laps. Crowding also varies for any one individual with circumstance. As our moods change, so does our definition of crowding. We have all enjoyed being with large crowds at times, and yet we may have all been bothered at one time or another by the presence of one or two other hikers. We are all aware that there are times when *three* is a particularly large crowd.

Despite the subjective qualities of crowding, we could probably all agree that at the extreme there are certain conditions that nearly everyone would find ugly, crowded, oppressive, or unpleasant. While we may lapse into subjective qualification throughout this chapter, we will proceed with the notion that when we say "ugly" and when we say "crowded," we are talking about whatever enters the reader's mind upon hearing these adjectives.

Crowding by Choice?

In Chapter 4 we introduced the concept of population distribution and discussed such things as clumping. Most human beings apparently opt for clumping. Nearly everyone in the United States, for example, can be found within only 1% of its land area. If the entire population of the United States were uniformly distributed over its entire area, there would be only 50 persons per square mile. Yet in residential parts of Manhattan, densities reach a quarter of a million people per square mile. This

Crowding is subjective. On some occasions we enjoy getting together with large numbers of other people.

pattern makes it difficult to attach much significance to densities figured over large areas and adds a major dimension to any discussion of crowding.

We would like to point out that although the United States is not as densely populated as many other countries of the world, our degree of urbanization and in particular our highly developed communication systems put us into direct and indirect contact with many, many members of our species every day. Perhaps we long ago passed the limit of our species' ability to cope with the numbers of individuals into which we come into contact, and many of our species are now stressed and strained by it all.

Studies of the Effects of Crowding on Animals in the Wild

In his review of studies of the physiological effects of crowding on animals, Porteous (1977) concludes that overcrowding causes reduced reproductive capacity in animals. This lowered capacity is sometimes caused by lower ovulation rates and sometimes more indirectly via deterioration of other organs like the liver, spleen, and kidney and the adrenal glands. The writings of Christian (1950), Selye (1956), Calhoon (1962), Hogland (1964), Southwick (1971), and others suggest that the reproductive effects are consequences of a crowding-induced stress syndrome. The implication is that while the type of stress involved most often simply serves as a stimulus to members of the same species to move apart and distribute themselves in an optimal way, it can have gross pathological effects if for some reason the redistribution does not occur.

It has been suggested that the crowding-induced stress syndrome is derived from the same biological roots as territoriality and pecking order (see Chapter 4). Wynne-Edwards (1964) was one of the first to hypothesize that territoriality and social hierarchy in animals is an important form of biological population control. The activities that subserve territoriality and pecking order and even the singing of birds may all serve to alert members of the same species and perhaps even related species of *presence,* influencing behavior in a way that ultimately limits population density. Perhaps in species like *Homo sapiens* the same kind of intraspecific stress, in some vestigial if not functional form, continues to provide a source of biological stress.

A *crowding-induced stress syndrome* has been reported in many species of animals including rabbits, deer, and lemmings and even in certain other more exotic species in animals housed in zoos.

The first observation may well have been made in snowshoe hares after a number of hypotheses were tested and proven false concerning the reason for an 11-year cycle in snowshoe hare populations. Ultimately, it was found that during the decline phase of these cycles, hares were found not to die from predation or from infectious diseases, but from the effects of a syndrome characterized by large adrenal glands, fatty livers, blood vessel changes, and even heart disease. This shock disease, or crowding-induced stress disease, has been described as a kind of hyperinsulinism, that is, like an oversecretion of insulin by the pancreas (Deevey, 1960).

The sequence of physiological events in this syndrome goes something like this: glucose (sugar) is stored in the liver, not as glucose itself but as glycogen. Glycogen is a complex polymer that can be broken down into sugar and serves as a reserve. Throughout evolution a number of mechanisms of control of **glycogenolysis**, the release of this stored sugar, have been installed to keep the concentration of sugar in the blood at an optimal constant level. Among the things involved in this control are hormones secreted by the adrenal glands that sit atop each kidney. Under conditions of stress the cortex of the adrenal gland secretes a hormone called cortisone. Cortisone causes glycogen to be released as sugar from the liver. It also suppresses the immune system.

The ability of the adrenal gland to secrete cortisone is determined by the adrenocorticotropic hormone (ACTH) secreted by the pituitary gland. The pituitary, a pea-sized gland located in the center of the head at the base of the cerebral cortex, is sometimes called the master endocrine gland because it secretes hormones that regulate the secretions of other endocrine glands—including the adrenal gland. Stress causes the pituitary to secrete more ACTH than it "should," and the effect of this, if it continues for very long, is to keep cortisone levels high and to cause the cortex of the adrenal gland to become larger so that it can secrete even more cortisone in response to stress. A vicious type of cycle develops quickly if stress is persistent, the result being that the pituitary/adrenocortical axis begins to pull the body out of balance. If the stress goes on long enough, the pituitary eventually pays nearly full attention to the adrenal cortex and begins to neglect other important duties. Among the neglected governing functions are those that have to do with hormonal control of reproduction and reproductive behavior.

Continual stress plus the generalized hormonal imbalance created by this adrenopituitary escalation makes great demands on the sugar stored in the liver. According to Selye (1956), this can proceed until the sugar reserve is nearly exhausted. The system for dealing with the movement of sugar into and out of storage in the liver is brought to a breaking point. Just one extra stress, such as a loud noise or the sight of or confrontation with a member of the same species, can drain the liver of its last reserves of glycogen. Then the level of sugar in the blood drops to critically low levels, and this leads to the death of cells in the brain, heart, and blood vessels in a rapidly deteriorating downward course for the unfortunate victim of this sequence.

The unusual behavior of lemmings, known for centuries, may be another kind of reaction to overcrowding. Lemmings captured during their celebrated pathological marches into the sea reveal many of the symptoms of the stress syndrome in snowshoe hare rabbits described above. Hogland (1964) has observed that the lemmings' misguided attempts to swim across oceans is stimulated by fighting among males and a winter of crowding under the snow.

Hogland also described an experiment in which deer were placed on an island in the Chesapeake Bay. Although the deer were well fed, they began to die after they had reached a density of about one deer per acre. Autopsies revealed the same kind of stress syndrome as was described above.

A number of studies in animals in the wild suggest that a kind of stress syndrome resulting from overcrowding may be one of the most important factors regulating the distribution and abundance of many species of animals. Careful laboratory studies in which such other factors as disease and predation were absolutely ruled out seem to support this hypothesis.

Crowding in Animals Under Controlled Laboratory Conditions

Charles Southwick (1955) and John Calhoun's (1962) reports of studies of animals deliberately crowded under laboratory conditions have become classics in the environmental literature. The design of Calhoun's initial studies was based on the simple concept of a limiting enclosure and providing rats confined therein with unlimited amounts of food and water. The rats were allowed to increase in numbers as much as they would, or they were allowed to reach certain high densities, well above what had previously been determined to be optimal. In his initial experiments, Calhoun used wild Norway Rats; in later experiments he used more domesticated albino strains. In experiments with the latter group, Calhoun made increasingly complex modifications of his enclosures, fashioning them with interconnections, burrows, ramps, and nest boxes.

Calhoun and his colleagues observed that when animals reached levels of overpopulation, there was a high incidence of reproductive pathology. There were numerous spontaneous abortions among pregnant females, and infant mortality rates eventually exceeded 80%. There was evidence of social pathology and disturbances in normal mating and courtship patterns. Females generally did poorly in taking care of their young and in nest building. Males exhibited abnormal behavior patterns that extended to homosexuality, hypoactivity, hypersexuality, and hyposexuality, to name a few. Calhoun's studies seemed to suggest that a direct connection between crowding-induced stress and reproductive behavior might work to control population densities in nature.

Calhoun and others have observed that not all members of a given population are equally susceptible to crowding induced stress. Apparently, the socially dominant members of a population are affected least, while those most subservient or lowest in the pecking order are affected most (Christian, 1968). Another interesting laboratory observation, one that may be relevant to the human condition, is that crowding produces high blood pressure in mice, much more so when the crowd consists of strange mice than when the crowd consists of familiar members of the species (Henry et al., 1967).

Crowding and Its Effects on Human Beings

The reader may have already begun to extrapolate the things mentioned above to human beings. Indeed, a limited amount of data on the effects of crowding in humans seem to suggest that the effects may be similar. Hogland (1964) suggests that actual observations of human beings under chronic stressful conditions indicate that the human pituitary-adrenal complex responds in a very similar way to that found in mice, rats, and deer. Much has been written about cities as agents of stress, deviant be-

havior, and various forms of mental illness. If such connections are found to be real, perceived crowding could well turn out to be part of the problem.

Crowding and Mental Illness. Throughout this book we have presented aspects of the urban environment as agents of disease in human beings. We discussed this in Chapter 14, where we indicated that certain types of cancer occur twice as frequently in cities as in rural areas. We have discussed numerous relationships to other city diseases related to air and water pollution. We will now briefly consider the problem of crowding-induced stress and its effect on the immune system, on health status in general, and in particular on mental health. The reader should be aware, as pointed out by Casswill (1971), that many attempts to prove that high population densities are indeed important factors in mental illness and other diseases have produced often confusing and conflicting interpretations.

There are only very few detailed studies of the effects of crowding on human beings. For reasons that we have cited many times, such studies are arduous and complicated, and interpreting them is difficult. A large part of this problem has to do with the fine line between crowding and what people seem to want in the way of interaction with other people. Cities where most of the studies take place that relate social pathology and mental illness to crowding simultaneously represent stress and tremendous opportunities for all sorts of desirable activities.

Crowding apparently induces stress even in relatively well-to-do communities.

Van R. Potter (1971) defines an optimum environment as one that delivers an optimum amount of stress. People apparently need a certain amount of stress or stimulation that requires some kind of reaction. Nevertheless, Porteous (1977) cites numerous studies indicating that many kinds of disease—mental disease in particular—occur with highest frequencies in the central parts of cities. There may be many reasons for this; overcrowding appears to be at least one of the reasons. In a study by Faris and Dunham cited by Porteous, schizophrenia, depression, senility, psychoses, and other kinds of mental disorders were found to be most frequent in the central city—in Chicago, Illinois, and Providence, Rhode Island, to be exact. This was true in both relatively poor and relatively well-to-do parts of the cities. In another study cited by Porteous, one done in Nottingham, England (Giggs, 1973), nearly 70% of mental hospital patients were found to live within four kilometers of the center of the city.

Does the city produce mental illness or do mentally ill people congregate in the city? In a study of the residents of midtown Manhattan published in a report called *Mental Health in the Metropolis* (Srole et al., 1962), only 20% of the people interviewed were found to be relatively free of significant symptoms of mental illness, although only about 3% of the remainder were really incapacitated by their mental disabilities. This makes one wonder about the definition of normal. In his comprehensive review of such studies, Porteous (1977) concludes that mental illnesses and the social pathology characteristic of cities can be attributed in large part to the environment. Apparently, noise, pollution, and poor housing along with the social disorganization characteristic of cities is responsible. The picture is extremely complicated, however.

Focusing on social pathology for a moment, just as there was social and reproductive pathology in Calhoun's rats, crime, drug abuse, and other forms of social pathology seem to be more profound and pronounced in urban areas and may well be linked to the crowding that exists there. Perhaps the anonymity of the city brings deviant behavior out in people who have no formal part to play in the superstructure as they perceive it. Perhaps criminals feel freer to do criminal things. Many varieties of social pathology including murder, suicide, rape, assault, domestic quarrels, and infant mortality are highly correlated with urban environments as cited in a number of the studies reported by Porteous. While these studies do not unequivocally implicate crowding as a cause, we cannot help but note that the symptoms of social pathology prevalent in cities are the very symptoms Calhoun saw in his rats.

Personal Space. Perhaps part of the crowding problem is related to the concept of personal space. **Personal space** is the area immediately around a person, the invasion of which causes stress; the size of personal space varies according to circumstances and also from culture to culture. The sanctity of our personal space becomes fully operational at early ages and can be seen in the behavior of people seating themselves on buses, in bars, and on park benches.

Perhaps the stress impact of crowding is partly related to the frequency of violations of personal space. Defining the exact extent to which this might be true is confounded by a number of variables in addition to cultural background. These include age, sex, affinity (familiarity), and social influence—the more important a person is, the bigger his or her personal space. At any rate, it is easy to imagine that in city subways, in elevators, and on sidewalks, personal space is violated often with stress as a result.

One final, somewhat frightening note: Keeley (1972) reported that when comparisons were made of mice born and reared in normal uncrowded conditions, mice born crowded and raised crowded, and mice crowded and raised uncrowded, *both* of the latter groups exhibited low survival, less activity among the offspring, and less responsiveness. These results suggest that some sort of stressing factor may, in fact, even pass through the placenta to the embryo.

The Impact of Ugly Surroundings

You know how bad you feel when you see litter and trash where you do not want to see it. You know the feelings of revulsion you experience when you see a contaminated stream, and unreclaimed strip mine spoil bank, or a beach stained with oil. You know how good you feel walking in the woods or even down a clean city street in the spring, swimming in a clear stream, or breathing air that looks and smells clean. We know what we like to see and what we do not like to see, but how does one quantify such things?

As far as we know, there are no good controlled studies of the impact of ugly environments on human beings. We wonder how such a study could even be done. If we could somehow all get together and pick some ugly places by consensus, we could compare the people living there with people living in

Though it is hard to determine the actual impact of ugly surroundings on human beings, ugliness can be considered a form of pollution.

"nice" places. But what would this show? People in ugly places might also be affected by poverty, poor nutrition, and poor health for reasons correlated with—but without any cause-and-effect relationships to—the ugliness of their environment.

We could hook up average people to monitor their blood pressure, heart rate, peripheral circulation, and the like while we showed them pictures of a lot of different kinds of ugly things and interspersed these with travel posters. We could do this with people from ugly places and with people from not so ugly places and see whether they had different reactions. We would probably learn that one can become acclimated to ugliness after a while.

Any studies of this sort that might be done would surely confirm some things that we all intuitively know. Whatever it is that we individually consider ugly—a littered vacant lot, a dilapidated house, polluted water, polluted skies, urban blight, or billboards—they are ugly to most of us. Ugliness is a form of stress or discomfort; it causes physiological and psychological tension in us. It makes us unhappy or less happy than we would otherwise be. Ugliness is a visual form of pollution.

CONCEPTS TO REMEMBER

1. Noise—unwanted, loud, or otherwise irritating sound—is a genuine pollutant. It is a human-generated feature of the environment that causes human health problems.
2. Noise harms people in three basic ways: (a) loud sounds can impair hearing; (b) loud and otherwise irritating sounds can elicit physiological changes, for example, in blood-pressure, in heart rate, and in digestive function; and (c) irritating sounds can also serve as a source of psychological stress.
3. The fact that noise has physiological and psychological impacts is related to the importance to survival of sound and hearing.
4. The decibel is a relative measure of sound intensity based on the reference sound pressure of the quietest sound that can be heard by a normal human.
5. Hearing damage associated with loud sound occurs in the inner ear and is permanent.
6. The psychological impact of sounds below the threshold of physical damage is almost entirely dependent on the listener. One listener's symphony is another listener's noise.
7. The impact of noise on wildlife is unknown.
8. Noise control technology is well developed, but motivation to apply this technology is lacking or even negative—people equate loud machinery with power and may actually seek out loudness.
9. As a general rule, people also seek crowds, even though there is some evidence that crowding can be a source of negative stress.

10. Stress is not necessarily all bad; humans need a certain amount of stress to function optimally.
11. Estimates of the social cost of noise range up to hundreds of billions of dollars annually.
12. Although crowding is relative, experiments with animals have demonstrated a connection between crowding and social pathology. There is some limited evidence that the connection may hold for human beings as well.
13. Environmental ugliness is another partly subjective form of pollution.

DISCUSSION QUESTIONS AND FOOD FOR THOUGHT

1. As a class or individual project, obtain a decibel meter from the physics department or wherever you can get one. After you have learned how to use it and have planned where to go and when, visit various locations in your community and make measurements at various distances from sound sources. Make a presentation, discussing the results in light of the material in this chapter.
2. Have your hearing tested.
3. As a group, use the information in this chapter and whatever else you can find and draft a noise ordinance for your city or town.
4. Debate: It should be illegal to play music above 85 decibels.
5. Ask your congressional representative for a copy of The Noise Control Act of 1972 as amended by The Quiet Communities Act of 1978 (Public Law 95-609; Nov. 8, 1978). Review it and prepare a written or oral synopsis.
6. Collect pictures of environmental scenes you consider ugly. Try to rank them in terms of ugliness. Have a classmate rank the same pictures. How do the results compare? Do not include any pictures of individual human beings (especially classmates).

REFERENCES AND FURTHER READING

References marked with an asterisk are cited in the chapter.

*Abey-Wickrama, I.; A'Brook, M. F.; Gattoni, F. E.; and Herridge, C. F., 1969. "Mental-Hospital Admissions and Aircraft Noise," *Lancet* **7633**:1275–1277.

American Speech and Hearing Association, 1968. *Proceedings, Conference on Noise as a Public Health Hazard.* Washington, D.C.

Aniansson, G., and Peterson, Y., 1983. "Speech Intelligibility of Normal Listeners and Persons with Impaired Hearing in Traffic Noise," *J. Sound Vib.* **90**(3):341–360.

Boranic, M., and Poljak-Blazi, M., 1983. "Effect of the Overcrowding Stress on Hematopoietic Colony Formation in Mice," *Exp. Hematol. (Lawrence)* **11**(9):873–877.

*Brody, J. E., 1979. "A Quiet Protest Against Noise," *New York Times News Service,* Jan. 28.

*Calhoun, J. B., 1962. "Population Density and Social Pathology," *Scientific American* **206**:139–148.

Carrighar, S., 1965. "Natural Balance, the Teetering See-Saw," reprinted in *Population in Perspective*, p. 359, Young, L. B., ed. New York: Oxford University Press, 1968.

*Casswill, J. C., 1971. "Health Consequences of Population Density and Crowding," in *Rapid Population Growth*, prepared by a study of the Office of the Foreign Secretary, National Academy of Sciences. Baltimore: The Johns Hopkins Press, pp. 462–478.

*Christian, J. J., 1950. "The Adreno-pituitary System and Population Cycles in Mammals," *J. Mammology* **31**:247–259.

*Christian, J. J., 1968. "The Potential Role of the Adrenal Cortex as Affected by Social Rank and Population Density in Experimental Epidemics," *American Journal of Epidemiology* **87**:255–264.

Chung, O., and Gannon, P., 1980. "Hearing Loss Due to Noise Trauma," *J. Laryngol. Otol.* **94**(4):419–420.

Cody, A., and Robertson, D., 1983. "Variability of Noise-induced Damage in Guinea Pig Cochlea," *Hear. Res.* **9**(1):55–70.

Cohen, S.; Krantz, D. S.; Evans, G. W.; and Stokols, D., 1981. "Cardiovascular and Behavioral Effects of Community Noise," *American Scientist* **69**:528–535.

Craig, J. V., 1982. "Behavioral and Genetic Adaptation of Laying Hens to High-density Environments," *Bioscience* **32**(1):33–37.

Crocker, M., and Price, A., 1975. *Noise and Noise Control,* Volumes I and II, Boca Raton, Fla.: CRC Press.

*Deevey, E. S., 1960. "The Hare and the Haruspex: A Cautionary Tale," *American Scientist* **48**:415–429.

*Detwyler, T. R.; and Marcus, M. G., 1972. *Urbanization and Environment.* Belmont, Calif.: Duxbury Press.

Dey, F. L., 1970. "Auditory Fatigue and Predicted Permanent Hearing Defects from Rock-and-roll Music," *N. Eng. J. Med.* **282**:467–479.

Engstrom, B.; Flock, A.; and Borg, E., 1983. "Ultrastructural Studies of Stereocilia in Noise-exposed Rabbits," *Hearing Res.* **12**(2):251–264.

*Fletcher, J. L., and Busnel, R. G., eds., 1978. *Effects of Noise on Wildlife.* New York: Academic Press.

*Environmental Education Group, 1973. *Noise Pollution and Solutions for Silencing the Problem.* A Public Interest Report. Los Angeles: Environmental Education Group.

*Giggs, J. A., 1973. "The Distribution of Schizophrenics in Nottingham," *Transactions of the Institute of British Geographers* **59**:55–76.

Gruenberg, E. M; Turns, D. M.; and Pepper, B., 1976. "The Epidemiology of Mental Disorders," in *The Social Setting of Mental Health*, Dean, A.; Kraft, A.; and Pepper, B., eds. New York: Basic Books.

Gyr, S., and Grandjean, E., 1984. "Industrial Noise in Residential Areas: Effects on Residents," *Int. Arch. Occup. Env. Health* **53**(3):219–232.

*Henry, J. P.; Meehan, J. P.; and Stephans, P. M., 1967. "The Use of Psychosocial Stimuli to Induce Prolonged Hypertension in Mice," *Psychosomatic Medicine* **29**:408–432.

Hiramatsu, K.; Takagi, K., and Yamamoto, T., 1983. "Experimental Investigation of the Effect of Some Temporal Factors of Nonsteady Noise on Annoyance," *J. Acoust. Soc. Am.* **74**(6):1782–1793.

*Hogland, H., 1964. "Cybernetics of Population Control," *Bull. Atom. Sci.* February: 1–6.

Holding, D.; Loeb, M.; and Baker, M., 1983. "Effects and After Effects of Continuous Noise and Computation Work on Risk and Effort Choices," *Motiv. Emotion* **7**(4):331–344.

Ising, H.; Dienel, D.; Guenther, T.; and Markert, B., 1981. "Health Effects of Traffic Noise," *Int. Arch. Occup. Env. Health* **47**(2):179–190.

*Keeley, K., 1972. "Prenatal Influence on Behavior in Offspring of Crowded Mice," *Science* **135**:44–45.

*Kupchella, C. E., 1976. "Noise, I Can't Stand It," in *Sights and Sounds—The Very Special Senses,* pp. 78–87. Indianapolis: Bobbs-Merrill Co.

Lebo, C. P.; Kenward, S.; Ouphant, E. E.; and Garrett, J., 1967. "Acoustic Trauma from Rock-and-roll Music," *Calif. Med.* **107**:378–380.

McElroy, J., and Middlemist, R., 1983. "Personal Space, Crowding, and the Interference Model of Test Anxiety," *Psychol. Rep.* **53**(2):419–424.

*Meyer, A. F., 1971. *EPA's Noise Abatement Program, Presented at the Second National Meeting of the National Organization to Insure a Sound-controlled Environment.* Washington, D.C.: Environmental Protection Agency.

Milosevic, S., 1983. "Effects of Noise on Signal Detection," *Ergonomics* **26**(10):939–946.

*Moller, A. R., 1975. "Noise as a Health Hazard," *Ambio* **4**(1):6–13.

Neus, H.; Schirmer, G.; Rueddel, H.; and Schultz, W., 1980. "Reaction of Finger-pulse Amplitude to Noise," *Int. Arch. Occup. Env. Health* **47**(1):9–20.

National Academy of Sciences, 1981. *Effects on Human Health from Long-Term Exposures to Noise.* Washington, D.C.: National Academy of Sciences.

Neus, H.; Rueddel, H.; and Schulte, W., 1983. "Traffic Noise and Hypertension: An Epidemiological Study on the Role of Subjective Reactions," *Int. Arch. Occup. Env. Health* **51**(3):223–230.

Nilsson, R., and Borg, E., 1983. "Noise Induced Hearing Loss in Shipyard Workers with Unilateral Conductive Hearing Loss," *Scand. Audiol.* **12**(2):135–140.

O'Donnell, P. A., and Lavaroni, C. W., 1971. *Noise Pollution.* Reading, Mass.: Addison-Wesley Publishing Co.

Pearce, D.; Bard, J.; and Lambert, J., 1984. "Estimating the Cost of Noise Pollution in France," *Ambio* **13**(1):27–29.

Peterson, A. P., 1980. *Handbook of Noise Measurement,* 9th ed. Concord, Mass.: Genrad.

*Porteous, J. D., 1977. *Environment and Behavior.* Reading, Mass.: Addison-Wesley Publishing Co.

*Potter, V. R., 1971. *Bioethics: Bridge to the Future.* Englewood Cliffs, N.J.: Prentice-Hall.

*ReVelle, C., and ReVelle, P., 1974. *Sourcebook on the Environment: The Scientific Perspective.* Boston: Houghton Mifflin.

*Rosen, S.; Bergman, M.; Plestor, D.; El-Mofti, A.; and Hamad-Falti, M., 1962. "Presbycusis Study of a Relatively Noise-free Population in the Sudan." *Ann. Otol. Rhinol. and Laryngol.* **71**:727–743.

*Selye, H., 1956. *The Stress of Life.* New York: McGraw-Hill.

*Smith, L. K., 1970. "Noise as a Pollutant," *Can. J. Public Health* **61**:475–480.

Smith, R. J., 1980. "Government Weakens Airport Noise Standards," *Science* **207**:1189–1190.

*Southwick, C. H., 1955. "The Population Dynamics of Confined House Mice Supplied with Unlimited Food," *Ecology* **36**:212–225.

*Southwick, C. H., 1971. "The Biology and Psychology of Overcrowding," *Ohio J. Sci.* **71**(2):65–72.

*Srole, L.; Langner, T.; Michael, S.; Opler, M.; and Rennie, T., 1962. *Mental Health in the Metropolis: The Midtown Manhattan Study.* New York: McGraw-Hill.

Stevens, S. S., and Warshofsky, F., 1970. *Sound and Hearing.* New York: Time-Life Books (Life Science Library Series).

*Still, H., 1970. *In Quest of Quiet.* Harrisburg, Pa.: Stackpole Books.

U.S. Environmental Protection Agency, 1971a. *Effects of Noise on People.* Washington, D.C.: Office of Noise Abatement and Control. (NTID 300.7)

U.S. Environmental Protection Agency, 1971b. *Report to the President and Congress on Noise.* Washington, D.C.: Office of Noise Abatement and Control. (NRC 500.0)

*Walton, S., 1980. "Noise Pollution: Environmental Battle of the 1980's" *Bioscience* **30**(3):205–207.

Welch, B. L., and Welch, A. S. 1970. *Physiological Effects of Noise.* NY: Plenum Press.

Wynne-Edwards, V. C., 1962. *Animal Dispersion in Relation to Social Behavior.* London: Oliver and Boyd.

*Wynne-Edwards, V. C., 1964. "Population Control in Animals," *Scientific American,* August. Reprinted in *Population in Perspective,* Young, L. B., ed., 1968, New York: Oxford University Press.

Young, L. B., 1968. *Population in Perspective.* New York: Oxford University Press.

*Zuremstehung, J. G., 1959. "Vegitative Funktionsstörungen durch Lärmeinwirkung," *Arch. Gewehrpathol. Hyg.* **17**: 238–261.

CHAPTER 17

Land and Resource Management

L and brings forth a variety of plant life, supports animal life, and yields the minerals that provide us with food, energy, and shelter. What is good for the land and the biotic communities supported by it is good for humankind. This was expressed well by Aldo Leopold in *The Sand County Almanac* published in the 1940s:

> A thing is right when it tends to preserve the integrity, stability, and beauty of the biotic community. It is wrong when it tends otherwise.

Leopold's book called attention to the need for a rational land ethic. (An **ethic** is a system of values by which decisions are made and on which actions are based.) It was an appeal that land decisions be based on the ecological importance of the land.

Land is taken for granted in modern U.S. society; historically, our use of land has been mostly haphazard and exploitive. Our present ethic treats land as a commodity to be bought and sold to the highest bidder, to be used at its highest economic value for the landowner. The problem is that this may not always coincide with what is best over the long run. Land is a finite resource; we must make wise decisions about its use that will satisfy our competing needs for eons to come.

In the first part of this chapter we explore how far we have come and how far we still have to go in developing a sound approach to land as a resource. We look at all the competing demands for land use—for cities, farms, roads, wilderness, forests, mining, and recreation—and we examine various land management theories and techniques. Although our orientation will be global in a few instances, we focus mainly on the United States.

LAND USE AND MISUSE

There are about 2264 million acres of land in the United States. Of this, almost one third is owned by the federal government. The rest is privately owned (59%) or owned by state or local governments (7%) or by Indian tribes (3%). These facts of ownership make regulating land very different from regulating air and water. Air and water are largely perceived as belonging to everyone; land, however, is owned by individuals and groups, who have deeds to prove it. How individuals and groups decide to use their land is a function of ever-changing population and economic shifts and cultural trends. Table 17.1 shows how non-federal lands in the United States are currently used.

Although there are a variety of possible uses for any one parcel of land, all land is not suitable for all uses because of topography, location, soils, or climatic factors. It is also a fact that some land uses are, for all practical purposes, irreversible.

Table 17.1 Use of Nonfederal Land

Use	Amount (Millions of Acres)	Percent of total Nonfederal Acreage
Urban	69	5
Water	9	1
Rural transport	26	2
Other nonfarm rural	47	3
Other farmland	23	2
Pasture	133	9
Forest	376	25
Rangeland	414	27
Cropland	413	27
Total	1512	100

The United States Soil Conservation Service (SCS) has developed a relatively simple system for generally classifying the capability of soils (land) for farming (see Figure 17.1). In this system a piece of land falls into one of eight classes. The SCS divides each class further on the basis of characteristics such as erosion potential, wetness, shallowness of root zones, or climatic limitations. Class I lands are those best for farming; Class VIII lands are not suitable for farming.

Figure 17.1 also shows how well farmers are doing in using land for farming. At first glance it appears that farmers are doing a good job of cropping the most suitable lands. Most Class I land is being used to grow crops. There is more Class II and Class III land available, and so most of our food is grown on these types of lands. According to the Soil Conservation Service, the quality of land used for cropping has improved over the last 30 years. In addition, there is a fair amount of land now in pasture, range, or forest that could be converted to crop use (Figure 17.2).

The problem is that although the land being farmed is generally good land, the total number of acres of good land available for farming is diminishing. Good Class I–III land is being used for places to live, places to work, and roads. Once land is given over to these uses, it cannot realistically be converted back to farmland. Strong economic forces come into play in this type of land use conversion.

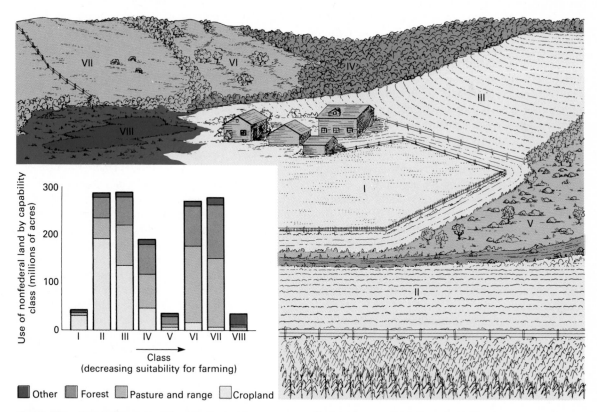

Figure 17.1 The Soil Conservation Service Land Classification System. There are eight groups based on suitability for farming. Class I land is the best for growing crops; Class VIII is not suitable for cropping owing to its soil type, topography, and wetness. A sample of each class type is shown here.

Chapter 17 Land and Resource Management

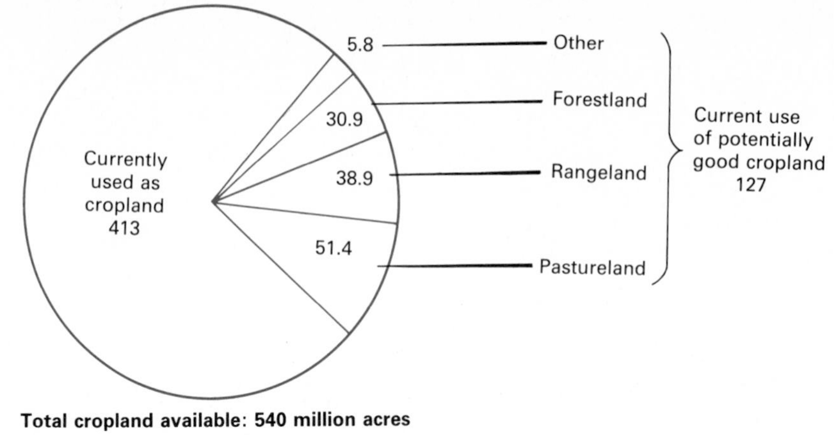

Figure 17.2 Uses of cropland in the United States. Numbers are in millions of acres. The National Agricultural Lands Study completed in 1981 estimates that the U.S. has a potential cropland base of 540 million acres. About three fourths of that is currently cropped.

Total cropland available: 540 million acres

Farmers in rural areas on urban fringes find it increasingly more profitable to sell their land to developers than to farm.

About one third of all of the land that is developed annually is land taken out of crop production. About one million acres of prime farmland is being converted to nonagricultural uses each year. One million acres is equivalent to a half-mile-wide strip of land across the country from New York to California (National Wildlife Federation, 1981). Other "less prime" farmland is being converted to nonagricultural use at a rate of two million acres per year. This means that a total of three million acres of agricultural land is lost to development annually, three million acres of agricultural land that will not be available for cultivation for many, many years, if ever.

In response to the need for a more useful tool to measure suitability of land for agriculture, in 1981 the SCS created the agricultural Land Evaluation and Site Assessment (LESA) system. The rating produced from this system is based on both physical and economic factors, which include the land capability classification, soil productivity, soil potential, location of the land, distance to market, uses of adjacent land, zoning, and the availability of water and sewer lines.

LESA provides a comprehensive approach to evaluating agricultural land use. It is flexible and adaptable to local conditions; it provides the potential for site-specific rankings that can be used to compare parcels of land instead of broad classifications less useful for comparison and land use decision making. Pilot projects throughout the country will eventually prove its usefulness in land use decision making.

It is not enough that land be used for a suitable purpose. The use must also be soundly managed. Suitability can, after all, change over time. According to the U.S. Department of Agriculture, soil loss from erosion threatens the productivity of one third of the nation's cropland. Although some of this is the result of using land for the wrong purposes, much is the result of poor land management for short-term gains. Some studies estimate that as much as four billion tons of topsoil are lost annually. This translates into 50 million tons of phosphorus, nitrogen, and potassium lost from U.S. cropland; the cost to restore these nutrients would run in excess of 18 billion dollars (1979 dollars). Since soil cannot be truly lost from the ecosphere, it must go somewhere. Soil out of place can cause air pollution, water pollution and/or land pollution.

There are still other kinds of land resource problems. We have tried to create more usable land by draining and filling wetlands; as a consequence, we have destroyed wetland habitat. With increasing demand for diminishing plant, animal, and mineral resources we have developed recovery techniques such as clearcutting of timber and surface mining of minerals that provide for a large return but are not always ecologically sound. We have harvested plant and animal resources of the land in a way that has brought many plant and animal species to extinction or near-extinction. In other cases, especially in recent times, we have brought some species to the same point indirectly by destroying their habitats.

Because land, like air and water, is essential to the common good, the points raised in the foregoing discussion suggest that we need land resource management plans. The challenge is how to regulate the use and management of land, especially privately owned land, and how to decide among competing land uses.

LAND USE: THE ECOLOGICAL CONNECTION

Before looking specifically at the problems and tools associated with managing land and land resources, let's review some relevant ecological concepts.

Everything Is Related

In the early pages of this text we discussed the interrelationships between the great spheres—land, air, water—and the biosphere. When an area that was once farmland is converted to an industrial park, each of the great spheres and the relationships between them are affected in some way. Among the questions that should be asked are: How will this change affect the quality of the air? Will the industries release pollutants? What effect will the change have on the watershed in which it lies? What wastes will be produced by the industrial plants and where will they go? How will drainage and runoff change?

In a somewhat less drastic change—for example, converting a farm woodlot to cropland—the questions might be: Once the trees are gone, what precautions will be taken to prevent erosion? What wildlife species might be eliminated? What new species might be attracted? How will air temperatures and humidity be affected? How will drainage patterns be altered? The point is that any change in land use will have some direct effects on the air and water and on living systems as well.

Thus it is important for land use planners and managers to have some familiarity with ecological interactions and with the concept of **assimilative capacity**. By this we mean that land, air, and water have the ability to cleanse themselves by physical, chemical, and biological reaction. They can assimilate or neutralize pollutants. For example, bacteria can break down organic matter that might enter waterways or be deposited on the land. However, self-cleansing is limited and is subject to overload. When an area is developed, bringing concentrations of people, animals, industry, and associated wastes, it is important that the assimilative capacity of the great spheres be taken into account as part of the planning process.

Diversity

The role of diversity in maintaining an ecosystem's stability is discussed in Chapter 4. As

more and more land is used for human settlements and the trappings of civilization, the habitats of some other organisms are destroyed. These organisms will be fewer in number henceforth or may even disappear. Some may become extinct. Human settlements actually provide niches for other species such as dandelions, chicory, pigeons, squirrels, and cockroaches, but the important factor is the net effect of the change on the stability of the system. Good decisions can be made about the use of land only with appreciation of how changing habitat affects species mix and of the importance of diversity in an ecosystem.

Irreversibility

The length of time needed for a succession from high-rise apartment house to woodlot is many hundreds of times more than the succession time from woodlot to high-rise. Cooper and Vlasen (1973) list six irreversible things that society can do to land and its bounty:

1. cause extinction,
2. introduce foreign plant and animal species that then become established,
3. contaminate local areas or the whole globe,
4. physically degrade critical areas,
5. deplete concentrated resources, and
6. use up critical environmental resources.

When a land use decision will result in such irreversible changes, it must be made with full knowledge that future generations are bound and limited by that decision. Good land use decisions require long-range vision—something our species has yet to master.

LAND ECONOMICS

Economics plays a big part in the way land is used. From an economic perspective the value of land depends on many factors, including the physical characteristics of the land, its location, climate, topography, institutional factors, public opinion, and technological ability to use the land. All of these affect the price of a given piece of real estate. When we talk about land use capacity from an economic perspective, we are referring to the ability of that parcel of land to return a net profit. The highest and best use in economic terms is the use that will provide the landowner with the greatest economic return. All other uses are lower uses, economically speaking. The economics of land and land use are based on the concepts of supply and demand. A unique economic characteristic of land is that the supply of land is ultimately inelastic. There is only so much land area on the surface of the earth; land is located in a given spot, and there is no relocating it. From an economic perspective the supply of land is elastic only through variation in the ways in which it is used.

It may well be that in most cases the highest and best immediate use of land for the landowner coincides also with what is best for society. Theoretically, as the needs of society change, this is matched by changes in the uses of land that return the highest profit, (see Figure 17.3). The problem is that certain land use decisions made out of immediate considerations may be irreversible. What then?

Just how sacred is the right of landowners to do anything with land? Should one be permitted to sell good farmland for an apartment complex when land nearby that is unsuitable for farming would do just as well for the apartments? Should a builder be permitted to build new houses in an area that is likely to flood every five years—perhaps creating a general tax burden later? Should the owners of "nice" houses be able to block the construction of low-cost houses nearby? Should a landowner be permitted to drain a swamp to bring extra acres into production during a time of high soybean prices? Should one be permitted to build a tavern in a residential neighborhood? Should a farmer be permitted to bring extremely hilly land into production even though the topsoil will almost certainly erode away within a few years? Some of these questions have been dealt with by governments and the courts, and the answer to many of these questions is *no*. The question of whether landowners should be permitted to do *anything* with their land is moot. They are not so permitted. The question now before us seems to be, How should decisions related to the best uses of land best be made and who should be involved in making them?

THE HISTORY OF LAND USE PLANNING

There are several important historical concepts at the heart of the land use issue. An appreciation of these is important to an understanding of where we have been and where we might be going.

The Fifth Amendment to the U.S. Constitution states, "No person shall . . . be deprived of life, liberty, or property without due process of law; nor shall private property be taken for public use without just compensation." Most of the original European immigrants who came to the United States were not landowners; they were peasants, debtors, and others looking for a better life. Their right to own land and use it as they saw fit was of prime importance.

As times changed and neighbors lived closer and closer to one another, it became necessary to place some restrictions on land use by zoning in order to protect the public interest. Zoning is a tool that can be used by a community to limit the development or use of land to ensure that its use is compatible with surrounding uses. For example, areas that are zoned residential cannot be used for industrial development. This public interest was for the most part wrapped up in protecting land values; a secondary application was to protect people from dust, smoke, and noise (Council on State Governments, 1975).

The essence of the controversy over placing re-

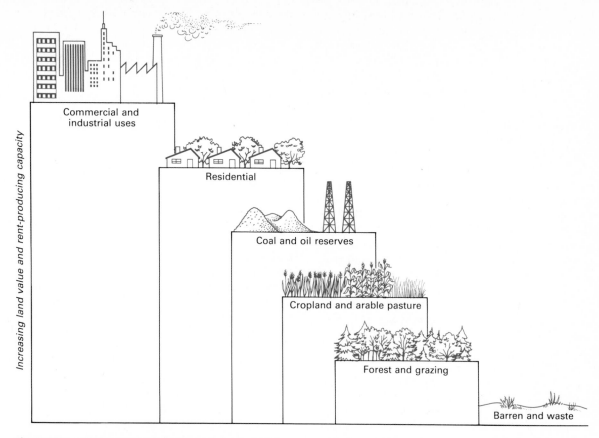

Figure 17.3 Valuing Land Uses. Economically, the highest and best use of land is that which is the most profitable to the landowner. The problem is that what is most economically profitable is not always the most ecologically sound and may not always coincide with the long-term general welfare.

strictions on land use was the issue of *taking*. Governments have the right of **eminent domain**, that is, the right to take private property for public use. In exercising this power the government must compensate the landowner (although landowners often feel that the compensation is not sufficient). This occurs, for example, when a dam is built and lands will be flooded by the reservoir formed by the dam. But the question of taking without just compensation also arises when restrictions are placed on land use. How many restrictions can be placed on a landowner before it is necessary to compensate the person for the land because the uses left are very limited? The courts have historically decided taking issues on a case-by-case basis. (See the references for more information on the issue of taking.)

Most current laws let land use decision making powers rest at the local level, where the people have the most control. This concept has become firmly entrenched as land use restrictions become increasingly inevitable. From an environmental perspective the limitations of the local approach lie in the fact that land resources, like air and water resources, are not always best managed within arbitrary political boundaries.

A concept that is firmly entrenched in the American way is that land is a commodity; bought and sold as such it can be used, and even exploited (U.S. General Accounting Office, 1977). Now that the frontier is closed, there is increasing concern that the land on which we all depend is finite and is misused and overused in many cases. We are also finding that changing an institution is at best a formidable undertaking.

FEDERAL INVOLVEMENT IN LAND USE PLANNING

Although land use decision making has traditionally been done at the local levels, both the federal government and the states have had some influence on land use planning. The Northwest Ordinances of 1785 and 1787 instituted a rectangular survey system for land and a system for land records. As is readily apparent by the rectangular configurations, most of the states west of the Mississippi were carved out after these ordinances were established. In the early 1800s the federal government began a system of land grants to states for educational purposes and for development of railroads, roads, and lands. For example, swamps needing improvement might be granted to the states for development. By the end of the nineteenth century, few grants of land were available; federal cash grants followed in their place (Clawson, 1973).

Perhaps the most wide-ranging federal land use planning effort came in 1934, when President Franklin D. Roosevelt created the National Resources Planning Board. This was a data-gathering group concerned with the development of natural resources, cities, and growth. This board was to work with all levels of government. However, concern grew over the power it seemed to wield, and it was abolished in 1943. Emphasis shifted again to the state level (Council of State Governments, 1974; Clawson, 1973).

Today we can best summarize federal involvement in land use planning in these ways: First of all, the federal government owns approximately one third of the land area of the United States; federal lands amount to about 760 million acres. Second, the federal government continues to use its traditional carrot-and-stick approach with regard to land use planning. That is, it provides incentives to get states to move in certain directions.

Numerous federal legislative acts affect land use; for example, in 1962 the Federal Highway Act required regional transportation planning as a prerequisite to granting federal highway money. In 1966 the Demonstration Cities and Metropolitan Development Act instituted the Budget Bureau Circular No. A-95 process. A so-called A-95 review means that projects using federal monies must go through a regional or state clearinghouse for review and comment before submittal to the appropriate federal agency. This was intended to align federal grants with overall regional and state plans and goals. This A-95 review process has essentially been eliminated under the Reagan Administration. Other examples include the National Flood Insurance Program, which requires participating communities to issue flood plain zoning ordinances.

Federal environmental laws also tend to force land use planning. Section 208 of the Federal Water Pollution Control Act requires areawide waste man-agement planning. Noise control by land use control is part of the Noise Control Act of 1973.

Perhaps one of the most controversial of major federal laws governing land use is the law regulating surface mining.

Surface Mining Regulation

Surface extraction is a method used for the mining of rocks, phosphates, and copper as well as coal. There are several methods of surface mining (see Figure 17.4); topography, depth and size of the coal seam, and other factors determine which type of mining will be used. When a coal seam is very deep, underground mining is the most practical method of extraction. If a coal seam is located near the surface, it is easier and cheaper to remove the earth above the coal seam (the **overburden**) and extract the coal from the surface. Surface mining of coal is common in the eastern, central, and western United States.

Because of the distinct differences in each region, the environmental problems associated with surface mining in each region vary. In the eastern coal region, erosion and acid mine drainage are the ecological problems of greatest importance. Degradation of the landscape has been another consideration; it is addressed in current federal law, which requires backfilling to eliminate high walls left after mining is completed. Chemical pollution of surface areas is the primary ecological problem resulting from surface mining in the central coal fields. Water—or rather the lack of it—dominates the ecological problems associated with surface mining in the West. Lack of rainfall hinders revegetation and permits wind erosion.

Potential strip mine land in the western region is now primarily in pasture and rangeland. In the central region, many potential surface mining areas are currently used as timberland, pasture, and cropland. In the eastern region, most of the land area overlying coal deposits is mountainous.

Because of its highly visible ecological effects on the landscape and water quality, strip mining is an old environmental issue. Perspectives on surface mining range from a call for a total, unqualified ban to the feeling that because of the energy crisis, coal resources should be developed at all costs.

On August 3, 1977, the federal **Surface Mining Control and Reclamation Act**, Public Law 95-87, was passed. In P.L. 95-87, Congress states that it is the purpose of the act to "strike a balance between protection of the environment and agricultural productivity and the nation's need for coal as an essential source of energy."

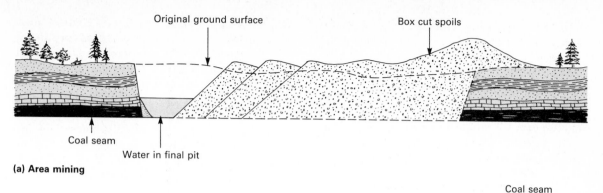

Original ground surface   Box cut spoils

Coal seam

Water in final pit

(a) Area mining

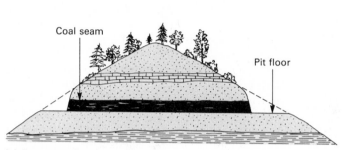

Coal seam

Pit floor

(b) Steep slope contour mining

Coal seam

(c) Mountaintop removal mining

Figure 17.4   Three Types of Surface Mining. (a) Area mining is used to get at shallow seams in gently rolling terrain. (b) Steep slope contour mining is used to mine relatively deep-lying seams in steep slope areas. It recovers only the outer edge of the seam. (c) Mountaintop removal is used to mine high-lying seams by completely shearing off the mountaintop. Federal law requires careful placement of the overburden (not shown here).

The aspects of the law that affect land use include some of its most controversial provisions:

1. Postmining land use must be described in the application for a permit to mine and is the basis for determining some variances. (**Variances** grant permission to vary, with justification, from the letter of the law or regulation.)
2. Prime farmland may not be mined unless the operator can restore the land to an equivalent or higher level of yield. Also the secretary of the U.S. Department of Agriculture will issue specific directives for soil removal, storage, and replacement.
3. Return to approximate original contour will be the general rule. Land must be restored to a condition capable of supporting the premining land use or a higher or better use. A variance from return to original contour may be requested by the surface landowner if the postmining use is industrial, commercial, residential, or public or if the variance would improve the watershed.
4. Each state, in order to assume **primacy** (authority) for the program, must establish a mechanism for declaring lands unsuitable for mining. Lands may be considered unsuitable if the reclamation is not technologically or economically feasible, if it is contrary to local land use plans, or if the mining affects fragile or historic lands. Under this provision other lands, the loss of which would affect water, food, or fiber supply or endanger life or property by disturbing flood-prone or geologically active areas, could also be considered unsuitable.
5. Mountaintop removal of coal is permitted if the postmining land use is for industrial, commercial, agricultural, residential, or public facilities use. Mountaintop removal is used in areas with steep slopes where it is easiest to shear off the top of the mountain as the coal is being removed, leaving a flat-topped mountain. It must be shown that the new use is an equal or better economic or public use.
6. The act places a severance tax on coal, a large percentage of which will go into an Abandoned Mine Reclamation Fund for the reclamation of **orphan lands,** that is, lands that were mined in the past and improperly reclaimed. This may turn

some now spoiled land into land of some productivity. It will also eliminate some of the environmental quality problems such as acid drainage and erosion.

Challenges to the strip mine law have been made in the courts and are aimed to a large extent at land use issues. They are based on the premise that the law amounts to an unjust taking of land without compensation, especially in the area of declaring land unsuitable for mining and in the requirement that land be returned to its approximate original contour even if the landowner would prefer a different postmining contour. According to the advocates of this position, mining operations in steep slope areas could produce a bench of flat land for housing and development if the slope did not have to be returned to the approximate original contour. The U.S. Supreme Court has upheld the constitutionality of P.L. 95-87. Other individual court challenges to the law in specific circumstances will no doubt be made.

Protecting Critical Land Areas: The Coasts and Other Wetlands

Another example of federal involvement in land use has been the management of coastal lands and other wetlands. These are considered to be critical natural areas for shore protection, flood protection, recreational opportunities, and spawning grounds for marine life. The **Coastal Zone Management Act of 1972** was designed to encourage states to regulate development of coastal areas in order to protect them from degradation. The bill was set up to provide planning and implementation grants to states with coastal areas.

Wetlands have been lost at an amazing rate since the 1950s. Estimates of the original wetland acreage range from 185 to 215 million acres. Around 50% of the original wetlands in the 48 coterminous states may have already been irreversibly altered or destroyed. From the mid-1950s to the mid-1970s, net annual wetland losses averaged around 500,000 acres. In the past ten years, losses averaged around 300,000 acres a year. About 95% of all wetland losses are attributable to human activity and 5% to the natural process of succession. The primary human activity resulting in inland drainage of wetlands is agriculture.

Inland freshwater marshes, swamps, bogs, and ponds make up 95% of U.S. mainland wetlands; coastal marshes comprise the rest. Because wetlands have no visible "use" and because dry lands do, management of wetlands has been basically nonexistent

and filling in of wetlands has been a common practice. The fact is, however, that wetlands are among the most biologically important and productive ecosystems on earth. Wetlands are important as stopping-off points and wintering and nesting areas for migratory waterfowl and other birds and as spawning grounds for fish and shellfish. It has been estimated that two thirds of the commercially important fish and shellfish along the Atlantic coast and the Gulf of Mexico and 50% along the Pacific coast depend on wetlands for their food sources and spawning grounds.

Wetlands also play a role in protecting shorelines and banks from erosion. In some cases they may store floodwater and moderate the level of the floodwater. Purchasing wetlands along the Charles River in eastern Massachusetts proved a more economic means for flood control than developing a system of dams (Turner, 1981). Florida has an 11-mile demonstration project to return a canal to marshland along the Kissimmee River. In the 1960s the area was drained and channelized; now the proposal is to plug the canal and return the area to wetlands.

Wetlands also play a role in the maintenance of groundwater supplies and in the purification of water. Runoff containing nutrients feeds into wetlands, which can then hold and utilize the nutrients. Bulrushes and cattails, common wetland plants, utilize nutrients from sewage and absorb some toxic chemicals. Wetlands help buffer temperature changes and are important in Florida and other citrus-growing areas that are susceptible to drastic temperature fluctuations. Some environmental economists have estimated that replacing all of the functions one wetland acre provides would cost society $50,000–80,000 (Eberhart, 1983).

Other federal policies have been promoted to protect wetlands. In 1977, President Carter issued an Executive Order making it the policy of the nation and all federal agencies to conserve wetlands and to assist in construction projects on wetlands only as a last practical resort. Several federal agencies are involved in wetlands. The Corps of Engineers is charged with issuing permits for placing dredge or fill material in wetlands. In its decision to issue or not issue a permit, the Corps consults with the Fish and Wildlife Service, the Environmental Protection Agency, and the National Marine Fisheries Service. Generally, however, the Corps does not consider agricultural expansion into wetlands to be within its jurisdiction.

Federal monies for wetlands protection have

Wetlands are not vacant, useless areas, as they might seem. Besides serving as spawning and nesting grounds, wetlands are buffer zones that minimize flooding and erosion and moderate temperature changes.

come from the Department of Housing and Urban Development for purchase of wetlands through revenue sharing, the Department of Interior through purchase of outdoor recreational areas, and the Fish and Wildlife Service for fish and wildlife restoration projects. However, pressures to develop wetlands continue.

Thus land use is being addressed and encouraged in bits and pieces, rather than in an overall, comprehensive land use plan at the federal level. Federal grants are also influential in housing, highways, airports, mass transit, and sewers—the so-called infrastructure of urban development. However, little has been done with these as tools in limiting urban sprawl and in land use planning.

A federal land use bill was debated in Congress several times in the 1970s. Most versions called for states to define state roles in land use decision making, to plan for the regulation of projects with regional impacts, and to protect the agricultural use of land.

STATE INVOLVEMENT IN LAND USE PLANNING

For many years, almost the only role of the states in land use planning was the enactment of legislation permitting local communities to plan and

zone. The U.S. Department of Commerce developed model laws in 1924 and 1928 called the **Standard Zoning Enabling Act** and the **Standard City Planning Enabling Act**, respectively. These model laws were prototypes for the states to use in drafting their own specific legislation authorizing planning and zoning.

In time, the states became more involved in land use management. A few states, beginning with Hawaii in 1962, passed state land use plans. Several different approaches to statewide plans have emerged. In some states—Hawaii, Connecticut, and New Jersey, for example—the state plan is only advisory. Local governments are encouraged to make planning decisions consistent with the state plan, which may go so far as to label areas in the state as suitable or not suitable for development. However, the state has no enforcement authority. Another approach is to set up statewide standards that local governments are required to meet in their planning and regulation of development. For example, there may be specific standards set for subdivision plans, and the local planning body is required to disapprove a plan that does not meet these standards. Colorado requires a developer to show that adequate water and sewer service is available to support the proposed development; a local authority would have to disapprove any plan not containing such information.

There are also states that use a combination of state zoning maps, state goals, and state mandatory standards. In Oregon, state goals and guidelines were set up in 1974. Local governments are required to develop land use plans consistent with these guidelines. This comprehensive approach remains the exception rather than the rule, however. Rather than dealing with the overall uses of land, many states have narrowly focused on the management of "special" or specific land resources. Generally, these are areas in which impacts are felt beyond local jurisdictions. Examples of how states have acted with regard to critical areas include siting legislation establishing guidelines for the locating of power plants. Control of state-owned lands and parks is a direct means by which states affect land management.

REGIONAL PLANNING

Regional planning within states and between states has also emerged. Some states—Kentucky, for example—have divided the state into area development districts. These multicounty districts are involved in acquiring data and planning for growth and services in the areas included in the district.

Perhaps one of the earliest, and still ongoing, attempts at regional land use planning within a state has been the agency set up to control land use in the Adirondack Park in New York state. In 1971, as a result of concern over development in the Park and the potential for degradation of a unique recreational resource, the New York legislature established a commission to develop a land use plan for the park. In 1973 a plan was approved by the New York state legislature. Zoning classifications were set up for private and public lands within the park based primarily on the intensity of use. A wilderness classification on state lands would prohibit high-intensity use such as off-road vehicles (ORVs); the intensity of use of private lands is controlled by restricting the number of buildings in a given area.

Under the plan, authority for land use decisions rests in some cases at the local level. This is true if the magnitude of the proposed development is small. For example, the expansion of an existing town in a hamlet zone would have a negligible overall impact on the park resources. Most decisions, however, rest with the state commission, the Adirondack Park Agency. Developers must apply for permits, and projects are reviewed on an individual basis. A project must be compatible with the zone but must also meet certain environmental standards within the zone, based on the exact location of the proposed development. Development on steep slope areas subject to erosion would have more strict standards than development on less steep slopes in the same zone. Local governments could assume some of these additional permit powers by submitting a land use plan for the local jurisdiction to the state commission. Upon approval by the commission the local agency is given the authority to approve more projects consistent with their approved plan.

The success of this regional land use program has been mixed. There has been local opposition; there have been permits granted at times on what some claim to be more political grounds than sound land use policy. Although private and municipal development is regulated, the Adirondack Park Agency is only advisory when it comes to projects of state agencies such as highway development. This double standard further aggravates some local residents. Development around the 2300 lakes and ponds is not well controlled; staff is lacking to follow up on permittees to be sure they are in compliance with the conditions of their permits. Perhaps the greatest accomplishment is that the agency and the plan are still in existence, guarding a valuable resource for the citizens of New York state. No one will agree with all of the decisions that have been made. But in a complicated area such as land use, a prototype of state involvement in resource protection has proved that it can survive and at least direct development, if not control it. The lessons learned from the record of this regional prototype may prove helpful to other states as natural resources become increasingly valuable to the general citizenry.

Regional planning involving several states by the formation of interstate compacts has been tried for a long time. The Ohio River Valley Water Sanitation Commission (ORSANCO) is a coalition of states bordering the Ohio River that seeks to coordinate water quality standards and provide for some consistency in the approach to the quality of water in the Ohio River. As a rule, states join such compacts without relinquishing any of their sovereignty; that is, the multistate compact has no authority over a participating state. Compliance with compact goals or guidelines is purely voluntary on the part of each state. A tougher compact has been suggested numerous times. It would be similar to ORSANCO but designed to address more politically sensitive issues such as power plant siting in the Ohio River Valley. However, the lack of enforcement or sanction powers and incompatible state interests, would make the formation of effective compacts difficult.

From an environmental perspective, regional approaches are especially important because watersheds and airsheds do not follow political boundaries. States' rights make it difficult to deal with problems such as acid rain in New York state that might originate in coal-fired power plants in states as far away as Illinois and Kentucky.

However, new efforts at regional approaches to dealing with environmental problems are likely. One key area will be state cooperative efforts to deal with problems of siting hazardous and low-level radioactive waste facilities. Already, Congress has sanctioned and discussions are underway for interstate compacts relating to the disposal of low-level radioactive waste (Chapter 15). We should see new developments in the interstate regional management concept in the future.

LOCAL PLANNING AND PLANNING TOOLS

Often when land use planning is discussed, one of the most critical areas omitted is urban land planning. As we saw in earlier chapters, the impact of noise, crowding, air pollution, and waste disposal is most critical in cities. Cities are home to too many people for urban planning not to be included in a discussion of land use. The concept of land use planning includes zoning in both urban and rural areas. Land use planning on a nationwide or global scale can be thought of as an extension of the concept of zoning.

Traditionally, urban land use planning has been left to the local communities. Several mechanisms are used generally by localities for such planning. The **planning board** or planning commission is an advisory group that analyzes available data and develops a comprehensive plan for directing growth in the community on the basis of this data. The plan is primarily a policy statement. In order to see that the master plan is implemented, a locality has other tools. The most common of these are zoning and subdivision regulations. In the past 15 years, other management tools have developed. We will examine these also.

Zoning and Subdivision Regulation

In 1926 the Supreme Court held that zoning was a legitimate use of a government's police power, that is, its right to protect the health, safety, and welfare of its citizens as specified in the Tenth Amendment to the U.S. Constitution (*Village of Euclid* v. *Ambler Realty Co.*). Zoning is implemented by zoning ordinances that consist of a zoning map, a narrative to accompany the map, and a listing of regulations that apply in each district such as building size and parking requirements. Basically, zoning ordinances set forth what uses are permissible and where. The districts or zones are usually classified as commercial, industrial, and residential (see Table 17.2). In recent years, agricultural and other categories have been added.

In general, zoning ordinances are developed by the planning boards or commissions but are approved and passed by local elected governing bodies. Zoning laws allow for zoning appeals in cases in which zoning ordinances are alleged to cause undue hardship. This and the fact that planning boards are purely advisory often allow political decisions to override administrative ones.

Related to zoning is the regulation of subdivisions through the specification of certain physical parameters such as minimum lot size, street design, open space, and service lines. The developer is usually required to follow a step-by-step procedure, and approval by a planning board is required before the lots are recorded with the county.

Table 17.2 Some Zoning Categories and Restrictions for Use

Zoning District	Principal Permitted Use
Residential	
R-2	Low density, not to exceed two dwellings per acre
R-4	Medium-low-density, single and two family dwellings not to exceed four per acre
R-8	Medium-density, single- and two-family dwellings; mobile homes parks; not to exceed eight dwellings per acre
RMF-16	Medium high density, multifamily; not to exceed 16 dwellings per acre
HRR-32	High-density, high-rise not to exceed 32 dwellings per acre
Business or Commercial	
PRD (or C-1)	Professional, research, office
LBD	Local business district (convenience businesses serving an immediate neighborhood)
GBD	General business district (shopping centers and other large-space uses)
Industrial	
I-1	Light industry
I-2	Heavy industry
I-3	Extractive industry (mining activities)
Special	
A	Agricultural districts
FP	Floodplain districts
OS	Open-space districts (recreation and conservation)

Is Zoning Good or Bad?

Not everyone agrees that zoning works as well as it should. Some critics of zoning think that it restricts innovative development. Zoning does not compensate a landowner for the restrictions placed on the use of the land. However, the courts have upheld the legality and constitutionality of zoning. Land development is not a right, and compensation for restricting development is not always necessary. Zoning is also described as too much of a negative tool; it *prohibits* certain uses in certain areas but is traditionally not geared to encouraging specific kinds of development.

A sociological criticism of zoning is that it may be used to preserve the status quo and to prevent the integration of neighborhoods. Minimum lot sizes and prohibitions on multiple dwellings put certain areas out of reach of middle- and low-income families and prevent development of low- and moderate-

Zoning laws help communities to regulate population density, preserve green space, and encourage the best use of land.

cost housing in certain areas. Critics claim that zoning has not halted urban sprawl. Another problem is that governments depend on property taxes for revenue, and this influences zoning decisions.

Even with all its limitations, zoning is one of the most widely used land use planning tools.

Other Land Use Planning Tools

Additional standard tools at the local level for influencing land use include so called "official maps" (maps that designate future rights-of-way for streets, drainage systems, parks, and other public lands) and building and housing codes that serve to regulate building size, frontage, and the like.

Localities can provide positive incentives for development via tax incentives, low-interest loans, aids in land acquisition, and many other stimuli to businesses locating in a specific area. For example, a local government may establish a special district such as in a center city area where industrial development is needed but not likely to occur and offer various economic incentives to encourage business to locate there.

DIRECTING THE USE OF PRIVATE LAND: ALTERNATIVES TO ZONING

There have been numerous proposals for methods of regulating use of private lands in rural areas and controlling urban sprawl.

Taxation

With the need to encourage the keeping of good agricultural land in agricultural production, the concept of **differential assessment** for land use was developed. Under this system, agricultural land is taxed (assessed) on the basis of its use as agricultural land rather than at its fair **market value**, that is, rather than at its economically highest potential land use. This offers some relief to farmers with land near suburban areas. If such land were taxed at its market value as subdivision lots, it would become too great a financial burden on the farmer. Differential assessments for agricultural lands give farmers a tax break as long as the land is in production. Differential assessments may be absolute, or they can have roll back provisions. **Roll back** means that the full tax payment based on market value is only deferred and becomes due when the land use is changed from agriculture to some other use. Such a provision is included to discourage speculators from purchasing and holding agricultural land. Land is more likely to be developed immediately if the speculator is required to pay deferred back taxes. Under roll back, the farmer is still protected indefinitely as long as the land stays in agricultural use.

A problem with the roll back concept is that it tends to encourage leapfrogging development. Since land farther from the city would tend to have a smaller deferred tax than that closer to the city, developers would be likely to jump over some agricultural areas with high deferred taxes to areas a little farther from the city. This, of course, means increasing urban sprawl. Further applications of the differential assessment are under consideration by various government bodies as a tool for encouraging land use other than agricultural—such as providing for open green space. Differential assessments in those cases would be based on a landowner's agreement to restrict development. As green space and open space become more and more desirable commodities, use of taxes to encourage their maintenance will be more likely. To date, 48 states have some type of differential assessment of farmland.

Limiting Growth or Development

In 1636, Boston passed one of the first ordinances relating to limiting population growth in an area. Boston required that any resident must obtain permission for any stranger or house guest who intended to stay more than two weeks. At various times, other cities have tried a somewhat similar action. In recent times, cities have restricted the number of new residences that can be built in an area, thus restricting population growth. Courts have given various interpretations of such ordinances. There is great controversy over whether or not such laws accomplish their intended purpose. Some seem to think they bear the old zoning stigmas associated with restricting lot size—that is, they result in increasing land prices because of the simple laws of supply and demand, thus stifling the poor and moderate income family. There is also the side effect that growth outside the restricted area is encouraged—people must go somewhere.

Development Rights

One of the most innovative approaches to land use control is that of transferable development rights. Under this system a unit or large parcel of land is assigned a certain degree of **development right**, that is, the right to change the use of the land from a natural area or an agricultural one to a commercial, residential, or industrial use. Such rights go with the land just like mineral rights and air rights (the right to use the air and space above one's land). Just as mineral rights can be sold, so can development rights. The system involves the sale of development rights by owners of land that will not or cannot be developed to owners who can and who wish to develop their own land. This is done by requiring developers to buy so many "rights" from other landowners in the area before a given type of development can take place. For example, if you owned land zoned multiple-residential and wanted to build condominiums, you would have to purchase development rights from landowners who will not be using their land for development. In this way an owner of undevelopable land is compensated for the fact that the land cannot be developed, and development is limited.

In other development rights programs, state or local governments may purchase development rights. Money for these purchases might come from a bond issue supported by the community as occurred in King County, Washington. In other cases such as the state of Maryland, state appropriations and county funds are used to purchase development rights. Problems with the development rights system lie primarily in lack of experience with it. There are no simple answers to how many development rights should be assigned to a particular use—for example, how many rights are needed for an apartment complex versus an industrial park or what the going price for a development right should be. However, the concept is promising and will probably become more common.

Easements

Another legal means of providing for the balanced use of land is the acquisition by a public group or agency of easements. Easements are a legal means by which permission is obtained to use land for a specific purpose when that land is owned by another person. Easements are required for installing sewer or gas lines by a public utility. Easements for public purposes usually give the landowner no option on whether to grant the easement or not. The utility offers the landowner monetary compensation, although landowners often question its adequacy. Ultimately, the land in question can be taken by use of eminent domain powers. Scenic easements are tools used to keep a land area from being developed from its natural state. The landowner keeps the title to the land but is given a tax break rather than any direct monetary compensation for agreeing to keep the land in an undeveloped state through a scenic easement. Organizations such as the Nature Conservancy use this as a tool when purchase of the land is not economically feasible. In the strict legal sense, the purchase of a development right could be considered a type of easement.

Let the Market Do It

There is another perspective at the opposite end of the spectrum of ideas on land use regulation. This view holds that regulation is not necessary and that economic forces alone will lead to a balanced use of land. The city of Houston, Texas, has used such a nonzoning approach. The concept underlying it is that if certain uses are economically advantageous, landowners will enter into "restrictive agreements or covenants" to preclude an uneconomic use. For example, under a nonzoning approach a developer interested in changing a large tract of land from a residential to a business development would not have to apply to a zoning board for a zoning change and be subject to a public hearing and formal public input. Under the nonzoning approach, a developer who can acquire a tract of land can then proceed with the project. Residents who are concerned about the potential for commercial development in their residential area could formally covenant or contract with each other not to sell for a use that may be incompatible with the single-family dwelling.

Studies of the Houston nonzoning approach (Siegan, 1970) did indicate that a separation of land uses occurs without formal zoning. Preservation of large areas of single-family residences was less likely than under zoning; however, this could have been the result of poorly developed restrictive covenants. Multiple-family developments under the nonzoning approach were found to be easier to locate than under the zoning process. However, planning for sewer and other utility services to commercial areas was much more difficult and in some cases more costly to the taxpayers initially. A nonzoning approach is less political and more responsive to economics, since there is no board to approach for a decision. If and when a particular development can be justified economically, it is likely to occur. Supply and demand dictate land use. The danger is that longer-term environmental considerations and social impacts may take a back seat.

As an example of the abuse of restricted covenants, some covenants still barred the lease or sale of real estate to nonwhites as late as December 1984. Although such provisions became illegal in 1968 when the Fair Housing Law was passed, lawsuits had not yet been filed to overturn all existing racially restrictive real estate deed covenants.

FEDERAL LANDS AND LAND USE MANAGEMENT

So far we have looked primarily at how the use of *private* lands can be directed toward the use that is the best for the common good, and we have talked primarily in terms of economics. However, at least one third of the land in the United States is part of the **public domain**, that is, land owned and managed by the federal government. Because the federal government is primarily concerned with the general welfare of the public, values other than purely monetary ones come into consideration in managing public lands. Let us now look at the federal policy on managing public lands, alternative uses, and competing interests and values.

Land Use Policies on Federal Lands

Approximately one third of the almost 2.3 billion acres of land in the United States is publicly owned. They are lands rich in resources. About one third of U.S. timber production occurs on federal lands. The federal government may lease minerals for extraction by the private sector, provide for the grazing of livestock on the land, and use the land for public recreation and protection of fish and wildlife resources.

Public lands are managed by several federal agencies. The Bureau of Land Management in the Department of Interior has control over the greatest fraction of the land—almost 50%. The Forest Service in the Department of Agriculture manages around 25%. The National Park Service and the Fish and Wildlife Service each manage about 10%. The Department of Defense manages 4–5%, and the remainder is parceled out among several other agencies.

In looking at land use on private lands we focused on techniques for providing incentives for the landowner to use land for the general welfare and not necessarily its highest economic return. In looking at land use on public lands we find that federal agencies are directed to manage the land in a way that will provide the greatest good to the greatest number of people in the long run. The issue that arises here is that as resources on private lands become scarce, the pressure for development and use of resources on public lands increases. Finding the balance among the conflicting uses that best serves the general welfare is the key.

Another controversy that has arisen because of increased competition for limited land resources and dissatisfaction with federal management of the land is the challenge by the states and by native Americans (Indians) to the federal title to many of these public lands. In the states west of the Rockies, the United States manages about 60% of the land–no insignificant amount. Consequently, in the western part of the nation, land management by the U.S. government is coming under increasing scrutiny. Typical of such reaction to federal land ownership is the **Sagebrush Rebellion**. This refers to the challenge the Western states such as Nevada, Arizona, Utah, New Mexico, and Wyoming have made to the federal title to millions of acres in these states. The federal government has provided payments to the state for federal land in lieu of taxes, since federal land is not taxable by the states and consequently deprives the states of revenue. This is becoming less and less satisfactory. States want the land and its resources for development as they see fit.

Multiple Use/Sustained Yield

Valid uses of public land include grazing, timber production, fish and wildlife management, watershed protection, outdoor recreation, mining, research, wilderness protection, education, and protection of historical, cultural, and archaeological artifacts. All of these purposes are to be served by our federal lands. The question is, How much for each?

The policy for public lands set down by statute in 1960 is that they be managed under the principle of **multiple use/sustained yield**. Public lands are to be used in a variety of noncompeting fashions (multiple use). For example, timber harvesting can coincide with recreational activities and can be done in a way that protects the watershed. Renewable resources are to be managed in such a way that future

generations can rely on these same resources (sustained yield); management of fish, wildlife and timber is to be done in a manner that does not deplete the resource over time.

To ensure that land and land resources are conserved as well as used, Congress has set up four programs that are aimed at keeping the land in its natural state. These four programs are the National Park System—set up to protect lands for recreation; the National Wildlife Refuge System—set up to protect wildlife species; the Wild and Scenic Rivers Systems—set up to protect these resources in their natural flowing state; and the National Forest System—set up to maintain forest resources. Then, consistent with the concept of multiple use, Congress has specifically allowed certain other subclassifications within each system and permitted activities to occur in lands dedicated to these systems as long as these activities are consistent with the primary purpose of the land designation. The national programs and the activities permitted within each classification are shown in Table 17.3. For example, under the National Park System a land area may be designated a park, a monument, a preserve, or a recreation area. Hunting is not allowed in a park or monument but is allowed in a preserve or recreation area.

Table 17.3   Federal Land Systems and Restrictions on Land Use

	National Park System				National Wildlife Refuge System			Wild and Scenic Rivers System		National Forest System
	Park	Monument	Preserve	Recreation Area	Refuge	Range	Monument	Wild Rivers	Scenic or Recreational Rivers	
Sport/trophy hunting	no	no	yes	yes	yes[2]	yes[2]	yes[2]	yes	yes	yes
New mining claims	no	no	no	yes	no[1]	no[1]	no	no	yes	yes
New oil and gas leasing	no	no	no	yes	yes[2]	yes[2]	no	no	no	yes
Commercial timber cutting	no	no	no	no	yes[2]	yes[2]	yes[2]	no	no	yes
Commercial cultivation	no	no	no	no	yes[2]	yes[2]	yes[2]	no	no	yes
Sport fishing	yes	yes	yes	yes	yes	yes	yes	yes	yes	yes
Commercial fishing	yes	yes	yes	yes	yes	yes	yes	yes	yes	yes

1. Some existing units are open to new mining claims to the extent allowed in Secretarial or Presidential order establishing the unit. H.R. 39, Gudger Substitute, and Huckaby Substitute, statutorily close all refuge units.

2. Permitted as long as it is found by Secretary to be compatible with purposes of the unit.

Note: Wilderness classification, by law, is supplemental to the purposes for which National Parks, National Wildlife Refuges and National Forests are established and administered and does not change those purposes. Wilderness designation does preclude developments and consumptive uses, such as commercial timber harvest, which would infringe upon the wilderness character of an area.

In Coronado National Forest in Arizona, recreation is compatible with forest conservation, an example of multiple use.

Realizing the importance of keeping some federal lands in a state relatively untouched by human activities, Congress has called for another designation to be added to all of the four major federal land protection systems just described. This is the designation of **wilderness**. If an area within any of these major programs is designated as wilderness, all development and consumptive uses of the land and its resources are prohibited. Wilderness areas are to be used in a manner that results in no, or very little, human impact. Because use of wilderness lands is so restricted, wilderness designations are strongly fought by those concerned with resource development.

With this general background on federal lands and federal management policies, let us look specifically at the management programs of certain federal agencies and some of the controversies surrounding them.

The Bureau of Land Management: Managing Rangelands

The largest public landowner, the Bureau of Land Management (BLM), has managed public lands for decades. Its management has been controversial. Generally, the BLM was directed to follow the policy of multiple use and sustained yield. Many people question its success in doing this.

A prime example of controversy over BLM has been its management of federal rangelands. BLM rangelands have been open to grazing by privately owned livestock. It has been estimated that about 25,000 ranchers graze eight million head of livestock on public lands. It has also been estimated that one quarter of the grazing is done by livestock owned by fewer than 2% of the ranchers. BLM does charge these ranchers a nominal grazing fee, but this fee has traditionally been about one third the fee charged for grazing on private lands. It has provided a few large ranchers with very inexpensive grazing opportunities. This has led to deterioration and overgrazing of public rangelands. Lawsuits requiring the BLM to assess the environmental impact of grazing on public lands led to the passage of the **Public Rangelands Improvement Act of 1978**. This act directs that grazing fees be increased and that a study be done to arrive at an equitable formula for assessing grazing fees after 1986. Half of all monies collected from the fees are to go into rangeland improvement. Time will tell how well new grazing policies and management techniques will be implemented.

The BLM has also been criticized for not allowing more development in some areas—primarily in its mineral leasing activities. In reaction to these pressures and in order to assess public lands and plan for their best overall use, the United States Congress passed the **Federal Land Policy and Management Act**, also called the BLM Organic Act, in 1976. This act for the first time set down in one piece of legislation a mechanism for managing federal lands under the jurisdiction of the BLM. Basically, the act calls for the management of those lands according to the policy of multiple use and sustained yield. Along with this the act calls for the development of comprehensive land use plans for these public lands including an inventory of the resources associated with these lands and, specifically, mineral surveys. Categories of public land use to be considered in the overall plans include:

1. mineral leasing and extraction;
2. intensive land use such as commercial, agricultural, industrial, and urban;
3. timber harvesting;
4. grazing lands;
5. water supply and water quality management;
6. wildlife habitat protection;
7. preservation of environmental and historical resources and recreation and wilderness values.

Mining on Federal Lands

The history of the leasing of federal coal lands has also been controversial. The leasing of federal lands for mining is administered by the Department of the Interior. The original legislation regulating this leasing was the **Minerals Licensing Act of 1920**. This law was enacted at a time when Western coal resources were not in demand, and from 1920–1960, relatively few leases were granted. In the 1960s, demand for Western coal increased, and the provisions of the 1920 act were found to be inadequate. A moratorium on the leasing of federal coal reserves was formally adopted in 1973, although it was informally in effect as early as 1971. In 1976, Congress passed the **Federal Coal Leasing Act**, which was designed to discourage speculative acquisition of coal resources. The same Congress enacted the Federal Land Policy and Management Act mentioned earlier, which placed land use planning requirements on the leasing process. The following year the **Federal Surface Mining Act** was passed.

Litigation relative to these laws and their regulations followed for several years. In 1981 the moratorium on coal leasing on federal lands was lifted. Shortly after the Department of the Interior began granting new leases, concern over the size of leases being offered for sale and outright allegations that information was divulged on valuation of the leases before their sale resulted in September 1983 in Congressional action establishing another moratorium on coal leasing. A Commission on Fair Market Value for Federal Coal Leasing was established to help address the problems with obtaining a fair price for the sale of minerals on public lands. In May 1984 the leasing ban expired. Congress is continuing to monitor coal-leasing policies and has threatened another moratorium if irregularities persist. The Department of the Interior is developing an overall plan for future lease sales.

U.S. Forest Service: To Clearcut or Not to Clearcut

Whereas the Federal Land Policy and Management Act addresses land use on federal lands controlled by the BLM, lands under the Forest Service are governed by other laws. The Forest Service regulates both forest and grasslands. In recent years the policy for managing forest lands has been set by the **Forest and Rangeland Renewable Resources Planning Act (RPA) of 1974** and the **National Forest Management Act (NFMA) of 1976**. Like the BLM Organic Act, these acts direct that a long-range plan for the management of U.S. Forest Service lands, including some rangelands, be developed so that these resources will be available on a sustained basis. The acts also set up a process for evaluating the status of forest and range resources, that is, a method for assessing how well the plan is working. Before this act, plans for the forests were localized, and no comprehensive overall program was in operation. According to the act, comprehensive multiple-use plans were to have been developed for all forests and grasslands by 1985.

The U.S. Forest Service has been criticized over the years primarily because it has been perceived as being overly concerned with timber production and less concerned with its other charges, including watershed protection. The issue of clearcutting of national forests epitomizes this controversy.

Clearcutting is a forest-harvesting technique whereby all of the trees in a given area are leveled. The land is scraped, and trees are replanted, resulting in an "even-age" stand of timber (a stand where all of the trees are about the same age) for the next cutting cycle. This technique provides an environment for the regeneration of sun-tolerant species, especially evergreens. Timber harvesters like it because it is relatively quick and easy and accommodating to machinery in comparison to **selective cutting**, whereby the stand of timber must be surveyed to mark mature trees of economic value, which then are cut, leaving a mix of tree sizes and types for the next cutting cycle.

Clearcutting mars the landscape aesthetically; this is what brought it to the attention of the public. It has been used inappropriately for hardwood species, resulting in a shift from mixed hardwood (deciduous) to softwood (evergreens) species. Clearcutting over large expanses causes destruction of habitat, erosion, and sedimentation in streams. Although the even-age stand resulting from the replanting of a clearcut area is beneficial in terms of the next harvest, the benefits can be short lived. Monocultures lack diversity and are susceptible to pest invasions. This fact and soil loss will eventually catch up with the timber owner of a consistently clearcut patch of woodland.

It should be noted that on a small scale (30 acres or less), when utilized in a staggered or checkerboard fashion and where erosion is not a major problem, clearcutting may not result in significant environmental damage. Clearcutting may even provide habitat, expanding edge effects within large wooded expanses (see Chapter 4). However, use of this technique in inappropriate locations and other large-scale misuses have resulted in major environmental

When done carefully, on a small scale, clearcutting may be a useful forest-harvesting technique. However, it can lead to erosion, sedimentation, and habitat destruction.

damage and the call by many for the banning of all clearcutting. In the long run, better management practices at the expense of convenient harvesting will allow for a longer-term timber operation—sustained yield as Congress has mandated.

Parks and Recreation

In 1983 there were over 243 million recreational visits to lands administered by the National Park Service. The lands administered by the U.S. Forest Service actually receive more recreational visits; Corps of Engineer facilities run second, and National Park lands are third. Americans need and use outdoor recreational opportunities.

Deterioration of federal recreational lands is a major concern. Recreation is low on the list of budget priorities, and this has led to a deterioration in facilities at National Parks. The use of off-road vehicles (ORVs) has also contributed to the deterioration of federal recreational lands. ORVs include snowmobiles, motorcycles, and four-wheel-drive vehicles. ORVs tend to destroy vegetative cover, leading to erosion and other environmental damage. By Executive Order in 1977, President Carter directed federal agencies to control the use of ORVs to reduce environmental damage. Implementation has been and will continue to be difficult. There may be over ten million ORVs in operation in the United States, and the expanses and types of land involved are not

easily patrolled. To help address some of the problems, Congress passed the National Park Access Act in 1978 to improve access to the parks consistent with preservation and good energy conservation. The act calls for the development of plans for mass transit within the parks and discouragement of private vehicles.

With the need for recreational lands increasing, Congress in 1978 also passed the National Parks and Recreation Act, which added to the lands designated as national parks and wild and scenic rivers. With a new administration, policy changes in the early 1980s focused on upgrading and maintaining existing federal parks and recreation areas rather than designating new areas. Proponents of new land designations cautioned that such a policy leaves potential future parklands open to development and aggravates the existing problem of park land overuse.

Thus the management of federal lands—*our* lands—is a struggle over what use is the best use for most of us over the long run. There are no simple answers; but Congress is moving to force federal management agencies to plan on a comprehensive basis for use of these lands. Land use planning at the federal level—planning that attempts to look at the whole picture—appears to be coming of age. But what about planning for land use in a way that is "nonuse," that is, planning for wilderness preservation. What are the benefits? What are the costs? What are the issues?

WILDERNESS

Wilderness Versus Multiple Use

In order to assure that an increasing population, accompanied by expanding settlement and growing mechanization, does not occupy and modify all areas within the United States and its possessions, leaving no lands designated for preservation and protection in their natural condition, it is hereby declared to be the policy of the Congress to secure for the American people of present and future generations the benefits of an enduring resource of wilderness. For this purpose there is hereby established a National Wilderness Preservation System to be composed of federally owned areas designated by Congress as "wilderness areas," and these shall be administered for the use and enjoyment of the American people in such manner as will leave them unimpaired for future use and enjoyment as wilderness, and so as to provide for the protection of these areas, the preservation of their wilderness character, and for the gathering and dissemination of information regarding their use and enjoyment as wilderness; and no federal lands shall be designated as "wilderness areas" except as provided for in this Act. (P.L. 88-577, enacted September 3, 1964, Section 2(a)).

Thus the U.S. Congress set forth the policy governing wilderness areas in the United States. By its designation as a wilderness area a given parcel of land is automatically eliminated from some land uses such as timber cutting and mining. Land is effectively taken out of production (in the common sense) and used entirely intact for educational, research, aesthetic, and limited recreational purposes. There are some who in an age of shortages think that too much area is being designated wilderness and that the concept of multiple use, which calls for the use of federal land to accommodate many uses at one time rather than a single use, is a more realistic and sensible approach. Others see the use of true wilderness lands for mining or timber harvesting or developed recreation as an irreversible land use decision. By statutory definition, **wilderness** is those areas "where the earth and its community of life are untrammeled by man (sic), where man himself is a visitor who does not remain."

The need for wilderness is difficult to document or to quantify. Consequently, challenges to wilderness designations have been loud and long.

There were a number of monumental battles over the issue of wilderness versus development during the 1970s. We will examine two: the Alaska lands issue and the designation of wilderness areas in the National Forests.

The Alaska Lands Issue

Perhaps the major battle of the 1970s over an imminent wilderness designation was the battle of Alaska. Alaska encompasses an area of 375 million acres, an area so large that at one time it spanned four time zones. (In 1983, Alaska consolidated these into two zones.) Alaska's coastline is longer than that of the continental United States, and it has 365,000 miles of streams and rivers. The only U.S. populations of dall sheep, polar bear, and musk oxen are found in Alaska. The state has numerous mineral deposits and expansive areas of forests. It has a population of little more than 400,000 persons. These features all combined to put Alaska in the middle of a national controversy involving conservationists and developers and raised questions extending to states' rights and national security.

The controversy began sometime after the **Alaska Native Claims Settlement Act (ANCSA)** became law in 1971. This act had come about because

the purchase of Alaska by the United States from Russia did not provide for the land rights of native Alaskans. When oil was discovered in the arctic slope in 1968, the natives formed a coalition and filed land claim suits. ANCSA was enacted to deal with the issues raised. Under the provisions of the act, native Alaskans including Aleuts, Indians, and Eskimos were given the authority to select 44 million acres of land from the public domain.

Two especially controversial sections of that act are sections 7(d) (1) and 7(d) (2), known popularly as D-1 and D-2. Under Section D-1 the Secretary of the Interior is to review all public lands in Alaska to see whether in the public interest any of them should be withdrawn from the native selections and from state selections that were authorized when Alaska became a state in 1959. (Alaska was given 25 years to select 104 million acres of land from the federal public domain for state lands. These selections were not complete when ANCSA was enacted.) Under Section D-2 the Secretary was to designate 80 million acres for inclusion in the National Park, National Forest, National Wildlife Refuge, and National Wild and Scenic Rivers Systems.

Numerous ways of designating the Alaska lands were debated in the Congress. The Alaska lands bill was finally signed into law in December 1980. Facing a new president to be inaugurated in January 1981, Congress settled for a compromise. As enacted, the bill set aside 56.4 million acres as wilderness and 49 million acres for various other designations including national parks, wildlife refuges, and wild river areas. The act also completed distribution of federal lands to the state of Alaska and the 44 million acres to Alaskan native groups. Although neither side—those in favor of protecting Alaska wilderness and those concerned with developing its natural resources—were completely satisfied, all concerned considered it a landmark after years of debate. The final decisions will lead to irrevocable changes in land areas heretofore substantially untouched.

Wilderness and the National Forest System

There are 187 million acres of land in the U.S. Forest System. Under the 1964 Wilderness Preservation Act, the U.S. Forest Service was directed to inventory the 60 million acres of roadless areas and to make recommendations for designation of these lands as part of the wilderness system. Finally, in January of 1973 the recommendations for RARE I (Roadless Area Review and Evaluation) were announced. They included 12.3 million acres to be designated wilderness, only 45,000 acres of which were east of the Rockies. Environmentalists challenged the findings in court. A second study, RARE II, was undertaken. More liberal criteria for "human impact" were used in eastern forests so that areas with some human impact could still be designated wilderness; the act provides only that humankind's imprint be "substantially" unnoticed. RARE II recommended that 15.4 million acres (577,000 east of the Mississippi) be declared wilderness areas, 36 million acres be nonwilderness and open for timber production, and 11 million acres remain under study with a final designation to come by 1985.

Generally, Congress has dealt with the wilderness designations on a state-by-state basis. By October 1984, over six million acres of new wilderness areas had been designated. Over 40 million acres of roadless national forest lands were released for potential commercial logging, mining, and petroleum production. Pending legislation will require the Forest Service to review wilderness designations for nondesignated roadless areas every 10–15 years when the forest management plans are revised. Between revisions the Forest Service could, but would not be required to, manage potential wilderness areas so as to protect them for future wilderness designation.

The Problem of Species Preservation

Extinction is a natural phenomenon (see Chapter 5), and most of the species that have existed during the evolution of the earth are now extinct. Why, then, are we concerned with **endangered species**, that is, species that appear to be near extinction (see Figure 17.5)? The problem is that the rate at which species are vanishing from the earth is in-

creasing. Species of mammals and birds now appear to be moving to extinction at the rate of one per year. This compares with an estimated rate of one species per 1000 years during the period of dying out of the dinosaurs (Reisner, 1977) and one species every four years between 1600 and 1900. If one looks not just at mammals and birds, but at all plant and animal species, the Council on Environmental Quality estimates that as many as three species vanish every day. If existing trends continue, the Council estimates that this will increase to one species every hour in ten years. At such a rate, 15–20% of all species on earth could be lost in the next 20 years—well within a lifetime!

Habitat Destruction: Tropical Deforestation

The main cause of the current problem of species loss appears to be the disappearance of adequate habitat because of human activities. Natural habitats are, after all, becoming rapidly displaced by agriculture, silviculture (the growing and harvesting of timber), industry, and human settlements. Recent trends toward development and exploitation of the tropics may increase the extinction rate even more because the tropics are estimated to contain two thirds of all living species. Ten acres of tropical forest contains 300 species of trees, compared to 20 or so species in ten acres of temperate forest. A report by the National Research Council estimates that nearly all of the remaining tropical rain forests in the world will disappear within the next generation (Holden, 1980). Only about 20% of the species in these tropical forests have been classified.

Tropical forests have been shown to play a significant role in limiting erosion, protecting soil quality, moderating seasonal flooding, and protec-

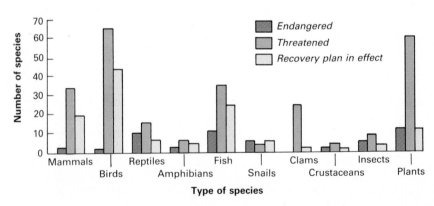

Figure 17.5 Endangered and Threatened Species in the U.S., 1984. This depicts the number of species by category on the threatened or endangered lists in 1984 in the U.S. The small number of invertebrates listed can be misleading. Not as much emphasis has been placed on these groups.

ting waterways from silt buildup. In addition to wood products, tropical forests produce oils, spices, and rattan used in worldwide commerce. Tropical forests provide habitat for many native and migratory species. Last but not least, the diversity of plants hold untold treasures in their gene pools for medicinal, agricultural, and other benefits for humankind.

The rate at which tropical forests are disappearing is of significant environmental concern, since some of its impacts, including loss of species, are irrevocable. On a global scale it is not known what impact deforestation will have on atmospheric conditions, in particular on the hydrologic cycle.

Pressures leading to increased deforestation include agricultural needs, areas for livestock grazing, and need for timber and fuel. Less than one tenth of land that is cleared each year is reforested.

Some techniques for lessening the problem of massive deforestation include the encouragement of agroforestry systems, that is, combining farming and forestry; the development of forest management plans; and new approaches to park design and management. However, the solutions also involve social, political, and economic considerations. If the forests are to be saved, sustained utilization of resources must become an essential component of development policy.

Species Preservation: The Rationale

Given the increasing pressures of growing human populations and growing, often conflicting, demands for goods and recreational vacationing spots, on what grounds can one justify protecting wilderness in order to preserve a variety of species of living things? There are several elements to the rationale for species preservation; these can be categorized as ecological, technological, and philosophical.

If humans are indeed part of the natural system, then what is good for the system is good for humankind. As we know by now, the stability of the ecosphere is related at least partially to diversity (Chapter 4). As species disappear, ecosystems become simpler and thus, in some respects, less stable. Losing species is like losing a part of a finely tuned machine that provides our food, water, and energy. As parts are lost—a screw here, a bolt there, a spring somewhere else—a machine might still be able to run. At some point, however, a part will be lost that is the last of a kind to perform an essential function in the system.

How much less stable does an ecosystem become when a species is lost? It depends; the specific species, the circumstances, and other factors are important. Certainly, the importance of a species to a system is *not* a function of whether or not a species can walk on two legs or be seen without a microscope. Without decomposers like fungi and bacteria, the nutrient cycles in the ecosystem would soon come to a halt. Clearly, we cannot prioritize the species to be protected on the basis of size or complexity.

The problem is that we still know very little about all the relationships in the ecosphere. This lack of understanding provides part of the basis for habitat and whole-system preservation. Preservation of habitats protects *all* of the species in given areas and allows them to be studied further.

Species preservation can also be argued from a human-centered technological perspective. If a species becomes extinct, we have lost the chance of using that species for improvement of the human condition. Plants, for example, may contain undiscovered antibiotics, anticancer drugs, and other drugs. Digitalis, a drug used by patients with heart disease, is made from the foxglove plant. The evening primrose has been found to contain a compound previously thought to be found naturally only in human milk. It has potential benefits in treating hardening of the arteries and arthritis. The wildflower periwinkle produces a substance used in treating Hodgkin's disease, a cancer of the lymphatic system. The medicinal potential of yet-undiscovered substances in discovered species and yet-to-be-discovered species could be immense. About 50% of the drugs sold in the United States today are derived from wild plants and animals.

Another economic and technological benefit of species preservation lies in the fact that the ability to transfer hereditary traits from one species to another is now coming of age. Through what is termed **genetic engineering** a gene carrying a desired characteristic can be lifted from one type of organism and inserted in the genetic material of another type of organism. The ability to transfer traits for resistance to pests and disease could transform the entire agricultural system and end its dependence on synthetic pesticides. The potential of such genetic transfer capability is awe-inspiring. For example, a variety of wild corn was recently found in Mexico that is a perennial; it grows every year and does not have to be replanted. This offers some intriguing possibilities for agriculture. Ironically, the only known patch of this wild corn was located on a hillside just about to be plowed under.

Some people argue for species preservation

from the position that all components of the eco-sphere have a right to be and that they do not exist solely for purposes useful to humankind. Do trees have rights? At a minimum, this kind of question brings us face to face with our perception of the real place of humankind in relation to other species. Can any one element really have special standing in a complex system in which all elements depend on each other?

Demands for land and resources will no doubt continue to conflict with species preservation. The Houston toad, the Furbish lousewort, and the Devil's Hole pupfish are obscure examples of this conflict. The Tellico Dam versus the snail darter is perhaps one of the more famous.

The Tellico Dam Versus the Snail Darter

In 1973, Congress passed the **Endangered Species Act**. This act sets out procedures for having species listed as endangered or threatened. The Endangered Species Act defines **endangered** as any species that is in danger of extinction throughout all or a significant portion of its range and **threatened** as any species that is likely to become an endangered species within the foreseeable future throughout all or a significant portion of its range. The act also provides that federal agencies may not proceed with or initiate projects that "jeopardize the continued existence" of endangered or threatened species. This includes private projects utilizing federal monies or requiring federal permits. That same year the snail darter, a small fish belonging to the perch family, was discovered in the Tennessee River in an area to be impounded by the Tellico Dam—a multimillion dollar TVA project in Tennessee. In 1975 the snail darter became listed as an endangered species. Soon lawsuits were filed to stop the completion of the Tellico Dam because impounding the water would allegedly lead to the disappearance of the snail darter, which is adapted to running stream water. Attempts were made at that time to transplant the snail darter to the Hiwassee River. In June 1978 the Supreme Court ruled in favor of the snail darter and against the TVA. As a result of this and other controversies, Congress amended the Endangered Species Act to establish a special committee to resolve such conflicts. In January 1979 this committee also ruled in favor of the snail darter and against completion of the dam, primarily on *economic* grounds—the costs of the dam did not justify the benefit.

After the Supreme Court decision, after the amendment to the law, and after the committee finding, Congress passed legislation exempting the Tellico Dam from the Endangered Species Act and funded the dam's completion. The provision was attached as an unobtrusive amendment to an appropriations bill for energy and water projects. In late 1979 the gates of the Tellico Dam were closed, and the reservoir began to fill.

The transplant of the snail darter to the Hiwassee River was a success. In 1984 the snail darter was also found to be thriving in four branches of the Tennessee River and in streams in Alabama and Georgia. The U.S. Fish and Wildlife Service has since upgraded the status of the darter from endangered to threatened.

Species Protection

Part of the problem with justifying wilderness preservation is the lack of scientific data on how much is enough? How large a population of a given species must be maintained to ward off premature extinction? How much habitat is required to maintain a certain type of stable ecosystem, given the potential for outside disturbance? These questions are only beginning to be addressed by the scientific community, and much needs to be done.

Mechanisms are in place at state, federal, and international levels to protect species. Some states regulate the taking of certain plant species as well as the taking of game species. For example, Arizona regulates the taking of cacti. Florida has a state endangered species list and requires a permit for collecting these. The problem with state regulation of species lies in the states' lack of authority over interstate and foreign trade.

We have already mentioned the federal Endangered Species Act passed by Congress in 1973. Some of the species protected by the act have included the peregrine falcon, the whooping crane, and the American alligator.

The Endangered Species Act was reauthorized in 1982. Opponents of the act wanted only "higher life forms" protected and organisms such as mosses, molds, algae, and invertebrates excluded from protection. Others wanted economic and not just biological factors considered in whether or not a species should be protected. Others proposed weakening of the restriction on federal projects that jeopardize protected species. These proposals threatened the very essence and spirit of the act and would have made it much less valuable in protecting the environment.

Congress did not weaken the act. The 1982 reauthorization streamlined the process for listing species. It allowed greater flexibility in regulating incidental taking of species when continued existence of species was not at stake. It provided for protection of endangered plants on public lands. And it provided for citizens lawsuits in defense of endangered species.

In 1980, Congress passed the **Fish and Wildlife Conservation Act**, providing matching funds to states on a 75% federal and 25% state basis for the protection of nongame species. About half of the states now have programs in place to participate in this program.

Regulation of endangered species is also conducted at the international level. In 1973 the **Convention on International Trade in Endangered Species of Wild Flora and Fauna (CITES)** was written to prohibit commercial trade in endangered species, restrict trade in threatened species, and regulate trade in protected species. Applicable species are listed as appendices in the agreement. Currently, 60 countries, including the United States, have ratified the agreement. Its effectiveness will obviously depend on how well it is enforced.

A concern over species preservation and wilderness preservation develops from a fundamental understanding that *Homo sapiens* is part of a system composed of numerous other species. It is a basic component of Aldo Leopold's land ethic. Where land cannot be preserved, it must be managed to provide for human needs, sustained yield, and species protection.

LAND, FOREST, AND WILDLIFE MANAGEMENT PRACTICES

The Basics

Good management of forests or other plant life and of wildlife begins with good managment of the land. In its most basic form, good management of land means keeping land in place. This is an obvious part of good farmland management, but good land management is just as important to a continued good harvest of trees year after year. Management by those involved in construction of highways, buildings, or homes is also important to protect streams from sediment runoff and to leave some soil for landscaping purposes.

Good land produces rich plant life, which in turn provides food, cover, and habitat for wildlife. The key to good land management is disturbing the land as little as necessary and, when it must be disturbed, to take steps to minimize erosion and repair the disturbance as quickly as possible.

Habitat Management

As we saw in Chapter 4, areas undergo succession from one type of plant life to another over time. The pace of succession can be altered by various techniques. Mowing, grazing, and plowing all slow succession by maintaining a given transitional stage. One tool of nature for slowing succession has been fire. This same tool can be used by humankind. One can speed up succession by soil improvements and

Contour plowing and strip cropping are good land management practices.

plantings, by selective cutting of plants, by draining marshes, or by protecting an area from grazing and fire.

Fire

Although we usually think of fire as a destroyer of plant and animal life, it can actually play a very positive role in the maintenance of certain habitats and consequently in the support of certain wildlife species. Fire is a natural occurrence in some habitats and can, when properly controlled, be used by humans for habitat management.

Forest fires have been around much longer than humankind. Fires caused by lightning are natural phenomena that serve to clear out dead forest debris. At the same time, fire provides a mechanism for a rapid return of nutrients to the soil. As material burns, it releases carbon dioxide and water, and its nutrients remain as ash. Destruction by fire results in a surge of nutrients for the next generation. Fire also allows for reestablishment of some sun-tolerant species. Certain pines, for example, have cones that do not open to disperse the seeds unless certain fire temperatures are reached. The open area from a controlled burn also provides an edge where a variety of transitional species may grow (see Chapter 4).

Burning of prairie land is another example of fire helping to maintain an ecosystem. Because these areas are grazed so closely today, such fires are less likely to occur. In some preserved prairie areas, fires may be set intentionally to maintain the system.

The chaparral areas in the southwestern United States are composed of dense, scrubby brush and low vegetation. Characteristically, chaparrals ignite and burn every eight to ten years when the vegetation becomes extremely dense. This prevents succession to taller tree species and thus perpetuates what would otherwise be a transitional stage.

Species Management

Species are managed indirectly by good land and habitat management; populations can also be managed directly. Good wildlife management is concerned with the production and harvesting of game species, the maintenance and protection of nongame species, and the control of all species. The purpose of such management is to prevent conflict with human health and human activities such as crop and livestock production. Two species population management tools are particularly controversial. Let us look in turn at the roles of predators and hunting in wildlife species management.

Predator Control

Perhaps the role in the ecosystem that is most misunderstood by the public is the predator (see Chapter 4). Predators have traditionally been seen as villains and their prey as innocent victims. Humans have spent much time and energy attempting to control or eliminate predators. We have at times put bounties on predators or promoted large-scale poisonings.

A prime example of modern-day attitudes toward predators is the controversy over coyotes in the West. Ranchers are convinced that coyotes are costing them millions of dollars by attacking their herds. Others believe that coyotes only cull the old and sickly from herds or that only a few individual coyotes in certain areas are to blame and not the whole species. Nevertheless, large poisoning campaigns were conducted in the 1960s. They succeeded in killing not only coyotes but also prairie dogs, eagles, and vultures. Poisoned bait was eaten indiscriminately by many species, not just the target species or the individual animal causing the problem. Some of the poisons such as "1080" (sodium fluoroacetate) were distributed in dead carcasses. Not only the animal that ate the carcass died but also any animal that fed on the animal that ate the carcass.

Public outrage resulted in the establishment of a committee to look into the problem; the committee was headed by Aldo Leopold's son, Starker. This committee adopted two principles regarding predator control. It concluded that all native animals should be considered resources and that control programs should be local and aimed at the individual animal causing the problem. However, it was not until 1972 that the coyote-poisoning campaigns were prohibited on public lands. Even now, the attitudes expressed by Leopold's group have not fully taken hold in predator management and in the minds of the public. In late 1983 the ban on "1080" was modified to allow its use in single lethal doses.

There are alternatives to poisoning for managing predator-prey relationships. Managing for wildlife may involve the provision of good cover habitat for the prey species. For management of game species it might involve the enhancement of nongame buffer species—species that are not hunted by humans but that a given predator would find satisfactory. Rodents are often buffer species. Care must be taken, however, to ensure that the buffer species does not compete with the game species for its food or habitat, carry disease, or interfere in any other way with the life cycle of the desired species. Care

Control of predators like coyotes is more conducive to good ecological balance than completely eliminating them.

must also be exercised so that the buffer species does not proliferate to the extent that it draws more predators. In addition, the buffer species must not have a hibernating stage, at which time it would leave the desired species even more vulnerable for a period of time.

Hunting

Although some deplore hunting as a sport, if it is managed properly, hunting not only does not adversely affect natural systems, it may in fact help. Any healthy animal population produces a surplus. The taking of this surplus will have no adverse effect on the population.

Hunting regulations determine what can be hunted (even what sex), when, and for how long. Bag limits are set to ensure that a population is not overhunted. Seasons ensure that hunting does not occur at times when a species is carrying its young or is unable to escape—for example, in certain periods, ducks' plumage hinders their flight.

Fall is a prime hunting season because populations largely contain adults at a maximum in size and numbers before the winter. The length of the hunting season may vary on the basis of updated population surveys. The amount of the take is recorded annually for large game species, and age and sex are determined when possible. Every effort is made to gauge the condition of the species so that the take can be properly controlled or prohibited for

the next season. Some species such as the dodo bird and passenger pigeon were overhunted, and this contributed to their extinction. It should be pointed out that 33% of all mammals and 42% of all birds that have become extinct since 1600 have disappeared because of overkill.

Problems arise when hunting goes unregulated as it did before 1900. Animals were shot strictly for sport, for their plumage, or for their taste. The American bison and the passenger pigeon are two examples. In the late 1800s and early 1900s, however, legislation was enacted to control some of these abuses.

Ecologically, hunters assume the role of predators, which are now missing in many cases. Hunting of deer may prevent overpopulation and later starvation within a herd. Thus hunting does have a place in the scheme of things.

CONFLICTS

The American Society of Planning Officials (now merged with the American Institute of Planners to form the American Planning Association) listed the major conflict areas or issues related to land use planning as follows (Listoken, 1974, pp. 35–37):

1. Regional versus local: Who should make land use decisions? As such decisions affect larger and larger areas, some jurisdictional guidelines will have to be set.
2. Public interest versus private interests: How shall the rights of the individual be weighed against the common good?
3. Conservation versus change: What is wrong with the way things are being done? What is progress?
4. Quality versus quantity: How much housing and for whom—low-, moderate-, or high-income residents? This concept can be expanded to other issues as well, such as open space and recreational areas.

At the moment there seem to be three conflicting philosophies related to land use. At one extreme there are those who hold that land should remain as it is; they are strict preservationists. At the opposite extreme are those who feel that land should be used for its highest immediate profit. A broad spectrum of positions lie in between. Most people express the desire to preserve some land and use the rest wisely.

CONCEPTS TO REMEMBER

1. Land is a finite resource.
2. Land possesses some elastic qualities; its use can and does change over time with the demands of society.
3. Not all land is suitable for all uses because of its location, soil type, topography, or climatic conditions.
4. Some changes in land use are, for all practical purposes, irreversible.
5. Loss of prime farmland to development is a serious problem facing humankind.
6. Land use is to a great extent governed by economics.
7. The best use of land from society's long-term perspective may not be the use that will provide the greatest immediate economic benefit to the landowner.
8. Certain government programs are designed to give a landowner incentive to use land in the best way for the public good over the long run.
9. The notion that any person should be able to do anything with his or her own land is outdated.
10. By being familiar with the tools of land use planning in urban and suburban areas and by being familiar with legal alternatives for preserving farmland in rural areas, an individual can become involved in effective land use management in his or her own community.
11. The increased destruction of natural areas in order to provide food, shelter, and energy for humans is being done at the expense of other species. It is an act of potential self-destruction, since loss of species may weaken the web of life and jeopardize the human species.
12. There are ways to manage land resources to provide for sustained yields, to protect the diversity of species, and to meet other human needs all at the same time.
13. Federal policy requires that federal lands be used and managed for multiple uses and sustained yields to ensure resources for future generations. The designation as wilderness prevents many developmental uses and so is often opposed by developmental interests.
14. Sound methods for managing the resources of the land are likely to be appreciated and practiced best by those who have an understanding of ecological relationships.
15. If we fail as a society to develop an ecologically sound land ethic, land will continue to be abused and will eventually no longer produce what humans need.
16. We all have responsibility as stewards of the land.

DISCUSSION QUESTIONS AND FOOD FOR THOUGHT

1. Contact your local planning board to obtain information on the zoning plan for your locality. Attend a zoning meeting.
2. Read Aldo Leopold's *Sand County Almanac* and determine how much of what he says is applicable today.
3. Role playing: Check the local paper for a land use issue in your community. Divide the class to present the various viewpoints and to debate the issue. Include viewpoints of members of the planning board, the developer, and residents from the affected area.
4. Find out what tools are authorized by your state or by federal law for land use planning, including development rights, scenic easements, and differential tax assessment.
5. Defend or criticize the addition of land to the wilderness system.
6. Debate: Land that cannot be returned to its original condition should not be strip-mined for coal.
7. Read *Night Comes to the Cumberlands* by H. Caudill and discuss some of the social implications of strip mining.
8. Competition for land will continue to increase and uses of land will intensify. Discuss life-style alternatives that may result.
9. Debate: Resolved: We must uphold the right of landowners to use their land as they see fit.
10. Draw diagrams as follows:
    (a) Trace some of the ecological impacts that will result from clearcutting a parcel of timberland in the watershed of a small creek. (Review Chapter 12.)
    (b) Trace some of the ecological impacts that will result from converting this clearcut area into an airport.
11. Discuss the factors that govern the use of marginal land.
12. Gifford Pinchot under President Theodore Roosevelt was largely responsible for administering the national forest program. His philosophy was embedded in the phrase "the greatest good for the greatest number over the long run." How would his philosophy apply in these cases:
    (a) Clearcutting versus selective cutting of timberland?
    (b) Single use versus multiple use of federal lands?

13. A plot of land in your community is being proposed for low-rent housing for the elderly. The land contains some rare species. Assign roles and present your case to the local board that will decide the fate of the area.

14. Discuss:

a. All species have a right to protection.
b. Only higher life forms should be protected.

15. See whether you have a local chapter of the Nature Conservancy. Find out what habitat preservation activities are going on in your state.

REFERENCES AND FURTHER READING

References marked with an asterisk are cited in the chapter.

Booth, R., and Hullar, T., 1980. "Has the Adirondack Park Agency Made a Difference?" *The Amicus Journal,* **1**(4):12–23.

Bosselman, F.; Callies, D.; and Banta, J., 1973. *Taking Issue: Analysis of Constitutional Limits of Land Use Control.* Washington, D.C.: Council on Environmental Quality.

Bury, R., and Lapotka, G., 1979. "The Making of Wilderness," *Environment* **21**(10):12–20.

Campbell, F. T., 1980. "Conserving Our Wild Plant Heritage," *Environment* **22**(9):14–20.

*Clawson, M., 1973. "Historical Overview of Land Use Planning in the United States," pp. 23–54. in *Environment: A New Focus for Land Use Planning.* Washington, D.C.: National Science Foundation.

Cook, F. and Kelly, W., 1976. *Evaluation of Current Surface Coal Mining Overburden Handling Techniques and Reclamation Practices.* Washington, D.C.: U.S. Department of Interior, Bureau of Mines. (Contract S0144081)

*Cooper, W. E., and Vlasen, R. D., 1973. "Ecological Concepts and Applications to Planning," pp. 183–206 in *Environment: A New Focus for Land Use Planning.* Washington, D.C.: National Science Foundation.

*Council of State Governments, 1974. *Guide to Land Management.* Lexington, Ky.: Council of State Governments.

*Council of State Governments, 1975. *Land: State Alternatives for Planning and Management.* Lexington, Ky.: Council of State Governments.

*Council on Environmental Quality, 1977. *Eighth Annual Report.*

*Council on Environmental Quality, 1979. *Tenth Annual Report.*

Dunford, R. W.; Roe, R. D.; Steiner, F. R.; Wagner, W. R.; and Wright, L. E., 1983. "Implementing LESA in Whitman County, Washington," *Journal of Soil and Water Conservation,* March–April: 87–89.

*Eberhardt, R., 1983. "Ecologically Valuable Wetlands Are Falling Victim to Progress,'" *The Louisville Courier-Journal,* December 4.

Healy, R. G., and Rosenberg, J. S., 1979. *Land Use and the States: A Book from Resources for the Future.* 2nd ed. Baltimore: Johns Hopkins University Press.

Held, R. B., and Visser, D. W., 1984. *Rural Land Uses and Planning: A Comparative Study of the Netherlands and the United States.* New York: Elsevier Science Publishers.

*Holden, C., 1980. "Rain Forests Vanishing," *Science* **208**:378.

Horwitz, E. L., 1978. *Our Nation's Wetlands: An Interagency Task Force Report.* Coordinated by the Council on Environmental Quality. Washington, D.C.: U.S. Government Printing Office.

Land Use Planning Report. Silver Spring, Md.: Business Publishers. (1978).

*Leopold, A., 1949. *A Sand County Almanac.* New York: Oxford University Press.

*Listokin, D., ed., 1974. *Land Use Controls: Present Problems and Future Reform,* N.J.: Center for Policy Research, Rutgers University.

Lyday, N., 1976. *The Law of the Land: Debating National Land Use Legislation 1970–1975.* Washington, D.C.: The Urban Institute.

Martin, P. S., and Klein, R. G., eds., 1984. *Quaternary Extinctions.* Tucson: University of Arizona Press.

McHarg, I., 1969. *Design with Nature.* Garden City, New York: Natural History Press.

Montana Legislative Council, 1976. *Preservation of Agricultural Lands: Alternative Approaches.* Helena, Mt.: Interim study by the Subcommittee on Agricultural Lands.

*National Wildlife Federation, 1981. *Environmental Quality Index* (updated annually). Washington, D.C.: NWF Educational Services.

Norman, C., 1981. "The Threat to One Million Species," *Science* **214**(4525):1105–1107.

Office of Technology Assessment, 1984. *Wetlands: Their Use and Regulation.* Washington, D.C.: U.S. Government Printing Office.

*Reisner, M., 1977. "The Garden of Eden to Weed Path: The Earth's Vanishing Genetic Heritage," *NRDC Newsletter* **6**(1):1–15.

Reisner, M., 1978. "The End of the Wilderness: The Future of Our National Forests," *NRDC Newsletter* **7**(5):1–20.

Ritter, M. K., 1979. "Alaska: Our Last Great First Chance," *NRDC Newsletter* **8**(1):1–5ff.

Rosenbaum, N., 1976. *Land Use and the Legislatures.* Washington, D.C.: The Urban Institute.

Shaffer, M. L., 1981. "Minimum Population Sizes for Species Conservation," *Bioscience* **31**(2):131–134.

*Siegan, B., 1970. "Nonzoning in Houston," *Journal of Law and Economics,* April: 129–144.

Steiner, F. R., 1983. "Regional Planning in the United States: Historic and Contemporary Examples," *Landscape Planning,* **10**:297–315.

Steiner, F. R., and Theilacker, J., eds., 1984. *Protecting Farmlands.* Westport Conn.: The AVI Publishing Co.

Tiner, R. W., Jr., 1984. *Wetlands of the United States: Current Status and Recent Trends.* Washington, D.C.: U.S. Fish and Wildlife Service.

*Turner, E. R., 1981. "Managing Wetlands," *Science* **212**: 795–796.

U.S. Department of Agriculture, 1977. *Handbook of Agricultural Charts.* Washington, D.C.: U.S. Government Printing Office.

U.S. Department of Agriculture and Council on Environmental Quality, 1981. *National Agricultural Lands Study: Final Report.* Washington, D.C.: U.S. Government Printing Office.

*U.S. General Accounting Office, 1977. *Land Use Planning Management and Control.* (CED-77-101) Washington, D.C.: U.S. Government Printing Office.

U.S. General Accounting Office, 1980. *Land Use Issues.* (CED-80-108) Washington, D.C.: U.S. Government Printing Office.

Waldrop, M. M., 1982. "Imaging the Earth (I): The Troubled First Decade of Landsat," *Science* **215**:1600–1603.

PART IV

Points of View

In Chapters 18 and 19 we summarize what we have covered up to this point, focusing on the roots of our environmental problems and our prospects for solving them in the future. Among the questions to be explored are: How has each of our institutions contributed to our most pressing environmental problems and to our failure to head them off? In what ways will these institutions be likely to help and/or hinder us in our search for solutions? In summary, just what *are* our most important environmental problems? How shall we deal with them in the future. What are the prospects for success?

CHAPTER 18

Human Institutions:
Problems and Solutions

While the word **institution** may conjure up images of hospitals, schools, or big buildings, we use the word here in a more general way. We refer to the formal ways in which human beings organize civilization and the things that make it up. We will use the word here to refer to religion, government, law, economics, education, science, medicine, and cities. We are devoting a chapter to institutions because (1) the way in which our institutions function have much to do with the fact that we have environmental problems, and (2) they will also have a lot to do with our prospects for dealing with these problems effectively.

The degree to which institutions are important as causes and potential solutions to environmental problems is suggested by the roles some of them have had in our "energy crises." As we saw in Chapter 6, the mid-1970s crises was certainly not a result of any absolute shortage of energy worldwide. We have immense reserves of coal and other forms of energy in many parts of the world. The crisis may have resulted, as suggested by Ridker (1973), from inappropriate institutional policies governing the use of energy. Regulation of oil and gas prices, for example, played a significant role by retarding conservation efforts, retarding exploration for new sources of energy, and retarding the search for new ways of using existing supplies.

It is important that we appreciate the general role of institutions in human affairs in order to appreciate their relationship to our environmental problems.

Institutions serve to stabilize and ease human interaction, making it orderly and more civilized. Institutions can also hamper interaction and stand in the way of needed changes. Civilizing human interaction while preserving flexibility is an extremely difficult balance to achieve. Some institutions achieve it better than others.

The U.S. system of government is thought by some to be a good example of an institution that has carefully spelled out, built-in mechanisms that provide for change and at the same time ensure that change will not be capricious, arbitrary, or too sudden. In other types of institutions—education, for example—mechanisms for change are not nearly so well established, and response to the need for change occurs via less formal mechanisms.

History indicates that, in general, institutions typically lack sufficient flexibility to persist for very long without change. Forces that are constantly at odds and partly account for this historical pattern are the inevitability of change and a strong human drive to live by institutions. Change or replacement of existing institutions is nearly always difficult because not all of the elements of the culture or society recognize the need for adaptation at the same time. If the natural resistance to change holds sway too long, pressures build up until needed change can no longer be accommodated by the existing structure. Then new institutions replace the old, sometimes traumatically. Institutions work best when permitted to evolve gradually.

Our ability to cope with the future will be determined in part by how adaptable our institutions are and how readily they can conform to new circumstances, new pressures, new opportunities, and new dangers related to the environment. It is somewhat encouraging, then, that clean, nonpolluted, well-planned environments are starting to become fixed within our institutions and our institutional value systems. The pace is not so encouraging. Some say that the pace is too slow and that our only hope is to recast some of our institutions—to bring about an abrupt change to a new way of living and relating to one another and to the environment. We are now going to look at some institutions that are important to the environment. We will spend more time on some than on others, not necessarily in direct proportion to their importance.

RELIGION

Early in the environmental movement the historian Lynn White wrote a widely reproduced and widely quoted essay blaming much of the environmental crisis on elements of the Judeo-Christian ethic. White and other writers have suggested that the notion featured in many religions that the earth is only a place we will use temporarily and then move on accounts for a basic disregard for the natural world and its life support systems. The attitude that we are simply passing through makes the world a disposable item.

Moncrief (1970), among others, disagrees with White, claiming that Judeo-Christian teaching has had only indirect influence on how the Western world treats the environment. He claims that religious tradition accounts for only a small part of the environmental problem and that other factors including rapidly changing technology, urbanization, and especially increased individual wealth are considerably more important.

Regardless of what has been true in the past, perhaps Western religious institutions could serve humankind better by putting more emphasis on ecological responsibility.

SCIENCE AND TECHNOLOGY

Is Science a "First Cause"?

Many observers have blamed science for the sad state of our environment. The reasoning is that science begets technology, and technology often causes problems more serious than those it solves. Science does provide the basic information out of which new technologies emerge. It is also generally true that nearly all of our environmental problems can be traced directly to technology—to the ways we have of doing things. But new technologies and ways of doing things have been good at the same time. This being the case, it would seem that our strategy for the future should be to be much more careful and less blindly willing to embrace new technologies.

Do We Need a Watchdog over Science and Technology?

A pretty generally held opinion up to now is that all new knowledge is good—that knowledge is better than ignorance. While this might well be true in the purest form, it is not equally true that all *technology* is good. We clearly need a system whereby reviews are made of the possible consequence of new technologies well before they are allowed to become established and recognized, by their effects, for what they are.

Obviously, no institution can be relied upon to police itself very well with the interests of all society in mind. We may need, as suggested by Paul Ehrlich and his colleagues (1977), to find new and better ways of involving all parts of society in evaluating new technologies. An example of such a review process is the system of **human studies review** now entrenched in U.S. biomedical research.

By law, any U.S. federally funded study involving human beings in which drugs will be given or that will involve risk must have its aims, objectives, and methods reviewed and certified by a duly constituted committee in each research institution or medical school. The composition of these committees is also specified by law and must include lay people, ministers, and lawyers as well as medical doctors and scientists. Such committees are charged with evaluating the risks and societal benefits to be derived from human studies. They also must assure themselves that the research subjects will be systematically informed of all the risks and the benefits they face by their participation in the study.

Human studies review systems emerged from concern about abuses in human research studies that came to light in recent decades. In one study, for example, healthy human beings were inoculated with cancer cells at a time when it was not known whether such cells would develop into cancers and it was known there were no cures for such cancers. Although the bureaucratic aspects of human studies review has given individual researchers fits and may well have retarded progress a little, some kind of systematic review is clearly needed.

Our reason for bringing this up here is to suggest that this concept should be extended to deal with all technological activities—all new ventures that amount to ecological experiments. Perhaps all we need is an extension of the concept of the environmental impact statement described in Chapter 12. Perhaps we need something more.

Scientific and Technical Solutions

Science obviously also holds promise with regard to environmental problems. Perhaps the major hurdle here is that not much of the scientific establishment has been set to work on our environmental problems. Ehrlich, Ehrlich, and Holden (1977) note a fact that makes this point well and at the same time tells us something else about ourselves: Half of the scientific and technical community of the world is now at work on weapons of war.

Still, science does have an important part to play in more clearly defining our environmental problems and outlining environmentally sound solutions. One important area in which considerable research remains to be done is environmental health. The Department of Health, Education and Welfare has cataloged research needs in this area in a report entitled *Human Health and the Environment: Some Research Needs* (1977). The group of people responsible for the report considered the general goals of environmental health research to be: (1) to identify currently unknown health effects of substances introduced by *Homo sapiens* and (2) to provide a better basis from which to establish exposure limits for various environmental contaminants. This, they say, can be done only by getting better information about the dosages of contaminants to which humans are exposed and the disease rates among people exposed at various dose levels. The group cited the fact that thousands of workers die annually as a result of exposure to occupational hazards and cite an "abysmal lack of information about many occupational exposures and the relationship to disease."

The task force also recommended that the health effects of such seemingly innocuous practices as the recycling of materials and the use of waste in agriculture be studied very intensively. Other needs cited by the task group included better information about alterations of chemicals in the environment; better ways of screening chemicals for their ability to cause cancer and/or mutations; more complete information on the effects of various kinds of chemicals and combinations of chemicals on human fetal development; and better information on the behavorial effects of chemical contaminants in our environment. The task group also concluded that increased training must be provided to generate specialists in environmental health in the future.

Training and research require funding; and at the moment, expenditures for environmental research worldwide fall significantly short of what is needed to do the job. The *increase* in the 1985 defense budget was three times the *total* budget for natural resources and environmental programs in all federal agencies combined (*Outdoor News Bulletin,* 1984).

As we have seen throughout this book, environmental problems are not limited to the borders of individual nations; they are global in scope and resources, and data are also needed on this level. Efforts are being made to establish an International Geosphere-Biosphere Program (IGBP) to collect data concerning climate, the biosphere, and biogeochemical cycles. There are big gaps in our knowledge of how the natural system operates on the global scale. The hope is that the International Council of Scientific Union (ICSU), which coordinated the International Geophysical year (IGY) in 1957–1958, will agree to coordinate the undertaking. The idea of the IGBP, however, is that it will continue to collect data for a 10- to 20-year period or more because many global processes take place on an extended time scale. The global nature of environmental problems was acknowledged in 1984 when the U.S. federal government established a Task Force on Nuclear Winter to study the global impact of a nuclear confrontation. Some scientists believe that regardless of where they happened, nuclear explosions beyond a certain total magnitude would produce long-lasting negative environmental effects worldwide.

MEDICINE

Individual physicians in the United States and elsewhere have been at the forefront of the environmental movement, studying environmental problems and warning societies of the hazards of various forms of pollution. However, the medical establishment is really not set up to deal with environmental health problems. Physicians have been admonished throughout recorded history to treat the sick and leave the well alone. The problem with this is that for the most part the diseases (most of which have clear environmental relationships) that are killing people in advanced countries today cannot be treated effectively *after they have emerged*. Some cannot be treated at all. Clearly, medicine must adopt more of a prevention format.

Carnow (1971) and many others since have recommended that physicians become knowledgeable about environmental factors in disease and that physicians change their way of looking for the cause of disease to include environmental causes. Physicians must not only support, but also participate in the search for complex environmental, physical, biological, pyschological, and causal factors in disease. They should be prepared to assume leadership roles in the effort to identify environmental problems and deal with them once they have been defined. The philosophical basis of medical practice and medical training must be reconsidered and restructured. Unfortunately, few institutions are as resistant to change as the U.S. medical establishment.

AGRICULTURE

We have little more to say about agriculture than what was already said elsewhere in this book. We do feel that the trend away from the small family farm and rural life in America has in part caused humankind to become estranged from the environment. This surely accounts for part of the environmental problem. The family farm in many ways epitomizes the relationship between humans and the environment. When this relationship was predominantly in the form of family units directly interacting with the land, an understanding of the importance of this interaction was reinforced daily.

What we lament here is the fact that most people now have no direct connection to the land. Something of an "out of sight, out of mind" problem may well have emerged as farm families have sold their farms and moved to the cities throughout this century.

The reader is referred to the books by Wendell Berry (1977, 1981) cited at the end of this chapter for an in-depth review of the significance of the demise of the family farm.

CITIES

Although we sometimes think of urbanization as a recent phenomenon, it is a pattern that has been building momentum for quite some time. Between the end of the Civil War and 1890, the number of people living in U.S. cities of 25,000 or more had already doubled (Greenwood and Edwards, 1973). Today, more than one in five people in the world live in urban areas of more than 100,000 people. More than half the people of developed nations live in cities. In recent years, urbanization has become increasingly important, particularly with respect to the relationship between humankind and the environment, and worldwide trends toward urbanization will probably continue for some time. Among less developed nations, the urban population is expected to double between 1960 and the turn of the century (Newcombe, Kalma, and Asta, 1978), and it is expected that by the end of the century, 38% of the world's population will be urban. What does this mean?

In a very real sense the city concentrates all the impacts humans have on nature. Cities are places in which most goods and services are consumed and in which nearly all of the by-products of civilization are concentrated.

Lets look at some of the specifics.

Many U.S. cities are beginning to coalesce into supercities or megapolises such as those in Figure 18.1. This development is a direct consequence of what we know of in the United States as **suburbanization**—moving to the suburbs. In 1950, one in four people lived in suburbs; in 1970 the number was more than one in three. It is still roughly one in three. Suburbanization presents special problems of governance, lack of community, and lack of control over such things as zoning and planning.

Suburbanization presents a political dilemma. Suburbanites are able to benefit from having a city adjacent but, because of tax structures and political boundaries, may contribute little if anything to the upkeep of the cities. The erosion of the tax base is the single most important problem facing American cities. It is clearly a problem that stands in the way

of city governments being able to improve the urban environment. Many of today's so-called metropolitan areas are made up of dozens of quasi-independent municipalities forming an ungovernable patchwork of law enforcement and zoning.

A second major problem with suburbs is that they are really not communities in the strict sense of the word. Many are just large collections of houses with no community identity—people working in different places in the city and having only a zip code in common. This is a problem because some sense of community must certainly be a prerequisite to any interest in looking after the community environment.

How Does Haphazard Happen?

The pattern is very familiar. Farmers at the edge of the city, because of rising taxes and sheer exasperation from trying to make a living working 16 hours a day, realize that the best thing they have going for them is the value of their land. As highways and other trappings of "civilization" begin to encroach around them, taxes are raised, and farmers decide to sell to a developer. Members of the family take jobs in the city. The farm is subdivided, and some of the trees are cut down and the gullies filled. Little streams whose capriciousness can no longer be tolerated are straitjacketed in storm sewers. Traffic gets worse. Service stations spring up on corners; ham-

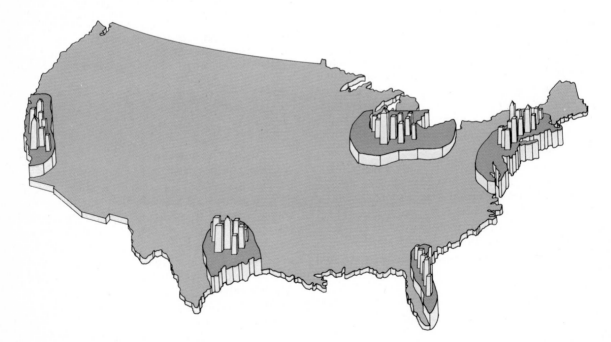

Figure 18.1 Megapolises. Much of the U.S. population is concentrated in five supercities.

burger stands appear along the main drags. Traffic lights are added. Government accommodates all of this by building a beltway, then an outer beltway. More shopping centers are built, largely without rhyme or reason. The patterns of growth and development proceed along lines that are determined primarily by who is willing to pay how much. As this goes on, little advance thought is given to the systems needed to support such developments—for example, providing for sewage and waste disposal, fire protection, and schools.

Cities As Ecological Problems

As incomplete ecosystems, cities are all part of larger wholes encompassing outside areas that are needed to support the city, that is, land "out there" on which grain is grown to feed the chickens that lay the eggs that are brought to the city to be sold for city breakfasts every morning. The unchecked growth of cities, especially the coalescing of many of them into large megapolises, creates the threat of a breakdown in the ecological exchange between cities and their support areas. There are problems getting food to these cities and getting wastes away

from them. Air pollution becomes a logarithmically increasing problem as cities get larger.

In general, as cities grow, efficiencies of ecological exchange drop. It has been suggested that the urban environment requires a much larger supply of energy and material per person than the small town or rural environment to satisfy even basic human needs (Newcombe, Kalma, and Asta, 1978). Water supplies (see Figure 18.2) have long been a problem in Southern California cities and are now becoming problems in cities of the Northeast. New York is a city that has had problems recently in getting rid of its wastes in ways other than ocean dumping. Many other cities face similar problems. The larger cities get, the longer and more inefficient the supply and waste removal lines become.

Some of the ways in which cities interact with the environment are summarized in Figure 18.3.

Cities and Artificial Impressions

Cities surely contribute to the artificial and incorrect impression held by many people that humankind is independent of the natural environment. How could it be obvious to a person born and raised

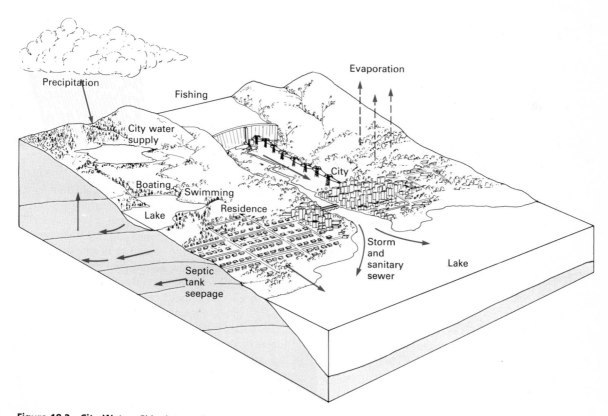

Figure 18.2 City Water. Cities interact in many ways with the hydrologic cycle.

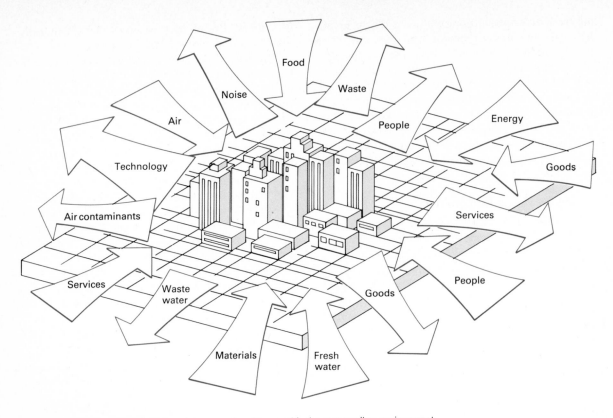

Figure 18.3 Urban Metabolism. High rates of exchange with the surrounding environment are necessary to keep cities viable.

in the city, a person who sees a world that is largely paved and who rarely encounters a tree, that he or she has any fundamental connection to the earth? It could be argued that two kinds of influences might balance one another out, that city dwellers see the most concentrated effects of the human impact on the environment and thus might have their consciousness raised by this experience—at the same time that they tend to lose the perspective of being connected to the land.

It is more likely, we think, that those who experience the concentrated effects of pollution come to accept them as *the* reality. Perhaps there is a special need for environmental education of city dwellers.

What Can Be Done?

There are obviously some things that can be done to improve cities that already exist. There are such things as redevelopment and urban renewal, and when these are done, they should incorporate all that we know about our relationship with the environment. New cities offer even more promise.

New Cities: Avoiding Old Mistakes. It seems inevitable that new cities will be built. We simply cannot go very far by expanding the ones we already have. According to Newcombe, Kalma, and Asta (1978), somewhere on the order of 5000 new cities, each with a half million people (if current demographic trends continue for long), will be built between now and the year 2000, mostly in the developing countries. Others feel that few if any new cities will be built. Cities, they say, require disproportionate energy and resource input; urban life-styles require rates of resource consumption that cannot be sustained—let alone extended. If we assume that there will be new cities, even if they simply rise from the ashes of the old ones, it is worthwhile to consider how old mistakes might be avoided.

First of all, a lot of obvious mistakes have been made in our cities that could be avoided or minimized in new cities. We would surely plan such cities to eliminate ugliness and to minimize pollution. It is encouraging that plans we hear about and see discussed in print for new cities seem to take into account the need for communities within communities, that is, to provide for self-regulating neighborhood groups within cities. We cannot help but feel that such units with clear identities will constitute optimal interacting units with the environment.

New Cities: In Concert with Nature. New cities will have to be developed as more integral parts of larger living systems. Cities, after all, are very much like multicellular organisms requiring energy and the means of excreting wastes. Newcombe, Kalma, and Asta (1978) suggest that new cities be treated as if they had a metabolism. Cities should be designed not as parasites on the land around them, but as symbionts with the life systems that support them—cities whose wastes do not represent an insult to the surroundings but are incorporated into the environment in accordance with the principles of nutrient cycling.

Cities might be designed to fit into natural systems without sharp boundaries. There should be more integration along the lines of the greenbelt concept long advocated by urban planners. Perhaps a green salad concept—the green mixed throughout—would be better. Trees and plants add a dimension to life that goes beyond aesthetics. Trees create cool environments, they dampen noise, they remove certain impurities from the air, and they serve as a reminder that nature is still there and that we are dependent on it.

It should be recognized that there is undoubtedly an optimum size for a city. New towns could have predetermined sizes, enabling more complete planning for all the activities and inter-relationships within the city and between the city and the adjacent environment.

A primary consideration will be the location of new cities. In the past, cities were located along rivers, mostly as a spin-off of the use of rivers in transportation. River banks do make nice locations, but as was suggested by Greenwood and Edwards (1973), plans for new cities and their locations should also include such factors as climate, topography, the existence of other cities, and the ability of the environment to support a city and assimilate its related wastes. There are places that should be avoided for positive reasons: Why build a new city on good farmland if nonproductive locations could serve just as well?

Perhaps the most important factors to be taken into account in building new cities is that they must be built with resource conservation and resource cycling in mind. Existing cities were built at times when energy and material were available in relatively unlimited amounts. This is no longer the case.

It is exciting to think about all the possibilities. There are different ways of building buildings and laying out residential areas that would conserve natural resources better than we have done in cities today. Buckminster Fuller described the house of the future, for example, as one that could be deposited on any site and that would not have any lines for sewage or electricity coming to them because the houses would be "energy-harvesting and growing machines." He envisioned energy-self-sufficient units, drawing energy locally from sources such as

When people spend almost all of their time in cities, they may lose sight of their connection to the natural environment.

the sun and the wind. Many houses could be built underground so that heat can be conserved and maintenance will be less of a problem.

Planning with Nature Is a Good Idea Anyway. According to the environmental planner Ian McHarg, planning with nature can be sold on the basis that it is economical. By going with the natural "grain," so to speak, by taking ecological principles into account, such problems as land erosion and flood damage can be minimized. Overall, our prospects for extended survival should be enhanced at the same time. Paraphrasing McHarg, in the final analysis it is not so much seeking a better, more pleasant environment as surviving that should be our motivation in the design or redesign of the cities of the future.

TRANSPORTATION

Although transportation-associated environmental problems are especially acute in cities, their magnitude and universal importance require that they be considered in a separate section. However, we will focus on the urban transportation problem.

First, as we have discussed in other chapters, the automobile is responsible for much of the air pollution problem and other general problems of the urban environment. Second, automobile-dominated transportation systems do not work very well. Most cities have poor systems of *intraurban* transit and poorly integrated systems of *interurban* transit; it can take more time to get to an airport than it does to fly from one airport to another. Beyond the development of new systems of integrated transportation, what we really need—particularly in the United States—is to recast our cities so that the number of automobile passenger miles can be reduced.

The Automobile As a Nonsolution

We emphasize again that the automobile is the greatest single contributor to dirty air, contributing large fractions of the carbon monoxide, hydrocarbons, and nitrogen dioxide in the air of cities (see Chapters 9 and 10). Because the layout of cities has been determined largely by patterns of automobile

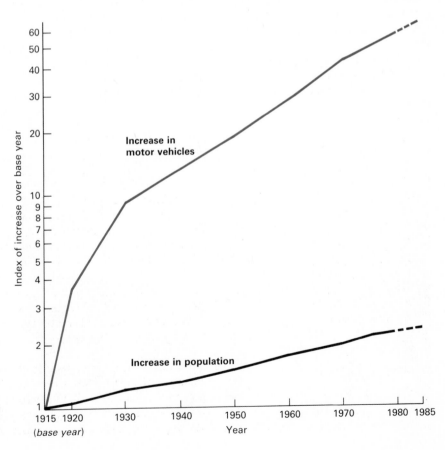

Figure 18.4 Automobilization and Population Growth. Comparison of population and the growth of automobilization in the U.S., 1915–1985. During the base year, 1915, there were 100 million Americans and only 2.5 million automobiles.

It takes more than physical components to make a mass transit system successful. People's attitudes are also important. They must believe that the system is convenient, economical, and safe.

use, the automobile is also largely, though indirectly, responsible for many other problems, including the dissolution of neighborhoods and the general decline of cities.

Many urban problems in the last half century have been the result of a rapid increase in automobilization (use of the automobile). According to Greenwood and Edwards (1973), automobilization has increased 20 times faster than population in the United States since 1915 (Figure 18.4). Since 1940, the number of auto passenger miles traveled per person in the United States rose from about 1800 per year to more than 4000 per year. Most of these miles have been traversed within cities. Today, more than 80% of all commuters use the private automobile as their means of transportation, and over half of commuting cars carry only the driver.

Environmental considerations suggest that in relation to transportation we need to reduce the number of auto miles traveled and reduce the per-mile impact of the automobile. The latter is a problem of law and automotive engineering. The former may be approached by developing integrated mass transit systems, improving alternative modes of interurban transportation, and/or bringing about drastic changes in the patterns of where people live in relation to where they work.

Mass Transit

The mass transit problem is more than one of building up integrated systems; transit systems have actually been in decline for many decades. More than 200 transit companies went out of business in the last 25 years in the United States. Between 1947 and 1970, private automobile travel increased 5.8% per year; during the same period, travel on public transit systems increased much less than 1%. Rail travel decreased almost 6% during the same period. What we have on our hands, then, is the problem of reversing a trend that has momentum in the "wrong" direction.

How will we go about restoring mass transit? Will it be expensive? Is it possible? Some believe that we will be able to improve ridership and the systems of mass transit only by generating negative pressures on the use of automobiles—making it more expensive for cars to be brought into cities. Mass mobilization will be expensive in any case. The institution of rapid urban mass transit systems will require that 50 miles of track be laid for every million people, and this could be done at present for about $25–30 million per mile. If we were to establish such systems in, let's say, 25–30 metropolitan areas with a million inhabitants in each, the total price tag would approach 50 billion dollars.

Auto Impact Reduction

Even with alternative long-range improvement and new developments in our future, we should plan on having the automobile around for the indefinite future, since it is such an important part of the American way of life. Accordingly, we should continue to direct our attention to ways of improving the automobile and reducing the impact of the automobile on urban life. In other sections of this book we discussed various approaches to this problem including electric automobiles, new types of engines, restrictions on the size of automobiles, and new kinds of fuel. These should all continue to be pursued with vigor.

Interurban Transit

Although there have been many years of decline in American rail transportation, it is an efficient mode of transportation and should be reinstituted as a primary means of getting people and freight from one place to another. European systems that are much more highly developed than U.S. systems could be studied as models.

Recasting an Institution

Perhaps our cultural practice of commuting to work and in effect having enormous "home ranges" is so out of tune with ecological constraints that the entire system will have to be scrapped, melted down, and recast over the long term.

As the realities of the laws of ecology become incorporated into our world view, it may well be that the design of our cities will change, and our way of life will change so as to render the automobile, and even the need to get around so much, obsolete. Education should help ease us along in this direction.

EDUCATION

Change in human behavior requires that there first be an inward change. "Learning is a process of emergence from within" (McInnis and Albrecht, 1975). To change human behavior so that it is aligned better with ecological reality will require a major adjustment of the philosophy underlying education in the United States. The task will be to generate more ecologically appropriate values, attitudes, and ethics. Our current "ethic" or "world view"— the way we look at things—developed when resources were plentiful and when environmental problems were not seen as problems. This ethic no longer serves us well.

But an ethic does not change quickly. Adjustment does not immediately follow awareness of a problem. This is because adjustments in ethics run deep. As Aldo Leopold pointed out (1949, pp. 209–210),

> No important change in ethics was ever accomplished without an internal change in intellectual emphasis, loyalties, affections, and convictions.

Much needs to be done in education to accelerate the necessary shift to a more ecologically sound world view or ethical framework and way of life.

An Environmental Ethic

"A thing is right when it tends to preserve the integrity, stability, and beauty of the biotic community. It is wrong when it tends otherwise." This is how Aldo Leopold (1949, pp. 224–225) defined a "land ethic" or, as we now call it, an "environmental ethic." Leopold also stated that an ethic is a limitation on freedom of action in the struggle for existence. Any ethic puts some constraints on total freedom. The frontier ethic that carried us well into this century emphasized freedom, including the freedom to bring about environmental degradation. We have learned that freedom in this extreme is at odds with more basic freedoms or rights to breathe, drink, eat, and enjoy a clean environment. A sound **environmental ethic** would cause us to go about the business of being human such that everything we did would be measured consciously and even unconsciously by how well it conformed to the laws of ecology. Actions would be judged by whether they were bad or good ecologically.

The development and application of an environmental ethic and the ethic itself have been the subject of much discussion and writing since Leopold. Additional sources of current thought are included at the end of this chapter.

An environmental ethic is what we need. Environmental education is a means by which we can develop one.

Environmental Education: What Is It?

In the fall of 1975 an international environmental education workshop was held at Belgrade, Yugoslavia. The Charter that resulted from that meeting established the goal of environmental education (p. 2):

> To develop a world population that is aware of and concerned about, the environment and its associated problems, and which has the knowledge, skills, attitudes, motivations, and commitment to work individually and collectively toward solutions of current problems and the prevention of new ones.

Acknowledging that this is much easier said than done, the conference also set forth some guiding principles for environmental education programs (p. 2):

1. Environmental education should consider the environment in its totality—natural and human-

made, ecological, political, economic, technological, social, legislative, cultural, and esthetic.

2. Environmental education should be a continuous, lifelong process, both in school and out of school.
3. Environmental education should be interdisciplinary in its approach.
4. Environmental education should emphasize active participation in preventing and solving environmental problems.
5. Environmental education should examine major environmental issues from a world point of view while paying due regard to regional differences.
6. Environmental education should focus on current and future environmental situations.
7. Environmental education should examine all development and growth from an environmental perspective.
8. Environmental education should promote the value and necessity of local, national, and international cooperation in the solution of environmental problems.

As established by the U.S. Office of Education (adapted from the Educational Facilities Laboratory as cited in *Guidelines for Environmental Education,* 1975), the official definition of environmental education is as follows:

> Environmental education is the education process dealing with humankind's relationship with the natural and human made surroundings, and includes the relation of population, pollution, resource allocation and depletion, conservation, transportation, technology, economic impact and urban and rural planning to the total human environment.

There is a general consensus that environmental education is:

— an approach to teaching about the relationship of humans to the rest of the environment, how humans affect and are affected by the world around them;
— an integrated process dealing with the natural and human-made surroundings;
— experience-based learning using the total human, natural, and physical resources of the school and surrounding community as an educational laboratory;
— an interdisciplinary approach that relates all subject areas to a whole earth, a "oneness of purpose";
— oriented toward survival in an urban society;
— life centered and oriented toward community development;
— an approach for developing self-reliance in responsible, motivated members of society;

— a rational approach to improve the quality of life;
— geared toward developing behavior patterns that will endure throughout life.

The consensus is that environmental education is *not:*

— conservation, outdoor resource management, or nature study (although these areas may be included in an environmental education program);
— a cumbersome new program requiring vast outlays of capital and operating funds;
— a self-contained course to be added to the already crowded curriculum;
— merely getting out of the classroom.

Above all, environmental education is not concerned with indoctrinating students on *what* to think, but rather on helping them develop skills on *how* to include environmental considerations in their thinking. Environmental issues provide ideal dilemmas that can be used by teachers to develop the reasoning process of their students.

Environmental Education: The Task and the Target Groups

There are three categories of environmental education. First of all, the public is generally not well informed about the way the natural world operates and how things fit together. While the environmental movement in the 1960s and early 1970s raised the general level of environmental awareness, there has not yet been much general improvement in the public's understanding of the environment and its significance for *Homo sapiens.* Second, a particularly important subset of the first category is that environmentalists—the prime movers in getting things done—have at times proceeded with a less than adequate understanding of the environmental issues at hand and have run into problems by overstating cases and by advocating inappropriate solutions. A third general category is that our educational institutions, geared toward specialization, have not produced graduates who are able to deal with the complexities and the broad scope of problems of the environment.

Public Education: Reading, 'Riting, 'Rithmetic, and Ecology

Early efforts to clean up public drinking water supplies late in the last century and early in this century were stymied for a long time because the public did not appreciate the germ theory of disease. As the story goes, once the public was won over, cleaning up public water supplies proceeded with haste. There is obviously an important general lesson here. Our educational institutions must work harder and more effectively to help the general public appreciate and understand the natural interrelationships that tell us how environmental problems came to be and how they might best be corrected. The current generally poor understanding of environmental issues by the public came about because in the past there was little in the way of environmental education. Now environmental education must become the keystone of general education; environmental principles must become the paradigms upon which *all* education is based. Curricula in public schools from kindergarten through graduate education should be restructured to feature core concepts and fundamental principles having to do with the human relationship with the environment.

Higher Education: The Need for Renaissance People

One would expect our universities to be front-runners in the attempt to "environmentalize" the American ethic. One reason why universities have not done more than they have is that environmental education does not fit the university department structure very well. This initial constraint has been and is being dealt with in several ways. In a few cases an entire university or college has been structured around an environmental core. In other cases, new departments have emerged that are composed of representatives of various disciplines coordinating a particular course or set of courses. In other cases, team teaching or guest lecturers have been the means of achieving an interdisciplinary perspective.

Another problem with higher education is the trend in recent years, particularly at the graduate and doctoral levels, to produce superspecialists in exceedingly narrow disciplines. This trend has reached the point at which many people with doctoral degrees have limited views of even the fields in which they work. Spending lifetimes dealing with single enzymes may well produce significant narrow advances. But unless there are also people trained to distill a new, interdisciplinary understanding and apply it to the broad, multifaceted problems, who will help us see the big picture?

Academia has always been slow to recognize and formalize new areas of inquiry as the need for new approaches and new disciplines is fashioned by

the times. In this age of rapid changes and new and complex problems, this is an especially serious defect. There must be provisions by which new specialists can be broadly as well as narrowly trained. We need big picture people who can see ramifications and interconnections and, in general, help society deal with problems involving many disciplines. We need rational people—people who know ecology, who know a little demography, who know anthropology, and who have some degree of common sense working on our environmental problems. The maintenance of sharp boundaries between academic disciplines is clearly out of date and gets in the way of solving many important human problems.

Informal Environmental Education and Environmentalists

Those who carry the cause of environmentalism forward, those at the forefront in the advocacy of a clean environment, have a special responsibility to inform themselves (see Kupchella and Levy, 1975). We have already experienced counterecological backlash resulting from announcements of imminent disasters that never come to pass, from overstatement of cases, and from the expending of great amounts of energy for inappropriate or low-priority purposes. To be effective, environmental advocates must be able to relate their cause to the operating principles of the ecosphere in order to be able to establish the cause's priority, to clarify the nature of the conflict, and to then proceed to change the status quo. Environmentalists must first be environmentally educated.

Federal Involvement

The implementation of the **Federal Environmental Education Act**, which was passed in 1970, acknowledged the fact that environmental education is for everyone. Federal funds were made available for elementary and secondary education, for curriculum development, for teacher training, and for community workshops for leaders of business, labor, and government.

In 1974 a Federal Interagency Commission on Education (FICE) was created by executive order to improve communication and coordination at the federal level. A subcommittee on environmental education was established as a part of FICE. Many federal agencies have formal environmental education programs. Among these are the Tennessee Valley Authority, the National Park Service, the Soil Conservation Service, and the Forest Service.

The States

In many states, environmental education has been integrated into the basic public school curriculum. Many states have laws requiring that environmental education be taught; some states have laws or policies requiring that textbooks contain environmental perspectives. Some states have policy statements on environmental education.

LAW

Environmental laws as such began to appear in abundance in the 1960s and 1970s. Before that, arguments on behalf of environmental protection had to be based on various general points of law. Environmental law is our focus in this section; we examine some of the underlying concepts and constitutional basis of environmental law.

Constitutional Provisions for Environmental Protection

Several arguments are given for interpreting the U.S. Constitution as providing for protection of the environment. The "general welfare" clause in the Constitution, for example, can be construed to apply to the environment. The Ninth Amendment to the Constitution states, "The enumeration in the Constitution of certain rights, shall not be construed to deny or disparage others retained by the people." The right to a decent environment may be one such right.

The Fourteenth Amendment says that no state shall "deprive any person of life, liberty, or property, without due process of law." To diminish human prospects for survival is to deprive unnamed persons of life—by the extra cancers that result from carcinogen contamination of the environment, for example. To deprive humans of clean air or water is to deprive them of a very basic dimension of freedom. Interestingly, the very same constitutional provisions have been used by those who are opposed to environmental regulation. It depends on how one interprets liberty and property.

General Grounds for Environmental Litigation

Long before there were specific environmental laws, legal mechanisms for challenging polluters existed through "nuisance," "trespass," and "negligence" laws. In its broadest sense, **trespass** includes intrusion by "visible or invisible pieces of matter or by energy which can be measured only in the mathematical language of the physicist" (Sloan, 1971). In all three categories the burden of proof is on the **plaintiff**, the one bringing the charges. Often in environmental suits the plaintiff is seeking **injunctive relief**, that is, the plaintiff wants the source of the harm to be stopped. In order to successfully enjoin a defendant the plaintiff must identify a legally defensible interest to be protected and demonstrate irreparable harm—which makes long-range or cumulative effects very poor bases for such suits—and show that the damage is greater than the benefits to be derived by continued action by the defendant.

Generally speaking, nuisance, trespass, and negligence are private remedies for special legal wrongs (Applegate, 1976). In some cases, **class action suits** are brought against polluters. Such suits are filed on behalf of all persons affected in the same negative way that the named plaintiff is affected. Such a mechanism makes it possible for small damages to a number of individuals to be added together and thus make the harm larger than any benefit. Also, if found guilty, defendants have greater damage assessments. The value of this approach was restricted in 1973 when the U.S. Supreme Court declared that in order for a *federal* class action suit to be filed, each member of the class must suffer damages greater than $10,000 (*Zahn* v. *International Paper Company*).

Another limitation on the use of common law remedies for environmental purposes has resulted from U.S. Supreme Court decisions relating to the federal Clean Water Act. In 1981 in a case involving Milwaukee and the state of Illinois, the Supreme Court ruled that Illinois could not sue under federal common law on the basis of "public nuisance" to force Milwaukee to meet certain water quality standards that were stricter than federal standards; according to the Supreme Court, federal statutes displaced federal common law. What impact this ruling will have on environmental litigation over the long run remains to be seen.

The right to bring a case to court is known as **standing**. Generally, to establish standing, a plaintiff must show that he or she is aggrieved, and a specific statute indicating Congressional recognition of the plaintiff's cause must be found (Sloan, 1971).

The classic court case that established the precedent for granting standing to environmentalists was *Scenic-Hudson Preservation Conference* v. *Federal Power Commission*. The Consolidated Edison Company of New York wanted to construct a hydroelectric project on Storm King Mountain. When the standing of the environmental group was challenged, the court ruled that an aggrieved or adversely affected party did not have to have "a personal economic interest," that a noneconomic injury was sufficient to establish standing (Sloan, 1971). The precedent was refined further in *Sierra Club* v. *Morton* in 1972 (known as the Mineral King case). The Sierra Club sued to prevent Walt Disney Productions from developing an area in the Sierra Nevadas. The Supreme Court held that members of the Club had to use the area in order to have standing. Many states have passed **citizen suit** legislation, which guarantees citizens standing in matters of environmental protection. Some people argue that the next step is to grant standing to natural objects—rocks, trees, and the like. They argue that inanimate objects such as corporations, trusts, and ships already are given legal rights (Ehrlich, Ehrlich, and Holdren, 1977).

The Public Trust

A so-called **public trust concept** has been used in environmental protection. The public trust concept or doctrine is based on the premise that the government holds public resources (such as air, water, and land) in trust for the public and that there are limits on the power of government to dispose of these resources (Sloan, 1971). Government is the trustee; the citizenry, both present and future, are the beneficiaries. When the trustee fails to carry out its responsibility, beneficiaries may force the trustee to protect their interest through litigation (Applegate, 1976).

Federal law now spells out a public trust doctrine in the National Environmental Policy Act (NEPA), which states:

> it is the continuing responsibility of the Federal Government to use all practical means, consistent with other essential considerations of national policy, to improve and coordinate Federal plans, functions, programs, and resources to the end that the Nation may . . .
>
> 1) Fulfill the responsibilities of each generation as trustee of the environment for succeeding generations . . . (NEPA, Section 101 (b)(1)).

By constitutional amendment, Pennsylvania has embraced a public trust doctrine at the state level:

> The people have a right to clean air, pure water, and to the preservation of the natural, scenic, historic and aesthetic values of the environment. Pennsylvania's public natural resources are the common property of all the people, including generations yet to come. As a trustee of these resources, the Commonwealth shall conserve and maintain them for the benefit of all the people (Article i, Section 27).

Michigan, Wisconsin, and other states also have public trust legislation on the books.

Environmental Laws

Environmental legislation has been enacted at the national level in the United States to deal specifically with the air, waste, water, and public health. Generally, the federal laws provide broad outlines that are filled in by administrative regulations. The enactment of these laws has been an uphill battle for many reasons:

> public-interest legislation poses many political difficulties because, as a rule, the benefits are often intangible, long-range, and distributed among a very large public, while the costs are often tangible, immediate, and imposed on a specific set of organized interests (Rosenbaum, 1973, p. 104).

Special interest groups traditionally have fought such legislation with the objective of blocking or weakening emerging laws. Vocal active public support for environmental concerns has been the key to passage of environmental legislation. Public "watchdogging" and follow-through have also been—and will continue to be—important. Laws can be amended, and laws can go unfunded. A law may contain authorizations for funding, but it must be followed by sustained *appropriation* before the legislation has any real meaning.

The environmental movement has largely been a popular grass roots movement. It is fitting then that environmental laws have explicit provisions by which citizen participation is to be encouraged, solicited, and made part of the administrative process. Citizens' rights to sue government officials for failing to carry out their mandates are spelled out in many environmental laws. A problem that citizens' groups face is that they are usually poorly financed volunteer organizations; this can and does limit their effectiveness.

GOVERNMENT

Ours is a government of more than laws. It is a government of law making, law enforcing, and law interpreting. It is a government of executive, legislative, and judicial branches, each with its own powers. It is a government of federal, state, and local levels, each with executive, legislative, and judicial components, each level having its own sometimes overlapping powers. It is a government by the people—a government of elections and election campaigns, of Democrats and Republicans. Space limitations do not permit us to attempt even a

The public interest may not coincide with special interests. We all owe it to ourselves to become informed about environmental issues and to stand up for our interests.

superficial analysis of how government works or does not work. Rather, we would like to discuss some selected general characteristics of our system of government and how they bear on our ability or inability to deal with environmental problems.

The Role of Government

It should be intuitively obvious that environmental improvement can be brought about only at some high level of human organization. One person cannot bring about a clean environment by cleaning up or protecting the air in his or her yard. Similarly, a citizen with riverfront property cannot make much headway cleaning up the river by doing anything to the part of the river that sweeps by his or her property. Environmental improvement can come only through concerted, highly organized efforts by all people along rivers. This is where government comes in.

Government is an institution by which we spread responsibility over the whole for the whole. It can also be thought of as a device for ensuring that actions take not only existing people into account, but also those who will come in the future. Government is the principal institution by which a society can protect the **commons**—those things that belong to everyone and yet belong to no one.

There are different approaches to rationalizing government's role in environmental protection. We touched on one under the heading of environmental law:

> there is a definite ethical basis to a national policy for the environment. This centers upon the responsibility of government as the agent of the peo-

ple to manage the environment in the role of steward or protective custodian for posterity. It requires the abandonment of government's role as umpire among conflicting and competing resource interests and the adoption of the total environment as a focus for public policy (Wandesforde-Smith, 1970, p. 208).

According to this view, government is the ultimate steward or trustee for the environment for present and future generations.

Another view is based on government's role in reconciling conflicting views. No one will deny that environmental issues are fraught with conflicting views and often require a referee. Sometimes the role of referee is at odds with the stewardship role. Government—the courts, law makers, and executive officers—must often consider whether or not a straight compromise among those with conflicting views is in the best public interest. "Government's greatest peril arises when the views ought not to be compromised because one view is in error" (Murphy, 1967, p. 290).

Government has and ought to have an important role in environmental protection. The complexity of environmental problems requires personnel, money, authority, and large-scale coordination that can be provided only by government.

Administering Environmental Law

As we indicated earlier, once laws have been enacted, they are further defined and implemented by administrative regulation. Many environmental laws are under the administrative jurisdiction of the Environmental Protection Agency (EPA).

The EPA was established in December 1970 by Executive Order of the President. The EPA has ten regional offices, and each state is in one of the ten regions. The EPA has broad administrative and coordinating responsibilities for environmental affairs. Its statutory responsibilities cut across those of many other agencies in the executive branch of the federal government and reach down to the local level. Environmental statutes covering air, water, and solid and hazardous waste call for state and local programs to be established but give the EPA the responsibility for guiding, reviewing, and ultimately approving and monitoring programs (see Chapter 12).

Many other federal agencies have direct environmental responsibilities. The Department of the Interior carries out laws dealing with public lands (among other things); within the Department of the Interior, specific offices have particular responsibilities. The Office of Surface Mining, Reclamation and Enforcement (OSMRE), for example, oversees the Federal Surface Mining Act. The Department of Agriculture administers forest and pesticide programs. Even the Department of Commerce and the Department of Defense (Corps of Engineers) administer environmental programs dealing with oceans and dams, respectively.

It has periodically been proposed that a Department for Natural Resources be established at the federal level combining programs from the Department of the Interior, the U.S. Forest Service, the Department of Agriculture, the National Oceanic and Atmospheric Administration (NOAA), and the Department of Commerce among others to help streamline the administration of natural resources policy. Currently, both the Bureau of Land Management and the Forest Service regulate activities on federal lands, though they are in different departments. The NOAA protects the endangered sea turtle when it is in the ocean; the Fish and Wildlife Service protects it when it comes ashore to lay its eggs. Action to streamline federal agencies and programs is always easier described than done, and little movement in this direction has occurred.

State Government and the Environment

The role of the states in administering environmental laws has changed over the last few decades. Before 1972, most federal acts established general environmental goals and provided research, technical assistance, and funding to the states to carry out state programs. Federal environmental legislation enacted after 1972 was much more specific and exacting. For example, recent federal environmental legislation tends to establish compulsory compliance deadlines and quantifiable standards.

Federal environmental laws of the last 15–20 years give specific responsibilities to the states. These laws contain "carrot and stick" incentives in the form of significant federal financial assistance, the threat of general cutoff of federal funds, and clauses that say "if you don't do it, we will."

In some cases, states have modeled their laws after federal laws. Some states require environmental impact statements for projects using state monies just as NEPA requires them for projects using federal monies. Some states designate wild rivers for protection, just as there are federal designations. In other cases, states have initiated environmental protection laws of their own as a result of public pressure and lack of action at the federal level. Many have established stringent state controls in the area of solid and hazardous waste management. States have also initiated their own programs to authorize the granting of scenic easements, to deal with nonreturnable bottles, and to grant citizen standing in environmental matters, among other things. Most states have special agencies for environmental matters.

Regulatory Approaches

Government has many tools for bringing about the results it desires in environmental control. As we have already discussed, the federal government uses a subsidy approach, providing money for irrigation, drainage, and water and sewage treatment. Another type of subsidy is the tax break for pollution control equipment. Such an approach has been criticized for promoting pollution control equipment over changes in processing that might be more effective. Later environmental laws used a more direct regulatory approach by which the government set standards and maximum discharge levels. This approach has been criticized for its lack of flexibility and for allowing polluters to pollute to a given level without charge. A third approach, which we will take up at some length in the section on economics, is that of disposal charges. By this approach, a fee or charge for each unit of pollution is set; the amount is set high enough that it is more economical for the polluter to reduce the discharge than to continue paying the disposal charge.

In all of these approaches, what government does is to cause needed change to take place in *other* institutions, using the time-honored methods of reward and punishment. Change does not come easily to institutions like "free enterprise"; sometimes government has to make things happen.

Economics can deal easily enough with a straightforward situation such as a person wanting to buy a ticket to a concert. Someone who is unwilling to bear his or her portion of the cost of the concert cannot get through the door. Hueckel (1975) points out that this is in sharp contrast to a situation in which a person wants some air—for breathing. People have never paid for air, and they surely cannot be excluded from using it very easily. This is where government comes in. Government finds a way through taxes, assessments, laws, and the like to create circumstances in which individuals must pay the cost of keeping air clean. Another example offered by Hueckel (1975) is the situation in which one person believes that airplanes are a nuisance and should not be permitted to exist because of the particulate pollution and noise. The role of government here might be to ensure that all of the costs of air travel, including the cost of abating noise pollution, the cost of minimizing particulate pollution, and other assorted indirect cost be taken into account and divided among those who feel that air travel is necessary. Government can force the inclusion of various indirect and external factors into cost-benefit equations and cause air travelers to consider them in deciding exactly how necessary air travel is.

Can Government Deal with the Long Range?

Democratic government is supposed to reflect consensus attitudes and feelings of the people it serves. If this is true, governments should be able to deal with long-range problems only to the extent that "the people" are able to perceive the need for such considerations. Herein lies the rub. It seems that most human beings are unable to deal in a very effective way with the long range. The stresses, pressures, and problems faced by people day to day are such that all most people can do is deal with the immediate. While it might be easy to say that governments *must* take the long range into account despite this obvious limitation, this is far easier said than done.

First of all, if the government goes very far beyond devoting its attention to immediate problems, it runs into the danger of being called unresponsive, and a new administration quickly takes the place of the old. Consider the dilemma. A U.S. congressional representative elected for a two-year term knows that if he or she is not reelected, he or she will not be able to do *any* good for the people. (We will

disregard the further complexity caused by the fact that corporations, political action groups, and other organized special interest groups play a significant role in the election of representatives.) While that representative might know that deregulation of gas prices would allow the price to rise, cause a drop in the demand for natural gas, and give the country more time to find new sources of energy, he or she also knows that a vote in favor of deregulation will gain the displeasure of constituents who would have to pay higher prices for gas at a time when all prices are high and getting higher. This, it seems, tends to strap us with a seat-of-the-pants system of management by government at a time when such management is increasingly less appropriate.

International Government?

There are signs of environmental awareness and conscience throughout the world—in Western Europe, Japan, the Soviet Union, and various developing countries. It is also becoming increasingly recognized that many environmental problems must be dealt with on a worldwide basis. The U.S. National Environmental Policy Act (NEPA) directed federal agencies to support efforts to maximize international cooperation to prevent decline in the quality of humankind's world environment.

As a member of the United Nations, the United States promotes the U.N. Environmental Program (UNEP). In 1972 the United Nations held a conference on the Human Environment in Stockholm; representatives of 114 nations attended from the industrialized world and the Third World. The group agreed on a number of principles and promulgated these in its Declaration of the Human Environment. Achieving such agreement was no small task; the Declaration had to contain principles assuring Third World Nations that environmental concerns would not restrain development. Among the outcomes of this important conference was a proposal that an environmental assessment system, "**Earthwatch,**" be established to look after water pollution, air pollution, endangered species, and the like on an international scale.

In May 1982 a ten-year follow-up conference was held in Nairobi. Out of that conference came an effort by representatives of six continents to establish a "World Campaign for the Biosphere." The objectives of this campaign are to promote educational programs on the operation of the biosphere, to promote enhanced scientific understanding of the biosphere, and to promote governmental action relative to worldwide environmental problems.

The Man and the Biosphere Program, (MAB) is an intergovernmental organization established through the U.N. Educational, Scientific, and Cultural Organization (UNESCO) to focus research, technical training, and public education on the need to know more about the intricacies of the whole-world biosphere. In its most basic form the purpose of MAB is to study the earth's ecosystems and how we relate to them. The work of MAB is coordinated by an International Council composed of representatives from 30 nations elected by the UNESCO General conference.

One of the projects of MAB is the Biosphere Reserve Project. This project recognizes that each of the earth's ecosystem types is different and that each must be preserved and studied if we are to understand the whole. Through this project, reserves are being established and recognized throughout the world (28 had been officially recognized in the United States as of the end of the 1970s; see Risser and Cornelison, 1979).

The eighth session of the Man and the Biosphere Program was held at UNESCO Headquarters in Paris in December 1984. There are now Man and The Biosphere National Committees in 105 member countries, and more than 1000 field research projects are underway or completed. The Biosphere network now includes nearly 250 biosphere reserves in 65 different countries.

Perhaps problems of the environment will bring on more international cooperation in general. Perhaps environmental problems and the effort to solve them will help humankind to understand that there are more similarities among people than there are differences.

ECONOMICS

In Chapters 9 and 10 we discussed the significance of economic factors to air and water pollution. Elsewhere we have suggested that economics is an extremely important factor in all of our environmental problems. Because of the pervasive importance of economics, we devote a section here to economics and business and how these relate to both the state of the environment and our environmental future.

Some Relevant Economic Principles

Perhaps *the* chief fact relating economics and the environment is that *in the past, ecological and environmental factors were not taken into account as part of the cost of doing business, and in the future they must be.* This means that there must be a transition from environmental protection being an external factor to its being fully included in the cost accounting that leads to the determination of the prices of products that are bought and sold in our society.

Among the important principles and concepts in economics that bear on the need for this transition is the so-called *law of supply and demand* and the concept of *margin.*

Supply and Demand

It is said that almost every economic system, and the one operative in the United States in particular, is based on **supply and demand** or some kind of market system. In this system a need is expressed in terms of willingness to pay, which in turn serves as a stimulus to someone else to meet the need—in exchange for money. There are many believers in the market system who claim that it is unmatchable in terms of satisfying countless different, ever-changing tastes and needs at minimum resource costs. Ideally, if consumers buy less, either because they do not want the product or because the prices are too high, demand falls, and producers quit producing. If, on the other hand, something is demanded by many people, prices rise, serving as an incentive for the producer to produce more, or to find more, and the result is an increased output of the things that people want. The system works to achieve a balance between supply and demand through feedback. As more and more is produced, supply increases, prices drop, and some stable state is reached wherein that which is needed is provided. The reader may appreciate the fact that, in theory anyway, the law of supply and demand operates through feedback much in the same way that feedback operates in ecological systems.

Some observers question the "purity" of the concept of supply and demand, believing that the market system itself often sets up distorted demand through devices such as advertising. Economists like John K. Galbraith argue that consumers tend to buy what is made, advertised, and put before them in shop windows. Producers, according to this view, are not simply providing people with what they want; they are taking an active part in defining what people can or cannot have. The counterpoint of view is that competition is an extremely strong force operating within systems of supply and demand, and competition brings into consideration all the information necessary for making optimal decisions about what should be produced (Ruff, 1970).

Marginalism

Although the economic concept of **marginalism** is quite complicated and grounded in differential calculus and the mathematics of maximization and minimization, it is in basic outline a straightforward concept and one that is important to our discussion (Figure 18.5). Perhaps it can be illustrated by an example.

Consider a patch of blueberries. If I hired a blueberry picker to pick the blueberries in a certain patch, set this picker to work, and paid him or her an hourly wage, the plentifulness of the blueberries would ensure that for a certain period of time the picker could sustain a high rate of blueberry harvesting—let's say 4000 blueberries per hour. If I could sell 4000 blueberries for $5 and paid the picker $3 an hour, I would be able to make a $2 per hour profit (disregarding for the moment any cost associated with growing the blueberries). After a while, as the blueberries became increasingly scarce, the yield per hour would decline, and inevitably, at some point the picker would be hard pressed to gather $3 worth of blueberries in a given hour. It would be at this point that I would maximize the gain I derive from my blueberry patch, and any additional time spent by the blueberry picker in that patch should give me more cost than benefit even though some blueberries remained to be picked (see Figure 18.5). If I had to include some of the other costs that sustained growing blueberries, the point at which maximization occurs would be earlier. Obviously, I would do well as a manager to know, to the second, the point at which my costs began to exceed benefits. To consider environmental problems appropriately, this concept has to be kept well in mind. It does not do in the real world to advocate that all pollutants be removed from the air. Our economic system—any system, in fact—demands that all the costs of removing or controlling pollutants be considered in relationship to the costs of not removing them.

On the Internalization of Externalities

One of the most important adjustments to be made in our economic system is the internalization of social costs or the inclusion of environmental cost in calculating the ratio of cost to benefit.

Economic theory has historically been far more concerned with private transactions and how these lead to the establishment of value than it has with social costs. There are many examples of how vari-

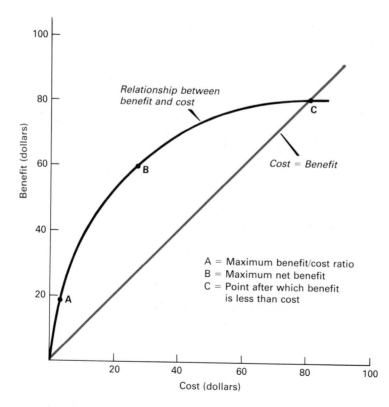

A = Maximum benefit/cost ratio
B = Maximum net benefit
C = Point after which benefit is less than cost

Figure 18.5 Cost-Benefit Ratio. This can vary significantly with such factors as level or intensity of economic activity. After some point (B), cost increases faster than benefit.

ous costs of doing business are ignored—treated as **externalities**. Perhaps one example here would help.

A chemical company that had to dispose of a waste product might find that the cheapest way to do it would be pay somebody to haul it away, no questions asked. By "no questions asked" we mean that any moral responsibility to see to it that the waste is disposed of properly is transferred by the company to the hauler. After the point of transfer to the hauler, any additional cost, to whomever or to whatever, becomes an externality as far as the chemical company is concerned. The hauler might (if able to circumvent the federal tracking system) simply drive the chemical drums to a relatively unpopulated area and just dump them without regard to what might happen after that. Then the chemicals might leak into a stream and/or render that particular piece of land and surrounding area unsuitable for many purposes. In effect, this would transfer the cost of having generated the waste product to people who might move there in the near or distant future.

Externalization has often been accomplished with the complete acquiescence of the citizens affected. One of us can remember growing up in a town with a mine-acid-polluted stream. Although the stream was remembered by old-timers as once good for fishing and most of the town's people were outdoor-oriented, no one ever seemed to mind the loss of the stream—apparently because people saw it as directly related to their livelihood. Pollution was something accepted as necessary to their being able to exist there at all. They went on accepting this as a social cost, driving many miles to fish and paying more than they would have had to otherwise to pipe their drinking water in from another stream. Social costs have often been accepted willingly, and this is precisely why more of them have not been internalized before now.

The divergence between private and social costs of doing business has been a fundamental factor in many types of pollution. The divergence occurred because managers traditionally have had to deal only with private cost to arrive at the profit-maximizing output levels and prices in their business. Dumping wastes into air or into water has, until now, been free. At first these practices were free because few if any people were affected by them, and then, for a long time, those who were affected by them did not care. What must be done now is clear. Private and social costs of doing business must be made to converge.

It is obvious that as long as our economics neglects the external costs of doing business, it will be a science of illusion, and business will continue to be a game of transferring external costs onto the shoulders of society and the citizens of the future. What we have had in the past could really be called institutionalized inhumanity to humankind. What we must have in the future is **ecological impacts costing**—an economic system in which ecological costs are reflected in prices. Many economists have made many proposals as to how this might be done. Some have outlined the problems that get in the way of doing it. We would like to take up some of these problems first.

Factors Operating Against the Internalization of Ecological Costs

Among the factors operating against bringing ecological costs into the price/output equations are (1) the inertial resistance built into our present economic and political system, (2) the magnitude of the costs and whether they can be passed along to consumers without any fatal skips in economic heartbeats, and (3) the problem of determining long-term and even short-term social costs (in terms of dollars).

Resistance to Internalization. It seems likely that from now on there will always be a conflict between forces tending to maximize profits and forces that would tend to minimize environmental impact. It has become a rigidly institutionalized business principle that managers will try to externalize as many costs as possible. It is useless to blame managers for this; they are simply players in a game, the rules of which have been established for some time, that is won by managers who are best at cutting costs.

Predictably, managers of plants and corporation presidents resist every suggested internalization, and it is highly unlikely that the business system will adopt the concept of internalization quietly. The record already indicates that players cite every sort of economic disaster when internalization is forced upon them.

The Magnitude of the Cost of Avoiding Social Costs. It is being argued that the magnitude of the cost of protecting the environment as goods and services are produced will be staggering to the point of bringing an end to civilization. The facts simply have not born such fears out. While it has been estimated that between 1981 and 1990 it will cost $526 billion dollars in tax money and corporate money to install required environmental protection devices and to adopt environmental protection prac-

Why Do a Cost-Benefit Analysis When We Know in Our Hearts What Is Right?

In many places throughout this book we have cited reasons why it is difficult to do cost-benefit analyses when environmental impacts are involved. A few of these reasons can be paraphrased as follows:

1. Since clean air is not something that is regularly bought and sold, we really do not know what it is worth.
2. In cases involving toxic substances, human health and lives are at stake. We do not know how much a human life is worth.
3. We do not know how to place a value on things such as being able to see trees or, inversely, on the psychological impact of not being able to see them.
4. The environmental consequences of proposed projects are often uncertain when the projects are being considered.

We have also implied and explicitly stated that we *must* try to establish such values in spite of the difficulty in doing so. We reiterate here some of the reasons why:

1. Dollar costs are the only things many people understand and act upon.
2. Being able to establish dollar costs and to perform cost-benefit analysis would simplify environmental decision making. The simplification would come from converting what would otherwise be multidimensional problems into those with fewer dimensions. The effect would be similar to simplifying a mathematical expression by applying a common denominator.

Bohm and Henry (1979) cite three cases illustrating how environmental cost-benefit analyses can be useful in making environmental decisions. We will paraphrase the case of the beltway around Paris, France, as an example.

Initially, the transportation-minded Department of Equipment performed an analysis of the need for a highway and how this need might be met by using the simplified approach of minimizing construction costs and maximizing the savings in driving time for French drivers. The equation placed the right of way through some of the most beautiful parks and forests west of Paris.

The French Department of Agriculture, which is responsible for preserving public forests, insisted that the loss of parkland and forestland had to be factored into the equation as well. This, as it turned out, had the effect of illustrating that while a certain route A was longer than another route B, route A would destroy less forest than route B. This in turn raised the question: How many miles of road is an acre of forest worth? In this particular case, since some forest would be lost with all route options, a more far-reaching question was raised: If the value of the forest is high enough, should the highway be built at all? The ensuing evaluation yielded three alternatives for President Giscard d'Estaing to consider:

1. no motorway at all,
2. an underground motorway, or
3. a longer motorway than was originally proposed—one that avoided the heart of the forest.

The reader should be aware that, as was pointed out by Bohm and Henry, while it would be a respectable goal to do this sort of analysis with all environmental issues, the difficulties should not be underestimated.

---

tices in the United States, this is expected to amount to only about 2% of the U.S. Gross National Product. The reader may remember that our estimates in Chapter 11 of the cost of environmental damage from air pollution alone during the same decade would amount to 250 billion dollars if present practices were allowed to continue. This seems to indicate that the cost of not cleaning up will more than outweigh the cost of keeping the environment clean.

It has also been argued that the cost of pollution control equipment will not add value to the goods being produced and thus the worker hours and dollars that go into pollution control will not show up in increased productivity. It would seem that the best way to counter this argument would be to find ways to assess the value of improved air and water and somehow add this to the GNP, using whatever formulas and methods seem appropriate.

Environmental Blackmail. There is a thing called **environmental blackmail**. This is a practice in which companies argue that if they are forced to clean up their act, they will shut down, and therefore a clean environment will come only at the expense of jobs. There no doubt have been and will be some plants closed as a result of new and future environmental protection measures. But this is as it should be—it is natural selection. In the past, the fact that social costs were unrecognized made environmental considerations nonfactors in natural selection. Environmental quality simply has not been a factor in determining what types of industries and what quality of industries would spring up and thrive in various places.

When we woke up this morning, we faced a world with an array of devices, practices, and patterns that have been determined by factors other than the social costs of doing business. We have loud lawn mowers, noisy airplanes, and loud trucks because heretofore no pressures have existed to select against them. We have dirty factories that cause disease or death in workers and render less than optimal the lives of people in the communities in which these plants are located. While a plant closing might cause pain and suffering at the local level, society has to look at the big picture. Overall, a pollution control industry has grown up around the new environmental laws; this industry could mean more jobs than have been lost as a result of the closing of inefficient, polluting plants (see Chapter 11).

The Impact of Environmental Protection Costs on the Poor. Among the problems of economic readjustment to include environmental costs is the idea that relatively poor people can have more of the "better" things in life only if social costs are not passed along to them. Presumably, if various environmental externalities were internalized and cost increases had to be borne by consumers, this would have an especially serious effect on the poor—those only marginally able to accumulate food, shelter, and clothing under present conditions. It is a sobering thought that there may be some people who are alive today only because technology has been able to borrow against nature and the people of the future. Governmental mechanisms can be used to ameliorate the impact of cost internalization on the poor. Continuing to borrow against nature is no solution. It will only lead to greater problems in the future.

The Political Problem. The fear is sometimes expressed that a very important short-term danger for the environmental movement is that the public will be faced with some of the very high and real costs of protecting the environment before any real benefit of the cleanup become evident. The public has never been very open to the idea of paying for the comfort—or even the survival—of generations yet to come.

The Problem of Determining Social Cost. Given the nature of our economic system, it would be best if clean air, clean water, unspoiled landscapes, and quiet had physical form and could be subdivided and transferred from one person to another. We would then be able to develop more complete assessments of the value of these commodities. We would be able to see how many dollars changed hands for these commodities. All the rest would fall into place. Our legal and economic systems could handle this kind of transaction in a straightforward manner; we

would be much better able to assess damage and the extent of various impairments. As was pointed out by Mishan (1969), just because the environment is not divisible in this way is no reason to treat environmental resources as if they were not valuable and as if they were not scarce. The problem is that we have very little basis on which to determine social cost and assign value to things like clean air and water (see Chapters 9 and 10).

How Can Internalization Be Accomplished?

Up to now we have assumed that there are ways of internalizing what have heretofore been externalities. In his essay "Not Peace, But Ecology," Garrett Hardin gives an example of how this might be done. He cites the following case: Before the appearance of the insurance industry, accidents in industry were thought of as the fault of workers. They were unexpected, and they happened as a result of random and miscellaneous causes. They certainly could not be planned for and certainly could not always be blamed on the company. The cost of accidents was therefore an externality.

In more recent years we have come to appreciate that while accidents are somewhat capricious, over large numbers of companies and large numbers of workers they are predictable consequences of people working. Because they happen with a certain frequency, they can be cost accounted, and the risk can be spread over industry by means of worker's compensation insurance. With worker's compensation the cost of covering accidents became assimilated into the cost of doing business. All companies now either pay insurance premiums or make plans and provisions for insuring themselves. The cost of accidents has thus been internalized. Some economists suggest that there are actually several ways by which environmental and social costs have been, and can be, internalized. These are:

1. appeal to reason—seeking voluntary internalization of costs;
2. use of the courts, relying on the threat of fines, suits, and judgments to serve as the pressure leading to internalization;
3. government regulation using a combination of the threat of economic sanction and imprisonment to force internalization;
4. taxing pollutants and granting pollution rights; and
5. using various subsidies and incentives.

Many economists argue that it would be better

Economic pressures are one of the few things to which people consistently respond.

to put price tags on pollution and to incorporate the environment into standard pricing practices in economics than to muddy the waters with regulations and prohibitions that would be subject to abuse. They see a system of taxing pollution as more compatible with existing economic theory. It seems worth discussing this particular approach at some length.

Paying for the Privilege of Polluting

This approach would actually allow an industry to pollute, provided that it pays a fee based on volume—so many dollars per ton of sulfur dioxide, so many per ton of particulate matter, and so on. Those who trust our existing economic system say that while this does say to the polluter, "Pollute all you want—but it's going to cost you," market forces will eventually cause the environment to be brought into the cost of doing business. Why? Because it would become each manager's responsibility to reduce the amount of money the firm has to pay for pollution, and managers would find ways to cut down on pollution.

Possible variations on this approach make it even more intriguing. The more toxic a substance is, the higher the prices that could be put on it. A very toxic substance could have a prohibitively high price for even a little pollution. There would be problems to be worked out. What about such vagaries as thermal inversions? Would the dollar price vary with the time of the year? With the hour of the day? Should it cost more to generate a given amount of pollution close to a population center? This might be effective in causing industries to be located where the cost

would be lower. There would be an economic incentive for the polluter to move or to build a plant in places remote from population centers so as to generate less social cost.

A system such as this would require that regulatory agencies be charged with metering the output of all sources of pollution and collecting fees.

The Problem of Uniformity

The major problem with what we have just discussed is that for it to be done right, it would have to be carried out on a global scale. It would not do, after all, to have the steel industry in the United States internalize its social costs if another country can make steel without such internalization and sell the steel in the United States at a much cheaper price, creating an unfair advantage. Such problems could be partially solved within a large country through a system of tariffs, but it would obviously be best if this type of approach were undertaken at the international level.

Is It Good to Have a High Gross National Product?

It is important to appreciate that economics merely keeps score of things that are exchanged for other things and that there is really no place for value judgment in keeping score. The dollar value of goods and services generated in a country—its **Gross National Product (GNP)**—is a valueless numerical expression of the total number of dollars paid for goods and services. Good and bad are not distinguished.

As was pointed out by Wallace (1972), much of the GNP in the United States consists of junk and of services that are of marginal importance. What this means is that GNP *does not necessarily reflect quality of life*; in other words: GNP is not a measure of (1) personal freedom, (2) natural resources left, (3) happiness, or (4) quality and stability of life in the immediate or long-range future.

The British economist, John M. Keynes, first articulated the economic theory that led to the economic ideology that is credited with taking the world out of the Great Depression wherein maximum production would be ensured by government spending to stimulate the economy. This ideology, which has dominated economic policy making for most of the last 50 years, apparently allowed the concept of production for production's sake to establish some place in our economic thinking. An example actually used in setting forth this theory is that it would be better to pay people to dig holes and pay other people to fill them up than for the diggers and fillers to be out of work. Although such make-work approaches had some value during the Depression, many economists believe that the concept actually allowed productivity to become established in our economic system as an end in itself. The fact that we still use an ill-defined concept like GNP in itself suggests that we do indeed have a problem.

Economics As a Descriptive Science

Economics is a science of identifying the factors that have relevance in making maximization decisions; it is, as we said, value-free. Economics generally has nothing to say about whether certain definitions of values are better than others. If the law still recognized indentured servitude, the cost of labor in economics would be no more than that necessary to indenture and maintain a servant. If, on the other hand, the law required that workers be looked after and have worker's compensation and other benefits, then the cost of labor would include these factors. As another example, suppose we were trying to determine the cost-benefit ratio for producing coal. Being environmentally minded, we might want to include the cost of avoiding contaminating streams and certain costs to minimize the health and safety problems faced by coal miners. Depending on the value assigned to a human life, the coal industry might be required by the unions and the government to establish safety conditions to the point at which it would be absolutely impossible for anyone ever to be killed or injured in mining coal. Somewhere short of this, however, the cost of providing this safety would

well surpass any economic benefit that might be derived from mining coal. This, of course, would be unacceptable to coal companies, unions, employees, and just about everybody else.

Economic Growth and the Environment

A major question that has much to do with the relationship between economics and ecology is the question of whether or not sustained economic growth is a requisite for a strong, healthy economy. Many economists are growth oriented and feel that continued economic growth is necessary for the survival of any economic system. Increasing numbers of economists feel otherwise, however. Ecologists know that anything—any piece of goods or any type of service that is based in some way on production by ecosystems—will have an upper limit to growth.

To Grow or Not to Grow

When Growth Is Not Really Growth. When the advocates of sustained economic growth speak of growth, they are referring to real increases in GNP. That is, growth over and above the illusion due to inflation. But there is another relativistic quality about GNP worth mentioning here. Human beings do not seem to be satisfied as much by the absolute value of the goods and services they command as by their relatively high standing in relationship to other people. Third World nations tend to see their need to experience real growth as the difference between what they have and what they see in the so-called developed countries.

Why Real Growth in the Numerical Sense Cannot be Sustained. On the basis of what we know about ecosystems as described in the first several chapters of this book, it is not clearly and definitely within the natural order of things that the growth of anything can be sustained indefinitely. All living systems—and all economic activity has something to do with ecosystems either directly or indirectly—have finite capacities to yield products and to absorb by-products. Economic growth must be an exceptional state. Whatever economic growth there has been in the past, for however long, has been a reflection of exploitation of space and resources and expanding populations with expanding needs. We have now reached the point, or will shortly, at which either world population growth will level off—bringing the stimulus for sustained economic growth to the level with it—or there will be catastrophe that will rewrite the script entirely.

We seem to have developed two conclusions:

1. It is an absurdity, at least in terms of the limits of what the human brain can comprehend, to assume that economic growth or the growth of anything can be sustained indefinitely.
2. Growth is not necessarily all that great anyway, and we would probably do well to develop a new breed of economics and economists whose instincts have not been developed during a period when economic health and growth occurred simultaneously for so long as to give the impression that they are related.

Growth or Change?

We might take the last section a step further. If it is true that economic and business activities are biological activities, we must conclude that change in economic activity is inevitable. Change, development, and improvement all fall into a category that can be described very well by another connotation of the word "growth." A person can grow in height (quantitatively) and can also grow in stature, maturity, and wisdom (qualitatively). If we can be permitted to use both senses of the word "growth" at the same time, we tend to agree with those who feel that some form of economic growth may be inevitable and perhaps even desirable. The time has come to discard the concept of growth embodied in current economic models for the United States and many other parts of the world—the model that permits planned obsolescence, inefficiency, and waste to be considered part of growth. It seems clear that the relevant ecological question is: How can economic activities be directed so as to improve the quality of life for all human beings.

To paraphrase William Ruckelshaus, two-time Administrator of the EPA, the question is not whether there will be growth because there will always be some kind of growth as long as humans have the inherent drive to achieve perfection. What we really must do is define growth and understand both what will happen as growth takes place and how to limit or avoid any deleterious consequences of growth. In other words, we must know where we are growing and go in that direction only if we wish to go in that direction.

The Fall of Boosterism

If the need is to emphasize quality rather than quantity, then it is encouraging that there are some visible signs of increased attention to the quality and planning of economic growth and development in

In centrally planned economies like the People's Republic of China, consumers now have more choices of clothing and other goods. What impact is this likely to have on the environment?

U.S. cities and in the cities and countries of the rest of the world. Many communities have moved away from the insane practice of the 1940s and 1950s that might be called "boosterism." The development syndrome that brought industry into many communities in a helter-skelter fashion is increasingly being recognized as the cause of more chaos than comfort and more problems than benefits.

Capitalist Versus Socialist Economic Systems

It has been suggested that the capitalist system of rewards via profits and higher salaries is very heavily oriented toward growth and that any form of control of this economic system by government would be inconsistent with capitalistic philosophy. Others suggest that capitalism has gradually moved away from the pure, free-market capitalist system. Similarly, many central-planning types of economic systems have drifted toward capitalism. The overall result has been a decrease in the economic difference between these ideologies.

In any case, the issue of capitalism versus socialism has little to do with the relationship between economics and the environment. Both systems are based on productivity and are made even more similar by competition in the same world market. Environmental problems related to economics are therefore similar under both systems.

Some Concluding Remarks

We have two points to make in conclusion. One is that in the past, many environmentalists have scorned economics, and this has not served the environmental movement well. Rather, it has tended to stereotype environmentalists as radical, out of tune with reality, and ignorant of the facts of life.

Environmental activists must learn as much as they can about the system by which things that people value are exchanged in our society. Economics is too important to the environment to be left to economists. The other side of this is that the economists must also develop a more complete understanding of the environment and the relationship it has to economics. A better understanding of this relationship is obviously needed by all. The world of the future may well look back and label this the "age of exploitation." We hope that what we are now moving into is an age of "eco-economic" adjustment.

A number of economists, notably Kenneth Boulding, William Nordhouse, and James Tobin, have begun to describe a new economics, one more in tune with ecology and natural laws and one encompassing the notion that the ultimate derivation of value has to be based in part on the natural environment. Georgescu'-Roegen (1977) has gone so far as to suggest that the new order might well begin with a bioeconomic program that takes into account not only contemporary fellow human beings, but future generations of human beings as well.

CONCEPTS TO REMEMBER

1. Our social institutions reflect our world view; as such, they also reflect the roots of our environmental difficulties. These institutions are being restructured as we adjust our world view in search of solutions.
2. Science and technology tend to offer us choices before the consequences of the choices are fully appreciated. We must continue to improve our ability to screen our technologies before they drag us unwittingly into problems in the future.
3. Medicine has historically focused on the sick and has left the well alone. Today's chronic diseases, some of which are connected to environmental quality, require that medicine adopt more of a preventive approach to keeping people well.
4. Nearly all of our cities were developed haphazardly, without regard to many important environmental realities. The cities of the future will have to be designed in harmony with the environment.
5. Ecological constraints suggest the need for more highly integrated, more energy-efficient, and less polluting forms of transportation.
6. Education is a key to creating in all citizens a world view that is compatible with the laws of ecology. Education must give us environmental specialists with a good general view of the operation of the ecosphere.
7. The constitutional basis of the government's role in environmental protection is, among other places, found in the directives to "provide for the general welfare . . . life, . . . liberty [to breathe and drink water without getting sick], . . . and the pursuit of happiness."
8. Government by the people—like the people—has trouble dealing with the long term.
9. Only too recently have we begun to include the protection of the general environment in the cost of doing business.
10. Science can help us diminish our environmental problems by providing the basis for non-polluting technologies. It can also help less directly but no less importantly by documenting the connections between environmental quality and the quality of life, thereby adding to our motivation to clean up the environment and keep it clean.
11. The laws of ecology say that quantitative economic growth—or any kind of quantitative growth for that matter—must be a temporary state.

DISCUSSION QUESTIONS AND FOOD FOR THOUGHT

1. Redesign a city to make it more livable and to improve the quality of life therein. Pick any city and discuss how it could be reconstructed while retaining some of its best features.
2. List and then discuss some of the environmental social costs associated with (a) owning and operating an air conditioner, (b) owning and operating a big automobile, and (c) taking a 30-minute shower.

3. Make a list of the most important environmental problems in your state. Contact local, state, and/or national legislative representatives and ask for their views on the most important problems.
4. Find out when your state legislature meets. Attend a committee meeting and a legislative session. Invite a state legislator to address the class on ways to influence the legislative process.
5. Get a copy of the U.S. Constitution and write a paper describing how the Constitution could be interpreted as providing for environmental protection or why you think it may not.
6. What is the relationship between law and regulation?
7. Find out what agencies in your state administer environmental laws. Ask them to provide information on opportunities for public participation.
8. Find out what environmental groups are active in your area. Invite a representative to speak to the class about his or her organization's activities.

9. Write an essay describing how you think a society would function if it had as its basis an environmental ethic rather than an economic ethic. Consider in your own mind how your life-style reflects the underlying ethic of your society. Which ethic is most predominant in your everyday decision making?
10. Survey the status of environmental education in your community by finding out the following:
   a. How does your public or private school system approach environmental education. What courses and programs are offered?
   b. What programs do your local elementary and secondary school systems have?
   c. What does state law or the state board of education require in the way of environmental education?
   d. What programs are available to civic groups or professionals? What is your overall evaluation of the status of environmental education in your community?

REFERENCES AND FURTHER READING

References marked with an asterisk are cited in the chapter.

Anglemeyer, M., Seagraves, E. R., and LeMaistre, C., eds., 1980. *A Search for Environmental Ethics: An Initial Bibliography.* Washington, D.C.: Smithsonian Institution Press Books.
*Applegate, R., 1976. *Public Trusts: A New Approach to Environmental Protection.* Washington, D.C.: Exploratory Project for Economic Alternatives.
Bardach, E., and Kagan, R., eds., 1982. *Social Regulation: Strategies for Reform.* San Francisco: Institute for Contemporary Studies.
"The Belgrade Charter: A Global Framework for Environmental Education," *Connect* 1(1):1–2 (1976).
*Berry, W., 1977. *The Unsettling of America: Culture and Agriculture.* San Francisco: Sierra Club Books.
*Berry, W., 1981. *The Gift of Good Land.* San Francisco: North Point Press.
*Bohm, P., and Henry, C., 1979. "Cost-Benefit Analysis and Environmental Effects," *Ambio* 8(1):18–24.
Butzer, K., 1980. "Civilizations: Organisms or Systems?" *American Scientist* 68:517–536.
*Carnow, B. W., 1971. "Air Pollution and Physician Responsibility," *Arch. Int. Med.* 127:91–95.
Catton, W., Jr., 1982. *Overshoot: The Ecological Bases of Revolutionary Change.* Champaign, Ill.: University of Illinois Press.
Cobb, J. B., Jr., 1971. *Is It Too Late: A Theology of Ecology.* New York: Glencoe Publishing Co.
Dorfman, R., and Dorfman, N. S., eds. 1972. *Economics of the Environment: Selected Readings.* New York: W. W. Norton.
Dunlap, T. R., 1981. *DDT: Scientists, Citizens, and Public Policy.* Princeton, N.J.: Princeton University Press.
Eichbaum, W. M., 1978. "State and Federal Environmental Enforcement," pp. 8–9 in *Environmental Enforcement;* sponsored by the American Bar Association's Standing Committee on Environmental Law. Washington, D.C.: American Bar Association.
*Ehrlich, P. R.; Ehrlich, A. H.; and Holdren, J. P., 1977.

Ecoscience: Population, Resources, Environment. San Francisco: W. H. Freeman and Company.
Elgin, D., 1981. *Voluntary Simplicity: Toward a Way of Life That Is Outwardly Simple, Inwardly Rich.* New York: Marrow, William, & Co.
The Environment Comes of Age: State Environmental Issues. Lexington, Ky.: Council of State Governments, 1977.
"EPA Memorandum: Draft Policy on Federal Oversight of Environmental Programs Delegated to States," *Environment Reporter* 14:1449–1453. (1983)
Eskridge, N. K., 1978. "Pell Pushes for International Treaty on Environment," *BioScience* 28(7):429–432.
Freund, W. C., 1979. "How Keynes Would Do It Now," *Newsweek,* Jan. 29, 13.
Gappert, G., and Knight, R., eds., 1982. *Cities in the 21st Century.* Beverly Hills, Calif.: Sage Publications.
*Georgescu'-Roegen, N., 1977. "The Steady State and Ecological Salvation: A Thermodynamic Analysis," *BioScience* 27(4):266–270.
Gibbons, B., 1981. "A Durable Scale of Values," *National Geographic,* November, 682–708.
*Greenwood, M. H., and Edwards, J. M. B., 1973. *Human Environments and Natural Systems: A Conflict of Dominion.* North Scituate, Mass.: Duxbury Press.
Guidelines for Environmental Education: The Kentucky Plan. Frankfort, Ky.: The Kentucky Department of Education and Advisory Council for Environmental Education. (1975)
Hardin, G., 1980. *Promethean Ethics: Living with Death, Competition, and Triage.* Seattle: University of Washington Press.
Hemmer, W. B., 1976. "Developing Environmental Values in the Classroom," Presentation at the Fifth Annual Conference of the National Association for Environmental Education, April 25–27.
Hock, I., 1976. "City Size Effects, Trends, and Policies," *Science* 193:856–863.
*Hueckel, G., 1975. "A Historical Approach to Future Economic Growth," *Science* 187:925–931.
Iozzi, L. A., 1978. "The Environmental Issues Test: A New

Assessment Instrument for Environmental Education," Presented at the Seventh Annual Conference of the National Association for Environmental Education, May 1.

Jarrett, H., ed., 1966. *Environmental Quality in a Growing Economy.* Baltimore, Md.: Resources for the Future, Johns Hopkins Press.

Keys, D., 1982. *Earth at Omega: Passage to Planetization.* Boston: Branden Press.

Komarov, B., 1980. *The Destruction of Nature in the Soviet Union.* White Plains, New York: Sharpe.

Kupchella, C. E., and Hyland, M. C., 1974. "Essential Curriculum Components in Environmental Education," *Journal of Environmental Education* **8**(3):11–16.

*Kupchella, C. E., and Levy, G. F., 1975. "Basic Principles in the Education of Environmentalists," *Journal of Environmental Education* **6**(3):2–6.

Kupchella, C. E., and Hyland, M. C., 1976. *Environmental Education: The Forest and the Farm. Selected papers from the Fifth Annual Conference of the National Association for Environmental Education.* Columbus, Ohio: Education Resources Information Center.

Laszlo, E., ed., 1977. *Goals in a Global Community: Studies on the Conceptual Foundation.* Elmsford, New York: Pergamon Press.

Laszlo, E., 1981. *Regionalism and a New World Order: A Strategy for Progress.* Elmsford, New York: Pergamon Press.

Lave, L., 1981. "Conflicting Objectives in Regulating the Automobile," *Science* **212**:893–899.

Lefcoe, G., 1979. *Land Development in Crowded Places: Lessons from Abroad.* Washington, D.C.: Conservation Foundation.

*Leopold, A., 1949. *The Sand County Almanac.* New York: Oxford University Press.

*McInnis, N., and Albrecht, D., eds, 1975. *What Makes Education Environmental?* Copublished by Environmental Educators, Inc. (Washington, D.C.) and Data Courier, Inc. (Louisville, Ky.).

Meier, R. L., 1976. "A Stable Urban Ecosystem," *Science* **192**:962–968.

Milbrath, L. W., and Inscho, F. R., eds., 1975. *The Politics of Environmental Policy.* Beverly Hills, Calif.: Sage Publications.

*Mishan, E. J., 1972. "Property Rights and Amenity Rights," pp. 187–193 in *Economics of the Environment: Selected Readings,* Dorfman, R. and Dorfman, N. S., eds. New York: W. W. Norton.

*Moncrief, L. W., 1970. "The Cultural Basis for Our Environmental Crisis," *Science* **170** (Oct. 30, 1970):508–512.

*Murphy, E. F., 1967. *Governing Nature.* Chicago: Quadrangle Books.

*Newcombe, K.; Kalma, J. D.; and Aston, A. R., 1978. "The Metabolism of a City: The Case of Hong Kong," *Ambio* **7** (1):3–15.

"A New Strategy for Environmental Control," *Resources,* a publication of *Resources for the Future,* No. 59 (April–July, 1978):1–5.

Outdoor News Bulletin **38**(4):5. (1984)

Pacey, A., 1983. *The Culture of Technology.* Cambridge, Mass.: MIT Press.

*Ridker, R. G., 1973. "To Grow or Not to Grow: That's Not the Relevant Question," *Science* **183**:1315–1318.

*Risser, P. and Cornelison, K., 1979. *Man and the Biosphere.* Norman, Okla.: University of Oklahoma Press.

Robertson, J., 1980. *The Sane Alternative: A Choice of Futures.* St. Paul, Minn.: River Basin Publishing Co.

*Rosenbaum, W. A., 1973. *The Politics of Environmental Concern.* New York: Praeger Publishers.

*Ruff, L. E., 1970. "The Economic Common Sense of Pollution," *The Public Interest* **19**(Spring 1970):69–85.

Schafer, R., and Disinger, J. T., eds., 1975. *Environmental Education: Perspectives and Prospectives.* Columbus, Ohio: ERIC Center.

Schultz, R., and Hughes, D., 1980. *Ecological Consciousness: Essays from the Earth Day X Colloquium.* Lanham, Md.: University Press of America.

Shrader-Frechette, K., 1982. *Environmental Ethics.* Pacific Grove, Calif.: The Boxwood Press.

Simon, S. B.; Howe, L. W.; and Kirschenbaum, H., 1972. *Values Clarification.* New York: Hart Publishing Company.

Skolimowski, H., 1981. *Eco-philosophy.* Salem, N.H.: Merrimack Book Service.

*Sloan, I. J., 1971. *Environment and the Law.* Dobbs Ferry, N.Y.: Oceana Publications. (Legal Almanac Series No. 65)

Smith, T. T., 1978. "Federal Environmental Statutes—Dilemmas for the Regulated," pp. 3–5 in *Environmental Enforcement,* sponsored by the American Bar Association's Standing Committee on Environmental Law, Washington, D.C.: The American Bar Association.

Standish, L., 1979. "A Measure of Morality," *Louisville Courier Journal and Times Magazine,* Sunday, February 4.

Sun, M., 1983. "China Faces Environmental Challenge," *Science* **221**:1271–72.

Swartznam, D., Liroff, R. A., and Croke, K. G., eds., 1982. *Cost-benefit Analysis and Environmental Regulations: Politics, Ethics, and Methods.* Washington, D.C.: Conservation Foundation.

Tweeten, L., 1983. "The Economics of Small Farms," *Science* **219**:1037–1041.

*U. S. Department of Health, Education and Welfare, 1977. *Human Health and the Environment: Some Research Needs.* Washington, D.C.: U.S. Department of Health, Education and Welfare, Public Health Service. (DHEW Publication No. NIH-77-1277, 1977)

Volk, T. L.; Hungerford, H. R.; and Tomera, A. N., 1983. *Curricular Needs in EE as Perceived by Professional Environmental Educators: A Report on a National Survey.* Carbondale, Ill.: Southern Illinois University.

Waldrop, M. M., 1984. "An Inquiry into the State of the Earth," *Science* **226**:33–35.

*Wallace, B., 1972. *People, Their Needs, Environment Ecology: Essays in Social Biology,* Vol. 1. Englewood Cliffs, N.J.: Prentice Hall.

*Wandesforde-Smith, G., 1970. "National Policy for the Environment: Politics and the Concept of Stewardship," in *Congress and the Environment,* Cooley, R. A., and Wandesforde-Smith, G., eds. Seattle: University of Washington Press, 205–226.

Winner, L., 1977. *Autonomous Technology: Technics-out-of-control as a Theme in Political Thought.* Cambridge, Mass.: MIT Press.

Worthington, E. B., 1983. *Ecology Around the World.* New York: Clarendon (Oxford University Press).

Whyte, W., 1980. *The Social Life of Small Urban Spaces.* Washington, D.C.: Conservation Foundation.

From Problems to Promise:

An Assessment

In 1972 a group of 18 internationally known ecologists met in Stockholm and identified what they considered to be the world's ten most important environmental problems. Their list is as follows:

1. Too many people creating impossible demands on all natural resources.
2. Pollution of the waters of the world.
3. Pollution of the air.
4. Lack of any significant worldwide research programs on food production.
5. Lack of workable programs to preserve and protect the endangered wildlife of our planet.
6. Worldwide inability to limit the indiscriminate use of persistent toxic substances.
7. Failure to develop systems by which raw materials can be recycled and the effective loss of these resources to the people of the future.
8. Failure to research and develop a plan for the use of various forms of energy in the future to improve living conditions for the people of the world.
9. Inability to find ways to invest wisely, both public and private funds, in the improvement of the general environment.
10. Inability of nations and their political subdivisions to develop workable systems of environmental control and cooperation.

This is still basically a good list, but it is obviously only one of many ways to describe the most general problems of the environment. Our intention in this chapter is to carry this form of generalization a bit further, annotating and expanding the list with some of our opinions and the opinions of others concerning the general and philosophical nature of these problems and the prospects for diminishing them.

This chapter is intended as an editorialized summary. It has four sections. The first deals with the nature of the environmental problem. The second deals in a general way with some of the basic truths that will have to be taken into account in formulating solutions to our environmental problems. A third section deals with more of the specifics of what must be done and why. In the final section we will peer into the future by guessing where present day momentum is likely to carry us. Within each section we will present a series of individual statements with supporting discussion.

ON THE NATURE OF THE ENVIRONMENTAL PROBLEM

We use energy in highly inefficient ways. Among the many problems that stem from our inefficient use of energy are the following:

1. depletion of key energy resources
2. acid rain
3. acid mine drainage
4. CO_2 buildup in the atmosphere
5. sulfur dioxide, ozone, particulate, and nitrogen oxide pollution of the air
6. strip-mine-ravaged land
7. destruction of national forests
8. oil pollution
9. imbalances in international trade
10. thermal pollution
11. increased contamination of the environment by radioactive materials

We use mineral resources in a one-way pattern. This flies in the face of the principles of material cycling found in the rest of nature. Predictably, this pattern has led to resource depletion at one end and waste disposal problems at the other end of the line.

We not only pollute water, we waste it. We waste water by using it in a linear fashion and by using so much of it that water resources are being depleted in many places. Water pollution renders water less useful for humans directly and jeopardizes the aquatic ecosystems on which we depend indirectly. Water resource depletion will be a key environmental problem in our future.

People are getting sick and dying as a direct result of the contamination of air, water, land, and food by toxic substances. Cancer, birth defects, emphysema, and acute poisoning have all been linked to specific environmental contaminants. Some toxic materials reach us as a result of accidental leaks or spills, some as a consequence of war (dioxin in defoliants and fallout from weapons testing), and some as a result of deliberate illegal dumping. Still other toxic substances get to us because they were made, distributed, used, and scattered before we knew enough about their toxicities and ecological impacts (for example, PCBs, dioxin, certain pesticides).

We use land and abuse land in ways that irreversibly diminish this vital resource. Could there be a more fundamental problem of human ecology than rendering good land unproductive? Nothing can take the place of land. We should, as suggested by Wendell Berry, not tolerate any loss of good farmland.

We have altered and continue to alter global ecosystems in ways that destabilize them. Through habitat destruction, through contamination of the environment, through inadvertent manipulations (e.g. species introduction), and through deliberate killing (e.g., pesticide overuse, predator poisoning, and overfishing) we have changed our life-support system, often without any thought of long-term consequences to that system.

There are more people on earth than our ecological, social, economic, and agricultural systems can handle. Too many people? Too much per capita impact? Too little food? Inappropriate life-styles? All of these are factors, but there is no doubt that we have a problem. Starvation, malnutrition, and related diseases constitute an enormous problem of human ecology.

Our surroundings are unnecessarily ugly, noisy, and cramped. This too is a very basic environmental problem. We do things in ways that unnecessarily diminish the quality of life. Perhaps if our surroundings were more pleasant, we would begin to see the environment more as something we are part of than as something to be dealt with or to overcome.

The people of the world are largely ignorant of the laws of ecology and the workings of the system of nature. How can we expect the things people do to be ecologically sound when the average citizen is largely ignorant of ecological principles? All citizens must be better educated about the system of nature.

National security and world peace are related to resource scarcity and vulnerability. We depend on large amounts of mineral and energy resources from other countries, many of which depend on the United States for foodstuffs and other products. Interdependence such as this among nations is both a stimulus for enhanced cooperation and a source of potentially explosive instability. Increasing global interdependence and awareness of this interdependence can work for us or against us; it cannot be ignored.

There is a growing gap between the rich and the poor at a time when it is being realized that there are not enough resources to go around. International environmental meetings point up the fact that the "haves" and the "have nots" are separated by a wide breech. Developing countries want what the developed countries have and got at tremendous environmental expense and jeopardy. The wants and needs of developing countries cannot be ignored. A similar disparity exists within many countries in which some individuals "have" and others "have not." Ways must be found to reverse these trends of wid-

Forty-Seven Issues

During the early 1980s there were several attempts to rank the major current and future environmental issues—by the Royal Swedish Academy of Sciences, the EPA, the government of France, the University of Michigan (with the EPA), the Congressional Clearinghouse for the Future, and the Conservation Foundation. In the volume *State of the Environment: An Assessment at Mid-Decade*, the Conservation Foundation consolidated the results of all of these surveys into a list of 47 "consensus" environmental issues as of 1985. Compared to the 1972 list given below, the 1985 list is more comprehensive and more specific, but it is basically the same list.

Wars, accidents, and natural disasters
— Wars
— Nuclear accidents, terrorism
— Chemical plant explosions
— Failure of aging infrastructure (for example, dams, reservoirs, navigation channels, water supply systems, water treatment systems, sewers, highways, and bridges)
— Intentional weather modification (unintentional effects)
— Droughts
— Floods
— Earthquakes, volcanoes, and other natural disasters

Population growth and distribution
— Population growth
— Crowding and impacts of urbanization
— Sprawl problems
— Mass migration, immigration

Contaminants (chemical, physical, and biological)
— Radioactive waste disposal (including decommissioning of nuclear power plants)
— Debris from space (especially, radioactive debris scattered by satellites reentering the atmosphere
— Microwave radiation
— Electronic pollution
— Solid waste disposal (including municipal waste management; landfills, incineration, and ocean disposal; sludge disposal or treatment; reduction at the source, resource recovery, and recycling; and littering and city cleanliness)
— Noise
— Pathogens from human wastes
— Proliferation of biological organisms, bioengineering wastes, and mistakes

— Genetic mutation
— Carbon dioxide accumulation in the atmosphere (caused primarily by deforestation and the burning of fossil fuels; widely expected to absorb much of the solar heat escaping the earth's surface, thereby making the climate significantly warmer through the "greenhouse effect")
— Acid deposition
— Depletion of the ozone layer
— Hazardous waste management
— Conventional pollutants, ambient air
— Toxic pollutants in air
— Indoor air pollution (including carbon monoxide from stoves, heaters, and appliances; formaldehyde insulation; radon gas from building materials; and chemicals in household cleaners)
— Conventional pollutants in water, from point sources
— Nonpoint-source water pollution (including agricultural runoff of sediment, fertilizers, pesticides, and animal wastes; nonpoint municipal and industrial discharges; acid mine drainage; accelerated runoff from urban streets; storm-water and sewer overflows)
— Toxic pollutants in surface water
— Groundwater, drinking-water contaminants
— Pesticides
— Chemical fertilizers
— Chemicals in food chains

Natural resource depletion
— Water scarcity
— Loss of agricultural land because of salinization, desertification, or urbanization
— Soil erosion and overexploitation of agricultural soils
— Ocean fisheries depletion
— Plant and animal species loss
— Energy scarcity
— Critical-materials scarcity
— Damage to the marine environment (including damage caused by oil spills, ocean dumping, and ocean mining)
— Loss of tropical forests
— Degradation of coastal areas
— Loss of wetlands
— Degradation of wilderness areas, parks, and wild and scenic rivers

---

ening disparity. Distribution of food and resources is a major problem that humankind must face up to and move to resolve.

Certain kinds of environmental deterioration are, for all practical purposes, irreversible. While certain negative things humans do to the environment can

be cleaned up within reasonable periods of time, many things that humans can do and have done to the environment can never really be restored, practically speaking. When farmland is given over to surburban development, that farmland is lost "forever." When especially rich ores are used and important minerals are dispersed rather than recy-

Because we did not plan ahead, we have cramped, unattractive cities that cover what used to be productive farmland.

cled, these materials are "lost," even though the absolute amounts remain unchanged. When areas of land are dedicated to hazardous or radioactive waste disposal, their use is restricted for generations to come.

Problems of the environment are the result of the kinds of things people do and the numbers of people doing them. We agree with Barry Commoner that the environmental problem in the United States is a result of the kinds of technology we now have more than it is a problem of overpopulation. Commoner attributes most of the increase in environmental deterioration that has occurred since 1946 in the United States to the new kinds of technology that have emerged since the late 1930s and early 1940s. Commoner cites irrefutable evidence that the ratio of pollution generated to population size has increased sharply since the end of World War II. Although population and urbanization have increased in the past several decades, the rates of increase have been small in comparison to the rise in pollution levels.

ON THE NATURE OF HUMAN MOTIVATION

Establishing the social cost of environmental deterioration is difficult. In the preceding chapter we considered this problem in some detail, the major point being that many of the social and environmental costs of various kinds of human activity are not easily brought into the equations used to determine the relationship between cost and benefit. It is easier to determine the value of ecosystem components like trees than it is to determine the value of the *function* of ecosystems (see Westman, 1977). Economic assessment of such marketable products as fish, minerals, and forest products is straightforward and relatively easily done. It is also relatively easy to assess the various standing elements of an ecosystem, for example, a forest used for recreation or other forms of enjoyment by people. On the other hand, what ecosystems do for humankind in less obvious ways—for example, absorbing and breaking down pollutants, cycling nutrients, degrading organic wastes, maintaining the balance of gases in the atmosphere, and converting solar energy into chemical substances—are more difficult to appreciate in terms of dollars.

Westman suggests that perhaps the only way of getting at the dollar value of an ecosystem function is to use the cost of restoring damaged systems to normal function. He cites as an example the provisions of the 1972 Federal Water Pollution Control Act in which it is estimated that cleaning up the effluents going into the nation's water supplies could cost as much as 594 billion dollars (Westman, 1977). Westman admits that this approach leaves something to be desired, especially since we really do not know that we have the ability to restore ecosystems once they are impaired.

In any case, we often hear how much it will cost to clean our air, water, and land and to keep it clean. Not often enough do we hear the costs of not cleaning up these resources—costs to health, property, ecosystem stability, quality of life, and human survival. For too long, air and water have been a free commons for polluters. Polluters gained individually by increased production or consumption while everyone shared in the deterioration of the air, water, and land.

Inertia is part of the problem. Throughout this book we have talked about things like the power of population growth. If we think of human existence on earth as a process, what we focus on here is the fact that this process has momentum as well as an inertia—it is difficult to get new things started, and it is difficult to get old things stopped. More than a few prophets of doom have predicted that these features of humanity will be its downfall now that rapidly changing times require quick starts and quick stops.

An especially important corollary to this point is that not all of what now has momentum is very good

Global 2000

In President Jimmy Carter's message to Congress on May 23, 1977, he directed the Council on Environmental Quality and the State Department to work with other federal agencies to study "probable changes in the world's population, natural resources, and environment through the end of the century" to serve as "the foundation of our longer-term planning." Three years later the Global 2000 report was published in three volumes. The first volume was a summary (see *The Global 2000 Report to the President*, Penguin Books, New York, 1982); Volume II contained expanded technical detail; and Volume III documented the models used in the projection.

Among the notable projections in the report are the following:

— World population will grow to 6.35 billion in 2000, with 90% of the growth in the poorest countries.
— Most of the 90% increase in world food production between 1975 and 2000 will occur in countries that already have high per capita food consumption, and the price of food will generally double.
— Arable land will increase only a few percentage points; increases in food production will come from increasingly intense use of existing farmland.
— We will not run out of fuel, but uneven distribution of supplies will continue to cause serious problems.
— Water supplies will become increasingly scarce; population growth alone will account for a doubling in the demand for water in nearly half the world.
— About 40% of the forests now standing in the undeveloped countries will be gone by 2000.

— There will be serious deterioration of agricultural soils worldwide.
— During the 1990s, world oil production will approach estimated maximum capacity—even with great increases in oil prices.
— The world's climate will be impacted by increases in carbon dioxide in the atmosphere and atmospheric ozone-depleting chemicals.
— There will be dramatic increases in the rate of extinction of plants and animals.

Needless to say, the report was generally pessimistic, although the writers of the report say that the models used tend to produce an optimistic bias. Since its publication, a debate has raged over whether or not the "optimistic" pessimism is justified (see Walton, 1980; Tangley 1984; Holden, 1983).

The Global 2000 Report itself acknowledges that there are inconsistencies in the projections, calling this a consequence of the methods used in the study (for example, how can seriously deteriorated agricultural soils yield most of the expected 90% increase in food production?). As with all projections derived from whatever models, the projections of Global 2000 are only as good as the accuracy of the assumptions upon which the model is based—and this, of course, remains to be seen. Projections are meant to be challenged, and even some of the harshest critics of the report acknowledge that it has engendered a healthy continuing dialog about global environmental issues.

---

or positive. A lot of it simply happened because of an infinite number of small decisions. Many of our problems are the results of individually insignificant decisions by large numbers of people. As an example, even though a single automobile is not a pollution problem, if 60 million people each make a decision to buy an automobile, then society has a problem with traffic and pollution. The inertia established as millions of people adopt an automobile-centered life-style makes the associated pollution problem difficult to attack.

Homo sapiens is a natural agent. We are sometimes led to believe that the differences between our species and the other elements of the system of nature are more important than the similarities. In our opinion, this stands in the way of recognizing and dealing with our environmental problems for what they are. We do not cause environmental problems because we are different from other species; many if not all of our impacts are the result of the fact that

we are similar. The ways in which we are different account mainly for the extra extent of our impact.

Homo sapiens is by nature exploitive. This is an important principle, one that must be kept in mind by those who want to understand how humankind interacts with nature. Many animal species do things to the environment that would ultimately render it inhospitable whenever and wherever certain restraints are temporarily removed. Habitat destruction by the species occupying a habitat is not unheard of in nature. It may help as we try to address environmental problems to appreciate that *H. sapiens* may well still be driven by the same forces of biological drive, aggressiveness, selfishness, and competitive spirit that brought us out of the dark ages of the human past.

People cannot live on earth without having a negative impact. It should be realized that human beings cannot live on this planet without causing some

Chapter 19   From Problems to Promise: An Assessment

form of environmental changes, some of which qualify as deterioration. This stems from biological principles unique neither to the human species nor to modern women, men, and children. The fact that it would be a problem for Americans to learn to live within the beauty of nature without somehow destroying that beauty bothered some of the earliest settlers. It is useless to expect that we can live on this planet and leave the environment in a condition absolutely free of impact.

Nature may not always know best. In his book *The Closing Circle,* Barry Commoner says that the third law of ecology is that nature knows best. He anticipated, however, that this principle was likely to encounter significant resistance. We would like to resist it.

First, the implied distinction between nature and humankind is inappropriate. Humankind is an integal part of nature. Nature without us cannot be assumed to be more all-knowing than nature with us. Beyond this, Commoner's analogy that human impact on nature is equivalent to random poking into the works of a watch is worse than most analogies. The fact is that much human intervention into the environment is *not* random. It is often done with careful consideration of nature—though sometimes not careful enough. Environmental laws and regulations are making this even more common. The human intellect and human capacity to learn being what they are, we feel confident that human beings can improve on nature from a human point of view at times and in certain places in concert with nature's own laws.

In sharp contrast to the view that nature knows best, Rene Dubos (1976) presents a picture of nature as a great river of forces that can be directed or channeled in certain positive ways by human intervention. Dubos points out that nearly every part of the globe has humanized areas that have remained attractive, pleasing, productive, and ecologically sound for long periods of time. He cites as particularly notable examples China, Holland, Japan, Italy, and Sweden. These offer what Rene Dubos calls evidence for a symbiotic relationship between humankind and environment—evidence that we can have environmental impacts that, though profound, do not desecrate the environment or render it worthless. He goes on to argue that natural channels are not always best, particularly for the human species itself and not always even for other species. Certainly, learning to control population size is preferable to an otherwise inevitable population crash brought only by war, famine, or disease. Nature is

really quite mindless. It works well because the parts that have not worked well have gradually been lost through natural selection, but this does not mean that new things cannot constitute subjective improvement.

We will probably always have difficulty dealing with the long term and the big picture. The history of humankind has been a long series of trials and tribulations, always seeming to have to do with the immediate problem of survival. Our species has never risen very far above crisis management. As long as there are large numbers of human beings having trouble ensuring their existence today, there will probably not be any concerted effort to deal with long-range and or even intermediate-range problems. Humans seem to have been bred to crisis management. There are many examples of our inability to deal with long-term effects; we have discussed some of these in other chapters.

Similarly, humankind has a problem dealing with the big picture. This is another harmful form of narrowness, although it may well be that nature's general pattern has been to favor the survival of the species by selecting for selfishness and narrowness in each individual member. In almost all aspects of our institutional approaches to science and education we seem to work from a reductionist viewpoint rather than a holistic one. We have far more lung specialists, kidney specialists, heart specialists, and cancer researchers than we have medical generalists or other types of generalists. Similarly, there are too few specialists in the relationship between humans and the environment who are paid to study, understand, and derive a better general understanding of the interaction between humans and the environment. This is significant in that, as Odum (1977) points out, every level of organization adds a dimension to that which is being studied. The adage that a forest is more than a collection of trees is offered by Odum as a first working principle in the holistic study of *Homo sapiens*.

We need more facts and less emotion. We need more and better data about the impacts of humans on the natural systems on which they depend and how some of these impacts actually affect us. Only with such data will we be able to continue to show that environmentalism is *not* an emotional movement based on exaggerated and unfounded claims. Perhaps emotion was the proper first step toward getting involved and getting the data collected. However, there is little place for emotion in formal discourse about problems of the environment. The new values many say must be established will have to be defended on the basis of ecological facts. Research that documents specific cause-and-effect relationships and that can help define thresholds for environmental impacts are crucial to the establishment of sound environmental policies.

Most environmental problems are complicated and have no perfect solutions. Those who want to work toward an improved environment should realize that we must work to diminish problems and to learn more about them rather than to solve them straightaway. Many problems of the environment are unsolvable in the absolute sense. They can be minimized, but they cannot be eliminated.

There will be no ultimate technical solution. In 1968, Garrett Hardin proposed that there is no technical solution to the population problem and acknowledged the difficulty in modern times of admitting the fact that there may not be a technical solution. We would like to extend this concept to say that there will be no strictly technical solutions to any of our environmental problems. What we have now is a need for changes in values and attitudes. As long as we cling to the assumption that technology alone will provide the answer, we simply delay the inevitable point at which we will be forced into a new world view.

Whatever solutions are proposed for our environmental problems must take into consideration how the natural system operates. Unless our solutions operate in concert with the natural system, they will inevitably lead to other problems and eventually to failure. Likewise, when new technologies are proposed, they must be weighed in terms of their compatibility with the operating laws of the universe.

Environmental improvement can be approached within the system. The United States has constitutional provisions for changing the ways things are done. Our form of democracy certainly has the mechanisms by which environmentally oriented laws can be passed and enforced once a large enough group of people sees it as falling under the parts of the Constitution providing that government protect the general welfare of its people. Environmentalists should become as familiar as possible with how things work—how the business system, the economic system, and the system of government work—and to proceed as any member of society to try to bring changes that conform to one's personal point of view.

People are not moved much by things "experts" know. The public, and here we mean the public of the world, has to be educated to the *need* to deal with environmental problems before anything significant can be done about them. It has never been effective for a group of informed individuals to say to the rest of the world, "Look, I know what needs to be done; please let's do it." The ineffectiveness of such appeals is perhaps best illustrated by the small impact that warnings about smoking and health have had on cigarette consumption. It is now generally considered to be a fact that cigarette smoking has a gross negative impact on health. Even though the effects of cigarette smoking are self-imposed as far as the smoker is concerned, the habit continues almost unabated, each person perhaps believing that he or she will not be one of those affected. How much more difficult it will be to convince people to make changes in their behavior out of concern for the environment—when the connection to health is much less visible and less direct.

ON THE NATURE OF WHAT MUST BE DONE

We must establish systems of review of emergent and existing technologies. Our ability to alter the environment has grown much faster than our understanding of the environment. Many negative environmental impacts are the results of unanticipated side effects. New technologies that have emerged in recent decades have been particularly troublesome. We now need systematic control on the emergence of new technologies, controls that insist that such technologies be ecologically sound. There is after all nothing inherently bad about technologies. The task is clearly one of taking stock of where we are and where we would like to go with our technologies and to consider new possibilities carefully—to assume control of our destiny, in other words.

Many factors must be considered in evaluating the safety and benefits of new and existing technologies. While many of these factors relate to direct and immediate impacts on humankind and its life-support systems, we must come to better appreciate and anticipate important effects that are neither direct nor immediate. We have to learn how to consider the relative importance of 100 people being killed in an explosion and 100 people being killed by a cancer initiated insidiously by exposure to some chemical. We have to develop equations to take into account the relative irreversibility of certain kinds of impacts like the accidental discharge of radioactive isotopes. The Toxic Substances Control Act exemplifies the sort of thing we have in mind. But we must go further.

We must establish more environmentally cognizant approaches to technology transfer from "developed" to "developing" countries. We live in a diverse world—diverse in biomes, cultures and development. All human beings obviously have similar needs for food, clothing, and shelter. There are also similar desires for a high standard of living that now constitute a conflict between what is fair and what is possible. Like it or not, the world cannot stand the spread of energy-intensive, material-intensive cultural practices to places where they do not yet exist, nor will these technologies be sustainable at current levels over time.

Technologies and economies must be developed that are more ecologically appropriate and sustainable. The current level of production and consumption in the United States cannot be maintained indefinitely. Our technologies are too environmentally costly. It seems that we must now begin to move to smaller-scale and more environmentally appropriate technologies, as are advocated for developing nations. It is unfortunate that we have for a time put all of our eggs in the fossil fuel basket. And it would be unfortunate if we placed too heavy an emphasis on any one new energy source. We must begin to diversify again—to have technologies and ways of doing things that differ from place to place according to differences in local environments.

We need environmental multidisciplinarians. The task before us requires that some of us become trained to deal with multidisciplinary problems. The optimal format for such training would probably consist of a solid grounding in one major discipline, but with training in a number of others as well. As harmless as this might sound, it does go against the grain of the education and occupational trends of the last several decades. We should encourage multidisciplinism and not discourage it by calling those who want to become involved in more than one narrow field "dilettantes." We can think of many desirable combinations—environmental lawyers who know something about ecological principles, ecologists who know more than a little about environmental law, and urban planners who are conversant with the principles of ecology, for example. Perhaps for the immediate future the most important will be the hybrid between economics and ecology. Here we agree with Barry Commoner that

despite all the inherent risks of professional sanction and disdain, both economists and environmentalists must risk reaching across the boundaries of their respective disciplines to deal with the necessary extension into the other.

Population growth for the world cannot continue. We are not sure where the population problem fits into the order of priorities of our environmental problems. We disagree with those who say that the population problem is *the* environmental problem. In industrialized nations like the United States the problem is more one of how we do things than the number of people. But regional population problems will be with us for some time; population control programs must be encouraged.

Recycling must become a way of life. We know that our energy problem is a problem mainly because once energy is used, it is gone. While the consumption of minerals and ores is a different kind of problem, thermodynamically speaking, ore also tends to "disappear" as it is "used up." The problem with material resources is one of keeping materials in forms in which they are usable. There has been some movement toward recycling in industry, but what we have accomplished so far really amounts to just a tentative first step. If we can make recycling an important part of all of the things we do in society, we will have solved several kinds of problems:

1. We will not have to destroy large expanses of territory searching for less rich ores as fast as we would otherwise.
2. The reuse of materials would diminish the solid waste problem.
3. Reuse would obviate or lessen the problems of increasing shortages of various raw materials.

We must develop strategies to encourage source reduction of pollution. Many of our pollution problems are the result of systems that exploit resources and add nothing to our standard of living. Much of our present packaging falls into this category. An example is jars packaged in boxes that are promptly tossed away, adding to the solid waste problem. Disposable containers are another example.

Likewise, many of our industrial processes that generate pollutants and hazardous wastes can be altered to produce less waste and less toxic by-products without altering the final product to any great extent. We must begin to find ways to encourage these kinds of changes at the source.

Mechanisms must be found to internalize environmental costs into the cost of doing business. We must make it more expensive to pollute. If the environmental costs are included in the price of the product, consumers are more likely to buy the less expensive, more environmentally compatible product. Ways must be found to internalize environmental costs along with other production costs.

Environmentalists must get their act together. Environmentalists must see to it that they are all informed. We discussed this at some length in the last chapter. There are a few other points about environmentalism we would like to make here.

The institutionalization of environmental concerns in the past 15 years has given environmentalism credibility and permanence. At the same time, the vocal environmental activists, with the exception of nuclear activists, have become less visible. We worry about this. Politics in a democracy is based on compromise. Government responds to pressure—economic, social, and public—such that the final compromise is determined by the pressures. The final compromise is also a function of where the points of the two extremes lie.

Environmental activist groups have long served as rallying points for public opinion, and environmental special interests have served the public well in competition with other special interests.

Environmentalists are a varied and a diverse lot. Some are interested in safe working conditions in factories, some in saving a single threatened or endangered species, some in preserving the wilderness, some in cleaning up air or water, and some in protecting us from radioactive materials, to name just a few.

Some have proposed that a coalition of many of the movements—labor, women, organic foods—could help to coalesce and mobilize common support for environmental issues. Perhaps a coalition of environmental groups would be a first step toward this broader end. Whatever the approach, it is time to consider bringing order into this diversity of environmental concerns if we are to move ahead and win the important battles.

Where conflicts exist between individual freedom and the quality of the human environment, individual freedom must give way. In many places throughout this book we have described our traditional reverence for individual freedom and how this sometimes obstructs intelligent stewardship of the environment. We have implied that (despite its not being a popular notion) government might actually have to assume a larger role in human affairs if the environment is to be looked after properly. If there are

The biggest obstacle to recycling is habit.

critics who would brand this attitude as an environmental form of socialism, so be it. We recognize that societies are made up of individuals and that, in general, as an individual goes, so goes the society. This is true only up to a point, however, and we believe that many of the environmental problems we face have happened because we have carried this ideal past the point of optimization. It may well be, as suggested by B. F. Skinner, that individual freedom has outlived its usefulness and will be replaced by philosophies that place the welfare of all people over the freedom of an individual.

Ecological paradigms must become the basis for all ethical systems. In the previous chapter we advocated the establishment of ecological principles as the core of general education. In other words, all training and education should emanate from the concepts having to do with human-environment relationships. Here we would like to carry this concept a step further. Clearly, our most impressive hope for the future is that we will find new ways to think about our environment and our relationship with it. A new philosophical attitude must emerge. Van R. Potter (1971, 1977) has suggested that since ethical values cannot be separated from biological facts and since the survival of ecosystems really is the ultimate test for any system of values, bioethics or environmental ethics constitute an appropriate base for the ethical systems by which humans express humanity.

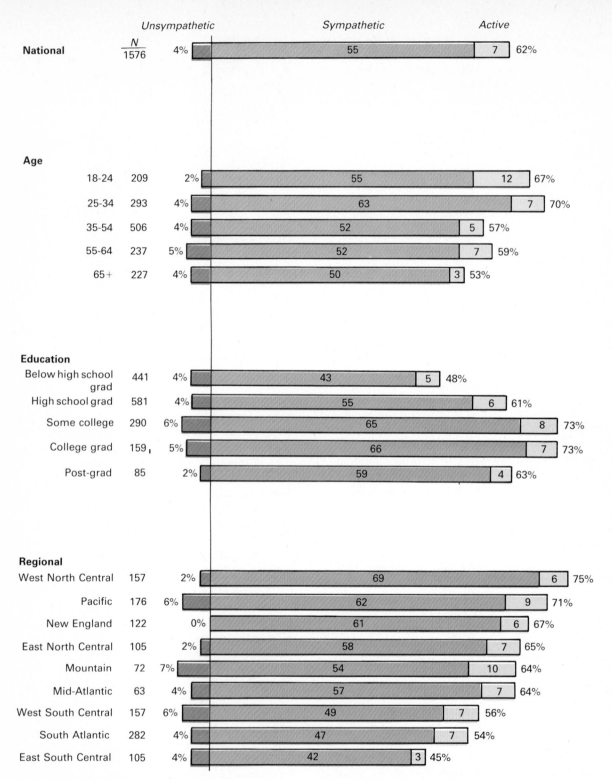

Figure 19.1   Views on the Environmental Movement. A government survey conducted in early 1980 indicates that there is broad-based support for a clean environment, despite growing economic pressures. The question was whether respondents considered themselves active participants in the environmental movement, sympathetic toward it but not active, or unsympathetic toward it. Differences between combined totals on a line and 100% are due to responses that were neutral or not sure.

Our religions must place more emphasis on environmental stewardship. The basis of our system of laws must change from its emphasis on property ownership and possession to an emphasis on property stewardship and responsibility. Under such a system, destruction of "one's own" land so that future generations are deprived of it, should be considered an act of theft. The decision makers in a corporation that pollutes a groundwater resource should be held legally accountable and be appropriately penalized.

We must proceed with environmental protection measures and cleaning up the environment even though there will be temporary negative impacts. We have touched on this idea in several places throughout the book. There are workers who will be displaced from jobs when plants are shutdown because the operations are too dirty. Passing certain environmental costs along to consumers will undoubtedly have disproportionate impacts on the poor. It is clear that no method of pollution control and cleanup will be easy, and it is also certain that the cost will not be equally borne by everyone. These problems cannot be given as a reason why nothing should be done; rather they must be addressed via institutional mechanisms designed to assist those in need (see the section on the role of government in Chapter 18). We must proceed; the bullet must be bitten.

There is a broad based corps of U.S. citizens concerned about the environment that must be sustained. Two major criticisms are often made of "environmentalists." One is that they represent only a small portion of the total population. The second is that concern for environmental protection will wane as the crunch of inflation continues. Recent surveys dispel both of these criticisms. A survey commissioned by the Council on Environmental Quality, the Department of Agriculture, the Department of Energy, and the EPA conducted between January 26 and February 9, 1980, indicated that while the people lying down in front of bulldozers were getting the attention, a majority of Americans were quietly developing a genuine concern for the environment. As Figure 19.1 shows, support for environmental protection cuts across racial, age, education, and geographic boundaries. There is now a solid, broad-based corps of U.S. citizens concerned about the environment.

What about the impact of the economy on attitudes toward the environment? Figure 19.2 shows how attitudes about this issue changed from 1977 to 1980. Interestingly, the percentage favoring the strongest environmental control decreased, as did the percentage supporting the strongest cost control option. Attitudes moved toward a maintenance option. The survey concludes overall that "there is no sign of the backlash which had been predicted once the costs of significant environmental protection became known" and that far from being a fad, environmental concerns show "every sign of remaining for the foreseeable future."

Some significant environmental progress has been made. This important point has been made throughout this book, but it may have gotten lost among litanies of environmental wrongs and environmental problems. We take heart at the progress we have seen, and we mean to call this progress to the attention of the reader now as we near the end of this volume.

According to the Environmental Protection Agency, since the Clean Air Act was passed in the

Some environmental progress has been made by people who keep the long term in mind. These Douglas fir trees were planted in the 1930s.

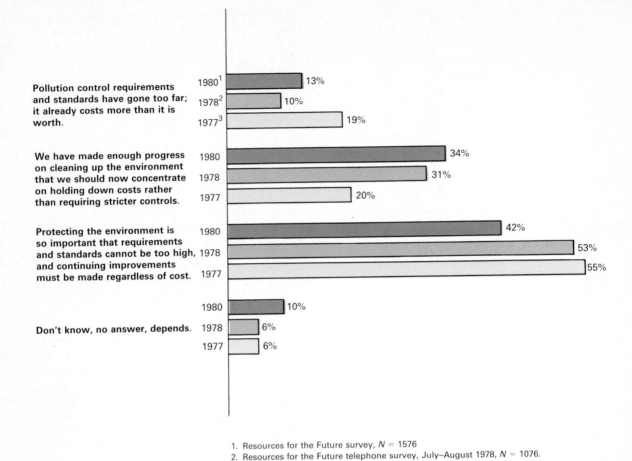

Pollution control requirements and standards have gone too far; it already costs more than it is worth.
- 1980[1] — 13%
- 1978[2] — 10%
- 1977[3] — 19%

We have made enough progress on cleaning up the environment that we should now concentrate on holding down costs rather than requiring stricter controls.
- 1980 — 34%
- 1978 — 31%
- 1977 — 20%

Protecting the environment is so important that requirements and standards cannot be too high, and continuing improvements must be made regardless of cost.
- 1980 — 42%
- 1978 — 53%
- 1977 — 55%

Don't know, no answer, depends.
- 1980 — 10%
- 1978 — 6%
- 1977 — 6%

1. Resources for the Future survey, $N = 1576$
2. Resources for the Future telephone survey, July–August 1978, $N = 1076$.
3. Opinion Research Corporation telephone survey, January 1977, $N = 1003$.

Figure 19.2 Views About Pollution Control. This figure shows how responses to survey questions on the environment and economics changed from 1977 to 1980. The question was which statement best represented the respondent's opinion.

early 1970s, sulfur dioxide levels, carbon monoxide levels, and particulate levels have declined considerably. There has also been significant improvement in water quality in many places; in many others there has been a halt in the trend toward further deterioration of water quality. Billions of dollars have been invested in waste treatment plants; and while this has not provided the ultimate solution, it has already carried us a significant distance in the right direction.

ON THE FUTURE

It sometimes strikes us as every bit as ludicrous to discuss what life will be like in the future as a discussion about a dish that none of those discussing it has tasted or seen. Knowing this full well, we cannot resist the logic of ending this text with a look into the future. First, we would like to drive home the point that the future cannot *really* be known. Second, we would like to make the related point that even if the future could be known, it could not be appreciated. Third, we would like to make a few points about the general significance and usefulness and dangers of predictions. Finally, we will risk a few predictions.

The future cannot be known. The future cannot really be known because there is not, for example, any way to know what raw materials will be used in the future. We are all well aware that humankind has historically made use of resources that had in years earlier been unrecognized as resources. We see in print on occasion the concept of "proved reserves" being used as a basis for making future projections —even though proved reserves are, by definition,

National Environmental Survey Results

Commissioned by the President's Council on Environmental Quality (CEQ), the Department of Energy, the Department of Agriculture, and the Environmental Protection Agency, Resources for the Future (RFF) conducted a comprehensive national survey of public opinion regarding a variety of environmental and energy issues.

The RFF survey was conducted with the assistance of the Roper Organization and Cantril Research, Inc. Roper and Cantril interviewed 1576 adults representing a cross section of the American population. Most of the interviews took place between January 26 and February 9 of 1980.

Study director Robert Cameron Mitchell, a senior fellow at RFF, also analyzed a large number of previous surveys in an effort to identify trends in public opinion on environmental issues over the past ten years.

Among the RFF survey's findings are:

— Although 81 percent of those surveyed said they are worried "a great deal" about inflation, only 13 percent chose the option which stated "pollution control requirements and standards have gone too far; it already costs more than it is worth." Thirty-four percent believed we should "now concentrate on holding down costs," and 42 percent declared, "Continuing improvements must be made regardless of cost."

— One in five chose the statement, "We must relax environmental standards in order to achieve economic growth." A plurality (39 percent) said we could achieve both goals at the same time, while 27 percent were willing to accept slower growth to protect the environment.

— A solid majority (62 percent) said they were sympathetic with the environmental movement; and an even larger majority (73 percent) said the term environmentalist applied to them at least "somewhat."

— Two out of three people said they were worried "a great deal" about the disposal of hazardous chemical wastes, a level of concern higher than that expressed in the early 1970s about air and water pollution.

— Seventy percent would "want to move to another place or to actively protest" if a government-approved and -inspected disposal site for hazardous waste chemicals were located within 20 miles of their home. An almost identical percentage felt that way about a new nuclear power plant, whereas only 34 percent said they would oppose a new coal-fired power plant at that distance from their home.

— While most polls show majorities willing to sacrifice some environmental quality to ensure an adequate energy supply, the RFF survey and other polls found a strong preference for environmentally benign sources like solar energy and conservation. Solar was chosen by 61 percent as the energy source which the nation should "concentrate on most" over the next twenty years, and nuclear energy was least preferred.

— Eighty-one percent believed "Technology will find a way of solving the problem of shortages and natural resources." Fewer than one out of three respondents agreed with the statement that "Future scientific research is more likely to cause problems than to find solutions to our problems."

In his analysis of trends since 1970, Mitchell found that "the intensity of public concern about environmental problems has lessened somewhat since its peak on Earth Day 1970." Other problems—in particular, national defense and inflation—are more urgent now. "Nevertheless," Mitchell states "at the beginning of the 1980s the answers to a broad range of probing questions posing sharp tradeoffs show continued strong support for national efforts to protect environmental quality."

---

the amount of a resource that can be profitably recovered and used with *present* technology. The fallacy here is that the future is being measured in terms of the present. Indeed, while this is really the only way we can ever look into the future and even though we may qualify what it is we are doing when we do it, everyone should be aware of the inherent shortcoming of this approach.

To take the example a bit further, Ridker (1973) points out that iron ore reserves increased five times between 1954 and 1965 and estimates of copper reserves increased $2\frac{1}{2}$ times since 1935. According to Hueckel (1975), the lowest grade of copper ore that could be used has gone from 3% copper in 1880 to about four tenths of a percent copper today. He suggests that similar reductions in the lowest feasible grade of ore have taken place in the production of iron, aluminum, and numerous other minerals. Of course, this is not to say that there is not some limit to what we will be able to recover, but it is to say that no one knows what the limit really is, and no one knows how much energy we have and want to use to get there. The raw material of the industry and activities of the future may well be water, air, rocks, soil, and sunlight.

The future could not be appreciated even if it could be known. Buckminster Fuller said that within a short time we might see the disappearance of private property, the end of the use of hydrocarbons as fuel, and the end of sovereign nations and certain religions. He admitted that these are incomprehensible changes to those of us alive today. But the future has always been incomprehensible. We should expect that some of the most sacred tenets of our way of life in this country and other countries and our attitudes toward free enterprise, religion, government, and other relationships between human beings will all change in ways that would be judged by those reading this textbook as terrible and even unspeakable. We are all prisoners of our own time, of the current climate of opinion. The things we read today, the people we talk to today, and the people among whom we live and from whom we derive our perspective and our points of view would keep us from understanding and appreciating the future even if we were somehow miraculously given a crystal clear picture of what will come to pass. It seems to be a common error among those who make projections and predictions about the future that they inevitably introduce their own personal perferences, tacitly assuming that these preferences are those of all members of society and will continue to be held dear by the people of tomorrow. This is an inexcusable error and one that was illustrated very well in a classroom discussion not long ago. During a session in which a scenario was being developed of the future and what it might be like to live 100 years hence, one student said that he would rather die than live in the world being described. Another student pointed out that this wish would probably be granted. Still another student remarked that if Daniel Boone could somehow be brought back to life to catch a glimpse of the world of today, he might well opt to remain dead.

On the significance and usefulness of predictions. The foregoing notwithstanding, there might be some utility in trying to project the future. It could be argued that our present-day problems came about because our forbears did *not* consider the future—or that most present-day progress has been the result of people trying to see the future and to understand and anticipate it.

Now for some low-risk predictions.

There will be better ways. The imaginations of the people of the immediate future will be tested— but not very much—in trying to come up with improvements on our ways of doing things. A lot of things we have done in the past and continue to do are pro-ugly and environmentally ignorant. Tele-phone poles offer one pedestrian example of the former; automobiles that get eight miles per gallon exemplify the latter. The people of the future will come up with new views of the world and humankind's place within the scheme.

Health implications of environmental deterioration will grow in importance. Two aspects of our daily existence will increasingly force the individual to stop short and take notice of problems of the environment. One aspect relates to our wallet; the second to our health. To date, much time and energy has been devoted to bemoaning the costs relating to environmental protection. But as we have pointed out, more needs to be done about the costs associated with *not* cleaning up and protecting the environment. Gradually, research has brought the health ramifications of pollution into sharper focus in the public eye. As these health implications are brought more and more to the forefront, they will provide a favorable impetus to increased environmental protection.

There is room for optimism, but there is no room for blind faith. Despite the many contraindications scattered throughout this volume, we must say in summary that our position is one of optimism concerning the future. We have emphasized the frailty of the system of nature. But we have also stressed the fact the system of nature is, above all else, highly resilient. Even when we speak of imminent disasters, we have the local scale in mind. *Homo sapiens* is not in any immediate great danger of disappearing from the face of the earth. Secondarily, while *Homo sapiens* may have gotten into a lot of environmental trouble following the dictates of biological nature, we foresee the emergence of the more rational side of this species, bringing unique skills and abilities to solve some of these very same problems. It is clear to us that we are now beginning to make such applications. We expect that, given the pattern of human history, the phases we have gone through with respect to our environment and that we will go through in the future reflect a common general pattern of (1) recognition, (2) overreaction, (3) backlash, and (4) getting down to business. In the late 1960s we went through a phase in which our awareness of the environment increased significantly. This was followed by a period of mixed overreaction—some progress and some reversals. This in turn is being followed by a period of quiet determination and steady progress. Concern for the environment has now become part of our way of thinking, has begun to form a baseline of care for the systems that support us, and has moved our institutions in an appropriate direction in a subtle but significant manner.

Our general purpose in writing this book was to describe from a natural sciences perspective the principal environmental problems facing the human species. Our specific main purpose was to expose and illuminate the underlying principles that have to be considered in order to recognize environmental problems for exactly what they are. Those of you that have stayed with us through these pages are now among those who will be counted on to continue to make a difference.

DISCUSSION QUESTIONS AND FOOD FOR THOUGHT

1. As a class exercise, come up with a list of your own top ten environmental problems and rank them in order of importance by consensus.
2. Make a list of human actions that amount to irreversible alteration of the environment.
3. Choose up sides and debate. Resolved: Nature does not always know best.
4. Choose up sides and debate. Resolved: Humans are no more exploitive than locusts, black flies, rabbits, or algae.
5. Natural selection and thus evolution are driven by the here and now—or are they? Can you come up with examples of things that might pass for foresight or planning that have survival value in nature—other than in human beings?

6. As a class exercise, paint a picture of your preferred future for the year 2050. How would you like to see it in terms of such things as business, technology, government, population, cities, farms, environmental quality, and education?
7. You have just finished a course intended to help enlighten you concerning the intricacies of humankind's interaction with the environment. Has your attitude changed? What are you going to do differently now as a direct result of taking this course? How do you see your role in the future relative to the quality of the human environment?

REFERENCES AND FURTHER READING

References marked with an asterisk are cited in the chapter.

Cast, R. M., 1975. "Thoughts on the Nature of Naturalism," *Bioscience* **24**(5):307–309.
Council on Environmental Quality, 1980. *Public Opinion on Environmental Issues: Results of a National Public Opinion Survey*. Washington, D.C.: U.S. Government Printing Office.
Dickson, D., 1984. "EPA Seeks Unified Approach to Risk," *Science* **225**:152.
Dubos, R., and Ward, D., 1972. *Only One Earth: The Care and Maintenance of a Small Planet*. New York: W. W. Norton.
*Dubos, R., 1976. "Symbiosis between Earth and Humankind," *Science* **193**:459–462.
"Ecology and National Security," *Science* **198**:712. (November 18, 1977)
Green, R., and Ronald, M., 1977. "Intergenerational Distributive Justice and Environmental Responsibility," *Bioscience* **27**(4):260–265.
*Hardin, G., 1968. "The Tragedy of the Commons," *Science* **162**:1243–1248.
Healy, R., 1982. *America's Industrial Future: An Environmental Perspective (An Issue Report)*. Washington, D.C.: Conservation Foundation.
Hohenemeser, C.; Kates, R.; and Slovic, P., 1983. "The Nature of Technological Hazard," *Science* **220**:376–384.
Hohenemeser, K. H., 1978. "Can High Technology Solve Our Energy Problem?" *Environment* (9):4–5.
*Holden, C., 1983. "Simon and Kahn Versus Global 2000," *Science* **221**:341–343.
*Hueckel, G., 1975. "A Historical Approach to Future Economic Growth," *Science* **187**:925–931.

Leonard, H., 1983. *Managing Oregon's Growth: The Politics of Development Planning*. Washington, D.C.: Conservation Foundation.
Mitchell, R. C., 1978. "The Public Speaks Again: A New Environmental Survey," *Resources for the Future* (60):1–6.
*Odum, E. P., 1977. "The Emergence of Ecology as a New Integrative Discipline," *Science* **195**(4284):1289–1293.
Odum, W., 1982. "Environmental Degradation and the Tyranny of Small Decisions," *Bioscience* **32**(9):728–729.
*Potter, V. R., 1971. *Bioethics*. Englewood Cliffs, N.J.: Prentice Hall.
*Potter, V. R., 1977. "Evolving Ethical Concepts," *Bioscience* **27** (4):251–253.
Pryde, P., 1983. "The 'Decade of the Environment' in the U.S.S.R.," *Science* **220**:274–279.
*Ridker, R. G., 1973. "To Grow or Not to Grow, That's Not the Relevant Question," *Science* **182**:1315–1318.
Skinner, B. F., 1971. *Beyond Freedom and Dignity*. New York: Alfred A. Knopf.
Spaeth, R. L., 1979. "Global Pessimism (Review of *The Human World Revisited: The World Predicament and Possible Solutions*, by Harrison Brown)," *Environment* **21** (1):43.
*Tangley, L., 1984. "Life After 2000—The Debate Goes on," *Bioscience* **34**(8):477–479.
*Walton, S., 1980. "Global 2000 Projects Grim Future," *Bioscience* **30**(9):619–632.
Weiss, C., Jr., 1979. "Mobilizing Technology for Developing Countries," *Science* (203):1083–1089.
*Westman, W. R., 1977. "How Much Are Nature's Services Worth?" *Science* **193**:960–964.

Interpreting Tables
and Graphs

Tables and graphs are very concise ways of describing relationships between two or more things or categories of things. They can hold more information than a casual glance will reveal. The reader simply has to know how to look at them.

As an example, the table below shows the relationship between the emission of various kinds of air pollutants and time from 1975 to 1982.

Obviously, many conclusions can be drawn from these data. For example, from 1975 to 1982:

— the emission of all pollutants except oxides of nitrogen declined;
— particulate emissions declined most (by 27% to be exact);
— emissions of oxides of nitrogen increased by more than 5%, while emissions of other pollutants decreased;
— the smallest percent change was in the oxides of nitrogen;
— carbon monoxide is the most prevalent pollutant emitted—on a weight basis, about three times more is emitted than the next most prevalent pollutant shown.

The same data could be presented as a graph. The advantage of a graph over a table is that a graph illustrates trends better; the disadvantage is that some of the exactness of the numbers is lost.

Traditionally, graphs begin with a horizontal or X axis and a vertical or Y axis.

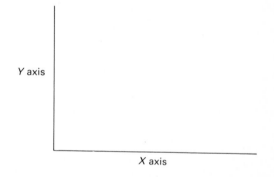

The X axis is used to represent the independent variable—for example, the years the measurements were made. Independent variables are variables picked out by the person doing the study. For example, to determine how emissions varied over time, the evaluator would select the years for which measurement was to be made. These years become the fixed or independent variable, and the pollution levels in the chosen years become the dependent vari-

Emissions (millions of metric tons)

Year	Particulate Pollutants	Oxides of Sulfur	Oxides of Nitrogen	Volatile Organic Compounds	Carbon Monoxide
1975	10.3	25.7	19.2	21.0	82.4
1976	9.6	26.3	20.4	22.1	87.2
1977	9.0	26.3	21.0	21.9	83.0
1978	8.9	24.6	21.2	22.4	82.3
1979	9.0	24.6	21.3	21.9	79.5
1980	8.6	23.3	20.7	20.8	77.6
1981	8.1	22.5	20.9	19.4	75.3
1982	7.5	21.4	20.2	18.2	73.6

able. For the table on page A-1, the X axis would look like this:

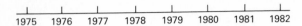

Note that the time span to be represented covers the entire length of the X axis. The Y or vertical axis, which will represent the pollution levels, usually begins with 0 at the bottom and should end at the top with a round number just above the highest value to be represented on the graph. If we were going to graph only the particulates in the table, the Y axis might look like this:

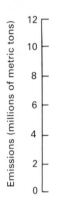

A graph on which we could plot all but the carbon monoxide emissions might look like this:

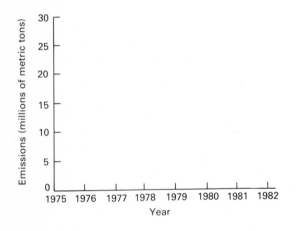

If we wished to plot and compare particulate and nitrogen oxide (NO$_x$) emissions, we would first place points on the graph showing the relationship between particulate matter and year and then connect the points with a line to emphasize the trends.

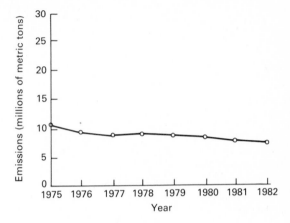

We would then repeat these steps—using different symbols for the points—for the oxides of nitrogen. The final graph would look like this:

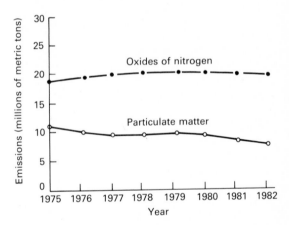

Notice how much more apparent the trends are here than in the table. Notice also how difficult it would be to determine the exact value of emissions each year if the graph were all you had.

Keeping Up to Date

*I*t is literally impossible to publish a *completely* up-to-date chapter on energy, air pollution, or many of the other topics covered in this book. In mid-1984 the United Nations was sending out questionnaires to collect world energy data for 1983. As of May 1, 1984, the U.S. Energy Information Administration had not yet released its 1983 *Annual Energy Review*. This pattern, which is fairly typical, means that much of the data about 1986 will not get into easily accessible reports and summaries until 1988. Because it may take up to 18 months for textbooks to go from finished manuscript to copyright date, they may be several years out of date even when they are updated at the last possible moment. This places the burden of getting the very latest information on instructors and their students. But getting this information is easy if you know the key sources.

THE FEDERAL DEPOSITORY LIBRARY PROGRAM

The Federal Depository Library Program places publications of the federal government in libraries. *Selective* Depository Libraries take those government publications selected by the librarian in charge. *Full* Depositories get all—yes, all—federal publications, but they do not have to keep them all. *Regional* Depositories receive and must keep all government publications in one form or another. For a list of Federal Depository Libraries, write:

U.S. Government Printing Office
Library Programs Service (SL)
Washington, D.C. 20401

To find publications of the federal government in a library, go to the *Government Documents Section* and ask the librarian for help. Many libraries have publications shelved according to department or agency of the federal government. A number of Guides to U.S. Government Publications are available to help you find particular publications or topics. One of these is published by the federal govern-

ment, and several are published by private firms. There is even a "Monthly Catalog of U.S. Government Publications" with a subject index. Additional *subject* bibliographies are published irregularly.

GENERAL SOURCES OF INFORMATION

The following government and private organizations can be contacted for current information on the status of the general environment, mineral and water resources, air and water pollution, land use, solid and hazardous waste, pesticides and toxic substances, food supply, and environmental resource policy and management:

Council on Environmental Quality
722 Jackson Place, N.W.
Washington, DC 20006

Environmental Protection Agency
401 M Street, S.W.
Washington DC 20460

U.S. General Accounting Office
441 G Street, N.W.
Washington, DC 20548
Publishes reports on the effectiveness of government programs and the implementation of public laws. An independent agency in the legislative branch of the federal government.

Publications Office
Office of Technology Assessment (OTA)
U.S. Congress
Washington, DC 20510
Publishes reports on issues and problems relating to technology and the environment. This agency is advisory to Congress.

Chamber of Commerce of the U.S.
Resources Policy Department
1615 H Street, N.W.
Washington, DC 20062
Local chambers of commerce may also have data on more environmental problems.

The Conservation Foundation
1717 Massachusetts Avenue, N.W.
Washington, DC 20036
A nonprofit environmental research organization. The Conservation Foundation conducts independent analyses of environmental policy issues and communicates its findings to policy makers and opinion leaders in government, business, academia, and the press.

Natural Resources Defense Council
122 E. 42nd Street
New York, NY 10168

The National Wildlife Federation
1412 16th Street, N.W.
Washington, DC 20036
A nonprofit conservation organization whose goals are conservation of natural resources and protection of environmental quality. Publishes many environmental books and brochures including an Annual Conservation Directory *listing government agencies and private organizations in the United States and Canada concerned with conservation and resource management.*

Resources for the Future
1616 P Street, N.W.
Washington, DC 20036
Performs research and publishes reports on public policy issues concerning energy and minerals, environmental quality, and renewable natural resources with emphasis on food and agricultural. Resources *is a free quarterly publication of this organization.*

United Nations Environment Programme
New York Liaison Office
Room DC2-0816
United Nations 10017
Generates annual analytical reports on global environmental problems.

World Environment Center, Inc.
605 Third Avenue
17th Floor
New York, NY 10158
A private nonprofit, nonadvocacy organization that provides information on international environmental and development issues.

Worldwatch Institute
1776 Massachusetts Avenue, N.W.
Washington, DC 20036
Issues publications on an irregular basis on environmental problems with a worldwide focus. An annual report, State of the World, *focuses on the interplay between the changing resource base and the economic system.*

THE FOLLOWING LIST OF SOURCES IS GIVEN BY CHAPTER TOPIC.

Energy (Chapter 6)

The following are published by the U.S. Department of Energy's Information Administration (EIA), National Energy Information Center (Forrestal Building, Room IF-048, Washington, DC 20585).

— *Annual Energy Review,* published in late spring or early summer, provides data on energy production, consumption, reserves, and prices for different forms of energy, domestic, and international, for the preceding year and usually the 10–20 years leading up to that year.
— *Annual Energy Outlook* (for projections)
— *Coal Production Annual*
— *EIA Annual Report to Congress*
— *Electric Power (Monthly)* (there is also a *Quarterly*)
— *International Energy Annual* (covers energy production, consumption, and reserves on a global scale.)
— *Monthly Energy Review* (a complete overview of the U.S. energy picture).
— *Natural Gas Monthly* (also *Annual*)
— *Petroleum Marketing Monthly*
— *Quarterly Coal Report* (production, consumption, stocks, etc.)
— *Short-Term Energy Outlook, Vol. I* (a quarterly short-term energy forecast. (Vol. II is published biannually and describes the methods used to make the forecasts.)
— For other periodicals, see: *EIA Publications: New Releases,* described below.

The EIA also publishes an *Energy Information Directory* every six months. This directory gives the names, addresses, and telephone numbers of information resource people within the DOE and other federal agencies (EPA, Department of Transportation, Bureau of the Census, etc.) listed by energy types—for example, natural gas, fusion technology, uranium. This directory also lists state energy offices and DOE research labs and includes both *subject* and *name* indices. The *Energy Information Directory* is free.

The EIA also publishes a free *EIA Publications: New Releases.* This is a bimonthly report on the latest EIA publications and upcoming reports. An *EIA Publications Directory: A Users Guide* annually identifies all of the EIA publications generated in the latest

Appendix B   Keeping Up to Date

calendar year. This directory includes abstracts, subject index, and article-ordering information.

A useful, nonfederal publication, *Annual Review of Energy,* is published every October by Annual Reviews Inc., (a nonprofit scientific publisher) 4139 El Camino Way, Palo Alto, CA 94306. Volume 1 was published in 1976; Volume 10 was published in 1985. Still another particularly useful publication is the annual *Statistical Abstracts of the United States,* published by the Department of Commerce (Bureau of the Census.)

Mineral and Water Resources (Chapter 7)

The two government agencies to contact for information on minerals and mineral consumption are the U.S. Bureau of Mines and the U.S. Geological Survey.

The Bureau of Mines collects and publishes data on mineral resources, including information on production, consumption, prices, shipments, imports, and exports. It also conducts research on all phases of mineral resource technology, including mining, mineral processing, waste disposal, and recycling, as well as on improving health and safety conditions for miners and reducing the environmental impact of the mineral industries.

Bureau of Mines
U.S. Department of Interior
2401 E Street, N.W.
Washington, DC 20241

The U.S. Geological Survey (U.S.G.S.) Geologic Division has information relating to mineral resources.

U.S.G.S. Geologic Division
12201 Sunrise Valley Drive,
Reston, VA 22092

The U.S.G.S. (Interior Department) also has data on water resources. The National Water Data Exchange, located at the U.S.G.S. address above, assists the public in obtaining data on water resources availability. There are 64 local offices assisting in this function as well. Also write:

American Water Resources Association
5410 Grosvenor Lane, Suite 220
Bethesda, MD 20814

Publishes the Water Resources Bulletin, Hydrata-News and Views Newsletter, *and a Technical Proceedings Series.*

See electronic information databases below under "water pollution."

Population and Food Production (Chapter 8)

Population Reference Bureau
2213 M Street N.W.
Washington, DC 20037
This is a private, nonprofit organization aimed at providing educational materials on population trends and policies both national and worldwide.

U.S. Department of Commerce
Bureau of the Census
Washington, DC 22161
Publishes the Statistical Abstracts of the U.S. *annually. Conducts a general census of the U.S. population annually.*

American Association for World Health
515 22nd Street, N.W.
Washington, DC 20037
This agency has general information on international health problems and publishes a quarterly newsletter.

U.S. Department of Agriculture
Soil Conservation Service
12th Street and Independence Avenue, S.W.
P.O. Box 2890
Washington, DC 20013
Soil Conservation employees work with local soil and water conservation districts to convince landowners to use soil and water conservation measures on their lands. Publications on a variety of topics are available to the public.

U.S. International Development Cooperation Agency
Agency for International Development
Office of Public Inquiries
21st and C Street N.W.
Washington, DC 20523
Publishes numerous country-specific reports and evaluations.

Air Pollution (Chapters 9–11)

Air pollution is another fast-changing topic. New studies and experiments are being conducted continuously. The results of studies on the health effects of air pollutants, studies on the effects of pollutants on materials and vegetation, and studies on the effects of air pollutants (e.g., acid precipitation) on ecosystems are summarized in occasional reports, criteria documents, and periodicals published by the EPA and various conservation organizations. The following regular reports and periodicals should be particularly useful:

Annual Reports Of the Council On Environmental Quality (The 14th Annual report covering 1983 was released in 1984.)
Council on Environmental Quality
722 Jackson Place, N.W.
Washington, DC 20006
The Annual Reports are available from the U.S. Government Printing Office, Washington, DC 20402.

Annual National Monitoring, Air Quality, and Emission Trends Reports
EPA Office of Air Quality Planning and Standards
Research Triangle Park, NC 27709
These are also available via the National Technical Information Service (see below).

EPA Publications Bibliography a quarterly bulletin (with an annual cumulation) identifying and abstracting publications released by the EPA. Available only from the National Technical Information Service (see below).

Canadian Publications
Environmental Protection Service Inquiries and Publications
Environment Canada
Ottawa, Ontario, KIA 1C8, Canada

Air Pollution Titles: A Guide to the Current Air Pollution Literature (issued bimonthly)
Center for Air Environment Studies
Pennsylvania State University
226 Fenske Laboratory
University Park, PA 16802

Acid Precipitation Digest (monthly)
Summarizes current news, research, and events related to acid rain. Published in conjunction with the Acid Rain Information Clearinghouse, which is a project of the:
Center for Environmental Information
33 S. Washington Street
Rochester, NY 14608

The Government Documents section of your nearest Federal Depository Library will have guides to *all* federal air pollution publications.

Electronic Databases and Reference Sources

Air pollution publications are included in the following reference sources and electronic databases:

— National Technical Information Service
— Chemical Abstracts
— Biological Abstracts
— Enviroline
— Pollution Abstracts
— Water Resources Abstracts
— Environmental Law Reporter

This is only a partial list of the databases available. Ask your reference librarian for help.

WRITE FOR THE LATEST INFORMATION

The interested reader might also write to the following organizations and groups for lists of recent publications and or for more specific information:

Congressional Research Service
101 Independence Avenue, S.E.
Washington, DC 20540

Distributes information packets on acid rain and other pollution topics. Although this organization works exclusively for the members of Congress, it publishes "Info Packs" as briefing aids for members of Congress; these may be passed along to constituents in response to inquiries. The CRS also publishes summaries of legislation and issues before the Congress; these are available to the general public through the Superintendent of Documents.

Environmental Protection Agency
(*see above*)

National Technical Information Service
5285 Port Royal Road
Springfield, VA 22161

Emission Control Technology Division
Office of Mobile Sources
Environmental Protection Agency
2565 Plymouth Road
Ann Arbor, MI 48105
Responsible for developing regulations for the federal government's motor vehicle emission control program; distributes information on emission standards for cars, trucks, and buses.

The Conservation Foundation
(*see above*)

Air Pollution Control Association
P.O. Box 2861
Pittsburgh, PA 15230

Natural Resources Defense Council
(*see above*)

Water Pollution (Chapter 12)

For up-to-date information, consult Environmental Protection Agency publications in the Government Documents section of your Federal Depository Library. Here are some places to which you can write for recent information:

American Water Resources Association
(*see above*)

Office of Water
Environmental Protection Agency
(*see above*)

U.S. Department of Commerce
National Technical Information Service
(*see above*)

Water Pollution Control Federation
Technical Services Department
2626 Pennsylvania Avenue
Washington, DC 20037

Other reference sources and electronic databases (ask your reference librarian for help in getting access to these):

— Aqualine (Water Research Center, England)
— Chemical Abstracts
— Enviroline
— "IRIS" (EPA)
— National Technical Information Service (NTIS)
— Pollution Abstracts
— Selected Water Resources Abstracts
— Water Resources Abstracts

Pesticides, Toxic Chemicals, and Radioisotopes (Chapter 13)

Contact the following agencies for more information on persistent chemicals.

U.S. Department of Agriculture (Pesticides)
Agriculture Research Service
14th Street and Independence Avenue, S.W.
Washington, DC 20250
This division coordinates the pesticide program.

U.S. EPA
(*see above*)

Also the American Organization for World Health and the U.S. General Accounting Office (address above).

For periodic environmental assessments, see the Council on Environmental Quality (annual) and The Conservation Foundation (biannual) (Addresses above).

Solid and Hazardous Waste Disposal (Chapter 15)

Contact the following agencies for current information on solid and hazardous waste:

U.S. Environmental Protection Agency
Office of Solid Waste
Office of Program Management and Support
401 M Street, S.W.
Washington, DC 20460

National Solid Waste Management Association
1730 Rhode Island Avenue, N.W.
Suite 100
Washington, DC 20036
An organization composed of people working in the waste management industry (collection, processing, and disposal). Compiles statistics and provides information on waste management and resource recovery.

Also see general environmental listing above.

Noise (Chapter 16)

See the Occupational Safety and Health Administration Section in the Government Documents section of your library. Write: National Association of Noise-Control Officials, c/o Edward J. DiPolvere, 65 Prospect Street, Trenton, NJ 08618.

Land and Resource Management (Chapter 17)

Bureau of Land Management
Renewable Resources (210)
U.S. Department of the Interior
Washington, DC 20240
Programs include management of forests, rangelands, wildlife habitat, and endangered species.

Fish and Wildlife Service
U.S. Department of the Interior
Main Interior Building
Washington, DC 20240

Forest Service
U.S. Department of Agriculture
14th Street and Independence Avenue, S.W.
Washington, DC 20013

Surface Mining Reclamation and Enforcement
U.S. Department of Interior
1951 Constitution Avenue, N.W.
Washington, DC 20240
See also listings in Chapter 7.

Think Metric

As a nation, we use both metric and English units of measurement. Depending on what you read, you may encounter either system. Scientists use the metric system, but many federal agencies report data in English units. We have used both in this book in the interests of clarity and familiarity. In most places we have provided conversion equivalents.

The conversion charts included here will be useful in putting comparable volumes, weights, distances, areas, or temperatures into perspective.

Temperature Conversion

Celsius, °C	Fahrenheit, °F
160	320
100	212 (water boils)
60	140°
37	98.6 (body temp)
32	90
20	68
10	50
0	32 (freezing)

(Celsius temperature × 1.8) + 32 = Fahrenheit temperature
(Fahrenheit temperature − 32) × 0.56 = Celsius temperature

FROM METRIC
(approximate to within 2%)

TO METRIC

To Convert			To Convert		
From	To	Multiply by	From	To (Symbol)	Multiply by
millimeters	inches	0.04	inches	millimeters (mm)	25
centimeters	inches	0.4	inches	centimeters (cm)	2.5
meters	feet	3.3	feet	meters (m)	0.3
meters	yards	1.1	yards	meters (m)	0.9
kilometers	miles	0.62	miles	kilometers (km)	1.6
square centimeters	square inches	0.155	square inches	square centimeters (cm^2)	6.5
square meters	square yards	1.2	square yards	square meters (m^2)	0.84
hectares	acres	2.5	acres	hectares (ha)	0.4
square kilometers	square miles	0.39	square miles	square kilometers (km^2)	2.6
cubic centimeters	cubic inches	0.06	cubic inches	cubic centimeters (cm^3)	16.4
cubic meters	cubic feet	35	cubic feet	cubic meters (m^3)	0.028
cubic meters	cubic yards	1.3	cubic yards	cubic meters (m^3)	0.76
liters	pints	2.1	pints	liters (L)	0.47
liters	quarts	1.06	quarts	liters (L)	0.95
liters	gallons	0.26	gallons	liters (L)	3.8
grams	ounces	0.035	ounces	grams (g)	28
kilograms	pounds	2.2	pounds	kilograms (kg)	0.45
metric tons	short tons (2000 lb)	1.1	short tons (2000 lb)	metric tons (t)	0.91
metric tons	long tons (2240 lb)	1.0	long tons (2240 lb)	metric tons (t)	1.0

Credits*

PART OPENER I
Main photo, Philip Gendreau, Bettman Archives. Insert, Tom Stack/TOM STACK AND ASSOCIATES.

CHAPTER ONE

Photographs
P. 6, National Oceanic and Atmospheric Administration. P. 8, United States Forest Service. P. 11, Grant Heilman Photography. P. 12, United States Department of Agriculture. P. 17, United States Department of Agriculture, Soil Conservation Service.

CHAPTER TWO

Photographs
P. 23, United States Department of Agriculture, Office of Governmental and Public Affairs. P. 33, Grant Heilman Photography, Runk/Schoenberger. P. 33, Grant Heilman Photography, Hal Harrison. P. 37. United States Department of Agriculture, Office of Governmental and Public Affairs. P. 40, United States Department of Agriculture, Office of Governmental and Public Affairs.

Figures
P. 25, Fig. 2.4: Data from Kormondy, 1984; Odum, 1983. P. 26: graph on right from *Life: The Science of Biology* (1983) by W. K. Purves and G. H. Orians. P. 27: From Purves and Orians, *Life: The Science of Biology* (1983). P. 32, Fig. 2.8: Data from Odum, 1983; Kormondy, 1984; Woodwill, 1970.

Tables
P. 29, Table 2.1: From Odum, 1983; Monteith, 1965. Adapted with permission from *Basic Ecology* by Eugene P. Odum. Copyright © 1983 by CBS College Publishing. Reprinted by permissions of Saunders College, CBS College Publishing; and with permission from *Annals of Botany,* Vol. 29, pp. 17–37, 1965. Copyright by Academic Press, Inc. (London) Ltd.

CHAPTER THREE

Photographs
P. 45, Courtesy of National Parks Service. P. 52, Grant Heilman Photography. P. 58, Grant Heilman Photography, Runk/Schoenberger.

Figures
P. 59, Fig. 3.10: From *Limnology,* By William H. Amos, 1969, published by LaMotte Chemical Co., Box 329, Chestertown, MD 21620. P. 60, Fig. 3.11: Mertz, 1981. P. 61, Fig. 3.12: Brush, 1982, p. 23.

Tables
P. 44, Table 3.1: Data from Kormondy, 1984.

CHAPTER FOUR

Photographs
P. 65, United States Department of the Interior, Fish and Wildlife Service. P. 68, United States Forest Service. P. 75, United States Department of the Interior, National Park Service. P. 81, Jeff Foott/TOM STACK AND ASSOCIATES. P. 82, Grant Heilman Photography.

Figures
p. 78, Fig. 4.11: Data from Gause, 1934.

Tables
P. 70, Table 4.1: Adapted from Deavey (1947), used with permission of the *Quarterly Review of Biology,* Vol. 22, p. 296, 1947. P. 77, Table 4.3: Reprinted with permission from *National Ecosystems* by W. B. Clapham, Jr. (copyright 1973 by W. B. Clapham, Jr.) as adapted from G. L. Clark, *Elements of Ecology,* New York: John Wiley and Sons, Inc., 1954.

CHAPTER FIVE

Photographs
P. 103, United States Department of the Interior. P. 104, Kenneth W. Fink, Bruce Coleman, Inc., New York. P. 108, Department of Economic Development and Planning, Alaska Travel Division. P. 108, Neg. #330830 Courtesy Department Library Services, American Museum of Natural History.

Figures
P. 90, Fig. 5.2: Swanson, 1973. P. 91, Fig. 5.3: From Volpe, E. Peter, UNDERSTANDING EVOLUTION 5th ed. © 1967, 1970, 1977, 1981, 1985 Wm. C. Brown Publishers, Dubuque, Iowa. All Rights Reserved. Reprinted by permission. P. 100: From Purves and Orians, *Life: The Science of Biology* (1983). P. 101, Fig. 5.7: Swanson, 1973. P. 105: © The Washington Post.

Tables
P. 110, Table 5.1: R. Dasmann, *Environmental Science,* © John Wiley & Sons, Inc.

PART OPENER II
Main Photo, United States Department of Interior, National Park Service. Insert, P. G. and E. News Bureau.

CHAPTER SIX

Photographs
P. 133, Courtesy of Boston Edison Company. P. 138, Jim McNee/TOM STACK AND ASSOCIATES. P. 144, Alyeska Pipeline Service Company. P. 144, Department of Energy. P. 148, Courtesy of Solar One Visitor Center, Daggett, CA. P. 154, Department of Energy, National Laboratory at Oak Ridge, TN. P. 158, Gary Millburn/TOM STACK AND ASSOCIATES. P. 163, Stock Boston, John Running. P. 166, Courtesy of Camp Dresser and McKee, Inc., Boston, MA. P. 169, Department of Energy, Dick Peabody. P. 170, United States Department of Energy, Lockheed Missiles and Space Company, Inc. P. 173, Dave Baird/TOM STACK AND ASSOCIATES. P. 181, Associated Press Photo. P. 186, Courtesy of Solaron Corporation, Englewood, CO.

Figures
P. 117, Fig. 6.1: Adapted from Hubbert, 1962. P. 118, Fig. 6.2: Adapted from Cook, 1971. Reprinted with permission from *Technology Review,* copyright 1971. P. 118, Fig. 6.3: DOE/EIA, 1983, *Annual Energy Review,* and the Conservation Foundation, 1982. P. 120, Fig. 6.4: DOE/EIA, *Monthly Energy Review,* De-

*For complete sources of figures and tables, see chapter reference lists.

cember 1983. P. 121, Fig.6.5: Adapted from Population Reference Bureau, *Interchange*, Vol. 6, No. 1, January 1977; United Nations, *World Energy Supplies, 1950–1974*, 1976, and *Selected World Demographic Indicators by Countries, 1950–2000*, May 1975. P. 121, Fig. 6.6: Department of Economics and Social Affairs, United Nations, *World Energy Supplies, 1950–1974*, 1976, *World Energy Supplies, 1973–1978*, 1979, After Population Reference Bureau, *Interchange*, Vol. 6, No. 1, January 1977. P. 122, Fig. 6.7: United States Bureau of Census and United States Bureau of Mines. P. 123, Fig. 6.8: DOE/EIA, 1982. P. 124, Fig. 6.9: DOE/EIA, *Annual Energy Review*, 1983. P. 125, Fig. 6.10: Dorf, 1978; DOE/EIA, *Annual Energy Review*, 1983. P. 127, Fig. 6.11: DOE/EIA, *Annual Energy Review*, 1983. P. 128, Fig. 6.12: DOE/EIA, *Annual Energy Review*, 1982. P. 128, Fig. 6.13: Department of Energy, 1980. P. 129, Fig. 6.14: DOE/EIA, *Annual Energy Review*, 1982. P. 130, Fig. 6.15: Adapted from Steinhart and Steinhart, 1974, p. 312. P. 133, Fig. 6.16: Federal Energy Administration, Office of Conservation, *Energy Conservation*, 1975. P. 134, Fig. 6.17: Dupree, Herman, Miller, and Hillier, 1976; DOE/EIA, *International Energy Annual*, 1979; and *Annual Energy Review*, 1983. P. 135, Fig. 6.18: DOE/EIA, *Annual Energy Review*, 1983. P. 135, Fig. 6.19: DOE/EIA, *Coal Production Annual*, 1982. P. 138, Fig. 6.20: Adapted from Tennessee Valley Authority. Copyright © 1983. The Courier-Journal. Reprinted with permission. P. 139, Fig. 6.21: Office of Fossil Energy, Quarterly Reports, Coal Gasification, 1976 and 1977, Energy Research and Development Administration. P. 140, Fig. 6.22: Data from M. K. Hubbert in Duggan and Cloutier, 1975. P. 141, Fig. 6.23: DOE/EIA, *Annual Energy Review*, 1983. P. 141, Fig. 6.24: Data from Dolton et al., 1982. P. 142, Fig. 6.25: Environmental Quality, 1982. P. 145, Fig. 6.26: *Fossil Energy Research Program of the Energy Research and Development Administration,* 1977, illustration adapted from *Exxon USA*. Courtesy Exxon Corporation, © 1982. P. 146, Fig. 6.27: DOE/EIA, *Annual Energy Review*, 1983. P. 161, Fig. 6.33: DOE/EIA, *Annual Energy Review*, 1983; DOE/EIA, *International Energy Annual*, 1982; and the Nuclear Regulatory Commission, direct communication. P. 162, Fig. 6.34: Data from Organization for Economic Cooperation and Development. P. 166, Fig. 6.37: Bjork and Granelli, *Ambio*, Vol. 7, No. 4, 1978. P. 167, Fig. 6.38: Reed and Lerner, 1973. Copyright 1973 by the AAAS. Courtesy of authors. P. 177, Fig. 6.43: DOE/EIA, *Annual Energy Review*, 1983. P. 180, Fig. 6.44: DOE/EIA, *Annual Energy Review*, 1982. P. 184, Fig. 6.45: DOE/EIA, *Annual Energy Outlook*, 1983.

Tables
P. 119, Table 6.1: Adapted from "The American Energy Consumer," Copyright the Ford Foundation, 1975. P. 124, Table 6.2: Up to 1960, Dorf (1978); after 1960, United States Department of Energy, 1983a. P. 125, Table 6.3: Department of Energy/Energy Information Administration, *Annual Energy Review*, 1982, and *Annual Energy Review*, 1983. P. 125, Table 6.4: Up to 1940, Dorf (1978); after 1940, Department of Energy, 1983a; projected year, United States Department of Energy, 1984b. P. 127, Table 6.5: Dorf (1978) and Department of Energy/Energy Information Administration, *Annual Energy Review*, 1982. P. 130, Table 6.6: Pimentel and Dazhong, "Technological Changes in Energy Use in U.S. Agricultural Production," in Gliessman, S., ed., *Research Approaches in Agricultural Ecology: An Approach.* New York, Springer, 1985. P. 132, Table 6.7: Congressional Budget Office, 1982. P. 132, Table 6.8: United States Department of Transportation. P. 133, Table 6.9: Department of Energy, *Monthly Energy Review*, July 1980. P. 151, Table 6.10: Department of Energy/Energy Information Administration, *Annual Energy Review*, 1983. P. 155, Table 6.11: National Academy of Sciences. P. 175, Table 6.12: Adapted from Snell, Achenbach, and Petersen, "Energy Conser-

vation in New Housing Design," *Science,* Vol. 192, pp. 1305–1311, 1976. Copyright 1976 by the AAAS.

Cartoons
P. 160, (A) Don Wright, *The Miami News;* (B) Reprinted by permission of the Courier-Journal and Hugh Haynie.

Quote
P. 159: Quote from Dr. Alfvén reprinted by permission of *The Bulletin of Atomic Scientists,* a magazine of science and world affairs. Copyright © 1972 by the Educational Foundation for Nuclear Science, Chicago, IL 60637.

CHAPTER SEVEN

Photographs
P. 196, Courtesy of Reynolds Aluminum. P. 205, Fredrik D. Bodin. P. 217, Courtesy of Los Angeles Department of Water and Power. P. 219, United States Department of Agriculture, Office of Governmental and Public Affairs.

Figures
P. 177, Fig. 7.3: Council on Environmental Quality, 1980. P. 198, Fig. 7.4: Council on Environmental Quality, 1980, Vol. II, p. 28. P. 199, Fig. 7.5: Data from Tilton, 1977. P. 203, Fig. 7.8: United States Bureau of Mines, 1979a, p. 18. P. 204, Fig. 7.9: National Commission on Materials Policy, 1973, p. 4D-5. P. 206, Fig. 7.10: United States Environmental Protection Agency, *Environmental Outlook,* 1980, Fig. II.1, p. 611; and Federal Reserve Board. P. 207, Fig. 7.11: United States Bureau of Mines, 1979a, p. 36. P. 208, Fig. 7.12: United States Geological Survey, 1977. P. 209, Fig. 7.13: United States Environmental Protection Agency, 1980, p. 449. P. 210, Fig. 7.14: United States Water Resources Council, 1978, Vol. I, pp. 30, 31. P. 211, Fig. 7.15: United States Water Resources Council, 1978, Vol. 2, Part IV, p. 6. P. 212, Fig. 7.17: Data from James, Kammerer, and Murray, 1976. P. 213, Fig. 7.18: United States Water Resources Council, 1978, p. 5. P. 216, Fig. 7.20: After Gerald Meyer, 1979, in United States Water Resources Council, 1980.

Tables
P. 194, Table 7.1: Data from Dasmann, 1972. P. 198, Table 7.2: Council on Environmental Quality, 1980; United States Bureau of Mines, 1979.

CHAPTER EIGHT

Photographs
P. 226, Courtesy of the United Nations. P. 236, Taurus Photos, Inc. P. 240, Taurus Photos, Inc., Richard J. Quataeri. P. 242, Eric Kroll, Joel Gordon Photography, 1974. P. 248, Courtesy of the Canadian Government Travel Bureau. P. 249, Taurus Photos, Inc., J. Somers.

Figures
P. 228, Bonus 8.1: World Bank, 1980. P. 230, Fig. 8.2: Council on Environmental Quality, 1980b, Vol. II, p. 17. P. 231, Fig. 8.3: T. Frejka, and W. P. Mauldin in Mauldin, 1980, p. 156. Copyright 1980 by the AAAS. P. 233, Fig. 8.5: Mauldin, 1980, p. 152. Copyright 1980 by the AAAS. P. 234, Fig. 8.6: Council on Environmental Quality, 1980b, Vol. II, p. 13. P. 234, Fig. 8.7: Coale, 1983, p. 829. P. 235, Fig. 8.8: United States Department of Commerce, Bureau of Census. P. 238, Fig. 8.10: Council on Environmental Quality, 1980b, Vol. II, p. 41. P. 245, Fig. 8.12: Council on Environmental Quality, 1980b, Vol. II, p. 87. P. 247, Fig. 8.13: Council on Environmental Quality, 1980b, Vol. II, p. 106.

Tables
P. 227, Table 8.1: Brown, 1984a, 1984b. Data from Worldwatch

Institute estimates. P. 241, Table 8.2: Berelson, 1969. P. 243, Table 8.3: Brown, 1984. Data from United Nations Food and Agriculture Organization, *Production Yearbook* (Rome: Various Years); United States Department of Agriculture, *Foreign Agriculture Circular,* August 1983; author's estimates.

PART OPENER III
Main photo, United States Department of Interior, National Park Service. Insert, Courtesy of Camp Dresser and McKee, Inc., Boston, MA.

CHAPTER NINE

Photographs
P. 259, Grant Heilman Photography. P. 260, Clerk of the Works, Dean and Chapter of London. P. 261, Clerk of the Works, Dean and Chapter of London. P. 268, Grant Heilman Photography, Barry L. Runk. P. 273, Dr. Roger Cheng, Atmospheric Sciences Research Center, SUNY, Albany. P. 282, Courtesy of Camp Dresser and McKee, Inc., Boston, MA.

Figures
P. 266, Fig. 9.2: *Air Quality Criteria for Nitrogen Oxide,* United States Environmental Protection Agency, April 1977b, p. 4.4–2. P. 270, Fig. 9.4: *Air Quality Criteria for Photochemical Oxidants,* United States Department HEW, National Air Pollution Control Administration, March 1970, and Air Quality Criteria for Ozone and Other Photochemical Oxidants, EPA 600/8–87–004, 1978. P. 275, Fig. 9.5: Conservation Foundation, 1984. P. 274, Fig. 9.6: Peterson and Salvia, *Environment,* Vol. 19, pp. 66–79, 1968; a publication of the Helen Dwight Reid Educational Foundation. P. 284, Fig. 9.8: United States Environmental Protection Agency, 1977.

Tables
P. 265: Adapted from a compilation by Dr. Warren B. Crummett, Dow Chemical Co. P. 279, Table 9.2: From Various Sources as Reported by Schlesinger, 1979. P. 281, Table 9.4: United States Environmental Protection Agency, 1984b. P. 283, Table 9.5, Reproduced by permission from G. L. Waldbott, *Health Effects of Environmental Pollution,* 2nd ed., St. Louis, 1978, The C.V. Mosby Co.

CHAPTER TEN

Photographs
P. 310, Grant Heilman Photography, Alan Pitcairn. P. 311, Taurus Photos, Inc., E. S. Beckwith. P. 317, The Columbia Daily Spectator/Art Resource, NY.

Figures
P. 298, Fig. 10.6: Reproduced by permission from G.L. Waldbott, *Health Effects of Environmental Pollution,* 2nd ed., St. Louis, 1978, The C.V. Mosby Co. P. 309. Fig. 10.7 (b), (c), (d), (e): Patrick et al., *Science,* Vol. 211, pp. 446–448, 1981. P. 311, Fig. 10.8: United States Environmental Protection Agency, 1980. P. 312, Fig. 10.9: Adapted from Ontario Ministry of the Environment and Commission on Air Quality, 1981. P. 313, Fig. 10.10: Adapted from United States Environmental Protection Agency, 1981. P. 316, Fig. 10.12: (a) Herrmann and Johnson, "Acid Rain: A Water Resources Issue for the '80's" *Proceedings of the Water Resources Association International Symposium on Hydrometeorology,* 1983; (b) Brookhaven National Laboratory. Reprinted with permission from *Technological Review,* copyright 1982. P. 319, Fig. 10.14: Council on Environmental Quality, 1983; From G. M. Woodwell et al., "The Carbon Dioxide Question." Copyright © 1978 by Scientific American, Inc. All rights reserved.

Tables
P. 297, Table 10.4: From *Chemical Contamination in the Human Environment* by M. Lippmann and R. B. Schlesinger. Copyright © 1979 by Oxford University Press, Inc. Reprinted by permission. P. 302, Table 10.5: Mausner and Bahn, 1974. P. 306, Table 10.6: From *Chemical Contamination in the Human Environment* by M. Lippmann and R. B. Schlesinger. Copyright © 1979 by Oxford University Press, Inc. Adapted by permission. P. 317, Table 10.7: From *Chemical Contamination in the Human Environment* by M. Lippmann and R. B. Schelsinger. Copyright © 1979 by Oxford University Press, Inc. Reprinted by permission.

CHAPTER ELEVEN

Photographs
P. 333, Courtesy of Carnegie Library, Pittsburgh. P. 337, Dave Baird/TOM STACK AND ASSOCIATES. P. 347, Courtesy of Bethlehem Steel. P. 349, Dave Davidson/TOM STACK AND ASSOCIATES.

Figures
P. 326, Fig. 11.1: 1979 Annual Report of the Council on Environmental Quality. P. 327, Fig. 11.2: United States Department of Commerce, Environmental Protection Agency 230/3–79–001, p. 44. Cost of all forms of pollution control, 1972–1982. P. 328, Fig. 11.3: United States Department of Commerce. P. 329, Fig. 11.4: Environmental Protection Agency; data from Data Resources, Inc. P. 330, Fig. 11.5: Environmental Protection Agency; data from Data Resources, Inc. P. 331, Fig. 11.6: Barrett and Waddell, *Cost of Air Pollution Damage: A Status Report,* United States Environmental Protection Agency, 1973, pp. 59–60. P. 340, Figs. 11.9, 11.10: Conservation Foundation, 1984. P. 341, Fig. 11.11: Data from *United States News & World Report,* February 28, 1983. P. 344, Fig. 11.12: Reproduced by permission from G.L. Waldbott, *Health Effects of Environmental Pollution,* 2nd ed., St. Louis, 1978, The C. V. Mosby Co.

Tables
P. 332, Table 11.1: Barrett and Waddell, 1973, p. 9. P. 333, Table 11.2: Barrett and Waddell, 1973, p. 35. P. 338, Table 11.3: Annual Reports of the Council on Environmental Quality and various Environmental Protection Agency publications. P. 342, Table 11.4: Tenth Annual Report, Council on Environmental Quality. P. 345, Table 11.6: Environmental Protection Agency.

CHAPTER TWELVE

Photographs
P. 359, United States Environmental Protection Agency–Documerica. P. 365, Courtesy of the Bureau of Sport Fisheries and Wildlife. P. 367, United States Department of Agriculture. P. 371, United States Department of Energy. P. 372, Courtesy of the Bureau of Sport Fisheries and Wildlife.

Figures
P. 363, Fig. 12.6: *Man and the Environment,* by R. H. Wagner, W. W. Norton & Company, Inc., 1971. P. 371, Fig. 12.8: Reproduced from "Petroleum in the Marine Environment," 1975, with permission of the National Academy of Sciences, Washington, DC. P. 377, Fig. 12.9: Environmental Protection Agency. P. 379, Fig. 12.10: Redrawn from Environmental Protection Agency publications. P. 390, Fig. 12.17: The Conservation Foundation, 1984. P. 391, Fig. 12.18: Council on Environmental Quality, 1980, p. 667. P. 392, Fig. 12.19: Freeman, 1979.

Tables
P. 358, Table 12.1: Lund, *Ambio,* Vol. 7, No. 2, 1978. P. 364, Table 12.3: *Report of the Committee on Water Quality Criteria.* Federal Water Pollution Control Administration, Washington,

D.C., 1968. P. 367, Table 12.4: From Nelson L. Nemerow, *Industrial Water Pollution,* © 1978, Addison-Wesley, Reading Massachusetts. Table 5.3. Reprinted with permission. Also *Statistical Abstract of the United States,* 140th Edition, United States Department of Commerce, Washington, D.C., 1984. P. 367, Table 12.5: Wadleigh, 1968. *Wastes in Relations to Agriculture and Forestry,* United States Department of Agriculture, Miscellaneous Publication No. 1065, March 1968. P. 369, Table 12.6: "Acid Mine Water: Its Control Reduces Stream Pollution," *Mechanization,* Parts I and II, Vol. 15. Data for Natural Waterways from Lippmann and Schlesinger, 1979. P. 380, Table 12.7: Schlesinger, 1979, pp. 97 and 99. P. 383, Table 12.8: Adapted from American Chemical Society, *Cleaning Our Environment: The Chemical Basis for Action,* 1969.

Mini-Glossary
Pp. 384–385: United States Environmental Protection Agency, Water Quality Office Superintendent of Documents, *A Primer on Waste Water Treatment,* 1971.

CHAPTER THIRTEEN

Photographs
P. 404, Grant Heilman Photography. P. 408, United States Department of Agriculture. P. 417, Woodfin Camp & Associates, Inc., Wendy Watriss.

Figures
P. 403, Fig. 13.1: Data from Cottam, 1965, "The ecologists role in problems of pesticide pollution," *Bioscience,* Vol. 15, pp. 457–463, and Rudd, 1964, *Pesticides and the Living Landscape,* University of Wisconsin Press. P. 407, Fig. 13.2: United States Department of Health, Education and Welfare, *Report of the Secretary's Commission on Pesticides,* Parts I and II, 1969. P. 409, Fig. 13.3: United States Environmental Protection Agency, *Environmental Outlook 1980,* p. 378. P. 411, Fig. 13.4: Grier, 1982. Copyright 1982 by the AAAS. P. 413, Fig. 13.5: The Conservation Foundation, *State of the Environment: An Assessment at Mid-Decade,* 1984, p. 57. P. 415, Fig. 13.6: Westöö and Norén, *Ambio,* Vol. 7, No. 2, 1978. P. 416, Fig. 13.7: National Academy of Science as found in Conservation Foundation, *State of the Environment: An Assessment at Mid-Decade,* 1984. Reproduced with permission from *Toxicity Testing: Strategies to Determine Needs and Priorities,* (1984) National Academy Press, Washington, D.C. P. 420, Fig. 13.8: Adkisson et al., 1982. Copyright 1982 by the AAAS. P. 423, Fig. 13.9: *EPA Journal,* July/August, 1979, Washington, D.C.: Office of Public Affairs.

Tables
P. 405, Table 13.1: *From Chemical Contamination in the Human Environment,* by M. Lippmann and R. B. Schlesinger, Copyright © 1979 by Oxford University Press, Inc. Adapted with permission; compiled from Salvato, J. A., Jr., *Environmental Engineering and Sanitation,* New York: Wiley-Interscience, 1972. P. 410, Table 13.2: Courtesy: Scientists Institute for Public Information, New York, NY. Reprinted from *Pesticides,* 1970. P. 412, Table 13.3: Campbell, A. D., Horwitz, W., Burke, J. A., Jelinek, C. F., Rodricks, J. V., and Shibko, S. I., "Food Additives and Contaminants," pp. 167–69 in *Handbook of Physiology, Section 9, Reaction to Environmental Agents.* D. H. K. Lee, H. L. Falk, and S. D. Murphy (eds.), Bethesda, Md: American Physiological Society, 1977. Pp. 413, 414, Tables 13.4, 13.5: S. McKerchner and F. W. Plapp, Jr., "Measuring the Residue," *Environment,* Vol. 22, pp. 10 and 12. P. 415, Table 15.6: Environmental Protection Agency.

CHAPTER FOURTEEN

Photographs
P. 429 (both), Taurus Photos, Inc., Martin M. Rotker, P. 442,

Taurus Photos, Inc., Alfred Pasieka. P. 445 (left), Grant Heilman Photography. P. 445 (right), Taurus Photos, Inc., Laimute E. Druskis. P. 541, Stock Boston, R. P. Kingston.

Figures
p. 428, Fig. 14.1: Data from United States National Cancer Center for Health Statistics and United States Bureau of Census. Reprinted by permission from *CA-A Cancer Journal for Clinicians,* ©1985, American Cancer Society, Inc. P. 429, Fig. 14.2: Adapted from Suss, Kinzel, and Scribner, *Cancer—Experiments and Concepts,* Springer Verlag, 1973. P. 437, Fig. 14.4: Courtesy American Cancer Society, *Cancer News,* 1983. P. 437, Fig. 14.5: Mason et al., 1975. P. 438, Fig. 14.6: Mason et al., 1975. Pp. 439, 443, Figs. 14.7, 14.8: From J.Cairns, "The Cancer Problem," Copyright © 1975 by Scientific American, Inc. All rights reserved. P. 446, Fig. 14.10: Data from Harris, Page, and Reiches, 1977. Pp. 447, 448, Figs. 14.11, 14.12: Suss, Kinzel, and Scribner, *Cancer—Experiments and Concepts,* Springer Verlag, 1973. P. 449, Fig. 14.13: From J. Cairns, "The Cancer Problem," Copyright © 1975 by Scientific American, Inc. All rights reserved. P. 450, Fig. 14.14: Lyon et al., 1976. Reprinted by permission of the New England Journal of Medicine, Vol. 294, No. 3, p. 131.

Tables
P. 432, Table 14.1: Data from Vaughn, 1976; Waldbott, 1978. Pp. 435, 436, Tables 14.2, 14.3: Adapted from L. Tomatis et al., "Evaluation of the Carcinogenicity of Chemicals: A Review of the Monograph Program of the International Agency for Research on Cancer (1971–1977)," *Cancer Research,* Vol. 38, pp. 877–885, 1978, Table 2. P. 441, Table 14.4: National Cancer Institute.

CHAPTER FIFTEEN

Photographs
P. 466, Dave Baird/TOM STACK AND ASSOCIATES. P. 479, Courtesy of Camp Dresser and McKee, Inc., Boston, MA. P. 485, Taurus Photos, Inc., Eric Kroll. P. 490, Taurus Photos, Inc., Eric Kroll.

Figures
P. 461, Fig. 15.2: Franklin Associates, Ltd. for United States Environmental Protection Agency, Office of Solid Waste as shown in The Council of Environmental Quality Annual Report, 1979, pp. 259. P. 462, Fig. 16.3: *Outlook 1980,* United States Environmental Protection Agency. P. 463, Fig. 15.4: Franklin Associates, Ltd. for United States Environmental Protection Agency, Office of Solid Waste as shown in The Council on Environmental Quality Annual Report, 1979, p. 258. P. 468, Fig. 15.7: Lahey and Connor, 1983. Reprinted with permission from *Technology Review,* copyright 1983. P. 470, Fig. 15.9: Franklin Associates, 1979, p. 21. P. 471, Fig. 15.10: Copyright © 1977. *The Courier Journal.* Reprinted with permission. Adapted from schematic by Grumman Ecosystems Corporation. P. 476, Fig. 15.12: Copyright © 1979. *The Courier Journal.* Reprinted with permission. P. 478, Fig. 15.13: United States Environmental Protection Agency, Review of Activities of Major Firms in the Commercial Hazardous Waste Management Industry, 1981 Update, May 7, 1982. P. 484, Fig. 15.15: Lash, 1979. Reprinted with the permission of *The Amicus Journal.* P. 488, Fig. 15.16: United States General Accounting Office, 1977.

Tables
P. 467, Table 15.1: United States General Accounting Office, 1977. P. 469, Table 15.2: Lahey and Connor, 1983. Reprinted with permission from *Technology Review,* copyright 1983. P. 470, Table 15.3: Nichols, Douglas R., Jr., "Are We Ready to Convert Solid Waste to Energy—Profitably?" *Resource Recovery and Energy Review,* Vol. 4, No. 4, Fall 1977, p. 9. P. 477, Table

Credits

15.4: United States Environmental Protection Agency, Office of Water and Waste Management, 1980. P. 478, Table 15.5: United States Office of Technology Assessment. P. 483, Table 15.6: United States Environmental Protection Agency, Office of Solid Waste and Emergency Response, *Using Compensation and Incentives When Siting Hazardous Waste Management Facilities,* July 1982, p. 4.

CHAPTER SIXTEEN

Photographs
P. 499, Taurus Photos, Inc., Eric Kroll. P. 505, Ulrike Welsch. P. 509, Grant Heilman Photography, Barry L. Runk. P. 511, Tom Stack/TOM STACK AND ASSOCIATES. P. 513, Taurus Photos, Inc., Eric Kroll.

Figures
P. 500, Fig. 16.5: Adapted from Moller, 1975, *Ambio,* Vol. 4, No. 1. P. 501, Fig. 16.6: Adapted from Moller, 1975, *Ambio,* Vol. 4, No. 1. p.12. P. 502, Fig. 16.7: Adapted from Moller, 1975, *Ambio,* Vol. 4, No. 1. p.12.

Cartoon
P. 506, By permission of Johnny Hart and News Group Chicago, Inc.

CHAPTER SEVENTEEN

Photographs
P. 525, Grant Heilman Photography. P. 528, Grant Heilman Photography. P. 532, Courtesy of the United States Forest Service. P. 534, Grant Heilman Photography. P. 539, United States Department of Agriculture, Soil Conservation Service. P. 541, Leonard Lee Rue III.

Figures
P. 517, Fig. 17.1: United States Soil Conservation Service, *America's Soil and Water: Conditions and Trends,* December 1980. P. 518, Fig. 17.2: United States Department of Agriculture and Council on Environmental Quality, *National Agricultural Lands Study,* 1981. P. 521, Fig. 17.3: Adapted from R. Barlowe, *Land Resource Economics: The Political Economy of Rural and Urban Land Use,* © 1958, p. 14. Adapted by permission of Prentice-Hall, Inc., Englewood Cliffs, N.J. P. 536, Fig. 17.5: Adapted from The Conservation Foundation, *State of the Environment,* 1984, p. 182. Data from U. S. Fish and Wildlife Service.

Tables
P. 517, Table 17.1: Council on Environmental Quality, *National Agricultural Land Study,* U.S. Department of Agriculture, 1981. P. 531, Table 17.3: Martha K. Ritter, *National Resources Defense Council Newsletter,* March/April, 1979, p. 25.

PART OPENER
Main Photo, Tom Stack/TOM STACK AND ASSOCIATES. Insert, National Aeronautics and Space Administration.

CHAPTER EIGHTEEN

Photographs
P. 553, Taurus Photos, Inc., Richard Wood, P. 555, Taurus Photos, Inc., Russell Thompson. P. 561, Courtesy of Camp Dresser and McKee, Inc., Boston, MA. P. 571, Taurus Photos, Inc., Eric Kroll.

Figures
P. 554, Fig. 18.4: After M. H. Greenwood and J. M. B. Edwards, *Human Environments and Natural Systems: A Conflict of Dominion,* Duxbury Press, 1973.

Cartoon
P. 569, By permission of Johnny Hart and News Group Chicago, Inc.

CHAPTER NINETEEN

Photographs
P. 583, United States Environmental Protection Agency. P. 585, Courtesy of United States Forest Service.

Figures
P. 584, Fig. 19.1: Council on Environmental Quality, 1980. P. 586, Fig. 19.2: Council on Environmental Quality, 1980.

Bonus
P. 577, Bonus 19.1: Reprinted from STATE OF THE ENVIRONMENT: AN ASSESSMENT AT MID-DECADE, with permission of The Conservation Foundation, Washington. P. 587, Bonus 19.3: Resources for the Future, *Resources,* No. 66, Spring 1981, p. 13.

INSERT ONE

Opening: National Aeronautics and Space Administration.
Spread: *Verso*: Top, Dave Millert/TOM STACK AND ASSOCIATES. Bottom, Courtesy of Mike Penney. *Recto*: Top Left, Taurus Photos, Inc., Lancelot Davis. Top Right, Courtesy of Mike Penney. Bottom, Taurus Photos, Inc., D. Wallin.

INSERT TWO

Opening: NASA, Grant Heilman.
Spread: *Verso*: Top, Image Workshop, Charles E. Zirkle. Center, Grant Heilman Photography. Bottom, Tom Stack/TOM STACK AND ASSOCIATES. *Recto*: Top, Stock Boston, Peter Menzel. Bottom, Stewart Green/TOM STACK AND ASSOCIATES. Closing: National Aeronautics and Space Administration.

Index*